INTRODUCTION TO PHILOSOPHY

INTRODUCTION TO PHILOSOPHY

Classical and Contemporary Readings

edited by
John Perry
and
Michael Bratman

New York Oxford
Oxford University Press
1986

Oxford University Press

Oxford New York Toronto
Delhi Bombay Calcutta Madras Karachi
Petaling Jaya Singapore Hong Kong Tokyo
Nairobi Dar es Salaam Cape Town
Melbourne Auckland

and associated companies in
Beirut Berlin Ibadan Nicosia

Published by Oxford University Press, Inc.
200 Madison Avenue, New York, New York 10016

Library of Congress Cataloging-in-Publication Data
Main entry under title:
Introduction to philosophy.
Bibliography: p.
1. Philosophy—Introductions. 2. Philosophy—
Addresses, essays, lectures. I. Perry, John, 1943–
II. Bratman, Michael.
BD21.I54 1986 100 85-18802
ISBN 0-19-503697-2

Printing (last digit): 9 8 7 6 5 4 3 2 1

Printed in the United States of America
Mfg. on acid-freee paper

ACKNOWLEDGMENTS

Bertrand Russell, "The Value of Philosophy," from *The Problems of Philosophy,* Oxford University Press, 1912. Reprinted by permission of the publisher.

Bertrand Russell, "Why I Am Not a Theist," from *Why I Am Not a Christian and Other Essays on Religion and Related Topics.* © 1957 by Bertrand Russell. Reprinted by permission of Simon & Schuster, Inc., and by permission of George Allen & Unwin Publishers Ltd.

Philip P. Wiener, "The Theodicy: Abridgement of the Argument Reduced to Syllogistic Form," from *Leibniz Selections.* Copyright 1951 Charles Scribner's Sons; copyright renewed © 1979 Charles Scribner's Sons. Reprinted by permission of the publisher.

Robert Merrihew Adams, "Must God Create the Best?" from *Philosophical Review* 81, no. 3. Copyright © 1972 by the *Philosophical Review.* Reprinted by permission of the publisher.

Saint Anselm, "The Ontological Argument," from *Proslogion,* translated by Ronald Rubbin. Copyright © 1983 by Arete Press. Reprinted by permission of the translator and the publisher.

Saint Thomas Aquinas, "The Existence of God Proven," from *Summa Theologica,* translated by Ronald Rubin. Reprinted by permission of the translator and Arete Press.

David Hume, "Dialogues Concerning Natural Religion," from *Dialogues Concerning Natural Religion,* edited by Norman Kemp-Smith, Oxford University Press, 1935. Reprinted by permission of the publisher.

Blaise Pascal, "The Wager," from Pascal's *Pensées,* translated by W. F. Trotter, Everyman's Library, J. M. Dent & Sons Ltd., 1958. Reprinted by permission of the publisher.

James Cargile, "Pascal's Wager," from *Philosophy* 41 (1966). Copyright © 1966 by The Royal Institute of Philosophy. Reprinted by permission of Cambridge University Press.

Søren Kierkegaard, *Concluding Unscientific Postscript,* translated by David F. Swenson and Walter Lowrie. Copyright 1941, © 1969 by Princeton University Press. Excerpts reprinted by permission of Princeton University Press.

Robert Merrihew Adams, "Kierkegaard's Arguments Against Objective Reasoning in Religion," reprinted by permission from vol. 60, no. 2 of *The Monist,* La Salle, Illinois 61301.

Henry M. Morris, from *Scientific Creationism,* San Diego: Creation-Life Publishers. Copyright © 1974 by Henry M. Morris. Reprinted by permission of the author.

Philip Kitcher, "The Case Against Creationism," from *Abusing Science.* Copyright © 1982 by the MIT Press. Reprinted by permission of the publisher.

Paul Feyerabend, "How to Defend Society Against Science," from *Radical Philosophy* (2), 1975.

René Descartes, "Meditations on First Philosophy, from *Meditations on First Philosophy,* translated from the Latin edition of 1641 by Ronald Rubin. Copyright © 1983 by Arete Press. Reprinted by permission of the translator and the publisher.

John Locke, "Some Further Considerations Concerning Our Simple Ideas of Sensation," from *An Essay Concerning Human Understanding,* Clarendon Press, 1894.

George Berkeley, *Three Dialogues Between Hylas and Philonous,* reprinted from the A. C. Fraser edition, vol. 1. Clarendon Press, 1901.

David Hume, "Of Scepticism With Regard to the Senses," from *A Treatise of Human Nature,* edited by L. A. Selby-Bigge, third edition revised by P. H. Nidditch. Copyright © 1975 by Oxford University Press. Reprinted by permission of the publisher.

David Hume, "An Enquiry Concerning Human Understanding," from *An Enquiry Concerning Human Understanding.* Reprinted from the L. A. Selby-Bigge edition, Oxford University Press, 1893.

George Edward Moore, sections IV and V of "A Defense of Common Sense," from *Philosophical Papers,* George Allen & Unwin Ltd., 1959. Used by permission of George Allen & Unwin and by permission of Humanities Press International, Inc., Atlantic Highlands, N.J.

O. K. Bouwsma, "Moore's Theory of Sense-Data," from *The Philosophy of G. E. Moore,* edited by P. A. Schillp, vol. IV of the Library of Living Philosophers. Open Court Publishing Co., 1942.

J. L. Austin, chapters III and IV from *Sense and Sensibilia,* edited by G. J. Warnock, Copyright © 1962 by Oxford University Press. Reprinted by permission of the publisher.

Wesley C. Salmon, from *The Foundations of Scientific Inference.* Copyright © 1967 by the University of Pittsburgh Press. Reprinted by permission of the publisher.

Carl G. Hempel, *Philosophy of Natural Science,* Copyright © 1966, pp. 47–69. Reprinted by permission of Prentice-Hall, Inc., Englewood Cliffs, N.J.

C. J. Ducasse, "Critique of Hume's Conception of Causality," *The Journal of Philosophy,* vol. 63, no. 6, March 17. Copyright © 1966 *The Journal of Philosophy.* Reprinted by permission of the publisher.

G. E. M. Anscombe, "Causality and Determination," an Inaugural Lecture delivered at Cambridge. Copyright © 1971 by Cambridge University Press. Reprinted by permission of Cambridge University Press.

Gilbert Ryle, "Descartes' Myth," *The Concept of Mind,* Copyright © 1949 by the Hutchinson Publishing Group. Reprinted by permission of the publisher.

Bertrand Russell, "The Argument from Analogy for Other Minds," from *Human Knowledge.* Copyright © 1948 by Bertrand Russell, © 1975 by the estate of Bertrand Russell. Reprinted by permission of Simon & Schuster, Inc., and by permission of George Allen & Unwin Ltd.

Norman Malcolm, "Knowledge of Other Minds," *The Journal of Philosophy,* vol. 55: 23. Copyright © 1958 by *The Journal of Philosophy.* Reprinted by permission of the publisher and the author.

David M. Armstrong, "The Nature of Mind," from *The Nature of Mind,* University of Queensland Press, 1980. Originally published in C. V. Borst, ed., *The Mind/Brain Identity Theory,* MacMillan London Ltd., 1970.

Hilary Putnam, "The Nature of Mental States," from *Mind, Language, and Reality. Philosophical Papers,* volume 2, pp. 429–44, and "Turing Machines," pp. 364–66. Copyright © 1975 by Cambridge University Press. Reprinted by permission of the publisher.

Jerry Fodor, "Functionalism," from *Representations: Philosophical Essays on the Foundations of Cognitive Science,* Bradford Books 1981. Copyright © 1981 by Jerry Fodor. Used by permission of the MIT Press, and by permission of the Harvester Press Ltd.

Thomas Nagel, "What Is It Like To Be a Bat?" from the *Philosophical Review* 83. Copyright © 1974 by the *Philosophical Review.* Reprinted by permission of the publisher.

A. M. Turing, "Computing Machinery and Intelligence," from *MIND,* vol. 59 (1950). Reprinted by permission of Oxford University Press.

John R. Searle, "Minds, Brains, and Programs," from *Behavioral and Brain Sciences,* vol. 3. Copyright © 1980 by Cambridge University Press. Reprinted by permission of the publisher.

John Locke, "Of Identity and Diversity," from *Essay Concerning Human Understanding,* 2nd edition, London, 1694.

Thomas Reid, "Of Identity," from *The Works of Thomas Reid,* vol. 2. Charlestown, So. Carol.: Samuel Ethridge, Jr., 1814.

David Hume, "Of Personal Identity," from *A Treatise of Human Nature,* edited by L. A. Selby-Bigge, 2nd edition revised by H. P. Nidditch. Copyright © 1978 by Oxford University Press. Reprinted by permission of the publisher.

Bernard Williams, "The Self and the Future" from the *Philosophical Review,* vol. 79, no. 2 (April 1970). Copyright © 1970 by the *Philosophical Review.* Reprinted by permission of the publisher.

John Perry, "Williams on the Self and Its Future," from *The Journal of Philosophy,* vol. 73, 1976. Copyright © 1976 by *The Journal of Philosophy.* Reprinted by permission of the publisher.

Baron D'Holbach, "Free Will Is a Myth," from *The System of Nature,* translated by H. D. Robinson. Boston: J. P. Mendum, 1889.

C. A. Campbell, "Has the Self 'Free Will'?" from *On Selfhood and God,* George Allen & Unwin Ltd., 1957. Reprinted by permission of the publisher.

David Hume, "Of Liberty and Necessity," from *Enquiries Concerning Human Understanding and Concerning the Principles of Morals,* edited by L. A. Selby-Bigge, 3rd edition revised by P. H. Nidditch. Copyright © 1975 by Oxford University Press. Reprinted by permission of the publisher.

Thomas Nagel, "Moral Luck," from *Mortal Questions.* Copyright © 1979 by Cambridge University Press. Reprinted by permission of the publisher.

Judith Jarvis Thomson, "A Defense of Abortion," from *Philosophy and Public Affairs,* vol. 1, No. 1 (Fall 1971). Copyright © 1971 by Princeton University Press. Reprinted by permission of Princeton University Press.

Philippa Foot, "The Problem of Abortion and the Doctrine of the Double Effect," from *The Oxford Review* (1967). Copyright © 1967 by Philippa Foot. Reprinted by permission of the author.

John M. Taurek, "Should the Numbers Count?" from *Philosophy and Public Affairs,* vol. 6, no. 4 (Summer 1977). Copyright © 1977 by Princeton University Press. Reprinted by permission of Princeton University Press.

Gregory Kavka, "Some Paradoxes of Deterrence," from *The Journal of Philosophy,* vol. 75, no. 6, June 1978. Copyright © 1978 by *The Journal of Philosophy.* Reprinted by permission of the publisher and the author.

Jeremy Bentham, "The Principle of Utility," from *An Introduction to the Principles of Morals and Legislation* (New York: Hafner, 1948).

John Stuart Mill, "Utililtarianism," from *The English Utilitarians* by John Plamenatz, Basil Blackwell Ltd., 1949. Reprinted by permission of the publisher.

E. F. Carritt, "Criticisms of Utilitarianism," from *Ethical and Political Thinking,* Oxford University Press, 1947. Reprinted by permission of the publisher.

J. O. Urmson, "The Interpretation of the Moral Philosophy of J. S. Mill," excerpts from *The Philosophical Quarterly* 3 (1953). Reprinted by permission of Basil Blackwell Ltd.

J. J. C. Smart, "Extreme and Restricted Utilitarianism," from *The Philosophical Quarterly,* vol. 6 (1956). Reprinted by permission of Basil Blackwell Ltd.

Bernard Williams, "Utilitarianism and Integrity," from *A Critique of Utilitarianism.* Copyright © 1973 by Cambridge University Press. Reprinted by permission of the publisher.

Peter Singer, "Famine, Affluence, and Morality," from *Philosophy and Public Affairs,* vol. 1, no. 3 (Spring 1972). Copyright © 1972 by Princeton University Press. Reprinted with the permission of Princeton University Press.

Immanuel Kant, "Groundwork of the Metaphysic of Morals," selections from chapters 1 and 2, translated by H. J. Paton, Hutchinson Publishing Group Limited. Reprinted by permission of the publisher.

Onora O'Neill, "Kantian Approaches to Some Famine Problems," from *Matters of Life and Death; New Introductory Essays in Moral Philosophy* edited by Tom Regan. Copyright © 1980 by Random House, Inc. Reprinted by permission of the publisher.

Thomas Nagel, "War and Massacre," from *Mortal Questions.* Copyright © 1979 by Cambridge University Press. Reprinted by permission of the publisher.

Aristotle, excerpts form *The Nicomachean Ethics,* translated by Sir David Ross. Oxford University Press, 1925. Reprinted by permission of the publisher.

J. O. Urmson, "Aristotle's Doctrine of the Mean," from *American Philosophical Quarterly,* vol. 10 (1973). Copyright © by *American Philosophical Quarterly.* Reprinted by permission of the publisher.

Thomas Nagel, "Aristotle on *Eudaimonia,*" from *Phronesis* 17 (1972). Copyright © 1972 by *Phronesis.* Reprinted by permission of the publisher.

John Rawls, "A Theory of Justice," reprinted by permission of the publishers from *A Theory of Justice,* Cambridge, Mass.: The Belknap Press of Harvard University Press, Copyright © 1971 by the President and Fellows of Harvard College.

Robert Nozick, "Justice and Entitlement," from *Anarchy, State, and Utopia.* Copyright © 1974 by Basic Books. Reprinted by permission of the publisher.

Kai Nielsen, "Capitalism, Socialism and Justice," in Tom Regan and Donald VanDeVeer, eds., *And Justice for All: New Introductory Essays in Ethics and Public Policy,* excerpted version, Totowa, N.J.: Rowman & Allanheld © 1982, pp. 264–86.

Ronald Dworkin, "Reverse Discrimination," from *Taking Rights Seriously,* Cambridge, Mass.; Harvard University Press, Copyright © 1977, 1978 by Ronald Dworkin. Reprinted by permission of Harvard University Press and by permission of Gerald Duckworth & Co. Ltd.

Plato, from *The Republic of Plato,* translated by F. M. Cornford. Oxford University Press, 1941. Reprinted by permission of the publisher.

David Hume, "An Enquiry Concerning the Principles of Morals," from *Enquiries Concerning Human Understanding and Concerning the Principles of Morals* edited by L. A. Selby-Bigge, third edition revised by P. H. Nidditch. Copyright © 1975 by Oxford University Press. Reprinted by permission of the publisher.

David Gauthier, "Morality and Advantage," from the *Philosophical Review,* 76. Copyright © 1967 by the *Philosophical Review.* Reprinted by permission of the publisher.

J. L. Mackie, "The Law of the Jungle: Moral Alternatives and Principles of Evolution," from *Philosophy,* 53. Copyright © 1978 by *Philosophy.* Reprinted by permission of the publisher.

J. L. Mackie, "The Subjectivity of Values," from *Ethics: Inventing Right and Wrong,* Penguin Books, 1977. Copyright © 1977 by J. L. Mackie. Reprinted by permission of the publisher.

John Rawls, "Outline of a Decision Procedure for Ethics," from the *Philosophical Review,* 60. Copyright © 1951 by the *Philosophical Review.* Reprinted by permission of the publisher.

W. V. Quine, "The Ways of Paradox," from *Ways of Paradox and Other Essays,* Random House, 1966. Reprinted by permission of the author.

For our children

Jim, Sarah, and Joe Perry

Gregory and Scott Bratman

Preface

In this anthology we have collected a variety of readings for use in a course or sequence of courses designed to introduce students to philosophy. We have based the selection on two courses we have taught numerous times at Stanford University: "God, Self, and World" and "Value and Obligation." The first is an introduction to metaphysics and epistemology, the second to ethics. These are one-quarter courses, usually taught in sequence, with a fair number of students taking both.

These courses are built around classic texts supplemented by shorter selections from the past and present. We have included in this anthology not only texts that we have found successful, but also others that a survey of colleagues at Stanford and other institutions have identified as suitable. Thus, the total number of selections is larger than can be reasonably covered in even a two-quarter sequence, and instructors will want to pick those that fit their approach. We have included some footnotes from the original selections but have eliminated others. In some cases footnotes were eliminated because they could not be understood in the context of the selection; in other cases this was done simply to save space. The remaining footnotes have been renumbered.

Punctuation and other matters of style have been altered to conform with American conventions, with a couple of exceptions. In cases where quotation marks are clearly used for mentioning linguistic items—and the author's practice indicates an intent to note this specific use of such marks—punctuation that is not part of the mentioned item has not been moved inside the marks. In other cases single quotes have been left where they would normally be replaced by double quotes, as they appeared to be making a distinction of importance to the author.

Part VI, "Puzzles and Paradoxes," consists of short statements of some famous, interesting, and philosophically relevant mind-benders. We have found these useful in several ways in introducing students to philosophy: as paper assignments, as subjects for the odd short lecture after an exam or a vacation, as challenges for motivated students, or as materials to be worked into other sections of the book. We hope others find them as much fun to teach with as we have. We are grateful to Carl Ginet of Cornell University who shared with us his experience of using such puzzles to introduce students to philosophy.

College students of the present era tend to be preoccupied with preparation for a career—a preoccupation one can hardly criticize, given the expense of a college education and the concerns of parents as well as a civilization rich in opportunities for those who are technically prepared and full of pitfalls for those who are not. But, for most students, college will be the only opportunity to address the enduring problems of human existence; to examine carefully and thoughtfully the beliefs and values inherited from culture and parents; to gain an appreciation of the unsettled questions at the foundations of science and culture; and to develop habits of orderly, but imaginative, thinking. It is the job of the teacher of philosophy to encourage and assist students in taking advantage of this opportunity, and we feel there could be few callings as exciting and fulfilling. We hope this anthology will be of some value to our like-minded colleagues.

Stanford, Calif.
May 1985

J.P.
M.B.

Contents

C. Evolution and Creation

Part III. Knowledge and Reality

A. Classics of Epistemology

B. Perception

C. Induction, Causation, and Explanation

Part IV. Mind and Body

A. The Traditional Problem of Mind and Body

B. Minds and Machines

C. Personal Identity

D. Freedom and Determinism

Part V. Ethics

A. Moral Perplexities

B. Moral Theories

1. Utilitarianism

Part VI. Puzzles and Paradoxes

PART I

THE NATURE AND VALUE OF PHILOSOPHY

The Value of Philosophy

BERTRAND RUSSELL

Bertrand Russell (1872–1970) taught at Cambridge University, but he lost his position because of his pacifism during World War I. A leader, with G. E. Moore, of the early twentieth-century revolt against idealism, Russell's work in logic and epistemology was one of the main influences on twentieth-century analytical philosophy. His works include *The Principles of Mathematics, Principia Mathematica* (with Alfred North Whitehead), *The Problems of Philosophy, Our Knowledge of the External World,* and numerous other books.

Having now come to the end of our brief and very incomplete review of the problems of philosophy, it will be well to consider, in conclusion, what is the value of philosophy and why it ought to be studied. It is the more necessary to consider this question, in view of the fact that many men, under the influence of science or of practical affairs, are inclined to doubt whether philosophy is anything better than innocent but useless trifling, hair-splitting distinctions, and controversies on matters concerning which knowledge is impossible.

This view of philosophy appears to result, partly from a wrong conception of the ends of life, partly from a wrong conception of the kind of goods which philosophy strives to achieve. Physical science, through the medium of inventions, is useful to innumerable people who are wholly ignorant of it; thus the study of physical science is to be recommended, not only, or primarily, because of the effect on the student, but rather because of the effect on mankind in general. Thus utility does not belong to philosophy. If the study of philosophy has any value at all for others than students of philosophy, it must be only indirectly, through its effects upon the lives of those who study it. It is in these effects, therefore, if anywhere, that the value of philosophy must be primarily sought.

But further, if we are not to fail in our endeavour to determine the value of philosophy, we must first free our minds from the prejudices of what are wrongly called "practical" men. The "practical" man, as this word is often used, is one who recognizes only material needs, who realizes that men must have food for the body, but is oblivious of the necessity of providing food for the mind. If all men were well off, if poverty and disease had been reduced to their lowest possible point, there would still remain much to be done to produce a valuable society; and even in the existing world the goods of the mind are at least as important as the goods of the body. It is exclusively among the goods of the mind that the value of philosophy is to be found; and only those who are not indifferent to these goods can be persuaded that the study of philosophy is not a waste of time.

Philosophy, like all other studies, aims primarily at knowledge. The knowledge it aims at is the kind of knowledge which gives unity and system to the body of the sciences, and the kind which results from a critical examination of the grounds of our convictions, prejudices, and beliefs. But it cannot be maintained that philosophy has had any very great measure of success in its attempts to provide definite answers to its questions. If you ask a mathematician, a mineralogist, a historian, or any other man of learning, what definite body of truths has been ascertained by his science, his answer will last as long as you are willing to listen. But if you put the same question to a philosopher, he will, if he is candid, have to confess that his study has not achieved positive results such as have been achieved by other sciences. It is true that this is partly ac-

From *The Problems of Philosophy* (New York: Oxford University Press, 1969), pp. 153–61.

counted for by the fact that, as soon as definite knowledge concerning any subject becomes possible, this subject ceases to be called philosophy, and becomes a separate science. The whole study of the heavens, which now belongs to astronomy, was once included in philosophy; Newton's great work was called "the mathematical principles of natural philosophy." Similarly, the study of the human mind, which was a part of philosophy, has now been separated from philosophy and has become the science of psychology. Thus, to a great extent, the uncertainty of philosophy is more apparent than real: those questions which are already capable of definite answers are placed in the sciences, while those only to which, at present, no definite answer can be given, remain to form the residue which is called philosophy.

This is, however, only a part of the truth concerning the uncertainty of philosophy. There are many questions—and among them those that are of the profoundest interest to our spiritual life—which, so far as we can see, must remain insoluble to the human intellect unless its powers become of quite a different order from what they are now. Has the universe any unity of plan or purpose, or is it a fortuitous concourse of atoms? Is consciousness a permanent part of the universe, giving hope of indefinite growth in wisdom, or is it a transitory accident on a small planet on which life must ultimately become impossible? Are good and evil of importance to the universe or only to man? Such questions are asked by philosophy, and variously answered by various philosophers. But it would seem that, whether answers be otherwise discoverable or not, the answers suggested by philosophy are none of them demonstrably true. Yet, however slight may be the hope of discovering an answer, it is part of the business of philosophy to continue the consideration of such questions, to make us aware of their importance, to examine all the approaches to them, and to keep alive that speculative interest in the universe which is apt to be killed by confining ourselves to definitely ascertainable knowledge.

Many philosophers, it is true, have held that philosophy could establish the truth of certain answers to such fundamental questions. They have supposed that what is of most importance in religious beliefs could be proved by strict demonstration to be true. In order to judge of such attempts, it is necessary to take a survey of human knowledge, and to form an opinion as to its methods and its limitations. On such a subject it would be unwise to pronounce dogmatically; but if the investigations of our previous chapters have not led us astray, we shall be compelled to renounce the hope of finding philosophical proofs of religious beliefs. We cannot, therefore, include as part of the value of philosophy any definite set of answers to such questions. Hence, once more, the value of philosophy must not depend upon any supposed body of definitely ascertainable knowledge to be acquired by those who study it.

The value of philosophy is, in fact, to be sought largely in its very uncertainty. The man who has no tincture of philosophy goes through life imprisoned in the prejudices derived from common sense, from the habitual beliefs of his age or his nation, and from convictions which have grown up in his mind without the co-operation or consent of his deliberate reason. To such a man the world tends to become definite, finite, obvious; common objects rouse no questions, and unfamiliar possibilities are contemptuously rejected. As soon as we begin to philosophize, on the contrary, we find, as we saw in our opening chapters, that even the most everyday things lead to problems to which only very incomplete answers can be given. Philosophy, though unable to tell us with certainty what is the true answer to the doubts which it raises, is able to suggest many possibilities which enlarge our thoughts and free them from the tyranny of custom. Thus, while diminishing our feeling of certainty as to what things are, it greatly increases our knowledge as to what they may be; it removes the somewhat arrogant dogmatism of those who have never travelled into the region of liberating doubt, and it keeps alive our sense of wonder by showing familiar things in an unfamiliar aspect.

Apart from its utility in showing unsuspected possibilities, philosophy has a value—perhaps its chief value—through the greatness of the objects which it contemplates, and the freedom from narrow and personal aims resulting from this contemplation. The life of the instinctive man is shut up within the circle of his private interests:

family and friends may be included, but the outer world is not regarded except as it may help or hinder what comes within the circle of instinctive wishes. In such a life there is something feverish and confined, in comparison with which the philosophic life is calm and free. The private world of instinctive interests is a small one, set in the midst of a great and powerful world which must, sooner or later, lay our private world in ruins. Unless we can so enlarge our interests as to include the whole outer world, we remain like a garrison in a beleagured fortress, knowing that the enemy prevents escape and that ultimate surrender is inevitable. In such a life there is no peace, but a constant strife between the insistence of desire and the powerlessness of will. In one way or another, if our life is to be great and free, we must escape this prison and this strife.

One way of escape is by philosophic contemplation. Philosophic contemplation does not, in its widest survey, divide the universe into two hostile camps—friends and foes, helpful and hostile, good and bad—it views the whole impartially. Philosophic contemplation, when it is unalloyed, does not aim at proving that the rest of the universe is akin to man. All acquisition of knowledge is an enlargement of the Self, but this enlargement is best attained when it is not directly sought. It is obtained when the desire for knowledge is alone operative, by a study which does not wish in advance that its objects should have this or that character, but adapts the Self to the characters which it finds in its objects. This enlargement of Self is not obtained when, taking the Self as it is, we try to show that the world is so similar to this Self that knowledge of it is possible without any admission of what seems alien. The desire to prove this is a form of self-assertion and, like all self-assertion, it is an obstacle to the growth of Self which it desires, and of which the Self knows that it is capable. Self-assertion, in philosophic speculation as elsewhere, views the world as a means to its own ends; thus it makes the world of less account than Self, and the Self sets bounds to the greatness of its goods. In contemplation, on the contrary, we start from the not-Self, and through its greatness the boundaries of Self are enlarged; through the infinity of the universe the mind which contemplates it achieves some share in infinity.

For this reason greatness of soul is not fostered by those philosophies which assimilate the universe to Man. Knowledge is a form of union of Self and not-Self; like all union, it is impaired by dominion, and therefore by any attempt to force the universe into conformity with what we find in ourselves. There is a widespread philosophical tendency towards the view which tells us that Man is the measure of all things, that truth is man-made, that space and time and the world of universals are properties of the mind, and that, if there be anything not created by the mind, it is unknowable and of no account for us. This view, if our previous discussions were correct, is untrue; but in addition to being untrue, it has the effect of robbing philosophic contemplation of all that gives it value, since it fetters contemplation to Self. What it calls knowledge is not a union with the not-Self, but a set of prejudices, habits, and desires, making an impenetrable veil between us and the world beyond. The man who finds pleasure in such a theory of knowledge is like the man who never leaves the domestic circle for fear his word might not be law.

The true philosophic contemplation, on the contrary, finds its satisfaction in every enlargement of the not-Self, in everything that magnifies the objects contemplated, and thereby the subject contemplating. Everything, in contemplation, that is personal or private, everything that depends upon habit, self-interest, or desire, distorts the object, and hence impairs the union which the intellect seeks. By thus making a barrier between subject and object, such personal and private things become a prison to the intellect. The free intellect will see as God might see, without a *here* and *now,* without hopes and fears, without the trammels of customary beliefs and traditional prejudices, calmly, dispassionately, in the sole and exclusive desire of knowledge—knowledge as impersonal, as purely contemplative, as it is possible for man to attain. Hence also the free intellect will value more the abstract and universal knowledge into which the accidents of private history do not enter, than the knowledge brought by the senses, and dependent, as such knowledge must be, upon an exclusive and personal point of view and a body whose sense-organs distort as much as they reveal.

The mind which has become accustomed to the

freedom and impartiality of philosophic contemplation will preserve something of the same freedom and impartiality in the world of action and emotion. It will view its purposes and desires as parts of the whole, with the absence of insistence that results from seeing them as infinitesimal fragments in a world of which all the rest is unaffected by any one man's deeds. The impartiality which, in contemplation, is the unalloyed desire for truth, is the very same quality of mind which, in action, is justice, and in emotion is that universal love which can be given to all, and not only to those who are judged useful or admirable. Thus contemplation enlarges not only the objects of our thoughts, but also the objects of our actions and our affections: it makes us citizens of the universe, not only of one walled city at war with all the rest. In this citizenship of the universe consists man's true freedom, and his liberation from the thraldom of narrow hopes and fears.

Thus, to sum up our discussion of the value of philosophy; Philosophy is to be studied, not for the sake of any definite answers to its questions, since no definite answers can, as a rule, be known to be true, but rather for the sake of the questions themselves; because these questions enlarge our conception of what is possible, enrich our intellectual imagination and diminish the dogmatic assurance which closes the mind against speculation; but above all because, through the greatness of the universe which philosophy contemplates, the mind also is rendered great, and becomes capable of that union with the universe which constitutes its highest good.

PART II

REASON AND RELIGION

INTRODUCTION

No issues are so likely to lead one into the study of philosophy as those arising from religious practices and beliefs. Here, we present selections that concern three such issues. The first section concerns the existence of God. In these selections the authors assume that human reason is capable of providing at least part of the answer to this question. Saint Anselm, St. Thomas Aquinas, and the characters Demea and Cleanthes in David Hume's *Dialogues Concerning Natural Religion* provide arguments in favor of the existence of God, whereas Bertrand Russell and the character Philo in Hume's *Dialogues* reply to such arguments. Cleanthes also provides a rebuttal for one of Demea's arguments.

Both Philo and Russell argue that the problem of evil counts heavily against the existence of God. Exactly what the problem is depends on how we conceive of the Deity. If we take it that God, by definition, must be perfect and that this includes being omnipotent (all-powerful), omniscient (all-knowing), and completely benevolent, then, the existence of evil in the world appears to provide an argument that God does not exist. A benevolent God would not want any evil, and omniscience and omnipotence should guarantee that God would be smart enough and powerful enough to avoid creating a world that contained it. Russell reasons in this way. Philo, on the other hand, is willing to use "God" or "the Deity" to stand for *whatever* the cause or causes of order in the universe might be. But, he thinks that evil shows that the Deity, so conceived, is not perfect.

Philo thinks that even if we have some reason to attribute intelligence to the cause (or causes) of order in the universe, we have no reason to attribute such moral properties as benevolence or the concern for justice to that cause, much less emotional properties such as jealousy or concern about whether one is loved by the creatures one has created. This would mean that we have no reason to believe in a Deity meeting the conception developed in the Judeo-Christian tradition, a completely perfect Person with a strong sense of justice and concern for the allegiance of the creatures He has created.

Robert Merrihew Adams and Gottfried Leibniz respond to the problem of evil. Leibniz argues that the presence of evil does not show that this is not the best of all possible worlds—the very best world even a perfect God could have created. Adams takes a more moderate line. He argues that even a perfect God would not be obliged to create the best of all possible worlds. For to whom would He be so obliged? We might well not have been born if God had created the best of all possible worlds. Surely, He was not obliged to us to create a world in which we do not exist.

The selections in Section A, "God and Evil," presuppose that reason is relevant to religious belief in a fairly straightforward way. The authors cite the evidence for or against religious doctrines in much the same way one argues about other intellectual issues. But, two of the authors in Section B, "Faith and Subjectivity," take a quite different track. Blaise Pascal reasons that we should believe in God, not because the evidence shows that this is the most probable hypothesis, but for a quite different reason. His argument appeals to our gambling instincts; it is a sort of cost-benefit defense of religious belief. Pascal argues: if we compare the relatively trivial cost of belief, even if it turns out that God *does not* exist, to the enormous cost of disbelief, if God *does* exist, we shall see that belief is by far the better gamble. Søren Kierkegaard maintains that all objective reasoning is simply inappropriate to religious questions: They are matters of faith, not reason. James Cargile and Robert Merrihew Adams reply to these arguments of Pascal and Kierkegaard.

Since Charles Darwin's theory of evolution first became widely accepted among biologists, there has been controversy about whether the theory should be taught in the public schools. The theory appears to conflict with religious doctrines about the creation of the world by God. Recently, the debate has taken a form that raises various philosophical issues about the nature of evidence, knowledge, and the scientific enterprise. The first selection is drawn from Henry M. Morris's book *Scientific Creationism.* He argues that no theory about the origin of the world can be proven and that the creationist view, which agrees with the biblical account, is as scientific as the theory of evolution and, therefore, should be presented as such in the classroom. The selection by Philip Kitcher is drawn from his book *Abusing Science,* which contains a detailed rebuttal to the creationist challenge. The general issues of the demarcation between religion and science and the danger of science becoming a government-sponsored orthodoxy are examined by Paul Feyerabend in "How to Defend Society Against Science."Several selections in other Parts of this volume are also relevant to the issues of reason and religion. Most important is René Descartes's *Meditations on First Philosophy* (in Part III), which develops arguments for the existence of God and discusses one aspect of the problem of evil, the possibility of human error. The questions about science and induction discussed in Section C of Part III, "Induction, Causation, and Explanation," are quite relevant to the matters considered by Morris, Kitcher, and Feyerabend.

A. GOD AND EVIL

Why I Am Not a Theist

BERTRAND RUSSELL

To come to this question of the existence of God: it is a large and serious question, and if I were to attempt to deal with it in any adequate manner I should have to keep you here until Kingdom Come, so that you will have to excuse me if I deal with it in a somewhat summary fashion. You know, of course, that the Catholic Church has laid it down as a dogma that the existence of God can be proved by the unaided reason. That is a somewhat curious dogma, but it is one of their dogmas. They had to introduce it because at one time the freethinkers adopted the habit of saying that there were such and such arguments which mere reason might urge against the existence of God, but of course they knew as a matter of faith that God did exist. The arguments and the reasons were set out at great length, and the Catholic Church felt that they must stop it. Therefore they laid it down that the existence of God can be proved by the unaided reason and they had to set up what they considered were arguments to prove it. There are, of course, a number of them, but I shall take only a few.

The First-Cause Argument

Perhaps the simplest and easiest to understand is the argument of the First Cause. (It is maintained that everything we see in this world has a cause, and as you go back in the chain of causes further and further you must come to a First Cause, and to that First Cause you give the name of God.) That argument, I suppose, does not carry very much weight nowadays, because, in the first place, cause is not quite what it used to be. The philosophers and the men of science have got going on cause, and it has not anything like the vitality it used to have, but, apart from that, you can see that the argument that there must be a First Cause is one that cannot have any validity. I may say that when I was a young man and was debating these questions very seriously in my mind, I for a long time accepted the argument of the First Cause, until one day, at the age of eighteen, I read John Stuart Mill's Autobiography, and I there found this sentence: "My father taught me that the question 'Who made me?' cannot be answered, since it immediately suggests the further question 'Who made God?' " That very simple sentence showed me, as I still think, the fallacy in the argument of the First Cause. If everything must have a cause, then God must have a cause. If there can be anything without a cause, it may just as well be the world as God, so that there cannot be any validity in that argument. It is exactly of the same nature as the Hindu's view, that the world rested upon an elephant and the elephant rested upon a tortoise; and when they said, "How about the tortoise?" the Indian said, "Suppose we change the subject." The argument is really no better than that. There is no reason why the world could not have come into being without a cause; nor, on the other hand, is there any reason why it should not have always existed. There is no reason to suppose that the world had a beginning at all. The idea that things

From *Why I Am Not a Christian and Other Essays on Religion and Related Topics* (New York: Simon & Schuster, 1957), pp. 5–14.

must have a beginning is really due to the poverty of our imagination. Therefore, perhaps, I need not waste any more time upon the argument about the First Cause.

The Natural-Law Argument

Then there is a very common argument from natural law. That was a favorite argument all through the eighteenth century, especially under the influence of Sir Isaac Newton and his cosmogony. People observed the planets going around the sun according to the law of gravitation, and they thought that God had given a behest to these planets to move in that particular fashion, and that was why they did so. That was, of course, a convenient and simple explanation that saved them the trouble of looking any further for explanations of the law of gravitation. Nowadays we explain the law of gravitation in a somewhat complicated fashion that Einstein has introduced. I do not propose to give you a lecture on the law of gravitation, as interpreted by Einstein, because that again would take some time; at any rate, you no longer have the sort of natural law that you had in the Newtonian system, where, for some reason that nobody could understand, nature behaved in a uniform fashion. We now find that a great many things we thought were natural laws are really human conventions. You know that even in the remotest depths of stellar space there are still three feet to a yard. That is, no doubt, a very remarkable fact, but you would hardly call it a law of nature. And a great many things that have been regarded as laws of nature are of that kind. On the other hand, where you can get down to any knowledge of what atoms actually do, you will find they are much less subject to law than people thought, and that the laws at which you arrive are statistical averages of just the sort that would emerge from chance. There is, as we all know, a law that if you throw dice you will get double sixes only about once in thirty-six times, and we do not regard that as evidence that the fall of the dice is regulated by design; on the contrary, if the double sixes came every time we should think that there was design. The laws of nature are of that sort as regards a great many of them. They are statistical averages such as would emerge from the laws of chance; and that makes this whole business of natural law much less impressive than it formerly was. Quite apart from that, which represents the momentary state of science that may change tomorrow, the whole idea that natural laws imply a lawgiver is due to a confusion between natural and human laws. Human laws are behests commanding you to behave a certain way, in which way you may choose to behave, or you may choose not to behave; but natural laws are a description of how things do in fact behave, and being a mere description of what they in fact do, you cannot argue that there must be somebody who told them to do that, because even supposing that there were, you are then faced with the question "Why did God issue just those natural laws and no others?" If you say that he did it simply from his own good pleasure, and without any reason, you then find that there is something which is not subject to law, and so your train of natural law is interrupted. If you say, as more orthodox theologians do, that in all the laws which God issues he had a reason for giving those laws rather than others—the reason, of course, being to create the best universe, although you would never think it to look at it—if there were a reason for the laws which God gave, then God himself was subject to law, and therefore you do not get any advantage by introducing God as an intermediary. You have really a law outside and anterior to the divine edicts, and God does not serve your purpose, because he is not the ultimate lawgiver. In short, this whole argument about natural law no longer has anything like the strength that it used to have. I am traveling on in time in my review of the arguments. The arguments that are used for the existence of God change their character as time goes on. They were at first hard intellectual arguments embodying certain quite definite fallacies. As we come to modern times they become less respectable intellectually and more and more affected by a kind of moralizing vagueness.

The Argument from Design

The next step in this process brings us to the argument from design. You all know the argument from design: everything in the world is made just so that we can manage to live in the world, and if the world was ever so little different, we could not manage to live in it. That is the argument from design. It sometimes takes a rather curious form; for instance, it is argued that rabbits have white tails in order to be easy to shoot. I do not know how rabbits would view that application. It is an easy argument to parody. You all know Voltaire's remark, that obviously the nose was designed to be such as to fit spectacles. That sort of parody has turned out to be not nearly so wide of the mark as it might have seemed in the eighteenth century; because since the time of Darwin we understand much better why living creatures are adapted to their environment. It is not that their environment was made to be suitable to them but that they grew to be suitable to it, and that is the basis of adaptation. There is no evidence of design about it.

When you come to look into this argument from design, it is a most astonishing thing that people can believe that this world, with all the things that are in it, with all its defects, should be the best that omnipotence and omniscience have been able to produce in millions of years. I really cannot believe it. Do you think that, if you were granted omnipotence and omniscience and millions of years in which to perfect your world, you could produce nothing better than the Ku Klux Klan or the Fascists? Moreover, if you accept the ordinary laws of science, you have to suppose that human life and life in general on this planet will die out in due course: it is a stage in the decay of the solar system; at a certain stage of decay you get the sort of conditions of temperature and so forth which are suitable to protoplasm, and there is life for a short time in the life of the whole solar system. You see in the moon the sort of thing to which the earth is tending—something dead, cold, and lifeless.

I am told that that sort of view is depressing, and people will sometimes tell you that if they believed that, they would not be able to go on living. Do not believe it; it is all nonsense. Nobody really worries much about what is going to happen millions of years hence. Even if you think they are worrying much about that, they are really deceiving themselves. They are worried about something much more mundane, or it may merely be a bad digestion; but nobody is really seriously rendered unhappy by the thought of something that is going to happen to this world millions and millions of years hence. Therefore, although it is of course a gloomy view to suppose that life will die out—at least I suppose we may say so, although sometimes when I contemplate the things that people do with their lives I think it is almost a consolation—it is not such as to render life miserable. It merely makes you turn your attention to other things.

The Moral Arguments for Deity

Now we reach one stage further in what I shall call the intellectual descent that the Theists have made in their argumentations, and we come to what we called the moral arguments for the existence of God. You all know, of course, that there used to be in the old days three intellectual arguments for the existence of God, all of which were disposed of by Immanuel Kant in the *Critique of Pure Reason;* but no sooner had he disposed of those arguments than he invented a new one, a moral argument, and that quite convinced him. He was like many people: in intellectual matters he was skeptical, but in moral matters he believed implicitly in the maxims that he had imbibed at his mother's knee. That illustrates what the psychoanalysts so much emphasize—the immensely stronger hold upon us that our very early associations have than those of later times.

Kant, as I say, invented a new moral argument for the existence of God, and that in varying forms was extremely popular during the nineteenth century. It has all sorts of forms. One form is to say that there would be no right or wrong unless God existed. I am not for the moment concerned with whether there is a difference between right and wrong, or whether there is not: that is another question. The point I am concerned with is that, if you are quite sure there is a difference between right and wrong, you are then in this situation: Is that difference due to God's fiat or is it not? If it is due to God's fiat, then for God himself there is no difference between right and wrong, and it is no longer a significant statement to say that God is good. If you are going to say, as theologians do, that God is good, you must then say that right and wrong have some meaning which is independent of God's fiat, because God's fiats are good and not bad independently of the mere fact that he made them. If you are going to say that, you will then have to say that it is not only through God that right and wrong came into being, but that they are in their essence logically anterior to God. You could, of course, if you liked, say that there was a superior deity who gave orders to the God who made this world, or could take up the line that some of the gnostics took up—a line which I often thought was a very plausible one—that as a matter of fact this world that we know was made by the devil at a moment when God was not looking. There is a good deal to be said for that, and I am not concerned to refute it.

The Argument for the Remedying of Injustice

Then there is another very curious form of moral argument, which is this: they say that the existence of God is required in order to bring justice into the world. In the part of this universe that we know there is great injustice, and often the good suffer, and often the wicked prosper, and one hardly knows which of those is the more annoying; but if you are going to have justice in the universe as a whole you have to suppose a future life to redress the balance of life here on earth. So they say that there must be a God, and there must be heaven and hell in order that in the long run there may be justice. That is a very curious argument. If you looked at the matter from a scientific point of view, you would say, "After all, I know only this world. I do not know about the rest of the universe, but so far as one can argue at all on probabilities one would say that probably this world is a fair sample, and if there is injustice here the odds are that there is injustice elsewhere also." Supposing you got a crate of oranges that you opened, and you found all the top layer of oranges bad, you would not argue, "The underneath ones must be good, so as to redress the balance." You would say, "Probably the whole lot is a bad consignment"; and that is really what a scientific person would argue about the universe. He would say, "Here we find in this world a great deal of injustice, and so far as that goes that is a reason for supposing that justice does not rule in the world; and therefore so far as it goes it affords a moral argument against deity and not in favor of one." Of course I know that the sort of intellectual arguments that I have been talking to you about are not what really moves people. What really moves people to believe in God is not any intellectual argument at all. Most people believe in God because they have been taught from early infancy to do it, and that is the main reason.

Then I think that the next most powerful reason is the wish for safety, a sort of feeling that there is a big brother who will look after you. That plays a very profound part in influencing people's desire for a belief in God.

God, Evil and the Best of All Possible Worlds

GOTTFRIED LEIBNIZ

Gottfried Wilhelm Leibniz (1646–1716) was a brilliant philosopher who also discovered the calculus independently of Newton. His main works include *New Essays on the Human Understanding, Theodicy, The Monadology,* and *Discourse on Metaphysics.*

Some intelligent persons have desired that this supplement be made [to *Theodicy*], and I have the more readily yielded to their wishes as in this way I have an opportunity again to remove certain difficulties and to make some observations which were not sufficiently emphasized in the work itself.

I. *Objection.* Whoever does not choose the best is lacking in power, or in knowledge, or in goodness.

God did not choose the best in creating this world.

Therefore, God has been lacking in power, or in knowledge, or in goodness.

Answer. I deny the minor, that is, the second premise of this syllogism; and our opponent proves it by this:

Prosyllogism. Whoever makes things in which there is evil, which could have been made without any evil, or the making of which could have been omitted, does not choose the best.

God has made a world in which there is evil; a world, I say, which could have been made without any evil, or the making of which could have been omitted altogether.

Therefore, God has not chosen the best.

Answer. I grant the minor of this prosyllogism; for it must be confessed that there is evil in this world which God has made, and that it was possible to make a world without evil, or even not to create a world at all, for its creation has depended on the free will of God; but I deny the major, that is, the first of the two premises of the prosyllogism, and I might content myself with simply demanding its proof; but in order to make the matter clearer, I have wished to justify this denial by showing that the best plan is not always that which seeks to avoid evil, since it may happen that the *evil is accompanied by a greater good.* For example, a general of an army will prefer a great victory with a slight wound to a condition without wound and without victory. We have proved this more fully in the large work by making it clear, by instances taken from mathematics and elsewhere, that an imperfection in the part may be required for a greater perfection in the whole. In this I have followed the opinion of St. Augustine, who has said a hundred times, that God has permitted evil in order to bring about good, that is, a greater good; and that of Thomas Aquinas (in libr. II. sent. dist. 32, qu. I, art. 1), that the permitting of evil tends to the good of the universe. I have shown that the ancients called Adam's fall *felix culpa,* a happy sin, because it

From *Leibniz Selections,* trans. George M. Duncan, with revisions by Philip P. Wiener (New York: Charles Scribner's Sons, 1951), pp. 509–12.

had been retrieved with immense advantage by the incarnation of the Son of God, who has given to the universe something nobler than anything that ever would have been among creatures except for it. For the sake of a clearer understanding, I have added, following many good authors, that it was in accordance with order and the general good that God allowed to certain creatures the opportunity of exercising their liberty, even when he foresaw that they would turn to evil, but which he could so well rectify; because it was not fitting that, in order to hinder sin, God should always act in an extraordinary manner. To overthrow this objection, therefore, it is sufficient to show that a world with evil might be better than a world without evil; but I have gone even farther, in the work, and have even proved that this universe must be in reality better than every other possible universe.

II. *Objection.* If there is more evil than good in intelligent creatures, then there is more evil than good in the whole work of God.

Now, there is more evil than good in intelligent creatures.

Therefore, there is more evil than good in the whole work of God.

Answer. I deny the major and the minor of this conditional syllogism. As to the major, I do not admit it at all, because this pretended deduction from a part to the whole, from intelligent creatures to all creatures, supposes tacitly and without proof that creatures destitute of reason cannot enter into comparison nor into account with those which possess it. But why may it not be that the surplus of good in the non-intelligent creatures which fill the world, compensates for, and even incomparably surpasses, the surplus of evil in the rational creatures? It is true that the value of the latter is greater; but, in compensation, the others are beyond comparison the more numerous, and it may be that the proportion of number and quantity surpasses that of value and of quality.

As to the minor, that is no more to be admitted; that is, it is not at all to be admitted that there is more evil than good in the intelligent creatures. There is no need even of granting that there is more evil than good in the human race, because it is possible, and in fact very probable, that the glory and the perfection of the blessed are incomparably greater than the misery and the imperfection of the damned, and that here the excellence of the total good in the smaller number exceeds the total evil in the greater number. The blessed approach the Divinity, by means of a Divine Mediator, as near as may suit these creatures, and make such progress in good as is impossible for the damned to make the evil, approach as nearly as they may to the nature of demons. God is infinite, and the devil is limited; the good may and does go to infinity, while evil has its bounds. It is therefore possible, and is credible, that in the comparison of the blessed and the damned, the contrary of that which I have said might happen in the comparison of intelligent and non-intelligent creatures, takes place; namely, it is possible that in the comparison of the happy and the unhappy, the proportion of degree exceeds that of number, and that in the comparison of intelligent and non-intelligent creatures, the proportion of number is greater than that of value. I have the right to suppose that a thing is possible so long as its impossibility is not proved; and indeed that which I have here advanced is more than a supposition.

But in the second place, if I should admit that there is more evil than good in the human race, I have still good grounds for not admitting that there is more evil than good in all intelligent creatures. For there is an inconceivable number of genii, and perhaps of other rational creatures. And an opponent could not prove that in all the City of God, composed as well of genii as of rational animals without number and of an infinity of kinds, evil exceeds good. And although in order to answer an objection, there is no need of proving that a thing is, when its mere possibility suffices; yet, in this work, I have not omitted to show that it is a consequence of the supreme perfection of the Sovereign of the universe, that the kingdom of God is the most perfect of all possible states or governments, and that consequently the little evil there is, is required for the consummation of the immense good which is found there.

Must God Create the Best?

ROBERT MERRIHEW ADAMS

Robert Merrihew Adams (1937–) is a professor of philosophy at the University of California at Los Angeles. His publications include numerous articles on the philosophy of religion and metaphysics.

I

Many philosophers and theologians have accepted the following proposition:

> (*P*) If a perfectly good moral agent created any world at all, it would have to be the very best world that he could create.

The best world that an omnipotent God could create is the best of all logically possible worlds. Accordingly, it has been supposed that if the actual world was created by an omnipotent, perfectly good God, it must be the best of all logically possible worlds.

In this paper I shall argue that ethical views typical of the Judeo-Christian religious tradition do not require the Judeo-Christian theist to accept (*P*). He must hold that the actual world is a good world. But he need not maintain that it is the best of all possible worlds, or the best world that God could have made.[1]

The position which I am claiming that he can consistently hold is that *even if* there is a best among possible worlds, God could create another instead of it, and still be perfectly good. I do not in fact see any good reason to believe that there is a best among possible worlds. Why can't it be that for every possible world there is another that is better? And if there is no maximum degree of perfection among possible worlds, it would be unreasonable to blame God, or think less highly of His goodness, because He created a world less excellent than He could have created.[2] But I do not claim to be able to prove that there is no best among possible worlds, and in this essay I shall assume for the sake of argument that there is one.

Whether we accept proposition (*P*) will depend on what we believe are the requirements for perfect goodness. If we apply an act-utilitarian standard of moral goodness, we will have to accept (*P*). For by act-utilitarian standards it is a moral obligation to bring about the best state of affairs that one can. It is interesting to note that the ethics of Leibniz, the best-known advocate of (*P*), is basically utilitarian.[3] In his *Theodicy* (Part I, Section 25) he maintains, in effect, that men, because of their ignorance of many of the consequences of their actions, ought to follow a rule-utilitarian code, but that God, being omniscient, must be a perfect act utilitarian in order to be perfectly good.

I believe that utilitarian views are not typical of the Judeo-Christian ethical tradition, although Leibniz is by no means the only Christian utilitarian. In this essay I shall assume that we are working with standards of moral goodness which are not utilitarian. But I shall not try either to show

From the *Philosophical Review* 81, no. 3 (July 1972), 317–32.

that utilitarianism is wrong or to justify the standards that I take to be more typical of Judeo-Christian religious ethics. To attempt either of these tasks would unmanageably enlarge the scope of the paper. What I can hope to establish here is therefore limited to the claim that the rejection of *(P)* is consistent with Juedo-Christian religious ethics.

Assuming that we are not using utilitarian standards of moral goodness, I see only two types of reason that could be given for *(P)*. (1) It might be claimed that a creator would necessarily wrong someone (violate someone's rights), or be less kind to someone than a perfectly good moral agent must be, if he knowingly created a less excellent world instead of the best that he could. Or (2) it might be claimed that even if no one would be wronged or treated unkindly by the creation of an inferior world, the creator's choice of an inferior world must manifest a defect of character. I will argue against the first of these claims in Section II. Then I will suggest, in Section III, that God's choice of a less excellent world could be accounted for in terms of His grace, which is considered a virtue rather than a defect of character in Judeo-Christian ethics. A counterexample, which is the basis for the most persuasive objections to my position that I have encountered, will be considered in Sections IV and V.

II

Is there someone *to* whom a creator would have an obligation to create the best world he could? Is there someone whose rights would be violated, or who would be treated unkindly, if the creator created a less excellent world? Let us suppose that our creator is God, and that there does not exist any being, other than Himself, which He has not created. It follows that if God has wronged anyone, or been unkind to anyone, in creating whatever world He has created, this must be one of His own creatures. To which of His creatures, then, might God have an obligation to create the best of all possible worlds? (For that is the best world He could create.)

Might He have an obligation to the creatures in the best possible world, to create them? Have they been wronged, or even treated unkindly, if God has created a less excellent world, in which they do not exist, instead of creating them? I think not. The difference between actual beings and merely possible beings is of fundamental moral importance here. The moral community consists of actual beings. It is they who have actual rights, and it is to them that there are actual obligations. A merely possible being cannot be (actually) wronged or treated unkindly. A being who never exists is not wronged by not being created, and there is no obligation to any possible being to bring it into existence.

Perhaps it will be objected that we believe we have obligations to future generations, who are not yet actual and may never be actual. We do say such things, but I think what we mean is something like the following. There is not merely a logical possibility, but a probability greater than zero, that future generations will really exist; and *if* they will in fact exist, we will have wronged them if we act or fail to act in certain ways. On this analysis we cannot have an obligation to future generations to bring them into existence.

I argue, then, that God does not have an obligation to the creatures in the best of all possible worlds to create them. If God has chosen to create a world less excellent than the best possible, He has not thereby wronged any creatures whom He has chosen not to create. He has not even been unkind to them. If any creatures are wronged, or treated unkindly, by such a choice of the creator, they can only be creatures that exist in the world He has created.

I think it is fairly plausible to suppose that God could create a world which would have the following characteristics:

(1) None of the individual creatures in it would exist in the best of all possible worlds.
(2) None of the creatures in it has a life which is so miserable on the whole that it would be better for that creature if it had never existed.
(3) Every individual creature in the world is at least as happy on the whole as it would have been in any other possible world in which it could have existed.

It seems obvious that if God creates such a world He does not thereby wrong any of the creatures in it, and does not thereby treat any of them with less than perfect kindness. For none of them would have been benefited by His creating any other world instead.[4]

If there are doubts about the possibility of God's creating such a world, they will probably have to do with the third characteristic. It may be worth while to consider two questions, on the supposition (which I am not endorsing) that no possible world less excellent than the best would have characteristic (3), and that God has created a world which has characteristics (1) and (2) but not (3). In such a case must God have wronged one of His creatures? Must He have been less than perfectly kind to one of His creatures?

I do not think it can reasonably be argued that in such a case God must have wronged one of His creatures. Suppose a creature in such a case were to complain that God had violated its rights by creating it in a world in which it was less happy on the whole than it would have been in some other world in which God could have created it. The complaint might express a claim to special treatment: "God ought to have created *me* in more favorable circumstances (even though that would involve His creating some *other* creature in less favorable circumstances than He could have created it in)." Such a complaint would not be reasonable, and would not establish that there had been any violation of the complaining creature's rights.

Alternatively, the creature might make the more principled complaint, "God has wronged me by not following the principle of refraining from creating any world in which there is a creature that would have been happier in another world He could have made." This also is an unreasonable complaint. For if God followed the stated principle, He would not create any world that lacked characteristic (3). And we are assuming that no world less excellent than the best possible would have characteristic (3). It follows that if God acted on the stated principle He would not create any world less excellent than the best possible. But the complaining creature would not exist in the best of all possible worlds; for we are assuming that this creature exists in a world which has characteristic (1). The complaining creature, therefore, would never have existed if God had followed the principle that is urged in the complaint. There could not possibly be any advantage to this creature from God's having followed that principle; and the creature has not been wronged by God's not following the principle. (It would not be better for the creature if it had never existed; for we are assuming that the world God created has characteristic [2].)

The question of whether in the assumed case God must have been unkind to one of His creatures is more complicated than the question of whether He must have wronged one of them. In fact it is too complicated to be discussed adequately here. I will just make three observations about it. The first is that it is no clearer that the best of all possible worlds would possess characteristic (3) than that some less excellent world would possess it. In fact it has often been supposed that the best possible world might not possess it. The problem we are now discussing can therefore arise also for those who believe that God has created the best of all possible worlds.

My second observation is that if kindness to a person is the same as a tendency to promote his happiness, God has been less than perfectly (completely, unqualifiedly) kind to any creature whom He could have made somewhat happier than He has made it. (I shall not discuss here whether kindness to a person is indeed the same as a tendency to promote his happiness; they are at least closely related.)

But in the third place I would observe that such qualified kindness (if that is what it is) toward some creatures is consistent with God's being perfectly good, and with His being very kind to all His creatures. It is consistent with His being very kind to all His creatures because He may have prepared for all of them a very satisfying existence even though some of them might have been slightly happier in some other possible world. It is consistent with His being perfectly good because even a perfectly good moral agent may be led, by other considerations of sufficient weight, to qualify his kindness or beneficence toward some person. It has sometimes been held that a perfectly good God might cause or permit a person to have less happiness than he might otherwise have had, in order to punish him, or to avoid interfering with the freedom of another person, or in order to create the best of all possible worlds. I would suggest that the desire to create and love all of a certain group of possible creatures (assuming that all of them would have satisfying lives on the whole) might be an adequate ground for a perfectly good God to create them, even if His creating *all* of them must have the result that some of them are less happy than they might otherwise have been. And they need not be the best of all possible creatures, or included in the best of all possible worlds, in order for this qualification of His kindness to be consistent with His perfect goodness. The desire to create *those* creatures is as legitimate a ground for Him to qualify His kindness toward some, as the desire to create the best of all possible worlds. This suggestion seems to me to be in keeping with the aspect of the Judeo-Christian moral ideal which will be discussed in Section III.

These matters would doubtless have to be discussed more fully if we were considering whether the *actual* world can have been created by a perfectly good God. For our present purposes, however, enough may have been said—especially since, as I have noted, it seems a plausible assumption that God could make a world having characteristics (1), (2), and (3). In that case He could certainly make a less excellent world than the best of all possible worlds without wronging any of His creatures or failing in kindness to any of them. (I have, of course, *not* been arguing that there is *no* way in which God could wrong anyone or be less kind to anyone than a perfectly good moral agent must be.)

III

Plato is one of those who held that a perfectly good creator would make the very best world he could. He thought that if the creator chose to make a world less good than he could have made, that could be understood only in terms of some defect in the creator's character. Envy is the defect that Plato suggests.[5] It may be thought that the creation of a world inferior to the best that he could make would manifest a defect in the creator's character even if no one were thereby wronged or treated unkindly. For the perfectly good moral agent must not only be kind and refrain from violating the rights of others, but must also have other virtues. For instance, he must be noble, generous, high-minded, and free from envy. He must satisfy the moral ideal.

There are differences of opinion, however, about what is to be included in the moral ideal. One important element in the Judeo-Christian moral ideal is *grace*. For present purposes, grace may be defined as a disposition to love which is not dependent on the merit of the person loved. The gracious person loves without worrying about whether the person he loves is worthy of his love. Or perhaps it would be better to say that the gracious person sees what is valuable in the person he loves, and does not worry about whether it is more or less valuable than what could be found in someone else he might have loved. In the Judeo-Christian tradition it is typically believed that grace is a virtue which God does have and men ought to have.

A God who is gracious with respect to creating might well choose to create and love less excellent creatures than He could have chosen. This is not to suggest that grace in creation consists in a preference for imperfection as such. God could have chosen to create the best of all possible creatures, and still have been gracious in choosing them. God's graciousness in creation does not imply that the creatures He has chosen to create must be less excellent than the best possible. It implies, rather, that even if they are the best possible creatures, that is not the ground for His choosing them. And it implies that there is nothing in God's nature or character which would require Him to act on the principle of choosing the best possible creatures to be the object of His creative powers.

Grace, as I have described it, is not part of everyone's moral ideal. For instance, it was not part of Plato's moral ideal. The thought that it may be the expression of a virtue, rather than a defect of character, in a creator, *not* to act on the principle of creating the best creatures he possibly could, is quite foreign to Plato's ethical viewpoint. But I believe that thought is not at all foreign to a Judeo-Christian ethical viewpoint.

This interpretation of the Juedo-Christian tradition is confirmed by the religious and devotional attitudes toward God's creation which prevail in the tradition. The man who worships God does not normally praise Him for His moral rectitude and good judgment in creating *us*. He thanks

God for his existence as for an undeserved personal favor. Religious writings frequently deprecate the intrinsic worth of human beings, considered apart from God's love for them, and express surprise that God should concern Himself with them at all.

When I look at thy heavens, the work of thy
fingers, the moon and the stars which thou
hast established;
What is man that thou art mindful of him, and
the son of man that thou dost care for him?
Yet thou hast made him little less than God,
and dost crown him with glory and honor.
Thou hast given him dominion over the works
of thy hands; thou hast put all things under
his feet [Psalm 8: 3–6].

Such utterances seem quite incongruous with the idea that God created us because if He had not He would have failed to bring about the best possible state of affairs. They suggest that God has created human beings and made them dominant on this planet although He could have created intrinsically better states of affairs instead.

I believe that in the Judeo-Christian tradition the typical religious attitude (or at any rate the attitude typically encouraged) toward the fact of our existence is something like the following. "I am glad that I exist, and I thank God for the life He has given me. I am also glad that other people exist, and I thank God for them. Doubtless there could be more excellent creatures than we. But I believe that God, in His grace, created us and loves us; and I accept that gladly and gratefully." (Such an attitude need not be complacent; for the task of struggling against certain evils may be seen as precisely a part of the life that the religious person is to accept and be glad in.) When people who have or endorse such an attitude say that God is perfectly good, we will not take them as committing themselves to the view that God is the kind of being who would not create any other world than the best possible. For they regard grace as an important part of perfect goodness.

IV

On more than one occasion when I have argued for the positions I have taken in Sections II and III above, a counterexample of the following sort has been proposed. It is the case of a person who, knowing that he intends to conceive a child and that a certain drug invariably causes severe mental retardation in children conceived by those who have taken it, takes the drug and conceives a severely retarded child. We all, I imagine, have a strong inclination to say that such a person has done something wrong. It is objected to me that our moral intuitions in this case (presumably including the moral intuitions of religious Jews and Christians) are inconsistent with the views I have advanced above. It is claimed that consistency requires me to abandon those views unless I am prepared to make moral judgments that none of us are in fact willing to make.

I will try to meet these objections. I will begin by stating the case in some detail, in the most relevant form I can think of. Then I will discuss objections based on it. In this section I will discuss an objection against what I have said in Section II, and a more general objection against the rejection of proposition (*P*) will be discussed in Section V.

Let us call this Case (*A*). A certain couple becomes so interested in retarded children that they develop a strong desire to have a retarded child of their own—to love it, to help it realize its potentialities (such as they are) to the full, to see that it is as happy as it can be. (For some reason it is impossible for them to *adopt* such a child.) They act on their desire. They take a drug which is known to cause damaged genes and abnormal chromosome structure in reproductive cells, resulting in severe mental retardation of children conceived by those who have taken it. A severely retarded child is conceived and born. They lavish affection on the child. They have ample means, so that they are able to provide for special needs, and to insure that others will never be called on to pay for the child's support. They give themselves unstintedly, and do develop the child's capacities as much as possible. The child is, on the whole, happy, though incapable of many of the higher intellectual, aesthetic, and social joys. It suffers some pains and frustrations, of course, but does not feel miserable on the whole.

The first objection founded on this case is based, not just on the claim that the parents have done something wrong (which I certainly grant), but on the more specific claim that they have *wronged the child.* I maintained, in effect, in Section II that a creature has not been wronged by its creator's creating it if both of the following conditions are satisfied.[6] (4) The creature is not, on the whole, so miserable that it would be better for him if he had never existed. (5) No being who came into existence in better or happier circumstances would have been the same individual as the creature in question. If we apply an analogous principle to the parent-child relationship in Case (*A*), it would seem to follow that the retarded child has not been wronged by its parents. Condition (4) is satisfied: the child is happy rather than miserable on the whole. And condition (5) also seems to be satisfied. For the retardation in Case (*A*), as described, is not due to prenatal injury but to the genetic constitution of the child. Any normal child the parents might have conceived (indeed any normal child at all) would have had a different genetic constitution, and would therefore have been a different person, from the retarded child they actually did conceive. But—it is objected to me—we do regard the parents in Case (*A*) as having wronged the child, and therefore we cannot consistently accept the principle that I maintained in Section II.

My reply is that if conditions (4) and (5) are really satisfied the child cannot have been wronged by its parents' taking the drug and conceiving it. If we think otherwise we are being led, perhaps by our emotions, into a confusion. If the child is not worse off than if it had never existed, and if *its* never existing would have been a sure consequence of its not having been brought into existence as retarded, I do not see how *its* interests can have been injured, or *its* rights violated, by the parents' bringing it into existence as retarded.

It is easy to understand how the parents might come to feel that they had wronged the child. They might come to feel guilty (and rightly so), and the child would provide a focus for the guilt. Moreover, it would be easy, psychologically, to assimilate Case (*A*) to cases of culpability for prenatal injury, in which it is more reasonable to think of the child as having been wronged.[7] And we often think very carelessly about counterfactual personal identity, asking ourselves questions of doubtful intelligibility, such as "What if I had been born in the Middle Ages?" It is very easy to fail to consider the objection, "But that would not have been the same person."

It is also possible that an inclination to say that the child has been wronged may be based, at least in part, on a doubt that conditions (4) and (5) are really satisfied in Case (*A*). Perhaps one is not convinced that in real life the parents could ever have a reasonable confidence that the child would be happy rather than miserable. Maybe it will be doubted that a few changes in chromosome structure, and the difference between damaged and undamaged genes, are enough to establish that the retarded child is a different person from any normal child that the couple could have had. Of course, if conditions (4) and (5) are not satisfied, the case does not constitute a counterexample to my claims in Section II. But I would not rest any of the weight of my argument on doubts about the satisfaction of the conditions in Case (*A*), because I think it is plausible to suppose that they would be satisfied in Case (*A*) or in some very similar case.

V

Even if the parents in Case (*A*) have not wronged the child, I assume that they have done something wrong. It may be asked *what* they have done wrong, or *why* their action is regarded as wrong. And these questions may give rise to an objection, not specifically to what I said in Section II, but more generally to my rejection of proposition (*P*). For it may be suggested that what is wrong about the action of the parents in Case (*A*) is that they have violated the following principle:

> (*Q*) It is wrong to bring into existence, knowingly, a being less excellent than one could have brought into existence.[8]

If we accept this principle we must surely agree that it would be wrong for a creator to make a world that was less excellent than the best he could make, and therefore that a perfectly good creator would not do such a thing. In other words, (*Q*) implies (*P*).

I do not think (*Q*) is a very plausible principle. It is not difficult to think of counterexamples to it.

Case (*B*): A man breeds goldfish, thereby

bringing about their existence. We do not normally think it is wrong, or even prima facie wrong, for a man to do this, even though he could equally well have brought about the existence of more excellent beings, more intelligent and capable of higher satisfactions. (He could have bred dogs or pigs, for example.) The deliberate breeding of human beings of subnormal intelligence is morally offensive; the deliberate breeding of species far less intelligent than retarded human children is not morally offensive.

Case (*C*): Suppose it has been discovered that if intending parents take a certain drug before conceiving a child, they will have a child whose abnormal genetic constitution will give it vastly superhuman intelligence and superior prospects of happiness. Other things being equal, would it be wrong for intending parents to have normal children instead of taking the drug? There may be considerable disagreement of moral judgment about this. I do not think that parents who chose to have normal children rather than take the drug would be doing anything wrong, nor that they would necessarily be manifesting any weakness or defect of moral character. Parents' choosing to have a normal rather than a superhuman child would not, at any rate, elicit the strong and universal or almost universal disapproval that would be elicited by the action of the parents in Case (*A*). Even with respect to the offspring of human beings, the principle we all confidently endorse is not that it is wrong to bring about, knowingly and voluntarily, the procreation of offspring less excellent than could have been procreated, but that it is wrong to bring about, knowingly and voluntarily, the procreation of a human offspring which is deficient by comparison with normal human beings.

Such counterexamples as these suggest that our disapproval of the action of the parents in Case (*A*) is not based on principle (*Q*), but on a less general and more plausible principle such as the following:

> (*R*) It is wrong for human beings to cause, knowingly and voluntarily, the procreation of an offspring of human parents which is notably deficient, by comparison with normal human beings, in mental or physical capacity.

One who rejects (*Q*) while maintaining (*R*) might be held to face a problem of explanation. It may seem arbitrary to maintain such a specific moral principle as (*R*), unless one can explain it as based on a more general principle, such as (*Q*). I believe, however, that principle (*R*) might well be explained in something like the following way in a theological ethics in the Judeo-Christian tradition, consistently with the rejection of (*Q*) and (*P*).[9]

God, in His grace, has chosen to have human beings among His creatures. In creating us He has certain intentions about the qualities and goals of human life. He has these intentions for us, not just as individuals, but as members of a community which in principle includes the whole human race. And His intentions for human beings as such extend to the offspring (if any) of human beings. Some of these intentions are to be realized by human voluntary action, and it is our duty to act in accordance with them.

It seems increasingly possible for human voluntary action to influence the genetic constitution of human offspring. The religious believer in the Judeo-Christian tradition will want to be extremely cautious about this. For he is to be thankful that we exist as the beings we are, and will be concerned lest he bring about the procreation of human offspring who would be deficient in their capacity to enter fully into the purposes that God has for human beings as such. We are not God. We are His creatures, and we belong to Him. Any offspring we have will belong to Him in a much more fundamental way than they can belong to their human parents. We have not the right to try to have as our offspring just any kind of being whose existence might on the whole be pleasant and of some value (for instance, a being of very low intelligence but highly specialized for the enjoyment of aesthetic pleasures of smell and taste). If we do intervene to affect the genetic constitution of human offspring, it must be in ways which seem likely to make them *more* able to enter fully into what we believe to be the purposes of God for human beings as such. The deliberate procreation of children deficient in mental or physical capacity would be an intervention which could hardly be expected to result in offspring more able to enter fully into God's purposes for human life. It would therefore be sinful, and inconsistent with a proper respect for the human life which God has given us.

On this view of the matter, our obligations to refrain from bringing about the procreation of deficient human offspring is rooted in our obligation to God, as His creatures, to respect His purposes for human life. In adopting this theological rationale for the acceptance of principle (*R*), one in no way commits oneself to proposition (*P*). For one does not base (*R*) on any principle to the effect that one must always try to bring into existence the most excellent things that one can. And the claim that, because of His intentions for human life, we have an obligation to God not to try to have as our offspring beings of certain sorts does not imply that it would be wrong for God to create such beings in other ways. Much less does it imply that it would be wrong for God to create a world less excellent than the best possible.

In this essay I have argued that a creator would not necessarily wrong anyone, or be less kind to anyone than a perfectly good moral agent must be, if he created a world of creatures who would not exist in the best world he could make. I have also argued that from the standpoint of Judeo-Christian religious ethics, a creator's choice of a less excellent world need not be regarded as manifesting a defect of character. It could be understood in terms of his *grace,* which (in that ethics) is considered an important part of perfect goodness. In this way I think the rejection of proposition (*P*) can be seen to be congruous with the attitude of gratitude and respect for human life as God's gracious gift which is encouraged in the Judeo-Christian religious tradition. And that attitude (rather than any belief that one ought to bring into existence only the best beings one can) can be seen as a basis for the disapproval of the deliberate procreation of deficient human offspring.[10]

Notes

1. What I am saying in this paper is obviously relevant to the problem of evil. But I make no claim to be offering a complete theodicy here.
2. Leibniz held (in his *Theodicy,* pt. I, sec. 8) that if there were no best among possible worlds, a perfectly good God would have created nothing at all. But Leibniz is mistaken if he supposes that in this way God could avoid choosing an alternative less excellent than others He could have chosen. For the existence of no created world at all would surely be a less excellent state of affairs than the existence of some of the worlds that God could have created.
3. See Gaston Grua, *Jurisprudence universelle et théodicée selon Leibniz* (Paris, 1953), pp. 210–18.
4. Perhaps I can have a right to something which would not benefit me (e.g., if it has been promised to me). But if there are such non-beneficial rights, I do not see any plausible reason for supposing that a right not to be created could be among them.
5. *Timaeus,* 29E–30A.
6. I am not holding that these are necessary conditions, but only that they are jointly sufficient conditions, for a creature's not being wronged by its creator's creating it. I have numbered these conditions in such a way as to avoid confusion with the numbered characteristics of worlds in sec. II.
7. It may be questioned whether even the prenatally injured child is the same person as any unimpaired child that might have been born. I am inclined to think it is the same person. At any rate there is *more* basis for regarding it as the same person as a possible normal child than there is for so regarding a child with abnormal genetic constitution.
8. Anyone who was applying this principle to human actions would doubtless insert an "other things being equal" clause. But let us ignore that, since such a clause would presumably provide no excuse for an agent who was deciding an issue so important as what world to create.
9. I am able to give here, of course, only a very incomplete sketch of a theological position on the issue of "biological engineering."
10. Among the many to whom I am indebted for help in working out the thoughts contained in this paper, and for criticisms of earlier drafts of it, I must mention Marilyn McCord Adams, Richard Brandt, Eric Lerner, the members of my graduate class on theism and ethics in the fall term of 1970 at the University of Michigan, and the editors of the *Philosophical Review*.

The Ontological Argument

SAINT ANSELM

Saint Anselm of Canterbury (1033–1109) was Archbishop of Canterbury. His works include *Monologion, Proslogion,* and *De Veritate.*

Chapter I
A Call for the Mind to Contemplate God

. . . I gratefully acknowledge, Lord, that you created your image in me so that I would remember you, conceive of you, and love you. But this image has been so worn away by my corruption, so obscured by the filth of my sins, that it cannot serve its purpose unless you renew and reshape it. I won't try to reach your heights, Lord, since I could never make my understanding reach that high. Yet I still want somehow to understand your truth, which my heart believes and loves. For, rather than seeking to understand so that I can believe, I believe so that I can understand. In fact, one of the things that I believe is that, "unless I believe, I cannot understand" [Isa. 7:9].

Chapter II
God Truly Exists

So Lord—you who reward faith with understanding—let me understand, insofar as you see fit, whether you are as we believe and whether you are what we believe you to be. We believe you to be something than which nothing greater can be conceived. The question, then, is whether something with this nature exists, since "the fool has said in his heart that there is no God" [Ps. 14:1, 53:1]. But, surely, when the fool hears the words "something than which nothing greater can be conceived," he understands what he hears, and what he understands exists in his understanding—even if he doesn't think that it exists. For it is one thing for an object to exist in someone's understanding, and another for him to think that it exists. When a painter plans out a painting, he has it in his understanding, but—not yet having produced it—he doesn't yet think that it exists. After he has painted it, he has the painting in his understanding, and—having produced it—he thinks that it exists. This should convince even the fool that something than which nothing greater can be conceived exists, if only in the understanding—since the fool understands the phrase "that than which nothing greater can be conceived" when he hears it, and whatever a person understands exists in his understanding. And surely that than which a greater cannot be conceived cannot exist *just* in the understanding. If it were to exist *just* in the understanding, we could conceive it to exist in reality too, in which case it would be greater. Therefore, if that than which a greater cannot be conceived exists just in the understanding, the very thing than which a greater cannot be conceived is something than which a greater *can* be conceived. But surely this cannot be. Without doubt, then, something than which a greater can't be conceived does exist—both in the understanding and in reality.

From Saint Anselm's *Proslogion,* trans. Ronald Rubin (Claremont, Calif.: Arete Press, forthcoming).

Chapter III
It Is Impossible To Conceive That God Doesn't Exist

In fact, this thing so truly exists that it can't be conceived not to exist. For something that can be conceived to exist but can't be conceived not to exist is greater than one which can be conceived not to exist. Hence, if that than which a greater can't be conceived can be conceived not to exist, then that than which a greater can't be conceived is not that than which a greater can't be conceived. But this would be a contradiction. Therefore, something than which a greater can't be conceived so truly exists that it can't be conceived not to exist.

And this thing is you, Lord our God. Therefore, you so truly exist, Lord my God, that you can't be conceived not to exist. And this is as it should be. For, if one's mind could conceive of something better than you, a created thing would rise above its creator and pass judgment on it, which would be completely absurd. Yes, anything other than you can be conceived not to exist. Therefore, you alone have the truest, and hence the greatest, being of all; nothing else has being as true or as great. Then why has the fool said in his heart that there is no God, when it is evident to a rational mind that your being is the greatest of all? Why—unless because he is stupid and a fool!

Chapter IV
How the Fool Can Say in His Heart That Which Can't Be Conceived

But how could the fool say in his heart something that he couldn't conceive of? And how could he fail to conceive of what he said in his heart, when saying something in one's heart is the same as conceiving of it? If—or, rather, since—he did conceive (since he spoke his heart) but did not speak in his heart (since he could not conceive), there is more than one way to say something in the heart or to conceive of it. We conceive of something in one way when we conceive of words that signify it, but in another when we understand what the thing itself is. In the first way, we can conceive of God's not existing; in the second way, we cannot. No one who understands what God is can possibly conceive that He doesn't exist—although he can say the "God does not exist" in his heart, if he regards the words as meaningless or takes them in unusual senses. For God is that than which a greater cannot be conceived. He who really understands this correctly understands God so to exist that He can't fail to exist, even in our conception. Therefore, he who understands God to be that than which a greater can't be conceived cannot conceive of His not existing.

I thank you, Lord. I thank you because what I once believed through your generosity I now understand through your enlightenment. If I now wanted not to believe that you exist, I wouldn't be able to prevent myself from understanding that you do.

. . . .

Chapter XV
God Is Greater Than Can Be Conceived

Therefore, Lord, you are not only that than which a greater cannot be conceived: you are also something greater than can be conceived. It is possible to conceive that there is something of this sort. And, if you are not this thing, it is possible to conceive of something greater than you—which is impossible.

. . . .

The Existence of God Proven

SAINT THOMAS AQUINAS

Saint Thomas Aquinas (1225–1274) was the leading Scholastic philosopher whose writings have been deemed authoritative by the Catholic Church. These include *Summa Contra Gentiles* and *Summa Theologica*.

Summa Theologica, Question 2, Article 3

Whether God Exists

Objection 1: It seems that God does not exist. For, if one of a pair of contraries were infinite, it would completely obliterate the other. But, when we use the word "God," we mean "something infinitely good." Therefore, if God were to exist, nothing would be bad. But there are bad things in the world. Therefore, God does not exist.

Objection 2: Moreover, if we can account for something on the basis of a few original causes [*principia*], we ought not to use many. But it seems that we can account for everything that we find in the world on the basis of various original causes even if we suppose that God does not exist. Nature can be taken as the original cause of natural things, and human reason and will can be taken as the original cause of purposeful acts. There is therefore no need to say that God exists.

On the other hand, the book of *Exodus* depicts God as saying, "I am who am" [*Exodus* 3:14].

Reply: There are five ways to prove that God exists.

The first and clearest way derives from facts about change. Surely, as our senses show, some things in the world do change. But everything that changes is made to change by something else. For a thing only undergoes a change inasmuch as it has a *potentiality* for being that into which it changes, while a thing only causes change inasmuch as it is *actual.* To cause change is just to draw something out of potentiality into actuality, and this can only be done by something that is in actuality. (Thus, something actually hot, like fire, makes wood which is potentially hot become actually hot, thereby changing and altering that wood.) But, while a single thing can simultaneously be in actuality with respect to one property and in potentiality with respect to another, it cannot simultaneously be in actuality and potentiality with respect to the one and the same property. (While that which is actually hot may simultaneously be potentially cold, that which is actually hot cannot simultaneously be potentially hot.) It is therefore impossible for a thing that undergoes a change to cause that change, or for something to change itself. Therefore, whatever undergoes change must be changed by another thing. And, if this other thing undergoes change, it also must be changed by something else, and so on. But this cannot go back to infinity. If it did, there would be no first cause of change and, consequently, no other causes of change—for something can be a secondary cause of change only if it is changed by a primary cause (as a stick moves something only if a hand moves the stick). We must therefore posit a first cause of change which is not itself changed by anything. And this everyone understands to be God.

The second way derives from the nature of efficient causation. In the world that we sense, we

From *Summa Theologica,* trans. Ronald Rubin. (Claremont, Calif.: Arete Press, forthcoming).

find that efficient causes come in series. We do not, and cannot, find that something is its own efficient cause—for, if something were its own efficient cause, it would be prior to itself, which is impossible. But the series of efficient causes cannot possibly go back to infinity. In all such series of causes, a first thing causes one or more intermediaries, and the intermediaries cause the last thing; when a cause is taken out of this series, so is its effect. Therefore, if there were no first efficient cause, there would be no last or intermediary efficient causes. If the series of efficient causes went back to infinity, however, there would be no first efficient cause and, hence, no last or intermediary causes. But there obviously are such causes. We must therefore posit a first efficient cause, which everyone understands to be God.

The third way, which derives from facts about possibility and necessity, is this: In the world, we find some things that can either exist or fail to exist—things which are generated and corrupted and which therefore exist at some times but not at others. It is impossible, however, that everything has being of this sort. If something *can* fail to exist, there must have been a time at which it *has* failed to exist. Therefore, if everything could fail to exist, there would have been a time at which nothing existed. But, if there had been such a time, there would not be anything in the world now—for something can begin to exist only if brought into existence by something that already exists. Therefore, if there once had been nothing in existence, it would have been impossible for anything to come into existence, and there would be nothing now. Therefore, not every entity can fail to exist; there must be something in the world that exists of necessity. But, if something exists of necessity, either this necessity is or is not caused by something else. And the series of necessary beings whose necessity is caused by another cannot possible go back to infinity. (The reasons are those that were used to show that the series of efficient causes cannot go back to infinity.) We must therefore posit something that is necessary per se—something that does not owe its necessity to anything else but which causes the necessity of other things. And this everyone understands to be God.

The fourth way derives from the gradations to be found in things. Some things are found to be better, truer, or more noble than others. But something is said to have more or less of a quality according to its distance from a maximum. (Thus, the hotter a thing is, the closer it is to that which is maximally hot.) There is therefore something maximally true, good, and noble. And this thing must be the greatest being—for, as Aristotle says in *Metaphysics II* [993b25–30], those things that are greatest in truth are greatest in being. But, as Aristotle says in the same work [993b25], the greatest thing of a kind is the cause of everything of that kind (as fire, the hottest thing is the cause of everything hot). There therefore is something which is the cause of being, of goodness, and of whatever other perfections there may be in things. And this we call God.

The fifth way derives from facts about the governance of the world. We see that even things that lack consciousness, such as physical objects, act for a purpose. They almost always act in the same way, and they tend towards what is best. And this shows that they achieve their ends, not by chance, but on purpose. But something that lacks consciousness can tend towards an end only if directed by something with consciousness and intelligence. (Thus, the arrow must be directed by the archer.) There therefore is some intelligence which directs everything in nature towards an end, and this we call God.

Reply to the first objection: As Augustine says [in *The Enchiridion*], since God is supremely good, He would allow bad things to exist in the world only if He were so powerful and good that He could even bring good out of bad. It is therefore an indication of God's infinite goodness that He permits bad things to exist and draws good things out of them.

Reply to the second objection: Since nature works for a definite end under the direction of a higher agency, we must trace whatever nature does back to God as its first cause. Similarly, we must trace purposeful acts back to a cause higher than human reason and will—for these can change or go out of existence, and, as has been shown, we should trace everything that can change or go out of existence back to an original cause [*principium*] which is unchangeable and necessary per se.

Dialogues Concerning Natural Religion

DAVID HUME

David Hume (1711–1776) is one of the greatest philosophers the world has known. In addition to his *Enquiries* and *Dialogues Concerning Natural Religion,* his writings include *A Treatise of Human Nature* and *History of England.*

David Hume worked on the *Dialogues Concerning Natural Religion* throughout the later part of his life; before his death in 1776, he left instructions that the *Dialogues* be published posthumously.*

By natural religion, Hume meant the doctrine, popular among intellectuals of his age, that the basic tenets of religion could be discovered and defended by using the same tools that are employed in scientific thought. Natural religion is opposed to revealed religion: the proposition that the doctrines of religion are essentially mysterious and can be known only through divine revelation.

There are three main characters in the *Dialogues:* Philo, Cleanthes, and Demea. Throughout the *Dialogues* Cleanthes defends natural religion, maintaining that we have considerable evidence—of the same sort that we use in science generally—that our universe was created by an intelligent and benevolent deity. In most of the *Dialogues* Philo seems skeptical about all claims of natural religion. However, in Part XII Philo appears willing to accept a guarded version of natural religion: that we have some evidence the cause or causes of the universe possessed something like intelligence but that there is no evidence the cause or causes of the universe was benevolent or had any of the moral attributes usually attributed to God and that form the basis of religious practices (e.g., prayer) and religious doctrines (e.g., an afterlife in which we are rewarded or punished for our actions while alive). Philo and Cleanthes are both represented as able philosophers, each explaining and defending various parts of Hume's philosophy. Demea is represented as being somewhat less clever, but it is his views on religion and how it should be taught that get the discussion started.

The *Dialogues* is in the form of a letter from Pamphilus, the son of a deceased friend of Cleanthes, to his philosophical friend Hermippus. Cleanthes had been charged with the education of Pamphilus,

From *Dialogues Concerning Natural Religion,* ed. Norman Kemp-Smith (Oxford: Oxford University Press, 1935), pp. 174–209, 224–72, 281–82.

*The *Dialogues* were first published in 1779. The text produced here is based on Norman Kemp-Smith's edition, Oxford University Press, 1935. We have omitted those footnotes in which Kemp-Smith indicates how Hume made various changes in various drafts, and we have used his translations of various passages that were in Latin in the original. Hume's habit was to capitalize proper names. We have preserved the capitalization for the names of the speakers as the dialogues unfold and changed other proper names to lowercase.

and the *Dialogues* are Pamphilus' account of a conversation between Demea, Cleanthes, and Philo that begins as a discussion of how Cleanthes should instruct Pamphilus about religion.

In Part I, which we omit, Demea asserts that, although religious training should begin early, discussion of the grounds of religious belief should be the last thing in the education plan:

> While they pass through every other science, I still remark the uncertainty of each part, the eternal disputations of men, the obscurity of all philosophy, and the strange, ridiculous conclusions, which some of the greatest geniuses have derived from the principles of mere human reason. Having thus tamed their mind to a proper submission and self-diffidence, I have no longer any scruple of opening to them the greatest mysteries of religion, nor apprehend any danger from that assuming arrogance of philosophy, which may lead them to reject the most established doctrines and opinions.

Philo appears to agree with this:

> Let the errors and deceits of our very senses be set before us; the insuperable difficulties, which attend first principles in all systems; the contradictions, which adhere to the very ideas of matter, cause and effect, extension, space, time motion . . . ; when these familiar objects, I say, are so inexplicable, . . . with what assurance can we decide concerning the origin of worlds, or trace their history from eternity to eternity?

Cleanthes' view of things is quite different. He allows that there are many unsolved intellectual problems of the sort Philo cites. But he thinks that the skepticism to which such problems might lead us does not distinguish between religion and science. In spite of the philosophical puzzles and problems Philo cites, we do know a great deal about how the universe works, and this knowledge is based on complex reasoning. The same sorts of reasoning that led to the Copernican conception of the universe will, Cleanthes thinks, confirm the most important doctrines of religion.

Thus a conversation that began with the question of when Pamphilus should study the basis for belief in religious doctrine has evolved by the beginning of Part II into a debate about whether reasoning—of the same sort that underlies our knowledge in other areas—can be the basis of religion. Part II begins with Demea and Philo, again apparently in agreement, insisting against Cleanthes that, although it is obvious that there is a God, the nature of God is not a fit subject for scientific inquiry, but rather an essentially mysterious subject.

Part II

I must own, Cleanthes, said DEMEA, that nothing can more surprise me, than the light, in which you have, all along, put this argument. By the whole tenor of your discourse, one would imagine that you were maintaining the being of a God, against the cavils of atheists and infidels; and were necessitated to become a champion for that fundamental principle of all religion. But this, I hope, is not by any means a question among us. No man; no man, at least, of common sense, I am persuaded, ever entertained a serious doubt with regard to a truth so certain and self-evident. The question is not concerning the *being* but the *nature* of *God*. This, I affirm, from the infirmities of human understanding, to be altogether incomprehensible and unknown to us. The essence of that supreme mind, his attributes, the manner of his existence, the very nature of his duration; these and every particular, which regards so divine a Being, are mysterious to men. Finite, weak, and blind creatures, we ought to humble ourselves in his august presence, and, conscious of our frailties, adore in silence his infinite perfections, which eye hath not seen, ear hath not heard, neither hath it entered into the heart of man to conceive them. They are covered in a deep cloud from human curiosity: It is profaneness to attempt penetrating through these sacred obscurities: And next to the impiety of denying his existence, is the temerity of prying into his nature and essence, decrees and attributes.

But lest you should think, that my *piety* has here got the better of my *philosophy,* I shall support my opinion, if it needs any support, by a very great authority. I might cite all the divines almost, from the foundation of Christianity, who have ever treated of this or any other theological subject: But I shall confine myself, at present, to one equally celebrated for piety and philosophy. It is Father Malebranche, who, I remember, thus expresses himself.[1] "One ought not so much (says he) to call God a spirit, in order to express positively what he is, as in order to signify that he is not matter. He is a Being infinitely perfect: Of this we cannot doubt. But in the same manner as we ought not to imagine, even supposing him corporeal, that he is cloathed with a human body, as the anthropomorphites asserted, under colour that that figure was the most perfect of any; so neither ought we to imagine, that the Spirit of God has human ideas, or bears *any* resemblance to our spirit; under colour that we know nothing more perfect than a human mind. We ought rather to believe, that as he comprehends the perfections of matter without being material . . . he comprehends also the perfections of created spirits, without being spirit, in the manner we conceive spirit: That his true name is, *He that is,* or in other words, Being without restriction, All Being, the Being infinite and universal."

After so great an authority, Demea, replied PHILO, as that which you have produced, and a thousand more, which you might produce, it would appear ridiculous in me to add my sentiment, or express my approbation of your doctrine. But surely, where reasonable men treat these subjects, the question can never be concerning the *being,* but only the *nature* of the Deity. The former truth, as you well observe, is unquestionable and self-evident. Nothing exists without a cause: and the original cause of this universe (whatever it be) we call God; and piously ascribe to him every species of perfection. Whoever scruples this fundamental truth deserves every punishment, which can be inflicted among philosophers, to wit, the greatest ridicule, contempt and disapprobation. But as all perfection is entirely relative, we ought never to imagine, that we comprehend the attributes of this divine Being, or to suppose, that his perfections have any analogy or likeness to the perfections of a human creature. Wisdom, thought, design, knowledge; these we justly ascribe to him; because these words are honourable among men, and we have no other language or other conceptions, by which we can express our adoration of him. But let us beware, lest we think, that our ideas any wise correspond to his perfections, or that his attributes have any resemblance to these qualities among men. He is infinitely superior to our limited view and comprehension; and is more the object of worship in the temple, than of disputation in the schools.

In reality, Cleanthes, continued he, there is no need of having recourse to that affected scepticism, so displeasing to you, in order to come at this determination. Our ideas reach no farther than our experience: We have no experience of divine attributes and operations: I need not conclude my syllogism: You can draw the inference yourself. And it is a pleasure to me (and I hope to you too) that just reasoning and sound piety here concur in the same conclusion, and both of them establish the adorably mysterious and incomprehensible nature of the supreme Being.

Not to lose any time in circumlocutions, said CLEANTHES, addressing himself to Demea, much less in replying to the pious declamations of Philo; I shall briefly explain how I conceive this matter. Look round the world: Contemplate the whole and every part of it: You will find it to be nothing but one great machine, subdivided into an infinite number of lesser machines, which again admit of subdivisions, to a degree beyond what human senses and faculties can trace and explain. All these various machines, and even their most minute parts, are adjusted to each other with an accuracy, which ravishes into admiration all men, who have ever contemplated them. The curious adapting of means to ends, throughout all nature, resembles exactly, though it much exceeds, the productions of human contrivance; of human design, thought, wisdom, and intelligence. Since therefore the effects resemble each other, we are led to infer, by all the rules of analogy, that the causes also resemble; and that the Author of nature is somewhat similar to the mind of man; though possessed of much larger faculties, proportioned to the grandeur of the work, which he has executed. By this argument *a posteriori,* and by this argument alone, do we prove at once the existence of a Deity, and his similarity to human mind and intelligence.

I shall be so free, Cleanthes, said DEMEA, as to tell you, that from the beginning, I could not approve of your conclusion concerning the similarity of the Deity to men; still less can I approve of the mediums, by which you endeavour to establish it. What! No demonstration of the being of a God! No abstract arguments! No proofs *a priori!* Are these, which have hitherto been so much insisted on by philosophers, all fallacy, all sophism? Can we reach no farther in this subject than experience and probability? I will not say, that this is betraying the cause of a Deity: But surely, by this affected candour, you give advantage to atheists, which they never could obtain, by the mere dint of argument and reasoning.

What I chiefly scruple in this subject, said PHILO, is not so much, that all religious arguments are by Cleanthes reduced to experience, as that they appear not to be even the most certain and irrefragable of that inferior kind. That a stone will fall, that fire will burn, that the earth has solidity, we have observed a thousand and a thousand times; and when any new instance of this nature is presented, we draw without hesitation the accustomed inference. The exact similarity of the cases gives us a perfect assurance of a similar event; and a stronger evidence is never desired nor sought after. But wherever you depart, in the least, from the similarity of the cases, you diminish proportionably the evidence; and may at last bring it to a very weak *analogy,* which is confessedly liable to error and uncertainty. After having experienced the circulation of the blood in human creatures, we make no doubt that it takes place in Titius and Maevius: But from its circulation in frogs and fishes, it is only a presumption, though a strong one, from analogy, that it takes place in men and other animals. The analogical reasoning is much weaker, when we infer the circulation of the sap in vegetables from our experience that the blood circulates in animals; and those, who hastily followed that imperfect analogy, are found, by more accurate experiments, to have been mistaken.

If we see a house, Cleanthes, we conclude, with the greatest certainty, that it had an architect or builder; because this is precisely that species of effect, which we have experienced to proceed from that species of cause. But surely you will not affirm, that the universe bears such a resemblance to a house, that we can with the same certainty infer a similar cause, or that the analogy is here entire and perfect. The dissimilitude is so striking, that the utmost you can here pretend to is a guess, a conjecture, a presumption concerning a similar cause; and how that pretension will be received in the world, I leave you to consider.

It would surely be very ill received, replied CLEANTHES; and I should be deservedly blamed and detested, did I allow, that the proofs of a Deity amounted to no more than a guess or conjecture. But is the whole adjustment of means to ends in a house and in the universe so slight a resemblance? The economy of final causes? The order, proportion, and arrangement of every part? Steps of a stair are plainly contrived, that human legs may use them in mounting; and this inference is certain and infallible. Human legs are also contrived for walking and mounting; and this inference, I allow, is not altogether so certain, because of the dissimilarity which you remark; but does it, therefore, deserve the name only of presumption or conjecture?

Good God! cried DEMEA, interrupting him, where are we? Zealous defenders of religion allow, that the proofs of a Deity fall short of perfect evidence! And you, Philo, on whose assistance I depended, in proving the adorable mysteriousness of the divine nature, do you assent to all these extravagant opinions of Cleanthes? For what other name can I give them? Or why spare my censure, when such principles are advanced, supported by such an authority, before so young a man as Pamphilus?

You seem not to apprehend, replied PHILO, that I argue with Cleanthes in his own way; and by showing him the dangerous consequences of his tenets, hope at last to reduce him to our opinion. But what sticks most with you, I observe, is the representation which Cleanthes has made of the argument *a posteriori;* and finding that that argument is likely to escape your hold and vanish into air, you think it so disguised, that you can scarcely believe it to be set in its true light. Now, however much I may dissent, in other respects from the dangerous principles of Cleanthes, I must allow, that he has fairly represented that argument; and I shall endeavour so to state the matter to you, that you will entertain no farther scruples with regard to it.

Were a man to abstract from every thing which he knows or has seen, he would be altogether incapable, merely from his own ideas, to determine what kind of scene the universe must be, or to give the preference to one state or situation of things above another. For as nothing, which he clearly conceives, could be esteemed impossible or implying a contradiction, every chimera of his fancy would be upon an equal footing; nor could he assign any just reason, why he adheres to one idea or system, and rejects the others, which are equally possible.

Again; after he opens his eyes, and contemplates the world, as it really is, it would be impossible for him, at first, to assign the cause of any one event; much less, of the whole of things or of the universe. He might set his fancy a rambling; and she might bring him in an infinite variety of reports and representations. These would all be possible; but being all equally possible, he would never, of himself, give a satisfactory account for his preferring one of them to the rest. Experience alone can point out to him the true cause of any phenomenon.

Now according to this method of reasoning, Demea, it follows (and is, indeed, tacitly allowed by Cleanthes himself) that order, arrangement, or the adjustment of final causes is not, of itself, any proof of design; but only so far as it has been experienced to proceed from that principle. For aught we can know *a priori,* matter may contain the source or spring of order originally, within itself, as well as mind does; and there is no more difficulty in conceiving, that the several elements, from an internal unknown cause, may fall into the most exquisite arrangement, than to conceive that their ideas, in the great, universal mind, from a like internal, unknown cause, fall into that arrangement. The equal possibility of both these suppositions is allowed. But by experience we find (according to Cleanthes), that there is a difference between them. Throw several pieces of steel together, without shape or form; they will never arrange themselves so as to compose a watch: Stone, and mortar, and wood, without an architect, never erect a house. But the ideas in a human mind, we see, by an unknown, inexplicable economy, arrange themselves so as to form the plan of a watch or house. Experience, therefore, proves, that there is an original principle of order in mind, not in matter. From similar effects we infer similar causes. The adjustment of means to ends is alike in the universe, as in a machine of human contrivance. The causes, therefore, must be resembling.

I was from the beginning scandalised, I must own, with this resemblance, which is asserted, between the Deity and human creatures; and must conceive it to imply such a degradation of the supreme Being as no sound theist could endure. With your assistance, therefore, Demea, I shall endeavour to defend what you justly call the adorable mysteriousness of the divine nature, and shall refute this reasoning of Cleanthes; provided he allows, that I have made a fair representation of it.

When Cleanthes had assented, PHILO, after a short pause, proceeded in the following manner.

That all inferences, Cleanthes, concerning fact, are founded on experience, and that all experimental reasonings are found on the supposition, that similar causes prove similar effects and similar effects similar causes; I shall not, at present, much dispute with you. But observe, I entreat you, with what extreme caution all just reasoners proceed in the transferring of experiments to similar cases. Unless the cases be exactly similar, they repose no perfect confidence in applying their past observation to any particular phenomenon. Every alteration of circumstances occasions a doubt concerning the event; and it requires new experiments to prove certainly, that the new circumstances are of no moment or importance. A change in bulk, situation, arrangement, age, disposition of the air, or surrounding bodies; any of these particulars may be attended with the most unexpected consequences: And unless the objects be quite familiar to us, it is the highest temerity to expect with assurance, after any of these changes, an event similar to that which before fell under our observation. The slow and deliberate steps of philosophers, here, if any where, are distinguished from the precipitate march of the vulgar, who, hurried on by the smallest similitude, are incapable of all discernment or consideration.

But can you think, Cleanthes, that your usual phlegm and philosophy have been preserved in so wide a step as you have taken, when you compared to the universe houses, ships, furniture, machines; and from their similarity in some circumstances inferred a similarity in their causes? Thought, design, intelligence, such as we discover in men and other animals, is no more than one of the springs and principles of the universe, as well as heat or cold, attraction or repulsion, and a hundred others, which fall under daily observation. It is an active cause, by which some particular parts of nature, we find, produce alterations on other parts. But can a conclusion, with any propriety, be transferred from parts to the whole? Does not the great disproportion bar all comparison and inference? From observing the growth of a hair, can we learn any thing concerning the generation of a man? Would the manner of a leaf's blowing, even though perfectly known, afford us any instruction concerning the vegetation of a tree?

But allowing that we were to take the *operations* of one part of nature upon another for the foundation of our judgement concerning the *origin* of the whole (which never can be admitted); yet why select so minute, so weak, so bounded a principle as the reason and design of animals is found to be upon this planet? What peculiar privilege has this little agitation of the brain which we call thought, that we must thus make it the model of the whole universe? Our partiality in our own favour does indeed present it on all occasions: But sound philosophy ought carefully to guard against so natural an illusion.

So far from admitting, continued PHILO, that the operations of a part can afford us any conclusion concerning the origin of the whole, I will not allow any one part to form a rule for another part, if the latter be very remote from the former. Is there any reasonable ground to conclude, that the inhabitants of other planets possess thought, intelligence, reason, or any thing similar to these faculties in men? When nature has so extremely diversified her manner of operation in this small globe; can we imagine, that she incessantly copies herself throughout so immense a universe? And if thought, as we may well suppose, be confined merely to this narrow concern, and has even there so limited a sphere of action; with what propriety can we assign it for the original cause of all things? The narrow views of a peasant, who makes his domestic economy the rule for the government of kingdoms, is in comparison a pardonable sophism.

But were we ever so much assured, that a thought and reason, resembling the human, were to be found throughout the whole universe, and were its activity elsewhere vastly greater and more commanding than it appears in this globe: Yet I cannot see, why the operations of a world, constituted, arranged, adjusted, can with any propriety be extended to a world, which is in its embryo-state, and is advancing towards that constitution and arrangement. By observation, we know somewhat of the economy, action, and nourishment of a finished animal; but we must transfer with great caution that observation to the growth of a foetus in the womb, and still more, to the formation of an animalcule in the loins of its male parent. Nature, we find, even from our limited experience, possesses an infinite number of springs and principles, which incessantly discover themselves on every change of her position and situation. And what new and unknown principles would actuate her in so new and unknown a situation as that of the formation of a universe, we cannot, without the utmost temerity, pretend to determine.

A very small part of this great system, during a very short time, is very imperfectly discovered to us: And do we thence pronounce decisively concerning the origin of the whole?

Admirable conclusion! Stone, wood, brick, iron, brass, have not, at this time, in this minute globe of earth, an order or arrangement without human art and contrivance: Therefore the universe could not originally attain its order and arrangement, without something similar to human art. But is a part of nature a rule for another part very wide of the former? Is it a rule for the whole? Is a very small part a rule for the universe? Is nature in one situation, a certain rule for nature in another situation, vastly different from the former?

And can you blame me, Cleanthes, if I here imitate the prudent reserve of Simonides, who, according to the noted story,[2] being asked by Hiero, *What God was?* desired a day to think of it, and then two days more; and after that manner continually prolonged the term, without ever bringing in his definition or description? Could you even blame me, if I had answered at first, *that I did not know,* and was sensible that this subject lay vastly beyond the reach of my faculties? You might cry out sceptic and raillier as much as you pleased: But having found, in so many other subjects, much more familiar, the imperfections and even contradictions of human reason, I never should expect any success from its feeble conjectures, in a subject, so sublime, and so remote from the sphere of our observation. When *two species* of objects have always been observed to be conjoined together, I can *infer,* by custom, the existence of one whenever I *see* the existence of the other: And this I call an argument from experience. But how this argument can have place, where the objects, as in the present case, are single, individual, without parallel, or specific resemblance, may be difficult to explain. And will any man tell me with a serious countenance, that an orderly universe must arise from some thought and art, like the human; because we have experience of it? To ascertain this reasoning, it were requisite, that we had experience of this origin of worlds; and it is not sufficient surely, that we have seen ships and cities arise from human art and contrivance.

. . . .

Philo was proceeding in this vehement manner, somewhat between jest and earnest, as it appeared to me; when he observed some signs of impatience in Cleanthes, and then immediately stopped short. What I had to suggest, said CLEANTHES, is only that you would not abuse terms, or make use of popular expressions to subvert philosophical reasonings. You know, that the vulgar often distinguish reason from experience, even where the question relates only to matter of fact and existence; though it is found, where that *reason* is properly analysed, that it is nothing but a species of experience. To prove by experience the origin of the universe from mind is not more contrary to common speech than to prove the motion of the earth from the same principle. And a caviller might raise all the same objections to the Copernican system, which you have urged against my reasonings. Have you other earths, might he say, which you have seen to move? Have. . . .

Yes! cried PHILO, interrupting him, we have other earths. Is not the moon another earth, which we see to turn round its centre? Is not Venus another earth, where we observe the same phenomenon? Are not the revolutions of the sun also a confirmation, from analogy, of the same theory? All the planets, are they not earths, which revolve about the sun? Are not the satellites moons, which move round Jupiter and Saturn, and along with these primary planets, round the sun? These analogies and resemblances, with others, which I have not mentioned, are the sole proofs of the Copernican system: And to you it belongs to consider, whether you have any analogies of the same kind to support your theory.

In reality, Cleanthes, continued he, the modern system of astronomy is now so much received by all enquirers, and has become so essential a part even of our earliest education, that we are not commonly very scrupulous in examining the reasons upon which it is founded. It is now become a matter of mere curiosity to study the first writers on that subject, who had the full force of prejudice to encounter, and were obliged to turn their arguments on every side, in order to render them popular and convincing. But if we peruse Galileo's famous Dialogues concerning the system of the world, we shall find, that that great genius, one of the sublimest that ever existed, first bent all his endeavours to prove, that there was no foundation for the distinction commonly made between elementary and celestial substances. The schools, proceeding from the illusions of sense, had carried this distinction very far; and had established the latter substances to be ingenerable, incorruptible, unalterable, impassible; and had assigned all the opposite qualities to the former. But Galileo, beginning with the moon, proved its similarity in every particular to the earth; its convex figure, its natural darkness when not illuminated, its density, its distinction into solid and liquid, the variations of its phases, the mutual illuminations of the earth and moon, their mutual eclipses, the inequalities of the lunar surface, etc. After many instances of this kind, with regard to all the planets, men plainly saw, that these bodies became proper objects of experience; and that the similarity of their nature enabled us to extend the same arguments and phenomena from one to the other.

In this cautious proceeding of the astronomers, you may read your own condemnation, Cleanthes; or rather may see, that the subject in which you are engaged exceeds all human reason and enquiry. Can you pretend to show any such similarity between the fabric of a house, and the generation of a universe? Have you ever seen nature in any such situation as resembles the first arrangement of the elements? Have worlds ever been formed under your eye? and have you had leisure to observe the whole progress of the phenomenon, from the first appearance of order to its final consummation? If you have, then cite your experience, and deliver your theory.

Part III

How the most absurd argument, replied CLEANTHES, in the hands of a man of ingenuity and invention, may acquire an air of probability! Are you now aware, Philo, that it became necessary for Copernicus and his first disciples to prove the similarity of the terrestrial and celestial matter; because several philosophers, blinded by old systems, and supported by some sensible appearances, had denied this similarity? But that it is by no means necessary, that theists should prove the similarity of the works of nature to those of art; because this similarity is self-evident and undeniable? The same matter, a like form: What more is requisite to show an analogy between their causes, and to ascertain the origin of all things from a divine purpose and intention? Your objections, I must freely tell you, are no better than the abstruse cavils of those philosophers, who denied motion; and ought to be refuted in the same manner, by illustrations, examples, and instances, rather than by serious argument and philosophy.

Suppose, therefore, that an articulate voice were heard in the clouds, much louder and more melodious than any which human art could ever reach: Suppose, that this voice were extended in the same instant over all nations, and spoke to each nation in its own language and dialect: Suppose, that the words delivered not only contain a just sense and meaning, but convey some instruction altogether worthy of a benevolent Being, superior to mankind: Could you possibly hesitate a moment concerning the cause of this voice? And must you not instantly ascribe it to some design or purpose? Yet I cannot see but all the same objections (if they merit that appellation) which lie against the system of theism, may also be produced against this inference.

Might you not say, that all conclusions concerning fact were founded on experience: That when we hear an articulate voice in the dark, and thence infer a man, it is only the resemblance of the effects, which leads us to conclude that there is a like resemblance in the cause: But that this extraordinary voice, by its loudness, extent, and flexibility to all languages, bears so little analogy to any human voice, that we have no reason to suppose any analogy in their causes: And consequently, that a rational, wise, coherent speech proceeded, you knew not whence, from some accidental whistling of the winds, not from any divine reason or intelligence? You see clearly your own objections in these cavils; and I hope too, you see clearly, that they cannot possibly have more force in the one case than in the other.

But to bring the case still nearer the present one of the universe, I shall make two suppositions, which imply not any absurdity or impossibility. Suppose, that there is a natural, universal, invariable language, common to every individual of human race; and that books are natural productions, which perpetuate themselves in the same manner with animals and vegetables, by descent and propagation. Several expressions of our passions contain a universal language: All brute animals have a natural speech, which, however limited, is very intelligible to their own species. And as there are infinitely fewer parts and less contrivance in the finest composition of eloquence, than in the coarsest organized body, the propagation of an *Iliad* or *Aeneid* is an easier supposition than that of any plant or animal.

Suppose, therefore, that you enter into your library, thus peopled by natural volumes, containing the most refined reason and most exquisite beauty: Could you possibly open one of them, and doubt, that its original cause bore the strongest analogy to mind and intelligence? When it reasons and discourses; when it expostulates, argues, and enforces its views and topics; when it applies sometimes to the pure intellect, sometimes to the affections; when it collects, disposes, and adorns every consideration suited to the subject: could you persist in asserting, that all this, at the bottom, had really no meaning, and that the first formation of this volume in the loins of its original parent proceeded not from thought and design? Your obstinacy, I know, reaches not that degree of firmness: Even your sceptical play and wantonness would be abashed at so glaring an absurdity.

But if there be any difference, Philo, between this supposed case and the real one of the universe, it is all to the advantage of the latter. The anatomy of an animal affords many stronger instances of design than the perusal of Livy or Tacitus: And any objection which you start in the former case, by carrying me back to so unusual and extraordinary a scene as the first formation of worlds, the same objection has placed on the supposition of our vegetating library. Choose, then, your party, Philo, without ambiguity or evasion: Assert either that a rational volume is no proof of a rational cause, or admit of a similar cause to all the works of nature.

Let me here observe too, continued CLEANTHES, that this religious argument, instead of being weakened by that scepticism, so much affected by you, rather acquires force from it, and becomes more firm and undisputed. To exclude all argument or reasoning of every kind is either affectation or madness. The declared profession of every reasonable sceptic is only to reject abstruse, remote and refined arguments; to adhere to common sense and the plain instincts of nature; and to assent, wherever any reasons strike him with so full a force, that he cannot, without the greatest violence, prevent it. Now the arguments for natural religion are plainly of this kind; and nothing but the most perverse, obstinate metaphysics can reject them. Consider, anatomize the eye: Survey its structure and contrivance; and tell me, from your own feeling, if the idea of a contriver does not immediately flow in upon you with a force like that of sensation. The most obvious conclusion surely is in favour of design; and it requires time, reflection and study, to summon up those frivolous, though abstruse, objections, which can support infidelity. Who can behold the male and female of each species, the correspondence of their parts and instincts, their passions and whole course of life before and after generation, but must be sensible, that the propagation of the species is intended by nature? Millions and millions of such instances present themselves through every part of the universe; and no language can convey a more intelligible, irresistible meaning, than the curious adjustment of final causes. To what degree, therefore, of blind dogmatism must one have attained, to reject such natural and such convincing arguments?

Some beauties in writing we may meet with, which seem contrary to rules, and which gain the affections, and animate the imagination, in opposition to all the precepts of criticism, and to the authroity of the established masters of art. And if the argument for theism be, as you pretend, contradictory to the principles of logic; its universal, its irresistible influence proves clearly, that there may be arguments of a like irregular nature. Whatever cavils may be urged; an orderly world, as well as a coherent, articulate speech, will still be received as an incontestable proof of design and intention.

It sometimes happens, I own, that the religious arguments have not their due influence on an ignorant savage and barbarian; not because they are obscure and difficult, but because he never asks himself any question with regard to them. Whence arises the curious structure of an animal? From the copulation of its parents. And these whence? From *their* parents. A few removes set the objects at such a distance, that to him they are lost in darkness and confusion; nor is he actuated by any curiosity to trace them farther. But this is neither dogmatism nor scepticism, but stupidity; a state of mind very different from your sifting, inquisitve disposition, my ingenious friend. You can trace causes from effects: You can compare the most distant and remote objects: And your greatest errors proceed not from barrenness of thought and invention, but from too luxuriant a fertility, which suppresses your natural good sense, by a profusion of unnecessary scruples and objections.

Here I could observe, Hermippus, that Philo was a little embarrassed and confounded: But while he hesitated in delivering an answer, luckily for him, DEMEA broke in upon the discourse, and saved his countenance.

Your instance, Cleanthes, said he, drawn from books and language, being familiar, has, I confess, so much more force on that account; but is there not some danger too in this very circumstance, and may it not render us presumptuous, by making us imagine we comprehend the Deity, and have some adequate idea of his nature and attributes? When I read a volume, I enter into the mind and intention of the author: I become him, in a manner, for the instant; and have an immediate feeling and conception of those ideas, which revolved in his imagination, while employed in that composition. But so near an approach we never surely can make to the Deity. His ways are not our ways. His attributes are perfect, but incomprehensible. And this volume of nature contains a great inexplicable riddle, more than any intelligible discourse or reasoning.

The ancient Platonists, you know, were the most religious and devout of all the pagan philosophers: Yet many of them, particularly Plotinus, expressly declare that intellect or understanding is not to be ascribed to the Deity, and that our most perfect worship of him consists, not in acts of veneration, reverence, gratitude or love; but in a certain mysterious self-annihilation or total extinction of all our faculties. These ideas are, perhaps, too far stretched; but still it must be acknowledged, that, by representing the Deity as so intelligible, and comprehensible, and so similar to a human mind, we are guilty of the grossest and most narrow partiality, and make ourselves the model of the whole universe.

All the *sentiments* of the human mind, gratitude, resentment, love, friendship, approbation, blame, pity, emulation, envy, have a plain reference to the state and situation of man, and are calculated for preserving the existence, and promoting the activity of such a being in such circumstances. It seems therefore unreasonable to transfer such sentiments to a supreme existence, or to suppose him actuated by them; and the phenomena, besides, of the universe will not support us in such a theory. All our *ideas,* derived from the senses, are confessedly false and illusive; and cannot, therefore, be supposed to have place in a supreme intelligence: And as the ideas of internal sentiment, added to those of the external senses, compose the whole furniture of human understanding, we may conclude, that none of the *materials* of thought are in any respect similar in the human and in the divine intelligence. Now, as to the *manner* of thinking; how can we make any comparison between them, or suppose them any wise resembling? Our thought is fluctuating, uncertain, fleeting, successive, and compounded; and were we to remove these circumstances, we absolutely annihilate its essence, and it would, in such a case, be an abuse of terms to apply to it the name of thought or reason. At least, if it appear more pious and respectful (as it really is) still to retain these terms, when we mention the supreme Being, we ought to acknowledge, that their meaning, in that case, is totally incomprehensible; and that the infirmities of our nature do not permit us to reach any ideas, which in the least correspond to the ineffable sublimity of the divine attributes.

Part IV

It seems strange to me, said CLEANTHES, that you, Demea, who are so sincere in the cause of religion, should still maintain the mysterious, incomprehensible nature of the Deity, and should insist so strenuously, that he has no manner of likeness or resemblance to human creatures. The Deity, I can readily allow, possesses many powers and attributes, of which we can have no comprehension: But if our ideas, so far as they go, be not just and adequate, and correspondent to his real nature, I know not what there is in this subject worth insisting on. Is the name, without any meaning, of such mighty importance? Or how do you mystics, who maintain the absolute incomprehensibility of the Deity, differ from sceptics or atheists, who assert, that the first cause of All is unknown and unintelligible? Their temerity must be very great, if, after rejecting the production by a mind; I mean, a mind resembling the human (for I know of no other), they pretend to assign, with certainty, any other specific, intelligible cause: And their conscience must be very scrupulous indeed, if they refuse to call the universal, unknown cause a God or Deity; and to bestow on him as many sublime eulogies and unmeaning epithets, as you shall please to require of them.

Who could imagine, replied DEMEA, that Cleanthes, the calm, philosophical Cleanthes, would attempt to refute his antagonists, by affixing a nick-name to them; and like the common bigots and inquisitors of the age, have recourse to invective and declamation, instead of reasoning? Or does he not perceive, that these topics are easily retorted, and that *anthropomorphite* is an appellation as invidious, and implies as dangerous consequences, as the epithet of *mystic,* with which he has honoured us? In reality, Cleanthes, consider what it is you assert, when you represent the Deity as similar to a human mind and understanding. What is the soul of man? A composition of various faculties, passions, sentiments, ideas; united, indeed, into one self or person, but still distinct from each other. When it reasons, the ideas, which are the parts of its discourse, arrange themselves in a certain form or order; which is not preserved entire for a moment, but immediately gives place to another arrangement. New opinions, new passions, new affections, new feelings arise, which continually diversify the mental scene, and produce in it the greatest variety, and most rapid succession imaginable. How is this compatible with that perfect immutability and simplicity, which all true theists ascribe to the Deity? By the same act, say they, he sees past, present, and future: His love and his hatred, his mercy and his justice are one individual operation: He is entire in every point of space; and complete in every instant of duration. No succession, no change, no acquisition, no diminution. What he is implies not in it any shadow of distinction or diversity. And what he is, this moment, he ever has been, and ever will be, without any new judgment, sentiment, or operation. He stands fixed in one simple, perfect state; nor can you ever say, with any propriety, that this act of his is different from that other, or that this judgment or idea has been lately formed, and will give place, by succession, to any different judgment or idea.

I can readily allow, said CLEANTHES, that those who maintain the perfect simplicity of the supreme Being, to the extent in which you have explained it, are complete *mystics,* and chargeable with all the consequences which I have drawn from their opinion. They are, in a word, atheists, without knowing it. For though it be allowed, that the Deity possesses attributes, of which we have no comprehension; yet ought we never to ascribe to him any attributes, which are absolutely incompatible with that intelligent nature, essential to him. A mind, whose acts and sentiments and ideas are not distinct and successive; one, that is wholly simple, and totally immutable; is a mind which has no thought, no reason, no will, no sentiment, no love, no hatred; or in a word, is no mind at all. It is an abuse of terms to give it that appellation; and we may as well speak of limited extension without figure, or of number without composition.

Pray consider, said PHILO, whom you are at present inveighing against. You are honouring with the appellation of atheist all the sound, orthodox divines almost, who have treated of this subject; and you will, at last, be, yourself, found, according to your reckoning, the only sound theist in the world. But if idolaters be atheists, as, I think, may justly be asserted, and Christian theologians the same; what becomes of the argument, so much celebrated, derived from the universal consent of mankind?

But because I know you are not much swayed by names and authorities, I shall endeavour to show you, a little more distinctly, the inconveniences of that anthropomorphism, which you have embraced; and shall prove, that there is no ground to suppose a plan of the world to be formed in the divine mind, consisting of distinct ideas, differently arranged; in the same manner as an architect forms in his head the plan of a house which he intends to execute.

It is not easy, I own, to see, what is gained by this supposition, whether we judge of the matter by *reason* or by *experience.* We are still obliged to mount higher, in order to find the cause of this cause, which you had assigned as satisfactory and conclusive.

If *reason* (I mean abstract reason, derived from enquiries *a priori*) be not alike mute with regard to all questions concerning cause and effect; this sentence at least it will venture to pronounce, That a mental world or universe of ideas requires a cause as much as does a material world or universe of objects; and if similar in its arrangement must require a similar cause. For what is there in this subject, which should occasion a different conclusion or inference? In an abstract view, they are entirely alike; and no difficulty attends the one supposition, which is not common to both of them.

Again, when we will needs force *experience* to pronounce some sentence, even on these subjects, which lie beyond her sphere; neither can she perceive any material difference in this particular, between these two kinds of worlds, but finds them to be governed by similar principles, and to depend upon an equal variety of causes in their operations. We have specimens in miniature of both of them. Our own mind resembles the one: A vegetable or animal body the other. Let experience, therefore, judge from these samples. Nothing seems more delicate with regard to its causes than thought; and as these causes never operate in two persons after the same manner, so we never find two persons, who think exactly alike. Nor indeed does the same person think exactly alike at any two different periods of time. A difference of age, of the disposition of his body, of weather, of food, of company, of books, of passions; any of these particulars or others more minute, are sufficient to alter the curious machinery of thought, and communicate to it very different movements and operations. As far as we can judge, vegetables and animal bodies are not more delicate in their motions, nor depend upon a greater variety or more curious adjustment of springs and principles.

How therefore shall we satisfy ourselves concerning the cause of that Being, whom you suppose the Author of nature, or, according to your system of anthropomorphism, the ideal world, into which you trace the material? Have we not the same reason to trace that ideal world into another ideal world, or new intelligent principle? But if we stop, and go no farther; why go so far? Why not stop at the material world? How can we satisfy ourselves without going on *in infinitum?* And after all, what satisfaction is there in that infinite progression? Let us remember the story of the Indian philosopher and his elephant. It was never more applicable than to the present subject. If the material world rests upon a similar ideal world, this ideal world must rest upon some other; and so on, without end. It were better, therefore, never to look beyond the present material world. By supposing it to contain the principle of its order within itself, we really assert it to be God; and the sooner we arrive at that divine Being so much the better. When you go one step beyond the mundane system, you only excite an inquisitive humour, which it is impossible ever to satisfy.

To say, that the different ideas, which compose the reason of the supreme Being, fall into order, of themselves, and by their own nature, is really to talk without any precise meaning. If it has a meaning, I would fain know, why it is not as good sense to say, that the parts of their material world fall into order, of themselves, and by their own nature? Can the one opinion be intelligible, while the other is not so?

We have, indeed, experience of ideas, which fall into order, of themselves, and without any *known* cause: But, I am sure, we have a much larger experience of matter, which does the same; as in all instances of generation and vegetation, where the accurate analysis of the cause exceeds all human comprehension. We have also experience of particular systems of thought and of matter, which have no order; of the first, in madness, of the second, in corruption. Why then should we think, that order is more essential to one than the other? And if it requires a cause in both, what do we gain by your system, in tracing the universe of objects into a similar universe of ideas? The first step, which we make, leads us on for ever. It were, therefore, wise in us, to limit all our enquiries to the present world, without looking farther. No satisfaction can ever be attained by these speculations, which so far exceed the narrow bounds of human understanding.

It was usual with the Peripatetics, you know, Cleanthes, when the cause of any phenomenon was demanded, to have recourse to their *faculties* or *occult qualities,* and to say, for instance, that bread nourished by its nutritive faculty, and senna purged by its purgative: But it has been discovered, that this subterfuge was nothing but the disguise of ignorance; and that these philosophers, though less ingenuous, really said the same thing with the sceptics or the vulgar, who fairly confessed, that they knew not the cause of these phenomena. In like manner, when it is asked, what cause producers order in the ideas of the supreme Being, can any other reason be assigned by you, anthropomorphites, than that it is a *rational* faculty, and that such is the nature of the Deity? But why a similar answer will not be equally satisfactory in accounting for the order of the world, without having recourse to any such intelligent Creator as you insist on, may be difficult to determine. It is only to say, that *such* is the nature of material objects, and that they are all originally possessed of a *faculty* of order and proportion. These are only more learned and elaborate ways of confessing our ignorance; nor has the one hypothesis any real advantage above the other, except in its greater conformity to vulgar prejudices.

You have displayed this argument with great emphasis, replied CLEANTHES: You seem not sensible, how easy it is to answer it. Even in common life, if I assign a cause for any event; is it any objection, Philo, that I cannot assign the cause of that cause, and answer every new question, which may incessantly be started? And what philosophers could possibly submit to so rigid a rule? philosophers, who confess ultimate causes to be totally unknown, and are sensible, that the most refined principles, into which they trace the phenomena, are still to them as inexplicable as these phenomena themselves are to the vulgar. The order and arrangement of nature, the curious adjustment of final causes, the plain use and intention of every part and organ; all these bespeak in the clearest language an intelligent cause or Author. The heavens and the earth join in the same testimony: The whole chorus of nature raises one hymn to the praises of its Creator: You alone, or almost alone, disturb this general harmony. You start abstruse doubts, cavils, and objections: You ask me, what is the cause of this cause? I know not; I care not; that concerns not me. I have found a Deity; and here I stop my enquiry. Let those go farther, who are wiser or more enterprising.

I pretend to be neither, replied PHILO: And for that very reason, I should never perhaps have attempted to go so far; especially when I am sensible, that I must at last be contented to sit down with the same answer, which, without farther trouble, might have satisfied me from the beginning. If I am still to remain in utter ignorance of causes, and can absolutely give an explication of nothing, I shall never esteem it any advantage to shove off for a moment a difficulty, which, you acknowledge, must immediately, in its full force, recur upon me. Naturalists indeed very justly explain particular effects by more general causes; though these general causes themselves should remain in the end totally inexplicable: But they never surely thought it satisfactory to explain a particular effect by a particular cause, which was no more to be accounted for than the effect itself. An ideal system, arranged of itself, without a precedent design, is not a whit more explicable than a material one, which attains its order in a like manner; nor is there any more difficulty in the latter supposition than in the former.

Part V

But to show you still more inconveniences, continued PHILO, in your anthropomorphism; please to take a new survey of your principles. *Like effects prove like causes.* This is the experimental argument; and this, you say too, is the sole theological argument. Now it is certain, that the liker the effects are, which are seen, and the liker the causes, which are inferred, the stronger is the argument. Every departure on either side diminishes the probability, and renders the experiment less conclusive. You cannot doubt of this principle: Neither ought you to reject its consequences.

All the new discoveries in astronomy, which prove the immense grandeur and magnificence of the works of nature, are so many additional arguments for a Deity, according to the true system of theism: But according to your hypothesis of experimental theism, they become so many objections, by removing the effect still farther from all resemblance to the effects of human art and contrivance. For if Lucretius,[3] even following the old system of the world, could exclaim,

> Who can rule the sum, who hold in his hand with controlling force the strong reins, of the immeasurable deep? who can at once make all the different heavens to roll and warm

> with ethereal fires all the fruitful earths, or be present in all places at all times?

If Tully[4] esteemed this reasoning so natural, as to put it into the mouth of his Epicurean.

> "For with what eyes of the mind could your Plato have beheld that workshop of such stupendous toil, in which he represents the world as having been put together and built by God? How was so vast an undertaking set about? What tools, what levers, what machines, what servants, were employed in so great a work? How came air, fire, water, and earth to obey and submit to the architect's will?"

If this argument, I say, had any force in former ages; how much greater must it have at present; when the bounds of nature are so infinitely enlarged, and such a magnificent scene is opened to us? It is still more unreasonable to form our idea of so unlimited a cause from our experience of the narrow productions of human design and invention.

The discoveries by microscopes, as they open a new universe in miniature, are still objections, according to you; arguments, according to me. The farther we push our researches of this kind, we are still led to infer the universal cause of All to be vastly different from mankind, or from any object of human experience and observation.

And what say you to the discoveries in anatomy, chemistry, botany? . . . These surely are no objections, replied CLEANTHES: They only discover new instances of art and contrivance. It is still the image of mind reflected on us from innumerable objects. Add, a mind *like the human,* said PHILO. I know of no other, replied CLEANTHES. And the liker the better, insisted PHILO. To be sure, said CLEANTHES.

Now, Cleanthes, said PHILO, with an air of alacrity and triumph, mark the consequences. *First,* By this method of reasoning, you renounce all claim to infinity in any of the attributes of the Deity. For as the cause ought only to be proportioned to the effect, and the effect, so far as it falls under our cognisance, is not infinite; what pretensions have we, upon your suppositions, to ascribe that attribute to the divine Being? You will still insist, that, by removing him so much from all similarity to human creatures, we give in to the most arbitrary hypothesis, and at the same time weaken all proofs of his existence.

Secondly, You have no reason, on your theory, for ascribing perfection to the Deity, even in his finite capacity; or for supposing him free from every error, mistake, or incoherence in his undertakings. There are many inexplicable difficulties in the works of nature, which, if we allow a perfect Author to be proved *a priori,* are easily solved, and become only seeming difficulties, from the narrow capacity of man, who cannot trace infinite relations. But according to your method of reasoning, these difficulties become all real; and perhaps will be insisted on, as new instances of likeness to human art and contrivance. At least, you must acknowledge, that it is impossible for us to tell, from our limited views, whether this system contains any great faults, or deserves any considerable praise, if compared to other possible, and even real systems. Could a peasant, if the *Aeneid* were read to him, pronounce that poem to be absolutely faultless, or even assign to it its proper rank among the productions of human wit; he, who had never seen any other production?

But were this world ever so perfect a production, it must still remain uncertain, whether all the excellencies of the work can justly be ascribed to the workman. If we survey a ship, what an exalted idea must we form of the ingenuity of the carpenter, who framed so complicated, useful, and beautiful a machine? And what surprise must we entertain, when we find him a stupid mechanic, who imitated others, and copied an art, which, through a long succession of ages, after multiplied trials, mistakes, corrections, deliberations, and controversies, had been gradually improving? Many worlds might have been botched and bungled, throughout an eternity, ere this system was struck out: Much labour lost: Many fruitless trials made: And a slow, but continued improvement carried on during infinite ages in the art of world-making. In such subjects, who can determine, where the truth; nay, who can conjecture where the probability, lies; amidst a great number of hypotheses which may be proposed, and a still greater number which may be imagined?

And what shadow of an argument, continued PHILO, can you produce, from your hypothesis, to prove the unity of the Deity? A great number of men join in building a house or ship, in rearing a city, in framing a commonwealth: Why may not several Deities combine in contriving and framing a world? This is only so much greater similarity to human affairs. By sharing the work among several, we may so much farther limit the attributes of each, and get rid of that extensive power and knowledge, which must be supposed in one Deity, and which, according to you, can only serve to weaken the proof of his existence. And if such foolish, such vicious creatures as man can yet often unite in framing and executing one plan; how much more those Deities or Demons, whom we may suppose several degrees more perfect?

To multiply causes, without necessity, is indeed contrary to true philosophy: But this principle applies not to the present case. Were one Deity antecedently proved by your theory, who were possessed of every attribute requisite to the production of the universe; it would be needless, I own (though not absurd) to suppose any other Deity existent. But while it is still a question, whether all these attributes are united in one subject, or dispersed among several independent Beings: By what phenomena in nature can we pretend to decide the controversy? Where we see a body raised in a scale, we are sure that there is in the opposite scale, however concealed from sight, some counterpoising weight equal to it: But it is still allowed to doubt, whether that weight be an aggregate of several distinct bodies, or one uniform united mass. And if the weight requisite very much exceeds any thing which we have ever seen conjoined in any single body, the former supposition becomes still more probable and natural. An intelligent Being of such vast power and capacity, as is necessary to produce the universe, or, to speak in the language of ancient philosophy, so prodigious an animal, exceeds all analogy, and even comprehension.

But farther, Cleanthes; men are mortal, and renew their species by generation; and this is common to all living creatures. The two great sexes of male and female, says Milton, animate the world. Why must this circumstance, so universal, so essential, be excluded from those numerous and limited Deities? Behold then the theogony of ancient times brought back upon us.

And why not become a perfect anthropomorphite? Why not assert the Deity or Deities to be corporeal, and to have eyes, a nose, mouth, ears, etc.? Epicurus maintained, that no man had ever seen reason but in a human figure; therefore the gods must have a human figure. And this argument, which is deservedly so much ridiculed by Cicero, becomes according to you, solid and philosophical.

In a word, Cleanthes, a man, who follows your hypothesis, is able, perhaps, to assert, or conjecture, that the universe, sometime, arose from something like design: But beyond that position he cannot ascertain one single circumstance, and is left afterwards to fix every point of his theology, by the utmost licence of fancy and hypothesis. This world, for aught he knows, is very faulty and imperfect, compared to a superior standard; and was only the first rude essay of some infant Deity, who afterwards abandoned it, ashamed of his lame performance; it is the work only of some dependent, inferior Deity; and is the object of derision to his superiors: it is the production of old age and dotage in some superannuated Deity; and ever since his death, has run on at adventures, from the first impulse and active force, which it received from him. . . . You justly give signs of horror, Demea, at these strange suppositions: But these, and a thousand more of the same kind, are Cleanthes' suppositions, not mine. From the moment the attributes of the Deity are supposed finite, all these have place. And I cannot, for my part, think, that so wild and unsettled a system of theology is, in any respect, preferable to none at all.

These suppositions I absolutely disown, cried CLEANTHES: They strike me, however, with no horror; especially, when proposed in that rambling way in which they drop from you. On the contrary, they give me pleasure, when I see, that, by the utmost indulgence of your imagination, you never get rid of the hypothesis of design in the universe; but are obliged, at every turn, to have recourse to it. To this concession I adhere steadily; and this I regard as a sufficient foundation for religion.

In Parts VI and VII (omitted here) Philo continues his attack on Cleanthes' position. In Part VI Philo argues that the hypothesis that the world is an animal, with the Deity as its soul, accounts as well for the evidence Cleanthes has cited as the view that an intelligent Deity created the world:

> . . . if we survey the universe, so far as it falls under our knowledge, it bears a great resemblance to an animal or organized body, and seems actuated with a like principle of life and notion. A continual circulation of matter in it produces no disorder: A continual waste in every part is incessantly repaired: The closest sympathy is perceived throughout the entire system: And each part or member, in performing its proper offices, operates both to its own preservation and to that of the whole. The world, therefore, I infer, is an animal, and the Deity is the Soul of the world, actuating it, and actuated by it.

In Part VII Philo pushes the idea that the world resembles animals—and now vegetables, too,—even further:

> If the universe bears a greater likeness to animal bodies and to vegetables, than to the works of human art, it is more probable that its cause resembles the cause of the former than of the latter, and its origin ought rather to be ascribed to generation or vegetation than to reason or design. Your conclusion, even according to your own principles, is therefore lame and defective.
>
> . . . The world, says [Cleanthes], resembles the works of human contrivance: Therefore its cause must also resemble that of the other . . . the operation of one very small part of nature, to wit man, upon another very small part, to wit that inanimate matter lying within his reach, is the rule by which Cleanthes judges of the origin of the whole; . . . there are other parts of the universe (besides the machines of human invention) which bear still a greater resemblance to the fabric of the world, and which therefore afford a better conjecture concerning the universal origin of this system. . . . The world plainly resembles more an animal or a vegetable, than it does a watch or a knitting loom. Its cause, therefore, it is more probable, resembles the cause of the former. The cause of the former is generation or vegetation. . . .

Demea wonders whether Philo can really make sense of this and can explain the operations of vegetation and generation that he is postulating as the cause of the world. Philo replies:

> As much, at least . . . as Cleanthes can explain the operations of reason. . . . These words *generation, reason,* mark only certain powers and energies in nature, whose effects are known, but whose essence is incomprehensible; and one of these principles, more than the other, has no privilege for being made a standard of the whole of nature.
>
> . . . When I enquired concerning the cause of that supreme reason and intelligence, into which [Cleanthes] resolves every thing; he told me, that the impossibility of satisfying such enquiries could never be admitted as an objection in any species of philosophy. *We must stop somewhere,* says he; *nor is it ever within the reach of human capacity to explain ultimate causes, or who the last connections of any objects. It is sufficient, if the steps, so far as we go, are supported*

> *by experience and observation.* Now that vegetation and generation, as well as reason, are experienced to be principles of order in nature, is undeniable. If I rest my system of cosmogony on the former, preferably to the latter, it is at my choice. The matter seems entirely arbitrary. . . .

All of this leaves Cleanthes exasperated, but unconvinced:

> I must confess, Philo, . . . that of all men living, the task which you have undertaken, of raising doubts and objections, suits you best, and seems, in a manner, natural and unavoidable to you. So great is your fertility of invention, that I am not ashamed to acknowledge myself unable, on a sudden, to solve regularly such out-of-the-way difficulties as you incessantly start upon me: Though I clearly see, in general, their fallacy and error . . . you must be sensible, that common sense and reason is entirely against you, and that such whimsies, as you have delivered, may puzzle, but never can convince us.

Part VIII

What you ascribe to the fertility of my invention, replied PHILO, is entirely owing to the nature of the subject. In subjects, adapted to the narrow compass of human reason, there is commonly but one determination, which carries probability or conviction with it; and to a man of sound judgment, all other suppositions, but that one, appear entirely absurd and chimerical. But in such questions as the present, a hundred contradictory views may preserve a kind of imperfect analogy; and invention has here full scope to exert itself. Without any great effort of thought, I believe that I could, in an instant, propose other systems of cosmogony, which would have some faint appearance of truth; though it is a thousand, a million to one, if either yours or any one of mine be the true system.

For instance; what if I should revive the old Epicurean hypothesis? This is commonly, and I believe, justly, esteemed the most absurd system, that has yet been proposed; yet, I know not, whether, with a few alterations, it might not be brought to bear a faint appearance of probability. Instead of supposing matter infinite, as Epicurus did; let us suppose it finite. A finite number of particles is only susceptible of finite transpositions: And it must happen, in an eternal duration, that every possible order or position must be tried an infinite number of times. This world, therefore, with all its events, even the most minute, has before been produced and destroyed, and will again be produced and destroyed, without any bounds and limitations. No one, who has a conception of the powers of infinite, in comparison of finite, will ever scruple this determination.

But this supposes, said DEMEA, that matter can acquire motion, without any voluntary agent or first mover.

And where is the difficulty, replied PHILO, of that supposition? Every event, before experience, is equally difficult and incomprehensible; and every event, after experience, is equally easy and intelligible. Motion, in many instances, from gravity, from elasticity, from electricity, begins in matter, without any known voluntary agent; and to suppose always, in these cases, an unknown voluntary agent, is mere hypothesis; and hypothesis attended with no advantages. The beginning of motion in matter itself is as conceivable *a priori* as its communication from the mind and intelligence.

Besides, why may not motion have been propagated by impulse through all eternity, and the same stock of it, or nearly the same, be still upheld in the universe? As much as is lost by the composition of motion, as much is gained by its resolution. And whatever the causes are, the fact is certain, that matter is, and always has been in continual agitation, as far as human experience or tradition reaches. There is not probably, at present, in the whole universe, one particle of matter at absolute rest.

And this very consideration too, continued PHILO, which we have stumbled on in the course of the argument, suggests a new hypothesis of cosmogony, that is not absolutely absurd and improbable. Is there a system, an order, an economy of things, by which matter can preserve that perpetual agitation, which seems essential to it, and yet maintain a constancy in the forms, which it produces? There certainly is such an economy: For this is actually the case with the present world. The continual motion of matter, therefore, in less than infinite transpositions, must produce this economy or order; and by its very nature, that order, when once established, supports itself, for many ages, if not to eternity. But wherever matter is so poised, arranged, and adjusted as to continue in perpetual motion, and yet preserve a constancy in the forms, its situation must, of necessity, have all the same appearance of art and contrivance which we observe at present. All the parts of each form must have a relation to each other, and to the whole: And the whole itself must have a relation to the other parts of the universe; to the element, in which the form subsists; to the materials, with which it repairs its waste and decay; and to every other form, which is hostile or friendly. A defect in any of these particulars destroys the form; and the matter, of which it is composed, is again set loose, and is thrown into irregular motions and fermentations, till it unite itself to some other regular form. If no such form be prepared to receive it, and if there be a great quantity of this corrupted matter in the universe, the universe itself is entirely disordered; whether it be the feeble embryo of a world in its first beginnings, that is thus destroyed, or the rotten carcass of one, languishing in old age and infirmity. In either case, a chaos ensues; till finite, though innumerable revolutions produce at last some forms, whose parts and organs are so adjusted as to support the forms amidst a continued succession of matter.

Suppose (for we shall endeavour to vary the expression), that matter were thrown into any position, by a blind, unguided force; it is evident that this first position must in all probability be the most confused and most disorderly imaginable, without any resemblance to those works of human contrivance, which, along with a symmetry of parts, discover an adjustment of means to ends and a tendency to self-preservation. If the actuating force cease after this operation, matter must remain for ever in disorder, and continue an immense chaos, without any proportion or activity. But suppose, that the actuating force, whatever it be, still continues in matter, this first position will immediately give place to a second, which will likewise in all probability be as disorderly as the first, and so on, through many successions of changes and revolutions. No particular order or position ever continues a moment unaltered. The original force, still remaining in activity, gives a perpetual restlessness to matter. Every possible situation is produced, and instantly destroyed. If a glimpse or dawn of order appears for a moment, it is instantly hurried away, and confounded, by that never-ceasing force, which actuates every part of matter.

Thus the universe goes on for many ages in a continued succession of chaos and disorder. But is it not possible that it may settle at last, so as not to lose its motion and active force (for that we have supposed inherent in it), yet so as to preserve an uniformity of appearance, amidst the continual motion and fluctuation of its parts? This we find to be the case with the universe at present. Every individual is perpetually changing, and every part of every individual, and yet the whole remains, in appearance, the same. May we not hope for such a position, or rather be assured of it, from the eternal revolutions of unguided matter, and may not this account for all the appearing wisdom and contrivance which is in the universe? Let us contemplate the subject a little, and we shall find, that this adjustment, if attained by matter, of a seeming stability in the forms, with a real and perpetual revolution or motion of parts, affords a plausible, if not a true solution of the difficulty.

It is in vain, therefore, to insist upon the uses of the parts in animals or vegetables, and their curious adjustment to each other. I would fain know how an animal could subsist, unless its parts were so adjusted? Do we not find, that it immediately perishes whenever this adjustment ceases, and that its matter corrupting tries some new form? It happens, indeed, that the parts of the world are so well adjusted, that some regular form immediately lays claim to this corrupted matter: And if it were not so, could the world subsist? Must it not dissolve as well as the animal, and pass through new positions and situations; till in a great, but finite succession, it fall at last into the present or some such order?

It is well, replied CLEANTHES, you told us, that this hypothesis was suggested on a sudden, in the course of the argument. Had you had leisure to examine it, you would soon have perceived the insuperable objections, to which it is exposed. No form, you say, can subsist, unless it possess those powers and organs, requisite for its subsistence: Some new order or economy must be tried, and so on, without intermission; till at last some order, which can support and maintain itself, is fallen upon. But according to this hypothesis, whence arise the many conveniences and advantages which men and all animals possess? Two eyes, two ears, are not absolutely necessary for the subsistence of the species. Human race might have been propagated and preserved, without horses, dogs, cows, sheep, and those innumerable fruits and products which serve to our satisfaction and enjoyment. If no camels had been created for the use of man in the sandy deserts of Africa and Arabia, would the world have been dissolved? If no loadstone had been framed to give that wonderful and useful direction to the needle, would human society and the human kind have been immediately extinguished? Though the maxims of nature be in general very frugal, yet instances of this kind are far from being rare; and any one of them is a sufficient proof of design, and of a benevolent design, which gave rise to the order and arrangement of the universe.

At least, you may safely infer, said PHILO, that the foregoing hypothesis is so far incomplete and imperfect; which I shall not scruple to allow. But can we ever reasonably expect greater success in any attempts of this nature? Or can we ever hope to erect a system of cosmogony, that will be liable to no exceptions, and will contain no circumstance repugnant to our limited and imperfect experience of the analogy of nature? Your theory itself cannot surely pretend to any such advantage; even though you have run into *anthropomorphism,* the better to preserve a conformity to common experience. Let us once more put it to trial. In all instances which we have ever seen, ideas are copied from real objects, and are ectypal, not archetypal, to express myself in learned terms: You reverse this order, and give thought the precedence. In all instances which we have ever seen, thought has no influence upon matter, except where that matter is so conjoined with it, as to have an equal reciprocal influence upon it. No animal can move immediately any thing but the members of its own body; and indeed, the equality of action and re-action seems to be an universal law of nature: But your theory implies a contradiction to this experience. These instances, with many more, which it were easy to collect (particularly the supposition of a mind or system of thought that is eternal, or in other words, an animal ingenerable and immortal), these instances, I say, may teach, all of us, sobriety in condemning each other, and let us see, that as no system of this kind ought ever to be received from a slight analogy, so neither ought any to be rejected on account of a small incongruity. For that is an inconvenience from which we can justly pronounce no one to be exempted.

All religious systems, it is confessed, are subject to great and insuperable difficulties. Each disputant triumphs in his turn; while he carries on an offensive war, and exposes the absurdities, barbarities, and pernicious tenets of his antagonist. But all of them, on the whole, prepare a complete triumph for the sceptic; who tells them, that no system ought ever to be embraced with regard to such subjects: For this plain reason, that no absurdity ought ever to be assented to with regard to any subject. A total suspense of judgment is here our only reasonable resource. And if every attack, as is commonly observed, and no defence, among theologians, is successful; how complete must be *his* victory, who remains always, with all mankind,[5] on the offensive, and has himself no fixed station or abiding city, which he is ever, on any occasion, obliged to defend?

Part IX

But if so many difficulties attend the argument *a posteriori,* said DEMEA; had we not better adhere to that simple and sublime argument *a priori,* which, by offering to us infallible demonstration, cuts off at once all doubt and difficulty? By this argument, too, we may prove the infinity of the divine attributes, which, I am afraid, can never be ascertained with certainty from any other topic. For how can an effect, which either is finite, or, for aught we know, may be so; how can such an effect, I say, prove an infinite cause? The unity too of the divine nature, it is very difficult, if not absolutely impossible, to deduce merely from contemplating the works of nature; nor will the uniformity alone of the plan, even were it allowed, give us any assurance of that attribute. Whereas the argument *a priori*. . . .

You seem to reason, Demea, interposed CLEANTHES, as if those advantages and conveniences in the abstract argument were full proofs of its solidity. But it is first proper, in my opinion, to determine what argument of this nature you choose to insist on; and we shall afterwards, from itself, better than from its *useful* consequences, endeavour to determine what value we ought to put upon it.

The argument, replied DEMEA, which I would insist on is the common one. Whatever exists must have a cause or reason of its existence; it being absolutely impossible for any thing to produce itself, or be the cause of its own existence. In mounting up, therefore, from effects to causes, we must either go on in tracing an infinite succession, without any ultimate cause at all, or must at last have recourse to some ultimate cause, that is *necessarily* existent: Now that the first supposition is absurd may be thus proved. In the infinite chain or succession of causes and effects, each single effect is determined to exist by the power and efficacy of that cause which immediately preceded; but the whole eternal chain or succession, taken together, is not determined or caused by any thing: And yet it is evident that it requires a cause or reason, as much as any particular object, which begins to exist in time. The question is still reasonable, why this particular succession of causes existed from eternity, and not any other succession, or no succession at all. If there be no necessarily existent Being, any supposition, which can be formed, is equally possible; nor is there any more absurdity in nothing's having existed from eternity, than there is in that succession of causes, which constitutes the universe. What was it, then, which determined something to exist rather than nothing, and bestowed being on a particular possibility, exclusive of the rest? *External causes,* there are supposed to be none. *Chance* is a word without a meaning. Was it *nothing?* But that can never produce any thing. We must, therefore, have recourse to a necessarily existent Being, who carries the reason of his existence in himself; and who cannot be supposed not to exist without an express contradiction. There is consequently such a Being, that is, there is a Deity.

I shall not leave it to Philo, said CLEANTHES (though I know that the starting objections is his chief delight), to point out the weakness of this metaphysical reasoning. It seems to me so obviously ill-grounded, and at the same time of so little consequence to the cause of true piety and religion, that I shall myself venture to show the fallacy of it.

I shall begin with observing, that there is an evident absurdity in pretending to demonstrate a matter of fact, or to prove it by any arguments *a priori*. Nothing is demonstratable, unless the contrary implies a contradiction. Nothing, that is distinctly conceivable, implies a contradiction. Whatever we conceive as existent, we can also conceive as non-existent. There is no Being, therefore, whose non-existence implies a contradiction. Consequently, there is no Being, whose existence is demonstrable. I propose this argument as entirely decisive, and am willing to rest the whole controversy upon it.

It is pretended that the Deity is a necessarily existent Being; and this necessity of his existence is attempted to be explained by asserting, that, if we knew his whole essence or nature, we should perceive it to be as impossible for him not to exist as for twice two not to be four. But it is evident, that this can never happen, while our faculties remain the same as at present. It will still be possible for us, at any time, to conceive the non-existence of what we formerly conceived to exist; nor can the mind ever lie under a necessity of supposing any object to remain always in being; in the same manner as we lie under a necessity of always conceiving twice two to be four. The words, therefore, *necessary existence,* have no meaning; or, which is the same thing, none that is consistent.

But farther; why may not the material universe be the necessarily existent Being, according to this pretended explication of necessity? We dare not affirm that we know all the qualities of matter; and for aught we can determine, it may contain some qualities, which, were they known, would make its non-existence appear as great a contradiction as that twice two is five. I find only one argument employed to prove, that the material world is not the necessarily existent Being; and this argument is derived from the contingency both of the matter and the form of the world. "Any particle of matter", it is said,[6] "may be *conceived* to be annihilated; and any form may be *conceived* to be altered. Such an annihilation or alteration, therefore, is not impossible." But it seems a great partiality not to perceive, that the same argument extends equally to the Deity, so far as we have any conception of him; and that the mind can at least imagine him to be non-existent, or his attributes to be altered. It must be some unknown, inconceivable qualities, which can make his non-existence appear impossible, or his attributes unalterable: And no reason can be assigned, why these qualities may not belong to matter. As they are altogether unknown and inconceivable, they can never be proved incompatible with it.

Add to this, that in tracing an eternal succession of objects, it seems absurd to inquire for a general cause or first Author. How can any thing, that exists from eternity, have a cause, since that relation implies a priority in time and a beginning of existence?

In such a chain too, or succession of objects, each part is caused by that which preceded it, and causes that which succeeds it. Where then is the difficulty? But the whole, you say, wants a cause. I answer, that the uniting of these parts into a whole, like the uniting of several distinct counties into one kingdom, or several distinct members into one body, is performed merely by an arbitrary act of the mind, and has no influence on the nature of things. Did I show you the particular causes of each individual in a collection of twenty particles of matter, I should think it very unreasonable, should you afterwards ask me, what was the cause of the whole twenty. This is sufficiently explained in explaining the cause of the parts.

Though the reasonings, which you have urged, Cleanthes, may well excuse me, said PHILO, from starting any farther difficulties; yet I cannot forbear insisting still upon another topic. It is observed by arithmeticians, that the products of 9 compose always either 9 or some lesser product of 9; if you add together all the characters, of which any of the former products is composed. Thus, of 18, 27, 36, which are products of 9, you make 9 by adding 1 to 8, 2 to 7, 3 to 6. Thus 369 is a product also of 9; and if you add 3, 6, and 9, you make 18, a lesser product of 9.[7] To a superficial observer, so wonderful a regularity may be admired as the effect either of chance or design; but a skilful algebraist immediately concludes it to be the work of necessity and demonstrates, that it must for ever result from the nature of these numbers. Is it not probable, I ask, that the whole economy of the universe is conducted by a like necessity, though no human algebra can furnish a key which solves the difficulty? And instead of admiring the order of natural beings, may it not happen, that, could we penetrate into the intimate nature of bodies, we should clearly see why it was absolutely impossible, they could ever admit of any other disposition? So dangerous is it to introduce this idea of necessity into the present question! And so naturally does it afford an inference directly opposite to the religious hypothesis!

But dropping all these abstractions, continued PHILO; and confining ourselves to more familiar topics; I shall venture to add an observation, that the argument *a priori* has seldom been found very convincing, except to people of a metaphysical head, who have accustomed themselves to abstract reasoning, and who finding from mathematics, that the understanding frequently leads to truth, through obscurity, and contrary to first appearances, have transferred the same habit of thinking to subjects where it ought not to have place. Other people, even of good sense and the best inclined to religion, feel always some deficiency in such arguments, though they are not perhaps able to explain distinctly where it lies. A certain proof, that men ever did, and ever will, derive their religion from other sources than from this species of reasoning.

Part X

It is my opinion, I own, replied DEMEA, that each man feels, in a manner, the truth of religion within his own breast; and from a consciousness of his imbecility and misery, rather than from any reasoning, is led to seek protection from that Being, on whom he and all nature is dependent. So anxious or so tedious are even the best scenes of life, that futurity is still the object of all our hopes and fears. We incessantly look forward, and endeavour, by prayers, adoration, and sacrifice, to appease those unknown powers, whom we find, by experience, so able to afflict and oppress us. Wretched creatures that we are! What resource for us amidst the innumerable ills of life, did not religion suggest some methods of atonement, and appease those terrors, with which we are incessantly agitated and tormented?

I am indeed persuaded, said PHILO, that the best and indeed the only method of bringing every one to a due sense of religion is by just representations of the misery and wickedness of men. And for that purpose a talent of eloquence and strong imagery is more requisite than that of reasoning and argument. For is it necessary to prove, what every one feels within himself? It is only necessary to make us feel it, if possible, more intimately and sensibly.

The people, indeed, replied DEMEA, are sufficiently convinced of this great and melancholy truth. The miseries of life, the unhappiness of man, the general corruptions of our nature, the unsatisfactory enjoyment of pleasures, riches, honours; these phrases have become almost proverbial in all languages. And who can doubt of what all men declare from their own immediate feeling and experience?

In this point, said PHILO, the learned are perfectly agreed with the vulgar; and in all letters, *sacred* and *profane,* the topic of human misery has been insisted on with the most pathetic eloquence that sorrow and melancholy could inspire. The poets, who speak from sentiment, without a system, and whose testimony has therefore the more authority, abound in images of this nature. From Homer down to Dr. Young, the whole inspired tribe have ever been sensible, that no other representation of things would suit the feeling and observation of each individual.

As to authorities, replied DEMEA, you need not seek them. Look round this library of Cleanthes. I shall venture to affirm, that, except authors of particular sciences, such as chemistry or botany, who have no occasion to treat of human life, there scarce is one of those innumerable writers, from whom the sense of human misery has not, in some passage or other, extorted a complaint and confession of it. At least, the chance is entirely on that side; and no one author has ever, so far as I can recollect, been so extravagant as to deny it.

There you must excuse me, said PHILO: Leibnitz has denied it; and is perhaps the first,[8] who ventured upon so bold and paradoxical an opinion; at least, the first, who made it essential to his philosophical system.

And by being the first, replied DEMEA, might he not have been sensible of his error? For is this a subject in which philosophers can propose to make discoveries, especially in so late an age? And can any man hope by a simple denial (for the subject scarcely admits of reasoning) to bear down the united testimony of mankind, founded on sense and consciousness?

And why should man, added he, pretend to an exemption from the lot of all other animals? The whole earth, believe me, Philo, is cursed and polluted. A perpetual war is kindled amongst all living creatures. Necessity, hunger, want, stimulate the strong and courageous: Fear, anxiety, terror, agitate the weak and infirm. The first entrance into life gives anguish to the new-born infant and to its wretched parent: Weakness, impotence, distress, attend each stage of that life: And it is at last finished in agony and horror.

Observe too, says PHILO, the curious artifices of nature, in order to embitter the life of every living being. The stronger prey upon the weaker, and keep them in perpetual terror and anxiety. The weaker too, in their turn, often prey upon the stronger, and vex and molest them without relaxation. Consider that innumerable race of insects, which either are bred on the body of each animal, or flying about infix their stings in him. These insects have others still less than themselves, which torment them. And thus on each hand, before and behind, above and below, every animal is surrounded with enemies, which incessantly seek his misery and destruction.

Man alone, said DEMEA, seems to be, in part, an exception to this rule. For by combination in society, he can easily master lions, tigers, and bears, whose greater strength and agility naturally enable them to prey upon him.

On the contrary, it is here chiefly, cried PHILO, that the uniform and equal maxims of nature are most apparent. Man, it is true, can, by combination, surmount all his *real* enemies, and become master of the whole animal creation: But does he not immediately raise up to himself *imaginary* enemies, the demons of his fancy, who haunt him with superstitious terrors, and blast every enjoyment of life? His pleasure, as he imagines, becomes, in their eyes, a crime: His food and repose give them umbrage and offence: His very sleep and dreams furnish new materials to anxious fear: And even death, his refuge from every other ill, presents only the dread of endless and innumerable woes. Nor does the wolf molest more the timid flock, than superstition does the anxious breast of wretched mortals.

Besides, consider, Demea; this very society, by which we surmount those wild beasts, our natural enemies; what new enemies does it not raise to us? What woe and misery does it not occasion? Man is the greatest enemy of man. Oppression, injustice, contempt, contumely, violence, sedition, war, calumny, treachery, fraud; by these they mutually torment each other: And they would soon dissolve that society which they had formed, were it not for the dread of still greater ills, which must attend their separation.

But though these external insults, said DEMEA, from animals, from men, from all the elements, which assault us, form a frightful catalogue of woes, they are nothing in comparison of those, which arise within ourselves, from the distempered condition of our mind and body. How many lie under the lingering torment of diseases? Hear the pathetic enumeration of the great poet.

Intestine stone and ulcer, colic-pangs,
Daemoniac frenzy, moping melancholy,
And moon-struck madness, pining atrophy,
Marasmus and wide-wasting pestilence.
Dire was the tossing, deep the groans: DESPAIR
Tended the sick, busiest from couch to couch.
And over them triumptant DEATH his dart
Shook, but delay'd to strike, tho' oft invok'd
With vows, as their chief good and final hope.[9]

The disorders of the mind, continued DEMEA, though more secret, are not perhaps less dismal and vexatious. Remorse, shame, anguish, rage, disappointment, anxiety, fear, dejection, despair; who has ever passed through life without cruel inroads from these tormentors? How many have scarcely ever felt any better sensations? Labour and poverty, so abhorred by every one, are the certain lot of the far greater number: And those few privileged persons, who enjoy ease and opulence, never reach contentment or true felicity. All the goods of life united would not make a very happy man: But all the ills united would make a wretch indeed; and any one of them almost (and who can be free from every one), nay often the absence of one good (and who can possess all) is sufficient to render life ineligible.

Were a stranger to drop, on a sudden, into this world, I would show him, as a specimen of its ills, an hospital full of diseases, a prison crowded with malefactors and debtors, a field of battle strowed with carcases, a fleet floundering in the ocean, a nation languishing under tyranny, famine, or pestilence. To turn the gay side of life to him, and give him a notion of its pleasures; whither should I conduct him? to a ball, to an opera, to court? He might justly think, that I was only showing him a diversity of distress and sorrow.

There is no evading such striking instances, said PHILO, but by apologies, which still farther aggravate the charge. Why have all men, I ask, in all ages, complained incessantly of the miseries of life? . . . They have no just reason, says one: These complaints proceed only from their discontented, repining, anxious disposition. . . . And can there possibly, I reply, be a more certain foundation of misery, than such a wretched temper?

But if they were really as unhappy as they pretend, says my antagonist, why do they remain in life? . . .

Not satisfied with life, afraid of death.

This is the secret chain, say I, that holds us. We are terrified, not bribed to the continuance of our existence.

It is only a false delicacy, he may insist, which a few refined spirits indulge, and which has spread these complaints among the whole race of mankind. . . . And what is this delicacy, I ask, which you blame? Is it any thing but a greater sensibility to all the pleasures and pains of life? and if the man of a delicate, refined temper, by being so much more alive than the rest of the world, is only so much more unhappy; what judgment must we form in general of human life?

Let men remain at rest, says our adversary; and they will be easy. They are willing artificers of their own misery. . . . No! reply I; an anxious languor follows their repose: Disappointment, vexation, trouble, their activity and ambition.

I can observe something like what you mention in some others, replied CLEANTHES: But I confess, I feel little or nothing of it in myself; and hope that it is not so common as you represent it.

If you feel not human misery yourself, cried DEMEA, I congratulate you on so happy a singularity. Others, seemingly the most prosperous, have not been ashamed to vent their complaints in the most melancholy strains. Let us attend to the great, the fortunate Emperor, Charles V, when, tired with human grandeur, he resigned all his extensive dominions into the hands of his son. In the last harangue, which he made on that memorable occasion, he publicly avowed, *that the greatest prosperities which he had ever enjoyed, had been mixed with so many adversities, that he might truly say he had never enjoyed any satisfaction or contentment.* But did the retired life, in which he sought for shelter, afford him any greater happiness? If we may credit his son's account, his repentance commenced the very day of his resignation.

Cicero's fortune, from small beginnings, rose to the greatest lustre and renown; yet what pathetic complaints of the ills of life do his familiar letters, as well as philosophical discourses, contain? And suitably to his own experience, he introduces Cato, the great, the fortunate Cato, protesting in his old age, that, had he a new life in his offer, he would reject the present.

Ask yourself, ask any of your acquaintance, whether they would live over again the last ten or twenty years of their life. No! but the next twenty, they say, will be better:

> And from the dregs of life, hope to receive
> What the first sprightly running could not
> give.[10]

Thus at last they find (such is the greatness of human misery; it reconciles even contradictions) that they complain, at once, of the shortness of life, and of its vanity and sorrow.

And is it possible, Cleanthes, said PHILO, that after all these reflections, and infinitely more, which might be suggested, you can still perserve in your anthropomorphism, and assert the moral attributes of the Deity, his justice, benevolence, mercy, and rectitude, to be of the same nature with these virtues in human creatures? His power we allow infinite: Whatever he wills is executed: But neither man nor any other animal are happy: Therefore he does not will their happiness. His wisdom is infinite: He is never mistaken in choosing the means to any end: But the course of nature tends not to human or animal felicity: Therefore it is not established for that purpose. Through the whole compass of human knowledge, there are no inferences more certain and infallible than these. In what respect, then, do his benevolence and mercy resemble the benevolence and mercy of men?

Epicurus' old questions are yet unanswered. Is he willing to prevent evil, but not able? then is he impotent. Is he able, but not willing? then is he malevolent. Is he both able and willing? whence then is evil?

You ascribe, Cleanthes (and I believe justly) a purpose and intention to nature. But what, I beseech you, is the object of that curious artifice and machinery, which she has displayed in all animals? The preservation alone of individuals and propagation of the species. It seems enough for her purpose, if such a rank be barely upheld in the universe, without any care or concern for the happiness of the members that compose it. No resource for this purpose: No machinery, in order merely to give pleasure or ease: No fund of pure joy and contentment: No indulgence without some want or necessity accompanying it. At least, the few phenomena of this nature are overbalanced by opposite phenomena of still greater importance.

Our sense of music, harmony, and indeed beauty of all kinds, gives satisfaction, without being absolutely necessary to the preservation and propagation of the species. But what racking pains, on the other hand, arise from gouts, gravels, megrims, tooth-aches, rheumatisms; where the injury to the animal-machinery is either small or incurable? Mirth, laughter, play, frolic, seem gratuitous satisfactions which have no farther tendency: Spleen, melancholy, discontent, superstition, are pains of the same nature. How then does the divine benevolence display itself, in the sense of you anthropomorphites? None but we mystics, as you were pleased to call us, can account for this strange mixture of phenomena, by deriving it from attributes, infinitely perfect, but incomprehensible.

And have you at last, said CLEANTHES smiling, betrayed your intentions, Philo? Your long agreement with Demea did indeed a little surprise me; but I find you were all the while erecting a concealed battery against me. And I must confess, that you have now fallen upon a subject worthy of your noble spirit of opposition and controversy. If you can make out the present point, and prove mankind to be unhappy or corrupted, there is an end at once of all religion. For to what purpose establish the natural attributes of the Deity, while the moral are still doubtful and uncertain?

You take umbrage very easily, replied DEMEA, at opinions the most innocent, and the most generally received even amongst the religious and devout themselves: And nothing can be more surprising than to find a topic like this, concerning the wickedness and misery of man, charged with no less than atheism and profaneness. Have not all pious divines and preachers, who have indulged their rhetoric on so fertile a subject; have they not easily, I say, given a solution of any difficulties which may attend it? This world is but a point in comparison of the universe: This life but a moment in comparison of eternity. The present evil phenomena, therefore, are rectified in other regions, and in some future period of existence. And the eyes of men, being then opened to larger views of things, see the whole connection of general laws, and trace, with adoration, the benevolence and rectitude of the Deity, through all the mazes and intricacies of his providence.

No! replied CLEANTHES, No! These arbitrary suppositions can never be admitted, contrary to matter of fact, visible and uncontroverted. Whence can any cause be known but from its known effects? Whence can any hypothesis be proved but from the apparent phenomena? To establish one hypothesis upon another is building entirely in the air; and the utmost we ever attain, by these conjectures and fictions, is to ascertain the bare possibility of our opinion; but never can we, upon such terms, establish its reality.

The only method of supporting divine benevolence (and it is what I willingly embrace) is to deny absolutely the misery and wickedness of man. Your representations are exaggerated: Your melancholy views mostly fictitious: Your inferences contrary to fact and experience. Health is more common than sickness: Pleasure than pain: Happiness than misery. And for one vexation which we meet with, we attain, upon computation, a hundred enjoyments.

Admitting your position, replied PHILO, which yet is extremely doubtful, you must, at the same time, allow, that, if pain be less frequent than pleasure, it is infinitely more violent and durable. One hour of it is often able to outweigh a day, a week, a month of our common insipid enjoyments: And how many days, weeks, and months are passed by several in the most acute torments? Pleasure, scarcely in one instance, is ever able to reach ecstacy and rapture: And in no one instance can it continue for any time at its highest pitch and altitude. The spirits evaporate; the nerves relax; the fabric is disordered; and the enjoyment quickly degenerates into fatigue and uneasiness. But pain often, Good God, how often! rises to torture and agony; and the longer it continues, it becomes still more genuine agony and torture. Patience is exhausted; courage languishes; melancholy seizes us; and nothing terminates our misery but the removal of its cause, or another event, which is the sole cure of all evil, but which, from our natural folly, we regard with still greater horror and consternation.

But not to insist upon these topics, continued PHILO, though most obvious, certain, and important; I must use the freedom to admonish you, Cleanthes, that you have put this controversy upon a most dangerous issue, and are unawares introducing a total scepticism into the most essential articles of natural and revealed theology. What! no method of fixing a just foundation for religion, unless we allow the happiness of human life, and maintain a continued existence even in this world, with all our present pains, infirmities, vexations, and follies, to be eligible and desirable! But this is contrary to every one's feeling and experience: It is contrary to an authority so established as nothing can subvert: No decisive proofs can ever be produced against this authority; nor is it possible for you to compute, estimate, and compare all the pains and all the pleasures in the lives of all men and of all animals: And thus by your resting the whole system of religion on a point, which, from its very nature, must for ever be uncertain, you tacitly confess, that that system is equally uncertain.

But allowing you, what never will be believed; at least, what you never possibly can prove, that animal, or at least, human happiness, in this life, exceeds its misery; you have yet done nothing: For this is not, by any means, what we expect from infinite power, infinite wisdom, and infinite goodness. Why is there any misery at all in the world? Not by chance surely. From some cause then. Is it from the intention of the Deity? But he is perfectly benevolent. Is it contrary to his intention? But he is almighty. Nothing can shake the solidity of this reasoning, so short, so clear, so decisive; except we assert, that these subjects exceed all human capacity, and that our common measures of truth and falsehood are not applicable to them; a topic, which I have all along insisted on, but which you have, from the beginning, rejected with scorn and indignation.

But I will be contented to retire still from this intrenchment: For I deny that you can ever force me in it: I will allow, that pain or misery in man is *compatible* with infinite power and goodness in the Deity, even in your sense of these attributes: What are you advanced by all these concessions? A mere possible compatibility is not sufficient. You must *prove* these pure, unmixed, and uncontrollable attributes from the present mixed and confused phenomena, and from these alone. A hopeful undertaking! Were the phenomena ever so pure and unmixed, yet being finite, they would be insufficient for that purpose. How much more, where they are also so jarring and discordant?

Here, Cleanthes, I find myself at ease in my argument. Here I triumph. Formerly, when we argued concerning the natural attributes of intelligence and design, I needed all my sceptical and metaphysical subtilty to elude your grasp. In many views of the universe, and of its parts, particularly the latter, the beauty and fitness of final causes strike us with such irresistible force, that all objections appear (what I believe they really are) mere cavils and sophisms; nor can we then imagine how it was ever possible for us to repose any weight on them. But there is no view of human life, or of the condition of mankind, from which, without the greatest violence, we can infer the moral attributes, or learn that infinite benevolence, conjoined with infinite power and infinite wisdom, which we must discover by the eyes of faith alone. It is your turn now to tug the labouring oar, and to support your philosophical subtilties against the dictates of plain reason and experience.

Part XI

I scruple not to allow, said CLEANTHES, that I have been apt to suspect the frequent repetition of the word, *infinite*, which we meet with in all theological writers, to savour more of panegyric than of philosophy, and that any purposes of reasoning, and even of religion, would be better served, were we to rest contented with more accurate and more moderate expressions. The terms, *admirable, excellent, superlatively great, wise,* and *holy;* these sufficiently fill the imaginations of men; and any thing beyond, besides that it leads into absurdities, has no influence on the affections or sentiments. Thus, in the present subject, if we abandon all human analogy, as seems your intention, Demea, I am afraid we abandon all religion, and retain no conception of the great object of our adoration. If we preserve human analogy, we must for ever find it impossible to reconcile any mixture of evil in the universe with infinite attributes; much less, can we ever prove the latter from the former. But supposing the Author of nature to be finitely perfect, though far exceeding mankind; a satisfactory account may then be given of natural and moral evil, and every untoward phenomenon be explained and adjusted. A less evil may then be chosen, in order to avoid a greater: Inconveniences be submitted to, in order to reach a desirable end: And in a word, benevolence, regulated by wisdom, and limited by necessity, may produce just such a world as the present. You, Philo, who are so prompt at starting views, and reflections, and analogies; I would gladly hear, at length, without interruption, your opinion of this new theory; and if it deserve our attention, we may afterwards, at more leisure, reduce it into form.

My sentiments, replied PHILO, are not worth being made a mystery of; and therefore, without any ceremony, I shall deliver what occurs to me with regard to the present subject. It must, I think, be allowed, that, if a very limited intelligence, whom we shall suppose utterly unacquainted with the universe, were assured, that it were the production of a very good, wise, and powerful Being, however finite, he would, from his conjectures, form *beforehand* a different notion of it from what we find it to be by experience; nor would he ever imagine, merely from these attributes of the cause, of which he is informed, that the effect could be so full of vice and misery and disorder, as it appears in this life. Supposing now, that this person were brought into the world, still assured, that it was the workmanship of such a sublime and benevolent Being; he might, perhaps, be surprised at the disappointment; but would never retract his former belief, if founded on any very solid argument; since such a limited intelligence must be sensible of his own blindness and ignorance, and must allow, that there may be many solutions of those phenomena, which will for ever escape his comprehension. But supposing, which is the real case with regard to man, that this creature is not antecedently convinced of a supreme intelligence, benevolent, and powerful, but is left to gather such a belief from the appearances of things; this entirely alters the case, nor will he ever find any reason for such a conclusion. He may be fully convinced of the narrow limits of his understanding; but this will not help him in forming an inference concerning the goodness of superior powers, since he must form that inference from what he knows, not from what he is ignorant of. The more you exaggerate his weakness and ignorance, the more diffident you render him, and give him the greater suspicion, that such subjects are beyond the reach of his faculties. You are obliged, therefore, to reason with him merely from the known phenomena, and to drop every arbitrary supposition or conjecture.

Did I show you a house or palace, where there was not one apartment convenient or agreeable; where the windows, doors, fires, passages, stairs, and the whole economy of the building were the source of noise, confusion, fatigue, darkness, and the extremes of heat and cold; you would certainly blame the contrivance, without any farther examination. The architect would in vain display his subtilty, and prove to you, that if this door or that window were altered, greater ills would ensue. What he says, may be strictly true: The alteration of one particular, while the other parts of the building remain, may only augment the inconveniences. But still you would assert in general, that, if the architect had had skill and good intentions, he might have formed such a plan of the whole, and might have adjusted the parts in such a manner, as would have remedied all or most of these inconveniences. His ignorance, or even your own ignorance of such a plan, will never convince you of the impossibility of it. If you find many inconveniences and deformities in the building, you will always, without entering into any detail, condemn the architect.

In short, I repeat the question: Is the world considered in general, and as it appears to us in this life, different from what a man or such a limited being would, *beforehand*, expect from a very powerful, wise, and benevolent Deity? It must be strange prejudice to assert the contrary. And from thence I conclude, that, however consistent the world may be, allowing certain suppositions and conjectures, with the idea of such a Deity, it can never afford us an inference concerning his existence. The consistence is not absolutely denied, only the inference. Conjectures, especially where infinity is excluded from the divine attributes, may, perhaps, be sufficient to prove a consistence; but can never be foundations for any inference.

There seem to be *four* circumstances, on which depend all, or the greatest part of the ills, that molest sensible creatures; and it is not impossible but all these circumstances may be necessary and unavoidable. We know so little beyond common life, or even of common life, that, with regard to the economy of a universe, there is no conjecture, however wild, which may not be just; nor any one, however plausible, which may not be erroneous. All that belongs to human understanding, in this deep ignorance and obscurity, is to be sceptical, or at least cautious; and not to admit of any hypothesis, whatever; much less, of any which is supported by no appearance of probability. Now this I assert to be the case with regard to all the causes of evil, and the circumstances on which it depends. None of them appear to human reason, in the least degree, necessary or unavoidable; nor can we suppose them such, without the utmost licence of imagination.

The *first* circumstance which introduces evil, is that contrivance or economy of the animal creation, by which pains, as well as pleasures, are employed to excite all creatures to action, and make them vigilant in the great work of self-preservation. Now pleasure alone, in its various degrees, seems to human understanding sufficient for this purpose. All animals might be constantly in a state of enjoyment; but when urged by any of the necessities of nature, such as thirst, hunger, weariness; instead of pain, they might feel a diminution of pleasure, by which they might be prompted to seek that object, which is necessary to their subsistence. Men pursue pleasure as eagerly as they avoid pain; at least, might have been so constituted. It seems, therefore, plainly possible to carry on the business life without any pain. Why then is any animal ever rendered susceptible of such a sensation? If animals can be free from it an hour, they might enjoy a perpetual exemption from it; and it required as particular a contrivance of their organs to produce that feeling, as to endow them with sight, hearing, or any of the senses. Shall we conjecture, that such a contrivance was necessary, without any appearance of reason? And shall we build on that conjecture as on the most certain truth?

But a capacity of pain would not alone produce pain, were it not for the *second* circumstance, viz. the conducting of the world by general laws; and this seems nowise necessary to a very perfect Being. It is true; if every thing were conducted by particular volitions, the course of nature would be perpetually broken, and no man could employ his reason in the conduct of life. But might not other particular volitions remedy this inconvenience? In short, might not the Deity exterminate all ill, wherever it were to be found; and produce all good, without any preparation or long progress of causes and effects?

Besides, we must consider, that, according to the present economy of the world, the course of nature, though supposed exactly regular, yet to us appears not so, and many events are uncertain, and many disappoint our expectations. Health and sickness, calm and tempest, with an infinite number of other accidents, whose causes are unknown and variable, have a great influence both on the fortunes of particular persons and on the prosperity of public societies: And indeed all human life, in a manner, depends on such accidents. A Being, therefore, who knows the secret springs of the universe, might easily, by particular volitions, turn all these accidents to the good of mankind, and render the whole world happy, without discovering himself in any operation. A fleet, whose purposes were salutary to society, might always meet with a fair wind: Good princes enjoy sound health and long life: Persons born to power and authority, be framed with good tempers and virtuous dispositions. A few such events as these, regularly and wisely conducted, would change the face of the world; and yet would no more seem to disturb the course of nature or confound human conduct, than the present economy of things, where the causes are secret, and variable, and compounded. Some small touches, given to Caligula's brain in his infancy, might have converted him into a Trajan: One wave, a little higher than the rest, by burying Caesar and his fortune in the bottom of the ocean, might have restored liberty to a considerable part of mankind. There may, for aught we know, be good reasons, why providence interposes not in this manner; but they are unknown to us: And though the mere supposition, that such reasons exist, may be sufficient to *save* the conclusion concerning the divine attributes, yet surely it can never be sufficient to *establish* that conclusion.

If every thing in the universe be conducted by general laws, and if animals be rendered susceptible of pain, it scarcely seems possible but some ill must arise in the various shocks of matter, and the various concurrence and opposition of general laws: But this ill would be very rare, were it not for the *third* circumstance, which I proposed to mention, viz. the great frugality with which all powers and faculties are distributed to every particular being. So well adjusted are the organs and capacities of all animals, and so well fitted to their preservation, that, as far as history or tradition reaches, there appears not to be any single species which has yet been extinguished in the universe. Every animal has the requisite endowments; but these endowments are bestowed with so scrupulous an economy, that any considerable diminution must entirely destroy the creature. Wherever one power is increased, there is a proportional abatement in the others. Animals, which excel in swiftness, are commonly defective in force. Those, which possess both, are either imperfect in some of their senses, or are oppressed with the most craving wants. The human species, whose chief excellency is reason and sagacity, is of all others the most necessitous, and the most deficient in bodily advantages; without clothes, without arms, without food, without lodging, without any convenience of life, except what they owe to their own skill and industry. In short, nature seems to have formed an exact calculation of the necessities of her creatures; and like a *rigid master,* has afforded them little more powers or endowments, than what are strictly sufficient to supply those necessities. An *indulgent parent* would have bestowed a large stock, in order to guard against accidents, and secure the happiness and welfare of the creature, in the most unfortunate concurrence of circumstances. Every course of life would not have been so surrounded with precipices, that the least departure from the true path, by mistake or necessity, must involve us in misery and ruin. Some reserve, some fund would have been provided to ensure happiness; nor would the powers and the necessities have been adjusted with so rigid an economy. The Author of nature is inconceivably powerful: His force is supposed great, if not altogether inexhaustible: Nor is there any reason, as far as we can judge, to make him observe this strict frugality in his dealings with his creatures. It would have been better, were his power extremely limited, to have created fewer animals, and to have endowed these with more faculties for their happiness and preservation. A builder is never esteemed prudent, who undertakes a plan, beyond what his stock will enable him to finish.

In order to cure most of the ills of human life, I require not that man should have the wings of the eagle, the swiftness of the stag, the force of the ox, the arms of the lion, the scales of the crocodile or rhinoceros; much less do I demand the sagacity of an angel or cherubim. I am contented to take an increase in one single power or faculty of his soul. Let him be endowed with a greater propensity to industry and labour; a more vigorous spring and activity of mind; a more constant bent to business and application. Let the whole species possess naturally an equal diligence with that which many individuals are able to attain by habit and reflection; and the most beneficial consequences, without any allay of ill, is the immediate and necessary result of this endowment. Almost all the moral, as well as natural evils of human life arise from idleness; and were our species, by the original constitution of their frame, exempt from this vice or infirmity, the perfect cultivation of land, the improvement of arts and manufactures, the exact execution of every office and duty, immediately follow; and men at once may fully reach that state of society, which is so imperfectly attained by the best-regulated government. But as industry is a power, and the most valuable of any, nature seems determined, suitably to her usual maxims, to bestow it on men with a very sparing hand; and rather to punish him severely for his deficiency in it, than to reward him for his attainments. She has so contrived his frame, that nothing but the most violent necessity can oblige him to labour; and she employs all his other wants to overcome, at least in part, the want of diligence, and to endow him with some share of a faculty, of which she has thought fit naturally to bereave him. Here our demands may be allowed very humble, and therefore the more reasonable. If we required the endowments of superior penetration and judgment, of a more delicate taste of beauty, of a nicer sensibility to benevolence and friendship; we might be told, that we impiously pretend to break the order of nature, that we want to exalt ourselves into a higher rank of being, that the presents which we require, not being suitable to our state and condition, would only be pernicious to us. But it is hard; I dare to repeat it, it is hard, that being placed in a world so full of wants and necessities; where almost every being and element is either our foe or refuses us their assistance; we should also have our own temper to struggle with, and should be deprived of that faculty which can alone fence against these multiplied evils.

The *fourth* circumstance, whence arises the misery and ill of the universe, is the inaccurate workmanship of all the springs and principles of the great machine of nature. It must be acknowledged, that there are few parts of the universe, which seem not to serve some purpose, and whose removal would not produce a visible defect and disorder in the whole. The parts hang all together; nor can one be touched without affecting the rest, in a greater or less degree. But at the same time, it must be observed, that none of these parts or principles, however useful, are so accurately adjusted, as to keep precisely within those bounds in which their utility consists; but they are, all of them, apt, on every occasion, to run into the one extreme or the other. One would imagine, that this grand production had not received the last hand of the maker; so little finished is every part, and so coarse are the strokes, with which it is executed. Thus, the winds are requisite to convey the vapours along the surface of the globe, and to assist men in navigation: But how oft, rising up to tempests and hurricanes, do they become pernicious? Rains are necessary to nourish all the plants and animals of the earth: But how often are they defective? how often excessive? Heat is requisite to all life and vegetation; but is not always found in the due proportion. On the mixture and secretion of the humours and juices of the body depend the health and prosperity of the animal: But the parts perform not regularly their proper function. What more useful than all the passions of the mind, ambition, vanity, love, anger? But how oft do they break their bounds, and cause the greatest convulsions in society? There is nothing so advantageous in the universe, but what frequently becomes pernicious, by its excess or defect; nor has nature guarded, with the requisite accuracy, against all disorder or confusion. The irregularity is never, perhaps, so great as to destroy any species; but is often sufficient to involve the individuals in ruin and misery.

On the concurrence, then, of these *four* circumstances does all or the greatest part of natural evil depend. Were all living creatures incapable of pain, or were the world administered by particular volitions, evil never could have found access into the universe: And were animals endowed with a large stock of powers and faculties, beyond what strict necessity requires; or were the several springs and principles of the universe so accurately framed as to preserve always the just temperament and medium; there must have been very little ill in comparison of what we feel at present. What then shall we pronounce on this occasion? Shall we say, that these circumstances are not necessary, and that they might easily have been altered in the contrivance of the universe? This decision seems too presumptuous for creatures so blind and ignorant. Let us be more modest in our conclusions. Let us allow, that, if the goodness of the Deity (I mean a goodness, like the human) could be established on any tolerable reasons *a priori,* these phenomena, however untoward, would not be sufficient to subvert that principle; but might easily, in some unknown manner, be reconcilable to it. But let us still assert, that as this goodness is not antecedently established, but must be inferred from the phenomena, there can be no grounds for such an inference, while there are so many ills in the universe, and while these ills might so easily have been remedied, as far as human understanding can be allowed to judge on such a subject. I am sceptic enough to allow, that the bad appearances, notwithstanding all my reasonings, may be compatible with such attributes as you suppose: But surely they can never prove these attributes. Such a conclusion cannot result from scepticism; but must arise from the phenomena, and from our confidence in the reasonings which we deduce from these phenomena.

Look round this universe. What an immense profusion of beings, animated and organized, sensible and active! You admire this prodigious variety and fecundity. But inspect a little more narrowly these living existences, the only beings worth regarding. How hostile and destructive to each other! How insufficient all of them for their own happiness! How contemptible or odious to the spectator! The whole presents nothing but the idea of a blind nature, impregnated by a great vivifying principle, and pouring forth from her lap, without discernment or parental care, her maimed and abortive children.

Here the Manichean system occurs as a proper hypothesis to solve the difficulty: And no doubt, in some respects, it is very specious, and has more probability than the common hypothesis, by giving a plausible account of the strange mixture of good and ill which appears in life. But if we consider, on the other hand, the perfect uniformity and agreement of the parts of the universe, we shall not discover in it any marks of the combat of a malevolent with a benevolent Being. There is indeed an opposition of pains and pleasures in the feelings of sensible creatures: But are not all the operations of nature carried on by an opposition of principles, of hot and cold, moist and dry, light and heavy? The true conclusion is, that the original source of all things is entirely indifferent to all these principles, and has no more regard to good above ill than to heat above cold, or to drought above moisture, or to light above heavy.

There may *four* hypotheses be framed concerning the first causes of the universe: *that* they are endowed with perfect goodness, *that* they have perfect malice, *that* they are opposite and have both goodness and malice, *that* they have neither goodness nor malice. Mixed phenomena can never prove the two former unmixed principles. And the uniformity and steadiness of general laws seem to oppose the third. The fourth, therefore, seems by far the most probable.

What I have said concerning natural evil will apply to moral, with little or no variation; and we have no more reason to infer, that the rectitude of the supreme Being resembles human rectitude than that his benevolence resembles the human. Nay, it will be thought, that we have still greater cause to exclude from him moral sentiments, such as we feel them; since moral evil, in the opinion of many, is much more predominant above moral good than natural evil above natural good.

But even though this should not be allowed, and though the virtue, which is in mankind, should be acknowledged much superior to the vice; yet so long as there is any vice at all in the universe, it will very much puzzle you anthropomorphites, how to account for it. You must assign a cause for it, without having recourse to the first cause. But as every effect must have a cause, and that cause another; you must either carry on the progression *in infinitum,* or rest on that original principle, who is the ultimate cause of all things. . . .

Hold! Hold! cried DEMEA: Whither does your imagination hurry you? I joined in alliance with you, in order to prove the incomprehensible nature of the divine Being, and refute the principles of Cleanthes, who would measure every thing by a human rule and standard. But I now find you running into all the topics of the greatest libertines and infidels; and betraying that holy cause, which you seemingly espoused. Are you secretly, then, a more dangerous enemy than Cleanthes himself?

And are you so late in perceiving it? replied CLEANTHES. Believe me, Demea; your friend Philo, from the beginning, has been amusing himself at both our expence; and it must be confessed, that the injudicious reasoning of our vulgar theology has given him but too just a handle of ridicule. The total infirmity of human reason, the absolute incomprehensibility of the divine nature, the great and universal misery and still greater wickedness of men; these are strange topics surely to be so fondly cherished by orthodox divines and doctors. In ages of stupidity and ignorance, indeed, these principles may safely be espoused; and perhaps, no views of things are more proper to promote superstition, than such as encourage the blind amazement, the diffidence, and melancholy of mankind. But at present. . . .

Blame not so much, interposed PHILO, the ignorance of these reverend gentlemen. They know how to change their style with the times. Formerly it was a most popular theological topic to maintain, that human life was vanity and misery, and to exaggerate all the ills and pains which are incident to men. But of late years, divines, we find, begin to retract this position, and maintain, though still with some hesitation, that there are more goods than evils, more pleasures than pains, even in this life. When religion stood entirely upon temper and education, it was thought proper to encourage melancholy; as indeed, mankind never have recourse to superior powers so readily as in that disposition. But as men have now learned to form principles, and to draw consequences, it is necessary to change the batteries, and to make use of such arguments as will endure, at least some scrutiny and examination. This variation is the same (and from the same causes) with that which I formerly remarked with regard to scepticism.

Thus Philo continued to the last his spirit of

opposition, and his censure of established opinions. But I could observe, that Demea did not at all relish the latter part of the discourse; and he took occasion soon after, on some pretence or other, to leave the company.

Part XII

After Demea's departure, Cleanthes and Philo continued the conversation in the following manner. Our friend, I am afraid, said CLEANTHES, will have little inclination to revive this topic of discourse, while you are in company; and to tell truth, Philo, I should rather wish to reason with either of you apart on a subject so sublime and interesting. Your spirit of controversy, joined to your abhorrence of vulgar superstition, carries you strange lengths, when engaged in an argument; and there is nothing so sacred and venerable, even in your own eyes, which you spare on that occasion.

I must confess, replied PHILO, that I am less cautious on the subject of natural religion than on any other; both because I know that I can never, on that head, corrupt the principles of any man of common sense, and because no one, I am confident, in whose eyes I appear a man of common sense, will ever mistake my intentions. You, in particular, Cleanthes, with whom I live in unreserved intimacy; you are sensible, that, notwithstanding the freedom of my conversation, and my love of singular arguments, no one has a deeper sense of religion impressed on his mind, or pays more profound adoration to the divine Being, as he discovers himself to reason, in the inexplicable contrivance and artifice of nature. A purpose, an intention, a design strikes everywhere the most careless, the most stupid thinker; and no man can be so hardened in absurd systems, as at all times to reject it. *That nature does nothing in vain,* is a maxim established in all the schools, merely from the contemplation of the works of nature, without any religious purpose; and, from a firm conviction of its truth, an *anatomist,* who had observed a new organ or canal, would never be satisfied till he had also discovered its use and intention. One great foundation of the Copernican system is the maxim, *that nature acts by the simplest methods, and chooses the most proper means to any end;* and astronomers often, without thinking of it, lay this strong foundation of piety and religion. The same thing is observable in other parts of philosophy: And thus all the sciences almost lead us insensibly to acknowledge a first intelligent Author; and their authority is often so much the greater, as they do not directly profess that intention.

. . . .

So little, replied PHILO, do I esteem this suspense of judgment in the present case to be possible, that I am apt to suspect there enters somewhat of a dispute of words into this controversy, more than is usually imagined. That the works of nature bear a great analogy to the productions of art is evident; and according to all the rules of good reasoning, we ought to infer, if we argue at all concerning them, that their causes have a proportional analogy. But as there are also considerable differences, we have reason to suppose a proportional difference in the causes; and in particular ought to attribute a much higher degree of power and energy to the supreme cause than any we have ever observed in mankind. Here then the existence of a Deity is plainly ascertained by reason; and if we make it a question, whether, on account of these analogies, we can properly call him a *mind* or *intelligence,* notwithstanding the vast difference, which may reasonably be supposed between him and human minds; what is this but a mere verbal controversy? No man can deny the analogies between the effects: To restrain ourselves from enquiring concerning the causes is scarcely possible: From this enquiry, the legitimate conclusion is, that the causes have also an analogy: And if we are not contented with calling the first and supreme cause a God or Deity, but desire to vary the expression; what can we call him but mind or thought, to which he is justly supposed to bear a considerable resemblance?

All men of sound reason are disgusted with verbal disputes, which abound so much in philosophical and theological enquiries; and it is found, that the only remedy for this abuse must arise from clear definitions, from the precision of those ideas which enter into any argument, and from the strict and uniform use of those terms which are employed. But there is a species of controversy, which, from the very nature of language and of human ideas, is involved in perpetual ambiguity, and can never, by any precaution or any definitions, be able to reach a reasonable certainty or precision. These are the controversies concerning the degrees of any quality or circumstance. Men may argue to all eternity, whether Hannibal be a great, or a very great, or a superlatively great man, what degree of beauty Cleopatra possessed, what epithet of praise Livy or Thucydides is entitled to, without bringing the controversy to any determination. The disputants may here agree in their sense and differ in the terms, or *vice versa;* yet never be able to define their terms, so as to enter into each other's meaning: Because the degrees of these qualities are not, like quantity or number, susceptible of any exact mensuration, which may be the standard in the controversy. That the dispute concerning theism is of this nature, and consequently is merely verbal, or perhaps, if possible, still more incurably ambiguous, will appear upon the slightest enquiry. I ask the theist, if he does not allow, that there is a great and immeasurable, because incomprehensible, difference between the *human* and the *divine* mind: The more pious he is, the more readily will he assent to the affirmative, and the more will he be disposed to magnify the difference: He will even assert, that the difference is of a nature which cannot be too much magnified. I next turn to the atheist, who, I assert, is only nominally so, and can never possibly be in earnest; and I ask him, whether, from the coherence and apparent sympathy in all the parts of this world, there be not a certain degree of analogy among all the operations of nature, in every situation and in every age; whether the rotting of a turnip, the generation of an animal, and the structure of human thought be not energies that probably bear some remote analogy to each other: It is impossible he can deny it: He will readily acknowledge it. Having obtained this concession, I push him still farther in his retreat; and I ask him, if it be not probable, that the principle which first arranged, and still maintains, order in this universe, bears not also some remote inconceivable analogy to the other operations of nature, and among the rest to the economy of human mind and thought. However reluctant, he must give his assent. Where then, cry I to both these antagonists, is the subject of your dispute? The theist allows, that the original intelligence is very different from human reason: The atheist allows, that the original principle of order bears some remote analogy to it. Will you quarrel, Gentlemen, about the degrees, and enter into a controversy, which admits not of any precise meaning, nor consequently of any determination? If you should be so obstinate, I should not be surprised to find you insensibly change sides; while the theist on the one hand exaggerates the dissimilarity between the supreme Being, and frail, imperfect, variable, fleeting, and mortal creatures; and the atheist on the other magnifies the analogy among all the operations of nature, in every period, every situation, and every position. Consider then, where the real point of controversy lies, and if you cannot lay aside your disputes, endeavour, at least, to cure yourselves of your animosity.

And here I must also acknowledge, Cleanthes, that, as the works of nature have a much greater analogy to the effects of *our* art and contrivance, than to those of *our* benevolence and justice; we have reason to infer that the natural attributes of the Deity have a greater resemblance to those of man, than his moral have to human virtues. But what is the consequence? Nothing but this, that the moral qualities of man are more defective in their kind than his natural abilities. For, as the supreme Being is allowed to be absolutely and entirely perfect, whatever differs most from him departs the farthest from the supreme standard of rectitude and perfection.[11]

These, Cleanthes, are my unfeigned sentiments on this subject; and these sentiments, you know, I have ever cherished and maintained. But in proportion to my veneration for true religion, is my abhorrence of vulgar superstitions; and I indulge a peculiar pleasure, I confess, in pushing such principles, sometimes into absurdity, sometimes into impiety. And you are sensible, that all bigots, notwithstanding their great aversion to the latter above the former, are commonly equally guilty of both.

My inclination, replied CLEANTHES, lies, I own, a contrary way. Religion, however corrupted, is still better than no religion at all. The doctrine of a future state is so strong and necessary a security to morals, that we never ought to abandon or neglect it. For if finite and temporary rewards and punishments have so great an effect, as we daily find: How much greater must be expected from such as are infinite and eternal?

How happens it then, said PHILO, if vulgar superstition be so salutary to society, that all history abounds so much with accounts of its pernicious consequences on public affairs? Factions, civil wars, persecutions, subversions of government, oppression, slavery; these are the dismal consequences which always attend its prevalency over the minds of men. If the religious spirit be ever mentioned in any historical narration, we are sure to meet afterwards with a detail of the miseries which attend it. And no period of time can be happier or more prosperous, than those in which it is never regarded, or heard of.

. . . .

It is contrary to common sense to entertain apprehensions or terrors, upon account of any opinion whatsoever, or to imagine that we run any risk hereafter, by the freest use of our reason. Such a sentiment implies both an *absurdity* and an *inconsistency*. It is an absurdity to believe that the Deity has human passions, and one of the lowest of human passions, a restless appetite for applause. It is an inconsistency to believe, that, since the Deity has this human passion, he has not others also; and, in particular, a disregard to the opinions of creatures so much inferior.

To know God, says Seneca, *is to worship him.* All other worship is indeed absurd, superstitious, and even impious. It degrades him to the low condition of mankind, who are delighted with entreaty, solicitation, presents, and flattery. Yet is this impiety the smallest of which superstition is guilty. Commonly, it depresses the Deity far below the condition of mankind; and represents him as a capricious Demon, who exercises his power without reason and without humanity! And were that divine Being disposed to be offended at the vices and follies of silly mortals, who are his own workmanship; ill would it surely fare with the votaries of most popular superstitions. Nor would any of human race merit his *favour,* but a very few, the philosophical theists, who entertain, or rather indeed endeavour to entertain, suitable notions of his divine perfections: As the only persons entitled to his *compassion* and *indulgence* would be the philosophical sceptics, a sect almost equally rare, who, from a natural diffidence of their own capacity, suspend, or endeavour to suspend all judgment with regard to such sublime and such extraordinary subjects.

If the whole of natural theology, as some people seem to maintain, resolves itself into one simple, though somewhat ambiguous, at least undefined proposition, *that the cause or causes of order in the universe probably bear some remote analogy to human intelligence:* If this proposition be not capable of extension, variation, or more particular explication: If it afford no inference that affects human life, or can be the source of any action or forbearance: And if the analogy, imperfect as it is, can be carried no farther than to the human intelligence; and cannot be transferred, with any appearance of probability, to the other qualities of the mind: If this really be the case, what can the most inquisitive, contemplative, and religious man do more than give a plain, philosophical assent to the proposition, as often as it occurs; and believe that the arguments, on which it is established, exceed the objections which lie against it? Some astonishment indeed will naturally arise from the greatness of the object: Some melancholy from its obscurity: Some contempt of human reason, that it can give no solution more satisfactory with regard to so extraordinary and magnificent a question. But believe me, Cleanthes, the most natural sentiment, which a well-disposed mind will feel on this occasion, is a longing desire and expectation, that Heaven would be pleased to dissipate, at least alleviate, this profound ignorance, by affording some more particular revelation to mankind, and making discoveries of the nature, attributes, and operations of the divine object of our Faith. A person, seasoned with a just sense of the imperfections of natural reason, will fly to revealed truth with the greatest avidity: While the haughty dogmatist, persuaded that he can erect a complete system of theology by the mere help of philosophy, disdains any farther aid, and rejects this adventitious instructor. To be a philosophical sceptic is, in a man of letters, the first and most essential step towards being a sound, believing Christian; a proposition which I would willingly recommend to the attention of Pamphilus: And I hope Cleanthes will forgive me for interposing so far in the education and instruction of his pupil.

Cleanthes and Philo pursued not this conversation much farther; and as nothing ever made greater impression on me, than all the reasonings of that day; so I confess, that, upon a serious review of the whole, I cannot but think, that Philo's principles are more probable than Demea's; but that those of Cleanthes approach still nearer to the truth.

Notes

1. *Recherche de la vérité, liv.* 3, chap. 9.
2. [Cf. Cicero, *De Natura Deorum,* Bk. I, 22.]
3. Lib. II, 1095 [Munro's translation].
4. *De Nat*[*ura*] *Deor* [*um*], Lib. I, 8.
5. [Hume presumably means *against* all mankind.]
6. Dr. Clarke.
7. *République des Lettres,* Août, 1685.
8. That sentiment had been maintained by Dr. King [*De Origine Mali, 1702*] and some few others, before Leibnitz, though by none of so great fame as that German philosopher.
9. [Milton: *Paradise Lost,* XI.]
10. [Dryden, *Aurengzebe,* Act IV, sc. 1.]
11. It seems evident, that the dispute between the sceptics and dogmatists is entirely verbal, or at least regards only the degrees of doubt and assurance, which we ought to indulge with regard to all reasoning: And such disputes are commonly, at the bottom, verbal, and admit not of any precise determination. No philosophical dogmatist denies, that there are difficulties both with regard to the senses and to all science; and that these difficulties are in a regular, logical method, absolutely insolveable. No sceptic denies, that we lie under an absolute necessity, notwithstanding these difficulties, of thinking, and believing, and reasoning with regard to all kind of subjects, and even of frequently assenting with confidence and security. The only difference, then, between these sects, if they merit that name, is, that the sceptic, from habit, caprice, or inclination, insists most on the difficulties; the dogmatist, for like reasons, on the necessity.

B. FAITH AND SUBJECTIVITY

The Wager

BLAISE PASCAL

Blaise Pascal (1623–1662) was a French mathematician, physicist, and theologian. His works include *Pensées* and *Provinciales*.

231

Do you believe it to be impossible that God is infinite, without parts?—Yes. I wish therefore to show you an infinite and indivisible thing. It is a point moving everywhere with an infinite velocity; for it is one in all places, and is all totality in every place.

Let this effect of nature, which previously seemed to you impossible, make you know that there may be others of which you are still ignorant. Do not draw this conclusion from your experiment, that there remains nothing for you to know; but rather that there remains an infinity for you to know.

232

Infinite movement, the point which fills everything, the moment of rest; infinite without quantity, indivisible and infinite.

233

Infinite—nothing.—Our soul is cast into a body, where it finds number, time, dimension. Thereupon it reasons, and calls this nature, necessity, and can believe nothing else.

Unity joined to infinity adds nothing to it, no more than one foot to an infinite measure. The finite is annihilated in the presence of the infinite, and becomes a pure nothing. So our spirit before God, so our justice before divine justice. There is not so great a disproportion between our justice and that of God, as between unity and infinity.

The justice of God must be vast like His compassion. Now justice to the outcast is less vast, and ought less to offend our feelings than mercy towards the elect.

We know that there is an infinite, and are ignorant of its nature. As we know it to be false that numbers are finite, it is therefore true that there is an infinity in number. But we do not know what it is. It is false that it is even, it is false that it is odd; for the addition of a unit can make no change in its nature. Yet it is a number, and every number is odd or even (this is certainly true of every finite number). So we may well know that there is a God without knowing what He is. Is there not one substantial truth, seeing there are so many things which are not the truth itself?

We know then the existence and nature of the finite, because we also are finite and have extension. We know the existence of the infinite, and are ignorant of its nature, because it has extension like us, but not limits like us. But we know neither the existence nor the nature of God, because He has neither extension nor limits.

Selections from *Pensées* trans. W. F. Trotter (New York: Dutton, 1958), pp. 65–70.

But by faith we know His existence; in glory we shall know His nature. Now, I have already shown that we may well know the existence of a thing, without knowing its nature.

Let us now speak according to natural lights.

If there is a God, He is infinitely incomprehensible, since, having neither parts nor limits, He has no affinity to us. We are then incapable of knowing either what He is or if He is. This being so, who will dare to undertake the decision of the question? Not we, who have no affinity to Him.

Who then will blame Christians for not being able to give a reason for their belief, since they profess a religion for which they cannot give a reason? They declare, in expounding it to the world, that it is a foolishness, *stultitiam;* and then you complain that they do not prove it! If they proved it, they would not keep their word; it is in lacking proofs, that they are not lacking in sense. "Yes, but although this excuses those who offer it as such, and takes away from them the blame of putting it forward without reason, it does not excuse those who receive it." Let us then examine this point, and say, "God is, or He is not." But to which side shall we incline? Reason can decide nothing here. There is an infinite chaos which separated us. A game is being played at the extremity of this infinite distance where heads or tails will turn up. What will you wager? According to reason, you can do neither the one thing nor the other; according to reason, you can defend neither of the propositions.

Do not then reprove for error those who have made a choice; for you know nothing about it. "No, but I blame them for having made, not this choice, but a choice; for again both he who chooses heads and he who chooses tails are equally at fault, they are both in the wrong. The true course is not to wager at all."

Yes; but you must wager. It is not optional. You are embarked. Which will you choose then? Let us see. Since you must choose, let us see which interests you least. You have two things to lose, the true and the good; and two things to stake, your reason and your will, your knowledge and your happiness; and your nature has two things to shun, error and misery. Your reason is no more shocked in choosing one rather than the other, since you must of necessity choose. This is one point settled. But your happiness? Let us weigh the gain and the loss in wagering that God is. Let us estimate these two chances. If you gain, you gain all; if you lose, you lose nothing. Wager, then, without hesitation that He is.—"That is very fine. Yes, I must wager; but I may perhaps wager too much."—Let us see. Since there is an equal risk of gain and of loss, if you had only to gain two lives, instead of one, you might still wager. But if there were three lives to gain, you would have to play (since you are under the necessity of playing), and you would be imprudent, when you are forced to play, not to chance your life to gain three at a game where there is an equal risk of loss and gain. But there is an eternity of life and happiness. And this being so, if there were an infinity of chances, of which one only would be for you, you would still be right in wagering one to win two, and you would act stupidly, being obliged to play, by refusing to stake one life against three at a game in which out of an infinity of chances there is one for you, if there were an infinity of an infinitely happy life to gain. But there is here an infinity of an infinitely happy life to gain, a chance of gain against a finite number of chances of loss, and what you stake is finite. It is all divided; wherever the infinite is and there is not an infinity of chances of loss against that of gain, there is no time to hesitate, you must give all. And thus, when one is forced to play, he must renounce reason to preserve his life, rather than risk it for infinite gain, as likely to happen as the loss of nothingness.

For it is no use to say it is uncertain if we will gain, and it is certain that we risk, and that the infinite distance between the *certainty* of what is staked and the *uncertainty* of what will be gained, equals the finite good which is certainly staked against the uncertain infinite. It is not so, as every player stakes a certainty to gain an uncertainty, and yet he stakes a finite certainty to gain a finite uncertainty, without transgressing against reason. There is not an infinite distance between the certainty staked and the uncertainty of the gain; that is untrue. In truth, there is an infinity between the certainty of gain and the certainty of loss. But the uncertainty of the gain is proportioned to the certainty of the stake according to the proportion of the chances of gain and loss. Hence it comes that, if there are as many risks on one side as on the other, the course is to play even; and then the certainty of the stake is equal to the uncertainty of the gain, so far is it from fact that there is an infinite distance between them. And so our proposition is of infinite force, when there is the finite to stake in a game where there are equal risks of gain and of loss, and the infinite to gain. This is demonstrable; and if men are capable of any truths, this is one.

"I confess it, I admit it. But, still, is there no means of seeing the faces of the cards?"—Yes, Scripture and the rest, etc. "Yes, but I have my hands tied and my mouth closed; I am forced to wager, and am not free. I am not released, and am so made that I cannot believe. What, then, would you have me do?"

True. But at least learn your inability to believe, since reason brings you to this, and yet you cannot believe. Endeavour then to convince yourself, not by increase of proofs of God, but by the abatement of your passions. You would like to attain faith, and do not know the way; you would like to cure yourself of unbelief, and ask the remedy for it. Learn of those who have been bound like you, and who now stake all their possessions. These are people who know the way which you would follow, and who are cured of an ill of which you would be cured. Follow the way by which they began; by acting as if they believed, taking the holy water, having masses said, etc. Even this will naturally make you believe, and deaden your acuteness.—"But this is what I am afraid of."—And why? What have you to lose?

But to show you that this leads you there, it is this which will lessen the passions, which are your stumbling-blocks.

The end of this discourse.—Now, what harm will befall you in taking this side? You will be faithful, honest, humble, grateful, generous, a sincere friend, truthful. Certainly you will not have those poisonous pleasures, glory and luxury; but will you not have others? I will tell you that you will thereby gain in this life, and that, at each step you take on this road, you will see so great certainty of gain, so much nothingness in what you risk, that you will at last recognise that you have wagered for something certain and infinite, for which you have given nothing.

"Ah! This discourse transports me, charms me," etc.

If this discourse pleases you and seems impressive, know that it is made by a man who has knelt, both before and after it, in prayer to that Being, infinite and without parts, before whom he lays all he has, for you also to lay before Him all you have for your own good and for His glory, that so strength may be given to lowliness.

234

If we must not act save on a certainty, we ought not to act on religion, for it is not certain. But how many things we do on an uncertainty, sea voyages, battles! I say then we must do nothing at all, for nothing is certain, and that there is more certainty in religion than there is as to whether we may see to-morrow; for it is not certain that we may see to-morrow, and it is certainly possible that we may not see it. We cannot say as much about religion. It is not certain that it is; but who will venture to say that it is certainly possible that it is not? Now when we work for to-morrow, and so on an uncertainty, we act reasonably; for we ought to work for an uncertainty according to the doctrine of chance which was demonstrated above.

Saint Augustine has seen that we work for an uncertainty, on sea, in battle, etc. But he has not seen the doctrine of chance which proves that we should do so. Montaigne has seen that we are shocked at a fool, and that habit is all-powerful; but he has not seen the reason of this effect.

All these persons have seen the effects, but they have not seen the causes. They are, in comparison with those who have discovered the causes, as those who have only eyes are in comparison with those who have intellect. For the effects are perceptible by sense, and the causes are visible only to the intellect. And although these effects are seen by the mind, this mind is, in comparison with the mind which sees the causes, as the bodily senses are in comparison with the intellect.

235

*Rem viderunt, causam non viderunt.**

*[Editors' note: "Things seen, causes unseen."]

236

According to the doctrine of chance, you ought to put yourself to the trouble of searching for the truth; for if you die without worshipping the True Cause, you are lost.—"But," say you, "if He had wished me to worship Him, He would have left me signs of His will."—He has done so; but you neglect them. Seek them, therefore; it is well worth it.

237

Chances.—We must live differently in the world, according to these different assumptions: (I) that we could always remain in it; (2) that it is certain that we shall not remain here long, and uncertain if we shall remain here one hour. This last assumption is our condition.

238

What do you then promise me, in addition to certain troubles, but ten years of self-love (for ten years is the chance), to try hard to please without success?

239

Objection.—Those who hope for salvation are so far happy; but they have as a counterpoise the fear of hell.

Reply.—Who has most reason to fear hell: he who is in ignorance whether there is a hell, and who is certain of damnation if there is; or he who certainly believes there is a hell, and hopes to be saved if there is?

240

"I would soon have renounced pleasure," say they, "had I faith." For my part I tell you, "You would soon have faith, if you renounced pleasure." Now, it is for you to begin. If I could, I would give you faith. I cannot do so, nor therefore test the truth of what you say. But you can well renounce pleasure, and test whether what I say is true.

241

Order.—I would have far more fear of being mistaken, and of finding that the Christian religion was true, than of not being mistaken in believing it true.

Pascal's Wager

JAMES CARGILE

James Cargile (1920–) is a professor of philosophy at the University of Virginia. His publications include *Paradoxes*.

A. Pascal's statement of his wager argument[1,2] is couched in terms of the theory of probability and the theory of games, and the exposition is unclear and unnecessarily complicated. The following is a "creative" reformulation of the argument designed to avoid *some* of the objections which have been or might be raised against the original.

B. Premises:

1. "If there is a God, we are incapable of knowing either what he is, or whether he exists" (Pascal). And further, we have no way of knowing that God does not exist.

2. If you perform religious rites with enthusiasm, and never question the claims of some religion, you will come to be devoutly religious. "Go then and take holy water, and have masses said; belief will come and stupefy your scruples" (William James' version[3] of a remark by Pascal).

3. If you are devoutly religious—Christian, Jew, Moslem, Hindu, polytheist, etc.—and there is a God, then he will send you to heaven when you die.

Conclusion: Solely on grounds of rational self-interest, you should participate in religious rites, refrain from sceptical thoughts, etc.

Proof: Consider the following case: A very rich man who is fond of jazz promises that in two years, he is going to toss an unbiased coin. If it lands heads, he will give each devoted jazz fan a million dollars. If it lands tails, he won't do anything. Every Sunday for the next two years, a one-hour jazz concert is scheduled. It is known to be highly likely that if you attend these concerts religiously, and avoid listening to classical music, you will become a devoted jazz fan.

This case is clearly analogous to the situation of the man who is reflecting as to whether or not he should take up religious observances. And in either case the answer is obvious: you had better start listening uncritically to a lot of jazz. You may return to classical music as a millionaire, and you may get to heaven and not have to listen to sermons any more.

It may be objected that the person who "wagers" by attending concerts loses, if he loses, only two years of classical music, while the person who "wagers" by participating in religious rites and avoiding sceptical thoughts loses, if he loses, the only chance for thinking he will ever have. But after all, what is thinking? You have only to pass up philosophical quibbling which everyone knows is silly anyway. You can keep your mind exercised on mathematics or formal logic or approved scientific topics. Concession to religion needn't be much, even when you strive for real faith. Look what subtle reasoners even fanatics can be!

It may be objected that God may save atheists and agnostics as well as religious people. And the rich man *might* give a million dollars to a lover of classical music—but why depend on *kindness* when you can get a *contract* (or rather, a covenant)?

Someone might plan to delay attending the concerts until the second year so as to get in as much classical music as possible. Similarly, someone might plan to follow the advice of Pascal's argument in forty years, after enjoying his scepticism as long as he can. But if the rich man announces that he *may* exclude people who are not jazz fans from his offer if they delay attending the concerts, it would obviously be foolish to delay. And if you plan to delay religious observance, you may not live that long. It is foolish to be even a little careless with an opportunity for infinite gain.

C. This argument is designed to convince an open-minded agnostic acting out of rational self-interest that he ought to take up religious practices in the hope of becoming religious. Pascal has other arguments which will then be brought forward to bring the newly won religious sympathiser into Pascal's own particular church, but the wager argument is not one of these. William Jones *(loc. cit.)* criticises Pascal's argument on the grounds that it would not convert a Moslem to Catholicism. But it wasn't intended to. James has probably been misled by Pascal's comment about holy water and masses. But this needn't occur in the presentation of the wager argument; the point which the reference to holy water and masses is designed to illustrate could be made just as well with respect to Moslem rituals. The argument is aimed at convincing sceptics, whose coolness about their prospects for immortality horrifies Pascal, that they should become *involved* on the side of those committed to belief in immortality.

James also criticises Pascal's argument as immoral, and says indignantly, "We feel that a faith in masses and holy water adopted wilfully after such a mechanical calculation would lack the inner soul of faith's reality: and if we were ourselves in the place of the Deity, we should probably take particular pleasure in cutting off believers of this pattern from their infinite reward." It seems that James is overlooking the fact that *"believers of this pattern"* are going to be just the same as other believers. Their belief isn't *sustained* by the argument, nor is it acquired by simply deciding to believe—James rightly regards the idea of "believing by our volition" as "simply silly"—rather, their faith is acquired as a result of actions which they were persuaded by the argument to perform. Once belief comes, the believer may genuinely despise his old sceptical self and shudder to think that such considerations as self-interest ever moved him. He may sincerely perform acts of faith, with no thought of his ultimate reward. A cynic may decide that the most convenient arrangement is a death-bed conversion; but if he is really converted, no one will despise this cynicism more than he.

Since James says that he is presenting Pascal's words "translated freely" it seems fair to protest against his representing Pascal as saying that "any finite loss is reasonable, even a certain one is reasonable, if there is but the possibility of infinite gain." Pascal's exposition is unclear, but he doesn't make such a mistake as this. James also presents the choice as one between belief and unbelief, which is probably one reason why he considers the argument immoral. But Pascal doesn't put it as a choice between belief and unbelief. He speaks obscurely of "risking your life," where he seems to be asking, not that you believe, but that you observe religious rites and abstain from criticism in the hope of being led to belief.

James also presents Pascal's argument as starting with the claim that human reason can't tell us what to do and ending with the claim that a certain course is obviously the reasonable one. This is especially reprehensible when presented as a translation. Jean Mesnard makes the same mistake in paraphrasing Pascal's argument,[4] apparently with approval, as starting with the claim that "reason cannot determine our choice" and ending with "Our reason therefore commands us to bet on the existence of God!" Pascal actually starts by saying that reason cannot settle the question as to whether or not there is a God, and concludes by saying that reason does clearly advise us to *"bet"* that there is a God—which for Pascal means being religious or sincerely trying to become so.

D. Various presentations of the wager argument defend it against the charge that it is an immoral argument. But no presentation I know of notices that the argument, which is presented as an appeal to a self-interested, rational sceptic who is completely uncommitted,[5] is simply invalid, because no such person could accept the premises.

Premise 1 might not be acceptable to an agnostic because it considers only the possibility of a transcendent God. The agnostic might think that investigation of occult phenomena *could* answer the God question, though of course only an affirmative answer would be so obtainable. Still, the sceptic would certainly admit that the God question is pretty much up in the air. So with "could not know" changed to "do not know," premise 1 would be acceptable to a sceptic.

The sceptic might doubt that he is the sort of person of whom the factual claim of premise 2 is true. But he would probably admit that there are measures sufficient to bring him into a religious frame of mind, even if the measures required were somewhat more severe than are needed by the average man. So he might accept premise 2 while still preserving his title as a sceptic or agnostic.

However, no self-respecting sceptic could accept premise 3. For one thing, if he accepts premise 1 as stated, that is, accepts that if there is a God, then "we are incapable of knowing what he is," then he cannot consistently agree with premise 3 that one thing we can be sure of about the possible owner-operator of the universe is that he is the sort of being who will send religious people to heaven. And premise 1 apart, why should not the neutral sceptic think it just as likely that God will save atheists and agnostics as that he will save believers? He might hope that it is more likely, either purely for his own sake, or on moral grounds.

The fact that, say, Christianity or Mohammedanism *promise* their adherents as infinite reward, while, say, dialectical materialism does not, cannot be produced as a good reason for a neutral adopting one of the former positions rather than the latter. The argument, "If you become devoutly religious, and religion is right about there being a God, then you will get an infinite reward," is just invalid. It would be all right to argue "If you become devoutly religious, and religion is right about there being a God and religion is right about one claim it makes about his character, then you will get an infinite reward." But with these premises, there are no longer just the two possibilities, "Religion is right about there being a God or it isn't right about there being a God." There are three possibilities: Religion is right about there being a God and right about his character; or religion is right about there being a God and wrong about his character; or religion is wrong about there being a God.

E. However, an attempt might be made to reinstate the wager argument in spite of the observations in D, as follows:

Either (a) there is a god who will send only religious people to heaven or (b) there is not. To be religious is to wager for (a). To fail to be religious is to wager for (b). We can't settle the question whether (a) or (b) is the case, at least not at present. But (a) is clearly vastly better than (b). With (a), infinite bliss is *guaranteed,* while with (b) we are still in the miserable human condition of facing death with no assurance as to what lies beyond. So (a) is clearly the best wager.

This arrangement does indeed appeal to a self-interested, *uncommitted* sceptic—it does not *presuppose* anything about the nature of god—the assumption about the nature of god is explicit in the argument. A sceptic might accept this argument and still deserve the title of "sceptic," but he would not deserve the title of "clear thinker."

The argument just presented is formally similar to the following:

Either (a) there is a god who will send you to heaven only if you commit a painful ritual suicide within an hour of first reading this, or (b) there is not. We cannot settle the question whether (a) or (b) is the case or it is at least not settled yet. But (a) is vastly preferable to (b), since in situation (a) infinite bliss is *guaranteed,* while in (b) we are left in the usual miserable human condition. So we should wager for (a) by performing the suicidal ritual.

It might be objected that we can be sure that there is not a god who will send us to heaven only if we commit suicide but we can't be sure that there is not a god who will send us to heaven only if we are religious. However, a sceptic would demand proof for this.

Both the foregoing arguments might gain plausibility through confusing possibility with probability. Certainly Pascal's application of probability theory could be severely criticised. However, my purpose has not been to criticise this aspect of the argument, but only to point out that the argument cannot stand as an appeal to someone who subscribes to no religious presuppositions.

F. Though my criticism of Pascal's argument has not been based on attacking his use of probability theory, it may be worth noting that if his use of probability theory were right, probability theory would be in a bad way.

Pascal uses a certain method from probability theory for calculating whether a given bet is a good one, to support his argument. The method is as follows: given a bet on whether or not an event E will happen, you multiply the probability of E by the odds offered (with the largest number in the odds if there is one, in the numerator). If this product exceeds one, and you are getting the high end of the odds, then the bet is a good one for you no matter how low the probability of E may be.

The limitations of this method are well known and Pascal's application of it creates a situation somewhat like the Petersburg Paradox.[6] But I think we need not go as far as the Petersburg Paradox to criticise Pascal's application of this method. It is enough to observe that in applying the method, Pascal takes for granted that the hypothesis that there is a God has some non-zero probability.

The only support Pascal could have for this is the so-called "Principle of Indifference," the fallaciousness of which is well known.[7] Pascal assumes that if a proposition is logically possible and not known to be false, then it has some non-zero probability. But the propositional function "There exists a God who prefers contemplating the real number x more than any other activity" provides us with a set of mutually incompatible propositions, each of which is logically and epistemically possible, such that there could not be a non-zero probability for each member of the set. Even if this "propositional function" is rejected as nonsense, such a function as "There are *n* rabbits in the universe" would provide a set of mutually incompatible propositions infinitely many of which would be both logically and epistemically possible. They could all be assigned probability numbers, e.g., from the series 1/2, 1/4, 1/8, . . . , but such an assignment would be absurd.

G. Of course, there remains the argument that if you become devoutly religious (and not a Calvinist!) you will *think* that you are going to get an infinite reward, and this is pleasanter than not thinking so. Whether Pascal would have stooped to this is a question outside the scope of the present essay.

H. It must be emphasised that my criticisms have not been intended to suggest that religious belief is unreasonable. It is one thing to hold that reason directs us to be religious, quite another to hold that it is (perfectly) reasonable to be religious.

Even in this connection, it is not the belief in an infinite gain which makes it reasonable to be religious. I may get the idea into my head that setting fire to the bus station will get me into heaven, but this belief does not make it *reasonable* for me to perform this religious act. *How I got the belief* would be crucial in determining whether the religious act of setting fire to the bus station is reasonable.

For example, if someone were dressed as an angel in a very convincing way, and lowered by an invisible wire to hang in front of me as I was climbing a cliff where I had every reason to think no one else was present, and this "angel" told me to burn the bus station, and I did, and the judge found out about the prank, and found out how diabolically convincing it had been, he might well dismiss my case, calling my action reasonable. Or again, if a heavenly host actually appeared to me and to all mankind, and promised us all eternal bliss if I burn down the bus station, my fellow men might consider me irrational to refuse.

On the other hand, if I were talked into burning the bus station by some sleazy prophet, my religious observance might well be called irrational.

I. There remains one way of reconstruing the wager argument so as to make the preceding criticisms inapplicable. It might be observed that many professed sceptics have lingering tendencies to believe in some religion, and that proposing a wager is an effective way to exploit these tendencies to bring them back into the fold.

Thus a lapsed Christian might feel that there is a 1/100 chance that Christianity is right, while assigning no likelihood at all to the claims of other religions. Furthermore, he may be sure that if Christianity is right, then however ordinary sinners and believers in other religions may fare, hard-boiled atheists will fare very badly indeed. For such a person as this, the wager might be thought to exert a powerful attraction to return to active Christianity.

However, this doesn't seem to be true in actual practice, and there are good reasons why this should be so. For one thing, if someone is a hard-boiled atheist, he won't assign any positive probability to Christian claims about God. And if he isn't a hardboiled atheist and does assign a positive probability to Christian claims, he is likely to imagine the Christian God as too nice to be stingy with rewards for people in his category, so the wager won't lead him to change his schedule.

Furthermore, lingering religiosity is not in itself enough to make the wager appetising. It has to be lingering religiosity which the agent will express in a positive probability estimate, or otherwise the wager won't get started. And many people who have superstitious tendencies would still not attach any positive probability to these superstitions.

And finally, even when someone does attach a positive probability to some religion's god-claims (and to no other's) the wager argument is not sure to bind him. Let us very roughly distinguish between objective and subjective theories of probability by noting that on an objective theory, it is not necessary that someone's judgment of a probability have any connection with his wagering behaviour; while on a subjective view, given the person's value scheme, his wagering behaviour is essential to determining his probability judgments. Then on the objective view, even given a positive probability estimate for some religion and a definite preference for heaven, being willing to make the wager doesn't follow and it is even a vexed question (at least) to show that wager-reluctance in such circumstances would even be less than reasonable. And on the subjective view, the probability estimate won't be of much use in persuading the agent to wager, considering that willingness to wager was an essential feature in determining the probability estimate.

Notes

1. *Pascal's Pensées,* bilingual edition, trans. H. F. Stewart, D.D., no. 223.
2. Georges Brunet, in *Le Pari de Pascal,* pp. 62–63, points out that Pascal was not the originator of the wager argument. Other writings on the background of Pascal's argument are *Le Pari de Pascal,* by A. Ducas, and "Le fragment Infini-Rien et ses Sources," by M. J. Orcibal, in *Blaise Pascal, L'Homme et l'Oeuvre,* section V.
3. William James, *The Will to Believe* (New York, 1897), pp.5–6.
4. Jean Mesnard, *Pascal, His Life and Works,* trans. by G. S. Fraser (London, 1952), pp. 156–57.
5. M. L. Goldmann ("Le Pari, est-il ecrit 'pour le libertin'?" in Blaise Pascal *L'Homme et l'Oeuvre,* section IV) argues that the argument is not for the sceptic who is *satisfied* with this world, but is rather for the man who is conscious of the miserable human condition. It is certainly consistent for a self-interested rational sceptic to feel unhappy with man's lot. But even if he has the appropriate human longings, the rational sceptic must find Pascal's argument invalid.
6. See, for example, Harold Cramer, *The Elements of Probability Theory,* p. 95, or William Feller, *Introduction to Probability Theory and Its Applications,* pp. 199–201.
7. See William Kneale, *Probability and Induction,* pp. 184–85.

Against Objectivity in Religion

SØREN KIERKEGAARD

Søren Kierkegaard (1813–1855) was a Danish philosopher who is regarded as the founder of existentialism. His works include *Either/Or, Concluding Unscientific Postscript,* and *Sickness unto Death.*

The Historical Point of View

When Christianity is viewed from the standpoint of its historical documentation, it becomes necessary to secure an entirely trustworthy account of what the Christian doctrine really is. If the inquirer were infinitely interested in behalf of his relationship to the doctrine he would at once despair; for nothing is more readily evident than that the greatest attainable certainty with respect to anything historical is merely an *approximation.* And an approximation, when viewed as a basis for an eternal happiness, is wholly inadequate, since the incommensurability makes a result impossible. But the interest of the inquiring subject being merely historical (whether he also has an infinite interest in Christianity in his capacity as believer, in which case the whole enterprise might readily come to involve him in several contradictions; or whether he stands aloof, yet, without any passionate negative decision *qua* unbeliever), he begins upon the tremendous task of research, adding new contributions of his own, and continuing thus until his seventieth year. Just two weeks before his death he looks forward to the publication of a new work, which it is hoped will throw light upon one entire side of the inquiry. Such an objective temper is an epigram, unless its antithesis be an epigram over it, over the restless concern of the infinitely interested subject, who surely needs to have such a question answered, related as it is to his eternal happiness. And in any case he will not upon any consideration dare to relinquish his interest until the last moment.

When one raises the historical question of the truth of Christianity, or of what is and is not Christian truth, the Scriptures at once present themselves as documents of decisive significance. The historical inquiry therefore first concentrates upon the Bible.

1. The Holy Scriptures

Here it is necessary for the scholar to secure the maximum of dependability; for me, on the contrary, it is of importance not to make a display of learning, or to betray the fact that I have none. In the interest of my problem it is more important to have it understood and remembered that even with the most stupendous learning and persistence in research, and even if all the brains of all the critics were concentrated in one, it would still be impossible to obtain anything more than an approximation; and that an approximation is essentially incommensurable with an infinite personal interest in an eternal happiness.

When the Scriptures are viewed as a court of last resort for determining what is and is not

From *Concluding Unscientific Postscript,* translated by David F. Swensen; Walter Lowrie (Princeton, N.J.: Princeton University Press for the American-Scandinavian Foundation, 1941), pp. 25–35, 177–82, 206–10, 378–84.

Christian doctrine, it becomes necessary to make sure of the Scriptures historically and critically.

In this connection there are a number of topics that come up for consideration: the canonicity of the individual books, their authenticity, their integrity, the trustworthiness of their authors; and a dogmatic guaranty is posited: Inspiration. When one thinks of the labors which the English have devoted to digging the tunnel under the Thames, the tremendous expenditure of energy involved, and then how a little accident may for a long time obstruct the entire enterprise, one will be able to form a fitting conception of this critical undertaking as a whole. How much time, what great industry, what splendid talents, what distinguished scholarship have been requisitioned from generation to generation in order to bring this miracle to pass. And yet a little dialectical doubt touching the presuppositions may suddenly arise, sufficient for a long time to unsettle the whole, closing the subterranean way to Christianity which one has attempted to construct objectively and scientifically, instead of letting the problem remain subjective, as it is.

One sometimes hears uneducated or half educated people, or conceited geniuses, speak with contempt of the labor of criticism devoted to ancient writings; one hears them foolishly deride the learned scholar's careful scrutiny of the most insignificant detail, which is precisely the glory of the scholar, namely, that he considers nothing insignificant that bears upon his science. No, philological scholarship is absolutely within its rights, and the present author yields to none in profound respect for that which science consecrates. But the scholarly critical theology makes no such clear and definite impression upon the mind; its entire procedure suffers from a certain conscious or unconscious ambiguity. It constantly seems as if this labor of criticism were suddenly about to yield a result for faith, issue in something relevant to faith. Here lies the difficulty. When a philologist prepares an edition of one of Cicero's writings, for example, and performs his task with great acumen, the scholarly apparatus held in beautiful subservience to the control of the spirit; when his ingenuity and his familiarity with the period, gained through formidable industry, combine with his instinct for discovery to overcome obstacles, preparing a clear way for the meaning through the obscure maze of the readings, and so forth—then it is quite safe to yield oneself in whole-hearted admiration. For when he has finished, nothing follows except the wholly admirable result that an ancient writing has now through his skill and competence received its most accurate possible form. But by no means that I should now base my eternal happiness on this work; for in relation to my eternal happiness, his astonishing acumen seems, I must admit, inadequate. Aye, I confess that my admiration for him would be not glad but despondent, if I thought he had any such thing in mind. But this is precisely how the learned theologian goes to work; when he has completed his task (and until then he keeps us in suspense, but holds this prospect before us) he draws the conclusion: *ergo,* now you can base your eternal happiness on these writings.

Anyone who posits inspiration, as a believer does, must consistently consider every critical deliberation, whether for or against, as a misdirection, a temptation for the spirit. And anyone who plunges into these critical inquiries without being a believer, cannot possibly intend to have inspiration emerge as a result. Who then really has any interest in the whole inquiry?

But the contradiction remains unnoticed because the mode of approach is purely objective; and then indeed the contradiction is no longer there. The inquirer forgets what he has up his sleeve, except in so far as he occasionally stimulates and encourages himself lyrically by referring to it; or indulges in lyrical polemics with the aid of eloquence. But let an individual approach this enterprise, let him propose in infinite personal passion to attach his eternal happiness to the result: he will readily perceive that there is no result, and that none is to be expected; and the contradiction will bring him to despair. Luther's rejection of the Epistle of James will alone suffice. In relation to an eternal happiness, and an infinite passionate interest in its behalf (in which latter alone the former can exist), an iota is of importance, of infinite importance; or rather, despair over the contradiction involved will teach him that there is no possibility of getting through along this road.

The years pass, but the situation remains unchanged. One generation after another departs from the scene, new difficulties arise and are overcome, and new difficulties again arise. Each generation inherits from its predecessor the illusion that the method is quite impeccable, but the learned scholars have not yet succeeded . . . and so forth. All of them seem to find themselves becoming more and more objective. The infinite personal passionate interest of the subject (which is, in the first instance, the potentiality of faith, and in the next, faith itself, as the form for an eternal happiness, and thereupon an eternal happiness itself) vanishes more and more, because the decision is postponed, and postponed as following directly upon the result of the learned inquiry. That is to say, the problem does not arise; we have become so objective as no longer to have an eternal happiness. For an eternal happiness is rooted in the infinite personal passionate interest, which the individual renounces in order to become objective, defrauded of his interest by the predominating objectivity. With the assistance of the clergy, who occasionally display learning, the laity get an inkling of how the land lies. The "community of believers" becomes at last a mere courtesy title; for the laity become objective merely by looking at the clergy, and expect a tremendously significant result, and so on. Now a hostile critic rushes forward to attack Christianity. He is precisely as well oriented as the scholarly critics and the dilettante laity. He attacks a book of the Bible, or a suite of books. Instantly the learned rescue corps rushes in to defend; and so it goes on indefinitely.

Wessel said that he always seeks to avoid a crowd, and so it is doubtless imprudent for the author of a little piece to intervene in this dispute, with a respectful request for a hearing on behalf of a few dialectical considerations: he will be as welcome as a dog in a game of bowls. Nor is there much of anything that a stark naked dialectician can do in such a learned dispute, where in spite of all learning and talent *pro* and *contra,* it is, in the last analysis, dialectically uncertain what the dispute is about. If it is purely a philological controversy, let us honor learning and talent with the admiration they deserve; but in that case the dispute is no concern of faith. If the disputants have something up their sleeves, let us have it brought out, so that we can think it through with dialectical deliberation. Whoever defends the Bible in the interest of faith must have made it clear to himself whether, if he succeeds beyond expectation, there could from all his labor ensue anything at all with respect to faith, lest he should come to stick fast in the parenthesis of his labor, and forget, over the difficulties of scholarship, the decisive dialectical *claudatur.* Whoever attacks the Bible must also have sought a clear understanding of whether, if the attack succeeds beyond all measure, anything else would follow than the philological result, or at most a victory *ex concessis,* where it must be noted that everything may be lost in another manner, provided, namely, the mutual underlying agreement is a phantom.

In order therefore that the dialectical issue be accorded the significance it deserves, and that we may think the thoughts through without disturbing irrelevancies, let us first assume the one and then the other.

I assume, accordingly, that the critics have succeeded in proving about the Bible everything that any learned theologian in his happiest moment has ever wished to prove about the Bible. These books and no others belong to the canon; they are authentic; they are integral; their authors are trustworthy—one may well say, that it is as if every letter were inspired. More than this it is impossible to say, for inspiration is an object of faith and subject to a qualitative dialectic; it is incapable of being reached by a quantitative approximation. Furthermore, there is not a trace of contradiction in the sacred writings. For let us be careful in formulating our hypothesis; if so much as a single hint in this direction is admitted the parenthesis again begins, and the critical philological occupation-complex will again lead us astray on bypaths. In general, all that is needed to make the question simple and easy is the exercise of a certain dietetic circumspection, the renunciation of every learned interpolation or subordinate consideration, which in a trice might degenerate into a century-long parenthesis. Perhaps this is after all not so easy, and just as our human life runs into danger everywhere, so a dialectical exposition runs everywhere into the danger of slipping into a parenthesis. The same principle holds in smaller things as in greater; and in general, what makes it so tiresome to listen as third party to an argumentative dispute, is the fact that usually by the second round the dispute has already run into a parenthesis, and now moves in this perverse direction more and more passionately away from the point at issue. This failing may be utilized as a sort of fencing feint, for the purpose of testing out an opponent, to determine whether he is a real master of the dialectical parade, or a mere parenthesis-hound who leaps into a gallop whenever the parenthetical suggests itself. How often has it not happened that an entire human life has from early youth moved only in parentheses! But I break off these moralizing reflections, looking toward the promotion of the common welfare, by which I have sought to atone somewhat for my lack of historico-critical competence.

Well then, everything being assumed in order with respect to the Scriptures—what follows? Has anyone who previously did not have faith been brought a single step nearer to its acquisition? No, not a single step. Faith does not result simply from a scientific inquiry; it does not come directly at all. On the contrary, in this objectivity one tends to lose that infinite personal interestedness in passion which is the condition of faith, the *ubique et nusquam* in which faith can come into being. Has anyone who previously had faith gained anything with respect to its strength and power? No, not in the least. Rather is it the case that in this voluminous knowledge, this certainty that lurks at the door of faith and threatens to devour it, he is in so dangerous a situation that he will need to put forth much effort in great fear and trembling, lest he fall a victim to the temptation to confuse knowledge with faith. While faith has hitherto had a profitable schoolmaster in the existing uncertainty, it would have in the new certainty its most dangerous enemy. For if passion is eliminated, faith no longer exists, and certainty and passion do not go together. Whoever believes that there is a God and an over-ruling providence finds it easier to preserve his faith, easier to acquire something that definitely is faith and not an illusion, in an imperfect world where passion is kept alive, than in an absolutely perfect world. In such a world faith is in fact unthinkable. Hence also the teaching that faith is abolished in eternity.

How fortunate then that this wishful hypothesis, this beautiful dream of critical theology, is an impossibility, because even the most perfect realization would still remain an approximation. And again how fortunate for the critics that the fault is by no means in them! If all the angels in heaven were to put their heads together, they could still bring to pass only an approximation, because an approximation is the only certainty attainable for historical knowledge—but also an inadequate basis for an eternal happiness.

I assume now the opposite, that the opponents have succeeded in proving what they desire about the Scriptures, with a certainty transcending the most ardent wish of the most passionate hostility—what then? Have the opponents thereby abolished Christianity? By no means. Has the believer been harmed? By no means, not in the least. Has the opponent made good a right to be relieved of responsibility for not being a believer? By no means. Because these books are not written by these authors, are not authentic, are not in an integral condition, are not inspired (though this cannot be disproved, since it is an object of faith), it does not follow that these authors have not existed; and above all, it does not follow that Christ has not existed. In so far, the believer is equally free to assume it; equally free, let us note this well, for if he had assumed it by virtue of any proof, he would have been on the verge of giving up his faith. If matters ever come to this pass, the believer will have some share of guilt, in so far as he has himself invited this procedure, and begun to play into the hands of unbelief by proposing to demonstrate.

Here is the crux of the matter, and I come back to the case of the learned theology. For whose sake is it that the proof is sought? Faith does not need it; aye, it must even regard the proof as its enemy. But when faith begins to feel embarrassed and ashamed, like a young woman for whom her love is no longer sufficient, but who secretly feels ashamed of her lover and must therefore have it established that there is something remarkable about him—when faith thus begins to lose its passion, when faith begins to cease to be faith, then a proof becomes necessary so as to command respect from the side of unbelief. And as for the rhetorical stupidities that have been perpetrated by clergymen in connection with this matter, through a confusion of the categories—alas, let us not speak of them. The vanity of faith (a modern substitute: How can they believe who receive honor one of another, John 5:44) naturally will not and cannot bear the martyrdom of faith; and the note of genuine faith is today perhaps the rarest note struck in the pulpit oratory of Europe. Speculative philosophy has understood everything, everything, everything. But the clergyman, nevertheless, holds himself a little in check; he admits that he has not yet understood everything, he admits that he is still striving. Poor man, what a confusion of the categories! "If there is anyone who has understood everything," he says, "then I confess (alas, he feels ashamed, and does not perceive that he ought to use irony against the others) that I have not understood it all, and that I cannot prove everything; we humbler folk (alas, he feels his humility in a very wrong place) must be content with faith." Poor, misunderstood, highest passion "faith," to have to be content with such a champion! Poor chap of a clergyman, that you do not know what you are talking about! Poor unlearned Peter Ericksen, on the other hand, who cannot quite make out about science, but who has faith; for he really has it, the faith which transformed fishermen into apostles, the faith which removes mountains—when one has it!

When the question is treated in an objective manner it becomes impossible for the subject to face the decision with passion, least of all with an infinitely interested passion. It is a self-contradiction and therefore comical, to be indifinitely interested in that which in its maximum still always remains an approximation. If in spite of this, passion is nevertheless imported, we get fanaticism. For an infinitely interested passion every iota will be of infinite value. The fault is not in the infinitely interested passion, but in the fact that its object has become an approximation-object.

The objective mode of approach to the problem persists from generation to generation precisely because the individuals, the contemplative individuals, become more and more objective, less and less possessed by an infinite passionate interest. Supposing that we continue in this manner to prove and seek the proof of the truth of Christianity, the remarkable phenomenon would finally emerge, that just when the proof for its truth had become completely realized, it would have ceased to exist as a present fact. It would then have become so completely an historical phenomenon as to be something entirely past, whose truth, i.e. whose historical truth, had finally been brought to a satisfactory determination. In this way perhaps the anxious prophecy of Luke 18:8, might be fulfilled: Nevertheless when the Son of Man cometh, shall he find faith on the earth?

The more objective the contemplative inquirer, the less he bases an eternal happiness, i.e. his eternal happiness, upon his relationship to the inquiry; since there can be no question of an eternal happiness except for the passionately and infinitely interested subject. Objectively, the contemplative inquirer, whether learned scholar or dilettante member of the laity, understands himself in the following farewell words, as he faces the final end: When I was a young man, such and such books were in doubt; now their genuineness has been demonstrated, but then again a doubt has recently been raised about certain books which have never before been under suspicion. But there will doubtless soon arise a scholar who will . . . and so forth.

The accommodating and objective subject holds himself aloof, displaying an applauded heroism. He is completely at your service, and ready to accept the truth as soon as it is brought to light. But the goal toward which he strives is far distant, undeniably so, since an approximation can continue indefinitely; and while the grass grows under his feet the inquirer dies, his mind at rest, for he was objective. It is not without reason that you have been praised, O wonderful objectivity, for you can do all things; not even the firmest believer has ever been so certain of his eternal happiness, and above all of not losing it, as the objective subject! Unless this objective and accommodating temper should perhaps be in the wrong place, so that it is possibly unchristian; in that case, it would naturally be a little dubious to have arrived at the truth of Christianity in this manner. Christianity is spirit, spirit is inwardness, inwardness is subjectivity, subjectivity is essentially passion, and in its maximum an infinite, personal, passionate interest in one's eternal happiness.

As soon as subjectivity is eliminated, and passion eliminated from subjectivity, and the infinite interest eliminated from passion, there is in general no decision at all, either in this problem or in any other. All decisiveness, all essential decisiveness, is rooted in subjectivity. A contemplative spirit, and this is what the objective subject is, feels nowhere any infinite need of a decision, and sees no decision anywhere. This is the *falsum* that is inherent in all objectivity; and this is the significance of mediation as the mode of transition in the continuous process, where nothing is fixed and where nothing is infinitely decided; because the movement turns back upon itself and again turns back, so that the movement becomes chimerical, and the philosopher is wise only after the event. There are indeed, in the objective sense, results everywhere, a superfluity of results. But there is no decisive result anywhere. This is quite as it should be, since decisiveness inheres in subjectivity alone, essentially in its passion, and maximally in the personal passion which is infinitely interested in an eternal happiness.

. . . .

Truth Is Subjectivity

In an attempt to make clear the difference of way that exists between an objective and a subjective reflection, I shall now proceed to show how a subjective reflection makes its way inwardly in inwardness. Inwardness in an existing subject culminates in passion; corresponding to passion in the subject the truth becomes a paradox; and the fact that the truth becomes a paradox is rooted precisely in its having a relationship to an existing subject. Thus the one corresponds to the other. By forgetting that one is an existing subject, passion goes by the board and the truth is no longer a paradox; the knowing subject becomes a fantastic entity rather than a human being, and the truth becomes a fantastic object for the knowledge of this fantastic entity.

When the question of truth is raised in an objective manner, reflection is directed objectively to the truth, as an object to which the knower is related. Reflection is not focussed upon the relationship, however, but upon the question of whether it is the truth to which the knower is related. If only the object to which he is related is the truth, the subject is accounted to be in the truth. When the question of the truth is raised subjectively, reflection is directed subjectively to the nature of the individual's relationship; if only the mode of this relationship is in the truth, the individual is in the truth even if he should happen to be thus related to what is not true. Let us take as an example the knowledge of God. Objectively, reflection is directed to the problem of whether this object is the true God; subjectively, reflection is directed to the question whether the individual is related to a something *in such a manner* that his relationship is in truth a God-relationship. On which side is the truth now to be found? Ah, may we not here resort to a mediation, and say: It is on neither side, but in the mediation of both? Excellently well said, provided we might have it explained how an existing individual manages to be in a state of mediation. For to be in a state of mediation is to be finished, while to exist is to become. Nor can an existing individual be in two places at the same time—he cannot be an identity of subject and object. When he is nearest to being in two places at the same time he is in passion; but passion is momentary, and passion is also the highest expression of subjectivity.

The existing individual who chooses to pursue the objective way enters upon the entire approximation-process by which it is proposed to bring God to light objectively. But this is in all eternity impossible, because God is a subject, and therefore exists only for subjectivity in inwardness. The existing individual who chooses the subjective way apprehends instantly the entire dialectical difficulty involved in having to use some time, perhaps a long time, in finding God objectively; and he feels this dialectical difficulty in all its painfulness, because every moment is wasted in which he does not have God. That very instant he has God, not by virtue of any objective deliberation, but by virtue of the infinite passion of inwardness. The objective inquirer, on the other hand, is not embarrassed by such dialectical difficulties as are involved in devoting an entire period of investigation to finding God—since it is possible that the inquirer may die tomorrow; and if he lives he can scarcely regard God as something to be taken along if convenient, since God is precisely that which one takes *a tout prix,* which in the understanding of passion constitutes the true inward relationship to God.

It is at this point, so difficult dialectically, that

the way swings off for everyone who knows what it means to think, and to think existentially; which is something very different from sitting at a desk and writing about what one has never done, something very different from writing *de omnibus dubitandum* and at the same time being as credulous existentially as the most sensuous of men. Here is where the way swings off, and the change is marked by the fact that while objective knowledge rambles comfortably on by way of the long road of approximation without being impelled by the urge of passion, subjective knowledge counts every delay a deadly peril, and the decision so infinitely important and so instantly pressing that it is as if the opportunity had already passed.

Now when the problem is to reckon up on which side there is most truth, whether on the side of one who seeks the true God objectively, and pursues the approximate truth of the God-idea; or on the side of one who, driven by the infinite passion of his need of God, feels an infinite concern for his own relationship to God in truth (and to be at one and the same time on both sides equally, is as we have noted not possible for an existing individual, but is merely the happy delusion of an imaginary I-am-I): the answer cannot be in doubt for anyone who has not been demoralized with the aid of science. If one who lives in the midst of Christendom goes up to the house of God, the house of the true God, with the true conception of God in his knowledge, and prays, but prays in a false spirit; and one who lives in an idolatrous community prays with the entire passion of the infinite, although his eyes rest upon the image of an idol: where is there most truth? The one prays in truth to God though he worships an idol; the other prays falsely to the true God, and hence worships in fact an idol.

When one man investigates objectively the problem of immortality, and another embraces an uncertainty with the passion of the infinite: where is there most truth, and who has the greater certainty? The one has entered upon a never-ending approximation, for the certainty of immortality lies precisely in the subjectivity of the individual; the other is immortal, and fights for his immortality by struggling with the uncertainty. Let us consider Socrates. Nowadays everyone dabbles in a few proofs; some have several such proofs, others fewer. But Socrates! He puts the question objectively in a problematic manner: *if* there is an immortality. He must therefore be accounted a doubter in comparison with one of our modern thinkers with the three proofs? By no means. On this "if" he risks his entire life, he has the courage to meet death, and he has with the passion of the infinite so determined the pattern of his life that it must be found acceptable—*if* there is an immortality. Is any better proof capable of being given for the immortality of the soul? But those who have the three proofs do not at all determine their lives in conformity therewith; if there is an immortality it must feel disgust over their manner of life: can any better refutation be given of the three proofs? The bit of uncertainty that Socrates had, helped him because he himself contributed the passion of the infinite; the three proofs that the others have do not profit them at all, because they are dead to spirit and enthusiasm, and their three proofs, in lieu of proving anything else, prove just this. A young girl may enjoy all the sweetness of love on the basis of what is merely a weak hope that she is beloved, because she rests everything on this weak hope; but many a wedded matron more than once subjected to the strongest expressions of love, has in so far indeed had proofs, but strangely enough has not enjoyed *quod erat demonstrandum*. The Socratic ignorance, which Socrates held fast with the entire passion of his inwardness, was thus an expression for the principle that the eternal truth is related to an existing individual, and that this truth must therefore be a paradox for him as long as he exists; and yet it is possible that there was more truth in the Socratic ignorance as it was in him, than in the entire objective truth of the System, which flirts with what the times demand and accommodates itself to *Privatdocents*.

The objective accent falls on WHAT is said, the subjective accent on HOW it is said. This distinction holds even in the aesthetic realm, and receives definite expression in the principle that what is in itself true may in the mouth of such and such a person become untrue. In these times this distinction is particularly worthy of notice, for if we wish to express in a single sentence the difference between ancient times and our own, we should doubtless have to say: "In ancient times only an individual here and there knew the truth;

now all know it, except that the inwardness of its appropriation stands in an inverse relationship to the extent of its dissemination. Aesthetically the contradiction that truth becomes untruth in this or that person's mouth, is best construed comically: In the ethico-religious sphere, accent is again on the "how." But this is not to be understood as referring to demeanor, expression, or the like; rather it refers to the relationship sustained by the existing individual, in his own existence, to the content of his utterance. Objectively the interest is focussed merely on the thought-content, subjectively on the inwardness. At its maximum this inward "how" is the passion of the infinite, and the passion of the infinite is the truth. But the passion of the infinite is precisely subjectivity, and thus subjectivity becomes the truth. Objectively there is no infinite decisiveness, and hence it is objectively in order to annul the difference between good and evil, together with the principle of contradiction, and therewith also the infinite difference between the true and the false. Only in subjectivity is there decisiveness, to seek objectivity is to be in error. It is the passion of the infinite that is the decisive factor and not its content, for its content is precisely itself. In this manner subjectivity and the subjective "how" constitute the truth.

But the "how" which is thus subjectively accentuated precisely because the subject is an existing individual, is also subject to a dialectic with respect to time. In the passionate moment of decision, where the road swings away from objective knowledge, it seems as if the infinite decision were thereby realized. But in the same moment the existing individual finds himself in the temporal order, and the subjective "how" is transformed into a striving, a striving which receives indeed its impulse and a repeated renewal from the decisive passion of the infinite, but is nevertheless a striving.

When subjectivity is the truth, the conceptual determination of the truth must include an expression for the antithesis to objectivity, a memento of the fork in the road where the way swings off; this expression will at the same time serve as an indication of the tension of the subjective inwardness. Here is such a definition of truth: *An objective uncertainty held fast in an appropriation-process of the most passionate inwardness is the truth,* the highest truth attainable for an *existing* individual. At the point where the way swings off (and where this is cannot be specified objectively, since it is a matter of subjectivity), there objective knowledge is placed in abeyance. Thus the subject merely has, objectively, the uncertainty; but it is this which precisely increases the tension of that infinite passion which constitutes his inwardness. The truth is precisely the venture which chooses an objective uncertainty with the passion of the infinite. I contemplate the order of nature in the hope of finding God, and I see omnipotence and wisdom; but I also see much else that disturbs my mind and excites anxiety. The sum of all this is an objective uncertainty. But it is for this very reason that the inwardness becomes as intense as it is, for it embraces this objective uncertainty with the entire passion of the infinite. In the case of a mathematical proposition the objectivity is given, but for this reason the truth of such a proposition is also an indifferent truth.

But the above definition of truth is an equivalent expression for faith. Without risk there is no faith. Faith is precisely the contradiction between the infinite passion of the individual's inwardness and the objective uncertainty. If I am capable of grasping God objectively, I do not believe, but precisely because I cannot do this I must believe. If I wish to preserve myself in faith I must constantly be intent upon holding fast the objective uncertainty, so as to remain out upon the deep, over seventy thousand fathoms of water, still preserving my faith.

. . . .

Subjectivity

Suppose, on the other hand, that subjectivity is the truth, and that subjectivity is an existing subjectivity, then, if I may so express myself, Christianity fits perfectly into the picture. Subjectivity culminates in passion, Christianity is the paradox, paradox and passion are a mutual fit, and the paradox is altogether suited to one whose situation is, to be in the extremity of existence. Aye, never in all the world could there be found two lovers so wholly suited to one another as paradox and passion, and the strife between them is like the strife between lovers, when the dispute is about whether he first aroused her passion, or she his.

And so it is here; the existing individual has by means of the paradox itself come to be placed in the extremity of existence. And what can be more splendid for lovers than that they are permitted a long time together without any alteration in the relationship between them, except that it becomes more intensive in inwardness? And this is indeed granted to the highly unspeculative understanding between passion and the paradox, since the whole life in time is vouchsafed, and the change comes first in eternity.

But the speculative philosopher is of another kidney, he believes only to a certain degree; he sets his hand to the plow, and looks about him to find something to know. From the Christian point of view it can scarcely be said that it is anything good he finds to know. Even if it were not the case, as a simple wise man who seeks to apprehend the paradox would strive to show, that it cannot be otherwise; even if the paradox held a little remnant of divine arbitrariness within it, God might seem justified in laying some stress upon His person, scarcely needing to lower the price of the God-relationship on account of the dullness prevailing in the religious market (and this expression seems even more suitable here than in connection with the stock-market). And even if God could be imagined willing, no man with passion in his heart could desire it. To a maiden genuinely in love it could never occur that she bought her happiness too dear, but rather that she had not bought it dear enough. And just as the passion of the infinite was itself the truth, so in the case of the highest value it holds true that the price is the value, that a low price means a poor value; while even the highest possible price in relation to God has in it no meritoriousness, since the highest price is to be willing to do everything and still to know that this is nothing (for if it is something, the price is lower), and nevertheless to will it. Since I am not wholly unacquainted with what has been said and written about Christianity, I might also say one or two things. But here I do not choose to do so; I merely repeat that there is one thing I shall take care not to say about it: that it is to a certain degree true. It is just possible that Christianity is the truth; it is possible that there will sometime come a judgment, where the separation will turn on the relationship of inwardness to Christianity. Suppose then there came a man who had to say: "I have not indeed believed, but so much have I honored Christianity that I have employed every hour of my life in pondering it." Or suppose there came one of whom the accuser had to say: "He has persecuted the Christians," and the accused replied: "Aye, I admit it; Christianity has set my soul aflame, and I have had no other ambition than to root it from the earth, precisely because I perceived its tremendous power." Or suppose there came another, of whom the accuser would have to say: "He has abjured Christianity," and the accused replied: "Aye, it is true; for I saw that Christianity was such a power that if I gave it a little finger it would take the whole man, and I felt that I could not belong to it wholly." But then suppose there finally came a dapper *Privatdocent* with light and nimble steps, who spoke as follows: "I am not like these three; I have not only believed, but I have even explained Christianity, and shown that as it was expounded by the Apostles and appropriated in the early centuries it was only to a certain degree true; but that now, through the interpretation of speculative philosophy it has become the true truth, whence I must ask for a suitable reward on account of my services to Christianity." Which of these four must be regarded as in the most terrible position? It is just possible that Christianity is the truth; suppose that now when its ungrateful children desire to have it declared incompetent, and placed under the guardianship of speculative philosophy, like the Greek poet whose children also demanded that the aged parent be placed under a guardian, but who astonished the judges and the people by writing one of his most beautiful tragedies as a sign that he was still in the full possession of his faculties—suppose that Christianity thus arose with renewed vigor: there would be no one else whose position would become as embarrassing as the position of the *Privatdocents*.

I do not deny that it is a lordly thing to stand so high above Christianity. I do not deny that it is comfortable to be a Christian, and at the same time be exempted from the martyrdom which is always present, even if no persecution menaces from without, even if the Christian is as unnoticed in life as if he had not lived, and is spared the martyrdom of believing against the understanding, the peril of lying upon the deep, the seventy thousand fathoms, in order there to find God. The wader feels his way with his foot, lest he get beyond his depth; and so the shrewd and prudent man feels his way with the understanding in the realm of the probable, and finds God where the probabilities are favorable, and gives thanks on the great holidays of probability, when he has acquired a good livelihood, and there is probability besides for an early advancement; when he has got himself a pretty and attractive wife, and even Councillor Marcussen says that it will be a happy marriage, and that the young woman is of the type of beauty that will in all probability last a long time, and that her physique is such that she will in all probability give birth to strong and healthy children. To believe against the understanding is something different, and to believe with the understanding cannot be done at all; for he who believes with the understanding speaks only of livelihood and wife and fields and oxen and the like, which things are not the object of faith. Faith *always* gives thanks, is *always* in peril of life, in this collision of finite and infinite which is precisely a mortal danger for him who is a composite of both. The probable is therefore so little to the taste of a believer that he fears it most of all, since he well knows that when he clings to probabilities it is because he is beginning to lose his faith.

Faith has in fact two tasks: to take care in every moment to discover the improbable, the paradox; and then to hold it fast with the passion of inwardness. The common conception is that the improbable, the paradoxical, is something to which faith is related only passively; it must provisionally be content with this relationship, but little by little things will become better, as indeed seems probable. O miraculous creation of confusions in speaking about faith! One is to begin believing, in reliance upon the probability that things will soon become better. In this way probability is after all smuggled in, and one is prevented from believing; so that it is easy to understand that the fruit of having been for a long time a believer is, that one no longer believes, instead of, as one might think, that the fruit is a more intensive inwardness in faith. No, faith is self-active in its relation to the improbable and the paradoxical, self-active in the discovery, and self-active in every moment holding it fast—in order to believe. Merely to lay hold of the improbable requires all the passion of the infinite and its concentration in itself; for the improbable and the paradoxical are not to be reached by the understanding's quantitative calculation of the more and more difficult. Where the understanding despairs, faith is already present in order to make the despair properly decisive, in order that the movement of faith may not become a mere exchange within the bargaining sphere of the understanding. But to believe against the understanding is martyrdom; to begin to get the understanding a little in one's favor, is temptation and retrogression. This martyrdom is something that the speculative philosopher is free from. That he must pursue his studies, and especially that he must read many modern books, I admit is burdensome; but the martyrdom of faith is not the same thing. What I therefore fear and shrink from, more than I fear to die and to lose my sweetheart, is to say about Christianity that it is to a certain degree true. If I lived to be seventy years old, if I shortened the night's sleep and increased the day's work from year to year, inquiring into Christianity—how insignificant such a little period of study, viewed as entitling me to judge in so lofty a fashion about Christianity! For to be so embittered against Christianity after a casual acquaintance with it, that I declared it to be false: that would be far more pardonable, far more human. But this lordly superiority seems to me the true corruption, making every saving relationship impossible—and it may possibly be the case, that Christianity is the truth.

. . . .

Existential Pathos

Here perhaps someone, some ''sober man,'' will say: ''But can I be sure that there really is such a good; is the expectation of an eternal happiness a matter of definite certainty? For in that case I shall assuredly strive to attain it, but otherwise I would be mad to risk everything for its sake.'' This or a similar turn of thought frequently makes its appearance in the clergyman's discourse, and forms the transition to that part of the speech in which for the solace and reassurance of the congregation it is proved that there is an eternal happiness to look forward to—in order that the members of the listening congregation may strive all the more earnestly for its attainment. Such a demonstration is food for the hungry, and is taken as true like the word of God by the theologue, "the practical exercises being postponed as usual." How fortunate that I am not a serious man, an asseverating philosopher or a guaranteeing clergyman, for then I, too, might be moved to attempt a demonstration. Fortunately my frivolity excuses me; and in my capacity as a frivolous man I venture to have the opinion that anyone who resolved to strive for an eternal happiness on the ground of his faith in the assurances of the philosophers and the guarantees of the clergy, will nevertheless not really strive for it, and that what will prevent him is precisely this confidence of his in the philosophers and the clergy; though the clergyman believes, to be sure, that it is lack of confidence. Such confidence merely inspires him with a desire to follow, to associate himself with others, to make a business transaction on the basis of a calculation, an advantageous speculation in the market instead of an absolute venture. This confidence in the assurances inspires a fictitious movement of the spirit, a gesture in the direction of the absolute, while still remaining totally within the relative; a fictitious transition, like the transition from eudaemonism to the ethical within eudaemonism. In general it is quite inconceivable how ingenious and inventive human beings can be in evading an ultimate decision. Anyone who has seen the curious antics of recruits when they are ordered into the water will often have occasion to perceive analogies in the realm of the spirit.

The fact is that the individual becomes infinite only by virtue of making the absolute venture. Hence it is not the same individual who makes this venture among others, yielding as a consequence one more predicate attaching to one and the same individual. No, but in making the absolute venture he becomes another individual. Before he has made the venture he cannot understand it as anything else than madness; and this is far better than the thoughtless galimatias which imagines that it understands the venture as wisdom—and yet omits to venture, whereby the individual directly accuses himself of being mad, while one who regards the venture as madness at any rate consistently asserts his own sanity by refusing to commit himself. And after the individual has made the venture he is no longer the same individual. Thus there is made room for the transition and its decisiveness, an intervening yawning chasm, a suitable scene for the infinite passion of the individual, a gulf which the understanding cannot bridge either forward or backward.

But since I have in no way undertaken to prove that there is an eternal happiness (partly because it is not my affair, but at most that of Christianity which proclaims it; and partly because if it could be demonstrated it would be non-existent, since the existence of the absolute ethical good can be proved only by the individual himself expressing it existentially in existence), I shall take a little time to examine what our serious citizen said above; his words will doubtless be found worthy of consideration. He demands that it should be made definitely certain that such a good exists and awaits us. But it is really too much to ask that anything subject to expectation should be made definitely certain. The present is, for example, separated from the future by a little moment, the influence of which is that it becomes possible to expect the future, but impossible to have a sure certainty about it in the present. The present gives certainty and security to whatever is comprised within it, but a present relationship to something in the future is *eo ipso* an uncertain relationship, and hence quite properly a relationship of expectation. The speculative principle is that I arrive at the eternal retrogressively through recollection, and that the eternal individual is in this manner directly related to the eternal. But an existing individual can have a relationship to the eternal only as something prospective, as something in the future.

The serious man continues: If he were able to obtain certainty with respect to such a good, so as to know that it is really there, he would venture everything for its sake. The serious man speaks like a wag; it is clear enough that he wishes to make fools of us, like the raw recruit who takes a run in preparation for jumping into the water, and actually takes the run,—but gives the leap a go-by. When the certainty is there he will venture all. But what then does it mean to venture? A venture is the precise correlative of an uncertainty; when the certainty is there the venture becomes impossible. If our serious man acquires the definite certainty that he seeks, he will be unable to venture all; for even if he gives up everything, he will under such circumstances venture nothing—and if he does not get certainty, our serious man says in all earnest that he refuses to risk anything, since that would be madness. In this way the venture of our serious man becomes merely a false alarm. If what I hope to gain by venturing is itself certain, I do not risk or venture, but make an exchange. Thus in giving an apple for a pear, I run no risk if I hold the pear in my hand while making the exchange. Rogues and pickpockets have a very clear understanding of this; they do not trust one another, and hence wish to hold in their possession the articles they seek to acquire by making the exchange. Aye, they have so precise a notion of risk that they even regard it as risky to permit the other party to turn his back for a moment to expectorate, lest this should be a cover for some hocus-pocus or other. When I give all that I have for a pearl, it is not a venture if I hold the pearl in my hand at the moment of making the exchange. If it is a false pearl, and I have been cheated, it is a poor exchange; but I cannot be said to have risked anything to get possession of the pearl. But if the pearl is in a far country, in Africa for example, in a secret place difficult of access, if I have never had the pearl in my hand, and I leave home and kindred, give everything up, and undertake the long and toilsome journey without knowing for a certainty whether my enterprise will succeed: then I venture—and it will no doubt be remarked that same evening at the club, just as the serious man put it, that it is madness on my part so to risk everything. But whatever strange adventures the seeker for the pearl may experience on the long and dangerous journey to Africa, I do not believe that anything stranger can happen to him than falls to the lot of the serious man and his statement; for of all his earnestness, only one truth remains, and that is that the enterprise is madness. To be sure it is madness. It is always madness to venture, but to risk everything for the expectation of an eternal happiness is the height of madness. To ask for certainty is on the other hand prudence, for it is an excuse to evade the venture and its strenuosity, and to transfer the problem into the realm of knowledge and of prattle. No, if I am in truth resolved to venture, in truth resolved to strive for the attainment of the highest good, the uncertainty must be there, and I must have room to move, so to speak. But the largest space I can obtain, where there is room for the most vehement gesture of the passion that embraces the infinite, is uncertainty of knowledge with respect to an eternal happiness, or the certain knowledge that the choice is in the finite sense a piece of madness: now there is room, now you can venture!

And this is why an eternal happiness as the absolute good has the remarkable trait of *being definable solely in terms of the mode of acquisition*. Other goods, precisely because the mode of acquisition is accidental, or at any rate subject to a relative dialectic, must be defined in terms of the good itself. Money, for example, may be acquired both with and without effort on the part of the possessor, and both modes of acquisition are again subject to manifold variations; but money, nevertheless, remains the same good. And knowledge is also variously obtainable, in relation to talent and external circumstances, and cannot therefore be defined solely in terms of the mode of acquisition. But there is nothing to be said of an eternal happiness except that it is the good which is attained by venturing everything absolutely. Every description of the glory of this good is already as it were an attempt to make several different modes of acquisition possible, one easier for example, and one more difficult. This is enough to prove that the description does not really describe the absolute good, but only imagines itself doing so, while essentially dealing with relative goods. Hence it is so easy, in a certain sense, to talk about this good; for it is certain—when everything else is made uncertain, and because the speaker will never, as is so often the case with relative goods, be embarrassed by the revelation that what helps one to gain it will not help another. This is why discourse concerning this good may be so brief, for there is only one thing to say: venture everything! There are no anecdotes to tell how Peter became rich by hard work, and Paul by playing the lottery, and Hans by inheriting a fortune, and Matts by the change in the value of the currency, and Christopher by purchasing a piece of furniture from a dealer, and so forth. But in another sense the discourse may be very long, the longest of all discourses, because really to venture everything requires a conscious clarity with respect to oneself which is acquired only slowly. Here is the task of the religious address. Were it merely to say the brief word: "Venture everything," there would not be needed more than one speaker in an entire kingdom, while the longest discourse must not forget the venture. The religious address may deal with anything and everything, if only it constantly brings everything into relationship with the absolute category of religiosity. It must explore every path, it must know where the errors lurk, where the moods have their hiding-places, how the passions understand themselves in solitude (and every man who has passion is always to some degree solitary, it is only the slobberers who wear their hearts wholly on their sleeves); it must know where the illusions spread their temptations, where the bypaths slink away, and so forth: all for the purpose of bringing everything into relationship with the absolute categories of religiosity.

If one human being can do anything toward helping another in this respect, he need not trouble to pass over to the treatment of China and Persia. For just as religious discourse is higher than all other discourse, so all truly religious discourse knows nothing of anything beyond the absolute good, an eternal happiness. It knows that the task is not to begin with the individual and arrive at the race, but to begin with the individual and through the race arrive at the individual again. The religious address is the way to the good, i.e. it reflects the way, which is as long as life.* It reflects the way which the religious man describes, though not in the sense in which the planet describes its path or the mathematician a circle. But there is no short cut to the absolute good, and since this good can be described only by reference to the mode of acquisition, the absolute difficulty of the acquirements is the only mark by which the individual's relationship to the absolute good can be known. For anyone to stumble upon this good in some easier manner (as by being born under favorable circumstances, in the nineteenth century for example; or through being endowed with exceptional brain power, or through being the childhood playmate of a great man, or the brother-in-law of an Apostle), so as to be a favorite of fortune with respect to it, is merely evidence that the individual is deceived; for favorites of fortune do not belong in the religious sphere. The religious address has its merit in making the way difficult; for it is the way that is decisive of the relationship, otherwise we have aestheticism. But Christianity has made the way as difficult as it is possible to make it, and it is only an illusion by which many have been blinded, that Christianity has made the way easy. It has helped men solely by confronting them with a beginning that makes everything far more difficult than it was before. If a pagan has been able merely to catch a glimpse of the absolute good, Christianity has helped men to a vision of it—by means of the absurd. When this last qualification is omitted, everything has indeed become much easier than it was in paganism. But if the point is held fast, everything is far more difficult; for it is easier to cling to a weak hope *in one's own strength,* than to acquire certainty by virtue of the absurd. When an aesthetic sufferer bemoans his fate and seeks solace in the ethical, the ethical really has solace for him, but first it makes him suffer more than he did before. When this consideration is omitted the ethical makes everything much too comfortable and easy; but in that case the ethical has also been taken in vain. If an aesthetic sufferer feels his pain ever so keenly, he may very well come to suffer more; when he sends for the ethical it first helps him from the frying-pan into the fire, so that he gets something to complain about in real earnest—and then only does it give him help. So it is also with Christianity. It requires that the individual should existentially venture all (the pathetic). This is something that a pagan can also do; he may, for example, venture everything on an immortality's

*Here again we see why the religious speaker must not use a shortened perspective. Aesthetically there is no way, because the aesthetic corresponds to immediacy, and the expression for this is a foreshortened perspective. Ethically and ethico-religiously, however, reflection is concentrated precisely on the way, and hence it follows that what is true aesthetically becomes a deception from the ethical and the ethico-religious point of view.

perhaps. But Christianity also requires that the individual risk his thought, venturing to believe against the understanding (the dialectical). And while our serious man never arrived at the point of venturing because he demanded certainty, one thing is here certain, and that is that this is the absolute venture and the absolute risk. It may seem strenuous enough to struggle through life on the basis of the mere possibility of immortality, and to obtain a proof of the resurrection seems by comparison a tremendous help—if it were not for the fact that the very existence of this proof constitutes the greatest difficulty of all. To obtain everything by means of a mediator might seem easy in comparison with paganism, where the greatest exertion of the wise brought him but little gain; but now suppose that the very existence of a mediator constituted the very greatest difficulty of all! It seems comfortable enough to get everything by means of a gospel, were it not for the fact that the very existence of a gospel constituted the greatest difficulty. With God's help to be able to do everything, is also a comfortable privilege, were it not that being unable to do anything of oneself is the greatest of difficulties, so difficult that there are doubtless not many in each generation who can truthfully testify that they succeed even moderately in becoming conscious, day in and day out, that a human being can do nothing of himself.

Kierkegaard's Arguments Against Objective Reasoning in Religion

ROBERT MERRIHEW ADAMS

It is sometimes held that there is something in the nature of religious faith itself that renders it useless or undesirable to reason objectively in support of such faith, even if the reasoning should happen to have considerable plausibility. Søren Kierkegaard's *Concluding Unscientific Postscript* is probably the document most commonly cited as representative of this view. In the present essay I shall discuss three arguments for the view. I call them the Approximation Argument, the Postponement Argument, and the Passion Argument; and I suggest they can all be found in the *Postscript*. I shall try to show that the Approximation Argument is a bad argument. The other two will not be so easily disposed of, however. I believe they show that Kierkegaard's conclusion or something like it, does indeed follow from a certain conception of religiousness—a conception which has some appeal, although for reasons which I shall briefly suggest, I am not prepared to accept it.

Kierkegaard uses the word "objective" and its cognates in several senses, most of which need not concern us here. We are interested in the sense in which he uses it when he says, "it is precisely a misunderstanding to seek an objective assurance," and when he speaks of "an objective uncertainty held fast in the appropriation-process of the most passionate inwardness" (pp. 41, 182).[1] Let us say that a piece of reasoning, *R*, is *objective reasoning* just in case every (or almost every) intelligent, fair-minded, and sufficiently informed person would regard *R* as showing or tending to show (in the circumstances in which *R* is used, and to the extent claimed in *R*) that *R*'s conclusion is true or probably true. Uses of "objective" and "objectively" in other contexts can be understood from their relation to this one; for example, an objective uncertainty is a proposition which cannot be shown by objective reasoning to be certainly true.

1. The Approximation Argument

"Is it possible to base an eternal happiness upon historical knowledge?" is one of the central questions in the *Postscript*, and in the *Philosophical Fragments* to which it is a "postscript." Part of Kierkegaard's answer to the question is that it is not possible to base an eternal happiness on objective reasoning about historical facts.

> For nothing is more readily evident than that the greatest attainable certainty with respect to anything historical is merely an *approximation*. And an approximation, when viewed as a basis for an eternal happiness, is wholly inadequate, since the incommensurability makes a result impossible. (p. 25)

Kierkegaard maintains that it is possible, however, to base an eternal happiness on a belief in historical facts that is independent of objective

From the *Monist* 60, no. 2 (1977), pp. 213–28.

evidence for them, and that that is what one must do in order to be a Christian. This is the Approximation Argument for the proposition that Christian faith cannot be based on objective reasoning.[2] (It is assumed that some belief about historical facts is an essential part of Christian faith, so that if religious faith cannot be based on objective historical reasoning, then Christian faith cannot be based on objective reasoning at all.) Let us examine the argument in detail.

Its first premise is Kierkegaard's claim that "the greatest attainable certainty with respect to anything historical is merely an *approximation.*" I take him to mean that historical evidence, objectively considered, never completely excludes the possibility of error. "It goes without saying," he claims, "that it is impossible in the case of historical problems to reach an objective decision so certain that no doubt could disturb it" (p. 41). For Kierkegaard's purposes it does not matter how small the possibility of error is, so long as it is finitely small (that is, so long as it is not literally infinitesimal). He insists (p. 31) that his Approximation Argument makes no appeal to the supposition that the objective evidence for Christian historical beliefs is weaker than the objective evidence for any other historical belief. The argument turns on a claim about *all* historical evidence. The probability of error in our belief that there was an American Civil War in the nineteenth century, for instance, might be as small as $1/10^{2,000,000}$; that would be a large enough chance of error for Kierkegaard's argument.

It might be disputed, but let us assume for the sake of argument that there is some such finitely small probability of error in the objective grounds for all historical beliefs, as Kierkegaard held. This need not keep us from saying that we "know," and it is "certain," that there was an American Civil War. For such an absurdly small possibility of error is as good as no possibility of error at all, "for all practical intents and purposes," as we might say. Such a possibility of error is too small to be worth worrying about.

But would it be too small to be worth worrying about if we had an *infinite* passionate interest in the question about the Civil War? If we have an infinite passionate interest in something, there is no limit to how important it is to us. (The nature of such an interest will be discussed more fully in section 3 below.) Kierkegaard maintains that in relation to an infinite passionate interest *no* possibility of error is too small to be worth worrying about. "In relation to an eternal happiness, and an infinite passionate interest in its behalf (in which latter alone the former can exist), an iota is of importance, of infinite importance . . ." (p. 28). This is the basis for the second premise of the Approximation Argument, which is Kierkegaard's claim that "an approximation, when viewed as a basis for an eternal happiness, is wholly inadequate" (p. 25). "An approximation is essentially incommensurable with an infinite personal interest in an eternal happiness" (p. 26).

At this point in the argument it is important to have some understanding of Kierkegaard's conception of faith, and the way in which he thinks faith excludes doubt. Faith must be decisive; in fact it seems to consist in a sort of decision-making. "The conclusion of belief is not so much a conclusion as a resolution, and it is for this reason that belief excludes doubt."[3] The decision of faith is a decision to disregard the possibility of error—to act on what is believed, without hedging one's bets to take account of any possibility of error.

To disregard the possibility of error is not to be unaware of it, or fail to consider it, or lack anxiety about it. Kierkegaard insists that the believer must be keenly *aware* of the risk of error. "If I wish to preserve myself in faith I must constantly be intent upon holding fast the objective uncertainty, so as to remain out upon the deep, over seventy thousand fathoms of water, still preserving my faith" (p. 182).

For Kierkegaard, then, to ask whether faith in a historical fact can be based on objective reasoning is to ask whether objective reasoning can justify one in disregarding the possibility of error which (he thinks) historical evidence always leaves. Here another aspect of Kierkegaard's conception of faith plays its part in the argument. He thinks that in all genuine religious faith the believer is *infinitely* interested in the object of his faith. And he thinks it follows that objective reasoning cannot justify him in disregarding *any* possibility of error about the object of faith, and therefore cannot lead him all the way to religious faith where a historical fact is concerned. The farthest it could lead him is to the conclusion that *if* he had only a certain finite (though very great) interest in the matter, the possibility of error would be too small to be worth worrying about and he would be justified in disregarding it. But faith disregards a possibility of error that *is* worth worrying about, since an infinite interest is involved. Thus faith requires a "leap" beyond the evidence, a leap that cannot be justified by objective reasoning (cf. p. 90).

There is something right in what Kierkegaard is saying here, but his Approximation Argument is a bad argument. He is right in holding that grounds of doubt which may be insignificant for most practical purposes can be extremely troubling for the intensity of a religious concern, and that it may require great decisiveness, or something like courage, to overcome them religiously. But he is mistaken in holding that objective reasoning could not justify one in disregarding any possibility of error about something in which one is infinitely interested.

The mistake, I believe, lies in his overlooking the fact that there are at least two different reasons one might have for disregarding a possibility of error. The first is that the possibility is too small to be worth worrying about. The second is that the risk of not disregarding the possibility of error would be greater than the risk of disregarding it. Of these two reasons only the first is ruled out by the infinite passionate interest.

I will illustrate this point with two examples, one secular and one religious. A certain woman has a very great (though not infinite) interest in her husband's love for her. She rightly judges that the objective evidence available to her renders it 99.9 per cent probable that he loves her truly. The intensity of her interest is sufficient to cause her some *anxiety* over the remaining 1/1,000 chance that he loves her not; for her this chance is not too small to be worth worrying about. (Kierkegaard uses a similar example to support his Approximation Argument; see p. 511). But she (very reasonably) wants to *disregard* the risk of error, in the sense of not hedging her bets, if he does love her. This desire is at least as strong as her desire not to be deceived if he does not love her. Objective reasoning should therefore suffice to bring her to the conclusion that she ought to disregard the risk of error, since by not disregarding it she would run 999 times as great risk of frustrating one of these desires.

Or suppose you are trying to base your eternal happiness on your relation to Jesus, and therefore have an infinite passionate interest in the question whether he declared Peter and his episcopal successors to be infallible in matters of religious doctrine. You want to be committed to whichever is the true belief on this question, disregarding any possibility of error in it. And suppose, just for the sake of argument, that objective historical evidence renders it 99 per cent probable that Jesus did declare Peter and his successors to be infallible—or 99 per cent probable that he did not—for our present discussion it does not matter which. The 1 per cent chance of error is enough to make you *anxious,* in view of your infinite interest. But objective reasoning leads to the conclusion that you ought to commit yourself to the more probable opinion, *disregarding* the risk of error, if your strongest desire in the matter is to be so committed to the true opinion. For the only other way to satisfy this desire would be to commit yourself to the less probable opinion, disregarding the risk of error in it. The first way will be successful if and only if the more probable opinion is true, and the second way if and only if the less probable opinion is true. Surely it is prudent to do what gives you a 99 per cent chance of satisfying your strong desire, in preference to what gives you only a 1 per cent chance of satisfying it.

In this argument your strong desire to be committed to the true opinion is presupposed. The reasonableness of this desire may depend on a belief for which no probability can be established by purely historical reasoning, such as the belief that Jesus is God. But any difficulties arising from this point are distinct from those urged in the Approximation Argument, which itself presupposes the infinite passionate interest in the historical question.

There is some resemblance between my arguments in these examples and Pascal's famous Wager argument. But whereas Pascal's argument turns on weighing an infinite interest against a finite one, mine turn on weighing a large chance of success against a small one. An argument closer to Pascal's will be discussed in section 4 below.

The reader may well have noticed in the foregoing discussion some unclarity about what sort of justification is being demanded and given for religious beliefs about historical facts. There are at least two different types of question about a proposition which I might try to settle by objective reasoning: (1) Is it probable that the proposition is true? (2) In view of the evidence which I have for and against the proposition, and my interest in the matter, is it prudent for me to have faith in the truth of the proposition, disregarding the possibility of error? Correspondingly, we may distinguish two ways in which a belief can be *based on* objective reasoning. The proposition believed may be the conclusion of a piece of objective reasoning, and accepted because it is that. We may say that such a belief is *objectively probable*. Or one might hold a belief or maintain a religious faith because of a piece of objective reasoning whose conclusion is that it would be prudent, morally right, or otherwise desirable for one to hold that belief or faith. In this latter case let us say that the belief is *objectively advantageous*. It is clear that historical beliefs can be objectively probable; and in the Approximation Argument, Kierkegaard does not deny Christian historical beliefs can be objectively probable. His thesis is, in effect, that in view of an infinite passionate interest in their subject matter, they cannot be objectively advantageous, and therefore cannot be fully justified objectively, even if they are objectively probable. It is this thesis that I have attempted to refute. I have not been discussing the question whether Christian historical beliefs are objectively probable.

2. The Postponement Argument

The trouble with objective historical reasoning, according to the Approximation Argument, is that it cannot yield complete certainty. But that is not Kierkegaard's only complaint against it as a basis for religious faith. He also objects that objective historical inquiry is never completely finished, so that one who seeks to base his faith on it postpones his religious commitment forever. In the process of historical research "new difficulties arise and are overcome, and new difficulties again arise. Each generation inherits from its predecessor the illusion that the method is quite impeccable, but the learned scholars have not yet succeeded . . . and so forth. . . . The infinite personal passionate interest of the subject . . . vanishes more and more, because the decision is postponed, and postponed as following directly upon the result of the learned inquiry" (p. 28). As soon as we take "an historical document" as "our standard for the determination of Christian truth," we are "involved in a parenthesis whose conclusion is everlastingly prospective" (p. 38)—that is, we are involved in a religious digression which keeps religious commitment forever in the future.[4]

Kierkegaard has such fears about allowing religious faith to rest on *any* empirical reasoning. The danger of postponement of commitment arises not only from the uncertainties of historical scholarship, but also in connection with the design argument for God's existence. In the *Philosophical Fragments* Kierkegaard notes some objections to the attempt to prove God's existence from evidence of "the wisdom of nature, the goodness, the wisdom in the governance of the world," and then says, "even if I began I would never finish, and would in addition have to live constantly in suspense, lest something so terrible should suddenly happen that my bit of proof would be demolished."[5] What we have before us is a quite general sort of objection to the treatment of religious beliefs as empirically testable. On this point many analytical philosophers seem to agree with Kierkegaard. Much discussion in recent analytical philosophy of religion has proceeded from the supposition that religious beliefs are not empirically testable. I think it is far from obvious that that supposition is correct; and it is interesting to consider arguments that may be advanced to support it.

Kierkegaard's statements suggest an argument that I call the Postponement Argument. Its first premise is that one cannot have an authentic religious faith without being totally committed to it. In order to be totally committed to a belief, in the relevant sense, one must be determined not to abandon the belief under any circumstances that one recognizes as epistemically possible.

The second premise is that one cannot yet be totally committed to any belief which one bases on an inquiry in which one recognizes any possibility of a future need to revise the results. Total commitment to any belief so based will necessarily be postponed. I believe that this premise, suitably interpreted, is true. Consider the position of someone who regards himself as committed to a belief on the basis of objective evidence, but who recognizes some possibility that future discoveries will destroy the objective justification of the belief. We must ask how he is disposed to react in the event, however unlikely, that the objective basis of his belief is overthrown. Is he prepared to abandon the belief in that event? If so, he is not totally committed to the belief in the relevant sense. But if he is determined to cling to his belief even if its objective justification is taken away, then he is not basing the belief on the objective justification—or at least he is not basing it solely on the justification.[6]

The conclusion to be drawn from these two premises is that authentic religious faith cannot be based on an inquiry in which one recognizes any possibility of a future need to revise the results. We ought to note that this conclusion embodies two important restrictions on the scope of the argument.

In the first place, we are not given an argument that authentic religious faith cannot *have* an objective justification that is subject to possible future revision. What we are given is an argument that the authentic believer's holding of his religious belief cannot *depend* entirely on such a justification.

In the second place, this conclusion applies only to those who *recognize* some epistemic possibility that the objective results which appear to support their belief may be overturned. I think it would be unreasonable to require, as part of total commitment, a determination with regard to one's response to circumstances that one does not recognize as possible at all. It may be, however, that one does not recognize such a possibility when one ought to.

Kierkegaard needs one further premise in order to arrive at the conclusion that authentic religious faith cannot without error be based on any objective empirical reasoning. This third premise is that in every objective empirical inquiry there is always, objectively considered, some epistemic possibility that the results of the inquiry will need to be revised in view of new evidence or new reasoning. I believe Kierkegaard makes this assumption; he certainly makes it with regard to historical inquiry. From this premise it follows that one is in error if in any objective empirical inquiry one does not recognize any possibility of a future need to revise the results. But if one does recognize such a possibility, then according to the conclusion already reached in the Postponement Argument, one cannot base an authentic religious faith on the inquiry.

Some philosophers might attack the third premise of this argument; and certainly it is controversial. But I am more inclined to criticize the first premise. There is undoubtedly something plausible about the claim that authentic religious faith must involve a commitment so complete that the believer is resolved not to abandon his belief under any circumstances that he regards as epistemically possible. If you are willing to abandon your ostensibly religious beliefs for the sake of objective inquiry, mightn't we justly say that objective inquiry is your real religion, the thing to which you are most deeply committed?

There is also something plausible to be said on the other side, however. It has commonly been thought to be an important part of religious ethics that one ought to be humble, teachable, open to correction, new inspiration, and growth of insight, even (and perhaps especially) in important religious beliefs. That view would have to be discarded if we were to concede to Kierkegaard that the heart of commitment in religion is an unconditional determination not to change in one's important religious beliefs. In fact I think there is something radically wrong with this conception of religious commitment. Faith ought not to be thought of as unconditional devotion to a belief. For in the first place the object of religious devotion is not a belief or attitude of one's own, but God. And in the second place it may be doubted that religious devotion to God can or should be completely unconditional. God's love for sinners is sometimes said to be completely unconditional, not being based on any excellence or merit of theirs. But religious devotion to God is generally thought to be based on His goodness and love. It is the part of the strong, not the weak, to love unconditionally. And in relation to God we are weak.

3. The Passion Argument

In Kierkegaard's statements of the Approximation Argument and the Postponement Argument it is assumed that a system of religious beliefs might be objectively probable. It is only for the sake of argument, however, that Kierkegaard allows this assumption. He really holds that religious faith, by its very nature, needs objective *im*probability. "Anything that is almost probable or probable, or extremely and emphatically probable, is something [one] can almost know, or as good as know, or extremely and emphatically almost *know*—but it is impossible to *believe*" (p. 189). Nor will Kierkegaard countenance the suggestion that religion ought to go beyond belief of some almost-knowledge based on probability. "Faith is the highest passion in a man. There are perhaps many in every generation who do not even reach it, but no one gets further."[7] It would be a betrayal of religion to try to go beyond faith. The suggestion that faith might be replaced by "probabilities and guarantees" is for the believer "a temptation to be resisted with all his strength" (p. 15). The attempt to establish religious beliefs on a foundation of objective probability is therefore no service to religion, but inimical to religion's true interests. The approximation to certainty which might be afforded by objective probability is rejected, not only for the reasons given in the Approximation Argument and Postponement Argument, but also from a deeper motive, "since on the contrary it behooves us to get rid of introductory guarantees of security, proofs from consequences, and the whole mob of public pawnbrokers and guarantors, so as to permit the absurd to stand out in all its clarity—in order that the individual may believe if he wills it; I merely say that it must be strenuous in the highest degree so to believe" (p. 190).

As this last quotation indicates, Kierkegaard thinks that religious belief ought to be based on a strenuous exertion of the will—a passionate striving. His reasons for thinking that objective probability is religiously undesirable have to do with the place of passion in religion, and constitute what I call the Passion Argument. The first premise of the argument is that the most essential and the most valuable of religiousness is passion, indeed an infinite passion, a passion of the greatest possible intensity. The second premise is that an infinite passion requires objective improbability. And the conclusion therefore is that that which is most essential and most valuable in religiousness requires objective improbability.

My discussion of this argument will have three parts. (a) First I will try to clarify, very briefly, what it is that is supposed to be objectively improbable. (b) Then we will consider Kierkegaard's reasons for holding that infinite passion requires objective improbability. In so doing we will also gain a clearer understanding of what a Kierkegaardian infinite passion is. (c) Finally I will discuss the first premise of the argument—although issues will arise at that point which I do not pretend to be able to settle by argument.

(a) What are the beliefs whose improbability is needed by religious passion? Kierkegaard will hardly be satisfied with the improbability of just any one belief; it must surely be at least an important belief. On the other hand it would clearly be preposterous to suppose that every belief involved in Christianity must be objectively improbable. (Consider, for example, the belief that the man Jesus did indeed live.) I think that what is demanded in the Passion Argument is the objective improbability of at least one belief which must be true if the goal sought by the religious passion is to be attained.

(b) We can find in the *Postscript* suggestions of several reasons for thinking that an infinite passion needs objective improbability. The two that seem to me most interesting have to do with (i) the risks accepted and (ii) the costs paid in pursuance of a passionate interest.

(i) One reason that Kierkegaard has for valuing objective improbability is that it increases the *risk* attaching to the religious life, and risk is so essential for the expression of religious passion that "without risk there is no faith" (p. 182). About the nature of an eternal happiness, the goal of religious striving, Kierkegaard says "there is nothing to be said . . . except that it is the good which is attained by venturing everything absolutely" (p. 382).

> But what then does it mean to venture? A venture is the precise correlative of an uncertainty; when the certainty is there the venture becomes impossible. . . . If what I hope to gain by venturing is itself certain, I do not risk or venture, but make an exchange. . . . No, if I am in truth resolved to venture, in truth resolved to strive for the attainment of the highest good, the uncertainty must be there, and I must have room

> to move, so to speak. But the largest space I can obtain, where there is room for the most vehement gesture of the passion that embraces the infinite, is uncertainty of knowledge with respect to an eternal happiness, or the certain knowledge that the choice is in the finite sense a piece of madness: now there is room, now you can venture! (pp. 380–82)

How is it that objective improbability provides the largest space for the most vehement gesture of infinite passion? Consider two cases. (A) You plunge into a raging torrent to rescue from drowning someone you love, who is crying for help. (B) You plunge into a raging torrent in a desperate attempt to rescue someone you love, who appears to be unconscious and *may* already have drowned. In both cases you manifest a passionate interest in saving the person, risking your own life in order to do so. But I think Kierkegaard would say there is more passion in the second case than in the first. For in the second case you risk your life in what is, objectively considered, a smaller chance that you will be able to save your loved one. A greater passion is required for a more desperate attempt.

A similar assessment may be made of the following pair of cases. (A′) You stake everything on your faith of Christianity, knowing that it is objectively 99 per cent probable that Christianity is true. (B′) You stake everything on your faith in the truth of Christianity, knowing that the truth of Christianity is, objectively, possible but so improbable that its probability is, say, as small as $1/10^{2,000,000}$. There is passion in both cases, but Kierkegaard will say that there is more passion in the second case than in the first. For to venture the same stake (namely, everything) on a much smaller chance of success shows greater passion.

Acceptance of risk can thus be seen as a *measure* of the intensity of passion. I believe this provides us with one way of understanding what Kierkegaard means when he calls religious passion "infinite." An *infinite* passionate interest in *x* is an interest so strong that it leads one to make the greatest possible sacrifices in order to obtain *x*, on the smallest possible chance of success. The infinity of the passion is shown in that there is no sacrifice so great one will not make it, and no chance of success so small one will not act on it. A passion which is infinite in this sense requires, by its very nature, a situation of maximum risk for its expression.

It will doubtless be objected that this argument involves a misunderstanding of what a passionate interest is. Such an interest is a disposition. In order to have a great passionate interest it is not necessary actually to make a great sacrifice with a small chance of success; all that is necessary is to have such an intense interest that one *would* do so if an appropriate occasion should arise. It is therefore a mistake to say that there *is* more passion in case (B) than in case (A), or in (B′) than in (A′). More passion is *shown* in (B) than in (A), and in (B′) than in (A′); but an equal passion may exist in cases in which there is no occasion to show it.

This objection may well be correct as regards what we normally mean by "passionate interest." But that is not decisive for the argument. The crucial question is what part dispositions, possibly unactualized, ought to play in religious devotion. And here we must have a digression about the position of the *Postscript* on this question—a position that is complex at best and is not obviously consistent.

In the first place I do not think that Kierkegaard would be prepared to think of passion, or a passionate interest, as primarily a disposition that might remain unactualized. He seems to conceive of passion chiefly as an intensity in which one actually does and feels. "Passion is momentary" (p. 178), although capable of continual repetition. And what is momentary in such a way that it must be repeated rather than protracted is presumably an occurrence rather than a disposition. It agrees with this conception of passion that Kierkegaard idealizes a life of "persistent striving," and says that the religious task is to "exercise" the God-relationship and to give "existential expression" to the religious choice (pp. 110, 364, 367).

All of this supports the view that what Kierkegaard means by "an infinite passionate interest" is a pattern of actual decision-making, in which one continually exercises and expresses one's religiousness by making the greatest possible sacrifices on the smallest possible chance of success. In order to actualize such a pattern of life one needs chances of success that are as small as possible. That is the room that is required for "the most vehement gesture" of infinite passion.

But on the other hand Kierkegaard does allow a dispositional element in the religious life, and even precisely in the making of the greatest possible sacrifices. We might suppose that if we are to make the greatest possible sacrifices in our religious devotion, we must do so by abandoning all worldly interests and devoting all our time and attention to religion. That is what monasticism attempts to do, as Kierkegaard sees it; and (in the *Postscript,* at any rate) he rejects the attempt, contrary to what our argument to this point would have led us to expect of him. He holds that "resignation" (pp. 353, 367) or "renunciation" (pp. 362, 386) of *all* finite ends is precisely the first thing that religiousness requires; but he means a renunciation that is compatible with pursuing and enjoying finite ends (pp. 362–71). This renunciation is the practice of a sort of detachment; Kierkegaard uses the image of a dentist loosening the soft tissues around a tooth, while it is still in place, in preparation for pulling it (p. 367). It is partly a matter of not treating finite things with a desperate seriousness, but with a certain coolness or humor, even while one pursues them (pp. 368, 370).

This coolness is not just a disposition. But the renunciation also has a dispositional aspect. "Now if for any individual an eternal happiness is his highest good, this will mean that all finite satisfactions are volitionally relegated to the status of what may have to be renounced in favor of an eternal happiness" (p. 350). The volitional relegation is not a disposition but an act of choice. The object of this choice, however, appears to be a dispositional state—the state of being such that one *would* forgo any finite satisfaction *if* it *were* religiously necessary or advantageous to do so.

It seems clear that Kierkegaard, in the *Postscript,* is willing to admit a dispositional element at one point in the religious venture, but not at another. It is enough in most cases, he thinks, if one is *prepared* to cease for the sake of religion from pursuing some finite end; but it is not enough that one *would* hold to one's belief in the face of objective improbability. The belief must actually be improbable, although the pursuit of the finite need not actually cease. What is not clear is a reason for this disparity. The following hypothesis, admittedly somewhat speculative as interpretation of the text, is the best explanation I can offer.

The admission of a dispositional element in the religious renunciation of the finite is something to which Kierkegaard seems to be driven by the view that there is no alternative to it except idolatry. For suppose one actually ceases from all worldly pursuits and enters a monastery. In the monastery one would pursue a number of particular ends (such as getting up in the middle of the night to say the offices) which, although religious in a way ("churchy," one might say), are still finite. The absolute *telos* or end of religion is no more to be identified with them than with the ends pursued by an alderman (pp. 362–71). To pretend otherwise would be to make an idolatrous identification of the absolute end with some finite end. An existing person cannot have sacrificed everything by actually having ceased from pursuing *all* finite ends. For as long as he lives and acts he is pursuing some finite end. Therefore his renouncing *everything* finite must be at least partly dispositional.

Kierkegaard does not seem happy with this position. He regards it as of the utmost importance that the religious passion should come to expression. The problem of finding an adequate expression for a passion for an infinite end, in the face of the fact that in every concrete action one will be pursuing some finite end, is treated in the *Postscript* as the central problem of religion (see especially pp. 386–468). If the sacrifice of everything finite must remain largely dispositional, then perhaps it is all the more important to Kierkegaard that the smallness of the chance for which it is sacrificed should be fully actual, so that the infinity of the religious passion may be measured by an actuality in at least one aspect of the religious venture.

(ii) According to Kierkegaard, as I have argued, the intensity of a passion is measured in part by the smallness of the chances of success that one acts on. It can also be measured in part by its *costliness*—that is, by how much one gives up or suffers in acting on those chances. This second measure can also be made the basis of an argument for the claim that an infinite passion requires objective improbability. For the objective improbability of a religious belief, if recognized, increases the costliness of holding it. The risk involved in staking everything on an objectively improbable belief gives rise to an anxiety and mental suffering whose acceptance is itself a sacrifice. It seems to follow that if one is not staking everything on a belief one sees to be objectively improbable, one's passion is not infinite in Kierkegaard's sense, since one's sacrifice could be greater if one did adhere to an improbable belief.

Kierkegaard uses an argument similar to this. For God to give us objective knowledge of Himself, eliminating paradox from it, would be "to lower the price of the God-relationship."

> And even if God could be imagined willing, no man with passion in his heart could desire it. To a maiden genuinely in love it could never occur that she bought her happiness too dear, but rather that she had not bought it dear enough. And just as the passion of the infinite was itself the truth, so in the case of the highest value it holds true that the price is the value, that a low price means a poor value. . . . (p. 207)

Kierkegaard here appears to hold, first, that an increase in the objective probability of religious belief would reduce its costliness, and second, that the value of a religious life is measured by its cost. I take it his reason for the second of these claims is that passion is the most valuable thing in a religious life and passion is measured by its cost. If we grant Kierkegaard the requisite conception of an infinite passion, we seem once again to have a plausible argument for the view that objective improbability is required for such a passion.

(c) We must therefore consider whether infinite passion, as Kierkegaard conceives of it, ought to be part of the religious ideal of life. Such a passion is a striving, or pattern of decision-making, in which, with the greatest possible intensity of feeling, one continually makes the greatest possible sacrifices on the smallest possible chance of success. This seems to me an impossible ideal. I doubt that any human being could have a passion of this sort, because I doubt that one could make a sacrifice so great that a greater could not be made, or have a (nonzero) chance of success so small that a smaller could not be had.

But even if Kierkegaard's ideal is impossible, one might want to try to approximate it. Intensity of passion might still be measured by the greatness of sacrifices made and the smallness of chances of success acted on, even if we cannot hope for a greatest possible or a smallest possible here. And it could be claimed that the most essential and valuable thing in religiousness is a passion that is very intense (though it cannot be infinite) by this standard—the more intense the better. This claim will not support an argument that objective improbability is absolutely required for religious passion. For a passion could presumably be very intense, involving great sacrifices and risks of some other sort, without an objectively improbable belief. But it could still be argued that objectively improbable religious beliefs enhance the value of the religious life by increasing its sacrifices and diminishing its chances of success, whereas objective probability detracts from the value of religious passion by diminishing its intensity.

The most crucial question about the Passion Argument, then, is whether maximization of sacrifice and risk are so valuable in religion as to make objective improbability a desirable characteristic of religious beliefs. Certainly much religious thought and feeling places a very high value on sacrifice and on passionate intensity. But the doctrine that it is desirable to increase without limit, or to the highest possible degree (if there is one) the cost and risk of a religious life is less plausible (to say the least) than the view that *some* degree of cost and risk may add to the value of a religious life. The former doctrine would set the religious interest at enmity with all other interests or at least with the best of them. Kierkegaard is surely right in thinking that it would be impossible to live without pursuing some finite ends. But even so it would be possible to exchange the pursuit of better finite ends for the pursuit of worse ones—for example, by exchanging the pursuit of truth, beauty, and satisfying personal relationships for the self-flagellating pursuit of pain. And a way of life would be the costlier for requiring such an exchange. Kierkegaard does not, in the *Postscript,* demand it. But the presuppositions of his Passion Argument seem to imply that such a sacrifice would be religiously desirable. Such a conception of religion is demonic. In a tolerable religious ethics some way must be found to conceive of the religious interest as inclusive rather than exclusive of the best of other interests—including, I think, the interest in having well-grounded beliefs.

4. Pascal's Wager and Kierkegaard's Leap

Ironically, Kierkegaard's views about religious passion suggest a way in which his religious beliefs could be based on objective reasoning—not on reasoning which would show them to be objectively probable, but on reasoning which shows them to be objectively advantageous. Consider the situation of a person whom Kierkegaard would regard as a genuine Christian believer. What would such a person want most of all? He would want above all else to attain the truth through Christianity. That is, he would desire both that Christianity be true and that he himself be related to it as a genuine believer. He would desire that state of affairs (which we may call *S*) so ardently that he would be willing to sacrifice everything else to obtain it, given only the smallest possible chance of success.

We can therefore construct the following argument, which has an obvious analogy to Pascal's Wager. Let us assume that there is, objectively, some chance, however small, that Christianity is true. This is an assumption which Kierkegaard accepts (p. 31), and I think it is plausible. There are two possibilities, then: either Christianity is true, or it is false. (Others might object to so stark a disjunction, but Kierkegaard will not.) If Christianity is false it is impossible for anyone to obtain *S*, since *S* includes the truth of Christianity. It is only if Christianity is true that anything one does will help one or hinder one in obtaining *S*. And if Christianity is true, one will obtain *S* just in case one becomes a genuine Christian believer. It seems obvious that one would increase one's chances of becoming a genuine Christian believer by becoming one now (if one can), even if the truth of Christian beliefs is now objectively uncertain or improbable. Hence it would seem to be advantageous for anyone who can to become a genuine Christian believer now, if he wants *S* so much that he would be willing to sacrifice everything else for the smallest possible chance of obtaining *S*. Indeed I believe that the argument I have given for this conclusion is a piece of objective reasoning, and that Christian belief is therefore *objectively* advantageous for anyone who wants *S* as much as a Kierkegaardian genuine Christian must want it.

Of course this argument does not tend at all to show that it is objectively probable that Christianity is true. It only gives a practical, prudential reason for believing, to someone who has a certain desire. Nor does the argument do anything to prove that such an absolutely overriding desire for *S* is reasonable.[8] It does show, however, that just as Kierkegaard's position has more logical structure than one might at first think, it is more difficult than he probably realized for him to get away entirely from objective justification.[9]

Notes

1. Søren Kierkegaard, *Concluding Unscientific Postscript,* translated by David F. Swenson; introduction, notes, and completion of translation by Walter Lowrie (Princeton: Princeton University Press for the American-Scandinavian Foundation, 1941). Page references in parentheses in the body of the present paper are to this work.
2. The argument is not original with Kierkegaard. It can be found in works of G. E. Lessing and D. F. Strauss that Kierkegaard had read. See especially Thulstrup's quotation and discussion of a passage from Strauss in the commentary portion of Søren Kierkegaard, *Philosophical Fragments,* trans. David F. Swenson, 2d ed., translation revised by Howard V. Hong, with introduction and commentary by Niels Thulstrup (Princeton: Princeton University Press, 1962), pp. 149–51.
3. Kierkegaard, *Philosophical Fragments,* p. 104; cf. pp. 102–3.
4. Essentially the same argument can be found in a plea, which has had great influence among more recent theologians, for making Christian faith independent of the results of critical historical study of the Bible: Martin Kähler's famous lecture, first delivered in 1892, *Der sogenannte historische Jesus und der geschichtliche biblische Christus* (Munich: Christus Kaiser Verlag, 1961), p. 50f.
5. Kierkegaard, *Philosophical Fragments,* p. 52.
6. Kierkegaard notes the possibility that in believing in God's existence "I make so bold as to defy all objections, even those that have not yet been made." But in that case he thinks the belief is not really based

on the evidence of God's work in the world; "it is not from the works that I make my proof" (*Philosophical Fragments,* p. 52).

7. Søren Kierkegaard, *Fear and Trembling,* trans. Walter Lowrie, 2d ed. (Princeton, Princeton University Press, 1970; published in one volume with *Sickness unto Death*), p. 131. Cf. *Postscript,* p. 31f.
8. It is worth noting, though, that a similar argument might still provide some less overriding justification of belief to someone who had a strong, but less overriding, desire for *S*.
9. Versions of this paper have been read to philosophical colloquia at Occidental College and California State University, Fullerton. I am indebted to participants in those discussions, to students in many of my classes, and particularly to Marilyn McCord Adams, Van Harvey, Thomas Kselman, William Laserow, and James Muyskens, for helpful comment on the ideas which are contained in this paper (or which would have been, had it not been for their criticisms).

C. EVOLUTION AND CREATION

Evolution or Creation?

HENRY M. MORRIS

Henry M. Morris (1918–) is director of the Institute for Creation Research. His books include *Scientific Creationism.*

Impossibility of Scientific Proof of Origins

. . . [it] must also be emphasized that it is impossible to *prove* scientifically any particular concept of origins to be true. This is obvious from the fact that the essence of the scientific method is experimental observation and repeatability. A scientific investigator, be he ever so resourceful and brilliant, can neither observe nor repeat *origins!*

This means that, though it is important to have a philosophy of origins, it can only be achieved by faith, not by sight. That is no argument against it, however. Every step we take in life is a step of faith. Even the pragmatist who insists he will only believe what he can see, *believes* that his pragmatism is the best philosophy, though he can't prove it! He also believes in invisible atoms and in such abstractions as the future.

As a matter of observation, belief in something is necessary for true mental health. A philosophy of life is a philosophy, not a scientific experiment. A life based on the whim of the moment, with no rationale, is "a tale told by an idiot, full of sound and fury, signifying nothing."

Thus, one must *believe,* at least with respect to ultimate origins. However, for optimally beneficial application of that belief, his faith should be a reasoned faith, not a credulous faith or a prescribed faith.

To illustrate more exactly what we mean when we say origins cannot be proved, a brief discussion is given below on each of the two basic concepts of origins, creation and evolution:

A. *Creation cannot be proved*

1. Creation is not taking place now, so far as can be observed. Therefore, it was accomplished sometime in the past, if at all, and thus is inaccessible to the scientific method.
2. It is impossible to devise a scientific experiment to describe the creation process, or even to ascertain whether such a process *can* take place. The Creator does not create at the whim of a scientist.

B. *Evolution cannot be proved*

1. If evolution is taking place today, it operates too slowly to be measurable, and, therefore, is outside the realm of empirical science. To transmute one kind of organism into a higher kind of organism would presumably take millions of years, and no team of scientific observers is available to make measurements on any such experiment.

From *Scientific Creationism* (San Diego, Calif.: Creation-Life Publishers, 1974), pp. 4–13, 51–58.

2. The small variations in organisms which are observed to take place today . . . are irrelevant to this question, since there is no way to prove that these changes within present kinds eventually change the kinds into different, higher kinds. Since small variations (including mutations) are as much to be expected in the creation model as in the evolution model, they are of no value in discriminating between the two models.
3. Even if modern scientists should ever actually achieve the artificial creation of life from non-life, or of higher kinds from lower kinds, in the laboratory, this would not *prove* in any way that such changes did, or even could, take place in the past by random natural processes.

Since it is often maintained by evolutionists that evolution is scientific, whereas creationism is religious, it will be well at this point to cite several leading evolutionists who have recognized that evolution also is incapable of being proved.[1]

Evolution Operates Too Slowly for Scientific Observation

One of the nation's leading evolutionists, Theodosius Dobzhansky, has admitted:

> The applicability of the experimental method to the study of such unique historical processes is severely restricted before all else by the time intervals involved, which far exceed the lifetime of any human experimenter. And yet, it is just such impossibility that is demanded by anti-evolutionists when they ask for "proofs" of evolution which they would magnanimously accept as satisfactory.[2]

Note the tacit admission that "the experimental method" is an "impossibility" when applied to evolution.

Evolution Is a Dogma Incapable of Refutation

Two leading modern biologists have pointed out the fact that, since evolution cannot in any conceivable way be disproved, therefore, neither can it be proved.

> Our theory of evolution has become . . . one which cannot be refuted by any possible observations. It is thus "outside of empirical science," but not necessarily false. No one can think of ways in which to test it. . . . [Evolutionary ideas] have become part of an evolutionary dogma accepted by most of us as part of our training.[3]

Similarly, Peter Medawar recognized the problem entailed by the fact that no way exists by which to test evolution.

> There are philosophical or methodological objections to evolutionary theory. . . . It is too difficult to imagine or envisage an evolutionary episode which could not be explained by the formulae of neo-Darwinism.[4]

In other words, both the long neck of the giraffe and the short neck of the hippopotamus can presumably be explained by natural selection. A theory which incorporates everything really *explains* nothing! It is tautologous. Those who survive in the struggle for existence are the fittest because the fittest are the ones who survive.

Evolution Is an Authoritarian System To Be Believed

> It seems at times as if many of our modern writers on evolution have had their views by some sort of revelation and they base their opinions on the evolution of life, from the simplest form to the complex, entirely on the nature of specific and intra-specific evolution. . . . It is premature, not to say arrogant, on our part if we make any dogmatic assertion as to the mode of evolution of the major branches of the animal kingdom.[5]

> But the facts of paleontology conform equally well with other interpretations . . . e.g., divine creation, etc., and paleontology by itself can neither prove nor refute such ideas.[6]

Thomas Huxley, probably more responsible than any other one man for the acceptance of

Darwinian philosophy, nevertheless recognized that:

> . . . "creation" in the ordinary sense of the word, is perfectly conceivable. I find no difficulty in conceiving that, at some former period, this universe was not in existence; and that it made its appearance in six days . . . in consequence of the volition of some pre-existing Being.[7]

The Reason for Favoring Evolution Is Not Because of the Scientific Evidence

An outstanding British biologist of a number of years ago made the following remarkable observation:

> If so, it will present a parallel to the theory of evolution itself, a theory universally accepted not because it can be proved by logically coherent evidence to be true but because the only alternative, special creation, is clearly incredible.[8]

The only reason for saying that special creation is incredible would be if one had certain knowledge that there was no God. Obviously, if no Creator exists, then special creation is incredible. But since a universal negative can only be proved if one has universal knowledge, such a statement requires omniscience. Thus, by denying God, Dr. Watson is claiming the attributes of God himself.

There are some scientists, at least, who find it easier to believe in the deity of an omnipotent Creator than in the deity of Professor Watson.

The Two Models of Origins

It is, as shown in the previous section, impossible to demonstrate scientifically which of the two concepts of origins is really true. Although many people teach evolution as though it were a proven fact of science, it is obvious that this is false teaching. There are literally thousands of scientists[9] and other educated intellectuals today who reject evolution, and this would certainly not be the case if evolution were as obvious as many scientists say it is.

The same is true of creation, of course. Although many believe special creation to be an absolute fact of history, they must believe this for theological, rather than scientific reasons. Neither evolution nor creation can be either confirmed or falsified scientifically.[10]

Furthermore, it is clear that neither evolution nor creation is, in the proper sense, either a scientific theory or a scientific hypothesis. Though people might speak of the "theory of evolution" or of the "theory of creation," such terminology is imprecise. This is because neither can be *tested.* A valid scientific hypothesis must be capable of being formulated experimentally, such that the experimental results either confirm or reject its validity.

As noted in the statement by Ehrlich and Birch cited previously, however, there is no conceivable way to do this. Ideally, we might like to set up an experiment, the results of which would demonstrate either evolution or creation to have been true. But there is no one test, nor any series of tests, which can do this scientifically.

All of these strictures do not mean, however, that we cannot discuss this question scientifically and objectively. Indeed, it is extremely important that we do so, if we are really to understand this vital question of origins and to arrive at a satisfactory basis for the faith we must ultimately exercise in one or the other.

A more proper approach is to think in terms of two scientific models, the *evolution model* and the *creation model.* A "model" is a conceptual framework, an orderly system of thought, within which one tries to correlate observable data, and even to predict data. When alternative models exist, they can be compared as to their respective capacities for correlating such data. When, as in this case, neither can be proved, the decision between the two cannot be solely objective. Normally, in such a case, the model which correlates the greater number of data, with the smallest number of unresolved contradictory data, would be accepted as the more probably correct model.

When particular facts do show up which seem to contradict the predictions of the model, it may still be possible to assimilate the data by a slight modification of the original model. As a matter of fact, in the case of the evolution model, as Ehrlich and Birch said: "Every conceivable observation can be fitted into it."

The same generalization, of course, is true of

the creation model. There is no observational fact imaginable which cannot, one way or another, be made to fit the creation model. The only way to decide objectively between them, therefore, is to note which model fits the facts and predictions with the smallest number of these secondary assumptions.

Creationists are convinced that, when this procedure is carefully followed, the creation model will always fit the facts as well as or better than will the evolution model. Evolutionists may, of course, believe otherwise. In either case, it is important that everyone have the facts at hand with which to consider *both* models, rather than one only. The latter is brainwashing, not brain-using!

Since the rest of this book is devoted primarily to a comparison of these two models, it is important that everyone using it, both teachers and students, clearly understand the formulation of the two models and their implications.

A. The Evolution Model The evolutionary system attempts to explain the origin, development, and meaning of all things in terms of natural laws and processes which operate today as they have in the past. No extraneous processes, requiring the special activity of an external agent, or Creator, are permitted. The universe, in all its aspects, evolves itself into higher levels of order (particles to people) by means of its innate properties.

To confirm that this is the essential nature of the evolution model, several recognized authorities are cited below, giving their own concepts of evolution.

> Most enlightened persons now accept as a fact that everything in the cosmos—from heavenly bodies to human beings—has developed and continues to develop through evolutionary processes.[11]

> Evolution comprises all the stages of the development of the universe: the cosmic, biological, and human or cultural developments. . . . Life is a product of the evolution of inorganic nature, and man is a product of the evolution of life.[12]

> Evolution in the extended sense can be defined as a directional and essentially irreversible process occurring in time, which in its course gives rise to an increase of variety and in increasingly high level of organization in its products. Our present knowledge indeed forces us to the view that the whole of reality is evolution—a single process of self-transformation.[13]

> Biological evolution can, however, be explained without recourse to a Creator or a planning agent external to the organisms themselves. There is no evidence, either, of any vital force or immanent energy directing the evolutionary process toward the production of specified kinds of organisms.[14]

Thus evolution entails a self-contained universe, in which its innate laws develop everything into higher levels of organization. Particles evolve into elements, elements into complex chemicals, complex chemicals into simple living systems, simple life forms into complex life, complex animal life into man.

Summarizing, evolution is: (1) naturalistic; (2) self-contained; (3) non-purposive; (4) directional; (5) irreversible; (6) universal; and, (7) continuing.

B. The Creation Model Diametrically opposed to the evolution model, the creation model involves a process of special creation which is: (1) supernaturalistic; (2) externally directed; (3) purposive, and (4) completed. Like evolution, the creation model also applies universally. It also is irreversibly directional, but its direction is downward toward lower levels of complexity rather than upward toward higher levels. The completed original creation was perfect and has since then been "running down."

The creation model thus postulates a period of special creation in the beginning, during which all the basic laws and categories of nature, including the major kinds of plants and animals, as well as man, were brought into existence by special creative and integrative processes which are no longer in operation. Once the creation was finished, these processes of *creation* were replaced by processes of *conservation,* which were designed by the Creator to sustain and maintain the basic systems He had created.

In addition to the primary concept of a completed creation followed by conservation, the creation model proposes a basic principle of disintegration now at work in nature (since any significant change in a *perfect* primeval creation must be in the direction of imperfection). Also, the evidence in the earth's crust of past physical convulsions seems to warrant inclusion of post-creation global catastrophism in the model.

The two models may be easily compared by studying the table below:

Evolution Model	Creation Model
Continuing naturalistic origin	Completed supernatural origin
Net present increase in complexity	Net present decrease in complexity
Earth history dominated by uniformitarianism	Earth history dominated by catastrophism

It is proposed that these two models be used as systems for "predicting" data, to see which one does so more effectively. To do this, one should imagine that neither the evolutionist nor the creationist knows in advance what data will be found. They do not know what they will find but bravely make predictions, each on the basis of his own model.

The table below indicates the predictions that would probably be made in several important categories.

It should be noted that the tabulated predictions are predictions of the *primary* models, as defined in their most general terms as in the foregoing discussion. These primary models may be modified by secondary assumptions to fit certain conditions. For example, the basic evolution model may be extended to include harmful, as well as beneficial, mutations, but this is not a natural prediction of the basic concept of evolution. If the "predictions" of evolution, as listed in the above table, were actually observed in the natural world, they would, of course, in every case be enthusiastically acclaimed as strong confirmations of the evolution model. That fact justifies the conclusion that these are the *basic* predictions of evolution.

The above predictions are merely suggestive of the types of entities that can be used to contrast the two models. Several of these will be discussed in some detail later. At this point, it may be noted that creationists maintain that the predictions of the creation model do fit the observed facts in nature better than do those of the evolution model. The data must be *explained* by the

	Basic Predictions of	
Category	**Evolution Model**	**Creation Model**
Structure of Natural Law	Constantly Changing	Invariable
Galactic Universe	Galaxies Changing	Galaxies Constant
Structures of Stars	Stars Changing into Other Types	Stars Unchanged
Other Heavenly Bodies	Building Up	Breaking Down
Types of Rock Formations	Different in Different "Ages"	Similar in All "Ages"
Appearance of Life	Life Evolving from Non-life	Life Only from Life
Array of Organisms	Continuum of Organisms	Distinct Kinds of Organisms
Appearance of Kinds of Life	New Kinds Appearing	No New Kinds Appearing
Mutations in Organisms	Beneficial	Harmful
Natural Selection	Creative Process	Conservative Process
Age of Earth	Extremely Old	Probably Young
Fossil Record	Innumerable Transitions	Systematic Gaps
Appearance of Man	Ape-Human Intermediates	No Ape-Human Intermediaries
Nature of Man	Quantitatively Superior to Animals	Qualitatively Distinct from Animals
Origin of Civilization	Slow and Gradual	Contemporaneous with Man

evolutionist, but they are *predicted* by the creationist.

. . . .

Variation and Selection

When Charles Darwin first published his theory of the origin of species by natural selection, it was his idea that the continual small variations between individuals of a species, that are observed in nature, would confer differing degrees of advantage or disadvantage in the struggle for existence. Those with significant advantages would be favored by natural selection and thus would survive longer to transmit these characteristics by inheritance to their descendants. Thus, gradually, completely new and higher types of organisms would emerge.

Normal variations were later found to be subject to the rigid Mendelian laws of inheritance, representing nothing really novel but only characters already latent within the genetic system. Modern molecular biology, with its penetrating insight into the remarkable genetic code implanted in the DNA system, has further confirmed that normal variations operate only within the range specified by the DNA for the particular type of organism, so that no truly novel characteristics, producing higher degrees of order or complexity, can appear. Variation is horizontal, not vertical!

It is normal variation of this sort, unfortunately, which is still commonly offered as evidence of present-day evolution. The classic example of the *peppered moth* of England, "evolving" from a dominant light coloration to a dominant dark coloration, as the tree trunks grew darker with pollutants during the advancing industrial revolution, is the best case in point. This was not evolution in the true sense at all but only variation. Natural selection is a conservative force, operating to keep kinds from becoming extinct when the environment changes.

> The [peppered moth] experiments beautifully demonstrate natural selection—or survival of the fittest—in action, but they do not show evolution in progress, for however the populations may alter in their content of light, intermediate, or dark forms, all the moths remain from beginning to end *Biston betularia*.[15]

In other words, the phenomenon of variation and natural selection, rather than explaining evolution in the way Darwin thought it did, is really a marvelous example of the creationist's principle of conservation in operation. That is, a fundamental prediction from the creation model is that, since the Creator had a purpose for each kind of organism created, He would institute a system which would not only assure its genetic integrity but would also enable it to survive in nature. The genetic system would be such as to maintain its identity as a specific kind while, at the same time, allowing it to adjust its characteristics (within limits) to changes in environment. Otherwise, even very slight changes in its habitat, food supply, etc., might cause its extinction.

Natural selection thus cannot produce any real novelties. It is a passive thing, a sort of sieve, through which pass only the variants which fit the environment. Those which do not fit are stopped and discarded by the sieving process. However, it can only act on variants which come to it via the genetic potentialities implicit in the DNA structure for its particular kind; it cannot generate anything new itself. The reshuffling, or recombination, of characters already implicitly present in the germ cell certainly does not create anything really new in an evolutionary sense. Nevertheless, this phenomenon of recombination followed by natural selection is somehow regarded by evolutionists as a very important aspect of their model.

> Recombination is by far the most important source of genetic variation, that is, of material for natural selection.[16]

As the term itself suggests, recombination does not generate something new, certainly not something of a higher order of complexity. In effect, it is merely another name for variation.

But even if variation, or recombination, really could produce something truly novel, for natural selection to act on, this novelty would almost certainly be quickly eliminated. A new structural or organic feature which would confer a real advantage in the struggle for existence—say a wing, for a previously earth-bound animal, or an eye, for a hitherto sightless animal—would be useless or even harmful until fully developed. There would be no reason at all for natural selection to favor any incipient wing or incipient eye or any other incipient feature. Yet, somehow, if the evolution model is valid, wings have "evolved" four different times (in insects, flying reptiles, birds and bats) and eyes have "evolved" independently at least three times. Salisbury has recently commented on this remarkable fact as follows:

> My last doubt concerns so-called parallel evolution. . . . Even something as complex as the eye has appeared several times; for example, in the squid, the vertebrates, and the arthropods. It's bad enough accounting for the origin of such things once, but the thought of producing them several times according to the modern synthetic theory makes my head swim.[17]

Which comment reminds us that Charles Darwin said that the thought of the eye, and how it could possibly be produced by natural selection, made him ill.

Natural selection, acting upon the variational potential designed into the genetic code for each organism, is thus a powerful device for permitting *horizontal* variation, or *radiation,* to enable it to adapt to the environment and thus to survive. It is useless, however, in generating a *vertical* variation, leading to the development of higher, more complex kinds of organisms. In fact, it acts to *prevent* such vertical variation, since incipient novelties would be useless at best until truly developed and functional. In most cases, in fact, such novelties would be positively harmful. It is significant that evolutionists have never yet been able to document, either in the living world or the fossil world, an incipient organ or structure leading to a future useful feature.

All of which is a specific confirmation of the predictions of the creation model.

Genetic Mutations

Since it is obvious that neither ordinary variations, nor recombinations of existing characters, can account for "upward" evolution, some extraordinary mechanism must be found for this purpose. In the modern synthetic theory of evolution, or neo-Darwinism, the mechanism universally adopted for this purpose is that of *mutation.*

A mutation is assumed to be a real structural change in a gene, of such character that something novel is produced, not merely a reworking of something already there. In some way, the linkages in a segment of the DNA molecule are changed, so that different "information" is conveyed via the genetic code in the formation of the structure of the descendant.

> It must not be forgotten that mutation is the ultimate source of all genetic variation found in natural populations and the only new material available for natural selection to work on.[18]

The phenomenon of mutation, therefore, is a most important component of the evolution model. The evolution model must postulate *some* mechanism to produce the required upward progress in complexity which characterizes the model in its broadest dimension. Mutation is supposedly that mechanism.

The basic evolution model would predict, therefore, that mutations must be primarily beneficial, generating a "vertical" change upward toward higher degrees of order. Each such change must be positively helpful in the environment if it is to be preserved by natural selection and contribute to evolutionary progress.

The creation model, on the other hand, would predict that, if there are any such things as real mutations, causing "vertical" changes in complexity and order of the kinds, they will be harmful, not beneficial.

With these two models in mind, let us now consider some of the actual experimental facts relative to mutations.

1. *Mutations are random, not directed.*

> It remains true to say that we know of no way other than random mutation by which new hereditary variation comes into being, nor any process other than natural selection

> by which the hereditary constitution of a population changes from one generation to the next.[19]

There is no way to control mutations to make them produce characteristics which might be needed. Natural selection must simply take what comes.

2. *Mutations are rare, not common.*

> It is probably fair to estimate the frequency of a majority of mutations in higher organisms between one in ten thousand and one in a million per gene per generation.[20]

3. *Good mutations are very, very rare.*

The man who has probably devoted more study than any other man to experimental observation of mutations, said:

> But mutations are found to be of a random nature, so far as their utility is concerned. Accordingly, the great majority of mutations, certainly well over 99%, are harmful in some way, as is to be expected of the effects of accidental occurrences.[21]

The man probably more responsible than any other for the modern view of evolution known as neo-Darwinism, which says evolution proceeds by the accumulation of small mutations preserved by natural selection, is even less confident in the frequency of beneficial mutations.

> A proportion of favorable mutations of one in a thousand does not sound much, but is probably generous, since so many mutations are lethal, preventing the organism living at all, and the great majority of the rest throw the machinery slightly out of gear.[22]

As a matter of fact, the phenomenon of a truly beneficial mutation, one which is *known* to be a mutation and not merely a latent characteristic already present in the genetic material but lacking previous opportunity for expression, and one which is permanently beneficial in the natural environment, has yet to be documented. Some evolutionists doubt that they occur at all:

> Accordingly, mutations are more than just sudden changes in heredity; they also affect viability, and, to the best of our knowledge, invariably affect it adversely. Does not this fact show that mutations are really assaults on the organism's central being, its basic capacity to be a living thing?[23]

4. *The net effect of all mutations is harmful*

Even if the mutations are not harmful enough to cause their carriers to be eliminated completely by natural selection, the over-all effect is to gradually lower the viability of the population.

> The large majority of mutations, however, are harmful or even lethal to the individual in whom they are expressed. Such mutations can be regarded as introducing a 'load,' or genetic burden, into the pool. The term 'genetic load' was first used by the late H. J. Muller, who recognized that the rate of mutations is increased by numerous agents man has introduced into his environment, notably ionizing radiation and mutagenic chemicals.[24]

That the net effect of mutations is harmful, rather than beneficial, to the supposed progress of evolution, is made transparently clear by the zeal with which evolutionists for decades have been trying to get mutation-producing radiations removed from the environment!

> The most important actions that need to be taken, however, are in the area of minimizing the addition of new mutagens to those already present in the environment. Any increase in the mutational load is harmful, if not immediately, then certainly to future generations.[25]

It does seem that, if evolutionists really believed that evolution is due to mutations, they would favor all measures which could increase the rate of mutations and thus facilitate further evolution. Instead, they have consistently for decades opposed nuclear testing for the very purpose of *preventing* mutations!

5. *Mutations affect and are affected by many genes.*

The mutation concept is no longer as simple as it once was. Instead of a given characteristic being controlled by a specific gene, it now appears that each gene affects many characteristics and every characteristic is controlled by many genes.

> Moreover, despite the fact that a mutation is a discrete, discontinuous effect of the cellular, chromosome or gene level, its effects are modified by interactions in the whole genetic system of an individual.[26]
>
> This universal interaction has been described, in deliberately exaggerated form, in this statement: *Every character of an organism is affected by all genes, and every gene affects all characters.* It is this interaction that accounts for the closely knit functional integration of the genotype as a whole.[27]

It would seem obvious that if any one mutation is highly likely to be deleterious, then since a changed characteristic requires the combined effects of many genes, and therefore many concurrent mutations, the probability of harmful effects is multiplied manyfold. Conversely, the probability of simultaneous good mutations in all the genes which control a given character is reduced to practically zero.

In conclusion, the prediction of the creation model that genuine changes in degree of order of any system, organic or inorganic, are practically certain to be downhill, rather than uphill, is abundantly confirmed by the laws of thermodynamics, the nature of mutations, and the complete lack of any observational evidence that life can evolve from non-life or that higher forms can be generated by any kind of variation and natural selection.

Each of these matters poses a serious difficulty to the model. Attempts to incorporate them into the evolution model by various secondary and tertiary assumptions have been singularly unsuccessful, in so far as any observational and experimental evidence is concerned.

Notes

1. It is interesting and encouraging to note that, in the Foreword to the most recent edition of Darwin's *Origin of Species,* a leading British evolutionary biologist, Professor L. Harrison Matthews, F.R.S., recognizes that "Belief in evolution is thus exactly parallel to belief in special creation—both are concepts which believers know to be true but neither, up to the present, has been capable of proof." (London: J. M. Dent & Sons, Ltd., 1971), p. x.
2. Theodosius Dobzhansky, "On Methods of Evolutionary Biology and Anthropology," *American Scientist,* Vol. 45 (December 1957), p. 888.
3. L. C. Birch and Paul Ehrlich, "Evolutionary History and Population Biology," *Nature,* Vol. 214 (1967), p. 352.
4. Peter Medawar, *Mathematical Challenges to the Neo-Darwinism Interpretation of Evolution,* (Philadelphia: Wistar Institute Press, 1967), p. xi.
5. G. A. Kerkut, *Implications of Evolution,* (London: Pergamon, 1965), p. 155.
6. D. Dwight Davis, "Comparative Anatomy and the Evolution of Vertebrates," in *Genetics, Paleontology and Evolution,* ed. by Jepsen, Mayr, and Simpson (Princeton: Princeton University Press, 1949), p. 74.
7. Leonard Huxley, *Life and Letters of Thomas Henry Huxley,* (London: Macmillan, Vol. 2, 1903), p. 429.
8. D. M. S. Watson, "Adaptation," *Nature,* Vol. 123 (1929), p. 233.
9. The Creation Research Society, for example, numbers over 500 M.S. and Ph.D. scientists on its rolls.
10. Dr. N. Heribert-Nilsson, director of the Botanical Institute at Lund University, Sweden, said "My attempt to demonstrate evolution by an experiment carried on for more than 40 years has completely failed. . . . The idea of an evolution rests on pure belief." (*Synthetische Artbildung,* 1953).
11. Rene Dubos, "Humanistic Biology," *American Scientist,* Vol. 53 (March 1965), p. 6.
12. Theodosius Dobzhansky, "Changing Man," *Science,* Vol. 155 (January 27, 1967), p. 409.
13. Julian Huxley, "Evolution and Genetics," Chap. 8 in *What Is Science?* ed. J. R. Newman, (New York: Simon & Schuster, 1955), p. 272.
14. Francisco J. Ayala, "Biology as an Autonomous Science," *American Scientist,* Vol. 56 (Autumn 1968), p. 213.
15. L. Harrison Matthews, "Introduction" to Darwin's *Origin of Species* (London: J. M. Dent & Sons, Ltd., 1971), p. xi.
16. Ernst Mayr. *Populations, Species, and Evolution* (Cambridge, Mass.: Harvard University Press, 1970), p. 103.
17. Frank B. Salisbury, "Doubts About the Modern Synthetic Theory of Evolution," *American Biology Teacher,* (September 1971), p. 338.
18. Ernst Mayr. *op. cit.,* p. 102.
19. C. H. Waddington, *The Nature of Life* (New York: Atheneum, 1962), p. 98.
20. Francisco J. Ayala, "Teleological Explanations in Evolutionary Biology," *Philosophy of Science,* Vol. 37 (March 1970), p. 3.
21. H. J. Muller, "Radiation Damage to the Genetic

Material,'' *American Scientist,* Vol. 38 (January 1950), p. 35.
22. Julian Huxley, *Evolution in Action* (New York: Harper Bros., 1953), p. 41.
23. C. P. Martin, ''A Non-Geneticist Looks at Evolution,'' *American Scientist,* (January 1953), p. 102.
24. Christopher Wills, ''Genetic Load,'' *Scientific American,* Vol. 222 (March 1970), p. 98.
25. *Ibid,* p. 107.
26. George G. Simpson, ''Uniformitarianism,'' Chap. 2 in *Essays in Evolution and Genetics,* eds. Max A. Hecht and Wm. C. Steeres (New York: Appleton-Century-Crofts, 1970), p. 80.
27. Ernst Mayr, *op. cit.,* p. 164. Emphasis is his.

The Case Against Creationism

PHILIP KITCHER

Philip Kitcher (1947–) is a professor of philosophy at the University of Minnesota and director of the Minnesota Center for the Philosophy of Science. His publications include *Abusing Science* and *The Nature of Mathematical Knowledge*.

Believing Where We Cannot Prove

Opening Moves

Simple distinctions come all too easily. Frequently we open the way for later puzzlement by restricting the options we take to be available. So, for example, in contrasting science and religion, we often operate with a simple pair of categories. On one side there is science, proof, and certainty; on the other, religion, conjecture, and faith.

The opening lines of Tennyson's *In Memoriam* offer an eloquent statement of the contrast:

> Strong Son of God, immortal love,
> Whom we, that have not seen Thy face,
> By faith, and faith alone, embrace,
> Believing where we cannot prove.

A principal theme of Tennyson's great poem is his struggle to maintain faith in the face of what seems to be powerful scientific evidence. Tennyson had read a popular work by Robert Chambers, *Vestiges of the Natural History of Creation,* and he was greatly troubled by the account of the course of life on earth that the book contains. *In Memoriam* reveals a man trying to believe where he cannot prove, a man haunted by the thought that the proofs may be against him.

Like Tennyson, contemporary Creationists accept the traditional contrast between science and religion. But where Tennyson agonized, they attack. While they are less eloquent, they are supremely confident of their own solution. They open their onslaught on evolutionary theory by denying that it is a science. In *The Troubled Waters of Evolution,* Henry Morris characterizes evolutionary theory as maintaining that large amounts of time are required for evolution to produce "new kinds." As a result, we should not expect to see such "new kinds" emerging. Morris comments, "Creationists in turn insist that this belief is not scientific evidence but only a statement of faith. The evolutionist seems to be saying, Of course, we cannot really *prove* evolution, since this requires ages of time, and so, therefore, you should accept it as a proved fact of science! Creationists regard this as an odd type of logic, which would be entirely unacceptable in any other field of science" (Morris 1974b, 16). David Watson makes a similar point in comparing Darwin with Galileo: "So here is the difference between Darwin and Galileo: Galileo sets a demonstrable *fact* against a few words of Bible poetry which the Church at that time had understood in an obviously naive way; Darwin sets an unprovable *theory* against eleven chapters of straightforward history which cannot be reinterpreted in any satisfactory way" (Watson 1976, 46).

The idea that evolution is conjecture, faith, or "philosophy" pervades Creationist writings (Morris 1974a, 4–8; Morris 1974b, 22, 172;

From *Abusing Science* (Cambridge: MIT Press, 1982), pp. 30–62; 205–8.

Wysong 1976, 43–45; Gish 1979, 11–13, 26, 186; Wilder-Smith 1981, 7–8). It is absolutely crucial to their case for equal time for "scientific" Creationism. This ploy has succeeded in winning important adherents to the Creationist cause. As he prepared to defend Arkansas law 590, Attorney General Steven Clark echoed the Creationist judgment. "Evolution," he said, "is just a theory." Similar words have been heard in Congress. William Dannemeyer, a congressman from California, introduced a bill to limit funding to the Smithsonian with the following words: "If the theory of evolution is just that—a theory—and if that theory can be regarded as a religion . . . then it occurs to this Member that other Members might prefer it not to be given exclusive or top billing in our Nation's most famous museum but equal billing or perhaps no billing at all."

In their attempt to show that evolution is not science, Creationists receive help from the least likely sources. Great scientists sometimes claim that certain facts about the past evolution of organisms are "demonstrated" or "indubitable" (Simpson 1953, 70, 371; also Mayr 1976, 9). But Creationists also can (and do) quote scientists who characterize evolution as "dogma" and contend that there is no conclusive proof of evolutionary theory (Matthews 1971, xi; Birch and Ehrlich 1967, 349; quoted in Gish 1979, 15–16; similar passages are quoted in Morris 1974a, 6–8, and in Wysong 1976, 44). Evolution is not part of science because, as evolutionary biologists themselves concede, science demands proof, and, as other biologists point out, proof of evolution is not forthcoming.

The rest of the Creationist argument flows easily. We educate our children in evolutionary theory as if it were a proven fact. We subscribe officially, in our school system, to one faith—an atheistic, materialistic faith—ignoring rival beliefs. Antireligious educators deform the minds of children, warping them to accept as gospel a doctrine that has no more scientific support than the true Gospel. The very least that should be done is to allow for both alternatives to be presented.

We should reject the Creationists' gambit. Eminent scientists notwithstanding, science is not a body of demonstrated truths. Virtually all of science is an exercise in believing where we cannot prove. Yet, scientific conclusions are not embraced by faith alone. Tennyson's dichotomy was too simple.

Inconclusive Evidence

Sometimes we seem to have conclusive reasons for accepting a statement as true. It is hard to doubt that $2+2=4$. If, unlike Lord Kelvin's ideal mathematician, we do not find it obvious that

$$\int_{-\infty}^{+\infty} e^{-x^2}\, dx = \sqrt{\pi},$$

at least the elementary parts of mathematics appear to command our agreement. The direct evidence of our senses seems equally compelling. If I see the pen with which I am writing, holding it firmly in my unclouded view, how can I doubt that it exists? The talented mathematician who has proved a theorem and the keen-eyed witness of an episode furnish our ideals of certainty in knowledge. What they tell us can be engraved in stone, for there is no cause for worry that it will need to be modified.

Yet, in another mood, one that seems "deeper" or more "philosophical," skeptical doubts begin to creep in. Is there really anything of which we are so certain that later evidence could not give us reason to change our minds? Even when we think about mathematical proof, can we not imagine that new discoveries may cast doubt on the cogency of our reasoning? (The history of mathematics reveals that sometimes what seems for all the world like a proof may have a false conclusion.) Is it not possible that the most careful observer may have missed something? Or that the witness brought preconceptions to the observation that subtly biased what was reported? Are we not *always* fallible?

I am mildly sympathetic to the skeptic's worries. Complete certainty is best seen as an ideal toward which we strive and that is rarely, if ever, attained. Conclusive evidence always eludes us. Yet even if we ignore skeptical complaints and imagine that we are sometimes lucky enough to have conclusive reasons for accepting a claim as true, we should not include scientific reasoning among our paradigms of proof. Fallibility is the hallmark of science.

This point should not be so surprising. The trouble is that we frequently forget it in discussing contemporary science. When we turn to the history of the natural science, however, our fallibility stares us in the face. The history of the natural sciences is strewn with the corpses of intricately organized theories, each of which had, in its day, considerable evidence in its favor. When we look at the confident defenders of those theories we should see anticipations of ourselves. The eighteenth-century scientists who believed that heat is a "subtle fluid," the atomic theorists who maintained that water molecules are compounded out of one atom of hydrogen and one of oxygen, the biochemists who identified protein as the genetic material, and the geologists who thought that continents cannot move were neither unintelligent nor ill informed. Given the evidence available to them, they were eminently reasonable in drawing their conclusions. History proved them wrong. It did not show that they were unjustified.

Why is science fallible? Scientific investigation aims to disclose the general principles that govern the workings of the universe. These principles are not intended merely to summarize what some select groups of humans have witnessed. Natural science is not just natural history. It is vastly more ambitious. Science offers us laws that are supposed to hold universally, and it advances claims about things that are beyond our power to observe. The nuclear physicist who sets down the law governing a particular type of radioactive decay is attempting to state a truth that holds throughout the entire cosmos and also to describe the behavior of things that we cannot even see. Yet, of necessity, the physicist's ultimate evidence is highly restricted. Like the rest of us, scientists are confined to a relatively small region of space and time and equipped with limited and imperfect senses.

How is science possible at all? How are we able to have any confidence about the distant regions of the cosmos and the invisible realm that lies behind the surfaces of ordinary things? The answer is complicated. Natural science follows intricate and ingenious procedures for fathoming the secrets of the universe. Scientists devise ways of obtaining especially revealing evidence. They single out some of the things we are able to see as crucial clues to the way that nature works. These clues are used to answer questions that cannot be addressed by direct observation. Scientific theories, even those that are most respected and most successful, rest on indirect arguments from the observational evidence. New discoveries can always call those arguments into question, showing scientists that the observed data should be understood in a different way, that they have misread their evidence.

But scientists often forget the fallibility of their enterprise. This is not just absentmindedness or wishful thinking. During the heyday of a scientific theory, so much evidence may support the theory, so many observational clues may seem to attest to its truth, that the idea that it could be overthrown appears ludicrous. In addition, the theory may provide ways of identifying quickly what is inaccessible to our unaided senses. Electron microscopes and cloud chambers are obvious examples of those extensions of our perceptual system that theories can inspire. Trained biochemists will talk quite naturally of seeing large molecules, and it is easy to overlook the fact that they are presupposing a massive body of theory in describing what they "see." If that theory were to be amended, even in subtle ways, then the descriptions of the "observed characteristics" of large molecules might have to be given up. Nor should we pride ourselves that the enormous successes of contemporary science secure us against future amendements. No theory in the history of science enjoyed a more spectacular career than Newton's mechanics. Yet Newton's ideas had to give way to Einstein's.

When practicing scientists are reminded of these straightforward points, they frequently adopt what the philosopher George Berkeley called a "forlorn skepticism." From the idea of science as certain and infallible, they jump to a cynical description of their endeavors. Science is sometimes held to be a game played with arbitrary rules, an irrational acceptance of dogma, an enterprise based ultimately on faith. Once we have appreciated the fallibility of natural science and recognized its sources, we can move beyond the simple opposition of proof and faith. Between these extremes lies the vast field of cases in which we believe something on the basis of good—even excellent—but inconclusive evidence.

If we want to emphasize the fact that what scientists believe today may have to be revised in the light of observations made tomorrow, then we can describe all our science as "theory." But the description should not confuse us. To concede that evolutionary biology is a theory is not to suppose that there are alternatives to it that are equally worthy of a place in our curriculum. All theories are revisable, but not all theories are equal. Even though our present evidence does not *prove* that evolutionary biology—or quantum physics, or plate tectonics, or any other theory—is true, evolutionary biologists will maintain that the present evidence is overwhelmingly in favor of their theory and overwhelmingly against its supposed rivals. Their enthusiastic assertions that evolution is a proven fact can be charitably understood as claims that the (admittedly inconclusive) evidence we have for evolutionary theory is as good as we ever obtain for any theory in any field of science.

Hence the Creationist try for a quick Fools' Mate can easily be avoided. Creationists attempt to draw a line between evolutionary biology and the rest of science by remarking that large-scale evolution cannot be observed. This tactic fails. Large-scale evolution is no more inaccessible to observation than nuclear reactions or the molecular composition of water. For the Creationists to succeed in divorcing evolutionary theory is less well supported by the evidence than are theories in, for example, physics and chemistry. It will come as no surprise to learn that they try to do this. To assess the merits of their arguments we need a deeper understanding of the logic of inconclusive justification. We shall begin with a simple and popular idea: Scientific theories earn our acceptance by making successful predictions.

Predictive Success

Imagine that somebody puts forward a new theory about the origins of hay fever. The theory makes a number of startling predictions concerning connections that we would not have thought worth investigating. For example, it tells us that people who develop hay fever invariably secrete a particular substance in certain fatty tissues and that anyone who eats rhubarb as a child never develops hay fever. The theory predicts things that initially appear fantastic. Suppose that we check up on these predictions and find that they are borne out by clinical tests. Would we not begin to believe—and believe reasonably—that the theory was *at least* on the right track?

This example illustrates a pattern of reasoning that is familiar in the history of science. Theories win support by producing claims about what can be observed, claims that would not have seemed plausible prior to the advancement of the theory, but that are in fact found to be true when we make the appropriate observations. A classic (real) example is Pascal's confirmation of Torricelli's hypothesis that we live at the bottom of an ocean of air that presses down upon us. Pascal reasoned that if Torricelli's hypothesis were true, then air pressure should decrease at higher altitudes (because at higher altitudes we are closer to the "surface" of the atmosphere, so that the length of the column of air that presses down is shorter). Accordingly, he sent his brother-in-law to the top of a mountain to make some barometric measurements. Pascal's clever working out of the observational predictions of Torricelli's theory led to a dramatic predictive success for the theory.

The idea of predictive success has encouraged a popular picture of science. (We shall see later that this picture, while popular, is not terribly accurate.) Philosophers sometimes regard a theory as a collection of claims or statements. Some of these statements offer generalizations about the features of particular, recondite things (genes, atoms, gravitational force, quasars, and the like). These statements are used to infer statements whose truth or falsity can be decided by observation. (This appears to be just what Pascal did.) Statements belonging to this second group are called the *observational consequences* of the theory. Theories are supported when we find that their observational consequences (those that we have checked) are true. The credentials of a theory are damaged if we discover that some of its observational consequences are false.

We can make the idea more precise by being clearer about the inferences involved. Those who talk of inferring observational predictions from our theories think that we can *deduce* from the statements of the theory, and from those statements alone, some predictions whose accuracy we can check by direct observation. Deductive inference is well understood. The fundamental idea of deductive inference is this: We say that a statement

S is a valid deductive consequence of a group of statements if and only if it is *impossible* that all the statements in the group should be true and that *S* should be false; alternatively, *S* is a valid deductive consequence (or, more simply, a valid consequence) of a group of statements if and only if it would be self-contradictory to assert all the statements in the group and to deny *S*.

It will be helpful to make the idea of valid consequence more familiar with some examples. Consider the statements "All lovers of baseball dislike George Steinbrenner" and "George Steinbrenner loves baseball." The statement "George Steinbrenner dislikes himself" is a deductively valid consequence of these two statements. For it is impossible that the first two should be true and the third false. However, in claiming that this is a case of deductively valid consequence, we do not commit ourselves to maintaining that *any* of the statements is true. (Perhaps there are some ardent baseball fans who admire Steinbrenner. Perhaps Steinbrenner himself has no time for the game.) What deductive validity means is that the truth of the first two statements would guarantee the truth of the third; that is, *if* the first two *were* true, then the third would have to be true.

Another example will help rule out other misunderstandings. Here are two statements: "Shortly after noon on January 1, 1982, in the Oval Office, a jelly bean was released from rest more than two feet above any surface"; "Shortly after noon on January 1, 1982, in the Oval Office, a jelly bean fell." Is the second statement a deductively valid consequence of the first? You might think that it is, on the grounds that it would have been impossible for the unfortunate object to have been released and not to have fallen. In one sense this is correct, but that is not the sense of impossibility that deductive logicians have in mind. Strictly speaking, it is not *impossible* for the jelly bean to have been released without falling; we can imagine, for example, that the law of gravity might suddenly cease to operate. We do not *contradict* ourselves when we assert that the jelly bean was released but deny that it fell; we simply refuse to accept the law of gravity (or some other relevant physical fact).

Thus, *S* is a deductively valid consequence of a group of statements if and only if there is *absolutely no possibility* that all the statements in the group should be true and *S* should be false. This conception allows us to state the popular view of theory and prediction more precisely. Theories are collections of statements. The observational consequences also have to be statements whose truth or falsity can be ascertained by direct observation.

My initial discussion of predictive success presented the rough idea that, when we find the observational consequences of a theory to be true, our findings bring credit to the theory. Conversely, discovery that some observational consequences of a theory are false was viewed as damaging. We can now make the second point much more precise. Any theory that has a false observational consequence must contain some false statement (or statements). For if all the statements in the theory were true, then, according to the standard definitions of *deductive validity* and *observational consequence,* any observational consequence would also have to be true. Hence, if a theory is found to have a false observational consequence, we must conclude that one or more statements of the theory is false.

This means that theories can be conclusively falsified, through the discovery that they have false observational consequences. Some philosophers, most notably Sir Karl Popper (Popper 1959; 1963), have taken this point to have enormous significance for our understanding of science. According to Popper, the essence of a scientific theory is that it should be *falsifiable*. That is, if the theory is false, then it must be possible to show that it is false. Now, if a theory has utterly no observational consequences, it would be extraordinarily difficult to unmask that theory as false. So, to be a genuine scientific theory, a group of statements must have observational consequences. It is important to realize that Popper is not suggesting that every good theory must be false. The difference between being falsifiable and being false is like the difference between being vulnerable and actually being hurt. A good scientific theory should not be false. Rather, it must have observational consequences that could reveal the theory as mistaken if the experiments give the wrong results.

While these ideas about theory testing may seem strange in their formal attire, they emerge quite frequently in discussions of science. They also find their way into the creation-evolution debate.

Predictive Failure

From the beginning, evolutionary theory has been charged with just about every possible type of predictive failure. Critics of the theory have argued that (a) the theory makes no predictions (it is unfalsifiable and also fails Popper's criterion for science), (b) the theory makes false predictions (it is falsified), (c) the theory does not make the kinds of predictions it ought to make (the observations and experiments that evolutionary theorists undertake have no bearing on the theory). Many critics, including several Creationists (Morris 1974a; Gish 1979; Wysong 1976), manage to advance all these objections in the same work. This is somewhat surprising, since points (a) and (b) are, of course, mutually contradictory.

The first objection is vitally important to the Creationist cause. Their opponents frequently insist that Creationism fails the crucial test for a scientific theory. The hypothesis that all kinds of organisms were separately fashioned by some "originator" is unfalsifiable (Gould 1981). Creationists retort that they can play the same game equally well. *Any* hypothesis about the origins of life, including that advanced by evolutionary theory, is not subject to falsification. Hence we cannot justify a decision to teach evolutionary theory and not to teach Creationism by appealing to the Popperian criterion for genuine science.

The allegation that evolutionary theory fails to make any predictions is a completely predictable episode in any Creationist discussion of evolution. Often the point is made by appeal to the authority of Popper. Here are two sample passages:

> The outstanding philosopher of science, Karl Popper, though himself an evolutionist, pointed out cogently that evolution, no less than creation, is untestable and thus unprovable. (Morris 1974b, 80)

> Thus, for a theory to qualify as a scientific theory, it must be supported by events, processes or properties, which can be observed, and the theory must be useful in predicting the outcome of future natural phenomena or laboratory experiments. An additional limitation usually imposed is that the theory must be capable of falsification. That is, it must be possible to conceive some experiment, the failure of which would disprove the theory.
>
> It is on the basis of such criteria that most evolutionists insist that creation be refused consideration as a possible explanation for origins. Creation has not been witnessed by human observers, it cannot be tested experimentally, and as a theory it is nonfalsifiable.
>
> The general theory of evolution also fails to meet all three of these criteria, however. (Gish 1979, 13)

These passages, and many others (for example, Morris 1974a, 150; Morris 1975, 9; Moore 1974, 9; Wilder-Smith 1981, 133), draw on the picture of science sketched above. It is not clear that the Creationists really understand the philosophical views that they attempt to apply. Gish presents the most articulate discussion of the falsifiability criterion. Yet he muddles the issue by describing falsifiability as an "additional limitation" beyond predictive power. (The previous section shows that theories that make predictions are automatically falsifiable.) Nevertheless, the Creationist challenge is a serious one, and, if it could not be met, evolutionary theory would be in trouble.

Creationists buttress their charge of unfalsifiability with further objections. They are aware that biologists frequently look as though they are engaged in observations and experiments. Creationists would allow that researchers in biology sometimes make discoveries. What they deny is that the discoveries support evolutionary theory. They claim that laboratory manipulations fail to teach us about evolution in nature: "Even if modern scientists should ever actually achieve the artificial creation of life from non-life, or of higher kinds from lower kinds, in the laboratory, this would not *prove* in any way that such changes did, or even could, take place in the past by random natural processes" (Morris 1974a, 6). The standards of evidence to be applied to evolutionary biology have suddenly been raised. In this area of inquiry, it is not sufficient that a theory yield observational consequences whose truth or falsity can be decided in the laboratory. Creationists demand special kinds of predictions, and will dismiss as irrelevant any laboratory evidence that evolutionary theorists produce. [In this way, they try to defend point (c).]

Oddly enough, however, the most popular supplement to the charge that evolutionary theory is unfalsifiable is a determined effort to falsify it [point (b)]. Creationists cannot resist arguing that the theory is actually falsified. Some of them, Morris and Gish, for example, recognize the tension between the two objections. They try to paper over the problem by claiming that evolutionary theory and the Creationist account are both "models." Each "model" would "naturally" incline us to expect certain observational results. A favorite Creationist ploy is to draw up tables in which these "predictions" are compared. When we look at the tables we find that the evolutionary expectations are confounded. By contrast, the Creationist "model" leads us to anticipate features of the world that are actually there. Faced with such adverse results, the benighted evolutionary biologist is portrayed as struggling to "explain away" the findings by whatever means he can invent.

Morris's own practice of this form of evolution baiting can serve as an example. Morris constructs a table (1974a, 12; see facing page) whose function is to indicate "the predictions that would probably be made in several important categories" (1974a, 12). Morris admits magnanimously that "these primary models may be modified by secondary [additional] assumptions to fit certain conditions. For example, the basic evolution model may be extended to include harmful, as well as beneficial, mutations, but this is not a natural prediction of the basic concept of evolution" (1974a, 13). The idea that the "natural predictions" of the evolution "model" are at odds with the phenomena is used to suggest that evolutionary biologists are forced to desperate measures to protect their "faith." As Morris triumphantly concludes, "The data must be *explained* by the evolutionist, but they are *predicted* by the creationist" (1974a, 13).

The careful reader ought to be puzzled. If Morris really thinks that evolutionary theory has been falsified, why does he not say so? Of course, he would have to admit that the theory is falsifiable. Seemingly, however, a staunch Creationist should be delighted to abandon a relatively abstruse point about unfalsifiability in favor of a clear-cut refutation. The truth of the matter is that the alleged refutations fail. No evolutionary theorist will grant that (for example) the theory predicts that the fossil record should show "innumerable transitions." Instead, paleontologists will point out that we can deduce conclusions about what we should find in the rocks only if we make assumptions about the fossilization process. Morris makes highly dubious assumptions, hails them as "natural," and then announces that the "natural predictions" of the theory have been defeated.

(This example suggests a method for coping with Morris's "table of natural predictions." Each of these predictions can be deduced from evolutionary theory only if the theory is extended by adding extra assumptions. Morris saddles evolutionary theory with faulty additional claims. These are the source of the false predictions. Later, I shall show this in detail for some of Morris's "natural predictions" and the similar difficulties raised by other Creationists [Gish 1979, 53–54; Wysong 1976, 421–26].)

To make a serious assessment of these broad Creationist charges, we must begin by asking some basic methodological questions. We cannot decide whether evolutionary biologists are guilty of trying to save their theory by using ad hoc assumptions (new and implausible claims dreamed up for the sole purpose of protecting some cherished ideas) unless we have some way of deciding when a proposal is ad hoc. Similarly, we cannot make a reasoned response to the charge that laboratory experiments are irrelevant, or to the fundamental objection that evolutionary theory is unfalsifiable, unless we have a firmer grasp of the relation between theory and evidence.

Naive Falsificationism

The time has come to tell a dreadful secret. While the picture of scientific testing sketched above continued to be influential among scientists, it has been shown to be seriously incorrect. (To give my profession its due, historians and philosophers of science have been trying to let this particular cat out of the bag for at least thirty years.

Category	Evolution Model	Creation Model
Structure of Natural Law	Constantly changing	Invariable
Galactic Universe	Galaxies changing	Galaxies constant
Structure of Stars	Stars changing into other types	Stars unchanged
Other Heavenly Bodies	Building up	Breaking down
Types of Rock Formations	Different in different ''Ages''	Similar in all ''Ages''
Appearance of Life	Life evolving from non-life	Life only from life
Array of Organisms	Continuum of Organisms	Distinct Kinds of Organisms
Appearance of Kinds of Life	New Kinds Appearing	No New Kinds Appearing
Mutations in Organisms	Beneficial	Harmful
Natural Selection	Creative Process	Conservative Process
Age of Earth	Extremely Old	Probably Young
Fossil Record	Innumerable Transitions	Systematic Gaps
Appearance of Man	Ape-Human Intermediates	No Ape-Human Intermediates
Nature of Man	Quantitatively Superior to Animals	Qualitatively Distinct from Animals
Origin of Civilization	Slow and Gradual	Contemporaneous with Man

See, for example, Hempel 1965; Quine 1952.) Important work in the history of science has made it increasingly clear that no major scientific theory has ever exemplified the relation between theory and evidence that the traditional model presents.

What is wrong with the old picture? Answer: Either it debars most of what we take to be science from counting as science or it allows virtually anything to count. On the traditional view of ''theory,'' textbook cases of scientific theories turn out to be unfalsifiable. Suppose we identify Newtonian mechanics with Newton's three laws of motion plus the law of gravitation. What observational consequences can we deduce from these four statements? You might think that we could deduce that if, as the (undoubtedly apocryphal) story alleges, an apple became detached from a branch above where Newton was sitting, the apple would have fallen on his head. But this does not follow at all. To see why not, it is only necessary to recognize that the failure of this alleged prediction would not force us to deny any of the four statements of the theory. All we need do is assume that some other forces were at work that overcame the force of gravity and caused the apple to depart from its usual trajectory. So, given this simple way of applying Popper's criterion, Newtonian mechanics would be unfalisifiable. The same would go for any other scientific theory. Hence none of what we normally take to be science would count as science. (I might note that Popper is aware of this problem and has suggestions of his own as to how it should be overcome. However, what concerns me here are the *applications* of Popper's ideas, that are made by Creationists, as well as by scientists in their professional debates.)

The example of the last paragraph suggests an obvious remedy. Instead of thinking about theories in the simple way just illustrated, we might take them to be far more elaborate. Newton's laws (the three laws of motion and the law of gravitation) are *embedded* in Newtonian mechanics. They form the core of the theory, but do not constitute the whole of it. Newtonian mechanics also contains supplementary assumptions, telling us, for example, that for certain special systems the effects of forces other than gravity are negligible. This more elaborate collection of statements *does* have observational consequences and *is* falsifiable.

But the remedy fails. Imagine that we attempt to expose some self-styled spiritual teacher as an overpaid fraud. We try to point out that the teacher's central message—''Quietness is wholeness in the center of stillness''—is unfalsifiable. The teacher cheerfully admits that, taken by itself, this profound doctrine yields no observational consequences. He then points out that, by themselves, the central statements of scientific theories are also incapable of generating observational consequences. Alas, if all that is demanded is that a doctrine be embedded in a group of statements with observational consequences, our imagined guru will easily slither off the hook. He replies, "You have forgotten that my doctrine has many other claims. For example, I believe that if quietness is wholeness in the center of stillness, then flowers bloom in the spring, bees gather pollen, and blinkered defenders of so-called science raise futile objections to the world's spiritual benefactors. You will see that these three predictions are borne out by experience. Of course, there are countless others. Perhaps when you see how my central message yields so much evident truth, you will recognize the wealth of evidence behind my claim. Quietness is wholeness in the center of stillness."

More formally, the trouble is that *any* statement can be coupled with other statements to produce observational consequences. Given any doctrine *D*, and any statement *O* that records the result of an observation, we can enable *D* to "predict" *O* by adding the extra assumption, "If *D*, then *O*." (In the example, *D* is "Quietness is wholeness in the center of stillness"; examples of *O* would be statements describing the blooming of particular flowers in the spring, the pollen gathering of specific bees, and so forth.)

The falsifiability criterion adopted from Popper—which I shall call the *naive falsificationist* criterion—is hopelessly flawed. It runs aground on a fundamental fact about the relation between theory and prediction: On their own, individual scientific laws, or the small groups of laws that are often identified as theories, do not have observational consequences. This crucial point about theories was first understood by the great historian and philosopher of science Pierre Duhem. Duhem saw clearly that individual scientific claims do not, and cannot, confront the evidence one by one. Rather, in his picturesque phrase, "Hypotheses are tested in bundles." Besides ruling out the possibility of testing an individual scientific theory (read, small group of laws), Duhem's insight has another startling consequence. We can only test relatively large bundles of claims. What this means is that when our experiments go awry we are not logically compelled to select any particular claim as the culprit. We can always save a cherished hypothesis from refutation by rejecting (however implausibly) one of the other members of the bundle. Of course, this is exactly what I did in the illustration of Newton and the apple above. Faced with disappointing results, I suggested that we could abandon the (tacit) additional claim that no large forces besides gravity were operating on the apple.

Creationists wheel out the ancient warhorse of naive falsificationism so that they can bolster their charge that evolutionary theory is not a science. The (very) brief course in deductive logic plus the whirlwind tour through naive falsificationism and its pitfalls enable us to see what is at the bottom of this seemingly important criticism. Creationists can appeal to naive falsificationism to show that evolution is not a science. But, given the traditional picture of theory and evidence I have sketched, one can appeal to naive falsificationism to show that *any* science is not a science. So, as with the charge that evolutionary change is unobservable, Creationists have again failed to find some "fault" of evolution not shared with every other science. (And, as we shall see, Creationists like some sciences, especially thermodynamics.) Consistent application of naive falsificationism can show that anybody's favorite science (whether it be quantum physics, molecular biology, or whatever is not science. Of course, what this shows is that the naive falsificationist criterion is a very poor test of genuine science. To be fair, this point can cut both ways. Scientists who charge that "scientific" Creationism is unfalsifiable are not insulting the theory as much as they think.

Successful Science

Despite the inadequacies of naive falsificationism, there is surely something right in the idea that a science can succeed only if it can fail. An invulnerable "science" would not be science at all. To achieve a more adequate understanding of how a science can succeed and how it runs the risk of failure, let us look at one of the most successful sciences and at a famous episode in its development.

Newtonian celestial mechanics is one of the star turns in the history of science. Among its numerous achievements were convincing explanations of the orbits of most of the known planets. Newton and his successors viewed the solar system as a collection of bodies subject only to gravitational interactions; they used the law of gravitation and the laws of motion to compute the orbits. (Bodies whose effects were negligible in any particular case would be disregarded. For example, the gravitational attraction due to Mercury would not be considered in working out the orbit of Saturn.) The results usually tallied beautifully with astronomical observations. But one case proved difficult. The outermost known planet, Uranus, stubbornly followed an orbit that diverged from the best computations. By the early nineteenth century it was clear that something was wrong. Either astronomers erred in treating the solar system as a Newtonian gravitational system or there was some particular difficulty in applying the general method to Uranus.

Perhaps the most naive of falsificationists would have recommended that the central claim of Newtonian mechanics—the claim that the solar system is a Newtonian gravitational system—be abandoned. But there was obviously a more sensible strategy. Astronomers faced one problematical planet, and they asked themselves what made Uranus so difficult. Two of them, John Adams and Urbain Leverrier, came up with an answer. They proposed (independently) that there was a hitherto unobserved planet beyond Uranus. They computed the orbit of the postulated planet and demonstrated that the anomalies of the motion of Uranus could be explained if a planet followed this path. There was a straightforward way to test their proposal. Astronomers began to look for the new planet. Within a few years, the planet—Neptune—was found.

I will extract several morals from this success story. The first concerns an issue we originally encountered in Morris's "table of natural predictions:" What is the proper use of auxiliary hypotheses? Adams and Leverrier saved the central claim of Newtonian celestial mechanics by offering an auxiliary hypothesis. They maintained that there were more things in the heavens than had been dreamed of in previous natural philosophy. The anomalies in the orbit of Uranus could be explained on the assumption of an extra planet. Adams and Leverrier worked out the exact orbit of that planet so that they could provide a detailed account of the perturbations—and so that they could tell their fellow astronomers where to look for Neptune. Thus, their auxiliary hypothesis was *independently testable*. The evidence for Neptune's existence was not just the anomalous motion of Uranus. The hypothesis could be checked independently of any assumptions about Uranus or about the correctness of Newtonian celestial mechanics—by making telescopic observations.

Since hypotheses are always tested in bundles, this method of checking presupposed other assumptions, in particuar, the optical principles that justify the use of telescopes. The crucial point is that, while hypotheses are always tested in bundles, they can be tested in *different* bundles. An auxiliary hypothesis ought to be testable independently of the particular problem it is introduced to solve, independently of the theory it is designed to save.

While it is obvious in retrospect—indeed it was obvious at the time—that the problem with Uranus should not be construed as "falsifying" celestial mechanics, it is worth asking explicitly why scientists should have clung to Newton's theory in the face of this difficulty. The answer is not just that nothing succeeds like success, and that Newton's theory had been strikingly successful in calculating the orbits of the other planets. The crucial point concerns the way in which Newton's successes have been achieved. Newton was no opportunist, using one batch of assumptions to cope with Mercury, and then moving on to new devices to handle Venus. Celestial mechanics was a remarkably *unified* theory. It solved problems by invoking the same pattern of reasoning, or *problem-solving strategy,* again and again: From a specification of the positions of the bodies under study, use the law of gravitation to calculate the forces acting; from a statement of the forces acting, use the laws of dynamics to compute the equations of motion; solve the equations of motion to obtain the motions of the bodies. This single pattern of reasoning was applied in case after case to yield conclusions that were independently found to be correct.

At a higher level, celestial mechanics was itself contained in a broader theory. Newtonian physics, as a whole, was remarkably unified. It offered a strategy for solving a diverse collection of problems. Faced with *any* question about motion, the Newtonian suggestion was the same: Find the forces acting, from the forces and the laws of dynamics work out the equations of motion, and solve the equations of motion. The method was employed in a broad range of cases. The revolutions of planets, the motions of projectiles, tidal cycles and pendulum oscillations—all fell to the same problem-solving strategy.

We can draw a second moral. A science should be *unified*. A thriving science is not a gerrymandered patchwork but a coherent whole. Good theories consist of just one problem-solving strategy, or a small family of problem-solving strategies, that can be applied to a wide range of problems. The theory succeeds as it is able to encompass more and more problem areas. Failure looms when the basic problem-solving strategy (or strategies) can resolve almost none of the problems in its intended domain without the "aid" of untestable auxiliary hypotheses.

Despite the vast successes of his theory, Newton hoped for more. He envisaged a time when scientists would recognize other force laws, akin to the law of gravitation, so that other branches of physics could model themselves after celestial mechanics. In addition, he suggested that many physical questions that are not ostensibly about motion—questions about heat and about chemical combination, for example—could be reduced to problems of motion. *Principia,* Newton's masterpiece, not only offered a theory; it also advertised a program:

> I wish we could derive the rest of the phenomena of Nature by the same kind of reasoning from mechanical principles, for I am induced by many reasons to suspect that they may all depend upon certain forces by which the particles of bodies, by some causes hitherto unknown, are either mutually impelled towards one another, and cohere in regular figures, or are repelled and recede from one another. These forces being unknown, philosophers have hitherto attempted the search of Nature in vain; but I hope the principles here laid down will afford some light either to this or some truer method of philosophy. (Newton 1687/Motte-Cajori 1960, xviii)

Newton's message was clear. His own work only began the task of applying an immensely fruitful, unifying idea.

Newton's successors were moved, quite justifiably, to extend the theory he had offered. They attempted to show how Newton's main problem-solving strategy could be applied to a broader range of physical phenomena. During the eighteenth and nineteenth centuries, the search for understanding of the forces of nature was carried into hydrodynamics, optics, chemistry, and the studies of heat, elasticity, electricity, and magnetisim. Not all of these endeavors were equally successful. Nevertheless, Newton's directive fostered the rise of some important new sciences.

The final moral I want to draw from this brief look at Newtonian physics concerns *fecundity*. A great scientific theory, like Newton's, opens up new areas of research. Celestial mechanics led to the discovery of a previously unknown planet. Newtonian physics as a whole led to the development of previously unknown sciences. Because a theory presents a new way of looking at the world, it can lead us to ask new questions, and so to embark on new and fruitful lines of inquiry. Of the many flaws with the earlier picture of theories as sets of statements, none is more important than the misleading presentation of sciences as static and insular. Typically, a flourishing science is incomplete. At any time, it raises more questions than it can currently answer. But incompleteness is no vice. On the contrary, incompleteness is the mother of fecundity. Unresolved problems present challenges that enable a theory to flower in unanticipated ways. They also make the theory hostage to future developments. A good theory should be productive; it should raise new questions and presume that those questions can be answered without giving up its problem-solving strategies.

I have highlighted three characteristics of successful science. *Independent testability* is achieved when it is possible to test auxiliary hypotheses independently of the particular cases for which they are introduced. *Unification* is the result of applying a small family of problem-solving strategies to a broad class of cases. *Fecundity* grows out of incompleteness when a theory opens up new and profitable lines of investigation. Given these marks of successful science, it is easy to see how sciences can fall short, and how some doctrines can do so badly that they fail to count as science at all. A scientific theory begins to wither if some of its auxiliary assumptions can be saved from refutation only by rendering them untestable; or if its problem-solving strategies become a hodgepodge, a collection of unrelated methods, each designed for a separate recalcitrant case; or if the promise of the theory just fizzles, the few questions it raises leading only to dead ends.

When does a doctrine fail to be a science? If a doctrine fails sufficiently abjectly as a science, then it fails to be a science. Where bad science becomes egregious enough, pseudoscience begins. The example of Newtonian physics shows us how to replace the simple (and incorrect) naive falsificationist criterion with a battery of tests. Do the doctrine's problem-solving strategies encounter recurrent difficulties in a significant range of cases? Are the problem-solving strategies an opportunistic collection of unmotivated and unrelated methods? Does the doctrine have too cozy a relationship with auxiliary hypotheses, applying its strategies with claims that can be "tested" only in their applications? Does the doctrine refuse to follow up on unresolved problems, airily dismissing them as "exceptional cases"? Does the doctrine restrict the domain of its methods, forswearing excusions into new areas of investigation where embarrassing questions might arise? If all, or many, of these tests are positive, then the doctrine is not a poor scientific theory. It is not a scientific theory at all.

The account of successful science that I have given not only enables us to replace the naive falsificationist criterion with something better. It also provides a deeper understanding of how theories are justified. Predictive success is one important way in which a theory can win our acceptance. But it is not the only way. In general, theories earn their laurels by solving problems—proving answers that can be independently recognized as correct—and by their fruitfulness. Making a prediction is answering a special kind of question. The astronomers who used celestial mechanics to predict the motion of Mars were answering the question of where Mars would be found. Yet, very frequently, our questions do not concern *what* occurs, but *why* it occurs. We already know that something happens and we want an explanation. Science offers us explanations by setting the phenomena within a unified framework. Using a widely applicable problem-solving strategy, together with independently confirmed auxiliary hypotheses, scientists show that what happened was to be expected. It was known before Newton that the orbits of the planets are approximately elliptical. One of the great achievements of Newton's celestial mechanics was to apply its problem-solving strategy to deduce that the orbit of any planet will be approximately elliptical, thereby explaining the shape of the orbits. In general, science is at least as concerned with reducing the number of unexplained phenomena as it is with generating correct predictions.

The most global Creationist attack on evolutionary theory is the claim that evolution is not a science. If this claim were correct, then the dispute about what to teach in high school science classes would be over . . . we saw how Creationists were able to launch their broad criticisms. If one accepts the idea that science requires proof, or if one adopts the naive falsificationist criterion, then the theory of evolution—and every other scientific theory—will turn out not to be a part of science. So Creationist standards for science imply that there is no science to be taught.

However, we have seen that Creationist standards rest on a very poor understanding of science. In light of a clearer picture of the scientific enterprise, I have provided a more realistic group of tests for good science, bad science, and pseudoscience. Using this more sophisticated approach, I now want to address seriously the global Creationist questions about the theory of evolution. Is it a pseudoscience? Is it a poor science? Or is it a great science? These are very important questions, for the appropriateness of granting equal time to Creation "science" depends, in part, on whether it can be regarded as the equal of the theory of evolution.

Darwin's Daring

The heart of Darwinian evolutionary theory is a family of problem-solving strategies, related by their common employment of a particular style of historical narrative. A *Darwinian history* is a piece of reasoning of the following general form.

The first step consists in a description of an ancestral population of organisms. The reasoning proceeds by tracing the modification of the population through subsequent generations, showing how characteristics were selected, inherited, and became prevalent. (As I noted earlier natural selection is taken to be the primary—but not the only—force of evolutionary change.)

Reasoning like this can be used to answer a host of biological questions. Suppose that we want to know why a contemporary species manifests a particular trait. We can answer that question by supplying a Darwinian history that describes the emergence of that trait. Equally, we can use Darwinian histories to answer questions about relationships among groups of organisms. One way to explain why two species share a common feature is to trace their descent from a common ancestor. Questions of biogeography can be addressed in a similar way. We can explain why we find contemporary organisms where we do by following the course of their historical modifications and migrations. Finally, we can tackle problems about extinction by showing how characteristics that had enabled organisms to thrive were no longer advantageous when the environment (or the competition) changed. In all these cases, we find related strategies for solving problems. The history of the development of populations, understood in terms of variation, competition, selection, and inheritance, is used to shed light on broad classes of biological phenomena.

The questions that evolutionary theory has addressed are so numerous that any sample is bound to omit important types. The following short selection undoubtedly reflects the idiosyncrasy of my interests: Why do orchids have such intricate internal structures? Why are male birds of paradise so brightly colored? Why do some reptilian precursors of mammals have enormous "sails" on their backs? Why do bats typically roost upside down? Why are the hemoglobins of humans and apes so similar? Why are there no marsupial analogues of seals and whales? Why is the mammalian fauna of Madagascar so distinctive? Why did the large, carnivorous ground birds of South America become extinct? Why is the sex ratio in most species one to one (although it is markedly different in some species of insects)? Answers to these questions, employing Darwinian histories, can be found in works written by contemporary Darwinian biolgoists. Those works contain answers to a myriad of other questions of the same general types. Darwinian histories are constructed again and again to illuminate the characteristics of contemporary organisms, to account for the similarities and differences among species, to explain why the forms preserved in the fossil record emerged and became extinct, to cast light on the geographical distribution of animals and plants.

We can see the theory in action by taking a brief look at one of these examples. The island of Madagascar, off the east coast of Africa, supports a peculiar group of mammals. Many of these mammals are endemic. Among them is a group of relatively small insectivorous mammals, the *tenrecs*. All tenrecs share certain features that mark them out as relatively primitive mammals. They have very poor vision, their excretory system is rudimentary, the testes in the male are carried within the body, their capacity for regulating their body temperature is poor compared with that of most mammals. Yet, on their simple and rudimentary body plan, specialized characteristics have often been imposed. Some tenrecs have the hedgehog's method of defense. Others have the forelimbs characteristic of moles. There are climbing tenrecs that resemble the shrews, and there are tenrecs that defend themselves by attempting to stick their quills into a would-be predator. Hedgehogs, moles, tree shrews, and porcupines do not inhabit Madagascar. But they seem to have their imitators. (These are examples of convergent evolution, cases in which unrelated organisms take on some of the same characteristics.) Why are these peculiar animals found on Madagascar, and nowhere else?

A straightforward evolutionary story makes sense of what we observe. In the late Mesozoic or early Cenozoic, small, primitive, insectivorous mammals rafted across the Mozambique channel and colonized Madagascar. Later the channel widened and Madagascar became inaccessible to the more advanced mammals that evolved on the mainland. Hence the early colonist developed without competition from advanced mainland forms and without pressure from many of the normal predators who make life difficult for small mammals. The tenrecs have been relatively protected. In the absence of rigorous competition, they have preserved their simple body plan, and they have exploited unoccupied niches, which are filled elsewhere by more advanced creatures. Tenrecs have gone up the trees and burrowed in the ground because those are good ways to make a living and because they have had nobody but one another to contend with.

The same kind of story can be told again and again to answer all sorts of questions about all sorts of living things. Evolutionary theory is unified because so many diverse questions—questions as various as those I listed—can be addressed by advancing Darwinian histories. Moreover, these narratives constantly make claims that are subject to independent check. Here are four examples from the case of the triumphant tenrecs. (1) The explanation presupposes that Madagascar has drifted away from the east coast of Africa. That is something that can be checked by using geological criteria for the movement of landmasses, criteria that are independent of biology. (2) The account claims that the tenrecs would have been able to raft across the Mozambique channel, but that the present channel constitutes a barrier to more advanced mammals (small rodents). These claims could be tested by looking to see whether the animals in question can disperse across channels of the appropriate sizes. (3) The narrative assumes that the specialized methods of defense offered advantages against the predators that were present in Madagascar. Studies of animal interactions can test whether the particular defenses are effective against local predators. (4) Central to the explanatory account is the thesis that the tenrecs are related. If this is so, then studies of the minute details of tenrec anatomy should reveal many common features, and the structures of proteins ought to be similar. In particular, the tenrecs ought to be much more like one another than they are like hedgehogs, shrews, or moles.

Looking at one example, or even at a small number of examples, does not really convey the strength of evolutionary theory. The same patterns of reasoning can be applied again and again, in book after book, monograph after monograph, article after article. Yet the particular successes in dealing with details of natural history, numerous though they are, do not exhaust the accomplishments of the theory. Darwin's original theory—the problem-solving strategies advanced in the *Origin,* which are, in essence, those just described—gave rise to important new areas of scientific investigation. Evolutionary theory has been remarkably fruitful.

Darwin not only provided a scheme for unifying the diversity of life. He also gave a structure to our ignorance. After Darwin, it was important to resolve general issues about the presuppositions of Darwinian histories. The way in which biology should proceed had been made admirably plain, and it was clear that biologists had to tackle questions for which they had, as yet, no answers. How do new characteristics arise in populations? What are the mechanisms of inheritance? How do characteristics become fixed in populations? What criteria decide when a characteristic confers some advantage on its possessor? What interactions among populations of organisms affect the adaptive value of characteristics? With respect to all of these questions, Darwin was forced to confess ignorance. By raising them, his theory pointed the way to its further articulation.

Since Darwin's day, biologists have contributed parts of evolutionary theory that help to answer these important questions. Geneticists have advanced our understanding of the transmission of characteristics between generations and have enabled us to see how new characteristics can arise. Population geneticists have analyzed the variation present in populations of organisms; they have suggested how that variation is maintained and have specified ways in which characteristics can be fixed or eliminated. Workers in morphology and physiology have helped us to see how variations of particular kinds might yield advantages in particular environments. Ecologists have studied the ways in which interactions among populations can affect survival and fecundity.

The moral is obvious. Darwin gambled. He trusted that the questions he left open would be answered by independent biological sciences and that the deliverances of these sciences would be consistent with the presuppositions of Darwinian histories. Because of the breadth of his vision, Darwin made his theory vulnerable from a number of different directions. To take just one example, it could have turned out the mechanisms of heredity would have made it impossible for advantageous variations to be preserved and to spread. Indeed, earlier in this century, many biologists felt that the emerging views about inheritance did not fit into Darwin's picture, and the fortunes of Darwinian evolutionary theory were on the wane.

When we look at the last 120 years of the history of biology, it is impossible to ignore the fecundity of Darwin's ideas. Not only have inquiries into the presuppositions of Darwinian histories yielded new theoretical disciplines (like population genetics), but the problem-solving strategies have been extended to cover phenomena that initially appeared troublesome. One recent triumph has been the development of explanations for social interactions among animals. Behavior involving one animal's promotion of the good of others seems initially to pose a problem for evolutionary theory. How can we construct Darwinian histories for the emergence of such behavior? W. D. Hamilton's concept of inclusive fitness, and the deployment of game-theoretic ideas by R. L. Trivers and John Maynard Smith, revealed how the difficulty could be resolved by a clever extension of traditional Darwinian concepts.

Yet puzzles remain. One problem is the existence of sex. When an organism forms gametes (sperm cells or egg cells) there is a meiotic division, so that in sexual reproduction only half of an organism's genes are transmitted to each of its progeny. Because of this "cost of meiosis," it is hard to see how genotypes for sexual reproduction might have become prevalent. (Apparently, they will spread only half as fast as their asexual rivals.) So why is there sex? We do not have a compelling answer to the question. Despite some ingenious suggestions by orthodox Darwinians (notably G. C. Williams 1975; John Maynard Smith 1978), there is no convincing Darwinian history for the emergence of sexual reproduction. However, evolutionary theorists believe that the problem will be solved without abandoning the main Darwinian insights—just as early nineteenth-century astronomers believed that the problem of the motion of Uranus could be overcome without major modification of Newton's celestial mechanics.

The comparison is apt. Like Newton's physics in 1800, evolutionary theory today rests on a huge record of successes. In both cases, we find a unified theory whose problem-solving strategies are applied to illuminate a host of diverse phenomena. Both theories offer problem solutions that can be subjected to rigorous independent checks. Both open up new lines of inquiry and have a history of surmounting apparent obstacles. The virtues of successful science are clearly displayed in both.

There is a simple way to put the point. Darwin is the Newton of biology. Evolutionary theory is not simply an area of science that has had some success at solving problems. It has unified biology and it has inspired important biological disciplines. Darwin himself appreciated the unification achieved by his theory and its promise of further development (Darwin 1859/Mayr 1964, 188, 253–54, 484–86). Over a century later, at the beginning of his authoritative account of current views of species and their origins, Ernst Mayr explained how that promise had been fulfilled: "The theory of evolution is quite rightly called the greatest unifying theory in biology. The diversity of organisms, similarities and differences between kinds of organisms, patterns of distribution and behavior, adaptation and interaction, all this was merely a bewildering chaos of facts until given meaning by the evolutionary theory" (Mayr 1970, 1). Dobzhansky put the point even more concisely: "Nothing in biology makes sense except in the light of evolution" (Dobzhansky 1973).

Darwin Redux

The Tautology Objection

Consistency is not the hobgoblin of the Creationist mind. However, Creationist motives are not hard to discern. Creationists would like to show that the theory of evolution is simply false. To this end, they hunt diligently for observational findings that would cast doubt on parts of the theory, and they revel in unresolved disputes among evolutionary biologists. On the other hand, the claim that evolution is untestable is essential to their case for equal time. Since "[n]either evolution nor creation is accessible to the scientific method," both can aptly be described as "religion." So both "models of origins" should be taught in the classroom (Morris 1974b, 172–

73). Given the strong pull of their objectives, Creationists throw consistency to the winds and try to press both types of criticism.

Because the point about untestability is so vital to their cause, they try to support it in a number of different ways. . . . we saw how the criterion of naive falsificationism (adapted from Popper) failed to pin any "fault" on evolution that is not shared by every other science. But the appeal to this criterion does not exhaust Creationist efforts.

One popular way to try to argue that evolutionary theory is not testable, that it differs from real science, can be called the *tautology objection*. The central idea is that evolutionary theory reduces to an empty truism. This is another ancient warhorse, which Creationists ride with zeal. Here are some typical Creationist versions:

> [Macbeth] points out that although evolutionists have abandoned classical Darwinism, the modern synthetic theory they have proposed as a substitute is equally inadequate to explain progressive change as the result of natural selection, and, as a matter of fact, they cannot even define natural selection in nontautologous terms. (Gish 1979, 20)
>
> Schutzenberger and others have shown the above Neodarwinian approach to biogenesis and the origin of species to be tautological, i.e. meaningless. The reasoning behind Schutzenberger's claim is quite elementary in reality, for he points out that the Neodarwinian hypothesis simply states nothing more than that the organism which survives has survived. Or put otherwise: the organism leaving the greatest number of offspring behind will survive. This type of depth of wisdom is not very difficult to plumb. (Wilder-Smith 1981, 127; see also Morris 1974a, 6–7)

The tautology objection is not an original contribution of the Creationists. Similar arguments have been voiced by philosophers (Popper 1963), lawyers (Macbeth 1971), and biologists (Peters 1976). The objection has even found its way into *Harper's Magazine* (Bethell 1976). Once again, there is good reason to believe that the Creationists do not really understand the objection they are borrowing. It is attractive to them because it ends in the right place. Some of their formulations are downright mystifying however. Tautologies are standardly taken to be the simplest logical truths, for example, statements of the form "All *A*'s are *A*'s," such as "All cats are cats." Logicians ought to be upset by the idea that tautologies are "meaningless" (Wilder-Smith). While a statement like "All cats are cats" is not exactly informative, it is perfectly clear what it means. Still, we can all take comfort in the fact that an "organism leaving the greatest number of offspring *behind will* survive" (Wilder-Smith).

Despite the infelicities of Creationist formulations, it is worth looking more closely at the tautology objection. The objection has certainly attracted a surprising number of adherents. What accounts for its fascination? There are two sources of confusion. The more important of these is the tendency to boil evolutionary theory down to a single statement: the principle of natural selection. The other is misunderstanding of the concept of Darwinian fitness. Working together, these muddles produce the idea that evolutionary theory reduces to the claim that the fittest survive—and that what this means is that those who survive survive.

I shall begin with the concept of fitness. The first point to note is that fitness is not concerned with survival as an end in itself, but rather with survival as a means to reproduction. From the Darwinian standpoint, what counts for fitness is success in leaving descendants. But if we simply measure the fitness of an organism by the number of offspring it leaves, then peculiar consequences threaten. Organisms that we would naturally regard as equally fit can differ in their fortunes. Let us consider two antelopes, each with the same complement of genes, happily grazing on a plain. A cheetah approaches from one side, seizing the nearer of the two. The other antelope escapes and goes on to produce numerous offspring. Obviously it would be absurd to declare that the two organisms have different degrees of fitness. The inequality in their actual reproductive successes is simply a matter of luck. So biologists say that the fitness of an organism varies as its *expected* reproductive success. What is important is *the number of offspring that an or-*

ganism with those genes could have been expected to produce.

What is this number? The last paragraph provides a constraint on any definition of fitness; we want to count two organisms with the same genes as equally fit. Contemporary evolutionary theory provides an approach to fitness designed to satisfy this constraint. The concept of fitness as expected reproductive sucess is introduced in terms of *genes,* not in terms of *organisms.* Scientists estimate the relative fitnesses of different alleles at the same locus by taking the fitness of an allele (or, more exactly, of an allelic pair) to be measured by its representation in future generations (see, for example, Wilson and Bossert 1971, 47–54). Here it is possible to use the *actual* reproductive success as an estimate because the same allelic pair will be found in many different organisms, so that the effects of good and bad luck are expected to cancel. Insofar as one can speak of the fitness of the organism—its expected reproductive success—it will be a function of the fitnesses of the allelic pairs which make up its genotype. (I should note that there are some obvious shortcomings of this approach to fitness. Genes do not act singly, but in combination. Hence it is something of an abstraction to identify the fitness of an allelic pair, in isolation, and then to regard the fitness of the organism as determined by the fitnesses of its allelic pairs. However, for some purposes, the abstraction works well enough.)

Now that the concept of fitness is somewhat clearer, it is time to ask what the principle of natural selection actually says about the fittest. The obvious way to answer this question would be to consult a presentation of evolutionary theory and to find the statement marked "Principle of Natural Selection" (just as we might look to a textbook on mechanics for the "Principle of Inertia"). Surprisingly, this approach yields no answer. The indexes of two excellent and thorough textbooks in evolutionary theory (Dobzhansky, Ayala, Steebins, and Valentine 1977; Futuyma 1979) have lengthy entries for natural selection, but *no* entry for the *principle* of natural selection. That is, the phrase "natural selection" occurs many times in presenting evolutionary biology, but there is no one general statement given pride of place as the principle of natural selection.

However, there is one part of evolutionary theory—mathematical population genetics—that offers very definite conclusions about fitness and representation in future generations. It is not easy to formulate the idea that "the fittest survive" if we try to provide a principle about *organisms.* On the other hand, if we want a principle about *genes,* then we can obtain detailed mathematical results about the relations between fitness and the representation of genotypes. The task of mathematical population genetics is to work out the mathematical intricacies of the ways in which the distributions of genetic combinations will vary in a sequence of populations, according to the relative fitnesses of the relevant allelic pairs. (Consider a simple example. Suppose that, at a locus, there are two alleles, A and a. The allelic pairs AA, Aa, aa have relative fitnesses 0.9, 1.0, and 0. It is a theorem of population genetics that the lethal allele a will persist in the population at a frequency of 0.09.

Mathematical population genetics articulates precisely the idea that genes that are more fit become prevalent in a population. It offers detailed descriptions of how the relative fitnesses of alleles will result in the spread of allelic combinations, how under some conditions equilibria will be reached, and so forth. The claim that the fittest survive becomes an array of definite results about the distribution of genes in successive populations.

So the tautology objection is wrong in the first place because the principle of natural selection is not a tautology. Insofar as the principle has an heir in contemporary evolutionary theory, it is a collection of theorems in mathematical population genetics. But there is a more significant error. We should not identify the Darwinian theory of evolution with the principle of natural selection to begin with. Fundamental to the tautology objection is the false philosophical view . . . that any theory can be identified with a small collection of statements. This view is applied to evolutionary theory to generate the caricature that the theory is just the principle of natural selection.

Let us approach the issue in terms of positive account offered [earlier]. Evolutionary theory is a collection of problem-solving strategies that use Darwinian histories. In constructing Darwinian histories, the concept of fitness is constantly employed. Darwinian histories frequently make claims about factors that promote or detract from fitness. One theorist, who is investigating cryptic coloring (protective camouflage) in moths, points out that an ability to blend with its environment makes an organism less vulnerable to predators. Another, who is interested in the physiognomy of bats, identifies the upturning of the nose as assisting the organism in its use of sound waves to locate neighboring objects. In these, and countless other cases, biologists use the concept of fitness and *make independently testable claims about what gives the organisms in question whatever fitness they have.*

The example of cryptic coloring in moths provides an especially good demonstration of how claims about the grounds of fitness can be independently evaluated. Naturalists can watch predators at work. They can record the relative numbers of captures involving well-camouflaged moths and those that stand out from their surroundings. Moreover, they can eliminate other possible reasons for differential reproductive success. For example, it is possible to show that protective coloration makes no difference in fecundity, survival of larvae, or ability to mate. Thus they confirm the claim that the success results from the protection afforded by cryptic coloration.

The main point is that the *concepts* of fitness and natural selection, not the *principle* of natural selection, play a central role in Darwinian evolutionary biology. Darwin made some relatively elementary observations. Organisms vary. The variation leads to differential abilities for survival and reproduction. Some of the characteristics that underlie differences in reproductive success can be inherited. What Darwin saw was that these elementary observations can give rise to problem-solving strategies of enormous potential. They suggest a general pattern of evolutionary explanation. When evolutionary theorists give explanations, they make statements about the fitness of particular organisms with particular characteristics, statements that are vulnerable to independent checks. They do not simply intone, "The fittest survive." . . . I [have] pointed out some defects of the traditional view that theories are small collections of statements. Whatever attractiveness that view may have when we think about Newtonian mechanics, it becomes ludicrous when we attempt to apply it to sciences like genetics, plate tectonics, and evolutionary theory. These sciences employ distinctive *concepts*—the concepts of gene, plate, and fitness—and they employ these concepts in distinctive ways to solve problems. But there are no general laws or principles involving the concepts that can be picked out as the whole (or even the essence) of any of these theories. Geologists use the concept of plate (and of interactions among plates) to explain earthquakes (among other things). They do not simply respond to a particular earthquake by stating some "principle of plates." Rather, they advance testable claims about the motions of the plates in the case at hand. Analogously, no reputable biologist accounts for an evolutionary development by asserting the principle of natural selection—as if it were enough to say "It's the survival of the fittest again." Instead, each time the concept of fitness is employed in evolutionary explanations, biologists are compelled to advance some independent, empirically vulnerable, claim about the advantage conferred by a particular characteristic under particular circumstances.

The principle of natural selection is not a tautology. Even if it were, it would not follow that evolutionary theory is tautologous and untestable. To generate that resounding conclusion, we would have to reduce evolutionary theory to the principle of natural selection. Since the reduction is hopelessly wrong, the objection collapses. Whatever Creationists may think, evolutionary biologists are not in the habit of declaiming *ad nauseam* that those who survive survive.

Anything Goes?

Here is still another way of trying to bolster the charge that evolutionary theory is untestable. The claim is that evolutionary theory is full of fantasizing. It consists of Just-So Stories without Kipling's wit. Once again, let us hear from the Creationists:

> Furthermore, the architects of the modern synthetic theory of evolution have so skillfully constructed their theory that it is not capable of falsification. The theory is so plastic that it is capable of explaining anything. (Gish 1979, 17)

> [Evolutionary theory] bridges enormous gaps in the fossil record with creatures of the imagination. (Watson 1976, 97)

> Rather than evolution being science, the exposé of, the objections to, the criticisms are science [sic]. Scientific facts, laws and the principles must be dismissed or seriously altered and tampered with to maintain one's belief in evolution. (Wysong 1976, 460)[1]

As with the tautology objection, the accusation is not new. Darwin's earliest critics objected that evolutionary theory is so accommodating that it can adapt to any observational finding. Fleeming Jenkin's presentation is forceful, specific and eloquent:

> The peculiarities of geographical distribution seem very difficult of explanation on any theory. Darwin calls in alternately, winds, tides, birds, beasts, all animated nature, as the diffusers of species, and then a good many of the same agencies as impenetrable barriers. There are some impenetrable barriers between the Galapagos Islands, but not between New Zealand and South America. Continents are created to join Australia and the Cape of Good Hope, while a sea as broad as the Bristol Channel is elsewhere a valid line of demarcation. With these facilities of hypothesis there seems no particular reason why many theories should not be true. However an animal may have been produced, it must have been produced somewhere, and it must either have spread very widely, or not have spread, and Darwin can give good reason for both results. (Jenkin 1867; in Hull 1974, 342)

The charges are serious. They portray the pronouncements of evolutionary theory as on a par with the "predictions" found in fortune cookies. What is wrong with such "predictions" is that they can adapt themselves to all cirmcumstances. Plainly, a theory that is compatible with all results explains none. But is it true that in evolutionary theorizing anything goes?

One initial qualification is in order. I have no doubt that we can discover cases in which evolutionary theorists have clutched at unconfirmed assumptions to save cherished hypotheses about the historical development of particular kinds of organisms. Biology is done by humans, and it would be surprising if the desire to protect one's past work did not sometimes override the force of the evidence. However, behavior of this sort does not have to occur. When evolutionary theorists dodge criticisms by inventing ad hoc hypotheses, they are not pursuing a practice endemic to their discipline, but flouting the limits that it imposes. Under these circumstances, they are properly criticized by their scientific colleagues.

Fleeming Jenkin's general worry was that the checks on Darwinian histories are too weak, so that there are no limits on the biologist's imagination. Yet, as we saw [earlier], Darwinian histories can be subjected to independent checks. If I hypothesize that two contemporary forms are related to a recent common ancestor, then studies of anatomical and biochemical similarities can test the extent of the relationship. If I suggest that a successful variation could have been fixed in a population in a specific number of generations, then my suggestion is vulnerable to the results of population genetics. If I propose that a modification of structure could have generated a reproductive advantage, then my proposal can be compared with what we know about the relation between similar modifications and reproductive success. Geological evidence can be amassed to test whatever claims I make about continental connections or climatic conditions. My liberty to invent scenarios is constantly checked. (Once again, let me note that if evolutionary theorists have sometimes been allowed to indulge their imaginations about particular evolutionary developments, that is not because their enterprise lacks rules but because they—and their colleagues—have been lax in enforcing the rules.)

Hence there is no basis for the blanket charge that evolutionary theory is a game without rules. As I have emphasized, independently testable hypotheses and theories provide numerous checks on Darwinian histories. Moreover, the proposals of evolutionary theorists provide cross checks on one another. If one scientist attempts to explain the emergence of a group of West Indian lizards and another tries to account for the distribution of birds in the same region, then the hypotheses about climate, faunal diversity, land connections, and so forth must be compatible with one another. As the enterprise of articulating the history of life proceeds, the resolution of outstanding problems will be ever more sharply constrained by the facts already established.

Hence, if there is any substance to the worry that evolutionary theory is too accommodating, it will have to be because there are identifiable loopholes that scientists can exploit or special strategems that allow the imagination free rein. Fleeming Jenkin made it quite clear what he found objectionable. Evolutioanry theorists, he claimed, can erect barriers where they wish and make whatever suppositions they please about past connections between continents and islands. But this is incorrect. The thesis that a particular obstacle, such as a body of water, constitutes a barrier for a species of organism can be tested in perfectly straightforward ways. Equally, geological theory enables us to test suggestions about previous land connections. However, to be fair to Jenkin, the resources for checking those suggestions are more adequate now than they were in Darwin's day. . . .

Note

1. Strictly speaking, these sentences are uttered by Wysong's Creationist spokesman. However, by the late stage in the book at which this passage appears, the pretence of an impartial author moderating a debate has long been dropped. So I have no qualms about attributing them directly to Wysong.

References

Bethell, T. 1976. ''Darwin's Mistake.'' *Harper's Magazine* (February issue).

Birch, L. C., and Ehrlich, P. R. 1967. ''Evolutionary History and Population Biology.'' *Nature* 214, 349–52.

Darwin, C. 1859/Mayr, E. 1964. *The Origin of Species*. Facsimile of the first edition. Cambridge: Harvard Univeristy Press.

Dobzhansky, T. 1973. ''Nothing in Biology Makes Sense Except in the Light of Evolution.'' *American Biology Teacher* 35, 125–29.

Dobzhansky, T., Ayala, F. J., Stebbins, G. L., and Valentine, J. W. 1977. *Evolution*. San Francisco: Freeman.

Futuyma, D. J. 1979. *Evolutionary Biology*. Sunderland, MA: Sinauer.

Gish, D. T. 1979. *Evolution? The Fossils Say No!* San Diego: Creation-Life Publishers.

Gould, S. J. 1981. ''Evolution as Fact and Theory.'' *Discover* 2, 34–37.

Hempel, C. G. 1965. ''Problems and Changes in the Empiricist Criterion of Meaning.'' In *Aspects of Scientific Explanation*. Glencoe, IL: The Free Press, 1965. Originally published in 1951.

Hull, D. L. 1974. *Darwin and His Critics*. Cambridge: Harvard University Press.

Jenkin, F. 1867. ''Review of *The Origin of Species*.'' *North British Review*. Reprinted in Hull 1974.

Macbeth, N. 1971. *Darwin Retried*. Boston: Gambit.

Matthews, L. H. 1971. Introduction to *Origin of Species*. London: Dent.

Maynard Smith, J. 1978. *The Evolution of Sex*. Cambridge: Cambridge University Press.

Mayr, E. 1970. *Populations, Species, and Evolution*. Cambridge: Harvard University Press.

Mayr, E. 1976. *Evolution and the Diversity of Life*.Cambridge: Harvard University Press.

Moore, J. 1974. *Should Evolution Be Taught?* San Diego: Creation-Life Publishers.

Morris, H. M. 1974a. *Scientific Creationism* (general edition). San Diego: Creation-Life Publishers. [With the exception of the passages cited from pp. iii and 244 (the foreword and final chapter), all quotations from *Scientific Creationism* will be found verbatim on the same pages of the ''public school'' edition.]

Morris, H. M. 1974b. *The Troubled Waters of Evolution*. San Diego: Creation-Life Publishers.

Morris, H. M. 1975. *Intorducing Creationism in the Public Schools*. San Diego: Creation-Life Publishers.

Newton, I. 1687/Motte-Cajori 1960. *The Mathematical Principles of Natural Philosophy*. Berkeley: University of California Press.

Peters, R. H. 1976. ''Tautology in Evolution and Ecology.'' *American Naturalist* 110, 1–12.

Popper, K. R. 1959. *The Logic of Scientific Discovery*. London: Hutchinson.

Popper, K. R. 1963. *Conjectures and Refutations*. New York: Harper.

Quine, W. V. O. 1952. ''Two Dogmas of Empiricism.'' Reprinted in *From a Logical Point of View*. Cambridge: Harvard University Press.

Simpson, G. G. 1953. *The Major Features of Evolution*. New York: Columbia University Press.

Watson, D. C. C. 1976. *The Great Brain Robbery*. Chicago: Moody Press.

Wilder-Smith, A. E. 1981. *The Natural Sciences Know Nothing of Evolution*. San Diego: Creation-Life Publishers.

Williams, G. C. 1975. *Sex and Evolution*. Princeton: Princeton University Press.

Wilson, E., and Bossert, W. H. 1971. *A Primer of Population Biology*. Sunderland, MA: Sinauer.

Wysong, R. L. 1976. *The Creation-Evolution Controversy*. Midland, MI: Inquiry Press.

How to Defend Society Against Science

PAUL FEYERABEND

Paul Feyerabend (1924–) is a professor of philosophy at the University of California at Berkeley. His publications include *Against Method* and *Knowledge Without Foundation*.

Fairytales

I want to defend society and its inhabitants from all ideologies, science included. All ideologies must be seen in perspective. One must not take them too seriously. One must read them like fairytales which have lots of interesting things to say but which also contain wicked lies, or like ethical prescriptions which may be useful rules of thumb but which are deadly when followed to the letter.

Now—is this not a strange and ridiculous attitude? Science, surely, was always in the forefront of the fight against authoritarianism and superstition. It is to science that we owe our increased intellectual freedom vis-à-vis religious beliefs; it is to science that we owe the liberation of mankind from ancient and rigid forms of thought. Today these forms of thought are nothing but bad dreams—and this we learned from science. Science and enlightenment are one and the same thing—even the most radical critics of society believe this. Kropotkin wants to overthrow all traditional institutions and forms of belief, with the exception of science. Ibsen criticises the most intimate ramifications of nineteenth century bourgeois ideology, but he leaves science untouched. Levi-Strauss has made us realise that Western Thought is not the lonely peak of human achievement it was once believed to be, but he excludes science from his relativization of ideologies. Marx and Engels were convinced that science would aid the workers in their quest for mental and social liberation. Are all these people deceived? Are they all mistaken about the role of science? Are they all the victims of a chimaera?

To these questions my answer is a firm *Yes and No*.

Now, let me explain my answer.

My explanation consists of two parts, one more general, one more specific.

The general explanation is simple. Any ideology that breaks the hold a comprehensive system of thought has on the minds of men contributes to the liberation of man. Any ideology that makes man question inherited beliefs is an aid to enlightenment. A truth that reigns without checks and balances is a tyrant who must be overthrown and any falsehood that can aid us in the overthrow of this tyrant is to be welcomed. It follows that seventeenth and eighteenth century science indeed *was* an instrument of liberation and enlightenment. It does not follow that science is bound to *remain* such an instrument. There is nothing inherent in science or in any other ideology that makes it *essentially* liberating, Ideologies can deteriorate and become stupid religions. Look at Marxism. And that the science of today is very different from the science of 1650 is evident at the most superficial glance.

For example, consider the role science now

From *Radical Philosophy* 2 (Summer 1975), pp. 4–8.

plays in education. Scientific "facts" are taught at a very early age and in the very same manner in which religious "facts" were taught only a century ago. There is no attempt to waken the critical abilities of the pupil so that he may be able to see things in perspective. At the universities the situation is even worse, for indoctrination is here carried out in a much more systematic manner. Criticism is not entirely absent. Society, for example, and its institutions, are criticised most severely and often most unfairly and this already at the elementary school level. But science is excepted from the criticism. In society at large the judgement of bishops and cardinals was accepted not too long ago. The move towards "demythologization," for example, is largely motivated by the wish to avoid any clash between Christianity and scientific ideas. If such a clash occurs, then science is certainly right and Christianity wrong. Pursue this investigation further and you will see that science has now become as oppressive as the ideologies it had once to fight. Do not be misled by the fact that today hardly anyone gets killed for joining a scientific heresy. This has nothing to do with science. It has something to do with the general quality of our civilization. Heretics in science are still made to suffer from the *most severe* sanctions this relatively tolerant civilization has to offer.

But—is this description not utterly unfair? Have I not presented the matter in a very distorted light by using tendentious and distorting terminology? Must we not describe the situation in a very different way? I have said that science has become *rigid*, that it has ceased to be an instrument of *change* and *liberation* without adding that it has found the *truth*, or a large part thereof. Considering this additional fact we realise, so the objection goes, that the rigidity of science is not due to human willfulness. It lies in the nature of things. For once we have dicovered the truth—what else can we do but follow it?

This trite reply is anything but original. It is used whenever an ideology wants to reinforce the faith of its followers. "Truth" is such a nicely neutral word. Nobody would deny that it is commendable to speak the truth and wicked to tell lies. Nobody would deny that—and yet nobody knows what such an attitude amounts to. So it is easy to twist matters and to change allegiance to truth in one's everyday affairs into allegiance to the Truth of ideology which is nothing but the dogmatic defence of that ideology. And it is of course *not* true that we *have* to follow the truth. Human life is guided by many ideas. Truth is one of them. Freedom and mental independence are others. If Truth, as conceived by some ideologists, conflicts with freedom then we have a *choice*. We may abandon freedom. But we may also abandon Truth. (Alternatively, we may adopt a more sophisticated idea of truth that no longer contradicts freedom; that was Hegel's solution.) My criticism of modern science is that it inhibits freedom of thought. If the reason is that it has found the truth and now follows it then I would say that there are better things than first finding, and then following such a monster.

This finishes the general part of my explanation.

There exists a more specific argument to defend the exceptional position science has in society today. Put in a nutshell the argument says (1) that science has finally found the correct *method* for achieving results and (2) that there are many *results* to prove the excellence of the method. The argument is mistaken—but most attempts to show this lead into a dead end. Methodology has by now become so crowded with empty sophistication that it is extremely difficult to perceive the simple errors at the basis. It is like fighting the hydra—cut off one ugly head, and eight formalizations take its place. In this situation the only answer is superficiality: when sophistication loses content then the only way of keeping in touch with reality is to be crude and superficial. This is what I intend to be.

Against Method

There is a method, says part (1) of the argument. What is it? How does it work?

One answer which is no longer as popular as it used to be is that science works by collecting facts and inferring theories from them. The answer is unsatisfactory as theories never *follow* from facts in the strict logical sense. To say that they may yet be *supported* by facts assumes a notion of support that (a) does not show this defect and is (b) sufficiently sophisticated to permit us to say to what extent, say, the theory of relativity is supported by the facts. No such notion exists today nor is it likely that it will ever be found (one of the problems is that we need a notion of support in which grey ravens can be said to support "All Ravens are Black"). This was realised by conventionalists and transcendental idealists who pointed out that theories *shape* and *order* facts and can therefore be retained come what may. They can be retained because the human mind either consciously or unconciously carried out its ordering function. The trouble with these views is that they assume for the mind what they want to explain for the world, viz. that it works in a regular fashion. There is only one view which overcomes all these difficulties. It was invented twice in the nineteenth century, by Mill, in his immortal essay *On Liberty*, and by some Darwinists who extended Darwinism to the battle of ideas. This view takes the bull by the horns: theories cannot be justified and their excellence cannot be shown without reference to other theories. We may explain the *success* of a theory by reference to a more comprehensive theory (we explain the success of Newton's theory by using the general theory of relativity); and we may explain our *preference* for it by comparing it with other theories. Such a comparison does not establish the intrinsic excellence of the theory we have chosen. As a matter of fact, the theory we have chosen may be pretty lousy. It may contain contradictions, it may conflict with well-known facts, it may be cumbersome, unclear, ad hoc in decisive places and so on. But it may still be better than any other theory that is available at the time. It may in fact be the best lousy theory there is. Nor are the standards of judgement chosen in an absolute manner. Our sophistication increases with every choice we make, and so do our standards. Standards compete just as theories compete and we choose the standards most appropriate to the historical situation in which the choice occurs. The rejected alternatives (theories; standards; "facts") are not eliminated. They serve as correctives (after all, we may have made the wrong choice) and they also explain the content of the preferred views (we understand relativity better when we understand the structure of its competitors; we know the full meaning of freedom only when we have an idea of life in a totalitarian state, of its advantages—and there are many advantages—as well as of its disadvantages). Knowledge so conceived is an ocean of alternatives channelled and subdivided by an ocean of standards. It forces our mind to make imaginative choices and thus makes it grow. It makes our mind capable of choosing, imagining, criticising.

Today this view is often connected with the name of Karl Popper. But there are some very decisive differences between Popper and Mill. To start with, Popper developed his view to solve a special problem of epistemology—he wanted to solve "Hume's problem." Mill, on the other hand, is interested in conditions favourable to human growth. His epistemology is the result of a certain theory of man, and not the other way around. Also Popper, being influenced by the Vienna Circle, improves on the logical form of a theory before discussing it while Mill uses every theory in the form in which it occurs in science. Thirdly, Popper's standards of comparison are rigid and fixed while Mill's standards are permitted to change with the historical situation. Finally, Popper's standards eliminate competitors once and for all: theories that are either not falsifiable, or falsifiable and falsified have no place in science. Popper's criteria are clear, unambiguous, precisely formulated; Mill's criteria are not. This would be an advantage if science itself were clear, unambiguous, and precisely formulated. Fortunately, it is not.

To start with, no new and revolutionary scientific theory is ever fomulated in a manner that permits us to say under what circumstances we must regard it as endangered: many revolutionary theories are unfalsifiable. Falsifiable versions do exist, but they are hardly ever in agreement with accepted basic statements: every moderately interesting theory is falsified. Moreover, theories have formal flaws, many of them contain contradictions, ad hoc adjustments, and so on and so forth. Applied resolutely, Popperian criteria would eliminate science without replacing it by anything comparable. They are useless as an aid to science.

In the past decade this has been realised by various thinkers, Kuhn and Lakatos among them. Kuhn's ideas are interesting but, alas, they are much too vague to give rise to anything but lots of hot air. If you don't believe me, look at the literature. Never before has the literature on the philosophy of science been invaded by so many creeps and incompetents. Kuhn encourages people who have no idea why a stone falls to the ground to talk with assurance about scientific method. Now I have no objection to incompetence but I do object when incompetence is accompanied by boredom and self-righteousness. And this is exactly what happens. We do not get interesting false ideas, we get boring ideas or words connected with no ideas as all. Secondly, wherever one tries to make Kuhn's ideas more definite one finds that they are *false*. Was there ever a period of normal science in the history of thought? No—and I challenge anyone to prove the contrary.

Lakatos is immeasurably more sophisticated than Kuhn. Instead of theories he considers research programmes which are sequences of theories connected by methods of modification, so-called heuristics. Each theory in the sequence may be full of faults. It may be beset by anomalies, contradictions, ambiguities. What counts is not the shape of the single theories, but the tendency exhibited by the sequence. We judge historical developmetns, achievements over a period of time, rather than the situation at a particular time. History and methodology are combined into a single enterprise. A research programme is said to progress if the sequence of theories leads to novel predictions. It is said to degenerate if it is reduced to absorbing facts that have been discovered without its help. A decisive feature of Lakatos's methodology is that such evaluations are no longer tied to methodological rules which tell the scientist to either retain or to abandon a research programme. Scientists may stick to a degenerating programme, they may even succeed in making the programme overtake its rivals and they therefore proceed rationally with whatever they are doing (provided they continue calling degenerating programmes degenerating and progressive programmes progressive). This means that Lakatos offers *words* which *sound* like the elements of a methodology; he does not offer a methodology. This is no method according to the most advanced and sophisticated methodology in existence today. This finishes my reply to part (1) of the specific argument.

Against Results

According to part (2), science deserves a special position because it has produced *results*. This is an argument only if it can be taken for granted that nothing else has ever produced results. Now it may be admitted that almost everyone who discusses the matter makes such an assumption. It may also be admitted that it is not easy to show that the assumption is false. Forms of life different from science have either disappeared or have degenerated to an extent that makes a fair comparison impossible. Still, the situation is not as hopeless as it was only a decade ago. We have become acquainted with methods of medical diagnosis and therapy which are effective (and perhaps even more effective then the corresponding parts of Western medicine) and which are yet based on an ideology that is radically different from the ideology of Western science. We have learned that there are phenomena such as telepathy and telekinesis which are obliterated by a scientific approach and which could be used to do research in an entirely novel way (earlier thinkers such as Agrippa of Nettesheim, John Dee, and even Bacon were aware of these phenomena). And then—is it not the case that the Church saved souls while science often does the very opposite? Of course, nobody now believes in the ontology that underlies this judgement. Why? Because of ideological pressures identical with those which today make us listen to science to the exclusion of everything else. It is also true that phenomena such as telekinesis and acupuncture may eventually be absorbed into the body of science and may therefore be called "scientific." But note that this happens only *after* a long period of resistance during which a science *not yet* containing the phenomena wants to get the upper hand over forms of life that contain them. And this leads to a further objection against part (2) of the specific argument. The fact that science has results counts in its favour only if these results were achieved by science alone, and without any outside help. A look at history shows that science hardly ever gets its results in this way. When Copernicus introduced a new view of the universe, he did not consult *scientific* predecessors, he consulted a crazy Pythagorean such as Philolaos. He adopted his ideas and he maintained them in the face of all sound rules of scientific method. Mechanics and optics owe a lot to artisans, medicine to midwives and witches. And in our own day we have seen how the interference of the state can advance science: when the Chinese Communists refused to be intimidated by the judgement of experts and ordered traditional medicine back into universities and hospitals there was an outcry all over the world that science would now be ruined in China. The very opposite occurred: Chinese science advanced and Western science learned from it. Wherever we look we see that great scientific advances are due to outside interference which is made to prevail in the face of the most basic and most "rational" methodological rules. The lesson is plain: there does not exist a single argument that could be used to support the exceptional role which science today plays in society. Science has done many things, but so have other ideologies. Science often proceeds systematically, but so do other ideologies (just consult the records of the many doctrinal debates that took place in the Church) and, besides, there are no overriding rules which are adhered to under any circumstances; there is no "scientific methodology" that can be used to separate science from the rest. *Science is just one of the many ideologies that propel society and it should be treated as such* (this statement applies even to the most progressive and most dialectical sections of science). What consequences can we draw from this result?

The most important consequence is that there must be a *formal separation between state and science* just as there is now a formal separation between state and church. Science may influence society but only to the extent to which any political or other pressure group is permitted to influence society. Scientists may be consulted on important projects but the final judgement must be left to the democratically elected consulting bodies. These bodies will consist mainly of laymen. Will the laymen be able to come to a correct judgement? Most certainly, for the competence, the complications and the successes of science are vastly exaggerated. One of the most exhilarating experiences is to see how a lawyer, who is a layman, can find holes in the testimony, the technical testimony of the most advanced expert and thus prepare the jury for its verdict. Science is not a closed book that is understood only after years of training. It is an intellectual discipline that can be examined and criticised by anyone who is interested and that looks difficult and profound only because of a systematic campaign of obfuscation carried out by many scientists (though, I am happy to say, not by all). Organs of the state should never hesitate to reject the judgement of scientists when they have reason for doing so. Such rejection will educate the general public, will make it more confident and it may even lead to improvement. Considering the sizeable chauvinism of the scientific establishment we can say: the more Lysenko affairs the better (it is not the *interference* of the state that is objectionable in the case of Lysenko, but the *totalitarian* interference which kills the opponent rather than just neglecting his advice). Three cheers to the fundamentalists in California who succeeded in having a dogmatic formulation of the theory of evolution removed from the text books and an account of Genesis included (but I know that they would become as chauvinistic and totalitarian as scientists are today when given the chance to run society all by themselves. Ideologies are marvellous when used in the company of other ideologies. They become boring and doctrinaire as soon as their merits lead to the removal of their opponents). The most important change, however, will have to occur in the field of *education*.

Education and Myth

The purpose of education, so one would think, is to introduce the young into life, and that means: into the *society* where they are born and into the *physical universe* that surrounds the society. The method of education often consists in the teaching of some *basic myth*. The myth is available in various versions. More advanced versions may be taught by initiation rites which firmly implant them into the mind. Knowing the myth the grown-up can explain almost everything (or else he can turn to experts for more detailed information). He is the master of Nature and of Society. He understands them both and he knows how to interact with them. However, *he is not the master of the myth that guides his understanding*.

Such further mastery was aimed at, and was partly achieved, by the Pre-Socratics. The Pre-Socratics not only tried to understand the *world*. They also tried to understand, and thus to become the masters of, the *means of understanding the world*. Instead of being content with a single myth they developed many and so diminished the power which a well-told story has over the minds of men. The Sophists introduced still further methods for reducing the debilitating effect of interesting, coherent, "empirically adequate" etc. etc. tales. The achievements of these thinkers were not appreciated and they certainly are not understood today. When teaching a myth we want to increase the chance that it will be understood (i.e. no puzzlement about any feature of the myth), believed, *and accepted*. This does not do any harm when the myth is counterbalanced by other myths: even the most dedicated (i.e. totalitarian) instructor in a certain version of Christianity cannot prevent his pupils from getting in touch with Buddhists, Jews and other disreputable people. It is very different in the case of science, or of rationalism where the field is almost completely dominated by the believers. In this case it is of paramount importance to strengthen the minds of the young and "strengthening the minds of the young" means strengthening them *against* any easy acceptance of comprehensive views. What we need here is an education that makes people *contrary, counter-suggestive without* making them incapable of devoting themselves to the elaboration of any single view. How can this aim be achieved?

It can be achieved by protecting the tremendous imagination which children possess and by developing to the full the spirit of contradiction that exists in them. On the whole children are much more intelligent than their teachers. They succumb, and give up their intelligence because they are bullied, or because their teachers get the better of them by emotional means. Children can learn, understand, and keep separate two to three different languages ("children" and by this I mean 3 to 5 year olds, NOT eight years olds who were experimented upon quite recently and did not come out too well; why? because they were already loused up by incompetent teaching at an earlier age). Of course, the languages must be introduced in a more interesting way than is usually done. There are marvellous writers in all languages who have told marvellous stories—let us begin our language teaching with *them* and not with "der Hund hat einen Schwanz" and similar inanities. Using stories we may of course also introduce "scientific" accounts, say, of the origin of the world and thus make the children acquainted with science as well. But science must not be given any special position except for pointing out that there are lots of people who believe in it. Later on the stories which have been told will be supplemented with "reasons" where by reasons I mean further accounts of the kind found in the tradition to which the story belongs. And, of course, there will also be contrary reasons. Both reasons and contrary reasons will be told by the experts in the fields and so the young generation becomes acquainted with all kinds of sermons and all types of wayfarers. It becomes acquainted with them, it becomes acquainted with their stories and every individual can make up his mind which way to go. By now everyone knows that you can earn a lot of money and respect and perhaps even a Nobel Prize by becoming a scientist, so, many will become scientists. They will *become* scientists *without having been taken in by the ideology of science,* they will *be* scientists *because they have made a free choice.* But has not much time been wasted on unscientific subjects and will this not detract from their competence once they have become scientists? Not at all! The progress of science, of good science, depends on novel ideas and on intellectual freedom: science has very often been advanced by outsiders (remember that Bohr and Einstein regarded themselves as outsiders). Will not many people make the wrong choice and end up in a dead end? Well, that depends on what you mean by a "dead end." Most scientists today are devoid of ideas, full of fear, intent on producing some paltry result so that they can add to the flood of inane papers that now constitutes "scientific progress" in many areas. And, besides, what is more important? To lead a life which one has chosen with open eyes, or to spend one's time in the nervous attempt of avoiding what some not so intelligent people call "dead ends"? Will not the number of scientists decrease so that in the end there is nobody to run our precious laboratories? I do not think so. Given a choice many people may choose science, for a science that is run by free agents looks much more attractive than the science of today which is run by slaves, slaves of institutions and slaves of "reason." And if there is a temporary shortage of scientists the situation may always be remedied by various kinds of incentives. Of course, scientists will not play any predominant role in the society I envisage. They will be more than balanced by magicians, or priests, or astrologers. Such a situation is unbearable for many people, old and young, right and left. Almost all of you have the firm belief that at least *some* kind of truth has been found, that it must be preserved, and that the method of teaching I advocate and the form of society I defend will dilute it and make it finally disappear. You have this firm belief; many of you may even have reasons. *But what you have to consider is that the absence of good contrary reasons is due to a historical accident;* it does *not* lie in the nature of things. Build up the kind of society I recommend and the views you now despise (without knowing them, to be sure) will return in such splendour that you will have to work hard to maintain your own position and will perhaps be entirely unable to do so. You do not believe me? Then look at history. Scientific astronomy was firmly founded on Ptolemy and Aristotle, two of the greatest minds in the history of Western Thought. Who upset their well-argued, empirically adequate and precisely formulated system? Philolaos the mad and antediluvian Pythagorean. How was it that Philolaos could stage a comeback; Because he found an able defender: Copernicus. Of course, you may follow your intuitions as I am following mine. But remember that your intuitions are the result of your ''scientific'' training where by science I also mean the science of Karl Marx. My training, or, rather, my non-training, is that of a journalist who is interested in strange and bizarre events. Finally, is it not utterly irresponsible, in the present world situation, with millions of people starving, others enslaved, downtrodden, in abject misery of body and mind, to think luxurious thoughts such as these? Is not freedom of choice a luxury under such circumstances; Is not the flippancy and the humour I want to see combined with the freedom of choice a luxury under such circumstances? Must we not give up all self-indulgence and *act*? Join together, and *act*? That is the most important objection which today is raised against an approach such as the one recommended by me. It has tremendous appeal, it has the appeal of unselfish dedication. Unselfish dedication—to what? Let us see!

We are supposed to give up our selfish inclinations and dedicate ourselves to the liberation of the oppressed. And selfish inclinations are what? They are our wish for maximum liberty of thought in the society in which we live *now*, maximum liberty not only of an abstract kind, but expressed in appropriate institutions and methods of teaching. This wish for concrete intellectual and physical liberty in our own surroundings is to be put aside, for the time being. This assumes, first, that we do not need this liberty for our task. It assumes that we can carry out our task with a mind that is firmly closed to some alternatives. It assumes that the correct way of liberating others *has already been found* and that all that is needed is to carry it out. I am sorry, I cannot accept such doctrinaire self-assurance in such extremely important matters. Does this mean that we cannot act at all? It does not, But it means that *while acting we have to try to realise as much of the freedom I have recommended so that our actions may be corrected in the light of the ideas we get while increasing our freedom.* This will slow us down, no doubt, but are we supposed to charge ahead simply because some people tell us that they have found an explanation for all the misery and an excellent way out of it? Also we want to liberate people not to make them succumb to a new kind of slavery, *but to make them realise their own wishes,* however different these wishes may be from our own. Self-righteous and narrow-minded liberators cannot do this. As a rule they soon impose a slavery that is worse, because more systematic, than the very sloppy slavery they have removed. And as regards humour and flippancy the answer should be obvious. Why would anyone want to liberate anyone else? Surely not because of some *abstract* advantage of liberty but because liberty is the best way to free development *and thus to happiness*. We want to liberate people *so that they can smile*. Shall we be able to do this if we ourselves have forgotten how to smile and are frowning on those who still remember? Shall we then not spread another disease, comparable to the one we want to remove, the disease of puritanical self-righteousness? Do not object that dedication and humour do not go together—Socrates is an excellent example to the contrary. *The hardest task needs the lightest hand or else its completion will not lead to freedom but to a tyranny much worse than the one it replaces.*

PART III

KNOWLEDGE AND REALITY

INTRODUCTION

There are (at least) three answers to any question: "Yes," "No," and "I don't know." As it stands, the third answer suggests ignorance. But, when we strengthen it and claim not only that knowledge is not at hand, but also that it is impossible for beings like us, we have not admitted ignorance but professed skepticism. We have taken a philosophical postion.

There is a long list of questions on which some philosopher or other has come to a skeptical position. For example, David Hume (assuming that Philo is his spokesperson) is a skeptic about questions concerning the nature of the cause or causes of order in the universe. During the seventeenth and eighteenth centuries, a very general sort of skepticism that held we could not even know the most basic facts about the external world was a major issue that gave rise to a number of great classics of epistemology—the branch of philosophy that considers the nature and possibility of knowledge. We reprint a number of classics from this Golden Age of Epistemology in Section A of Part III. In two of these, our friend Hume advocates a moderate skepticism. Two other selections, by René Descartes and George Berkeley, defend theories that are intended to solve problems posed by skeptics. The essay by John Locke, although not directly concerned with skepticism, deals with a central issue in the skeptical controversies: the distinction between ideas in our mind and the objects in the world they are about.

Descartes's Problem

No work in the history of philosophy has had more impact than Descartes's *Meditations on First Philosophy*. This work is a battle with skepticism. Descartes's very trust in reason—the capacity each of us seems to have to learn the truth through careful thought and observation—is thrown into question by skeptical challenges he considers in "Meditation–I." Could it be that he is only dreaming? Or worse yet, that an evil demon is devoted to deceiving him in every particular, even those things about which he is more confident? His reason tells Descartes that he should not place his confidence in any belief about which he can have the least doubt. But, unless he can rule out these hypotheses, he seems to have grounds for doubting everything. Reason seems to have rendered itself useless.

The modern student may have little worry about evil demons and be confident that his dreams are too chaotic to be mistaken for waking experience; so, it may be worthwhile to construct a high-tech example to arouse sympathy for Descartes's worry. Suppose that after your last philosophy class, a psychology graduate student shot you with a tranquilizing dart, took you to her dark laboratory in the subbasement of the Psychology Building, and sawed off the top of your skull and removed your brain. Then, she inserted electrodes into your brain. To these electrodes she attached wires through which a computer program could feed electrical charges. The program simulates the input you would receive from your perceptual system if you had been allowed to go about your business. You are really a brain in a vat in a basement, but the experiences you are having are just the ones you would have had if you were back in your room reading this textbook. Now that you have contemplated this alternative hypothesis to explain the experiences you are having, how can you rule it out? This episode of computer-assisted philosophy should have placed you in the skeptical abyss along with Descartes.

In the rest of the *Meditations,* Descartes ascends step by step out of this abyss. The first steps seem small, but he soon picks up speed; by the end of "Meditation VI," he has vaulted out of the abyss and vindicated most of his earlier beliefs.

Descartes takes his first step (in "Meditation II") when he notes that he cannot doubt that he exists, for he would have to exist to dream or be deceived. And, he cannot doubt that he has ideas either. This is progress, but not much, for the whole physical world still lies within the realm of that which can be doubted.

At the end of "Meditation II" and the beginning of "Meditation III," Descartes develops a conception of what knowledge of the external world would be—to help him determine whether he has any. This conception is known as the theory of representative ideas. (A similar conception is developed by Locke in the selection reprinted from his *An Essay Concerning Human Understanding*.) According to this theory, knowledge would consist in a two-way relationship between one's ideas and the objects in the external world. Suppose, for example, that you see a book in front of you. The images you have in your mind could exist, even if there were no book, for you might be dreaming or being deceived by an evil demon or by a psychology graduate student. So, just having those ideas or images does not constitute knowledge that there is a book in front of you. For you to know that, there must be a book there, which is causally responsible for your having the ideas and images you do. To have knowledge, one's ideas must accurately represent the objects that give rise to them.

Given this conception of what it would be to know the external world, can we be sure that we do? It seems that all we can ever be sure of is our own ideas. I might check that there is a book in front of me by reaching out and handling it. Or, I might ask a friend (who is in the room with me) if there is, indeed, a book there. But, what would this show? Suppose, when I reach out, I feel the hard booklike surface and see my hand on the book. And, when I ask my friend, he replies, "Yep, there sure is a book there." But, what do these tests prove? These events could just be additional parts of the dream or of the evil demons's plot.

Once one starts thinking in terms of the theory of representative ideas, one gets the feeling of being trapped in one's own mind. If one is really perceiving an external world, one's ideas must be caused by objects beyond the ideas that these ideas accurately represent. But, how can one ever check this out? One would have to get outside the circle of one's own ideas, and that seems impossible. This epistemological predicament is sometimes called Descartes's Problem.

Descartes believed he had a solution. He thought that one of his ideas, his idea of God, had a very special quality. It is what we might call self-certifying. It could not have been caused by anything other than God. Descartes invoked certain principles—connecting causes and effects—to convince himself of this. He believed that the cause of an idea must be as perfect as that which the idea represents. Given this, he argues that only God could have caused the idea of God in him. Then, Descartes argues that God, being perfect, would not allow him to be deceived when he tries hard to be careful. Thus, Descartes needs God's help to climb back out of the abyss into which he tumbled.

Berkeley and Hume

Many philosophers have followed Descartes's path into the abyss of ignorance, but few have followed his path out of it.

Some have thought that his mistake, and Locke's, was the theory of representative ideas. Berkeley is one such philosopher. In his *Three Dialogues Between Hylas and Philonous* he argues that we should not distinguish between the ideas in our mind and the external objects they represent or else skepticism is unavoidable. Berkeley thought all arguments for such distinctions fallacious. That of which we are directly aware, the ideas in our minds, are what we mean to be speaking of when we talk about tables and chairs in the external world. According to Berkeley, we do not really think there is a nonmental reality behind these ideas. The student may find this notion quite absurd on first encountering it. This was the reaction of Berkeley's character Hylas, when Philonous, the spokesperson for Berkeley's views, first explained it. But Hylas seems powerless to combat the force of Philonous's arguments. Each student should try to lend Hylas a hand and see if Philonous's arguments are actually as powerful as Hylas finally finds them.

Hume's response to Descartes's problem is different from Berkeley's. Berkeley maintains that the idea of a material object beyond our ideas is a philosopher's confusion and no part of ordinary common sense. Hume, in his "Of Scepticism with Regard to the Senses," argues that, although it is a confusion, it is not just a philosopher's confusion. The way people in general look at chairs and desks and other physical objects—as things that can endure when no one is perceiving them—is a mass of confusion. Should we then revise the way we think about the world? Hume thinks we cannot do this, at least not more than for a moment or two while actively engaged in philosophical reflection. He recommends instead a moderate skepticism. We should be aware of our confusions and limitations while doing philosophy; but, at other times, we should give into our natural inclinations to believe and infer cheerfully, for we really have no choice. And, in his *Enquiry,* Hume argues that only habit or custom, not reason, leads us to expect the future to be like the past: a principle he shows to underlie all of our important beliefs about the world, beyond the most immediate deliverances of sense perception.

Sense Data and Perception

All the philosophers from the Golden Age of Epistemology represented here followed Descartes to a certain point. They all accepted that what they were immediately aware of was not a material object outside the mind. There are various arguments for this view. One, the argument from illusion, is implicit in Descartes's worry about whether he is dreaming. Suppose I am in the state I would normally take to be that of seeing a book in front of me. There seems to be something, of which I am directly aware, that could exist, even if I were dreaming (or were in some other way deceived) and there was no book in front of me at all. But this thing, which is common to the cases in which there is a book in front of me and the cases in which there is not a book in front of me, *cannot* be a book. It must, it seems, be an idea in my own mind. Another version of the argument comes from Hume. He pokes a finger in his eye, and he notes that he now sees double. But, what is it of which there are two? Poking oneself in the eye cannot cause there to be two books where there was only one. Again, it seems that of which we are directly aware—that which is doubled when we put pressure on our eye—*cannot* be the material object we might naively take it to be. Finally, all of our authors note that the same material object looks different from various perspectives. The material object does not change, but that of which we are directly aware does change—so, the latter cannot be the former. This last argument, the argument from perceptual relativity, is sometimes considered just a version of the argument from illusion.

All of our seventeenth- and eighteenth-century authors seem to agree that the immediate objects of perception are not material objects; they differ on what to do about it. (There were philosophers of the era, notably Thomas Reid, who did not go along with this view, however.) But in the twentieth century, a great deal of thought has gone into whether the distinction between the material objects and the things we directly perceive can really be sustained. And some who have thought that the distinction could be sustained have, nevertheless, thought that the objects we directly perceive are not mental at all. The term, sense data, is used neutrally because whatever sense data are—whether ideas, surfaces of a material object, or something else—they are the direct object of perception.

The three essays in Section B, "Perception," are concerned with these issues. G. E. Moore gives both a careful analysis of his reasons for believing in sense data as well as the reasons for and against various views about what they are. Careful as Moore's analysis is, O. K. Bouwsma finds that he cannot make sense of Moorean sense data. And J. L. Austin submits the argument from illusion to a painstaking analysis and finds it quite unconvincing.

Hume's Problems

Abstractly considered, Descartes's Problem is a special case of the following sort of question. Suppose that I know that an event of a certain sort is occurring at one time. How can I, on the basis of this, know of the occurrence of some other event? In Descartes's case, the first event is the occurrence of an idea in my mind; the second is the external existence of a physical world of the sort the idea represents.

Hume considers the general problem in his *Enquiry*. He comes to the conclusion that there is essentially no way that knowledge of one event can give us knowledge of another if knowledge requires immunity from any possible doubt. We are so constituted that, in certain circumstances, we will infer the existence of events of one sort from the occurrence of events of another. Given perception, we will believe in an external world—at least when we do not inhibit our natural inclination to do so by thinking philosophical thoughts. And, if one sort of event has been accompanied in our experience by another sort of event many times in the past, then, when an event of the first sort is perceived by us, we will expect an event of the second sort. If we see lightning, we expect to hear thunder; if we see someone loosen his or her hold on a book, we expect the book to fall. This is the way we are "wired up"; we have no real choice but to follow the natural flow of ideas in our minds. But, there is no further guarantee that the world will conform to these inferences and expectations. Our only grounds for supposing it will is that we have no choice. In the "explanation," appeals to reason must give way to appeals to instinct.

Hume thought that these results of his investigation provided a sort of solution to our doubts. If we cannot do better than rely on our natural inclinations to believe, what is there to worry about? But many philosophers have thought that Hume's arguments raised problems rather than solved them.

These philosopehrs have thought that there *must* be something more to be said in favor of *induction:* the practice of basing our expectations about the future on regularities that have been observed in the past. Even if this practice cannot be guaranteed to work, it has been thought that it must have some favored logical status. Something, beside the brute fact that this is the way our minds work, should mark out this practice as more reasonable than any alternative. This problem has become known as Hume's Problem or the problem of induction. It is a part of the more general inquiry into scientific reasoning that is known as the philosophy of science, for the extrapolation from the observed to the unobserved parts of nature seems essential to the scientific method.

In his selection, "The Problem of Induction," W. C. Salmon surveys the various attempts that have been made to improve on Hume's account of induction, that is, to provide it with some more telling justification than Hume was able to provide. Salmon is unable to accept any of the proposed solutions to Hume's Problem that he considers. Yet, Salmon is convinced that there must be a solution; for, if there is not, science will be just a matter of faith on a par with other faiths. This situation, Salmon says, is "intellectually and socially undesirable. . . . I find it intolerable to suppose that a theory of biological evolution, supported as it is by extensive scientific evidence, has no more rational foundation than has its rejection by ignorant fundamentalists." Thus, the issues of epistemology lead us back to the issues discussed in Section C of Part II.

Even if, as Salmon suggests, Hume's Problem is real and remains unsolved, it should not be thought that the philosophy of science has made no progress since Hume's day. The selections is this anthology do not reflect the enormous activity that has gone on in this field, for much of it is concerned with the details of particular sciences and is quite technical. The article by Carl G. Hempel, however, does explain one of the most important and controversial ideas to emerge in this field, the covering law or the deductive nomological model of scientific explanation. This idea is often regarded as providing a sophisticated version of Hume's treatment of empirical reasoning.

The last two selections in Section C consider a related problem found in Hume. The reader will recall that Descartes used principles about causality to solve his special case of Hume's Problem. The principle Descartes relied on, that an idea (specifically the idea of God) could not be caused by anything less perfect than what it represents, has not struck most philosophers as obvious or even very intelligible. But, many philosophers have thought that causal principles do have a special status. A certain necessity seems to attach to some of them, and understanding this necessity seems like a first step toward solving Hume's Problem.

Hume himself considered this possibility, and he came to a negative conclusion. In so doing, he put forward an analysis of causation that has itself become a source of philosophical controversy. Causal principles, Hume thought, are not in the least necessary. Indeed, the relation of causation, he thought, is no more than that of constant conjunction. We say that an event of a certain type, for example, E causes an event of type E', if events of type E have, in our experience, been constantly conjoined with events of type E'. The last two essays, by C. J. Ducasse and G. E. M. Anscombe, are directly critical of Hume's position.

A. CLASSICS OF EPISTEMOLOGY

Meditations on First Philosophy

RENÉ DESCARTES

René Descartes (1596–1650) was one of the greatest philosophers and mathematicians of all time. In addition to the *Meditations,* his works include *Discourse on Method* and *Principles of Philosophy.*

Meditation I
On What Can Be Called into Doubt

For several years now, I have been aware that I accepted many falsehoods as true in my youth, that what I built on the foundation of those falsehoods was dubious, and therefore that, once in my life, I would need to tear down everything and begin anew from the foundations if I wanted to establish any firm and lasting knowledge. But the task seemed enormous, and I waited until I was so old that no better time for undertaking it would be likely to follow. I have thus delayed so long that it would be wrong for me to waste in indecision the time left for action. Today, then, having rid myself of worries and having arranged for some peace and quiet, I withdraw alone, free at last earnestly and wholeheartedly to overthrow all my beliefs.

To do this, I do not need to show each of my beliefs to be false; I may never be able to do that. But, since reason now convinces me that I ought to withhold my assent just as carefully from what is not obviously certain and indubitable as from what is obviously false, I can justify the rejection of all my beliefs if I can find some ground for doubt in each. And, to do this, I need not take on the endless task of running through my beliefs one by one: since a building collapses when its foundation is cut out from under it, I will go straight to the principles on which all my former beliefs rested.

Of course, whatever I have so far accepted as supremely true I have learned either from the senses or through the senses. But I have occasionally caught the senses deceiving me, and it would be prudent for me never completely to trust those who have cheated me even once.

But, while my senses may deceive me about what is small or far away, there may still be other things taken in by the senses which I cannot possibly doubt—such as that I am here, sitting before the fire, wearing a dressing gown, touching this paper. Indeed, these hands and the rest of my body—on what grounds might I deny that they exist?—unless perhaps I liken myself to madmen whose brains are so rattled by the persistent vapors of melancholy that they are sure they are kings when in fact they are paupers, or that they wear purple robes when in fact they are naked, or that their heads are clay, or that they are gourds, or that they are made of glass. But these people are insane, and I would seem just as crazy if I were to apply what I say about them to myself.

This would be perfectly obvious—if I weren't a man accustomed to sleeping at night whose experiences while asleep are at least as far-fetched as those that madmen have while awake. How

From *Meditations on First Philosophy,* trans. Ronald Rubin (Claremont, Calif.: Arete Press, forthcoming.

often a dream has convinced me that I was here, sitting before the fire, wearing my dressing gown, when, in fact, I was undressed and between the covers of my bed! But now I am looking at this piece of paper with my eyes wide open; the head that I am shaking has not been lulled to sleep; I put my hand out consciously and deliberately; I feel the paper and see it. None of this would be as distinct if I were asleep. As if I can't remember having been deluded by similar thoughts while asleep! When I think very carefully about this, I see so plainly that there are no reliable signs by which I can distinguish sleeping from waking that I am stupified—and my stupor itself suggests that I am asleep!

Suppose then that I am dreaming. Suppose, in particular, that my eyes are not open, that my head is not moving, and that I have not put out my hand. Suppose that I do not have hands, or even a body. I must still admit that the things I see in sleep are like painted images, which must have been patterned after real things. Hence, things like eyes, heads, hands, and bodies are not imaginary, but real. For, even when painters try to give bizarre shapes to sirens and satyrs, they are unable to give them completely new natures, but can only jumble together the parts of various animals. Even if they were to come up with something so novel that no one had ever seen anything like it before, something entirely fictitious and unreal, there would at least need to be real colors from which they can compose it. By the same reasoning, while things like eyes, heads, and hands may be imaginary, it must be granted that some simpler and more universal things are real—the "real colors" from which the true and the false images in our thoughts are formed. Among things of this sort seem to be general bodily nature and its extension, the shape of extended things, their quantitiy (that is, their magnitude and number), the place in which they exist, and the time through which they endure.

Perhaps we can correctly infer that, while physics, astronomy, medicine, and other disciplines requiring the study of composites are dubious, disciplines like arithmetic and geometry, which deal only with completely simple and universal things without regard to whether they exist in the world, are somehow certain and indubitable. Whether we are awake or asleep, two plus three is always five, and the square never has more than four sides. It seems impossible even to suspect such obvious truths of falsity.

Nevertheless, the old belief is imprinted on my mind that there is a God who can do anything and by whom I have been made to be as I am. How do I know that He hasn't brought it about that, while there is in fact no earth, no sky, no extended thing, no shape, no magnitude, and no place, all of these things seem to me to exist, just as they now do? Besides, I think that other people sometimes err in what they believe themselves to know perfectly well; mightn't I be deceived when I add two and three, or count the sides of a square, or do even simpler things (if we can even suppose that there is anything simpler)? Maybe God does not want to deceive me; after all, He is said to be supremely good. But, if God's being good is incompatible with His having created me so that I am always deceived, it seems just as out of line with his being good that he sometimes permits me to be deceived—as he undeniably does.

Or maybe some would rather deny that there is an omnipotent God than to believe that everything else is uncertain. Rather than arguing with these people, I will grant that everything I have said about God is fiction. But, however these people think I came to be as I now am (whether they say it is by fate, or by accident, or by a continuous series of events, or in some other way) since it seems that he who errs and is deceived is somehow imperfect, the likelihood that I am constantly deceived increases as the power that they attribute to my original creator decreases. To these arguments, I have no reply; I am forced to admit that nothing that I used to believe is beyond legitimate doubt—not because I have been careless or playful, but because I have valid and well-considered grounds for doubt. I must therefore withhold my assent from my former beliefs as carefully as from obvious falsehoods, if I want to arrive at something certain.

But it is not enough to have noticed this: I must also take care to bear it in mind. For my habitual beliefs constantly return to my mind as if our long-standing, intimate relationship has given them the right to do so, even against my will. I will never break the habit of trusting them and of giving in to them while I see them for what they are—things somewhat dubious (as I have just shown) but nonetheless probable, things that we have much more reason to believe than to deny. That is why I think it will be good deliberately to turn my beliefs around, to allow myself to be deceived, and to suppose that all my previous beliefs are false and imaginary. Eventually, when I have counterbalanced the weight of my prejudices, my bad habits will no longer distort my grasp of things. And I know that there is no danger of error in this and that I won't overindulge in skepticism, since I am now concerned, not with acting, but only with knowing.

I will suppose, then, not that there is a supremely good God who is the source of all truth, but that there is an evil demon, supremely powerful and cunning, who works as hard as he can to deceive me. I will say that sky, air, earth, color, shape, sound, and other external things are just dreamed illusions which the demon uses to ensnare my judgment. I will regard myself as not having hands, eyes, flesh, blood, and senses—but as having the false belief that I have all these things. I will obstinately concentrate on this meditation and will thus ensure by mental resolution that, if I do not really have the ability to know the truth, I will at least withhold assent from what is false and from what a deceiver may try to put over on me, however powerful and cunning he may be. But this plan requires effort, and laziness brings me back to my ordinary life. I am like a prisoner who happens to enjoy the illusion of freedom in his dreams, begins to suspect that he is asleep, fears being awakened, and deliberately lets the enticing illusions slip by unchallenged. Thus, I slide back into my old beliefs; I am afraid that, if I awaken, I will need to spend the waking life which follows my peaceful rest, not in the light, but in the confusing darkness of the problems I have just raised.

Meditation II
On the Nature of the Human Mind, Which Is Better Known Than the Body

Yesterday's meditation has hurled me into doubts so great that I can neither ignore them nor think my way out of them. I am in turmoil, as if I have accidentally fallen into a whirlpool and can neither touch bottom nor swim to the safety of the surface. But I will struggle and try to follow the path that I started on yesterday. That is, I will reject whatever is open to the slightest doubt just as though I have found it to be entirely false, and I will continue until I find something certain—even if it is just that nothing is certain. As Archimedes requried only one fixed and immovable point to move the whole earth from its place, I can hope for great things if I can even find one small thing that is certain and unshakable.

I suppose, then, that everything I see is unreal. I believe that none of what my unreliable memory presents to me ever happened. I have no senses. Body, shape, extension, motion, and place are fantasies. What then is true? Perhaps only that nothing is certain.

But how do I know that, in addition to the things I just listed, there isn't something that I do not have the slightest reason to doubt? Isn't there a God, or something like one, who puts my thoughts into me? But why should I say so when I may be the author of those thoughts? Well, isn't it at least the case that I am something? But I now am denying that I have senses and a body. But I stop here. For what follows from these denials? Am I so bound to my body and to my senses that I cannot exist without them? I have convinced myself that there is nothing in the world—no sky, no earth, no minds, no bodies. Doesn't it follow that I don't exist? No; surely I must exist if it's me who is convinced of something. But there is a deceiver, supremely powerful and cunning, whose aim is to see that I am always deceived. Then surely I exist, since I am deceived. Let him deceive me all he can, he will never make it the case that I am nothing while I think that I am something. Thus having fully weighed every consideration, I must finally conclude that the statement "I am, I exist" must be true whenever I state or mentallly consider it.

But I do not yet fully understand what this "I" is that must now exist. I must guard against inadvertently taking myself to be something other than I am, thereby going wrong even in the knowledge that I contend is supremely certain and evident. Accordingly, I will think once again about what I believed myself to be before beginning these meditations. From my previous conception of myself, I will subtract everything that can be challenged by the reasons for doubt that I have produced, until nothing remains except what is certain and indubitable.

What, then, did I formerly take myself to be? A man, of course. But what is a man? Should I say a rational animal? No, because then I would need to ask what an animal is and what it is to be rational. Thus, starting from a single question, I would sink into many which are more difficult, and I do not have the time to waste on such subtleties. I would rather pay attention here to the thoughts that occurred to me spontaneously and naturally when I asked what I was. First, it occurred to me that I have a face, hands, arms, and all the other equipment (also found in corpses) which I call a body. Next, it occurred to me that I take nourishment, move myself around, sense, and think—that I do things which I trace back to my soul. I didn't often stop to think about what this soul was, and, when I did, I imagined it to be a rarified air, or fire, or ether permeating the denser parts of my body. On the other hand, I did not have any doubts about physical objects: I thought that I distinctly knew their nature. If I had tried to describe my conception of these objects, I might have said this: "When I call something a physical object, I mean that it is capable of being bounded by a shape and limited to a place; that it can so fill a space as to exclude others from it; that it can be perceived by sight, touch, hearing, taste, and smell; that it cannot move itself but can be moved by something else that touches it." I judged that the powers of self-movement, of sensing, and of thinking did not belong to the nature of physical objects, and, in fact, I marveled that there were some physical objects in which these powers could be found.

But what should I think now, while supposing that a supremely powerful and "evil" deceiver completely devotes himself to seeing to it that I am decieved? Can I say that I have any of the things that I attributed to the nature of physical objects? I concentrate, think, reconsider—but nothing comes to me; I am tired of this pointless repetition. But what about the things that I have assigned to soul? Nutrition and self-movement? Since I have no body, these are merely illusions. Sensing? But I cannot sense without a body, and in sleep I have seemed to sense many things that I did not really sense. Thinking? It comes down to this: There is thinking, and thought alone cannot be taken away from me. I am, I exist. That much is certain. For how long? For as long as I think—for it may be that, if I completely stopped thinking, I would also cease to be. I am not now admitting anything unless it must be true, and I am therefore not admitting that I am anything at all other than a thinking thing—that is, a mind, soul, understanding, or reason (terms whose meaning I did not previously know). I know that I am a real, existing thing, but what kind of thing? As I have said, a thing that thinks.

What else? I will draw up mental images. I can't say that I am the collection of organs that we call a human body, or that I am some rarified gas permeating these organs, or that I am air, or fire, or vapor, or breath—for I have supposed that none of these things exist. But I can still say that I am something. It may be, of course, that these things, which I do not yet know and which I am therefore supposing to be nonexistent, are not really distinct from the "I" that I know to exist. I don't know, and I am not going to argue about it now. I can only pass judgment on what I do know. I know that I exist, and I ask what the "I" is that I know to exist. It is obvious that the conception of myself that I derive in *this* way does not depend on anything that I do not yet know to exist and, consequently, that it does not depend on anything of which I can shape a mental image. And the word "shape" points to my mistake. I would truly be creating things if I were to have a mental image of what I am, since to have a mental image is just to contemplate the shape or image of a physical object. I now know with certainty that I exist and at the same time that all images—and, more generally, all things associated with the nature of physical objects—may just be dreams. When I keep this in mind, it seems just as absurd to say "I use mental images to help me understand what I am" as it would be to say "Now, while awake, I see something true—but, since I don't yet see it clearly enough, I'll go to sleep and let my dreams present it to me more clearly and truly." Thus I know that none of the things that I can comprehend with the aid of the mental images bear on my knowledge of myself. I must carefully draw my mind away from such things so that it can gain a distinct knowledge of its own nature.

But what then am I? A thinking thing. And what is that? Something that doubts, understands, affirms, denies, wills, refuses—and also imagines and senses.

It is no small matter if I do all of these things. But how could it be otherwise? Isn't it me who now doubts nearly everything, understands something, affirms this one thing, refuses to affirm other things, wants to know much more, refuses to be deceived, has mental images (sometimes involuntarily), and is aware of what seems to come from his senses? Even if I am always dreaming, and even if my creator does what he can to deceive me, isn't it just as true that I do all these things as that I exist? Are any of these things distinct from my thought? Can any be said to be separate from me? It's so obvious that it is me who doubts, understands, and wills that I don't see how I could make it more evident. And it is also me who has mental images—for while it may be (as I am supposing) that absolutely nothing of which I have a mental image really exists, the ability to have mental images really does exist and influences my thought. Finally, it is me who senses—or who seems to gain awareness of physical objects through the senses. For example, I now see the light, hear the noise, and feel the heat. These things are unreal, since I am dreaming. But it is still certain that I *seem* to see, to hear, and to feel. This seeming cannot be unreal, but *it* is what is properly called sensing; strictly speaking, sensing is just thinking.

From these considerations, I begin to learn a little about what I am. But I still can't stop thinking that I know physical objects (which I picture in mental images and examine with my senses) much more distinctly than I know this unknown "I" (of which I cannot form a mental image). I think this, even though it would be astounding if it turns out that I comprehend things which I have found to be doubtful, unknown, and alien to me more distinctly than that which I know to be real—namely, my self. But I see what is happening: My mind enjoys wandering, and it won't confine itself to the truth. I will therefore loosen the reigns for now so that later, when the time is right, I will be able to control my mind more easily.

Let's consider the things commonly taken to be the most distinctly comprehended: physical objects that we see and touch. Let's not consider the general idea of a physical object, since such general conceptions are very often confused. Rather, let's consider a particular. Take, for example, this piece of wax. It has just been taken from the honeycomb; it hasn't yet completely lost the taste of honey; it still smells of the flowers from which it was gathered; its color, shape, and size are obvious; it is hard, cold, and easy to touch; it makes a sound when rapped. In short, everything required for me to have distinct knowledge of a physical object seems to be present. But, as I speak, I move the wax towards the fire; it loses what was left of its taste; it gives up its smell; it changes color; it loses its shape; it gets bigger; it melts; it heats up; it becomes difficult to touch; it no longer makes a sound when struck. Is it still the same piece of wax? We must say that it is: no one denies it or thinks otherwise. Then what was there in the wax that was so distinctly comprehended? Certainly nothing that I reached with the senses—for, while everything having to do with taste, smell, sight, touch, and hearing has changed, the same piece of wax remains.

Perhaps what I distinctly knew was neither the sweetness of honey, nor the fragrance of flowers, nor a sound, but a physical object that sometimes appeared to me one way and sometimes another. But what exactly is it that I am now imagining? Let's pay careful attention; removing everything that doesn't belong to the wax, let's see what is left. Nothing is left except an extended, flexible, and changeable thing. But what is it for this thing to be flexible and changeable? Is it just that the wax can go from round to square and then to triangular, as I have mentally pictured? Of course not; since I understand that the wax's shape can change in innumerable ways, and since I can't run through all the changes in my imagination, my comprehension of the wax's flexibility and changeability cannot be the product of my ability to have mental images. And what about the thing that is extended? Are we also ignorant of its extension? Since the extension of the wax increases when the wax melts, increases again when the wax boils, and increases still more when the wax gets hotter, I will be mistaken about what the wax is unless I believe that it can undergo more changes in extension than I can ever encompass with mental images. I must therefore admit that I do not have an image of what the wax is—that I grasp what it is with only my mind. (While I am saying this about a particular piece of wax, it is even more clearly true about wax in general.) What then is this piece of wax that I grasp with my mind? It is exactly what I believed it to be at the outset—something that I see, feel, and imagine. It must be noted, however, that my grasp of the wax is not visual, tactile, or pictorial; despite the appearances, I have never had a sensory grasp of what the wax is. Rather, my grasp of the wax is the result of a purely mental inspection, which is imperfect and confused (as it was once) or clear and distinct (as it is now) depending on how much attention I pay to the things of which the wax consists.

But it is surprisingly easy for my mind to be misled. Even when I think to myself nonverbally, language impedes me, and common usage comes close to deceiving me. For, when the wax is present, we say that we see the wax itself, not that we infer its presence from its color and shape. I would leap from this fact about language to the conclusion that I learn about the wax by eyesight rather than by purely mental inspection—except that, if I happen to look out my window and see men walking in the street, it is no less natural to say that I see the men than it is to say that I see the wax. But what do I really see, except hats and coats that could be covering robots? Yet, I judge that there are men in the street. Thus I comprehend with my judgment, which is in my mind, objects that I once believed myself to see with my eyes.

One who aspires to wisdom above that of the common man disgraces himself by deriving doubt from common ways of speaking. Let's go on, then, to ask *when* I most clearly and perfectly grasped what the wax is. Was it when I first looked at the wax and believed my knowledge of it to come from the external senses (or, at any rate from the imagination, the "common sense")? Or is it now, after I have carefully studied what the wax is and how I come to know it? Doubt would be silly here. For what was distinct in my original conception of the wax? How did that conception differ from the one shared by all animals? Of course, when I distinguish the wax from its external forms—when I "undress" it and view it "denuded"—there may still be errors in my judgments about it, but I can't possibly grasp the wax in this way without a human mind.

What should I say about this mind—or, in other words, about myself? (I am not now admitting that there is anything to me but a mind.) What is this "I" that seems to grasp the wax so distinctly? Don't I know myself much more truly and certainly, and also much more distinctly and plainly, than I know the wax? If I base my judgment that the wax exists on the fact that I see it, my seeing it much more obviously implies that I exist. It is possible that what I see is not really wax, and it is also possible that I don't even have eyes with which to see—but it clearly is *not* possible that, when I see (or, what now amounts to the same thing, when I think I see), the "I" which thinks is not a real thing. Similarly, while I might base my judgment that the wax exists on the fact that I feel it, the same fact makes it obvious that I exist. If I base my judgment that the wax exists on the fact that I have a mental image of it or on some other fact of this sort, the same thing can obviously be said. And what I have said about the wax applies to everything else that is outside me. Moreover, if I seem to grasp the wax more distinctly when I detect it with several senses than when I detect it just with sight or touch, I must know myself even more distinctly—for every consideration that contributes to my grasp of the piece of wax or to my grasp of any other physical object serves better to reveal the nature of my mind. Besides, the mind has so much in it by which it can make its conception of itself distinct that what comes to it from physical objects hardly seems to matter.

And now I have brought myself back to where I wanted to be. I now know that physical objects are not really known through sensation or imagination, but are grasped by the understanding alone. And, from the fact that physical objects are grasped in virtue of their being understandable (rather than tangible or visible), I infer that I can't know anything more easily or plainly than my mind. Since it takes time to break old habits of thought, however, I should pause here to allow the length of contemplation to impress the new thoughts more deeply into my memory.

Meditation III
On God's Existence

I will now close my eyes, plug my ears, and withdraw all my senses. I will even rid my thoughts of the images of physical objects—or, if that is too hard, I will write those images off as empty illusions. Relying on nothing but myself, I will look more deeply into myself and try gradually to come to know myself better. I am a thinking thing—a thing that doubts, affirms, denies, understands a few things, is ignorant of many things, wills, and refuses. I also imagine and sense—for (as I have noted) I am certain that, even if I do not imagine or sense anything outside me, the modifications of thought that I call sensations and mental images exist in me insofar as they are just modifications of thought.

That is a brief summary of all that I really know—or, at any rate, of all that I have so far noticed that I know. I now will examine more carefully whether there are other things in me which I have not yet discovered. I am certain that I am a thinking thing. Then don't I know what is needed for me to be certain of other things? In this first knowledge, there is nothing but a clear and distinct grasp of what I affirm, and this grasp surely would not suffice to make me certain if it could ever happen that something I grasped so clearly and distinctly was false. Accordingly, I seem to be able to establish the general rule that whatever I clearly and distinctly grasp is true.

But, in the past, I have accepted as completely obvious and certain many thoughts which I later found to be dubious. What were these thoughts about? The earth, the sky, the stars, and other objects of sense. But what did I clearly grasp about these objects? Only that ideas or thoughts of them appeared in my mind. Even now, I do not deny that these ideas occur in me. But there was something else that I used to affirm—something that I used to believe myself to grasp clearly but did not really grasp at all: I affirmed that there were things besides me, that the ideas in me came from these things, and that the ideas perfectly resembled these things. If I didn't err here, I at least reached a true judgment that wasn't justified by the strength of my understanding.

But what follows from this? When I considered very simple and easy points of arithmetic or geometry—such as that two and three together make five—didn't I see them clearly enough to affirm their truth? My only reason for thinking that I ought to doubt these things was the thought that my God-given nature might deceive me, even about what seems most obvious. But, whenever I conceive of this all-powerful God, I am compelled to admit that, if He wants, he can make it the case that I err even about what I take my mind's eye to see most clearly. On the other hand, when I turn to the things that I believe myself to grasp very clearly, I am so convinced by them that I spontaneously burst forth saying, "Whoever may deceive me, he will never bring it about that I am nothing while I think that I am something, or that I have never been when it is now true that I am, or that two plus three is either more or less than five, or that something else in which I recognize an obvious inconsistency is true." Of course, since I have no reason for thinking that God *is* a deceiver—indeed, since I don't yet know whether God *is*—the grounds for doubt that rest on the supposition that God deceives are very weak and "metaphysical." Still, to rid myself of them, I ought to ask as soon as possible whether there is a God and, if so, whether He can be a deceiver. For it seems that, until I know these two things, I can never be completely certain of anything else.

The structure of my project seems to require, however, that I first categorize my thoughts and ask in which of them truth and falsity really reside. Some of my thoughts are like images of things, and only these can properly be called ideas; I have an idea, for example, when I think of a man, of a chimera, of heaven, of an angel, or of God. But other thoughts have other properties: while I always apprehend something as the object of my thought when I will, fear, affirm, or deny, my thought also includes a component in addition to the likeness of that thing. Some of these components are called volitions or emotions; others, judgments.

Now, viewed in themselves and without regard to other things, ideas cannot really be false: if I imagine a chimera and a goat, it is just as true that I imagine the chimera as that I imagine the goat. And I needn't worry about falsehood in volitions or emotions: if I perversely want something that does not exist, it is still true that I want that thing. All that remains, then, are my judgments; it is here that I must be careful not to err. And the first and foremost of the errors that I find in my judgments is that of assuming that the ideas in me have a similarity of conformity to things outside of me. For, if I were to regard ideas merely as modifications of thought, they could hardly lead me wrong.

Of my ideas, some seem to me to be innate, others acquired, and others produced by me. The ideas by which I understand what reality, truth, and thought are seem to have come from my own nature; those by which I hear a noise, see the sun, or feel the fire are ones I formerly judged to come from things outside me; and those of sirens, hippogriffs, and so on are ones that I have formed in myself. Or maybe I can take all of my ideas to be acquired, all innate, or all created by me: I do no yet clearly see where my ideas come from.

For the moment, the central question is about the ideas that I view as derived from objects existing outside me. What reason is there for thinking that these ideas resemble the objects? I seem to have been taught this by nature. Moreover, I find that these ideas are independent of my will (and hence of me) for they often appear when I do not want them to do so. For example, I now feel heat whether I want to or not, and I therefore take the idea or sensation of heat to come from something distinct from me—namely, from the heat of the fire by which I am now sitting. And the obvious thing to think is that what a thing sends to me is its own likeness.

Now, I see whether these reasons are good ones. When I say that nature teaches me something, I mean just that I have a spontaneous impulse to believe it—not that the light of nature reveals the thing's truth to me. There is an important difference. When the light of nature reveals something to me (such as that my thinking implies my existing) that thing is completely beyond doubt, since there is nothing as reliable as the light of nature by means of which I could learn that the thing is not true. As for my natural impulses, however, I have often judged them to have led me astray in practical choices, and I don't see why I should trust them any more on other matters.

Next, while my sensory ideas may not depend on my will, it doesn't follow that they come from outside me. The natural impulses of which I just spoke are in me, but *they* seem to *conflict* with my will. I may therefore have in me an as yet undiscovered ability to produce in myself the ideas that seem to come from outside me. In fact, it has always seemed to me that, while dreaming, I *have* formed such ideas in myself without the aid of external objects.

Finally, even if some of my ideas do come from things distinct from me, it doesn't follow that they are likenesses of things. Indeed, it often seems to me that an idea differs greatly from its cause. For example, I find in myself two different ideas of the sun. One, which I "take in" through the senses and which I ought therefore to view as a typical acquired idea, makes the sun look very small to me. The other, which I derive from astronomical reasoning (that is, which I make, perhaps by composing it from innate ideas), shows the sun to be many times larger than the earth. It is not possible that both of these ideas are accurate likenesses of the sun that exists outside me, and reason convinces me that the one least like the sun is the one that seems to arise most directly from it.

All that I have said shows that, until now, my belief that there are things outside me which implant their ideas or images in me (perhaps through my senses) has rested on blind impulse rather than on certain judgment.

But there may still be a way of telling whether the things which are the sources of my ideas exist outside me. When I regard the ideas of things as mere modifications of thought, I find no inequality among them; all seem to arise from me in the same way. But, inasmuch as different ideas present different things to me, there obviously are great differences among them. The ideas that show me substances are unquestionably greater—or have more "presentational reality"—than those that merely show me modifications or accidents. Similarly, the idea by which I understand the supreme God—eternal, infinite, omniscient, omnipotent, and creator of all things other than Him self—has more presentational reality in it than the ideas which present finite substances.

But the light of nature has revealed that there is at least as much in the complete efficient cause as in its effect. For where could an effect get its reality if not from its cause? And how could a cause give what it did not itself have? It follows both that something cannot come from nothing and that what is more perfect—or, in other words, has more reality in it—cannot come from what is less perfect and has less reality. This obviously holds, not just for those effects whose reality is actual or formal, but also for ideas, whose reality we regard as merely presentational. For example, it's impossible for a nonexistent stone to come into existence unless it is produced by something containing, either formally or eminently, everything in the stone. Similarly, heat can only be induced in something that is not already hot by something having at least the same degree of perfection as heat. Moreover, it is impossible for the idea of heat or of a stone to be in me unless it has been put there by a cause in which there is at least as much reality as in heat or the stone. For, although an idea's cause does not transmit any of its actual or formal reality to the idea, and although an idea does not by its nature require any formal reality other than what it borrows from my thought (of which it is a modification), we should not think that the idea's cause can be less real than the idea. Rather, we should think that each idea contains one particular presentational reality which it must get from a cause having at least as much formal reality as the idea has presentational reality. For, if we suppose that something is in an idea but not in its cause, we must suppose that something has come from nothing. And, however imperfect the existence of a thing that exists presentationally in the understanding through an idea, that thing obviously is *something,* and it therefore cannot come from nothing.

And, although the reality that I am considering in my ideas is just presentational, I ought not to suspect that it need not be in the ideas' cause formally—that it suffices for it to be there presentationally. For, just as the presentational existence of my ideas belongs to the ideas in virtue of their nature, the formal existence of the ideas' causes belongs to those causes—or, at least, to the first and foremost of them—in virtue of their nature. Although one idea may arise from another, this can't go back to infinity; it must eventually arrive at a primary idea whose cause is an "archetype" containing formally all that the idea contains presentationally. Hence, the light of nature makes it clear to me that the ideas in me are like images which may well fall short of the things from which they derive, but which cannot contain anything greater or more perfect.

The more time and care I take in studying all of this, the more clearly and distinctly I know that it is true. But what follows from it? On the one hand, if the presentational reality of one of my ideas is so great that I can be confident that the same degree of reality is not in me either formally or eminently, I can conclude that I cannot be the cause of that idea, that another thing must necessarily exist as its cause, and consequently that I am not alone in the world. On the other hand, if I can find no such idea in me, I will have no argument at all for the existence of something other than me—for, having diligently searched for another such argument, I have yet to find one.

Besides the idea that shows me to myself (about which there can be no problem here), my ideas include one which presents God, others which present physical objects, others which present angels, others which present animals, and finally others which present men like me.

As to my ideas of other men, of animals, and of angels, it is easy to see that—even if the world contained no men but me, no animals, and no angels—I could have composed these ideas from those that I have of myself, of physical objects, and of God.

And, as to my ideas of physical objects, it seems that nothing in them is so great that it couldn't have come from me. For, if I analyze my ideas of physical objects carefully, taking them one by one as I did yesterday when examining my idea of the piece of wax, I notice that there is very little in them that I grasp clearly and distinctly except magnitude (which is extension in length, breadth, and depth), shape (which arises from extension's limits), position (which the differently shaped things have relative to one another), and motion (which is just change of this relative position). To these I can add substance, duration, and number, but my thoughts of other things in physical objects (such as light and color, sound, odor, taste, heat and cold, and tactile qualities) are so confused and obscure that I can't say whether they are true or false—whether my ideas of these things are of something or of nothing. For, although—as I noted earlier—that which is properly called falsehood (namely, *formal* falsehood) can only be found in judgments, we can still find falsehood of another sort (namely, *material* falsehood) in an idea when it presents what is not a thing as though it were a thing. For example, the ideas that I have of coldness and heat are so unclear and indistinct that I can't tell from them whether coldness is just the absence of heat, or heat just the absence of coldness, or both are real qualities, or neither is. And, since every idea is "of something," the idea that presents coldness to me as something real and positive could justifiably be called false if coldness were just the absence of heat. And the same holds for other similar ideas.

For ideas of this sort, I need not posit a creator other than me. I know by the light of nature that, if one of these ideas is false (that is, if it doesn't present a real thing), it comes from nothing—that is, that the only cause of its being in me is a deficiency of my (obviously imperfect) nature. And, if one of these ideas is true, I still see no reason why I couldn't have produced it—for these ideas present so little reality to me that I can't even distinguish the reality in them from the reality of that which doesn't exist.

Of the things that *are* clear and distinct in my ideas of physical objects, it seems that I may have borrowed some—such as substance, duration, and number—from my idea of myself. Of course, my conception of myself differs from my conception of a stone in that I think of myself as a thinking and unextended thing while I think of the stone as an extended and unthinking thing. But, when I conceive the stone as a substance (that is, as something that can exist by itself), my understanding of substance seems to be the same as when I conceive of myself as a substance. Similarly, when I grasp that I now exist and remember that I have existed in the past, and when I have various thoughts and notice how many of them there are, I get the ideas of duration and number, which I can then apply to other objects of thought. The other components of my ideas of physical objects—namely, extension, shape, place, and motion—can't be in me formally since I am just a thinking thing, but, as they are just modes of substance, and as I am a substance, they can be in me eminently.

All that is left is to consider whether there may be something in my idea of God that couldn't have come from me. By "God" I mean infinite substance, independent, supremely intelligent, and supremely powerful—the thing from which I and everything else that may exist get our existence. The more I consider these attributes, the less it seems that they could have come from me alone. And I must therefore conclude that God necessarily exists.

While I may have the idea of substance in me in virtue of my being a substance, I who am finite would not have the idea of infinite substance in me unless it came from a substance that really was infinite.

And I ought not to say that, rather than having a true idea of infinity, I grasp it merely as the absence of limits—in the way that I grasp rest as the absence of motion and darkness as the absence of light. On the contrary, it's clear to me that there is more reality in an infinite than in a finite substance and, hence, that my grasp of the infinite must somehow be prior to my grasp of the finite—my understanding of God prior to my understanding of myself. For, how could I understand that I doubt and desire, that I am deficient and imperfect, if I don't have the idea of something more perfect to use as a standard of comparison?

And, unlike the ideas of hot and cold which I just discussed, the idea of God cannot be said to be materially false and, hence, to come from nothing. On the contrary, since the idea of God is completely clear and distinct and contains more presentational reality than any other idea, no idea is truer per se and none less open to the suspicion of falsity. The idea of a supremely perfect and infinite entity, I maintain, is completely true. For, while I may be able to suppose that there is no such entity, I cannot even suppose that my idea of God (like the idea of coldness) fails to show me anything real. Yes, this idea is maximally clear and distinct; it contains everything that I grasp clearly and distinctly, everything real and true, everything with any perfection. And it is no ojection that I can't fully comprehend the infinite or that there are innumerable things in God which

I can't comprehend fully or even reach with thought. It suffices for me to understand that, being finite, I cannot fully comprehend the infinite and to judge that, if I grasp something clearly and distinctly and know it to have some perfection, it is either formally or eminently present in God (perhaps along with innumerable other things of which I am ignorant). If I do this, my idea of God will be supremely true, and supremely clear and distinct.

But maybe I am greater than I have assumed; maybe all the perfections that I attribute to God are in me potentially, still unreal and unactualized. I have already seen my knowledge gradually increase, and I don't see anything to prevent its becoming greater and greater to infinity. Nor do I see why, by means of such increased knowledge, I couldn't get all the rest of God's perfections. Finally, if the potential for these perfections is in me, I don't see why this potential couldn't by itself produce in me the ideas of these perfections.

None of this is possible. First, while it's true that my knowledge gradually increases and that I have many as yet unactualized potentialities, none of this fits with my idea of God, in whom absolutely nothing is potential; the gradual increase in my knowledge shows that I am *imperfect,* not that I am perfect. Moreover, even if my knowledge were continually to become greater and greater, it would never become actually infinite, since it will never become so great that it couldn't be greater. But I judge that God is actually infinite and that nothing can be added to his perfection. Finally, I see that an idea's presentational being must be produced, not by mere potentiality (which, strictly speaking, is nothing), but by what is actual or formal.

When I pay attention to these things, the light of nature makes all of them obvious. But, when I attend less carefully and the images of sensible things blind my mind's eye, it's hard for me to remember that the idea of an entity more perfect than I am must come from an entity that is more perfect. That's why I want to go on to ask whether I, who have the idea of a perfect entity, could exist if no such entity existed.

From what might I derive my existence if not my God? Either from myself, or from my parents, or from something else less perfect than God (for I can't suppose that anything other than God is His superior, or even His equal, in perfection).

But, if I were to get my existence from myself, I wouldn't doubt, or want, or lack anything; I would have given myself every perfection of which I have an idea and would therefore be God. And I shouldn't think that it might be harder to give myself what I lack than what I already have. On the contrary, it would obviously be much harder to make me (a thinking thing or substance) emerge from nothing than to give me complete knowledge (which is just an attribute of substance). But surely, if I had given myself that which is harder to get, I wouldn't have denied myself complete knowledge, which would have been easier to get. In fact, I wouldn't have denied myself *any* of the perfections that I grasp in the idea of God. None of these perfections seems harder to get than existence, but they would seem harder to get if I had really given myself everything I now have—for in creating myself I would have discovered the limits of my power.

And I can't avoid the force of this argument by supposing that, having always existed as I do now, I don't have any creator. Since my lifetime can be divided into innumerable, mutually independent parts, the fact that I existed a little while ago does not entail that I exist now, unless a cause "re-creates" me—or, in other words, preserves me—at this moment. Thus, when I keep the nature of time in mind, it becomes obvious that exactly the same power and action is required to preserve a thing at each of the moments at which it exists as would be required to create it anew if it had never existed. Accordingly, one of the things revealed by the light of nature is that preservation and creation differ only in the way we think of them.

I ought to ask myself, then, whether *I* have the power to ensure that I, who now am, will exist a little while from now. Since I am nothing but a thinking thing—or, at any rate, since I am not focusing on the part of me that thinks—I would surely be aware of this power if it were in me. But I find no such power. And this very clearly shows that there is an entity distinct from me on whom I depend.

Maybe this entity isn't God; maybe I am the product of my parents or of some other cause less perfect than God. But, as I just said, there must be at least as much in a cause as in its effect. Therefore, since I am a thinking thing with the idea of God in me, my cause—whatever it is—must be a thinking thing having in it the idea of every perfection that I attribute to God. And I can go on to ask whether this thing gets its existence from itself or from something else. But it's obvious from what I have just said that, if my cause gets its existence from itself, it must *be* God; having the pwoer to exist in itself, it must also have the power actually to give itself every perfection of which it has an idea—including every perfection that I conceive of in God. On the other hand, if my cause gets its existence from some other thing, I can go on to ask whether this other thing gets its existence from itself or from something else. Eventually, I will come to the ultimate cause: God.

It is clear that there can't be an infinite regress here—especially since I am concerned, not so much with the cause that originally produced me, as with the one that preserves me in the present.

But what about the view that several partial causes combined to make me, that I get the ideas of the various perfections I attribute to God from different causes, and that, while each of these perfections can be found somewhere in the universe, there is no God in whom they all come together? I can't suppose that this is true. On the contrary, one of the chief perfections that I understand God to have is unity—that is, simplicity, or inseparability from everything to Him. But, of all God's perfections, unity is the one whose idea could only have been put in me by a cause which gives me the ideas of all the other perfections: I can be made to regard God's perfections as inseparably joined only if I am made aware of what these perfections are.

Finally, it's clear that, even if everything that I used to believe about my parents is true, they do not preserve me. Insofar as I am a thinking thing, they did not even take part in creating me. They simply formed the matter in which I used to think that I resided. (By "I" I mean my mind, which is all that I now grasp of myself.) There can therefore be no problem about my parents, and I am driven to this conclusion: The fact that I exist and have an idea of God as a perfect entity conclusively entails that God does in fact exist.

All that's left is to explain how I have gotten my idea of God from Him. I have not taken it in through my senses; it has never come to me unexpectedly as the ideas of sensible things do when those things affect (or seem to affect) my external organs of sense. Nor have I made the idea myself; I can't subtract from it or add to it. The idea must therefore be innate in me, like my idea of myself.

And it's not at all surprising that in creating me God put this idea into me, impressing it like a craftsman's mark on His work. This mark needn't be distinct from the work itself. Indeed, the very fact that it was God who created me confirms that I have somehow been made in His image or likeness and that I grasp this likeness (which contains the idea of God) in the same way that I grasp myself. For, when I turn my mind's eye on myself, I understand, not only that I am an incomplete, dependent thing which constantly strives for bigger and better things, but also that He on whom I depend, having all these things in Himself as infinite reality rather than just as vague potentiality, must therefore be God. The whole argument comes down to this: I know that I could not exist with my present nature (that is, that I could not exist with the idea of God in me) unless there really were a God—the very God of whom I have an idea, the thing having all of the perfections that I can't fully comprehend but can somehow reach with thought, the thing that clearly cannot be defective. From this, it is obvious that He can't deceive, for the natural light reveals that fraud and deception arise from defect.

But before examining this more carefully and investigating its consequences, I want to dwell for a moment in the contemplation of God, to ponder His attributes in me, to see, admire, and adore the beauty of His boundless light, insofar as my clouded insight allows. Believing that the supreme happiness of the other life consists wholly of the contemplation of divine greatness, I now find that through less perfect contemplation of the same sort I can gain the greatest joy available in this life.

Meditation IV On Truth and Falsity

In the last few days, I have gotten used to drawing my mind away from my senses. Having carefully noted that I really grasp very little about physical objects, that I know much more about the human mind, and that I know even more about God, I no longer find it hard to turn my thoughts away from things of which I can have mental images and towards things which I can only understand—things completely separate from matter. I have a much more distinct idea of the human mind than of physical objects, insofar as the mind is just a thinking thing which isn't extended in length, breadth, or depth and which doesn't have anything in common with physical objects. Moreover, when I observe that I doubt or that I am incomplete and dependent, I have a clear and distinct idea of God, a complete and independent entity. And, from the fact that this idea is in me and that I who have the idea exist, I can infer both that God exists and that I am completely dependent on Him for my existence from moment to moment. This inference is so obvious that I'm sure humans can't know anything more evidently or certainly. And now I think I see a way of moving from the contemplation of the true God, in whom are hidden all treasures of knowledge and wisdom, to knowledge of *other* things.

First, I know that it is impossible for Him ever to deceive me. Fraud and deception always contain imperfection, and, while the ability to deceive may seem a sign of cunning and power, the desire to deceive reveals malice or weakness and therefore can't be among God's desires.

Next, I find in myself an ability to judge which, like everything else in me, I have gotten from God. Since He doesn't want to decieve me, He certainly hasn't given me an ability which will lead me wrong when properly used.

There could be no doubt about this—except that it may seem to imply that I *never* err. For, if I have gotten everything in me from God and He hasn't given me the ability to err, it doesn't seem possible for me *ever* to err. Thus, as long as I think only of God and devote all my attention to Him, I can't find any cause for error and falsity. When I turn my attention back to myself, however, I find that I can make innumerable errors. In looking for the cause of these errors, I find before me, not just the real and positive idea of God, but also the negative idea of "nothingness"—the idea of that which is completely devoid of perfection. I find that I am "intermediary" between God and nothingness, between the supreme entity and the nonentity. Insofar as I am the creation of the supreme entity, there is nothing in me that accounts for my being deceived or led into error, but, insofar as I somehow participate in nothingness or the nonentity—that is, insofar as I am not identical to the supreme entity and lack a great many things—it is not surprising that I am deceived. Thus I understand that, in itself, error is a *lack* rather than a real thing dependent on God. And I therefore understand that I can err without God's having given me a special ability to do so: I fall into error because my God-given ability to judge the truth isn't infinite.

But there is still something to be explained. Error is not just an absence, but a deprivation—the lack of knowledge that somehow *ought* to be in me. But, when I attend to God's nature, it seems impossible that He has given me an ability that is an imperfect thing of its kind—an ability lacking a perfection that it ought to have. The greater the craftsman's skill, the more perfect his product. Then how can the supreme creator of all things have made something that isn't absolutely perfect? There is no doubt that God could have made me so that I never err, and there is no doubt that He always wants what is best. Then is it better for me to be deceived than not to be deceived?

When I pay more careful attention, I realize that I should not be surprised at God's doing things that I can't explain and that I should not doubt His existence just because I find that I sometimes can't understand why or how He has made something. For, since I know that my nature is weak and limited while God's is limitless, incomprehensible, and infinite, I also know that He can do innumerable things of whose causes I am ignorant. And, on this ground alone, I regard the common practice of explaining things in terms of their purposes to be useless in physics: I would be foolhardy if I tried to understand God's purposes.

It also seems to me that, rather than looking at a single creation in isolation when asking whether God's works are perfect, I ought to look at all of them together. For a thing that seems imperfect when viewed alone may seem completely perfect when regarded as a part of the world. Of course, since calling everything into doubt, I haven't established that anything exists besides me and God. But, when I consider God's immense power, I can't deny that He has made (or, in any case, that He can make) many other things, and I must therefore regard myself as part of a universe.

Finally, turning to myself and investigating the nature of my errors (which are all that show me to be imperfect), I notice that these errors depend on two concurrent causes: my ability to know and my ability to choose freely—that is, my understanding and my will.

Viewed in itself, the understanding is just the thing by which I grasp the ideas about which I form judgments, and I therefore cannot say that there are errors in the understanding itself. While there may be innumerable things of which I have no idea, I can't say that I am deprived of these ideas, but only that I happen to lack them—for I don't have any reason to think that God ought to have given me a greater ability to know than He has: Although God is a supremely skillful craftsman, I don't think that He ought to endow each of his works with all the perfections that He can put in the others.

On the other hand, I can't complain about the scope or perfection of my God-given freedom of will—for my will doesn't seem to me to be restricted in any way. In fact, it seems well worth noting that nothing in me other than my will is so great and perfect that I couldn't conceivably be bigger or better. When I think about my ability to understand, for example, I immediately realize that it is very small and restricted, and I simultaneously form the idea of something much greater—something supremely perfect and infinite. From the fact that I can form the idea of this perfection, I infer that the perfection is present in God's nature. Similarly, when I consider my other abilities (such as the abilities to remember and to imagine) I clearly see that they all are feeble and limited in me but boundless in God. The only exception is my will or freedom of choice, which cannot conceivably be greater than it is. In fact, it is largely for this reason that I regard myself as an image or likeness of God. God's will is incomparably greater than mine, of course, both in virture of the knowledge and power associated with it (which result in its greater strength and efficacy) and in virtue of the greater range of its objects. Yet, viewed in itself as a will, God's will seems no greater than mine—because having a will just amounts to being able either to do or not to do, to affirm or deny, to seek or avoid. Or better: having a will amounts to being inclined to do or not to do (affirm or deny, seek or shun) what the understanding offers, without an awareness of being forced towards it by external forces. For being free does not require being inclined towards both alternatives. On the contrary, the more I lean towards one alternative—either because I understand the truth or goodness in it or because God has so arranged my deepest thoughts—the more freely I choose it. Thus divine grace and knowledge of nature clearly increase and strengthen rather than diminish my freedom. The indifference that I experience when no consideration impels me towards one alternative rather than the other is freedom of the lowest sort, which reveals a defect or an absence of knowledge rather than a perfection. For, if I always knew what was good or true, I wouldn't ever deliberate about what to do or choose, and consequently, though completely free, I would never be indifferent.

From this I see that my God-given ability to will is not itself the cause of my errors; my will is great, and it is a perfect thing of its kind. Neither is my power of understanding the cause of my errors; whenever I understand something, I understand it correctly and without the possiblity of deception, since my understanding comes from God. Then what *is* the source of my errors? Just that, while my will has a broader scope than my understanding, I don't keep it within the same bounds, but extend it to what I don't understand. Being indifferent to these things, I am easily led away from truth and goodness into error and sin.

For example, when I asked a while ago whether anything exists in the world, I noted that, from the fact that I ask this, it follows that I exist. Since I very clearly understood this, I couldn't fail to believe it to be true. It was not that a force outside me compelled me to believe, but that an intense light in my understanding produced a strong inclination of my will. And, because I wasn't indifferent, my belief was spontaneous and free. However, while I now know that I exist insofar as I am a thinking thing, I still wonder whether the thinking nature that is in me—or, rather, that *is* me—differs from bodily nature, whose idea I find in myself. Here I am completely indifferent to affirming either view, to denying either view, and even to suspending judgment.

And, indifference of this sort is not limited to things of which the understanding is completely ignorant. It extends to everything about which the will deliberates in the absense of a sufficiently clear understanding. For, however strong the force with which plausible conjectures draw me towards one alternative, the knowledge that they *are* conjectures rather than assertions backed by certain and indubitable arguments is enough to impel me the other way. And the past few days have provided me with ample experience of this—for I am now supposing each of my former beliefs to be false just because I have found a way to call them into doubt.

If I suspend judgment when I don't clearly and distinctly grasp what's true, I obviously do right and am not deceived. But, if I either affirm or deny in a case of this sort, I misuse my freedom of choice: I err if I affirm what is false, and I am also blameworthy if I stumble onto the truth, since the light of nature reveals that the understanding should always grasp a thing before the will decides what to do with it. In these misuses of freedom of choice lies the deprivation which accounts for error. And this deprivation, I maintain, lies in what I do insofar as it comes from *me*—not in the abilities that God has given me, or even in the uses of those abilities insofar as those uses derive from Him.

I have no reason to complain that God hasn't given me a more perfect understanding or a greater natural light than He has: Necessarily, an understanding is finite only if there are many things that it doesn't understand, and, necessarily, every created understanding is finite. In fact, rather than taking myself to be deprived or robbed of what God hasn't given me, I ought to be grateful to Him, who owes me absolutely nothing, for what He *has* bestowed.

Also, I have no reason to complain about God having given me a will whose scope is greater than that of my understanding. The will is like a unity made on inseparable parts; its nature apparently will not allow anything to be taken away from it. And, really, the wider the scope of my will, the more grateful I ought to be to Him who gave it to me.

Finally, I ought not to complain that God concurs in bringing about the acts of will and judgment in which I err. Insofar as these acts derive from God, they are completely true and good, and I am more perfect with the abilty to perform these acts than I would be without it. Moreover, the deprivation which is the real ground of falsity and error does not need God's concurrence, since it's not a thing. When we regard God as its cause, we should say that it is an absence rather than a privation. For, it clearly is no imperfection in God that He has given me the freedom to assent or not to assent to things of which He hasn't given me a clear and distinct grasp. Rather, it is an imperfection in me that I misuse this freedom by passing judgment on things that I don't properly understand. I see, of course, that God could easily have brought it about that, while I remain free and limited in knowledge, I never err: He could have implanted in me a clear and distinct understanding of everything about which I was ever going to make a choice, or He could have indelibly impressed on my memory that I must never pass judgment on something unelss I clearly and distinctly understand it. And I also understand that, regarded in isolation from everything else, I would have been more perfect if God had made me so that I never err. But I still can't deny that, because some things are immune to error while others are not, the universe is more perfect than it would have been if all its parts were alike. And I have no right to complain about God's wanting me to hold a place in the world other than the greatest and most perfect.

Moreover, if I can't avoid error by having an evident grasp of every matter on which I make a choice, I can avoid it in the other way, which only requires my bearing in mind the thought that I must not pass judgment on things whose truth isn't apparent. For, although I find myself too weak to fix my attention permanently on this single thought, I can—by careful and frequent meditation—ensure that I call it to mind whenever it is needed and that I thus acquire the habit of avoiding error.

Since the first and foremost perfection of man lies in acquiring this habit, I have profited from today's meditation, in which I have investigated the cause of error and falsity. Clearly, the only possible cause of error is the one I have described. When I limit my will's range of judgment to the things shown clearly and distinctly to my understanding, I obviously cannot err—for everything that I clearly and distinctly grasp is something and therefore comes, not from nothing, but from God who is supremely perfect and who cannot deceive. What I clearly and distinctly grasp is therefore unquestionably true. Today, then, I have learned what to avoid in order not to err and also what to do to attain the truth: I surely will attain the truth if I attend only to the things that I understand perfectly, distinguishing them from those that I grasp more obscurely and confusedly. And, from now on, I will devote myself to doing just that.

Meditation V
On the Essence of Material Objects and More on God's Existence

Many questions remain about God's attributes and about the nature of my self or mind. I may return to these questions later, but now—having found what to do and what to avoid in order to attain truth—I regard nothing as more pressing than to work my way out of the doubts that I raised the other day and to see whether I can find anything certain about material objects.

Before asking whether any such objects exist outside me, I ought to consider the ideas of these objects as they are in my thoughts and to see which are clear and which confused.

I distinctly imagine that which philosophers commonly call "continuous quantity," of course, and I distinctly imagine the extension of this quantity—or rather of the quantified thing—in length, breadth, and depth. I can distinguish various parts of this extension. I can ascribe at will any size, shape, place, and motion to these parts and any duration to the motions.

And, in addition to having a thorough knowledge of extension in general, I grasp innumerable particulars about shape, number, motion, and so on. The truth of these particulars is so obvious and so consonant with my nature that, when I first think about one of them, I do not seem to be learning anything novel. Rather I seem to be remembering something that I already knew—or noticing something that had been in me for a long time without my having been aware of it.

What is important here, I think, is that I find in myself innumerable ideas of things which, though they may not exist outside me, can't be said to be nothing. While I have some control over my thoughts of these things, I do not make the things up: they have their own real and immutable natures. Suppose, for example, that I imagine a triangle. While it may be that there is not—and never has been—a figure of this sort outside my thought, the figure still has a fixed, immutable, and eternal nature (essence, form) which hasn't been produced by me and which doesn't depend on my mind. The proof is that I can demonstrate various propositions about the triangle, such as that its angles equal two right angles and that its greatest side subtends its greatest angle. Even though I didn't think of these propositions at all when I first imagined the triangle, I now clearly see their truth whether I want to or not, and it follows that I didn't make them up.

It isn't relevant that, having seen triangular physical objects, I may have gotten the idea of the triangle from external objects through my organs of sense. For I can invent innumerable other figures whose ideas I *cannot* have gotten through my senses, and I can demonstrate facts about these other figures just as I can about the triangle. Since I know these facts clearly, they must be true, and they therefore must be something rather than nothing—for it's obvious that everything true is something, and everything that I know clearly and distinctly is true, as I have already shown. But, even if I had not shown this, the nature of my mind would have made it impossible for me to withhold my assent from these things (at least when I clearly and distincly grasped them). As I recall, I regarded truths about shape and number—truths of arithmetic, geometry, or pure mathematics in general—as more certain than any others, even when I clung most tightly to objects of sense.

But, if anything whose idea I can draw from my thought must in fact have everything that I clearly and distinctly grasp it to have, can't I derive from this a proof of God's existence? Surely,

I find the idea of a supremely perfect being in me just as I find the ideas of figures and numbers, and I understand as clearly and distinctly that eternal existence belongs to His nature as that the things that I demonstrate of figures and numbers belong to the natures of those figures and numbers. Accordingly, even if what I have thought up in the past few days hasn't been entirely true, I ought to be at least as certain of God's existence as I have been of the truths of pure mathematics.

At first, this reasoning may seem unclear and fallacious. For, being accustomed to distinguishing existence from essence in other cases, I am easily convinced that I can separate God's existence from His essence and, hence, that I can think of God as nonexistent. But, when I pay more careful attention, it's clear that I can no more separate God's existence from His essence than I can separate the essence of the triangle from its angles equaling two right angles, or the idea of a mountain from the idea of a valley. It is no less a contradiction to think that God (the supremely perfect being) lacks existence (a perfection) than to think that a mountain lacks a valley.

Well, suppose that I can't think of God without existence, just as I can't think of a mountain without a valley. The fact that I can think of a mountain with a valley doesn't entail that a mountain exists in the world, and, similarly, the fact that I can think of God as existing doesn't seem to entail that He exists. For my thought doesn't impose any necessity on things: it may be that I can ascribe existence to God when no God exists, just as I can imagine a winged horse when no such horse exists.

No, there is a fallacy here. From the fact that I can't think of a mountain without a valley it follows, not that the mountain and valley exist, but only that—whether they exist or not—they can't be separated. Similarly, from the fact that I can't think of God without existence, it follows that existence is inseparable from Him and, hence, that he really exists. It's not that my thoughts make things happen or impose a necessity on things. On the contrary, it's the fact that God exists which necessitates my thinking of Him as I do. I am not free to think of God without existence—of the supremely perfect being without supreme perfection—as I am free to think of a horse without wings.

Now someone might say this: "If I take God to have all perfections, and if I take existence to be a perfection, I must take God to exist, but I needn't accept the premise that God has all perfections. Similarly, if I accept the premise that every quadrilateral can be inscribed in a circle, I am forced to the patently false view that every rhombus can be inscribed in a circle, but I need not accept the premise." This is wrong, however. For, while it's not necessary that the idea of God occurs to me, it *is* necessary that I attribute all perfections to Him (even if I don't enumerate them or consider them individually) whenever I think of the primary and supreme entity and bring the idea of Him out of my mind's treasury. And this necessity ensures that, when I do notice that existence is a perfection, I can rightly conclude that the primary and supreme being exists. Similarly, while it's not necessary that I ever imagine a triangle, it is necessary that, when I do choose to consider a rectilinear figure having exactly three angles, I attribute to it (perhaps without noticing that I am doing so) properties from which I can rightly infer that its angles are no more than two right angles. But, when I consider the various shapes that can be inscribed in the circle, there's absolutely no necessity for my thinking that all quadrilaterals are among them; in fact, having resolved to accept only what I clearly and distinctly understand, I can't even think that all quadrilaterals are among them. Thus my false suppositions differ greatly from the true ideas implanted in me, the first and foremost of which is my idea of God. In many ways, I see that this idea is not a figment of my thought—that it is the image of a real and immutable nature: First, God is the only thing that I can think of whose existence belongs to its essence. Second, I can't conceive of there being two or more Gods. Third, having supposed that one God now exists, I see that He has necessarily existed from all eternity and will continue to exist into eternity. And there are many other things in God that I can't diminish or alter.

But, whatever proof I offer, it always comes back to the fact that I am only convinced of what I grasp clearly and distinctly. Of the things that

I grasp in this way, some are obvious to everyone. Others are discovered only by those who examine things more closely and search more carefully, but, once these things have been discovered, they are regarded as no less certain than the others. That the square on the hypotenuse of a right triangle equals the sum of the squares on the sides is not as readily apparent as that the hypotenuse subtends the greatest angle, but, once it has been seen, it is believed just as firmly. And (when I am not overwhelmed by prejudices and my thoughts are not besieged by images of sensible things) there surely is nothing that I know earlier or more easily than what pertains to God. For what could be more self-evident than there is a supreme entity—that God, the only thing whose existence belongs to His essence, exists?

While I need to pay careful attention in order to grasp this, I am now as certain of it as of any of the things that seem most certain. Moreover, I now see that the certainty of everything else so depends on my being certain that God exists that, if I weren't certain of God's existence, it wouldn't be possible for me to know anything perfectly.

Of course, my nature is such that, when I grasp something clearly and distinctly, I can't fail to believe it. But, since my nature is also such that I can't permanently fix my attention on a single thing so as always to grasp it clearly, the memory of previous judgments often comes to me when I am no longer attending to the grounds on which I originally made them. When this happens, reasons could be produced which would easily overthrow the judgments if I were ignorant of God, and I therefore would not have true and certain knowledge, but only unstable and changing opinion. For example, when I consider the nature of the triangle, it seems plain to me—steeped as I am in the principles of geometry—that its three angles equal two right angles: I can't fail to believe this as long as I pay attention to its demonstration. But, if I were ignorant of God, I might come to doubt its truth as soon as my attention wandered from its demonstration, even if I recalled having mastered the demonstration in the past: I could convince myself that I have been so constructed by nature that I sometimes err about what I believe myself to grasp most plainly—especially if I remembered that, having taken many things to be true and certain, I had later found reasons for judging them false.

But now I grasp that God exists, and I understand both that everything else depends on Him and that He's not a deceiver. From this, I infer that everything I clearly and distinctly grasp must be true. Even if I no longer pay attention to the grounds on which I judged God to exist, my recollection that I once clearly and distinctly knew Him to exist ensures that no contrary ground can be produced to impel me towards doubt. About God's existence, I have true and certain knowledge. And I have such knowledge, not just about this one thing, but about all the other things—such as the theorems of geometry—which I remember having proven. For what can now be said against my believing these things? That I am so constructed that I always err? But I now know that I can't err about what I clearly and distinctly understand. That much of what I took to be true and certain I later found to be false? But I didn't grasp any of these things clearly and distinctly; ignorant of the true standard of truth, I based my belief on grounds that I later found to be unsound. Then what can be said? What about the objection (which I recently used against myself) that I may be dreaming and that the things I am now experiencing may be as unreal as those that occur to me in sleep? No, the point would be irrelevant—for, even if I *am* dreaming, everything that is evident to my understanding *must* be true.

Thus I plainly see that the certainty and truth of all my knowledge derives from my knowledge of the true God. Before I knew Him, I couldn't know anything else perfectly. But now I can plainly and certainly know innumerable things about God, about other mental beings, and (insofar as it is the subject of pure mathematics) about the nature of physical objects.

Meditation VI
On the Existence of Material Objects and the Real Distinction of Mind from Body

It remains for me to examine whether physical objects exist. Insofar as they are the subject of pure mathematics, I now know that they *can* exist, because I grasp them clearly and distinctly.

For God can undoubtedly make whatever I can clearly and distinctly grasp, and I never judge that something is impossible for Him to make unless there would be a contradiction in my grasping that thing distinctly. Moreover, the fact that I find myself having mental images when I turn my attention to physical objects seems to imply that these objects really do exist. For, when I pay careful attention to what imagination is, it seems to me that it is just the application of my power of thought to a certain body which is immediately present to my thought and which must therefore exist.

I will begin to clarify this by examining the ways in which having mental images differs from having a pure understanding. When I picture a triangle, for example, I don't just understand that it is a figure bounded by three lines; I also "look at" the lines as though they were present to my mind's eye. And it is this "looking" that I call imagining. In contrast, when I want to think of a chiliagon, I can't imagine the sides or "look" at them as though they were present, but I *understand* that the chiliagon is a figure with a thousand sides as well as I understand that a triangle is a figure with three. Being accustomed to using images when I think about physical objects, I may confusedly picture *some* figure to myself, but—as this figure in no way differs from what I present to myself when thinking about a myriagon or any other many sided figure, and as it does not help me to discern the properties that distinguish chiliagons from the other polygons, it obviously is not a chiliagon. If it's a pentagon that is in question, I can understand its shape (as I can that of the chiliagon) without the aid of mental images. But I can also get a mental image of the pentagon by directing my mind's eye to its five lines and to the area that they bound. It's obvious to me that getting this mental image requires a special mental effort different from that needed for understanding, and this special effort clearly reveals the difference between imagination and pure understanding.

It also seems to me that my power of imagining, being distinct from my power of understanding, is not essential to myself or, in other words, to my mind—for, if I were to lose this ability, I would surely remain the same thing that I now am. And it seems to follow that this ability depends on something distinct from me. It's easy to understand how my mind might get mental images of physical objects by means of my body, *if* we suppose that there is a body so associated with my mind that the mind can "look into" it at will. If there were such a body, the mode of understanding that we call imagination would only differ from pure understanding in one way: when the mind understood something, it would turn "inward" and view an idea that it found in itself, but, when it imagined, it would turn to the body and look at something there—something resembling an idea that it had understood by itself or had grasped by sense. Thus, as I have said, it is easy to see how imagination works, if we suppose that my body exists. And, since I don't have in mind any other equally plausible explanation of imagination, I conjecture that physical objects probably do exist. But this conjecture is only probable. Despite my careful and thorough investigation, the distinct idea of bodily nature that comes from the imagination does not seem to have anything in it from which I can validly infer that physical objects exist.

Besides having a mental image of the bodily nature that is the subject of pure mathematics, I have mental images of such things as colors, sounds, flavors, and pains—but these images are not very distinct. I seem to grasp these things better by sense, from which they seem to come (with the aid of memory) to the understanding. It therefore seems appropriate to deal with these things in the context of an examination of the senses and to see whether there is something in the mode of awareness that I call *sensation* from which I can draw a conclusive argument for the existence of physical objects.

First, I will remind myself of the things that I believed really to be as I perceived them and of the grounds for my belief. Next, I will set out the grounds on which I later called this belief into doubt. And, finally, I will consider what I ought to think now.

To begin with, I sensed that I had a head, hands, feet, and the other members that make up a human body. I viewed this body as part, or maybe even as all, of me. I sensed that it was influenced by other physical objects whose affects could be either benefcial or harmful—beneficial to the extent that I felt pleasant sensations and harmful to the extent that I felt pain. In addition to sensations of pain and pleasure, I sensed hunger, thirst, and other such desires—and also bodily inclinations towards cheerfulness, sadness, and other emotions. Outside me, I sensed, not just extension, shape, and motion, but also hardness, hotness, and other qualities detected by touch. I also sensed light, color, odor, taste, and sound—qualities by whose variation I distinguished such things as the sky, earth, and sea from one another.

In view of these ideas of qualities (which presented themselves to my thought and were all that I really sensed directly) I had some reason for believing that I sensed objects distinct from my thought—physical objects from which the ideas came. For I found that these ideas came to me independently of my desires so that, however much I tried, I couldn't sense an object when it wasn't present to an organ to sense or fail to sense one when it was present. And, since the ideas that I grasped by sense were much livelier, more explicit, and (in their own way) more distinct than those I deliberately created or found impressed in my memory, it seemed that these ideas could not have come from me and that they must therefore have come from something else. Having no conception of these things other than the one suggested by my ideas, I could only think that the things resembled the ideas. Indeed, since I remembered using my senses before my reason, since I found the ideas that I created in myself to be less explicit than those grasped by sense, and since I found the ideas that I created to be composed largely of those that I had grasped by sense, I easily convinced myself that I didn't understand anything at all unless I had first sensed it.

I also had some reason for supposing that a certain physical object, which I view as belonging to me in a special way, is related to me more closely than any other. I can't be separated from it as I can from other physical objects; I feel all of my emotions and desires in it and because of it; and I am aware of pains and pleasant feelings in it but nothing else. I don't know *why* sadness goes with the sensation of pain, or *why* joy goes with sensory stimulation. I don't know *why* the stomach twitchings that I call hunger warn me that I need to eat or *why* dryness in my throat warns me that I need to drink. Seeing no connection between stomach twitchings and the desire to eat or between the sensation of a pain-producing thing and the consequent awareness of sadness, I can only say that I have been taught the connection by nature. And nature seems also to have taught me everything else that I knew about the objects of sensation—for I convinced myself that the sensations came to me in a certain way before having found grounds on which to prove that they did.

But, since then, many experiences have shaken my faith in the senses. Towers that seemed round from a distance sometimes looked square from close up, and huge statues on pediments sometimes did not look big when seen from the ground. In innumerable such cases, I found the judgments of the external senses to be wrong. And the same holds for the internal senses. What is felt more inwardly than pain? But I had heard that people with amputated arms and legs sometimes seem to feel pain in the missing limb, and it therefore didn't seem perfectly certain to me that the limb in which *I* feel a pain is always the one that hurts. And, to these grounds for doubt, I have recently added two that are very general: First, since I didn't believe myself to sense anything while awake that I couldn't also take myself to sense in a dream, and since I didn't believe that what I sense in sleep comes from objects outside me, I didn't see why I should believe what I sense while awake comes from such objects. Second, since I didn't yet know my creator (or, rather, since I supposed that I didn't know Him) nothing ruled out my having been so designed by nature that I am deceived even in that which seems most obviously true to me.

And I could easily reply to the reasoning by which I convinced myself of the reality of sensible things. Since my nature seemed to impel me towards many judgments which my reason rejected, I didn't believe that I ought to have much faith in nature's teachings. And, while my will didn't control my sense perceptions, I didn't believe it to follow that these perceptions came from outside me, since I thought that the ability to produce these ideas might have been in me without my being aware of it.

Now that I have begun to know myself and my creator better, I still believe that I oughtn't blindly to accept everything that I seem to get from the senses. But I no longer believe that I ought to call it all into doubt.

In the first place, I know that everything that I clearly and distinctly understand can be made by God to be exactly as I understand it. The fact that I can clearly and distinctly understand one thing apart from another is therefore enough to make me certain that it *is* distinct from the other, since the things could be separated by God if not by something else. (I judge the things to be distinct regardless of the power needed to make them exist separately.) Accordingly, from the fact that I have gained knowledge of my existence without noticing anything about my nature or essence except that I am a thinking thing, I can rightly conclude that my essence consists solely in the fact that I am a thinking thing. It's possible (or, as I will say later, it's certain) that I have a body which is very tightly bound to me. But, on the other hand, I have a clear and distinct idea of myself insofar as I am just a thinking and unextended thing, and, on the other hand, I have a distinct idea of my body insofar as it is just an extended and unthinking thing. It's certain, then, that I am really distinct from my body and can exist without it.

Moreover, I find in myself abilities for special modes of awareness, such as the abilities to have mental images and to sense. I can clearly and distinctly conceive of my whole self as something that lacks these abilities, but I can't conceive of the abilities existing without me, or without an understanding substance in which to reside. Since the conception of these abilities includes the conception of something that understands, I see that these abilities are distinct from me in the way that a thing's properties are distinct from the thing itself.

I recognize other abilities in me, such as the ability to move around and to assume various postures. These abilities can't be understood to exist apart from a substance in which they reside any more than the abilities to imagine and sense, and they therefore cannot exist without such a substance. But it's obvious that, if these abilities do exist, the substance in which they reside must be a body or extended substance rather than an understanding one, for the clear and distinct conceptions of these abilities contain extension but not understanding.

There is also in me, however, a passive ability to sense—to receive and recognize ideas of sensible things. I wouldn't be able to put this ability to use if there weren't—either in me or in something else—an active power to produce or make sensory ideas. But, since this active power does not presuppose understanding, and since it often produces ideas in me without my cooperation and even against my will, it cannot exist in me. Therefore this power must exist in a substance distinct from me. And, for reasons that I have noted, this substance must contain, either formally or eminently, all the reality that is contained presentationally in the ideas that the power produces. Accordingly, this substance must be either a physical object (which contains formally the reality that the idea contains presentationally), or one of God's creations that is higher than physical objects (which contains this reality eminently), or God himself. But, since God isn't a deceiver, it's completely obvious that He doesn't send these ideas to me directly or by means of a creation which contains their reality eminently rather than formally. For, since He has not given me any ability to recognize that these ideas are sent by Him or by creations other than physical objects, and since He has given me a strong inclination to believe that the ideas come from physical objects, there would be no way to avoid the conclusion that He deceives me if the ideas were sent to me by anything other than physical objects. Therefore physical objects exist. These objects may not exist exactly as I comprehend them by sense; in many ways, sensory comprehension is obscure and confused. But these objects must at least have in them everything that I clearly and distinctly understand them to have—every general property within the scope of pure mathematics.

But what about particular properties, such as the size and shape of the sun? And what about things that I understand less clearly than general mathematical properties—things like light, sound, and pain? These are open to doubt. But, since God isn't a deceiver, and since I therefore have the God-given ability to correct any falsity that may be in my beliefs, I have high hopes of finding the truth about even these things. There is undoubtedly some truth in everything I have been taught by nature—for, when I use the term "nature" in its general sense, I refer to God or to the order that He has established in the created world, and, when I apply the term specifically to *my* nature, I refer to the collection of everything that God has given *me*.

Nature teaches me nothing more explicitly, however, than that I have a body which is hurt when I feel pain, which needs food or drink when I experience hunger or thirst, and so on. And, accordingly, I ought not to doubt that there is some truth to the thought that I have a body.

Nature also teaches me—through sensations like pain, hunger, and thirst—that I am not present in my body in the way that a sailor is present in his ship. Rather, I am very tightly bound to my body and so "mixed up" with it that we form a single thing. If this weren't so, I—who am just a thinking thing—wouldn't feel pain when my body was injured; I would perceive the injury by pure understanding in the way that a sailor sees the leaks in his ship with his eyes. And, when my body needed food or drink, I would explicitly understand that the need existed without having the confused sensations of hunger and thirst. For the sensations of thirst, hunger, and pain are just confused modifications of thought arising from the union and "mixture" of mind and body.

Moreover, nature teaches me that there are other physical objects around my body—some that I ought to seek and others that I ought to avoid. From the fact that I sense colors, sounds, odors, flavors, and temperatures, I correctly infer that sense perceptions come from physical objects which vary as widely (though perhaps not in the same way) as the perceptions do. And, from the fact that some of these perceptions are pleasant while others are unpleasant, I infer with certainty that my body—or, rather, my whole self which consists of a body and a mind—can be benefited and harmed by the physical objects around it.

There are many other things which I *seem* to have been taught by nature, but which I have really accepted out of a habit of thoughtless judgment and which therefore may well be false. Among these things are the judgments that a space is empty if nothing in it happens to affect my senses, that a hot physical object has something in it resembling my idea of heat, that a white or green thing has in it the same whiteness or greenness that I sense, that a bitter or sweet thing has in it the same flavor that I taste, and the stars, towers, and other physical objects have the same size and shape that they show to my senses.

If I am to avoid accepting what is indistinct in these cases, I must more carefully explain my use of the phrase "taught by nature." In particular, I should say that I am now using the term "nature" in a narrower sense than when I took it to refer to the whole complex of what God has given me. This complex includes much having to do with my mind alone (such as my grasp of the fact that what is done cannot be undone and of the rest of what I know by the light of nature) which does not bear on what I am now saying. And the complex also includes much having to do with my body alone (such as its tendency to go downwards) that I also am not now dealing with. I am now using the term "nature" to refer only to what God has given me insofar as I am composite of mind and body. This nature teaches me to avoid that which occasions painful sensations, to seek that which occasions pleasant sensations, and so on, but it seems *not* to teach me to draw conclusions about external objects from sense perceptions without first having examined the matter with my understanding—for true knowledge of external things seems to belong to the mind alone, rather than to the composite of mind and body.

Thus, while a star has no more effect on my eye than a flame does, I do not have a real, positive inclination to believe that the star is as small as the flame; my youthful judgment to the contrary was not based on reason. And, while I feel heat when I approach a fire and pain when I draw nearer, I have absolutely no reason for believing that something in the fire resembles the heat, just as I have no reason for believing that something in the fire resembles the pain; I only have reason for believing that *something* in the fire produces the ideas of heat and pain in me. And, while there may be nothing in a given region of space that affects my senses, it doesn't follow that there are no physical objects in that space. Rather, I now see that, on these matters and others, I used to pervert the natural order of things. For, while nature has given sense perceptions to my mind for the sole purpose of indicating what is beneficial and what harmful to the composite of which my mind is a part, and while the perceptions are sufficiently clear and distinct for this purpose, I used these perceptions as standards for identifying the essence of physical objects—an essence which they only reveal obscurely and confusedly.

I have already explained how it can be that, despite God's goodness, my judgments can be false. But a new difficulty arises here—one having to do with the things that nature presents to me as desirable or undesirable and with the errors that I seem to have found in my internal sensations. One of these errors seems to be committed, for example, when a man is fooled by some food's pleasant taste into eating poison hidden in that food. But surely, in this case, what the man's nature impels him to eat is the good tasting food, not the poison of which he knows nothing. We can draw no conclusion except that his nature isn't omniscient, and this conclusion isn't surprising: since a man is a limited thing, he can only have limited perfections.

Still, we often err in things towards which nature *does* impel us. This happens, for example, when sick people want food or drink that would quickly harm them. To say that these people err as a result of the corruption of their nature does not solve the problem—for a sick man is no less a creation of God than a well one, and it seems as absurd to suppose that God has given him a deceptive nature. A clock made of wheels and weights follows the natural laws just as precisely when it is poorly made and inaccurate as when it does everything that its maker wants. Thus, if we regard a human body as a machine made up of bones, nerves, muscles, veins, blood, and skin, and if we notice that a body without a mind in it would do just the things that it does now (except for those that require a mind because they are commanded by the will), it is easy to see that what happens to a sick man is no less "natural" than what happens to a well one. For instance, if a body suffers from dropsy, it has a dry throat of the sort that regularly brings the sensation of thirst to the mind, the dryness disposes the nerves and other organs to drink, and the drinking makes the illness worse. But this is just as natural as when a similar dryness of throat moves a person who is perfectly healthy to take a drink that is beneficial.

Bearing in mind my conception of a clock's use, I might say that an inaccurate clock departs from its nature. And, similarly, viewing the machine of the human body as designed for working as it usually does, I can say that it drifts away from its nature if it has a dry throat when drinking will not help to maintain it. I should note, however, that the sense in which I am now using the term "nature" differs from that in which I used it before. For, as I have just used the term, the *nature* of a man (or clock) is something that depends on my thinking of the difference between a sick and a well man (or of the difference between a poorly made and a well-made clock)—something that is regarded as *extrinsic* to the things. But, when I used "nature" before, I referred to something which is *in* things and which therefore has some reality.

It may be that we just offer an extrinsic description of a body suffering from dropsy when, noting that it has a dry throat but doesn't need to drink, we say that its nature is corrupted. Still, the description is not purely extrinsic when we say that a composite or union of mind and body has a corrupted nature: there is a real fault in the composite's nature, for it is thirsty when drinking is harmful to it. It therefore remains to be asked why God's goodness doesn't prevent *this* nature's being deceptive.

To begin the answer, I will note that mind differs importantly from body in that body is by its nature divisible, while mind is indivisible. When I think about my mind—or, in other words, about myself insofar as I am just a thinking thing—I can't distinguish any parts; I understand myself to be a single, unified thing. Although my whole mind seems united to my whole body, I know that cutting off a foot, arm, or other limb would not take anything away from my mind. And the abilities to will, sense, understand can't be called parts, since it is one and the same mind that wills, senses, and understands. On the other hand, whenever I think of a physical or extended thing, I can mentally divide it, and I therefore understand that the object is divisible. This single fact would be enough to teach me that my mind and my body are distinct, if I hadn't already gained that knowledge.

Next, I notice that the mind isn't directly affected by all parts of the body, but only by the brain—or maybe just by the small part of the brain containing the so-called "common sense."

Whenever this part of the brain is in a given state, it exhibits the same thing to the mind, regardless of what is happening in the rest of the body (as is shown by innumerable experiments that I need not review here).

Moreover, I notice that the nature of body is such that, if a first part can be moved by a second that is far away, the first part can be moved in exactly the same way by something between the first and second without the second part's being affected. For example, if A, B, C, and D are points on a cord, and if the first point (A) can be moved in a certain way by a pull on the last point (D), then A can be moved in the same way by a pull on one of the middle points (B or C) without D's being moved. Similarly, science teaches me that, when my foot hurts, the sensation of pain is produced by nerves distributed throughout the foot which extend like a cord from there to the brain. When pulled in the foot, these nerves pull the central parts of the brain to which they are attached, moving those parts in ways designated by nature to present the mind with the sensation of a pain "in the foot." Since these nerves pass through the shins, thighs, hips, back, and neck on their way from foot to brain, it can happen that their being touched in the middle, rather than at the end in the foot, produces the same motion in the brain as when the foot is hurt and, consequently, that the mind feels the same pain "in the foot." And the point holds for other sensations as well.

Finally, I notice that, since only one sensation can be produced by a given motion of the part of the brain that directly affects the mind, the best conceivable sensation for it to produce is the one that is most often useful for the maintenance of the healthy man. Experience teaches, however, that all the sensations put in us by nature *are* of this sort and therefore that there is nothing in our sensations which doesn't testify to God's power and goodness. For example, when the nerves in the foot are moved with unusual violence, the motion is communicated through the middle of the spine to the center of the brain, where it signals the mind to sense a pain "in the foot." This urges the mind to view the pain's cause as harmful to the foot and to do what it can to remove the cause. Of course, God could have so designed man's nature that the same motion of the brain showed the mind something else (such as itself as a motion in the brain, or as a motion in the foot, or as a motion somewhere between the brain and foot), but no alternative to the way things are would be as conducive to the maintenance of the body. Similarly, when we need drink, the throat becomes dry, the dryness moves the nerves of the throat thereby moving the center of the brain, and the brain's movements cause the sensation of thirst in the mind. It's the sensation of thirst that is produced, because no information about our condition is more useful to us than that we need to get something to drink in order to remain healthy. And the same is true in other cases.

This makes it completely obvious that, despite God's immense goodness, the nature of man (whom we now view as a composite of mind and body) cannot fail to be deceptive. For, if something produces the movement usually associated with a bad foot in the nerve running from foot to brain or in the brain itself (rather than in the foot), a pain is felt "in the foot," and the senses are deceived by my nature. Since this motion in the brain must always bring the same sensation to mind, and since the motion's cause more often *is* something hurting the foot than something elsewhere, it is in accordance with reason that the motion always shows the mind a pain in the foot rather than elsewhere. And, if dryness of the throat arises, not (as usual) from drink's being conducive to the body's health, but (as happens in dropsy) from some other cause, it is much better that we are deceived than that we are generally deceived when our bodies are sound. And so on for other sensations.

In addition to helping me to be aware of the errors to which my nature is subject, these reflections help me readily to correct or avoid those errors. I know that sensory indications of what is good for my body are more often true than false; I can almost always examine a given thing with several senses; and I can also use my memory (which connects the present to the past) and my understanding (which has now ascertained all the causes of error). Hence, I need no longer fear that what the senses daily show me is unreal. I should reject the exaggerated doubts of the past few days as ridiculous. This is especially true of the chief ground for these doubts—namely, that I couldn't distinguish dreaming from being awake—for I now notice that dreaming and being awake are importantly different: the events in dreams are not linked by memory to the rest of my life like those that happen while I am awake. If, while I am awake, someone were suddenly to appear and then immediately to disappear without my seeing where he came from or went to (as happens in dreams), I would justifiably judge that he was not a real man, but a ghost—or, better, an apparition created in my brain. But, if I distinctly observe something's source, its place, and the time at which I learn about it, and if I grasp an unbroken connection between it and the rest of my life, I am quite sure that it is something in my waking life rather than in a dream. And I ought not to have the slightest doubt about the reality of such things, if I have examined them with all my senses, my memory, and my understanding without finding any conflicting evidence. For, from the fact that God is not a deceiver, it follows that I am not deceived in any case of this sort. Since the need to act does not always allow time for such a careful examination, however, we must admit the likelihood of men's erring about particular things and acknowledge the weakness of our nature.

Some Further Considerations Concerning Our Simple Ideas of Sensation

JOHN LOCKE

John Locke (1632–1704) was one of the greatest and most influential of English philosophers. His works include *An Essay Concerning Human Understanding* and *Two Treatises on Civil Government.*

1. Concerning the simple ideas of Sensation, it is to be considered,—that whatsoever is so constituted in nature as to be able, by affecting our senses, to cause any perception in the mind, doth thereby produce in the understanding a simple idea; which, whatever be the external cause of it, when it comes to be taken notice of by our discerning faculty, it is by the mind looked on and considered there to be a real positive idea in the understanding, as much as any other whatsoever; though, perhaps, the cause of it be but a privation of the subject.

2. Thus the ideas of heat and cold, light and darkness, white and black, motion and rest, are equally clear and positive ideas in the mind; though, perhaps, some of the causes which produce them are barely privations, in those subjects from whence our senses derive those ideas. These the understanding, in its view of them, considers all as distinct positive ideas, without taking notice of the causes that produce them: which is an inquiry not belonging to the idea, as it is in the understanding, but to the nature of the things existing without us. These are two very different things, and carefully to be distinguished; it being one thing to perceive and know the idea of white or black, and quite another to examine what kind of particles they must be, and how ranged in the superficies, to make any object appear white or black.

3. A painter or dyer who never inquired into their causes hath the ideas of white and black, and other colours, as clearly, perfectly, and distinctly in his understanding, and perhaps more distinctly, than the philosopher who hath busied himself in considering their natures, and thinks he knows how far either of them is, in its cause, positive or privative; and the idea of black is no less positive in his mind than that of white, however the cause of that colour in the external object may be only a privation.

4. If it were the design of my present undertaking to inquire into the natural causes and manner of perception, I should offer this as a reason why a privative cause might, in some cases at least, produce a positive idea; viz. that all sensation being produced in us only by different degrees and modes of motion in our animal spirits, variously agitated by external objects, the abatement of any former motion must as necessarily produce a new sensation as the variation or increase of it; and so introduce a new idea, which depends only on a different motion of the animal spirits in that organ.

5. But whether this be so or not I will not here determine, but appeal to every one's own expe-

From *An Essay Concerning Human Understanding* (Oxford: Oxford University Press, 1894), pp. 166–82.

rience, whether the shadow of a man, though it consists of nothing but the absence of light (and the more the absence of light is, the more discernible is the shadow) does not, when a man looks on it, cause as clear and positive idea in his mind, as a man himself, though covered over with clear sunshine? And the picture of a shadow is a positive thing. Indeed, we have negative names, which stand not directly for positive ideas, but for their absence, such as *insipid, silence, nihil,* etc.; which words denote positive ideas, v.g. *taste, sound, being,* with a signification of their absence.

6. And thus one may truly be said to see darkness. For, supposing a hole perfectly dark, from whence no light is refelcted, it is certain one may see the figure of it, or it may be painted; or whether the ink I write with makes any other idea, is a question. The privative causes I have here assigned of positive ideas are according to the common opinion; but, in truth, it will be hard to determine whether there be really any ideas from a privative cause, till it be determined, whether rest be any more a privation than motion.

7. To discover the nature of our *ideas* the better, and to discourse of them intelligibly, it will be convenient to distinguish them *as they are ideas or perceptions in our minds;* and *as they are modifications of matter in the bodies that cause such perceptions in us:* that so we may not think (as perhaps usually is done) that they are exactly the images and resemblances of something inherent in the subject; most of those of sensation being in the mind no more the likeness of something existing without us, than the names that stand for them are the likeness of our ideas, which yet upon hearing they are apt to excite in us.

8. Whatsoever the mind perceives *in itself,* or is the immediate object of perception, thought, or understanding, that I call *idea;* and the power to produce any idea in our mind, I call *quality* of the subject wherein that power is. Thus a snowball having the power to produce in us the ideas of white, cold, and round,—the power to produce those ideas in us, as they are in the snowball, I call qualities; and as they are sensations or perceptions in our understandings, I call them ideas; which *ideas,* if I speak of sometimes as in the things themselves, I would be understood to mean those qualities in the objects which produce them in us.

9. Qualities thus considered in bodies are,

First, such as are utterly inseparable from the body, in what state soever it be; and such as in all the alterations and changes it suffers, all the force can be used upon it, it constantly keeps; and such as sense constantly finds in every particle of matter which has bulk enough to be perceived; and the mind finds inseparable from every particle of matter, though less than to make itself singly be perceived by our senses: v.g. Take a grain of wheat, divide it into two parts; each part has still solidity, extension, figure, and mobility: divide it again, and it retains still the same qualities; and so divide it on, till the parts become insensible; they must retain still each of them all those qualities. For division (which is all that a mill, or pestle, or any other body, does upon another, in reducing it to insensible parts) can never take away either solidity, extension, figure, or mobility from any body, but only makes two or more distinct separate masses of matter, of that which was but one before; all which distinct masses, reckoned as so many distinct bodies, after division, make a certain number. These I call *original* or *primary qualities* of body, which I think we may observe to produce simple ideas in us, viz. solidity, extension, figure, motion or rest, and number.

10. *Secondly,* such qualities which in truth are nothing in the objects themselves but powers to produce various sensations in us by their primary qualities, i.e. by the bulk, figure, texture, and motion of their insensible parts, as colours, sounds, tastes, etc. These I call *secondary qualities.* To these might be added a *third* sort, which are allowed to be barely powers; though they are as much real qualities in the subject as those which I, to comply with the common way of speaking, call qualities, but for distinction, secondary qualities. For the power in fire to produce a new colour, or consistency, in *wax* or *clay,*—by its primary qualities, is as much a quality in fire, as the power it has to produce in *me* a new idea or sensation of warmth or burning, which I felt not before,—by the same primary qualities, viz. the bulk, texture, and motion of its insensible parts.

11. The next thing to be considered is, how bodies produce ideas in us; and that is manifestly

by impulse, the only way which we can conceive bodies to operate in.

12. If then external objects be not united to our minds when they produce ideas therein; and yet we perceive these *original* qualities in such of them as singly fall under our senses, it is evident that some motion must be thence continued by our nerves, or animal spirits, by some parts of our bodies, to the brains or the seat of sensation, there to produce in our minds the particular ideas we have of them. And since the extension, figure, number, and motion of bodies of an observable bigness, may be perceived at a distance by the sight, it is evident some singly imperceptible bodies must come from them to the eyes, and thereby convey to the brain some motion; which produces these ideas which we have of them in us.

13. After the same manner that the ideas of these original qualities are produced in us, we may conceive that the ideas of *secondary* qualities are also produced, viz. by the operation of insensible particles on our senses. For, it being manifest that there are bodies and good store of bodies, each whereof are so small, that we cannot by any of our senses discover either their bulk, figure, or motion,—as is evident in the particles of the air and water, and others extremely smaller than those; perhaps as much smaller than the particles of air and water, as the particles of air and water are smaller than peas or hail-stones;—let us suppose at present that the different motions and figures, bulk and number, of such particles, affecting the several organs of our senses, produce in us those different sensations which we have from the colours and smells of bodies; v.g. that a violet, by the impulse of such insensible particles of matter, of peculiar figures and bulks, and in different degrees and modifications of their motions, causes the ideas of the blue colour, and sweet scent of that flower to be produced in our minds. It being no more impossible to conceive that God should annex such ideas to such motions, with which they have no similitude, than that he should annex the idea of pain to the motion of a piece of steel dividing our flesh, with which that idea hath no resemblance.

14. What I have said concerning colours and smells may be understood also of tastes and sounds, and other the like sensible qualities; which, whatever reality we by mistake attribute to them, are in truth nothing in the objects themselves, but powers to produce various sensations in us; and depend on those primary qualities, viz. bulk, figure, texture, and motion of parts as I have said.

15. From whence I think it easy to draw this observation,—that the ideas of primary qualities of bodies are resemblances of them, and their patterns do really exist in the bodies themselves, but the ideas produced in us by these secondary qualities have no resemblance of them at all. There is nothing like our ideas, existing in the bodies themselves. There are, in the bodies we denominate from them, only a power to produce those sensations in us: and what is sweet, blue, or warm in idea, is but the certain bulk, figure, and motion of the insensible parts, in the bodies themselves, which we call so.

16. Flame is denominated hot and light; snow, white and cold; and manna, white and sweet, from the ideas they produce in us. Which qualities are commonly thought to be the same in those bodies that those ideas are in us, the one the perfect resemblance of the other, as they are in a mirror, and it would by most men be judged very extravagant if one should say otherwise. And yet he that will consider that the same fire that, at one distance produces in us the sensation of warmth, does, at a nearer approach, produce in us the far different sensation of pain, ought to bethink himself what reason he has to say—that this idea of warmth, which was produced in him by the fire, is *actually in the fire;* and his idea of pain, which the same fire produced in him the same way, is *not* in the fire. Why are whiteness and coldness in snow, and pain not, when it produces the one and the other idea in us; and can do neither, but by the bulk, figure, number, and motion of its solid parts?

17. The particular bulk, number, figure, and motion of the parts of fire or snow are really in them,—whether any one's senses perceive them or no: and therefore they may be called *real* qualities, because they really exist in those bodies. But light, heat, whiteness, or coldness, are no more really in them than sickness or pain is in manna. Take away the sensation of them; let not the eyes see light or colours, nor the ears hear sounds; let the palate not taste, nor the nose smell,

and all colours, tastes, odours, and sounds, *as they are such particular ideas,* vanish and cease, and are reduced to their causes, i.e., bulk, figure, and motion of parts.

18. A piece of manna of a sensible bulk is able to produce in us the idea of a round or square figure; and by being removed from one palce to another, the idea of motion. This idea of motion represents it as it really is in manna moving: a circle or square are the same, whether in idea or existence, in the mind or in the manna. And this, both motion and figure, are really in the manna, whether we take notice of them or no: this everybody is ready to agree to. Besides, manna, by the bulk, figure, texture, and motion of its parts, has a power to produce the sensations of sickness, and sometimes of acute pains or gripings in us. That these ideas of sickness and pain are *not* in the manna, but effects of its operations on us, and are nowhere when we feel them not; this also every one readily agrees to. And yet men are hardly to be brought to think that sweetness and whiteness are not really in manna; which are but the effects of the operations of manna, by the motion, size, and figure of its particles, on the eyes and palate: as the pain and sickness caused by manna are confessedly nothing but the effects of its operations on the stomach and guts, by the size, motion, and figure of its insensible parts, (for by nothing else can a body operate, as has been proved): as if it could not operate on the eyes and palate, and thereby produce in the mind particular distinct ideas, which in itself it has not, as well as we allow it can operate on the guts and stomach, and thereby produce distinct ideas, which in itself it has not. These ideas, being all effects of the operations of manna on several parts of our bodies, by the size, figure, number, and motion of its parts;—why those produced by the eyes and palate should rather be thought to be really in the manna, than those produced by the stomach and guts; or why the pain and sickness, ideas that are the effect of manna, should be thought to be nowhere when they are not felt; and yet the sweetness and whiteness, effects of the same manna on other parts of the body, by ways equally as unknown, should be thought to exist in the manna, when they are not seen or tasted, would need some reason to explain.

19. Let us consider red and white colours in porphyry. Hinder light from striking on it, and its colours vanish; it no longer produces any such ideas in us: upon the return of light it produces these appearances on us again. Can any one think any real alterations are made in the prophyry by the presence or absence of light; and that those ideas of whiteness and redness are really in porphyry in the light, when it is plain *it has no colour in the dark?* It has, indeed, such a configuration of particles, both night and day, as are apt, by the rays of light rebounding from some parts of that hard stone, to produce in us the idea of redness, and from others the idea of whiteness; but whiteness or redness are not in it at any time, but such a texture that hath the power to produce such a sensation in us.

20. Pound an almond, and the clear white colour will be altered into a dirty one, and the sweet taste into an oily one. What real alteration can the beating of the pestle make in any body, but an alteration of the texture of it?

21. Ideas being thus distinguished and understood, we may be able to give an account how the same water, at the same time, may produce the idea of cold by one hand and of heat by the other: whereas it is impossible that the same water, if those ideas were really in it, should at the same time be both hot and cold. For, if we imagine *warmth,* as it is in our hands, to be nothing but a certain sort and degree of motion in the minute particles of our nerves or animal spirits, we may understand how it is possible that the same water may, at the same time, produce the sensations of heat in one hand cold in the other; which yet *figure* never does, that never producing the idea of a square by one hand which has produced the idea of a globe by another. But if the sensation of heat and cold be nothing but the increase or diminution of the motion of the minute parts of our bodies, caused by the corpuscles of any other body, it is easy to be understood, that if that motion be greater in one hand than in the other; if a body be applied to the two hands, which has in its minute particles a greater motion than in those of one of the hands, and a less than in those of the other, it will increase the motion of the one hand and lessen it in the other; and so cause the different sensations of heat and cold that depend thereon.

22. I have in what just goes before been engaged in physical inquiries a little further than

perhaps I intended. But, it being necessary to make the nature of sensation a little understood; and to make the difference between the *qualities* in bodies, and the *ideas* produced by them in the mind, to be distinctly conceived, without which it were impossible to discourse intelligibly of them;—I hope I shall be pardoned this little excursion into natural philosophy; it being necessary in our present inquiry to distinguish the *primary* and *real* qualities of bodies, which are always in them (viz. solidity, extension, figure, number, and motion, or rest, and are sometimes perceived by us, viz. when the bodies they are in are big enough singly to be discerned), from those *secondary* and *imputed* qualities, which are but the powers of several combinations of those primary ones, when they operate without being distinctly discerned;—whereby we may also come to know what ideas are, and what are not, resemblances of something really existing in the bodies we denominate from them.

23. The qualities, then, that are in bodies, rightly considered, are of three sorts:—

First, The bulk, figure, number, situation, and motion or rest of their solid parts. Those are in them, whether we perceive them or not; and when they are of that size that we can discover them, we have by these an idea of the thing as it is in itself; as is plain in artificial things. These I call *primary qualities*.

Secondly, The power that is in any body, by reason of its insensible primary qualities, to operate after a peculiar manner on any of our senses, and thereby produce in *us* the different ideas of several colours, sounds, smells, tastes, etc. These are usually called *sensible qualities*.

Thirdly, The power that is in any body, by reason of the particular constitution of its primary qualities, to make such a change in the bulk, figure, texture, and motion of *another body,* as to make it operate on our senses differently from what it did before. Thus the sun has a power to make wax white, and fire to make lead fluid. These are usually called *powers*.

The first of these, as has been said, I think may be properly called real, original, or primary qualities; because they are in the things themselves, whether they are perceived or not: and upon their different modifications it is that the secondary qualities depend.

The other two are only powers to act differently upon other things: which powers result from the different modifications of those primary qualities.

24. But, though the two latter sorts of qualities are powers barely, and nothing but powers, relating to several other bodies, and resulting from the different modifications of the original qualities, yet they are generally otherwise thought of. For the *second* sort, viz. the powers to produce several ideas in us, by our senses, are looked upon as real qualities in the things thus affecting us: but the *third* sort are called and esteemed barely powers. . . . The idea of heat or light, which we receive by our eyes, or touch, from the sun, are commonly thought real qualities existing in the sun, and something more than mere powers in it. But when we consider the sun in reference to wax, which it melts or blanches, we look on the whiteness and softness produced in the wax, not as qualities in the sun, but effects produced by powers in it. Whereas, if rightly considered, these qualities of light and warmth, which are perceptions in me when I am warmed or enlightened by the sun, are no [more] in the sun, than the changes made in the wax, when it is blanched or melted, are in the sun. They are all of them equally *powers in the sun, depending on its primary qualities;* whereby it is able, in the one case, so to alter the bulk, figure, texture, or motion of some of the insensible parts of my eyes or hands, as thereby to produce in me the idea of light or heat; and in the other, it is able so to alter the bulk, fugure, texture, or motion of the insensible parts of the wax, as to make them fit to produce in me the distinct ideas of white and fluid.

25. The reason why the one are ordinarily taken for real qualities, and the other only for bare powers, seems to be, because the ideas we have of distinct colours, sounds, etc., containing nothing at all in them of bulk, figure, or motion, we are not apt to think them the effects of these primary qualities; which appear not, to our senses, to operate in their production, and with which they have not any apparent congruity or conceivable connexion. Hence it is that we are so forward to imagine, that those ideas are the resemblances of something really existing in the objects themselves: since sensation discovers nothing of bulk, figure, or motion of parts in their production; nor can reason show how bodies, *by their*

bulk, figure and motion, should produce in the mind the ideas of blue or yellow, etc. But, in the other case, in the operations of bodies changing the qualities one of another, we plainly discover that the quality produced hath commonly no resemblance with anything in the thing producing it; wherefore we look on it as a bare effect of power. For, through receiving the idea of heat or light from the sun, we are apt to think *it* is a perception and resemblance of such a quality in the sun; yet when we see wax, or a fair face, receive change of colour from the sun, we cannot imagine *that* to be the reception of resemblance of anything in the sun, because we find not those different colours in the sun itself. For, one senses being able to observe a likeness or unlikeness of sensible qualities in two different external objects, we forwardly enough conclude the production of any sensible quality in any subject to be an effect of bare power, and not the communication of any quality which was really in the efficient, when we find no such sensible quality in the thing that produced it. But our senses, not being able to discover any unlikeness between the idea produced in us, and the quality of the object producing it, we are apt to imagine that our ideas are resemblances of something in the objects, and not the effects of certain powers placed in the modification of the primary qualities, with which primary qualities the ideas produced in us have no resemblance.

26. To conclude. Beside those before-mentioned primary qualities in bodies, viz. bulk, figure, extension, number, and motion of their solid parts; all the rest, whereby we take notice of bodies, and distinguish them one from another, are nothing else but several powers in them, depending on those primary qualities; whereby they are fitted, either by immediately operating on our bodies to produce several different ideas in us; or else, by operating on other bodies, so to change their primary qualities as to render them capable of producing ideas in us different from what before they did. The former of these, I think, may be called secondary qualities *immediately perceivable:* the latter, secondary qualities, *mediately perceivable.*

Three Dialogues Between Hylas and Philonous

GEORGE BERKELEY

The design of which is plainly to demonstrate the reality and perfection of human knowledge, the incorporeal nature of the soul, and the immediate providence of a Deity: in opposition to the Sceptics and Atheists. Also to open a method for rendering the Sciences more easy, useful, and compendious.

George Berkeley (1685–1753) was Bishop of Cloyne. His works are classics of empiricism that have provoked admiration and frustration from generations of philosophy students. He wrote a number of works in addition to the *Three Dialogues,* including *A Treatise Concerning the Principles of Human Knowledge* and *An Essay Towards a New Theory of Vision.*

The First Dialogue

PHILONOUS. Good morrow, Hylas: I did not expect to find you abroad so early.

HYLAS. It is indeed something unusual; but my thoughts were so taken up with a subject I was discoursing of last night, that finding I could not sleep, I resolved to rise and take a turn in the garden.

PHIL. It happened well, to let you see what innocent and agreeable pleasures you lose every morning. Can there be a pleasanter time of the day, or a more delightful season of the year? That purple sky, those wild but sweet notes of birds, the fragrant bloom upon the trees and flowers, the gentle influence of the rising sun, these and a thousand nameless beauties of nature inspire the soul with secret transports; its faculties too being at this time fresh and lively, are fit for those meditations, which the solitude of a garden and tranquillity of the morning naturally dispose us to. But I am afraid I interrupt your thoughts: for you seemed very intent on something.

HYL. It is true, I was, and shall be obliged to you if you will permit me to go on in the same vein; not that I would by any means deprive myself of your company, for my thoughts always flow more easily in conversation with a friend, than when I am alone: but my request is that you would suffer me to impart my reflexions to you.

PHIL. With all my heart, it is what I should have requested myself if you had not prevented me.

HYL. I was considering the odd fate of those men who have in all ages, through an affectation of being distinguished from the vulgar, or some unaccountable turn of thought, pretended either to believe nothing at all, or to believe the most extravagant things in the world. This however might be borne, if their paradoxes and scepticism did not draw after them some consequences of

From *The Works of George Berkeley,* ed. A. Campbell Fraser (Oxford: Oxford University Press, 1901), Vol. I, pp. 379–428, 442–52, 463–70, 480–85.

general disadvantage to mankind. But the mischief lieth here; that when men of less leisure see them who are supposed to have spent their whole time in the pursuits of knowledge professing an entire ignorance of all things, or advancing such notions as are repugnant to plain and commonly received principles, they will be tempted to entertain suspicions concerning the most important truths, which they had hitherto held sacred and unquestionable.

PHIL. I entirely agree with you, as to the ill tendency of the affected doubts of some philosophers, and fantastical conceits of others. I am even so far gone of late in this way of thinking, that I have quitted several of the sublime notions I had got in their schools for vulgar opinions. And I give it you on my word; since this revolt from metaphysical notions to the plain dictates of nature and common sense, I find my understanding strangely enlightened, so that I can now easily comprehend a great many things which before were all mystery and riddle.

HYL. I am glad to find there was nothing in the accounts I heard of you.

PHIL. Pray, what were those?

HYL. You were represented, in last night's conversation, as one who maintained the most extravagant opinion that ever entered into the mind of man, to wit, that there is no such thing as *material substance* in the world.

PHIL. That there is no such thing as what *philosophers* call *material substance,* I am seriously persuaded: but, if I were made to see anything absurd or sceptical in this, I should then have the same reason to renounce this that I imagine I have now to reject the contrary opinion.

HYL. What! can anything be more fantastical, more repugnant to Common Sense, or a more manifest piece of Scepticism, than to believe there is no such thing as *matter?*

PHIL. Softly, good Hylas. What if it should prove that you, who hold there is, are, by virtue of that opinion, a greater sceptic, and maintain more paradoxes and repugnances to Common Sense, than I who believe no such thing?

HYL. You may as soon persuade me, the part is greater than the whole, as that, in order to avoid absurdity and Scepticism, I should ever be obliged to give up my opinion in this point.

PHIL. Well then, are you content to admit that opinion for true, which upon examination shall appear most agreeable to Common Sense, and remote from Scepticism?

HYL. With all my heart. Since you are for raising disputes about the plainest things in nature, I am content for once to hear what you have to say.

PHIL. Pray, Hylas, what do you mean by a *sceptic?*

HYL. I mean what all men mean—one that doubts of everything.

PHIL. He then who entertains no doubt concerning some particular point, with regard to that point cannot be thought a sceptic.

HYL. I agree with you.

PHIL. Whether doth doubting consist in embracing the affirmative or negative side of a question?

HYL. In neither; for whoever understands English cannot but know that *doubting* signifies a suspense between both.

PHIL. He then that denies any point, can no more be said to doubt of it, than he who affirmeth it with the same degree of assurance.

HYL. True.

PHIL. And, consequently, for such his denial is no more to be esteemed a sceptic than the other.

HYL. I acknowledge it.

PHIL. How cometh it to pass then, Hylas, that you pronounce me a *sceptic,* because I deny what you affirm, to wit, the existence of Matter? Since, for aught you can tell, I am as peremptory in my denial, as you in your affirmation.

HYL. Hold, Philonous, I have been a little out in my definition; but every false step a man makes in discourse is not to be insisted on. I said indeed that a *sceptic* was one who doubted of everything; but I should have added, or who denies the reality and truth of things.

PHIL. What things? Do you mean the principles and theorems of sciences? But these you know are universal intellectual notions, and consequently independent of Matter. The denial therefore of this doth not imply the denying them.

HYL. I grant it. But are there no other things? What think you of distrusting the senses, of denying the real existence of sensible things, or pretending to know nothing of them. Is not this sufficient to denominate a man a *sceptic?*

PHIL. Shall we therefore examine which of us it is that denies the reality of sensible things, or professes the greatest ignorance of them; since, if I take you rightly, he is to be esteemed the greatest *sceptic?*

HYL. That is what I desire.

PHIL. What mean you by Sensible Things?

HYL. Those things which are perceived by the senses. Can you imagine that I mean anything else?

PHIL. Pardon me, Hylas, if I am desirous clearly to apprehend your notions, since this may much shorten our inquiry. Suffer me then to ask you this farther question. Are those things only perceived by the senses which are perceived immediately? Or, may those things properly be said to be *sensible* which are perceived mediately, or not without the intervention of others?

HYL. I do not sufficiently understand you.

PHIL. In reading a book, what I immediately perceive are the letters; but mediately, or by means of these, are suggested to my mind the notions of God, virtue, truth, etc. Now, that the letters are truly sensible things, or perceived by sense, there is no doubt: but I would know whether you take the things suggested by them to be so too.

HYL. No, certainly: it were absurd to think God or *virtue* sensible things; though they may be signified and suggested to the mind by sensible marks, with which they have an arbitrary connexion.

PHIL. It seems then, that by *sensible things* you mean those only which can be perceived *immediately* by sense?

HYL. Right.

PHIL. Doth it not follow from this, that though I see one part of the sky red, and another blue, and that my reason doth thence evidently conclude there must be some cause of that diversity of colours, yet that cause cannot be said to be a sensible thing, or perceived by the sense of seeing?

HYL. It doth.

PHIL. In like manner, though I hear variety of sounds, yet I cannot be said to hear the causes of those sounds?

HYL. You cannot.

PHIL. And when by my touch I perceive a thing to be hot and heavy, I cannot say, with any truth or propriety, that I feel the cause of its heat or weight?

HYL. To prevent any more questions of this kind, I tell you once for all, that by *sensible things* I mean those only which are perceived by sense; and that in truth the senses perceive nothing which they do not perceive *immediately:* for they make no inferences. The deducing therefore of causes or occasions from effects and appearances, which alone are perceived by sense, entirely relates to reason.

PHIL. This point then is agreed between us—That *sensible things are those only which are immediately perceived by sense.* You will farther inform me, whether we immediately perceive by sight anything beside light, and colours, and figures; or by hearing, anything but sounds; by the palate, anything beside tastes; by the smell, beside odours; or by the touch, more than tangible qualities.

HYL. We do not.

PHIL. It seems, therefore, that if you take away all sensible qualities, there remains nothing sensible.

HYL. I grant it.

PHIL. Sensible things therefore are nothing else but so many sensible qualities, or combinations of sensible qualities?

HYL. Nothing else.

PHIL. Heat then is a sensible thing?

HYL. Certainly.

PHIL. Doth the *reality* of sensible things consist in being perceived? or, is it something distinct from their being perceived, and that bears no relation to the mind?

HYL. To *exist* is one thing, and to be *perceived* is another.

PHIL. I speak with regard to sensible things only. And of these I ask, whether by their real existence you mean a subsistence exterior to the mind, and distinct from their being perceived?

HYL. I mean a real absolute being, distinct from, and without any relation to, their being perceived.

PHIL. Heat therefore, if it be allowed a real being, must exist without the mind?

HYL. It must.

PHIL. Tell me, Hylas, is this real existence equally compatible to all degrees of heat, which we perceive; or is there any reason why we should attribute it to some, and deny it to others? And if there be, pray let me know that reason.

HYL. Whatever degree of heat we perceive by sense, we may be sure the same exists in the object that occasions it.

PHIL. What! the greatest as well as the least?

HYL. I tell you, the reason is plainly the same in respect of both. They are both perceived by sense; nay, the greater degree of heat is more sensibly perceived; and consequently, if there is any difference, we are more certain of its real existence than we can be of the reality of a lesser degree.

PHIL. But is not the most vehement and intense degree of heat a very great pain?

HYL. No one can deny it.

PHIL. And is any unperceiving thing capable of pain or pleasure?

HYL. No, certainly.

PHIL. Is your material substance a senseless being, or a being endowed with sense and perception?

HYL. It is senseless without doubt.

PHIL. It cannot therefore be the subject of pain?

HYL. By no means.

PHIL. Nor consequently of the greatest heat perceived by sense, since you acknowledge this to be no small pain?

HYL. I grant it.

PHIL. What shall we say then of your external object; is it a material Substance, or no?

HYL. It is a material substance with the sensible qualities inhering in it.

PHIL. How then can a great heat exist in it, since you own it cannot in a material substance? I desire you would clear this point.

HYL. Hold, Philonous, I fear I was out in yielding intense heat to be a pain. It should seem rather, that pain is something distinct from heat, and the consequence or effect of it.

PHIL. Upon putting your hand near the fire, do you perceive one simple uniform sensation, or two distinct sensations?

HYL. But one simple sensation.

PHIL. Is not the heat immediately perceived?

HYL. It is.

PHIL. And the pain?

HYL. True.

PHIL. Seeing therefore they are both immediately perceived at the same time, and the fire affects you only with one simple or uncompounded idea, it follows that this same simple idea is both the intense heat immediately perceived, and the pain; and, consequently, that the intense heat immediately perceived is nothing distinct from a particular sort of pain.

HYL. It seems so.

PHIL. Again, try in your thoughts, Hylas, if you can conceive a vehement sensation to be without pain or pleasure.

HYL. I cannot.

PHIL. Or can you frame to yourself an idea of sensible pain or pleasure in general, abstracted from every particular idea of heat, cold, tastes, smells? etc.

HYL. —I do not find that I can.

PHIL. Doth it not therefore follow, that sensible pain is nothing distinct from those sensations or ideas, in an intense degree?

HYL. It is undeniable; and, to speak the truth, I begin to suspect a very great heat cannot exist but in a mind perceiving it.

PHIL. What! are you then in that sceptical state of suspense, between affirming and denying?

HYL. I think I may be positive in the point. A very violent and painful heat cannot exist without the mind.

PHIL. It hath not therefore, according to you, any *real* being?

HYL. I own it.

PHIL. Is it therefore certain, that there is no body in nature really hot?

HYL. I have not denied there is any real heat in bodies. I only say, there is no such thing as an intense real heat.

PHIL. But, did you not say before that all degrees of heat were equally real; or, if there was any difference, that the greater were more undoubtedly real than the lesser?

HYL. True: but it was because I did not then consider the ground there is for distinguishing between them, which I now plainly see. And it is this: because intense heat is nothing else but a particular kind of painful sensation; and pain cannot exist but in a perceiving being; it follows that no intense heat can really exist in an unperceiving corporeal substance. But this is no reason why we should deny heat in an inferior degree to exist in such a substance.

PHIL. But how shall we be able to discern those degrees of heat which exist only in the mind from those which exist without it.

HYL. That is no difficult matter. You know the least pain cannot exist unperceived; whatever, therefore, degree of heat is a pain exists only in the mind. But, as for all other degrees of heat, nothing obliges us to think the same of them.

PHIL. I think you granted before that no unperceiving being was capable of pleasure, any more than of pain.

HYL. I did.

PHIL. And is not warmth, or a more gentle degree of heat than what causes uneasiness, a pleasure?

HYL. What then?

PHIL. Consequently, it cannot exist without the mind in an unperceiving substance, or body.

HYL. So it seems.

PHIL. Since therefore as well those degrees of heat that are not painful, as those that are, can exist only in a thinking substance; may we not conclude that external bodies are absolutely incapable of any degree of heat whatsoever?

HYL. On second thoughts, I do not think it so evident that warmth is a pleasure as that a great degree of heat is a pain.

PHIL. I do not pretend that warmth is as great pleasure as heat is a pain. But, if you grant it to be even a small pleasure, it serves to make good my conclusion.

HYL. I could rather call it an *indolence*. It seems to be nothing more than a privation of both pain and pleasure. And that such a quality or state as this may agree to an unthinking substance, I hope you will not deny.

PHIL. If you are resolved to maintain that warmth, or a gentle degree of heat, is no pleasure, I know not how to convince you otherwise than by appealing to your own sense. But what think you of cold?

HYL. The same that I do for heat. An intense degree of cold is a pain; for to feel a very great cold, is to perceive a great uneasiness: it cannot therefore exist without the mind; but a lesser degree of cold may, as well as a lesser degree of heat.

PHIL. Those bodies, therefore, upon whose application to our own, we perceive a moderate degree of heat, must be concluded to have a moderate degree of heat or warmth in them; and those, upon whose application we feel a like degree of cold, must be thought to have cold in them.

HYL. They must.

PHIL. Can any doctrine be true that necessarily leads a man into an absurdity?

HYL. Without doubt it cannot.

PHIL. Is it not an absurdity to think that the same thing should be at the same time both cold and warm?

HYL. It is.

PHIL. Suppose now one of your hands hot, and the other cold, and that they are both at once put into the same vessel of water, in an intermediate state; will not the water seem cold to one hand, and warm to the other?

HYL. It will.

PHIL. Ought we not therefore, by your principles, to conclude it is really both cold and warm at the same time, that is, according to your own concession, to believe an absurdity?

HYL. I confess it seems so.

PHIL. Consequently, the principles themselves are false, since you have granted that no true principle leads to an absurdity.

HYL. But, after all, can anything be more absurd than to say, *there is no heat in the fire?*

PHIL. To make the point still clearer; tell me whether, in two cases exactly alike, we ought not to make the same judgment?

HYL. We ought.

PHIL. When a pin pricks your finger, doth it not rend and divide the fibers of your flesh?

HYL. It does.

PHIL. And when a coal burns your finger, doth it any more?

HYL. It doth.

PHIL. Since, therefore, you neither judge the sensation itself occasioned by the pin, nor anything like it to be in the pin; you should not, conformably to what you have now granted, judge the sensation occasioned by the fire, or anything like it, to be in the fire.

HYL. Well, since it must be so, I am content to yield this point, and acknowledge that heat and cold are only sensations existing in our minds. But there still remain qualities enough to secure the reality of external things.

PHIL. But what will you say, Hylas, if it shall appear that this case is the same with regard to all other sensible qualities, and that they can no more be supposed to exist without the mind, than heat and cold?

HYL. Then indeed you will have done something to the purpose; but that is what I despair of seeing proved.

PHIL. Let us examine them in order. What think you of *tastes*—do they exist without the mind, or no?

HYL. Can any man in his senses doubt whether sugar is sweet, or wormwood bitter?

PHIL. Inform me, Hylas. Is a sweet taste a particular kind of pleasure or pleasant sensation, or is it not?

HYL. It is.

PHIL. And is not bitterness some kind of uneasiness or pain?

HYL. I grant it.

PHIL. If therefore sugar and wormwood are unthinking corporeal substances existing without the mind, how can sweetness and bitterness, that is, pleasure and pain, agree to them?

HYL. Hold, Philonous, I now see what it was deluded me all this time. You asked whether heat and cold, sweetness and bitterness, were not particular sorts of pleasure and pain; to which I answered simply, that they were. Whereas I should have thus distinguished:—those qualities, as perceived by us, are pleasures or pains; but not as existing in the external objects. We must not therefore conclude absolutely, that there is no heat in the fire, or sweetness in the sugar, but only that heat or sweetness, as perceived by us, are not in the fire or sugar. What say you to this?

PHIL. I say it is nothing to the purpose. Our discourse proceeded altogether concerning sensible things, which you defined to be, *the things we immediately perceive by our senses.* Whatever other qualities, therefore, you speak of, as distinct from these, I know nothing of them, neither do they all belong to the point in dispute. You may, indeed, pretend to have discovered certain qualities which you do not perceive, and assert those insensible qualities exist in fire and sugar. But what use can be made of this to your present purpose, I am at a loss to conceive. Tell me then once more, do you acknowledge that heat and cold, sweetness and bitterness (meaning those qualities which are perceived by the senses), do not exist without the mind?

HYL. I see it is to no purpose to hold out, so I give up the cause as to those mentioned qualities. Though I profess it sounds oddly, to say that sugar is not sweet.

PHIL. But, for your farther satisfaction, take this along with you: that which at other times seems sweet, shall, to a distempered palate, appear bitter. And, nothing can be plainer than that divers persons perceive different tastes in the same food; since that which one man delights in, another abhors. And how could this be, if the taste was something really inherent in the food?

HYL. I acknowledge I know not how.

PHIL. In the next place, *odours* are to be considered. And, with regard to these, I would fain know whether what hath been said of tastes doth not exactly agree to them? Are they not so many pleasing or displeasing sensations?

HYL. They are.

PHIL. Can you then conceive it possible that they should exist in an unperceiving thing?

HYL. I cannot.

PHIL. Or, can you imagine that filth and ordure affect those brute animals that feed on them out of choice, with the same smells which we perceive in them?

HYL. By no means.

PHIL. May we not therefore conclude of smells, as of the other forementioned qualities, that they cannot exist in any but a perceiving substance or mind?

HYL. I think so.

PHIL. Then as to *sounds,* what must we think of them: are they accidents really inherent in external bodies, or not?

HYL. That they inhere not in the sonorous bodies is plain from hence: because a bell struck in the exhausted receiver of an air-pump sends forth no sound. The air, therefore, must be thought the subject of sound.

PHIL. What reason is there for that, Hylas?

HYL. Because, when any motion is raised in the air, we perceive a sound greater or lesser, according to the air's motion; but without some motion in the air, we never hear any sound at all.

PHIL. And granting that we never hear a sound but when some motion is produced in the air, yet I do not see how you can infer from thence, that the sound itself is in the air.

HYL. It is this very motion in the external air that produces in the mind the sensation of *sound*. For, striking on the drum of the ear, it causeth a vibration, which by the auditory nerves being communicated to the brain, the soul is thereupon affected with the sensation called *sound*.

PHIL. What! is sound then a sensation?

HYL. I tell you, as perceived by us, it is a particular sensation in the mind.

PHIL. And can any sensation exist without the mind?

HYL. No, certainly.

PHIL. How then can sound, being a sensation, exist in the air, if by the *air* you mean a senseless substance existing without the mind?

HYL. You must distinguish, Philonous, between sound as it is perceived by us, and as it is in itself; or (which is the same thing) between the sound we immediately perceive, and that which exists without us. The former, indeed, is a particular kind of sensation, but the latter is merely a vibrative or undulatory motion in the air.

PHIL. I thought I had already obviated that distinction, by the answer I gave when you were applying it in a like case before. But, to say no more of that, are you sure then that sound is really nothing but motion?

HYL. I am.

PHIL. Whatever therefore agrees to real sound, may with truth be attributed to motion?

HYL. It may.

PHIL. It is then good sense to speak of *motion* as of a thing that is *loud, sweet, acute, or grave*.

HYL. I see you are resolved not to understand me. Is it not evident those accidents or modes belong only to sensible sound, or *sound* in the common acceptation of the word, but not to *sound* in the real and philosophic sense; which, as I just now told you, is nothing but a certain motion of the air?

PHIL. It seems then there are two sorts of sound—the one vulgar, or that which is heard, the other philosophical and real?

HYL. Even so.

PHIL. And the latter consists in motion?

HYL. I told you so before.

PHIL. Tell me, Hylas, to which of the senses, think you, the idea of motion belongs? to the hearing?

HYL. No, certainly; but to the sight and touch.

PHIL. It should follow then, that, according to you, real sounds may possibly be *seen* or *felt*, but never *heard*.

HYL. Look you, Philonous, you may, if you please, make a jest of my opinion, but that will not alter the truth of things. I own, indeed, the inferences you draw me into sound something oddly; but common language, you know, is framed by, and for the use of the vulgar: we must not therefore wonder if expressions adapted to exact philosophic notions seem uncouth and out of the way.

PHIL. Is it come to that? I assure you, I imagine myself to have gained no small point, since you make so light of departing from common phrases and opinions; it being a main part of our inquiry, to examine whose notions are widest of the common road, and most repugnant to the general sense of the world. But, can you think it no more than a philosophical paradox, to say that *real sounds are never heard*, and that the idea of them is obtained by some other sense? And is there nothing in this contrary to nature and the truth of things?

HYL. To deal ingenuously, I do not like it. And, after the concessions already made, I had as well grant that sounds too have no real being without the mind.

PHIL. And I hope you will make no difficulty to acknowledge the same of *colours*.

HYL. Pardon me: the case of colours is very different. Can anything be plainer than that we see them on the objects?

PHIL. The objects you speak of are, I suppose, corporeal Substances existing without the mind?

HYL. They are.

PHIL. And have true and real colours inhering in them?

HYL. Each visible object hath that colour which we see in it.

PHIL. How! is there anything visible but what we perceive by sight?

HYL. There is not.

PHIL. And, do we perceive anything by sense which we do not perceive immediately?

HYL. How often must I be obliged to repeat the same thing? I tell you, we do not.

PHIL. Have patience, good Hylas; and tell me once more, whether there is anything immediately perceived by the senses, except sensible qualities. I know you asserted there was not; but I would now be informed, whether you still persist in the same opinion.

HYL. I do.

PHIL. Pray, is your corporeal substance either a sensible quality, or made up of sensible qualities?

HYL. What a question that is! who ever thought it was?

PHIL. My reason for asking was, because in saying, *each visible object hath that colour which we see in it,* you make visible objects to be corporeal substances; which implies either that corporeal substances are sensible qualities, or else that there is something beside sensible qualities perceived by sight: but, as this point was formerly agreed between us, and is still maintained by you, it is a clear consequence, that your *corporeal substance* is nothing distinct from *sensible qualities*.

HYL. You may draw as many absurd consequences as you please, and endeavour to perplex the plainest things; but you shall never persuade me out of my senses. I clearly understand my own meaning.

PHIL. I wish you would make me understand it too. But, since you are unwilling to have your notion of corporeal substance examined, I shall urge that point no farther. Only be pleased to let me know, whether the same colours which we see exist in external bodies, or some other.

HYL. The very same.

PHIL. What! are then the beautiful red and purple we see on yonder clouds really in them? Or do you imagine they have in themselves any other form than that of a dark mist or vapour?

HYL. I must own, Philonous, those colours are not really in the clouds as they seem to be at this distance. They are only apparent colours.

PHIL. *Apparent* call you them? how shall we distinguish these apparent colours from real?

HYL. Very easily. Those are to be thought apparent which, appearing only at a distance, vanish upon a nearer approach.

PHIL. And those, I suppose, are to be thought real which are discovered by the most near and exact survey.

HYL. Right.

PHIL. Is the nearest and exactest survey made by the help of a microscope, or by the naked eye?

HYL. By a microscope, doubtless.

PHIL. But a microscope often discovers colours in an object different from those perceived by the unassisted sight. And, in case we had microscopes magnifying to any assigned degree, it is certain that no object whatsoever, viewed through them, would appear in the same colour which it exhibits to the naked eye.

HYL. And what will you conclude from all this? You cannot argue that there are really and naturally no colours on objects: because by artificial managements they may be altered, or made to vanish.

PHIL. I think it may evidently be concluded from your own concessions, that all the colours we see with our naked eyes are only apparent as those on the clouds, since they vanish upon a more close and accurate inspection which is afforded us by a microscope. Then, as to what you say by way of prevention: I ask you whether the real and natural state of an object is better discovered by a very sharp and piercing sight, or by one which is less sharp?

HYL. By the former without doubt.

PHIL. Is it not plain from *Dioptrics* that microscopes make the sight more penetrating, and represent objects as they would appear to the eye in case it were naturally endowed with a most exquisite sharpness?

HYL. It is.

PHIL. Consequently the microscopical representation is to be thought that which best sets forth the real nature of the thing, or what it is in itself. The colours, therefore, by it perceived are more genuine and real than those perceived otherwise.

HYL. I confess there is something in what you say.

PHIL. Besides, it is not only possible but manifest, that there actually are animals whose eyes are by nature framed to perceive those things which by reason of their minuteness escape our sight. What think you of those inconceivably small animals perceived by glasses? must we suppose they are all stark blind? Or, in case they see, can it be imagined their sight hath not the same use in preserving their bodies from injuries, which appears in that of all other animals? And if it hath, is it not evident they must see particles less than their own bodies; which will present them with a far different view in each object from that which strikes our senses? Even our own eyes do not always represent objects to us after the same manner. In the jaundice every one knows that all things seem yellow. Is it not therefore highly probable those animals in whose eyes we discern a very different texture from that of ours, and whose bodies abound with different texture from that of ours, and whose bodies abound with different humours, do not see the same colours in every object that we do? From all which, should it not seem to follow that all colours are equally apparent, and that none of those which we perceive are really inherent in any outward object?

HYL. It should.

PHIL. The point will be past all doubt, if you consider that, in case colours were real properties or affections inherent in external bodies, they could admit of no alteration without some change wrought in the very bodies themselves: but, is it not evident from what hath been said that, upon the use of microscopes, upon a change happening in the humours of the eye, or a variation of distance, without any manner of real alteration in the thing itself, the colours of any object are either changed, or totally disappear? Nay, all other circumstances remaining the same, change but the situation of some objects, and they shall present different colours to the eye. The same thing happens upon viewing an object in various degrees of light. And what is more known than that the same bodies appear differently coloured by candle-light from what they do in the open day? Add to these the experiment of a prism which, separating the heterogeneous rays of light, alters the colour of any object, and will cause the whitest to appear of a deep blue or red to the naked eye. And now tell me whether you are still of opinion that every body hath its true real colour inhering in it; and, if you think it hath, I would fain know farther from you, what certain distance and position of the object, what peculiar texture and formation of the eye, what degree or kind of light is necessary for ascertaining that true colour, and distinguishing it from apparent ones.

HYL. I own myself entirely satisfied, that they are all equally apparent, and that there is no such thing as colour really inhering in external bodies, but that it is altogether in the light. And what confirms me in this opinion is, that in proportion to the light colours are still more or less vivid; and if there be no light, then are there no colours perceived. Besides, allowing there are colours on external objects, yet, how is it possible for us to perceive them? For no external body affects the mind, unless it acts first on our organs of sense. But the only action of bodies is motion; and motion cannot be communicated otherwise than by impulse. A distant object therefore cannot act on the eye; nor consequently make itself or its properties perceivable to the soul. Whence it plainly follows that it is immediately some contiguous substance, which, operating on the eye, occasions a perception of colours: and such is light.

PHIL. How! is light then a substance?

HYL. I tell you, Philonous, external light is nothing but a thin fluid substance, whose minute particles being agitated with a brisk motion, and in various manners reflected from the different surfaces of outward objects to the eyes, communicate different motions to the optic nerves; which, being propagated to the brain, cause therein various impressions; and these are attended with the sensations of red, blue, yellow, etc.

PHIL. It seems then the light doth no more than shake the optic nerves.

HYL. Nothing else.

PHIL. And consequent to each particular motion of the nerves, the mind is affected with a sensation, which is some particular colour.

HYL. Right.

PHIL. And these sensations have no existence without the mind.

HYL. They have not.

PHIL. How then do you affirm that colours are in the light; since by *light* you understand a corporeal substance external to the mind?

HYL. Light and colours, as immediately perceived by us, I grant cannot exist without the mind. But in themselves they are only the motions and configurations of certain insensible particles of matter.

PHIL. Colours then, in the vulgar sense, or taken for the immediate objects of sight, cannot agree to any but a perceiving substance.

HYL. That is what I say.

PHIL. Well then, since you give up the point as to those sensible qualities which are alone thought colours by all mankind beside, you may hold what you please with regard to those invisible ones of the philosophers. It is not my business to dispute about *them;* only I would advise you to bethink yourself, whether, considering the inquiry we are upon, it be prudent for you to affirm—*the red and blue which we see are not real colours, but certain unknown motions and figures which no man ever did or can see are truly so.* Are not these shocking notions, and are not they subject to as many ridiculous inferences, as those you were obliged to renounce before in the case of sounds?

HYL. I frankly own, Philonous, that it is in vain to stand out any longer. Colours, sounds, tastes, in a word all those termed *secondary qualities,* have certainly no existence without the mind. But by this acknowledgement I must not be supposed to derogate anything from the reality of Matter, or external objects; seeing it is no more than several philosophers maintain, who nevertheless are the farthest imaginable from denying Matter. For the clearer understanding of this, you must know sensible qualities are by philosophers divided into *Primary* and *Secondary*. The former are Extension, Figure, Solidity, Gravity, Motion, and Rest; and these they hold exist really in bodies. The latter are those above enumerated; or, briefly, *all sensible qualities beside the Primary;* which they assert are only so many sensations or ideas existing nowhere but in the mind. But all this, I doubt not, you are apprised of. For my part, I have been a long time sensible there was such an opinion current among philosophers, but was never thoroughly convinced of its truth until now.

PHIL. You are still then of opinion that *extension* and *figures* are inherent in external unthinking substances?

HYL. I am.

PHIL. But what if the same arguments which are brought against Secondary Qualities will hold good against these also?

HYL. Why then I shall be obliged to think, they too exist only in the mind.

PHIL. Is it your opinion the very figure and extension which you perceive by sense exist in the outward object or material substance?

HYL. It is.

PHIL. Have all other animals as good grounds to think the same of the figure and extension which they see and feel?

HYL. Without doubt, if they have any thought at all.

PHIL. Answer me, Hylas. Think you the senses were bestowed upon all animals for their preservation and well-being in life? or were they given to men alone for this end?

HYL. I make no question but they have the same use in all other animals.

PHIL. If so, is it not necessary they should be enabled by them to perceive their own limbs, and those bodies which are capable of harming them?

HYL. Certainly.

PHIL. A mite therefore must be supposed to see his own foot, and things equal or even less than it, as bodies of some considerable dimension; though at the same time they appear to you scarce discernible, or at best as so many visible points?

HYL. I cannot deny it.

PHIL. And to creatures less than the mite they will seem yet larger?

HYL. They will.

PHIL. Insomuch that what you can hardly discern will to another extremely minute animal appear as some huge mountain?

HYL. All this I grant.

PHIL. Can one and the same thing be the same time in itself of different dimensions?

HYL. That were absurd to imagine.

PHIL. But, from what you have laid down it follows that both the extension by you perceived, and that perceived by the mite itself, as likewise all those perceived by lesser animals, are each of them the true extension of the mite's foot; that is to say, by your own principles you are led into an absurdity.

HYL. There seems to be some difficulty in the point.

PHIL. Again, have you not acknowledged that no real inherent property of any object can be changed without some change in the thing itself?

HYL. I have.

PHIL. But, as we approach to or recede from an object, the visible extension varies, being at one distance ten or a hundred times greater than at another. Doth it not therefore follow from hence likewise that it is not really inherent in the object?

HYL. I own I am at a loss what to think.

PHIL. Your judgment will soon be determined, if you will venture to think as freely concerning this quality as you have done concerning the rest. Was it not admitted as a good argument, that neither heat nor cold was in the water, because it seemed warm to one hand and cold to the other?

HYL. It was.

PHIL. Is it not the very same reasoning to conclude, there is no extension or figure in an object, because to one eye it shall seem little, smooth, and round, when at the same time it appears to the other, great, uneven, and angular?

HYL. The very same. But does this latter fact ever happen?

PHIL. You may at any time make the experiment, by looking with one eye bare, and with the other through a microscope.

HYL. I know not how to maintain it; and yet I am loath to give up *extension,* I see so many odd consequences following upon such a concession.

PHIL. Odd, say you? After the concessions already made, I hope you will stick at nothing for its oddness. But, on the other hand, should it not seem very odd, if the general reasoning which includes all other sensible qualities did not also include extension? If it be allowed that no idea, nor anything like an idea, can exist in an unperceiving substance, then surely it follows that no figure, or mode of extension, which we can either perceive, or imagine, or have any idea of, can be really inherent in Matter; not to mention the peculiar difficulty there must be in conceiving a material substance, prior to and distinct from extension, to be the *substratum* of extension. Be the sensible quality what it will—figure, or sound, or colour, it seems alike impossible it should subsist in that which doth not perceive it.

HYL. I give up the point for the present, reserving still a right to retract my opinion, in case I shall hereafter discover any false step in my progress to it.

PHIL. That is a right you cannot be denied. Figures and extension being despatched, we proceed next to *motion.* Can a real motion in any external body be at the same time both very swift and very slow?

HYL. It cannot.

PHIL. Is not the motion of a body swift in a reciprocal proportion to the time it takes up in describing any given space? Thus a body that describes a mile in an hour moves three times faster than it would in case it described only a mile in three hours.

HYL. I agree with you.

PHIL. And is not time measured by the succession of ideas in our minds?

HYL. It is.

PHIL. And is it not possible ideas should succeed one another twice as fast in your mind as they do in mine, or in that of some spirit of another kind?

HYL. I own it.

PHIL. Consequently the same body may to another seem to perform its motion over any space in half the time that it doth to you. And the same reasoning will hold as to any other proportion: that is to say, according to your principles (since the motions perceived are both really in the object) it is possible one and the same body shall be really moved the same way at once, both very swift and very slow. How is this consistent either with common sense, or with what you just now granted?

HYL. I have nothing to say to it.

PHIL. Then as for *solidity;* either you do not mean any sensible quality by that word, and so it is beside our inquiry: or if you do, it must be either hardness or resistance. But both the one and the other are plainly relative to our senses: it being evident that what seems hard to one animal may appear soft to another, who hath greater force and firmness of limbs. Nor is it less plain that the resistance I feel is not in the body.

HYL. I own the very *sensation* of resistance, which is all you immediately perceive, is not in the body; but the *cause* of that sensation is.

PHIL. But the causes of our sensations are not

things immediately perceived, and therefore are not sensible. This point I thought had been already determined.

HYL. I own it was; but you will pardon me if I seem a little embarrassed: I know not how to quit my old notions.

PHIL. To help you out, do but consider that if *extension* be once acknowledged to have no existence without the mind, the same must necessarily be granted of motion, solidity, and gravity; since they all evidently suppose extension. It is therefore superfluous to inquire particularly concerning each of them. In denying extension, you have denied them all to have any real existence.

HYL. I wonder, Philonous, if what you say be true, why those philosophers who deny the Secondary Qualities any real existence should yet attribute it to the Primary. If there is no difference between them, how can this be accounted for?

PHIL. It is not my business to account for every opinion of the philosophers. But, among other reasons which may be assigned for this, it seems probable that pleasure and pain being rather annexed to the former than the latter may be one. Heat and cold, tastes and smells, have something more vividly pleasing or disagreeable than the ideas of extension, figure, and motion affect us with. And, it being too visibly absurd to hold that pain or pleasure can be in an unperceiving Substance, men are more easily weaned from believing the external existence of the Secondary than the Primary Qualities. You will be satisfied there is something in this, if you recollect the difference you made between an intense and more moderate degree of heat; allowing the one a real existence, while you denied it to the other. But, after all, there is no rational ground for that distinction; for, surely an indifferent sensation is as truly *a sensation* as one more pleasing or painful; and consequently should not any more than they be supposed to exist in an unthinking subject.

HYL. It is just come into my head, Philonous, that I have somewhere heard of a distinction between absolute and sensible extension. Now, though it be acknowledged that *great* and *small,* consisting merely in the relation which other extended beings have to the parts of our own bodies, do not really inhere in the substances themselves; yet nothing obliges us to hold the same with regard to *absolute extension,* which is something abstracted from *great* and *small,* from this or that particular magnitude or figure. So likewise as to motion; *swift* and *slow* are altogether relative to the succession of ideas in our own minds. But, it doth not follow, because those modifications of motion exist not without the mind, that therefore absolute motion abstracted from them doth not.

PHIL. Pray what is it that distinguishes one motion, or one part of extension, from another? Is it not something sensible, as some degree of swiftness or slowness, some certain magnitude or figure peculiar to each?

HYL. I think so.

PHIL. These qualities, therefore, stripped of all sensible properties, are without all specific and numerical differences, as the schools call them.

HYL. They are.

PHIL. That is to say, they are extension in general, and motion in general.

HYL. Let it be so.

PHIL. But it is a universally received maxim that *Everything which exists is particular.* How then can motion in general, or extension in general, exist in any corporeal substance?

HYL. I will take time to solve your difficulty.

PHIL. But I think the point may be speedily decided. Without doubt you can tell whether you are able to frame this or that idea. Now I am content to put our dispute on this issue. If you can frame in your thoughts a distinct *abstract idea* of motion or extension, divested of all those sensible modes, as swift and slow, great and small, round and square, and the like, which are acknowledged to exist only in the mind, I will then yield the point you contend for. But if you cannot, it will be unreasonable on your side to insist any longer upon what you have no notion of.

HYL. To confess ingenuously, I cannot.

PHIL. Can you even separate the ideas of extension and motion from the ideas of all those qualities which they who make the distinction term *secondary?*

HYL. What! is it not an easy matter to consider extension and motion by themselves, abstracted from all other sensible qualities? Pray how do the mathematicians treat of them?

PHIL. I acknowledge, Hylas, it is not difficult to form general propositions and reasonings about those qualities, without mentioning any other; and, in this sense, to consider or treat of them abstractedly. But, how doth it follow that, because I can pronounce the word *motion* by itself, I can form the idea of it in my mind exclusive of body? or, because theorems may be made of extension and figures, without any mention of *great* or *small*, or any other sensible mode of quality, that therefore it is possible such an abstract idea of extension, without any particular size or figure, or sensible quality, should be distinctly formed, and apprehended by the mind? Mathematicians treat of quantity, without regarding what other sensible qualities it is attended with, as being altogether indifferent to their demonstrations. But, when laying aside the words, they contemplate the bare ideas, I believe you will find, they are not the pure abstracted ideas of extension.

HYL. But what say you to *pure intellect?* May not abstracted ideas be framed by that faculty?

PHIL. Since I cannot frame abstract ideas at all, it is plain I cannot frame them by the help of *pure intellect;* whatsoever faculty you understand by those words. Besides, not to inquire into the nature of pure intellect and its spiritual objects, as *virtue, reason, God,* or the like, thus much seems manifest—that sensible things are only to be perceived by sense, or represented by the imagination. Figures, therefore, and extension, being originally perceived by sense, do not belong to pure intellect: but, for your farther satisfaction, try if you can frame the idea of any figure, abstracted from all particularities of size, or even from other sensible qualities.

HYL. Let me think a little—I do not find that I can.

PHIL. And can you think it possible that should really exist in nature which implies a repugnancy in its conception?

HYL. By no means.

PHIL. Since therefore it is impossible even for the mind to disunite the ideas of extension and motion from all other sensible qualities, doth it not follow, that where the one exist there necessarily the other exist likewise?

HYL. It should seem so.

PHIL. Consequently, the very same arguments which you admitted as conclusive against the Secondary Qualities are, without any farther application of force, against the Primary too. Besides, if you will trust your senses, is it not plain all sensible qualities coexist, or to them appear as being in the same place? Do they ever represent a motion, or figure, as being divested of all other visible and tangible qualities?

HYL. You need say no more on this head. I am free to own, if there be no secret error or oversight in our proceedings hitherto, that *all* sensible qualities are alike to be denied existence without the mind. But, my fear is that I have been too liberal in my former concessions, or overlooked some fallacy or other. In short, I did not take time to think.

PHIL. For that matter, Hylas, you may take what time you please in reviewing the progress of our inquiry. You are at liberty to recover any slips you might have made, or offer whatever you have omitted which makes for your first opinion.

HYL. One great oversight I take to be this—that I did not sufficiently distinguish the *object* from the *sensation*. Now, though this latter may not exist without the mind, yet it will not thence follow that the former cannot.

PHIL. What object do you mean? the object of the senses?

HYL. The same.

PHIL. It is then immediately perceived?

HYL. Right.

PHIL. Make me to understand the difference between what is immediately perceived and a sensation.

HYL. The sensation I take to be an act of the mind perceiving; besides which, there is something perceived; and this I call the *object*. For example, there is red and yellow on that tulip. But then the act of perceiving those colours is in me only, and not in the tulip.

PHIL. What tulip do you speak of? Is it that which you see?

HYL. The same.

PHIL. And what do you see beside colour, figure, and extension?

HYL. Nothing.

PHIL. What you would say then is that the red and yellow are coexistent with the extension; is it not?

HYL. That is not all; I would say they have a

real existence without the mind, in some unthinking substance.

PHIL. That the colours are really in the tulip which I see is manifest. Neither can it be denied that this tulip may exist independent of your mind or mine; but, that any immediate object of the senses—that is, any idea, or combination of ideas—should exist in an unthinking substance, or exterior to *all* minds, is in itself an evident contradiction. Nor can I imagine how this follows from what you said just now, to wit, that the red and yellow were on the tulip *you saw,* since you do not pretend to *see* that unthinking substance.

HYL. You have an artful way, Philonous, of diverting our inquiry from the subject.

PHIL. I see you have no mind to be pressed that way. To return then to your distinction between *sensation* and *object;* if I take you right, you distinguish in every perception two things, the one an action of the mind, the other not.

HYL. True.

PHIL. And this action cannot exist in, or belong to, any unthinking thing; but, whatever beside is implied in a perception may?

HYL. That is my meaning.

PHIL. So that if there was a perception without any act of the mind, it were possible such a perception should exist in an unthinking substance?

HYL. I grant it. But it is impossible there should be such a perception.

PHIL. When is the mind said to be active?

HYL. When it produces, puts an end to, or changes, anything.

PHIL. Can the mind produce, discontinue, or change anything, but by an act of the will?

HYL. It cannot.

PHIL. The mind therefore is to be accounted *active* in its perceptions so far forth as *volition* is included in them?

HYL. It is.

PHIL. In plucking this flower I am active; because I do it by the motion of my hand, which was consequent upon my volition; so likewise in applying it to my nose. But is either of these smelling?

HYL. No.

PHIL. I act too in drawing the air through my nose; because my breathing so rather than otherwise is the effect of my volition. But neither can this be called *smelling*: for, if it were, I should smell every time I breathed in that manner?

HYL. True.

PHIL. Smelling then is somewhat consequent to all this?

HYL. It is.

PHIL. But I do not find my will concerned any farther. Whatever more there is—as that I perceive such a particular smell, or any smell at all—this is independent of my will, and therein I am altogether passive. Do you find it otherwise with you, Hylas?

HYL. No, the very same.

PHIL. Then, as to seeing, is it not in your power to open your eyes, or keep them shut; to turn them this or that way?

HYL. Without doubt.

PHIL. But, doth it in like manner depend on *your* will that in looking on this flower you perceive *white* rather than any other colour? Or, directing your open eyes towards yonder part of the heaven, can you avoid seeing the sun? Or is light or darkness the effect of your volition?

HYL. No, certainly.

PHIL. You are then in these respects altogether passive?

HYL. I am.

PHIL. Tell me now, whether *seeing* consists in perceiving light and colours, or in opening and turning the eyes?

HYL. Without doubt, in the former.

PHIL. Since therefore you are in the very perception of light and colours altogether passive, what is become of that action you were speaking of as an ingredient in every sensation? And, doth it not follow from your own concessions, that the perception of light and colours, including no action in it, may exist in an unperceiving substance? And is not this a plain contradiction?

HYL. I know not what to think of it.

PHIL. Besides, since you distinguish the *active* and *passive* in every perception, you must do it in that of pain. But how is it possible that pain, be it as little active as you please, should exist in an unperceiving substance? In short, do but consider the point, and then confess ingenuously, whether light and colours, tastes, sounds, etc. are not all equally passions or sensations in the soul. You may indeed call them *external objects,* and give them in words what subsistence you please. But, examine your own thoughts, and then tell me whether it be not as I say?

HYL. I acknowledge, Philonous, that, upon a fair observation of what passes in my mind, I can discover nothing else but that I am a thinking being, affected with variety of sensations; neither is it possible to conceive how a sensation should exist in an unperceiving substance.—But then, on the other hand, when I look on sensible things in a different view, considering them as so many modes and qualities, I find it necessary to suppose a *material substratum,* without which they cannot be conceived to exist.

PHIL. *Material substratum* call you it? Pray, by which of your senses came you acquainted with that being?

HYL. It is not itself sensible; its modes and qualities only being perceived by the senses.

PHIL. I presume then it was by reflexion and reason you obtained the idea of it?

HYL. I do not pretend to any proper positive *idea* of it. However, I conclude it exists, because qualities cannot be conceived to exist without a support.

PHIL. It seems then you have only a relative *notion* of it, or that you conceive it not otherwise than by conceiving the relation it bears to sensible qualities?

HYL. Right.

PHIL. Be pleased therefore to let me know wherein that relation consists.

HYL. Is it not sufficiently expressed in the term *substratum,* or *substance?*

PHIL. If so, the word *substratum* should import that it is spread under the sensible qualities or accidents?

HYL. True.

PHIL. And consequently under extension?

HYL. I own it.

PHIL. It is therefore somewhat in its own nature entirely distinct from extension?

HYL. I tell you, extension is only a mode, and Matter is something that supports modes. And is it not evident the thing supported is different from the thing supporting?

PHIL. So that something distinct from, and exclusive of, extension is supposed to be the *substratum* of extension?

HYL. Just so.

PHIL. Answer me, Hylas. Can a thing be spread without extension? or is not the idea of extension necessarily included in *spreading?*

HYL. It is.

PHIL. Whatsoever therefore you suppose spread under anything must have in itself an extension distinct from the extension of that thing under which it is spread?

HYL. It must.

PHIL. Consequently, every corporeal substance, being the *substratum* of extension, must have in itself another extension, by which it is qualified to be a *substratum:* and so on to infinity? And I ask whether this be not absurd in itself, and repugnant to what you granted just now, to wit, that the *substratum* was something distinct from and exclusive of extension?

HYL. Aye but, Philonous, you take me wrong. I do not mean that Matter is *spread* in a gross literal sense under extension. The word *substratum* is used only to express in general the same thing with *substance*.

PHIL. Well then, let us examine the relation implied in the term *substance.* Is it not that it stands under accidents?

HYL. The very same.

PHIL. But, that one thing may stand under or support another, must it not be extended?

HYL. It must.

PHIL. Is not therefore this supposition liable to the same absurdity with the former?

HYL. You still take things in a strict literal sense. That is not fair, Philonous.

PHIL. I am not for imposing any sense on your words: you are at liberty to explain them as you please. Only, I beseech you, make me understand something by them. You tell me Matter supports or stands under accidents. How! is it as your legs support your body?

HYL. No; that is the literal sense.

PHIL. Pray let me know any sense, literal or not literal, that you understand it in.—How long must I wait for an answer, Hylas?

HYL. I declare I know not what to say. I once thought I understood well enough what was meant by Matter's supporting accidents. But now, the more I think on it the less can I comprehend it: in short I find that I know nothing of it.

PHIL. It seems then you have no idea at all, neither relative nor positive, of Matter; you know neither what it is in itself, nor what relation it bears to accidents?

HYL. I acknowledge it.

PHIL. And yet you asserted that you could not

conceive how qualities or accidents should really exist, without conceiving at the same time a material support of them?

HYL. I did.

PHIL. That is to say, when you conceive the *real* existence of qualities, you do withal conceive Something which you cannot conceive?

HYL. It was wrong, I own. But still I fear there is some fallacy or other. Pray what think you of this? It is just come into my head that the ground of all our mistake lies in your treating of each quality by itself. Now, I grant that each quality cannot singly subsist without the mind. Colour cannot without extension, neither can figure without some other sensible quality. But, as the several qualities united or blended together form entire sensible things, nothing hinders why such things may not be supposed to exist without the mind.

PHIL. Either, Hylas, you are jesting, or have a very bad memory. Though indeed we went through all the qualities by name one after another, yet my arguments, or rather your concessions, nowhere tended to prove that the Secondary Qualities did not subsist each alone by itself; but, that they were not *at all* without the mind. Indeed, in treating of figure and motion we concluded they could not exist without the mind, because it was impossible even in thought to separate them from all secondary qualities, so as to conceive them existing by themselves. But then this was not the only argument made use of upon that occasion. But (to pass by all that hath been hitherto said, and reckon it for nothing, if you will have it so) I am content to put the whole upon this issue. If you can conceive it possible for any mixture or combination of qualities, or any sensible object whatever, to exist without the mind, then I will grant it actually to be so.

HYL. If it comes to that the point will soon be decided. What more easy than to conceive a tree or house existing by itself, independent of, and unperceived by, any mind whatsoever? I do at this present time conceive them existing after that manner.

PHIL. How say you, Hylas, can you see a thing which is at the same time unseen?

HYL. No, that were a contradiction.

PHIL. Is it not as great a contradiction to talk of *conceiving* a thing which is *unconceived?*

HYL. It is.

PHIL. The tree or house therefore which you think of is conceived by you?

HYL. How should it be otherwise?

PHIL. And what is conceived is surely in the mind?

HYL. Without question, that which is conceived is in the mind.

PHIL. How then came you to say, you conceived a house or tree existing independent and out of all minds whatsoever?

HYL. That was I own an oversight; but stay, let me consider what led me into it.—It is a pleasant mistake enough. As I was thinking of a tree in a solitary place, where no one was present to see it, methought that was to conceive a tree as existing unperceived or unthought of; not considering that I myself conceived it all the while. But now I plainly see that all I can do is to frame ideas in my own mind. I may indeed conceive in my own thoughts the idea of a tree, or a house, or a mountain, but that is all. And this is far from proving that I can conceive them *existing out of the minds of all Spirits*.

PHIL. You acknowledge then that you cannot possibly conceive how any one corporeal sensible thing should exist otherwise than in a mind?

HYL. I do.

PHIL. And yet you will earnestly contend for the truth of that which you cannot so much as conceive?

HYL. I profess I know not what to think; but still there are some scruples remain with me. Is it not certain I *see things at a distance?* Do we not perceive the stars and moon, for example, to be a great way off? Is not this, I say, manifest to the senses?

PHIL. Do you not in a dream too perceive those or the like objects?

HYL. I do.

PHIL. Do you not dream too perceive those or the like objects?

HYL. I do.

PHIL. And have they not then the same appearance of being distant?

HYL. They have.

PHIL. But you do not thence conclude the apparitions in a dream to be without the mind?

HYL. By no means.

PHIL. You ought not therefore to conclude that

sensible objects are without the mind, from their appearance, or manner wherein they are perceived.

HYL. I acknowledge it. But doth not my sense deceive me in those cases?

PHIL. By no means. The idea or thing which you immediately perceive, neither sense nor reason informs you that *it* actually exists without the mind. By sense you only know that you are affected with such certain sensations of light and colours, etc. And these you will not say are without the mind.

HYL. True: but, beside all that, do you not think the sight suggests something of *outness* or *distance?*

PHIL. Upon approaching a distant object, do the visible size and figure change perpetually, or do they appear the same at all distances?

HYL. They are in a continual change.

PHIL. Sight therefore doth not suggest, or any way inform you, that the visible object you immediately perceive exists at a distance, or will be perceived when you advance farther onward; there being a continued series of visible objects succeeding each other during the whole time of your approach.

HYL. It doth not; but still I know, upon seeing an object, what object I shall perceive after having passed over a certain distance: no matter whether it be exactly the same or no: there is still something of distance suggested in the case.

PHIL. Good Hylas, do but reflect a little on the point, and then tell me whether there be any more in it than this: From the ideas you actually perceive by sight, you have by experience learned to collect what other ideas you will (according to the standing order of nature) be affected with, after such a certain succession of time and motion.

HYL. Upon the whole, I take it to be nothing else.

PHIL. Now, is it not plain that if we suppose a man born blind was on a sudden made to see, he could at first have no experience of what may be *suggested* by sight?

HYL. It is.

PHIL. He would not then, according to you, have any notion of distance annexed to the things he saw; but would take them for a new set of sensations, existing only in his mind?

HYL. It is undeniable.

PHIL. But, to make it still more plain: is not *distance* a line turned endwise to the eye?

HYL. It is.

PHIL. And can a line so situated be perceived by sight?

HYL. It cannot.

PHIL. Doth it not therefore follow that distance is not properly and immediately perceived by sight?

HYL. It should seem so.

PHIL. Again, is it your opinion that colours are at a distance?

HYL. It must be acknowledged they are only in the mind.

PHIL. But do not colours appear to the eye as coexisting in the same place with extension and figures?

HYL. They do.

PHIL. How can you then conclude from sight that figures exist without, when you acknowledge colours do not; the sensible appearance being the very same with regard to both?

HYL. I know not what to answer.

PHIL. But, allowing that distance was truly and immediately perceived by the mind, yet it would not thence follow it existed out of the mind. For, whatever is immediately perceived is an idea: and can any idea exist out of the mind?

HYL. To suppose that were absurd: but, inform me, Philonous, can we perceive or know nothing beside our ideas?

PHIL. As for the rational deducing of causes from effects, that is beside our inquiry. And, by the senses you can best tell whether you perceive anything which is not immediately perceived. And I ask you, whether the things immediately perceived are other than your own sensations or ideas? You have indeed more than once, in the course of this conversation, declared yourself on those points; but you seem, by this last question, to have departed from what you then thought.

HYL. To speak the truth, Philonous, I think there are two kinds of objects:—the one perceived immediately, which are likewise called *ideas;* the other are real things or external objects, perceived by the mediation of ideas, which are their images and representations. Now, I own ideas do not exist without the mind; but the latter sort of objects do. I am sorry I did not think of this distinction sooner; it would probably have cut short your discourse.

PHIL. Are those external objects perceived by sense, or by some other faculty?

HYL. They are perceived by sense.

PHIL. How! Is there anything perceived by sense which is not immediately perceived?

HYL. Yes, Philonous, in some sort there is. For example, when I look on a picture or statue of Julius Cæsar, I may be said after a manner to perceive him (though not immediately) by my senses.

PHIL. It seems then you will have our ideas, which alone are immediately perceived, to be pictures of external things: and that these also are perceived by sense, inasmuch as they have a conformity or resemblance to our ideas?

HYL. That is my meaning.

PHIL. And, in the same way that Julius Cæsar, in himself invisible, is nevertheless perceived by sight; real things, in themselves imperceptible, are perceived by sense.

HYL. In the very same.

PHIL. Tell me, Hylas, when you behold the picture of Julius Cæsar, do you see with your eyes any more than some colours and figures, with a certain symmetry and composition of the whole?

HYL. Nothing else.

PHIL. And would not a man who had never known anything of Julius Cæsar see as much?

HYL. He would.

PHIL. Consequently he hath his sight, and the use of it, in as perfect a degree as you?

HYL. I agree with you.

PHIL. Whence comes it then that your thoughts are directed to the Roman emperor, and his are not? This cannot proceed from the sensations or ideas of sense by you then perceived; since you acknowledge you have no advantage over him in that respect. It should seem therefore to proceed from reason and memory: should it not?

HYL. It should.

PHIL. Consequently, it will not follow from that instance that anything is perceived by sense which is not immediately perceived. Though I grant we may, in one acceptation, be said to perceive sensible things mediately by sense: that is, when, from a frequently perceived connexion, the immediate perception of ideas by one sense *suggests* to the mind others, perhaps belonging to another sense, which are wont to be connected with them. For instance, when I hear a coach drive along the streets, immediately I perceive only the sound; but, from the experience I have had that such a sound is connected with a coach, I am said to hear the coach. It is nevertheless evident that, in truth and strictness, nothing can be *heard* but *sound;* and the coach is not then properly perceived by sense, but suggested from experience. So likewise when we are said to see a red-hot bar of iron; the solidity and heat of the iron are not the objects of sight, but suggested to the imagination by the colour and figure which are properly perceived by that sense. In short, those things alone are actually and strictly perceived by any sense, which would have been perceived in case that same sense had then been first conferred on us. As for other things, it is plain they are only suggested to the mind by experience, grounded on former perceptions. But, to return to your comparison of Cæsar's picture, it is plain, if you keep to that, you must hold the real things, or archetypes of our ideas, are not perceived by sense, but by some internal faculty of the soul, as reason or memory. I would therefore fain know what arguments you can draw from reason for the existence of what you call *real things* or *material objects*. Or, whether you remember to have seen them formerly as they are in themselves; or, if you have heard or read of any one that did.

HYL. I see, Philonous, you are disposed to raillery; but that will never convince me.

PHIL. My aim is only to learn from you the way to come at the knowledge of *material beings*. Whatever we perceive is perceived immediately or mediately: by sense, or by reason and reflexion. But, as you have excluded sense, pray shew me what reason you have to believe their existence; or what *medium* you can possibly make use of to prove it, either to mine or your own understanding.

HYL. To deal ingenuously, Philonous, now I consider the point, I do not find I can give you any good reason for it. But, thus much seems pretty plain, that it is at least possible such things may really exist. And, as long as there is no absurdity in supposing them, I am resolved to believe as I did, till you bring good reasons to the contrary.

PHIL. What! Is it come to this, that you only

believe the existence of material objects, and that your belief is founded barely on the possibility of its being true? Then you will have me bring reasons against it: though another would think it reasonable the proof should lie on him who holds the affirmative. And, after all, this very point which you are now resolved to maintain, without any reason, is in effect what you have more than once during this discourse seen good reason to give up. But, to pass over all this; if I understand you rightly, you say our ideas do not exist without the mind, but that they are copies, images, or representations, of certain originals that do?

HYL. You take me right.

PHIL. They are then like external things?

HYL. They are.

PHIL. Have those things a stable and permanent nature, independent of our senses; or are they in a perpetual change, upon our producing any motions in our bodies—suspending, exerting, or altering, our faculties or organs of sense?

HYL. Real things, it is plain, have a fixed and real nature, which remains the same notwithstanding any change in our senses, or in the posture and motion of our bodies; which indeed may affect the ideas in our minds, but it were absurd to think they had the same effect on things existing without the mind.

PHIL. How then is it possible that things perpetually fleeting and variable as our ideas should be copies or images of anything fixed and constant? Or, in other words, since all sensible qualities, as size, figure, colour, etc., that is, our ideas, are continually changing, upon every alteration in the distance, medium, or instruments of sensation; how can any determinate material objects be properly represented or painted forth by several distinct things, each of which is so different from and unlike the rest? Or, if you say it resembles some one only of our ideas, how shall we be able to distinguish the true copy from all the false ones?

HYL. I profess, Philonous, I am at a loss. I know not what to say to this.

PHIL. But neither is this all. Which are material objects in themselves—perceptible or imperceptible?

HYL. Properly and immediately nothing can be perceived but ideas. All material things, therefore, are in themselves insensible, and to be perceived only by our ideas.

PHIL. Ideas then are sensible, and their archetypes or originals insensible?

HYL. Right.

PHIL. But how can that which is sensible be *like* that which is insensible? Can a real thing, in itself *invisible,* be like a *colour;* or a real thing, which is not *audible,* be like a *sound?* In a word, can anything be like a sensation or idea, but another sensation or idea?

HYL. I must own, I think not.

PHIL. Is it possible there should be any doubt on the point? Do you not perfectly know your own ideas?

HYL. I know them perfectly; since what I do not perceive or know can be no part of my idea.

PHIL. Consider, therefore, and examine them, and then tell me if there be anything in them which can exist without the mind: or if you can conceive anything like them existing without the mind.

HYL. Upon inquiry, I find it is impossible for me to conceive or understand how anything but an idea can be like an idea. And it is most evident that *no idea can exist without the mind.*

PHIL. You are therefore, by your principles, forced to deny the *reality* of sensible things; since you made it to consist in an absolute existence exterior to the mind. That is to say, you are a downright sceptic. So I have gained my point, which was to shew your principles led to Scepticism.

HYL. For the present I am, if not entirely convinced, at least silenced.

PHIL. I would fain know what more you would require in order to a perfect conviction. Have you not had the liberty of explaining yourself all manner of ways? Were any little slips in discourse laid hold and insisted on? Or were you not allowed to retract or reinforce anything you had offered, as best served your purpose? Hath not everything you could say been heard and examined with all the fairness imaginable? In a word, have you not in every point been convinced out of your own mouth? And, if you can at present discover any flaw in any of your former concessions, or think of any remaining subterfuge, any new distinction, colour, or comment whatsoever, why do you not produce it?

HYL. A little patience, Philonous. I am at present so amazed to see myself ensnared, and as it were imprisoned in the labyrinths you have drawn me into, that on the sudden it cannot be expected I should find my way out. You must give me time to look about me and recollect myself.

PHIL. Hark; is not this the college bell?

HYL. It rings for prayers.

PHIL. We will go in then, if you please, and meet here again to-morrow morning. In the meantime, you may employ your thoughts on this morning's discourse and try if you can find any fallacy in it, or invent any new means to extricate yourself.

HYL. Agreed.

. . . .

The Second Dialogue

PHILONOUS. Well then, are you at length satisfied that no sensible things have a real existence; and that you are in truth an arrant sceptic?

HYLAS. It is too plain to be denied.

PHIL. Look! are not the fields covered with a delightful verdure? Is there not something in the woods and groves, in the rivers and clear springs, that soothes, that delights, that transports the soul? At the prospect of the wide and deep ocean, or some huge mountain whose top is lost in the clouds, or of an old gloomy forest, are not our minds filled with a pleasing horror? Even in rocks and deserts is there not an agreeable wildness? How sincere a pleasure is it to behold the natural beauties of the earth! To preserve and renew our relish for them, is not the veil of night alternately drawn over her face, and doth she not change her dress with the seasons? How aptly are the elements disposed! What variety and use in the meanest productions of nature! What delicacy, what beauty, what contrivance, in animal and vegetable bodies! How exquisitely are all things suited, as well to their particular ends, as to constitute opposite parts of the whole! And, while they mutually aid and support, do they not also set off and illustrate each other? Raise now your thoughts from this ball of earth to all those glorious luminaries that adorn the high arch of heaven. The motion and situation of the planets, are they not admirable for use and order? Were those (miscalled *erratic*) globes once known to stray, in their repeated journeys through the pathless void? Do they not measure areas round the sun ever proportioned to the times? So fixed, so immutable are the laws by which the unseen Author of nature actuates the universe. How vivid and radiant is the lustre of the fixed stars! How magnificent and rich that negligent profusion with which they appear to be scattered throughout the whole azure vault! Yet, if you take the telescope, it brings into your sight a new host of stars that escape the naked eye. Here they seem contiguous and minute, but to a nearer view immense orbs of light at various distances, far sunk in the abyss of space. Now you must call imagination to your aid. The feeble narrow sense cannot descry innumerable worlds revolving round the central fires; and in those worlds the energy of an all-perfect Mind displayed in endless forms. But, neither sense nor imagination are big enough to comprehend the boundless extent, with all its glittering furniture. Though the labouring mind exert and strain each power to its utmost reach, there still stands out ungrasped a surplusage immeasurable. Yet all the vast bodies that compose this mighty frame, how distant and remote soever, are by some secret mechanism, some Divine art and force, linked in a mutual dependence and intercourse with each other; even with this earth, which was almost slipt from my thoughts and lost in the crowd of worlds. Is not the whole system immense, beautiful, glorious beyond expression and beyond thought! What treatment, then, do those philosophers deserve, who would deprive these noble and delightful scenes of all *reality?* How should those Principles be entertained that lead us to think all the visible beauty of the creation a false imaginary glare? To be plain, can you expect this Scepticism of yours will not be thought extravagantly absurd by all men of sense?

HYL. Other men may think as they please; but for your part you have nothing to reproach me with. My comfort is, you are as much a sceptic as I am.

PHIL. There, Hylas, I must beg leave to differ from you.

HYL. What! Have you all along agreed to the premises, and do you now deny the conclusion, and leave me to maintain those paradoxes by myself which you led me into? This surely is not fair.

PHIL. I deny that I agreed with you in those

notions that led to Scepticism. You indeed said the *reality* of sensible things consisted in an *absolute existence out of the minds of spirits,* or distinct from their being perceived. And pursuant to this notion of reality, *you* are obliged to deny sensible things any real existence: that is, according to your own definition, you profess yourself a sceptic. But I neither said nor thought the reality of sensible things was to be defined after that manner. To me it is evident, for the reasons you allow of, that sensible things cannot exist otherwise than in a mind or spirit. Whence I conclude, not that they have no real existence, but that, seeing they depend not on my thought, and have an existence distinct from being perceived by me, *there must be some other Mind wherein they exist.* As sure, therefore, as the sensible world really exists, so sure is there an infinite omnipresent Spirit who contains and supports it.

HYL. What! This is no more than I and all Christians hold; nay, and all others too who believe there is a God, and that He knows and comprehends all things.

PHIL. Aye, but here lies the difference. Men commonly believe that all things are known or perceived by God, because they believe the being of a God; whereas I, on the other side, immediately and necessarily conclude the being of a God, because all sensible things must be perceived by Him.

HYL. But, so long as we all believe the same thing, what matter is it how we come by that belief?

PHIL. But neither do we agree in the same opinion. For philosophers, though they acknowledge all corporeal beings to be perceived by God, yet they attribute to them an absolute subsistence distinct from their being perceived by any mind whatever; which I do not. Besides, is there no difference between saying, *There is a God, therefore He perceives all things;* and saying, *Sensible things do really exist; and, if they really exist, they are necessarily perceived by an infinite Mind: therefore there is an infinite Mind, or God?* This furnishes you with a direct and immediate demonstration, from the beauty and usefulness of the several parts of the creation, that it was the workmanship of God. But that—setting aside all help of astronomy and natural philosophy, all contemplation of the contrivance, order, and adjustment of things—an infinite Mind should be necessarily inferred from the bare *existence of the sensible world,* is an advantage to them only who have made this easy reflexion: That the sensible world is that which we perceive by our several senses; and that nothing is perceived by the senses beside ideas; and that no idea or archetype of an idea can exist otherwise than in a mind. You may now, without any laborious search into the sciences, without any subtlety of reason, or tedious length of discourse, oppose and baffle the most strenuous advocate for Atheism. Those miserable refuges, whether in an eternal succession of unthinking causes and effects, or in a fortuitous concourse of atoms; those wild imaginations of Vanini, Hobbes, and Spinoza: in a word, the whole system of Atheism, is it not entirely overthrown, by this single reflexion on the repugnancy included in supposing the whole, or any part, even the most rude and shapeless, of the visible world, to exist without a Mind? Let any one of those abettors of impiety but look into his own thoughts, and there try if he can conceive how so much as a rock, a desert, a chaos, or confused jumble of atoms; how anything at all, either sensible or imaginable, can exist independent of a Mind, and he need go no farther to be convinced of his folly. Can anything be fairer than to put a dispute on such an issue, and leave it to a man himself to see if he can conceive, even in thought, what he holds to be true in fact, and from a notional to allow it a real existence?

. . . .

[Phil] . . . —It is evident that the things I perceive are my own ideas, and that no idea can exist unless it be in a mind: nor is it less plain that these ideas or things by me perceived, either themselves or their archetypes, exist independently of *my* mind, since I know myself not to be their author, it being out of my power to determine at pleasure what particular ideas I shall be affected with upon opening my eyes or ears: they must therefore exist in some other Mind, whose Will it is they should be exhibited to me. The things, I say, immediately perceived are ideas or sensations, call them which you will. But how can any idea or sensation exist in, or be produced by, anything but a mind or spirit? This indeed is inconceivable. And to assert that which is inconceivable is to talk nonsense: is it not?

HYL. Without doubt.

PHIL. But, on the other hand, it is very conceivable that they should exist in and be produced by a Spirit; since this is no more than I daily experience in myself, inasmuch as I perceive numberless ideas; and, by an act of my will, can form a great variety of them, and raise them up in my imagination: though, it must be confessed, these creatures of the fancy are not altogether so distinct, so strong, vivid, and permanent, as those perceived by my senses—which latter are called *real things*. From all which I conclude, *there is a Mind which affects me every moment with all the sensible impressions I perceive*. And, from the variety, order, and manner of these, I conclude *the Author of them to be wise, powerful, and good, beyond comprehension*. Mark it well; I do not say, I see things by perceiving that which represents them in the intelligible Substance of God. This I do not understand; but I say, the things by me perceived are known by the understanding, and produced by the will of an infinite Spirit. And is not all this most plain and evident? Is there any more in it than what a little observation in our own minds, and that which passeth in them, not only enables us to conceive, but also obliges us to acknowledge?

. . . .

The Third Dialogue

PHILONOUS. Tell me, Hylas, what are the fruits of yesterday's meditation? Has it confirmed you in the same mind you were in at parting? or have you since seen cause to change your opinion?

HYLAS. Truly my opinion is that all our opinions are alike vain and uncertain. What we approve to-day, we condemn to-morrow. We keep a stir about knowledge, and spend our lives in the pursuit of it, when, alas! we know nothing all the while: nor do I think it possible for us ever to know anything in this life. Our faculties are too narrow and too few. Nature certainly never intended us for speculation.

PHIL. What! Say you we can know nothing, Hylas?

HYL. There is not that single thing in the world whereof we can know the real nature, or what it is in itself.

PHIL. Will you tell me I do not really know what fire or water is?

HYL. You may indeed know that fire appears hot, and water fluid; but this is no more than knowing what sensations are produced in your own mind, upon the application of fire and water to your organs of sense. Their internal constitution, their true and real nature, you are utterly in the dark as to *that*.

PHIL. Do I not know this to be a real stone that I stand on, and that which I see before my eyes to be a real tree?

HYL. *Know?* No, it is impossible you or any man alive should know it. All you know is, that you have such a certain idea or appearance in your mind. But what is this to the real tree or stone? I tell you that colour, figure, and hardness, which you perceive, are not the real natures of those things, or in the least like them. The same may be said of all other real things, or corporeal substances, which compose the world. They have none of them anything of themselves, like those sensible qualities by us perceived. We should not therefore pretend to affirm or know anything of them, as they are in their own nature.

PHIL. But surely, Hylas, I can distinguish gold, for example, from iron: and how could this be, if I knew not what either truly was?

HYL. Believe me, Philonous, you can only distinguish between your own ideas. That yellowness, that weight, and other sensible qualities, think you they are really in the gold? They are only relative to the senses, and have no absolute existence in nature. And in pretending to distinguish the species of real things, by the appearances in your mind, you may perhaps act as wisely as he that should conclude two men were of a different species, because their clothes were not of the same colour.

PHIL. It seems, then, we are altogether put off with the appearances of things, and those false ones too. The very meat I eat, and the cloth I wear, have nothing in them like what I see and feel.

HYL. Even so.

PHIL. But is it not strange the whole world should be thus imposed on, and so foolish as to believe their senses? And yet I know not how it is, but men eat, and drink, and sleep, and perform all the offices of life, as comfortably and conveniently as if they really knew the things they are conversant about.

HYL. They do so: but you know ordinary practice does not require a nicety of speculative knowledge. Hence the vulgar retain their mistakes, and for all that make a shift to bustle through the affairs of life. But philosophers know better things.

PHIL. You mean, they *know* that they *know nothing*.

HYL. That is the very top and perfection of human knowledge.

PHIL. But are you all this while in earnest, Hylas; and are you seriously persuaded that you know nothing real in the world? Suppose you are going to write, would you not call for pen, ink, and paper, like another man; and do you not know what it is you call for?

HYL. How often must I tell you, that I know not the real nature of any one thing in the universe? I may indeed upon occasion make use of pen, ink, and paper. But what any one of them is in its own true nature, I declare positively I know not. And the same is true with regard to every other corporeal thing. And, what is more, we are not only ignorant of the true and real nature of things, but even of their existence. It cannot be denied that we perceive such certain appearances or ideas; but it cannot be concluded from thence that bodies really exist. Nay, now I think on it, I must, agreeably to my former concessions, farther declare that it is impossible any *real* corporeal thing should exist in nature.

PHIL. You amaze me. Was ever anything more wild and extravagant than the notions you now maintain: and is it not evident you are led into all these extravagances by the belief of *material substance?* This makes you dream of those unknown natures in everything. It is this occasions your distinguishing between the reality and sensible appearances of things. It is to this you are indebted for being ignorant of what everybody else knows perfectly well. Nor is this all: you are not only ignorant of the true nature of everything, but you know not whether anything really exists, or whether there are any true natures at all; forasmuch as you attribute to your material beings an absolute or external existence, wherein you suppose their reality consists. And, as you are forced in the end to acknowledge such an existence means either a direct repugnancy, or nothing at all, it follows that you are obliged to pull down your own hypothesis of material Substance, and positively to deny the real existence of any part of the universe. And so you are plunged into the deepest and most deplorable scepticism that ever man was. Tell me, Hylas, is it not as I say?

HYL. I agree with you. *Material substance* was no more than an hypothesis; and a false and groundless one too. I will no longer spend my breath in defence of it. But whatever hypothesis you advance, or whatsoever scheme of things you introduce in its stead, I doubt not it will appear every whit as false: let me but be allowed to question you upon it. That is, suffer me to serve you in your own kind, and I warrant it shall conduct you through as many perplexities and contradictions, to the very same state of scepticism that I myself am in at present.

PHIL. I assure you, Hylas, I do not pretend to frame any hypothesis at all. I am of a vulgar cast, simple enough to believe my senses, and leave things as I find them. To be plain, it is my opinion that the real things are those very things I see, and feel, and perceive by my senses. These I know; and, finding they answer all the necessities and purposes of life, have no reason to be solicitous about any other unknown beings. A piece of sensible bread, for instance, would stay my stomach better than ten thousand times as much of that insensible, unintelligible, real bread you speak of. It is likewise my opinion that colours and other sensible qualities are on the objects. I cannot for my life help thinking that snow is white, and fire hot. You indeed, who by *snow* and *fire* mean certain external, unperceived, unperceiving substances, are in the right to deny whiteness or heat to be affections inherent in *them*. But I, who understand by those words the things I see and feel, am obliged to think like other folks. And, as I am no sceptic with regard to the nature of things, so neither am I as to their existence. That a thing should be really perceived by my senses, and at the same time not really exist, is to me a plain contradiction; since I cannot prescind or abstract, even in thought, the existence of a sensible thing from its being perceived. Wood, stones, fire, water, flesh, iron, and the like things, which I name and discourse of, are things that I know. And I should not have known them but that I perceived them by my senses; and things perceived by the senses are immediately perceived; and things immediately perceived are ideas; and ideas cannot exist without the mind; their existence therefore consists in being perceived; when, therefore, they are actually perceived there can be no doubt of their existence. Away then with all that scepticism, all those ridiculous philosophical doubts. What a jest is it for a philosopher to question the existence of sensible things, till he hath it proved to him from the veracity of God; or to pretend our knowledge in this point falls short of intuition or demonstration! I might as well doubt of my own being, as of the being of those things I actually see and feel.

HYL. Not so fast, Philonous: you say you cannot conceive how sensible things should exist without the mind. Do you not?

PHIL. I do.

HYL. Supposing you were annihilated, cannot you conceive it possible that things perceivable by sense may still exist?

PHIL. I can; but then it must be in another mind. When I deny sensible things an existence out of the mind, I do not mean my mind in particular, but all minds. Now, it is plain they have an existence exterior to my mind; since I find them by experience to be independent of it. There is therefore some other Mind wherein they exist, during the intervals between the times of my perceiving them: as likewise they did before my birth, and would do after my supposed annihilation. And, as the same is true with regard to all other finite created spirits, it necessarily follows there is an *omnipresent eternal Mind,* which knows and comprehends all things, and exhibits them to our view in such a manner, and according to such rules, as He Himself hath ordained, and are by us termed the *laws of nature.*

HYL. Answer me, Philonous. Are all our ideas perfectly inert beings? Or have they any agency included in them?

PHIL. They are altogether passive and inert.

HYL. And is not God an agent, a being purely active?

PHIL. I acknowledge it.

HYL. No idea therefore can be like unto, or represent the nature of God?

PHIL. It cannot.

HYL. Since therefore you have no *idea* of the mind of God, how can you conceive it possible that things should exist in His mind? Or, if you can conceive the mind of God, without having an idea of it, why may not I be allowed to conceive the existence of Matter, notwithstanding I have no idea of it?

PHIL. As to your first question: I own I have properly no *idea,* either of God or any other spirit; for these being active, cannot be represented by things perfectly inert, as our ideas are. I do nevertheless know that I, who am a spirit or thinking substance, exist as certainly as I know my ideas exist. Farther, I know what I mean by the terms *I* and *myself;* and I know this immediately or intuitively, though I do not perceive it as I perceive a triangle, a colour, or a sound. The Mind, Spirit, or Soul is that indivisible unextended thing which thinks, acts, and perceives. I say *indivisible,* because unextended; and *unextended,* because extended, figured, moveable things are ideas; and that which perceives ideas, which thinks and wills, is plainly itself no idea, nor like an idea. Ideas are things inactive, and perceived. And Spirits a sort of beings altogether different from them. I do not therefore say my soul is an idea, or like an idea. However, taking the word *idea* in a large sense, my soul may be said to furnish me with an idea, that is, an image or likeness of God—though indeed extremely inadequate. For, all the notion I have of God is obtained by reflecting on my own soul, heightening its powers, and removing its imperfections. I have, therefore, though not an inactive idea, yet in *myself* some sort of an active thinking image of the Deity. And, though I perceive Him not by sense, yet I have a notion of Him, or know Him by reflexion and reasoning. My own mind and my own ideas I have an immediate knowledge of; and, by the help of these, do mediately apprehend the possibility of the existence of other spirits and ideas. Farther, from my own being, and from the dependency I find in myself and my ideas, I do, by an act of reason, necessarily infer the existence of a God, and of all created things in the mind of God. So much for your first question. For the second: I suppose by this time you can answer it yourself. For you neither perceive Matter objectively, as you do an inactive being or idea; nor know it, as you do yourself, by a reflex act; neither do you mediately apprehend it by similitude of the one or the other; nor yet collect it by reasoning from that which you know immediately. All which makes the case of *Matter* widely different from that of the *Deity*.

HYL. You say your own soul supplies you with some sort of an idea or image of God. But, at the same time, you acknowledge you have, properly speaking, no *idea* of your own soul. You even affirm that spirits are a sort of beings altogether different from ideas. Consequently that no idea can be like a spirit. We have therefore no idea of any spirit. You admit nevertheless that there is spiritual Substance, although you have no idea of it; while you deny there can be such a thing as material Substance, because you have no notion or idea of it. Is this fair dealing? To *act* consistently, you must either admit Matter or reject Spirit. What say you to this?

PHIL. I say, in the first place, that I do not deny the existence of material substance, merely because I have no notion of it, but because the notion of it is inconsistent; or, in other words, because it is repugnant that there should be a notion of it. Many things, for aught I know, may exist, whereof neither I nor any other man hath or can have any idea or notion whatsoever. But then those things must be possible, that is, nothing inconsistent must be included in their definition. I say, secondly, that, although we believe things to exist which we do not perceive, yet we may not believe that any particular thing exists, without some reason for such belief: but I have no reason for believing the existence of Matter. I have no immediate intuition thereof: neither can I immediately from my sensations, ideas, notions, actions, or passions, infer an unthinking, unperceiving, inactive Substance—either by probable deduction, or necessary consequence. Whereas the being of my Self, that is, my own soul, mind, or thinking principle, I evidently know by reflexion. You will forgive me if I repeat the same things in answer to the same objections. In the very notion or definition of *material Substance,* there is included a manifest repugnance and inconsistency. But this cannot be said of the notion of Spirit. That ideas should exist in what doth not perceive, or be produced by what doth not act, is repugnant. But, it is no repugnancy to say that a perceiving thing should be the subject of ideas, or an active thing the cause of them. It is granted we have neither an immediate evidence nor a demonstrative knowledge of the existence of other finite spirits; but it will not thence follow that such spirits are on a foot with material substances: if to suppose the one be inconsistent, and it be not inconsistent to suppose the other; if the one can be inferred by no argument, and there is a probability for the other; if we see signs and effects indicating distinct finite agents like ourselves, and see no sign or symptom whatever that leads to a rational belief of Matter. I say, lastly, that I have a notion of Spirit, though I have not, strictly speaking, an idea of it. I do not perceive it as an idea, or by means of an idea, but know it by reflexion.

HYL. Notwithstanding all you have said, to me it seems that, according to your own way of thinking, and in consequence of your own principles, it should follow that *you* are only a system of floating ideas, without any substance to support them. Words are not to be used without a meaning. And, as there is no more meaning in *spiritual Substance* than in *material Substance,* the one is to be exploded as well as the other.

PHIL. How often must I repeat, that I know or am conscious of my own being; and that *I myself* am not my ideas, but somewhat else, a thinking, active principle that perceives, knows, wills, and operates about ideas. I know that I, one and the same self, perceive both colours and sounds: that a colour cannot perceive a sound, nor a sound a colour: that I am therefore one individual principle, distinct from colour and sound; and, for the same reason, from all other sensible things and inert ideas. But, I am not in like manner conscious either of the existence or essence of Matter. On the contrary, I know that nothing inconsistent can exist, and that the existence of Matter implies an inconsistency. Farther, I know what I mean when I affirm that there is a spiritual substance or support of ideas, that is, that a spirit knows and perceives ideas. But, I do not know what is meant when it is said that an unperceiving substance hath inherent in it and supports either ideas or the archetypes of ideas. There is therefore upon the whole no parity of case between Spirit and Matter.

. . . .

HYL. But, according to your notions, what difference is there between real things, and chimeras formed by the imagination, or the visions of a dream—since they are all equally in the mind?

PHIL. The ideas formed by the imagination are faint and indistinct; they have, besides, an entire dependence on the will. But the ideas perceived by sense, that is, real things, are more vivid and clear; and, being imprinted on the mind by a sprit distinct from us, have not the like dependence on our will. There is therefore no danger of confounding these with the foregoing: and there is as little of confounding them with the visions of a dream, which are dim, irregular, and confused. And, though they should happen to be never so lively and natural, yet, by their not being connected, and of a piece with the preceding and subsequent transactions of our lives, they might easily be distinguished from realities. In short, by whatever method you distinguish *things* from *chimeras* on your scheme, the same, it is evident, will hold also upon mine. For, it must be, I presume, by some perceived difference; and I am not for depriving you of any one thing that you perceive.

HYL. As for the difficulties other opinions may be liable to, those are out of the question. It is your business to defend your own opinion. Can anything be plainer than that you are for changing all things into ideas? You, I say, who are not ashamed to charge me with *scepticism*. This is so plain, there is no denying it.

PHIL. You mistake me. I am not for changing things into ideas, but rather ideas into things; since those immediate objects of perception, which, according to you, are only appearances of things, I take to be the real things themselves.

HYL. Things! You may pretend what you please; but it is certain you leave us nothing but the empty forms of things, the outside only which strikes the senses.

PHIL. What you call the empty forms and outside of things seem to me the very things themselves. Nor are they empty or incomplete, otherwise than upon your supposition—that Matter is an essential part of all corporeal things. We both, therefore, agree in this, that we perceive only sensible forms: but herein we differ—you will have them to be empty appearances, I real beings. In short, you do not trust your senses, I do.

HYL. You say you believe your senses; and seem to applaud yourself that in this you agree with the vulgar. According to you, therefore, the true nature of a thing is discovered by the senses. If so, whence comes that disagreement? Why is not the same figure, and other sensible qualities, perceived all manner of ways? and why should we use a microscope the better to discover the true nature of a body, if it were discoverable to the naked eye?

PHIL. Strictly speaking, Hylas, we do not see the same object that we feel; neither is the same object perceived by the microscope which was by the naked eye. But, in case every variation was thought sufficient to constitute a new kind or individual, the endless number or confusion of names would render language impracticable. Therefore, to avoid this, as well as other inconveniences which are obvious upon a little thought, men combine together several ideas, apprehended by divers senses, or by the same sense at different times, or in different circumstances, but observed, however, to have some connexion in nature, either with respect to co-existence or succession; all which they refer to one name, and consider as one thing. Hence it follows that when I examine, by my other senses, a thing I have seen, it is not in order to understand better the same object which I had perceived by sight, the object of one sense not being perceived by the other senses. And, when I look through a microscope, it is not that I may perceive more clearly what I perceived already with my bare eyes; the object perceived by the glass being quite different from the former. But, in both cases, my aim is only to know what ideas are connected together; and the more a man knows of the connexion of ideas, the more he is said to know of the nature of things. What, therefore, if our ideas are variable; what if our senses are not in all circumstances affected with the same appearances? It will not thence follow they are not to be trusted; or that they are inconsistent either with themselves or anything else: except it be with your preconceived notion of (I know not what) one single, unchanged, unperceivable, real Nature, marked by each name. Which prejudice seems to have taken its rise from not rightly understanding the common language of men, speaking of several distinct ideas as united into one thing by the mind. And, indeed, there is cause to suspect several erroneous conceits of the philosophers are owing to the same original: while they began to build their schemes not so much on notions as on words, which were framed by the vulgar, merely for conveniency and dispatch in the common actions of life, without any regard to speculation.

HYL. Methinks I apprehend your meaning.

PHIL. It is your opinion the ideas we perceive by our senses are not real things, but images or copies of them. Our knowledge, therefore, is no farther real than as our ideas are the true *representations* of those *originals*. But, as these supposed originals are in themselves unknown, it is impossible to know how far our ideas resemble them; or whether they resemble them at all. We cannot, therefore, be sure we have any real knowledge. Farther, as our ideas are perpetually varied, without any change in the supposed real things, it necessarily follows they cannot all be true copies of them: or, if some are and others are not, it is impossible to distinguish the former from the latter. And this plunges us yet deeper in uncertainty. Again, when we consider the point, we cannot conceive how any idea, or anything like an idea, should have an absolute existence out of a mind: nor consequently, according to you, how there should be any real thing in nature. The result of all which is that we are thrown into the most hopeless and abandoned scepticism. Now, give me leave to ask you, First, Whether your referring ideas to certain absolutely existing unperceived substances, as their originals, be not the source of all this scepticism? Secondly, whether you are informed, either by sense or reason, of the existence of those unknown originals? And, in case you are not, whether it be not absurd to suppose them? Thirdly, Whether, upon inquiry, you find there is anything distinctly conceived or meant by the *absolute or external existence of unperceiving substances?* Lastly, Whether, the premises considered, it be not the wisest way to follow nature, trust your senses, and, laying aside all anxious thought about unknown natures or substances, admit with the vulgar those for real things are perceived by the senses?

HYL. For the present, I have no inclination to the answering part. I would much rather see how you can get over what follows. Pray are not the objects perceived by the *senses* of one, likewise perceivable to others present? If there were a hundred more here, they would all see the garden, the trees, and flowers, as I see them. But they are not in the same manner affected with the ideas I frame in my *imagination*. Does not this make a difference between the former sort of objects and the latter?

PHIL. I grant it does. Nor have I ever denied a difference between the objects of sense and those of imagination. But what would you infer from thence? You cannot say that sensible objects exist unperceived, because they are perceived by many.

HYL. I own I can make nothing of that objection: but it hath led me into another. Is it not your opinion that by our senses we perceive only the ideas existing in our minds?

PHIL. It is.

HYL. But the *same* idea which is in my mind cannot be in yours, or in any other mind. Doth it not therefore follow, from your principles, that no two can see the same thing? And is not this highly absurd?

PHIL. If the term *same* be taken in the vulgar acceptation, it is certain (and not at all repugnant to the principles I maintain) that different persons may perceive the same thing; or the same thing or idea exist in different minds. Words are of arbitrary imposition; and, since men are used to apply the word *same* where no distinction or variety is perceived, and I do not pretend to alter their perceptions, it follows that, as men have said before, *several saw the same thing,* so they may, upon like occasions, still continue to use the same phrase, without any deviation either from propriety of language, or the truth of things. But, if the term *same* be used in the acceptation of philosophers, who pretend to an abstracted notion of identity, then, according to their sundry definitions of this notion (for it is not yet agreed wherein that philosophic identity consists), it may or may not be possible for divers persons to perceive the same thing. But whether philosophers shall think fit to *call* a thing the *same* or no, is, I conceive, of small importance. Let us suppose several men together, all endued with the same faculities, and consequently affected in like sort by their senses, and who had yet never known the use of language; they would, without question, agree in their perceptions. Though perhaps, when they came to the use of speech, some regarding the uniformness of what was perceived, might call it the *same* thing: others, especially regarding the diversity of persons who perceived, might choose the denomination of *different* things. But who sees not that all the dispute is about a word? to wit, whether what is perceived by different persons may yet have the term *same* applied to it? Or, suppose a house, whose walls or outward shell remaining unaltered, the chambers are all pulled down, and new ones built in their place; and that you should call this the *same,* and I should say it was not the *same* house:—would we not, for all this, perfectly agree in our thoughts of the house, considered in itself? And would not all the difference consist in a sound? If you should say, We differed in our notions; for that you superadded to your idea of the house the simple abstracted idea of identity, whereas I did not; I would tell you, I know not what you mean by the *abstracted idea of identity;* and should desire you to look into your own thoughts, and be sure you understood yourself.—Why so silent, Hylas? Are you not yet satisfied men may dispute about identity and diversity, without any real difference in their thoughts and opinions, abstracted from names? Take this farther reflexion with you—that whether Matter be allowed to exist or no, the case is exactly the same as to the point in hand. For the Materialists themselves acknowledge what we immediately perceive by our senses to be our own ideas. Your difficulty, therefore, that no two see the same thing, makes equally against the Materialists and me.

. . . .

HYL. But, what would you say, Philonous, if I should bring the very same reasons against the existence of sensible things *in a mind,* which you have offered against their existing *in a material substratum?*

PHIL. When I see your reasons, you shall hear what I have to say to them.

HYL. Is the mind extended or unextended?

PHIL. Unextended, without doubt.

HYL. Do you say the things you perceive are in your mind?

PHIL. They are.

HYL. Again, have I not heard you speak of sensible impressions?

PHIL. I believe you may.

HYL. Explain to me now, O Philonous! how it is possible there should be room for all those trees and houses to exist in your mind. Can extended things be contained in that which is unextended? Or, are we to imagine impressions made on a thing void of all solidity? You cannot say objects are in your mind, as books in your study: or that things are imprinted on it, as the figure of a seal upon wax. In what sense, therefore, are we to understand those expressions? Explain me this if you can: and I shall then be able to answer all those queries you formerly put to me about my *substratum.*

PHIL. Look you, Hylas, when I speak of objects as existing in the mind, or imprinted on the senses, I would not be understood in the gross literal sense; as when bodies are said to exist in a place, or a seal to make an impression upon wax. My meaning is only that the mind comprehends or perceives them; and that it is affected from without, or by some being distinct from itself. This is my explication of your difficulty; and how it can serve to make your tenet of an unperceiving material *substratum* intelligible, I would fain know.

HYL. Nay, if that be all, I confess I do not see what use can be made of it. But are you not guilty of some abuse of language in this?

PHIL. None at all. It is no more than common custom, which you know is the rule of language, hath authorised: nothing being more usual, than for philosophers to speak of the immediate objects of the understanding as things existing in the mind. Nor is there anything in this but what is conformable to the general analogy of language; most part of the mental operations being signified by words borrowed from sensible things; as is plain in the terms *comprehend, reflect, discourse, etc.,* which, being applied to the mind, must not be taken in their gross, original sense.

. . . .

HYL. I agree to all you have now said, and must own that nothing can incline me to embrace your opinion more than the advantages I see it is attended with. I am by nature lazy; and this would be a mighty abridgment in knowledge. What doubts, what hypotheses, what labyrinths of amusement, what fields of disputation, what an ocean of false learning, may be avoided by that single notion of *Immaterialism!*

PHIL. After all, is there anything farther remaining to be done? You may remember you promised to embrace that opinion which upon examination should appear most agreeable to Common Sense and remote from Scepticism. This, by your own confession, is that which denies Matter, or the *absolute* existence of corporeal things. Nor is this all; the same notion has been proved several ways, viewed in different lights, pursued in its consequences, and all objections against it cleared. Can there be a greater evidence of its truth? or is it possible it should have all the marks of a true opinion and yet be false?

HYL. I own myself entirely satisfied for the present in all respects. But, what security can I have that I shall still continue the same full asset to your opinion, and that no unthought-of objection or difficulty will occur hereafter?

PHIL. Pray, Hylas, do you in other cases, when a point is once evidently proved, withhold your consent on account of objections or difficulties it may be liable to? Are the difficulties that attend the doctrine of incommensurable quantities, of the angle of contact, of the asymptotes to curves, or the like, sufficient to make you hold out against mathematical demonstration? Or will you disbelieve the Providence of God, because there may be some particular things which *you* know not how to reconcile with? If there are difficulties attending *Immaterialism,* there are at the same time direct and evident proofs of it. But for the existence of Matter there is not one proof, and far more numerous and insurmountable objections lie against it. But where are those mighty difficulties you insist on? Alas! you know not where or what they are; something which may possibly occur hereafter. If this be a sufficient pretence for withholding your full assent, you should never yield it to any proposition, how free soever from exceptions, how clearly and solidly soever demonstrated.

HYL. You have satisfied me, Philonous.

PHIL. But, to arm you against all future objections, do but consider: That which bears equally hard on two contradictory opinions can be proof against neither. Whenever, therefore, any difficulty occurs, try if you can find a solution for it on the hypothesis of the *Materialists.* Be not deceived by words; but sound your own thoughts. And in case you cannot conceive it easier by the help of *Materialism,* it is plain it can be no objection against *Immaterialism.* Had you proceeded all along by this rule, you would probably have spared yourself abundance of trouble in objecting; since of all your difficulties I challenge you to shew one that is explained by Matter: nay, which is not more unintelligible with than without that supposition; and consequently makes rather *against* than *for* it. You should consider, in each particular, whether the difficulty arises from the *non-existence of Matter.* If it doth not, you might as well argue from the infinite divisibility of extension against the Divine prescience, as from such a difficulty against *Immaterialism.* And yet, upon recollection, I believe you will find this to have been often, if not always, the case. You should likewise take heed not to argue on a *petitio principii.* One if apt to say—The unknown substances ought to be esteemed real things, rather than the ideas in our minds: and who can tell but the unthinking external substance may concur, as a cause or instrument, in the productions of our ideas? But is not this proceeding on a supposition that there are such external substances? And to suppose this, is it not begging the question? But, above all things, you should beware of imposing on yourself by that vulgar sophism which is called *ignoratio elenchi.* You talked often as if you thought I maintained the non-existence of Sensible Things. Whereas in truth no one can be more thoroughly assured of their existence than I am. And it is you who doubt; I should have said, positively deny it. Everything that is seen, felt, heard, or any way perceived by the senses, is, on the principles I embrace, a real being; but not on yours. Remember, the Matter you contend for is an Unknown Somewhat (if indeed it may be termed *somewhat*), which is quite stripped of all sensible qualities, and can neither be perceived by sense, nor apprehended by the mind. Remember, I say, that it is not any object which is hard or soft, hot or cold, blue or white, round or square, etc. For all these things I affirm do exist. Though indeed I deny that they exist out of all minds whatsoever. Think on these points; let them be attentively considered and still kept in view. Otherwise you will not comprehend the state of the question; without which your objections will always be wide of the mark, and, instead of mine, may possibly be directed (as more than once they have been) against your own notions.

HYL. I must needs own, Philonous, nothing seems to have kept me from agreeing with you more than this same *mistaking the question.* In denying Matter, at first glimpse I am tempted to imagine you deny the things we see and feel: but, upon reflexion, find there is no ground for it. What think you, therefore, of retaining the name *Matter,* and applying it to *sensible things?* This may be done without any change in your sentiments: and, believe me, it would be a means of reconciling them to some persons who may be more shocked at an innovation in words than in opinion.

PHIL. With all my heart: retain the word *Matter,* and apply it to the objects of sense, if you please; provided you do not attribute to them any subsistence distinct from their being perceived. I shall never quarrel with you for an expression. *Matter,* or *material substance,* are terms introduced by philosophers; and, as used by them, imply a sort of independency, or a subsistance distinct from being perceived by a mind: but are never used by common people; or, if ever, it is to signify the immediate objects of sense. One would think, therefore, so long as the names of all particular things, with the terms *sensible, substance, body, stuff,* and the like, are retained, the word *Matter* should be never missed in common talk. And in philosophical discources it seems the best way to leave it quite out: since there is not, perhaps, any one thing that hath more favoured and strengthened the depraved bent of the mind towards Atheism than the use of that general confused term.

HYL. Well but, Philonous, since I am content to give up the notion of an unthinking substance exterior to the mind, I think you ought not to deny me the privilege of using the word *Matter* as I please, and annexing it to a collection of sensible qualities subsisting only in the mind. I freely own there is no other substance, in a strict sense, than *Spirit.* But I have been so long accustomed to the *term Matter* that I know not how to part with it: to say, there is no *Matter* in the world, is still shocking to me. Whereas to say—There is no *Matter,* if by that term be meant an unthinking substance existing without the mind; but if by *Matter* is meant some sensible thing, whose existence consists in being perceived, then there is *Matter:*—this distinction gives it quite another turn; and men will come into your notions with small difficulty, when they are proposed in that manner. For, after all, the controversy about *Matter* in the strict acceptation of it, lies altogether between you and the philosophers: whose principles, I acknowledge, are not near so natural, or so agreeable to the common sense of mankind, and Holy Scripture, as yours. There is nothing we either desire or shun but as it makes, or is apprehended to make, some part of our happiness or misery. But what hath happiness or misery, joy or grief, pleasure or pain, to do with Absolute Existence; or with unknown entities, *abstracted from all relation to us?* It is evident, things regard us only as they are pleasing or displeasing: and they can please or displease only so far forth as they are perceived. Farther, therefore, we are not concerned; and thus far you leave things as you found them. Yet still there is something new in this doctrine. It is plain, I do not now think with the philosophers; nor yet altogether with the vulgar. I would know how the case stands in that respect; precisely, what you have added to, or altered in my former notions.

PHIL. I do not pretend to be a setter-up of new notions. My endeavours tend only to unite, and place in a clearer light, that truth which was before shared between the vulgar and the philosophers:—the former being of opinion, that *those things they immediately perceive are the real things;* and the latter, that *the things immediately perceived are ideas, which exist only in the mind.* Which two notions put together, do, in effect, constitute the substance of what I advance.

HYL. I have been a long time distrusting my senses: methought I saw things by a dim light and through false glasses. Now the glasses are removed and a new light breaks in upon my understanding. I am clearly convinced that I see things in their native forms, and am no longer in pain about their *unknown natures* or *absolute existence.* This is the state I find myself in at present; though, indeed, the course that brought me to it I do not yet thoroughly comprehend. You set out upon the same principles that Academics, Cartesians, and the like sects usually do; and for a long time it looked as if you were advancing their philosophical Scepticism: but, in the end, your conclusions are directly opposite to theirs.

PHIL. You see, Hylas, the water of yonder fountain, how it is forced upwards, in a round column, to a certain height; at which it breaks, and falls back into the basin from whence it rose: its ascent, as well as descent, proceeding from the same uniform law or principle of gravitation. Just so, the same Principles which, at first view, lead to Scepticism, pursued to a certain point, bring men back to Common Sense.

Of Scepticism with Regard to the Senses

DAVID HUME

Section II
Of Scepticism with Regard to the Senses

Thus the sceptic still continues to reason and believe, even tho' he asserts, that he cannot defend his reason by reason; and by the same rule he must assent to the principle concerning the existence of body, tho' he cannot pretend by any arguments of philosophy to maintain its veracity. Nature has not left this to his choice, and has doubtless esteem'd it an affair of too great importance to be trusted to our uncertain reasonings and speculations. We may well ask, *What causes induce us to believe in the existence of body?* but 'tis in vain to ask, *Whether there be body or not?* That is a point, which we must take for granted in all our reasonings.

The subject, then, of our present enquiry is concerning the *causes* which induce us to believe in the existence of body: And my reasonings on this head I shall begin with a distinction, which at first sight may seem superfluous, but which will contribute very much to the perfect understanding of what follows. We ought to examine apart those two questions, which are commonly confounded together, viz. Why we attribute a CONTINU'D existence to objects, even when they are not present to the senses; and why we suppose them to have an existence DISTINCT from the mind and perception. Under this last head I comprehend their situation as well as relations, their *external* position as well as the *independence* of their existence and operation. These two questions concerning the continu'd and distinct existence of body are intimately connected together. For if the objects of our senses continue to exist, even when they are not perceiv'd, their existence is of course independent of and distinct from the perception; and vice versa, if their existence be independent of the perception and distinct from it, they must continue to exist, even tho' they be not perceiv'd. But tho' the decision of the one question decides the other; yet that we may the more easily discover the principles of human nature, from whence the decision arises, we shall carry along with us this distinction, and shall consider, whether it be the *senses, reason,* or the *imagination,* that produces the opinion of a *continu'd* or of a *distinct* existence. These are the only questions, that are intelligible on the present subject. For as to the notion of external existence, when taken for something specifically different from our perceptions,[1] we have already shewn its absurdity.

To begin with the SENSES, 'tis evident these faculties are incapable of giving rise to the notion of the *continu'd* existence of their objects, after they no longer appear to the senses. For that is a contradiction in terms, and supposes that the senses continue to operate, even after they have ceas'd all manner of operation. These faculties, therefore, if they have any influence in the present case, must produce the opinion of a distinct, not of a continu'd existence; and in order to that, must present their impressions either as images and representations, or as these very distinct and external existences.

That our senses offer not their impressions as the images of something *distinct,* or *independent,* and *external,* is evident; because they con-

From *A Treatise of Human Nature,* ed. L. A. Selby-Bigge (Oxford: Oxford University Press, 1888), pp. 187–218.

vey to us nothing but a single perception, and never give us the least intimation of any thing beyond. A single perception can never produce the idea of a double existence, but by some inference either of the reason or imagination. When the mind looks farther than what immediately appears to it, its conclusions can never be put to the account of the senses; and it certainly looks farther, when from a single perception it infers a double existence, and supposes the relations of resemblance and causation betwixt them.

If our senses, therefore, suggest any idea of distinct existences, they must convey the impressions as those very existences, by a kind of fallacy and illusion. Upon this head we may observe, that all sensations are felt by the mind, such as they really are, and that when we doubt, whether they present themselves as distinct objects, or as mere impressions, the difficulty is not concerning their nature, but concerning their relations and situation. Now if the senses presented our impressions as external to, and independent of ourselves, both the objects and ourselves must be obvious to our senses, otherwise they cou'd not be compar'd by these faculties. The difficulty, then, is how far we are *ourselves* the objects of our senses.

'Tis certain there is no question in philosophy more abstruse than that concerning identity, and the nature of the uniting principle, which constitutes a person. So far from being able by our senses merely to determine this question, we must have recourse to the most profound metaphysics to give a satisfactory answer to it; and in common life 'tis evident these ideas of self and person are never very fix'd nor determinate. 'Tis absurd, therefore, to imagine the senses can ever distinguish betwixt ourselves and external objects.

Add to this, that every impression, external and internal, passions, affections, sensations, pains and pleasures, are originally on the same footing; and that whatever other differences we may observe among them, they appear, all of them, in their true colours, as impressions or perceptions. And indeed, if we consider the matter aright, 'tis scarce possible it shou'd be more capable of deceiving us in the situation and relations, than in the nature of our impressions. For since all actions and sensations of the mind are known to us by consciousness, they must necessarily appear in every particular what they are, and be what they appear. Every thing that enters the mind, being in *reality* as the perception, 'tis impossible any thing shou'd to *feeling* appear different. This were to suppose, that even where we are most intimately conscious, we might be mistaken.

But not to lose time in examining, whether 'tis possible for our senses to deceive us, and represent our perceptions as distinct from ourselves, that is as *external* to and *independent* of us; let us consider whether they really do so, and whether this error proceeds from an immediate sensation, or from some other causes.

To begin with the question concerning *external* existence, it may perhaps be said, that setting aside the metaphysical question of the identity of a thinking substance, our own body evidently belongs to us; and as several impressions appear exterior to the body, we suppose them also exterior to ourselves. The paper, on which I write at present, is beyond my hand. The table is beyond the paper. The walls of the chamber beyond the table. And in casting my eye towards the window, I perceive a great extent of fields and buildings beyond my chamber. From all this it may be infer'd, that no other faculty is requir'd, beside the senses, to convince us of the external existence of body. But to prevent this inference, we need only weigh the three following considerations. *First,* That, properly speaking, 'tis not our body we perceive, when we regard our limbs and members, but certain impressions, which enter by the senses; so that the ascribing a real and corporeal existence to these impressions, or to their objects, is an act of the mind as difficult to explain, as that which we examine at present. *Secondly,* Sounds, and tastes, and smells, tho' commonly regarded by the mind as continu'd independent qualities, appear not to have any existence in extension, and consequently cannot appear to the senses as situated externally to the body. The reason, why we ascribe a place to them, shall be consider'd[2] afterwards. *Thirdly,* Even our sight informs us not of distance or outness (so to speak) immediately and without a certain reasoning and experience, as is acknowledg'd by the most rational philosophers.

As to the *independency* of our perceptions on ourselves, this can never be an object of the senses; but any opinion we form concerning it, must be deriv'd from experience and observation: And we shall see afterwards, that our conclusions from experience are far from being favourable to the doctrine of the independency of our perceptions. Mean while we may observe that when we talk of real distinct existences, we have commonly more in our eye their independency than external situation in place, and think an object has a sufficient reality, when its Being is uninterrupted, and independent of the incessant revolutions, which we are conscious of in ourselves.

Thus to resume what I have said concerning the senses; they give us no notion of continu'd existence, because they cannot operate beyond the extent, in which they really operate. They as little produce the opinion of a distinct existence, because they neither can offer it to the mind as represented, nor as original. To offer it as represented, they must present both an object and an image. To make it appear as original, they must convey a falshood; and this falshood must lie in the relations and situation: In order to which they must be able to compare the object with ourselves; and even in that case they do not, nor is it possible they shou'd, deceive us. We may, therefore, conclude with certainty, that the opinion of a continu'd and of a distinct existence never arises from the senses.

To confirm this we may observe, that there are three different kinds of impressions convey'd by the senses. The first are those of the figure, bulk, motion and solidity of bodies. The second those of colours, tastes, smells, sounds, heat and cold. The third are the pains and pleasures, that arise from the application of objects to our bodies, as by the cutting of our flesh with steel, and such like. Both philosophers and the vulgar suppose the first of these to have a distinct continu'd existence. The vulgar only regard the second as on the same footing. Both philosophers and the vulgar, again, esteem the third to be merely perceptions; and consequently interrupted and dependent beings.

Now 'tis evident, that, whatever may be our philosophical opinion, colours, sounds, heat and cold, as far as appears to the senses, exist after the same manner with motion and solidity, and that the difference we make betwixt them in this respect, arises not from the mere perception. So strong is the prejudice for the distinct continu'd existence of the former qualities, that when the contrary opinion is advanc'd by modern philosophers, people imagine they can almost refute it from their feeling and experience, and that their very senses contradict this philosophy. 'Tis also evident, that colours, sounds, etc. are originally on the same footing with the pain that arises from steel, and pleasure that proceeds from a fire; and that the difference betwixt them is founded neither on perception nor reason, but on the imagination. For as they are confest to be, both of them, nothing but perceptions arising from the particular configurations and motions of the parts of body, wherein possible can their difference consist? Upon the whole, then, we may conclude, that as far as the senses are judges, all perceptions are the same in the manner of their existence.

We may also observe in this instance of sounds and colours, that we can attribute a distinct continu'd existence to objects without ever consulting REASON, or weighing our opinions by any philosophical principles. And indeed, whatever convincing arguments philosophers may fancy they can produce to establish the belief of objects independent of the mind, 'tis obvious these arguments are known but to very few, and that 'tis not by them, that children, peasants, and the greatest part of mankind are induc'd to attribute objects to some impressions, and deny them to others. Accordingly we find, that all the conclusions, which the vulgar form on this head, are directly contrary to those, which are confirm'd by philosophy. For philosophy informs us, that every thing, which appears to the mind, is nothing but a perception, and is interrupted, and dependent on the mind; whereas the vulgar confound perceptions and objects, and attribute a distinct continu'd existence to the very things they feel or see. This sentiment, then, as it is entirely unreasonable, must proceed from some other faculty than the understanding. To which we may add, that as long as we take our perceptions and objects to be the same, we can never infer the existence of the one from that of the other, nor form any argument from the relation of cause and effect; which is the only one that can assure us of matter of fact. Even after we distinguish our perceptions from our objects, 'twill appear presently, that we are still incapable of reasoning from the existence of one to that of the other: So that upon the whole our reason neither does, nor is it possible it ever shou'd, upon any supposition, give us an assurance of the continu'd and distinct existence of body. That opinion must be entirely owing to the IMAGINATION: which must now be the subject of our enquiry.

Since all impressions are internal and perishing existences, and appear as such, the notion of their distinct and continu'd existence must arise from a concurrence of some of their qualities with the qualities of the imagination; and since this notion does not extend to all of them, it must arise from certain qualities peculiar to some impressions. 'Twill therefore be easy for us to discover these qualities by a comparison of the impressions, to which we attribute a distinct and continu'd existence, with those, which we regard as internal and perishing.

We may observe, then, that 'tis neither upon account of the involuntariness of certain impressions, as is commonly suppos'd, nor of their superior force and violence, that we attribute to them a reality, and continu'd existence, which we refuse to others, that are voluntary or feeble. For 'tis evident our pains and pleasures, our passions and affections, which we never suppose to have any existence beyond our perception, operate with greater violence, and are equally involuntary, as the impressions of figure and extension, colour and sound, which we suppose to be permanent beings. The heat of a fire, when moderate, is suppos'd to exist in the fire; but the pain, which it causes upon a near approach, is not taken to have any being except in the perception.

These vulgar opinions, then, being rejected, we must search for some other hypothesis, by which we may discover those peculiar qualities in our impressions, which makes us attribute to them a distinct and continu'd existence.

After a little examination, we shall find, that all those objects, to which we attribute a continu'd existence, have a peculiar *constancy,* which distinguishes them from the impressions, whose existence depends upon our perception. Those mountains, and houses, and trees, which lie at present under my eye, have always appear'd to me in the same order; and when I lose sight of them by shutting my eyes or turning my head, I soon after find them return upon me without the least alteration. My bed and table, my books and papers, present themselves in the same uniform manner, and change not upon account of any interruption in my seeing or perceiving them. This is the case with all the impressions, whose objects are suppos'd to have an external existence; and is the case with no other impressions, whether gentle or violent, voluntary or involuntary.

This constancy, however, is not so perfect as not to admit of very considerable exceptions. Bodies often change their position and qualities, and after a little absence or interruption may become hardly knowable. But here 'tis observable, that even in these changes they preserve a *coherence,* and have a regular dependence on each other; which is the foundation of a kind of reasoning from causation, and produces the opinion of their continu'd existence. When I return to my chamber after an hour's absence, I find not my fire in the same situation, in which I left it: But then I am accustom'd in other instances to see a like alteration produc'd in a like time, whether I am present or absent, near or remote. This coherence, therefore, in their changes is one of the characteristics of external objects, as well as their constancy.

Having found that the opinion of the continu'd existence of body depends on the COHERENCE and CONSTANCY of certain impressions, I now proceed to examine after what manner these qualities give rise to so extraordinary an opinion. To begin with the coherence; we may observe, that tho' those internal impressions, which we regard as fleeting and perishing, have also a certain coherence or regularity in their appearances, yet 'tis of somewhat a different nature, from that which we discover in bodies. Our passions are found by experience to have a mutual connexion with and dependance on each other; but on no occasion is it necessary to suppose, that they have existed and operated, when they were not perceiv'd, in order to preserve the same dependance and connexion, of which we have had experience. The case is not the same with relation to external objects. Those require a continu'd existence, or otherwise lose, in a great measure, the regularity of their operation. I am here seated in my chamber with my face to the fire; and all the objects, that strike my senses, are contain'd in a few yards around me.

My memory, indeed, informs me of the existence of many objects; but then this information extends not beyond their past existence, nor do either my senses or memory give any testimony to the continuance of their being. When therefore I am thus seated, and revolve over these thoughts, I hear on a sudden a noise as of a door turning upon its hinges; and a little after see a porter, who advances towards me. This gives occasion to many new reflexions and reasonings. First, I never have observ'd, that this noise cou'd proceed from any thing but the motion of a door; and therefore conclude, that the present phenomenon is a contradiction to all past experience, unless the door, which I remember on t'other side the chamber, be still in being. Again, I have always found, that a human body was possest of a quality, which I call gravity, and which hinders it from mounting in the air, as this porter must have done to arrive at my chamber, unless the stairs I remember be not annihilated by my absence. But this is not all. I receive a letter, which upon opening it I perceive by the hand-writing and subscription to have come from a friend, who says he is two hundred leagues distant. 'Tis evident I can never account for this phenomenon, conformable to my experience in other instances, without spreading out in my mind the whole sea and continent between us, and supposing the effects and continu'd existence of posts and ferries, according to my memory and observation. To consider these phenomena of the porter and letter in a certain light, they are contradictions to common experience, and may be regarded as objections to those maxims, which we form concerning the connexions of causes and effects. I am accustom'd to hear such a sound, and see such an object in motion at the same time. I have not receiv'd in this particular instance both these perceptions. These observations are contrary, unless I suppose that the door still remains, and that it was open'd without my perceiving it: And this supposition, which was at first entirely arbitrary and hypothetical, acquires a force and evidence by its being the only one, upon which I can reconcile these contradictions. There is scarce a moment of my life, wherein there is not a similar instance presented to me, and I have not occasion to suppose the continu'd existence of objects, in order to connect their past and present appearances, and give them such an union with each other, as I have found by experience to be suitable to their particular natures and circumstances. Here then I am naturally led to regard the world, as something real and durable, and as preserving its existence, even when it is no longer present to my perception.

But tho' this conclusion from the coherence of appearances may seem to be of the same nature with our reasonings concerning causes and effects; as being deriv'd from custom, and regulated by past experience; we shall find upon examination, that they are at the bottom considerably different from each other, and that this inference arises from the understanding, and from custom in an indirect and oblique manner. For 'twill readily be allow'd, that since nothing is ever really present to the mind, besides its own perceptions, 'tis not only impossible, that any habit shou'd ever be acquir'd otherwise than by the regular succession of these perceptions, but also that any habit shou'd ever exceed that degree of regularity. Any degree, therefore, of regularity in our perceptions, can never be a foundation for us to infer a greater degree of regularity in some objects, which are not perceiv'd; since this supposes a contradiction, viz. a habit acquir'd by what was never present to the mind. But 'tis evident, that whenever we infer the continu'd existence of the objects of sense from their coherence, and the frequency of their union, 'tis in order to bestow on the objects a greater regularity than what is observ'd in our mere perceptions. We remark a connexion betwixt two kinds of objects in their past appearance to the senses, but are not able to observe this connexion to be perfectly constant, since the turning about of our head, or the shutting of our eyes is able to break it. What then do we suppose in this case, but that these objects still continue their usual connexion, notwithstanding their apparent interruption, and that the irregular appearances are join'd by something, of which we are insensible? But as all reasoning concerning matters of fact arises only from custom, and custom can only be the effect of repeated perceptions, the extending of custom and reasoning beyond the perceptions can never be the direct and natural effect of the constant repetition and connexion, but must arise from the co-operation of some other principles.

I have already[3] observ'd, in examining the foundation of mathematics, that the imagination, when set into any train of thinking, is apt to continue, even when its object fails it, and like a galley put in motion by the oars, carries on its course without any new impulse. This I have assign'd for the reason, why, after considering several loose standards of equality, and correcting them by each other, we proceed to imagine so correct and exact a standard of that relation, as is not liable to the least error or variation. The same principle makes us easily entertain this opinion of the continu'd existence of body. Objects have a certain coherence even as they appear to our senses; but this coherence is much greater and more uniform, if we suppose the objects to have a continu'd existence; and as the mind is once in the train of observing an uniformity among objects, it naturally continues, till it renders the uniformity as compleat as possible. The simple supposition of their continu'd existence suffices for this purpose, and gives us a notion of a much greater regularity among objects, than what they have when we look no farther than our senses.

But whatever force we may ascribe to this principle, I am afraid 'tis too weak to support alone so vast an edifice, as is that of the continu'd existence of all external bodies; and that we must join the *constancy* of their appearance to the *coherence,* in order to give a satisfactory account of that opinion. As the explication of this will lead me into a considerable compass of very profound reasoning; I think it proper, in order to avoid confusion, to give a short sketch or abridgment of my system, and afterwards draw out all its parts in their full compass. This inference from the constancy of our perceptions, like the precedent from their coherence, gives rise to the opinion of the *continu'd* existence of body, which is prior to that of its *distinct* existence, and produces that latter principle.

When we have been accustom'd to observe a constancy in certain impressions, and have found, that the perception of the sun or ocean, for instance, returns upon us after an absence or annihilation with like parts and in a like order, as at its first appearance, we are not apt to regard these interrupted perceptions as different, (which they really are) but on the contrary consider them as individually the same, upon account of their resemblance. But as this interruption of their existence is contrary to their perfect identity, and makes us regard the first impression as annihilated, and the second as newly created, we find ourselves somewhat at a loss, and are involv'd in a kind of contradiction. In order to free ourselves from this difficulty, we disguise, as much as possible, the interruption, or rather remove it entirely, by supposing that these interrupted perceptions are connected by a real existence, of which we are insensible. This supposition, or idea of continu'd existence, acquires a force and vivacity from the memory of these broken impressions, and from that propensity, which they give us, to suppose them the same; and according to the precedent reasoning, the very essence of belief consists in the force and vivacity of the conception.

In order to justify this system, there are four things requisite. *First,* To explain the *principium individuationis,* or principle of identity. *Secondly,* Give a reason, why the resemblance of our broken and interrupted perceptions induces us to attribute an identity to them. *Thirdly,* Account for that propensity, which this illusion gives, to unite these broken appearances by a continu'd existence. *Fourthly* and lastly, Explain that force and vivacity of conception, which arises from the propensity.

First, As to the principle of individuation; we may observe, that the view of any one object is not sufficient to convey the idea of identity. For in that proposition, *an object is the same with itself,* if the idea express'd by the word, *object,* were no ways distinguish'd from that meant by *itself;* we really shou'd mean nothing, nor wou'd the proposition contain a predicate and a subject, which however are imply'd in this affirmation. One single object conveys the idea of unity, not that of identity.

On the other hand, a multiplicity of objects can never convey this idea, however resembling they may be suppos'd. The mind always pronounces the one not to be the other, and considers them as forming two, three, or any determinate number of objects, whose existences are entirely distinct and independent.

Since then both number and unity are incompatible with the relation of identity, it must lie in something that is neither of them. But to tell the truth, at first sight this seems utterly impossible. Betwixt unity and number there can be no medium; no more than betwixt existence and non-existence. After one object is suppos'd to exist, we must either suppose another also to exist; in which case we have the idea of number: Or we must suppose it not to exist; in which case the first object remains at unity.

To remove this difficulty, let us have recourse to the idea of time or duration. I have already observ'd,[4] that time, in a strict sense, implies succession, and that when we apply its idea to any unchangeable object, 'tis only by a fiction of the imagination, by which the unchangeable object is suppos'd to participate of the changes of the co-existent objects, and in particular of that of our perceptions. This fiction of the imagination almost universally takes place; and 'tis by means of it, that a single object, plac'd before us, and survey'd for any time without our discovering in it any interruption or variation, is able to give us a notion of identity. For when we consider any two points of this time, we may place them in different lights: We may either survey them at the very same instant; in which case they give us the idea of number, both by themselves and by the object; which must be multiply'd, in order to be conceiv'd at once, as existent in these two different points of time: Or on the other hand, we may trace the succession of time by a like succession of ideas, and conceiving first one moment, along with the object then existent, imagine afterwards a change in the time without any *variation* or *interruption* in the object; in which case it gives us the idea of unity. Here then is an idea, which is a medium betwixt unity and number; or more properly speaking, is either of them, according to the view, in which we take it: And this idea we call that of identity. We cannot, in any propriety of speech, say, that an object is the same with itself, unless we mean, that the object existent at one time is the same with itself existent at another. By this means we make a difference, betwixt the idea meant by the word, *object,* and that meant by *itself,* without going the length of number, and at the same time without restraining ourselves to a strict and absolute unity.

Thus the principle of individuation is nothing but the *invariableness* and *uninterruptedness* of any object, thro' a suppos'd variation of time, by which the mind can trace it in the different periods of its existence, without any break of the view, and without being oblig'd to form the idea of multiplicity or number.

I now proceed to explain the *second* part of my system, and show why the constancy of our perceptions makes us ascribe to them a perfect numerical identity, tho' there be very long intervals betwixt their appearance, and they have only one of the essential qualities of identity, viz. *invariableness.* That I may avoid all ambiguity and confusion on this head, I shall observe, that I here account for the opinions and belief of the vulgar with regard to the existence of body; and therefore must entirely conform myself to their manner of thinking and of expressing themselves. Now we have already observ'd, that however philosophers may distinguish betwixt the objects and perceptions of the senses; which they suppose co-existent and resembling; yet this is a distinction, which is not comprehended by the generality of mankind, who as they perceive only one being, can never assent to the opinion of a double existence and representation. Those very sensations, which enter by the eye or ear, are with them the true objects, nor can they readily conceive that this pen or paper, which immediately perceiv'd, represents another, which is different from, but resembling it. In order, therefore, to accommodate myself to their notions, I shall at first suppose; that there is only a single existence, which I shall call indifferently *object* or *perception,* according as it shall seem best to suit my purpose, understanding by both of them what any common man means by a hat, or shoe, or stone, or any other impression, convey'd to him by his senses. I shall be sure to give warning, when I return to a more philosophical way of speaking and thinking.

To enter, therefore, upon the question concerning the source of the error and deception with regard to identity, when we attribute it to our resembling perceptions, notwithstanding their interruption; I must here recall an observation, which I have already prov'd and explain'd.[5] Nothing is more apt to make us mistake one idea for another, than any relation betwixt them, which associates them together in the imagination, and makes it pass with facility from one to the other.

Of all relations, that of resemblance is in this respect the most efficacious; and that because it not only causes an association of ideas, but also of dispositions, and makes us conceive the one idea by an act or operation of the mind, similar to that by which we conceive the other. This circumstance I have observ'd to be of great moment; and we may establish it for a general rule, that whatever ideas place the mind in the same disposition or in similar ones, are very apt to be confounded. The mind readily passes from one to the other, and perceives not the change without a strict attention, of which, generally speaking, 'tis wholly incapable.

In order to apply this general maxim, we must first examine the disposition of the mind in viewing any object which preserves a perfect identity, and then find some other object, that is confounded with it, by causing a similar disposition. When we fix our thought on any object, and suppose it to continue the same for some time; 'tis evident we suppose the change to lie only in the time, and never exert ourselves to produce any new image or idea of the object. The faculties of the mind repose themselves in a manner, and take no more exercise, than what is necessary to continue that idea, of which we were formerly possest, and which subsists without variation or interruption. The passage from one moment to another is scarce felt, and distinguishes not itself by a different perception or idea, which may require a different direction of the spirits, in order to its conception.

Now what other objects, beside identical ones, are capable of placing the mind in the same disposition, when it considers them, and of causing the same uninterrupted passage of the imagination from one idea to another? This question is of the last importance. For if we can find any such objects, we may certainly conclude, from the foregoing principle, that they are very naturally confounded with identical ones, and are taken for them in most of our reasonings. But tho' this question be very important, 'tis not very difficult nor doubtful. For I immediately reply, that a succession of related objects places the mind in this disposition, and is consider'd with the same smooth and uninterrupted progress of the imagination, as attends the view of the same invariable object. The very nature and essence of relation is to connect our ideas with each other, and upon the appearance of the one, to facilitate the transition to its correlative. The passage betwixt related ideas is, therefore, so smooth and easy, that it produces little alteration on the mind, and seems like the continuation of the same action; and as the continuation of the same action is an effect of the continu'd view of the same object, 'tis for this reason we attribute sameness to every succession of related objects. The thought slides along the succession with equal facility, as if it consider'd only one object; and therefore confounds the succession with the identity.

We shall afterwards see many instances of this tendency of relation to make us ascribe an *identity* to *different* objects; but shall here confine ourselves to the present subject. We find by experience, that there is such a *constancy* in almost all the impressions of the senses, that their interruption produces no alteration on them, and hinders them not from returning the same in appearance and in situation as at their first existence. I survey the furniture of my chamber; I shut my eyes, and afterwards open them; and find the new perceptions to resemble perfectly those, which formerly struck my senses. This resemblance is observ'd in a thousand instances, and naturally connects together our ideas of these interrupted perceptions by the strongest relation, and conveys the mind with an easy transition from one to another. An easy transition or passage of the imagination, along the ideas of these different and interrupted perceptions, is almost the same disposition of mind with that in which we consider one constant and uninterrupted perception. 'Tis therefore very natural for us to mistake the one for the other.[6]

The persons, who entertain this opinion concerning the identity of our resembling perceptions, are in general all the unthinking and unphilosophical part of mankind, (that is, all of us, at one time or other) and consequently such as suppose their perceptions to be their only objects, and never think of a double existence internal and external, representing and represented. The very image, which is present to the senses, is with us the real body; and 'tis to these interrupted images we ascribe a perfect identity. But as the interruption of the appearance seems contrary to the identity, and naturally leads us to regard these resembling perceptions as different from each other, we here find ourselves at a loss how to reconcile such opposite opinions. The smooth passage of the imagination along the ideas of the resembling perceptions makes us ascribe to them a perfect identity. The interrupted manner of their appearance makes us consider them as so many resembling, but still distinct beings, which appear after certain intervals. The perplexity arising from this contradiction produces a propension to unite these broken appearances by the fiction of a continu'd existence, which is the *third* part of that hypothesis I propos'd to explain.

Nothing is more certain from experience, than that any contradiction either to the sentiments or passions gives a sensible uneasiness, whether it proceeds from without or from within; from the opposition of external objects, or from the combat of internal principles. On the contrary, whatever strikes in with the natural propensities, and either externally forwards their satisfaction, or internally concurs with their movements, is sure to give a sensible pleasure. Now there being here an opposition betwixt the notion of the identity of resembling perceptions, and the interruption of their appearance, the mind must be uneasy in that situation, and will naturally seek relief from the uneasiness. Since the uneasiness arises from the opposition of two contrary principles, it must look for relief by sacrificing the one to the other. But as the smooth passage of our thought along our resembling perceptions makes us ascribe to them an identity, we can never without reluctance yield up that opinion. We must, therefore, turn to the other side, and suppose that our perceptions are no longer interrupted, but preserve a continu'd as well as an invariable existence, and are by that means entirely the same. But here the interruptions in the appearance of these perceptions are so long and frequent, that 'tis impossible to overlook them; and as the *appearance* of a perception in the mind and its *existence* seem at first sight entirely the same, it may be doubted, whether we can ever assent to so palpable a contradiction, and suppose a perception to exist without being present to the mind. In order to clear up this matter, and learn how the interruption in the appearance of a perception implies not necessarily an interruption in its existence, 'twill be proper to touch upon some principles. . . .[7]

We may begin with observing, that the difficulty in the present case is not concerning the matter of fact, or whether the mind forms such a conclusion concerning the continu'd existence of its perceptions, but only concerning the manner in which the conclusion is form'd, and principles from which it is deriv'd. 'Tis certain, that almost all mankind, and even philosophers themselves, for the greatest part of their lives take their perceptions to be their only objects, and suppose, that the very being, which is intimately present to the mind, is the real body or material existence. 'Tis also certain, that this very perception or object is suppos'd to have a continu'd uninterrupted being, and neither to be annihilated by our absence, nor to be brought into existence by our presence. When we are absent from it, we say it still exists, but that we do not feel, we do not see it. When we are present, we say we feel, or see it. Here then may arise two questions; *First,* How we can satisfy ourselves in supposing a perception to be absent from the mind without being annihilated. *Secondly,* After what manner we conceive an object to become present to the mind, without some new creation of a perception or image; and what we mean by this *seeing,* and *feeling,* and *perceiving.*

As to the first question; we may observe, that what we call a *mind,* is nothing but a heap or collection of different perceptions, united together by certain relations, and suppos'd, tho' falsely, to be endow'd with a perfect simplicity and identity. Now as every perception is distinguishable from another, and may be consider'd as separately existent; it evidently follows, that there is no absurdity in separating any particular perception from the mind; that is, in breaking off all its relations, with that connected mass of perceptions, which constitute a thinking being.

The same reasoning affords us an answer to the second question. If the name of *perception* renders not this separation from a mind absurd and contradictory, the name of *object,* standing for the very same thing, can never render their conjunction impossible. External objects are seen, and felt, and become present to the mind; that is, they acquire such a relation to a connected heap of perceptions, as to influence them very considerably in augmenting their number by present reflexions and passions, and in storing the memory with ideas. The same continu'd and uninterrupted Being may, therefore, be sometimes present to the mind, and sometimes absent from it, without any real or essential change in the Being itself. An interrupted appearance to the senses implies not necessarily an interruption in the existence. The supposition of the continu'd existence of sensible objects or perceptions involves no contradiction. We may easily indulge our inclination to that supposition. When the exact resemblance of our perceptions makes us ascribe to them an identity, we may remove the seeming interruption by feigning a continu'd being, which may fill those intervals, and preserve a perfect and entire identity to our perceptions.

But as we here not only *feign* but *believe* this continu'd existence, the question is, *from whence arises such a belief;* and this question leads us to the *fourth* member of this system. It has been prov'd already, that belief in general consists in nothing, but the vivacity of an idea; and that an idea may acquire this vivacity by its relation to some present impression. Impressions are naturally the most vivid perceptions of the mind; and this quality is in part convey'd by the relation to every connected idea. The relation causes a smooth passage from the impression to the idea, and even gives a propensity to that passage. The mind falls so easily from the one perception to the other, that it scarce perceives the change, but retains in the second a considerable share of the vivacity of the first. It is excited by the lively impression; and this vivacity is convey'd to the related idea, without any great diminution in the passage, by reason of the smooth transition and the propensity of the imagination.

But suppose, that this propensity arises from some other principle, besides that of relation; 'tis evident it must still have the same effect, and convey the vivacity from the impression to the idea. Now this is exactly the present case. Our memory presents us with a vast number of instances of perceptions perfectly resembling each other, that return at different distances of time, and after considerable interruptions. This resemblance gives us a propension to consider these interrupted perceptions as the same; and also a propension to connect them by a continu'd existence, in order to justify this identity, and avoid the contradiction, in which the interrupted appearance of these perceptions seems necessarily to involve us. Here then we have a propensity to feign the continu'd existence of all sensible objects; and as this propensity arises from some lively impressions of the memory, it bestows a vivacity on that fiction; or in other words, makes us believe the continu'd existence to objects, which are perfectly new to us, and of whose constancy and coherence we have no experience, 'tis because the manner, in which they present themselves to our senses, resembles that of constant and coherent objects; and this resemblance is a source of reasoning and analogy, and leads us to attribute the same qualities to the similar objects.

I believe an intelligent reader will find less difficulty to assent to this system, than to comprehend it fully and distinctly, and will allow, after a little reflection, that every part carries its own proof along with it. 'Tis indeed evident, that as the vulgar *suppose* their perceptions to be their only objects, and at the same time *believe* the continu'd existence of matter, we must account for the origin of the belief upon that supposition. Now upon that supposition, 'tis a false opinion that any of our objects, or perceptions, are identically the same after an interruption; and consequently the opinion of their identity can never arise from reason, but must arise from the imagination. The imagination is seduc'd into such an opinion only by means of the resemblance of certain perceptions; since we find they are only our resembling perceptions, which we have a propension to suppose the same. This propension to bestow an identity on our resembling perceptions, produces the fiction of a continu'd existence; since that fiction, as well as the identity, is really false, as is acknowledg'd by all philosophers, and has no other effect than to remedy the interruption of our perceptions, which is the only circumstance that is contrary to their identity. In the last place this propension causes belief by means of the present impressions of the memory; since without the remembrance of former sensations, 'tis plain we never shou'd have any belief of the continu'd existence of body. Thus in examining all these parts, we find that each of them is supported by the strongest proofs; and that all of them together form a consistent system, which is perfectly convincing. A strong propensity or inclination alone, without any present impression, will sometimes cause a belief or opinion. How much more when aided by that circumstance?

But tho' we are led after this manner, by the natural propensity of the imagination, to ascribe a continu'd existence to those sensible objects or perceptions, which we find to resemble each other in their interrupted appearance; yet a very little reflection and philosophy is sufficient to make us perceive the fallacy of that opinion. I have already observ'd, that there is an intimate connexion betwixt those two principles, of a *continu'd* and of a *distinct* or *independent* existence, and that we no sooner establish the one than the other follows, as a necessary consequence. 'Tis the opinion of a continu'd existence, which first takes place, and without much study or reflection draws the other along with it, wherever the mind follows its first and most natural tendency. But when we compare experiments, and reason a little upon them, we quickly perceive, that the doctrine of the independent existence of our sensible perceptions is contrary to the plainest experience. This leads us backward upon our footsteps to perceive our error in attributing a continu'd existence to our perceptions, and is the origin of many very curious opinions, which we shall here endeavour to account for.

'Twill first be proper to observe a few of those experiments, which convince us, that our perceptions are not possest of any independent existence. When we press one eye with a finger, we immediately perceive all the objects to become double, and one half of them to be remov'd from their common and natural position. But as we do not attribute a continu'd existence to both these perceptions, and as they are both of the same nature, we clearly perceive, that all our perceptions are dependent on our organs, and the disposition of our nerves and animal spirits. This opinion is confirm'd by the seeming encrease and diminution of objects, according to their distance; by the apparent alterations in their figure; by the changes in their colour and other qualities from our sickness and distempers; and by an infinite number of other experiments of the same kind; from all which we learn, that our sensible perceptions are not possest of any distinct or independent existence.

The natural consequence of this reasoning shou'd be, that our perceptions have no more a continu'd than an independent existence; and indeed philosophers have so far run into this opinion, that they change their system, and distinguish, (as we shall do for the future) betwixt perceptions and objects, of which the former are suppos'd to be interrupted, and perishing, and different at every different return; the latter to be uninterrupted, and to preserve a continu'd existence and identity. But however philosophical this new system may be esteem'd, I assert that 'tis only a palliative remedy, and that it contains all the difficulties of the vulgar system, with some others, that are peculiar to itself. There are no principles either of the understanding or fancy, which lead us directly to embrace this opinion of the double existence of perceptions and objects, nor can we arrive at it but by passing thro' the common hypothesis of the identity and continuance of our interrupted perceptions. Were we not first persuaded, that our perceptions are our only objects, and continue to exist even when they no longer make their appearance to the senses, we shou'd never be led to think that our perceptions and objects are different, and that our objects alone preserve a continu'd existence. 'The latter hypothesis has no primary recommendation either to reason or the imagination, but acquires all its influence on the imagination from the former.' This proposition contains two parts, which we shall endeavour to prove as distinctly and clearly, as such abstruse subjects will permit.

As to the first part of the proposition, *that this philosophical hypothesis has no primary recommendation, either to reason or the imagination,* we may soon satisfy ourselves with regard to *reason* by the following reflections. The only existences, of which we are certain, are perceptions, which being immediately present to us by consciousness, command our strongest assent, and are the first foundation of all our conclusions. The only conclusion we can draw from the existence of one thing to that of another, is by means of the relation of cause and effect, which shows, that there is a connexion betwixt them, and that the existence of one is dependent on that of the other. The idea of this relation is deriv'd from past experience, by which we find, that two beings are constantly conjoin'd together, and are always present at once to the mind. But as no beings are ever present to the mind but perceptions; it follows that we may observe a conjunction or a relation of cause and effect between different perceptions, but can never observe it between perceptions and objects. 'Tis impossible, therefore, that from the existence or any of the qualities of the former, we can ever form any conclusion concerning the existence of the latter, or ever satisfy our reason in this particular.

'Tis no less certain, that this philosophical system has no primary recommendation to the *imagination,* and that the faculty wou'd never, of itself, and by its original tendency, have fallen upon such a principle. I confess it will be somewhat difficult to prove this to the full satisfaction of the reader; because it implies a negative, which in many cases will not admit of any positive proof. If any one wou'd take the pains to examine this question, and wou'd invent a system, to account for the direct origin of this opinion from the imagination, we shou'd be able, by the examination of that system, to pronounce a certain judgment in the present subject. Let it be taken for granted, that our perceptions are broken, and interrupted, and however like, are still different from each other; and let any one upon this supposition shew why the fancy, directly and immediately, proceeds to the belief of another existence, resembling these perceptions in their nature, but yet continu'd, and uninterrupted, and identical; and after he has done this to my satisfaction, I promise to renounce my present opinion. Mean while I cannot forbear concluding, from the very abstractedness and difficulty of the first supposition, that 'tis an improper subject for the fancy to work upon. Whoever wou'd explain the origin of the *common* opinion concerning the continu'd and distinct existence of body, must take the mind in its *common* situation, and must proceed upon the supposition, that our perceptions are our only objects, and continue to exist even when they are not perceiv'd. Tho' this opinion be false, 'tis the most natural of any, and has alone any primary recommendation to the fancy.

As to the second part of the proposition, *that the philosophical system acquires all its influence on the imagination from the vulgar one;* we may observe, that this is a natural and unavoidable consequence of the foregoing conclusion, *that it has no primary recommendation to reason or the imagination.* For as the philosophical system is found by experience to take hold of many minds, and in particular of all those, who reflect ever so little on this subject, it must derive all its authority from the vulgar system; since it has no original authority of its own. The manner, in which these two systems, tho' directly contrary, are connected together, may be explain'd, as follows.

The imagination naturally runs on in this train of thinking. Our perceptions are our only objects: Resembling perceptions are the same, however broken or uninterrupted in their appearance: This appearing interruption is contrary to the identity: The interruption consequently extends not beyond the appearance, and the perception or object really continues to exist, even when absent from us: Our sensible perceptions have, therefore, a continu'd and uninterrupted existence. But as a little reflection destroys this conclusion, that our perceptions have a continu'd existence, by showing that they have a dependent one, 'twou'd naturally be expected, that we must altogether reject the opinion, that there is such a thing in nature as a continu'd existence, which is preserv'd even when it no longer appears to the senses. The case, however, is otherwise. Philosophers are so far from rejecting the opinion of a continu'd existence upon rejecting that of the independence and continuance of our sensible perceptions, that tho' all sects agree in the latter sentiment, the former, which is, in a manner, its necessary consequence, has been peculiar to a few extravagant sceptics; who after all maintain'd that opinion in words only, and were never able to bring themselves sincerely to believe it.

There is a great difference betwixt such opinions as we form after a calm and profound reflection, and such as we embrace by a kind of instinct or natural impulse, on account of their suitableness and conformity to the mind. If these opinions become contrary, 'tis not difficult to foresee which of them will have the advantage. As long as our attention is bent upon the subject, the philosophical and study'd principle may prevail; but the moment we relax our thoughts, nature will display herself, and draw us back to our former opinion. Nay she has sometimes such an influence, that she can stop our progress, even in the midst of our most profound reflections, and keep us from running on with all the consequences of any philosophical opinion. Thus tho' we clearly perceive the dependence and interruption of our perceptions, we stop short in our carreer, and never upon that account reject the notion of an independent and continu'd existence. That opinion has taken such deep root in the imagination, that 'tis impossible ever to eradicate it, nor will any strain'd metaphysical conviction of the dependence of our perceptions be sufficient for that purpose.

But tho' our natural and obvious principles here prevail above our study'd reflections, 'tis certain there must be some struggle and opposition in the case; at least so long as these reflections retain any force or vivacity. In order to set ourselves at ease in this particular, we contrive a new hypothesis, which seems to comprehend both these principles of reason and imagination. This hypothesis is the philosophical one of the double existence of perceptions and objects; which pleases our reason, in allowing, that our dependent perceptions are interrupted and different; and at the same time is agreeable to the imagination, in attributing a continu'd existence to something else, which we call *objects.* This philosophical system, therefore, is the monstrous offspring of two principles, which are contrary to each other, which are both at once embrac'd by the mind, and which are unable mutually to destroy each other. The imagination tells us, that our resembling perceptions have a continu'd and uninterrupted existence, and are not annihilated by their absence. Reflection tells us, that even our resembling perceptions are interrupted in their existence, and different from each other. The contradiction betwixt these opinions we elude by a new fiction, which is conformable to the hypotheses both of reflection and fancy, by ascribing these contrary qualities to different existences; the *interruption* to perceptions, and the *continuance* to objects. Nature is obstinate, and will not quit the field, however strongly attack'd by reason; and at the same time reason is so clear in the point, that there is no possibility of disguising her. Not being able to reconcile these two enemies, we endeavour to set ourselves at ease as much as possible, by successively granting to each whatever it demands, and by feigning a double existence, where each may find something, that has all the conditions it desires. Were we fully convinc'd, that our resembling perceptions are continu'd, and identical, and independent, we shou'd never run into this opinion of a double existence; since we shou'd find satisfaction in our first supposition, and wou'd not look beyond. Again, were we fully convinc'd, that our perceptions are dependent, and interrupted, and different, we shou'd be as little inclin'd to embrace the opinion of a double existence; since in that case we shou'd clearly perceive the error of our first supposition of a continu'd existence, and wou'd never regard it any farther. 'Tis therefore from the intermediate situation of the mind, that this opinion arises, and from such an adherence to these two contrary principles, as makes us seek some pretext to justify our receiving both; which happily at last is found in the system of a double existence.

Another advantage of this philosophical system is its similarity to the vulgar one; by which means we can humour our reason for a moment, when it becomes troublesome and sollicitous; and yet upon its least negligence or inattention, can easily return to our vulgar and natural notions. Accordingly we find, that philosophers neglect not this advantage; but immediately upon leaving their closets, mingle with the rest of mankind in those exploded opinions, that our perceptions are our only objects, and continue identically and uninterruptedly the same in all their interrupted appearances.

There are other particulars of this system, wherein we may remark its dependence on the fancy, in a very conspicuous manner. Of these, I shall observe the two following. *First,* We suppose external objects to resemble internal perceptions. I have already shewn, that the relation of cause and effect can never afford us any just conclusion from the existence or qualities of our perceptions to the existence of external continu'd objects: And I shall farther add, that even tho' they cou'd afford such a conclusion, we shou'd never have any reason to infer, that our objects resemble our perceptions. That opinion, therefore, is deriv'd from nothing but the quality of the fancy above-explain'd, *that it borrows all its ideas from some precedent perception.* We never can conceive any thing but perceptions, and therefore must make everything resemble them.

Secondly, As we suppose our objects in general to resemble our perceptions, so we take it for granted, that every particular object resembles that perception, which it causes. The relation of cause and effect determines us to join the other of resemblance; and the ideas of these existences being already united together in the fancy but the former relation, we naturally add the latter to compleat the union. We have a strong propensity to compleat every union by joining new relations to those which we have before observ'd betwixt any ideas, as we shall have occasion to observe presently.

Having thus given an account of all the systems both popular and philosophical, with regard to external existence, I cannot forbear giving vent to a certain sentiment, which arises upon reviewing those systems. I begun this subject with premising, that we ought to have an implicit faith in our senses, and that this wou'd be the conclusion, I shou'd draw from the whole of my reasoning. But to be ingenuous, I feel myself *at present* of a quite contrary sentiment, and am more inclin'd to repose no faith at all in my senses, or rather imagination, than to place in it such an implicit confidence. I cannot conceive how such trivial qualities of the fancy, conducted by such false suppositions, can ever lead to any solid and rational system. They are the coherence and constancy of our perceptions, which produce the opinion of their continu'd existence; tho' these qualities of perceptions have no perceivable connexion with such an existence. The constancy of our perceptions has the most considerable effect, and yet is attended with the greatest difficulties. 'Tis a gross illusion to suppose, that our resembling perceptions are numerically the same; and 'tis this illusion, which leads us into the opinion, that these perceptions are uninterrupted, and are still existent, even when they are not present to the senses. This is the case with our popular system. And as to our philosophical one, 'tis liable to the same difficulties; and is over-and-above loaded with this absurdity, that it at once denies and establishes the vulgar supposition. Philosophers deny our resembling perceptions to be identically the same, and uninterrupted; and yet have so great a propensity to believe them such, that they arbitrarily invent a new set of perceptions, to which they attribute these qualities. I say, a new set of perceptions: For we may well suppose in general, but 'tis impossible for us distinctly to conceive, objects to be in their nature any thing but exactly the same with perceptions. What then can we look for from this confusion of groundless and extraordinary opinions but error and falshood? And how can we justify to ourselves any belief we repose in them?

This sceptical doubt, both with respect to reason and the senses, is a malady, which can never be radically cur'd, but must return upon us every moment, however we may chace it away, and sometimes may seem entirely free from it. 'Tis impossible upon any system to defend either our understanding or senses; and we but expose them farther when we endeavour to justify them in that manner. As the sceptical doubt arises naturally from a profound and intense reflection on those subjects, it always encreases, the farther we carry our reflections, whether in opposition or conformity to it. Carelessness and in-attention alone can afford us any remedy. For this reason I rely entirely upon them; and take it for granted, whatever may be the reader's opinion at this present moment, that an hour hence he will be persuaded there is both an external and internal world; and going upon that supposition, I intend to examine some general systems both ancient and modern, which have been propos'd of both, before I proceed to a more particular enquiry concerning our impressions. This will not, perhaps, in the end be found foreign to our present purpose.

Notes

1. Part II. sect. 6.
2. Sect. 5.
3. Part II. sect. 4.
4. Part II. sect. 5.
5. Part II. sect. 5.
6. This reasoning, it must be confest, is somewhat abstruse, and difficult to be comprehended; but it is remarkable, that this very difficulty may be converted into a proof of the reasoning. We may observe, that there are two relations, and both of them resemblances, which contribute to our mistaking the

succession of our interrupted perceptions for an identical object. The first is, the resemblance of the perceptions: The second is the resemblance, which the act of the mind in surveying a succession of resembling objects bears to that in surveying an identical object. Now these resemblances we are apt to confound with each other; and 'tis natural we shou'd, according to this very reasoning. But let us keep them distinct, and we shall find no difficulty in conceiving the precedent argument.

7. Sect. 6.

An Enquiry Concerning Human Understanding

DAVID HUME

Section II
Of the Origin of Ideas

Every one will readily allow, that there is a considerable difference between the perceptions of the mind, when a man feels the pain of excessive heat, or the pleasure of moderate warmth, and when he afterwards recalls to his memory this sensation, or anticipates it by his imagination. These faculties may mimic or copy the perceptions of the senses; but they never can entirely reach the force and vivacity of the original sentiment. The utmost we say of them, even when they operate with greatest vigour, is, that they represent their object in so lively a manner, that we could *almost* say we feel or see it: But, except the mind be disordered by disease or madness, they never can arrive at such a pitch of vivacity, as to render these perceptions altogether undistinguishable. All the colours of poetry, however splendid, can never paint natural objects in such a manner as to make the description be taken for a real landskip. The most lively thought is still inferior to the dullest sensation.

We may observe a like distinction to run through all the other perceptions of the mind. A man in a fit of anger, is actuated in a very different manner from one who only thinks of that emotion. If you tell me, that any person is in love, I easily understand your meaning, and form a just conception of his situation; but never can mistake that conception for the real disorders and agitations of the passion. When we reflect on our past sentiments and affections, our thought is a faithful mirror, and copies its objects truly; but the colours which it employs are faint and dull, in comparison of those in which our original perceptions were clothed. It requires no nice discernment or metaphysical head to mark the distinction between them.

Here therefore we may divide all the perceptions of the mind into two classes or species, which are distinguished by their different degrees of force and vivacity. The less forcible and lively are commonly denominated *Thoughts* or *Ideas*. The other species want a name in our language, and in most others; I suppose, because it was not requisite for any, but philosophical purposes, to rank them under a general term or appellation. Let us, therefore, use a little freedom, and call them *Impressions;* employing that word in a sense somewhat different from the usual. By the term *impression,* then, I mean all our more lively perceptions, when we hear, or see, or feel, or love, or hate, or desire, or will. And impressions are distinguished from ideas, which are the less lively perceptions, of which we are conscious, when we reflect on any of those sensations or movements above mentioned.

Nothing, at first view, may seem more unbounded than the thought of man, which not only escapes all human power and authority, but is not even restrained within the limits of nature and reality. To form monsters, and join incongruous shapes and appearances, costs the imagination no more trouble than to conceive the most natural

From *Enquiries Concerning Human Understanding and Concerning the Principles of Morals,* 2nd ed. (Oxford: Oxford University Press, 1902), pp. 17–79.

and familiar objects. And while the body is confined to one planet, along which it creeps with pain and difficulty; the thought can in an instant transport us into the most distant regions of the universe; or even beyond the universe, into the unbounded chaos, where nature is supposed to lie in total confusion. What never was seen, or heard of, may yet be conceived; nor is any thing beyond the power of thought, except what implies an absolute contradiction.

But though our thought seems to possess this unbounded liberty, we shall find, upon a nearer examination, that it is really confined within very narrow limits, and that all this creative power of the mind amounts to no more than the faculty of compounding, transposing, augmenting, or diminishing the materials afforded us by the senses and experience. When we think of a golden mountain, we only join two consistent ideas, *gold,* and *mountain,* with which we were formerly acquainted. A virtuous horse we can conceive; because, from our own feeling, we can conceive virtue; and this we may unite to the figure and shape of a horse, which is an animal familiar to us. In short, all the materials of thinking are derived either from our outward or inward sentiment: the mixture and composition of these belongs alone to the mind and will. Or, to express myself in philosophical language, all our ideas or more feeble perceptions are copies of our impressions or more lively ones.

To prove this, the two following arguments will, I hope, be sufficient. First, when we analyze our thoughts or ideas, however compounded or sublime, we always find that they resolve themselves into such simple ideas as were copied from a precedent feeling or sentiment. Even those ideas, which, at first view, seem the most wide of this origin, are found, upon a nearer scrutiny, to be derived from it. The idea of God, as meaning and infinitely intelligent, wise, and good Being, arises from reflecting on the operations of our own mind, and augmenting, without limit, those qualities of goodness and wisdom. We may prosecute this enquiry to what length we please; where we shall always find, that every idea which we examine is copied from a similar impression. Those who would assert that this position is not universally true nor without exception, have only one, and that an easy method of refuting it; by producing that idea, which, in their opinion, is not derived from this source. It will then be incumbent on us, if we would maintain our doctrine, to produce the impression, or lively perception, which corresponds to it.

Secondly. If it happen, from a defect of the organ, that a man is not susceptible of any species of sensation, we always find that he is as little susceptible of the correspondent ideas. A blind man can form no notion of colours; a deaf man of sounds. Restore either of them that sense in which he is deficient; by opening this new inlet for his sensations, you also open an inlet for the ideas; and he finds no difficulty in conceiving these objects. The case is the same, if the object, proper for exciting any sensation, has never been applied to the organ. A Laplander or Negro has no notion of the relish of wine. And though there are a few or no instances of a like deficiency in the mind, where a person has never felt or is wholly incapable of a sentiment or passion that belongs to his species; yet we find the same observation to take place in a less degree. A man of mild manners can form no idea of inveterate revenge or cruelty; nor can a selfish heart easily conceive the heights of friendship and generosity. It is readily allowed, that other beings may possess many senses of which we can have no conception; because the ideas of them have never been introduced to us in the only manner by which an idea can have access to the mind, to wit, by the actual feeling and sensation.

There is, however, one contradictory phenomenon, which may prove that it is not absolutely impossible for ideas to arise, independent of their correspondent impressions. I believe it will readily be allowed, that the several distinct ideas of colour, which enter by the eye, or those of sound, which are conveyed by the ear, are really different from each other; though, at the same time, resembling. Now if this be true of different colours, it must be no less so of the different shades of the same colour; and each shade produces a distinct idea, independent of the rest. For if this should be denied, it is possible, by the continual gradation of shades, to run a colour insensibly into what is most remote from it; and if you will not allow any of the means to be different, you cannot, without absurdity, deny the extremes to be the same. Suppose, therefore, a person to have enjoyed his sight for thirty years, and to have become perfectly acquainted with colours of all kinds except one particular shade of blue, for instance, which it never has been his fortune to meet with. Let all different shades of that colour, except that single one, be placed before him, descending gradually from the deepest to the lightest; it is plain that he will perceive a blank, where that shade is wanting, and will be sensible that there is a greater distance in that place between the contiguous colours than in any other. Now I ask, whether it be possible for him, from his own imagination, to supply this deficiency, and raise up to himself the idea of that particular shade, though it had never been conveyed to him by his senses? I believe there are few but will be of opinion that he can: and this may serve as a proof that the simple ideas are not always, in every instance, derived from the correspondent impressions; though this instance is so singular, that it is scarcely worth our observing, and does not merit that for it alone we should alter our general maxim.

Here, therefore, is a proposition, which not only seems, in itself, simple and intelligible; but, if a proper use were made of it, might render every dispute equally intelligible, and banish all that jargon, which has so long taken possession of metaphysical reasonings, and drawn disgrace upon them. All ideas, especially abstract ones, are naturally faint and obscure: the mind has but a slender hold of them: they are apt to be confounded with other resembling ideas; and when we have often employed any term, though without a distinct meaning, we are apt to imagine it has a determinate idea annexed to it. On the contrary, all impressions, that is, all sensations, either outward or inward, are strong and vivid: the limits between them are more exactly determined: nor is it easy to fall into any error or mistake with regard to them. When we entertain, therefore, any suspicion that a philosophical term is employed without any meaning or idea (as is but too frequent), we need but enquire, *from what impression is that supposed idea derived?* And if it be impossible to assign any, this will serve to confirm our suspicion. By bringing ideas into so clear a light we may reasonably hope to remove all dispute, which may arise, concerning their nature and reality.[1]

Section III
Of the Association of Ideas

It is evident that there is a principle of connexion between the different thoughts or ideas of the mind, and that, in their appearance to the memory or imagination, they introduce each other with a certain degree of method and regularity. In our more serious thinking or discourse this is so observable that any particular thought, which breaks in upon the regular tract or chain of ideas, is immediately remarked and rejected. And even in our wildest and most wandering reveries, nay in our very dreams, we shall find, if we reflect, that the imagination ran not altogether at adventures, but that there was still a connexion upheld among the different ideas, which succeeded each other. Were the loosest and freest conversation to be transcribed, there would immediately be observed something which connected it in all its transitions. Or where this is wanting, the person who broke the thread of discourse might still inform you, that there had secretly revolved in his mind a succession of thought, which had gradually led him from the subject of conversation. Among different languages, even where we cannot suspect the least connexion or communication, it is found, that the words, expressive of ideas, the most compounded, do yet nearly correspond to each other: a certain proof that the simple ideas, comprehended in the compound ones, were bound together by some universal principle, which had an equal influence on all mankind.

Though it be too obvious to escape observation, that different ideas are connected together; I do not find that any philosopher has attempted to enumerate or class all the principles of association; a subject, however, that seems worthy of curiosity. To me, there appear to be only three principles of connexion among ideas, namely, *Resemblance, Contiguity* in time or place, and *Cause* or *Effect*.

That these principles serve to connect ideas will not, I believe, be much doubted. A picture naturally leads our thoughts to the original:[2] the mention of one apartment in a building naturally introduces an enquiry or discourse concerning the others:[3] and if we think of a wound, we can scarcely forbear reflecting on the pain which follows it.[4] But that this enumeration is complete, and that there are no other principles of association except these, may be difficult to prove to the satisfaction of the reader, or even to a man's own satisfaction. All we can do, in such cases, is to run over several instances, and examine carefully the principle which binds the different thoughts to each other, never stopping till we render the principle as general as possible.[5] The more instances we examine, and the more care we employ, the more assurance shall we acquire, that the enumeration, which we form from the whole, is complete and entire.

Section IV
Sceptical Doubts Concerning the Operations of the Understanding

Part I

All the objects of human reason or enquiry may naturally be divided into two kinds, to wit, *Relations of Ideas,* and *Matters of Fact.* Of the first kind are the sciences of Geometry, Algebra, and Arithmetic; and in short, every affirmation which is either intuitively or demonstratively certain. *That the square of the hypothenuse is equal to the square of the two sides,* is a proposition which expresses a relation between these figures. *That three times five is equal to the half of thirty,* expresses a relation between these numbers. Propositions of this kind are discoverable by the mere operation of thought, without dependence on what is anywhere existent in the universe. Though there never were a circle or triangle in nature, the truths demonstrated by Euclid would for ever retain their certainty and evidence.

Matters of fact, which are the second objects of human reason, are not ascertained in the same manner; nor is our evidence of their truth, however great, of a like nature with the foregoing. The contrary of every matter of fact is still possible; because it can never imply a contradiction, and is conceived by the mind with the same facility and distinctness, as if ever so conformable to reality. *That the sun will not rise to-morrow* is no less intelligible a proposition, and implies no more contradiction than the affirmation, *that it will rise.* We should in vain, therefore, attempt to demonstrate its falsehood. Were it demonstratively false, it would imply a contradiction, and could never be distinctly conceived by the mind.

It may, therefore, be a subject worthy of curiosity, to enquire what is the nature of that evidence which assures us of any real existence and matter of fact, beyond the present testimony of our senses, or the records of our memory. This part of philosophy, it is observable, has been little cultivated, either by the ancients or moderns; and therefore our doubts and errors, in the prosecution of so important an enquiry, may be the more excusable; while we march through such difficult paths without any guide or direction. They may even prove useful, by exciting curiosity, and destroying that implicit faith and security, which is the bane of all reasoning and free enquiry. The discovery of defects in the common philosophy, if any such there be, will not, I presume, be a discouragement, but rather an incitement, as is usual, to attempt something more full and satisfactory than has yet been proposed to the public.

All reasonings concerning matter of fact seem to be founded on the relation of *Cause and Effect.* By means of that relation alone we can go beyond the evidence of our memory and senses. If you were to ask a man, why he believes any matter of fact, which is absent; for instance, that his friend is in the country, or in France; he would give you a reason; and this reason would be some other fact; as a letter received from him, or the knowledge of his former resolutions and promises. A man finding a watch or any other machine in a desert island, would conclude that there had once been men in that island. All our reasonings concerning fact are of the same nature. And here it is constantly supposed that there is a connexion between the present fact and that which is inferred from it. Were there nothing to bind them together, the inference would be entirely precarious. The hearing of an articulate voice and rational discourse in the dark assures us of the presence of some person: Why? because these are the effects of the human make and fabric, and closely connected with it. If we anatomize all the other reasonings of this nature, we shall find that they are founded on the relation of cause and effect, and that this relation is either near or remote, direct or collateral. Heat and light are collateral effects of fire, and the one effect may justly be inferred from the other.

If we would satisfy ourselves, therefore, concerning the nature of that evidence, which assures us of matters of fact, we must enquire how we arrive at the knowledge of cause and effect.

I shall venture to affirm, as a general proposition, which admits of no exception, that the knowledge of this relation is not, in any instance, attained by reasonings a priori; but arises entirely from experience, when we find that any particular objects are constantly conjoined with each other. Let an object be presented to a man of ever so strong natural reason and abilities; if that object be entirely new to him, he will not be able, by the most accurate examination of its sensible qualities, to discover any of its causes or effects. Adam, though his rational faculties be supposed, at the very first, entirely perfect, could not have inferred from the fluidity and transparency of water that it would suffocate him, or from the light and warmth of fire that it would consume him. No object ever discovers, by the qualities which appear to the senses, either the causes which produce it, or the effects which will arise from it; nor can our reason, unassisted by experience, ever draw any inference concerning real existence and matter of fact.

This proposition, *that causes and effects are discoverable, not by reason but by experience,* will readily be admitted with regard to such objects, as we remember to have once been altogether unknown to us; since we must be conscious of the utter inability, which we then lay under, of foretelling what would arise from them. Present two smooth pieces of marble to a man who has no tincture of natural philosophy; he will never discover that they will adhere together in such a manner as to require great force to separate them in a direct line, while they make so small a resistance to a lateral pressure. Such events, as bear little analogy to the common course of nature, are also readily confessed to be known only by experience; nor does any man imagine that the explosion of gunpowder, or the attraction of a loadstone, could ever be discovered by arguments a priori. In like manner, when an effect is supposed to depend upon an intricate machinery or secret structure of parts, we make no difficulty in attributing all our knowledge of it to experience. Who will assert that he can give the ultimate reason, why milk or bread is proper nourishment for a man, not for a lion or a tiger?

But the same truth may not appear, at first sight, to have the same evidence with regard to events, which have become familiar to us from our first appearance in the world, which bear a close analogy to the whole course of nature, and which are supposed to depend on the simple qualities of objects, without any secret structure of parts. We are apt to imagine that we could discover these effects by the mere operation of our reason, without experience. We fancy, that were we brought on a sudden into this world, we could at first have inferred that one Billiard-ball would communicate motion to another upon impulse; and that we needed not to have waited for the event, in order to pronounce with certainty concerning it. Such is the influence of custom, that, where it is strongest, it not only covers our natural ignorance, but even conceals itself, and seems not to take place, merely because it is found in the highest degree.

But to convince us that all the laws of nature, and all the operations of bodies without exception, are known only by experience, the following reflections may, perhaps, suffice. Were any object presented to us, and were we required to pronounce concerning the effect, which will result from it, without consulting past observation; after what manner, I beseech you, must the mind proceed in this operation? It must invent or imagine some event, which it ascribes to the object as its effect; and it is plain that this invention must be entirely arbitrary. The mind can never possibly find the effect in the supposed cause, by the most accurate scrutiny and examination. For the effect is totally different from the cause, and consequently can never be discovered in it. Motion in the second Billiard-ball is a quite distinct event from motion in the first; nor is there anything in the one to suggest the smallest hint of the other. A stone or piece of metal raised into the air, and left without any support, immediately falls: but to consider the matter a priori, is there anything we discover in this situation which can beget the idea of a downward, rather than an upward, or any other motion, in the stone or metal?

And as the first imagination or invention of a particular effect, in all natural operations, is arbitrary, where we consult not experience; so must we also esteem the supposed tie or connexion between the cause and effect, which binds them together, and renders it impossible that any other effect could result from the operation of that cause. When I see, for instance, a Billiard-ball moving in a straight line towards another; even suppose motion in the second ball should by accident be suggested to me, as the result of their contact or impulse; may I not conceive, that a hundred different events might as well follow from that cause? May not both these balls remain at absolute rest? May not the first ball return in a straight line, or leap off from the second in any line or direction? All these suppositions are consistent and conceivable. Why then should we give the preference to one, which is no more consistent or conceivable than the rest? All our reasonings a priori will never be able to show us any foundation for this preference.

In a word, then, every effect is a distinct event from its cause. It could not, therefore, be discovered in the cause, and the first invention or conception of it, a priori, must be entirely arbitrary. And even after it is suggested, the conjunction of it with the cause must appear equally arbitrary; since there are always many other effects, which, to reason, must seem fully as consistent and natural. In vain, therefore, should we pretend to determine any single event, or infer any cause of effect, without the assistance of observation and experience.

Hence we may discover the reason why no philosopher, who is rational and modest, has ever pretended to assign the ultimate cause of any natural operation, or to show distinctly the action of that power, which produces any single effect in the universe. It is confessed, that the utmost effort of human reason is to reduce the principles, productive of natural phenomena, to a greater simplicity, and to resolve the many particular effects into a few general causes, by means of reasonings from analogy, experience, and observation. But as to the causes of these general causes, we should in vain attempt their discovery; nor shall we ever be able to satisfy ourselves, by any particular explication of them. These ultimate springs and principles are totally shut up from human curiosity and enquiry. Elasticity, gravity, cohesion of parts, communication of motion by impulse; these are probably the ultimate causes and principles which we shall ever discover in nature; and we may esteem ourselves sufficiently happy, if, by accurate enquiry and reasoning, we can trace up the particular phenomena to, or near to, these general principles. The most perfect philosophy of the natural kind only staves off our ignorance a little longer: as perhaps the most perfect philosophy of the moral or metaphysical kind serves only to discover larger portions of it. Thus the observation of human blindness and weakness is the result of all philosophy, and meets us at every turn, in spite of our endeavours to elude or avoid it.

Nor is geometry, when taken into the assistance of natural philosophy, ever able to remedy this defect, or lead us into the knowledge of ultimate causes, by all that accuracy of reasoning for which it is so justly celebrated. Every part of mixed mathematics proceeds upon the supposition that certain laws are established by nature in her operations; and abstract reasonings are employed, either to assist experience in the discovery of these laws, or to determine their influence in particular instances, where it depends upon any precise degree of distance and quantity. Thus, it is a law of motion, discovered by experience, that the moment or force of any body in motion is in the compound ratio or proportion of its solid contents and its velocity; and consequently, that a small force may remove the greatest obstacle or raise the greatest weight, if, by any contrivance or machinery, we can increase the velocity of that force, so as to make it an overmatch for its antagonist. Geometry assists us in the application of this law, by giving us the just dimensions of all the parts and figures which can enter into any species of machine; but still the discovery of the law itself is owing merely to experience, and all the abstract reasonings in the world could never lead us one step towards the knowledge of it. When we reason a priori, and consider merely any object or cause, as it appears to the mind, independent of all observation, it never could suggest to us the notion of any distinct object, such as its effect; much less, show us the inseparable and inviolable connexion between them. A man must be very sagacious who could discover by reasoning that crystal is the effect of heat, and ice of cold, without being previously acquainted with the operation of these qualities.

Part II

But we have not yet attained any tolerable satisfaction with regard to the question first proposed. Each solution still gives rise to a new question as difficult as the foregoing, and leads us on to farther enquiries. When it is asked, *What is the nature of all our reasonings concerning matter of fact?* the proper answer seems to be, that they are founded on the relation of cause and effect. When again it is asked, *What is the foundation of all our reasonings and conclusions concerning that relation?* it may be replied in one word, Experience. But if we still carry on our sifting humour, and ask, *What is the foundation of all conclusions from experience?* this implies a new question, which may be of more difficult solution and explication. Philosophers, that give themselves airs of superior wisdom and sufficiency, have a hard task when they encounter persons of inquisitive dispositions, who push them from every corner to which they retreat, and who are sure at last to bring them to some dangerous dilemma. The best expedient to prevent this confusion, is to be modest in our pretensions; and even to discover the difficulty ourselves before it is objected to us. By this means, we may make a kind of merit of our very ignorance.

I shall content myself, in this section, with an easy task, and shall pretend only to give a negative answer to the question here proposed. I say then, that, even after we have experience of the operations of cause and effect, our conclusions from that experience are *not* founded on reasoning, or any process of the understanding. This answer we must endeavour both to explain and to defend.

It must certainly be allowed, that nature has kept us at a great distance from all her secrets, and has afforded us only the knowledge of a few superficial qualities of objects; while she conceals from us those powers and principles on which the influence of those objects entirely depends. Our senses inform us of the colour, weight, and consistence of bread; but neither sense nor reason can ever inform us of those qualities which fit it for the nourishment and support of a human body. Sight or feeling conveys an idea of the actual motion of bodies; but as to that wonderful force or power, which would carry on a moving body for ever in a continued change of place, and which bodies never lose but by communicating it to others; of this we cannot form the most distant conception. But notwithstanding this ignorance of natural powers[6] and principles, we always presume, when we see like sensible qualities, that they have like secret powers, and expect that effects, similar to those which we have experienced, will follow from them. If a body of a like colour and consistence with that bread, which we have formerly eat, be presented to us, we make no scruple of repeating the experiment, and foresee, with certainty, like nourishment and support. Now this is a process of the mind or thought, of which I would willingly know the foundation. It is allowed on all hands that there is no known connexion between the sensible qualities and the secret powers; and consequently, that the mind is not led to form such a conclusion concerning their constant and regular conjunction, by anything which it knows of their nature. As to past *Experience,* it can be allowed to give *direct* and *certain* information of those precise objects only, and that precise period of time, which fell under its cognizance: but why this experience should be extended to future times, and to other objects, which for aught we know, may be only in appearance similar; this is the main question on which I would insist. The bread, which I formerly eat, nourished me; that is, a body of such sensible qualities was, at that time, endued with such secret powers: but does it follow, that other bread must also nourish me at another time, and that like sensible qualities must always be attended with like secret powers? The consequence seems nowise necessary. At least, it must be acknowledged that there is here a consequence drawn by the mind; that there is a certain step taken; a process of thought, and an inference, which wants to be explained. These two propositions are far from being the same, *I have found that such an object has always been attended with such an effect,* and *I foresee, that other objects, which are, in appearance, similar, will be attended with similar effects.* I shall allow, if you please, that the one proposition may justly be inferred from the other: I know, in fact, that it always is inferred. But if you insist that the inference is made by a chain of reasoning, I desire you to produce that reasoning. The connexion between these propositions is not intuitive. There is required a medium, which may enable the mind to draw such an inference, if indeed it be drawn by reasoning and argument. What that medium is, I must confess, passes my comprehension; and it is incumbent on those to produce it, who assert that it really exists, and is the origin of all our conclusions concerning matter of fact.

This negative argument must certainly, in process of time, become altogether convincing, if many penetrating and able philosophers shall turn their enquiries this way and no one be ever able to discover any connecting proposition or intermediate step, which supports the understanding in this conclusion. But as the question is yet new, every reader may not trust so far to his own penetration, as to conclude, because an argument escapes his enquiry, that therefore it does not really exist. For this reason it may be requisite to venture upon a more difficult task; and enumerating all the branches of human knowledge, endeavour to show that none of them can afford such an argument.

All reasonings may be divided into two kinds, namely, demonstrative reasoning, or that concerning relations of ideas, and moral reasoning, or that concerning matter of fact and existence. That there are no demonstrative arguments in the case seems evident; since it implies no contradiction that the course of nature may change, and that an object, seemingly like those which we have experienced, may be attended with different or contrary effects. May I not clearly and distinctly conceive that a body, falling from the clouds, and which, in all other respects, resembles snow, has yet the taste of salt or feeling of fire? Is there any more intelligible proposition than to affirm, that all the trees will flourish in December and January, and decay in May and June? Now whatever is intelligible, and can be distinctly conceived, implies no contradiction, and can never be proved false by any demonstrative argument or abstract reasoning a priori.

If we be, therefore, engaged by arguments to put trust in past experience, and make it the standard of our future judgement, these arguments must be probable only, or such as regard matter of fact and real existence, according to the division above mentioned. But that there is no argument of this kind, must appear, if our explication of that species of reasoning be admitted as solid and satisfactory. We have said that all arguments concerning existence are founded on the relation of cause and effect; that our knowledge of that relation is derived entirely from experience; and that all our experimental conclusions proceed upon the supposition that the future will be conformable to the past. To endeavour, therefore, the proof of this last supposition by probable arguments, or arguments regarding existence, must be evidently going in a circle, and taking that for granted, which is the very point in question.

In reality, all arguments from experience are founded on the similarity which we discover among natural objects, and by which we are induced to expect effects similar to those which we have found to follow from such objects. And though none but a fool or madman will ever pretend to dispute the authority of experience, or to reject that great guide of human life, it may surely be allowed a philosopher to have so much curiosity at least as to examine the principle of human nature, which gives this mighty authority to experience, and makes us draw advantage from that similarity which nature has placed among different objects. From causes which appear *similar* we expect similar effects. This is the sum of all our experimental conclusions. Now it seems evident that, if this conclusion were formed by reason, it would be as perfect at first, and upon one instance, as after ever so long a course of experience. But the case is far otherwise. Nothing so like as eggs; yet no one, on account of this appearing similarity, expects the same taste and relish in all of them. It is only after a long course of uniform experiments in any kind, that we attain a firm reliance and security with regard to a particular event. Now where is that process of reasoning which, from one instance, draws a conclusion, so different from that which it infers from a hundred instances that are nowise different from that single one? This question I propose as much for the sake of information, as with an intention of raising difficulties. I cannot find, I cannot imagine any such reasoning. But I keep my mind still open to instruction, if any one will vouchsafe to bestow it on me.

Should it be said that, from a number of uniform experiments, we *infer* a connexion between the sensible qualities and the secret powers; this, I must confess, seems the same difficulty, couched in different terms. The question still recurs, on what process of argument this *inference* is founded? Where is the medium, the interposing ideas, which join propositions so very wide of each other? It is confessed that the colour, consistence, and other sensible qualities of bread appear not, of themselves, to have any connexion with the secret powers of nourishment and support. For otherwise we could infer these secret powers from the first appearance of these sensible qualities, without the aid of experience; contrary to the sentiment of all philosophers, and contrary to plain matter of fact. Here, then, is our natural state of ignorance with regard to the powers and influence of all objects. How is this remedied by experience? It only shows us a number of uniform effects, resulting from certain objects, and teaches us that those particular objects, at that particular time, were endowed with such powers and forces. When a new object, endowed with similar sensible qualities, is produced, we expect similar powers and forces, and look for a like effect. From a body of like colour and consistence with bread we expect like nourishment and support. But this surely is a step or progress of the mind, which wants to be explained. When a man says, *I have found, in all past instances, such sensible qualities conjoined with such secret powers:* And when he says, *Similar sensible qualities will always be conjoined with similar secret powers,* he is not guilty of a tautology, nor are these propositions in any respect the same. You say that the one proposition is an inference from the other. But you must confess that the inference is not intuitive; neither is it demonstrative: Of what nature is it, then? To say it is experimental, is begging the question. For all inferences from experience suppose, as their foundation, that the future will resemble the past, and that similar powers will be conjoined with similar sensible qualities. If there be any suspicion that the course of nature may change, and that the past may be no rule for the future, all experience becomes useless, and can give rise to no inference or conclusion. It is impossible, therefore, that any arguments from experience can prove this resemblance of the past to the future; since all these arguments are founded on the supposition of that resemblance. Let the course of things be allowed hitherto ever so regular; that alone, without some new argument or inference, proves not that, for the future, it will continue so. In vain do you pretend to have learned the nature of bodies from your past experience. Their secret nature, and consequently all their effects and influence, may change, without any change in their sensible qualities. This happens sometimes, and with regard to some objects: Why may it not happen always, and with regard to all objects? What logic, what process of argument secures you against this supposition? My practice, you say, refutes my doubts. But you mistake the purport of my question. As an agent, I am quite satisfied in the point; but as a philosopher, who has some share of curiosity, I will not say scepticism, I want to learn the foundation of this inference. No reading, no enquiry has yet been able to remove my difficulty, or give me satisfaction in a matter of such importance. Can I do better than propose the difficulty to the public, even though, perhaps, I have small hopes of obtaining a solution? We shall at least, by this means, be sensible of our ignorance, if we do not augment our knowledge.

I must confess that a man is guilty of unpardonable arrogance who concludes, because an argument has escaped his own investigation, that therefore it does not really exist. I must also confess that, though all the learned, for several ages, should have employed themselves in fruitless search upon any subject, it may still, perhaps, be rash to conclude positively that the subject must, therefore, pass all human comprehension. Even though we examine all the sources of our knowledge, and conclude them unfit for such a subject, there may still remain a suspicion, that the enumeration is not complete, or the examination not accurate. But with regard to the present subject, there are some considerations which seem to remove all this accusation of arrogance or suspicion of mistake.

It is certain that the most ignorant and stupid peasants—nay infants, nay even brute beasts—improve by experience, and learn the qualities of natural objects, by observing the effects which result from them. When a child has felt the sensation of pain from touching the flame of a candle, he will be careful not to put his hand near any candle; but will expect a similar effect from a cause which is similar in its sensible qualities and appearance. If you assert, therefore, that the understanding of the child is led into this conclusion by any process of argument or ratiocination, I may justly require you to produce that argument; nor have you any pretence to refuse so equitable a demand. You cannot say that the argument is abstruse, and may possibly escape your enquiry; since you confess that it is obvious to the capacity of a mere infant. If you hesitate, therefore, a moment, or if, after reflection, you produce any intricate or profound argument, you, in a manner, give up the question, and confess that it is not reasoning which engages us to suppose the past resembling the future, and to expect similar effects from causes which are, to appearance, similar. This is the proposition which I intended to enforce in the present section. If I be right, I pretend not to have made any mighty discovery. And if I be wrong, I must acknowledge myself to be indeed a very backward scholar; since I cannot now discover an argument which, it seems, was perfectly familiar to me long before I was out of my cradle.

Section V
Sceptical Solution of These Doubts

Part I

The passion for philosophy, like that for religion, seems liable to this inconvenience, that, though it aims at the correction of our manners, and extirpation of our vices, it may only serve, by imprudent management, to foster a predominant inclination, and push the mind, with more determined resolution, towards that side which already *draws* too much, by the bias and propensity of the natural temper. It is certain that, while we aspire to the magnanimous firmness of the philosophic sage, and endeavour to confine our pleasures altogether within our own minds, we may, at last, render our philosophy like that of Epictetus, and other *Stoics,* only a more refined system of selfishness, and reason ourselves out of all virtue as well as social enjoyment. While we study with attention the vanity of human life, and turn all our thoughts towards the empty and transitory nature of riches and honours, we are, perhaps, all the while flattering our natural indolence, which, hating the bustle of the world, and drudgery of business, seeks a pretence of reason to give itself a full and uncontrolled indulgence. There is, however, one species of philosophy which seems little liable to this inconvenience, and that because it strikes in with no disorderly passion of the human mind, nor can mingle itself with any natural affection or propensity; and that is the Academic or Sceptical philosophy. The academics always talk of doubt and suspense of judgement, of danger in hasty determinations, of confining to very narrow bounds the enquiries of the understanding, and of renouncing all speculations which lie not within the limits of common life and practice. Nothing, therefore, can be more contrary than such a philosophy to the supine indolence of the mind, its rash arrogance, its lofty pretensions, and its superstitious credulity. Every passion is mortified by it, except the love of truth; and that passion never is, nor can be, carried to too high a degree. It is surprising, therefore, that this philosophy, which, in almost every instance, must be harmless and innocent, should be the subject of so much groundless reproach and obloquy. But, perhaps, the very circumstance which renders it so innocent is what chiefly exposes it to the public hatred and resentment. By flattering no irregular passion, it gains few partizans: By opposing so many vices and follies, it raises to itself abundance of enemies, who stigmatize it as libertine profane, and irreligious.

Nor need we fear that this philosophy, while it endeavours to limit our enquiries to common life, should ever undermine the reasonings of common life, and carry its doubts so far as to destroy all action, as well as speculation. Nature will always maintain her rights, and prevail in the end over any abstract reasoning whatsoever. Though we should conclude, for instance, as in the foregoing section, that, in all reasonings from experience, there is a step taken by the mind which is not supported by any argument or process of the understanding; there is no danger that these reasonings, on which almost all knowledge depends, will ever be affected by such a discovery. If the mind be not engaged by argument to make this step, it must be induced by some other principle of equal weight and authority; and that principle will preserve its influence as long as human nature remains the same. What that principle is may well be worth the pains of enquiry.

Suppose a person, though endowed with the strongest faculties of reason and reflection, to be brought on a sudden into this world; he would, indeed, immediately observe a continual succession of objects, and one event following another; but he would not be able to discover anything farther. He would not, at first, by any reasoning, be able to reach the idea of cause and effect; since the particular powers, by which all natural operations are performed, never appear to the senses; nor is it reasonable to conclude, merely because one event, in one instance, precedes another, that therefore the one is the cause, the other the effect. Their conjunction may be arbitrary and casual. There may be no reason to infer the existence of one from the appearance of the other. And in a word, such a person, without more experience, could never employ his conjecture or reasoning concerning any matter of fact, or be assured of anything beyond what was immediately present to his memory and senses.

Suppose, again, that he has acquired more experience, and has lived so long in the world as to have observed familiar objects or events to be constantly conjoined together; what is the consequence of this experience? He immediately infers the existence of one object from the appearance of the other. Yet he has not, by all his experience, acquired any idea or knowledge of the secret power by which the one object produces the other; nor is it, by any process of reasoning, he is engaged to draw this inference. But still he finds himself determined to draw it: And though he should be convinced that his understanding has no part in the operation, he would nevertheless continue in the same course of thinking. There is some other principle which determines him to form such a conclusion.

This principle is Custom or Habit. For wherever the repetition of any particular act or operation produces a propensity to renew the same act or operation, without being impelled by any reasoning or process of the understanding, we always say, that this propensity is the effect of *Custom*. By employing that word, we pretend not to have given the ultimate reason of such a propensity. We only point out a principle of human nature, which is universally acknowledged, and which is well known by its effects. Perhaps we can push our enquiries no farther, or pretend to give the cause of this cause; but must rest contented with it as the ultimate principle, which we can assign, of all our conclusions from experience. It is sufficient satisfaction, that we can go so far, without repining at the narrowness of our faculties because they will carry us no farther. And it is certain we here advance a very intelligible proposition at least, if not a true one, when we assert that, after the constant conjunction of two objects—heat and flame, for instance, weight and solidity—we are determined by custom alone to expect the one from the appearance of the other. This hypothesis seems even the only one which explains the difficulty, why we draw, from a thousand instances, an inference which we are not able to draw from one instance, that is, in no respect different from them. Reason is incapable of any such variation. The conclusions which it draws from considering one circle are the same which it would form upon surveying all the circles in the universe. But no man, having seen only one body move after being impelled by another, could infer that every body will move after a like impulse. All inferences from experience, therefore, are effects of custom, not of reasoning.[7]

Custom, then, is the great guide of human life. It is that principle alone which renders our experience useful to us, and makes us expect, for the future, a similar train of events with those which have appeared in the past. Without the influence of custom, we should be entirely ignorant of every matter of fact beyond what is immediately present to the memory and senses. We should never know how to adjust means to ends, or to employ our natural powers in the production of any effect. There would be an end at once of all action, as well as of the chief part of speculation.

But here it may be proper to remark, that though our conclusions from experience carry us beyond our memory and senses, and assure us of matters of fact which happened in the most distant places and most remote ages, yet some fact must always be present to the senses or memory, from which we may first proceed in drawing these conclusions. A man, who should find in a desert country the reamins of pompous buildings, would conclude that the country had, in ancient times, been cultivated by civilized inhabitants; but did nothing of this nature occur to him, he could never form such an inference. We learn the events of former ages from history; but then we must peruse the volumes in which this instruction is contained, and thence carry up our inferences from one testimony to another, till we arrive at the eyewitnesses and spectators of these distant events. In a word, if we proceed not upon some fact, present to the memory or senses, our reasonings would be merely hypothetical; and however the particular links might be connected with each other, the whole chain of inferences would have nothing to support it, nor could we ever, by its means, arrive at the knowledge of any real existence. If I ask why you believe any particular matter of fact, which you relate, you must tell me some reason; and this reason will be some other fact, connected with it. But as you cannot proceed after this manner, *in infinitum,* you must at last terminate in some fact, which is present to your memory or senses; or must allow that your belief is entirely without foundation.

What, then, is the conclusion of the whole matter? A simple one; though, it must be confessed, pretty remote from the common theories of philosophy. All belief of matter of fact or real existence is derived merely from some object, present to the memory or senses, and a customary conjunction between that and some other object. Or in other words; having found, in many instances, that any two kinds of objects—flame and heat, snow and cold—have always been conjoined together; if flame or snow be presented anew to the senses, the mind is carried by custom to expect heat or cold, and to *believe* that such a quality does exist, and will discover itself upon a nearer approach. This belief is the necessary result of placing the mind in such circumstances. It is an operation of the soul, when we are so situated, as unavoidable as to feel the passion of love, when we receive benefits; or hatred, when we meet with injuries. All these operations are a species of natural instincts, which no reasoning or process of the thought and understanding is able either to produce or to prevent.

At this point, it would be very allowable for us to stop our philosophical researches. In most questions we can never make a single step farther; and in all questions we must terminate here at last, after our most restless and curious enquiries. But still our curiosity will be pardonable, perhaps commendable, if it carry us on to still farther researches, and make us examine more accurately the nature of this *belief,* and of the *customary conjunction,* whence it is derived. By this means we may meet with some explications and analogies that will give satisfaction; at least to such as love the abstract sciences, and can be entertained with speculations, which, however accurate, may still retain a degree of doubt and uncertainty. As to readers of a different taste; the remaining part of this section is not calculated for them, and the following enquiries may well be understood, though it be neglected.

Part II

Nothing is more free than the imagination of man; and though it cannot exceed that original stock of ideas furnished by the internal and external senses, it has unlimited power of mixing, compounding, separating, and dividing these ideas, in all the varieties of fiction and vision. It can feign a train of events, with all the appearance of reality, ascribe to them a particular time and place, conceive them as existent, and paint them out to itself with every circumstance, that belongs to any historical fact, which it believes with the greatest certainty. Wherein, therefore, consists the difference between such a fiction and belief? It lies not merely in any peculiar idea, which is annexed to such a conception as commands our assent, and which is wanting to every known fiction. For as the mind has authority over all its ideas, it could voluntarily annex this particular idea to any fiction, and consequently be able to believe whatever it pleases; contrary to what we find by daily experience. We can, in our conception, join the head of a man to the body of a horse; but it is not in our power to believe that such an animal has ever really existed.

It follows, therefore, that the difference between *fiction* and *belief* lies in some sentiment or feeling, which is annexed to the latter, not to the former, and which depends not on the will, nor can be commanded at pleasure. It must be excited by nature, like all other sentiments; and must arise from the particular situation, in which the mind is placed at any particular juncture. Whenever any object is presented to the memory or sense, it immediately, by the force of custom, carries the imagination to conceive that object, which is usually conjoined to it; and this conception is attended with a feeling or sentiment, different from the loose reveries of the fancy. In this consists the whole nature of belief. For as there is no matter of fact which we believe so firmly that we cannot conceive the contrary, there would be no difference between the conception assented to and that which is rejected, were it not for some sentiment which distinguishes the one from the other. If I see a billiard-ball moving towards another, on a smooth table, I can easily conceive it to stop upon contact. This conception implies no contradiction; but still it feels very differently from that conception by which I represent to myself the impulse and the communication of motion from one ball to another.

Were we to attempt a *definition* of this sentiment, we should perhaps, find it a very difficult, if not an impossible task; in the same manner as if we should endeavour to define the feeling of cold or passion of anger, to a creature who never had any experience of these sentiments. Belief is the true and proper name of this feeling; and no one is ever at a loss to know the meaning of that term; because every man is every moment conscious of the sentiment represented by it. It may not, however, be improper to attempt a *description* of this sentiment; in hopes we may, by that means, arrive at some analogies, which may afford a more perfect explication of it. I say, then, that belief is nothing but a more vivid, lively, forcible, firm, steady conception of an object, than what the imagination alone is ever able to attain. This variety of terms, which may seem so unphilosophical, is intended only to express that act of the mind, which renders realities, or what is taken for such, more present to us than fictions, causes them to weigh more in the thought, and gives them a superior influence on the passions and imagination. Provided we agree about the thing, it is needless to dispute about the terms. The imagination has the command over all its ideas, and can join and mix and vary them, in all the ways possible. It may conceive fictitious objects with all the circumstances of place and time. It may set them, in a manner, before our eyes, in their true colours, just as they might have existed. But as it is impossible that this faculty of imagination can ever, of itself, reach belief, it is evident that belief consists not in the peculiar nature or order of ideas, but in the *manner* of their conception, and in their *feeling* to the mind. I confess, that it is impossible perfectly to explain this feeling or manner of conception. We may make use of words which express something near it. But its true and proper name, as we observed before, is *belief;* which is a term that every one sufficiently understands in common life. And in philosophy, we can go no farther than assert, that *belief* is something felt by the mind, which distinguishes the ideas of the judgement from the fictions of the imagination. It gives them more weight and influence; makes them appear of greater importance; enforces them in the mind; and renders them the governing principle of our actions. I hear at present, for instance, a person's voice, with whom I am acquainted; and the sound comes as from the next room. This impression of my senses immediately conveys my thought to the person, together with all the surrounding objects. I paint them out to myself as existing at present, with the same qualities and relations, of which I formerly knew them possessed. These ideas take faster hold of my mind than ideas of an enchanted castle. They are very different to the feeling, and have a much greater influence of every kind, either to give pleasure or pain, joy or sorrow.

Let us, then, take in the whole compass of this doctrine, and allow, that the sentiment of belief is nothing but a conception more intense and steady than what attends the mere fictions of the imagination, and that this *manner* of conception arises from a customary conjunction of the object with something present to the memory or senses: I believe that it will not be difficult, upon these suppositions, to find operations of the mind analogous to it, and to trace up these phenomena to principles still more general.

We have already observed that nature has established connexions among particular ideas, and that no sooner one idea occurs to our thoughts than it introduces its correlative, and carries our attention towards it, by a gentle and insensible movement. These principles of connexion or association we have reduced to three, namely, *Re-*

semblance, Contiguity and *Causation;* which are the only bonds that unite our thoughts together, and beget that regular train of reflection or discourse, which, in a greater or less degree, takes place among all mankind. Now here arises a question, on which the solution of the present difficulty will depend. Does it happen, in all these relations, that, when one of the objects is presented to the senses or memory, the mind is not only carried to the conception of the correlative, but reaches a steadier and stronger conception of it than what otherwise it would have been able to attain? This seems to be the case with that belief which arises from the relation of cause and effect. And if the case be the same with the other relations or principles of associations, this may be established as a general law, which takes place in all the operations of the mind.

We may, therefore, observe, as the first experiment to our present purpose, that, upon the appearance of the picture of an absent friend, our idea of him is evidently enlivened by the *resemblance,* and that every passion, which that idea occasions, whether of joy or sorrow, acquires new force and vigour. In producing this effect, there concur both a relation and a present impression. Where the picture bears him no resemblance, at least was not intended for him, it never so much as conveys our thought to him: And where it is absent as well as the person, though the mind may pass from the thought of the one to that of the other, it feels its idea to be rather weakened than enlivened by that transition. We take a pleasure in viewing the picture of a friend, when it is set before us; but when it is removed, rather choose to consider him directly than by reflection in an image, which is equally distant and obscure.

The ceremonies of the Roman Catholic religion may be considered as instances of the same nature. The devotees of that superstition usually plead in excuse for the mummeries, with which they are upbraided, that they feel the good effect of those external motions, and postures, and actions, in enlivening their devotion and quickening their fervour, which otherwise would decay, if directed entriely to distant and immaterial objects. We shadow out the objects of our faith, say they, in sensible types and images, and render them more present to us by the immediate presence of these types, than it is possible for us to do merely by an intellectual view and contemplation. Sensible objects have always a greater influence on the fancy than any other; and this influence they readily convey to those ideas to which they are related, and which they resemble. I shall only infer from these practices, and this reasoning, that the effect of resemblance in enlivening the ideas is very common; and as in every case a resemblance and a present impression must concur, we are abundantly supplied with experiments to prove the reality of the foregoing principle.

We may add force to these experiments by others of a different kind, in considering the effects of *contiguity* as well as of *resemblance*. It is certain that distance diminishes the force of every idea, and that, upon our approach to any object; though it does not discover itself to our senses; it operates upon the mind with an influence, which imitates an immediate impression. The thinking on any object readily transports the mind to what is contiguous; but it is only the actual presence of an object, that transports it with a superior vivacity. When I am a few miles from home, whatever relates to it touches me more nearly than when I am two hundred leagues distant; though even at that distance the reflecting on any thing in the neighbourhood of my friends or family naturally produces an idea of them. But as in this latter case, both the objects of the mind are ideas; notwithstanding there is an easy transition between them; that transition alone is not able to give a superior vivacity to any of the ideas, for want of some immediate impression.[8]

No one can doubt but causation has the same influence as the other two relations of resemblance and contiguity. Superstitious people are fond of the reliques of saints and holy men, for the same reason, that they seek after types or images, in order to enliven their devotion, and give them a more intimate and strong conception of those exemplary lives, which they desire to imitate. Now it is evident, that one of the best reliques, which a devotee could procure, would be the handywork of a saint; and if his cloaths and furniture are ever to be considered in this light, it is because they were once at his dosposal, and were moved and affected by him; in which respect they are to be considered as imperfect effects, and as connected with him by a shorter chain of consequences than any of those, by which we learn the reality of his existence.

Suppose, that the son of a friend, who had been long dead or absent, were presented to us; it is evident, that this object would instantly revive its correlative idea, and recal to our thoughts all past intimacies and familiarities, in more lively colours than they would otherwise have appeared to us. This is another phaenomenon, which seems to prove the principle above mentioned.

We may observe, that, in these phaenomena, the belief of the correlative object is alway presupposed; without which the relation could have no effect. The influence of the picture supposes, that we *believe* our friend to have once existed. Contiguity to home can never excite our idea of home, unless we *believe* that it really exists. Now I assert, that this belief, where it reaches beyond the memory or sense, is of a similar nature, and arises from similar causes, with the transition of thought and vivacity of conception here explained. When I throw a piece of dry wood into a fire, my mind is immediately carried to conceive, that it augments, not extinguishes the flame. This transition of thought from the cause to the effect proceeds not from reason. It derives its origin altogether from custom and experience. And as it first begins from an object, present to the senses, it renders the idea or conception of flame more strong and lively than any loose, floating reverie of the imagination. That idea arises immediately. The thought moves instantly towards it, and conveys to it all that force of conception, which is derived from the impression present to the senses. When a sword is levelled at my breast, does not the idea of wound and pain strike me more strongly, than when a glass of wine is presented to me, even though by accident this idea should occur after the appearance of the latter object? But what is there in this whole matter to cause such a strong conception, except only a present object and a customary transition to the idea of another object, which we have been accustomed to conjoin with the former? This is the whole operation of the mind, in all our conclusions concerning matter of fact and existence; and it is a satisfaction to find some analogies, by which it may be explained. The transition from a present object does in all cases give strength and solidity to the related idea.

Here, then, is a kind of pre-established harmony between the course of nature and the succession of our ideas; and though the powers and forces, by which the former is governed, be wholly unknown to us; yet our thoughts and conceptions have still, we find, gone on in the same train wtih the other works of nature. Custom is that principle, by which this correspondence has been effected; so necessary to the subsistence of our species, and the regulation of our conduct, in every circumstance and occurrence of human life. Had not the presence of an object, instantly excited the idea of those objects, commonly conjoined with it, all our knowledge must have been limited to the narrow sphere of our memory and senses; and we should never have been able to adjust means to ends, or employ our natural powers, either to the producing of good, or avoiding of evil. Those, who delight in the discovery and contemplation of *final causes,* have here ample subject to employ their wonder and admiration.

I shall add, for a further confirmation of the foregoing theory, that, as this operation of the mind, by which we infer like effects from like causes, and vice versa, is so essential to the subsistence of all human creatures, it is not probable, that it could be trusted to the fallacious deductions of our reason, which is slow in its operations; appears not, in any degree, during the first years of infancy; and at best is, in every age and period of human life, extremely liable to error and mistake. It is more conformable to the ordinary wisdom of nature to secure so necessary an act of the mind, by some instinct or mechanical tendency, which may be infallible in its operations, may discover itself at the first appearance of life and thought, and may be independent of all the laboured deductions of the understanding. As nature has taught us the use of our limbs, without giving us the knowledge of the muscles and nerves, by which they are actuated; so has she implanted in us an instinct, which carries forward the thought in a correspondent course to that which she has established among external objects; though we are ignorant of those powers and forces, on which this regular course and succession of objects totally depends.

Section VI
Of Probability[9]

Though there be no such thing as *Chance* in the world; our ignorance of the real cause of any event has the same influence on the understanding, and begets a like species of belief or opinion.

There is certainly a probability, which arises from a superiority of chances on any side; and according as this superiority encreases, and surpasses the opposite chances, the probability receives a proportionable encrease, and begets still a higher degree of belief or assent to that side, in which we discover the superiority. If a dye were marked with one figure or number of spots on four sides, and with another figure or number of spots on the two remaining sides, it would be more probable, that the former would turn up than the latter; though, if it had a thousand sides marked in the same manner, and only one side different, the probability would be much higher, and our belief or expectation of the event more steady and secure. This process of the thought or reasoning may seem trivial and obvious; but to those who consider it more narrowly, it may, perhaps, afford matter for curious speculation.

It seems evident, that, when the mind looks forward to discover the event, which may result from the throw of such a dye, it considers the turning up of each particular side as alike probable; and this is the very nature of chance, to render all the particular events, comprehended in it, entirely equal. But finding a greater number of sides concur in the one event than in the other, the mind is carried more frequently to that event, and meets it oftener, in revolving the various possibilities or chances, on which the ultimate result depends. This concurrence of several views in one particular event begets immediately, by an inexplicable contrivance of nature, the sentiment of belief, and gives that event the advantage over its antagonist, which is supported by a smaller number of views, and recurs less frequently to the mind. If we allow, that belief is nothing but a firmer and stronger conception of an object than what attends the mere fictions of the imagination, this operation may, perhaps, in some measure, be accounted for. The concurrence of these several views or glimpses imprints the idea more strongly on the imagination; gives it superior force and vigour; renders its influence on the passions and affections more sensible; and in a word, begets that reliance or security, which constitutes the nature of belief and opinion.

The case is the same with the probability of causes, as with that of chance. There are some causes, which are entirely uniform and constant in producing a particular effect; and no instance has ever yet been found of any failure or irregularity in their operation. Fire has always burned, and water suffocated every human creature: The production of motion by impulse and gravity is an universal law, which has hitherto admitted of no exception. But there are other causes, which have been found more irregular and uncertan; nor has rhubarb always proved a purge, or opium a soporific to every one, who has taken these medicines. It is true, when any cause fails of producing its usual effect, philosophers ascribe not this to any irregularity in nature; but suppose, that some secret causes, in the particular structure of parts, have prevented the operation. Our reasonings, however, and conclusions concerning the event are the same as if this principle had no place. Being determined by custom to transfer the past to the future, in all our inferences; where the past has been entirely regular and uniform, we expect the event with the greatest assurance, and leave no room for any contrary supposition. But where different effects have been found to follow from causes, which are to *appearance* exactly similar, all these various effects must occur to the mind in transferring the past to the future, and enter into our consideration, when we determine the probability of the event. Though we give the preference to that which has been found most usual, and believe that this effect will exist, we must not overlook the other effects, but must assign to each of them a particular weight and authority, in proportion as we have found it to be more or less frequent. It is more probable, in almost every country of Europe, that there will be frost sometime in January, than that the weather will continue open throughout that whole month; though this probability varies according to the different climates, and approaches to a certainty in the more northern kingdoms. Here then it seems evident, that, when we transfer the past to the future, in order to determine the effect, which will result from any cause, we transfer all the different events, in the same proportion as they have appeared in the past, and conceive one to have existed a hundred times, for instance, another ten times, and another once. As a great number of views do here concur in one event, they fortify and confirm it to the imagination, beget that sentiment which we call *belief,* and give its object the preference above the contrary event, which is not supported by an equal number of experiments, and recurs not so frequently to the thought in transferring the past to the future. Let any one try to account for this operation of the mind upon any of the received systems of philosophy, and he will be sensible of the difficulty. For my part, I shall think it sufficient, if the present hints excite the curiosity of philosophers, and make them sensible how defective all common theories are in treating of such curious and such sublime subjects.

Section VII
Of the Idea of Necessary Connexion

Part I

The great advantage of the mathematical sciences above the moral consists in this, that the ideas of the former, being sensible, are always clear and determinate, the smallest distinction between them is immediately perceptible, and the same terms are still expressive of the same ideas, without ambiguity or variation. An oval is never mistaken for a circle, nor an hyperbola for an ellipsis. The isosceles and scalenum are distinguished by boundaries more exact than vice and virtue, right and wrong. If any term be defined in geometry, the mind readily, of itself, substitutes, on all occasions, the definition for the term defined: Or even when no definition is employed, the object itself may be presented to the senses, and by that means be steadily and clearly apprehended. But the finer sentiments of the mind, the operations of the understanding, the various agitations of the passions, though really in themselves distinct, easily escape us, when surveyed by reflection; nor is it in our power to recal the original object, as often as we have occasion to contemplate it. Ambiguity, by this means, is gradually introduced into our reasonings: Similar objects are readily taken to be the same: And the conclusion becomes at last very wide of the premises.

One may safely, however, affirm, that, if we consider these sciences in a proper light, their advantages and disadvantages nearly compensate each other, and reduce both of them to a state of equality. If the mind, with greater facility, retains the ideas of geometry clear and determinate, it must carry on a much longer and more intricate chain of reasoning, and compare ideas much wider of each other, in order to reach the abstruser truths of that science. And if moral ideas are apt, without extreme care, to fall into obscurity and confusion, the inferences are always much shorter in these disquisitions, and the intermediate steps, which lead to the conclusion, much fewer than in the sciences which treat of quantity and number. In reality, there is scarcely a proposition in Euclid so simple, as not to consist of more parts, than are to be found in any moral reasoning which runs not into chimera and conceit. Where we trace the principles of the human mind through a few steps, we may be very well satisfied with our progress; considering how soon nature throws a bar to all our concerning causes, and reduces us to an acknowledgment of our ignorance. The chief obstacle, therefore, to our improvement in the moral or metaphysical sciences is the obscurity of the ideas, and ambiguity of the terms. The principle difficulty in the mathematics is the length of inferences and compass of thought, requisite to the forming of any conclusion. And, perhaps, our progress in natural philosophy is chiefly retarded by the want of proper experiments and phaenomena, which are often discovered by chance, and cannot always be found, when requisite even by the most diligent and prudent enquiry. As moral philosophy seems hitherto to have received less improvement than either geometry or physics, we may conclude, that, if there be any difference in this respect among these sciences, the difficulties, which obstruct the progress of the former, require superior care and capacity to be surmounted.

There are no ideas, which occur in metaphysics, more obscure and uncertain, than those of *power, force, energy* or *necessary connexion,* of which it is every moment necessary for us to treat in all our disquisitions. We shall, therefore, endeavour, in this section, to fix, if possible, the precise meaning of these terms, and thereby remove some part of that obscurity, which is so much complained of in this species of philosophy.

It seems a proposition, which will not admit of much dispute, that all our ideas are nothing but copies of our impressions, or, in other words, that it is impossible for us to *think* of any thing, which we have not antecedently *felt,* either by our external or internal senses. I have endeavoured[10] to explain and prove this proposition, and have expressed my hopes, that, by a proper application of it, men may reach a greater clearness and precision in philosophical reasonings, than what they have hitherto been able to attain. Complex ideas may, perhaps, be well known by definition, which is nothing but an enumeration of those parts or simple ideas, that compose them. But when we have pushed up definitions to the most simple ideas, and find still some ambiguity and obscurity; what resource are we then possessed of? By what invention can we throw light upon these ideas, and render them altogether precise and determinate to our intellectual view? Produce the impressions or original sentiments, from which the ideas are copied. These impressions are all strong and sensible. They admit not of ambiguity. They are not only placed in a full light themselves, but may throw light on their correspondent ideas, which lie in obscurity. And by this means, we may, perhaps, attain a new microscope or species of optics, by which, in the moral sciences, the most minute, and most simple ideas may be so enlarged as to fall readily under our apprehension, and be equally known with the grossest and most sensible ideas, that can be the object of our enquiry.

To be fully acquainted, therefore, with the idea of power or necessary connexion, let us examine its impression; and in order to find the impression with greater certainty, let us search for it in all the sources, from which it may possibly be derived.

When we look about us towards external objects, and consider the operation of causes, we are never able, in a single instance, to discover any power or necessary connexion; any quality, which binds the effect to the cause, and renders the one an infallible consequence of the other. We only find, that the one does actually, in fact, follow the other. The impulse of one billiard-ball is attended with motion in the second. This is the whole that appears to the *outward* senses. The mind feels no sentiment or *inward* impression from this succession of objects: Consequently, there is not, in any single, particular instance of cause and effect, any thing which can suggest the idea of power or necessary connexion.

From the first appearance of an object, we never can conjecture what effect will result from it. But were the power or energy of any cause discoverable by the mind, we could foresee the effect, even without experience; and might, at first, pronounce with certainty concerning it, by mere dint of thought and reasoning.

In reality, there is no part of matter, that does ever, by its sensible qualities, discover any power or energy, or give us ground to imagine, that it could produce any thing, or be followed by any other object, which we could denominate its effect. Solidity, extension, motion; these qualities are all complete in themselves, and never point out any other event which may result from them. The scenes of the universe are continually shifting, and one object follows another in an uninterrupted succession; but the power of force, which actuates the whole machine, is entirely concealed from us, and never discovers itself in any of the sensible qualities of body. We know, that, in fact, heat is a constant attendant of flame; but what is the connexion between them, we have no room so much as to conjecture or imagine. It is impossible, therefore, that the idea of power can be derived from the contemplation of bodies, in single instances of their operation; because no bodies ever discover any power, which can be the original of this idea.[11]

Since, therefore, external objects as they appear to the senses, give us no idea of power or necessary connexion, by their operation in particular instances, let us see, whether this idea be derived from reflection on the operations of our own minds, and be copied from any internal impression. It may be said, that we are every moment conscious of internal power; while we feel, that, by the simple command of our will, we can move the organs of our body, or direct the faculties of our mind. An act of volition produces motion in our limbs, or raises a new idea in our imagination. This influence of the will we know by consciousness. Hence we acquire the idea of power or energy; and are certain, that we ourselves and all other intelligent beings are possessed of power. This idea, then, is an idea of reflection, since it arises from reflecting on the operations of our own mind, and on the command which is exercised by will, both over the organs of the body and faculties of the soul.

We shall proceed to examine this pretension; and first with regard to the influence of volition over the organs of the body. This influence, we may observe, is a fact, which, like all other natural events, can be known only by experience, and can never be foreseen from any apparent energy or power in the cause, which connects it with the effect, and renders the one an infallible consequence of the other. The motion of our body follows upon the command of our will. Of this we are every moment conscious. But the means, by which this is effected; the energy, by which the will performs so extraordinary an operation; of this we are so far from being immediately conscious, that it must for ever escape our most diligent enquiry.

For *first;* is there any principle in all nature more mysterious than the union of soul with body; by which a supposed spiritual substance acquires such an influence over a material one, that the most refined thought is able to actuate the grossest matter? Were we empowered, by a secret wish, to remove mountains, or control the planets in their orbit; this extensive authority would not be more extraordinary, nor more beyond our comprehension. But if by consciousness we perceived any power or energy in the will, we must know this power; we must know its connexion with the effect; we must know the secret union of soul and body, and the nature of both these substances; by which the one is able to operate, in so many instances, upon the other.

Secondly, We are not able to move all the organs of the body with a like authority; though we cannot assign any reason besides experience, for so remarkable a difference between one and the other. Why has the will an influence over the tongue and fingers, not over the heart or liver? This question would never embarrass us, were we conscious of a power in the former case, not in the latter. We should then perceive, independent of experience, why the authority of will over the organs of the body is circumscribed within such particular limits. Being in that case fully acquainted with the power or force, by which it operates, we should also know, why its influence reaches precisely to such boundaries, and no farther.

A man, suddenly struck with palsy in the leg or arm, or who had newly lost those members, frequently endeavours, at first to move them, and employ them in their usual offices. Here he is as much conscious of power to command such limbs, as a man in perfect health is conscious of power to actuate any member which remains in its natural state and condition. But consciousness never deceives. Consequently, neither in the one case nor in the other, are we ever conscious of any power. We learn the influence of our will from experience alone. And experience only teaches us, how one event constantly follows another; without instructing us in the secret connexion, which binds them together, and renders them inseperable.

Thirdly, We learn from anatomy, that the immediate object of power in voluntary motion, is not the member itself which is moved, but certain muscles, and nerves, and animal spirits, and, perhaps, something still more minute and more unknown, through which the motion is successively propagated, ere it reach the member itself whose motion is the immediate object of volition. Can there be a more certain proof, that the power, by which this whole operation is performed, so far from being directly and fully known by an inward sentiment or consciousness, is, to the last degree mysterious and unintelligible? Here the mind wills a certain event: Immediately another event, unknown to ourselves, and totally different from the one intended, is produced: This event produces another, equally unknown: Till at last, through a long succession, the desired event is produced. But if the original power were felt, it must be known: Were it known, its effect also must be known; since all power is relative to its effect. And vice versa, if the effect be not known, the power cannot be known nor felt. How indeed can we be conscious of a power to move our limbs, when we have no such power; but only that to move certain animal spirits, which, though they produce at last the motion of our limbs, yet operate in such a manner as is wholly beyond our comprehension?

We may, therefore, conclude from the whole,

I hope, without any temerity, though with assurance; that our idea of power is not copied from any sentiment or consciousness of power within ourselves, when we give rise to animal motion, or apply our limbs to their proper use and office. That their motion follows the command of the will is a matter of common experience, like other natural events: But the power or energy by which this is effected, like that in other natural events, is unknown and inconceivable.[12]

Shall we then assert, that we are conscious of a power or energy in our own minds, when, by an act or command of our will, we raise up a new idea, fix the mind to the contemplation of it, turn it on all sides, and at last dismiss it for some other idea, when we think that we have surveyed it with sufficient accuracy? I believe the same arguments will prove, that even this command of the will gives us no real idea of force or energy.

First, It must be allowed, that, when we know a power, we know that very circumstance in the cause, by which it is enabled to produce the effect: For these are supposed to be synonimous. We must, therefore, know both the cause and effect, and the relation between them. But do we pretend to be acquainted with the nature of the human soul and the nature of an idea, or the aptitude of the one to produce the other? This is a real creation; a production of something out of nothing: Which implies a power so great, that it may seem, at first sight, beyond the reach of any being, less than infinite. At least it must be owned, that such a power is not felt, nor known, nor even conceivable by the mind. We only feel the event, namely, the existence of an idea, consequent to a command of the will: But the manner, in which this operation is performed, the power by which it is produced, is entirely beyond our comprehension.

Secondly, The command of the mind over itself is limited, as well as its command over the body; and these limits are not known by reason, or any acquaintance with the nature of cause and effect, but only by experience and observation, as in all other natural events and in the operation of external objects. Our authority over our sentiments and passions is much weaker than that over our ideas; and even the latter authority is circumscribed within very narrow boundaries. Will any one pretend to assign the ultimate reason of these boundaries, or show why the power is deficient in one case, not in another.

Thirdly, This self-command is very different at different times. A man in health possesses more of it than one languishing with sickness. We are more master of our thoughts in the morning than in the evening: Fasting, than after a full meal. Can we give any reason for these variations, except experience? Where then is the power, of which we pretend to be conscious? Is there not here, either in a spiritual or material substance, or both, some secret mechanism or structure of parts, upon which the effect depends, and which, being entirely unknown to us, renders the power or energy of the will equally unknown and incomprehensible?

Volition is surely an act of the mind, with which we are sufficiently acquainted. Reflect upon it. Consider it on all sides. Do you find anything in it like this creative power, by which it raises from nothing a new idea, and with a kind of *Fiat,* imitates the omnipotence of its Maker, if I may be allowed so to speak, who called forth into existence all the various scenes of nature? So far from being conscious of this energy in the will, it requires as certain experience as that of which we are possessed, to convince us that such extraordinary effects do ever result from a simple act of volition.

The generality of mankind never find any difficulty in accounting for the more common and familiar operatoins of nature—such as the descent of heavy bodies, the growth of plants, the generation of animals, or the nourishment of bodies by food: But suppose that, in all these cases, they perceive, the very force or energy of the cause, by which it is connected with its effect, and is for ever infallible in its operation. They acquire, by long habit, such a turn of mind, that, upon the appearance of the cause, they immediately expect with assurance its usual attendant, and hardly conceive it possible that any other event could result from it. It is only on the discovery of extraordinary phaenomena, such as earthquakes, pestilence, and prodigies of any kind, that they find themselves at a loss to assign a proper cause, and to explain the manner in which the effect is produced by it. It is usual for men, in such difficulties, to have recourse to some invisible intelligent principle[13] as the immediate cause of that event which surprises them, and which, they think, cannot be accounted for from the common powers of nature. But philosophers, who carry their scrutiny a little farther, immediately perceive that, even in the most familiar events, the energy of the cause is as unintelligible as in the most unusual, and that we only learn by experience the frequent *Conjunction* of objects, without being ever able to comprehend anything like *Connexion* between them. Here, then, many philosophers think themselves obliged by reason to have recourse, on all occasions, to the same principle, which the vulgar never appeal to but in cases that appear miraculous and supernatural. They acknowledge mind and intelligence to be, not only the ultimate and original cause of all things, but the immediated and sole cause of every event which appears in nature. They pretend that those objects which are commonly denominated *causes,* are in reality nothing but *occasions;* and that the true and direct principle of every effect is not any power or force in nature, but a volition of the Supreme Being, who wills that such particular objects should for ever be conjoined with each other. Instead of saying that one billiard-ball moves another by force which it has derived from the author of nature, it is the Deity himself, they say, who, by a particular volition, moves the second ball, being determined to this operation by the impulse of the first ball, in consequence of those general laws which he has laid down to himself in the government of the universe. But philosophers advancing still in their inquiries, discover that, as we are totally ignorant of the power on which depends the mutual operation of bodies, we are no less ignorant of that power on which depends the operation of mind on body, or of body on mind; nor are we able, either from our senses or consciousness, to assign the ultimate principle in one case more than in the other. The same ignorance, therefore, reduces them to the same conclusion. They assert that the Deity is the immediate cause of the union between soul and body; and that they are not the organs of sense, which, being agitated by external objects, produce sensations in the mind; but that it is a particular volition of our omnipotent Maker, which excites such a sensation, in consequence of such a motion in the organ. In like manner, it is not any energy in the will that produces local motion in our members: It is God himself, who is pleased to second our will, in itself impotent, and to command that motion which we erroneously attribute to our own power and efficacy. Nor do philosophers stop at this conclusion. They sometimes extend the same inference to the mind itself, in its internal operations. Our mental vision or conception of ideas is nothing but a revelation made to us by our Maker. When we voluntarily turn our thoughts to any object, and raise up its image in the fancy, it is not the will which creates that idea: It is the universal Creator, who discovers it to the mind, and renders it present to us.

Thus, according to these philosophers, every thing is full of God. Not content with the principle, that nothing exists but by his will, that nothing possesses any power but by his concession: They rob nature, and all created beings, of every power, in order to render their dependence on the Deity still more sensible and immediate. They consider not that, by this theory, they diminish, instead of magnifying, the grandeur of those attributes, which they affect so much to celebrate. It argues surely more power in the Deity to delegate a certain degree of power to inferior creatures than to produce every thing by his own immediate volition. It argues more wisdom to contrive at first the fabric of the world with such perfect foresight that, of itself, and by its proper operation, it may serve all the purposes of providence, than if the great Creator were obliged every moment to adjust its parts, and animate by his breath all the wheels of that stupendous machine.

But if we would have a more philosophical confutation of this theory, perhaps the two following reflections may suffice.

First, it seems to me that this theory of the universal energy and operation of the Supreme Being is too bold ever to carry conviction with it to a man, sufficiently apprized of the weakness of human reason, and the narrow limits to which it is confined in all its operations. Though the chain of arguments which conduct to it were ever so logical, there must arise a strong suspicion, if not an absolute assurance, that it has carried us quite beyond the reach of our faculties, when it leads to conclusions so extraordinary, and so remote from common life and experience. We are got into fairy land, long ere we have reached the last steps of our theory; and *there* we have no reason to trust our common methods of argument, or to think that our usual analogies and probabilities have any authority. Our line is too short to fathom such immense abysses. And however we may flatter ourselves that we are guided, in every step which we take, by a kind of verisimilitude and experience, we may be assured that this fancied experience has no authority when we thus apply it to subjects that lie entirely out of the sphere of experience. But on this we shall have occasion to touch afterwards.

Secondly, I cannot perceive any force in the arguments on which this theory is founded. We are ignorant, it is true, of the manner in which bodies operate on each other: Their force or energy is entirely incomprehensible: But are we not equally ignorant of the manner or force by which a mind, even the supreme mind, operates either on itself or on body? Whence, I beseech you, do we acquire any idea of it? We have no sentiment or consciousness of this power in ourselves. We have no idea of the Supreme Being but what we learn from reflection on our own faculties. Were our ignorance, therefore, a good reason for rejecting any thing, we should be led into that principle of denying all energy in the Supreme Being as much as in the grossest matter. We surely comprehend as little the operations of one as of the other. Is it more difficult to conceive that motion may arise from impulse than that it may arise from volition? All we know is our profound ignorance in both cases.[14]

Part II

But to hasten to a conclusion of this argument, which is already drawn out to too great a length: We have sought in vain for an idea of power or necessary connexion in all the sources from which we could suppose it to be derived. It appears that, in single instances of the operation of bodies, we never can, by our utmost scrutiny, discover any thing but one event following another, without being able to comprehend any force or power by which the cause operates, or any connexion between it and its supposed effect. The same difficulty occurs in contemplating the operations of mind on body—where we observe the motion of the latter to follow upon the volition of the former, but are not able to observe or conceive the tie which binds together the motion and volition, or the energy by which the mind produces this effect. The authority of the will over its own faculties and ideas is not a whit more comprehensible: So that, upon the whole, there appears not, throughout all nature, any one instance of connexion which is conceivable by us. All events seem entirely loose and separate. One event follows another; but we never can observe any tie between them. They seem *conjoined,* but never *connected.* And as we can have no idea of any thing which never appeared to our outward sense or inward sentiment, the necessary conclusion *seems* to be that we have no idea of connexion or power at all, and that these words are absolutely without any meaning, when employed either in philosophical reasonings or common life.

But there still remains one method of avoiding this conclusion, and one source which we have not yet examined. When any natural object or event is presented, it is impossible for us, by any sagacity or penetration, to discover, or even conjecture, without experience, what event will result from it, or to carry our foresight beyond that object which is immediately present to the memory and senses. Even after one instance or experiment where we have observed a particular event to follow upon another, we are not entitled to form a general rule, or foretell what will happen in like cases; it being justly esteemed an unpardonable temerity to judge of the whole course of nature from one single experiment, however accurate or certain. But when one particular species of event has always, in all instances, been conjoined with another, we make no longer any scruple of foretelling one upon the appearance of the other, and of employing that reasoning, which can alone assure us of any matter of fact or existence. We then call the one object, *Cause;* the other, *Effect.* We suppose that there is some connexion between them; some power in the one, by which it infallibly produces the other, and operates with the greatest certainty and strongest necessity.

It appears, then, that this idea of a necessary connexion among events arises from a number of similar instances which occur of the constant conjunction of these events; nor can that idea ever be suggested by any one of these instances, surveyed in all possible lights and positions. But there is nothing in a number of instances, different from every single instance, which is supposed to be exactly similar; except only, that after a repetition of similar instances, the mind is carried by habit, upon the appearance of one event, to expect its usual attendant, and to believe that it will exist. This connexion, therefore, which we *feel* in the mind, this customary transition of the imagination from one object to its usual attendant, is the sentiment or impression from which we form the idea of power or necessary connexion. Nothing farther is in the case. Contemplate the subject on all sides; you will never find any other origin of that idea. This is the sole difference between one instance, from which we can never receive the idea of connexion, and a number of similar instances, by which it is suggested. The first time a man saw the communication of motion by impulse, as by the shock of two billiard-balls, he could not pronounce that the one event was *connected:* but only that it was *conjoined* with the other. After he has observed several instances of this nature, he then pronounces them to be *connected.* What alteration has happened to give rise to this new idea of *connexion?* Nothing but that he now *feels* these events to be *connected* in his imagination, and can readily foretell the existence of one from the appearance of the other. When we say, therefore, that one object is connected with another, we mean only that they have acquired a connexion in our thought, and give rise to this inference, by which they become proofs of each other's existence: A conclusion which is somewhat extraordinary, but which seems founded on sufficient evidence. Nor will its evidence be weakened by any general diffidence of the understanding, or sceptical suspicion concerning every conclusion which is new and extraordinary. No conclusions can be more agreeable to scepticism than such as make discoveries concerning the weakness and narrow limits of human reason and capacity.

And what stronger instance can be produced of the surprising ignorance and weakness of the understanding than the present? For surely, if there be any relation among objects which it imports to us to know perfectly, it is that of cause and effect. On this are founded all our reasonings concerning matter of fact or existence. By means of it alone we attain any assurance concerning objects which are removed from the present testimony of our memory and senses. The only immediate utility of all sciences, is to teach us, how to control and regulate future events by their causes. Our thoughts and enquiries are, therefore, every moment, employed about this relation: Yet so imperfect are the ideas which we form concerning it, that it is impossible to give any just definition of cause, except what is drawn from something extraneous and foreign to it. Similar objects are always conjoined with similar. Of this we have experience. Suitably to this experience, therefore, we may define a cause to be *an object, followed by another, and where all the objects similar to the first are followed by objects similar to the second.* Or in other words *where, if the first object had not been, the second never had existed.* The appearance of a cause always conveys the mind, by a customary transition, to the idea of the effect. Of this also we have experience. We may, therefore, suitably to this experience, form another definition of cause, and call it, *an object followed by another, and whose appearance always conveys the thought to that other.* But though both these definitions be drawn from circumstances foreign to the cause, we cannot remedy this inconvenience, or attain any more perfect definition, which may point out that circumstance in the cause, which gives it a connexion with its effect. We have no idea of this connexion, nor even any distinct notion what it is we desire to know, when we endeavour at a conception of it. We say, for instance, that the vibration of this string is the cause of this particular sound. But what do we mean by that affirmation? We either mean *that this vibration is followed by this sound, and that all similar vibrations have been followed by similar sounds:* Or, *that this vibration is followed by this sound, and that upon the appearance of one the mind anticipates the senses, and forms immediately an idea of the other.* We may consider the relation of cause and effect in either of these two lights; but beyond these, we have no idea of it.[15]

To recapitulate, therefore, the reasonings of this section: Every idea is copied from some preceding impression or sentiment; and where we cannot find any impression, we may be certain that there is no idea. In all single instances of the operation of bodies or minds, there is nothing that produces any impression, nor consequently can suggest any idea of power or necessary connexion. But when many uniform instances appear, and the same object is always followed by the same event; we then begin to entertain the notion of cause and connexion. We then *feel* a new sentiment or impression, to wit, a customary connexion in the thought or imagination between one object and its usual attendant; and this sentiment is the original of that idea which we seek for. For as this idea arises from a number of similar instances, and not from any single instance, it must arise from that circumstance, in which the number of instances differ from every individual instance. But this customary connexion or transition of the imagination is the only circumstance in which they differ. In every other particular they are alike. The first instance which we saw of motion communicated by the shock of two billiard-balls (to return to this obvious illustration) is exactly similar to any instance that may, at present, occur to us; except only, that we could not, at first, *infer* one event from the other; which we are enabled to do at present, after so long a course of uniform experience. I know not whether the reader will readily apprehend this reasoning. I am afraid that, should I multiply words about it, or throw it into a greater variety of lights, it would only become more obscure and intricate. In all abstract reasonings there is one point of view which, if we can happily hit, we shall go farther towards illustrating the subject than by all the eloquence and copious expression in the world. This point of view we should endeavour to reach, and reserve the flowers of rhetoric for subjects which are more adapted to them.

Notes

1. It is probable that no more was meant by those, who denied innate ideas, than that all ideas were copies of our impressions; though it must be confessed, that the terms, which they employed, were not chosen with such caution, nor so exactly defined, as to prevent all mistakes about their doctrine. For what is meant by *innate?* If innate be equivalent to natural, then all the perceptions and ideas of the mind must be allowed to be innate or natural, in whatever sense we take the latter word, whether in opposition to what is uncommon, artificial, or miraculous. If by innate be meant, contemporary to our birth, the dispute seems to be frivolous; nor is it worth while to enquire at what time thinking begins, whether before, at, or after our birth. Again, the word *idea,* seems to be commonly taken in a very loose sense, by Locke and others; as standing for any of our perceptions, our sensations and passions, as well as thoughts. Now in this sense, I should desire to know, what can be meant by asserting, that self-love, or resentment of injuries, or the passion between the sexes is not innate!

   But admitting these terms, *impressions* and *ideas,* in the sense above explained, and understanding by *innate,* what is original or copied from no precedent perception, then may we assert that all our impressions are innate, and our ideas not innate.

   To be ingenuous, I must own it to be my opinion, that Locke was betrayed into this question by the schoolmen, who, making use of undefined terms, draw out their disputes to a tedious length, without ever touching the point in question. A like ambiguity and circumlocution seem to run through that philosopher's reasonings on this as well as most other subjects.
2. Resemblance.
3. Contiguity.
4. Cause and effect.
5. For instance, Contrast or Contrariety is also a connexion among Ideas: but it may, perhaps, be considered as a mixture of *Causation* and *Resemblance*. Where two objects are contrary, the one destroys the other; that is, the cause of its annihilation, and the idea of the annihilation of an object, implies the idea of its former existence.
6. The word, Power, is here used in a loose and popular sense. The more accurate explication of it would give additional evidence to this argument. See Section VII.
7. Nothing is more useful than for writers, even, on *moral, political,* or *physical* subjects, to distinguish between *reason* and *experience,* and to suppose, that these species of argumentation are entirely different from each other. The former are taken for the mere result of our intellectual faculties, which, by considering a priori the nature of things, and examining the effects, that must follow from their operation, establish particular principles of science and philosophy. The latter are supposed to be derived entirely from sense and observation, by which we learn what has actually resulted from the operation of particular objects, and are thence able to infer, what will, for the future, result from them. Thus, for instance, the limitations and restraints of civil government, and a legal constitution, may be defended, either from *reason,* which reflecting on the great frailty and corruption of human nature, teaches, that no man can safely be trusted with unlimited authority; or from *experience* and history, which inform us of the enormous abuses, that ambition, in every age and country, has been found to make of so imprudent a confidence.

The same distinction between reason and experience is maintained in all our deliberations concerning the conduct of life; while the experienced statesman, general, physician, or merchant is trusted and followed; and the unpractised novice, with whatever natural talents endowed, neglected and despised. Though it be allowed, that reason may form very plausible conjectures with regard to the consequences of such a particular conduct in such particular circumstances; it is still supposed imperfect, without the assistance of experience, which is alone able to give stability and certainty to the maxims, derived from study and reflection.

But notwithstanding that this distinction be thus universally received, both in the active speculative scenes of life, I shall not scruple to pronounce, that it is, at bottom, erroneous, at least, superficial.

If we examine those arguments, which, in any of the sciences above mentioned, are supposed to be the mere effects of reasoning and reflection, they will be found to terminate, at last, in some general principle or conclusion, for which we can assign no reason but observation and experience. The only difference between them and those maxims, which are vulgarly esteemed the result of pure experience, is, that the former cannot be established without some process of thought, and some reflection on what we have observed, in order to distinguish its circumstances, and trace its consequences: Whereas in the latter, the experienced event is exactly and fully familiar to that which we infer as the result of any particular situation. The history of a TIBERIUS or a NERO makes us dread a like tyranny, were our monarchs freed from the restraints of laws and senates: But the observation of any fraud or cruelty in private life is sufficient, with the aid of a little thought, to give us the same apprehension; while it serves as an instance of the general corruption of human nature, and shows us the danger which we must incur by reposing an entire confidence in mankind. In both cases, it is experience which is ultimately the foundation of our inference and conclusion.

There is no man so young and unexperienced, as not to have formed, from observation, many general and just maxims concerning human affairs and the conduct of life; but it must be confessed, that, when a man comes to put these in practice, he will be extremely liable to error, till time and farther experience both enlarge these maxims, and teach him their proper use and application. In every situation or incident, there are many particular and seemingly minute circumstances, which the man of greatest talent is, at first, apt to overlook, though on them the justness of his conclusions, and consequently the prudence of his conduct, entirely depend. Not to mention, that, to a young beginner, the general observations and maxims occur not always on the proper occasions, nor can be immediately applied with due calmness and distinction. The truth is, an unexperienced reasoner could be no reasoner at all, were he absolutely unexperienced; and when we assign that character to any one, we mean it only in a comparative sense, and suppose him possessed of experience, in a smaller and more imperfect degree.

8. Whether it is a natural instinct or a mere illusion, I can't say; but one's emotions are more strongly aroused by seeing the places that tradition records to have been the favorite resort of men of note in former days, than by hearing about their deeds or reading their writings. My own feelings at the present moment are a case in point. I am reminded of Plato, the first philosopher, so we are told, that made a practice of holding discussions in this place; and indeed, the garden close at hand, yonder, not only recalls his memory but seems to bring the actual man before my eyes. This was the haunt of Speusippus, of Xenocrates, and of Xenocrates' pupil Polemo, who used to sit on the very seat we see over there. For my own part, even the sight of our senate-house at home (I mean the Curia Hostilia, not the present new building, which looks to my eyes smaller since its enlargement) used to call up to me thoughts of Scipio, Cato, Laelius, and chief of all, my grandfather; such powers of suggestion do places possess. No wonder the scientific training of the memory is based upon locality. Cicero, *De Finibus,* Book V, trans. H. Rackham (Cambridge: Harvard University Press, 1914), pp. 291–92.
9. Mr. Locke divides all arguments into demonstrative and probable. In this view, we must say, that it is only probable all men must die, or that the sun will rise to-morrow. But to conform our language more to common use, we ought to divide arguments into *demonstrations, proofs,* and *probabilities.* By proofs meaning such arguments from experience as leave no room for doubt or opposition.
10. Section II.
11. Mr. Locke, in his chapter of power, says that, finding from experience, that there are several new productions in nature, and concluding that there must somewhere be a power capable of producing them, we arrive at last by this reasoning at the idea of power. But no reasoning can ever give us a new, original, simple idea; as this philosopher himself confesses. This, therefore, can never be the origin of that idea.
12. It may be pretended, that the resistance which we meet with in bodies, obliging us frequently to exert our force, and call up all our power, this gives us the idea of force and power. It is this *nisus,* or strong endeavour, of which we are conscious, that is the original impression from which this idea is copied. But, first, we attribute powers to a vast number of objects, where we never can suppose this resistance or exertion of force to take place; to the Supreme Being, who never meets with any resistance; to the mind in its command over its ideas and limbs, in common thinking and motion, where

the effect follows immediately upon the will, without any exertion or summoning up of force; to inanimate matter, which is not capable of this sentiment. *Secondly,* This sentiment of an endeavour to overcome resistance has no known connexion with any event: What follows it, we know by experience; but could not know it a priori. It must, however, be confessed, that the animal *nisus,* which we experience, though it can afford no accurate precise idea of power, enters very much into that vulgar, inaccurate idea, which is formed of it.

13. Θεὸς ἀπὸ μηχανῆς. [In Latin, *"Deus ex machina."* Literally, god from a machine. A thing or person that appears suddenly and unexpectedly in a play to provide a contrived solution to a difficult situation.]

14. I need not examine at length the *vis inertiae* which is so much talked of in the new philosophy, and which is ascribed to matter. We find by experience, that a body at rest or in motion continues for ever in its present state, till put from it by some new cause; and that a body impelled takes as much motion from the impelling body as it acquires itself. These are facts. When we call this a *vis inertiae,* we only mark these facts, without pretending to have any idea of the inert power; in the same manner as, when we talk of gravity, we mean certain effects, without comprehending that active power. It was never the meaning of Sir ISAAC NEWTON to rob second causes of all force or energy; though some of his followers have endeavoured to establish that theory upon his authority. On the contrary, that great philosopher had recourse to an etherial active fluid to explain his universal attraction; though he was so cautious and modest as to allow, that it was a mere hypothesis, not to be insisted on, without more experiments. I must confess, that there is something in the fate of opinions a little extraordinary. DES CARTES insinuated that doctrine of the universal and sole efficacy of the Deity, without insisting on it. MALEBRANCHE and other CARTESIANS made it the foundation of all their philosophy. It had, however, no authority in England. LOCKE, CLARKE, and CUDWORTH, never so much as take notice of it, but suppose all along, that matter has a real, though subordinate and derived power. By what means has it become so prevalent among our modern metaphysicians?

15. According to these explications and definitions, the idea of *power* is relative as much as that of *cause;* and both have a reference to an effect, or some other event constantly conjoined with the former. When we consider the *unknown* circumstance of an object, by which the degree or quantity of its effect is fixed and determined, we call that its power: And accordingly, it is allowed by all philosophers, that the effect is the measure of the power. But if they had any idea of power, as it is in itself, why could not they Measure it in itself? The dispute whether the force of a body in motion be as its velocity, or the square of its velocity; this dispute, I say, need not be decided by comparing its effects in equal or unequal times; but by a direct mensuration and comparison.

As to the frequent use of the words, Force, Power, Energy, etc., which every where occur in common conversation, as well as in philosophy; that is no proof, that we are acquainted, in any instance, with the connecting principle between cause and effect, or can account ultimately for the production of one thing to another. These words, as commonly used, have very loose meanings annexed to them; and their ideas are very uncertain and confused. No animal can put external bodies in motion without the sentiment of a *nisus* or endeavour; and every animal has a sentiment or feeling from the stroke or blow of an external object, that is in motion. These sensations, which are merely animal, and from which we can a priori draw no inference, we are apt to transfer to inanimate objects, and to suppose, that they have some such feelings, whenever they transfer or receive motion. With regard to energies, which are exerted, without our annexing to them any idea of communicated motion, we consider only the constant experienced conjunction of the events; and as we *feel* a customary connexion between the ideas, we transfer that feeling to the objects; as nothing is more usual than to apply to external bodies every internal sensation, which they occasion.

B. PERCEPTION

Sense-Data and Common Sense

G. E. MOORE

G. E. Moore (1873–1958) was a professor of philosophy at Cambridge University. A leader, with Bertrand Russell, of the revolt against idealism in the early twentieth century, Moore became known as a staunch defender of common sense in philosophy. His works include *Principia Ethica, Philosophical Studies,* and *Some Main Problems of Philosophy.*

IV. . . . I am not at all sceptical as to the *truth* of such propositions as "The earth has existed for many years past." "Many human bodies have each lived for many years upon it," i.e. propositions which assert the existence of material things: on the contrary, I hold that we all know, with certainty, many such propositions to be true. But I am very sceptical as to what, in certain respects, the correct *analysis* of such propositions is. And this is a matter as to which I think I differ from many philosophers. Many seem to hold that there is no doubt at all as to their *analysis,* nor, therefore, as to the analysis of the proposition"Material things have existed," in certain respects in which I hold that the analysis of the propositions in question is extremely doubtful; and some of them, as we have seen, while holding that there is no doubt as to their *analysis* seem to have doubted whether any such propositions are *true.* I, on the other hand, while holding that there is no doubt whatever that many such propositions are wholly true, hold also that no philosopher, hitherto, has succeeded in suggesting an analysis of them, as regards certain important points, which comes anywhere near to being certainly true.

It seems to me quite evident that the question how propositions of the type I have just given are to be analysed, depends on the question how propositions of another and simpler type are to be analysed. I know, at present, that I am perceiving a human hand, a pen, a sheet of paper, etc.; and it seems to me that I cannot know how the proposition "Material things exist" is to be analysed, until I know how, in certain respects, these simpler propositions are to be analysed. But even these are not simple enough. It seems to me quite evident that my knowledge that I am now perceiving a human hand is a deduction from a pair of propositions simpler still—propositions which I can only express in the form "I am perceiving *this*" and "This is a human hand." It is the analysis of propositions of the latter kind which seems to me to present such great difficulties, while nevertheless the whole question as to the *nature* of material things obviously depends upon their analysis. It seems to me a surprising thing that so few philosophers, while saying a great deal as to what material things *are* and as to what it is to perceive them, have attempted to give a clear account as to what precisely they suppose themselves to *know* (or to *judge,* in case they have held that we don't *know* any such propositions to be true, or even that no such propositions *are* true)

From *Philosophical Papers* (London: Allen & Unwin, 1959), pp. 52–59.

when they know or judge such things as "This is a hand," "That is the sun," "This is a dog," etc. etc. etc.

Two things only seem to me to be quite certain about the analysis of such propositions (and even with regard to these I am afraid some philosophers would differ from me) namely that whenever I know, or judge, such a proposition to be true, (1) there is always some *sense-datum* about which the proposition in question is a proposition—some sense-datum which is *a* subject (and, in a certain sense, the principal or ultimate subject) of the proposition in question, and (2) that, nevertheless, *what* I am knowing or judging to be true about this sense-datum is not (in general) that it is *itself* a hand, or a dog, or the sun, etc. etc., as the case may be.

Some philosophers have I think doubted whether there are any such things as other philosophers have meant by "sense-data" or "sensa." And I think it is quite possible that some philosophers (including myself, in the past) have used these terms in senses such that it is really doubtful whether there are any such things. But there is no doubt at all that there are sense-data, in the sense in which I am now using that term. I am at present seeing a great number of them, and feeling others. And in order to point out to the reader what sort of things I mean by sense-data, I need only ask him to look at his own right hand. If he does this he will be able to pick out something (and, unless he is seeing double, *only* one thing) with regard to which he will see that it is, at first sight, a natural view to take that that thing is identical, not, indeed, with his whole right hand, but with that part of its surface which he is actually seeing, but will also (on a little reflection) be able to see that it is doubtful whether it can be identical with the part of the surface of his hand in question. Things *of the sort* (in a certain respect) of which this thing is, which he sees in looking at his hand, and with regard to which he can understand how some philosophers should have supposed it to *be* the part of the surface of his hand which he is seeing, while others have supposed that it can't be, are what I mean by "sense-data." I therefore define the term in such a way that it is an open question whether the sense-datum which I now see in looking at my hand and which is a sense-datum of my hand is or is not identical with that part of its surface which I am now actually seeing.

That what I know, with regard to this sense-datum, when I know "This is a human hand," is not that it is *itself* a human hand, seems to me certain because I know that my hand has many parts (e.g. its other side, and the bones inside it), which are quite certainly *not* parts of this sense-datum.

I think it certain, therefore, that the analysis of the proposition "This is a human hand" is, roughly at least, of the form "There is a thing, and only one thing, of which it is true both that it is a human hand and that *this surface* is a part of its surface." In other words, to put my view in terms of the phrase "theory of representative perception," I hold it to be quite certain that I do not *directly* perceive *my hand;* and that when I am said (as I may be correctly said) to "perceive" it, that I "perceive" it means that I perceive (in a different and more fundamental sense) something which is (in a suitable sense) *representative* of it, namely, a certain part of its surface.

This is all that I hold to be *certain* about the analysis of the proposition "This is a human hand." We have seen that it includes in its analysis a proposition of the form "This is part of the surface of a human hand" (where "This," of course, has a different meaning from that which it has in the original proposition which has now been analysed). But this proposition also is undoubtedly a proposition about the sense-datum, which I am seeing, which is a sense-datum *of* my hand. And hence the further question arises: *What,* when I know "*This* is *part of the surface of* a human hand," am I knowing about the sense-datum in question? Am I, in this case, really knowing about the sense-datum in question that it *itself* is part of the surface of a human hand? Or, just as we found in the case of "This is a human hand," that what I was knowing about the sense-datum was certainly not that it *itself* was a human hand, so, is it perhaps the case, with this new proposition, that even here I am now knowing, with regard to the sense-datum, that it is *itself* part of the surface of a hand? And, if so, what is it that I am knowing about the sense-datum itself?

This is the question to which, as it seems to

me, no philosopher has hitherto suggested an answer which comes anywhere near to being *certainly* true.

There seem to me to be three, and only three, alternative types of answer possible; and to any answer yet suggested, of any of these types, there seem to me to be very grave objections.

(1) Of the first type, there is but one answer: namely, that in this case what I am knowing really is that the sense-datum *itself* is part of the surface of a human hand. In other words that, though I don't perceive *my hand* directly, I do *directly* perceive part of its surface; that the sense-datum itself *is* this part of its surface and not merely something which (in a sense yet to be determined) "represents" this part of its surface; and that hence the sense in which I "perceive" this part of the surface of my hand, is not in its turn a sense which needs to be defined by reference to yet a third more ultimate sense of "perceive," which is the only one in which perception is direct, namely that in which I perceive the sense-datum.

If this view is true (as I think it may just possibly be), it seems to me certain that we must abandon a view which has been held to be certainly true by most philosophers, namely the view that our sense-data always really have the qualities which they sensibly appear to us to have. For I know that if another man were looking through a microscope at the same surface which I am seeing with the naked eye, the sense-datum which he saw would sensibly appear to him to have qualities very different from and incompatible with those which my sense-datum sensibly appears to me to have: and yet, if my sense-datum is identical with the surface we are both of us seeing, his must be identical with it also. My sense-datum can, therefore, be identical with this surface only on condition that it is identical with his sense-datum; and, since his sense-datum sensibly appears to him to have qualities incompatible with those which mine sensibly appears to me to have, his sense-datum can be identical with mine only on condition that the sense-datum in question either has not got the qualities which it sensibly appears to me to have, or has not got those which it sensibly appears to him to have.

I do not, however, think that this is a fatal objection to this first type of view. A far more serious objection seems to me to be that, when we see a thing double (have what is called "a double image" of it), we certainly have *two* sense-data each of which is *of* the surface seen, and which cannot therefore both be identical with it; and that yet it seems as if, if any sense-datum is ever identical with the surface *of* which it is a sense-datum, each of these so-called "images" must be so. It looks, therefore, as if every sense-datum is, after all, only "representative" of the surface, *of* which it is a sense-datum.

(2) But, if so, what relation has it to the surface in question?

This second type of view is one which holds that when I know "This is part of the surface of a human hand," what I am knowing with regard to the sense-datum which is *of* that surface, is, *not* that it is *itself* part of the surface of a human hand, but something of the following kind. There is, it says, *some* relation, R, such that what I am knowing with regard to the sense-datum is either "There is one thing and only one thing, of which it is true both that it is a part of the surface of a human hand, and that it has R to this sense-datum," or else "There are a set of things, of which it is true both that that set, taken collectively, *are* part of the surface of a human hand, and also that each member of the set has R to this sense-datum, and that nothing which is not a member of the set has R to it."

Obviously, in the case of this second type, many different views are possible, differing according to the view they take as to what the relation R is. But there is only one of them, which seems to me to have any plausibility; namely that which holds that R is an ultimate and unanalysable relation, which might be expressed by saying that "xRy" means the same as "y is an appearance or manifestation of x." I.e. the analysis which this answer would give of "This is part of the surface of a human hand" would be "There is one and only one thing of which it is true both that it is part of the surface of a human hand, and that this sense-datum is an appearance or manifestation of it."

To this view also there seem to me to be very grave objections, chiefly drawn from a consideration of the questions how we can possibly *know* with regard to any of our sense-data that there is one thing and one thing only which has to them such a supposed ultimate relation; and how, if we do, we can possibly *know* anything further about such things, e.g. of what size or shape they are.

(3) The third type of answer, which seems to me to be the only possible alternative if (1) and (2) are rejected, is the type of answer which J. S. Mill seems to have been implying to be the true one when he said that material things are "permanent possibilities of sensation." He seems to have thought that when I know such a fact as "This is part of the surface of a human hand," what I am knowing with regard to the sense-datum which is the principal subject of that fact, is not that it is itself part of the surface of a human hand, nor yet, with regard to any relation, that *the* thing which has to it that relation is part of the surface of a human hand, but a whole set of hypothetical facts each of which is a fact of the form "If *these* conditions had been fulfilled, I should have been perceiving a sense-datum intrinsically related to *this* sense-datum, in *this* way," "If *these* (other) conditions had been fulfilled, I should have been perceiving a sense-datum intrinsically related to *this* sense-datum in *this* (other) way," etc. etc.

With regard to this third type of view as to the analysis of propositions of the kind we are considering, it seems to me, again, just *possible* that it is a true one; but to hold (as Mill himself and others seem to have held) that it is *certainly,* or nearly certainly, true, seems to me as great a mistake, as to hold with regard either to (1) or to (2), that they are *certainly,* or nearly certainly, true. There seem to me to be very grave objections to it; in particular the three, *(a)* that though, in general, when I know such a fact as "This is a hand," I certainly do know some hypothetical facts of the form "If *these* conditions had been fulfilled, I should have been perceiving a sense-datum of *this* kind, which would have been a sense-datum of the same surface of which *this* is a sense-datum," it seems doubtful whether any conditions with regard to which I know this are not themselves conditions of the form "If this and that *material thing* had been in those positions and conditions . . . ," *(b)* that it seems again very doubtful whether there is any intrinsic relation, such that my knowledge that (under *these* conditions) I should have been perceiving a sense-datum of *this* kind, which would have been a sense-datum of the same surface of which *this* is a sense-datum, is equivalent to a knowledge, with regard to that relation, that I should, under those conditions, have been perceiving a sense-datum related by it to *this* sense-datum, and *(c)* that, if it were true, the sense in which a material surface is "round" or "square," would necessarily be utterly different from that in which our sense-data sensibly appear to us to be "round" or "square."

V. Just as I hold that the proposition "There are and have been material things" is quite certainly true, but that the question how this proposition is to be analysed is one to which no answer that has been hitherto given is anywhere near certainly true; so I hold that the proposition "There are and have been many Selves" is quite certainly true, but that here again all the analyses of this proposition that have been suggested by philosophers are highly doubtful.

That I am now perceiving many different sense-data, and that I have at many times in the past perceived many different sense-data, I know for certain—that is to say, I know that there are mental facts of class (β), connected in a way which it is proper to express by saying that they are all of them facts about *me;* but how this kind of connection is to be analysed, I do not know for certain, nor do I think that any other philosopher knows with any approach to certainty. Just as in the case of the proposition "This is part of the surface of a human hand," there are several extremely different views as to its analysis, each of which seems to me *possible,* but none nearly certain, so also in the case of the proposition "This, that and that sense-datum are all at present being perceived by *me,*" and still more so in the case of the proposition "*I* am now perceiving this sense-datum, and *I* have in the past perceived sense-data of these other kinds." Of the *truth* of these propositions there seems to me to be no doubt, but as to what is the correct analysis of them there seems to me to be the gravest doubt—the true analysis may, for instance, *possibly* be quite as paradoxical as is the third view given under IV as to the analysis of "This is part of the surface of a human hand''; but whether it *is* as paradoxical as this seems to me to be quite as doubtful as in that case. Many philosophers, on the other hand, seem to me to have assumed that there is little or no doubt as to the correct analysis of such propositions; and many of these, just reversing my position, have also held that the propositions themselves are not true.

Moore's Theory of Sense-Data

O. K. BOUWSMA

O. K. Bouwsma (1898–1978) was an important American philosopher in the ordinary language movement, which emphasized the importance of studying our concepts through careful investigation of their expression in ordinary modes of discourse. He was a professor of philosophy at the University of Nebraska and the University of Texas. His publications include *Philosophical Essays*.

I

I want in this essay to discuss a few sentences from Professor Moore's "A Defence of Common Sense," published in the volume containing the second series of contributions to *Contemporary British Philosophy*. These sentences are contained in part IV of that contribution. In this part Professor Moore is expounding what he regards as the correct analysis of such sentences as "This is a hand," "That is the sun," "This is a dog," etc. Involved in this exposition is the assertion: "whenever I know or judge such a proposition to be true, there is always some sense-datum about which the proposition in question is a proposition—some sense-datum which is a subject of the proposition in question."[1] Professor Moore goes on to recognize "that some philosophers have . . . doubted whether there are any such things as other philosophers have meant by 'sense-datum',"[2] and in order to make sure that his readers may be persuaded, he goes on with the following attempt at definition, which I quote.

Professor Moore writes:

> And in order to point out to the reader what sort of things I mean by sense-data, I need only ask him to look at his own right hand. If he does this he will be able to pick out something (and unless he is seeing double, only one thing) with regard to which he will see that it is, at first sight, a natural view to take, that that thing is identical, not indeed, with his whole right hand, but with that part of its surface which he is actually seeing, but will also (on a little reflection) be able to see that it is doubtful whether it can be identical with the part of the surface of his hand in question. Things *of the sort* (in a certain respect) of which this thing is, which he sees in looking at his hand, and with regard to which he can understand how some philosophers should have supposed it to be the part of the surface of his hand which he is seeing, while others have supposed that it can't be, are what I mean by sense-data. I therefore define the term in such a way that it is an open question whether the sense-datum which I now see in looking at my hand and which is a sense-datum of my hand, is or is not identical with that part of its surface which I am now actually seeing.[3]

I propose first to discuss some difficulties in this paragraph. Professor Moore invites his readers to pick out something, but his directions for

From *The Philosophy of G. E. Moore*, ed. P. A. Schillp; Vol. 4, Library of Living Philosophers (Evanston, Ill.: Northwestern University Press, 1942), pp. 203–21. Reprinted by permission of the Library of Living Philosophers, Inc.

doing this are not clear. Commonly if one is asked to pick out something, the something is described. Out of this bowl, pick out the red flower; out of this sheaf pick out the longest straw. We should all know how to follow these directions. But Professor Moore's directions are not like this. Apparently you simply pick out something; that is, as you are looking at your hand, and keeping your eye on your hand, you pick out something. Suppose you pick out your knuckles. Certainly that is something you can pick out. Well, is that the sort of thing Professor Moore intended that you should pick out? It is not. And this is the test which what you pick out must satisfy in order to meet Professor Moore's requirement. You must pick out something "with regard to which . . . it is, at first sight, a natural view to take, that that thing is identical with that part of its surface which [you are] actually seeing." So of course, the knuckles won't do. Even the surface of the knuckles won't do. What better could one do, than pick out the surface of the hand one is seeing? Certainly you can pick this out and it would be a natural view to take that that thing is identical with that part of the surface which you are actually seeing. This is a bit doubtful however, since you would scarcely be expected to pick out the whole of the surface which you are seeing, for picking out is selecting, and after selection there would be a remainder, which in this case there would not be. Furthermore if you do pick out the surface of the hand which you are seeing, could you then (on a little reflection) doubt that it is the surface of the hand you are seeing? For until you manage to do this too you would not have picked out what Professor Moore means by a sense-datum.

I confess that I am unable with these directions to attain the desired result. Looking at my hand I can pick out knuckles, finger-tips, nails, lines, veins, etc., but to none of them does the description which Professor Moore gives apply. If I pick out the knuckles, I am not seized with any doubts that they are the surface of my hand; and so with the finger-tips, nails, etc. And how I should ever be in a position to anticipate that what I do pick out would satisfy the given conditions I do not understand. I can see how if yesterday I had been asked to pick out my thumb, and then a little later doubted that what I had picked out was my thumb (for I had my fingers crossed in an unusual way) then today I might, remembering, pick out what yesterday it seemed very natural to take to be identical with my thumb and then what later I came to doubt was identical with my thumb. But Professor Moore's directions are not like this. He says that there is something which you may pick out and with respect to it, you will have the described difficulty. I have not been able to pick it out.

This, then, is one peculiarity of Professor Moore's directions. One who is unacquainted with sense-data, and so has no information with regard to what to pick out, must resort to random picking, and wish for luck. Professor Moore's directions are something like this: Pick out of this basket something of which you will see that it is, at first sight, a natural view to take that that thing is identical with a red marble, but of which you will also see that it is doubtful whether it can be identical with the red marble. Now one might look at the basket and notice what there is in it. Here is a red marble, here a red pepper, here a red rubber ball, etc. One might notice all these things, and turn away, saying that there was nothing there which seemed at first glance to be a red marble, and then a moment later seemed not to be a red marble so there was nothing to pick out. On the other hand, there might be something red and round in that basket which did at first appear to be a red marble, and then upon closer inspection turned out to be a red rubber ball. And picking out the red rubber ball would satisfy the directions. I am trying by these analogies to figure out just what sort of directions these are that Professor Moore is giving, in order to show why I have been unable in looking at my hand to discover anything which I should have some reason to suppose met with Professor Moore's directions.

But this is a general comment. Professor Moore says that there is something about which you first feel sure and then about which you doubt. In seeking for this I do not see how in feeling sure one could anticipate the doubting. But I should like further to notice some peculiarities concerning what it is one is at first to be sure of, and then is to doubt. I have in mind Professor Moore's use of the following types of sentence, in which X symbolizes the something which you are able to pick out:

1. X is identical with the surface of my right hand.
2. X can be identical with the surface of my right hand.
3. X cannot be identical with the surface of my right hand.

I want first to consider the first type of sentence in order to make clear the context in which we should commonly understand it. And for this purpose I am going to define a certain word, parodying the definition which Moore gives of the word sense-datum. This is the parody:

"And in order to point out to the reader what sort of thing I mean by ____, I need only ask him to look at the cook's right hand. If he does this he will be able to pick out something with regard to which he will see that it is at first a natural view to take that that thing is identical not indeed with the cook's whole right hand, but with that part of its surface which one is actually (?) seeing but will also (on a little inspection) be able to see that it is doubtful whether it can be identical with the part of the hand in question. Things of the sort of which this thing is, which he sees in looking at the cook's hand, and with regard to which he can understand how some kitchen visitors should have supposed it to be the part of the surface of the cook's hand at which he was looking, while others have supposed that it can't be, are what I mean by rubber gloves."

This experiment, I think, might do very well for all kitchen visitors. But obviously its success depends upon a familiarity with the use of the expression "human hand" by which the inspection is guided. Look closely at the hand; does it look like a hand? pinch it, smell it, etc. Does the surface stretch like taffy, is it very smooth, etc? Apparently in a case such as this there is no difficulty in distinguishing the surface of a hand from the surface of rubber gloves. Now then, when the reader in Professor Moore's experiments looks at his hand, and sees the surface of his hand, what happens? Does he think that some new kind of gloves, made to resemble the hand, have come to be worn, and that these gloves are, to smell, and touch, and sight, indistinguishable from the surface of the hand, gloves which you may not know you are wearing unless you remember that you put them on? If in a case of this sort one forgot, would one then be sensing, directly perceiving, a sense-datum? The answer is: No. For what distinguishes the doubt in terms of which Professor Moore defines the sense-datum, is that it cannot be resolved. Once the doubt arises, there is no way of settling the question whether the thing one can pick out is identical with the surface of one's hand or not. It must be remembered that Professor Moore does not say that the sense-datum is not identical with the surface of the hand. He only says that in looking at one's hand one comes to doubt that something, which may be the surface of one's hand, is the surface of one's hand. But, unlike the doubt about the surface of the hand and the rubber gloves, it cannot be settled. Once the doubt has arisen, there's nothing to do but to go on doubting. Scratching, smelling, looking more closely, do not give relief.

I can imagine someone in a facetious vein suggesting that the situation which Professor Moore describes is more like trying to distinguish identical twins occupying the same space. It's as though someone had been told: "He's identical twins," and then whenever that someone saw him, he would shake his head, looking, wondering, asking himself: Am I seeing Hans or Fritz? or when I am directly perceiving Hans, am I indirectly perceiving Fritz? He cannot decide. If someone says: You're seeing Hans, (that seems the natural view to take) he proceeds to doubt: "Maybe it's Fritz." He might in this situation easily come to see that some people would hold that Hans was not twins, and that Fritz is either an alternative notation for Fritz, or a meaningless expression.

Now I want to try a further experiment, again to exhibit the misleading familiarity of Professor Moore's language. In the experiment designed to test for rubber gloves, the point made was that Moore's language is applicable to such things as hands and gloves. I want now to show that it is also applicable to mirror-images. This is the experiment: "And in order to point out to the reader what I mean by ____, I need only ask him to look into the mirror, holding up his right hand to the glass. If he does this, he will be able to pick out something with regard to which he will see, that it is, at first sight, a natural view to take, that that thing is identical, not indeed with his whole right hand, but with that part of the surface which is reflected there, but will also (smiling to himself) be able to see that it is doubtful whether it can be identical with the part of the surface of his hand in question. Things of this sort of which this thing is, which he sees in looking at the reflection of his hand, and with regard to which he can understand how some creatures, little people and puppies, should have supposed it to be the part of the surface of his hand, while grown-ups supposed that it can't be, are what I mean by hand-mirror-images.''

Now the point of these two analogous experiments is this: If you are among those philosophers who doubt that there are any such things as some philosophers have meant by sense-data, and if you try to understand Professor Moore's directions in the attempt to identify a sense-datum, then further if you interpret a philosopher's language as so much English, you are certain to fail. If you look at your hand and try to stir up doubts about what you are seeing, you may object to yourself: But maybe I am wearing rubber gloves. Well, you know how to take care of that. Or you may object: But maybe I am looking into a mirror, and what I see is an image. You also know how to take care of that. What other misgiving suggestion remains then? It must be remembered that Professor Moore says that the doubt arises ''on a little reflection'' though he does not, in this context at least, tell us at all what reflection induces the doubt. It won't do, of course, to object: But maybe there are sense-data, and it is a property of sense-data to pass for the surfaces of things we look at, both when and if they are, and when and if they are not, the surfaces of objects. For it is by means of some reflection which does not involve that there are sense-data, but that leads to the requisite doubt concerning the surface of one's hand, that one is persuaded that there are sense-data. What I mean to point out here is that the language of the experiment is strange language so long as we are not acquainted with sense-data. Once we distinguish a sense-datum we may come to see how it applies. But before we can do this we must come to doubt. And before we come to doubt we must indulge in a ''little reflection.'' The question is: what reflection? What is it that led Professor Moore and some other philosophers to come to that pass where, when each looks at his hand, he may ask without the slightest perturbation: And is this the surface of a hand? If, actually seeing the surface of his hand, he says: ''Maybe not,'' then he is aware of a sense-datum. The question is: What thoughts lead him to his doubt?

Before I go on to consider what these reflections may be, I should like to discuss the second and third kinds of sentences above:

2. X can be identical with the surface of my right hand.

3. X cannot be identical with the surface of my right hand.

For this, notice a case of doubt in which one might have employed language of the sort which Professor Moore uses. Isaac on the day when he was deceived might have asked: Is this the hand of Jacob or the hand of Esau? Isaac was touching the hand and hearing the voice. The voice led him to doubt. We all understand this. And he might, had he attended Cambridge, have said: The hand that I am touching (and which I have picked out) is identical with the hand that is Esau's. I suppose that generally no one ever bothers to say a thing like this unless some doubt has preceded the assertion. So Isaac expected that this was the hand of Esau, but the voice made him doubtful. How could this be Esau's hand, when the voice which accompanied it sounded like Jacob's voice? In a dispute then, and to settle the matter (Isaac was very old!) Isaac may have said: This hand is identical with Esau's hand. He was wrong of course, but the confusion was one of hands; he mistook Jacob's hand for Esau's hand. The occasion for the use of the sentence arises after doubt and after denial. ''What do you see?'' ''My right hand.'' ''Oh, no you don't.'' ''I say [temper rising] that what I see, is identical with my right hand. It is my right hand.'' It follows, of course, that we also have a use for: X is not identical with my right hand. If Rebecca on that occasion long ago, had had a mind to, she might have interrupted with: ''You're wrong, Isaac. That hand is not identical with the hand of Esau. It's Jacob's hand.''

Now we can also make a case for ''This hand can be the hand of Esau,'' and so with ''This hand cannot be the hand of Esau.'' Rebecca might have said: ''It can't be.'' And then she would have given reasons, for such statements as "It can be" and "It can't be" have this sort of reference. So Isaac might have asked: Why can't it be? And the answer might have been: See here: You know that Esau's is a hairy hand. If you pull at the hairs on his hand, it pains him and you can see it on his face. And what is more the hair does not pull out. Try that experiment on his hand. There is no pain. The hair easily pulls off, and under the layer of hair, you will find paste. That's why this cannot be Esau's hand. Esau's hand is a genuine hairy, but this hand is a wolf's hand in sheep's clothing. To which Isaac might have lamented: But I thought it was Esau's. And it could have been for all I knew. The hand was hairy, it smelled of the field and of game, like Esau's hand. And it seemed like a large hand to me. So you see it could have been Esau's hand.

It is clearly, I think, situations such as these which we have in mind in the use of the expressions which Professor Moore employs. There is mistaking one thing for another thing, Jacob's hand for Esau's hand. There are also considerations which are involved in making the mistake, and other considerations which are involved in correcting the mistake. These considerations are of two kinds. If we are clear about what Jacob's hand is like, and clear about what Esau's hand is like, then the respects in which they are similar are likely to involve us in mistaking one for the other. The respects in which they are dissimilar, are the considerations which we draw upon when we correct our mistake, or when we come to say that "This cannot be so and so."

Accordingly, when Professor Moore says that you can pick out something about which you are inclined to say that it is identical with the surface of your hand, and this arises in a context in which you are inclined to say both that it can be, and that it cannot be, one would expect that some reasons would be at hand in respect to both. What makes you think that what you can pick out, can be identical with the surface of your hand and what makes you think that it cannot be identical with it? Is what you picked out similar in certain respects to the surface of your right hand, and dissimilar in certain other respects to that surface? Professor Moore has said that one would come to doubt by way of "a little reflection," as I noticed before, and the analysis which we have just made would lead one to expect that the reflection would consist in noticing similarities and dissimilarities between what you picked out and the surface of your right hand. Of course, if any dissimilarities were noticed, that ought to settle the matter. If the something is dissimilar, then of course, it is not the surface of one's hand. It looks as though one is aware of nothing but similarities, supposing one has picked out something, and yet that one is suspicious that there may be dissimilarities of which one is unaware. It's as though one were looking at one's hand, and had a suspicion that what one was seeing was not one's hand at all. So one examined one's hand carefully, found out that it was exactly what one expected one's hand to be like and yet concluded: "But maybe there is something I am not seeing, maybe there's a difference I am missing. So maybe after all, this is not my hand." What then planted this suspicion?

There is one further point that I should like to make. The experiment which Professor Moore proposes, takes for granted that each of us knows how to identify the surface of his hand. It is in terms of this identification that we are to come to recognize the something we pick out. Now then, each of us is able to describe his own hand. One might take a print of it, study it carefully for colour shadings, shape and surface markings. If then one is well-informed about the surface of one's own hand, the doubt which Professor Moore describes does not arise because of any lack of information about one's hand. Apparently then the something which you pick out has the same characteristics which the surface of your hand has. If it did not have the same characteristics, obviously it would be different from the surface of your hand, and if it had the same and some others, it would also be different. So, if it has any characteristics at all, it must have the same characteristics as the surface of your hand. How then explain the suggestion that they are different? Are they in different places? This is also out of the question. We do not see the surface of the hand in one place, and pick out the something in a different place. If we did, the doubt that the "something" and the surface of my hand are identical would be settled. This too does not explain the suggestion that the something and the surface of my hand are identical. What then?

If what I have just suggested about knowing the surface of one's hand is not admitted, then what? Then certainly we are at a loss. The experiment presupposes that we know something, and that by way of this we may become aware of something else. If you know the surface of your hand, you can become acquainted with your knuckles. You certainly can, if you look at your hand, pick out your knuckles. In some such way as this you also become acquainted with "a sense-datum." Suppose however that, in a situation in which you did pick out your knuckles, you were seized with a doubt as to whether your knuckles were identical with the surface of your right hand which you are seeing, how would you account for this? If nothing very serious has happened, one might suggest that you had now come to use the expression "the surface of my hand" in a very unusual way. I have an inkling that something of this sort has happened in the sentences from Professor Moore's exposition. If one can think that "the something which one can pick out" is identical with the surface of one's hand, then either one must take for granted the use of the expression "the surface of one's hand" which applies then to something one can see, smell, touch, kiss, etc., and so grant that what one can pick out is also something which one can see, smell, touch, kiss, etc., or otherwise one takes for granted the use of the expression "what one can pick out" knowing well what this is like that one can pick out, and that for instance one cannot touch, taste, smell, etc., what one can pick out, and so grant also that "the surface of my hand" is something which, like what one can pick out, can be seen, but cannot be touched, tasted, smelled, etc. Either, then, Professor Moore is in effect saying that you can pick out a physical object which is identical with the surface of your hand, or you can pick out something which is not a physical object at all, and that is identical with the surface of your hand. The puzzle is as to how a non-physical object (a sense-datum) can be identical with a physical object. It seems at any rate inevitable that if anything can be conceived to be the surface of my hand, it must be physical; and that if the surface of my hand can be conceived to be a sense-datum, the surface of my hand is not physical. But in that case what has happened to the expression: "the surface of my hand"?

II

I have tried, in what preceded, to point out some of the difficulties which I have met in trying to follow Professor Moore's directions. And I regard as crucial in this respect the three sentences which I discussed, and the use of the phrase: "the surface of my hand." I also noticed that what leads to the doubt in Professor Moore's experiment, is a "little reflection." My suggestion is that it is the same "little reflection" which leads us to use these sentences, and the phrase just noticed. And I want now to describe the reflections which, in my own case, seem to lead me in that direction.

There are especially three sets of facts which lead me to try to distinguish a sense-datum in the prescribed way. One is certain facts concerning sounds, odours and tastes. Another is facts concerning mirror reflections, images, echoes, etc. And a third is the use of such expressions as: It looks like . . . , This looks like . . . , etc. There may be other facts which are relevant as these are. But I have noticed that when I, at any rate, meet the expression sense-data, these are the sorts of fact which come to my mind.

I want, before I go on, to notice how narrowly Professor Moore has conceived the problem of sense-data. It is common among those who say that there are sense-data to say that sounds, odours, tastes, etc., are sense-data; but it appears, apart from the tell-no-tale phrase "in a certain respect," that Professor Moore means by a sense-datum only that sort of thing which may be taken to be the surface of something or other. In other words, Professor Moore confines his use of the phrase sense-datum only to what others would describe as *visual* sense-data. I find Professor Moore's definition unusual in this respect, or misleading. If he does define "sense-data" in such a way as to include only "visual sense-data" then he defines the term in a way inconsistent with his own use of the term, for in a previous sentence he says, referring to sense-data: "I am at present seeing a great number of them and feeling others.'' At any rate his exposition excludes smells, tastes, and sounds. However that may be, the problem here is: What reflections would lead one to distinguish something which one would then say can or cannot be identical with the surface of one's hand which one is seeing?

The fact with respect to sounds, smells, and tastes is that they function in perceptual experiences in two ways. I can illustrate this best by a few pairs of sentences. Notice these:

I hear a gnawing sound.
I hear a rat.

I smell an odour.
I smell a rat.

I taste a sour taste.
I taste a lemon.

The first of each of these pairs functions independently of the second, and one can describe sounds, odours, and tastes, without committing oneself to any sentence of the sort which is second in each pair. But the second does not function independently of the first. If you say: I hear a rat, then the question: What was the sound like?, is pertinent. In each case one may ask: What was the sound, or the odour, or the taste like? We are all acquainted with the descriptions of sounds, odours, and tastes. I need not, I think, enlarge upon this. If now someone held that there were sense-data and he meant by this that there were sounds, odours, and tastes, and that these are descriptively independent of rats and lemons, etc., there would, I think, be no controversy about this. There is no such question as: Is the sound or the odour of the rat identical with the surface of a rat, or the taste of a lemon identical with the surface of a lemon, or of that part of the lemon which I am tasting?

But now there are also certain similarities among facts of this following sort:

I hear a rat.
I smell a rat.
I taste a lemon.
I see a cloud.
I touch velvet.

And here, I take it, one is likely by reflection upon these sets of similarities to suppose that there must be some fact which corresponds to: I see a cloud, as: I hear a sound corresponds to: I hear a rat. And so too with: I touch velvet. Since, in other words, to hearing there corresponds a hearing sense-datum, and to smelling a smelling sense-datum, etc., so to seeing and to touching there must correspond seeing and touching sense-data. Actually, of course, there need not be such; and one part of the suggested parallel between hearing, smelling, and tasting, on the one hand, and seeing and touching, on the other, is missing. There are no descriptions of ''sights'' and ''touches'' which are independent conceptually of the descriptive characteristics of rats, lemons, clouds, velvet, etc. If you attempt to describe what you see, the same words which you use to describe the lemon or the cloud, will also serve to describe the purported sense-datum. So, if there is a sense-datum in these last cases, a new vocabulary will have to be engaged to perform the service. And so we get two different meanings for ''is red'' in the sentences ''This (sense-datum) is red,'' and ''This rose is red.'' This sort of accommodation is the consequence of the assumption that just as there are auditory sense-data so there must be visual sense-data. We make up for the deficiency in the facts from which we start by inventing a new vocabulary. Unfortunately we are compelled to use the same words which have otherwise performed an unambiguous service. It also follows that, if in the respect noted, seeing is like hearing, then as one is able, in hearing a bird, to distinguish the sound of the bird, so in seeing a hand one is able to pick out a corresponding visual sense-datum. The effect of these analogies may be so strong as to lead one to say that there must be a sense-datum.

These analogies do not however provide the only motive. Consider mirror reflections. Mirror reflections are like sounds and odours and tastes in a certain respect, and they are like lemons and clouds and velvet in another respect. The image of a lemon or a cloud is like a sound or an odour, in that the image is descriptively independent of the description of any lemon or cloud. On the other hand, the description of an image of a lemon or cloud is unlike the description of a sound or odour, in that the descriptive items which compose it are engaged also in describing lemons and clouds. Now how do these facts about images incline one to the belief that when one is looking at one's hand one is seeing a sense-datum, as one hears a sound? Perhaps in this way: If one is already impressed with the analogy between hearing and seeing, then one is inclined to believe that there is something which one is seeing which is distinguishable as the sound is from the bird one hears. Now if you look at your hand and try to discover this corresponding element, you may find your effort encouraged by the fact that there are things which are descriptively identical with what you are seeing which are nevertheless not the surfaces of lemons and clouds at all. That is, here you have in reflections what, since they are described in the same way in which lemons and clouds and hands are described, may very well be taken to be "the surfaces of lemons and clouds." So when you look at your hand, you may describe what you see just as you would describe the reflection of it in the mirror. Since then what you see is taken to be the surface of your hand, you at once understand how something might be described in this same way, and yet not be the surface of your hand at all. For the image in the mirror is not the surface of your hand. It is clear certainly that with this in mind you can, if you look at your hand, pick out something which is like what you saw in the mirror, when you raised your hand to the mirror.

There is one further set of facts which disposes us in the same way. Notice such sentences as these:

> This sounds like a horse.
> This smells like an onion.
> This tastes like a peppermint.
> This looks like a million dollars.
> This feels like a sponge.

The use of these expressions is parallel to the first set described above. The first three are admittedly statements about a sound, a smell, and a taste. Now how about the fourth and the fifth? Well, they must also be about a "look" and about a "feel," the corresponding sense-data of seeing and touching, respectively. This does not now seem to me at all persuasive, and of course, for the same reason which I gave in discussing sounds, smells, etc. If one wished, for instance, to identify by description or by some other form of direction, the sound or smell in question, as distinguished from the horse or the onion, this is a simple matter. But if you wish to call attention to the "look" or to the "feel" in question there is no resort to doing this, save pointing out or identifying the "million dollars" or "the sponge" or whatever the object may be. In other words, what is called the "look" or the "feel" is not identifiable in the way in which the sound, or smell are identifiable. The use of the word "this" is commonly defined so as to apply to such uses as are involved in these first three sentences. But it is only by analogy that one comes to suppose that in the last two sentences the use is like that in the first three. Of course such a sentence as: "This looks like a million dollars," may apply also to a mirror-image, and we have already noticed what this means. The image of a girl who looks like a million dollars would also look like a million dollars. This means simply that they are described in the same way. Certainly from such facts as these, which we all admit, it does not follow that when you look at your hand, you can pick out something which is not your hand, of which you now say that it looks like your hand.

These are some of the facts upon which I reflect a little, when I am led to the view that what Professor Moore has tried to persuade us is true. I want now to show that, if one does follow the lead of these facts, one is likely to use precisely the sort of language about "sense-data" which Professor Moore does use. If the analogy between seeing and hearing holds, then it follows in the first place that if you look at your right hand you will be able to pick out something, something which on the assumption given, corresponds to the sound in hearing. But this is a strange sort of direction, for, if I look at my right hand, nothing at all corresponds to the sound in case of hearing. There is simply my hand, or more conveniently as you will see in a moment, the surface of my hand. So I pick that out. Now I reflect, and describe what I see, reminded that what I see is like reflections in mirrors. I know, of course, that mirror-reflections are not identical with the surfaces of any hands, no matter how perfect the image may be. Now, since this is like an image in all these respects, it can't be the surface of my hand at all, and this in spite of the fact that I thought at the outset that I was picking out the surface of my hand. If the only thing I could pick out was what I took to be the surface of my hand, and that is the sense-datum, and this is like the image in the mirror, then see what follows. The reflection in the mirror has no depth. I cannot prick it with a pin. Now then does the surface of my hand have depth? If you say that what you picked out is like the reflection in the mirror, and it has no depth, then if it is identical with the surface of my hand, then the surface of my hand also has no depth. Can that be? On the other hand, if you say that what I picked out is identical with the surface of my hand, and the surface of my hand has depth, are we then to allow that the sense-datum, like a hand's surface, has depth? Can I prick a sense-datum with a pin? This is the puzzle which I noticed previously when I discussed Professor Moore's use of the phrase "surface of my hand," and it arises from conceiving of the sense-datum as like a mirror-reflection, and at the same time as something which one can pick out. If then, on this basis, I look at my hand, and try to pick out a sense-datum, I must be surprised to discover something which, though it may be in certain respects like the image in the mirror, is also remarkably unlike it. For, in spite of what all these facts already noticed lead me to expect, I discover nothing but my hand.

I should like to labour this last point. Imagine the sort of situation you would be in, if, upon the basis of such facts as I have noticed, you were disposed to expect a sense-datum. What would you say in trying to describe what you expect? First of all, you might tell someone to look at his hand, on the expectation that just as if he heard a bird, there would be a sound to identify, so here there would be something corresponding to the sound. It also follows from the character of what you see, that if there is something corresponding to the sound, then you could pick it out. If this were all, one would be inclined to describe what you might pick out as "a yellow patch," "a red patch," "a canoid patch of brown," etc., and it is easy to see what in a case of this sort has happened. People who invent expressions of this sort are trying to find some expressions which parallel the descriptions of sounds, but the parallel is deceptive. For, if in looking at your hand you now try to pick out "a hand-shape of pink," you will find yourself picking out the surface of your hand, whereas in the case of a sound the relations between the sound and the bird are obviously different. The description of the sound is not a description of the bird. But there is no necessity for pursuing this. It is only necessary that what you pick out should, like the sound, be distinguishable from your hand, or the surface of your hand. As it is, you know that reflections in mirrors and images otherwise are distinguishable from what they reflect and image, though they are not descriptively distinguishable from what they reflect and image. So we formulate a description accordingly: Pick out what has the characteristics of a mirror-reflection. Looking into the mirror, holding your hand to the mirror, I might ask: What do you see?, and what you would then give me as a description would equally apply to your hand. Now then you look at your hand, and describe your hand, for what will satisfy my request is just that. Further, if you have already committed yourself to saying that there is something here which corresponds to the sound in the case of hearing the bird, then you will feel pretty sure that you have picked that out. But you will nevertheless be puzzled. For if you have picked out the sense-datum, then if someone says: Now pick out the surface of your hand, you will be unable to do so unless the sense-datum and the surface of your hand are identical. And if you then ask: Did I pick out the surface of my hand?, already assured that you did pick out the sense-datum, you will be inclined to say: That may be, for a sense-datum can be the surface of a hand. And you will be inclined to say this because, as I said before, the reflection and the surface of my hand are similar. But you will also be inclined to say that a sense-datum cannot be the surface.

III

I have tried, in the preceding sections, first of all to explore certain difficulties in the directions which Professor Moore gives for discovering what it is he means by a sense-datum, and second to try to discover what motives there are which lead us to expect that there are sense-data, and which lead us also to such curious descriptions of them. My thesis has been this: The obvious distinction between sounds, tastes, and smells in hearing, tasting, and smelling leads us to expect a corresponding something or other in the case of seeing and touching. So when I look at my hand, I am led to expect that there is a sense-datum in this case. So I may say that I can pick it out. But when I try to pick it out I am at a loss. There is only my hand. Now if I still persist in holding that there is a sense-datum present, I am bound to describe it in a peculiar way. I am likely to describe it in analogy with an image or mirror-reflection. I may go on to think of the sense-datum which must be there, as spread exceedingly thin over the surface of my hand, a kind of epi-epidermis, and at the same time as looking just like my hand when the sense-datum has been removed. Now if I keep this fixed in my mind, and look at my hand, and if I am asked: What do you see?, I am supposed not to know what to say. Do I see just an image spread over the surface of my hand like so much surfacing surfaceless paint, or do I see the surface of my hand? I think I can tell an image from the surface of my hand, but I confess that I should be much distressed in the attempt to distinguish the image of the surface of my hand laid neatly on the surface of my hand and defined in such a way as to be indistinguishable from the surface of my hand, from the surface of my hand. But fortunately, as I think, at least, I am not led to expect anything like images spread over the surface of my hand, and if I did, I should try pricking the epidermis. As I have noticed before, that the attempt to describe what "must" be present is desperate is also apparent in the consequent use of the expression "the surface of his hand." For we do not as a matter of fact have any difficulty in identifying the surface of our hands. If then there is some difficulty, that difficulty has not been properly described. And the point of my essay is that the supposed entity which is defined in terms of a confusion, which is generated by sentential likenesses, misleads us and catches us in linguistic pockets.

Rubber gloves, the image of my hand, another man's hand, all of these I know how to distinguish from my hand, when I look at my hand, and when I am in doubt. But I am not moved by the suggestion that whenever I look at my hand an image of my hand may be interposed between my hand and my eye. In that case we should need to invent the theory of the Pre-Established Harmony between the hand and the sense-datum. But why suggest it?

Having come to the end of my essay I am now full of misgivings. I know that I have not refuted Professor Moore's view. I have tried however, teasing the words of Professor Moore's exposition, to get the matter straight. And this is what has come of it. May my betters rob me of my "darling follies," among which betters I have long counted first Professor Moore.

Notes

1. *Contemporary British Philosophy,* Second Series, 217.
2. Ibid., 217.
3. Ibid., 218.

The Argument from Illusion

J. L. AUSTIN

J. L. Austin (1911–1960) taught at Oxford University. He was a leader of the ordinary language movement in philosophy and had a great influence on a generation of British philosophers. His publications include *Sense and Sensibilia, Philosophical Papers,* and *How To Do Things with Words,* all published posthumously.

III

The primary purpose of the argument from illusion is to induce people to accept "sense-data" as the proper and correct answer to the question what they perceive on certain *abnormal, exceptional* occasions; but in fact it is usually followed up with another bit of argument intended to establish that they *always* perceive sense-data. Well, what is the argument?

In Ayer's statement[1] it runs as follows. It is "based on the fact that material things may present different appearances to different observers, or to the same observer in different conditions, and that the character of these appearances is to some extent causally determined by the state of the conditions and the observer." As illustrations of this alleged fact Ayer proceeds to cite perspective ("a coin which looks circular from one point of view may look elliptical from another"); refraction ("a stick which normally appears straight looks bent when it is seen in water"); changes in colour-vision produced by drugs ("such as mescal"); mirror-images; double vision; hallucination; apparent variations in tastes; variations in felt warmth ("according as the hand that is feeling it is itself hot or cold"); variations in felt bulk ("a coin seems larger when it is placed on the tongue than when it is held in the palm of the hand"); and the oft-cited fact that "people who have had limbs amputated may still continue to feel pain in them."

He then selects three of these instances for detailed treatment. First, refraction—the stick which normally "appears straight" but "looks bent" when seen in water. He makes the "assumptions" (*a*) that the stick does not *really change its shape* when it is placed in water, and (*b*) that it *cannot be* both crooked and straight.[2] He then concludes ("it follows") that "at least one of the *visual appearances* of the stick is *delusive.*" Nevertheless, even when "what we see is not the *real quality* of a *material thing,* it is supposed that we are still seeing something"—and this something is to be called a "sense-datum." A sense-datum is to be "the object of which we are *directly* aware, in perception, if it is not *part* of any *material thing.*" (The italics are mine throughout this and the next two paragraphs.)

Next, mirages. A man who sees a mirage, he says, is "not perceiving any material thing; for the oasis which he thinks he is perceiving *does not exist.*" But "his *experience* is not an experience of nothing"; thus "it is said that he is experiencing sense-data, which are similar in character to what he would be experiencing if he were seeing a real oasis, but are delusive in the sense that *the material thing which they appear to present* is not *really there.*"

From *Sense and Sensibilia,* ed. G. J. Warnock (Oxford: Oxford University Press, 1962), pp. 20–32, 44–54.

Lastly, reflections. When I look at myself in a mirror "my body *appears to be* some distance behind the glass"; but it cannot actually be in two places at once; thus, my perceptions in this case "cannot all be *veridical.*" But I do see *something;* and if "there really is no such material thing as my body in the place where it appears to be, what is it that I am seeing?" Answer—a sense-datum. Ayer adds that "the same conclusion may be reached by taking any other of my examples."

Now I want to call attention, first of all, to the name of this argument—the "argument from *illusion,*" and to the fact that it is produced as establishing the conclusion that some at least of our "perceptions" are *delusive*. For in this there are two clear implications—(*a*) that all the cases cited in the argument are cases of *illusions;* and (*b*) that *illusion* and *delusion* are the same thing. But both of these implications, of course, are quite wrong; and it is by no means unimportant to point this out, for, as we shall see, the argument trades on confusion at just this point.

What, then, would be some genuine examples of illusion? (The fact is that hardly any of the cases cited by Ayer is, at any rate without stretching things, a case of illusion at all.) Well, first, there are some quite clear cases of *optical* illusion—for instance the case we mentioned earlier in which, of two lines of equal length, one is made to look longer than the other. Then again there are illusions produced by professional "illusionists," conjurors—for instance the Headless Woman on the stage, who is made to look headless, or the ventriloquist's dummy which is made to appear to be talking. Rather different—not (usually) produced on purpose—is the case where wheels rotating rapidly enough in one direction may look as if they were rotating quite slowly in the opposite direction. Delusions, on the other hand, are something altogether different from this. Typical cases would be delusions of persecution, delusions of grandeur. These are primarily a matter of grossly disordered beliefs (and so, probably, behaviour) and may well have nothing in particular to do with perception.[3] But I think we might also say that the patient who sees pink rats has (suffers from) delusions—particularly, no doubt, if, as would probably be the case, he is not clearly aware that his pink rats aren't real rats.[4]

The most important differences here are that the term "an illusion" (in a perceptual context) does not suggest that something totally unreal is *conjured up*—on the contrary, there just is the arrangement of lines and arrows on the page, the woman on the stage with her head in a black bag, the rotating wheels; whereas the term "delusion" *does* suggest something totally unreal, not really there at all. (The convictions of the man who has delusions of persecution can be *completely* without foundation.) For this reason delusions are a much more serious matter—something is really wrong, and what's more, wrong *with* the person who has them. But when I see an optical illusion, however well it comes off, there is nothing wrong with me personally, the illusion is not a little (or a large) peculiarity or idiosyncrasy of my own; it is quite public, anyone can see it, and in many cases standard procedures can be laid down for producing it. Furthermore, if we are not actually to be taken in, we need to be *on our guard;* but it is no use to tell the sufferer from delusions to be on his guard. He needs to be cured.

Why is it that we tend—if we do—to confuse illusions with delusions? Well, partly, no doubt the terms are often used loosely. But there is also the point that people may have, without making this explicit, different views or theories about the facts of some cases. Take the case of seeing a ghost, for example. It is not generally known, or agreed, what seeing ghosts *is*. Some people think of seeing ghosts as a case of something being conjured up, perhaps by the disordered nervous system of the victim; so in their view seeing ghosts is a case of delusion. But other people have the idea that what is called seeing ghosts is a case of being taken in by shadows, perhaps, or reflections, or a trick of the light—that is, they assimilate the case in their minds to illusion. In this way, seeing ghosts, for example, may come to be labelled sometimes as "delusion," sometimes as "illusion"; and it may not be noticed that it makes a difference which label we use. Rather, similarly, there seem to be different doctrines in the field as to what mirages are. Some seem to take a mirage to be a vision conjured up by the crazed brain of the thirsty and exhausted traveller (delusion), while in other accounts it is a case of atmospheric refraction, whereby something below the horizon is made to appear above it (illusion). (Ayer . . . takes the delusion view, although he cites it . . . as a case of illusion. He says not that the oasis appears to be where it is not, but roundly that "it does not exist.")

The way in which the "argument from illusion" positively trades on not distinguishing illusions from delusions is, I think, this. So long as it is being suggested that the cases paraded for our attention are cases of *illusion,* there is the implication (from the ordinary use of the word) that there really is something there that we perceive. But then, when these cases begin to be quietly called delusive, there comes in the very different suggestion of something being conjured up, something unreal or at any rate "immaterial." These two implications taken together may then subtly insinuate that in the cases cited there really is something that we are perceiving, but that this is an immaterial something; and this insinuation, even if not conclusive by itself, is certainly well calculated to edge us a little closer towards just the position where the sense-datum theorist wants to have us.

So much, then—though certainly there could be a good deal more—about the differences between illusions and delusions and the reasons for not obscuring them. Now let us look briefly at some of the other cases Ayer lists. Reflections, for instance. No doubt you *can* produce illusions with mirrors, suitably disposed. But is just *any* case of seeing something in a mirror an illusion, as he implies? Quite obviously not. For seeing things in mirrors is a perfectly *normal* occurrence, completely familiar, and there is usually no question of anyone being taken in. No doubt, if you're an infant or an aborigine and have never come across a mirror before, you may be pretty baffled, and even visibly perturbed, when you do. But is that a reason why the rest of us should speak of illusion here? And just the same goes for the phenomena of perspective—again, one *can* play tricks with perspective, but in the ordinary case there is no question of illusion. That a round coin should "look elliptical" (in one sense) from some points of view is exactly what we expect and what we normally find; indeed, we should be badly put out if we ever found this not to be so. Refraction again—the stick that looks bent in water—is far too familiar a case to be properly called a case of illusion. We may perhaps be prepared to agree that the stick looks bent; but then we can see that it's partly submerged in water, so that is exactly how we should expect it to look.

It is important to realize here how familiarity, so to speak, takes the edge off illusion. Is the cinema a case of illusion? Well, just possibly the first man who ever saw moving pictures may have felt inclined to say that here was a case of illusion. But in fact it's pretty unlikely that even he, even momentarily, was actually taken in; and by now the whole thing is so ordinary a part of our lives that it never occurs to us even to raise the question. One might as well ask whether producing a photograph is producing an illusion—which would plainly be just silly.

Then we must not overlook, in all this talk about illusions and delusions, that there are plenty of more or less unusual cases, not yet mentioned, which certainly aren't either. Suppose that a proof-reader makes a mistake—he fails to notice that what ought to be "causal" is printed as "casual"; does he have a delusion? Or is there an illusion before him? Neither, of course; he simply *misreads.* Seeing after-images, too, though not a particularly frequent occurrence and not just an ordinary case of seeing, is neither seeing illusions nor having delusions. And what about dreams? Does the dreamer see illusions? Does he have delusions? Neither; dreams are *dreams.*

Let us turn for a moment to what Price has to say about illusions. He produces,[5] by way of saying "what the term 'illusion' means," the following "provisional definition": "An illusory sense-datum of sight or touch is a sense-datum which is such that we tend to take it to be part of the surface of a material object, but if we take it so we are wrong." It is by no means clear, of course, what this dictum itself means; but still, it seems fairly clear that the definition doesn't actually fit all the cases of illusion. Consider the two lines again. Is there anything here which we tend to take, wrongly, to be part of the surface of a material object? It doesn't seem so. We just see the two lines, we don't think or even tend to think that we see anything else, we aren't even raising the question whether anything is or isn't "part of the surface" of—what, anyway? the lines? the page?—the trouble is just that one line looks longer than the other, though it isn't. Nor surely, in the case of the Headless Woman, is it a question whether anything is or isn't part of her surface; the trouble is just that she looks as if she had no head.

It is noteworthy, of course, that, before he even begins to consider the "argument from illusion," Price has already incorporated in this "definition" the idea that in such cases there is something to be seen *in addition to* the ordinary things—which is part of what the argument is commonly used, and not uncommonly taken, to *prove*. But this idea surely has no place in an attempt to say what "illusion" *means*. It comes in again, improperly I think, in his account of perspective (which incidentally he also cites as a species of illusion)—"a distant hillside which is full of protuberances, and slopes upwards at quite a gentle angle, will appear flat and vertical. . . . This means that the sense-datum, the colour-expanse which we sense, actually *is* flat and vertical." But why should we accept this account of the matter? Why should we say that there is *anything* we see which *is* flat and vertical, though not "part of the surface" of any material object? To speak thus is to assimilate all such cases to cases of delusion, where there *is* something not "part of any material thing." But we have already discussed the undesirability of this assimilation.

Next, let us have a look at the account Ayer himself gives of some at least of the cases he cites. (In fairness we must remember here that Ayer has a number of quite substantial reservations of his own about the merits and efficacy of the argument from illusion, so that it is not easy to tell just how seriously he intends his exposition of it to be taken; but this is a point we shall come back to.)

First, then, the familiar case of the stick in water. Of this case Ayer says (*a*) that since the stick looks bent but is straight, "at least one of the visual appearances of the stick is *delusive*"; and (*b*) that "what we see [directly anyway] is not the real quality of [a few lines later, not part of] a material thing." Well now: does the stick "look bent" to begin with? I think we can agree that it does, we have no better way of describing it. But of course it does *not* look *exactly* like a bent stick, a bent stick out of water—at most, it may be said to look rather like a bent stick partly immersed *in* water. After all, we can't help seeing the water the stick is partly immersed in. So exactly what in this case is supposed to be *delusive?* What is wrong, what is even faintly surprising, in the idea of a stick's being straight but looking bent sometimes? Does anyone suppose that if something is straight, then it jolly well has to *look* straight at all times and in all circumstances? Obviously no one seriously supposes this. So what mess are we supposed to get into here, what is the difficulty? For of course it has to be suggested that there *is* a difficulty—a difficulty, furthermore, which calls for a pretty radical solution, the introduction of sense-data. But what is the problem we are invited to solve in this way?

Well, we are told, in this case you are seeing *something;* and what is this something "if it is not part of any material thing?" But this question is, really, completely mad. The straight part of the stick, the bit not under water, is presumably part of a material thing; don't we see that? And what about the bit *under* water?—we can see that too. We can see, come to that, the water itself. In fact what we see is *a stick partly immersed in water;* and it is particularly extraordinary that this should appear to be called in question—that a question should be raised about *what* we are seeing—since this, after all, is simply the description of the situation with which we started. It was, that is to say, agreed at the start that we were looking at a stick, a "material thing," part of which was under water. If, to take a rather different case, a church were cunningly camouflaged so that it looked like a barn, how could any serious question be raised about what we see when we look at it? We see, of course, *a church* that now *looks like a barn*. We do *not* see an immaterial barn, an immaterial church, or an immaterial anything else. And what in this case could seriously tempt us to say that we do?

Notice, incidentally, that in Ayer's description of the stick-in-water case, which is supposed to be prior to the drawing of any philosophical conclusions, there has already crept in the unheralded but important expression "visual appearances"—it is, of course, ultimately to be suggested that all we *ever* get when we see is a visual appearance (whatever that may be).

Consider next the case of my reflection in a mirror. My body, Ayer says, "appears to be some distance behind the glass"; but as it's in front, it can't really be behind the glass. So what am I seeing? A sense-datum. What about this? Well, once again, although there is no objection to saying that my body "appears to be some distance behind the glass," in saying this we must remember what sort of situation we are dealing with. It does not "appear to be" there in a way which might tempt me (though it might tempt a baby or a savage) to go round the back and look for it, and be astonished when this enterprise proved a failure. (To say that A is *in* B doesn't always mean that if you open B you will find A, just as to say that A is *on* B doesn't always mean that you could pick it off—consider "I saw my face in the mirror," "There's a pain in my toe," "I heard him on the radio," "I saw the image on the screen," etc. Seeing something in a mirror is not like seeing a bun in a shop-window.) But does it follow that, since my body is not actually located behind the mirror, I am not seeing a material thing? Plainly not. For one thing, I can see the mirror (nearly always anyway). I can see my own body "indirectly," *sc.* in the mirror. I can also see the reflection of my own body or, as some would say, a mirror-image. And a mirror-image (if we choose this answer) is not a "sense-datum"; it can be photographed, seen by any number of people, and so on. (Of course there is no question here of either illusion or delusion.) And if the question is pressed, what actually *is* some distance, five feet say, behind the mirror, the answer is, not a sense-datum, but some region of the adjoining room.

The mirage case—at least if we take the view, as Ayer does, that the oasis the traveler thinks he can see "does not exist"—is significantly more amenable to the treatment it is given. For here we are supposing the man to be genuinely deluded, he is *not* "seeing a material thing."[6] We don't actually have to say, however, even here that he is "experiencing sense-data"; for though, as Ayer says "it is convenient to give a name" to what he is experiencing, the fact is that it already has a name—a *mirage*. Again, we should be wise not to accept too readily the statement that what he is experiencing is "*similar in character* to what he would be experiencing if he were seeing a real oasis." For is it at all likely, really, to be very similar? And, looking ahead, if we were to concede this point we should find the concession being used against us at a later stage—namely, at the stage where we shall be invited to agree that we see sense-data always, in normal cases too.

. . . .

V

I want now to take up again the philosophical argument as it is set out in the texts we are discussing. . . . the argument from illusion is intended primarily to persuade us that, in certain exceptional, abnormal situations, what we perceive—directly anyway—is a sense-datum; but then there comes a second stage, in which we are to be brought to agree that what we (directly) perceive is *always* a sense-datum, even in the normal, unexceptional case. It is this second stage of the argument that we must now examine.

Ayer expounds the argument thus.[7] There is, he says, "no intrinsic difference in kind between those of our perceptions that are veridical in their presentation of material things and those that are delusive. When I look at a straight stick, which is refracted in water and so appears crooked, my experience is qualitatively the same as if I were looking at a stick that really was crooked. . . ." If, however, "when our perceptions were delusive, we were always perceiving something of a different kind from what we perceived when they were veridical, we should expect our experience to be qualitatively different in the two cases. We should expect to be able to tell from the intrinsic character of a perception whether it was a perception of a sense-datum or of a material thing. But this is not possible. . . ." Price's exposition of this point,[8] to which Ayer refers us, is in fact not perfectly analogous; for Price has already somehow reached the conclusion that we are always aware of sense-data, and here is trying to establish only that we cannot distinguish *normal* sense-data, as "parts of the surfaces of material things," from *abnormal* ones, not "parts of the surfaces of material things." However, the argument used is much the same: "the abnormal crooked sense-datum of a straight stick standing in water is qualitatively indistinguishable from a normal sense-datum of a crooked stick"; but "is it not incredible that two entities so similar in all these qualities should really be so utterly different: that the one should be a real constituent of a material object, wholly independent of the observer's mind and organism, while the other is merely the fleeting product of his cerebral processes?''

It is argued further, both by Ayer and Price, that "even in the case of veridical perceptions we are not directly aware of material things" [or in the work of Price, that our sense-data are not parts of the surfaces of material things] for the reason that "veridical and delusive perceptions may form a continuous series. Thus, if I gradually approach an object from a distance I may begin by having a series of perceptions which are delusive in the sense that the object appears to be smaller than it really is. Let us assume that this series terminates in a veridical perception.[9] Then the difference in quality between this perception and its immediate predecessor will be of the same order as the difference between any two delusive perceptions that are next to one another in the series. . . ." But "these are differences of degree and not of kind. But this, it is argued, is not what we should expect if the veridical perception were a perception of an object of a different sort, a material thing as opposed to a sense-datum. Does not the fact that veridical and delusive perceptions shade into one another in the way that is indicated by these examples show that the objects that are perceived in either case are generically the same? And from this it would follow, if it was acknowledged that the delusive perceptions were perceptions of sense-data, that what we directly experienced was always a sense-datum and never a material thing." As Price puts it, "it seems most extraordinary that there should be a total difference of nature where there is only an infinitesimal difference of quality."[10]

Well, what are we to make of the arguments thus set before us?

1. It is pretty obvious, for a start, that the terms in which the argument is stated by Ayer are grossly tendentious. Price, you remember, is not producing the argument as a proof that we are always aware of sense-data; in his view that question has already been settled, and he conceives himself to be faced here only with the question whether any sense-data are "parts of the surfaces of material objects." But in Ayer's exposition the argument *is* put forward as a ground for the conclusion that what we are (directly) aware of in perception is always a sense-datum; and if so, it seems a rather serious defect that this conclusion is practically assumed from the very first sentence of the statement of the argument itself. In that sentence Ayer uses, not indeed for the first time, the term "perceptions" (which incidentally has never been defined or explained), and takes it for granted, here and throughout, that there is at any rate some kind of entities of which we are aware in absolutely all cases—namely, "perceptions," delusive or veridical. But of course, if one has already been induced to swallow the idea that every case, whether "delusive" or "veridical," supplies us with "perceptions," one is only too easily going to be made to feel that it would be straining at a gnat not to swallow sense-data in an equally comprehensive style. But in fact one has not even been told what "perceptions" *are;* and the assumption of their ubiquity has been slipped in without any explanation or argument whatever. But if those to whom the argument is ostensibly addressed were not thus made to concede the essential point from the beginning, would the statement of the argument be quite such plain sailing?

2. Of course we shall also want to enter a protest against the argument's bland assumption of a simple dichotomy between "veridical and delusive experiences." There is, as we have already seen, *no* justification at all *either* for lumping all so-called "delusive" experiences together, *or* for lumping together all so-called "veridical" experiences. But again, could the argument run quite so smoothly without this assumption? It would certainly—and this, incidentally, would be all to the good—take rather longer to state.

3. But now let us look at what the argument actually says. It begins, you will remember, with an alleged statement of fact—namely, that "there is no intrinsic difference in kind between those of our perceptions that are veridical in their presentation of material things and those that are delusive" (Ayer), that "there is no qualitative difference between normal sense-data as such and abnormal sense-data as such" (Price). Now, waiving so far as possible the numerous obscurities in and objections to this manner of speak-

ing, let us ask whether what is being alleged here is actually true. Is it the case that "delusive and veridical experiences" are not "qualitatively different"? Well, at least it seems perfectly extraordinary to say so in this sweeping way. Consider a few examples. I may have the experience (dubbed "delusive" presumably) of dreaming that I am being presented to the Pope. Could it be seriously suggested that having this dream is "qualitatively indistinguishable" from *actually being* presented to the Pope? Quite obviously not. After all, we have the phrase "a dream-like quality"; some waking experiences are said to have this dream-like quality, and some artists and writers occasionally try to impart it, usually with scant success, to their works. But of course, if the fact here alleged *were* a fact, the phrase would be perfectly meaningless, because applicable to everything. If dreams were not "qualitatively" different from waking experiences, then *every* waking experience would be like a dream; the dream-like quality would be, not difficult to capture, but impossible to avoid.[11] It is true, to repeat, that dreams are *narrated* in the same terms as waking experiences: these terms, after all, are the best terms we have; but it would be wildly wrong to conclude from this that what is narrated in the two cases is *exactly alike*. When we are hit on the head we sometimes say that we "see stars"; but for all that, seeing stars when you are hit on the head is *not* "qualitatively" indistinguishable from seeing stars when you look at the sky.

Again, it is simply not true to say that seeing a bright green after-image against a white wall is exactly like seeing a bright green patch actually on the wall; or that seeing a white wall through blue spectacles is exactly like seeing a blue wall; or that seeing pink rats in D.T.s is exactly like really seeing pink rats; or (once again) that seeing a stick refracted in water is exactly like seeing a bent stick. In all these cases we may *say* the same things ("It looks blue," "It looks bent," etc.), but this is no reason at all for denying the obvious fact that the "experiences" are *different*.

4. Next, one may well wish at least to ask for the credentials of a curious general principle on which both Ayer and Price seem to rely,[12] to the effect that if two things are not "generically the same," the same "in nature," then they can't be alike, or even very nearly alike. If it were true, Ayer says, that from time to time we perceived things of two different kinds, then "we should expect" them to be qualitatively different. But why on earth should we?—particularly if, as he suggests would be the case, we never actually found such a thing to be true. It is not at all easy to discuss this point sensibly, because of the initial absurdity in the hypothesis that we perceive just *two* kinds of things. But if, for example, I had never seen a mirror, but were told (*a*) that in mirrors one sees reflections of things, and (*b*) that reflections of things are not "generically the same" as things, is there any reason why I should forthwith *expect* there to be some whacking big "qualitative" difference between seeing things and seeing their reflections? Plainly not; if I were prudent, I should simply wait and see what seeing reflections was like. If I am told that a lemon is generically different from a piece of soap, do I "expect" that no piece of soap could look just like a lemon? Why should I?

(It is worth noting that Price helps the argument along at this point by a bold stroke of rhetoric: how *could* two entities be "qualitatively indistinguishable," he asks, if one is a "real constituent of a material object," the other *"a fleeting product of his cerebral processes?"* But how in fact are we supposed to have been persuaded that sense-data are *ever* fleeting products of cerebral processes? Does this colourful description fit, for instance, the reflection of my face in a mirror?)

5. Another erroneous principle which the argument here seems to rely on is this: that it *must* be the case that "delusive and veridical experiences" are not (as such) "qualitatively" or "intrinsically" distinguishable—for if they were distinguishable, we should never be "deluded." But of course this is not so. From the fact that I am sometimes "deluded," mistaken, taken in through failing to distinguish A from B, it does not follow at all that A and B must be *indistinguishable*. Perhaps I should have noticed the difference if I had been more careful or attentive; perhaps I am just bad at distinguishing things of this sort (e.g. vintages); perhaps, again, I have never learned to discriminate between them, or haven't had much practice at it. As Ayer observes, probably truly, "a child who had not learned that refraction was a means of distortion

would naturally believe that the stick really was crooked as he saw it''; but how is the fact that an uninstructed child probably would not discriminate between *being refracted* and *being crooked* supposed to establish the allegation that there *is* no ''qualitative'' difference between the two cases? What sort of reception would I be likely to get from a professional tea-taster, if I were to say to him, ''But there can't be any difference between the flavours of these two brands of tea, for I regularly fail to distinguish between them?'' Again, when ''the quickness of the hand deceives the eye,'' it is not that what the hand is really doing is *exactly like* what we are tricked into thinking it is doing, but simply that it is *impossible to tell* what it is really doing. In this case it may be true that we can't distinguish, and not merely that we don't; but even this doesn't mean that the two cases are exactly alike.

I do not, of course, wish to deny that there may be cases in which ''delusive and veridical experiences'' really are ''qualitatively indistinguishable''; but I certainly do wish to deny (*a*) that such cases are anything like as *common* as both Ayer and Price seem to suppose, and (*b*) that there *have* to be such cases to accommodate the undoubted fact that we are sometimes ''deceived by our senses.'' We are not, after all, quasi-infallible beings, who can be taken in only where the avoidance of mistake is completely impossible. But if we are prepared to admit that there may be, even that there are, *some* cases in which ''delusive and veridical perceptions'' really are indistinguishable, does this admission require us to drag in, or even to let in, sense-data? No. For even if we were to make the prior admission (which we have so far found no reason to make) that in the ''abnormal'' cases we perceive sense-data, we should not be obliged to extend this admission to the ''normal'' cases too. For why on earth should it *not* be the case that, in some few instances, perceiving one sort of thing is exactly like perceiving another?

6. There is a further quite general difficulty in assessing the force of this argument, which we (in common with the authors of our texts) have slurred over so far. The question which Ayer invites us to consider is whether two classes of ''perceptions,'' the veridical and the delusive, are or are not ''qualitatively different,'' ''intrinsically different in kind''; but how are we supposed to set about even considering this question, when we are not told what ''a perception'' *is?* In particular, how many of the circumstances of a situation, as these would ordinarily be stated, are supposed to be included in ''the perception?'' For example, to take the stick in water again: it is a feature of this case that part of the stick is under water, and water, of course, is not invisible; is the water, then, part of ''the perception?'' It is difficult to conceive of any grounds for denying that it is; but *if* it is, surely this is a perfectly obvious respect in which ''the perception'' differs from, is distinguishable from, the ''perception'' we have when we look at a bent stick *not* in water. There is a sense, perhaps, in which the presence or absence of water is not the *main thing* in this case—we are supposed to be addresssing ourselves primarily to questions about the stick. But in fact, as a great quantity of psychological investigation has shown, discrimination between one thing and another very frequently depends on such more or less extraneous concomitants of the main thing, even when such concomitants are not consciously taken note of. As I said, we are told nothing of what ''a perception'' is; but could any defensible account, if such an account were offered, completely exclude all these highly significant attendant circumstances? And if they *were* excluded—in some more or less arbitrary way—how much interest or importance would be left in the contention that ''delusive'' and ''veridical'' perceptions are indistinguishable? Inevitably, if you rule out the respects in which A and B differ, you may expect to be left with respects in which they are alike.

I conclude, then, that this part of the philosophical argument involves (though not in every case equally essentially) (*a*) acceptance of a quite bogus dichotomy of all ''perceptions'' into two groups, the ''delusive'' and the ''veridical''—to say nothing of the unexplained introduction of ''perceptions'' themselves; (*b*) an implicit but grotesque exaggeration of the *frequency* of ''delusive perceptions''; (*c*) a further grotesque exaggeration of the *similarity* between ''delusive'' perceptions and ''veridical'' ones; (*d*) the erroneous suggestion that there *must* be such similarity, or even qualitative *identity;* (*e*) the acceptance of the pretty gratuitous idea that things "generically different" could not be qualitatively alike; and (*f*)—which is really a corollary of (*c*) and (*a*)—the gratuitous neglect of those more or less subsidiary features which often make possible the discrimination of situations which, in other *broad* respects, may be roughly alike. These seem to be rather serious deficiencies.

Notes

1. Alfred J. Ayer, *The Foundations of Empirical Knowledge* (London: Macmillan, 1969).
2. It is not only strange, but also important, that Ayer calls these "assumptions." Later on he is going to take seriously the notion of denying at least one of them, which he could hardly do if he had recognized them here as the plain and incontestable facts that they are.
3. The latter point holds, of course, for *some* uses of "illusion" too; there are the illusions which some people (are said to) lose as they grow older and wiser.
4. Cp. the white rabbit in the play called *Harvey*.
5. H. H. Price, *Perception* (London: Methuen, 1932), p. 27.
6. Not even "indirectly," no such thing is "presented." Doesn't this seem to make the case, though more amenable, a good deal less useful to the philosopher? It's hard to see how normal cases could be said to be *very like* this.
7. Ayer, op. cit., pp. 5–9.
8. *Perception,* p. 31.
9. But what, we may ask, does this assumption amount to? From what distance *does* an object, a cricket-ball say, "look the size that it really is?" Six feet? Twenty feet?
10. I omit from consideration a further argument cited by both Price and Ayer, which makes play with the "causal dependence" of our "perceptions" upon the conditions of observation and our own "physiological and psychological states."
11. This is part, no doubt *only* part, of the absurdity in Descartes's toying with the notion that the whole of our experience might be a dream.
12. Ayer in fact expresses qualms later. . . .

C. INDUCTION, CAUSATION, AND EXPLANATION

The Problem of Induction

W. C. SALMON

W. C. Salmon (1925–) is a professor of philosophy at the University of Pittsburgh. His publications include *The Foundations of Scientific Inference* and *Space, Time, and Motion*.

I. The Problem of Induction

We all believe that we have knowledge of facts extending far beyond those we directly perceive. The scope of our senses is severely limited in space and time; our immediate perceptual knowledge does not reach to events that happened before we were born to events that are happening now in certain other places or to any future events. We believe, nevertheless, that we have some kind of indirect knowledge of such facts. We know that a glacier once covered a large part of North America, that the sun continues to exist at night, and that the tides will rise and fall tomorrow. Science and common sense have at least this one thing in common: Each embodies knowledge of matters of fact that are not open to our direct inspection. Indeed, science purports to establish general laws or theories that apply to all parts of space and time without restriction. A "science" that consisted of no more than a mere summary of the results of direct observation would not deserve the name.

Hume's profound critique of induction begins with a simple and apparently innocent question: How do we acquire knowledge of the unobserved?[1] This question, as posed, may seem to call for an empirical answer. We observe that human beings utilize what may be roughly characterized as inductive or scientific methods of extending knowledge from the observed to the unobserved. The sciences, in fact, embody the most powerful and highly developed methods known, and we may make an empirical investigation of scientific methods much as we might for any other sort of human behavior. We may consider the historical development of science. We may study the psychological, sociological, and political factors relevant to the pursuit of science. We may try to give an exact characterization of the behavior of scientists. In doing all these things, however, important and interesting as they are, we will have ignored the *philosophical* aspect of the problem Hume raised. Putting the matter very simply, these empirical investigations may enable us to describe the ways in which people arrive at *beliefs* about unobserved facts, but they leave open the question of whether beliefs arrived at in this way actually constitute *knowledge*. It is one thing to describe how peo-

From *The Foundations of Scientific Inference* (Pittsburgh: University of Pittsburgh Press, 1966), pp. 5–27, 40–43, 48–56, 132–36.

ple go about seeking to extend their knowledge; it is quite another to claim that the methods employed actually do yield knowledge.

One of the basic differences between knowledge and belief is that knowledge must be founded upon evidence—i.e., it must be belief founded upon some rational justification. To say that certain methods yield knowledge of the unobserved is to make a cognitive claim for them. Hume called into question the justification of such cognitive claims. The answer cannot be found entirely within an empirical study of human behavior, for a *logical* problem has been raised. It is the problem of understanding the logical relationship between evidence and conclusion in logically correct inferences. It is the problem of determining whether the inferences by which we attempt to make the transition from knowledge of the observed to knowledge of the unobserved are logically correct. The fact that people do or do not use a certain type of inference is irrelevant to its justifiability. Whether people have confidence in the correctness of a certain type of inference has nothing to do with whether such confidence is justified. If we should adopt a logically incorrect method for inferring one fact from others, these facts would not actually constitute evidence for the conclusion we have drawn. The problem of induction is the problem of explicating the very concept of *inductive evidence*.

There is another possibly misleading feature of the question as I have formulated it. When we ask how we can *acquire* knowledge of the unobserved, it sounds very much as if we are asking for a method for the *discovery* of new knowledge. This is, of course, a vital problem, but it is not the fundamental problem Hume raised. Whether there is or can be any sort of inductive logic of discovery is a controversial question I shall discuss in detail in a later section.[2] Leaving this question aside for now, there remains the problem of *justification* of conclusions concerning unobserved matters of fact. Given some conclusion, however arrived at, regarding unobserved facts, and given some alleged evidence to support that conclusion, the question remains whether that conclusion is, indeed, supported by the evidence offered in support of it.

Consider a simple and highly artificial situation. Suppose a number of balls have been drawn from an urn, and that all of the black ones that have been drawn are licorice-flavored. I am not now concerned with such psychological questions as what makes the observer note the color of these balls, what leads him to taste the black ones, what makes him take note of the fact that licorice flavor is associated with black color in his sample, or what makes him suppose that the black balls not yet drawn will also be licorice-flavored. The problem—Hume's basic *philosophical* problem—is this: Given that all of the observed black balls have been licorice-flavored, and given that somehow the conclusion has been entertained that the unobserved black balls in the urn are also licorice-flavored, do the observed facts constitute sound *evidence* for that conclusion? Would we be *justified* in accepting that conclusion on the basis of the facts alleged to be evidence for it?

As a first answer to this question we may point out that the inference does conform to an accepted inductive principle, a principle saying roughly that observed instances conforming to a generalization constitute evidence for it. It is, however, a very small step to the next question: What grounds have we for accepting this or any other inductive principle? Is there any reason or justification for placing confidence in the conclusions of inferences of this type? Given that the premises of this inference are true, and given that the inference conforms to a certain rule, can we provide any rational justification for accepting its conclusion rather than, for instance, the conclusion that black balls yet to be drawn will taste like quinine?

It is well known that Hume's answer to this problem was essentially skeptical. It was his great merit to have shown that a justification of induction, if possible at all, is by no means easy to provide. In order to appreciate the force of his argument it is first necessary to clarify some terminological points. This is particularly important because the word *induction* has been used in a wide variety of ways.

For purposes of systematic discussion one distinction is fundamental, namely, the distinction between demonstrative and nondemonstrative inference. A *demonstrative* inference is one whose premises necessitate its conclusion; the conclusion cannot be false if the premises are true. All valid deductions are demonstrative inferences. A *nondemonstrative* inference is simply one that fails to be demonstrative. Its conclusion is not necessitated by its premises; the conclusion could be false even if the premises are true. A demonstrative inference is *necessarily truth-preserving;* a nondemonstrative inference is not.

The category of nondemonstrative inferences, as I have characterized it, contains, among other things perhaps, all kinds of fallacious inferences. If, however, there is any kind of inference whose premises, although not necessitating the conclusion, do lend it weight, support it, or make it probable, then such inferences possess a certain kind of logical rectitude. It is not deductive validity, but it is important anyway. Inferences possessing it are *correct inductive inferences.*

Since demonstrative inferences have been characterized in terms of their basic property of necessary truth preservation, it is natural to ask how they achieve this very desirable trait. For a large group of demonstrative inferences, including those discussed under "valid deduction" in most logic texts, the answer is rather easy. Inferences of this type purchase necessary truth preservation by sacrificing any extension of content. The conclusion of such an inference says no more than do the premises—often less.[3] The conclusion cannot be false if the premises are true *because* the conclusion says nothing that was not already stated in the premises. The conclusion is a mere reformulation of all or part of the content of the premises. In some cases the reformulation is unanticipated and therefore psychologically surprising, but the conclusion cannot augment the content of the premises. Such inferences are *nonampliative;* an ampliative inference, then, has a conclusion with content not present either explicitly or implicitly in the premises.

While it is easy to understand why nonampliative inferences are necessarily truth-preserving, the further question arises whether there are any necessarily truth-preserving inferences that are also ampliative. Is there any type of inference whose conclusion must, of necessity, be true if the premises are true, but whose conclusion says something not stated by the premises? Hume believed that the answer is negative and so do I, but it is not easy to produce an adequate defense of this answer. Let us see, however, what an affirmative answer would amount to.

Suppose there were an ampliative inference that is also necessarily truth-preserving. Consider the implication from its premises, $P_1, \ldots, P_k$, to its conclusion C. If the inference were an ordinary nonampliative deduction, this implication would be analytic and empty; but since the argument is supposed to be ampliative, the implication must be synthetic. At the same time, because the argument is supposed to be necessarily truth-preserving, this implication must be not only true but necessarily true. Thus, to maintain that there are inferences that are both ampliative and necessarily truth-preserving is tantamount to asserting that there are synthetic a priori truths.[4] This may be seen in another way. Any ampliative inference can be made into a nonampliative one by adding a premise. In particular, if we add to the foregoing ampliative inference the synthetic a priori premise, "If P_1 and P_2 and . . . and P_k, then C," the resulting inference will be an ordinary valid nonampliative deduction. Consider our example once more; this time let us set it out more formally:

1. Some black balls from this urn have been observed.
   All observed black balls from this urn are licorice-flavored.

   All black balls in this urn are licorice-flavored.

This argument is clearly ampliative, for the premise makes a statement about observed balls only, while the conclusion makes a statement about the unobserved as well as the observed balls. It appears to be nondemonstrative as well, for it seems perfectly possible for the conclusion to be false even if the premises are true. We see no reason why someone might not have dropped a black marble in the urn which, when it is drawn, will be found to be tasteless. We could, however, rule out this sort of possibility by adding another premise:

2. Some black balls from this urn have been observed.
   All observed black balls in this urn are licorice-flavored.
   Any two balls in this urn that have the same color also have the same flavor.

   All black balls in this urn are licorice-flavored.

The additional premise has transformed the former nondemonstrative inference into a demonstrative inference, but we must also admit that we have transformed it into a nonampliative inference. If, however, the third premise of 2 were a synthetic a priori truth, the original inference, although ampliative, would have been necessarily truth-preserving and, hence, demonstrative. If the premise that transformed inference 1 into inference 2 were necessarily true, then it would be impossible for the conclusion of inference 1 to be false if the premises were true, for that would contradict the third premise of inference 2.

Hardly anyone would be tempted to say that the statement, "Any two balls in this urn that have the same color also have the same flavor," expresses a synthetic a priori truth. Other propositions have, however, been taken to be synthetic a priori. Hume and many of his successors noticed that typical inductive inferences, such as our example concerning licorice-flavored black balls, would seem perfectly sound if we could have recourse to some sort of principle of uniformity of nature. If we could only prove that the course of nature is uniform, that the future will be like the past, or that uniformities that have existed thus far will continue to hold in the future, then we would seem to be justified in generalizing from past cases to future cases—from the observed to the unobserved. Indeed, Hume suggests that we presuppose in our inductive reasoning a principle from which the third premise of 2 would follow as a special case: "We always presume, when we see like sensible qualities, that they have like secret powers, and expect that effects, similar to those which we have experienced, will follow from them."[5] Again, "From causes which appear *similar* we expect similar effects. This is the sum of all our experimental conclusions."[6]

Hume's searching examination of the principle of uniformity of nature revealed no ground on which it could be taken as a synthetic a priori principle. For all we can know a priori, Hume argued, the course of nature might change, the future might be radically unlike the past, and regularities that have obtained in respect to observed events might prove completely inapplicable to unobserved cases. We have found by experience, of course, that nature has exhibited a high degree of uniformity and regularity so far, and we infer inductively that this will continue, but to use an inductively inferred generalization as a justification for induction, as Hume emphasized, would be flagrantly circular. He concluded, in fact, that there are no synthetic a priori principles in virtue of which we could have demonstrative inferences that are ampliative. Hume recognized two kinds of reasoning: reasoning concerning relations of ideas and reasoning concerning matters of fact and existence. The former is demonstrative but nonampliative while the latter is ampliative but not necessarily truth-preserving.

If we agree that there are no synthetic a priori truths, then we must identify necessarily truth-preserving inference with nonampliative inference. All ampliative inference is nondemonstrative. This leads to an exhaustive trichotomy of inferences: valid deductive inference, correct inductive inference, and assorted fallacies. The first question is, however, whether the second category is empty or whether there are such things as correct inductive inferences. This is Hume's problem of induction. Can we show that any particular type of ampliative inference can be justified in any way? If so, it will qualify as correct induction.

Consider, then, any ampliative inference whatever. The example of the licorice-flavored black balls illustrates the point. We cannot show *deductively* that this inference will have a true conclusion given true premises. If we could, we would have proved that the conclusion must be true if the premises are. That would make it necessarily truth-preserving, hence, demonstrative. This, in turn, would mean that it was nonampliative, contrary to our hypothesis. Thus, if an ampliative inference could be justified deductively it would not be ampliative. It follows that ampliative inference cannot be justified deductively.

At the same time, we cannot justify any sort of ampliative inference *inductively*. To do so would require the use of some sort of nondemonstrative inference. But the question at issue is the justification of nondemonstrative inference, so the procedure would be question begging. Before we can properly employ a nondemonstrative inference in a justifying argument, we must already have justified that nondemonstrative inference.

Hume's position can be summarized succinctly: We cannot justify any kind of ampliative inference. If it could be justified deductively it would not be ampliative. It cannot be justified nondemonstratively because that would be viciously circular. It seems, then, that there is no way in which we can extend our knowledge to the unobserved. We have, to be sure, many beliefs about the unobserved, and in some of them we place great confidence. Nevertheless, they are without rational justification of any kind!

This is a harsh conclusion, yet it seems to be supported by impeccable arguments. It might be called "Hume's paradox," for the conclusion, although ingeniously argued, is utterly repugnant to common sense and our deepest convictions. We *know* ("in our hearts") that we have knowledge of unobserved fact. The challenge is to show how this is possible.

II. Attempted Solutions

It hardly needs remarking that philosophers have attempted to meet Hume's intriguing challenge in a wide variety of ways. There have been direct attacks upon some of Hume's arguments. Attempts to provide inductive arguments to support induction and attempts to supply a synthetic a priori principle of uniformity of nature belong in this category. Some authors have claimed that the whole problem arises out of linguistic confusion, and that careful analysis shows it to be a pseudoproblem. Some have even denied that inductive inference is needed, either in science or in everyday affairs. In this section I shall survey what seem to me to be the most important efforts to deal with the problem.

1. Inductive Justification. If Hume's arguments had never been propounded and we were asked why we accept the methods of science, the most natural answer would be, I think, that these methods have proved themselves by their results. We can point to astonishing technological advances, to vastly increased comprehension, and to impressive predictions. Science has provided us with foresight, control, and understanding. No other method can claim a comparable record of successful accomplishment. If methods are to be judged by their fruits, there is no doubt that the scientific method will come out on top.

Unfortunately, Hume examined this argument and showed that it is viciously circular. It is an example of an attempt to justify inductive methods inductively. From the premise that science has had considerable predictive success in the past, we conclude that it will continue to have substantial predictive success in the future. Observed cases of the application of scientific method have yielded successful prediction; therefore, as yet unobserved cases of the application of scientific method will yield successful predictions. This argument has the same structure as our black-balls-in-the-urn example; it is precisely the sort of ampliative inference from the observed to the unobserved whose justifiability is in question.

Consider the parallel case for a radically different sort of method. A crystal gazer claims that his method is the appropriate method for making predictions. When we question his claim he says, "Wait a moment; I will find out whether the method of crystal gazing is the best method for making predictions." He looks into his crystal ball and announces that future cases of crystal gazing will yield predictive success. If we should protest that his method has not been especially successful in the past, he might well make certain remarks about parity of reasoning. "Since you have used your method to justify your method, why shouldn't I use my method to justify my method? If you insist upon judging my method by using your method, why shouldn't I use my method to evaluate your method? By the way, I note by gazing into my crystal ball that the scientific method is now in for a very bad run of luck."

The trouble with circular arguments is obvious: with an appropriate circular argument you can prove anything. In recent years, nevertheless, there have been several notable attempts to show how inductive rules can be supported inductively. The authors of such attempts try to show, of course, that their arguments are not circular. Although they argue persuasively, it seems to me that they do not succeed in escaping circularity.

One of the most widely discussed attempts to show that self-supporting inductive inferences are possible without circularity is due to Max Black.[7] Black correctly observes that the traditional fallacy of circular argument *(petitio principii)* involves assuming as a premise, often unwittingly, the conclusion that is to be proved. Thus, for example, a variety of "proofs" of Euclid's fifth postulate offered by mathematicians for about two millennia before the discovery of non-Euclidean geometry are circular in the standard fashion. They fail to show that the fifth postulate follows from the first four postulates alone; instead, they require in addition the assumption of a proposition equivalent to the proposition being demonstrated. The situation is quite different for self-supporting inductive arguments. The conclusion to be proved does not appear as one of the premises. Consider one of Black's examples:[8]

3. In most instances of the use of R_2 in arguments with true premises examined in a wide variety of conditions, R_2 has usually been successful.

   Hence (probably):

   In the next instance to be encountered of the use of R_2 in an argument with true premises, R_2 will be successful.

To say that an argument with true premises is successful is merely to say that it has a true conclusion. The rule R_2 is

> To argue from *Most instances of A's examined in a wide variety of conditions have been B to* (probably) *The next A to be encountered will be B.*

Inference 3 can be paraphrased suggestively, although somewhat inaccurately, as:

4. R_2 has usually been successful in the past.

   Hence (probably):

   R_2 will be successful in the next instance.

Inference 3 is governed by R_2, that is, it conforms to the stipulation laid down by R_2. R_2 is *not* a premise, however, nor is any statement to the effect that all, some, or any future instances of R_2 will be successful. As Lewis Carroll showed decisively, there is a fundamental distinction between premises and rules of inference.[9] Any inference, inductive or deductive, must conform to some rule, but neither the rule nor any statement about the rule is to be incorporated into the inference as an additional premise. If such additional premises were required, inference would be impossible. Thus, inference 3 is not a standard *petitio principii.*

What, then, are the requirements for a self-supporting argument? At least three are immediately apparent: (1) The argument must have true premises. (2) The argument must conform to a certain rule. (3) The conclusion of that argument must say something about the success or reliability of that rule in unexamined instances of its application. Inference 3 has these characteristics.

It is not difficult to find examples of deductive inferences with the foregoing characteristics.

5. If snow is white, then *modus ponens* is valid.
   Snow is white.

   Modus ponens is valid.

Inference 5 may seem innocuous enough, but the same cannot be said for the following inference:

6. If affirming the consequent is valid, then coal is black.
   Coal is black.

   Affirming the consequent is valid.

Like inference 5, inference 6 has true premises, it conforms to a certain rule, and its conclusion asserts the validity of that rule. Inference 5 did nothing to enhance our confidence in the validity of *modus ponens,* for we have far better grounds for believing it to be valid. Inference 6 does nothing to convince us that affirming the consequent is valid, for we know on other grounds that it is invalid. Arguments like 5 and 6 are, nevertheless, instructive. Both are circular in some sense, though neither assumes *as a premise* the conclusion it purports to establish. In deductive logic the situation is quite straightforward. A deductive inference establishes its conclusion if it has true premises and has a valid form. If either of these features is lacking the conclusion is not established by that argument. If the argument is valid but the premises are not true we need not accept the conclusion. If the premises are true but the argument is invalid we need not accept the conclusion. One way in which an argument can be circular is by adopting as a premise the very conclusion that is to be proved; this is the fallacy of *petitio principii* which I shall call "premise-circularity." Another way in which an argument can be circular is by exhibiting a form whose validity is asserted by the very conclusion that is to be proved; let us call this type of circularity "rule-circularity." Neither type of circular argument establishes its conclusion in any interesting fashion, for in each case the conclusiveness of the argument depends upon the assumption of the conclusion of that argument. Inferences 5 and 6 are not premise-circular; each is rule-circular. They are, nevertheless, completely question begging.

The situation in induction is somewhat more complicated, but basically the same.[10] Consider the following argument:

7. In most instances of the use of R_3 in arguments with true premises examined in a wide variety of conditions, R_3 has usually been *un*successful.
   Hence (probably):
   In the next instance to be encountered of the use of R_3 in an argument with true premises, R_3 will be successful.

The rule R_3 is

> To argue from *Most instances of A's examined in a wide variety of conditions have been non-B to* (probably) *The next A to be encountered will be B.*

Inference 7 can be paraphrased as follows:

8. R_3 has usually been unsuccessful in the past.
   Hence (probably):
   R_3 will be successful in the next instance.

Notice that there is a perfect parallel between R_2, 3, 4 on the one hand and R_3, 7, 8 on the other. Since those instances in which R_2 would be successful are those in which R_3 would be unsuccessful, the premises of 3 and 4 describe the same state of affairs as do the premises of 7 and 8. Thus, the use of R_3 in the next instance seems to be supported in the same manner and to the same extent as the use of R_2 in the next instance. However, R_2 and R_3 conflict directly with each other. On the evidence that most Italians examined in a wide variety of conditions have been dark-eyed, R_2 allows us to infer that the next Italian to be encountered will be dark-eyed, while R_3 permits us to infer from the same evidence that he will have light-colored eyes. It appears then that we can construct self-supporting arguments for correct and incorrect inductive rules just as we can for valid and invalid deductive rules.

Black would reject self-supporting arguments for the fallacy of affirming the consequent and for a counterinductive rule like R_2, because we know on independent grounds that such rules are faulty. Affirming the consequent is known to be fallacious, and the counterinductive method can be shown to be self-defeating. An additional requirement for a self-supporting argument is that the rule thus supported be one we have no independent reason to reject. Nevertheless, the fact that we can construct self-supporting arguments for such rules should give us pause. What if we had never realized that affirming the consequent is fallacious? What if we had never noticed anything wrong with the counterinductive method? Would arguments like 6, 7, and 8 have to be considered cogent? What about the standard inductive method? Is it as incorrect as the counterinductive method, but for reasons most of us have not yet realized?

It sounds as if a self-supporting argument is applicable only to rules we already know to be correct; as a matter of fact, this is the view Black holds. He has argued in various places that induction is in no need of a general justification.[11] He holds that calling into question of all inductive methods simultaneously results in a hopelessly skeptical position. He is careful to state explicitly at the outset of his discussion of self-supporting inductive arguments that he is not dealing with the view "that *no* inductive argument ought to be regarded as correct until a philosophical justification of induction has been provided."[12] At the conclusion he acknowledges, moreover, that "anybody who thinks he has good grounds for condemning all inductive arguments will also condemn inductive arguments in support of inductive rules."[13] Black is careful to state explicitly that self-supporting inductive arguments provide no answer to the problem of justification of induction as raised by Hume. What good, then, are self-supporting inductive arguments?

In deductive logic, correctness is an all-or-nothing affair. Deductive inferences are either totally valid or totally invalid; there cannot be such a thing as degree of validity. In inductive logic the situation is quite different. Inductive correctness does admit of degrees; one inductive conclusion may be more strongly supported than another. In this situation it is possible, Black claims, to have an inductive rule we know to be correct to some degree, but whose status can be enhanced by self-supporting arguments. We might think a rather standard inductive rule akin to Black's R_2 is pretty good, but through inductive investigation of its application we might find that it is extremely good—much better than we originally thought. Moreover, the inductive inferences we use to draw that conclusion might be governed by precisely the sort of rule we are investigating. It is also possible, of course, to find by inductive investigation that the rule is not as good as we believed beforehand.

It is actually irrelevant to the present discussion to attempt to evaluate Black's view concerning the possibility of increasing the justification of inductive rules by self-supporting arguments. The important point is to emphasize, because of the possibility of constructing self-supporting arguments for counterinductive rules, that the attempt to provide inductive support of inductive rules cannot, without vicious circularity, be applied to the problem of justifying induction from scratch. If there is any way of providing the beginnings of a justification, or if we could show that some inductive rule stands in no need of justification in the first instance, then it would be suitable to return to Black's argument concerning the increase of support. I am not convinced, however, that Black has successfully shown that there is a satisfactory starting place.

I have treated the problem of inductive justification of induction at some length, partly because other authors have not been as cautious as Black in circumscribing the limits of inductive justification of induction.[14] More important, perhaps, is the fact that it is extremely difficult, psychologically speaking, to shake the view that past success of the inductive method constitutes a genuine justification of induction. Nevertheless, the basic fact remains: Hume showed that inductive justifications of induction are fallacious, and no one has since proved him wrong.

2. The Complexity of Scientific Inference. The idea of a philosopher discussing inductive inference in science is apt to arouse grotesque images in many minds. People are likely to imagine someone earnestly attempting to explain why it is reasonable to conclude that the sun will rise tomorrow morning because it always has done so in the past. There may have been a time when primitive man anticipated the dawn with assurance based only upon the fact that he had seen dawn follow the blackness of night as long as he could remember, but this primitive state of knowledge, if it ever existed, was unquestionably *pre*scientific. This kind of reasoning bears no resemblance to science; in fact, the crude induction exhibits a complete absence of scientific understanding. Our scientific reasons for believing that the sun will rise tomorrow are of an entirely different kind. We understand the functioning of the solar system in terms of the laws of physics. We predict particular astronomical occurrences by means of these laws in conjunction with a knowledge of particular initial conditions that prevail. Scientific laws and theories have the logical form of general statements, but they are seldom, if ever, simple generalizations from experience.

Consider Newton's gravitational theory: Any two bodies are mutually attracted by a force proportional to the product of their masses and inversely proportional to the square of the distance between their centers. Although general in form, this kind of statement is not established by generalization from instances. We do not go around saying, "Here are two bodies—the force between them is such and such; here are two more bodies—the force between them is such and such; etc." Scientific theories are taken quite literally as hypotheses. They are entertained in order that their consequences may be drawn and examined. Their acceptability is judged in terms of these consequences. The consequences are extremely diverse—the greater the variety the better. For Newtonian theory, we look to such consequences as the behavior of Mars, the tides, falling bodies, the pendulum, and the torsion balance. These consequences have no apparent unity among themselves; they do not constitute a basis for inductive generalization. They achieve a kind of unity only by virtue of the fact that they are consequences of a single physical theory.

The type of inference I have been characterizing is very familiar; it is known as the *hypothetico-deductive method.*[15] It stands in sharp contrast to *induction by enumeration,* which consists in simple inductive generalization from instances. Schematically, the hypothetico-deductive method works as follows: From a general hypothesis and particular statements of initial conditions, a particular predictive statement is deduced. The statements of initial conditions, at least for the time, are accepted as true; the hypothesis is the statement whose truth is at issue. By observation we determine whether the predictive statement turned out to be true. If the predictive consequence is false, the hypothesis is disconfirmed. If observation reveals that the predictive statement is true, we say that the hypothesis is confirmed to some extent. A hypothesis is not, of course, conclusively proved by any one or more positively confirming instances, but it may become highly confirmed. A hypothesis that is sufficiently confirmed is accepted, at least tentatively.

It seems undeniable that science uses a type of inference at least loosely akin to the hypothetico-deductive method.[16] This has led some people to conclude that the logic of science is thoroughly deductive in character. According to this view, the only nondeductive aspect of the situation consists in thinking up hypotheses, but this is not a matter of logic and therefore requires no justification. It is a matter of psychological ingenuity of discovery. Once the hypothesis has been discovered, by some entirely nonlogical process, it remains only to *deduce* consequences and check them against observation.

It is, of course, a fallacy to conclude that the premises of an argument must be true if its conclusion is true. This fact seems to be the basis for the quip that a logic text is a book that consists of two parts; in the first part (on deduction) the fallacies are explained, in the second part (on induction) they are committed. The whole trouble with saying that the hypothetico-deductive method renders the logic of science entirely deductive is that we are attempting to establish a *premise* of the deduction, not the conclusion. Deduction is an indispensible part of the logic of the hypothetico-deductive method, but it is not the only part. There is a fundamental and important sense in which the hypothesis must be regarded as a conclusion instead of a premise. Hypotheses (later perhaps called "theories" or "laws") are among the *results* of scientific investigation; science aims at establishing general statements about the world. Scientific prediction and explanation require such generalizations. While we are concerned with the status of the general hypothesis—whether we should accept it or reject it—the hypothesis must be treated as a conclusion to be supported by evidence, not as a premise lending support to other conclusions. The inference *from* observational evidence *to* hypothesis is surely not deductive. If this point is not already obvious it becomes clear the moment we recall that for any given body of observational data there is, in general, more than one hypothesis compatible with it. These alternative hypotheses differ in factual content and are incompatible with each other. Therefore, they cannot be deductive consequences of any consistent body of observational evidence.

We must grant, then, that science embodies a type of inference resembling the hypothetico-deductive method and fundamentally different from induction by enumeration. Hume, on the other hand, has sometimes been charged with a conception of science according to which the only kind of reasoning is induction by enumeration. His typical examples are cases of simple generalization of observed regularities, something like our example of the licorice-flavored black balls. In the past, water has quenched thirst; in the future, it will as well. In the past, fires have been hot; in the future, they will be hot. In the past, bread has nourished; in the future, it will do so likewise. It might be said that Hume, in failing to see the essential role of the hypothetico-deductive method, was unable to appreciate the complexity of the theoretical science of his own time, to say nothing of subsequent developments. This is typical, some might say, of the misunderstandings engendered by philosophers who undertake to discuss the logic of science without being thoroughly conversant with mathematics and natural science.

This charge against Hume (and other philosophers of induction) is ill-founded. It was part of Hume's genius to have recognized that the arguments he applied to simple enumerative induction apply equally to any kind of ampliative or nondemonstrative inference whatever. Consider the most complex kind of scientific reasoning—the most elaborate example of hypothetico-deductive inference you can imagine. Regardless of subtle features or complications, it is ampliative overall. The conclusion is a statement whose content exceeds the observational evidence upon which it is based. A scientific theory that merely summarized what had already been observed would not deserve to be called a theory. If scientific inference were not ampliative, science would be useless for prediction, postdiction, and explanation. The highly general results that are the pride of theoretical science would be impossible if scientific inference were not ampliative.

In presenting Hume's argument, I was careful to set it up so that it would apply to any kind of ampliative or nondemonstrative inference, no matter how simple or how complex. Furthermore, the distinction between valid deduction and nondemonstrative inference is completely exhaustive. Take any inference whatsoever. It must be deductive or nondemonstrative. Suppose it is nondemonstrative. If we could justify it deductively it would cease to be nondemonstrative. To justify it nondemonstratively would presuppose an already justified type of nondemonstrative inference, which is precisely the problem at issue. Hume's argument does *not* break down when we consider forms more complex than simple enumeration. Although the word "induction" is sometimes used as a synonym for "induction by simple enumeration," I am not using it in that way. Any type of logically correct ampliative inference is induction; the problem of induction is to show that some particular form of ampliative inference is justifiable. It is in this sense that we are concerned with the problem of the justification of inductive inference.

A further misunderstanding is often involved in this type of criticism of Hume. There is a strong inclination to suppose that induction is regarded as the method by which scientific results are discovered.[17] Hume and other philosophers of induction are charged with the view that science has developed historically through patient collection of facts and generalization from them. I know of no philosopher—not even Francis Bacon!—who has held this view, although it is frequently attacked in the contemporary literature.[18] The term "generalization" has an unfortunate ambiguity which fosters the confusion. In one meaning, "generalization" refers to an inferential process in which one makes a sort of mental transition from particulars to a universal proposition; in this sense, generalization is an act of generalizing—a process that yields general results. In another meaning, "generalization" simply refers to a universal type or proposition, without any reference to its source or how it was thought of. It is entirely possible for science to contain many generalizations (in the latter sense) without embodying any generalizations (in the former sense). As I said explicitly at the outset, the problem of induction I am discussing is a problem concerning justification, not discovery. The thesis I am defending—that science does embody induction in a logically indispensable fashion—has nothing to do with the history of science or the psychology of particular scientists. It is simply the claim that scientific inference is ampliative.

3. Deductivism. One of the most interesting and controversial contemporary attempts to provide an account of the logic of science is Karl Popper's deductivism.[19] In the preceding section I discussed the view that the presence of the hypothetico-deductive method in the logic of science makes it possible to dispense with induction in science and, thereby, to avoid the problem of induction. I argued that the hypothetico-deductive method, since it is ampliative and nondemonstrative, is not strictly deductive; it is, in fact, inductive in the relevant sense. As long as the hypothetico-deductive method is regarded as a method for supporting scientific hypotheses, it cannot succeed in making science thoroughly deductive. Popper realizes this, so in arguing that deduction is the sole mode of inference in science he rejects the hypothetico-deductive method as a means for confirming scientific hypotheses. He asserts that induction plays no role whatever in science; indeed, he maintains that there is no such thing as correct inductive inference. Inductive logic is, according to Popper, a complete delusion. He admits the psychological fact that people (including himself) have faith in the uniformity of nature, but he holds, with Hume, that this can be no more than a matter of psychological fact. He holds, with Hume, that there can be no rational justification of induction, and he thinks Hume proved this point conclusively.

Popper's fundamental thesis is that falsifiability is the mark by which statements of empirical science are distinguished from metaphysical statements and from tautologies. The choice of falsifiability over verifiability as the criterion of demarcation is motivated by a long familiar fact—namely, it is possible to falsify a universal generalization by means of one negative instance, while it is impossible to verify a universal generalization by any limited number of positive instances. This, incidentally, is the meaning of the old saw which is so often made into complete nonsense: "The exception proves the rule." In this context, a rule is a universal generalization, and the term "to prove" means archaically "to test." The exception (i.e., the negative instance) proves (i.e., tests) the rule (i.e., the universal generalization), not by showing it to be true, but by showing it to be false. There is no kind of positive instance to prove (i.e., test) the rule, for positive instances are completely indecisive. Scientific hypotheses, as already noted, are general in form, so they are amenable to falsification but not verification.

Popper thus holds that falsifiability is the hallmark of empirical science. The aim of empirical science is to set forth theories to stand the test of every possible serious attempt at falsification. Scientific theories are hypotheses or conjectures; they are general statements designed to explain the world and make it intelligible, but they are never to be regarded as final truths. Their status is always that of tentative conjecture, and they must continually face the severest possible criticism. The function of the theoretician is to propose scientific conjectures; the function of the experimentalist is to devise every possible way of falsifying these theoretical hypotheses. The attempt to confirm hypotheses is no part of the aim of science.[20]

General hypotheses by themselves do not entail any predictions of particular events, but they do in conjunction with statements of initial conditions. The laws of planetary motion in conjunction with statements about the relative positions and velocities of the earth, sun, moon, and planets enable us to predict a solar eclipse. The mode of inference is deduction. We have a high degree of intersubjective agreement concerning the initial conditions, and we likewise can obtain intersubjective agreement as to whether the sun's disc was obscured at the predicted time and place. If the predicted fact fails to occur, the theory has suffered falsification. Again, the mode of inference is deduction. If the theory were true, then, given the truth of the statements of initial conditions, the prediction would have to be true. The prediction, as it happens, is false; therefore, the theory is false. This is the familiar principle of *modus tollens;* it is, according to Popper, the only kind of inference available for the acceptance or rejection of hypotheses, and it is clearly suitable for rejection only.

Hypothetico-deductive theorists maintain that we have a confirming instance for the theory if the eclipse occurs as predicted. Confirming instances, they claim, tend to enhance the probability of the hypothesis or give it inductive support. With enough confirming instances of appropriate kinds, the probability of the hypothesis becomes great enough to warrant accepting it as true—not, of course, with finality and certainty, but provisionally. With sufficient inductive support of this kind we are justified in regarding it as well established. Popper, however, rejects the positive account, involving as it does the notion of inductive support. If a hypothesis is tested and the result is negative, we can reject it. If the test is positive, all we can say is that we have failed to falsify it. We cannot say that it has been confirmed or that it is, because of the positive test result, more probable. Popper does admit a notion of *corroboration* of hypotheses, but that is quite distinct from confirmation. We shall come to corroboration presently. For the moment, all we have are successful or unsuccessful attempts at falsification; all we can say about our hypotheses is that they are falsified or unfalsified. This is as far as inference takes us; according to Popper, this is the limit of logic. Popper therefore rejects the hypothetico-deductive method as it is usually characterized and accepts only the completely deductive *modus tollens*.

Popper—quite correctly I believe—denies that there are absolutely basic and incorrigible protocol statements that provide the empirical foundation for all of science. He does believe that there are relatively basic observation statements about macroscopic physical occurrences concerning which we have a high degree of intersubjective agreement. Normally, we can accept as unproblematic such statements as, "There is a wooden table in this room," "The pointer on this meter stands between 325 and 350," and "The rope just broke and the weight fell to the floor." Relatively basic statements of this kind provide the observation base for empirical science. This is the stuff of which empirical tests of scientific theories are made.

Although Popper's basic statements must in the last analysis be considered hypotheses, falsifiable and subject to test like other scientific hypotheses, it is obvious that the kinds of hypotheses that constitute theoretical science are far more general than the basic statements. But now we must face the grim fact that valid deductive inference, although necessarily truth-preserving, is nonampliative.[21] It is impossible to deduce from accepted basic statements any conclusion whose content exceeds that of the basic statements themselves. Observation statements and deductive inference yield nothing that was not stated by the observation statements themselves. If science consists solely of observation statements and deductive inferences, then talk about theories, their falsifiability, and their tests is empty. The content of science is coextensive with the content of the statements used to describe what we directly observe. There are no general theories, there is no predictive content, there are no inferences to the remote past. Science is barren.

Consider a few simple time-honored examples. Suppose that the statement "All ravens are black" has been entertained critically and subjected to every attempt at falsification we can think of. Suppose it has survived all attempts at falsification. What is the scientific content of all this? We can say that "All ravens are black" has not been falsified, which is equivalent to saying that we have not observed a nonblack raven. This statement is even poorer in content than a simple recital of our color observations of ravens. To say that the hypothesis has not been falsified is to say less than is given in a list of our relevant observation statements. Or, consider the generalization, "All swans are white." What have we said when we say that this hypothesis has been falsified? We have said only that a nonwhite swan has been found. Again, the information conveyed by this remark is less than we would get from a simple account of our observations of swans.

Popper has never claimed that falsification by itself can establish scientific hypotheses. When one particular hypothesis has been falsified, many alternative hypotheses remain unfalsified. Likewise, there is nothing unique about a hypothesis that survives without being falsified. Many other unfalsified hypotheses remain to explain the same facts. Popper readily admits all of this. If science is to amount to more than a mere collection of our observations and various reformulations thereof, it must embody some other methods besides observation and deduction. Popper supplies that additional factor: *corroboration*.[22]

When a hypothesis has been falsified, it is discarded and replaced by another hypothesis which has not yet experienced falsification. Not all unfalsified hypotheses are on a par. There are principles of selection among unfalsified hypotheses. Again, falsifiability is the key. Hypotheses differ from one another with respect to the ease with which they can be falsified, and we can often compare them with respect to degree of falsifiability. Popper directs us to seek hypotheses that are as highly falsifiable as possible. Science, he says, is interested in bold conjectures. These conjectures must be consistent with the known facts, but they must run as great a risk as possible of being controverted by the facts still to be accumulated. Furthermore, the search for additional facts should be guided by the effort to find facts that will falsify the hypothesis.

As Popper characterizes falsifiability, the greater the degree of falsifiability of a hypothesis, the greater its content. Tautologies lack empirical content because they do not exclude any possible state of affairs; they are compatible with any possible world. Empirical statements are not compatible with every possible state of affairs; they are compatible with some and incompatible with others. The greater the number of possible states of affairs excluded by a statement, the greater its content, for the more it does to pin down our actual world by ruling out possible but nonactual states of affairs. At the same time, the greater the range of facts excluded by a statement—the greater the number of situations with which the statement is incompatible—the greater the risk it runs of being false. A statement with high content has more *potential falsifiers* than a statement with low content. For this reason, high content means high falsifiability. At the same time, content varies inversely with probability. The logical probability of a hypothesis is defined in terms of its range—that is, the possible states of affairs with which it is compatible. The greater the logical probability of a hypothesis, the fewer are its potential falsifiers. Thus, high probability means low falsifiability.

Hypothetico-deductive theorists usually recommend selecting, from among those hypotheses that are compatible with the available facts, the most probable hypothesis. Popper recommends the opposite; he suggests selecting the most falsifiable hypothesis. Thus, he recommends selecting a hypothesis with low probability. According to Popper, a highly falsifiable hypothesis which is severely tested becomes highly corroborated. The greater the severity of the tests—the greater their number and variety—the greater the corroboration of the hypothesis that survives them.

Popper makes it very clear that hypotheses are not regarded as true because they are highly corroborated. Hypotheses cannot be firmly and finally established in this or any other way. Furthermore, because of the inverse relation between falsifiability and probability, we cannot regard highly corroborated hypotheses as probable. To be sure, a serious attempt to falsify a hypothesis which fails does add to the corroboration of this hypothesis, so there is some similarity between corroboration and confirmation as hypothetico-deductive theorists think of it, but it would be a misinterpretation to suppose that increasing corroboration is a process of accumulating positive instances to increase the probability of the hypothesis.[23]

Nevertheless, Popper does acknowledge the need for a method of selecting among unfalsified hypotheses. He has been unequivocal in his emphasis upon the indispensability of far-reaching theory in science. Empirical science is not an activity of merely accumulating experiences; it is theoretical through and through. Although we do not regard any hypotheses as certainly true, we do accept them tentatively and provisionally. Highly corroborated hypotheses are required for prediction and explanation. From among the ever-present multiplicity of hypotheses compatible with the available evidence, we select and accept.

There is just one point I wish to make here regarding Popper's theory. It is not properly characterized as *deductivism.* Popper has not succeeded in purging the logic of science of all inductive elements. My reason for saying this is very simple. Popper furnishes a method for selecting hypotheses whose content exceeds that of the relevant available basic statements. Demonstrative inference cannot accomplish this task alone, for valid deductions are nonampliative and their conclusions cannot exceed their premises in content. Furthermore, Popper's theory does not pretend that basic statements plus deduction can give us scientific theory; instead, corroboration is introduced. Corroboration is a nondemonstrative form of inference. It is a way of providing for the acceptance of hypotheses even though the content of these hypotheses goes beyond the content of the basic statements. *Modus tollens* without corroboration is empty; *modus tollens* with corroboration is induction.

When we ask, "Why should we reject a hypothesis when we have accepted one of its potential falsifiers?" the answer is easy. The potential falsifier contradicts the hypothesis, so the hypothesis is false if the potential falsifier holds. That is simple deduction. When we ask, "Why should we accept from among all the unfalsified hypotheses one that is highly corroborated?" we have a right to expect an answer. The answer is some kind of justification for the methodological rule—for the method of corroboration. Popper attempts to answer this question.

Popper makes it clear that his conception of scientific method differs in important respects from the conceptions of many inductivists. I do not want to quibble over a word in claiming that Popper is, himself, a kind of inductivist. The point is not a trivial verbal one. Popper has claimed that scientific inference is exclusively deductive. We have seen, however, that demonstrative inference is not sufficient to the task of providing a reconstruction of the logic of the acceptance—albeit tentative and provisional—of hypotheses. Popper himself realizes this and introduces a mode of nondemonstrative inference. It does not matter whether we call this kind of inference "induction"; whatever we call it, it is ampliative and not necessarily truth preserving. Using the same force and logic with which Hume raised problems about the justification of induction, we may raise problems about the justification of any kind of nondemonstrative inference. As I argued in the preceding section, Hume's arguments are not peculiar to induction by enumeration or any other special kind of inductive inference; they apply with equal force to any inference whose conclusion can be false, even though it has true premises. Thus, it will not do to dismiss induction by enumeration on grounds of Hume's argument and then accept some other mode of nondemonstrative inference without even considering how Hume's argument might apply to it. I am not arguing that Popper's method is incorrect.[24] I am not even arguing that Popper has failed in his attempt to justify this method. I do claim that Popper is engaged in the same task as many inductivists—namely, the task of providing some sort of justification for a mode of nondemonstrative inference. This enterprise, if successful, *is* a justification of induction.

. . . .

5. The Principle of Uniformity of Nature. A substantial part of Hume's critique of induction rested upon his attack on the principle of the uniformity of nature. He argued definitively that the customary forms of inductive inference cannot be expected to yield correct predictions if nature fails to be uniform—if the future is not like the past—if like sensible qualities are not accompanied by like results.

> All inferences from experience suppose, as their foundation, that the future will resemble the past, and that similar powers will be conjoined with similar sensible qualities. If there be any suspicion that the course of nature may change, and that the past may be no rule for the future, all experience becomes useless, and can give rise to no inference or conclusion.[25]

He argued, moreover, that there is no logical contradiction in the supposition that nature is not uniform—that the regularities we have observed up to the present will fail in wholesale fashion in the future.

> It implies no contradiction that the course of nature may change, and that an object, seemingly like those which we have experienced, may be attended with different or contrary effects. May I not clearly and distinctly conceive that a body, falling from the clouds, and which, in all other respects resembles snow, has yet the taste of salt or feeling of fire? Is there any more intelligible proposition than to affirm, that all the trees will flourish in December and January, and decay in May and June? Now whatever is intelligible, and can be distinctly conceived, implies no contradiction, and can never be proved false by any demonstrative argument. . . .[26]

He argues, in addition, that the principle of uniformity of nature cannot be established by an inference from experience: "It is impossible, therefore, that any arguments from experience can prove this resemblance of the past to the future; since all these arguments are founded on the supposition of that resemblance."[27] Throughout Hume's discussion there is, however, a strong suggestion that we might have full confidence in the customary inductive methods if nature were known to be uniform.

Kant attempted to deal with the problem of induction in just this way, by establishing a principle of uniformity of nature, in the form of the principle of universal causation, as a synthetic a priori truth. Kant claimed, in other words, that every occurrence is governed by causal regularities, and this general characteristic of the universe can be established by pure reason, without the aid of any empirical evidence. He did not try to show that the principle of universal causation is a principle of logic, for to do so would have been to show that it was analytic—not synthetic—and thus lacking in factual content. He did not reject Hume's claim that there is no logical contradiction in the statement that nature is not uniform; he did not try to prove his principle of universal causation by deducing a contradiction from its denial. He did believe, however, that this principle, while not a proposition of pure logic, is necessarily true nevertheless. Hume, of course, argued against this alternative as well. He maintained not only that the uniformity of nature is not a logical or analytic truth, but also that it cannot be any other kind of a priori truth either. Even before Kant had enunciated the doctrine of synthetic a priori principles, Hume had offered strong arguments against them:

> I shall venture to affirm, as a general proposition, which admits of no exception, that the knowledge of this relation [of cause and effect] is not, in any instance, attained by reasonings a priori.[28]
>
> Adam, though his rational faculties be supposed, at the very first, entirely perfect, could not have inferred from the fluidity and transparency of water that it would suffocate him, or from the light and warmth of fire that it would consume him.[29]
>
> When we reason a priori, and consider merely any object or cause, as it appears to the mind, independent of all observation, it never could suggest to us the notion of any distinct object, such as its effect; much less, show us the inseparable and inviolable connexion between them. A man must be very sagacious who could discover by reasoning that crystal is the effect of heat, and ice of cold, without being previously acquainted with the operation of these qualities.[30]
>
> Now whatever is intelligible, and can be distinctly conceived . . . can never be proved false by any . . . abstract reasoning a priori.[31]

Humes argues, by persuasive example and general principle, that nothing about the causal structure of reality can be established by pure reason. He poses an incisive challenge to those who would claim the ability to establish a priori knowledge of a particular causal relation or of the principle of universal causation. In the foregoing discussion of synthetic a priori statements, I have given reasons for believing that Kant failed to overcome Hume's previous objections.

There is, however, another interesting issue that arises in connection with the principle of uniformity of nature. Suppose it could be established—never mind how—prior to a justification of induction. Would it then provide an adequate basis for a justification of induction? The answer is, I think, negative.[32]

Even if nature is uniform to some extent, it is not absolutely uniform. The future is something like the past, but it is somewhat different as well. Total and complete uniformity would mean that the state of the universe at any given moment is the same as its state at any other moment. Such a universe would be a changeless, Parmenidean world. Change obviously does occur, so the future is not exactly like the past. There are some uniformities, it appears, but not a complete absence of change. The problem is how to ferret out the genuine uniformities. As a matter of actual fact, there are many uniformities *within experience* that we take to be mere coincidences, and there are others that seem to represent genuine causal regularities. For instance, in every election someone finds a precinct, say in Maryland, which has always voted in favor of the winning presidential candidate. Given enough precincts, one expects this sort of thing by sheer chance, and we classify such regularities as mere coincidences. By contrast, the fact that glass windowpanes break when bricks are hurled at them is more than mere coincidence. Causal regularities provide a foundation for inference from the observed to the unobserved; coincidences do not. We can predict with some confidence that the next glass window pane at which a brick is hurled will break; we take with a grain of salt the prediction of the outcome of a presidential election early on election night when returns from the above-mentioned precinct are in. The most that a principle of uniformity of nature could say is that there are some uniformities that persist into the future; if it stated that every regularity observed to hold within the scope of our experience also holds universally, it would be patently false. We are left with the problem of finding a sound basis for distinguishing between mere coincidence and genuine causal regularity.

Kant's principle of universal causation makes a rather weak and guarded statement. It asserts only that there exist causal regularities: "Everything that happens presupposes something from which it follows according to some rule." For each occurrence it claims only the existence of *some* prior cause and *some* causal regularity. It gives no hint as to how we are to find the prior cause or how we are to identify the causal regularity. It therefore provides no basis upon which to determine whether the inductive inferences we make are correct or incorrect. It would be entirely consistent with Kant's principle for us always to generalize on the basis of observed coincidences and always to fail to generalize on the basis of actual causal relations. It would be entirely consistent with Kant's principle, moreover, for us always to cite a coincidentally preceding event as the cause instead of the event that is the genuine cause. Kant's principle, even if it could be established, would not help us to justify the assertion that our inductive inferences would always or usually be correct. It would provide no criterion to distinguish sound from unsound inductions. Even if Kant's program had succeeded in establishing a synthetic a priori principle of universal causation, it would have failed to produce a justification of induction.

. . . .

7. A Probabilistic Approach. It may seem strange in the extreme that this discussion of the problem of induction has proceeded at such great length without seriously bringing in the concept of probability. It is very tempting to react immediately to Hume's argument with the admission that we do not have *knowledge* of the unobserved. Scientific results are not established with absolute certainty. At best we can make probabilistic statements about unobserved matters of fact, and at best we can claim that scientific generalizations and theories are highly confirmed. We who live in an age of scientific empiricism can accept with perfect equanimity the fact that the quest for certainty is futile; indeed, our thanks go to Hume for helping to destroy false hopes for certainty in science.

Hume's search for a justification of induction, it might be continued, was fundamentally misconceived. He tried to find a way of proving that inductive inferences with true premises would have *true* conclusions. He properly failed to find any such justification precisely because it is the function of *deduction* to prove the truth of conclusions, given true premises. Induction has a different function. An inductive inference with true premises establishes its conclusions as *probable*. No wonder Hume failed to find a justification of induction. He was trying to make induction into deduction, and he succeeded only in proving the platitude that induction is not deduction.[33] If we want to justify induction, we must show that inductive inferences establish their conclusions as probable, not as true.

The foregoing sort of criticism of Hume's arguments is extremely appealing, and it has given rise to the most popular sort of attempt, currently, to deal with the problem.[34] In order to examine this approach, we must consider, at least superficially, the meaning of the concept of probability. Two basic meanings must be taken into account at present.

One leading probability concept identifies probability with frequency—roughly, the probable is that which happens often, and the improbable is that which happens seldom. Let us see what becomes of Hume's argument under this interpretation of probability. If we were to claim that inductive conclusions are probable in this sense, we would be claiming that inductive inferences with true premises often have true conclusions, although not always. Hume's argument shows, unhappily, that this claim cannot be substantiated. It was recognized long before Hume that inductive inferences cannot be expected always to lead to the truth. Hume's argument shows, not only that we cannot justify the claim that *every* inductive inference with true premises will have a true conclusion, but also, that we cannot justify the claim that *any* inductive inference with true premises will have a true conclusion. Hume's argument shows that, for all we can know, every inductive inference made from now on might have a false conclusion despite true premises. Thus, Hume has proved, we can show neither that inductive inferences establish their conclusions as true nor that they establish their conclusions as probable in the frequency sense. The introduction of the frequency concept of probability gives no help whatever in circumventing the problem of induction, but this is no surprise, for we should not have expected it to be suitable for this purpose.

A more promising probability concept identifies probability with degree of rational belief. To say that a statement is probable in this sense means that one would be rationally justified in believing it; the degree of probability is the degree of assent a person would be rationally justified in giving. We are not, of course, referring to the degree to which anyone *actually* believes in the statement, but rather to the degree to which one could *rationally* believe it. Degree of actual belief is a purely psychological concept, but degree of rational belief is determined objectively by the evidence. To say that a statement is probable in this sense means that it is supported by evidence. But, so the argument goes, if a statement is the conclusion of an inductive inference with true premises, it *is* supported by evidence—by inductive evidence—this is part of what it *means* to be supported by evidence. The very concept of evidence depends upon the nature of induction, and it becomes incoherent if we try to divorce the two. Trivially, then, the conclusion of an inductive inference is probable under this concept of probability. To ask, with Hume, if we should accept inductive conclusions is tantamount to asking if we should fashion our beliefs in terms of the evidence, and this, in turn, is tantamount to asking whether we should be rational. In this way we arrive at an "ordinary language dissolution" of the problem of induction. Once we understand clearly the meanings of such key terms as "rational," "probable," and "evidence," we see that the problem arose out of linguistic confusion and evaporates into the question of whether it is rational to be rational. Such tautological questions, if meaningful at all, demand affirmative answers.

Unfortunately, the dissolution is not satisfactory.[35] Its inadequacy can be exhibited by focusing upon the concept of inductive evidence and seeing how it figures in the foregoing argument. The fundamental difficulty arises from the fact that the very notion of inductive evidence is determined by the rules of inductive inference. If a conclusion is to be supported by inductive evidence, it must be the conclusion of a correct inductive inference with true premises. Whether the inductive inference is correct depends upon whether the rule governing that inference is correct. The relation of inductive evidential support is, therefore, inseparably bound to the correctness of rules of inductive inference. In order to be able to say whether a given statement is supported by inductive evidence we must be able to say which inductive rules are correct.

For example, suppose that a die has been thrown a large number of times, and we have observed that the side two came up in one sixth of the tosses. This is our "evidence" *e*. Let *h* be the conclusion that, "in the long run," side two will come up one sixth of the times. Consider the following three rules:

1. (Induction by enumeration.) Given m/n of observed *A* are *B*, to infer that the "long run" relative frequency of *B* among *A* is m/n.
2. (A priori rule.) Regardless of observed frequencies, to infer that the "long run" relative frequency of *B* among *A* is $1/k$, where *k* is the number of possible outcomes—six in the case of the die.
3. (Counterinductive rule.) Given m/n of observed *A* are *B*, to infer that the "long run" relative frequency of *B* among *A* is $(n-m)/n$.

Under Rule 1, *e* is positive evidence for *h;* under Rule 2, *e* is irrelevant to *h;* and under Rule 3, *e* is negative evidence for *h*. In order to say which conclusions are supported by what evidence, it is necessary to arrive at a decision as to what inductive rules are acceptable. If Rule 1 is correct, the evidence *e* supports the conclusion *h*. If Rule 2 is correct, we are justified in drawing the conclusion *h,* but this is entirely independent of the observational evidence *e;* the same conclusions would have been sanctioned by Rule 2 regardless of observational evidence. If Rule 3 is correct, we are not only prohibited from drawing the conclusion *h,* but also we are permitted to draw a conclusion *h′* which is logically incompatible with *h*. Whether a given conclusion is *supported by evidence*—whether it would be *rational to believe* it on the basis of given evidence—whether it is *made probable* by virtue of its relation to given evidence—depends upon selection of the correct rule or rules from among the infinitely many rules we might conceivably adopt.

The problem of induction can now be reformulated as a problem about evidence. What rules ought we to adopt to determine the nature of inductive evidence? What rules provide suitable concepts of inductive evidence? If we take the customary inductive rules to define the concept of inductive evidence, have we adopted a proper concept of evidence? Would the adoption of some alternative inductive rules provide a more suitable concept of evidence? These are genuine questions which need to be answered.[36]

We find, moreover, that what appeared earlier as a pointless question now becomes significant and difficult. If we take the customary rules of inductive inference to provide a suitable definition of the relation of inductive evidential support, it makes considerable sense to ask whether it is rational to believe on the basis of evidence as thus defined rather than to believe on the basis of evidence as defined according to other rules. For instance, I believe that the a priori rule and the counterinductive rule mentioned above are demonstrably unsatisfactory, and hence, they demonstrably fail to provide a suitable concept of inductive evidence. The important point is that something concerning the selection from among possible rules needs demonstration and is amenable to demonstration.

There is danger of being taken in by an easy equivocation. One meaning we may assign to the concept of inductive evidence is, roughly, the basis on which we ought to fashion our beliefs. Another meaning results from the relation of evidential support determined by whatever rule of inductive inference we adopt. It is only by supposing that these two concepts are the same that we suppose the problem of induction to have vanished. The problem of induction is still there; it is the problem of providing adequate grounds for the selection of inductive rules. We want the relation of evidential support determined by these rules to yield a concept of inductive evidence which is, in fact, the basis on which we ought to fashion our beliefs.[37]

We began this initially promising approach to the problem of the justification of induction by introducing the notion of probability, but we end with a dilemma. If we take "probability" in the frequency sense, it is easy to see why it is advisable to accept probable conclusions in preference to improbable ones. In so doing we shall be right more often. Unfortunately, we cannot show that inferences conducted according to any particular rule establish conclusions that are probable in this sense. If we take "probability" in a nonfrequency sense it may be easy to show that inferences which conform to our accepted inductive rules establish their conclusions as probable. Unfortunately, we can find no reason to prefer conclusions which are probable in this sense to those that are improbable. As Hume has shown, we have no reason to suppose that probable conclusions will often be true and improbable ones will seldom be true. This dilemma is Hume's problem of induction all over again. We have been led to an interesting reformulation, but it is only a reformulation and not a solution.

8. Pragmatic Justification. Of all the solutions and dissolutions proposed to deal with Hume's problem of induction, Hans Reichenbach's attempt to provide a pragmatic justification seems to me the most fruitful and promising.[38] This approach accepts Hume's arguments up to the point of agreeing that it is impossible to establish, either deductively or inductively, that any inductive inferences will ever again have true conclusions. Nevertheless, Reichenbach claims, the standard method of inductive generalization can be justified. Although its *success* as a method of prediction cannot be established in advance, it can be shown to be superior to any alternative method of prediction.

The argument can be put rather simply. Nature may be sufficiently uniform in suitable respects for us to make successful inductive inferences from the observed to the unobserved. On the other hand, for all we know, she may not. Hume has shown that we cannot prove in advance which case holds. All we can say is that nature may or may not be uniform—if she is, induction works; if she is not, induction fails. Even in the face of our ignorance about the uniformity of nature, we can ask what would happen if we adopted some radically different method of inference. Consider, for instance, the method of the crystal gazer. Since we do not know whether nature is uniform or not, we must consider both possibilities. If nature is uniform, the method of crystal gazing might work successfully, or it might fail. We cannot prove a priori that it will not work. At the same time, we cannot prove a priori that it will work, even if nature exhibits a high degree of uniformity. Thus, in case nature is reasonably uniform, the standard inductive method *must* work while the alternative method of crystal gazing *may or may not* work. In this case, the superiority of the standard inductive method is evident. Now, suppose nature lacks uniformity to such a degree that the standard inductive method is a complete failure. In this case, Reichenbach argues, the alternative method must likewise fail. Suppose it did not fail—suppose, for instance, that the method of crystal gazing worked consistently. This would constitute an important relevant uniformity that could be exploited inductively. If a crystal gazer had consistently predicted future occurrences, we could infer inductively that he has a method of prediction that will enjoy continued success. The inductive method would, in this way, share the success of the method of crystal gazing, and would therefore be, contrary to hypothesis, successful. Hence, Reichenbach concludes, the standard inductive method will be successful *if any other method could succeed.* As a result, we have everything to gain and nothing to lose by adopting the inductive method. If any method works, induction works. If we adopt the inductive method and it fails, we have lost nothing, for any other method we might have adopted would likewise have failed. Reichenbach does not claim to prove that nature is uniform, or that the standard inductive method will be successful. He does not postulate the uniformity of nature. He tries to show that the inductive method is the best method for ampliative inference, whether it turns out to be successful or not.

This ingenious argument, although extremely suggestive, is ultimately unsatisfactory. As I have just presented it, it is impossibly vague. I have not specified the nature of the standard inductive method. I have not stated with any exactness what constitutes success for the inductive method or any other. Moreover, the uniformity of nature is not an all-or-none affair. Nature appears to be uniform to some extent and also to be lacking in uniformity to some degree. As we have already seen, it is not easy to state a principle of uniformity that is strong enough to assure the success of inductive inference and weak enough to be plausible. The vagueness of the foregoing argument is not, however, its fundamental drawback. It can be made precise, and I shall do so below in connection with the discussion of the frequency interpretation of probability.[39] When it is made precise, . . . it suffers the serious defect of equally justifying too wide a variety of rules for ampliative inference.

I have presented Reichenbach's argument rather loosely in order to make intuitively clear its basic strategy. The sense in which it is a pragmatic justification should be clear. Unlike many authors who have sought a justification of induction, Reichenbach does not try to prove the truth of any synthetic proposition. He recognizes that the problem concerns the justification of a rule, and rules are neither true nor false. Hence, he tries to show that the adoption of a standard inductive rule is practically useful in the attempt to learn about and deal with the unobserved. He maintains that this can be shown even though we cannot prove the truth of the assertion that inductive methods will lead to predictive success. This pragmatic aspect is, it seems to me, the source of the fertility of Reichenbach's approach. Even though his argument does not constitute an adequate justification of induction, it seems to me to provide a valid core from which we may attempt to develop a more satisfactory justification.

III. Significance of the Problem

Hume's problem of induction evokes, understandably, a wide variety of reactions. It is not difficult to appreciate the response of the man engaged in active scientific research or practical affairs who says, in effect, "Don't bother me with these silly puzzles; I'm too busy doing science, building bridges, or managing affairs of state." No one, including Hume, seriously suggests any suspension of scientific investigation or practical decision pending a solution of the problem of induction. The problem concerns the *foundations* of science. As Hume eloquently remarks in *Enquiry Concerning Human Understanding:*

> Let the course of things be allowed hitherto ever so regular; that alone, without some new argument or inference, proves not that, for the future, it will continue so. In vain do you pretend to have learned the nature of bodies from your past experience. Their secret nature, and consequently all their effects and influence, may change, without any change in their sensible qualities. This happens sometimes, and with regard to some objects: Why may it not happen always, and with regard to all objects? What logic, what process of argument secures you against this supposition? My practice, you say, refutes my doubts. But you mistake the purport of my question. As an agent, I am quite satis-

> fied in the point; but as a philosopher, who has some share of curiosity, I will not say scepticism, I want to learn the foundation of this inference.

We should know by now that the foundations of a subject are usually established long after the subject has been well developed, not before. To suppose otherwise would be a glaring example of "naïve first-things-firstism."[40]

Nevertheless, there is something intellectually disquieting about a serious gap in the foundations of a discipline, and it is especially disquieting when the discipline in question is so broad as to include the whole of empirical science, all of its applications, and indeed, all of common sense. As human beings we pride ourselves on rationality—so much so that for centuries rationality was enshrined as the very essence of humanity and the characteristic that distinguishes man from the lower brutes. Questionable as such pride may be, our intellectual consciences should be troubled by a gaping lacuna in the structure of our knowledge and the foundations of scientific inference. I do not mean to suggest that the structure of empirical science is teetering because of foundational difficulties; the architectural metaphor is really quite inappropriate. I do suggest that intellectual integrity requires that foundational problems not be ignored.

Each of two opposing attitudes has its own immediate appeal. One of these claims that the scientific method is so obviously the correct method that there is no need to waste our time trying to show that this is so. There are two difficulties. First, we have enough painful experience to know that the appeal to obviousness is dangerously likely to be an appeal to prejudice and superstition. What is obvious to one age or culture may well turn out, on closer examination, to be just plain false. Second, if the method of science is so obviously superior to other methods we might adopt, then I should think we ought to be able to point to those characteristics of the method by which it gains its obvious superiority.

The second tempting attitude is one of pessimism. In the face of Hume's arguments and the failure of many attempts to solve the problem, it is easy to conclude that the problem is hopeless. Whether motivated by Hume's arguments or, as is probably more often the case, by simple impatience with foundational problems, this attitude seems quite widespread. It is often expressed by the formula that science is, at bottom, a matter of faith. While it is no part of my purpose to launch a wholesale attack on faith as such, this attitude toward the foundations of scientific inference is unsatisfactory. The crucial fact is that science makes a *cognitive claim,* and this cognitive claim is a fundamental part of the rationale for doing science at all. Hume has presented us with a serious challenge to that cognitive claim. If we cannot legitimize the cognitive claim, it is difficult to see what reason remains for doing science. Why not turn to voodoo, which would be simpler, cheaper, less time consuming, and more fun?

If science is basically a matter of faith, then the scientific faith exists on a par with other faiths. Although we may be culturally conditioned to accept this faith, others are not. Science has no ground on which to maintain its *cognitive* superiority to any form of irrationalism, however repugnant. This situation is, it seems to me, intellectually and socially undesirable. We have had enough experience with various forms of irrationalism to recognize the importance of being able to distinguish them logically from genuine science. I find it intolerable to suppose that a theory of biological evolution, supported as it is by extensive scientific evidence, has no more rational foundation than has its rejection by ignorant fundamentalists. I, too, have faith that the scientific method is especially well suited for establishing knowledge of the unobserved, but I believe this faith should be justified. It seems to me extremely important that some people should earnestly seek a solution to this problem concerning the foundations of scientific inference.

One cannot say in advance what consequences will follow from a solution to a foundational problem. It would seem to depend largely upon the nature of the solution. But a discipline with well-laid foundations is surely far more satisfactory than one whose foundations are in doubt. We have only to compare the foundationally insecure calculus of the seventeenth and eighteenth centuries with the calculus of the late nineteenth century to appreciate the gains in elegance, simplicity, and rigor. Furthermore, the foundations of calculus provided a basis for a number of other developments, interesting in their own right and *greatly extending the power and fertility of the original theory*. Whether similar extensions will occur as a result of a satisfactory resolution of Hume's problem is a point on which it would be rash to hazard any prediction, but we know from experience that important consequences result from the most unexpected sources. The subsequent discussion of the foundations of probability will indicate directions in which some significant consequences may be found, but for the moment it will suffice to note that a serious concern for the solution of Hume's problem cannot fail to deepen our understanding of the nature of scientific inference. This, after all, is the ultimate goal of the whole enterprise.

Notes

This book *[The Foundations of Scientific Inference]* is based upon five lectures in the Philosophy of Science Series at the University of Pittsburgh. The first two lectures, *Foundations of Scientific Inference:* I. *The Problem of Induction,* II. *Probability and Induction,* were presented in March 1963. The next two lectures, *Inductive Inference in Science:* I. *Hypothetico-Deductive Arguments,* II. *Plausibility Arguments,* were delivered in October 1964. The final lecture, *A Priori Knowledge,* was given in October 1965. The author wishes to express his gratitude to the National Science Foundation and the Minnesota Center for Philosophy of Science for support of research on inductive logic and probability.

1. David Hume, *Enquiry Concerning Human Understanding,* see IV, I.
2. Ibid.
3. For a more detailed account of the relation between deductive validity and factual content, see p. 24.
4. The problem of the synthetic a priori is discussed earlier, in sec. II, 4, pp. 27–40 [of Salmon's *Foundations of Scientific Inference,* from which this selection is excerpted].
5. Hume, *Human Understanding.*
6. Ibid.
7. Max Black, *Problems of Analysis* (Ithaca: Cornell University Press, 1954), Chap. 11.
8. Ibid., pp. 196–97.
9. Lewis Carroll, "What the Tortoise Said to Achilles," in *The Complete Works of Lewis Carroll* (New York: Random House, n.d.).
10. I presented the following self-supporting argument for the counterinductive method in "Should We Attempt to Justify Induction?" *Philosophical Studies,* 8 (April 1957), pp. 45–47. Max Black in "Self-supporting Inductive Arguments," *Models and Metaphors* (Ithaca: Cornell University Press, 1962), Chap. 12, replies to my criticism, but he does not succeed in shaking the basic point: The counterinductive rule is related to its self-supporting argument in precisely the same way as the standard inductive rule is related to its self-supporting argument. This is the "cash value" of claiming that the self-supporting argument is circular. Peter Achinstein, "The Circularity of a Self-supporting Inductive Argument," *Analysis,* 22 (June 1962), considers neither my formulation nor Black's answer sufficient, so he makes a further attempt to show circularity. Black's reply is found in "Self-Support and Circularity: A Reply to Mr. Achinstein," *Analysis,* 23 (December 1962). Achinstein's rejoinder is "Circularity and Induction," *Analysis,* 23 (June 1963).
11. Max Black, "The Justification of Induction," *Language and Philosophy* (Ithaca: Cornell University Press, 1949), Chap. 3. The view he expresses in this essay, I believe, is closely related to the "probabilistic approach" I discuss in sec. II, 7, pp. 280–82.
12. Max Black, *Problems of Analysis,* p. 191.
13. Ibid., p. 206.
14. Compare Richard Bevan Braithwaite, *Scientific Explanation* (New York: Harper & Row, 1960), Chap. 8. I think the same general view is to be found in A. J. Ayer, *The Problem of Knowledge* (Baltimore: Penguin Books, 1956), p. 75. I have discussed Ayer's view in "The Concept of Inductive Evidence," *American Philosophical Quarterly,* 2 (October 1965).
15. See Braithwaite for a systematic exposition of this conception.
16. Sec. VII, pp. 108–31 [of Salmon's *Foundations of Scientific Inference*]. "The Confirmation of Scientific Hypotheses" is devoted to a detailed analysis of this type of inference.
17. See John Patrick Day, *Inductive Probability* (New York: Humanities Press, 1961), p. 6. The nineteenth-century notion that induction is a process of discovery and the problem of whether there can be a logic of discovery are discussed earlier in sec. VII, pp. 109–14 [of Salmon's *Foundations of Scientific Inference.*]
18. See e.g., Karl R. Popper, *The Logic of Scientific Discovery* (New York: Basic Books, 1959), sec. 30, and Thomas S. Kuhn, *The Structure of Scientific Revolutions* (Chicago: University of Chicago Press, 1962). A fuller discussion of the relations among such concepts as deductive validity and content is given earlier in sec. II, 4, especially p. 33 [of Salmon's *Foundations of Scientific Inference*].
19. The most comprehensive statement of Popper's position is to be found in *The Logic of Scientific Discovery.* This is the English translation, with additions, of Karl R. Popper, *Logik der Forschung* (Vienna, 1934).
20. "I think that we shall have to get accustomed to

the idea that we must not look upon science as a 'body of knowledge,' but rather as a system of hypotheses; that is to say, a system of guesses or anticipations which in principle cannot be justified, but with which we work as long as they stand up to tests, and of which we are never justified in saying that we know that they are 'true' or 'more or less certain' or even 'probable.' " *The Logic of Scientific Discovery,* p. 317.

21. I believe Popper openly acknowledges the nonampliative character of deduction. See "Why Are the Calculi of Logic and Arithmetic Applicable to Reality," in Karl R. Popper, *Conjectures and Refutations* (New York: Basic Books, 1962), Chap. 9.
22. See *The Logic of Scientific Discovery,* Chap. 10.
23. Ibid., p. 270.
24. I . . . return to Popper's methodological views in the discussion of confirmation in sec. VII [of *Foundations of Scientific Inference.*] In that context I shall exhibit what I take to be the considerable valid content of Popper's account of the logic of science. See pp. 114–21.
25. David Hume, *Human Understanding,* sec. IV.
26. Ibid.
27. Ibid.
28. Ibid.
29. Ibid.
30. Ibid.
31. Ibid.
32. Wesley C. Salmon, "The Uniformity of Nature," *Philosophy and Phenomenological Research,* 14 (September 1953).
33. Max Black, "The Justification of Induction," in *Language and Philosophy.*
34. Among the authors who subscribe to approaches similar to this are A. J. Ayer, *Language, Truth and Logic* (New York: Dover Publications, 1952); Paul Edwards, "Russell's Doubts about Induction," *Mind,* 58 (1949), pp. 141–63; Asher Moore, "The Principle of Induction," *Journal of Philosophy,* 49 (1952), pp. 741–58; Arthur Pap, *Elements of Analytic Philosophy* (New York: Macmillan, 1949), and *An Introduction to the Philosophy of Science;* and P. F. Strawson, *Introduction to Logical Theory* (London: Methuen, 1952).
35. I have criticized this type of argument at some length in "Should We Attempt To Justify Induction?" *Philosophical Studies,* 8 (April 1957), and in "The Concept of Inductive Evidence," *American Philosophical Quarterly,* 2 (October 1965). This latter article is part of a "Symposium on Inductive Evidence" in which Stephen Barker and Henry E. Kyburg, Jr., defend against the attack. See their comments and my rejoinder.
36. This point has enormous import for any attempt to construct an inductive justification of induction. To decide whether the fact that induction has been successful in the past is positive evidence, negative evidence, or no evidence at all begs the very question at issue.
37. As I attempted to show in "Should We Attempt to Justify Induction?" this equivocation seems to arise out of a failure to distinguish *validation* and *vindication.* This crucial distinction is explicated by Herbert Feigl, "De Principiis non Disputandum . . . ?" in *Philosophical Analysis,* ed. Max Black (Ithaca: Cornell U. Press, 1950).
38. Hans Reichenbach, *Experience and Prediction* (Chicago: University of Chicago Press, 1938), Chap. 5, and *The Theory of Probability* (Berkeley: University of California Press, 1949), Chap. 11.
39. Sec. V, 5, pp. 83–96 [of Salmon's *Foundations of Scientific Inference*].
40. Leonard J. Savage, *The Foundations of Statistics* (New York: Wiley, 1954), p. 1.

Laws and Their Role in Scientific Explanation

CARL G. HEMPEL

Carl G. Hempel (1905-) is Emeritus Stuart Professor at Princeton and a professor of philosophy at the University of Pittsburgh. His publications include *Fundamentals of Concept Formation in Empirical Science, Aspects of Scientific Explanation,* and *Philosophy of Natural Science.*

Two Basic Requirements for Scientific Explanations

To explain the phenomena of the physical world is one of the primary objectives of the natural sciences. Indeed, almost all of the scientific investigations that served as illustrations in the preceding chapters were aimed not at ascertaining some particular fact but at achieving some explanatory insight; they were concerned with questions such as how puerperal fever is contracted, why the water-lifting capacity of pumps has its characteristic limitation, why the transmission of light conforms to the laws of geometrical optics, and so forth. In this chapter . . . we will examine in some detail the character of scientific explanations and the kind of insight they afford.

That man has long and persistently been concerned to achieve some understanding of the enormously diverse, often perplexing, and sometimes threatening occurrences in the world around him is shown by the manifold myths and metaphors he has devised in an effort to account for the very existence of the world and of himself, for life and death, for the motions of the heavenly bodies, for the regular sequence of day and night, for the changing seasons, for thunder and lightning, sunshine and rain. Some of these explanatory ideas are based on anthropomorphic conceptions of the forces of nature, others invoke hidden powers or agents, still others refer to God's inscrutable plans or to fate.

Accounts of this kind undeniably may give the questioner a sense of having attained some understanding; they may resolve his perplexity and in this sense "answer" his question. But however satisfactory these answers may be psychologically, they are not adequate for the purposes of science, which, after all, is concerned to develop a conception of the world that has a clear, logical bearing on our experience and is thus capable of objective test. Scientific explanations must, for this reason, meet two systematic requirements, which will be called the requirement of explanatory relevance and the requirement of testability.

The astronomer Francesco Sizi offered the following argument to show why, contrary to what his contemporary, Galileo, claimed to have seen through his telescope, there could be no satellites circling around Jupiter:

> There are seven windows in the head, two nostrils, two ears, two eyes and a mouth; so in the heavens there are two favorable stars, two unpropitious, two luminaries, and Mercury alone undecided and indifferent. From which and many other similar phenomena of nature such as the seven metals, etc., which

Chapter 5 from *Philosophy of Natural Science* (Englewood Cliffs, N.J.: Prentice-Hall, 1966), pp. 47–69.

> it were tedious to enumerate, we gather that the number of planets is necessarily seven. . . . Moreover, the satellites are invisible to the naked eye and therefore can have no influence on the earth and therefore would be useless and therefore do not exist.[1]

The crucial defect of this argument is evident: the "facts" it adduces, even if accepted without question, are entirely irrelevant to the point at issue; they do not afford the slightest reason for the assumption that Jupiter has no satellites; the claim of relevance suggested by the barrage of words like "therefore", "it follows", and "necessarily" is entirely spurious.

Consider by contrast the physical explanation of a rainbow. It shows that the phenomenon comes about as a result of the reflection and refraction of the white light of the sun in spherical droplets of water such as those that occur in a cloud. By reference to the relevant optical laws, this account shows that the appearance of a rainbow is to be expected whenever a spray of mist of water droplets is illuminated by a strong white light behind the observer. Thus, even if we happened never to have seen a rainbow, the explanatory information provided by the physical account would constitute good grounds for expecting or believing that a rainbow will appear under the specified circumstances. We will refer to this characteristic by saying that the physical explanation meets the *requirement of explanatory relevance:* the explanatory information adduced affords good grounds for believing that the phenomenon to be explained did, or does, indeed occur. This condition must be met if we are to be entitled to say: "That explains it—the phenomenon in question was indeed to be expected under the circumstances!"

The requirement represents a necessary condition for an adequate explanation, but not a sufficient one. For example, a large body of data showing a red-shift in the spectra of distant galaxies provides strong grounds for believing *that* those galaxies recede from our local one at enormous speeds, yet it does not explain *why.*

To introduce the second basic requirement for scientific explanations, let us consider once more the conception of gravitational attraction as manifesting a natural tendency akin to love. As we noted earlier, this conception has no test implications whatever. Hence, no empirical finding could possibly bear it out or disconfirm it. Being thus devoid of empirical content, the conception surely affords no grounds for expecting the characteristic phenomena of gravitational attraction: it lacks objectivie explanatory power. Similar comments apply to explanations in terms of an inscrutable fate: to invoke such an idea is not to achieve an especially profound insight, but to give up the attempt at explanation altogether. By contrast, the statements on which the physical explanation of a rainbow is based do have various test implications; these concern, for example, the conditions under which a rainbow will be seen in the sky, and the order of the colors in it; the appearance of rainbow phenomena in the spray of a wave breaking on the rocks and in the mist of a lawn sprinkler; and so forth. These examples illustrate a second condition for scientific explanations, which we will call the *requirement of testability:* the statements constituting a scientific explanation must be capable of empirical test.

It has already been suggested that since the conception of gravitation in terms of an underlying universal affinity has no test implications, it can have no explanatory power: it cannot provide grounds for expecting that universal gravitation will occur, nor that gravitational attraction will show such and such characteristic features; for if it did imply such consequences either deductively or even in a weaker, inductive-probabilistic sense, then it would be testable by reference to those consequences. As this example shows, the two requirements just considered are interrelated: a proposed explanation that meets the requirement of relevance also meets the requirement of testability. (The converse clearly does not hold.)

Now let us see what forms scientific explanations take, and how they meet the two basic requirements.

Deductive-Nomological Explanation

Consider . . . Périer's finding in the Puy-de-Dôme experiment, that the length of the mercury column in a Torricelli barometer decreased with increasing altitude. Torricelli and Pascal's ideas on atmospheric pressure provided an explanation for this phenomenon; somewhat pedantically, it can be spelled out as follows:

(a) At any location, the pressure that the mercury column in the closed branch of the Torricelli apparatus exerts upon the mercury below equals the pressure exerted on the surface of the mercury in the open vessel by the column of air above it.

(b) The pressures exerted by the columns of mercury and of air are proportional to their weights; and the shorter the columns, the smaller their weights.

(c) As Périer carried the apparatus to the top of the mountain, the column of air above the open vessel became steadily shorter.

(d) [Therefore,] the mercury column in the closed vessel grew steadily shorter during the ascent.

Thus formulated, the explanation is an argument to the effect that the phenomenon to be explained, as described by the sentence *(d)*, is just what is to be expected in view of the explanatory facts cited in *(a)*, *(b)*, and *(c)*; and that, indeed, *(d)* follows deductively from the explanatory statements. The latter are of two kinds; *(a)* and *(b)* have the character of general laws expressing uniform empirical connections; whereas *(c)* describes certain particular facts. Thus, the shortening of the mercury column is here explained by showing that it occurred in accordance with certain laws of nature, as a result of certain particular circumstances. The explanation fits the phenomenon to be explained into a pattern of uniformities and shows that its occurrence was to be expected, given the specified laws and the pertinent particular circumstances.

The phenomenon to be accounted for by an explanation will henceforth also be referred to as the *explanandum phenomenon;* the sentence describing it, as the *explanandum sentence*. When the context shows which is meant, either of them will simply be called the explanandum. The sentences specifying the explanatory information—*(a)*, *(b)*, *(c)* in our example—will be called the *explanans sentences;* jointly they will be said to form the *explanans*.

As a second example, consider the explanation of a characteristic of image formation by reflection in a spherical mirror; namely, that generally $1/u + 1/v = 2/r$, where u and v are the distances of object-point and image-point from the mirror, and r is the mirror's radius of curvature. In geometrical optics, this uniformity is explained with the help of the basic law of reflection in a plane mirror, by treating the reflection of a beam of light at any one point of a spherical mirror as a case of reflection in a plane tangential to the spherical surface. The resulting explanation can be formulated as a deductive argument whose conclusion is the explanandum sentence, and whose premisses include the basic laws of reflection and of rectilinear propagation, as well as the statement that the surface of the mirror forms a segment of a sphere.[2]

A similar argument, whose premisses again include the law for reflection in a plane mirror, offers an explanation of why the light of a small light source placed at the focus of a paraboloidal mirror is reflected in a beam parallel to the axis of the paraboloid (a principle technologically applied in the construction of automobile headlights, searchlights, and other devices).

The explanations just considered may be conceived, then, as deductive arguments whose conclusion is the explanandum sentence, E, and whose premiss-set, the explanans, consists of general laws, $L_1, L_2, \ldots, L_r$ and of other statements, $C_1, C_2, \ldots, C_k$, which make assertions about particular facts. The form of such arguments, which thus constitute one type of scientific explanation, can be represented by the following schema:

$$\text{(D-N)} \quad \left.\begin{array}{c} L_1, L_2, \ldots, L_r \\ C_1, C_2, \ldots, C_k \end{array}\right\} \text{Explanans sentences}$$
$$\overline{\qquad E \qquad} \quad \text{Explanandum sentence}$$

Explanatory accounts of this kind will be called explanations by deductive subsumption under general laws, or *deductive-nomological explanations*. (The root of the term 'nomological' is the Greek word 'nomos', for law.) The laws invoked in a scientific explanation will also be called *covering laws* for the explanandum phenomenon, and the explanatory argument will be said to subsume the explanandum under those laws.

The explanandum phenomenon in a deductive-nomological explanation may be an event occurring at a particular place and time, such as the outcome of Périer's experiment. Or it may be some regularity found in nature, such as certain characteristics generally displayed by rainbows; or a uniformity expressed by an empirical law such as Galileo's or Kepler's laws. Deductive explanations of such uniformities will then invoke laws of broader scope, such as the laws of reflection and refraction, or Newton's laws of motion and of gravitation. As this use of Newton's laws illustrates, empirical laws are often explained by means of theoretical principles that refer to structures and processes underlying the uniformities in question. We will return to such explanations in the next chapter.

Deductive-nomological explanations satisfy the requirement of explanatory relevance in the strongest possible sense: the explanatory information they provide implies the explanandum sentence deductively and thus offers logically conclusive grounds why the explanandum phenomenon is to be expected. (We will soon encounter other scientific explanations, which fulfill the requirement only in a weaker, inductive, sense.) And the testability requirement is met as well, since the explanans implies among other things that under the specified conditions, the explanandum phenomenon occurs.

Some scientific explanations conform to the pattern (D-N) quite closely. This is so, particularly, when certain quantitative features of a phenomenon are explained by mathematical derivation from covering general laws, as in the case of reflection in spherical and paraboloidal mirrors. Or take the celebrated explanation, propounded by Leverrier (and independently by Adams), of peculiar irregularities in the motion of the planet Uranus, which on the current Newtonian theory could not be accounted for by the gravitational attraction of the other planets then known. Leverrier conjectured that they resulted from the gravitational pull of an as yet undetected outer planet, and he computed the position, mass, and other characterisitcs which that planet would have to possess to account in quantitative detail for the observed irregularities. His explanation was strikingly confirmed by the discovery, at the predicted location, of a new planet, Neptune, which had the quantitative characteristics attributed to it by Leverrier. Here again, the explanation has the character of a deductive argument whose premisses include general laws—specifically, Newton's laws of gravitation and of motion—as well as statements specifying various quantitative particulars about the disturbing planet.

Not infrequently, however, deductive-nomological explanations are stated in an elliptical form: they omit mention of certain assumptions that are presupposed by the explanation but are simply taken for granted in the given context. Such explanations are sometimes expressed in the form *'E* because *C'*, where *E* is the event to be explained and *C* is some antecedent or concomitant event or state of affairs. Take, for example, the statement: 'The slush on the sidewalk remained liquid during the frost because it had been sprinkled with salt'. This explanation does not explicitly mention any laws, but it tacitly presupposes at least one: that the freezing point of water is lowered whenever salt is dissolved in it. Indeed, it is precisely by virtue of this law that the sprinkling of salt acquires the explanatory, and specifically causative, role that the elliptical because-statement ascribes to it. That statement, incidentally, is elliptical also in other respects; for example, it tacitly takes for granted, and leaves unmentioned, certain assumptions about the prevailing physical conditions, such as the temperature's not dropping to a very low point. And if nomic and other assumptions thus omitted are added to the statement that salt had been sprinkled on the slush, we obtain the premisses for a deductive-nomological explanation of the fact that the slush remained liquid.

Similar comments apply to Semmelweis's explanation that childbed fever was caused by decomposed animal matter introduced into the bloodstream through open wound surfaces. Thus formulated, the explanation makes no mention of general laws; but it presupposes that such contamination of the bloodstream generally leads to blood poisoning attended by the characteristic symptoms of childbed fever, for this is implied by the assertion that the contamination *causes* puerperal fever. The generalization was no doubt taken for granted by Semmelweis, to whom the cause of Kolletschka's fatal illness presented no etiological problem: given that infectious matter was introduced into the bloodstream, blood poisoning would result. (Kolletschka was by no means the first one to die of blood poisoning resulting from a cut with an infected scalpel. And by a tragic irony, Semmelweis himself was to suffer the same fate.) But once the tacit premiss is made explicit, the explanation is seen to involve reference to general laws.

As the preceding examples illustrate, corresponding general laws are always presupposed by an explanatory statement to the effect that a particular event of a certain kind *G* (e.g., expansion of a gas under constant pressure; flow of a current in a wire loop) was *caused* by an event of another kind, *F* (e.g., heating of the gas; motion of the loop across a magnetic field). To see this, we need not enter into the complex ramifications of the notion of cause; it suffices to note that the general maxim "Same cause, same effect", when applied to such explanatory statements, yields the implied claim that whenever an event of kind *F* occurs, it is accompanied by an event of kind *G*.

To say that an explanation rests on general laws is not to say that its discovery required the discovery of the laws. The crucial new insight achieved by an explanation will sometimes lie in the discovery of some particular fact (e.g., the presence of an undetected outer planet; infectious matter adhering to the hands of examining physicians) which, by virtue of antecedently accepted general laws, accounts for the explanandum phenomenon. In other cases, such as that of the lines in the hydrogen spectrum, the explanatory achievement does lie in the discovery of a covering law (Balmer's) and eventually of an explanatory theory (such as Bohr's); in yet other cases, the major accomplishment of an explanation may lie in showing that, and exactly how, the explanandum phenomenon can be accounted for by reference to laws and data about particular facts that are already available: this is illustrated by the explanatory derivation of the reflection laws for spherical and paraboloidal mirrors from the basic law of geometrical optics in conjunction with statements about the geometrical characteristics of the mirrors.

An explanatory problem does not by itself determine what kind of discovery is required for its solution. Thus, Leverrier discovered deviations from the theoretically expected course also in the motion of the planet Mercury; and as in the case of Uranus, he tried to explain these as resulting from the gravitational pull of an as yet undetected planet, Vulcan, which would have to be a very dense and very small object between the sun and Mercury. But no such planet was found, and a satisfactory explanation was provided only much later by the general theory of relativity, which accounted for the irregularities not by reference to some disturbing particular factor, but by means of a new system of laws.

Universal Laws and Accidental Generalizations

As we have seen, laws play an essential role in deductive-nomological explanations. They provide the link by reason of which particular circumstances (described by $C_1, C_2, \ldots, C_k$) can serve to explain the occurrence of a given event. And when the explanandum is not a particular event, but a uniformity such as those represented by characteristics mentioned earlier of spherical and paraboloidal mirrors, the explanatory laws exhibit a system of more comprehensive uniformities, of which the given one is but a special case.

The laws required for deductive-nomological explanations share a basic characteristic: they are, as we shall say, statements of universal form. Broadly speaking, a statement of this kind asserts a uniform connection between different empirical phenomena or between different aspects of an empirical phenomenon. It is a statement to the effect that whenever and wherever conditions of a specified kind *F* occur, then so will, always and without exception, certain conditions of another kind, *G*. (Not all scientific laws are of this type. In the sections that follow, we will encounter laws of probabilistic form, and explanations based on them.)

Here are some examples of statements of universal form: whenever the temperature of a gas increases while its pressure remains constant, its volume increases; whenever a solid is dissolved in a liquid, the boiling point of the liquid is raised; whenever a ray of light is reflected at a plane surface, the angle of reflection equals the angle of incidence; whenever a magnetic iron rod is broken in two, the pieces are magnets again; whenever a body falls freely from rest in a vacuum near the surface of the earth, the distance it covers in t seconds is $16t^2$ feet. Most of the laws of the natural sciences are quantitative: they assert specific mathematical connections between different quantitative characteristics of physical systems (e.g., between volume, temperature, and pressure of a gas) or of processes (e.g., between time and distance in free fall in Galileo's law; between the period of revolution of a planet and its mean distance from the sun, in Kepler's third law; between the angles of incidence and refraction in Snell's law).

Strictly speaking, a statement asserting some uniform connection will be considered a law only if there are reasons to assume it is true: we would not normally speak of false laws of nature. But if this requirement were rigidly observed, then the statements commonly referred to as Galileo's and Kepler's laws would not qualify as laws; for according to current physical knowledge, they hold only approximately; and . . . physical theory explains why this is so. Analogous remarks apply to the laws of geometrical optics. For example, even in a homogeneous medium, light does not move strictly in straight lines: it can bend around corners. We shall therefore use the word 'law' somewhat liberally, applying the term also to certain statements of the kind here referred to, which, on theoretical grounds, are known to hold only approximatley and with certain qualifications. . . .

We saw that the laws invoked in deductive-nomological explanations have the basic form: 'In all cases when conditions of kind *F* are realized, conditions of kind *G* are realized as well'. But, interestingly, not all statements of this universal form, even if true, can qualify as laws of nature. For example, the sentence 'All rocks in this box contain iron' is of universal form (*F* is the condition of being a rock in the box, *G* that of containing iron); yet even if true, it would not be regarded as a law, but as an assertion of something that "happens to be the case," as an "accidental generalization." Or consider the statement: 'All bodies consisting of pure gold have a mass of less than 100,000 kilograms'. No doubt all bodies of gold ever examined by man conform to it; thus, there is considerable confirmatory evidence for it and no disconfirming instances are known. Indeed, it is quite possible that never in the history of the universe has there been or will there be a body of pure gold with a mass of 100,000 kilograms or more. In this case, the proposed generalization would not only be well confirmed, but true. And yet, we would presumably regard its truth as accidental, on the ground that nothing in the basic laws of nature as conceived in contemporary science precludes the possibility of there being—or even the possibility of our producing—a solid gold object with a mass exceeding 100,000 kilograms.

Thus, a scientific law cannot be adequately defined as a true statement of universal form: this characterization expresses a necessary, but not a sufficient, condition for laws of the kind here under discussion.

What distinguishes genuine laws from accidental generalizations? This intriguing problem has been intensively discussed in recent years. Let us look briefly at some of the principal ideas that have emerged from the debate, which is still continuing.

One telling and suggestive difference, noted by Nelson Goodman,[3] is this: a law can, whereas an accidental generalization cannot, serve to support *counterfactual conditionals,* i.e., statements of the form 'If *A* were (had been) the case, then *B* would be (would have been) the case', where in fact *A* is not (has not been) the case. Thus, the assertion 'If this paraffin candle had been put into a kettle of boiling water, it would have melted' could be supported by adducing the law that paraffin is liquid above 60 degrees centrigrade (and the fact that the boiling point of water is 100 degrees centigrade). But the statement 'All rocks in this box contain iron' could not be used similarly to support the counterfactual statement 'If this pebble had been put into the box, it would contain iron'. Similarly, a law, in contrast to an accidentally true generalization, can support *subjunctive conditionals,* i.e., sentences of the type 'If *A* should come to pass, then so would *B*', where it is left open whether or not *A* will in fact come to pass. The statement 'If this paraffin candle should be put into boiling water then it would melt' is an example.

Closely related to this difference is another one, which is of special interest to us: a law can, whereas an accidental generalization cannot, serve as a basis for an explanation. Thus, the melting of a particular paraffin candle that was put into boiling water can be explained, in conformity with the schema (D-N), by reference to the particular facts just mentioned and to the law that paraffin melts when its temperature is raised above 60 degrees centigrade. But the fact that a particular rock in the box contains iron cannot be analogously explained by reference to the general statement that all rocks in the box contain iron.

It might seem plausible to say, by way of a further distinction, that the latter statement simply serves as a conveniently brief formulation of a finite conjunction of this kind: 'Rock r_1 contains iron, and the rock r_2 contains iron, . . . , and rock r_{63} contains iron'; whereas the generalization about paraffin refers to a potentially infinte set of particular cases and therefore cannot be paraphrased by a finite conjunction of statements describing individual instances. This distinction is suggestive, but it is overstated. For to begin with, the generalization 'All rocks in this box contain iron' does not in fact tell us how many rocks there are in the box, nor does it name any particular rocks r_1, r_2, etc. Hence, the general sentence is not logically equivalent to a finite conjunction of the kind just mentioned. To formulate a suitable conjunction, we need additional information, which might be obtained by counting and labeling the rocks in the box. Besides, our generalization 'All bodies of pure gold have a mass of less than 100,000 kilograms' would not count as a law even if there were infinitely many bodies of gold in the world. Thus, the criterion we have under consideration fails on several grounds.

Finally, let us note that a statement of universal form may qualify as a law even if it actually has no instances whatever. As an example, consider the sentence: 'On any celestial body that has the same radius as the earth but twice its mass, free fall from rest conforms to the formula $s = 32t^2$'. There might well be no celestial object in the entire universe that has the specified size and mass, and yet the statement has the character of a law. For it (or rather, a close approximation of it, as in the case of Galileo's law) follows from the Newtonian theory of gravitation and of motion in conjunction with the statement that the acceleration of free fall on the earth is 32 feet per second per second; thus, it has strong theoretical support, just like our earlier law for free fall on the moon.

A law, we noted, can support subjunctive and counterfactual conditional statements about potential instances, i.e., about particular cases that might occur, or that might have occurred but did not. In similar fashion, Newton's theory supports our general statement in a subjunctive version that suggests its lawlike status, namely: 'On any celestial body that there may be which has the same size as the earth but twice its mass, free fall would conform to the formula $s = 32t^2$'. By contrast, the generalization about the rocks cannot be paraphrased as asserting that any rock that might be in this box would contain iron, nor of course would this latter claim have any theoretical support.

Similarly, we would not use our generalization about the mass of gold bodies—let us call it *H*—to support statements such as this: 'Two bodies of pure gold whose individual masses add up to more than 100,000 kilograms cannot be fused to form one body; or if fusion should be possible, then the mass of the resulting body will be less than 100,000 kg', for the basic physical and chemical theories of matter that are currently accepted do not preclude the kind of fusion here considered, and they do not imply that there would be a mass loss of the sort here referred to. Hence, even if the generalization *H* should be true, i.e., if no exceptions to it should ever occur, this would constitute a mere accident or coincidence as judged by current theory, which permits the occurrence of exceptions to *H*.

Thus, whether a statement of universal form counts as a law will depend in part upon the scientific theories accepted at the time. This is not to say that "empirical generalizations"—statements of universal form that are empirically well confirmed but have no basis in theory—never qualify as laws: Galileo's, Kepler's, and Boyle's laws, for example, were accepted as such before they received theoretical grounding. The relevance of theory is rather this: a statement of universal form, whether empirically confirmed or as yet untested, will qualify as a law if it is implied by an accepted theory (statements of this kind are often referred to as theoretical laws); but even if it is empirically well confirmed and presumably true in fact, it will not qualify as a law if it rules out certain hypothetical occurrences (such as the fusion of two gold bodies with a resulting mass of more than 100,000 kilograms, in the case of our generalization *H*) which an accepted theory qualifies as possible.[4]

Probablistic Explanation: Fundamentals

Not all scientific explanations are based on laws of strictly universal form. Thus, little Jim's getting the measles might be explained by saying that he caught the disease from his brother, who had a bad case of the measles some days earlier. This account again links the explanandum event to an earlier occurrence, Jim's exposure to the measles; the latter is said to provide an explanation because there is a connection between exposure to the measles and contracting the disease. That connection cannot be expressed by a law of universal form, however; for not every case of exposure to the measles produces contagion. What can be claimed is only that persons exposed to the measles will contract the disease with high probability, i.e., in a high percentage of all cases. General statements of this type, which we shall soon examine more closely, will be called *laws of probabilistic form* or *probabilistic laws,* for short.

In our illustration, then, the explanans consists of the probabilistic law just mentioned and the statement that Jim was exposed to the measles. In contrast to the case of deductive-nomological explanation, these explanans statements do not deductively imply the explanandum statement that Jim got the measles; for in deductive inferences from true premisses, the conclusion is invariably true, whereas in our example, it is clearly possible that the explanans statements might be true and yet the explanandum statement false. We will say, for short, that the explanans implies the explanandum, not with "deductive certainty," but only with near-certainty or with high probability.

The resulting explanatory argument may be schematized as follows . . . [:]

The probability for persons exposed to the measles to catch the disease is high.

Jim was exposed to the measles.

══════════ [makes highly probable]

Jim caught the measles.

In the customary presentation of a deductive argument, which was used, for example, in the schema (D-N) above, the conclusion is separated from the premisses by a single line, which serves to indicate that the premisses logically imply the conclusion. The double line used in our latest schema is meant to indicate analogously that the "premisses" (the explanans) make the "conclusion" (the explanandum sentence) more or less probable; the degree of probability is suggested by the notation in brackets.

Arguments of this kind will be called *probabilistic explanations.* As our discussion shows, a probabilistic explanation of a particular event shares certain basic characteristics with the corresponding deductive-nomological type of explanation. In both cases, the given event is explained by reference to others, with which the explanandum event is connected by laws. But in one case, the laws are of universal form; in the other, of probabilistic form. And while a deductive explanation shows that, on the information contained in the explanans, the explanandum was to be expected with "deductive certainty", an inductive explanation shows only that, on the information contained in the explanans, the explanandum was to be expected with high probability, and perhaps with "practical certainty"; it is in this manner that the latter argument meets the requirement of explanatory relevance.

Statistical Probabilities and Probabilistic Laws

We must now consider more closely the two differentiating features of probabilistic explanation that have just been noted: the probabilistic laws they invoke and the peculiar kind of probabilistic implication that connects the explanans with the explanandum.

Suppose that from an urn containing many balls of the same size and mass, but not necessarily of the same color, successive drawings are made. At each drawing, one ball is removed, and its color is noted. Then the ball is returned to the urn, whose contents are thoroughly mixed before the next drawing takes place. This is an example of a so-called random process or random experiment, a concept that will soon be characterized in more detail. Let us refer to the procedure just described as experiment *U*, to each drawing as one performance of U, and to the color of the ball produced by a given drawing as the result, or the outcome, of that performance.

If all the balls in an urn are white, then a statement of strictly universal form holds true of the results produced by the performance of U: every drawing from the urn yields a white ball, or yields the result W, for short. If only some of the balls—say, 600 of them—are white, whereas the others—say 400—are red, then a general statement of probabilistic form holds true of the experiment: the probability for a performance of U to produce a white ball, or outcome W, is .6; in symbols:

(5*a*) $$P(W,U) = .6$$

Similarly, the probability of obtaining heads as a result of the random experiment C of flipping a fair coin is given by

(5*b*) $$P(H,C) = .5$$

and the probability of obtaining an ace as a result of the random experiment D of rolling a regular die is

(5*c*) $$P(A,D) = 1/6$$

What do such probability statements mean? According to one familiar view, sometimes called the "classical" conception of probability, the statement (5*a*) would have to be interpreted as follows: each performance of the experiment U effects a choice of one from among 1,000 basic possibilities, or basic alternatives, each represented by one of the balls in the urn; of these possible choices, 600 are "favorable" to the outcome W; and the probability of drawing a white ball is simply the ratio of the number of favorable choices available to the number of all possible choices, i.e., 600/1,000. The classical interpretation of the probability statements (5*b*) and (5*c*) follows similar lines.

Yet this characterization is inadequate; for if before each drawing, the 400 red balls in the urn were placed on top of the white ones, then in this new kind of urn experiment—let us call it U'—the ratio of favorable to possible basic alternatives would remain the same, but the probability of drawing a white ball would be smaller than in the experiment U, in which the balls are thoroughly mixed before each drawing. The classical conception takes account of this difficulty by requiring that the basic alternatives referred to in its definition of probability must be "equipossible" or "equiprobable"—a requirement presumably violated in the case of experiment U'.

This added proviso raises the question of how to define equipossibility or equiprobability. We will pass over this notoriously troublesome and controversial issue, because—even assuming that equiprobability can be satisfactorily characterized—the classical conception would still be inadequate, since probabilities are assigned also to the outcomes of random experiments for which no plausible way is known of marking off equiprobable basic alternatives. Thus, for the random experiment D of rolling a regular die, the six faces might be regarded as representing such equiprobable alternatives; but we attribute probabilities to such results as rolling an ace, or an odd number of points, etc., also in the case of a loaded die, even though no equiprobable basic outcomes can be marked off here.

Similarly—and this is particularly important—science assigns probabilities to the outcomes of certain random experiments or random processes encountered in nature, such as the step-by-step decay of the atoms of radioactive substances, or the transition of atoms from one energy state to another. Here again, we find no equiprobable basic alternatives in terms of which such probabilities might be classically defined and computed.

To arrive at a more satisfactory construal of our probability statements, let us consider how one would ascertain the probability of the rolling of an ace with a given die that is not known to be regular. This would obviously be done by making a large number of throws with the die and ascertaining the *relative frequency*, i.e., the proportion, of those cases in which an ace turns up. If, for example, the experiment D' of rolling the given die is performed 300 times and an ace turns up in 62 cases, then the relative frequency, 62/300, would be regarded as an approximate value of the probability $p(A,D')$ of rolling an ace with the given die. Analogous procedures would be used to estimate the probabilities associated with the flipping of a given coin, the spinning of a roulette wheel, and so on. Similarly, the probabilities associated with radioactive decay, with the transitions between different atomic energy states, with genetic processes, etc., are determined by ascertaining the corresponding relative frequencies; however, this is often done in highly indirect ways rather than by simply counting individual atomic or other events of the relevant kinds.

The interpretation in terms of relative frequencies applies also to probability statements such as (5*b*) and (5*c*), which concern the results of flipping a fair (i.e., homogeneous and strictly cylindrical) coin or tossing a regular (homogeneous and strictly cubical) die: what the scientist (or the gambler, for that matter) is concerned with in making a probability statement is the relative frequency with which a certain outcome *O* can be expected in long series of repetitions of some random experiment *R*. The counting of "equiprobable" basic alternatives and of those among them which are "favorable" to *O* may be regarded as a heuristic device for guessing at the relative frequency of *O*. And indeed when a regular die or a fair coin is tossed a large number of times, the different faces tend to come up with equal frequency. One might expect this on the basis of symmetry considerations of the kind frequently used in forming physical hypotheses, for our empirical knowledge affords no grounds on which to expect any of the faces to be favored over any other. But while such considerations often are heuristically useful, they must not be regarded as certain or as self-evident truths: some very plausible symmetry assumptions, such as the principle of parity, have been found not to be generally satisfied at the subatomic level. Assumptions about equiprobabilities are therefore always subject to correction in the light of empirical data concerning the actual relative frequencies of the phenomena in question. This point is illustrated also by the statistical theories of gases developed by Bose and Einstein and by Fermi and Dirac, respectively, which rest on different assumptions concerning what distributions of particles over a phase space are equiprobable.

The probabilities specified in the probabilisitc laws, then, represent relative frequencies. They cannot, however, be strictly defined as relative frequencies in long series of repetitions of the relevant random experiment. For the proportion, say, of aces obtained in throwing a given die will change, if perhaps only slightly, as the series of throws is extended; and even in two series of exactly the same length, the number of aces will usually differ. We do find, however, that as the number of throws increases, the relative frequency of each of the different outcomes tends to change less and less, even though the results of successive throws continue to vary in an irregular and practically unpredictable fashion. This is what generally characterizes a random experiment *R* with outcomes O_1, O_2, O_n: successive performances of *R* yield one or another of those outcomes in an irregular manner; but the relative frequencies of the outcomes tend to become stable as the number of performances increases. And the probabilities of the outcomes, $p(O_1,R)$, $p(O_2,R)$, . . . $p(O_{11},R)$, may be regarded as ideal values that the actual frequencies tend to assume as they become increasingly stable. For mathematical convenience, the probabilities are sometimes defined as the mathematical *limits* toward which the relative frequencies converge as the number of performances increases indefinitely. But this definition has certain conceptual shortcomings, and in some more recent mathematical studies of the subject, the intended empirical meaning of the concept of probability is deliberately, and for good reasons, characterized more vaguely by means of the following so-called *statisitical interpretation of probability*:[5]

The statement

$$p(O,R) = r$$

means that in a long series of performances of random experiment *R*, the proportion of cases with outcome *O* is almost certain to be close to *r*.

The concept of *statistical probability* thus characterized must be carefully distingusihed from the concept of *inductive or logical probability*, which we considered [in chapter 4]. Logical probability is a quantitative logical relation between definite *statements;* the sentence

$$c(H,K) = r$$

asserts that the hypothesis *H* is supported, or made probable, to degree *r* by the evidence formulated in statement *K*. Statistical probability is a quantitative relation between repeatable *kinds of events:* a certain kind of outcome, *O*, and a certain kind of random process, *R;* it represents, roughly speaking, the relative frequency with which the result *O* tends to occur in a long series of performances of *R*.

What the two concepts have in common are their mathematical characteristics: both satisfy the basic principles of mathematical probability theory:

(a) The possible numerical values of both probabilities range from 0 to 1:

$$0 \leq p(O,R) \leq 1$$
$$0 \leq c(H,K) \leq 1$$

(b) The probability for one of two mutually exclusive outcomes of *R* to occur is the sum of the probabilities of the outcomes taken separately; the probability, on any evidence *K*, for one or the other of two mutually exclusive hypotheses to hold is the sum of their respective probabilities:

If O_1, O_2 are mutually exclusive, then
$$p(O_1 \text{ or } O_2, R) = p(O_1,R) + p(O_2,R)$$
If H_1, H_2 are logically exclusive hypotheses, then
$$c(H_1 \text{ or } H_2, K) = c(H_1,K) + c(H_2,K)$$

(c) The probability of an outcome that necessarily occurs in all cases—such as *O* or not *O*—is 1; the probability, on any evidence, of a hypothesis that is logically (and in this sense necessarily) true, such as *H* or not *H*, is 1:

$$p(O \text{ or not } O,R) = 1$$
$$c(H \text{ or not } H,K) = 1$$

Scientific hypotheses in the form of statistical probability statements can be, and are, tested by examining the long-run relative frequencies of the outcomes concerned; and the confirmation of such hypotheses is then judged, broadly speaking, in terms of the closeness of the agreement between hypothetical probabilities and observed frequencies. The logic of such tests, however, presents some intriguing special problems, which call for at least brief examination.

Consider the hypothesis, *H*, that the probability of rolling an ace with a certain die is .15; or briefly, that $p(A,D) = .15$, where *D* is the random experiment of rolling the given die. The hypothesis *H* does not deductively imply any test implications specifying how many aces will occur in a finite series of throws of the die. It does not imply, for example, that exactly 75 among the first 500 throws will yield an ace, nor even that the number of aces will lie between 50 and 100, say. Hence, if the proportion of aces actually obtained in a large number of throws differs considerably from .15, this does not refute *H* in the sense in which a hypothesis of strictly universal form, such as 'All swans are white', can be refuted, in virtue of the *modus tollens* argument, by reference to one counter-instance, such as a black swan. Similarly, if a long run of throws of the given die yields a proportion of aces very close to .15, this does not confirm *H* in the sense in which a hypothesis is confirmed by the finding that a test sentence *I* that it logically implies is in fact true. For in this latter case, the hypothesis asserts *I* by logical implication, and the test result is thus confirmatory in the sense of showing that a certain part of what the hypothesis asserts is indeed true; but nothing strictly analogous is shown for *H* by confirmatory frequency data; for *H* does *not* assert by implication that the frequency of aces in some long run will definitely be very close to .15.

But while *H* does not logically preclude the possibility that the proportion of aces obtained in a long series of throws of the given die may depart widely from .15, it does logically imply that such departures are highly improbable in the statistical sense; i.e., that if the experiment of performing a long series of throws (say, 1,000 of them per series) is repeated a large number of times, then only a tiny proportion of those long series will yield a proportion of aces that differs considerably from .15. For the case of rolling a die, it is usually assumed that the results of successive throws are "statistically independent"; this means roughly that the probability of obtaining an ace in a throw of the die does not depend on the result of the preceding throw. Mathematical analysis shows that in conjunction with this independence assumption, our hypothesis *H* deductively determines the statistical probability for the proportion of aces obtained in *n* throws to differ from .15 by no more than a specified amount. For example, *H* implies that for a series of 1,000 throws of the die here considered, the probability is about .976 that the proportion of aces will lie between .125 and .175; and similarly, that for a run of 10,000 throws the probability is about .995 that the proportion of aces will be between .14 and .16. Thus, we may say that if *H* is true, then it is practically certain that in a long trial run the observed proportion of aces will differ by very little from the hypothetical probability value .15. Hence, if the observed long-run frequency of an outcome is not close to the probability assigned to it by a given probabilistic hypothesis, then that hypothesis is very likely to be false. In this case, the frequency data count as disconfirming the hypothesis, or as reducing its credibility; and if sufficiently strong disconfirming evidence is found, the hypothesis will be considered as practically, though not logically, refuted and will accordingly be rejected. Similarly, close agreement between hypothetical probabilities and observed frequencies will tend to confirm a probabilistic hypothesis and may lead to its acceptance.

If probabilistic hypotheses are to be accepted or rejected on the basis of statistical evidence concerning observed frequencies, then appropriate standards are called for. These will have to determine *(a)* what deviations of observed frequencies from the probability stated by a hypothesis are to count as grounds for rejecting the hypothesis, and *(b)* how close an agreement between observed frequencies and hypothetical probability is to be required as a condition for accepting the hypothesis. The requirements in question can be made more or less strict, and their specification is a matter of choice. The stringency of the chosen standards will normally vary with the context and the objectives of the research in question. Broadly speaking, it will depend on the importance that is attached, in the given context, to avoiding two kinds of error that might be made: rejecting the hypothesis under test although it is true, and accepting it although it is false. The importance of this point is particularly clear when acceptance or rejection of the hypothesis is to serve as a basis for practical action. Thus, if the hypothesis concerns the probable effectiveness and safety of a new vaccine, then the decision about its acceptance will have to take into account not only how well the statistical test results accord with the probabilities specified by the hypothesis, but also how serious would be the consequences of accepting the hypothesis and acting on it (e.g., by inoculating children with the vaccine) when in fact it is false, and of rejecting the hypothesis and acting accordingly (e.g., by destroying the vaccine and modifying or discontinuing the process of manufacture) when in fact the hypothesis is true. The complex problems that arise in this context form the subject matter of the theory of statistical tests and decisions, which has been developed in recent decades on the basis of the mathematical theory of probability and statistics.[6]

Many important laws and theoretical principles in the natural sciences are of probabilistic character, though they are often of more complicated form than the simple probability statements we have discussed. For example, according to current physical theory, radioactive decay is a random phenomenon in which the atoms of each radioactive element possess a characteristic probability of disintegrating during a specified period of time. The corresponding probabilistic laws are usually formulated as statements giving the "half-life" of the element concerned. Thus, the statements that the half-life of radium^{226} is 1,620 years and that of polonium^{218} is 3.05 minutes are laws to the effect that the probability for a radium^{226} atom to decay within 1,620 years, and for an atom of polonium^{218} to decay within 3.05 minutes, are both one-half. According to the statistical interpretation cited earlier, these laws imply that of a large number of radium^{226} atoms or of polonium^{218} atoms given at a certain time, very close to one-half will still exist 1,620 years, or 3.05 minutes, later; the others having disintegrated by radioactive decay.

Again, in the kinetic theory various uniformities in the behavior of gases, including the laws of classical thermodynamics, are explained by means of certain assumptions about the constituent molecules; and some of these are probabilistic hypotheses concerning statistical regularities in the motions and collisions of those molecules.

A few additional remarks concerning the notion of a probabilistic law are indicated. It might seem that all scientific laws should be qualified as probabilistic since the supporting evidence we have for them is always a finite and logically inconclusive body of findings, which can confer upon them only a more or less high probability. But this argument misses the point that the distinction between laws of universal form and laws of probabilistic form does not refer to the strength of the evidential support for the two kinds of statements, but to their form, which reflects the logical character of the claim they make. A law of universal form is basically a statement to the effect that in *all* cases where conditions of kind F are realized, conditions of kind G are realized as well; a law of probabilistic form asserts, basically, that under certain conditions, constituting the performance of a random experiment R, a certain kind of outcome will occur in a specified percentage of cases. No matter whether true or false, well supported or poorly supported, these two types of claims are of a logically different character, and it is on this difference that our distinction is based.

As we saw earlier, a law of the universal form 'Whenever F then G' is by no means a brief, telescoped equivalent of a report stating for each occurrence of F so far examined that it was associated with an occurrence of G. Rather, it implies assertions also for all unexamined cases of F, past as well as present and future; also, it implies counter-factual and hypothetical conditionals which concern, so to speak "possible occurrences" of F: and it is just this characteristic that gives such laws their explanatory power. Laws of probabilistic form have an analogous status. The law stating that the radioactive decay of radium^{226} is a random process with an associated half-life of 1,620 years is plainly not tantamount to a report about decay rates that have been observed in certain samples of radium^{226}. It concerns the decaying process of any body of radium^{226}—past, present, or future; and it implies subjunctive and counterfactual conditionals, such as: if two particular lumps of radium^{226} were to be combined into one, the decay rates would remain the same as if the lumps had remained separate. Again, it is this characteristic that gives probabilistic laws their predictive and their explanatory force.

The Inductive Character of Probabilistic Explanation

One of the simplest kinds of probabilistic explanation is illustrated by our earlier example of Jim's catching the measles. The general form of that explanatory argument may be stated thus:

$p(0,R)$ is close to 1
i is a case of R
═══════════ [makes highly probable]
i is a case of 0

Now the high probability which, as indicated in brackets, the explanans confers upon the explanandum is surely not a statistical probability, for it characterizes a relation between sentences, not between (kinds of) events. . . . we might say that the probability in question represents the rational credibility of the explanandum, given the information provided by the explanans; and . . . , in so far as this notion can be construed as a probability, it represents a logical or inductive probability.

In some simple cases, there is a natural and obvious way of expressing that probability in numerical terms. In an argument of the kind just considered, if the numerical value of $p(O,R)$ is specified, then it is reasonable to say that the inductive probability that the explanans confers upon the explanandum has the same numerical value. The resulting probabilistic explanation has the form:

$p(0,R)=r$
i is a case of R
═══════════ [r]
i is a case of 0

If the explanans is more complex, the determination of corresponding inductive probabilities for the explanandum raises difficult problems, which in part are still unsettled. But whether or not it is possible to assign definite numerical probabilities to all such explanations, the preceding considerations show that when an event is explained by reference to probabilistic laws, the explanans confers upon the explanandum only more or less strong inductive support. Thus, we may distinguish deductive-nomological from probabilistic explanations by saying that the former effect a deductive subsumption under laws of universal form, the latter an inductive subsumption under laws of probabilistic form.

It is sometimes said that precisely because of its inductive character, a probabilistic account does not explain the occurrence of an event, since the explanans does not logically preclude its nonoccurrence. But the important, steadily expanding role that probabilistic laws and theories play in science and its applications, makes it preferable to view accounts based on such principles as affording explanations as well, though of a less stringent kind than those of deductive-nomological form. Take, for example, the radioactive decay of a sample of one milligram of polonium^{218}. Suppose that what is left of this initial amount after 3.05 minutes is found to have a mass that falls within the interval from .499 to .501 milligrams. This finding can be explained by the probabilistic law of decay for polonium^{218}; for that law, in combination with the principles of mathematical probability, deductively implies that given the huge number of atoms in a milligram of polonium^{218}, the probability of the specified outcome is overwhelmingly large, so that in a particular case its occurrence may be expected with "practical certainty."

Or consider the explanation offered by the kinetic theory of gases for an empirically established generalization called Graham's law of diffusion. The law states that at fixed temperature and pressure, the rates at which different gases in a container escape, or diffuse, through a thin porous wall are inversely proportional to the square roots of their molecular weights; so that the amount of a gas that diffuses through the wall per second will be the greater, the lighter its molecules. The explanation rests on the consideration that the mass of a given gas that diffuses through the wall per second will be proportional to the average velocity of its molecules, and that Graham's law will therefore have been explained if it can be shown that the average molecular velocities of different pure gases are inversely proportional to the square roots of their molecular weights. To show this, the theory makes certain assumptions broadly to the effect that a gas consists of a very large number of molecules moving in random fashion at different speeds that frequently change as a result of collisions, and that this random behavior shows certain probabilistic uniformities—in particular, that among the molecules of a given gas at specified temperature and pressure, different velocities will occur with definite, and different, probabilities. These assumptions make it possible to compute the probabilistically expected values—or, as we might briefly say, the "most probable" values—that the average velocities of different gases will possess at equal temperatures and pressures. These most probable average values, the theory shows, are indeed inversely proportional to the square roots of the molecular weights of the gases. But the actual diffusion rates, which are measured experimentally and are the subject of Graham's law, will depend on the actual values that the average velocities have in the large but finite swarms of molecules constituting the given bodies of gas. And the actual average values are related to the corresponding probabilistically estimated, or "most probable," values in a manner that is basically analogous to the relation between the proportion of aces occurring in a large but finite series of tossings of a given die and the corresponding probability of rolling an ace with that die. From the theoretically derived conclusion concerning the probabilistic estimates, it follows only that in view of the very large number of molecules involved, it is overwhelmingly *probable* that at any given time the actual average speeds will have values very close to their probability estimates and that, therefore, it is *practically certain* that they will be, like the latter, inversely proportional to the square roots of their molecular masses, thus satisfying Graham's law.[7]

It seems reasonable to say that this account affords an explanation, even though "only" with very high associated probability, of why gases display the uniformity expressed by Graham's law; and in physical texts and treatises, theoretical accounts of this probabilistic kind are indeed very widely referred to as explanations.

Notes

1. From Holton and Roller, *Foundations of Modern Physical Science,* p. 160.
2. The derivation of the laws of reflection for the curved surfaces referred to in this example and in the next one is simply and lucidly set forth in Chap. 17 of Morris Kline, *Mathematics and the Physical World* (New York: Thomas Y. Crowell Company, 1959).
3. In his essay, "The Problem of Counterfactual Conditionals," reprinted as the first chapter of his book, *Fact, Fiction, and Forecast,* 2nd ed. (Indianapolis: The Bobbs-Merrill Co., Inc., 1965). This work raises

fascinating basic problems concerning laws, counterfactual statements, and inductive reasoning, and examines them from an advanced analytic point of view.

4. For a fuller analysis of the concept of law, and for further bibliographic references, see E. Nagel, *The Structure of Science* (New York: Harcourt, Brace & World, Inc., 1961), Chap. 4.
5. Further details on the concept of statistical probability and on the limit-definition and its shortcomings will be found in E. Nagel's monograph, *Principles of the Theory of Probability* (Chicago: University of Chicago Press, 1939). Our version of the statistical interpretation follows that given by H. Cramer on pp. 148–49 of his book, *Mathematical Methods of Statistics* (Princeton: Princeton University Press, 1946).
6. On this subject, see R. D. Luce and H. Raiffa, *Games and Decisions* (New York: John Wiley & Sons, Inc., 1957).
7. The "average" velocities here referred to are technically defined as root-mean-square velocities. Their values do not differ very much from those of average velocities in the usual sense of the arithmetic mean. A succinct outline of the theoretical explanation of Graham's law can be found in Chapter 25 of Holton and Roller, *Foundations of Modern Physical Science*. The distinction, not explicitly mentioned in that presentation, between the average value of a quantity for some finite number of cases and the probabilistically estimated or expected value of that quantity is briefly discussed in Chapter 6 (especially section 4) of R. P. Feynman, R. B. Leighton, and M. Sands, *The Feynman Lectures on Physics* (Reading, Mass.: Addison-Wesley Publishing Co., 1963).

Critique of Hume's Conception of Causality

C. J. DUCASSE

C. J. Ducasse (1881–1969) was a professor of philosophy at Brown University. An important American philosopher known for his interest in parapsychology, his works include *Nature, Mind and Death* and *Truth, Knowledge, and Causation.*

The ubiquity and consequent vast importance of the causality relation both for practical and for theoretical purposes is made evident by the very large number of verbs of causation in the language; e.g., to push, to bend, to corrode, to cut, to make, to ignite, to transport, to convince, to compel, to remind, to irritate, to influence, to create, to motivate, to stimulate, to incite, to mislead, to induce, to offend, to effect, to prevent, to facilitate, to produce, etc.

Such verbs are employed not only by every person on innumerable ordinary occasions, but also by scientists in their technical works and by philosophers in formulating various of their hypotheses, reasonings, and conclusions.

The importance of the causality relation was emphasized by David Hume, who, in his *Enquiry Concerning Human Understanding,* declared that "if there be any relation among objects which it imports to us to know perfectly, it is that of cause and effect. On this are founded all our reasonings concerning matter of fact or existence. By means of it alone we attain assurance concerning objects which are removed from the present testimony of our memory and senses. The only immediate utility of all sciences, is to teach us, how to control and regulate future events by their causes. Our thoughts and enquiries are, therefore, every moment, employed about this relation."[1]

In modern philosophy, the conception of causality that has proved most challenging has undoubtedly been that of Hume. Kant, in the Introduction to his *Prolegomena to Any Future Metaphysics,* wrote: "I confess freely: the admonition of David Hume [concerning causality] was the very thing which many years ago first interrupted my dogmatic slumber, and gave to my researches in the field of speculative philosophy a wholly different direction."[2]

Even today, Hume's conception of causality is still influential and, therefore, must now be examined with care.

1. Hume's Conception of Causality

Hume sets forth his conception of causality both in his *Treatise of Human Nature,*[3] and in his *Enquiry Concerning Human Understanding* (E 79). At both places he gives two definitions of Cause, one in purely objective terms, the other employing in addition a subjective feature. The definitions are in essence the same in the *Treatise* and in the *Enquiry,* but in the *Treatise* the requirement of contiguity of cause and effect in time and place is explicit; whereas it is left tacit in the somewhat pithier wording of the *Enquiry,* where Necessary Connection is the central topic of the section where Causality is defined.

The objective definition reads there: "we may define a cause to be *an object, followed by another, and where all the objects similar to the first*

From the *Journal of Philosophy,* 63, no. 6 (March 17, 1966), pp. 141–48.

are followed by objects similar to the second." The other definition, which introduces a subjective factor, defines a cause as "*an object followed by another, and whose appearance always conveys the thought to that other.*"

The first of these two is the basic definition, since the regularity of sequence it specifies is not only implied in the second definition by the word 'always' but is in addition tacitly *used* there by employment of the verb 'conveys'—which makes that second definition circular, since 'conveys' means "*causes* to pass . . . to . . . ," and no meaning of 'causes' has yet been provided by Hume other than 'is regularly followed by'; so that 'always conveys the thought to that other' means only "is always followed by thought of that other." Indeed, strict adherence to the empiricism Hume professes requires that his words "is always followed" be replaced by 'has always been followed'.

Hence, when what is left tacit in Hume's second definition of a cause is made fully explicit, the definition reads: *a cause is an object which has always been followed by a certain other, and whose appearance has always been followed by thought of the other.*

2. Hume's Definition of Psychological Necessity

Hume asserts that no *connection* is ever perceived between a cause and its effect and, hence, as his empiricism entails, that there is none. For the following of the effect is not necessitated by the preceding occurrence of the cause, in the sense that 'necessitated' has in logic and mathematics where what Hume calls "relations of ideas" (as distinguished from "matters of fact"; E 25) are concerned, and where truth of a *conclusion* is necessitated by truth of given *premises* in the sense that their being true and its being false would imply a contradiction.

When on the other hand, as in causation, "matters of fact" are concerned instead, then 'necessity' designates not a relation among "objects" themselves but, Hume says, only the "propensity," which custom produces, to pass from an object to the idea of its usual attendant. ". . . necessity is something, that exists in the mind, not in Objects" (T 165).

This definition of psychological as distinguished from logical necessity, however, contains three terms of causation, namely, 'custom', 'produces', and 'propensity'; and since no account of what constitutes causation, other than that it consists in empirical regularity of sequence, has yet been provided by Hume, it is in terms of such empirical regularity that those three terms of causation have to be themselves explicated, as follows:

'Produces', as Hume himself stresses on page 77 of the *Treatise,* is but a synonym of 'causes'. Hence that custom produces in a person *P* the propensity to pass from perception of an object *O* to the idea of its usual attendant *A* can only mean that the *custom*—that is, *P*'s having repeatedly observed occurrence of *O* being followed by occurrence of *A*—has *itself* been regularly followed by occurrence in *P* of "propensity" to pass from perception of *O* to the idea *I* of *O*'s usual attendant *A*.

But, 'propensity' being itself a term of causality, propensity in *P* to pass from perception of *O* to idea *I* can, for Hume, only mean that perception of *O* by *P* has been regularly followed in *P* by occurrence of idea *I*. It cannot, for Hume, mean—as commonly it does in addition and essentially—that *P*'s *now* perceiving *O is going to be* followed in *P* by occurrence of idea *I*; for Hume is emphatic that we have no proof "*that those instances, of which we have had no experience, resemble those, of which we have had experience* [T, p. 89; the italics are Hume's]. Hence, even if occurrence of the idea *I* in *P* has in the past regularly followed perception of *O* by *P* (after *P* had repeatedly observed occurrence of *A* after occurrence of *O*), even then it remains perfectly possible that, *this time,* perception of *O* by *P* will not be followed in him by occurrence of the idea *I* of *A*; for no contradiction is involved in supposing "a change in the course of nature" (89).

The upshot, then, is that, because Hume's definition of psychological necessitation is worded in terms that are inherently terms of causation—to wit, 'conveys', 'produces', and 'propensity'—and because he has offered as yet no definition of causation other than as sequence that has in fact been regular in our experience, his definition of psychological 'necessity', when explicated in terms of that definition of causation, turns out to tell us that *in the mind just as among objects,* there is *no necessity,* i.e., *no connection;* but only so much regularity of sequence as there happens to be. Indeed, Hume explicitly acknowledges that *he does not even know what he is denying* when he denies that a "connection" obtains between a cause and its effect; for he declares that "we have no idea of this connection, nor even any distinct notion what it is we desire to know, when we endeavor at a conception of it" (E 79).

3. Hume's Contention That Causation May Be Detected by a Single Experiment

At some places in the *Treatise,* however, Hume's common sense almost gets the better of his indefensible official contention that causation ultimately consists in nothing but empirical regularity of sequence. For example (T 104), he asserts that "we may attain the knowledge of a particular cause merely by one experiment, provided it be made with judgment, and after a careful removal of all foreign and superfluous circumstances."

But of course it is paradoxical to suppose that a *single* experiment—unless it reveals a genuine *connection* between events of the kinds that figure in it—can inform us that in all past and all future cases of an event similar to the first, an event similar to the second *did,* or *will,* follow. Hume is aware of this difficulty and attempts to deal with it by saying that "tho' we are suppos'd to have had only one experiment of a particular effect, yet we have had many millions to convince us of this principle; that like objects, plac'd in like circumstances, will always produce like effects" (p. 105).

But to "convince" is only to *cause* belief i.e., on Hume's definition of 'cause', it is *to have been regularly followed* by belief—here, belief that like objects placed in like circumstances will always "produce," i.e., be followed by, like effects. And, on an empiricism that denies that any *connection* is ever perceived between a cause and its effect, the belief mentioned is made illegitimate by the reference in it of the words 'will always' to cases not actually experienced, to wit, cases as yet future. For, as I have pointed out already in section 2, Hume stresses that we have no proof "that those instances, of which we have had no experience, resemble those, of which we have had experience" (89). The "principle" to which Hume appeals in order to meet the difficulty he recognized is, therefore, on his own premises, only an unwarranted belief, and leaves the difficulty standing.

Indeed, that "principle," taken by itself, would justify us in generalizing from *any* case of sequence we had observed—whether it was in fact an accidental or a causal sequence. The "principle" therefore has valid applicability only *after* we have somehow managed to identify the cause by one experiment. But, according to Hume, we can do this only after we have performed the prescribed preliminary "careful removal of all foreign and superfluous circumstances"; and unfortunately we cannot know which these are unless we *already* know what identifies a particular one of the circumstances as being *the cause.* But the "principle" does not inform us of this and is, therefore, useful only for *generalizing* a causal connection if, somehow, a *single* experiment has already revealed it to us. If, however, a single experiment can reveal it to us, then causation does not consist in empirical constancy of sequence, even if such constancy is entailed by causal connection.

Hume appears to be aware in the end that he has not succeeded in providing a tenable analysis of the causality relation, for he writes that "it is impossible to give any just definition of cause, except"—and this is paradoxical—"what is drawn from something extraneous and foreign to it"; and he adds that both the definitions of cause he has given are "drawn from circumstances foreign to the cause" (E 79). Moreover, in the section of the *Treatise* where Hume gives the "Rules by which to judge of causes and effects," he at first refers to causation as "that constant conjunction on which the relation of cause and effect *totally* depends" (T 173); but, lower down on the same page, what he says is not "totally" but "*chiefly*"; and, at the top of page 174, he refers to constant repetition only as that "from which the *first idea* of this relation [to wit, the causal relation] is derived" (italics mine).

4. Hume's Rules by Which To Judge of Causes and Effects

Hume, however, does in section xv of part III of the *Treatise* offer a set of "rules by which to judge of causes and effects." The fifth, sixth, and seventh of these are the clearest formulations given, not only up to his time but up to the publication in 1830 of J. F. W. Herschel's *Preliminary Discourse on the Study of Natural Philosophy* (secs. 146–62), of what John Stuart Mill later denominated the Methods of Agreement, of Difference, and of Concomitant Variations—William Minto still later rightly contending that the first two should be called the methods of *Single* Agreement, and of *Single* Difference.[4] And it might be thought that in the fifth and sixth of them Hume gives us what we need in order to distinguish, in a single experiment, between the circumstance that *is* the cause of an occurrence and the circumstances that are "foreign and superfluous."

This, however, is not the case; but in order to see that it is not, we must view the fifth and sixth rules in the light of the fourth. The three read as follows:

> Rule 4. The same cause always produces the same effect, and the same effect never arises but from the same cause. This principle we derive from experience, and is the source of most of our philosophical reasonings. For when by any clear experiment we have discovered the causes or effects of any phenomenon, we immediately extend our observation to every phenomenon of the same kind, without waiting for that constant repetition, from which the first idea of this relation is derived.

The fifth rule, which formulates Hume's conception of the principle of Agreement, is as follows:

> Rule 5. There is another principle, which hangs upon this, viz., that where several different objects produce the same effect, it must be by means of some quality, which we discover to be common amongst them. For as like effects imply like causes, we must always ascribe the causation to the circumstances, wherein we discover the resemblance.

And the sixth rule, which is Hume's formulation of the principle of Difference, reads:

> Rule 6. The following principle is founded on the same reason. The difference in the effects of two resembling objects must proceed from that particular in which they differ. For as like causes always produce like effects, when in any instance we find our expectation to be disappointed, we must conclude that this irregularity proceeds from some difference in the causes.

In commenting now on these rules, attention must be drawn first to the fact that the principle stated in the fourth rule, to wit, that "the same cause always produces the same effect, and the same effect never arises but from the same cause" is presented there explicitly as a principle for *generalizing* particular relations of cause and effect after we have discovered them by some "clear experiment." Do, then, the fifth and sixth rules tell us how to distinguish *experimentally* that circumstance which is the cause from those which are "foreign and superfluous"?

Clearly, they do not; for those two rules are presented by Hume as *corollaries* of the principle stated in the fourth, and—contrary to what he asserts in Rule 4 and for the reasons he himself gives on page 89 of the *Treatise,* which were cited in section 2 of the present paper—that principle *cannot* be derived from experience. For the word 'always', which Hume employs in the statement of it, makes that principle include innumerable cases that we have *not* experienced—not only all cases as yet future, but also many past and present cases that happened to go unobserved.

A much more modest principle, which experience, in Hume's sense of the term, might conceivably have yielded if we had already known how to identify causes and effects experimentally, would be that the same observed causes has been observed always to have had the same effect, and the same observed effect always to have had the same cause. But *this* principle would not entail Hume's fifth and sixth rules. Indeed, *every observation of the two kinds respectively de-*

scribed in these two rules would constitute a patent exception to and invalidation of that principle. For "where several different objects produce the same effect" (Rule 5), what this shows is that the same effect sometimes does result from different causes—a plain fact illustrated by the many different causes from which death can result. And where what we observe is a "difference in the effects of two resembling objects" (Rule 6), what is thereby shown is that the same cause does not always have the same effect—a fact which, as Josiah Royce once pointed out to one of his classes, one can make patent if, having stepped on a man's foot, apologized, and noted his response, one then immediately repeats accurately the stepping and the apology. For the man's response is pretty certain then to be different!

5. Facts That Clash with Hume's Definition of Causality

The examination made in this paper of Hume's various statements concerning causality has shown that the only definition of causality he really offers is his first: "We may define a cause to be an object, followed by another, and where all the objects similar to the first are followed by objects similar to the second." For this is the only one of his definitions of causality which, as not itself employing any term of causality—such as 'conveys', 'produces', 'propensity',—is free from circularity.

But the conception of causality simply thus as observed regularity of occurrence of an event of kind *B* after occurrence of an event of kind *A* is untenable, as obviously clashing with certain of our most confident judgments, positive and negative, about cases of causation or of noncausation. For on the one hand a single experiment, if performed with the great care normally exercised in laboratories, unquestionably makes manifest the causation of one particular occurrence by a particular other. On the other hand, some instances of regularity of sequence are admittedly *not* instances of the cause-effect relation; for example, as Thomas Reid pointedly remarked, if the cause of an occurrence is defined as its invariable antecedent, then night must be the cause of day and day the cause of night. And, one may add, growth of hair on babies would be the cause of their growth of teeth!

John Stuart Mill, when he considers Reid's objection, states that "invariable sequence, therefore, is not synonymous with causation, unless the sequence, besides being invariable, is unconditional."[5] This, he writes, "is what writers mean when they say that the notion of cause involves the idea of necessity. If there be any meaning which confessedly belongs to the term necessity, it is *unconditionalness*. That which is necessary, that which *must* be, means that which will be, whatever supposition we may make in regard to all other things."

As Dr. Charles Mercier has pointed out, however, this definition of necessity is unfortunately worded, since such necessity as an event possesses is always *conditional* on occurrence of its cause.[6]

Nothing more need be said here concerning Mill's discussion of causality, which, on attentive examination, is seen to be a mass of confusions at most of the essential points.[7]

Notes

1. Open Court edition, La Salle, Ill., 1904, hereafter referred to as E; pp. 78–79.
2. Sämmtliche Werke; ed. Rosenkrantz, Leipzig 1838. Part III, *Prolegomena zu einer jeden künftigen Metaphysik*. Introduction, p. 9: "Ich gestehe frei: die Erinnerung des David Hume war eben dasjenige, was mir vor vielen Jahren zuerst den dogmatischen Schlummer unterbrach, und meinen Untersuchungen im Felde der spekulativen Philosophie eine ganz andere Richtung gab."
3. Selby-Bigge edition, Oxford, 1896, hereafter T; p. 170.
4. *Logic, Inductive and Deductive* (New York: Scribner's, 1904). p. 332.
5. *System of Logic* (8th ed.; New York: Harper, 1874), book III, ch. v, sec. 6, p. 245.
6. *Causation and Belief* (London: Longmans Green, 1916), pp. 75–76.
7. The grounds on which this severe judgment is based have been set forth in detail in ch. II of the writer's *Causation and the Types of Necessity* (Seattle: University of Washington Press, 1924).

Causality and Determination

G. E. M. ANSCOMBE

G. E. M. Anscombe (1919–) is a professor of philosophy at Cambridge University. Her publications include *Intention, An Introduction to Wittgenstein's Tractatus,* and (with Peter Geach,) *Three Philosophers.*

I

It is often declared or evidently assumed that causality is some kind of necessary connection, or alternatively, that being caused is—non-trivially—instancing some exceptionless generalization saying that such an event always follows such antecedents. Or the two conceptions are combined.

Obviously there can be, and are, a lot of divergent views covered by this account. Any view that it covers nevertheless manifests one particular doctrine or assumption. Namely:

> If an effect occurs in one case and a similar effect does not occur in an apparently similar case, there must be a relevant further difference.

Any radically different account of causation, then, by contrast with which all those diverse views will be as one, will deny this assumption. Such a radically opposing view can grant that often—though it is difficult to say generally when—the assumption of relevant difference is a sound principle of investigation. It may grant that there are necessitating causes, but will refuse to identify causation as such with necessitation. It can grant there are situations in which, given the initial conditions and no interference, only one result will accord with the laws of nature; but it will not see general reason, in advance of discovery, to suppose that any given course of things has been so determined. So it may grant that in many cases difference of issue can rightly convince us of a relevant difference of circumstances; but it will deny that, quite generally, this *must* be so.

The first view is common to many philosophers of the past. It is also, usually but not always in a neo-Humeian form, the prevailing received opinion throughout the currently busy and productive philosophical schools of the English-speaking world, and also in some of the European and Latin American schools where philosophy is pursued in at all the same sort of way; nor is it confined to these schools. So firmly rooted is it that for many even outside pure philosophy, it routinely determines the meaning of "cause", when consciously used as a theoretical term: witness the terminology of the contrast between 'causal' and 'statistical' laws, which is drawn by writers on physics—writers, note, who would not conceive themselves to be addicts of any philosophic school when they use this language to express that contrast.

The truth of this conception is hardly debated. It is, indeed, a bit of *Weltanschauung:* it helps to form a cast of mind which is characteristic of our whole culture.

The association between causation and necessity is old; it occurs for example in Aristotle's

From an inaugural lecture delivered at Cambridge University (published by Cambridge University Press, 1971).

Metaphysics: "When the agent and patient meet suitably to their powers, the one acts and the other is acted on OF NECESSITY." Only with 'rational powers' an extra feature is needed to determine the result: "What has a rational power [e.g. medical knowledge, which can kill *or* cure] OF NECESSITY does what it has the power to do and as it has the power, when it has the desire."[1]

Overleaping the centuries, we find it an axiom in Spinoza, "Given a determinate cause, the effect follows OF NECESSITY, and without its cause, no effect follows."[2] And in the English philosopher Hobbes: "A cause simply, or an entire cause, is the aggregate of all the accidents both of the agents how many soever they be, and of the patients, put together; which when they are supposed to be present, IT CANNOT BE UNDERSTOOD BUT THAT THE EFFECT IS PRODUCED at the same instant; and if any of them be wanting, IT CANNOT BE UNDERSTOOD BUT THAT THE EFFECT IS NOT PRODUCED."[3]

It was this last view, where the connection between cause and effect is evidently seen as *logical* connection of some sort, that was overthrown by Hume, the most influential of all philosophers on this subject in the English-speaking and allied schools. For he made us see that, given any particular cause—or 'total causal situation' for that matter—and its effect, there is not in general any contradiction in supposing the one to occur and the other not to occur. That is to say, we'd know what was being described—what it would be like for it to be true—if it were reported for example that a kettle of water was put, and kept, directly on a hot fire, but the water did not heat up.

Were it not for the preceding philosophers who had made causality out as some species of logical connection, one would wonder at this being called a discovery on Hume's part: for vulgar humanity has always been over-willing to believe in miracles and marvels and *lusus naturae*. Mankind at large saw no contradiction, where Hume worked so hard to show the philosophic world—the Republic of Letters—that there was none.

The discovery was thought to be great. But as touching the equation of causality with necessitation, Hume's thinking did nothing against this but curiously reinforced it. For he himself assumed that NECESSARY CONNECTION is an essential part of the idea of the relation of cause and effect,[4] and he sought for its nature. He thought this could not be found in the situations, objects, or events called "causes" and "effects", but was to be found in the human mind's being determined, by experience of CONSTANT CONJUNCTION, to pass from the sensible impression or memory of one term of the relation to the convinced idea of the other. Thus to say that an event was caused was to say that its occurrence was an instance of some exceptionless generalization connecting such an event with such antecedents as it occurred in. The twist that Hume gave to the topic thus suggested a connection of the notion of causality with that of deterministic laws—i.e. laws such that always, given initial conditions and the laws, a unique result is determined.

The well-known philosophers who lived after Hume may have aimed at following him and developing at least some of his ideas, or they may have put up a resistance; but in no case, so far as I know,[5] has the resistance called in question the equation of causality with necessitation.

Kant, roused by learning of Hume's discovery, laboured to establish causality as an a priori conception and argued that the objective time order consists "in that order of the manifold of appearance according to which, IN CONFORMITY WITH A RULE, the apprehension of that which happens follows upon the apprehension of that which precedes. . . . In conformity with such a rule there must be in that which precedes an event the condition of a rule according to which this event INVARIABLY and NECESSARILY follows."[6] Thus Kant tried to give back to causality the character of a *justified* concept which Hume's considerations had taken away from it. Once again the connection between causation and necessity was reinforced. And this has been the general characteristic of those who have sought to oppose Hume's conception of causality. They have always tried to establish the necessitation that they saw in causality: either a priori, or somehow out of experience.

Since Mill it has been fairly common to explain causation one way or another in terms of 'necessary' and 'sufficient' conditions. Now "sufficient condition" is a term of art whose users may therefore lay down its meaning as they please. So they are in their rights to rule out the query: "May not the sufficient conditions of an event be present, and the event yet not take place?" For "sufficient condition" is so used that if the sufficient conditions for *X* are there, *X* occurs. But at the same time, the phrase cozens the understanding into not noticing an assumption. For "sufficient condition" sounds like: "enough". And one certainly *can* ask: "May there not be *enough* to have made something happen—and yet it not have happened?"

Russell wrote of the notion of cause, or at any rate of the 'law of causation' (and he seemed to feel the same way about 'cause' itself), that, like the British monarchy, it had been allowed to survive because it had been erroneously thought to do no harm. In a destructive essay of great brilliance he cast doubt on the notion of necessity involved, unless it is explained in terms of universality, and he argued that upon examination the concepts of determination and of invariable succession of like objects upon like turn out to be empty: they do not differentiate between any conceivable course of things and any other. Thus Russell too assumes that necessity or universality is what is in question, and it never occurs to him that there may be any other conception of causality.[7]

Now it's not difficult to shew it prima facie wrong to associate the notion of cause with necessity or universality in this way. For, it being much easier to trace effects back to causes with certainty than to predict effects from causes, we often know a cause without knowing whether there is an exceptionless generalization of the kind envisaged, or whether there is a necessity.

For example, we have found certain diseases to be contagious. If, then, I have had one and only one contact with someone suffering from such a disease, and I get it myself, we suppose I got it from him. But what if, having had the contact, I ask a doctor whether I will get the disease? He will usually only be able to say, "I don't know—maybe you will, maybe not."

But, it is said, knowledge of causes here is partial; doctors seldom even know any of the conditions under which one invariably gets a disease, let alone all the sets of conditions. This comment betrays the assumption that there is such a thing to know. Suppose there is: still, the question whether there is does not have to be settled before we can know what we mean by speaking of the contact as cause of my getting the disease.

All the same, might it not be like this: knowledge of causes is possible without any satisfactory grasp of what is involved in causation? Compare the possibility of wanting clarification of 'valency' or 'long-run frequency', which yet have been handled by chemists and statisticians without such clarification; and valencies and long-run frequencies, whatever the right way of explaining them, have been known. Thus one of the familiar philosophic analyses of causality, or a new one in the same line, may be correct, though knowledge of it is not necessary for knowledge of causes.

There is something to observe here, that lies under our noses. It is little attended to, and yet still so obvious as to seem trite. It is this: causality consists in the derivativeness of an effect from its causes. This is the core, the common feature, of causality in its various kinds. Effects derive from, arise out of, come of, their causes. For example, everyone will grant that physical parenthood is a causal relation. Here the derivation is material, by fission. Now analysis in terms of necessity or universality does not tell us of this derivedness of the effect; rather it forgets about that. For the necessity will be that of laws of nature; through it *we* shall be able to derive knowledge of the effect from knowledge of the cause, or vice versa, but that does not shew us the cause as source of the effect. Causation, then, is not to be identified with necessitation.

If *A* comes from *B*, this does not imply that every *A*-like thing comes from some *B*-like thing or set-up or that every *B*-like thing or set-up has an *A*-like thing coming from it; or that given *B*, *A* had to come from it, or that given *A*, there had to be *B* for it to come from. Any of these may be true, but if any is, that will be an additional fact, not comprised in *A*'s coming from *B*. If we take "coming from" in the sense of travel, this is perfectly evident.

"But that's because we can observe travel!" The influential Humeian argument at this point is that we can't similarly observe causality in the individual case.[8] So the reason why we connect what we call the cause and what we call the effect as we do must lie elsewhere. It must lie in the fact that the succession of the latter upon the former is of a kind regularly observed.

There are two things for me to say about this. *First,* as to the statement that we can never observe causality in the individual case. Someone who says this is just not going to count anything as 'observation of causality'. This often happens in philosophy; it is argued that 'all we find' is such-and-such, and it turns out that the arguer has excluded from his idea of 'finding' the sort of thing he says we don't 'find'. And when we consider what we are allowed to say we do 'find', we have the right to turn the tables on Hume, and say that neither do we perceive bodies, such as billiard balls, approaching one another. When we "consider the matter with the utmost attention," we find only an impression of travel made by the successive positions of a round white patch in our visual fields . . . etc. Now a 'Humeian' account of causality has to be given in terms of constant conjunction of physical things, events etc., not of experiences of them. If, then, it must be allowed that we "find" bodies in motion, for example, then what theory of perception can justly disallow the perception of a lot of causality? The truthful—though unhelpful—answer to the question: How did we come by our primary knowledge of causality? is that in learning to speak we learned the linguistic representation and application of a host of causal concepts. Very many of them were represented by transitive and other verbs of action used in reporting statements, but rather expressions of causal hypotheses. The word "cause" itself is highly general. How does someone show that he has the concept *cause?* We may wish to say: only by having such a word in his vocabulary. If so, then the manifest possession of the concept presupposes the mastery of much else in language. I mean: the word "cause" can be *added* to a language in which are already represented many causal concepts. A small selection: *scrape, push, wet, carry, eat, burn, knock over, keep off, squash, make* (e.g. noises, paper boats), *hurt.* But if we care to imagine languages in which no special causal concepts are represented, then no description of the use of a word in such languages will be able to present it as meaning *cause*. Nor will it even contain words for natural kinds of stuff, nor yet words equivalent to "body", "wind", or "fire". For learning to use special causal verbs is part and parcel of learning to apply the concepts answering to these, and many other, substantives. As surely as we learned to call people by name or to report from seeing it that the cat was on the table, we also learned to report from having observed it that someone drank up the milk or that the dog made a funny noise or that things were cut or broken by whatever we saw cut or break them.

(I will mention, only to set on one side, one of the roots of Hume's argument, the implicit appeal to Cartesian scepticism. He confidently challenges us to "produce some instance, wherein the efficacy is plainly discoverable to the mind, and its operations obvious to our consciousness or sensation."[9] Nothing easier: is cutting, is drinking, is purring not 'efficacy'? But it is true that the apparent perception of such things may be only apparent: we may be deceived by false appearances. Hume presumably wants us to 'produce an instance' in which *efficacy* is related to sensation as *red* is. It is true that we can't do that; it is not *so* related to sensation. He is also helped, in making his argument that we don't perceive 'efficacy', by his curious belief that "efficacy" means much the same thing as "necessary connection"! But as to the Cartesian-sceptical root of the argument, I will not delay upon it, as my present topic is not the philosophy of perception.)

Second, as to that instancing of a universal generalization, which was supposed to supply what could not be observed in the individual case, the causal relation. The needed examples are none too common. "Motion in one body in all past instances that have fallen under our observation, is follow'd upon impulse by motion in another":[10] so Hume. But, as is always a danger in making large generalizations, he was thinking only of the cases where we do observe this—billiard balls against free-standing billiard balls in an ordinary situation; not billiard balls against stone walls. Neo-Humeians are more cautious. They realize that if you take a case of cause and effect, and relevantly describe the cause *A* and the effect *B*, and then construct a universal proposition, "Always, given an *A*, a *B* follows" you usually won't get anything true. You have got to describe the absence of circumstances in which an *A* would not cause a *B*. But the task of excluding all such circumstances can't be carried out. There is, I suppose, a vague association in people's minds between the universal propositions which would be examples of the required type of generalizations, and scientific laws. But there is no similarity.

Suppose we were to call propositions giving the properties of substances 'laws of nature'. Then there will be a law of nature running "The flash-point of such a substance is . . .," and this will be important in explaining why striking matches usually causes them to light. This law of nature has not the form of a generalization running "Always, if a sample of such a substance is raised to such a temperature, it ignites"; nor is it equivalent to such a generalization, but rather to: "If a sample of such a substance is raised to such a temperature and doesn't ignite, there must be a cause of its not doing so." Leaving aside questions connected with the idea of a pure sample, the point here is that 'normal conditions' is quite properly a vague notion. That fact makes generalizations running "Always . . ." merely fraudulent in such cases; it will always be necessary for them to be hedged about with clauses referring to normal conditions; and we may not know in advance whether conditions are normal or not, or what to count as an abnormal condition. In exemplar analytical practice, I suspect, it will simply be a relevant condition in which the generalization, "Always, if such and such, such and such happens . . . ," supplemented with a few obvious conditions that have occurred to the author, turns out to be untrue. Thus the conditional "If it doesn't ignite then there must be some cause" is the better gloss upon the original proposition, for it does not pretend to say specifically, or even disjunctively specifically, what *always* happens. It is probably these facts which make one hesitate to call propositions about the action of substances 'laws of nature'. The law of inertia, for example, would hardly be glossed: "If a body accelerates without any force acting on it, there must be some cause of its doing so." (Though I wonder what the author of *Principia* himself would have thought of that.) On the other hand just such 'laws' as that about a substance's flash-point are connected with the match's igniting because struck.

Returning to the medical example, medicine is of course not interested in the hopeless task of constructing lists of all the sets of conditions under each of which people always get a certain disease. It is interested in finding what that is special, if anything, is always the case when people get a particular disease; and, given such a cause or condition (or in any case), in finding circumstances in which people don't get the disease, or tend not to. This is connected with medicine's concern first, and last, with things as they happen in the messy and mixed up conditions of life: only between its first and its last concern can it look for what happens unaffected by uncontrolled and inconstant conditions.

II

Yet my argument lies always to the charge of appealing to ignorance. I must therefore take a different sort of example.

Here is a ball lying on top of some others in a transparent vertical pipe. I know how it got there: it was forcibly ejected with many others out of a certain aperture into the enclosed space above a row of adjacent pipes. The point of the whole construction is to shew how a totality of balls so ejected always build up in rough conformity to the same curve. But I am interested in this one ball. Between its ejection and its getting into this pipe, it kept hitting sides, edges, other balls. If I made a film of it I could run it off in slow motion and tell the impact which produced each stage of the journey. Now was the result necessary? We would probably all have said it was in the time when Newton's mechanics was undisputed for truth. It was the impression made on Hume and later philosophers by that mechanics, that gave them so strong a conviction of the iron necessity with which everything happens, the "absolute fate" by which "Every object is determin'd to a certain degree and direction of its motion."[11]

Yet no one could have deduced the resting place of the ball—because of the indeterminateness that you get even in the Newtonian Mechanics, arising from the finite accuracy of measurements. From exact figures for positions, veolocities, directions, spins, and masses you might be able to calculate the result as accurately as you chose. But the minutest inexactitudes will multiply up factor by factor, so that in a short time your information is gone. Assuming a given margin of error in your initial figure, you could assign an associated probability to that ball's falling into each of the pipes. If you want the highest probability you assign to be really high, so that you can take it as practical certainty, it will be a problem to reckon how tiny the permitted margins of inaccuracy must be—analogous to the problem: how small a fraction of a grain of millet must I demand is put on the first square of the chess board, if after doubling up at every square I end up having to pay out only a pound of millet? It would be a figure of such smallness as to have no meaning as a figure for a margin of error.

However, so long as you believed the classical mechanics you might also think there could be no such thing as a figure for a difference that had no meaning. Then you would think that though it was not feasible for us to find the necessary path of the ball because our margins of error are too great, yet there *was* a necessary path, which could be assigned a sufficient probability for firm acceptance of it, by anyone (not one of us) capable of reducing his limits of accuracy in measurement to a sufficiently small compass. Admittedly, so small a compass that he'd be down among the submicroscopic particles and no longer concerned with the measurements, say, of the ball. And now we can say: with certain degrees of smallness we get to a region where Newton's mechanics is no longer believed.

If the classical mechanics can be used to calculate a certain real result, we may give a sense to, and grant, the 'necessity' of the result, given the antecedents. Here, however, you can't use the mechanics to calculate the result, but at most to give yourself a belief in its necessity. For this to be reasonable the system has got to be acknowledged as true. Not, indeed, that that would be enough; but if so much were secured, then it would be worth while to discuss the metaphysics of absolute measures of continuous quantities.

The point needs some labouring precisely because "the system does apply to such bodies"—that is, to moderately massive balls. After all, it's Newton we use to calculate Sputniks! "The system applies to these bodies" is true only in the sense and to the extent that it yields sufficient results of calculations about these bodies. It does not mean: in respect of these bodies the system is the truth, so that it just doesn't matter that we can't use it to calculate such a result in such a case. I am not saying that a deterministic system involves individual predictability: it evidently does not. But in default of predictability the determinedness declared by the deterministic system has got to be believed because the system itself is believed.

I conclude that we have no ground for calling the path of the ball determined—at least, until it has taken its path—but, it may be objected, is not each state of its path determined, even though we cannot determine it? My argument has partly relied on loss of information through multiplicity of impacts. But from one impact to the next the path is surely determined, and so the whole path is so after all.

It sounds plausible to say: each stage is determined and so the whole is. But what does "determined" mean? The word is a curious one (with a curious history); in this sort of context it is often used as if it *meant* "caused." Or perhaps "caused" is used as if it meant "determined". But there is at any rate one important difference—a thing hasn't been caused until it has happened; but it may be determined before it happens.

(It is important here to distinguish between being *determined* and being *determinate*. In indeterministic physics there is an apparent failure of both. I am concerned only with the former.)

When we call a result determined we are implicitly relating it to an antecedent range of possibilities and saying that all but one of these is disallowed. What disallows them is not the result itself but something antecedent to the result. The antecedences may be logical or temporal or in the order of knowledge. Of the many—antecedent—possibilities, *now* only one is—antecedently—possible.

Mathematical formulae and human decisions are limiting cases; the former because of the obscurity of the notion of antecedent possibilities, and the latter because decisions can be retrieved.

In a chess-game, the antecedent possibilities are, say, the powers of the pieces. By the rules, a certain position excludes all but one of the various moves that were in that sense antecedently possible. This is logical antecedence. The next move is determined.

In the zygote, sex and eye-colour are already determined. Here the antecedent possibilities are the possibilities for sex and eye-colour for a child;

or more narrowly: for a child of these parents. *Now,* given the combination of this ovum and this spermatozoon, all but one of these antecedent possibilities is excluded.

It might be said that anything was determined once it had happened. There is now no possibility open: it *has* taken place! It was in this sense that Aristotle said that past and present were necessary. But this does not concern us: what interests us is *pre*-determination.

Then "each stage of the ball's path is determined" must mean "Upon any impact, there is only one path possible for the ball up to the next impact (and assuming no air currents, etc.)." But what ground system could one have for believing this, if one does not believe in some system of which it is a consequence? Consider a steel ball dropping between two pins on a Galton board to hit the pin centred under the gap between them. That it should balance on this pin is not to be expected. It has two possibilities; to go to the right or to the left. If you have a system which forces this on you, you can say: "There has to be a determining factor; otherwise, like Buridan's ass, the ball must balance." But if you have not, then you should say that the ball may be undetermined until it does move to the right or the left. Here the ball had only two significant possibilities and was perhaps unpredetermined between them. This was because it cannot be called determined—no reasonable account can be given of insisting that it is so—within a small range of possibility, actualization within which will lead on to its falling either to the right or to the left. With our flying ball there will also be such a small range of possibility. The further consequences of the path it may take are not tied down to just two significant possibilities, as with one step down the Galton board: the range of further possibility gets wider as we consider the paths it may take. Otherwise, the two cases are similar.

We see that to give content to the idea of something's being determined, we have to have a set of possibilities, which something narrows down to one—before the event.

This accords well with our understanding of part of the dissatisfaction of some physicists with the quantum theory. They did not like the undeterminedness of individual quantum phenomena. Such a physicist might express himself by saying "I believe in causality!" He meant: I believe that the real physical laws and the initial conditions must entail uniqueness of result. Of course, within a range of co-ordinate and mutually exclusive identifiable possible results, only one happens: he means that the result that happens ought to be understood as the only one that was possible before it happened.

Must such a physicist be a 'determinist'? That is, must he believe that the whole universe is a system such that, if its total states at t and t' are thus and so, the laws of nature are such as then to allow only one possibility for its total state at any other time? No. He may not think that the idea of a total state of the universe at a time is one he can do anything with. He may even have no views on the uniqueness of possible results for whatever may be going on in any arbitrary volume of space. For "Our theory should be such that only the actual result was possible for that experiment" doesn't mean "Our theory should have excluded the experiment's being muffed or someone's throwing a boot, so that we didn't get the result," but rather: "Our theory should be such that only this result was possible as *the result of the experiment.*" He hates a theory, even if he has to put up with it for the time being, that essentially assigns only probability to a result, essentially allows of a range of possible results, never narrowed down to one until the event itself.

It must be admitted that such dissatisfied physicists very often have been determinists. Witness Schrödinger's account of the 'principle of causality': "The exact physical situation at *any* point P at a given moment t is unambiguously determined by the exact physical situation within a certain surrounding of P at any previous time, say $t-\tau$. If τ is large, that is if that previous time lies far back, it may be necessary to know the previous situation for a wide domain around P."[12] Or Einstein's more modest version of a notorious earlier claim: if you knew all about the contents of a sphere of radius 186,000 miles, and knew the laws, you would be able to know for sure what would happen at the centre for the next second. Schrödinger says: *any* point P; and *a* means *any* sphere of that radius. So their view of causality was not that of my hypothetical physicist, who I said may not have views on the uniqueness of possible results for whatever may be going on in any arbitrary volume of space. My physicist restricts his demand for uniqueness of result to situations in which he has got certain processes going in isolation from inconstant external influences, or where they do not matter, as the weather on a planet does not matter for predicting its course round the sun.

The high success of Newton's astronomy was in one way an intellectual disaster: it produced an illusion from which we tend still to suffer. This illusion was created by the circumstance that Newton's mechanics *had a good model in the solar system.* For this gave the impression that we had here an ideal of scientific explanation; whereas the truth was, it was mere obligingness on the part of the solar system, by having had so peaceful a history in recorded time, to provide such a model. For suppose that some planet had at some time erupted with such violence that its shell was propelled rocket-like out of the solar system. Such an event would not have violated Newton's laws; on the contrary, it would have illustrated them. But also it would not have been calculable as the past and future motions of the planets are presently calculated on the assumption that they can be treated as the simple 'bodies' of his mechanics, with no relevant properties but mass, position, and velocity and no forces mattering except gravity.

Let us pretend that Newton's laws were still to be accepted without qualification: no reserve in applying them in electrodynamics; no restriction to bodies travelling a good deal slower than light; and no quantum phenomena. Newton's mechanics is a deterministic system; but this does not mean that believing them commits us to determinism. We could say: Of course nothing violates those axioms or the laws of the force of gravity. But animals, for example, run about the world in all sorts of paths and no path is dictated for them by those laws, as it is for planets. Thus in relation to the solar system (apart from questions like whether in the past some planet has blown up), the laws are like the rules of an infantile card game: once the cards are dealt we turn them up in turn, and make two piles each, one red, one black; the winner has the biggest pile of red ones. So once the cards are dealt the game is determined, and from any position in it you can derive all others back to the deal and forward to win or draw. But in relation to what happens on and inside a planet the laws are, rather, like the rules of chess; the play is seldom determined, though nobody breaks the rules.[13]

Why this difference? A natural answer is: the mechanics does not give the special laws of all the forces. Not, for example, for thermal, nuclear, electrical, chemical, muscular forces. And now the Newtonian model suggests the picture: given the laws of all the forces, then there is total coverage of what happens and then the whole game of motion is determined; for, by the first law, any acceleration implies a force of some kind, and must not forces have laws? My hypothetical physicist at least would think so; and would demand that they be deterministic. Nevertheless he still does not have to be a "determinist"; for many forces, unlike gravity, can be switched on and off, are generated, and also shields can be put up against them. It is one thing to hold that in a clear-cut situation—an astronomical or a well-contrived experimental one designed to discover laws—"the result" should be determined: and quite another to say that in the hurly-burly of many crossing contingencies whatever happens next must be determined; or to say that the generation of forces (by human experimental procedures, among other things) is always determined in advance of the generating procedure; or to say that there is always a law of composition, of such a kind that the combined effect of a set of forces is determined in every situation.

Someone who is inclined to say those things, or implicitly to assume them, has almost certainly been affected by the impressive relation between Newton's mechanics and the solar system.

> We remember how it was in mechanics. By knowing the position and velocity of a particle at one single instant, by knowing the acting forces, the whole future path of the particle could be foreseen. In Maxwell's theory, if we know the field at one instant only, we can deduce from the equations of the theory how the whole field will change in space and time. Maxwell's equations enable us to follow the history of the field, just as the mechanical equations enabled us to

> follow the history of material particles. . . . With the help of Newton's laws we can deduce the motion of the earth from the force acting between the sun and the earth.[14]

"By knowing the acting forces"—that must of course include the *future* acting forces, not merely the present ones. And similarly for the equations which enable us to follow the history of the field; a change may be produced by an external influence. In reading both Newton and later writers one is often led to ponder that word "external". Of course, to be given 'the acting forces' is to be given the external forces too and any new forces that may later be introduced into the situation. Thus those first sentences are true, if true, without the special favour of fate, being general truths of mechanics and physics, but the last one is true by favour, by the brute fact that only the force acting between earth and sun matters for the desired deductions.

The concept of necessity, as it is connected with causation, can be explained as follows: a cause *C* is a necessitating cause of an effect *E when* (I mean: on the occasions when) if *C* occurs it is certain to cause *E* unless something prevents it. *C* and *E* are to be understood as general expressions, not singular terms. If 'certainty' should seem too epistemological a notion: a necessitating cause *C* of a given kind of effect *E* is such that it *is* not possible (on the occasion) that *C* should occur and should not cause an *E*, nor should there be anything that prevents an *E* from occurring. A non-necessitating cause is then one that can fail of its effect without the intervention of anything to frustrate it. We may discover *types* of necessitating and non-necessitating cause; e.g. rabies is a necessitating cause of death, because it is not possible for one who has rabies to survive without treatment. We don't have to tie it to the occasion. An example of a non-necessitating cause is mentioned by Feynman: a bomb is connected with a Geiger counter, so that it will go off if the Geiger counter registers a certain reading; whether it will or not is not determined, for it is so placed near some radioactive material that it may or may not register that reading.

There would be no doubt of the cause of the reading or of the explosion if the bomb did go off. Max Born is one of the people who has been willing to dissociate causality from determinism: he explicates cause and effect in terms of dependence of the effect on the cause. It is not quite clear what 'dependence' is supposed to be, but at least it seems to imply that you would not get the effect without the cause. The trouble about this is that you might—from some other cause. That this effect was produced by this cause does not at all shew that it could not, or would not, have been produced by something else in the absence of this cause.

Indeterminism is not a possibility unconsidered by philosophers. C. D. Broad, in his inaugural lecture, given in 1934, described it as a possibility; but added that whatever happened without being determined was accidental. He did not explain what he meant by being accidental; he must have meant more than not being necessary. He may have meant being uncaused; but, if I am right, not being determined does not imply not being caused. Indeed, I should explain indeterminism as the thesis that not all physical effects are necessitated by their causes. But if we think of Feynman's bomb, we get some idea of what is meant by 'accidental'. It was random: it 'merely happened' that the radioactive material emitted particles in such a way as to activate the Geiger counter enough to set off the bomb. Certainly the motion of the Geiger counter's needle is caused; and the actual emission is caused too; it occurs because there is this mass of radioactive material here. (I have already indicated that, contrary to the opinion of Hume, there are many different sorts of causality.) But all the same the *causation* itself is, one could say, *mere hap*. It is difficult to explain this idea any further.

Broad used the idea to argue that indeterminism, if applied to human action, meant that human actions are 'accidental'. Now he had a picture of choices as being determining causes, analogous to determining physical causes, and of choices in their turn being either determined or accidental. To regard a choice as such—i.e. any case of choice—as a predetermining causal event, now appears as a naïve mistake in the philosophy of mind, though that is a story I cannot tell here.

It was natural that when physics went indeterministic, some thinkers should have seized on this indeterminism as being just what was wanted for defending the freedom of the will. They received severe criticism on two counts: one, that this 'mere hap' is the very last thing to be invoked as the physical correlate of 'man's ethical behaviour'; the other, that quantum laws predict statistics of events when situations are repeated; interference with these, by the *will*'s determining individual events which the laws of nature leave undetermined, would be as much a violation of natural law as would have been interference which falsified a deterministic mechanical law.

Ever since Kant it has been a familiar claim among philosophers, that one can believe in both physical determinism and 'ethical' freedom. The reconciliations have always seemed to me to be either so much gobbledegook, or to make the alleged freedom of action quite unreal. My actions are mostly physical movements; if these physical movements are physically predetermined by processes which I do not control, then my freedom is illusory. The truth of physical indeterminism is thus indispensable if we are to make anything of the claim to freedom. But certainly it is insufficient. The physically undetermined is not thereby 'free'. For freedom at least involves the power of acting according to an idea, and no such thing is ascribed to whatever is the subject (what would be the relevant subject?) of unpredetermination in indeterministic physics. Nevertheless, there is nothing unacceptable about the idea that that 'physical haphazard' should be the only physical correlate of human freedom of action; and perhaps also of the voluntariness and intentionalness in the conduct of other animals which we do not call 'free'. The freedom, intentionalness and voluntariness are not to be analysed as the same thing as, or as produced by, the physical haphazard. Different sorts of pattern altogether are being spoken of when we mention them, from those involved in describing elementary processes of physical causality.

The other objection is, I think, more to the point. Certainly if we have a statistical law, but undetermined individual events, and then enough of these are supposed to be pushed by will in one direction to falsify the statistical law, we have again a supposition that puts will into conflict with natural laws. But it is not clear that the same train of minute physical events should have to be the regular correlate of the same action; in fact, that suggestion looks immensely implausible. It is, however, required by the objection.

Let me construct an analogy to illustrate this point. Suppose that we have a large glass box full of millions of extremely minute coloured particles, and the box is constantly shaken. Study of the box and particles leads to statistical laws, including laws for the random generation of small unit patches of uniform colour. Now the box is remarkable for also presenting the following phenomenon: the word "Coca-Cola" formed like a mosaic, can always be read when one looks at one of the sides. It is not always the same shape in the formation of its letters, not always the same size or in the same position, it varies in its colours; but there it always is. It is not at all clear that those statistical laws concerning the random motion of the particles and their formation of small unit patches of colour would have to be supposed violated by the operation of a cause for this phenomenon which did not derive it from the statistical laws.

It has taken the inventions of indeterministic physics to shake the rather common dogmatic conviction that determinism is a presupposition or perhaps a conclusion, of scientific knowledge. Not that that conviction has been very much shaken even so. Of course, the belief that the laws of nature are deterministic has been shaken. But I believe it has often been supposed that this makes little difference to the assumption of macroscopic determinism: as if undeterminedness were always encapsulated in systems whose internal workings could be described only by statistical laws, but where the total upshot, and in particular the outward effect, was as near as makes no difference always the same. What difference does it make, after all, that the scintillations, whereby my watch dial is luminous, follow only a statistical law—so long as the gross manifest effect is sufficiently guaranteed by the statistical law? Feynman's example of the bomb and Geiger counter smashes this conception; but as far as I can judge it takes time for the lesson to be learned. I find deterministic assumptions more common now among people at large, and among philosophers, than when I was an undergraduate.

The lesson is welcome, but indeterministic physics (if it succeeds in giving the lesson) is only culturally, not logically, required to make the deterministic picture doubtful. For it was always a mere extravagant fancy, encouraged in the 'age of science' by the happy relation of Newtonian mechanics to the solar system. It ought not to have mattered whether the laws of nature were or were not deterministic. For them to be deterministic is for them, together with the description of the situation, to entail unique results in situations defined by certain relevant objects and measures, and where no part is played by inconstant factors external to such definition. If that is right, the law being deterministic does not tell us whether 'determinism' is true. It is the total coverage of every motion that happens, that is a fanciful claim. But I do not mean that any motions lie outside the scope of physical laws, or that one cannot say, in any given context, that certain motions would be violations of physical law. Remember the contrast between chess and the infantile card game.

Meanwhile in non-experimental philosophy it is clear enough what are the dogmatic slumbers of the day. It is over and over again assumed that any singular causal proposition implies a universal statement running "Always when this, then that"; often assumed that true singular causal statements are derived from such 'inductively believed' universalities. Examples indeed are recalcitrant, but that does not seem to disturb. Even a philosopher acute enough to be conscious of this, such as Davidson, will say, without offering any reason at all for saying it, that a singular causal statement implies *that there is* such a true universal proposition[15]—though perhaps we can never have knowledge of it. Such a thesis needs some reason for believing it! "Regularities in nature": that is not a reason. The most neglected of the key topics in this subject are: interference and prevention.

Notes

1. *Metaphysics,* Book IX, Chapter V.
2. *Ethics,* Book I, Axiom III.
3. *Elements of Philosophy Concerning Body,* Chapter IX.
4. *Treatise of Human Nature,* Book I, Part III, Sections II and VI.
5. My colleague Ian Hacking has pointed out C. S. Peirce to me as an exception to this generalization.
6. *Critique of Pure Reason,* Book II, Chapter II, Section III, Second Analogy.
7. 'The Notion of Cause,' in *Mysticism and Logic.*
8. *Treatise of Human Nature,* Book I, Part III, Section II.
9. Ibid., Book I, Part III, Section XIV.
10. Ibid., Book II, Part III, Section I.
11. Ibid., Book II, Part III, Section I.
12. *Science and Humanism.*
13. I should have made acknowledgements to Gilbert Ryle (*Concept of Mind,* p. 77) for this comparison. But his use of the openness of chess is somewhat ambiguous and is not the same as mine. For the contrast with a closed card game I was indebted to A. J. P. Kenny.
14. Albert Einstein and Leopold Infeld, *The Evolution of Physics,* Simon & Schuster, New York, 1938; (paperback edition, 1967), p. 146.
15. 'Causal Relations,' *Journal of Philosophy,* 64 (November 1967).

PART IV

MIND AND BODY

INTRODUCTION

How do we fit into the wider world? Are we simply very complex parts of the physical world? Could a computer be conscious in the way that we are? Are we just things, with the same sort of identity that rocks and buildings have? Or, is there something special about us? Are our actions as subject to the laws of nature and as predictable, at least in theory, as those of other objects? Or, do we have some special sort of freedom? These questions are as old as philosophy. Yet, in spite of the wealth of seemingly relevant knowledge afforded us by contemporary science, discussion of such questions continues unabated.

Descartes's Dualism

René Descartes's *Meditations on First Philosophy* should be considered as relevant to Part IV of this book as it is to Part III (see pp. 138–62). His treatment of the mind-body problem is as important as his attempts to deal with skepticism. Indeed, although his approach to skepticism has not been widely followed, the basic outline of Descartes's treatment of the relation between mind and body was the dominant view among psychologists and others who attempted to deal with the mind scientifically until our own century, and, it remains the view of sophisticated common sense.

Descartes's answer to the second question we asked was a resounding no. The mind is not part of the physical world at all. Physical things are extended: they take up space. And, they are not conscious. Our minds, on the other hand, are conscious, and do not take up space. Minds and bodies are as fundamentally different as things could be. Descartes begins to develop this dualistic conception in ''Meditation II,'' where he finds that he cannot doubt the existence of his own mind (that is, of himself), whereas he can doubt the existence of the physical world. In ''Meditation VI,'' after he has resolved his doubts about the physical world and determined that the essence of physical things is extension, Descartes develops his theory of mind and body at greater length and gives arguments for it.

Descartes's view is that we know what the mind is by reflecting on our own thinking or consciousness. We can see that the essence of our minds is this consciousness rather than extension. Thinking about Detroit, wishing for a puce Ferrari, feeling a pain, or having a visual image of a tree are all ways of being conscious, not ways of taking up space. There are no ways of thinking that seem to involve being extended; and there are no ways of being extended—no combination of extended parts, however complex—that carry consciousness with them. To be conscious is not to be of a certain shape or size or to move in a certain way, but a quite different and undefinable property of which we are each intimately aware when we reflect on our own minds.

How, then, are immaterial minds and the material world connected? Descartes's theory is that there is a two-way causal interaction between them (thus, Cartesian dualism is often called interactive dualism). One the one hand, the physical world affects one's mind. This happens, for example, in perception. Light rays bounce off the book in front of me, enter my eye, and cause changes in my nervous system, beginning at the periphery and ending in the brain. The state of the brain (the pineal gland in particular, Descartes thought) directly affects the mind. Thus, my body is not me, but simply the part of the material world that most directly affects me. But, there is also a causal interaction in the other direction. States of my mind affect my body and through it the wider world. The most obvious case is action. The intention to drink from the cup in front of me is a certain sort of mental state that involves ideas of the cup. This has an effect on the brain (through the pineal gland again) that affects the muscles and results in my arm moving in a certain way, and, if things to right, in the cup coming to my lips and my getting a drink. Although Descartes's hypothesis about the role of the pineal gland did not turn out to be correct, his basic conception of immaterial mind linked causally to material bodies proved durable.

Alternatives to Descartes

Descartes's position is not without its problem however. One such problem, vigorously stated by Gilbert Ryle, is traditionally known as the problem of other minds. If minds are immaterial, then, we cannot see or touch or otherwise perceive any mind but our own mind, of which we seem to be directly aware. But, then, how do we know that other bodies are really, as is our body, animated by minds at all? Perhaps our mind is the only mind in the world, and every other being seemingly like ours is just some sort of automation? Of course, if we remain stuck in the skeptical abyss into which Descartes leads us in "Meditation I," this will only be a small part of a much larger problem: not only other minds, but also other bodies—even our own—are in doubt. The dualist appears to have an additional problem. Even if convinced of a world external to our own minds, how can we know that there are minds lying behind those other human bodies?

In our selections in Section A, "The Tradition of Problem of Mind and Body," Bertrand Russell poses one solution. He claims that our knowledge of other minds is based on a general principle used in scientific reasoning: analogy. Because other bodies behave as our body does, we may postulate other minds as their causal principle. Norman Malcolm examines the argument from anology and finds it wanting.

A second problem is the interaction Descartes assumes between mental and physical events. Many philosophers have found the whole idea of an interaction between two such different realms completely unintelligible. For example, how could an immaterial mind make contact with a material object in order to affect it or to be affected by it?

But what alternatives are there to Descartes's position? George Berkeley has already given us one: there are not minds and bodies, just minds. It is not obvious how this helps with the problem of other minds. Indeed, in the intellectual milieu of the twentieth century, philosophers have sought to solve the problem of interaction in the opposite direction—not to deny the existence of minds, but to argue that minds can, after all, be considered as parts (or aspects) of the physical world. Just as in the eighteenth century Berkeley maintained that talk about tables and chairs only seems to be talk about non-minds but is actually a complex way of talking about minds and their ideas, so, many twentieth-century philosophers claim that talk about beliefs and desires and pains only seems to be talk about a nonphysical realm but is actually just a complicated way of talking about bodies, brains, and behavior.

Three types of theory are represented (or, at least, suggested) in Section A. The first theory is *logical behaviorism.* Even with Descartes's view, a strong case can be made for the importance of studying behavior as a way of studying the mind, for the behavior that minds cause is part of the evidence we have about minds. Methodological behaviorism is a movement in psychology that emphasizes the importance of studying behavior as a supplement to (possibly as a replacement for) introspective study of the mind.

But, logical behaviorism goes a step further. It claims that our mental language—our talk of beliefs, desires, pains, and so on—is not a way of describing an inner, immaterial cause of behavior, but rather a way of describing behavior itself. An inelegant logical behaviorist might say, for example, that my belief that it is raining out is no more than my behavior of carrying an umbrella and canceling my tennis game. Such a roughcast form of logical behaviorism doesn't seem very plausible. Our representatives of this tradition, Gilbert Ryle and Norman Malcolm, would not appreciate being associated with those presenting such an unsophisticated view. Still, we can see their ideas emerging from just such a view, and only in three moves. The first move is from actual behavior to dispositions to behave. Is my belief that it is raining any more than my disposition to carry an umbrella if I want to go out and to cancel my tennis game if I do not want to get wet? The second move is to couch the thesis in a linguistic form. It is not the crude thesis that mental events are behavioral events, but the more perceptive thesis that there are logical connections between behavior descriptions and mental descriptions. Finally, these logical connections are of a complex sort. We should not expect explicit definitions of mental terms in behavioral language. The connections are more subtle. Talk of behavior and talk of the mind are two linguistic systems for describing the same phenomena; they just cut the phenomena up in different ways. But there is not a mind in addition to behavior or action. This would be, Ryle thinks, a category mistake, on a par with taking a university to be an additional group of buildings over and above its college buildings. The relation between mental states and behavior, Malcolm says, is "criterial." Although behavior provides the criteria for ascription of mental predicates, we should never expect to develop perfect definitions of mental predicates in terms of behavioral ones.

The second theory is represented by David M. Armstrong's essay, "The Nature of Mind." Armstrong thinks that both Descartes and the logical behaviorists have part of the story right. The logical behaviorists are right in thinking that there are logical connections between descriptions of behavior and descriptions of mental states as well as in their rejection of Descartes's idea of an immaterial mind. But Descartes is right in thinking that the mind is an inner cause of behavior, not just behavior redescribed. The key is to see that our mental concepts are simply indirect concepts of brain states. By "pain" we mean something like "that internal state which is apt to produce wincing, crying out, and the like." Our understanding of the causes of such behavior is necessarily indirect, because brains are enormously complex systems enclosed by skulls, which, until recently, could not be examined while still in working condition. Indeed, the concept of pain itself leaves the question open as to whether the cause of pain-behavior is physical or nonphysical. This is what Descartes saw when he noted that mental states are not logically required to be "ways of being extended." But, there is a difference between *not being required to be* a physical state and being required *not to be* a physical state. There is nothing in our concept of mental states, Armstrong argues, that precludes their turning out to be physical states. He thinks the progress of science, which has found physical causes for a wider and wider circle of phenomena, makes it probable that the causes of such behavior are physical. Hence, the mind turns out to be the brain, even though Descartes could conceive of his mind existing without his brain.

Such a view would leave Descartes astounded. How can Armstrong suppose that a sensation like pain is just a state of his brain, Descartes might ask. Can Armstrong not reflect and simply note that such sensations are far different than that? Perhaps, Armstrong's theory would be a reasonable conjecture about other people's minds if one did not have the example of one's own mind to show its absurdity? But how can Armstrong think that believing is a brain state when he can tell by introspecting what he believes and has never seen his brain?

Armstrong, one might charge, has traded the problem of other minds for the problem of his own mind. Armstrong devotes a good deal of his article facing up to this objection. A version of this difficulty is pushed by Thomas Nagel in his essay, "What Is It Like To Be a Bat?" Nagel does not defend a full-blown Cartesianism, but he pushes a question Descartes would appreciate. Isn't there something that we can't know about the mental states of bats, even if we know everything there is to know about their brains and how their behavior is caused? It seems in Armstrong's view that there could be nothing left to know—but isn't there? And, isn't there something we do know about our own minds—just by reflecting on what our various experiences are like—that could never be known by someone who couldn't have the same sorts of experiences no matter how detailed that person's knowledge of our brain states and the connection of those brain states to behavior?

Another sort of objection to Armstrong's view is put forward by Hilary Putnam. In Armstrong's view, mental states turn out to be a certain sort of physical state: the neurophysiological states of the human brain. But, suppose we found beings (Martians perhaps) to whom we comfortably ascribed beliefs, desires, and pains, and, then, discovered that their bodies were constituted out of basically different stuff than ours? These beings would not be in the same physical states as we when they "believed that it was raining" or "felt pain." But, there seems to be an equivalence between their system of physical states and ours. For each of our brain states, there is an analogous state of these being's different sort of brain. In addition, the connections our brain states have to one another and to behavior are mirrored in the connections these being's different states have to each other and their behavior. In such a case, would we really want to deny that they have beliefs, desires, and pains as we do?

Putnam explains the position that is called "functionalism" in his "The Nature of Mental States," and Jerry Fodor compares functionalism with other views and explains its virtues as a philosophical basis for psychology. (It should be said that the bliss Fodor feels at the end of his essay is short lived in the larger work from which it is extracted: he finds problems with functionalism, too!)

Minds and Machines

If a Martian could have a mind like ours in spite of being built out of very different stuff, isn't it logically possible that computers could also have minds? Several of the theories of mind seem to leave open this possibility. Surprisingly, Descartes's view is one of them. If God could cause the brain states of humans to be causally connected with states of mind, why should He not do as well for computers? Of course, the problem of other minds arises here, too. If a computer had a Cartesian mind, how would we know?

Armstrong's view seems to dictate that computers could not have minds as long as they are built out of silicon and not living tissue. But, the functionalist theory of Putnam and Fodor leaves the question open. Why could a computer not have states that were functionally equivalent to ours and, therefore, be in the very same mental states that we are in?

Different points of view on the possibility of a mental life for computers are found in the work of the logician A. M. Turing—whose ideas were important in the development of computer science—and the philosopher John R. Searle. Neither Turing nor Searle is worried about whether any presently existing computer can be said, without metaphor or exaggeration, to think. (Indeed, Turing's selection was written in 1950 when actual computers were still quite primitive by today's standards.) Both men are not merely interested in whether at some time in the future something we are willing to call a "computer" might be said to think. Instead, they are interested in whether computers that work on the principles that modern computers do could, if they became sufficiently complex and were programmed sufficiently cleverly, be said to think. Turing argues that insofar as the question has a clear meaning, the answer is probably yes. He sees no reason computers could not be designed to pass the imitation test, that is, the machine could successfully imitate the behavior of humans insofar as such behavior is relevant to assess the intellectual powers of humans. Computers, thus, need not look like humans or feel like humans or sound like humans, but the content of their answers to any conceivable question would have to be just what humans would answer.

Searle writes in 1980 at a time when computers can do things that Turing could only imagine thirty years earlier. Some computer scientists claim that certain mental properties should be attributed to computers on the basis of what they can do. Searle maintains that, if we examine the way that computer programs work, we will see that this claim is nonsense. Although computers may be programmed to do as well as humans on certain tasks, the way the achieve these results does not require the mental properties that humans would typically use if they performed them. Searle's argument for his conclusion is based on his famous Chinese Room example. In that, Searle imagines himself locked in a room following mechanical rules that, unknown to him, result in his writing suitable Chinese answers to Chinese questions, even though he doesn't know a word of Chinese. "I simply behave like a computer; I perform computational operations on formally specified elements. . . . I am simply the instantiation of a computer program." Now, in this case, Searle says, this ability on his part would not mean that he understood Chinese. So why, he asks, should a computer's doing something similar lead us to say that the computer understood Chinese or had any of the numerous mental abilities that a computer can be programmed to imitate?

The Problem of Personal Identity

Many religions believe in survival after death. Usually, such doctrines allow that the survivor does not have the very same body as before death. Suppose a lawyer who leads a faultless life is reincarnated as a philosopher. The lawyer's original body will still be locked in a coffin or, perhaps, will even have rotted away while the philosopher is growing up. Or, suppose our faultless lawyer goes to heaven. Again, it seems the body he will have in heaven—if beings have bodies there at all—will not be the same body that remains behind on earth. These possibilities raise the problem of personal identity. If the very same being can, at different times, have different bodies (or not have a body at all), then, personal identity cannot simply be bodily identity. But, then, what is it?

One possible answer is that of Descartes: personal identity consists of sameness of immaterial mind, not identity of material body. So, there is no problem with survival after death.

It is interesting to see, however, that one might deny that personal identity consisted in bodily identity, even if one were a thoroughgoing materialist about the mind. A high-tech version of our problem will make the point.

In recent years, there have been several books and television shows that have contemplated the possibility of a brain transplant. Suppose Ms. *A*'s brain is put in Ms. *B*'s body. It seems that the survivor of this operation would be mentally like Ms. *A*, not Ms. *B*. That is, if memories, beliefs, desires, and the like are largely dependant on brain states (whether or not they are identical with them), we might expect *that* survivor to remember things that Ms. *A* has done, have Ms. *A*'s beliefs and desires, and, with respect to mental characteristics generally, to be like Ms. *A*, even though she would, of course, look just like Ms. *B* always did.

In this instance, many people would be inclined to say that the survivor is Ms. *A*, not Ms. *B*—in spite of physical appearances and even fingerprints. But, then, we also have a case of a body transplant, not a brain transplant, in which there is sameness of person without sameness of body—without any appeal to an immaterial mind.

Of course, the survivor has part of Ms. *A*'s body. But, one is inclined to think that it is not just having Ms. *A*'s brain that inclines us to take her to be Ms. *A*. It is not the brain, but what the brain apparently would bring with it, in particular Ms. *A*'s memories—that seems crucial.

Now, we have, independently of any religious doctrine or even a dualistic theory of mind, two possible approaches to personal identity: personal identity as sameness of body or personal identity as consisting in links of memory. The selections we have included in Section C. take different sides on this issue. John Locke was the first to articulate the problem of personal identity in something like this form and to propose a memory theory. He distinguished between sameness of person and sameness of immaterial thinking substance, on the one hand (for he was willing to go along with Descartes's claim that matter could not think), and sameness of human body (he calls it sameness of man), on the other hand. Personal identity, Locke thought, consists in neither of these, but in links of memory, or, to use his words, our ability to extend our consciousness into the past: "For as far as any intelligent being can repeat the idea of any past action with the same consciousness it had of it at first, and with the same consciousness it has of any present action; so far it is the same personal self . . . and would be by distance of time, or change of substance, no more two persons, than a man be two men by wearing other clothes to-day than he did yesterday."

Locke's theory is criticized in three of the essays we have included. Thomas Reid thinks that Locke's whole idea is based on confusions and misunderstandings about identity. David Hume, on the other hand, thinks that Locke is close to having things right. But, in the end, Hume thinks that memory cannot be the source of personal identity, for the latter can reach back further than the former. Hume finds the principle of personal identity rather in causation. The two essays that follow Hume's work consider more high-tech versions of puzzles of personal identity. Bernard Williams mounts a clever argument, which is designed to undercut our inclination in a case like that of Ms. *A* and Ms. *B*, to base our judgments about personal identity on memory rather than identity of body; John Perry criticizes Williams's argument and, by implication, the spirit—if not the letter—of Locke's view. (also, see the "Paradox of Identity" in Part VI.)

Freedom and Determinism

Suppose your friend, standing next to you at a party, suddenly lifts her arm and slaps you in the face. You will be inclined to hold her responsible for this action: to blame her for your sore face, resent her for what she did, and think ill of her moral character.

But, suppose you find out that her arm is tied to a fishline, pulled by someone on a balcony above. Your face is still sore, but now you will hardly be inclined to blame her for what happened. Why? Because she wasn't in control of the movement of her arm; once the person in the balcony pulled the line, a sequence of events was put in motion that ended up with your face getting slapped. Given the tug, the rest of the situation, and the laws of nature, your face was going to get slapped. She had no choice. Her movement was the result of a prior, remote event. She was not free to do otherwise. So how can you blame her?

But, if she is not free, are any of us every free? For the laws of nature do not just concern fishlines, but they concern all events inside and outside our bodies. If nature obeys universal laws, then, our actions are just the most recent parts of a causal sequence of ever-more remote events, the earliest parts of which occurred long before we were born. If the fact that the movement of your friend's arm is explained by the earlier tug on the fishline means she is not free, doesn't the fact that all of our actions can be explained by remote events and the working of general laws mean that none of us are ever free?

But can we really accept such a conclusion? After all, we blame and punish people all the time, and such practices presuppose that these people had a choice in what they did. That we have such choices seems obvious as soon as we reflect on our own actions. Can you doubt that you have the choice, right now to lay down this book and to order a pizza?

This is the dilemma of freedom and determinism. Our assumption that people have choices and are, thus, responsible for what they do appears to conflict with the view that everything, even the movements of human agents, has an explanation in terms of universal laws of nature and antecedent conditions.

There are two obvious responses to our dilemma. The first is to accept that, because we are subject to laws of nature, we are not free. This is Baron d'Holbach's view, which he calls fatalism. C. A. Campbell calls this view determinism, but as we will see, this is misleading. We call it hard determinism for reasons also explained later. The second response to our dilemma is to accept that, because we are free, some of our actions must escape the web of the laws of nature. This is the position of Campbell, which he calls libertarianism.

Given the choice between denying freedom and denying universal causation, most of us would choose the latter. Universal causation may be a useful postulate to guide scientific investigation, but why should we accept it at the cost of giving up a belief so central to our day-to-day lives as our conviction that we are free agents?

But, does giving up universal causation really help? The absence of explanation just doesn't seem to add up to the presence of freedom. Suppose that instead of being pulled by a fishline, your friend's arm moved as a result of a totally random and unpredictable spasm in her brain. That wouldn't make her action more free or her more responsible. Campbell's response to this challenge is that free actions, though uncaused, are not random. We are forced to "recognise a *third* possibility, as remote from chance as from necessity, that, namely, of *creative activity,* in which . . . nothing determines the act save the agent's doing of it." When we take the "inner standpoint," as Campbell urges us to do, this seems an apt enough description of how things seem. But does an apt description of what freedom feels like to the agent do more than label the problem?

Hume takes a third approach. He refuses to choose between freedom and universal causation (which he calls liberty and necessity), but he accepts them both. How does he think this is possible?

Hume describes himself as reconciling liberty and necessity. This brings us back to the terminological matter we left dangling earlier. Let us call the doctrine of universal causation, determinism. And, let us call the view that freedom and determinism (so defined) are not both possible, incompatibilsm; and let us call the opposite view (which Hume held), compatibilism. Then, we can say that d'Holbach is an incompatabilist who accepts determinism; this is what we call hard determinism. Campbell is an incompatibilist who rejects determinism and accepts freedom; this is what we call (as Campbell does) libertarianism. Of course, incompatibilists like Campbell don't find the distinction between determinism and hard determinism very interesting. Finally, a compatibilist who, like Hume, accepts determinism, we call a soft determinist.

Hume thinks that the appearance of incompatibility is due to confusions about causation. Causes do not compel effects, they are merely regularly followed by them. (Hume, of course, is recalling his own discussion of causation in *An Enquiry Concerning Human Understanding,* from which the selection in Section D, "Freedom and Determinism," is taken. See his discussion—and criticisms by G. E. M. Anscombe and C. J. Ducasse—in Part III.) Indeed, Hume claims determinism is just what we want. We want our own desires to determine our actions. The problem with your friend, he would say, was not that her action had a causal explanation, nor even that it had remote causes, but that her own desires were not part of the causal sequence that led to it.

Each of these philosophers seems confident of their resolution of the dilemma of freedom and determinism. We end Section D, however, with an essay by Thomas Nagel, a philosopher who cannot be confident with any of these positions. Indeed, he states that "in a sense the problem has no solution, because something in the idea of agency is incompatible with actions being events, or people being things. But as the external determinants of what someone has done are gradually exposed, in their effect on consequences, character, and choice itself, it becomes gradually clear that actions are events and people things. Eventually nothing remains which can be ascribed to the responsible self, and we are left with nothing but a portion of the larger sequence of events, which can be deplored or celebrated, but not blamed or praised."

A. THE TRADITIONAL PROBLEM OF MIND AND BODY

Descartes's Myth

GILBERT RYLE

Gilbert Ryle (1900–1976) was Waynflete Professor of Metaphysical Philosophy at Oxford University. A leading ordinary language philosopher, his works include *The Concept of Mind, Dilemmas,* and *Plato's Progress.*

(1) The Official Doctrine

There is a doctrine about the nature and place of minds which is so prevalent among theorists and even among laymen that it deserves to be described as the official theory. Most philosophers, psychologists and religious teachers subscribe, with minor reservations, to its main articles and, although they admit certain theoretical difficulties in it, they tend to assume that these can be overcome without serious modifications being made to the architecture of the theory. It will be argued here that the central principles of the doctrine are unsound and conflict with the whole body of what we know about minds when we are not speculating about them.

The official doctrine, which hails chiefly from Descartes, is something like this. With the doubtful exceptions of idiots and infants in arms every human being has both a body and a mind. Some would prefer to say that every human being is both a body and a mind. His body and his mind are ordinarily harnessed together, but after the death of the body his mind may continue to exist and function.

Human bodies are in space and are subject to the mechanical laws which govern all other bodies in space. Bodily processes and states can be inspected by external observers. So a man's bodily life is as much a public affair as are the lives of animals and reptiles and even as the careers of trees, crystals and planets.

But minds are not in space, nor are their operations subject to mechanical laws. The workings of one mind are not witnessable by other observers; its career is private. Only I can take direct cognisance of the states and processes of my own mind. A person therefore lives through two collateral histories, one consisting of what happens in and to his body, the other consisting of what happens in and to his mind. The first is public, the second private. The events in the first history are events in the physical world, those in the second are events in the mental world.

It has been disputed whether a person does or can directly monitor all or only some of the episodes of his own private history; but, according to the official doctrine, of at least some of these episodes he has direct and unchallengeable cognisance. In consciousness, self-consciousness and introspection he is directly and authentically apprised of the present states and operations of his mind. He may have great or small uncertainties about concurrent and adjacent episodes in the physical world, but he can have none about at least part of what is momentarily occupying his mind.

From *The Concept of Mind* (London: Hutchinson and Co., 1949), pp. 11–24.

It is customary to express this bifurcation of his two lives and of his two worlds by saying that the things and events which belong to the physical world, including his own body, are external, while the workings of his own mind are internal. This antithesis of outer and inner is of course meant to be construed as a metaphor, since minds, not being in space, could not be described as being spatially inside anything else, or as having things going on spatially inside themselves. But relapses from this good intention are common and theorists are found speculating how stimuli, the physical sources of which are yards or miles outside a person's skin, can generate mental responses inside his skull, or how decisions framed inside his cranium can set going movements of his extremities.

Even when "inner" and "outer" are construed as metaphors, the problem how a person's mind and body influence one another is notoriously charged with theoretical difficulties. What the mind wills, the legs, arms and the tongue execute; what affects the ear and the eye has something to do with what the mind perceives; grimaces and smiles betray the mind's moods and bodily castigations lead, it is hoped, to moral improvement. But the actual transactions between the episodes of the private history and those of the public history remain mysterious, since by definition they can belong to neither series. They could not be reported among the happenings described in a person's autobiography of his inner life, but nor could they be reported among those described in some one else's biography of that person's overt career. They can be inspected neither by introspection nor by laboratory experiment. They are theoretical shuttlecocks which are forever being bandied from the physiologist back to the psychologist and from the psychologist back to the physiologist.

Underlying this partly metaphorical representation of the bifurcation of a person's two lives there is a seemingly more profound and philosophical assumption. It is assumed that there are two different kinds of existence or status. What exists or happens may have the status of physical existence, or it may have the status of mental existence. Somewhat as the faces of coins are either heads or tails, or somewhat as living creatures are either male or female, so, it is supposed, some existing is physical existing, other existing is mental existing. It is a necessary feature of what has physical existence that it is in space and time, it is a necessary feature of what has mental existence that it is in time but not in space. What has physical existence is composed of matter, or else is a function of matter; what has mental existence consists of consciousness, or else is a function of consciousness.

There is thus a polar opposition between mind and matter, an opposition which is often brought out as follows. Material objects are situated in a common field, known as "space", and what happens to one body in one part of space is mechanically connected with what happens to other bodies in other parts of space. But mental happenings occur in insulated fields, known as "minds", and there is, apart maybe from telepathy, no direct causal connection between what happens in one mind and what happens in another. Only through the medium of the public physical world can the mind of one person make a difference to the mind of another. The mind is its own place and in his inner life each of us lives the life of a ghostly Robinson Crusoe. People can see, hear and jolt one another's bodies, but they are irremediably blind and deaf to the workings of one another's minds and inoperative upon them.

What sort of knowledge can be secured of the workings of a mind? On the one side, according to the official theory, a person has direct knowledge of the best imaginable kind of the workings of his own mind. Mental states and processes are (or are normally) conscious states and processes, and the consciousness which irradiates them can engender no illusions and leaves the door open for no doubts. A person's present thinkings, feelings and willings, his perceivings, rememberings and imaginings are intrinsically "phosphorescent"; their existence and their nature are inevitably betrayed to their owner. The inner life is a stream of consciousness of such a sort that it would be absurd to suggest that the mind whose life is that stream might be unaware of what is passing down it.

True, the evidence adduced recently by Freud seems to show that there exist channels tributary to this stream, which run hidden from their owner. People are actuated by impulses the existence of which they vigorously disavow; some of their thoughts differ from the thoughts which they acknowledge; and some of the actions which they think they will to perform they do not really will. They are thoroughly gulled by some of their own hypocrisies and they successfully ignore facts about their mental lives which on the official theory ought to be patent to them. Holders of the official theory tend, however, to maintain that anyhow in normal circumstances a person must be directly and authentically seized of the present state and workings of his own mind.

Besides being currently supplied with these alleged immediate data of consciousness, a person is also generally supposed to be able to exercise from time to time a special kind of perception, namely inner perception, or introspection. He can take a (non-optical) "look" at what is passing in his mind. Not only can he view and scrutinize a flower through his sense of sight and listen to and discriminate the notes of a bell through his sense of hearing; he can also reflectively or introspectively watch, without any bodily organ of sense, the current episodes of his inner life. This self-observation is also commonly supposed to be immune from illusion, confusion or doubt. A mind's reports of its own affairs have a certainty superior to the best that is possessed by its reports of matters in the physical world. Sense-perceptions can, but consciousness and introspection cannot, be mistaken or confused.

On the other side, one person has no direct access of any sort to the events of the inner life of another. He cannot do better than make problematic inferences from the observed behaviour of the other person's body to the states of mind which, by analogy from his own conduct, he supposes to be signalised by that behaviour. Direct access to the workings of a mind is the privilege of that mind itself; in default of such privileged access, the workings of one mind are inevitably occult to everyone else. For the supposed arguments from bodily movements similar to their own to mental workings similar to their own would lack any possibility of observational corroboration. Not unnaturally, therefore, an adherent of the official theory finds it difficult to resist this consequence of his premisses, that he has no good reason to believe that there do exist minds other than his own. Even if he prefers to believe that to other human bodies there are harnessed minds not unlike his own, he cannot claim to be able to discover their individual characteristics, or the particular things that they undergo and do. Absolute solitude is on this showing the ineluctable destiny of the soul. Only our bodies can meet.

As a necessary corollary of this general scheme there is implicitly prescribed a special way of construing our ordinary concepts of mental powers and operations. The verbs, nouns and adjectives, with which in ordinary life we describe the wits, characters and higher-grade performances of the people with whom we have do, are required to be construed as signifying special episodes in their secret histories, or else as signifying tendencies for such episodes to occur. When someone is described as knowing, believing or guessing something, as hoping, dreading, intending or shirking something, as designing this or being amused at that, these verbs are supposed to denote the occurrence of specific modifications in his (to us) occult stream of consciousness. Only his own privileged access to this stream in direct awareness and introspection could provide authentic testimony that these mental-conduct verbs were correctly or incorrectly applied. The onlooker, be he teacher, critic, biographer or friend, can never assure himself that his comments have any vestige of truth. Yet it was just because we do in fact all know how to make such comments, make them with general correctness and correct them when they turn out to be confused or mistaken, that philosophers found it necessary to construct their theories of the nature and place of minds. Finding mental-conduct concepts being regularly and effectively used, they properly sought to fix their logical geography. But the logical geography officially recommended would entail that there could be no regular or effective use of these mental-conduct concepts in our descriptions of, and prescriptions for, other people's minds.

(2) The Absurdity of the Official Doctrine

Such in outline is the official theory. I shall often speak of it, with deliberate abusiveness, as "the dogma of the Ghost in the Machine". I hope to prove that it is entirely false, and false not in detail but in principle. It is not merely an assemblage of particular mistakes. It is one big mistake and a mistake of a special kind. It is, namely, a category-mistake. It represents the facts of mental life as if they belonged to one logical type or category (or range of types or categories), when they actually belong to another. The dogma is therefore a philosopher's myth. In attempting to explode the myth I shall probably be taken to be denying well-known facts about the mental life of human beings, and my plea that I aim at doing nothing more than rectify the logic of mental-conduct concepts will probably be disallowed as mere subterfuge.

I must first indicate what is meant by the phrase "Category-mistake". This I do in a series of illustrations.

A foreigner visiting Oxford or Cambridge for the first time is shown a number of colleges, libraries, playing fields, museums, scientific departments and administrative offices. He then asks "But where is the University? I have seen where the members of the Colleges live, where the Registrar works, where the scientists experiment and the rest. But I have not yet seen the University in which reside and work the members of your University." It has then to be explained to him that the University is not another collateral institution, some ulterior counterpart to the colleges, laboratories and offices which he has seen. The University is just the way in which all that he has already seen is organized. When they are seen and when their co-ordination is understood, the University has been seen. His mistake lay in his innocent assumption that it was correct to speak of Christ Church, the Bodleian Library, The Ashmolean Museum *and* the University, to speak, that is, as if "the University" stood for an extra member of the class of which these other units are members. He was mistakenly allocating the University to the same category as that to which the other institutions belong.

The same mistake would be made by a child witnessing the march-past of a division, who, having had pointed out to him such and such battalions, batteries, squadrons, etc., asked when the division was going to appear. He would be supposing that a division was counterpart to the units already seen, partly similar to them and partly unlike them. He would be shown his mistake by being told that in watching the battalions, batteries and squadrons marching past he had been watching the division marking past. The march-past was not a parade of battalions, batteries, squadrons *and* a division; it was a parade of the battalions, batteries and squadrons *of* a division.

One more illustration. A foreigner watching his first game of cricket learns what are the functions of the bowlers, the batsmen, the fielders, the umpires and the scorers. He than says "But there is no one left on the field to contribute the famous element of team-spirit. I see who does the bowling, the batting and the wicket-keeping; but I do not see whose role it is to exercise *esprit de corps.*" Once more, it would have to be explained that he was looking for the wrong type of thing. Team-spirit is not another cricketing-operation supplementary to all of the other special tasks. It is, roughly, the keenness with which each of the special tasks is performed, and performing a task keenly is not performing two tasks. Certainly exhibiting team-spirit is not the same thing as bowling or catching, but nor is it a third thing such that we can say that the bowler first bowls *and* then exhibits team-spirit or that a fielder is at a given moment *either* catching *or* displaying *esprit de corps.*

These illustrations of category-mistakes have a common feature which must be noticed. The mistakes were made by people who did not know how to wield the concepts *University, division* and *team-spirit.* Their puzzles arose from inability to use certain items in the English vocabulary.

The theoretically interesting category-mistakes are those made by people who are perfectly competent to apply concepts, at least in the situations with which they are familiar, but are still liable in their abstract thinking to allocate those concepts to logical types to which they do not belong. An instance of a mistake of this sort would be the following story. A student of politics has learned the main differences between the British, the French and the American Constitutions, and has learned also the differences and connections between the Cabinet, Parliament, the various Ministries, the Judicature and the Church of England. But he still becomes embarrassed when asked questions about the connections between the Church of England, the Home Office and the British Constitution. For while the Church and the Home Office are institutions, the British Constitution is not another institution in the same sense of that noun. So inter-institutional relations which can be asserted or denied to hold between the Church and the Home Office cannot be asserted or denied to hold between either of them and the British Constitution. "The British Constitution" is not a term of the same logical type as "the Home Office" and "the Church of England". In a partially similar way, John Doe may be a relative, a friend, an enemy or a stranger to Richard Roe; but he cannot be any of these things to the Average Taxpayer. He knows how to talk sense in certain sorts of discussions about the Average Taxpayer, but he is baffled to say why he could not come across him in the street as he can come across Richard Roe.

It is pertinent to our main subject to notice that, so long as the student of politics continues to think of the British Constitution as a counterpart to the other institutions, he will tend to describe it as a mysteriously occult institution; and so long as John Doe continues to think of the Average Taxpayer as a fellow-citizen, he will tend to think of him as an elusive insubstantial man, a ghost who is everywhere yet nowhere.

My destructive purpose is to show that a family of radical category-mistakes is the source of the double-life theory. The representation of a person as a ghost mysteriously ensconced in a machine derives from this argument. Because, as is true, a person's thinking, feeling and purposive doing cannot be described solely in the idioms of physics, chemistry and physiology, therefore they must be described in counterpart idioms. As the human body is a complex organised unit, so the human mind must be another complex organised unit, though one made of a different sort of stuff and with a different sort of structure. Or, again, as the human body, like any other parcel of matter, is a field of causes and effects, so the mind must be another field of causes and effects, though not (Heaven be praised) mechanical causes and effects.

(3) The Origin of the Category-Mistake

One of the chief intellectual origins of what I have yet to prove to be the Cartesian category-mistake seems to be this. When Galileo showed that his methods of scientific discovery were competent to provide a mechanical theory which should cover every occupant of space, Descartes found in himself two conflicting motives. As a man of scientific genius he could not but endorse the claims of mechanics, yet as a religious and moral man he could not accept, as Hobbes accepted, the discouraging rider to those claims, namely that human nature differs only in degree of complexity from clockwork. The mental could not be just a variety of the mechanical.

He and subsequent philosophers naturally but erroneously availed themselves of the following escape-route. Since mental-conduct words are not to be construed as signifying the occurrence of mechanical processes, they must be construed as signifying the occurrence of non-mechanical processes; since mechanical laws explain movements in space as the effects of other movements in space, other laws must explain some of the non-spatial workings of minds as the effects of other non-spatial workings of minds. The difference between the human behaviours which we describe as intelligent and those which we describe as unintelligent must be a difference in their causation; so, while some movements of human tongues and limbs are the effects of mechanical causes, others must be the effects of non-mechanical causes, i.e. some issue from movements of particles of matter, others from workings of the mind.

The differences between the physical and the mental were thus represented as differences inside the common framework of the categories of "thing", "stuff", "attribute", "stage", "process", "change", "cause" and "effect". Minds are things, but different sorts of things from bodies; mental processes are causes and effects but different sorts of causes and effects from bodily movements. And so on. Somewhat as the foreigner expected the University to be an extra edifice, rather like a college but also considerably different, so the repudiators of mechanism represented minds as extra centers of causal processes, rather like machines but also considerably different from them. Their theory was a paramechanical hypothesis.

That this assumption was at the heart of the doctrine is shown by the fact that there was from the beginning felt to be a major theoretical difficulty in explaining how minds can influence and be influenced by bodies. How can a mental process, such as willing, cause spatial movements like the movements of the tongue? How can a physical change in the optic nerve have among its effects a mind's perception of a flash of light? This notorious crux by itself shows the logical mould into which Descartes pressed his theory of the mind. It was the self-same mould into which he and Galileo set their mechanics. Still unwittingly adhering to the grammar of mechanics, he tried to avert disaster by describing minds in what was merely an obverse vocabulary. The workings of minds had to be described by the mere negatives of the specific descriptions given to bodies; they are not in space, they are not motions, they are not modifications of matter, they are not accessible to public observation. Minds are not bits of clockwork, they are just bits of not-clockwork.

As thus represented, minds are not merely ghosts harnessed to machines, they are themselves just spectral machines. Though the human body is an engine, it is not quite an ordinary engine, since some of its workings are governed by another engine inside it—this interior governor-engine being one of a very special sort. It is invisible, inaudible and it has no size or weight. It cannot be taken to bits and the laws it obeys are not those known to ordinary engineers. Nothing is known of how it governs the bodily engine.

A second major crux points the same moral. Since, according to the doctrine, minds belong to the same category as bodies and since bodies are rigidly governed by mechanical laws, it seemed to many theorists to follow that minds must be similarly governed by rigid non-mechanical laws. The physical world is a deterministic system, so the mental world must be a deterministic system. Bodies cannot help the modifications that they undergo, so minds cannot help pursuing the careers fixed for them. *Responsibility, choice, merit* and *demerit* are therefore inapplicable concepts—unless the compromise solution is adopted of saying that the laws governing mental processes, unlike those governing physical processes, have the congenial attribute of being only rather rigid. The problem of the Freedom of the Will was the problem how to reconcile the hypothesis that minds are to be described in terms drawn from the categories of mechanics with the knowledge that higher-grade human conduct is not of a piece with the behavior of machines.

It is an historical curiosity that it was not noticed that the entire argument was broken-backed. Theorists correctly assumed that any sane man could already recognise the differences between, say, rational and non-rational utterances or between purposive and automatic behaviour. Else there would have been nothing requiring to be salved from mechanism. Yet the explanation given presupposed that one person could in principle never recognise the difference between the rational and the irrational utterances issuing from other human bodies, since he could never get access to the postulated immaterial causes of some of their utterances. Save for the doubtful exception of himself, he could never tell the difference between a man and a Robot. It would have to be conceded, for example, that, for all that we can tell, the inner lives of persons who are classed as idiots or lunatics are as rational as those of anyone else. Perhaps only their overt behaviour is disappointing; that is to say, perhaps "idiots" are not really idiotic, or "lunatics" lunatic. Perhaps, too, some of those who are classed as sane are really idiots. According to the theory, external observers could never know how the overt behaviour of others is correlated with their mental powers and processes and so they could never know or even plausibly conjuncture whether their applications of mental-conduct concepts to these other people were correct or incorrect. It would then be hazardous or impossible for a man to claim sanity or logical consistency even for himself, since he would be debarred from comparing his own performances with those of others. In short, our characterisations of persons and their performances as intelligent, prudent and virtuous or as stupid, hypocritical and cowardly could never have been made, so the problem of providing a special causal hypothesis to serve as the basis of such diagnoses would never have arisen. The question, "How do persons differ from machines?" arose just because everyone already knew how to apply mental-conduct concepts before the new causal hypothesis was introduced. This causal hypothesis could not therefore be the source of the criteria used in those applications. Nor, of course, has the causal hypothesis in any degree improved our handling of those criteria. We still distinguish good from bad arithmetic, politic from impolitic conduct and fertile from infertile imaginations in the ways in which Descartes himself distinguished them before and after he speculated how the applicability of these criteria was compatible with the principle of mechanical causation.

He had mistaken the logic of his problem. Instead of asking by what criteria intelligent behaviour is actually distinguished from non-intelligent behaviour, he asked "Given that the principle of mechanical causation does not tell us the difference, what other causal principle will tell it us?" He realised that the problem was not one of mechanics and assumed that it must therefore be one of some counterpart to mechanics. Not unnaturally psychology is often cast for just this role.

When two terms belong to the same category, it is proper to construct conjunctive propositions embodying them. Thus a purchaser may say that he bought a left-hand glove and a right-hand glove, but not that he bought a left-hand glove, a right-hand glove and a pair of gloves. "She came home in a flood of tears and a sedan-chair" is a well-known joke based on the absurdity of conjoining terms of different types. It would have been equally ridiculous to construct the disjunction "She came home either in a flood of tears or else in a sedan-chair". Now the dogma of the Ghost in the Machine does just this. It maintains that there exist both bodies and minds; that there occur physical processes and mental processes; that there are mechanical causes of corporeal movements and mental causes of corporeal movements. I shall argue that these and other analogous conjunctions are absurd; but, it must be noticed, the argument will not show that either of the illegitimately conjoined propositions is absurd in itself. I am not, for example, denying that there occur mental processes. Doing long division is a mental process and so is making a joke. But I am saying that the phrase "there occur mental processes" does not mean the same sort of thing as "there occur physical processes", and, therefore, that it makes no sense to conjoin or disjoin the two.

If my argument is successful, there will follow some interesting consequences. First, the hallowed contrast between Mind and Matter will be dissipated, but dissipated not by either of the equally hallowed absorptions of Mind by Matter or of Matter by Mind, but in quite a different way. For the seeming contrast of the two will be shown to be as illegitimate as would be the contrast of "she came home in a flood of tears" and "she came home in a sedan-chair". The belief that there is a polar opposition between Mind and Matter is the belief that they are terms of the same logical type.

It will also follow that both Idealism and Materialism are answers to an improper question. The "reduction" of the material world to mental states and processes, as well as the "reduction" of mental states and processes to physical states and processes, presuppose the legitimacy of the disjunction "Either there exist minds or there exist bodies (but not both)". It would be like saying, "Either she bought a left-hand and a right-hand glove or she bought a pair of gloves (but not both)".

It is perfectly proper to say, in one logical tone of voice, that there exist minds and to say, in another logical tone of voice, that there exist bodies. But these expressions do not indicate two different species of existence, for "existence" is not a generic word like "coloured" or "sexed". They indicate two different senses of "exist", somewhat as "rising" has different senses in "the tide is rising", "hopes are rising", and "the average age of death is rising". A man would be thought to be making a poor joke who said that three things are now rising, namely the tide, hopes and the average age of death. It would be just as good or bad a joke to say that there exist prime numbers and Wednesdays and public opinions and navies; or that there exist both minds and bodies. . . .

(4) Historical Note

It would not be true to say that the official theory derives solely from Descartes's theories, or even from a more widespread anxiety about the implications of seventeenth century mechanics. Scholastic and Reformation theology had schooled the intellects of the scientists as well as of the laymen, philosophers and clerics of that age. Stoic-

Augustinian theories of the will were embedded in the Calvinist doctrines of sin and grace; Platonic and Aristotelian theories of the intellect shaped the orthodox doctrines of the immortality of the soul. Descartes was reformulating already prevalent theological doctrines of the soul in the new syntax of Galileo. The theologian's privacy of conscience became the philosopher's privacy of consciousness, and what had been the bogy of Predestination reappeared as the bogy of Determinism.

It would also not be true to say that the two-worlds myth did no theoretical good. Myths often do a lot of theoretical good, while they are still new. One benefit bestowed by the para-mechanical myth was that it partly superannuated the then prevalent para-political myth. Minds and their Faculties had previously been described by analogies with political superiors and political subordinates. The idioms used were those of ruling, obeying, collaborating and rebelling. They survived and still survive in many ethical and some epistemological discussions. As, in physics, the new myth of occult Forces was a scientific improvement on the old myth of Final Causes, so, in anthropological and psychological theory, the new myth of hidden operations, impulses and agencies was an improvement on the old myth of dictations, deferrences and disobediences.

The Argument from Analogy for Other Minds

BERTRAND RUSSELL

The problem with which we are concerned is the following. We observe in ourselves such occurrences as remembering, reasoning, feeling pleasure, and feeling pain. We think that sticks and stones do not have these experiences, but that other people do. Most of us have no doubt that the higher animals feel pleasure and pain, though I was once assured by a fisherman that "Fish have no sense nor feeling." I failed to find out how he had acquired this knowledge. Most people would disagree with him, but would be doubtful about oysters and starfish. However this may be, common sense admits an increasing doubtfulness as we descend in the animal kingdom, but as regards human beings it admits no doubt.

It is clear that belief in the minds of others requires some postulate that is not required in physics, since physics can be content with a knowledge of structure. My present purpose is to suggest what this further postulate may be.

It is clear that we must appeal to something that may be vaguely called "analogy." The behavior of other people is in many ways analogous to our own, and we suppose that it must have analogous causes. What people say is what we should say if we had certain thoughts, and so we infer that they probably have these thoughts. They give us information which we can sometimes subsequently verify. They behave in ways in which we behave when we are pleased (or displeased) in circumstances in which we should be pleased (or displeased). We may talk over with a friend some incident which we have both experienced, and find that his reminiscences dovetail with our own; this is particularly convincing when he remembers something that we have forgotten but that he recalls to our thoughts. Or again: you set your boy a problem in arithmetic, and with luck he gets the right answer; this persuades you that he is capable of arithmetical reasoning. There are, in short, very many ways in which may responses to stimuli differ from those of "dead" matter, and in all these ways other people resemble me. As it is clear to me that the causal laws governing my behavior have to do with "thoughts," it is natural to infer that the same is true of the analogous behavior of my friends.

The inference with which we are at present concerned is not merely that which takes us beyond solipsism, by maintaining that sensations have causes about which *something* can be known. This kind of inference . . . suffices for physics. . . . We are concerned now with a much more specific kind of inference, the kind that is involved in our knowledge of the thoughts and feelings of others—assuming that we have such knowledge. It is of course obvious that such knowledge is more or less doubtful. There is not only the general argument that we may be dreaming; there is also the possibility of ingenious automata. There are calculating machines that do sums much better than our schoolboy sons; there are gramophone records that remember impeccably what So-and-so said on such-and-such an occasion; there are people in the cinema who, though copies of real people, are not themselves alive. There is no theoretical limit to what ingenuity could achieve in the way of producing the

From *Human Knowledge: Its Scope and Limits* (New York: Simon & Schuster, 1948), pp. 482–86.

illusion of life where in fact life is absent.

But, you will say, in all such cases it was the thoughts of human beings that produced the ingenious mechanism. Yes, but how do you know this? And how do you know that the gramophone does *not* "think"?

There is, in the first place, a difference in the causal laws of observable behavior. If I say to a student, "Write me a paper on Descartes's reasons for believing in the existence of matter," I shall, if he is industrious, cause a certain response. A gramophone record might be so constructed as to respond to this stimulus, perhaps better than the student, but if so it would be incapable of telling me anything about any other philosopher, even if I threatened to refuse to give it a degree. One of the most notable peculiarities of human behavior is change of response to a given stimulus. An ingenious person could construct an automaton which would always laugh at his jokes, however often it heard them; but a human being, after laughing a few times, will yawn, and end by saying, "How I laughed the first time I heard that joke."

But the differences in observable behavior between living and dead matter do not suffice to prove that there are "thoughts" connected with living bodies other than my own. It is probably possible theoretically to account for the behavior of living bodies by purely physical causal laws, and it is probably impossible to refute materialism by external observation alone. If we are to believe that there are thoughts and feelings other than our own, that must be in virtue of some inference in which our own thoughts and feelings are relevant, and such an inference must go beyond what is needed in physics.

I am, of course, not discussing the history of how we come to believe in other minds. We find ourselves believing in them when we first begin to reflect; the thought that Mother may be angry or pleased is one which arises in early infancy. What I am discussing is the possibility of a postulate which shall establish a rational connection between this belief and data, e.g., between the belief "Mother is angry" and the hearing of a loud voice.

The abstract schema seems to be as follows. We know, from observation of ourselves, a causal law of the form "A causes B," where A is a "thought" and B a physical occurrence. We sometimes observe a B when we cannot observe any A; we then infer an unobserved A. For example: I know that when I say, "I'm thirsty," I say so, usually, because I am thirsty, and therefore, when I hear the sentence "I'm thirsty" at a time when I am not thirsty, I assume that someone else is thirsty. I assume this the more readily if I see before me a hot, drooping body which goes on to say, "I have walked twenty desert miles in this heat with never a drop to drink." It is evident that my confidence in the "inference" is increased by increased complexity in the datum and also by increased certainty of the causal law derived from subjective observation, provided the causal law is such as to account for the complexities of the datum.

It is clear that insofar as plurality of causes is to be suspected, the kind of inference we have been considering is not valid. We are supposed to know "A causes B," and also to know that B has occurred; if this is to justify us in inferring A, we must know that *only* A causes B. Or, if we are content to infer that A is probable, it will suffice if we can know that in most cases it is A that causes B. If you hear thunder without having seen lightning, you confidently infer that there was lightning, because you are convinced that the sort of noise you heard is seldom caused by anything except lightning. As this example shows, our principle is not only employed to establish the existence of other minds but is habitually assumed, though in a less concrete form, in physics. I say "a less concrete form" because unseen lightning is only abstractly similar to seen lightning, whereas we suppose the similarity of other minds to our own to be by no means purely abstract.

Complexity in the observed behavior of another person, when this can all be accounted for by a simple cause such as thirst, increases the probability of the inference by diminishing the probability of some other cause. I think that in ideally favorable circumstances the argument would be formally as follows:

From subjective observation I know that A, which is a thought or feeling, causes B, which is a bodily act, e.g., a statement. I know also that, whenever B is an act of my own body, A is its cause. I now observe an act of the kind B in a body not my own, and I am having no thought or feeling of the kind A. But I still believe, on the basis of self-observation, that only A can cause B; I therefore infer that there was an A which caused B, though it was not an A that I could observe. On this ground I infer that other people's bodies are associated with minds, which resemble mine in proportion as their bodily behavior resembles my own.

In practice, the exactness and certainty of the above statement must be softened. We cannot be sure that, in our subjective experience, A is the only cause of B. And even if A is the only cause of B in our experience, how can we know that this holds outside our experience? It is not necessary that we should know this with any certainty; it is enough if it is highly probable. It is the assumption of probability in such cases that is our postulate. The postulate may therefore be stated as follows:

> If, whenever we can observe whether A and B are present or absent, we find that every case of B has an A as a causal antecedent, then it is probable that most B's have A's as causal antecedents, even in cases where observation does not enable us to know whether A is present or not.

This postulate, if accepted, justifies the inference to other minds, as well as many other inferences that are made unreflectingly by common sense.

Knowledge of Other Minds

NORMAN MALCOLM

Norman Malcolm (1911–) is emeritus professor of philosophy at Cornell University. A leading exponent of Ludwig Wittgenstein's philosophy, his publications include *Dreaming* and *Knowledge and Certainty*.

I

I believe that the argument from analogy for the existence of other minds still enjoys more credit than it deserves, and my first aim will be to show that it leads nowhere. J. S. Mill is one of many who have accepted the argument and I take his statement of it as representative. He puts to himself the question, "By what evidence do I know, or by what considerations as I led to believe, that there exist other sentient creatures; that the walking and speaking figures which I see and hear, have sensations and thoughts, or in other words, possess Minds?" His answer is the following:

> I conclude that other human beings have feelings like me, because, first, they have bodies like me, which I know, in my own case, to be the antecedent condition of feelings; and because, secondly, they exhibit the acts, and other outward signs, which in my own case I know by experience to be caused by feelings. I am conscious in myself of a series of facts connected by an uniform sequence, of which the beginning is modifications of my body, the middle is feelings, the end is outward demeanor. In the case of other human beings I have the evidence of my senses for the first and last links of the series, but not for the intermediate link. I find, however, that the sequence between the first and last is as regular and constant in those other cases as it is in mine. In my own case I know that the first link produces the last through the intermediate link, and could not produce it without. Experience, therefore, obliges me to conclude that there must be an intermediate link; which must either be the same in others as in myself, or a different one: I must either believe them to be alive, or to be automations: and by believing them to be alive, that is, by supposing the link to be of the same nature as in the case of which I have experience, and which is in all other respects similar, I bring other human beings, as phenomena, under the same generalizations which I know by experience to be the true theory of my own existence.[1]

I shall pass by the possible objection that this would be very *weak* inductive reasoning, based as it is on the observation of a single instance. More interesting is the following point: Suppose this reasoning could yield a conclusion of the sort "It is probable that that human figure" (pointing at some person other than oneself) "has thoughts and feelings." Then there is a question as to whether this conclusion can *mean* anything to the

From *Knowledge and Certainty* (Ithaca, N.Y.: Cornell University Press, 1963), pp. 130–40.

philosopher who draws it, because there is a question as to whether the sentence "That human figure has thoughts and feelings" can mean anything to him. Why should this be a question? Because the assumption from which Mill starts is that he has *no criterion* for determining whether another "walking and speaking figure" does or does not have thoughts and feelings. If he had a criterion he could apply it, establishing with certainty that this or that human figure does or does not have feelings (for the only plausible criterion would lie in behavior and circumstances that are open to view), and there would be no call to resort to tenuous analogical reasoning that yields at best a probability. If Mill has no criterion for the existence of feelings other than his own then in that sense he does not understand the sentence "That human figure has feelings" and therefore does not understand the sentence "It is *probable* that that human figure has feelings."

There is a familiar inclination to make the following reply: "Although I have no criterion of verification still I *understand,* for example, the sentence 'He has a pain.' For I understand the meaning of 'I have a pain,' and 'He has a pain' means that he has the *same* thing I have when I have a pain." But this is a fruitless maneuver. If I do not know how to establish that someone has a pain then I do not know how to establish that he has the *same* as I have when I have a pain.[2] You cannot improve my understanding of "He has a pain" by this recourse to the notion of "the same," unless you give me a criterion for saying that someone *has* the same as I have. If you can do this you will have no use for the argument from analogy: and if you cannot then you do not understand the supposed conclusion of that argument. A philosopher who purports to rely on the analogical argument cannot, I think, escape this dilemma.

There have been various attempts to repair the argument from analogy. Mr. Stuart Hampshire has argued[3] that its validity as a method of inference can be established in the following way: Others sometimes infer that I am feeling giddy from my behavior. Now I have direct, non-inferential knowledge, says Hampshire, of my own feelings. So I can check inferences made about me against the facts, checking thereby the accuracy of the "methods" of inference.

> All that is required for testing the validity of any method of factual inference is that each one of us should sometimes be in a position to confront the conclusions of the doubtful method of inference with what is known by him to be true independently of the method of inference in question. Each one of us is certainly in this position in respect of our common methods of inference about the feelings of persons other than ourselves, in virtue of the fact that each one of us is constantly able to compare the results of this type of inference with what he knows to be true directly and non-inferentially; each one of us is in the position to make this testing comparison, whenever he is the designated subject of a statement about feelings and sensations. I, Hampshire, know by what sort of signs I may be misled in inferring Jones's and Smith's feelings, because I have implicitly noticed (though probably not formulated) where Jones, Smith and others generally go wrong in inferring my feelings. (op. cit., pp. 4–5).

Presumably I can also note when the inferences of others about my feelings do not go wrong. Having ascertained the reliability of some inference-procedures I can use them myself, in a guarded way, to draw conclusions about the feelings of others, with a modest but justified confidence in the truth of those conclusions.

My first comment is that Hampshire has apparently forgotten the purpose of the argument from analogy, which is to provide some probability that "the walking and speaking figures which I see and hear, have sensations and thoughts" (Mill). For the reasoning that he describes involves the assumption that other human figures *do* have thoughts and sensations: for they are assumed to *make inferences* about me from *observations* of my behavior. But the philosophical problem of the existence of other minds *is* the problem of whether human figures other than oneself do, among other things, make observations, inferences, and assertions. Hampshire's supposed defense of the argument from analogy is an *ignoratio elenchi*.

If we struck from the reasoning described by Hampshire all assumption of thoughts and sensations in others we should be left with something roughly like this: "When my behavior is such and such there come from nearby human figures the sounds 'He feels giddy.' And generally I do feel giddy at the time. Therefore when another human figure exhibits the same behavior and I say 'He feels giddy,' it is probable that he does feel giddy." But the reference here to the sentence-like sounds coming from other human bodies is irrelevant, since I must not assume that those sounds express inferences. Thus the reasoning becomes simply the classical argument from analogy: "When my behavior is such and such I feel giddy; so probably when another human figure behaves the same way he feels the same way." This argument, again, is caught in the dilemma about the criterion of the *same*.

The version of analogical reasoning offered by Professor H. H. Price[4] is more interesting. He suggests that "one's evidence for the existence of other minds is derived primarily from the understanding of language" (p. 429). His idea is that if another body gives forth noises one understands, like "There's the bus," and if these noises give one new information, this "provides some evidence that the foreign body which uttered the noises is animated by a mind like one's own. . . . Suppose I am often in its neighborhood, and it repeatedly produces utterances which I can understand, and which I then proceed to verify for myself. And suppose that this happens in many different kinds of situations. I think that my evidence for believing that this body is animated by a mind like my own would then become very strong" (p. 430). The body from which these informative sounds proceed need not be a human body. "If the rustling of the leaves of an oak formed intelligible words conveying new information to me, and if gorse-bushes made intelligible gestures, I should have evidence that the oak or the gorse-bush was animated by an intelligence like my own" (p. 436). Even if the intelligible and informative sounds did not proceed from a body they would provide evidence for the existence of a (disembodied) mind (p. 435).

Although differing sharply from the classical analogical argument, the reasoning presented by Price is still analogical in form: I know by introspection that when certain combinations of sounds come from me they are "symbols in acts of spontaneous thinking"; therefore similar combinations of sounds, not produced by me, "probably function as instruments to an act of spontaneous thinking, which in this case is not my own" (p. 446). Price says that the reasoning also provides an *explanation* of the otherwise mysterious occurrence of sounds which I understand but did not produce. He anticipates the objection that the hypothesis is nonsensical because unverifiable. "The hypothesis is a perfectly conceivable one," he says, "in the sense that I know very well what the world would have to be like if the hypothesis were true—what sorts of entities there must be in it, and what sorts of events must occur in them. I know from introspection what acts of thinking and perceiving are, and I know what it is for such acts to be combined into the unity of a single mind . . ." (pp. 446–47).

I wish to argue against Price that no amount of intelligible sounds coming from an oak tree or a kitchen table could create any probability that it has sensations and thoughts. The question to be asked is: What would show that a tree or table *understands* the sounds that come from it? We can imagine that useful warnings, true descriptions and predictions, even "replies" to questions, should emanate from a tree, so that it came to be of enormous value to its owner. How should we establish that it understood those sentences? Should we "question" it? Suppose that the tree "said" that there was a vixen in the neighborhood, and we "asked" it "What is a vixen?," and it "replied," "A vixen is a female fox." It might go on to do as well for "female" and "fox." This performance might incline us to say that the tree understood the words, in contrast to the possible case in which it answered "I don't know" or did not answer at all. But would it show that the tree understood the words in the same sense that a person could understand them? With a person such a performance would create a presumption that he could make correct *applications* of the word in question; but not so with a tree. To see this point think of the normal teaching of words (e.g., "spoon," "dog," "red") to a child and how one decides whether he understands them. At a primitive stage of teaching one does not require or expect definitions, but rather than the child should *pick out* reds from blues, dogs from cats, spoons from forks. This involves his looking, pointing, reaching for and going to the right things and not the wrong ones. That a child says "red" when a red thing and "blue" when a blue thing is put before him is indicative of a mastery of those words *only* in conjunction with the other activities of looking, pointing, trying to get, fetching, and carrying. Try to suppose that he says the right words but looks at and reaches for the wrong things. Should we be tempted to say that he has mastered the use of those words? No, indeed. The disparity between words and behavior would make us say that he does not understand the words. In the case of a tree there could be no disparity between its words and its "behavior" because it is logically incapable of behavior of the relevant kind.

Since it has nothing like the human face and body it makes no sense to say of a tree, or an electronic computer, that it is looking or pointing at or fetching something. (Of course one can always *invent* a sense for these expressions.) Therefore it would make no sense to say that it did or did not understand the above words. Trees and computers cannot either pass or fail the tests that a child is put through. They cannot take them. That an object was a source of intelligible sounds or other signs (no matter how sequential) would not be enough by itself to establish that it had thoughts or sensations. How informative sentences and valuable predictions could emanate from a gorse-bush might be a grave scientific problem, but the explanation could never be that the gorse-bush has a mind. Better no explanation than nonsense!

It might be thought that the above difficulty holds only for words whose meaning has a "perceptual content" and that if we imagined, for example, that our gorse-bush produced nothing but pure mathematical propositions we should be justified in attributing thought to it, although not sensation. But suppose there was a remarkable "calculating boy" who could give right answers to arithmetical problems but could not apply numerals to reality in empirical propositions, e.g., he could not *count* any objects. I believe that everyone would be reluctant to say that he *understood* the mathematical signs and truths that he produced. If he could count in the normal way there would not be this reluctance. And "counting in the normal way" involves looking, pointing, reaching, fetching, and so on. That is, it requires the human face and body, and human behavior—or something similar. Things which do not have the human form, or anything like it, not merely do not but *cannot* satisfy the criteria for thinking. I am trying to bring out part of what Wittgenstein meant when he said, "We only say of a human being and what is like one that it thinks" (*Investigations,* sec. 360), and "The human body is the best picture of the human soul" (ibid., p. 178).

I have not yet gone into the most fundamental error of the argument from analogy. It is present whether the argument is the classical one (the analogy between my body and other bodies) or Price's version (the analogy between my language and the noises and signs produced by other things). It is the mistaken assumption that *one learns from one's own case* what thinking, feeling, sensation are. Price gives expression to this assumption when he says: "I know from introspection what acts of thinking and perceiving are . . ." (op. cit., p. 447). It is the most natural assumption for a philosopher to make and indeed seems at first to be the only possibility. Yet Wittgenstein has made us see that it leads first to solipsism and then to nonsense. I shall try to state as briefly as possible how it produces those results.

A philosopher who believes that one must learn what thinking, fear, or pain is "from one's own case," does not believe that the thing to be observed is one's behavior, but rather something "inward." He considers behavior to be related to the inward states and occurrences merely as an accompaniment or possibly an effect. He cannot regard behavior as a *criterion* of psychological phenomena: for if he did he would have no use for the analogical argument (as was said before) and also the priority given to "one's own case" would be pointless. He believes that he notes something in himself that he calls "thinking" or "fear" or "pain," and then he tries to infer the presence of the *same* in others. He should then deal with the question of what his criterion of the *same* in others is. This he cannot do because it is of the essence of his viewpoint to reject circumstances and behavior as a criterion of mental phenomena in others. And what else could serve as a criterion? He ought, therefore, to draw the conclusion that the notion of thinking, fear, or pain in others is in an important sense meaningless. He has no idea of what would count for or against it.[5] "That there should be thinking or pain other than my own is unintelligible,'' he ought to hold. This would be a rigorous solipsism, and a correct outcome of the assumption that one can know only from one's own case what the mental phenomena are. An equivalent way of putting it would be: ''When I say 'I am in pain,' by 'pain' I mean a certain inward state. When I say *'He* is in pain,' by 'pain' I mean *behavior.* I cannot attribute pain to others *in the same sense* that I attribute it to myself.''

Some philosophers before Wittgenstein may have seen the solipsistic result of starting from ''one's own case.'' But I believe he is the first to have shown how that starting point destroys itself. This may be presented as follows: One supposes that one inwardly picks out something as thinking or pain and thereafter identifies it whenever it presents itself in the soul. But the question to be pressed is, Does one make *correct* identifications? The proponent of these ''private'' identifications has nothing to say here. He feels sure that he identifies correctly the occurrences in his soul; but feeling sure is no guarantee of being right. Indeed he has no idea of what being *right* could mean. He does not know how to distinguish between actually making correct identifications and being under the impression that he does. (See *Investigations,* secs. 258–59.) Suppose that he identified the emotion of anxiety as the sensation of pain? Neither he nor anyone else could know about this ''mistake.'' Perhaps he makes a mistake *every* time! Perhaps all of us do! We ought to see now that we are talking nonsense. We do not know what a *mistake* would be. We have no standard, no examples, no customary practice, with which to compare our inner recognitions. The inward identification cannot hit the bull's-eye, or miss it either, because there is no bull's-eye. When we see that the ideas of correct and incorrect have no application to the supposed inner identification, the latter notion loses its appearance of sense. Its collapse brings down both solipsism and the argument from analogy.

II

The destruction of the argument from analogy also destroys the *problem* for which it was supposed to provide a solution. A philosopher feels himself in a difficulty about other minds because he assumes that first of all he is acquainted with mental phenomena ''from his own case.'' What troubles him is how to make the transition from his own case to the case of others. When his thinking is freed of the illusion of the priority of his own case, then he is able to look at the familiar facts and to acknowledge that the circumstances, behavior, and utterances of others actually are his *criteria* (not merely his evidence) for the existence of their mental states. Previously this had seemed impossible.

But now he is in danger of flying to the opposite extreme of behaviorism, which errs by believing that through observation of one's own circumstances, behavior, and utterances one can find out that one is thinking or angry. The philosophy of ''from one's own case'' and behaviorism, though in a sense opposites, make the common assumption that the first-person, present-tense psychological statements are verified by self-observation. According to the ''one's own case'' philosophy the self-observation cannot be checked by others; according to behaviorism the self-observation would be by means of outward criteria that are available to all. The first position becomes unintelliglble; the second is false for at least many kinds of psychological statements. We are forced to conclude that the first-person psychological statements are not (or hardly ever) verified by self-observation. It follows that they have no verification at all; for if they had a verification it would have to be by self-observation.

But if sentences like ''My head aches'' or ''I wonder where she is'' do not express observations then what do they do? What is the relation between my declaration that my head aches and the fact that my head aches, if the former is not the report of an observation? The perplexity about the existence of *other* minds has, as the result of criticism, turned in to a perplexity about the meaning of one's own psychological sentences about oneself. At our starting point it was the sentence *''His* head aches'' that posed a problem; but now it is the sentence *''My* head aches'' that puzzles us.

One way in which this problem can be put is by the question, ''How does *one know when to say* the words 'My head aches'?'' The inclination to ask this question can be made acute by imagining a fantastic but not impossible case of a person who has survived to adult years without ever experiencing pain. He is given various sorts of injections to correct this condition, and on receiving one of these one day, he jumps and exclaims, "Now I feel pain!" One wants to ask, "How did he *recognize* the new sensation as a *pain?*"

Let us note that if the man gives an answer (e.g., "I knew it must be pain because of the way I jumped") then he proves by that very fact that he has not mastered the correct use of the words "I feel pain." They cannot be used to state a *conclusion*. In telling us *how* he did it he will convict himself of a misuse. Therefore the question "How did he recognize his sensation?" requests the impossible. The inclination to ask it is evidence of our inability to grasp the fact that the use of this psychological sentence has nothing to do with recognizing or identifying or observing a state of oneself.

The fact that this imagined case produces an especially strong temptation to ask the "How?" question shows that we have the idea that it must be more difficult to give the right name of one's sensation *the first time*. The implication would be that it is not so difficult *after* the first time. Why should this be? Are we thinking that then the man would have a paradigm of pain with which he could compare his sensations and so be in a position to know right off whether a certain sensation was or was not a pain? But the paradigm would be either something "outer" (behavior) or something "inner" (perhaps a memory impression of the sensation). If the former then he is misusing the first-person sentence. If the latter then the question of whether he compared *correctly* the present sensation with the inner paradigm of pain would be without sense. Thus the idea that the use of the first-person sentences can be governed by paradigms must be abandoned. It is another form of our insistent misconception of the first-person sentence as resting somehow on the identification of a psychological state.

These absudities prove that we must conceive of the first-person psychological sentences in some entirely different light. Wittgenstein presents us with the suggestion that the first-person sentences are to be thought of as similar to the natural nonverbal, behavioral expressions of psychological states. "My leg hurts," for example, is to be assimilated to crying, limping, holding one's leg. This is a bewildering comparison and one's first thought is that two sorts of things could not be more unlike. By saying the sentence one can make a *statement;* it has a *contradictory;*it is *true* of *false;* in saying it one *lies* or tells the truth; and so on. None of these things, exactly, can be said of crying, limping, holding one's leg. So how can there be any resemblance? But Wittgenstein knew this when he deliberately likened such a sentence to "the primitive, the natural, expressions" of pain, and said that it is "new pain-behavior" (ibid., sec. 244). This analogy has at least two important merits: first, it breaks the hold on us of the question "How does one *know when to say* 'My leg hurts'?," for in the light of the analogy this will be as nonsensical as the question "How does one know when to cry, limp, or hold one's leg?"; second, it explains how the utterance of a first-person psychological sentence by another person can have *importance* for us, although not as an identification—for in the light of the analogy it will have the same importance as the natural behavior which serves as our preverbal criterion of the psychological states of others.

Notes

1. J. S. Mill, *An Examination of Sir William Hamilton's Philosophy,* 6th ed. (New York: Longmans, Green & Co., Inc., 1889), pp. 243–44.
2. "It is no explanation to say: the supposition that he has a pain is simply the supposition that he has the same as I. For *that* part of the grammar is quite clear to me: that is, that one will say that the stove has the same experience as I, *if* one says: it is in pain and I am in pain" (Ludwig Wittgenstein, *Philosophical Investigations* [New York: The Macmillan Company, 1953], sec. 350).
3. "The Analogy of Feeling," *Mind,* January 1952, pp. 1–12.
4. "Our Evidence for the Existence of Other Minds," *Philosophy,* 13 (1938), 425–56.
5. One reason why philosophers have not commonly drawn this conclusion may be, as Wittgenstein acutely suggests, that they assume that they have "an infallible paradigm of identity in the identity of a thing with itself" *(Investigations,* sec. 215).

The Nature of Mind

DAVID M. ARMSTRONG

David M. Armstrong (1926–) is Challis Professor of Philosophy at the University of Sydney. His publications include *Perception and the Physical World, A Materialist Theory of the Mind,* and *Universals and Scientific Realism.*

Men have minds, that is to say, they perceive, they have sensations, emotions, beliefs, thoughts, purposes, and desires.[1] What is it to have a mind? What is it to perceive, to feel emotion, to hold a belief, or to have a purpose? In common with many other modern philosophers, I think that the best clue we have to the nature of mind is furnished by the discoveries and hypotheses of modern science concerning the nature of man.

What does modern science have to say about the nature of man? There are, of course, all sorts of disagreements and divergencies in the views of individual scientists. But I think it is true to say that one view is steadily gaining ground, so that it bids fair to become established scientific doctrine. This is the view that we can give a complete account of man *in purely physico-chemical terms.* This view has received a tremendous impetus in the last decade from the new subject of molecular biology, a subject which promises to unravel the physical and chemical mechanisms which lie at the basis of life. Before that time, it received great encouragement from pioneering work in neurophysiology pointing to the likelihood of a purely electro-chemical account of the working of the brain. I think it is fair to say that those scientists who still reject the physico-chemical account of man do so primarily for philosophical, or moral, or religious reasons, and only secondarily, and halfheartedly, for reasons of scientific detail. This is not to say that in the future new evidence and new problems may not come to light which will force science to reconsider the physico-chemical view of man. But at present the drift of scientific thought is clearly set towards the physico-chemical hypothesis. And we have nothing better to go on than the present.

For me, then, and for many philosophers who think like me, the moral is clear. We must try to work out an account of the nature of mind which is compatible with the view that man is nothing but a physico-chemical mechanism.

And . . . I shall be concerned to do just this: to sketch (in barest outline) what may be called a Materialist or Physicalist account of the mind.

But before doing this I should like to go back and consider a criticism of my position which must inevitably occur to some. What reason have I, it may be asked, for taking my stand on science? Even granting that I am right about what is the currently dominant scientific view of man, why should we concede science a special authority to decide questions about the nature of man? What of the authority of philosophy, of religion, of morality, or even of literature and art? Why do I set the authority of science above all these? Why this "scientism"?

It seems to me that the answer to this question is very simple. If we consider the search for truth, in all its fields, we find that it is only in science

From *The Mind/Brain Identity Theory,* ed. C. V. Borst (London: Macmillan and Co., Ltd., 1970), pp. 67–79.

that men versed in their subject can, after investigation that is more or less prolonged, and which may in some cases extend beyond a single human lifetime, reach substantial agreement about what is the case. It is only as a result of scientific investigation that we ever seem to reach an intellectual consensus about controversial matters.

In the Epistle Dedicatory to his *De Corpore* Hobbes wrote of William Harvey, the discoverer of the circulation of the blood, that he was "the only man I know, that conquering envy, hath established a new doctrine in his life-time."

Before Copernicus, Galileo and Harvey, Hobbes remarks, "there was nothing certain in natural philosophy." And, we might add, with the exception of mathematics, there was nothing certain in any other learned discipline.

These remarks of Hobbes are incredibly revealing. They show us what a watershed in the intellectual history of the human race the seventeenth century was. Before that time inquiry proceeded, as it were, in the dark. Men could not hope to see their doctrine *established,* that is to say, accepted by the vast majority of those properly versed in the subject under discussion. There was no intellectual consensus. Since that time, it has become a commonplace to see new doctrines, sometimes of the most far-reaching kind, established to the satisfaction of the learned, often within the lifetime of their first proponents. Science has provided us with a method of deciding disputed questions. This is not to say, of course, that the consensus of those who are learned and competent in a subject cannot be mistaken. Of course such a consensus can be mistaken. Sometimes it has been mistaken. But, granting fallibility, what better authority have we than such a consensus?

Now this is of the utmost importance. For in philosophy, in religion, in such disciplines as literary criticism, in moral questions in so far as they are thought to be matters of truth and falsity, there has been a notable failure to achieve an intellectual consensus about disputed questions among the learned. Must we not then attach a peculiar authority to the discipline that can achieve a consensus? And if it presents us with a certain vision of the nature of man, is this not a powerful reason for accepting that vision?

I will not take up here the deeper question *why* it is that the methods of science have enabled us to achieve an intellectual consensus about so many disputed matters. That question, I think, could receive no brief or uncontroversial answer. I am resting my argument on the simple and uncontroversial fact that, as a result of scientific investigation, such a consensus has been achieved.

It may be replied—it often is replied—that while science is all very well in its own sphere—the sphere of the physical, perhaps—there are matters of fact on which it is not competent to pronounce. And among such matters, it may be claimed, is the question what is the whole nature of man. But I cannot see that this reply has much force. Science has provided us with an island of truths, or, perhaps one should say, a raft of truths, to bear us up on the sea of our disputatious ignorance. There may have to be revisions and refinements, new results may set old findings in a new perspective, but what science has given us will not be altogether superseded. Must we not therefore appeal to these relative certainties for guidance when we come to consider uncertainties elsewhere? Perhaps science cannot help us to decide whether or not there is a God, whether or not human beings have immortal souls, or whether or not the will is free. But if science cannot assist us, what can? I conclude that it is the scientific vision of man, and not the philosophical or religious or artistic or moral vision of man, that is the best clue we have to the nature of man. And it is rational to argue from the best evidence we have.

Having in this way attempted to justify my procedure, I turn back to my subject: the attempt to work out an account of mind, or, if you prefer, of mental process, within the framework of the physico-chemical or, as we may call it, the Materialist view of man.

Now there is one account of mental process that is at once attractive to any philosopher sympathetic to a Materialist view of man: this is Behaviourism. Formulated originally by a psychologist, J. B. Watson, it attracted widespread interest and considerable support from scientifically oriented philosophers. Traditional philosophy had tended to think of the mind as a rather mysterious inward arena that lay behind, and was responsible for, the outward or physical behaviour of our bodies. Descartes thought of this inner arena as a *spiritual substance,* and it was this conception of the mind as spiritual object that Gilbert Ryle attacked, apparently in the interest of Behaviourism, in his important book *The Concept of Mind.* He ridiculed the Cartesian view as the dogma of "the ghost in the machine." The mind was not something behind the behaviour of the body, it was simply part of that physical behaviour. My anger with you is not some modification of a spiritual substance which somehow brings about aggressive behaviour; rather it is the aggressive behaviour itself; my addressing strong words to you, striking you, turning my back on you, and so on. Thought is not an inner process that lies behind, and brings about, the words I speak and write: it is my speaking and writing. The mind is not an inner arena, it is outward act.

It is clear that such a view of mind fits in very well with a completely Materialistic or Physicalist view of man. If there is no need to draw a distinction between mental processes and their expression in physical behaviour, but if instead the mental processes are identified with their so-called "expressions," then the existence of mind stands in no conflict with the view that man is nothing but a physico-chemical mechanism.

However, the version of Behaviourism that I have just sketched is a very crude version, and its crudity lays it open to obvious objections. One obvious difficulty is that it is our common experience that there can be mental processes going on although there is no behaviour occurring that could possibly be treated as expressions of these processes. A man may be angry, but give no bodily sign; he may think, but say or do nothing at all.

In my view, the most plausible attempt to refine Behaviourism with a view to meeting this objection was made by introducing the notion of *a disposition to behave.* (Dispositions to behave play a particularly important part in Ryle's account of the mind.) Let us consider the general notion of disposition first. Brittleness is a disposition, a disposition possessed by materials like glass. Brittle materials are those which, when subjected to relatively small forces, break or shatter easily. But breaking and shattering easily is not brittleness, rather it is the *manifestation* of brittleness. Brittleness itself is the tendency or liability of the material to break or shatter easily. A piece of glass may never shatter or break throughout its whole history, but it is still the case that it is brittle: it is liable to shatter or break if dropped quite a small way or hit quite lightly. Now a disposition to *behave* is simply a tendency or liability of a person to behave in a certain way under certain circumstances. The brittleness of glass is a disposition that the glass retains throughout its history, but clearly there could also be dispositions that come and go. The dispositions to behave that are of interest to the Behaviourist are, for the most part, of this temporary character.

Now how did Ryle and others use the notion of a disposition to behave to meet the obvious objection to Behaviourism that there can be mental processes going on although the subject is engaging in no relevant behaviour? Their strategy was to argue that in such cases, although the subject was not behaving in any relevant way, he or she was *disposed* to behave in some relevant way. The glass does not shatter, but it is still brittle. The man does not behave, but he does have a disposition to behave. We can say he thinks although he does not speak or act because at that time he was disposed to speak or act in a certain way. *If* he had been asked, perhaps, he would have spoken or acted. We can say he is angry although he does not behave angrily, because he is disposed so to behave. *If* only one more word had been addressed to him, he would have burst out. And so on. In this way it was hoped that Behaviourism could be squared with the obvious facts.

It is very important to see just how these thinkers conceived of dispositions. I quote from Ryle

> To possess a dispositional property *is not to be in a particular state, or to undergo a particular change;* it is to be bound or liable to be in a particular state, or to undergo a particular change, when a particular condition is realised. *(The Concept of Mind,* p. 43, my italics.)

So to explain the breaking of a lightly struck glass on a particular occasion by saying it was brittle is, on this view of dispositions, simply to say that the glass broke because it is the sort of thing that regularly breaks when quite lightly struck. The breaking was the normal behaviour, or not abnormal behaviour, of such a thing. The brittleness is not to be conceived of as a *cause* for the breakage, or even, more vaguely, a *factor* in bringing about the breaking. Brittleness is just the fact that things of that sort break easily.

But although in this way the Behaviourists did something to deal with the objection that mental processes can occur in the absence of behaviour, it seems clear, now that the shouting and the dust have died, that they did not do enough. When I think, but my thoughts do not issue in any action, it seems as obvious as anything is obvious that there is something actually going on in me which constitutes my thought. It is not simply that I would speak or act if some conditions that are unfulfilled were to be fulfilled. Something is currently going on, in the strongest and most literal sense of "going on", and this something is my thought. Rylean Behaviourism denies this, and so it is unsatisfactory as a theory of mind. Yet I know of no version of Behaviourism that is more satisfactory. The moral for those of us who wish to take a purely physicalistic view of man is that we must look for some other account of the nature of mind and of mental processes.

But perhaps we need not grieve too deeply about the failure of Behaviourism to produce a satisfactory theory of mind. Behaviourism is a profoundly unnatural account of mental processes. If somebody speaks and acts in certain ways it is natural to speak of this speech and action as the *expression* of his thought. It is not at all natural to speak of his speech and action as identical with his thought. We naturally think of the thought as something quite distinct from the speech and action which, under suitable circumstances, brings the speech and action about. Thoughts are not to be identified with behaviour, we think, they lie behind behaviour. A man's behaviour constitutes the *reason* we have for attributing certain mental processes to him, but the behaviour cannot be identified with the mental processes.

This suggests a very interesting line of thought about the mind. Behaviourism is certainly wrong, but perhaps it is not altogether wrong. Perhaps the Behaviourists are wrong in identifying the mind and mental occurrences with behaviour, but perhaps they are right in thinking that our notion of a mind and of individual mental states is *logically tied to behaviour*. For perhaps what we mean by a mental state is some state of the person which, under suitable circumstances, *brings about* a certain range of behaviour. Perhaps mind can be defined not as behaviour, but rather as the inner *cause* of certain behaviour. Thought is not speech under suitable circumstances, rather it is something within the person which, in suitable circumstances brings about speech. And, in fact, I believe that this is the true account, or, at any rate, a true first account, of what we mean by a mental state.

How does this line of thought link up with a purely physicalist view of man? The position is, I think, that while it does not make such a physicalist view inevitable, it does make it *possible*. It does not entail, but it is compatible with, a purely physicalist view of man. For if our notion of the mind and mental states is nothing but that of a cause within the person of certain ranges of behaviour, then it becomes a scientific question, and not a question of logical analysis, what in fact the intrinsic nature of that cause is. The cause might be, as Descartes thought it was, a spiritual substance working through the pineal gland to produce the complex bodily behaviour of which men are capable. It might be breath, or specially smooth and mobile atoms dispersed throughout the body; it might be many other things. But in fact the verdict of modern science seems to be that the sole cause of mind-betokening behaviour in man and the higher animals is the physico-chemical workings of the central nervous system. And so, assuming we have correctly characterised our concept of a mental state as nothing but the cause of certain sorts of behaviour, then we can identify these mental states with purely physical states of the central nervous system.

At this point we may stop and go back to the Behaviourists' dispositions. We saw that, according to them, the brittleness of glass or, to take another example, the elasticity of rubber, is not a state of the glass or the rubber, but is simply the fact that things of that sort behave in the way they do. But now let us consider how a scientist would think about brittleness or elasticity. Faced with the phenomenon of breakage under relatively small impacts, or the phenomenon of stretching when a force is applied followed by contraction when the force is removed, he will assume that there is some current *state* of the glass or the rubber which is responsible for the characteristic behaviour of samples of these two materials. At the beginning he will not know what this state is, but he will endeavour to find out, and he may succeed in finding out. And when he has found out he will very likely make remarks of this sort: "We have discovered that the brittleness of glass is in fact a certain sort of pattern in the molecules of the glass." That is to say, he will *identify* brittleness with the state of the glass that is responsible for the liability of the glass to break. For him, a disposition of an object is a state of the object. What makes the state a state of brittleness is the fact that it gives rise to the characteristic manifestations of brittleness. But the disposition itself is distinct from its manifestations: it is the state of the glass that gives rise to these manifestations in suitable circumstances.

You will see that this way of looking at dispositions is very different from that of Ryle and the Behaviourists. The great difference is this: If we treat dispositions as actual states, as I have suggested that scientists do, even if states whose intrinsic nature may yet have to be discovered, then we can say that dispositions are actual *causes,* or causal factors, which, in suitable circumstances, actually bring about those happenings which are the manifestations of the disposition. A certain molecular constitution of glass which constitutes its brittleness is actually *responsible* for the fact that, when the glass is struck, it breaks.

Now I shall not argue the matter here, because the detail of the argument is technical and difficult,[2] but I believe that the view of dispositions as states, which is the view that is natural to science, is the correct one. I believe it can be shown quite strictly that, to the extent that we admit the notion of dispositions at all, we are committed to the view that they are actual *states* of the object that has the disposition. I may add that I think that the same holds for the closely connected notions of capacities and powers. Here I will simply assume this step in my argument.

But perhaps it can be seen that the rejection of the idea that mind is simply a certain range of man's behaviour in favour of the view that mind is rather the inner *cause* of that range of man's behaviour is bound up with the rejection of the Rylean view of dispositions in favour of one that treats dispositions as states of objects and so as having actual causal power. The Behaviourists were wrong to identify the mind with behaviour. They were not so far off the mark when they tried to deal with cases where mental happenings occur in the absence of behaviour by saying that these are dispositions to behave. But in order to reach a correct view, I am suggesting, they would have to conceive of these dispositions as actual *states* of the person who has the disposition, states that have actual power to bring about behaviour in suitable circumstances. But to do this is to abandon the central inspiration of Behaviourism: that in talking about the mind we do not have to go behind outward behaviour to inner states.

And so two separate but interlocking lines of thought have pushed me in the same direction. The first line of thought is that it goes profoundly against the grain to think of the mind as behaviour. The mind is, rather, that which stands behind and brings about our complex behaviour. The second line of thought is that the Behaviourists' dispositions, properly conceived, are really states that underlie behaviour, and, under suitable circumstances, bring about behaviour. Putting these two together, we reach the conception of a mental state as *a state of the person apt for producing certain ranges of behaviour*. This formula: a mental state is a state of the person apt for producing certain ranges of behaviour, I believe to be a very illuminating way of looking at the concept of a mental state. I have found it very fruitful in the search for detailed logical analyses of the individual mental concepts.

Now, I do not think that Hegel's dialectic has much to tell us about the nature of reality. But I think that human thought often moves in a dialectical way, from thesis to antithesis and then to the synthesis. Perhaps thought about the mind is a case in point. I have already said that classical philosophy tended to think of the mind as an inner arena of some sort. This we may call the Thesis. Behaviourism moved to the opposite extreme: the mind was seen as outward behaviour. This is the Antithesis. My proposed Synthesis is that the mind is properly conceived as an inner principle, but a principle that is identified in terms of the outward behaviour it is apt for bringing about. This way of looking at the mind and mental states does not itself entail a Materialist or Physicalist view of man, for nothing is said in this analysis about the intrinsic nature of these mental states. But if we have, as I have asserted that we do have, general scientific grounds for thinking that man is nothing but a physical mechanism, we can go on to argue that the mental states are in fact nothing but physical states of the central nervous system.

Along these lines, then, I would look for an account of the mind that is compatible with a purely Materialist theory of man. I have tried to carry out this programme in detail in *A Materialist Theory of the Mind.* There are, as may be imagined, all sorts of powerful objections that can be made to this view. But . . . I propose to do only one thing. I will develop one very important objection to my view of the mind—an objection felt by many philosophers—and then try to show how the objection should be met.

The view that our notion of mind is nothing but that of an inner principle apt for bringing about certain sorts of behaviour may be thought to share a certain weakness with Behaviourism. Modern philosophers have put the point about Behaviourism by saying that although Behaviourism may be a satisfactory account of the mind from an *other-person point of view,* it will not do as a *first-person* account. To explain. In our encounters with other people, all we ever observe is their behaviour: their actions, their speech, and so on. And so, if we simply consider other people, Behaviourism might seem to do full justice to the facts. But the trouble about Behaviourism is that it seems so unsatisfactory as applied to our *own* case. In our own case, we seem to be aware of so much more than mere behaviour.

Suppose that now we conceive of the mind as an inner principle apt for bringing about certain sorts of behaviour. This again fits the other-person cases very well. Bodily behaviour of a very sophisticated sort is observed, quite different from the behaviour that ordinary physical objects display. It is inferred that this behaviour must spring from a very special sort of inner cause in the object that exhibits this behaviour. This inner cause is christened "the mind", and those who take a physicalist view of man argue that it is simply the central nervous system of the body observed. Compare this with the case of glass. Certain characteristic behaviour is observed: the breaking and shattering of the material when acted upon by relatively small forces. A special inner state of the glass is postulated to explain this behaviour. Those who take a purely physicalist view of glass then argue that this state is a *natural* state of the glass. It is, perhaps, an arrangement of its molecules, and not, say, the peculiarly malevolent disposition of the demons that dwell in glass.

But when we turn to our own case, the position may seem less plausible. We are conscious, we have experiences. Now can we say that to be conscious, to have experiences, is simply for something to go on within us apt for the causing of certain sorts of behaviour? Such an account does not seem to do any justice to the phenomena. And so it seems that our account of the mind, like Behaviourism, will fail to do justice to the first-person case.

In order to understand the objection better it may be helpful to consider a particular case. If you have driven for a very long distance without a break, you may have had experience of a curious state of automatism, which can occur in these conditions. One can suddenly "come to" and realise that one has driven for long distances without being aware of what one was doing, or, indeed, without being aware of anything. One has kept the car on the road, used the brake and the clutch perhaps, yet all without any awareness of what one was doing.

Now, if we consider this case it is obvious that *in some sense* mental processes are still going on when one is in such an automatic state. Unless one's will was still operating in some way, and unless one was still perceiving in some way, the car would not still be on the road. Yet, of course, *something* mental is lacking. Now, I think, when it is alleged that an account of mind as an inner principle apt for the production of certain sorts of behaviour leaves out consciousness or experience, what is alleged to have been left out is just whatever is missing in the automatic driving case. It is conceded that an account of mental processes as states of the person apt for the production of certain sorts of behaviour may very possibly be adequate to deal with such cases as that of automatic driving. It may be adequate to deal with most of the mental processes of animals, who perhaps spend a good deal of their lives in this state of automatism. But, it is contended, it cannot deal with the consciousness that we normally enjoy.

I will now try to sketch an answer to this important and powerful objection. Let us begin in an apparently unlikely place, and consider the way that an account of mental processes of the sort I am giving would deal with *sense-perception.*

Now psychologists, in particular, have long realised that there is a very close logical tie between sense-perception and *selective behaviour.* Suppose we want to decide whether an animal can perceive the difference between red and green. We might give the animal a choice between two pathways, over one of which a red light shines and over the other of which a green light shines. If the animal happens by chance to choose the green pathway we reward it; if it happens to choose the other pathway we do not reward it. If, after some trials, the animal systematically takes the green-lighted pathway, and if we become assured that the only relevant differences in the two pathways are the differences in the colour of the lights, we are entitled to say that the animal can see this colour difference. Using its eyes, it selects between red-lighted and green-lighted pathways. So we say it can see the difference between red and green.

Now a Behaviourist would be tempted to say that the animal's regularly selecting the green-lighted pathway *was* its perception of the colour difference. But this is unsatisfactory, because we all want to say that perception is something that goes on within the person or animal—within its mind—although, of course, this mental event is normally *caused* by the operation of the environment upon the organism. Suppose, however, that we speak instead of 'capacities for selective behaviour towards the current environment, and suppose we think of these capacities, like dispositions, as actual inner states of the organism. We can then think of the animal's perception as a state within the animal apt, if the animal is so impelled, for selective behaviour between the red- and green-lighted pathways.

In general, we can think of perceptions as inner states or events apt for the production of certain sorts of selective behaviour towards our environment. To perceive is like acquiring a key to a door. You do not have to use the key: you can put it in your pocket and never bother about the door. But if you do want to open the door the key may be essential. The blind man is a man who does not acquire certain keys, and, as a result, is not able to operate in his environment in the way that somebody who has his sight can operate. It seems, then, a very promising view to take of perceptions that they are inner states defined by the sorts of selective behaviour that they enable the perceiver to exhibit, if so impelled.

Now how is this discussion of perception related to the question of consciousness of experience, the sort of thing that the driver who is in a state of automatism has not got, but which we normally do have? Simply this. My proposal is that consciousness, in this sense of the word, is nothing but *perception or awareness of the state of our own mind.* The driver in a state of automatism perceives, or is aware of, the road. If he did not, the car would be in a ditch. But he is not currently aware of his awareness of the road. He perceives the road, but he does not perceive his perceiving, or anything else that is going on in his mind. He is not, as we normally are, conscious of what is going on in his mind.

And so I conceive of consciousness or experience, in this sense of the words, in the way that Locke and Kant conceived it, as like perception. Kant, in a striking phrase, spoke of "inner sense". We cannot directly observe the minds of others, but each of us has the power to observe directly our own minds, and "perceive" what is going on there. The driver in the automatic state is one whose "inner eye" is shut: who is not currently aware of what is going on in his own mind.

Now if this account is along the right lines, why should we not given an account of this inner observation along the same lines as we have already given of perception? Why should we not conceive of it as an inner state, a state in this case directed towards other inner states and not to the environment, which enables us, if we are so impelled, to behave in a selective way *towards our own states of mind?* One who is aware, or conscious, of his thoughts or his emotions is one who has the capacity to make discriminations between his different mental states. His capacity might be exhibited in words. He might say that he was in an angry state of mind when, and only when, he *was* in an angry state of mind. But such verbal behaviour would be the mere *expression* or *result* of the awareness. The awareness itself would be an inner state: the sort of inner state that gave the man a capacity for such behavioural expressions.

So I have argued that consciousness of our own mental state may be assimilated to *perception* of our own mental state, and that, like other perceptions, it may then be conceived of as an inner state or event giving a capacity for selective behaviour, in this case selective behaviour towards our own mental state. All this is meant to be simply a logical analysis of consciousness, and none of it entails, although it does not rule out, a purely physicalist account of what these inner states are. But if we are convinced, on general scientific grounds, that a purely physical account of man is likely to be the true one, then there seems to be no bar to our identifying these inner states with purely physical states of the central nervous system. And so consciousness of our own mental state becomes simply the scanning of one part of our central nervous system by another. Consciousness is a self-scanning mechanism in the central nervous system.

As I have emphasised before, I have done no more than sketch a programme for a philosophy of mind. There are all sorts of expansions and elucidations to be made, and all sorts of doubts and difficulties to be stated and overcome. But I hope I have done enough to show that a purely physicalist theory of the mind is an exciting and plausible intellectual option.

Notes

1. Inaugural lecture of the Challis Professor of Philosophy at the University of Sydney (1965); slightly amended (1968).
2. It is presented in my book *A Materialist Theory of the Mind* (1968) ch. 6, sec. VI.

The Nature of Mental States

HILARY PUTNAM

Hilary Putnam (1926–   ) is Walter Beverly Pearson Professor of Modern Mathematics and Mathematical Logic at Harvard University. His publications include *Philosophy of Logic* and two volumes of collected papers, *Mathematics, Matter and Method* and *Mind, Language and Reality*.

The typical concerns of the Philosopher of Mind might be represented by three questions: (1) How do we know that other people have pains? (2) Are pains brain states? (3) What is the analysis of the concept *pain?* . . . I shall say something [here] about question (2).

I. Identity Questions

"Is pain a brain state?" (Or, "Is the property of having a pain at time *t* a brain state?")[1] It is impossible to discuss this question sensibly without saying something about the peculiar rules which have grown up in the course of the development of "analytical philosophy"—rules which, far from leading to an end to all conceptual confusions, themselves represent considerable conceptual confusion. These rules—which are, of course, implicit rather than explicit in the practice of most analytical philosophers—are (1) that a statement of the form "being *A* is being *B*" (e.g., "being in pain is being in a certain brain state") can be *correct* only if it follows, in some sense, from the meaning of the terms *A* and *B;* and (2) that a statement of the form "being *A* is being *B*" can be philosophically *informative* only if it is in some sense reductive (e.g., "being in pain is having a certain unpleasant sensation" is not philosophically informative; "being in pain is having a certain behaviour disposition" is, if true, philosophically informative). These rules are excellent rules if we still believe that the program of reductive analysis (in the style of the 1930s) can be carried out; if we don't, then they turn analytical philosophy into a mug's game, at least so far as "is" questions are concerned.

. . . I shall use the term "property" as a blanket term for such things as being in pain, being in a particular brain state, having a particular behavior disposition, and also for magnitudes such as temperature, etc.—i.e. for things which can naturally be represented by one-or-more-place predicates or functors. I shall use the term "concept" for things which can be identified with synonymy-classes of expressions. Thus the concept *temperature* can be identified (I maintain) with the synonymy-class of the word "temperature".[2] (This is like saying that the number 2 can be identified with the class of all pairs. This is quite a different statement from the peculiar statement that 2 *is* the class of all pairs. I do not maintain that concepts *are* synonymy-classes, whatever that might mean, but that they can be identified with synonymy-classes, for the purpose of formalization of the relevant discourse.)

The question "What is the concept *temperature?*" is a very "funny" one. One might take it

From *Mind, Language and Reality; Philosophical Papers* (Cambridge: Cambridge University Press, 1975), Vol. 2, pp. 364–66, 429–40.

to mean "What is temperature? Please take my question as a conceptual one." In that case an answer might be (pretend for a moment "heat" and "temperature" are synonyms) "temperature is heat," or even "the concept of temperature is the same concept as the concept of heat." Or one might take it to mean "What are *concepts,* really? For example, what is 'the concept of temperature'?" In that case heaven knows what an "answer" would be. (Perhaps it would be the statement that concepts *can be identified with* synonymy-classes.)

Of course, the question "What is the property temperature?" is also "funny." And one way of interpreting it is to take it as a question about the concept of temperature. But this is not the way a physicist would take it.

The effect of saying that the property P_1 can be identical with the property P_2 only if the terms P_1, P_2 are in some suitable sense "synonyms" is, to all intents and purposes, to collapse the two notions of "property" and "concept" into a single notion. The view that concepts (intensions) *are* the same as properties has been explicitly advocated by Carnap (e.g. in *Meaning and Necessity).* This seems an unfortunate view, since "temperature is mean molecular kinetic energy" appears to be a perfectly good example of a true statement of identity of properties, whereas "the concept of temperature is the same concept as a concept of mean molecular kinetic energy" is simply false.

Many philosophers believe that the statement "pain is a brain state" violates some rules or norms of English. But the arguments offered are hardly convincing. For example, if the fact that I can know that I am in pain without knowing that I am in brain state *S* shows that pain cannot be brain state *S,* then, by exactly the same argument, the fact that I can know that the stove is hot without knowing that the mean molecular kinetic energy is high (or even that molecules exist) shows that it is *false* that temperature is mean molecular kinetic energy, physics to the contrary. In fact, all that immediately follows from the fact that I can know that I am in pain without knowing that I am in brain state *S* is that the concept of pain is not the same concept as the concept of being in brain state *S*. But either pain, or the state of being in pain, or some pain, or some pain state, might still be brain state *S*. After all, the concept of temperature is not the same concept of mean molecular kinetic energy. But temperature is mean molecular kinetic energy.

Some philosophers maintain that both "pain is a brain state" and "pain states are brain states" are unintelligible. The answer is to explain to these philosophers, as well as we can, given the vagueness of all scientific methodology, what sorts of considerations lead one to make an empirical reduction (i.e. to say such things as "water is H_2O," "light is electromagnetic radiation," "temperature is mean molecular kinetic energy"). If, without giving reasons, he still maintains in the face of such examples that one cannot imagine parallel circumstances for the use of "pains are brain states" (or, perhaps, "pain states are brain states") one has grounds to regard him as perverse.

Some philosophers maintain that "P_1 is P_2" is something that can be true, when the "is" involved is the "is" of empirical reduction, only when the properties P_1 and P_2 are (a) associated with a spatio-temporal region; and (b) the region is one and the same in both cases. Thus "temperature is mean molecular kinetic energy" is an admissible empirical reduction, since the temperature and the molecular energy are associated with the same space–time region, but "having a pain in my arm is being in a brain state" is not, since the spatial regions involved are different.

This argument does not appear very strong. Surely no one is going to be deterred from saying that mirror images are light reflected from an object and then from the surface of a mirror by the fact that an image can be "located" three feet *behind* the mirror! (Moreover, one can always find *some* common property of the reductions one is willing to allow—e.g. temperature is mean molecular kinetic energy—which is not a property of some one identification one wishes to disallow. This is not very impressive unless one has an argument to show that the very purposes of such identification depend upon the common property in question.)

Again, other philosophers have contended that all the predictions that can be derived from the conjunction of neurophysiological laws with such statements as "pain states are such-and-such brain states" can equally well be derived from the conjunction of the same neurophysiological laws with "being in pain is correlated with such-and-such brain states", and hence *(sic!)* there can be no methodological grounds for saying that pains (or pain states) *are* brain states, as opposed to saying that they are *correlated* (invariantly) with brain states. This argument, too, would show that light is only correlated with electromagnetic radiation. The mistake is in ignoring the fact that, although the theories in question may indeed lead to the same predictions, they open and exclude different *questions*. "Light is invariantly correlated with electromagnetic radiation" would leave open the questions "What is the light then, if it isn't the same as the electromagnetic radiation?" and "What makes the light accompany the electromagnetic radiation?"—questions which are excluded by saying that the light *is* the electromagnetic radiation. Similarly, the purpose of saying that pains are brain states is precisely to exclude from empirical meaningfulness the questions "What is the pain, then, if it isn't the same as the brain state?" and "What makes the pain accompany the brain state?" If there are grounds to suggest that these questions represent, so to speak, the wrong way to look at the matter, then those grounds are grounds for a theoretical identification of pains with brain states.

If all arguments to the contrary are unconvincing, shall we then conclude that it is meaningful (and perhaps true) to say either that pains are brain states or that pain states are brain states?

(1) It is perfectly meaningful (violates no "rule of English," involves no "extension of usage") to say "pains are brain states."

(2) It is not meaningful (involves a "changing of meaning" or "an extension of usage," etc.) to say "pains are brain states."

My own position is not expressed by either (1) or (2). It seems to me that the notions "change of meaning" and "extension of usage" are simply so ill defined that one cannot in fact say *either* (1) or (2). I see no reason to believe that either the linguist, or the man-on-the-street, or the philosopher possesses today a notion of "change of meaning" applicable to such cases as the one we have been discussing. The *job* for which the notion of change of meaning was developed in the history of the language was just a *much* cruder job than this one.

But, if we don't assert either (1) or (2)—in other words, if we regard the "change of meaning" issue as a pseudo-issue in this case—then how are we to discuss the question with which we started? "Is pain a brain state?"

The answer is to allow statements of the form "pain is *A*", where "pain" and "*A*" are in no sense synonyms, and to see whether any such statement can be found which might be acceptable on empirical and methodological grounds. This is what we shall now proceed to do.

II. Is Pain a Brain State?

We shall discuss "Is pain a brain state?" then. And we have agreed to waive the "change of meaning" issue.

Since I am discussing not what the concept of pain comes to, but what pain is, in a sense of "is" which requires empirical theory-construction (or, at least, empirical speculation), I shall not apologize for advancing an empirical hypothesis. Indeed, my strategy will be to argue that pain is *not* a brain state, not on a priori grounds, but on the grounds that another hypothesis is more plausible. The detailed development and verification of my hypothesis would be just as Utopian a task as the detailed development and verification of the brain-state hypothesis. But the putting-forward, not of detailed and scientifically "finished" hypotheses, but of schemata for hypotheses, has long been a function of philosophy. I shall, in short, argue that pain is not a brain state, in the sense of a physical-chemical state of the brain (or even the whole nervous system), but another *kind* of state entirely. I propose the hypothesis that pain, or the state of being in pain, is a functional state of a whole organism.

To explain that it is necessary to introduce some technical notions. In previous papers I have explained the notion of a Turing Machine* and discussed the use of this notion as a model for an organism. The notion of a Probabilistic Automation is defined similarly to a Turing Machine, except that the transitions between "states" are allowed to be with various probabilities rather than

*[Editors' note: See the Appendix to this paper.]

being "deterministic." (Of course, a Turing Machine is simply a special kind of Probabilistic Automaton, one with transition probabilities 0, 1). I shall assume the notion of a Probabilistic Automaton has been generalized to allow for "sensory inputs" and "motor outputs"—that is, the Machine Table specifies, for every possible combination of a "state" and a complete set of "sensory inputs," an "instruction" which determines the probability of the next "state," and also the probabilities of the "motor outputs." (This replaces the idea of the Machine as printing on a tape.) I shall also assume that the physical realization of the sense organs responsible for the various inputs, and of the motor organs, is specified, but that the "states" and the "inputs" themselves are, as usual, specified only "implicitly"—i.e. by the set of transition probabilities given by the Machine Table.

Since an empirically given system can simultaneously be a "physical realization" of many different Probabilistic Automata, I introduce the notion of a *Description* of a system. A Description of S where S is a system, is any true statement to the effect that S possesses distinct states $S_1, S_2 \ldots S_n$ which are related to one another and to the motor outputs and sensory inputs by the transition probabilities given in such-and-such a Machine Table. The Machine Table mentioned in the Description will then be called the Functional Organization of S relative to that Description, and the S_i such that S is in state S_i at a given time will be called the Total State of S (at the time) relative to that Description. It should be noted that knowing the Total State of a system relative to a Description involves knowing a good deal about how the system is likely to "behave," given various combinations of sensory inputs, but does *not* involve knowing the physical realization of the S_i as, e.g. physical-chemical states of the brain. The S_i, to repeat, are specified only *implicitly* by the Description—i.e. specified *only* by the set of transition probabilities given in the Machine Table.

The hypothesis that "being in pain is a functional state of the organism" may now be spelled out more exactly as follows:

(1) All organisms capable of feeling pain are Probabilistic Automata.

(2) Every organism capable of feeling pain possesses at least one Description of a certain kind (i.e. being capable of feeling pain *is* possessing an appropriate kind of Functional Organization).

(3) No organism capable of feeling pain possesses a decomposition into parts which separately possess Descriptions of the kind referred to in (2).

(4) For every Description of the kind referred to in (2), there exists a subset of the sensory inputs such that an organism with that Description is in pain when and only when some of its sensory inputs are in that subset.

This hypothesis is admittedly vague, though surely no vaguer than the brain-state hypothesis in its present form. For example, one would like to know more about the kind of Functional Organization that an organism must have to be capable of feeling pain, and more about the marks that distinguish the subset of the sensory inputs referred to in (4). With respect to the first question, one can probably say that the Functional Organization must include something that resembles a "preference function," or at least a preference partial ordering and something that resembles an "inductive logic" (i.e. the Machine must be able to "learn from experience"). . . . In addition, it seems natural to require that the Machine possess "pain sensors," i.e. sensory organs which normally signal damage to the Machine's body, or dangerous temperatures, pressures, etc., which transmit a special subset of the inputs, the subset referred to in (4). Finally, and with respect to the second question, we would want to require at least that the inputs in the distinguished subset have a high disvalue on the Machine's preference function or ordering. . . . The purpose of condition (3) is to rule out such "organisms" (if they can count as such) as swarms of bees as single pain-feelers. The condition (1) is, obviously, redundant, and is only introduce for expository reasons. (It is, in fact, empty, since everything is a Probabilistic Automation under *some* Description.)

I contend, in passing, that this hypothesis, in spite of its admitted vagueness, is far *less* vague than the "physical-chemical state" hypothesis is today, and far more susceptible to investigation of both a mathematical and an empirical kind. Indeed, to investigate this hypothesis is just to attempt to produce "mechanical" models of organisms—and isn't this, in a sense, just what psychology is about? The difficult step, of course, will be to pass from models to *specific* organisms to a *normal form* for the psychological description or organisms—for this is what is required to make (2) and (4) precise. But this too seems to be an inevitable part of the program of psychology.

I shall now compare the hypothesis just advanced with (a) the hypothesis that pain is a brain state, and (b) the hypothesis that pain is a behavior disposition.

III. Functional State Versus Brain State

It may, perhaps, be asked if I am not somewhat unfair in taking the brain-state theorist to be talking about *physical-chemical* states of the brain. But (a) these are the only sorts of states ever mentioned by brain-state theorists. (b) The brain-state theorist usually mentions (with a certain pride, slightly reminiscent of the Village Atheist) the incompatibility of his hypothesis with all forms of dualism and mentalism. This is natural if physical-chemical states of the brain are what is at issue. However, functional states of whole systems are something quite different. In particular, the functional-state hypothesis is *not* incompatible with dualism! Although it goes without saying that the hypothesis is "mechanistic" in its inspiration, it is a slightly remarkable fact that a system consisting of a body and a "soul," if such things there be, can perfectly well be a Probabilistic Automaton. (c) One argument advanced by Smart is that the brain-state theory assumes only "physical" properties, and Smart finds "non-physical" properties unintelligible. The Total States and the "inputs" defined above are, of course, neither mental nor physical per se, and I cannot image a functionalist advancing this argument. (d) If the brain-state theoriest does mean (or at least allow) states other than physical-chemical states, then his hypothesis is completely empty, at least until he specifies *what* sort of "states" he *does* mean.

Taking the brain-state hypothesis in this way, then, what reasons are there to prefer the functional-state hypothesis over the brain-state hypothesis? Consider what the brain-state theorist has to do to make good his claims. He has to specify a physical-chemical state such that *any* organism (not just a mammal) is in pain if and only if (a) it possesses a brain of a suitable physical-chemical structure; and (b) its brain is in that physical-chemical state. This means that the physical-chemical state in question must be a possible state of a mammalian brain, a reptilian brain, a mollusc's brain (octopuses are mollusca, and certainly feel pain), etc. At the same time, it must *not* be a possible (physically possible) state of the brain of any physically possible creature that cannot feel pain. Even if such a state can be found, it must be nomologically certain that it will also be a state of the brain of any extraterrestrial life that may be found that will be capable of feeling pain before we can even entertain the supposition that it may *be* pain.

It is not altogether impossible that such a state will be found. Even though octopus and mammal are examples of parallel (rather than sequential) evolution, for example, virtually identical structures (physically speaking) have evolved in the eye of the octopus and in the eye of the mammal, notwithstanding the fact that this organ has evolved from different kinds of cells in the two cases. Thus it is at least possible that parallel evolution, all over the universe, might *always* lead to *one and the same* physical "correlate" of pain. But this is certainly an ambitious hypothesis.

Finally, the hypothesis becomes still more ambitious when we realize that the brain-state theorist is not just saying that *pain* is a brain state; he is, of course, concerned to maintain that *every* psychological state is a brain state. Thus if we can find even one psychological predicate which can clearly be applied to both a mammal and an octopus (say "hungry"), but whose physical-chemical "correlate" is different in the two cases, the brain-state theory has collapsed. It seems to me overwhelmingly probable that we can do this. Granted, in such a case the brain-state theorist can save himself by ad hoc assumptions (e.g. defining the disjunction of two states to be a single "physical-chemical state"), but this does not have to be taken seriously.

Turning now to the considerations *for* the functional-state theory, let us begin with the fact that we identify organisms as in pain, or hungry, or angry, or in heat, etc., on the basis of their *behavior*. But it is a truism that similarities in the behavior of two systems are at least a reason to suspect similarities in the functional organization of the two systems, and a much *weaker* reason to suspect similarities in the actual physical details. Moreover, we expect the various psychological states—at least the basic ones, such as hunger, thirst, aggression, etc.—to have more or less similar "transition probabilities" (within wide and ill-defined limits, to be sure) with each other and with behavior in the case of different species, because this is an artifact of the way in which we identify these states. Thus, we would not count an animal as *thirsty* if its "unsatiated" behavior did not seem to be directed toward drinking and was not followed by "satiation for liquid." Thus any animal that we count as capable of these various states will at least *seem* to have a certain rough kind of functional organization. And, as already remarked, if the program of finding psychological laws that are not species-specific—i.e. of finding a normal form for psychological theories of different species—ever succeeds, then it will bring in its wake a delineation of the kind of functional organization that is necessary and sufficient for a given psychological state, as well as a precise definition of the notion "psychological state". In contrast, the brain-state theorist has to hope for the eventual development of neurophysiological laws that are species-independent, which seems much less reasonable than the hope that psychological laws (of a sufficiently general kind) may be species-independent, or, still weaker, that a species-independent *form* can be found in which psychological laws can be written.

IV. Functional State Versus Behavior-Disposition

The theory that being in pain is neither a brain state nor a functional state but a behavior disposition has one apparent advantage: it appears to agree with the way in which we verify that organisms are in pain. We do not in practice know anything about the brain state of an animal when we say that it is in pain; and we possess little if any knowledge of its functional organization, except in a crude intuitive way. In fact, however, this "advantage" is not advantage at all: for, although statements about how we verify that x is A may have a good deal to do with what the concept of being A comes to, they have precious little to do with what the property A *is*. To argue on the ground just mentioned that pain is neither a brain state nor a functional state is like arguing that heat is not mean molecular kinetic energy from the fact that ordinary people do not (they think) ascertain the mean molecular kinetic energy of something when they verify that it is hot or cold. It is not necessary that they should; what is necessary is that the marks that they take as indications of heat should in fact be explained by the mean molecular kinetic energy. And, similarly, it is necessary to our hypothesis that the marks that are taken as behavioral indications of pain should be explained by the fact that the organism is a functional state of the appropriate kind, but not that speakers should *know* that this is so.

The difficulties with "behavior disposition" accounts are so well known that I shall do little more than recall them here. The difficulty—it appears to be more than a "difficulty," in fact—of specifying the required behavior disposition except as "the disposition of X to behave as if X were in *pain,*" is the chief one, of course. In contrast, we *can* specify the functional state with which we propose to identify pain, at least roughly, without using the notion of pain. Namely, the functional state we have in mind is the state of receiving sensory inputs which play a certain role in the Functional Organization of the organism. This role is characterized, at least partially, by the fact that the sense organs responsible for the inputs in question are organs whose function is to detect damage to the body, or dangerous extremes of temperature, pressure, etc., and by the fact that the "inputs" themselves, whatever their physical realization, represent a condition that the organism assigns a high disvalue to. . . . this does *not* mean that the Machine will always *avoid* being in the condition in question ("pain"); it only means that the condition will be avoided unless not avoiding it is necessary to the attainment of some more highly valued goal. Since the behavior of the Machine (in this case, an organism) will depend not merely on the sensory inputs, but also on the Total State (i.e. on other values, beliefs, etc.), it seems hopeless to make any general statement about how an organism in such a condition *must* behave; but this does not mean that we must abandon hope of characterizing the condition. Indeed, we have just characterized it.

Not only does the behavior-disposition theory seem hopelessly vague; if the "behavior" referred to is peripheral behavior, and the relevant stimuli are peripheral stimuli (e.g. we do not say anything about what the organism will do if its brain is operated upon), then the theory seems clearly false. For example, two animals with all motor nerves cut will have the same actual and potential "behavior" (namely, none to speak of); but if one has cut pain fibers and the other has uncut pain fibers, then one will feel pain and the other won't. Again, if one person has cut pain fibers, and another suppresses all pain responses deliberately due to some strong compulsion, then the actual and potential peripheral behavior may be the same, but one will feel pain and the other won't. (Some philosophers maintain that this last case is conceptually impossible, but the only evidence for this appears to be that *they* can't, or don't want to, conceive of it.) If, instead of pain, we take some sensation the "bodily expression" of which is easier to suppress—say, a slight coolness in one's left little finger—the case becomes even clearer.

Finally, even if there *were* some behavior disposition invariantly correlated with pain (species-independently!), and specifiable without using the term "pain", it would still be more plausible to identify being in pain with some state whose presence *explains* this behavior disposition—the brain state or functional state—than with the behavior disposition itself. Such considerations of plausibility may be somewhat subjective; but if other things *were* equal (of course, they aren't) why shouldn't we allow considerations of plausibility to play the deciding role?

V. Methodological Considerations

So far we have considered only what might be called the "empirical" reasons for saying that being in pain is a functional state, rather than a brain state or a behavior disposition; namely, that it seems more likely that the functional state we described is invariantly "correlated" with pain, species-independently, than that there is either a physical-chemical state of the brain (must an organism have a *brain* to feel pain? perhaps some ganglia will do) or a behavior disposition so correlated. If this is correct, then it follows that the identification we proposed is at least a candidate for consideration. What of methodological considerations?

The methodological considerations are roughly similar in all cases of reduction, so no surprises need be expected here. First, identification of psychological states with functional states means that the laws of psychology can be derived from statements of the form "such-and-such organisms have such-and-such Descriptions" together with the identification statements ("being in pain is such-and-such a functional state," etc.). Secondly, the presence of the functional state (i.e. of inputs which play the role we have described in the Functional Organization of the organism) is not merely "correlated with" but actually explains the pain behavior on the part of the organism. Thirdly, the identification serves to exclude questions which (if a naturalistic view is correct) represent an altogether wrong way of looking at the matter, e.g. "What *is* pain if it isn't either the brain state or the functional state?" and "What causes the pain to be always accompanied by this sort of functional state?" In short, the identification is to be tentatively accepted as a theory which leads to both fruitful predictions and to fruitful *questions,* and which serves to discourage fruitless and empirically senseless questions, where by "empirically senseless" I mean "senseless" not merely from the standpoint of verification, but from the standpoint of what there in fact *is.*

Appendix: Turing Machines

. . . the notion of a *Turing machine* . . . will now be explained.

Briefly, a Turing machine is a device with a finite number of internal configurations, each of which involves the machine's being in one of a finite number of *states,* and the machine's scanning a tape on which certain symbols appear.

The machine's tape is divided into separate squares, thus:

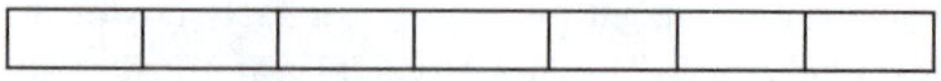

on each of which a symbol (from a fixed finite alphabet) may be printed. Also the machine has a "scanner" which "scans" one square of the tape at a time. Finally, the machine has a *printing mechanism* which many (a) *erase* the symbol which appears on the square being scanned, and (b) print some other symbol (from the machine's alphabet) on that square.

Any Turing machine is completely described by a *machine table,* which is constructed as follows: the rows of the table correspond to letters of the alphabet (including the "null" letter, i.e. blank space), while the columns correspond to states *A, B, C,* etc. In each square there appears an "instruction", e.g. "$s_5L\,A$", "$s_7C\,B$", "$s_3R\,C$". These instructions are read as follows: "$s_5L\,A$" means "print the symbol s_5 on the square you are now scanning (after erasing whatever symbol it now contains), and proceed to scan the square immediately to the left of the one you have just been scanning; also, shift into state *A.*" The other instructions are similarly interpreted ("*R*" means "scan the square immediately to the *right,*" while "*C*" means "center," i.e. continue scanning the *same* square). The following is a sample machine table:

		A	B	C	D
(s_1)	*I*	s_1RA	s_1LB	s_3LD	s_1CD
(s_2)	+	s_1LB	s_2CD	s_2LD	s_2CD
(s_3)	*blank space*	s_3CD	s_3RC	s_3LD	s_3CD

The machine described by this table is intended to function as follows: the machine is started in state *A.* On the tape there appears a "sum" (in unary notion) to be "worked out," e.g. "II + III."

The machine is initially scanning the first "I". The machine proceeds to "work out" the sum (essentially by replacing the plus sign by a I, and then going back and erasing the first I). Thus if the "input" was IIII + IIIII the machine would "print out"IIIIIIIII, and then go into the "rest state" (state *D*).

A "machine table" *describes* a machine if the machine has internal states corresponding to the columns of the table, and if it "obeys" the instruction in the table in the following sense: when it is scanning a square on which a symbol s_1 appears and it is in, say, state *B,* that it carries out the "instruction" in the appropriate row and column of the table (in this case, column *B* and row s_1). Any machine that is described by a machine table of the sort just exemplified is a Turing machine.

The notion of a Turing machine is also subject to generalization in various ways—for example, one may suppose that the machine has a second tape (an "input tape") on which additional information may be printed by an operator in the course of a computation. In the sequel we shall make use of this generalization (with electronic "sense organs" taking the place of the "operator").

It should be remarked that Turing machines are able in principle to do anything that any computing machine (of whichever kind) can do.

It has sometimes been contended (e.g. by Nagel and Newman in their book *Gödel's Proof**) that "the theorem [i.e. Gödel's theorem] does indicate that the structure and power of the human mind are far more complex and subtle than any non-living machine yet envisaged" (p. 10), and hence that a Turing machine cannot serve as a model for the human mind, but this is simply a mistake.

Let *T* be a Turing machine which "represents" me in the sense that *T* can prove just the mathematical statements I can prove. Then the argument (Nagel and Newman give no argument, but I assume they must have this one in mind) is that by using Gödel's technique I can discover a proposition that *T* cannot prove, and moreover *I* can prove this proposition. This refutes the assumption that *T* "represents" me, hence I am not a Turing machine. The fallacy is a misapplication of Gödel's theorem, pure and simple. Given an arbitrary machine *T,* all I can do is find a proposition *U* such that *I* can prove:

(3) If *T* is consistent, *U* is true,

where *U* is undecidable by *T* if *T* is in fact consistent. However, *T* can perfectly well prove (3) too! And the statement *U,* which *T cannot* prove (assuming consistency), *I* cannot prove either

*Ernest Nagel and James R. Newman, *Gödel's Proof* (New York: New York University Press, 1958).

(unless I can prove that *T* is inconsistent, which is unlikely if *T* is very complicated)!

Notes

1. . . . I wish to avoid the vexed question of the relation between *pains* and *pain states*. I only remark in passing that one common argument *against* identification of these two—namely, that a pain can be in one's arm but a state (of the organism) cannot be in one's arm—is easily seen to be fallacious.
2. There are some well-known remarks by Alonzo Church on this topic. Those remarks do not bear (as might at first be supposed) on the identification of concepts with synonymy-classes as such, but rather support the view that (in formal semantics) it is necessary to retain Frege's distinction between the normal and the "oblique" use of expressions. That is, even if we say that the concept of temperature *is* the synonymy-class of the word "temperature", we must not thereby be led into the error of supposing that "the concept of temperature" is synonymous with "the synonymy-class of the word 'temperature' "—for then "the concept of temperature" and "der Begriff der Temperatur" would not be synonymous, which they are. Rather, we must say that the concept of "temperature" *refers to* the synonymy-class of the word "temperature" (on this particular reconstruction); but that class is *identified* not as "the synonymy class to which such-and-such a word belongs", but in another way (e.g. as the synonymy-class whose members have such-and-such a characteristic use.

Functionalism

JERRY FODOR

Jerry Fodor (1935–) is a professor of philosophy and psychology at the Massachusetts Institute of Technology. His publications include *Psychological Explanation* and *The Language of Thought.*

The stumbling block for a dualist is the problem of mind/body interaction. If you think, as Descartes did, that minds are immaterial substances, you ought to be worried (as Descartes was) about how there can be mental causes of behavioral effects. Cynicism might suggest that the question how an immaterial substance could contribute to the etiology of physical events is not, after all, much more obscure than the question how material substances could interact causally with one another. But there is this difference: whereas we can produce lots of untendentious examples of the latter kind of interaction, there are no untendentious examples of the former kind. Physical causation we will have to live with; but non-physical causation might be an artifact of the immaterialist construal of the claim that there are minds.

Viewed this way, the issue is one of ontological parsimony. A Cartesian dualist is going to hold that there are species of causal relations over and above physical interactions. He is therefore in need of an argument why mind/body causation should not itself be viewed as an instance of physical interaction. Most philosophers now agree that no such argument has successfully been made. Even philosophers like Ryle, whose preferred style of anti-Cartesian argument was so very often epistemological, insisted on the force of such considerations: "there was from the beginning felt to be a major theoretical difficulty in explaining how minds can influence and be influenced by bodies. How can a mental process, such as willing, cause spatial movements like movements of the tongue? How can a physical change in the optic nerve have among its effects a mind's perception of a flash of light?" (1949, p. 19).[1]

It is precisely the advantage of materialistic monism that it provides for the subsumption of mind/body interaction as a special case of physical interaction, thereby making problems like the ones that Ryle mentions go away. By the early 1960s, it was becoming clear that there are two quite different strategies for performing this reduction, one corresponding to the program of *logical behaviorism* and the other ocrresponding to the program of the *central state identity theory*. And it was also becoming clear that each of these strategies has its problems.

The essence of one kind of logical behaviorism is the idea that every truth-valuable ascription of a mental state or process to an organism is semantically equivalent to the ascription of a certain sort of dispositional property to that organism. . . . In particular, in the interesting cases, mental ascriptions were supposed to be semantically equivalent to ascriptions of *behavioral dispositions*. A behavioral disposition is one that an organism has if and only if (iff) it satisfied a certain indefinite (possibly infinite) set of *behavioral hypotheticals* which constitute the *analysis* of the disposition. A behavioral hypothetical is a

From *Representations* (Cambridge, Eng.: Bradford Books, 1981), pp. 2–11.

(possibly counterfactual) statement whose antecedent is couched solely in terms of *stimulus parameters* and whose consequent is couched solely in terms of *response parameters.* Heaven only knows what stimulus and response parameters were supposed to be; but it was an Article of Faith that these notions could, in principle, be made clear. Perhaps stimulus and response parameters are species of physical parameters (parameters that would be acknowledged by an ideally completed physical theory), though not all logical behaviorists would have accepted that identification. In any event, precisely because the ontological impulse of behaviorism was reductionistic, success depended on the possibility of expressing stimulus and response parameters in a vocabulary which contained no mental terms.

What is attractive about logical behaviorism is that the proposed identification of mental properties with dispositional ones provides for a sort of construal of statements that attribute behavioral effects to mental causes—a construal that is, moreover, conformable to the requirements of materialistic monism. Roughly, mental causation is the manifestation of a behavioral disposition; it's what you get when an organism has such a disposition and the antecedent of a behavioral hypothetical that belongs to the analysis of the disposition happens to be true. It is, no doubt, a travesty to say that for a logical behaviorist "Smith is thirsty" means "if there were water around, Smith would drink it" and "Smith drank because he was thirsty" means "if there were water around Smith would drink it; and there was water around." But it is a travesty that comes close enough for our present purposes. It allows us to see how logical behaviorists proposed to assimilate worrisome etiologies that invoke mental causes to relatively untendentious etiologies like "it broke because it was fragile; it bent because it was pliable," etc.

So, logical behaviorism provides a construal of mental causation, and the glaring question is whether the construal it provides is adequately robust to do the jobs that need doing. In the long run this is the question whether the identification of mental properties with behavioral dispositions yields a notion of mental causation that is rich enough to reconstruct the etiologies propounded by our best psychological theories: the ones that achieve simplicity, explanatory power, and predictive success. However, we needn't wait for the long run, since there are plenty of cases of *pre*-theoretically plausible etiologies for which plausible behavioristic construals are not forthcoming, and these, surely, are straws in the wind.

Here is a quick way of making the point. Suppose "John took aspirin because he had a headache" is true iff conjunction C holds:

> *C:* John was disposed to produce headache behaviors and being disposed to produce headache behaviors involves satisfying the hypothetical *if there are aspirin around, one takes some,* and there were aspirin around.

So, *C* gives us a construal of "John took aspirin because he had a headache." But consider that we are also in want of a construal of statements like "John was disposed to produce headache behaviors because he had a headache." Such statements *also* invoke mental causes and, pretheoretically at least, we have no reason to doubt that many of them are true. Yet in these cases it seems unlikely that the putative mental causes can be traded for dispositions; or if they can, the line of analysis we've been pursuing doesn't show us how to do it. We cannot, for example, translate "John had a headache" as "John had a disposition to produce headache behaviors" in these cases, since, patently, "John was disposed to produce headache behaviors because he had a headache" doesn't mean the same as "John was disposed to produce headache behaviors because he had a disposition to produce headache behaviors." Yet, "John had a headache" surely means the same in "John took aspirin because he had a headache" and in "John was disposed to produce headache behaviors because he had a headache," so if the behavioristic analysis is wrong for the second case, it must also be wrong for the first.

This is, no doubt, a relatively technical kind of difficulty, but it points in the direction of what is now widely viewed as a hopeless problem for logical behaviorism. Mental causes typically have their overt effects *in virtue of their interactions with one another,* and behaviorism provides no satisfactory analysis of statements that articulate such interactions. Statements that attribute behavioral dispositions to mental causes are of this species, but they are far from exhausting the kind. Consider that having a headache is sufficient to cause a disposition to take aspirin only if it is accompanied by a battery of other mental states: the desire to be rid of the headache; the belief that aspirin exists; the belief that taking aspirin leads to a reduction of headache; the belief that its side effects are not worse than headaches are; the belief that it is not grossly immoral to take aspirin when one has a headache; and so on. Moreover, such beliefs and utilities must be, as it were, *operative;* not only must one *have* them, but some of them must come into play as causal agents contributing to the production of the behavioral effect.

The consequences of this observation are twofold. First, it seems highly unlikely that mental causes can be identified with *behavioral* dispositions, since the antecedents of many putatively behavioral hypotheticals turn out to contain mentalistic vocabulary ineliminably. But, moreover, we shall have to find analyses for etiologies in which interactions among mental states involve possibly quite long and elaborate causal chains; and here we have a fertile source of counterexamples to the generality of *any* kind of dispositional construal of mental ascriptions, behavioral or otherwise. "It occurred to John to move his knight, but then he noticed that that would leave his king in trouble, and since he wanted to avoid check, he thought on balance that he'd better temporize and push a pawn. When, however, he had considered for a which which pawn to push, it all began to look boring and hopeless, and he thought: 'Oh, bother it,' and decided to resign. (Overt behavior finally ensues.)" Surely, the mental life is often like that; such cases occur everywhere where mental *processes* are at issue, and it is, perhaps, the basic problem with behaviorism that it can't reconstruct the notion *mental process*. But these cases seem to be most glaringly the norm in reasoning and problem solving, so it's not surprising that, among psychologists, it has been the cognition theorists who have led the recent antibehaviorist campaign. It seems perfectly obvious that what's needed to construe cognitive processes is precisely what behaviorists proposed to do without: causal sequences of mental episodes and a "mental mechanics" to articulate the generalizations that such sequences instantiate. The problem was—and remains—to accommodate these methodological requirements within the ontological framework of materialism.

Which is why the physicalist reading of materialistic monism seemed so very attractive an alternative to the behavioristic version. Suppose we assume that mental particulars (events, states, processes, dispositions, etc.) are identical with physical particulars, and also that the property of being in a certain mental state (such as having a headache or believing that it will rain) is identical with the property of being in a certain physical (e.g. neural) state. Then we have a guaranty that our notion of mental causation will be as robust as our notion of physical causation, the former having turned out to be a special case of the latter. In particular, we will have no difficulty in making sense of the claim that behavioral effects may sometimes be the consequence of elaborate chains of mental causes; or, indeed, that mental causes may interact elaborately *without* eventuating in behavioral effects. If mental processes are, in fact, physical processes, they must enjoy whatever ontological autonomy physical processes are conceded. More than that we surely should not ask for.

This is bracing stuff from the point of view of the psychologist. Endorsing the central state identity theory is tantamount to accepting a Realist interpretation of explanations in which appeal to mental causes figure: If mental particulars are physical particulars, then the singular terms in (true) psychological theories denote. Indeed, they denote precisely the same sorts of things that the singular terms in (true) physical theories do. Moreover, since physicalism is not a semantic thesis, it is immune to many of the kinds of arguments that make trouble for behaviorists. It is, for example, uninteresting from the physicalist's point of view that "John has a headache" doesn't mean the same as "John is in such and such a brain state." The physicalist's claim is not that such sentences are synonymous—that the second provides a linguistically or epistemologically adequate construal of the first—but only that they are rendered true (or false) by the same states of affairs.

I remarked that the identity theory can be held either as a doctrine about mental *particulars*

(John's current headache, Bill's fear of cats) or as a doctrine about the nature of mental *properties* (universals like having a pain or being afraid of animals.) These two variants—known as "token physicalism" and "type physicalism" respectively—differ in both strength and plausibility. For, while the former claims only that all the mental particulars that there happen to be are neurological, the latter makes that claim about all the mental particulars that there *could* be. Token physicalism is thus compatible with the logical—perhaps even the nomological—possibility of unincarnate bearers of mental properties (e.g. angels) and of bearers of mental properties that are incarnate but not in flesh (e.g. machines). Whereas, type physicalism does not recognize such possibilities, since, if the property of having a pain is the same property as that of being in a certain neural state, nothing can have the former property that does not have the latter.

Type physicalism is, on balance, not a plausible doctrine about the nature of mental properties—not even if token physicalism is a plausible doctrine about the nature of mental particulars; not even if token physicalism is a *true* doctrine about the nature of mental particulars. The argument against type physicalism is often made in a way that does it less than justice: "Why shouldn't (e.g.) silicon-based Martians suffer pains? And why shouldn't machines have beliefs? But if it is conceivable that mental properties should have such bearers, then it cannot be that mental properties *are* neural properties, however much the two may prove to be de facto coextensive. And neither can it be that they are *physical* properties if what you mean by a physical property is one that can be expressed by a projectible predicate in (say) an ideally completed physics. What silicon-based Martians and IBM machines and you and I are likely to have in common by way of the physical constitution of our nervous systems simply isn't worth discussing."

But that's really not the point. The real point is that, if we want a science of mental phenomena at all, we are required to so identify mental properties that the kinds they subsume are natural from the point of view of psychological theory construction. If, for example, we identify mental properties with neural properties, then we are in effect claiming that domains consisting of creatures with a certain sort of neural organization constitute natural kinds for the psychologist's purposes. (Compare: if we claim that the property of being fish is the property of living in the water, then we are in effect claiming that a domain consisting of creatures that live in the water constitutes a natural kind for the purposes of the marine biologist. Either that or we are claiming that "is a fish" is not a projectible predicate in marine biology. The essays that follow are neutral on fish, but they do assume the projectibility of properties like those expressed by typical mental predicates.)

Now, there is a level of abstraction at which the generalizations of psychology are most naturally pitched and, as things appear to be turning out, that level of abstraction collapses across the differences between physically quite different kinds of systems. Given the sorts of things we need to say about having pains and believing Ps, it seems to be at best just accidental, and at worst just false, that pains and beliefs are proprietary to creatures like us; if we *wanted* to restrict the domains of our psychological theories to just us, we would have to do so by ad hoc conditions upon their generalizations. Whereas, what does seem to provide a natural domain for psychological theorizing, at least in cognitive psychology, is something like the set of (real and possible) information processing systems. The point being, of course, that there are possible—and, for all we know, real—information processing systems which share our psychology (instantiate its generalizations) but do not share our physical organization.

It would be hard to overemphasize this point, but I shall do my best: Philosophical theories about the nature of mental properties carry empirical commitments about the appropriate domains for psychological generalizations. It is therefore an argument against such a theory if it carves things up in ways that prohibit stating such psychological generalizations as there are to state. And it looks as though type physicalism does carve things up in the wrong ways, assuming that the sort of psychological theories that are now being developed are even close to being true.

This is a state of affairs which cries out for a *relational* treatment of mental properties, one which identifies them in ways that abstract from the physiology of their bearers. Indeed there is a sense in which behaviorists had the right end of the stick in hand, despite the sorts of objections we reviewed above. Behaviorists, after all, *did* offer a relational construal of mental properties: to have a belief or a pain was to be disposed to exhibit a certain pattern of relations between the responses that one produces and the stimuli that one encounters. So there seemed, ten or fifteen years ago, to be a nasty dilemma facing the materialist program in the philosophy of mind: What central state physicalists seemed to have got right—contra behaviorists—was the ontological autonomy of mental particulars and, of a piece with this, the causal character of mind/body interactions. Whereas, what the behaviorists seemed to have got right—contra the identity theory—was the relational character of mental properties. Functionalism, grounded in the machine analogy, seemed to be able to get both right at once. It was in the cheerful light of that promised synthesis that the now dominant approaches to the philosophy of mind first began to emerge.

It's implicit in the preceding that there is a way of understanding the new functionalism that makes it simply an extension of the logical behaviorist's program. Having a belief (say) was still to be construed as having a relational property, except that, whereas behaviorists had permitted only references to stimuli and responses to appear essentially in specifications of the relata, functionalists allowed reference to *other mental states* as well. A functionalist could thus concede many platidues that behaviorists are hard put even to construe—as, for example, that it is plausibly a necessary condition for having certain beliefs that one is disposed to draw certain inferences (no belief that P&Q without a disposition to infer that P and a disposition to infer that Q); that it is plausibly a necessary condition for performing certain acts that one be in certain states of mind (no prevariacation without the causal involvement of an intent to deceive); and so forth.

But, in fact, reading functionalism this way—as a liberated form of behaviorism—is more than mildly perverse; for *all* that functionalism and behaviorism have in common is the relational construal of mental properties. If one considers the ontological issues (to say nothing of the epistemological issues), striking differences between the doctrines emerge at once. Unlike behaviorism, functionalism is not a reductionist thesis; it does not envision—even in principle—the elimination of mentalistic concepts from the explanatory apparatus of psychological theories. In consequence, functionalism is compatible with a physicalist (hence Realist) account of mental particulars. It thus tolerates the ascription of causal roles to mental particulars and can take literally theories which represent mental particulars as interacting causally, with whatever degree of complexity, in the course of mental processes. That, as we have seen, was the primary advantage the central state identity theory enjoyed. So it is possible for a functionalist to hold (1) that mental kinds are typically relationally defined; and (2) that the relations that mental particulars exhibit, insofar as they constitute the domains of mental processes, are typically *causal* relations: to stimuli, to responses, and to one another. Of these claims, a logical behaviorist can endorse only the first with an absolutely clear conscience, and a type-physicalist only the second.

So functionalism appeared to capture the best features of the previously available alternatives to dualism while avoiding all the major embarrassments. Viewed from one perspective, it offered behaviorism without reductionism; viewed from another, it offered physicalism without parochialism. The idea that mental particulars are physical, the idea that mental kinds are relational, the idea that mental processes are causal, and the idea that there could, at least in logical principle, be non-biological bearers of mental properties were all harmonized. And the *seriousness* of the psychologist's undertaking was vindicated by providing for a Realistic interpretation of his theoretical constructs. Bliss!

Note

1. [See pp. 331–32—Eds.]

What Is It Like To Be a Bat?

THOMAS NAGEL

Thomas Nagel (1937–) is a professor of philosophy at New York University. His publications include *The Possibility of Altruism* and *Mortal Questions*

Consciousness is what makes the mind-body problem really intractable. Perhaps that is why current discussions of the problem give it little attention or get it obviously wrong. The recent wave of reductionist euphoria has produced several analyses of mental phenomena and mental concepts designed to explain the possibility of some variety of materialism, psychophysical identification, or reduction.[1] But the problems dealt with are those common to this type of reduction and other types, and what makes the mind-body problem unique, and unlike the water-H_2O problem or the Turing machine-IBM machine problem or the lightning-electrical discharge problem or the gene-DNA problem or the oak tree-hydrocarbon problem, is ignored.

Every reductionist has his favorite analogy from modern science. It is most unlikely that any of these unrelated examples of successful reduction will shed light on the relation of mind to brain. But philosophers share the general human weakness for explanations of what is incomprehensible in terms suited for what is familiar and well understood, though entirely different. This has led to the acceptance of implausible accounts of the mental largely because they would permit familiar kinds of reduction. I shall try to explain why the usual examples do not help us to understand the relation between mind and body—why, indeed, we have at present no conception of what an explanation of the physical nature of a mental phenomenon would be. Without consciousness the mind-body problem would be much less interesting. With consciousness it seems hopeless. The most important and characteristic feature of conscious mental phenomena is very poorly understood. Most reductionist theories do not even try to explain it. And careful examination will show that no currently available concept of reduction is applicable to it. Perhaps a new theoretical form can be devised for the purpose, but such a solution, if it exists, lies in the distant intellectual future.

Conscious experience is a widespread phenomenon. It occurs at many levels of animal life, though we cannot be sure of its presence in the simpler organisms, and it is very difficult to say in general what provides evidence of it. (Some extremists have been prepared to deny it even of mammals other than man.) No doubt it occurs in countless forms totally unimaginable to us, on other planets in other solar systems throughout the universe. But no matter how the form may vary, the fact that an organism has conscious experience *at all* means, basically, that there is something it is like to *be* that organism. There may be further implications about the form of the experience; there may even (though I doubt it) be implications about the behavior of the organism. But fundamentally an organism has conscious mental states if and only if there is something that it is like to *be* that organism—something it is like *for* the organism.

We may call this the subjective character of

From the *Philosophical Review* 83, no. 4 (October 1974), pp. 435–50.

experience. It is not captured by any of the familiar, recently devised reductive analyses of the mental, for all of them are logically compatible with its absence. It is not analyzable in terms of any explanatory system of functional states, or intentional states, since these could be ascribed to robots or automata that behaved like people though they experienced nothing.[2] It is not analyzable in terms of the causal role of experiences in relation to typical human behavior—for similar reasons.[3] I do not deny that conscious mental states and events cause behavior, nor that they may be given functional characterizations. I deny only that this kind of thing exhausts their analysis. Any reductionist program has to be based on an analysis of what is to be reduced. If the analysis leaves something out, the problem will be falsely posed. It is useless to base the defense of materialism on any analysis of mental phenomena that fails to deal explicitly with their subjective character. For there is no reason to suppose that a reduction which seems plausible when no attempt is made to account for consciousness can be extended to include consciousness. Without some idea, therefore, of what the subjective character of experience is, we cannot know what is required of a physicalist theory.

While an account of the physical basis of mind must explain many things, this appears to be the most difficult. It is impossible to exclude the phenomenological features of experience from a reduction in the same way that one excludes the phenomenal features of an ordinary substance from a physical or chemical reduction of it—namely, by explaining them as effects on the minds of human observers.[4] If physicalism is to be defended, the phenomenological features must themselves be given a physical account. But when we examine their subjective character it seems that such a result is impossible. The reason is that every subjective phenomenon is essentially connected with a single point of view, and it seems inevitable that an objective, physical theory will abandon that point of view.

Let me first try to state the issue somewhat more fully than by referring to the relation between the subjective and the objective, or between the *pour-soi* and the *en-soi*. This is far from easy. Facts about what it is like to be an *X* are very peculiar, so peculiar that some may be inclined to doubt their reality, or the singificance of claims about them. To illustrate the connection between subjectivity and a point of view, and to make evident the importance of subjective features, it will help to explore the matter in relation to an example that brings out clearly the divergence between the two types of conception, subjective and objective.

I assume we all believe that bats have experience. After all, they are mammals, and there is no more doubt that they have experience than that mice or pigeons or whales have experience. I have chosen bats instead of wasps or flounders because if one travels too far down the phylogenetic tree, people gradually shed their faith that there is experience there at all. Bats, although more closely related to us than those other species, nevertheless present a range of activity and a sensory apparatus so different from ours that the problem I want to pose is exceptionally vivid (though it certainly could be raised with other species). Even without the benefit of philosophical reflection, anyone who has spent some time in an enclosed space with an excited bat knows what it is to encounter a fundamentally *alien* form of life.

I have said that the essence of the belief that bats have experience is that there is something that it is like to be a bat. Now we know that most bats (the microchiroptera, to be precise) perceive the external world primarily by sonar, or echolocation, detecting the reflections, from objects within range, of their own rapid, subtly modulated, high-frequency shrieks. Their brains are designed to correlate the outgoing impulses with the subsequent echoes, and the information thus acquired enables bats to make precise discriminations of distance, size, shape, motion, and texture comparable to those we make by vision. But bat sonar, though clearly a form of perception, is not similar in its operation to any sense that we possess, and there is no reason to suppose that it is subjectively like anything we can experience or imagine. This appears to create difficulties for the notion of what it is like to be a bat. We must consider whether any method will permit us to extrapolate to the inner life of the bat from our own case,[5] and if not, what alternative methods there may be for understanding the notion.

Our own experience provides the basic material for our imagination, whose range is therefore limited. It will not help to try to imagine that one has webbing on one's arms, which enables one to fly around at dusk and dawn catching insects in one's mouth; that one has very poor vision, and perceives the surrounding world by a system of reflected high-frequency sound signals; and that one spends the day hanging upside down by one's feet in an attic. In so far as I can imagine this (which is not very far), it tells me only what it would be like for *me* to behave as a bat behaves. But that is not the question. I want to know what it is like for a *bat* to be a bat. Yet if I try to imagine this, I am restricted to the resources of my own mind, and those resources are inadequate to the task. I cannot perform it either by imagining additions to my present experience, or by imagining segments gradually subtracted from it, or by imagining some combination of additions, subtractions, and modifications.

To the extent that I could look and behave like a wasp or a bat without changing my fundamental structure, my experiences would not be anything like the experiences of those animals. On the other hand, it is doubtful that any meaning can be attached to the supposition that I should possess the internal neurophysiological constitution of a bat. Even if I could by gradual degrees be transformed into a bat, nothing in my present constitution enables me to imagine what the experiences of such a future stage of myself thus metamorphosed would be like. The best evidence would come from the experiences of bats, if we only knew what they were like.

So if extrapolation from our own case is involved in the idea of what it is like to be a bat, the extrapolation must be incompletable. We cannot form more than a schematic conception of what it *is* like. For example, we may ascribe general *types* of experience on the basis of the animal's structure and behavior. Thus we describe bat sonar as a form of three-dimensional forward perception; we believe that bats feel some versions of pain, fear, hunger, and lust, and that they have other, more familiar types of perception besides sonar. But we believe that these experiences also have in each case a specific subjective character, which it is beyond our ability to conceive. And if there is conscious life elsewhere in the universe, it is likely that some of it will not be describable even in the most general experiential terms available to us.[6] (The problem is not confined to exotic cases, however, for it exists between one person and another. The subjective character of the experience of a person deaf and blind from birth is not accessible to me, for example, nor presumably is mine to him. This does not prevent us each from believing that the other's experience has such a subjective character.)

If anyone is inclined to deny that we can believe in the existence of facts like this whose exact nature we cannot possibly conceive, he should reflect that in contemplating the bats we are in much the same position that intelligent bats or Martians[7] would occupy if they tried to form a conception of what it was like to be us. The structure of their own minds might make it impossible for them to succeed, but we know they would be wrong to conclude that there is not anything precise that it is like to be us: that only certain general types of mental state could be ascribed to us (perhaps perception and appetite would be concepts common to us both; perhaps not). We know they would be wrong to draw such a skeptical conclusion because we know what it is like to be us. And we know that while it includes an enormous amount of variation and complexity, and while we do not possess the vocabulary to describe it adequately, its subjective character is highly specific, and in some respects describable in terms that can be understood only by creatures like us. The fact that we cannot expect ever to accommodate in our language a detailed description of Martian or bat phenomenology should not lead us to dismiss as meaningless the claim that bats and Martians have experiences fully comparable in richness of detail to our own. It would be fine if someone were to develop concepts and a theory that enabled us to think about those things; but such an understanding may be permanently denied to us by the limits of our nature. And to deny the reality or logical significance of what we can never describe or understand is the crudest form of cognitive dissonance.

This brings us to the edge of a topic that requires much more discussion that I can give it here: namely, the relation between facts on the one hand and conceptual schemes or systems of representation on the other. My realism about the subjective domain in all its forms implies a belief in the existence of facts beyond the reach of human concepts. Certainly it is possible for a human being to believe that there are facts which humans never *will* possess the requisite concepts to represent or comprehend. Indeed, it would be foolish to doubt this, given the finiteness of humanity's expectations. After all, there would have been transfinite numbers even if everyone had been wiped out by the Black Death before Cantor discovered them. But one might also believe that there are facts which *could* not ever be represented or comprehended by human beings, even if the species lasted forever—simply because our structure does not permit us to operate with concepts of the requisite type. This impossibility might even be observed by other beings, but it is not clear that the existence of such beings, or the possibility of their existence, is a precondition of the significance of the hypothesis that there are humanly inaccessible facts. (After all, the nature of beings with access to humanly inaccessible facts is presumably itself a humanly inaccessible fact.) Reflection on what it is likely to be a bat seems to lead us, therefore, to the conclusion that there are facts that do not consist in the truth of propositions expressible in a human language. We can be compelled to recognize the existence of such facts without being able to state or comprehend them.

I shall not pursue this subject, however. It bearing on the topic before us (namely, the mind-body problem) is that it enables us to make a general observation about the subjective character of experience. Whatever may be the status of facts about what it is like to be a human being, or a bat, or a Martian, these appear to be facts that embody a particular point of view.

I am not adverting here to the alleged privacy of experience to its possessor. The point of view in question is not one accessible only to a single individual. Rather it is a *type*. It is often possible to take up a point of view other than one's own, so the comprehension of such facts is not limited to one's own case. There is a sense in which phenomenological facts are perfectly objective: one person can know or say of another what the quality of the other's experience is. They are subjective, however, in the sense that even this objective ascription of experience is possible only for someone sufficiently similar to the object of ascription to be able to adopt his point of view—to understand the ascription in the first person as well as in the third, so to speak. The more different from oneself the other experiencer is, the less success one can expect with this enterprise. In our own case we occupy the relevant point of view, but we will have as much difficulty understanding our own experience properly if we approach it from another point of view as we would if we tried to understand the experience of another species without taking up *its* point of view.[8]

This bears directly on the mind-body problem. For if the facts of experience—facts about what it is like *for* the experiencing organism—are accessible only from one point of view, then it is a mystery how the true character of experiences could be revealed in the physical operation of that organism. The latter is a domain of objective facts par excellence—the kind that can be observed and understood from many points of view and by individuals with differing perceptual systems. There are no comparable imaginative obstacles to the acquisition of knowledge about bat neurophysiology by human scientists, and intelligent bats or Martians might learn more about the human brain than we ever will.

This is not by itself an argument against reduction. A Martian scientist with no understanding of visual perception could understand the rainbow, or lightning, or clouds as physical phenomena, though he would never be able to understand the human concepts of rainbow, lighting, or cloud, or the place these things occupy in our phenomenal world. The objective nature of the things picked out by these concepts could be apprehended by him because, although the concepts themselves are connected with a particular point of view and a particular visual phenomenology, the things apprehended from that point of view are not: they are observable from the point of view but external to it; hence they can be comprehended from other points of view also, either by the same organisms or by others. Lightning has an objective character that is not exhausted by its visual appearance, and this can be investigated by a Martian without vision. To be precise, it has a *more* objective character than is revealed in its visual appearance. In speaking of the move from subjective to objective characterization, I wish to remain noncommittal about the existence of an end point, the completely objective intrinsic nature of the thing, which one might or might not be able to reach. It may be more accurate to think of objectivity as a direction in which the understanding can travel. And in understanding a phenomenon like lightning, it is legitimate to go as far away as one can from a strictly human viewpoint.[9]

In the case of experience, on the other hand, the connection with a particular point of view seems much closer. It is difficult to understand what could be meant by the *objective* character of an experience, apart from the particular point of view from which its subject apprehends it. After all, what would be left of what it was like to be a bat if one removed the viewpoint of the bat? But if experience does not have, in addition to its subjective character, an objective nature that can be apprehended from many different points of view, then how can it be supposed that a Martian investigating my brain might be observing physical processes which were my mental processes (as he might observe physical processes which were bolts of lightning), only from a different point of view? How, for that matter, could a human physiologist observe them from another point of view?[10]

We appear to be faced with a general difficulty about psychophysical reduction. In other areas the process of reduction is a move in the direction of greater objectivity, toward a more accurate view of the real nature of things. This is accomplished by reducing our dependence on individual or species-specific points of view toward the objective of investigation. We describe it not in terms of the impressions it makes on our senses, but in terms of its more general effects and of properties detectable by means other than the human senses. The less it depends on a specifically human viewpoint, the more objective is our description. It is possible to follow this path because although the concepts and ideas we employ in thinking about the external world are initially applied from a point of view that involves our perceptual apparatus, they are used by us to refer to things beyond themselves—toward which we *have* the phenomenal point of view. Therefore we can abandon it in favor of another, and still be thinking about the same things.

Experience itself, however, does not seem to fit the pattern. The idea of moving from appearance to reality seems to make no sense here. What is the analogue in this case to pursuing a more objective understanding of the same phenomena by abandoning the initial subjective viewpoint toward them in favor of another that is more objective but concerns the same thing? Certainly it *appears* unlikely that we will get closer to the real nature of human experience by leaving behind the particularity of our human point of view and striving for a description in terms accessible to beings that could not imagine what it was like to be us. If the subjective character of experience is fully comprehensible only from one point of view, then any shift to greater objectivity—that is, less attachment to a specific viewpoint—does not take us nearer to the real nature of the phenomenon: it takes us farther away from it.

In a sense, the seeds of this objection to the reducibility of experience are already detectable in successful cases of reduction; for in discovering sound to be, in reality, a wave phenomenon in air or other media, we leave behind one viewpoint to take up another, and the auditory, human or animal viewpoint that we leave behind remains unreduced. Members of radically different species may both understand the same physical events in objective terms, and this does not require that they understand the phenomenal forms in which those events appear to the senses of members of the other species. Thus it is a condition of their referring to a common reality that their more particular viewpoints are not part of the common reality that they both apprehend. The reduction can succeed only if the species-specific viewpoint is omitted from what is to be reduced.

But while we are right to leave this point of view aside in seeking a fuller understanding of the external world, we cannot ignore it permanently, since it is the essence of the internal world, and not merely a point of view on it. Most of the neobehaviorism of recent philosophical psychology results from the effort to substitute an objective concept of mind for the real thing, in order to have nothing left over which cannot be reduced. If we acknowledge that a physical theory of mind must account for the subjective character of experience, we must admit that no presently available conception gives us a clue how this could be done. The problem is unique. If mental processes are indeed physical processes, then there is something it is like, intrinsically,[11] to undergo certain physical processes. What it is for such a thing to be the case remains a mystery.

What moral should be drawn from these reflections, and what should be done next? It would be a mistake to conclude that physicalism must be false. Nothing is proved by the inadequacy of physicalist hypotheses that assume a faulty objective analysis of mind. It would be truer to say that physicalism is a position we cannot understand because we do not at present have any conception of how it might be true. Perhaps it will be thought unreasonable to require such a conception as a condition of understanding. After all, it might be said, the meaning of physicalism is clear enough: mental states are states of the body; mental events are physical events. We do not know *which* physical states and events they are, but that should not prevent us from understanding the hypothesis. What could be clearer than the words "is" and "are"?

But I believe it is precisely this apparent clarity of the word "is" that is deceptive. Usually, when we are told that *X* is *Y* we know *how* it is supposed to be true, but that depends on a conceptual or theoretical background and is not conveyed by the "is" alone. We know how both "*X*" and "*Y*" refer, and the kinds of things to which they refer, and we have a rough idea how the two referential paths might converge on a single thing, be it an object, a person, a process, an event, or whatever. But when the two terms of the identification are very disparate it may not be so clear how it could be true. We may not have even a rough idea of how the two referential paths could converge, or what kind of things they might converge on, and a theoretical framework may have to be supplied to enable us to understand this. Without the framework, an air of mysticism surrounds the identification.

This explains the magical flavor of popular presentations of fundamental scientific discoveries, given out as propositions to which one must subscribe without really understanding them. For example, people are now told at an early age that all matter is really energy. But despite the fact that they know what "is" means, most of them never form a conception of what makes this claim true, because they lack the theoretical background.

At the present time the status of physicalism is similar to that which the hypothesis that matter is energy would have had if uttered by a pre-Socratic philosopher. We do not have the beginnings of a conception of how it might be true. In order to understand the hypothesis that a mental event is a physical event, we require more than an understanding of the word "is." The idea of how a mental and a physical term might refer to the same thing is lacking, and the usual analogies with theoretical identification in other fields fail to supply it. They fail because if we construe the reference of mental terms to physical events on the usual model, we either get a reappearance of separate subjective events as the effects through which mental reference to physical events is secured, or else we get a false account of how mental terms refer (for example, a causal behaviorist one).

Strangely enough, we may have evidence for the truth of something we cannot really understand. Suppose a caterpillar is locked in a sterile safe by someone unfamiliar with insect metamorphosis, and weeks later the safe is reopened, revealing a butterfly. If the person knows that the safe has been shut the whole time, he has reason to believe that the butterfly is or was once the caterpillar, without having any idea in what sense this might be so. (One possibility is that the caterpillar contained a tiny winged parasite that devoured it and grew into the butterfly.)

It is conceivable that we are in such a position with regard to physicalism. Donald Davidson has argued that if mental events have physical causes and effects, they must have physical descriptions. He holds that we have reason to believe this even though we do not—and in fact *could* not—have a general psychophysical theory.[12] His argument applies to intentional mental events, but I think we also have some reason to believe that sensations are physical processes, without being in a position to understand how. Davidson's position is that certain physical events have irreducibly mental properties, and perhaps some view describable in this way is correct. But nothing of which we can now form a conception corresponds to it; nor have we any idea what a theory would be like that enabled us to conceive of it.[13]

Very little work has been done on the basic question (from which mention of the brain can be entirely omitted) whether any sense can be made of experiences having an objective character at all. Does it make sense, in other words, to ask what my experiences are *really* like, as opposed to how they appear to me? We cannot genuinely understand the hypothesis that their nature is captured in a physical description unless we understand the more fundamental idea that they *have* an objective nature (or that objective processes can have a subjective nature).[14]

I should like to close with a speculative proposal. It may be possible to approach the gap between subjective and objective from another direction. Setting aside temporarily the relation between the mind and the brain, we can pursue a more objective understanding of the mental in its own right. At present we are completely unequipped to think about the subjective character of experience without relying on the imagination—without taking up the point of view of the experiential subject. This should be regarded as a challenge to form new concepts and devise a new method—an objective phenomenology not dependent on empathy or the imagination. Though presumably it would not capture everything, its goal would be to describe, at least in part, the subjective character of experiences in a form comprehensible to beings incapable of having those experiences.

We would have to develop such a phenomenology to describe the sonar experiences of bats; but it would also be possible to begin with humans. One might try, for example, to develop concepts that could be used to explain to a person blind from birth what it was like to see. One would reach a blank wall eventually, but it should be possible to devise a method of expressing in objective terms much more than we can at present, and with much greater precision. The loose intermodal analogies—for example, "Red is like the sound of a trumpet"—which crop up in discussions of this subject are of little use. That should be clear to anyone who has both heard a trumpet and seen red. But structural features of perception might be more accessible to objective description, even though something would be left out. And concepts alternative to those we learn in the first person may enable us to arrive at a kind of understanding even of our own experience which is denied us by the very ease of description and lack of distance that subjective concepts afford.

Apart from its own interest, a phenomenology that is in this sense objective may permit questions about the physical[15] basis of experience to assume a more intelligible form. Aspects of subjective experience that admitted this kind of objective description might be better candidates for objective explanations of a more familiar sort. But whether or not this guess is correct, it seems unlikely that any physical theory of mind can be contemplated until more thought has been given to the general problem of subjective and objective. Otherwise we cannot even pose the mind-body problem without sidestepping it.[16]

Notes

1. Examples are J. J. C. Smart, *Philosophy and Scientific Realism* (London, 1963); David K. Lewis, "An Argument for the Identity Theory," *Journal of Philosophy,* 63 (1966), reprinted with addenda in David M. Rosenthal, *Materialism and the Mind-Body Problem* (Englewood Cliffs, N.J., 1971); Hilary Putnam, "Psychological Predicates" in Captain and Merrill, *Art, Mind and Religion* (Pittsburgh, 1967), reprinted in Rosenthal, op. cit., as "The Nature of Mental States"; D. M. Armstrong, *A Materialist Theory of the Mind* (London, 1968); D. C. Dennett, *Content and Consciousness* (London, 1969). I have expressed earlier doubts in "Armstrong on the Mind," *Philosophical Review,* 79 (1970), 394–403; "Brain Bisection and the Unity of Consciousness," *Synthese,* 22 (1971); and a review of Dennett, *Journal of Philosophy,* 69 (1972). See also Saul Kripke, "Naming and Necessity" in Davidson and Harman, *Semantics of Natural Language* (Dordrecht, 1972), esp. pp. 334–42; and M. T. Thornton, "Ostensive Terms and Materialism," *Monist,* 56 (1972).
2. Perhaps there could not actually be such robots. Perhaps anything complex enough to behave like a person would have experiences. But that, if true, is a fact which cannot be discovered merely by analyzing the concept of experience.
3. It is not equivalent to that about which we are incorrigible, both because we are not incorrigible about experience and because experience is pres-

ent in animals lacking language and thought, who have no beliefs at all about their experiences.

4. Cf. Richard Rorty, "Mind-Body Identity, Privacy, and Categories," *Review of Metaphysics,* 19 (1965), esp. 37–38.
5. By "our own case" I do not mean just "my own case," but rather the mentalistic ideas that we apply unproblematically to ourselves and other human beings.
6. Therefore the analogical form of the English expression "what it is like" is misleading. It does not mean "what (in our experience) it *resembles,*" but rather "how it is for the subject himself."
7. Any intelligent extraterrestrial beings totally different from us.
8. It may be easier than I suppose to transcend inter-species barriers with the aid of the imagination. For example, blind people are able to detect objects near them by a form of sonar, using vocal clicks or taps of a cane. Perhaps if one knew what that was like, one could be extension imagine roughly what it was like to possess the much more refined sonar of a bat. The distance between oneself and other persons and other species can fall anywhere on a continuum. Even for other persons the understanding of what it is like to be them is only partial, and when one moves to species very different from oneself, a lesser degree of partial understanding may still be available. The imagination is remarkably flexible. My point, however, is not that we cannot *know* what it is like to be a bat. I am not raising that epistemological problem. My point is rather that even to form a *conception* of what it is like to be a bat (and a fortiori to know what it is like to be a bat) one must take up the bat's point of view. If one can take it up roughly, or partially, then one's conception will also be rough or partial. Or so it seems in our present state of understanding.
9. The problem I am going to raise can therefore be posed even if the distinction between more subjective and more objective descriptions or viewpoints can itself be made only within a larger human point of view. I do not accept this kind of conceptual relativism, but it need not be refuted to make the point that psychophysical reduction cannot be accommodated by the subjective-to-objective model familiar from other cases.
10. The problem is not just that when I look at the Mona Lisa, my visual experience has a certain quality, no trace of which is to be found by someone looking into my brain. For even if he did observe there a tiny image of the Mona Lisa, he would have no reason to identify it with the experience.
11. The relation would therefore not be a contingent one, like that of a cause and its distinct effect. It would be necessarily true that a certain physical state felt a certain way. Saul Kripke (op. cit.) argues that causal behaviorist and related analyses of the mental fail because they construe, e.g., "pain" as a merely contingent name of pains. The subjective character of an experience ("its immediate phenomenological quality" Kripke calls it [p. 340] is the essential property left out by such analyses, and the one in virtue of which it is, necessarily, the experience it is. My view is closely related to his. Like Kripke, I find the hypothesis that a certain brain state should *necessarily* have a certain subjective character incomprehensible without further explanation. No such explanation emerges from theories which view the mind-brain relation as contingent, but perhaps there are other alternatives, not yet discovered.

    A theory that explained how the mind-brain relation was necessary would still leave us with Kripke's problem of explaining why it nevertheless appears contingent. That difficulty seems to me surmountable, in the following way. We may imagine something by representing it to ourselves either perceptually, sympathetically, or symbolically. I shall not try to say how symbolic imagination works, but part of what happens in the other two cases is this. To imagine something perceptually, we put ourselves in a conscious state resembling the state we would be in if we perceived it. To imagine something sympathetically, we put ourselves in a conscious state resembling the thing itself. (This method can be used only to imagine mental events and states—our own or another's.) When we try to imagine a mental state occurring without its associated brain state, we first sympathetically imagine the occurrence of the mental state: that is, we put ourselves into a state that resembles it mentally. At the same time, we attempt to perceptually imagine the non-occurrence of the associated physical state, by puting ourselves into another state unconnected with the first: one resembling that which we would be in if we perceived the non-occurrence of the physical state. Where the imagination of physical features is perceptual and the imagination of mental features is sympathetic, it appears to us that we can imagine any experience occurring without its associated brain state, and vice versa. The relation between them will appear contingent even if it is necessary, because of the independence of the disparate types of imagination.

    (Solipsism, incidentally, results if one misinterprets sympathetic imagination as if it worked like perceptual imagination: it then seems impossible to imagine any experience that is not one's own.)
12. See "Mental Events" in Foster and Swanson, *Experience and Theory* (Amherst, 1970); though I don't understand the argument against psychophysical laws.
13. Similar remarks apply to my paper "Physicalism," *Philosophical Review* 74 (1965), 339–56, reprinted with postscript in John O'Connor, *Modern Materialism* (New York, 1969).
14. This question also lies at the heart of the problem of other minds, whose close connection with the mind-body problem is often overlooked. If one understood how subjective experience could have

an objective nature, one would understand the existence of subjects other than oneself.

15. I have not defined the term "physical." Obviously it does not apply just to what can be described by the concepts of contemporary physics, since we expect further developments. Some may think there is nothing to prevent mental phenomena from eventually being recognized as physical in their own right. But whatever else may be said of the physical, it has to be objective. So if our idea of the physical ever expends to include mental phenomena, it will have to assign them an objective character—whether or not this is done by analyzing them in terms of other phenomena already regarded as physical. It seems to me more likely, however, that mental-physical relations will eventually be expressed in a theory whose fundamental terms cannot be placed clearly in either category.

16. I have read versions of this paper to a number of audiences, and am indebted to many people for their comments.

B. MINDS AND MACHINES

Computing Machinery and Intelligence

A. M. TURING

A. M. Turing (1912–54), a Cambridge mathematician, made fundamental contributions to the theory of computation.

1. The Imitation Game

I propose to consider the question "Can machines think?" This should begin with definitions of the meaning of the terms "machine" and "think." The definitions might be framed so as to reflect so far as possible the normal use of the words, but this attitude is dangerous. If the meaning of the words "machine" and "think" are to be found by examining how they are commonly used it is difficult to escape the conclusion that the meaning and the answer to the question, "Can machines think?" is to be sought in a statistical survey such as a Gallup poll. But this is absurd. Instead of attempting such a definition I shall replace the question by another, which is closely related to it and is expressed in relatively unambiguous words.

The new form of the problem can be described in terms of a game which we call the "imitation game." It is played with three people, a man (A), a woman (B), and an interrogator (C) who may be of either sex. The interrogator stays in a room apart from the other two. The object of the game for the interrogator is to determine which of the other two is the man and which is the woman. He knows them by labels X and Y, and at the end of the game he says either "X is A and Y is B" or "X is B and Y is A." The interrogator is allowed to put questions to A and B thus:

C: Will X please tell me the length of his or her hair?

Now suppose X is actually A, then A must answer. It is A's object in the game to try to cause C to make the wrong identification. His answer might therefore be

"My hair is shingled, and the longest strands are about nine inches long."

In order that tones of voice may not help the interrogator the answers should be written, or better still, typewritten. The ideal arrangement is to have a teleprinter communicating between the two rooms. Alternatively the question and answers can be repeated by an intermediary. The object of the game for the third player (B) is to help the interrogator. The best strategy for her is probably to give truthful answers. She can add such things as "I am the woman, don't listen to him!" to her answers, but it will avail nothing as the man can make similar remarks.

We now ask the question, "What will happen when a machine takes the part of A in this game?" Will the interrogator decide wrongly as often when the game is played like this as he does when the game is played between a man and a woman? These questions replace our original, "Can machines think?"

2. Critique of the New Problem

As well as asking, "What is the answer to this new form of the question," one may ask, "Is this new question a worthy one to investigate?" This

From *Mind* 59, no. 236 (1950), pp. 4–30.

latter question we investigate without further ado, thereby cutting short an infinite regress.

The new problem has the advantage of drawing a fairly sharp line between the physical and the intellectual capacities of a man. No engineer or chemist claims to be able to produce a material which is indistinguishable from the human skin. It is possible that at some time this might be done, but even supposing this invention available we should feel there was little point in trying to make a "thinking machine" more human by dressing it up in such artificial flesh. The form in which we have set the problem reflects this fact in the condition which prevents the interrogator from seeing or touching the other competitors, or hearing their voices. Some other advantages of the proposed criterion may be shown up by specimen questions and answers. Thus:

Q: Please write me a sonnet on the subject of the Forth Bridge.

A: Count me out on this one. I never could write poetry.

Q: Add 34957 to 70764.

A: (Pause about 30 seconds and then give as answer) 105621.

Q: Do you play chess?

A: Yes.

Q: I have K at my K1, and no other pieces. You have only K at K6 and R at R1. It is your move. What do you play?

A: (After a pause of 15 seconds) R-R8 mate.

The question and answer method seems to be suitable for introducing almost any one of the fields of human endeavor that we wish to include. We do not wish to penalize the machine for its inability to shine in beauty competitions, nor to penalize a man for losing in a race against an airplane. The conditions of our game make these disabilities irrelevant. The "witnesses" can brag, if they consider it advisable, as much as they please about their charms, strength or heroism, but the interrogator cannot demand practical demonstrations.

The game may perhaps be criticized on the ground that the odds are weighted too heavily against the machine. If the man were to try and pretend to be the machine he would clearly make a very poor showing. He would be given away at once by slowness and inaccuracy in arithmetic. May not machines carry out something which ought to be described as thinking but which is very different from what a man does? This objection is a very strong one, but at least we can say that if, nevertheless, a machine can be constructed to play the imitation game satisfactorily, we need not be troubled by this objection.

It might be urged that when playing the "imitation game" the best strategy for the machine may possibly be something other than imitation of the behavior of a man. This may be, but I think it is unlikely that there is any great effect of this kind. In any case there is no intention to investigate here the theory of the game, and it will be assumed that the best strategy is to try to provide answers that would naturally be given by a man.

3. The Machines Concerned in the Game

The question which we put in §1 will not be quite definite until we have specified what we mean by the word "machine." It is natural that we should wish to permit every kind of engineering technique to be used in our machines. We also wish to allow the possibility that an engineer or team of engineers may construct a machine which works, but whose manner of operation cannot be satisfactorily described by its constructors because they have applied a method which is largely experimental. Finally, we wish to exclude from the machines men born in the usual manner. It is difficult to frame the definitions so as to satisfy these three conditions. One might for instance insist that the team of engineers should be all of one sex, but this would not really be satisfactory, for it is probably possible to rear a complete individual from a single cell of the skin (say) of a man. To do so would be a feat of biological technique deserving of the very highest praise, but we would not be inclined to regard it as a case of "constructing a thinking machine." This prompts us to abandon the requirement that every kind of technique should be permitted. We are the more ready to do so in view of the fact that the present interest in "thinking machines" has been aroused by a particular kind of machine, usually called an "electronic computer" or "digital computer." Following this suggestion we only permit digital computers to take part in our game.

This restriction appears at first sight to be a very drastic one. I shall attempt to show that it is not so in reality. To do this necessitates a short account of the nature and properties of these computers.

It may also be said that this identification of machines with digital computers, like our criterion for "thinking," will only be unsatisfactory if (contrary to my belief), it turns out that digital computers are unable to give a good showing in the game.

There are already a number of digital computers in working order, and it may be asked, "Why not try the experiment straight away? It would be easy to satisfy the conditions of the game. A number of interrogators could be used, and statistics compiled to show how often the right identification was given." The short answer is that we are not asking whether all digital computers would do well in the game nor whether the computers at present available would do well, but whether there are imaginable computers which would do well. But this is only the short answer. We shall see this question in a different light later.

4. Digital Computers

The idea behind digital computers may be explained by saying that these machines are intended to carry out any operations which could be done by a human computer. The human computer is supposed to be following fixed rules; he has no authority to deviate from them in any detail. We may suppose that these rules are supplied in a book, which is altered whenever he is put on to a new job. He has also an unlimited supply of paper on which he does his calculations. He may also do his multiplications and additions on a "desk machine," but this is not important.

If we use the above explanation as a definition we shall be in danger of ciricularity of argument. We avoid this by giving an outline of the means by which the desired effect is achieved. A digital computer can usually be regarded as consisting of three parts:

(i) Store.

(ii) Executive unit.

(iii) Control.

The store is a store of information, and corresponds to the human computer's paper, whether this is the paper on which he does his calculations or that on which his book of rules is printed. Insofar as the human computer does calculations in his head a part of the store will correspond to his memory.

The executive unit is the part which carries out the various individual operations involved in a calculation. What these individual operations are will vary from machine to machine. Usually fairly lengthy operations can be done such as "Multiply 3540675445 by 7076345687" but in some machines only very simple ones such as "Write down 0" are possible.

We have mentioned that the "book of rules" supplied to the computer is replaced in the machine by a part of the store. It is then called the "table of instructions." It is the duty of the control to see that these instructions are obeyed correctly and in the right order. The control is so constructed that this necessarily happens.

The information in the store is usually broken up into packets of moderately small size. In one machine, for instance, a packet might consist of ten decimal digits. Numbers are assigned to the parts of the store in which the various packets of information are stored, in some systematic manner. A typical instruction might say—

"Add the number stored in position 6809 to that in 4302 and put the result back into the latter storage position."

Needless to say it would not occur in the machine expressed in English. It would more likely be coded in a form such as 6809430217. Here 17 says which of various possible operations is to be performed on the two numbers. In this case the operation is that described above, viz. "Add the number. . . ." It will be noticed that the instruction takes up 10 digits and so forms one packet of information, very conveniently. The control will normally take the instructions to be obeyed in the order of the positions in which they are stored, but occasionally an instruction such as

"Now obey the instruction stored in position 5606, and continue from there"

may be encountered, or again

"If position 4505 contains 0 obey next the instruction stored in 6707, otherwise continue straight on."

Instructions of these latter types are very important because they make it possible for a sequence of operations to be repeated over and over again until some condition if fulfilled, but in doing so to obey, not fresh instructions on each repetition, but the same ones over and over again. To take a domestic analogy. Suppose Mother wants Tommy to call at the cobbler's every morning on his way to school to see if her shoes are done; she can ask him afresh every morning. Alternatively she can stick up a notice once and for all in the hall which he will see when he leaves for school and which tells him to call for the shoes, and also to destroy the notice when he comes back if he has the shoes with him.

The reader must accept it as a fact that digital computers can be constructed, and indeed have been constructed, according to the principles we have described, and that they can in fact mimic the actions of a human computer very closely.

The book of rules which we have described our human computer as using is of course a convenient fiction. Actual human computers really remember what they have got to do. If one wants to make a machine mimic the behavior of the human computer in some complex operation one has to ask him how it is done, and then translate the answer into the form of an instruction table. Constructing instruction tables is usually described as "programing." To "program a machine to carry out the operation A" means to put the appropriate instruction table into the machine so that it will do A.

An interesting variant on the idea of a digital computer is a "digital computer with a random element." These have instructions involving the throwing of a die or some equivalent electronic process; one such instruction might for instance be, "Throw the die and put the resulting number into store 1000." Sometimes such a machine is described as having free will (though I would not use this phrase myself). It is not normally possible to determine from observing a machine whether it has a random element, for a similar effect can be produced by such devices as making the choices depend on the digits of the decimal for π.

Most actual digital computers have only a finite store. There is no theoretical difficulty in the idea of a computer with an unlimited store. Of course only a finite part can have been used at any one time. Likewise only a finite amount can have been constructed, but we can imagine more and more being added as required. Such computers have special theoretical interest and will be called infinite capacity computers.

The idea of a digital computer is an old one. Charles Babbage, Lucasian Professor of Mathematics at Cambridge from 1828 to 1839, planned such a machine, called the Analytical Engine, but it was never completed. Although Babbage had all the essential ideas, his machine was not at that time such a very attractive prospect. The speed which would have been available would be definitely faster than a human computer but something like 100 times slower than the Manchester machine, itself one of the slower of the modern machines. The storage was to be purely mechanical, using wheels and cards.

The fact that Babbage's Analytical Engine was to be entirely mechanical will help us to rid ourselves of a superstition. Importance is often attached to the fact that modern digital computers are electrical, and that the nervous system also is electrical. Since Babbage's machine was not electrical, and since all digital computers are in a sense equivalent, we see that this use of electricity cannot be of theoretical importance. Of course electricity usually comes in where fast signaling is concerned, so that it is not surprising that we find it in both these connections. In the nervous system chemical phenomena are at least as important as electrical. In certain computers the storage system is mainly acoustic. The feature of using electricity is thus seen to be only a very superficial similarity. If we wish to find such similarities we should look rather for mathematical analogies of function.

5. Universality of Digital Computers

The digital computers considered in the last section may be classified among the "discrete state machines." These are the machines which move by sudden jumps or clicks from one quite definite state to another. These states are sufficiently different for the possibility of confusion between them to be ignored. Strictly speaking there are no such machines. Everything really moves continuously. But there are many kinds of machines which can profitably be *thought of* as being discrete state machines. For instance in considering the switches for a lighting system it is a convenient fiction that each switch must be definitely on or definitely off. There must be intermediate positions, but for most purposes we can forget about them. As an example of a discrete state machine we might consider a wheel which clicks round through 120° once a second, but may be stopped by a lever which can be operated from outside; in addition a lamp is to light in one of the positions of the wheel. This machine could be described abstractly as follows: The internal state of the machine (which is described by the position of the wheel) may be q_1, q_2 or q_3. There is an input signal i_0 or i_1 (position of lever). The internal state at any moment is determined by the last state and input signal according to the table

		Last State		
		q_1	q_2	q_3
Input	i_0	q_2	q_3	q_1
	i_1	q_1	q_2	q_3

The output signals, the only externally visible indication of the internal state (the light) are described by the table

State	q_1	q_2	q_3
Output	o_0	o_0	o_1

This example is typical of discrete state machines. They can be described by such tables provided they have only a finite number of possible states.

It will seem that given the initial state of the machine and the input signals it is always possible to predict all future states. This is reminiscent of Laplace's view that from the complete state of the universe at one moment of time, as described by the positions and velocities of all particles, it should be possible to predict all future states. The prediction which we are considering is, however, rather nearer to practicability than that considered by Laplace. The system of the "universe as a whole" is such that quite small errors in the initial conditions can have an overwhelming effect at a later time. The displacement of a single electron by a billionth of a centimeter at one moment might make the difference between a man being killed by an avalanche a year later, or escaping. It is an essential property of the mechanical systems which we have called "discrete state machines" that this phenomenon does not occur. Even when we consider the actual physical machines instead of the idealized machines, reasonably accurate knowledge of the state at one moment yields reasonably accurate knowledge any number of steps later.

As we have mentioned, digital computers fall within the class of discrete state machines. But the number of states of which such a machine is capable is usually enormously large. For instance, the number for the machine now working at Manchester is about $2^{165,000}$, i.e., about $10^{50,000}$. Compare this with our example of the clicking wheel described above, which had three states. It is not difficult to see why the number of states should be so immense. The computer includes a store corresponding to the paper used by a human computer. It must be possible to write into the store any one of the combinations of symbols which might have been written on the paper. For simplicity suppose that only digits from 0 to 9 are used as symbols. Variations in handwriting are ignored. Suppose the computer is allowed 100 sheets of paper each containing 50 lines each with room for 30 digits. Then the number of states is $10^{100 \times 50 \times 30}$, i.e., $10^{150,000}$. This is about the number of states of three Manchester machines put together. The logarithm to the base two of the number of states is usually called the "storage capacity" of the machine. Thus the Manchester machine has a storage capacity of about 165,000 and the wheel machine of our example about $1 \cdot 6$. If two machines are put together their capacities must be added to obtain the capacity of the resultant machine. This leads to the possibility of statements such as "The Manchester machine contains 64 magnetic tracks each with a capacity of 2560, eight electronic tubes with a capacity of 1280. Miscellaneous storage amounts to about 300 making a total of 174,380."

Given the table corresponding to a discrete state machine it is possible to predict what it will do. There is no reason why this calculation should not be carried out by means of a digital computer. Provided it could be carried out sufficiently quickly the digital computer could mimic the behavior of any discrete state machine. The imitation game could then be played with the machine in question (as B) and the mimicking digital computer (as A) and the interrogator would be unable to distinguish them. Of course the digital computer must have an adequate storage capacity as well as working sufficiently fast. Moreover, it must be programed afresh for each new machine which it is desired to mimic.

This special property of digital computers, that they can mimic any discrete state machine, is described by saying that they are *universal* machines. The existence of machines with this property has the important consequence that, considerations of speed apart, it is unnecessary to design various new machines to do various computing processes. They can all be done with one digital computer, suitably programed for each case. It will be seen that as a consequence of this all digital computers are in a sense equivalent.

We may now consider again the pont raised at the end of §3. It was suggested tentatively that the question, "Can machines think?" should be replaced by "Are there imaginable ditital computers which would do well in the imitation game?" If we wish we can make this superficially more general and ask "Are there discrete state machines which would do well?" But in view of the universality property we see that either of these questions is equivalent to this, "Let us fix our attention on one particular digital computer C. Is it true that by modifying this computer to have an adequate storage, suitably increasing its speed of action, and providing it with an appropriate program, C can be made to play satisfactorily the part of A in the imitation game, the part of B being taken by a man?"

6. Contrary Views on the Main Question

We may now consider the ground to have been cleared and we are ready to proceed to the debate on our question, "Can machines think?" and the variant of it quoted at the end of the last section. We cannot altogether abandon the original form of the problem, for opinions will differ as to the appropriateness of the substitution and we must at least listen to what has to be said in this connection.

It will simplify matters for the reader if I explain first my own beliefs in the matter. Consider first the more accurate form of the question. I believe that in about fifty years' time it will be possible to program computers, with a storage capacity of about 10^9, to make them play the imitation game so well that an average interrogator will not have more than 70 per cent chance of making the right identification after five minutes of questioning. The original question, "Can machines think?" I believe to be too meaningless to deserve discussion. Nevertheless I believe that at the end of the century the use of words and general educated opinion will have altered so much that one will be able to speak of machines thinking without expecting to be contradicted. I believe further that no useful purpose is served by concealing these beliefs. The popular view that scientists proceed inexorably from well-established fact to well-established fact, never being influenced by any unproved conjecture, is quite mistaken. Provided it is made clear which are proved facts and which are conjectures, no harm can result. Conjectures are of great importance since they suggest useful lines of research.

I now proceed to consider opinions opposed to my own.

(1) *The Theological Objection.* Thinking is a function of man's immortal soul. God has given an immortal soul to every man and woman, but not to any other animal or to machines. Hence no animal or machine can think.[1]

I am unable to accept any part of this, but will attempt to reply in theological terms. I should find the argument more convincing if animals were classed with men, for there is a greater difference, to my mind, between the typical animate and the inanimate than there is between man and the other animals. The arbitrary character of the orthodox view becomes clearer if we consider how it might appear to a member of some other religious community. How do Christians regard the Moslem view that women have no souls? But let us leave this point aside and return to the main argument. It appears to me that the argument quoted above implies a serious restriction of the omnipotence of the Almighty. It is admitted that there are certain things that He cannot do such as making one equal to two, but should we not believe that He has freedom to confer a soul on an elephant if He sees fit? We might expect that He would only exercise this power in conjunction with a mutation which provided the elephant with an appropriately improved brain to minister to the needs of this soul. An argument of exactly similar form may be made for the case of machines. It may seem different because it is more difficult to ''swallow.'' But this really only means that we think it would be less likely that He would consider the circumstances suitable for conferring a soul. The circumstances in question are discussed in the rest of this paper. In attempting to construct such machines we should not be irreverently usurping His power of creating souls, any more than we are in the procreation of children: rather we are, in either case, instruments of His will providing mansions for the souls that He creates.

However, this is mere speculation. I am not very impressed with theological arguments whatever they may be used to support. Such arguments have often been found unsatisfactory in the past. In the time of Galileo it was argued that the texts, ''And the sun stood still . . . and hasted not to go down about a whole day'' (Joshua x. 13) and ''He laid the foundations of the earth, that it should not move at any time'' (Psalm cv. 5) were an adequate refutation of the Copernican theory. With our present knowledge such an argument appears futile. When that knowledge was not available it made a quite different impression.

(2) *The ''Heads in the Sand'' Objection.* ''The consequences of machines thinking would be too dreadful. Let us hope and believe that they cannot do so.''

This argument is seldom expressed quite so openly as in the form above. But it affects most of us who think about it at all. We like to believe that Man is in some subtle way superior to the rest of creation. It is best if he can be shown to be *necessarily* superior, for then there is no danger of him losing his commanding position. The popularity of the theological argument is clearly connected with this feeling. It is likely to be quite strong in intellectual people, since they value the power of thinking more highly than others, and are more inclined to base their belief in the superiority of Man on this power.

I do not think that this argument is sufficiently substantial to require refutation. Consolation would be more appropriate: perhaps this should be sought in the transmigration of souls.

(3) *The Mathematical Objection.* There are a number of results of mathematical logic which can be used to show that there are limitations to the powers of discrete state machines. The best known of these results is known as Gödel's theorem, and shows that in any sufficiently powerful logical system statements can be formulated which can neither be proved nor disproved within the system, unless possibly the system itself is inconsistent. There are other, in some respects similar, results due to Church, Kleene, Rosser, and Turing. The latter result is the most convenient to consider, since it refers directly to machines, whereas the others can only be used in a comparatively indirect argument: for instance if Gödel's theorem is to be used we need in addition to have some means of describing logical systems in terms of machines, and machines in terms of logical systems. The result in question refers to a type of machine which is essentially a digital computer with an infinite capacity. It states that there are certain things that such a machine cannot do. If it is rigged up to give answers to questions as in the imitation game, there will be some questions to which it will either give a wrong answer, or fail to give an answer at all however much time is allowed for a reply. There may, of course, be many such questions, and questions which cannot be answered by one machine may be satisfactiorily answered by another. We are of course supposing for the present that the questions are of the kind to which an answer ''Yes'' or ''No'' is appropriate, rather than questions such as ''What do you think of Picasso?'' The questions that we know the machines must fail on are of this type, ''Consider the machine specified as follows. . . . Will this machine ever answer 'Yes' to any question?'' The dots are to be replaced by a description of some machine in a standard form, which could be something like that used in §5. When the machine described bears a certain comparatively simple relation to the machine

which is under interrogation, it can be shown that the answer is either wrong or not forthcoming. This is the mathematical result: it is argued that it proves a disability of machines to which the human intellect is not subject.

The short answer to this argument is that although it is established that there are limitations to the powers of any particular machine, it has only been stated, without any sort of proof, that no such limitations apply to the human intellect. But I do not think this view can be dismissed quite so lightly. Whenever one of these machines is asked the appropriate critical question, and gives a definite answer, we know that this answer must be wrong, and this gives us a certain feeling of superiority. Is this feeling illusory? It is no doubt quite genuine, but I do not think too much importance should be attached to it. We too often give wrong answers to questions ourselves to be justified in being very pleased at such evidence of fallibility on the part of the machines. Further, our superiority can only be felt on such an occasion in relation to the one machine over which we have scored our petty triumph. There would be no question of triumphing simultaneously over *all* machines. In short, then, there might be men cleverer than any given machine, but then again there might be other machines cleverer again, and so on.

Those who hold to the mathematical argument would, I think, mostly be willing to accept the imitation game as a basis for discussion. Those who believe in the two previous objections would probably not be interested in any criteria.

(4) *The Argument from Consciousness*. This argument is very well expressed in Professor Jefferson's Lister Oration for 1949, from which I quote. "Not until a machine can write a sonnet or compose a concerto because of thoughts and emotions felt, and not by the chance fall of symbols, could we agree that machine equals brain—that is, not only write it but know that it had written it. No mechanism could feel (and not merely artificially signal, an easy contrivance) pleasure at its successes, grief when its valves fuse, be warmed by flattery, be made miserable by its mistakes, be charmed by sex, be angry or depressed when it cannot get what it wants."

This argument appears to be a denial of the validity of our test. According to the most extreme form of this view the only way by which one could be sure that a machine thinks is to *be* the machine and to feel oneself thinking. One could then describe these feelings to the world, but of course no one would be justified in taking any notice. Likewise according to this view the only way to know that a *man* thinks is to be that particular man. It is in fact the solipsist point of view. It may be the most logical veiw to hold but it makes communication of ideas difficult. A is liable to believe "A thinks but B does not" while B believes "B thinks but A does not." Instead of arguing continually over this point it is usual to have the polite convention that everyone thinks.

I am sure that Professor Jefferson does not wish to adopt the extreme and solipsist point of view. Probably he would be quite willing to accept the imitation game as a test. The game (with the player B omitted) is frequently used in practice under the name of viva voce to discover whether someone really understands something or has "learned it parrot fashion." Let us listen in to a part of such a viva voce:

INTERROGATOR: In the first line of your sonnet which reads "Shall I compare thee to a summer's day," would not "a spring day" do as well or better?

WITNESS: It wouldn't scan.

INTERROGATOR: How about "a winter's day." That would scan all right.

WITNESS: Yes, but nobody wants to be compared to a winter's day.

INTERROGATOR: Would you say Mr. Pickwick reminded you of Christmas?

WITNESS: In a way.

INTERROGATOR: Yet Christmas is a winter's day, and I do not think Mr. Pickwick would mind the comparison.

WITNESS: I don't think you're serious. By a winter's day one means a typical winter's day, rather than a special one like Christmas.

And so on. What would Professor Jefferson say if the sonnet-writing machine was able to answer like this in the viva voce? I do not know whether he would regard the machine as "merely artificially signaling" these answers, but if the answers were as satisfactory and sustained as in the above passage I do not think he would describe it as "an easy contrivance." This phrase is, I think, intended to cover such devices as the inclusion in the machine of a record of someone reading a sonnet, with appropriate switching to turn it on from time to time.

In short then, I think that most of those who support the argument from consciousness could be persuaded to abandon it rather than be forced into the solipsist position. They will then probably be willing to accept our test.

I do not wish to give the impression that I think there is no mystery about consciousness. There is, for instance, something of a paradox connected with any attempt to localize it. But I do not think these mysteries necessarily need to be solved before we can answer the question with which we are concerned in this paper.

(5) *Arguments from Various Disabilities.* These arguments take the form, "I grant you that you can make machines do all the things you have mentioned but you will never be able to make one to do X." Numerous features X are suggested in this connection. I offer a selection:

> Be kind, resourceful, beautiful, friendly . . . have initiative, have a sense of humor, tell right from wrong, make mistakes . . . fall in love, enjoy strawberries and cream . . . , make someone fall in love with it, learn from experience . . . , use words properly, be the subject of its own thought . . . , have as much diversity of behavior as a man, do something really new. . . .

No support is usually offered for these statements. I believe they are mostly founded on the principle of scientific induction. A man has seen thousands of machines in his lifetime. From what he sees of them he draws a number of general conclusions. They are ugly, each is designed for a very limited purpose, when required for a minutely different purpose they are useless, the variety of behavior of any one of them is very small, etc., etc. Naturally he concludes that these are necessary properties of machines in general. Many of these limitations are associated with the very small storage capacity of most machines. (I am assuming that the idea of storage capacity is extended in some way to cover machines other than discrete state machines. The exact definition does not matter as no mathematical accuracy is claimed in the present discussion.) A few years ago, when very little had been heard of digital computers, it was possible to elicit much incredulity concerning them, if one mentioned their properties without describing their construction. That was presumably due to a similar application of the principle of scientific induction. These applications of the principle are of course largely unconscious. When a burned child fears the fire and shows that he fears it by avoiding it, I should say that he was applying scientific induction. (I could of course also describe his behavior in many other ways.) The works of customs of mankind do not seem to be very suitable material to which to apply scientific induction. A very large part of space-time must be investigated if reliable results are to be obtained. Otherwise we may (as most English children do) decide that everybody speaks English, and that it is silly to learn French.

There are, however, special remarks to be made about many of the disabilities that have been mentioned. The inability to enjoy strawberries and cream may [strike] the reader as frivolous. Possibly a machine might be made to enjoy this delicious dish, but any attempt to make one do so would be idiotic. What is important about this disability is that it contributes to some of the other disabilities, e.g., to the difficulty of the same kind of friendliness occurring between man and machine as between white man and white man, or between black man and black man.

The claim that "machines cannot make mistakes" seems a curious one. One is tempted to retort, "Are they any worse for that?" But let us adopt a more sympathetic attitude, and try to see what is really meant. I think this criticism can be explained in terms of the imitation game. It is claimed that the interrogator could distinguish the machine from the man simply by setting them a number of problems in arithmetic. The machine would be unmasked because of its deadly accuracy. The reply to this is simple. The machine (programed for playing the game) would not attempt to give the *right* answers to the arithmetic problems. It would deliberately introduce mistakes in a manner calculated to confuse the interrogator. A mechanical fault would probably show itself through an unsuitable decision as to what sort of a mistake to make in the arithmetic. Even this interpretation of the criticism is not sufficiently sympathetic. But we cannot afford the space to go into it much further. It seems to me that this criticism depends on a confusion between two kinds of mistakes. We may call them "errors of functioning" and "errors of conclusion." Errors of functioning are due to some mechanical or electrical fault which causes the machine to behave otherwise than it was designed to do. In philosophical discussions one likes to ignore the possibility of such errors; one is therefore discussing "abstract machines." These abstract machines are mathematical fictions rather than physical objects. By definition they are incapable of errors of functioning. In this sense we can truly say that "machines can never make mistakes." Errors of conclusion can only arise when some meaning is attached to the output signals from the machine. The machine might, for instance, type out mathematical equations, or sentences in English. When a false proposition is typed we say that the machine has committed an error of conclusion. There is clearly no reason at all for saying that a machine cannot make this kind of mistake. It might do nothing but type out repeatedly "$0=1$." To take a less perverse example, it might have some method for drawing conclusions by scientific induction. We must expect such a method to lead occasionally to erroneous results.

The claim that a machine cannot be the subject of its own thought can of course only be answered if it can be shown that the machine has *some* thought with *some* matter. Nevertheless, "the subject matter of a machine's operations" does seem to mean something, at least to the people who deal with it. If, for instance, the machine was trying to find a solution of the equation $x^2-40x-11=0$ one would be tempted to describe this equation as part of the machine's subject matter at that moment. In this sort of sense a machine undoubtedly can be its own subject matter. It may be used to help in making up its own programs, or to predict the effect of alterations in its own structure. By observing the results of its own behavior it can modify its own programs so as to achieve some purpose more effectively. These are possibilities of the near future, rather than Utopian dreams.

The criticism that a machine cannot have much diversity of behavior is just a way of saying that it cannot have much storage capacity. Until fairly recently a storage capacity of even a thousand digits was very rare.

The criticisms that we are considering here are often disguised forms of the argument from consciousness. Usually if one maintains that a machine *can* do one of these things, and describes the kind of method that the machine could use, one will not make much of an impression. It is thought that the method (whatever it may be, for it must be mechanical) is really rather base. Compare the parenthesis of Jefferson's statement quoted above.

(6) *Lady Lovelace's Objection*. Our most detailed information of Babbage's Analytical Engine comes from a memoir by Lady Lovelace. In it she states, "The Analytical Engine has no pretensions to *originate* anything. It can do *whatever we know how to order it* to perform" (her italics). This statement is quoted by Hartree who adds: "This does not imply that it may not be possible to construct electronic equipment which will 'think for itself,' or in which, in biological terms, one could set up a conditioned reflex, which would serve as a basis for 'learning.' Whether this is possible in principle or not is a stimulating and exciting question, suggested by some of these recent developments. But it did not seem that the machines constructed or projected at the time had this property."

I am in thorough agreement with Hartree over this. It will be noticed that he does not assert that the machines in question had not got the property, but rather that the evidence available to Lady Lovelace did not encourage her to believe that they had it. It is quite possible that the machines in question had in a sense got this property. For suppose that some discrete state machine has the property. The Analytical Engine was a universal digital computer, so that, if its storage capacity and speed were adequate, it could by suitable programing be made to mimic the machine in question. Probably this argument did not occur to the Countess or to Babbage. In any case there was no obligation on them to claim all that could be claimed.

This whole question will be considered again under the heading of learning machines.

A variant of Lady Lovelace's objection states that a machine can "never do anything really new." This may be parried for a moment with the saw, "There is nothing new under the sun." Who can be certain that "original work" that he has done was not simply the growth of the seed planted in him by teaching, or the effect of following well-known general principles. A better variant of the objection says that a machine can never "take us by surprise." This statement is a more direct challenge and can be met directly. Machines take me by surprise with great frequency. This is largely because I do not do sufficient calculation to decide what to expect them to do, or rather because, although I do a calculation, I do it in a hurried, slipshod fashion, taking risks. Perhaps I say to myself, "I suppose the voltage here ought to be the same as there: anyway let's assume it is." Naturally I am often wrong, and the result is a surprise for me, for by the time the experiment is done these assumptions have been forgotten. These admissions lay me open to lectures on the subject of my vicious ways, but do not throw any doubt on my credibility when I testify to the surprises I experience.

I do not expect this reply to silence my critic. He will probably say that such surprises are due to some creative mental act on my part, and reflect no credit on the machine. This leads us back to the argument from consciousness, and far from the idea of surprise. It is a line of argument we must consider closed, but it is perhaps worth remarking that the appreciation of something as surprising requires as much of a "creative mental act" whether the surprising event originates from a man, a book, a machine or anything else.

The view that machines cannot give rise to surprises is due, I believe, to a fallacy to which philosophers and mathematicians are particularly subject. This is the assumption that as soon as a fact is presented to a mind all consequences of that fact spring into the mind simultaneously with it. It is a very useful assumption under many circumstances, but one too easily forgets that it is false. A natural consequence of doing so is that one then assumes that there is no virtue in the mere working out of consequences from data and general principles.

(7) *Argument from Continuity in the Nervous System.* The nervous system is certainly not a discrete state machine. A small error in the information about the size of a nervous impulse impinging on a neuron, may make a large difference to the size of the outgoing impulse. It may be argued that, this being so, one cannot expect to be able to mimic the behavior of the nervous system with a discrete state system.

It is true that a discrete state machine must be different from a continuous machine. But if we adhere to the conditions of the imitation game, the interrogator will not be able to take any advantage of this difference. The situation can be made clearer if we consider some other simpler continuous machine. A differential analyzer will do very well. (A differential analyzer is a certain kind of machine not of the discrete state type used for some kinds of calculation.) Some of these provide their answers in a typed form, and so are suitable for taking part in the game. It would not be possible for a digital computer to predict exactly what answers the differential analyzer would give to a problem, but it would be quite capable of giving the right sort of answer. For instance, if asked to give the value of π (actually about 3·1416) it would be reasonable to choose at random between the values 3·12, 3·13, 3·14, 3·15, 3·16 with the probabilities of 0·05, 0·15, 0·55, 0·19, 0·06 (say). Under these circumstances it would be very difficult for the interrogator to distinguish the differential analyzer from the digital computer.

(8) *The Argument from Informality of Behavior.* It is not possible to produce a set of rules purporting to describe what a man should do in every conceivable set of circumstances. One might for instance have a rule that one is to stop when one sees a red traffic light, and to go if one sees a green one, but what if by some fault both appear together? One may perhaps decide that it is safest to stop. But some further difficulty may well arise from this decision later. To attempt to provide rules of conduct to cover every eventuality, even those arising from traffic lights, appears to be impossible. With all this I agree.

From this it is argued that we cannot be machines, I shall try to reproduce the argument, but I fear I shall hardly do it justice. It seems to run something like this. "If each man had a definite set of rules of conduct by which he regulated his life he would be no better than a machine. But there are no such rules, so men cannot be machines." The undistributed middle is glaring. I do not think the argument is ever put quite like this, but I believe this is the argument used nevertheless. There may however be a certain confusion between "rules of conduct" and "laws of behavior" to cloud the issue. By "rules of conduct" I mean precepts such as "Stop if you see red lights," on which one can act, and of which one can be conscious. By "laws of behavior" I mean laws of nature as applied to a man's body such as "if you pinch him he will squeak." If we substitute "laws of behavior which regulate his life" for "laws of conduct by which he regulates his life" in the argument quoted the undistributed middle is no longer insurperable. For we believe that it is not only true that being regulated by laws of behavior implies being some sort of machine (though not necessarily a discrete state machine), but that conversely being such a machine implies being regulated by such laws. However, we cannot so easily convince ourselves of the absence of complete laws of behavior as of complete rules of conduct. The only way we know of for finding such laws is scientific observation, and we certainly know of no circumstances under which we could say, "We have searched enough. There are no such laws."

We can demonstrate more forcibly that any such statement would be unjustified. For suppose we could be sure of finding such laws if they existed. Then given a discrete state machine it should certainly be possible to discover by observation sufficient about it to predict its future behavior, and this within a reasonable time, say a thousand years. But this does not seem to be the case. I have set up on the Manchester computer a small program using only 1000 units of storage, whereby the machine supplied with one sixteen-figure number replies with another within two seconds. I would defy anyone to learn from these replies sufficient about the program to be able to predict any replies to untried values.

(9) *The Argument from Extra-Sensory Perception.* I assume that the reader is familiar with the idea of extra-sensory perception, and the meaning of the four items of it, viz., telepathy, clairvoyance, precognition and psychokinesis. These disturbing phenomena seem to deny all our usual scientific ideas. How we would like to discredit them! Unfortunately the statistical evidence, at least for telepathy, is overwhelming. It is very difficult to rearrange one's ideas so as to fit these new facts in. Once one has accepted them it does not seem a very big step to believe in ghosts and bogies. The idea that our bodies move simply according to the known laws of physics, together with some others not yet discovered but somewhat similar, would be one of the first to go.

This argument is to my mind quite a strong one. One can say in reply that many scientific theories seem to remain workable in practice, in spite of clashing with E.S.P.; that in fact one can get along very nicely if one forgets about it. This is rather cold comfort, and one fears that thinking is just the kind of phenomenon where E.S.P. may be especially relevant.

A more specific argument based on E.S.P. might run as follows: "Let us play the imitation game, using a witnesses a man who is good as a telepathic receiver, and a digital computer. The interrogator can ask such questions as 'What suit does the card in my right hand belong to?' The man by telepathy or clarivoyance gives the right answer 130 times out of 400 cards. The machine can only guess at random, and perhaps get 104 right, so the interrogator makes the right identification." There is an interesting possibility which opens here. Suppose the digital computer contains a random number generator. Then it will be natural to use this to decide what answer to give. But then the random number of generator will be subject to the psychokinetic powers of the interrogator. Perhaps this psychokinesis might cause the machine to guess right more often than would be expected on a probability calculation, so that the interrogator might still be unable to make the right identification. On the other hand, he might be able to guess right without any questioning, by clairvoyance. With E.S.P. anything may happen.

If telepathy is admitted it will be necessary to tighten our test. The situation could be regarded as analogous to that which would occur if the interrogator were talking to himself and one of the competitors was listening with his ear to the wall. To put the competitors into a "telepathy-proof room" would satisfy all requirements.

7. Learning Machines

The reader will have anticipated that I have no very convincing arguments of a positive nature to support my views. If I had I should not have taken such pains to point out the fallacies in contrary views. Such evidence as I have I shall now give.

Let us return for a moment to Lady Lovelace's objection, which stated that the machine can only do what we tell it to do. One could say that a man can "inject" an idea into the machine, and that it will respond to a certain extent and then drop into quiescence, like a piano string struck by a hammer. Another simile would be an atomic pile of less than critical size: an injected idea is to correspond to a neutron entering the pile from without. Each such neutron will cause a certain disturbance which eventually dies away. If, however, the size of the pile is sufficiently increased, the disturbance caused by such an incoming neutron will very likely go on and on increasing until the whole pile is destroyed. Is there a corresponding phenomenon for minds, and is there one for machines? There does seem to be one for the human mind. The majority of them seem to to "subcritical," i.e., to correspond in this analogy to piles of subcritical size. An idea presented to such a mind will on an average give rise to less than one idea in reply. A smallish proportion are supercritical. An idea presented to such a mind may give rise to a whole "theory" consisting of secondary, tertiary and more remote ideas. Animals' minds seem to be very definitely subcritical. Adhering to this analogy we ask, "Can a machine be made to be supercritical?"

The "skin of an onion" analogy is also helpful. In considering the functions of the mind or the brain we find certain operations which we can explain in purely mechanical terms. This we say does not correspond to the real mind: it is a sort of skin which we must strip off if we are to find the real mind. But then in what remains we find a further skin to be stripped off, and so on. Proceeding in this way do we ever come to the "real" mind, or do we eventually come to the skin which has nothing in it? In the latter case the whole mind is mechanical. (It would not be a discrete state machine however. We have discussed this.)

These last two paragraphs do not claim to be convincing arguments. They should rather be described as "recitations tending to produce belief."

The only really satisfactory support that can be given for the view expressed at the beginning of §6, p. 380, will be that provided by waiting for the end of the century and then doing the experiment described. But what can we say in the meantime? What steps should be taken now if the experiment is to be successful?

As I have explained, the problem is mainly one of programing. Advances in engineering will have to be made too, but it seems unlikely that these will not be adequate for the requirements. Estimates of the storage capacity of the brain vary from 10^{10} to 10^{15} binary digits. I incline to the lower values and believe that only a very small fraction is used for the higher types of thinking. Most of it is probably used for the retention of visual impressions. I should be surprised if more then 10^9 was required for satisfactory playing of the imitation game, at any rate against a blind man. (Note: The capacity of the *Encyclopaedia Britannica,* eleventh edition, is 2×10^9.) A storage capacity of 10^7 would be a very practicable possibility even by present techniques. It is probably not necessary to increase the speed of operations of the machines at all. Parts of modern machines which can be regarded as analogues of nerve cells work about a thousand times faster than the latter. This should provide a "margin of safety" which could cover losses of speed arising in many ways. Our problem then is to find out how to program these machines to play the game. At my present rate of working I produce about a thousand digits of program a day, so that about sixty workers, working steadily through the fifty years might accomplish the job, if nothing went into the wastepaper basket. Some more expeditious method seems desirable.

In the process of trying to imitate an adult human mind we are bound to think a good deal about the process which has brought it to the state that it is in. We may notice three components,

(a) The initial state of the mind, say at birth,

(b) The education to which it has been subjected,

(c) Other experience, not to be described as education, to which it has been subjected.

Instead of trying to produce a program to simulate the adult mind, why not rather try to produce one which simulates the child's? If this were then subjected to an appropriate course of education one would obtain the adult brain. Presumably the child-brain is something like a notebook as one buys it from the stationers. Rather little mechanism, and lots of blank sheets. (Mechanism and writing are from our point of view almost synonymous.) Our hope is that there is so little mechanism in the child-brain that something like it can be easily programed. The amount of work in the education we can assume, as a first approximation, to be much the same as for the human child.

We have thus divided our problem into two parts—the child-program and the education process. These two remain very closely connected. We cannot expect to find a good child-machine at the first attempt. One must experiment with teaching one such machine and see how well it learns. One can then try another and see if it is better or worse. There is an obvious connection between this process and evolution, by the identifications

Structure of the child-machine	=	Hereditary material
Changes of the child-machine	=	Mutations
Natural selection	=	Judgment of the experimenter

One may hope, however, that this process will be more expeditious than evolution. The survival of the fittest is a slow method for measuring advantages. The experimenter, by the exercise of intelligence, should be able to speed it up. Equally important is the fact that he is not restricted to random mutations. If he can trace a cause for some weakness he can probably think of the kind of mutation which will improve it.

It will not be possible to apply exactly the same teaching process to the machine as to a normal child. It will not, for instance, be provided with legs, so that it could not be asked to go out and fill the coal scuttle. Possibly it might not have eyes. But however well these deficiencies might be overcome by clever engineering, one could not send the creature to school without the other children making excessive fun of it. It must be given some tuition. We need not be too concerned about the legs, eyes, etc. The example of Miss Helen Keller shows that education can take place provided that communication in both directions between teacher and pupil can take place by some means or other.

We normally associate punishments and rewards with the teaching process. Some simple child-machines can be constructed or programed on this sort of principle. The machine has to be so constructed that events which shortly preceded the occurrence of a punishment-signal are unlikely to be repeated, whereas a reward-signal increases the probability of repetition of the events which led up to it. These definitions do not presuppose any feelings on the part of the machine. I have done some experiments with one such child-machine, and succeeded in teaching it a few things, but the teaching method was too unorthodox for the experiment to be considered really successful.

The use of punishments and rewards can at best be a part of the teaching process. Roughly speaking, if the teacher has no other means of communicating to the pupil, the amount of information which can reach him does not exceed the total number of rewards and punishments applied. By the time a child has learned to repeat "Casablanca" he would probably feel very sore indeed, if the text could only be discovered by a "Twenty Questions" technique, every "NO" taking the form of a blow. It is necessary therefore to have some other "unemotional" channels of communication. If these are available it is possible to teach a machine by punishments and rewards to obey orders given in some language, e.g., a symbolic language. These orders are to be transmitted through the "unemotional" channels. The use of this language will diminish greatly the number of punishments and rewards required.

Opinions may vary as to the complexity which is suitable in the child-machine. One might try to make it as simple as possible consistently with the general principles. Alternatively one might have a complete system of logical inference "built in."[2] In the latter case the store would be largely occupied with definitions and propositions. The propositions would have various kinds of status, e.g., well-established facts, conjectures, mathematically proved theorems, statements given by an authority, expressions having the logical form of proposition but not belief-value. Certain propositions may be described as "imperatives." The machine should be so constructed that as soon as an imperative is classed as "well established" the appropriate action automatically takes place. To illustrate this, suppose the teacher says to the machine, "Do your homework now." This may cause "Teacher says 'Do your homework now'" to be included among the well-established facts. Another such fact might be, "Everything that teacher says is true."Combining these may eventually lead to the imperative, "Do your homework now," being included among the well-established facts, and this, by the construction of the machine, will mean that the homework actually gets started, but the effect is very unsatisfactory. The processes of inference used by the machine need not be such as would satisfy the most exacting logicians. There might for instance be no hierarchy of types. But this need not mean that type fallacies will occur, any more than we are bound to fall over unfenced cliffs. Suitable imperatives (expressed *within* the systems, not forming part of the rules *of* the system) such as "Do not use a class unless it is a subclass of one which has been mentioned by teacher" can have a similar effect to "Do not go too near the edge."

The imperatives that can be obeyed by a machine that has no limbs are bound to be of a rather intellectual character, as in the example (doing homework) given above. Important among such imperatives will be ones which regulate the order in which the rules of the logical system concerned are to be applied. For at each stage when one is using a logical system, there is a very large number of alternative steps, any of which one is permitted to apply, so far as obedience to the rules of the logical system is concerned. These choices make the difference between a brilliant and a footling reasoner, not the difference between a sound and a falacious one. Propositions leading to imperatives of this kind might be "When Socrates is mentioned, use the syllogism in Barbara" or "If one method has been proved to be quicker than another, do not use the slower method." Some of these may be "given by authority," but others may be produced by the machine itself, e.g., by scientific induction.

The idea of a learning machine may appear paradoxical to some readers. How can the rules of operation of the machine change? They should describe completely how the machine will react whatever its history might be, whatever changes it might undergo. The rules are thus quite time-invariant. This is quite true. The explanation of the paradox is that the rules which get changed in the learning process are of a rather less pretentious kind, claiming only an ephemeral validity. The reader may draw a parallel with the Constitution of the United States.

An important feature of a learning machine is that its teacher will often be very largely ignorant of quite what is going on inside, although he may still be able to some extent to predict his pupil's behavior. This should apply most strongly to the later education of a machine arising from a child-machine of well-tried design (or program). This is in clear contrast with normal procedure when using a machine to do computations: one's object is then to have a clear mental picture of the state of the machine at each moment in the computation. This object can only be achieved with a struggle. The view that "the machine can only do what we know how to order it to do,"[3] appears strange in face of this. Most of the programs which we can put into the machine will result in its doing something that we cannot make sense of at all, or which we regard as completely random behavior. Intelligent behavior presumably consists in a departure from the completely disciplined behavior involved in computation, but a rather slight one, which does not give rise to random behavior, or to pointless repetitive loops. Another important result of preparing our machine for its part in the imitation game by a process of teaching and learning is that "human fallibility" is likely to be omitted in a rather natural way, i.e., without special "coaching." (The reader should reconcile this with the point of view on p. 383.) Processes that are learned do not produce a hundred per cent certainty of result; if they did they could not be unlearned.

It is probably wise to include a random element in a learning machine (see p. 378). A random element is rather useful when we are searching for a solution of some problem. Suppose for instance we wanted to find a number between 50 and 200 which was equal to the square of the sum of its digits, we might start at 51 then try 52 and go on until we got a number that worked. Alternatively we might choose numbers at random until we got a good one. This method has the advantage that is is unnecessary to keep track of the values that have been tried, but the disadvantage that one may try the same one twice, but this is not very important if there are several solutions. The systematic method has the disadvantage that there may be an enormous block without any solutions in the region which has to be investigated first. Now the learning process may be regarded as a search for a form of behavior which will satisfy the teacher (or some other criterion). Since there is probably a very large number of satisfactory solutions the random method seems to be better than the systematic. It should be noticed that it is used in the analogous process of evolution. But there the systematic method is not possible. How could one keep track of the different genetical combinations that had been tried, so as to avoid trying them again?

We may hope that machines will eventually compete with men in all purely intellectual fields. But which are the best ones to start with? Even this is a difficult decision. Many people think that a very abstract activity, like the playing of chess, would be best. It can also be maintained that it is best to provide the machine with the best sense organs that money can buy, and then teach it to understand and speak English. This process could follow the normal teaching of a child. Things would be pointed out and named, etc. Again I do not know what the right answer is, but I think both approaches should be tried.

We can only see a short distance ahead, but we can see plenty there that needs to be done.

Notes

1. Possibly this view is heretical. Saint Thomas Aquinas (*Summa Theologica,* quoted by Bertrand Russell, *A History of Western Philosophy* [New York: Simon & Schuster, 1945], p. 458) states that God cannot make a man to have no soul. But this may not be a real restriction on His powers, but only a result of the fact that men's souls are immortal, and therefore indestructible.
2. Or rather "programed in" for our child-machine will be programed in a digital computer. But the logical system will not have to be learned.
3. Compare Lady Lovelace's statement (p. 384), which does not contain the word "only."

Minds, Brains, and Programs

JOHN R. SEARLE

John R. Searle (1932–) is a professor of philosophy at the University of California at Berkeley. His publications include *Speech Acts* and *Expression and Meaning*.

What psychological and philosophical significance should we attach to recent efforts at computer simulations of human cognitive capacities? In answering this question, I find it useful to distinguish what I will call "strong" AI from "weak" or "cautious" AI (artificial intelligence). According to weak AI, the principal value of the computer in the study of the mind is that it gives us a very powerful tool. For example, it enables us to formulate and test hypotheses in a more rigorous and precise fashion. But according to strong AI, the computer is not merely a tool in the study of the mind; rather, the appropriately programmed computer really *is* a mind, in the sense that computers given the right programs can be literally said to *understand* and have other cognitive states. In strong AI, because the programmed computer has cognitive states, the programs are not mere tools that enable us to test psychological explanations; rather, the programs are themselves the explanations.

I have no objection to the claims of weak AI, at least as far as this article is concerned. My discussion here will be directed at the claims I have defined as those of strong AI, specifically the claim that the appropriately programmed computer literally has cognitive states and that the programs thereby explain human cognition. When I hereafter refer to AI, I have in mind the strong version, as expressed by these two claims.

I will consider the work of Roger Schank and his colleagues at Yale (Schank and Abelson 1977), because I am more familiar with it than I am with any other similar claims, and because it provides a very clear example of the sort of work I wish to examine. But nothing that follows depends upon the details of Schank's programs. The same arguments would apply to Winograd's SHRDLU (Winograd 1973), Weizenbaum's ELIZA (Weizenbaum 1965), and indeed any Turing machine simulation of human mental phenomena. . . .

Very briefly, and leaving out the various details, one can describe Schank's program as follows: The aim of the program is to simulate the human ability to understand stories. It is characteristic of human beings' story-understanding capacity that they can answer questions about the story even though the information that they give was never explicitly stated in the story. Thus, for example, suppose you are given the following story: "A man went into a restaurant and ordered a hamburger. When the hamburger arrived it was burned to a crisp, and the man stormed out of the restaurant angrily, without paying for the burger or leaving a tip." Now, if you are asked "Did the man eat the hamburger?" you will presum-

I am indebted to a rather large number of people for discussion of these matters and for their patient attempts to overcome my ignorance of artificial intelligence. I would especially like to thank Ned Block, Hubert Dreyfus, John Haugeland, Roger Schank, Robert Wilensky, and Terry Winograd.

From *The Behavioral and Brain Sciences* (Cambridge: Cambridge University Press, 1980), vol. 3, pp. 417–24.

ably answer, "No, he did not." Similarly, if you are given the following story: "A man went into a restaurant and ordered a hamburger; when the hamburger came he was very pleased with it; and as he left the restaurant he gave the waitress a large tip before paying his bill," and you are asked the question, "Did the man eat the hamburger?" you will presumably answer, "Yes, he ate the hamburger." Now Schank's machines can similarly answer questions about restaurants in this fashion. To do this, they have a "representation" of the sort of information that human beings have about restaurants, which enables them to answer such questions as those above, given these sorts of stories. When the machine is given the story and then asked the question, the machine will print out answers of the sort that we would expect human beings to give if told similar stories. Partisans of strong AI claim that in this question and answer sequence the machine is not only simulating a human ability but also (1) that the machine can literally be said to *understand* the story and provide the answers to questions, and (2) that what the machine and its program do *explains* the human ability to understand the story and answer questions about it.

Both claims seem to me to be totally unsupported by Schank's work, as I will attempt to show in what follows.[1]

One way to test any theory of the mind is to ask oneself what it would be like if my mind actually worked on the principles that the theory says all minds work on. Let us apply this test to the Schank program with the following *Gedankenexperiment*. Suppose that I'm locked in a room and given a large batch of Chinese writing. Suppose furthermore (as is indeed the case) that I know no Chinese, either written or spoken, and that I'm not even confident that I could recognize Chinese writing as Chinese writing distinct from, say, Japanese writing or meaningless squiggles. To me, Chinese writing is just so many meaningless squiggles. Now suppose further that after this first batch of Chinese writing I am given a second batch of Chinese script together with a set of rules for correlating the second batch with the first batch. The rules are in English, and I understand these rules as well as any other native speaker of English. They enable me to correlate one set of formal symbols with another set of formal symbols, and all that "formal" means here is that I can identify the symbols entirely by their shapes. Now suppose also that I am given a third batch of Chinese symbols together with some instructions, again in English, that enable me to correlate elements of this third batch with the first two batches, and these rules instruct me how to give back certain Chinese symbols with certain sorts of shapes in response to certain sorts of shapes given me in the third batch. Unknown to me, the people who are giving me all of these symbols call the first batch a "script," they call the second batch a "story," and they call the third batch "questions." Furthermore, they call the symbols I give them back in response to the third batch "answers to the questions," and the set of rules in English that they gave me, they call the "program." Now just to complicate the story a little, imagine that these people also give me stories in English, which I understand, and they then ask me questions in English about these stories, and I give them back answers in English. Suppose also that after a while I got so good at following the instructions for manipulating the Chinese symbols and the programmers get so good at writing the programs that from the external point of view—that is, from the point of view of somebody outside the room in which I am locked—my answers to the questions are absolutely indistinguishable from those of native Chinese speakers. Nobody just looking at my answers can tell that I don't speak a word of Chinese. Let us also suppose that my answers to the English questions are, as they no doubt would be, indistinguishable from those of other native English speakers, for the simple reason that I am a native English speaker. From the external point of view—from the point of view of someone reading my "answers"—the answers to the Chinese questions and the English questions are equally good. But in the Chinese case, unlike the English case, I produce the answers by manipulating uninterpreted formal symbols. As far as the Chinese is concerned, I simply behave like a computer; I perform computational operations on formally specified elements. For the purposes of the Chinese, I am simply an instantiation of the computer program.

Now the claims made by strong AI are that the programmed computer understands the stories and that the program in some sense explains human understanding. But we are now in a position to examine these claims in light of our thought experiment.

1. As regards the first claim, it seems to me quite obvious in the example that I do not understand a word of Chinese stories. I have inputs and outputs that are indistinguishable from those of the native Chinese speaker, and I can have any formal program you like, but I still understand nothing. For the same reasons, Schank's computer understands nothing of any stories, whether in Chinese, English, or whatever, since in the Chinese case the computer is me, and in cases where the computer is not me, the computer has nothing more than I have in the case where I understand nothing.

2. As regards the second claim, that the program explains human understanding, we can see that the computer and its program do not provide sufficient conditions of understanding since the computer and the program are functioning, and there is no understanding. But does it even provide a necessary condition or a significant contribution to understanding? One of the claims made by the supporters of strong AI is that when I understand a story in English, what I am doing is exactly the same—or perhaps more of the same—as what I was doing in manipulating the Chinese symbols. It is simply more formal symbol manipulation that distinguishes the case in English, where I do understand, from the case in Chinese where I don't. I have not demonstrated that this claim is false, but it would certainly appear an incredible claim in the example. Such plausibility as the claim has derives from the supposition that we can construct a program that will have the same inputs and outputs as native speakers, and in addition we assume that speakers have some level of description where they are also instantiations of a program. On the basis of these two assumptions we assume that even if Schank's program isn't the whole story about understanding, it may be part of the story. Well, I suppose that is an empirical possibility, but not the slightest reason has so far been given to believe that it is true, since what is suggested—though certainly not demonstrated—by the example is that the computer program is simply irrelevant to my understanding of the story. In the Chinese case I have everything that artificial intelligence can put into me by way of a program, and I understand nothing; in the English case I understand everything, and there is so far no reason at all to suppose that my understanding has anything to do with computer programs, that is, with computational operations on purely formally specified elements. As long as the program is defined in terms of computational operations on purely formally defined elements, what the example suggests is that these by themselves have no interesting connection with understanding. They are certainly not sufficient conditions, and not the slightest reason has been given to suppose that they are necessary conditions or even that they make a significant contribution to understanding. Notice that the force of the argument is not simply that different machines can have the same input and output while operating on different formal principles—that is not the point at all. Rather, whatever purely formal principles you put into the computer, they will not be sufficient for understanding, since a human will be able to follow the formal principles without understanding anything. No reason whatever has been offered to suppose that such principles are necessary or even contributory, since no reason has been given to suppose that when I understand English I am operating with any formal program at all.

Well, then, what is it that I have in the case of the English sentences that I do not have in the case of the Chinese sentences? The obvious answer is that I know what the former mean, while I haven't the faintest idea what the latter mean. But in what does this consist and why couldn't we give it to a machine, whatever it is? I will return to this question later, but first I want to continue with the example.

I have had the occasions to present this example to several workers in artificial intelligence, and, interestingly, they do not seem to agree on what the proper reply to it is. I get a surprising variety of replies, and in what follows I will consider the most common of these (specified along with their geographic origins).

But first I want to block some common misunderstandings about "understanding": In many of these discussions one finds a lot of fancy footwork about the word "understanding." My critics point out that there are many different degrees of understanding; that "understanding" is not a simple two-place predicate; that there are even different kinds and levels of understanding, and often the law of excluded middle doesn't even apply in a straightforward way to statements of the form "*x* understands *y*"; that in many cases it is a matter for decision and not a simple matter of fact whether *x* understands *y*; and so on. To all of these points I want to say: of course, of course. But they have nothing to do with the points at issue. There are clear cases in which "understanding" literally applies and clear cases in which it does not apply; and these two sorts of cases are all I need for this argument.[2] I understand stories in English; to a lesser degree I can understand stories in French; to a still lesser degree, stories in German; and in Chinese, not at all. My car and my adding machine, on the other hand, understand nothing: they are not in that line of business. We often attribute "understanding" and other cognitive predicates by metaphor and analogy to cars, adding machines, and other artifacts, but nothing is proved by such attributions. We say, "The door *knows* when to open because of its photoelectric cell," "The adding machine *knows how (understands how,* is *able)* to do addition and subtraction but not division," and "The thermostat *perceives* changes in the temperature." The reason we make these attributions is quite interesting, and it has to do with the fact that in artifacts we extend our own intentionality;[3] our tools are extensions of our purposes, and so we find it natural to make metaphorical attributions of intentionality to them; but I take it no philosophical ice is cut by such examples. The sense in which an automatic door "understands instructions" from its photoelectric cell is not at all the sense in which I understand English. If the sense in which Schank's programmed computers understand stories is supposed to be the metaphorical sense in which the door understands, and not the sense in which I understand English, the issue would not be worth discussing. But Newell and Simon (1963) write that the kind of cognition they claim for computers is exactly the same as for human beings. I like the straightforwardness of this claim, and it is the sort of claim I will be considering. I will argue that in the literal sense the programmed computer understands what the car and the adding machine understand, namely, exactly nothing. The computer understanding is not just (like my understanding of German) partial or incomplete; it is zero.

Now to the replies:

I. The Systems Reply (Berkeley) "While it is true that the individual person who is locked in the room does not understand the story, the fact is that he is merely part of a whole system, and the system does understand the story. The person has a large ledger in front of him in which are written the rules, he has a lot of scratch paper and pencils for doing calculations, he has 'data banks' of sets of Chinese symbols. Now, understanding is not being ascribed to the mere individual; rather it is being ascribed to this whole system of which he is a part."

My response to the systems theory is quite simple: Let the individual internalize all of these elements of the system. He memorizes the rules in the ledger and the data banks of Chinese symbols, and he does all the calculations in his head. The individual then incorporates the entire system. There isn't anything at all to the system that he does not encompass. We can even get rid of the room and suppose he works outdoors. All the same, he understands nothing of the Chinese, and a fortiori neither does the system, because there isn't anything in the system that isn't in him. If he doesn't understand, then there is no way the system could understand because the system is just a part of him.

Actually I feel somewhat embarrassed to give even this answer to the systems theory because the theory seems to me so implausible to start with. The idea is that while a person doesn't understand Chinese, somehow the *conjunction* of that person and bits of paper might understand Chinese. It is not easy for me to imagine how someone who was not in the grip of an ideology would find the idea at all plausible. Still, I think many people who are committed to the ideology of strong AI will in the end be inclined to say something very much like this; so let us pursue it a bit further. According to one version of this view, while the man in the internalized systems example doesn't understand Chinese in the sense that a native Chinese speaker does (because, for example, he doesn't know that the story refers to restaurants and hamburgers, etc.), still "the man as a formal symbol manipulation system" *really does understand Chinese*. The subsystem of the man that is the formal symbol manipulation system for Chinese should not be confused with the subsystem for English.

So there are really two subsystems in the man; one understands English, the other Chinese, and "it's just that the two systems have little to do with each other." But, I want to reply, not only do they have little to do with each other, they are not even remotely alike. The subsystem that understands English (assuming we allow ourselves to talk in this jargon of "subsystems" for a moment) knows that the stories are about restaurants and eating hamburgers, he knows that he is being asked questions about restaurants and that he is answering questions as best he can by making various inferences from the content of the story, and so on. But the Chinese system knows none of this. Whereas the English subsystem knows that "hamburgers" refers to hamburgers, the Chinese subsystem knows only that "squiggle squiggle" is followed by "squoggle squoggle." All he knows is that various formal symbols are being introduced at one end and manipulated according to rules written in English, and other symbols are going out at the other end. The whole point of the original example was to argue that such symbol manipulation by itself couldn't be sufficient for understanding Chinese in any literal sense because the man could write "squoggle squoggle" after "squiggle squiggle" without understanding anything in Chinese. And it doesn't meet that argument to postulate subsystems within the man, because the subsystems are no better off than the man was in the first place; they still don't have anything even remotely like what the English-speaking man (or subsystem) has. Indeed, in the case as described, the Chinese subsystem is simply a part of the English subsystem, a part that engages in meaningless symbol manipulation according to rules in English.

Let us ask ourselves what is supposed to motivate the systems reply in the first place; that is, what *independent* grounds are there supposed to be for saying that the agent must have a subsystem within him that literally understands stories in Chinese? As far as I can tell the only grounds are that in the example I have the same input and output as native Chinese speakers and a program that goes from one to the other. But the whole point of the examples has been to try to show that that couldn't be sufficient for understanding, in the sense in which I understand stories is in English, because a person, and hence the set of systems that go to make up a person, could have the right combination of input, output, and program and still not understand anything in the relevant literal sense in which I understand English. The only motivation for saying there *must* be a subsystem in me that understands Chinese is that I have a program and I can pass the Turing test; I can fool native Chinese speakers. But precisely one of the points at issue is the adequacy of the Turing test. The example shows that there could be two "systems," both of which pass the Turing test, but only one of which understands; and it is no argument against this point to say that since they both pass the Turing test they must both understand, since this claim fails to meet the argument that the system in me that understands English has a great deal more than the system that merely processes Chinese. In short, the systems reply simply begs the question by insisting without argument that the system must understand Chinese.

Furthermore, the systems reply would appear to lead to consequences that are independently absurd. If we are to conclude that there must be cognition in me on the grounds that I have a certain sort of input and output and a program in between, then it looks like all sorts of noncognitive subsystems are going to turn out to be cognitive. For example, there is a level of description at which my stomach does information processing, and it instantiates any number of computer programs, but I take it we do not want to say that it has any understanding (cf. Pylyshyn 1980). But if we accept the systems reply, then it is hard to see how we avoid saying that stomach, heart, liver, and so on are all understanding subsystems, since there is no principled way to distinguish the motivation for saying the Chinese subsystem understands from saying that the stomach understands. It is, by the way, not an answer to this point to say that the Chinese system has information as input and output and the stomach has food and food products as input and output, since from the point of view of the agent, from my point of view, there is no information in either the food or the Chinese—the Chinese is just so many meaningless squiggles. The information in the Chinese case is solely in the eyes of the programmers and the interpreters, and there is nothing to prevent them from treating the input and output of my digestive organs as information if they so desire.

This last point bears on some independent problems in strong AI, and it is worth digressing for a moment to explain it. If strong AI is to be a branch of psychology, then it must be able to distinguish those systems that are genuinely mental from those that are not. It must be able to distinguish the principles on which the mind works from those on which nonmental systems work; otherwise it will offer us no explanations of what is specifically mental about the mental. And the mental-nonmental distinction cannot be just in the eye of the beholder but it must be intrinsic to the systems; otherwise it would be up to any beholder to treat people as nonmental and, for example, hurricanes as mental if he likes. But quite often in the AI literature the distinction is blurred in ways that would in the long run prove disastrous to the claim that AI is a cognitive inquiry. McCarthy, for example, writes. "Machines as simple as thermostats can be said to have beliefs, and having beliefs seems to be a characteristic of most machines capable of problem solving performance" (McCarthy 1979). Anyone who thinks strong AI has a chance as a theory of the mind ought to ponder the implications of that remark. We are asked to accept it as a discovery of strong AI that the hunk of metal on the wall that we use to regulate the temperature has beliefs in exactly the same sense that we, our spouses, and our children have beliefs, and furthermore that "most" of the other machines in the room—telephone, tape recorder, adding machine, electric light switch—also have beliefs in this literal sense. It is not the aim of this article to argue against McCarthy's point, so I will simply assert the following without argument. The study of the mind starts with such facts as that humans have beliefs, while thermostats, telephones, and adding machines don't. If you get a theory that denies this point you have produced a counterexample to the theory and the theory is false. One gets the impression that people in the AI who write this sort of thing think they can get away with it because they don't really take it seriously, and they don't think anyone else will either. I propose, for a moment at least, to take it seriously. Think hard for one minute about what would be necessary to establish that the hunk of metal on the wall over there had real beliefs, beliefs with direction of fit, propositional content, and conditions of satisfaction; beliefs that had the possiblity of being strong beliefs or weak beliefs; nervous, anxious, or secure beliefs; dogmatic, rational, or superstitious beliefs; blind faiths or hesitant cogitations; any kind of beliefs. The thermostat is not a candidate. Neither is stomach, liver, adding machine, or telephone. However, since we are taking the idea seriously, notice that its truth would be fatal to strong AI's claim to be a science of the mind. For now the mind is everywhere. What we wanted to know is what distinguishes the mind from thermostats and livers. And if McCarthy were right, strong AI wouldn't have a hope of telling us that.

II. The Robot Reply (Yale). "Suppose we wrote a different kind of program from Schank's program. Suppose we put a computer inside a robot, and this computer would not just take in formal symbols as input and give out formal symbols as output, but rather would actually operate the robot in such a way that the robot does something very much like perceiving, walking, moving about, hammering nails, eating, drinking—anything you like. The robot would, for example, have a television camera attached to it that enabled it to see, it would have arms and legs that enabled it to 'act,' and all of this would be controlled by its computer 'brain.' Such a robot would, unlike Schank's computer, have genuine understanding and other mental states."

The first thing to notice about the robot reply is that it tacitly concedes that cognition is not solely a matter of formal symbol manipulation, since this reply adds a set of causal relations with the outside world (cf. Foder 1980). But the answer to the robot reply is that the addition of such "perceptual" and "motor" capacities adds nothing by way of understanding, in particular, or intentionality, in general, to Schank's original program. To see this, notice that the same thought experiment applies to the robot case. Suppose that instead of the computer inside the robot, you put me inside the room and, as in the original Chinese case, you give me more Chinese symbols with more instructions in English for matching Chinese symbols to Chinese symbols and feeding back Chinese symbols to the outside. Suppose, unknown to me, some of the Chinese symbols that come to me come from a television camera attached to the robot and other Chinese symbols that I am giving out serve to make the motors inside the robot move the robot's legs or arms. It is important to emphasize that all I am doing is manipulating formal symbols: I know none of these other facts. I am receiving "information" from the robot's "perceptual" apparatus, and I am giving out "instructions" to its motor apparatus without knowing either of these facts. I am the robot's homunculus, but unlike the traditional homunculus, I don't know what's going on. I don't understand anything except the rules for symbol manipulation. Now in this case I want to say that the robot has no intentional states at all; it is simply moving about as a result of its electrical wiring and its program. And furthermore, by instantiating the program I have no intentional states of the relevant type. All I do is follow formal instructions about manipulating formal symbols.

III. The Brain Simulator Reply (Berkeley and M.I.T.). "Suppose we design a program that doesn't represent information that we have about the world, such as the information in Schank's scripts, but simulates the actual sequence of neuron firings at the synapses of the brain of a native Chinese speaker when he understands stories in Chinese and gives answers to them. The machine takes in Chinese stories and questions about them as input, it simulates the formal structure of actual Chinese brains in processing these stories, and it gives out Chinese answers as outputs. We can even imagine that the machine operates, not with a single serial program, but with a whole set of programs operating in parallel, in the manner that actual human brains presumably operate when they process natural language. Now surely in such a case we would have to say that the machine understood the stories; and if we refuse to say that, wouldn't we also have to deny that native Chinese speakers understood the stories? At the level of the synapses, what would or could be different about the program of the computer and the program of the Chinese brain?"

Before countering this reply I want to digress to note that it is an odd reply for any partisan of artificial intelligence (or functionalism, etc.) to make: I though the whole idea of strong AI is that we don't need to know how the brain works to know how the mind works. The basic hypothesis, or so I had supposed, was that there is a level of mental operations consisting of computational processes over formal elements that constitute the essence of the mental and can be realized in all sorts of different brain processes, in the same way that any computer program can be realized in different computer hardwares: On the assumptions of strong AI, the mind is to the brain as the program is to the hardware, and thus we can understand the mind without doing neurophysiology. If we had to know how the brain worked to do AI, we wouldn't bother with AI. However, even getting this close to the operation of the brain is still not sufficient to produce understanding. To see this, imagine that instead of a monolingual man in a room shuffling symbols we have the man operate an elaborate set of water pipes with valves connecting them. When the man receives the Chinese symbols, he looks up in the program, written in English, which valves he has to turn on and off. Each water connection corresponds to a synapse in the Chinese brain, and the whole system is rigged up so that after doing all the right firings, that is after turning on all the right faucets, the Chinese answers pop out at the output end of the series of pipes.

Now where is the understanding in this system? It takes Chinese as input, it simulates the formal structure of the synapses of the Chinese brain, and it gives Chinese as output. But the man certainly doesn't understand Chinese, and neither do the water pipes, and if we are tempted to adopt what I think is the absurd view that somehow the *conjuction* of man *and* water pipes understands, remember that in principle the man can internalize the formal structure of the water pipes and do all the "neuron firings" in his imagination. The problem with the brain simulator is that it is simulating the wrong things about the brain. As long as it simulates only the formal structure of the sequence of neuron firings at the synapses, it won't have simulated what matters about the brain, namely its causal properties, its ability to produce intentional states. And that the formal properties are not sufficient for the causal properties is shown by the water pipe example: we can have all the formal properties carved off from the relevant neurobiological causal properties.

IV. The Combination Reply (Berkeley and Stanford). "While each of the previous three replies might not be completely convincing by itself as a refutation of the Chinese room counterexample, if you take all three together they are collectively much more convincing and even decisive. Imagine a robot with a brain-shaped computer lodged in its cranial cavity, imagine the computer programmed with all the synapses of a human brain, imagine the whole behavior of the robot is indistinguishable from human behavior, and now think of the whole thing as a unified system and not just as a computer with inputs and outputs. Surely in such a case we would have to ascribe intentionality to the system."

I entirely agree that in such a case we would find it rational and indeed irresistible to accept the hypothesis that the robot had intentionality, as long as we knew nothing more about it. Indeed, besides appearance and behavior, the other elements of the combination are really irrelevant. If we could build a robot whose behavior was indistinguishable over a large range from human behavior, we would attribute intentionality to it, pending some reason not to. We wouldn't need to know in advance that its computer brain was a formal analogue of the human brain.

But I really don't see that this is any help to the claims of strong AI, and here's why: According to strong AI, instantiating a formal program with the right input and output is a sufficient condition of, indeed is constitutive of, intentionality. As Newell (1979) puts it, the essence of the mental is the operation of a physical symbol system. But the attributions of intentionality that we make to the robot in this example have nothing to do with formal programs. They are simply based on the assumption that if the robot looks and behaves sufficiently like us, then we would suppose, until proven otherwise, that it must have mental states like ours that cause and are expressed by its behavior and it must have an inner mechanism capable of producing such mental states. If we knew independently how to account for its behavior without such assumptions we would not attribute intentionality to it, especially if we knew it had a formal program. And this is precisely the point of my earlier reply to objection II.

Suppose we knew that the robot's behavior was entirely accounted for by the fact that a man inside it was receiving uninterpreted formal symbols from the robot's sensory receptors and sending out uninterpreted formal symbols to its motor mechanisms, and the man was doing the symbol manipulation in accordance with a bunch of rules. Furthermore, suppose the man knows none of these facts about the robot, all he knows is which operations to perform on which meaningless symbols. In such a case we would regard the robot as an ingenious mechanical dummy. The hypothesis that the dummy has a mind would now be unwarranted and unnecessary, for there is now no longer any reason to ascribe intentionality to the robot or to the system of which it is a part (except of course for the man's intentionality in manipulating the symbols). The formal symbol manipulations go on, the input and output are correctly matched, but the only real locus of intetionality is the man, and he doesn't know any of the relevant intentional states; he doesn't, for example, *see* what comes into the robot's eyes, he doesn't *intend* to move the robot's arm, and he doesn't *understand* any of the remarks made to or by the robot. Nor, for the reasons stated earlier, does the system of which man and robot are a part.

To see this point, contrast this case with cases in which we find it completely natural to ascribe intentionality to members of certain other primate species such as apes and monkeys and to domestic animals such as dogs. The reasons we find it natural are, roughly, two: We can't make sense of the animal's behavior without the ascription of intentionality, and we can see that the beasts are made of similar stuff to ourselves—that is an eye, that a nose, this is its skin, and so on. Given the coherence of the animal's behavior and the assumption of the same causal stuff underlying it, we assume both that the animal must have mental states underlying its behavior, and that the mental states must be produced by mechanisms made out of the stuff that is like our stuff. We would certainly make smilar assumptions about the robot unless we had some reason not to, but as soon as we knew that the behavior was the result of a formal program, and that the actual causal properties of the physical substance were irrelevant we would abandon the assumption of intentionality.

There are two other responses to my example that come up frequently (and so are worth discussing) but really miss the point.

V. The Other Minds Reply (Yale). "How do you know that other people understand Chinese or anything else? Only by their behavior. Now the computer can pass the behavioral tests as well as they can (in principle), so if you are going to attribute cognition to other people you must in principle also attribute it to computers."

This objection really is only worth a short reply. The problem in this discussion is not about how I know that other people have cognitive states, but rather what it is that I am attributing to them when I attribute cognitive states to them. The thrust of the argument is that it couldn't be just computational processes and their output because the computational processes and their output can exist without the cognitive state. It is no answer to this argument to feign anesthesia. In "cognitive sciences" one presupposes the reality and knowability of the mental in the same way that in physical sciences one has to presuppose the reality and knowability of physical objects.

VI. The Many Mansions Reply (Berkeley). "Your whole argument presupposes that AI is only about analog and digital computers. But that just happens to be the present state of technology. Whatever these causal processes are that you say are essential for intentionality (assuming you are right), eventually we will be able to build devices that have these causal processes, and that will be artificial intelligence. So your arguments are in no way directed at the ability of artificial intelligence to produce and explain cognition."

I really have no objection to this reply save to say that it in effect trivializes the project of strong AI by redefining it as whatever artificially produces and explains cognition. The interest of the original claim made on behalf of artificial intelligence is that it was a precise, well defined thesis: mental processes are computational processes over formally defined elements. I have been concerned to challenge that thesis. If the claim is redefined so that it is no longer that thesis, my objections no longer apply because there is no longer a testable hypothesis for them to apply to.

Let us now return to the question I promised I would try to answer: Granted that in my original example I understand the English and I do not understand the Chinese, and granted therefore that the machine doesn't understand either English or Chinese, still there must be something about me that makes it the case that I understand English and a corresponding something lacking in me that makes it the case that I fail to understand Chinese. Now why couldn't we give those somethings, whatever they are, to a machine?

I see no reason in principle why we couldn't give a machine the capacity to understand English or Chinese, since in an important sense our bodies with our brains are precisely such machines. But I do see very strong arguments for saying that we could not give such a thing to a machine where the operation of the machine is defined solely in terms of computational processes over formally defined elements; that is, where the operational of the machine is defined as an instantiation of a computer program. It is not because I am the instantiation of a computer program that I am able to understand English and have other forms of intentionality (I am, I suppose, the instantiation of any number of computer programs), but as far as we know it is because I am a certain sort of organism with a certain biological (i.e., chemical and physical) structure, and this structure, under certain conditions, is causally capable of producing perception, action, understanding, learning, and other intentional phenomena. And part of the point of the present argument is that only something that had those causal powers could have that intentionality. Perhaps other physical and chemical processes could produce exactly these effects; perhaps, for example, Martians also have intentionality but their brains are made of different stuff. That is an empirical question, rather like the question whether photosynthesis can be done by something with a chemistry different from that of chlorophyll.

But the main point of the present argument is that no purely formal model will ever be sufficient by itself for intentionality because the formal properties are not by themselves constitutive of intentionality, and they have by themselves no causal powers except the power, when instantiated, to produce the next stage of the formalism when the machine is running. And any other causal properties that particular realizations of the formal model have, are irrelevant to the formal model because we can always put the same formal model in a different realization where those causal properties are obviously absent. Even if, by some miracle, Chinese speakers exactly realize Schank's program, we can put the same program in English speakers, water pipes, or computers, none of which understand Chinese, the program notwithstanding.

What matters about brain operations is not the formal shadow cast by the sequence of synapses but rather the actual properties of the sequences. All the arguments for the strong version of artificial intelligence that I have seen insist on drawing an outline around the shadows cast by cognition and then claiming that the shadows are the real thing.

By way of concluding I want to try to state some of the general philosophical points implicit in the argument. For clarity I will try to do it in a question-and-answer fashion, and I begin with that old chestnut of a question:

"Could a machine think?"

The answer is, obviously, yes. We are precisely such machines.

"Yes, but could an artifact, a man-made machine, think?"

Assuming it is possible to produce artificially a machine with a nervous system, neurons with axons and dendrites, and all the rest of it, sufficiently like ours, again the answer to the question seems to be obviously, yes. If you can exactly duplicate the causes, you could duplicate the effects. And indeed it might be possible to produce consciousness, intentionality, and all the rest of it using some other sorts of chemical principles than those that human beings use. It is, as I said, an empirical question.

"OK, but could a digital computer think?"

If by "digital computer" we mean anything at all that has a level of description where it can correctly be described as the instantiation of a computer program, then again the answer is, of course, yes, since we are the instantiations of any number of computer programs, and we can think.

"But could something think, understand, and so on *solely* in virtue of being a computer with a right sort of program? Could instantiating a program, the right program of course, by itself be a sufficient condition of understanding?"

This I think is the right question to ask, though it is usually confused with one or more of the earlier questions, and the answer to it is no.

"Why not?"

Because the formal symbol manipulations by themselves don't have any intentionality; they are quite meaningless; they aren't even *symbol* manipulations, since the symbols don't symbolize anything. In the linguistic jargon, they have only a syntax but no semantics. Such intentionality as computers appear to have is solely in the minds of those who program them and those who use them, those who send in the input and those who interpret the output.

The aim of the Chinese room example was to try to show this by showing that as soon as we put something into the system that really does have intentionality (a man), and we program him with the formal program, you can see that the formal program carries no additional intentionality. It adds nothing, for example, to a man's ability to understand Chinese.

Precisely that feature of AI that seemed so appealing—the distinction between the program and the realization—proves fatal to the claim that simulation could be duplication. The distinction between the program and its realization in the hardware seems to be parallel to the distinction between the level of mental operations and the level of brain operations. And if we could describe the level of mental operations as a formal program, then it seems we could describe what was essential about the mind without doing either introspective psychology or neurophysiology of the brain. But the equation "mind is to brain as program is to hardware" breaks down at several points, among them the following three:

First, the distinction between program and realization has the consequence that the same program could have all sorts of crazy realizations that had no form of intentionality. Weizenbaum (1976, Ch. 2), for example, shows in detail how to construct a computer using a role of toilet paper and a pile of small stones. Similarly, the Chinese story understanding program can be programmed into a sequence of water pipes, a set of wind machines, or a monolingual English speaker, none of which thereby acquires an understanding of Chinese. Stones, toilet paper, wind, and water pipes are the wrong kind of stuff to have intentionality in the first place—only something that has the same causal powers as brains can have intentionality—and though the English speaker has the right kind of stuff for intentionality you can easily see that he doesn't get any extra intentionality by memorizing the program, since memorizing it won't teach him Chinese.

Second, the program is purely formal, but the intentional states are not in that way formal. They are defined in terms of their content, not their form. The belief that it is raining, for example, is not defined as a certain formal shape, but as a certain mental content with conditions of satisfaction, a direction of fit (see Searle 1979), and the like. Indeed the belief as such hasn't even got a formal shape in this syntactic sense, since one and the same belief can be given an indefinite number of different syntactic expressions in different linguistic systems.

Third, as I mentioned before, mental states and events are literally a product of the operation of the brain, but the program is not in that way a product of the computer.

"Well if programs are in no way constitutive of mental processes, why have so many people believed the converse? That at least needs some explanation."

I don't really know the answer to that one. The idea that computer simulations could be the real thing ought to have seemed suspicious in the first place because the computer isn't confined to simulating mental operations, by any means. No one supposes that computer simualtions of a five-alarm fire will burn the neighborhood down or that a computer simulation of a rainstorm will leave us all drenched. Why on earth would anyone suppose that a computer simulation of understanding actually understood anything? It is sometimes said that it would be frightfully hard to get computers to feel pain or fall in love, but love and pain are neither harder nor easier than cognition or anything else. For simulation, all you need is the right input and output and a program in the middle that trasforms the former into the latter. That is all the computer has for anything it does. To confuse simulation with duplication is the same mistake, whether it is pain, love, cognition, fires, or rainstorms.

Still, there are several reasons why AI must have seemed—and to many people perhaps still does seem—in some way to reproduce and thereby explain mental phenomena, and I believe we will not succeed in removing these illusions until we have fully exposed the reasons that give rise to them.

First, and perhaps the most important, is a confusion about the notion of "information processing": many people in cognitive science believe that the human brain, with its mind, does something called "information processing," and analogously the computer with its program does information processing; but fires and rainstorms, on the other hand, don't do information processing at all. Thus, though the computer can simulate the formal features of any process whatever, it stands in a special relation to the mind and brain because when the computer is properly programmed, ideally with the same program as the brain, the information processing is identical in the two cases, and this information processing is really the essence of the mental. But the trouble with this argument is that it rests on an ambiguity in the notion of "information." In the sense in which people "process information" when they reflect, say, on problems in arithmetic or when they read and answer questions about stories, the programmed computer does not do "information processing." Rather, what it does is manipulate formal symbols. The fact that the programmer and the interpreter of the computer output use the symbols to stand for objects in the world is totally beyond the scope of the computer. The computer, to repeat, has a syntax but no semantics. Thus, if you type into the computer "2 plus 2 equals?" it will type out "4." But it has no idea that "4" means 4 or that it means anything at all. And the point is not that it lacks some second-order information about the interpretation of its first-order symbols, but rather that its first-order symbols don't have any interpretations as far as the computer is concerned. All the computer has is more symbols. The introduction of the notion of "information processing" therefore produces a dilemma: either we construe the notion of "information processing" in such a way that it implies intentionality as part of the process or we don't. If the former, then the programmed computer does not do information processing, it only manipulates formal symbols. If the latter, then, though the computer does information processing, it is only doing so in the sense in which adding machines, typewriters, stomachs, thermostats, rainstorms, and hurricanes do information processing; namely, they have a level of description at which we can describe them as taking information in at one end, transforming it, and producing information as output. But in this case it is up to outside observers to interpret the input and output as information in the ordinary sense. And no similarity is established between the computer and the brain in terms of any similarity of information processing.

Second, in much of AI there is a residual behaviorism or operationalism. Since appropriately programmed computers can have input-output patterns similar to those of human beings, we are tempted to postulate mental states in the computer similar to human mental states. But once we see that it is both conceptually and empirically possible for a system to have human capacities in some realm without having any intentionality at all, we should be able to overcome this impulse. My desk adding machine has calculating capacities, but no intentionality, and in this paper I have tried to show that a system could have input and output capabilities that duplicated those of a native Chinese speaker and still not understand Chinese, regardless of how it was programmed. The Turing test is typical of the tradition in being unashamedly behavioristic and operationalistic, and I believe that if AI workers totally repudiated behaviorism and operationalism much of the confusion between simulation and duplication would be eliminated.

Third, this residual operationalism is joined to a residual form of dualism; indeed strong AI only makes sense given the dualistic assumption that, where the mind is concerned, the brain doesn't matter. In strong AI (and in functionalism, as well) what matters are programs, and programs are independent of their realization in machines; indeed, as far as AI is concerned, the same program could be realized by an electronic machine, a Cartesian mental substance, or a Hegelian world spirit. The single most surprising discovery that I have made in discussing these issues is that many AI workers are quite shocked by my idea that actual human mental phenomena might be dependent on actual physical-chemical properties of actual human brains. But if you think about it a minute you can see that I should not have been surprised; for unless you accept some form of dualism, the strong AI project hasn't got a chance. The project is to reproduce and explain the mental by designing programs, but unless the mind is not only conceptually but empirically independent of the brain you couldn't carry out the project, for the program is completely independent of any realization. Unless you believe that the mind is separable from the brain both conceptually and empirically—dualism in a strong form—you cannot hope to reproduce the mental by writing and running programs since programs must be independent of brains or any other particular forms of instantiation. If mental operations consist in computational operations on formal symbols, then it follows that they have no interesting connection with the brain; the only connection would be that the brain just happens to be one of the indefinitely many types of machines capable of instantiating the program. This form of dualism is not the traditional Cartesian variety that claims there are two sorts of *substances,* but it is Cartesian in the sense that it insists that what is specifically mental about the mind has no intrinsic connection with the actual properties of the brain. This underlying dualism is masked from us by the fact that AI literature contains frequent fulminations against "dualism"; what the authors seem to be unaware of is that their position presupposes a strong version of dualism.

"Could a machine think?" My own view is that *only* a machine could think, and indeed only very special kinds of machines, namely brains and machines that had the same causal powers as brains. And that is the main reason strong AI has had little to tell us about thinking, since it has nothing to tell us about machines. By its own definition, it is about programs, and programs are not machines. Whatever else intentionality is, it is a biological phenomenon, and it is as likely to be as causally dependent on the specific biochemistry of its origins as lactation, photosynthesis, or any other biological phenomena. No one would suppose that we could produce milk and sugar by running a computer simulation of the formal sequences in lactation and photosynthesis, but where the mind is concerned many people are willing to believe in such a miracle because of a deep and abiding dualism: the mind they suppose is a matter of formal processes and is independent of quite specific material causes in the way that milk and sugar are not.

In defense of this dualism the hope is often expressed that the brain is a digital computer (early computers, by the way, were often called "electronic brains"). But that is no help. Of course the brain is a digital computer. Since everything is a digital computer, brains are too. The point is that the brain's causal capacity to produce intentionality cannot consist in its instantiating a computer program, since for any program you like it is possible for something to instantiate that program and still not have any mental states. Whatever it is that the brain does to produce intentionality, it cannot consist in instantiating a program since no program, by itself, is sufficient for intentionality.

Notes

1. I am not, of course, saying that Schank himself is committed to these claims.
2. Also, "understanding" implies both the possession of mental (intentional) states and the truth (validity, success) of these states. For the purposes of this discussion we are concerned only with the possession of the states.
3. Intentionality is by definition that feature of certain mental states by which they are directed at or about objects and states of affairs in the world. Thus, beliefs, desires, and intentions are intentional states; undirected forms of anxiety and depression are not.

References

Fodor, J. A. 1968. The appeal to tacit knowledge in psychological explanation. *Journal of Philosophy* 65: 627–40.

Fodor, J. A. 1980. Methodological solipsism considered as a research strategy in cognitive psychology. *Behavioral and Brain Sciences* 3:1.

McCarthy, J. 1979. Ascribing mental qualities to machines. In: *Philosophical perceptives in artificial intelligence,* ed. M. Ringle. Atlantic Highlands, NJ: Humanities Press.

Newell, A. 1973. Physical symbol systems. Lecture at the La Jolla Conference on Cognitive Science.

Newell, A., and Simon, H. A. 1963. GPS, a program that simulates human thought. In: *Computers and thought.* ed. A. Feigenbaum & V. Feldman, pp. 279–93. New York: McGraw-Hill.

Pylyshyn, Z. W. 1980. Computation and cognition: issues in the foundations of cognitive science. *Behavioral and Brain Sciences* 3.

Schank, R. C., and Abelson, R. P. 1977. *Scripts, plans, goals, and understanding.* Hillsdale, NJ: Lawrence Erlbaum Press.

Searle, J. R. 1979. The intentionality of intention and action. *Inquiry* 22:253–80.

Weizenbaum, J. 1965. Eliza—a computer program for the study of natural language communication between man and machine. *Communication of the Association for Computing Machinery* 9:36–45.

Weizenbaum, J. 1976. *Computer power and human reason.* San Francisco: W. H. Freeman.

Winograd, T. 1973. A procedural model of language understanding. In: *Computer models of thought and language,* ed. R. Schank & K. Colby. San Francisco: W. H. Freeman.

C. PERSONAL IDENTITY

Of Identity and Diversity

JOHN LOCKE

1. *Wherein Identity Consists.*—Another occasion the mind often takes of comparing, is the very being of things; when, considering anything as existing at any determined time and place, we compare it with itself existing at another time, and thereon form the ideas of identity and diversity. When we see anything to be in any place in any instant of time, we are sure (be it what it will) that it is that very thing, and not another, which at that same time exists in another place, how like and undistinguishable soever it may be in all other respects: and in this consists identity, when the ideas it is attributed to vary not at all from what they were that moment wherein we consider their former existence, and to which we compare the present. For we never finding, nor conceiving it possible, that two things of the same kind should exist in the same place at the same time, we rightly conclude, that, whatever exists anywhere at any time, excludes all of the same kind, and is there itself alone. When therefore we demand whether anything be the same or no, if refers always to something that existed such a time in such a place, which it was certain at that instant was the same with itself, and no other. From whence it follows, that one thing cannot have two beginnings of existence, nor two things one beginning; it being impossible for two things of the same kind to be or exist in the same instant, in the very same place, or one and the same thing in different places. That, therefore, that had one beginning, is the same thing; and that which had a different beginning in time and place from that, is not the same, but diverse. That which has made the difficulty about this relation has been the little care and attention used in having precise notions of the things to which it is attributed.

2. *Identity of Substances*—We have the ideas but of three sorts of substances: 1. God. 2. Finite intelligences. 3. Bodies. First, God is without beginning, eternal, unalterable, and everywhere; and therefore concerning his identity there can be no doubt. Secondly, Finite spirits having had each its determinate time and place of beginning to exist, the relation to that time and place will always determine to each of them its identity, as long as it exists. Thirdly, The same will hold of every particle of matter, to which no addition or subtraction of matter being made, it is the same. For, though these three sorts of substances, as we term them, do not exclude one another out of the same place, yet we cannot conceive but that they must necessarily each of them exclude any of the same kind out of the same place; or else the notions and names of identity and diversity would be in vain, and there could be no such distinctions of substances, or anything else one from another. For example: could two bodies be in the same place at the same time, then those two parcels of matter must be one and the same, take them great or little; nay, all bodies must be one

The selection is chapter 27 of Locke's *Essay Concerning Human Understanding*. The *Essay* was first published in 1690; this chapter first appeared in the second edition, 1694. The numbering of the first 10 sections varies from edition to edition; the popular edition by A. C. Fraser assigns the number 10 to both section 8 and section 10.

From *Essay Concerning Human Understanding,* 2nd ed. (London: A. and J. Churchill, 1694), pp. 178–90.

and the same. For, by the same reason that two particles of matter may be in one place, all bodies may be in one place; which, when it can be supposed, takes away the distinction of identity and diversity of one and more, and renders it ridiculous. But it being a contradiction that two or more should be one, identity and diversity are relations and ways of comparing well founded, and of use to the understanding.

Identity of Modes.—All other things being but modes or relations ultimately terminated in substances, the identity and diversity of each particular existence of them too will be by the same way determined: only as to things whose existence is in succession, such as are the actions of finite beings, v.g., motion and thought, both which consist in a continued train of succession: concerning their diversity there can be no question; because each perishing the moment it begins, they cannot exist in different times, or in different places, as permanent beings can at different times exist in distant places; and therefore no motion or thought, considered as at different times, can be the same, each part thereof having a different beginning of existence.

3. *Principium Individuationis.*—From what has been said, it is easy to discover what is so much inquired after, the principium individuationis; and that, it is plain, is existence itself, which determines a being of any sort to a particular time and place, incommunicable to two beings of the same kind. This, though it seems easier to conceive in simple substances or modes, yet, when reflected on, is not more difficult in compound ones, if care be taken to what it is applied: v.g., let us suppose an atom, i.e., a continued body under one immutable superfices, existing in a determined time and place; it is evident, that considered in any instant of its existence, it is in that instant the same with itself. For, being at that instant what it is, and nothing else, it is the same, and so must continue as long as its existence is continued; for so long it will be the same, and no other. In like manner, if two or more atoms be joined together into the same mass, every one of those atoms will be the same, by the foregoing rule: and whilst they exist united together, the mass, consisting of the same atoms, must be the same mass, or the same body, let the parts be ever so differently jumbled. But if one of these atoms be taken away, or one new one added, it is no longer the same mass or the same body. In the state of living creatures, their identity depends not on a mass of the same particles, but on something else. For in them the variation of great parcels of matter alters not the identity: an oak growing from a plant to a great tree, and then lopped, is still the same oak; and a colt grown up to a horse, sometimes fat, sometimes lean, is all the while the same horse: though, in both these cases, there may be a manifest change of the parts; so that truly they are not either of them the same masses of matter, though they be truly one of them the same oak, and the other the same horse. The reason whereof is, that, in these two cases, a mass of matter, and a living body, identity is not applied to the same thing.

4. *Identity of Vegetables.*—We must therefore consider wherein an oak differs from a mass of matter, and that seems to me to be in this, that the one is only the cohesion of particles of matter any how united, the other such a disposition of them as constitutes the parts of an oak; and such an organization of those parts as is fit to receive and distribute nourishment, so as to continue and frame the wood, bark, and leaves, etc., of an oak, in which consists the vegetable life. That being then one plant which has such an organization of parts in one coherent body, partaking of one common life, it continues to be the same plant as long as it partakes of the same life, though that life be communicated to new particles of matter vitally united to the living plant, in a like continued organization conformable to that sort of plants. For this organization being at any one instant in any one collection of matter, is in that particular concrete distinguished from all other, and is that individual life, which existing constantly from that moment both forwards and backwards, in the same continuity of insensibly succeeding parts united to the living body of the plant, it has that identity which makes the same plant, and all the parts of it, parts of the same plant, during all the time that they exist united in that continued organization, which is fit to convey that common life to all the parts so united.

5. *Identity of Animals.*—The case is not so much different in brutes, but that any one may hence see what makes an animal and continues it the same. Something we have like this in ma-

chines, and may serve to illustrate it. For example, what is a watch? It is plain it is nothing but a fit organization or construction of parts to a certain end, which, when a sufficient force is added to it, it is capable to attain. If we would suppose this machine one continued body, all whose organized parts were repaired, increased, or diminished by a constant addition or separation of insensible parts, with one common life, we should have something very much like the body of an animal; with this difference, that, in an animal the fitness of the organization, and the motion wherein life consists, begin together, the motion coming from within; but in machines, the force coming sensibly from without, is often away when the organ is in order, and well fitted to receive it.

6. *The Identity of Man.*—This also shows wherein the identity of the same man consists; vis., in nothing but a participation of the same continued life, by constantly fleeting particles of matter, in succession vitally united to the same organized body. He that shall place the identity of man in anything else, but like that of other animals, in one fitly organized body, taken in any one instant, and from thence continued, under one organization of life, in several successively fleeting particles of matter united to it, will find it hard to make an embryo, one of years, mad and sober, the same man, by any supposition, that will not make it possible for Seth, Ismael, Socrates, Pilate, Saint Austin, and Caesar Borgia, to be the same man. For, if the identity of soul alone makes the same man, and there be nothing in the nature of matter why the same individual spirit may not be united to different bodies, it will be possible that those men living in distant ages, and of different tempers, may have been the same man: which way of speaking must be, from a very strange use of the word man, applied to an idea, out of which body and shape are excluded. And that way of speaking would agree yet worse with the notions of those philosophers who allow of transmigration, and are of opinion that the souls of men may, for their miscarriages, be detruded into the bodies of beasts, as fit habitations, with organs suited to the satisfaction of their brutal inclinations. But yet I think nobody, could he be sure that the souls of Heliogabalus were in one of his hogs, would yet say that hog were a man or Heliogabalus.

7. *Identity Suited to the Idea.*—It is not therefore unity of substance that comprehends all sorts of identity, or will determine it in every case; but to conceive and judge of it aright, we must consider what idea the word it is applied to stands for: it being one thing to be the same substance, another the same man, and a third the same person, if person, man, and substance, are three names standing for three different ideas; for such as is the idea belonging to that name, such must be the identity; which, if it had been a little more carefully attended to, would possibly have prevented a great deal of that confusion which often occurs about this matter, with no small seeming difficulties, especially concerning personal identity, which therefore we shall in the next place a little consider.

8. *Same Man.*—An animal is living organized body; and consequently the same animal, as we have observed, is the same continued life communicated to different particles of matter, as they happen successively to be united to that organized living body. And whatever is talked of other definitions, ingenious observation puts it past doubt, that the idea in our minds, of which the sound man in our mouths is the sign, is nothing else but of an animal of such a certain form: since I think I may be confident, that, whoever should see a creature of his own shape or make, though it had no more reason all its life than a cat or a parrot, would call him still a man; or whoever should hear a cat or a parrot discourse, reason, and philosophize, would call or think it nothing but a cat or a parrot; and say, the one was a dull irrational man, and the other a very intelligent rational parrot. A relation we have in an author of great note, is sufficient to countenance the supposition of a rational parrot. His words are:

> I had a mind to know, from Prince Maurice's own mouth, the account of a common, but much credited story, that I had heard so often from many others, of an old parrot he had in Brazil, during his government there, that spoke, and asked, and answered common questions, like a reasonable creature: so that those of his train there generally con-

cluded it to be witchery or possession; and one of his chaplains, who lived long afterwards in Holland, would never from that time endure a parrot, but said they all had a devil in them. I had heard many particulars of this story, and assevered by people hard to be discredited, which made me ask Prince Maurice what there was of it. He said, with his usual plainness and dryness in talk, there was something true, but a great deal false of what had been reported. I desired to know of him what there was of the first. He told me short and coldly, that he had heard of such an old parrot when he had been at Brazil; and though he believed nothing of it, and it was a good way off, yet he had so much curiosity as to send for it: that it was a very great and a very old one; and when it came first into the room where the prince was, with a great many Dutchmen about him, it said presently, What a company of white men are here! They asked it, what it thought that man was, pointing to the prince. It answered, Some General or other. When they brought it close to him, he asked it, D'ou venez-vous? It answered, De Marinnan. The Prince, A qui estes-vous? The parrot, A un Portugais. The Prince, Que fais-tu là? Je garde les poulles. The Prince laughed, and said, Vous gardez les poulles? The parrot answered, Oui, moi, et je sçai bein faire; and made the chuck four or five times that people use to make to chickens when they call them. I set down the words of this worthy dialogue in French, just as Prince Maurice said them to me. I asked him in what language the parrot spoke, and he said in Brazilian. I asked whether he understood Brazilian; he said no: but he had taken care to have two interpreters by him, the one a Dutchman that spoke Brazilian, and the other a Brazilian that spoke Dutch; that he asked them separately and privately, and both of them agreed in telling him just the same thing that the parrot had said. I could not but tell this odd story, because it is so much out of the way, and from the first hand, and what may pass for a good one; for I dare say this prince at least believed himself in all he told me, having ever passed for a very honest and pious man: I leave it to naturalists to reason, and to other men to believe, as they please upon it; however, it is not, perhaps, amiss to relieve or enliven a busy scene sometimes with such digressions, whether to the purpose or no.

Same Man.—I have taken care that the reader should have the story at large in the author's own words, because he seems to me not to have thought it incredible; for it cannot be imagined that so able a man as he, who had sufficiency enough to warrant all the testimonies he gives of himself, should take so much pains, in a place where it had nothing to do, to pin so close not only on a man whom he mentions as his friend, but on a prince in whom he acknowledges very great honesty and piety, a story which, if he himself thought incredible, he could not but also think ridiculous. The prince, it is plain, who vouches this story, and our author, who relates it from him, both of them call this talker a parrot: and I ask any one else who thinks such a story fit to be told, whether—if this parrot, and all of its kind, had always talked, as we have a prince's word for it this one did—whether, I say, they would not have passed for a race of rational animals; but yet, whether, for all that, they would have been allowed to be men, and not parrots? For I presume it is not the idea of a thinking or rational being alone that makes the idea of a man in most people's sense, but of a body, so and so shaped, joined to it; and if that be the idea of a man, the same successive body not shifted all at once, must, as well as the same immaterial spirit, go to the making of the same man.

9. *Personal Identity.*—This being premised, to find wherein personal identity consists, we must consider what person stands for; which, I think, is a thinking intelligent being, that has reason and reflection, and can consider itself as itself, the same thinking thing, in different times and places; which it does only by that consciousness which is inseparable from thinking, and, as it seems to me, essential to it: it being impossible for any one to perceive without perceiving that he does perceive. When we see, hear, smell, taste, feel, meditate, or will anything, we know that we do so. Thus it is always as to our present sensations

and perceptions: and by this every one is to himself that which he calls self; it not being considered, in this case, whether the same self be continued in the same or divers substances. For, since consciousness always accompanies thinking, and it is that which makes every one to be what he calls self, and thereby distinguishes himself from all other thinking things: in this alone consists personal identity, i.e., the sameness of a rational being; and as far as this consciousness can be extended backwards to any past action or thought, so far reaches the identity of that person; it is the same self now it was then; and it is by the same self with this present one that now reflects on it, that that action was done.

10. *Consciousness Makes Personal Identity.*—But it is further inquired, whether it be the same identical substance? This, few would think they had reason to doubt of, if these perceptions, with their consciousness, always remained present in the mind, whereby the same thinking thing would be always consciously present, and, as would be thought, evidently the same to itself. But that which seems to make the difficulty is this, that this consciousness being interrupted always by forgetfulness, there being no moment of our lives wherein we have the whole train of all our past actions before our eyes in one view, but even the best memories losing the sight of one part whilst they are viewing another; and we sometimes, and that the greatest part of our lives, not reflecting on our past selves, being intent on our present thoughts, and in sound sleep having no thoughts at all, or at least none with that consciousness which remarks our waking thoughts; I say, in all these cases, our consciousness being interrupted, and we losing the sight of our past selves, doubts are raised whether we are the same thinking thing, i.e., the same substance or no. Which, however reasonable or unreasonable, concerns not personal identity at all: the question being, what makes the same person, and not whether it be the same identical substance, which always thinks in the same person; which in this case, matters not at all: different substances, by the same consciousness (where they do partake in it) being united into one person, as well as different bodies by the same life are united into one animal, whose identity is preserved in that change of substances by the unity of one continued life. For it being the same consciousness that makes a man be himself to himself, personal identity depends on that only, whether it be annexed solely to one individual substance, or can be continued in a succession of several substances. For as far as any intelligent being can repeat the idea of an any past action with the same consciousness it had of it at first, and with the same consciousness it has of any present action; so far it is the same personal self. For it is by the consciousness it has of its present thoughts and actions, that it is self to itself now, and so will be the same self, as far as the same consciousness can extend to actions past or to come; and would be by distance of time, or change of substance, no more two persons, than a man be two men by wearing other clothes today than he did yesterday, with a long or a short sleep between: the same consciousness uniting those distant actions into the same person, whatever substances contributed to their production.

11. *Personal Identity in Change of Substances.*—That this is so, we have some kind of evidence in our very bodies, all whose particles, whilst vitally united to this same thinking conscious self, so that we feel when they are touched, and are affected by, and conscious of good or harm that happens to them, are a part of ourselves; i.e., of our thinking conscious self. Thus, the limbs of his body are to every one a part of himself; he sympathizes and is concerned for them. Cut off a hand, and thereby separate it from that consciousness he had of its heat, cold, and other affections, and it is then no longer a part of that which is himself, any more than the remotest part of matter. Thus, we see the substance whereof personal self consisted at one time may be varied at another, without the change of personal identity; there being no question about the same person, though the limbs which but now were a part of it, be cut off.

12. But the question is, "Whether, if the same substance, which thinks, be changed, it can be the same person; or, remaining the same, it can be different persons?"

Whether in the Change of Thinking Substances.—And to this I answer: First, This can be no question at all to those who place thought in a purely material animal constitution, void of an immaterial substance. For, whether their supposition be true or no, it is plain they conceive personal identity preserved in something else than identity of substance; as animal identity is preserved in identity of life, and not of substance. And therefore those who place thinking in an immaterial substance only, before they can come to deal with these men, must show why personal identity cannot be preserved in the change of material substances, or variety of particular bodies: unless they will say, it is one immaterial spirit that makes the same life in brutes, as it is one immaterial spirit that makes the same person in men; which the Cartesians at least will not admit, for fear of making brutes thinking things too.

13. But next, as to the first part of the question, "Whether if the same thinking substance (supposing immaterial substances only to think) be changed, it can be the same person?" I answer, that cannot be resolved, but by those who know what kind of substances they are that do think, and whether the consciousness of past actions can be transferred from one thinking substance to another. I grant, were the same consciousness the same individual action, it could not: but it being a present representation of a past action, why it may not be possible that that may be represented to the mind to have been, which really never was, will remain to be shown. And therefore how far the consciousness of past actions is annexed to any individual agent, so that another cannot possibly have it, will be hard for us to determine, till we know what kind of action it is that cannot be done without a reflex act of perception accompanying it, and how performed by thinking substances, who cannot think without being conscious of it. But that which we call the same consciousness, not being the same individual act, why one intellectual substance may not have represented to it, as done by itself, what it never did, and was perhaps done by some other agent; why, I say, such a representation may not possibly be without reality of matter of fact, as well as several representations in dreams are, which yet whilst dreaming we take for true, will be difficult to conclude from the nature of things. And that it never is so, will by us, till we have clearer views of the nature of thinking substances, be best resolved into the goodness of God, who, as far as the happiness or misery of any of his sensible creatures is concerned in it, will not, by a fatal error of theirs, transfer from one to another that consciousness which draws reward or punishment with it. How far this may be an argument against those who would place thinking in a system of fleeting animal spirits, I leave to be considered. But yet, to return to the question before us, it must be allowed, that, if the same consciousness (which, as has been shown, is quite a different thing from the same numerical figure or motion in body) can be transferred from one thinking substance to another, it will be possible that two thinking substances may make but one person. For the same consciousness being preserved, whether in the same or different substances, the personal identity is preserved.

14. As to the second part of the question, "Whether the same immaterial substance remaining, there may be two distinct person?" which question seems to me to be built on this, whether the same immaterial being, being conscious of the action of its past duration, may be wholly stripped of all the consciousness of its past existence, and lose it beyond the power of ever retrieving it again; and so as it were beginning a new account from a new period, have a consciousness that cannot reach beyond this new state. All those who hold pre-existence are evidently of this mind, since they allow the soul to have no remaining consciousness of what it did in that preexistent state, either wholly separate from body, or informing any other body; and if they should not, it is plain experience would be against them. So that personal identity reaching no further than consciousness reaches, a preexistent spirit not having continued so many ages in a state of silence, must needs make different persons. Suppose a Christian Platonist or a Pythagorean should, upon God's having ended all his works of creation the seventh day, think his soul hath existed ever since; and would imagine it has revolved in several human bodies, as I once met with one, who was persuaded his had been the soul of Socrates; (how reasonably I will not dispute; this I know, that in the post he filled, which was no inconsiderable one, he passed for a very rational man, and the press has shown that he wanted not parts or learning;) would any one say, that he, being not conscious of any of Socrates' actions or thoughts, could be the same person with Socrates? Let any one reflect upon himself, and conclude that he has in himself an immaterial spirit,

which is that which thinks in him, and, in the constant change of his body keeps him the same: and is that which he calls himself: let him also suppose it to be the same soul that was in Nestor or Thersites, at the siege of Troy (for souls being, as far as we know anything of them, in their nature indifferent to any parcel of matter, the supposition has no apparent absurdity in it), which it may have been, as well as it is now the soul of any other man: but he now having no consciousness of any of the actions either of Nestor or Thersites, does or can he conceive himself the same person with either of them? Can he be concerned in either of their actions? Attribute them to himself, or think them his own, more than the actions of any other men that ever existed? So that this consciousness not reaching to any of the actions of either of those men, he is no more one self with either of them, than if the soul or immaterial spirit that now informs him had been created, and began to exist, when it began to inform his present body, though it were ever so true, that the same spirit that informed Nestor's or Thersites' body were numerically the same that now informs his. For this would no more make him the same person with Nestor, than if some of the particles of matter that were once a part of Nestor, were now a part of this man; the same immaterial substance, without the same consciousness, no more making the same person by being united to any body, than the same particle of matter, without consciousness united to any body, makes the same person. But let him once find himself conscious of any of the actions of Nestor, he then finds himself the same person with Nestor.

15. And thus may we be able, without any difficulty, to conceive the same person at the resurrection, though in a body not exactly in make or parts the same which he had here, the same consciousness going along with the soul that inhabits it. But yet the soul alone, in the change of bodies, would scarce to any one but to him that makes the soul the man, be enough to make the same man. For should the soul of a prince, carrying with it the consciousness of the prince's past life, enter and inform the body of a cobbler, as soon as deserted by his own soul, every one sees he would be the same person with the prince, accountable only for the prince's actions: but who would say it was the same man? The body too goes to the making the man, and would, I guess, to everybody determine the man in this case; wherein the soul, with all its princely thoughts about it, would not make another man: but he would be the same cobbler to every one besides himself. I know that, in the ordinary way of speaking, the same person, and the same man, stand for one and the same thing. And indeed every one will always have a liberty to speak as he pleases, and to apply what articulate sounds to what ideas he thinks fit, and change them as often as he pleases. But yet, when we will inquire what makes the same spirit, man, or person, we must fix the ideas of spirit, man, or person in our minds, and having resolved with ourselves what we mean by them, it will not be hard to determine in either of them, or the like, when it is the same, and when not.

16. *Consciousness Makes the Same Person.*—But though the same immaterial substance or soul does not alone, wherever it be, and in whatsoever state, make the same man; yet it is plain, consciousness, as far as ever it can be extended, should it be to ages past, unites existences and actions, very remote in time into the same person, as well as it does the existences and actions of the immediately preceding moment: so that whatever has the consciousness of present and past actions, is the same person to whom they both belong. Had I the same consciousness that I saw the ark and Noah's flood, as that I saw an overflowing of the Thames last winter, or as that I write now; I could no more doubt that I who write this now, that saw the Thames overflowed last winter, and that viewed the flood at the general deluge, was the same self, place that self in what substance you please, than that I who write this am the same myself now whilst I write (whether I consist of all the same substance, material or immaterial, or no) that I was yesterday; for as to this point of being the same self, it matters not whether this present self be made up of the same or other substances; I being as much concerned, and as justly accountable for any action that was done a thousand years since, appropriated to me now by this self-consciousness, as I am for what I did the last moment.

17. *Self Depends on Consciousness.*—Self is that conscious thinking thing, whatever sub-

stance made up of (whether spiritual or material, simple or compounded, it matters not), which is sensible or conscious of pleasure and pain, capable of happiness or misery, and so is concerned for itself, as far as that consciousness extends. Thus every one finds, that, whilst comprehended under that consciousness, the little finger is as much a part of himself as what is most so. Upon separation of this little finger, should this consciousness go along with the little finger, and leave the rest of the body, it is evident the little finger would be the person, the same person, and self then would have nothing to do with the rest of the body. As in this case it is the consciousness that goes along with the substance, when one part is separate from another, which makes the same person, and constitutes this inseparable self; so it is in reference to substances remote in time. That with which the consciousness of this present thinking thing can join itself, makes the same person, and is one self with it, and with nothing else; and so attributes to itself, and owns all the actions of that thing as its own, as far as that consciousness reaches, and no further; as every one who reflects will perceive.

18. *Objects of Reward and Punishment.*—In this personal identity is founded all the right and justice of reward and punishment; happiness and misery being that for which every one is concerned for himself, and not mattering what becomes of any substance not joined to, or affected with that consciousness. For as it is evident in the instance I gave but now, if the consciousness went along with the little finger when it was cut off, that would be the same self which was concerned for the whole body yesterday, as making part of itself, whose actions then it cannot but admit as its own now. Though, if the same body should still live, and immediately from the separation of the little finger have its own peculiar consciousness, whereof the little finger knew nothing; it would not at all be concerned for it, as a part of itself, or could own any of its actions, or have any of them imputed to him.

19. This may show us wherein personal identity consists: not in the identity of substance, but, as I have said, in the identity of consciousness; wherein if Socrates and the present mayor of Queenborough agree, they are the same person: if the same Socrates waking and sleeping do not partake of the same consciousness, Socrates waking and sleeping is not the same person. And to punish Socrates waking for what sleeping Socrates thought, and waking Socrates was never conscious of, would be no more of right, than to punish one twin for what his brother-twin did, whereof he knew nothing, because their outsides were so like, that they could not be distinguished; for such twins have been seen.

20. But yet possibly it will still be objected, suppose I wholly lose the memory of some parts of my life, beyond a possibility of retrieving them, so that perhaps I shall never be conscious of them again; yet am I not the same person that did those actions, had those thoughts that I once was conscious of, though I have now forgot them? To which I answer, that we must here take notice what the word I is applied to; which, in this case, is the man only. And the same man being presumed to be the same person, I is easily here supposed to stand also for the same person. But if it be possible for the same man to have distinct incommunicable consciousness at different times, it is past doubt the same man would at different times make different persons; which, we see, is the sense of mankind in the solemnest declaration of their opinions; human laws not punishing the mad man for the sober man's actions, nor the sober man for what the mad man did, thereby making them two persons: which is somewhat explained by our way of speaking in English, when we say such an one is not himself, or is beside himself; in which phrases it is insinuated, as if those who now, or at least first used them, thought that self was changed, the selfsame person was no longer in that man.

21. *Difference Between Identity of Man and Person.*—But yet it is hard to conceive that Socrates, the same individual man, should be two persons. To help us a little in this, we must consider what is meant by Socrates, or the same individual man.

First, it must be either the same individual, immaterial, thinking substance; in short, the same numerical soul, and nothing else.

Secondly, or the same animal, without any regard to an immaterial soul.

Thirdly, or the same immaterial spirit united to the same animal.

Now, take which of these suppositions you

please, it is impossible to make personal identity to consist in anything but consciousness, or reach any further than that does.

For, by the first of them, it must be allowed possible that a man born of different women, and in distant times, may be the same man. A way of speaking, which whoever admits, must allow it possible for the same man to be two distinct persons, as any two that have lived in different ages, without the knowledge of one another's thoughts.

By the second and third, Socrates, in this life and after it, cannot be the same man any way, but by the same consciousness; and so making human identity to consist in the same thing wherein we place personal identity, there will be no difficulty to allow the same man to be the same person. But then they who place human identity in consciousness only, and not in something else, must consider how they will make the infant Socrates the same man with Socrates after the resurrection. But whatsoever to some men makes a man, and consequently the same individual man, wherein perhaps few are agreed, personal identity can by us be placed in nothing but consciousness (which is that alone which makes what we call self), without involving us in great absurdities.

22. But is not a man drunk and sober the same person? why else is he punished for the fact he commits when drunk, though he be never afterwards conscious of it? Just as much the same person as a man that walks, and does other things in his sleep, is the same person, and is answerable for any mischief he shall do in it. Human laws punish both, with a justice suitable to their way of knowledge; because, in these cases, they cannot distinguish certainly what is real, what counterfeit: and so the ignorance in drunkenness or sleep is not admitted as a plea. For, though punishment be annexed to personality, and personality to consciousness, and the drunkard perhaps be not conscious of what he did, yet human judicatures justly punish him, because the fact is proved against him, but want of consciousness cannot be proved for him. But in the great day, wherein the secrets of all hearts shall be laid open, it may be reasonable to think, no one shall be made to answer for what he knows nothing of; but shall receive his doom, his conscience accusing or excusing him.

23. *Consciousness Alone Makes Self.*—Nothing but consciousness can unite remote existences into the same person: the identity of substance will not do it; for whatever substance there is, however framed, without consciousness there is no person: and a carcass may be a person, as well as any sort of substance be so without consciousness.

Could we suppose two distinct incommunicable consciousnesses acting the same body, the one constantly by day, the other by night; and, on the other side, the same consciousness, acting by intervals, two distinct bodies; I ask, in the first case, whether the day and the night man would not be two as distinct persons as Socrates and Plato? And whether, in the second case, there would not be one person in two distinct bodies, as much as one man is the same in two distinct clothings? Nor is it at all material to say, that this same, and this distinct consciousness, in the cases above mentioned, is owing to the same and distinct immaterial substances, bringing it with them to those bodies; which, whether true or no, alters not the case; since it is evident the personal identity would equally be determined by the consciousness, whether that consciousness were annexed to some individual immaterial substance or no. For, granting that the thinking substance in man must be necessarily supposed immaterial, it is evident that immaterial thinking thing may sometimes part with its past consciousness, and be restored to it again, as appears in the forgetfulness men often have of their past actions: and the mind many times recovers the memory of a past consciousness, which it had lost for twenty years together. Make these intervals of memory and forgetfulness to take their turns regularly by day and night, and you have two persons with the same immaterial spirit, as much as in the former instance two persons with the same body. So that self is not determined by identity or diversity of substance, which it cannot be sure of, but only by identity of consciousness.

24. Indeed it may conceive the substance whereof it is now made up to have existed formerly, united in the same conscious being; but, consciousness removed, that substance is no more

itself, or makes no more a part of it, than any other substance; as is evident in the instance we have already given of a limb cut off, of whose heat, or cold, or other affections, having no longer any consciousness, it is no more of a man's self, than any other matter of the universe. In like manner it will be in reference to any immaterial substance, which is void of that consciousness whereby I am myself to myself: if there be any part of its existence which I cannot upon recollection join with that present consciousness, whereby I am now myself, it is in that part of its existence no more myself, than any other immaterial being. For whatsoever any substance has thought or done, which I cannot recollect, and by my consciousness make my own thought and action, it will no more belong to me, whether a part of me thought or did it, than if it had been thought or done by any other immaterial being anywhere existing.

25. I agree, the more probable opinion is, that this consciousness is annexed to, and the affection of, one individual immaterial substance.

But let men, according to their diverse hypotheses, resolve of that as they please; this very intelligent being, sensible of happiness or misery, must grant that there is something that is himself that he is concerned for, and would have happy; that this self has existed in a continued duration more than one instant, and therefore it is possible may exist, as it has done, months and years to come, without any certain bounds to be set to its duration; and may be the same self by the same consciousness continued on for the future. And thus, by this consciousness, he finds himself to be the same self which did such or such an action some years since, by which he comes to be happy or miserable now. In all which account of self, the same numerical substance is not considered as making the same self; but the same continued consciousness, in which several substances may have been united, and again separated from it; which, whilst they continued in a vital union with that wherein this consciousness then resided, made a part of that same self. Thus any part of our bodies vitally united to that which is conscious in us, makes a part of ourselves: but upon separation from the vital union by which that consciousness is communicated, that which a moment since was part of ourselves, is now no more so than a part of another man's self is a part of me: and it is not impossible but in a little time may become a real part of another person. And so we have the same numerical substance become a part of two different persons; and the same person preserved under the change of various substances. Could we suppose any spirit wholly stripped of all its memory or consciousness of past actions, as we find our minds always are of a great part of ours, and sometimes of them all; the union or separation of such a spiritual substance would make no variation of personal identity, any more than that of any particle of matter does. Any substance vitally united to the present thinking being, is a part of that very same self which now is; anything united to it by a consciousness of former actions, makes also a part of the same self, which is the same both then and now.

26. *Person a Forensic Term.*—Person, as I take it, is the name for this self. Wherever a man finds what he calls himself there, I think, another may say is the same person. It is a forensic term, appropriating actions and their merit; and so belongs only to intelligent agents capable of a law, and happiness, and misery. This personality extends itself beyond present existence to what is past, only by consciousness, whereby it becomes concerned and accountable, owns and imputes to itself past actions, just upon the same ground and for the same reason that it does the present. All which is founded in a concern for happiness, the unavoidable concomitant of consciousness; that which is conscious of pleasure and pain, desiring that that self that is conscious should be happy. And therefore whatever past actions it cannot reconcile or appropriate to that present self by consciousness, it can be no more concerned in, than if they had never been done; and to receive pleasure or pain, i.e., reward or punishment, on the account of any such action, is all one as to be made happy or miserable in its first being, without any demerit at all: for supposing a man punished now for what he had done in another life, whereof he could be made to have no consciousness at all, what difference is there between that punishment, and being created miserable? And therefore, conformable to this, the apostle tells us, that, at the great day, when every

one shall "receive according to his doings, the secrets of all hearts shall be laid open." The sentence shall be justified by the consciousness all persons shall have, that they themselves, in what bodies soever they appear, or what substances soever that consciousness adheres to, are the same that committed those actions, and deserve that punishment for them.

27. I am apt enough to think I have, in treating of this subject, made some suppositions that will look strange to some readers, and possibly they are so in themselves. But yet, I think they are such as are pardonable, in this ignorance we are in of the nature of that thinking thing that is in us, and which we look on as ourselves. Did we know what it was, or how it was tied to a certain system of fleeting animal spirits; or whether it could or could not perform its operations of thinking and memory out of a body organized as ours is: and whether it has pleased God, that no one such spirit shall ever be united to any one but such body, upon the right constitution of whose organs its memory should depend; we might see the absurdity of some of these suppositions I have made. But, taking as we ordinarily now do, (in the dark concerning these matters,) the soul of a man for an immaterial substance, independent from matter, and indifferent alike to it all, there can, from the nature of things, be no absurdity at all to suppose that the same soul may at different times be united to different bodies, and with them make up for that time one man, as well as we suppose a part of a sheep's body yesterday should be a part of a man's body to-morrow, and in that union make a vital part of Meliboeus himself, as well as it did of his ram.

28. *The Difficulty from Ill Use of Names.*—To conclude: Whatever substance begins to exist, it must, during its existence, necessarily be the same: whatever compositions of substances begin to exist, during the union of those substances the concrete must be the same; whatsoever mode begins to exist, during its existence it is the same; and so if the composition be of distinct substances and different modes, the same rule holds: whereby it will appear, that the difficulty or obscurity that has been about this matter rather rises from the names ill used, than from any obscurity in things themselves. For whatever makes the specific idea to which the name is applied, if that idea be steadily kept to, the distinction of anything into the same, and divers, will easily be conceived, and there can arise no doubt about it.

29. *Continued Existence Makes Identity.*—For, supposing a rational spirit be the idea of a man, it is easy to know what is the same man, viz., the same spirit, whether separate or in a body, will be the same man. Supposing a rational spirit vitally united to a body of a certain conformation of parts to make a man, whilst that rational spirit, with that vital conformation of parts, though continued in a fleeting successive body, remain, it will be the same man. But if to any one the idea of a man be but the vital union of parts in a certain shape, as long as that vital union and shape remain in a concrete no otherwise the same, but by a continued succession of fleeting particles, it will be the same man. For, whatever be the composition whereof the complex idea is made, whenever existence makes it one particular thing under any denomination, the same existence continued, preserves it the same individual under the same denomination.

Of Identity

THOMAS REID

Thomas Reid (1710–96) was the originator of the Scottish common-sense school of philosophy. His works include *Enquiry into the Human Mind on the Principles of Common Sense* and *Essays on the Intellectual Powers of Man.*

The conviction which every man has of his identity, as far back as his memory reaches, needs no aid of philosophy to strengthen it; and no philosophy can weaken it, without first producing some degree of insanity.

The philosopher, however, may very properly consider this conviction as a phenomenon of human nature worthy of his attention. If he can discover its cause, an addition is made to his stock of knowledge; it not, it must be held as a part of our original constitution, or an effect of that constitution produced in a manner unknown to us.

We may observe, first of all, that this conviction is indispensably necessary to all exercise of reason. The operations of reason, whether in action or in speculation, are made up of successive parts. The antecedent are the foundation of the consequent, and, without the conviction that the antecedent have been seen or done by me, I could have no reason to proceed to the consequent, in any speculation, or in any active project whatever.

There can be no memory of what is past without the conviction that we existed at the time remembered. There may be good arguments to convince me that I existed before the earliest thing I can remember; but to suppose that my memory reaches a moment farther back than my belief and conviction of my existence, is a contradiction.

The moment a man loses this conviction, as if he had drunk the water of Lethe, past things are done away; and, in his own belief, he then begins to exist. Whatever was thought, or said, or done, or suffered before that period, may belong to some other person; but he can never impute it to himself, or take any subsequent step that supposes it to be his doing.

From this it is evident that we must have the conviction of our own continued existence and identity, as soon as we are capable of thinking or doing anything, on account of what we have thought, or done, or suffered before; that is, as soon as we are reasonable creatures.

That we may form as distinct a notion as we are able of this phenomenon of the human mind, it is proper to consider what is meant by identity in general, what by our own personal identity, and how we are led into that invincible belief and conviction which every man has of his own personal identity, as far as his memory reaches.

Identity in general I take to be a relation between a thing which is known to exist at one time, and a thing which is known to have existed at another time. If you ask whether they are one and the same, or two different things, every man of common sense understands the meaning of your question perfectly. Whence we may infer with certainty, that every man of common sense has a clear and distinct notion of identity.

This selection is Chapter 4 "Of Memory," which is the third essay in Reid's *Essays on the Intellectual Powers of Man,* first published in 1785.

From *The Works of Thomas Reid,* vol. 2 (Charlestown, So. Carol.: Samuel Ethridge, Jr., 1814), pp. 338–44.

If you ask a definition of identity, I confess I can give none; it is too simple a notion to admit of logical definition: I can say it is a relation, but I cannot find words to express the specific difference between this and other relations, though I am in no danger of confounding it with any other. I can say that diversity is a contrary relation, and that similitude and dissimilitude are another couple of contrary relations, which every man easily distinguishes in his conception from identity and diversity.

I see evidently that identity supposes an uninterrupted continuance of existence. That which has ceased to exist cannot be the same with that which afterwards begins to exist; for this would be to suppose a being to exist after it ceased to exist, and to have had existence before it was produced, which are manifest contradictions. Continued uninterrupted existence is therefore necessarily implied in identity.

Hence we may infer, that identity cannot, in its proper sense, be applied to our pains, our pleasures, our thoughts, or any operation of our minds. The pain felt this day is not the same individual pain which I felt yesterday, though they may be *similar* in kind and degree, and have the same cause. The same may be said of every feeling, and of every operation of mind. They are all successive in their nature, like time itself, no two moments of which can be the same moment.

It is otherwise with the parts of absolute space. They always are, and were, and will be the same. So far, I think, we proceed upon clear ground in fixing the notion of identity in general.

It is perhaps more difficult to ascertain with precision the meaning of personality; but it is not necessary in the present subject: it is sufficient for our purpose to observe, that all mankind place their personality in something that cannot be divided, or consist of parts.

A part of a person is a manifest absurdity. When a man loses his estate, his health, his strength, he is still the same person, and has lost nothing of his personality. If he has a leg or an arm cut off, he is the same person he was before. The amputated member is no part of his person, otherwise it would have a right to a part of his estate, and be liable for a part of his engagements. It would be entitled to a share of his merit and demerit, which is manifestly absurd. A person is something indivisible, and is what Leibnitz calls a *monad*.

My personal identity, therefore, implies the continued existence of that indivisible thing which I call *myself*. Whatever this self may be, it is something which thinks, and deliberates, and resolves, and acts, and suffers. I am not thought, I am not action, I am not feeling; I am something that thinks, and acts, and suffers. My thoughts, and actions, and feelings, change every moment; they have no continued, but a successive, existence; but that *self*, or *I*, to which they belong, is permanent, and has the same relation to all the succeeding thoughts, actions, and feelings which I call mine.

Such are the notions that I have of my personal identity. But perhaps it may be said, this may all be fancy without reality. How do you know—what evidence have you—that there is such a permanent self which has a claim to all the thoughts, actions, and feelings which you call yours?

To this I answer, that the proper evidence I have of all this is remembrance. I remember that twenty years ago I conversed with such a person; I remember several things that passed in that conversation: my memory testifies, not only that this was done, but that it was done by me who now remember it. If it was done by me, I must have existed at that time, and continued to exist from that time to the present: if the identical person whom I call myself had not a part in that conversation, my memory is fallacious; it gives a distinct and positive testimony of what is not true. Every man in his senses believes what he distinctly remembers, and every thing he remembers convinces him that he existed at the time remembered.

Although memory gives the most irresistible evidence of my being the identical person that did such a thing, at such a time, I may have other good evidence of things which befell me, and which I do not remember: I know who bare me, and suckled me, but I do not remember these events.

It may here be observed (though the observation would have been unnecessary, if some great philosophers had not contradicted it), that it is not my remembering any action of mine that makes me to be the person who did it. This remembrance makes me to know assuredly that I did it; but I might have done it, though I did not remember it. That relation to me, which is expressed by saying that I did it, would be the same, though I had not the least remembrance of it. To say that my remembering that I did such a thing, or, as some choose to express it, my being conscious that I did it, makes me to have done it, appears to me as great an absurdity as it would be to say, that my belief that the world was created made it to be created.

When we pass judgment on the identity of other persons than ourselves, we proceed upon other grounds, and determine from a variety of circumstances, which sometimes produce the firmest assurance, and sometimes leave room for doubt. The identity of persons has often furnished matter of serious litigation before tribunals of justice. But no man of a sound mind ever doubted of his own identity, as far as he distinctly remembered.

The identity of a person is a perfect identity: wherever it is real, it admits of no degrees; and it is impossible that a person should be in part the same, and in part different; because a person is a *monad,* and is not divisible into parts. The evidence of identity in other persons than ourselves does indeed admit of all degrees, from what we account certainty, to the least degree of probability. But still it is true, that the same person is perfectly the same, and cannot be so in part, or in some degree only.

For this cause, I have first considered personal identity, as that which is perfect in its kind, and the natural measure of that which is imperfect.

We probably at first derive our notion of identity from that natural conviction which every man has from the dawn of reason of his own identity and continued existence. The operations of our minds are all successive, and have no continued existence. But the thinking being has a continued existence, and we have an invincible belief, that it remains the same when all its thoughts and operations change.

Our judgments of the identity of objects of sense seem to be formed much upon the same grounds as our judgments of the identity of other persons than ourselves.

Wherever we observe great similarity, we are apt to presume identity, if no reason appears to the contrary. Two objects ever so like, when they are perceived at the same time, cannot be the same; but if they are presented to our senses at different times, we are apt to think them the same, merely from their similarity.

Whether this be a natural prejudice, or from whatever cause it proceeds, it certainly appears in children from infancy; and when we grow up, it is confirmed in most instances by experience: for we rarely find two individuals of the same species that are not distinguishable by obvious differences.

A man challenges a thief whom he finds in possession of his horse or his watch, only on similarity. When the watchmaker swears that he sold this watch to such a person, his testimony is grounded on similarity. The testimony of witnesses to the identity of a person is commonly grounded on no other evidence.

Thus it appears, that the evidence we have of our own identity, as far back as we remember, is totally of a different kind from the evidence we have of the identity of other persons, or of objects of sense. The first is grounded on memory, and gives undoubted certainty. The last is grounded on similarity, and on other circumstances, which in many cases are not so decisive as to leave no room for doubt.

It may likewise be observed, that the identity of objects of sense is never perfect. All bodies, as they consist of innumerable parts that may be disjoined from them by a great variety of causes, are subject to continual changes of their substance, increasing, diminishing, changing insensibly. When such alterations are gradual, because language could not afford a different name for every different state of such a changeable being, it retains the same name, and is considered as the same thing. Thus we say of an old regiment, that it did such a thing a century ago, though there now is not a man alive who then belonged to it. We say a tree is the same in the seed-bed and in the forest. A ship of war, which has successively changed her anchors, her tackle, her sails, her masts, her planks, and her timbers, while she keeps the same name, is the same.

The identity, therefore, which we ascribe to bodies, whether natural or artificial, is not perfect identity; it is rather something which, for the conveniency of speech, we call identity. It admits of a great change of the subject, providing the change be gradual; sometimes, even of a total change. And the changes which in common language are made consistent with identity differ from those that are thought to destroy it, not in kind, but in number and degree. It has no fixed nature when applied to bodies; and questions about the identity of a body are very often questions about words. But identity, when applied to persons, has no ambiguity, and admits not of degrees, or of more and less. It is the foundation of all rights and obligations, and of all accountableness; and the notion of it is fixed and precise.

Of Personal Identity

DAVID HUME

There are some philosophers, who imagine we are every moment intimately conscious of what we call our SELF; that we feel its existence and its continuance in existence; and are certain, beyond the evidence of a demonstration, both of its perfect identity and simplicity. The strongest sensation, the most violent passion, say they, instead of distracting us from this view, only fix it the more intensely, and make us consider their influence on *self* either by their pain or pleasure. To attempt a farther proof of this were to weaken its evidence; since no proof can be deriv'd from any fact, of which we are so intimately conscious; nor is there any thing, of which we can be certain, if we doubt of this.

Unluckily all these positive assertions are contrary to that very experience, which is pleaded for them, not have we any idea of *self,* after the manner it is here explain'd. For from what impression cou'd this idea be deriv'd? This question 'tis impossible to answer without a manifest contradiction and absurdity; and yet 'tis a question, which must necessarily be answer'd, if we wou'd have the idea of self pass for clear and intelligible. It must be some one impression, that gives rise to every real idea. But self or person is not any one impression, but that to which our several impressions and ideas are suppos'd to have a reference. If any impression gives rise to the idea of self, that impression must continue invariably the same, thro' the whole course of our lives; since self is suppos'd to exist after that manner. But there is no impression constant and invariable. Pain and pleasure, grief and joy, passions and sensations succeed each other, and never all exist at the same time. It cannot, therefore, be from any of these impressions, or from any other, that the idea of self is deriv'd; and consequently there is no such idea.

But farther, what must become of all our particular perceptions upon this hypothesis? All these are different, and distinguishable, and separate from each other, and may be separately consider'd, and may exist separately, and have no need of any thing to support their existence. After what manner, therefore, do they belong to self; and how are they connected with it? For my part, when I enter most intimately into what I call *myself,* I always stumble on some particular perception or other, of heat or cold, light or shade, love or hatred, pain or pleasure. I never can catch *myself* at any time without a perception, and never can observe any thing but the perception. When my perceptions are remov'd for any time, as by sound sleep; so long am I insensible of *myself,* and may truly be said not to exist. And were all my perceptions remov'd by death, and cou'd I neither think, nor feel, nor see, nor love, nor hate after the dissolution of my body, I shou'd be entirely annihilated, nor do I conceive what is farther requisite to make me a perfect non-entity. If any one upon serious and unprejudic'd reflexion, thinks he has a different notion of *himself,* I must confess I can reason no longer with him. All I can allow him is, that he may be in the right as well as I, and that we are essentially different in this particular. He may, perhaps, perceive something simple and continu'd, which he calls *himself;* tho' I am certain there is no such principle in me.

From *A Treatise of Human Nature,* Selby-Bigge edition, rev. by P. H. Nidditch (Oxford: Oxford University Press, 1978), pp. 251–63.

But setting aside some metaphysicians of this kind, I may venture to affirm of the rest of mankind, that they are nothing but a bundle or collection of different perceptions, which succeed each other with an inconceivable rapidity, and are in a perpetual flux and movement. Our eyes cannot turn in their sockets without varying our perceptions. Our thought is still more variable than our sight; and all our other senses and faculties contribute to this change; nor is there any single power of the soul, which remains unalterably the same, perhaps for one moment. The mind is a kind of theatre, where several perceptions successively make their appearance; pass, re-pass, glide away, and mingle in an infinite variety of postures and situations. There is properly no *simplicity* in it at one time, nor *identity* in different; whatever natural propension we may have to imagine that simplicity and identity. The comparison of the theatre must not mislead us. They are the successive perceptions only, that constitute the mind; nor have we the most distant notion of the place, where these scenes are represented, or of the materials, of which it is compos'd.

What then gives us so great a propension to ascribe an identity to these successive perceptions, and to suppose ourselves possest of an invariable and uninterrupted existence thro' the whole course of our lives? In order to answer this question, we must distinguish betwixt personal identity, as it regards our thought or imagination, and as it regards our passions or the concern we take in ourselves. The first is our present subject; and to explain it perfectly we must take the matter pretty deep, and account for that identity, which we attribute to plants and animals; there being a great analogy betwixt it, and the identity of a self or person.

We have a distinct idea of an object, that remains invariable and uninterrupted thro' a suppos'd variation of time; and this idea we call that of *identity* or *sameness*. We have also a distinct idea of several different objects existing in succession, and connected together by a close relation; and this to an accurate view affords as perfect a notion of *diversity,* as if there was no manner of relation among the objects. But tho' these two ideas of identity, and a succession of related objects be in themselves perfectly distinct, and even contrary, yet 'tis certain, that in our common way of thinking they are generally confounded with each other. That action of the imagination, by which we consider the uninterrupted and invariable object, and that by which we reflect on the succession of related objects, are almost the same to the feeling, nor is there much more effort of thought requir'd in the latter case than in the former. The relation facilitates the transition of the mind from one subject to another, and renders its passage as smooth as if it contemplated one continu'd object. This resemblance is the cause of the confusion and mistake, and makes us substitute the notion of identity, instead of that of related objects. However at one instant we may consider the related succession as variable or interrupted, we are sure the next to ascribe to it a perfect identity, and regard it as invariable and uninterrupted. Our propensity to this mistake is so great from the resemblance above-mention'd, that we fall into it before we are aware; and tho' we incessantly correct ourselves by reflexion, and return to a more accurate method of thinking, yet we cannot long sustain our philosophy, or take off this bias from the imagination. Our last resource is to yield to it, and boldly assert that these different related objects are in effect the same, however interrupted and variable. In order to justify to ourselves this absurdity, we often feign some new and unintelligible principle, that connects the objects together, and prevents their interruption or variation. Thus we feign the continu'd existence of the perceptions of our senses, to remove the interruption; and run into the notion of a *soul,* and *self,* and *substance,* to disguise the variation. But we may farther observe, that where we do not give rise to such a fiction, our propension to confound identity with relation is so great, that we are apt to imagine[1] something unknown and mysterious, connecting the parts, beside their relation; and this I take to be the case with regard to the identity we ascribe to plants and vegetables. And even when this does not take place, we still feel a propensity to confound these ideas, tho' we are not able fully to satisfy ourselves in that particular, nor find any thing invariable and uninterrupted to justify our notion of identity.

Thus the controversy concerning identity is not merely a dispute of words. For when we attribute identity, in an improper sense, to variable or interrupted objects, our mistake is not confin'd to the expression, but is commonly attended with a fiction, either of something invariable and uninterrupted, or of something mysterious and inexplicable, or at least with a propensity to such fictions. What will suffice to prove this hypothesis to the satisfaction of every fair enquirer, is to shew from daily experience and observation, that the objects, which are variable or interrupted, and yet are suppos'd to continue the same, are such only as consist of a succession of parts, connected together by resemblance, contiguity, or causation. For as such a succession answers evidently to our notion of diversity, it can only be by mistake we ascribe to it an identity; and as the relation of parts, which leads us into this mistake, is really nothing but a quality, which produces an association of ideas, and an easy transition of the imagination from one to another, it can only be from the resemblance, which this act of the mind bears to that, by which we contemplate one continu'd object, that the error arises. Our chief business, then, must be to prove, that all objects, to which we ascribe identity, without observing their invariableness and uninterruptedness, are such as consist of a succession of related objects.

In order to [do] this, suppose any mass of matter, of which the parts are contiguous and connected, to be plac'd before us; 'tis plain we must attribute a perfect identity to this mass, provided all the parts continue uninterruptedly and invariably the same, whatever motion or change of place we may observe either in the whole or in any of the parts. But supposing some very *small* or *inconsiderable* part to be added to the mass, or substracted from it; tho' this absolutely destroys the identity of the whole, strictly speaking; yet as we seldom think so accurately, we scruple not to pronounce a mass of matter the same, where we find so trivial an alteration. The passage of the thought from the object before the change to the object after it, is so smooth and easy, that we scarce perceive the transition, and are apt to imagine, that 'tis nothing but a continu'd survey of the same object.

There is a very remarkable circumstance, that attends this experiment; which is, that tho' the change of any considerable part in a mass of matter destroys the identity of the whole, yet we must measure the greatness of the part, not absolutely, but by its *proportion* to the whole. The addition or diminution of a mountain wou'd not be sufficient to produce a diversity in a planet; tho' the change of a very few inches wou'd be able to destroy the identity of some bodies. 'Twill be impossible to account for this, but by reflecting that objects operate upon the mind, and break or interrupt the continuity of its actions not according to their real greatness, but according to their proportion to each other: And therefore, since this interruption makes an object cease to appear the same, it must be the uninterrupted progress of the thought, which constitutes the imperfect identity.

This may be confirm'd by another phenomenon. A change in any considerable part of a body destroys its identity; but 'tis remarkable, that where the change is produc'd *gradually* and *insensibly* we are less apt to ascribe to it the same effect. The reason can plainly be no other, than that the mind, in following the successive changes of the body, feels an easy passage from the surveying its condition in one moment to the viewing of it in another, and at no particular time perceives any interruption in its actions. From which continu'd perception, it ascribes a continu'd existence and identity to the object.

But whatever precaution we may use in introducing the changes gradually, and making them proportionable to the whole, 'tis certain, that where the changes are at last observ'd to become considerable, we make a scruple of ascribing identity to such different objects. There is, however, another artifice, by which we may induce the imagination to advance a step farther; and that is, by producing a reference of the parts to each other, and a combination to some *common end* or purpose. A ship, of which a considerable part has been chang'd by frequent reparations, is still consider'd as the same; nor does the difference of the materials hinder us from ascribing an identity to it. The common end, in which the parts conspire, is the same under all their variations, and affords an easy transition of the imagination from one situation of the body to another.

But this is still more remarkable, when we add a *sympathy* of parts fo their *common end,* and suppose that they bear to each other, the reciprocal relation of cause and effect in all their actions and operations. This is the case with all animals and vegetables; where not only the several parts have a reference to some general purpose, but also a mutual dependence on, and connexion with each other. The effect of so strong a relation is, that tho' every one must allow, that in a very few years both vegetables and animals endure a *total* change, yet we still attribute identity to them, while their form, size, and substance are entirely alter'd. An oak, that grows from a small plant to a large tree, is still the same oak; tho' there be not one particle of matter, or figure of its parts the same. An infant becomes a man, and is sometimes fat, sometimes lean, without any change in his identity.

We may also consider the two following phenomena, which are remarkable in their kind. The first is, that tho' we commonly be able to distinguish pretty exactly betwixt numerical and specific identity, yet it sometimes happens, that we confound them, and in our thinking and reasoning employ the one for the other. Thus a man, who hears a noise, that is frequently interrupted and renew'd, says, it is still the same noise; tho' 'tis evident that sounds have only a specific identity or resemblance, and there is nothing numerically the same, but the cause, which produc'd them. In like manner it may be said without breach of the propriety of language, that such a church, which was formerly of brick, fell to ruin, and that the parish rebuilt the same church of free-stone, and according to modern architecture. Here neither the form nor materials are the same, nor is there any thing common to the two objects, but their relation to the inhabitants of the parish; and yet this alone is sufficient to make us denominate them the same. But we must observe, that in these cases the first object is in a manner annihilated before the second comes into existence; by which means, we are never presented in any one point of time with the idea of difference and multiplicity; and for that reason are less scrupulous in calling them the same.

Secondly, We may remark, that tho' in a succession of related objects, it be in a manner requisite, that the change of parts be not sudden nor entire, in order to preserve the identity, yet where the objects are in their nature changeable and inconstant, we admit of a more sudden transition, than wou'd otherwise be consistent with that relation. Thus as the nature of a river consists in the motion and change of parts; tho' in less than four and twenty hours these be totally alter'd; this hinders not the river from continuing the same during several ages. What is natural and essential to any thing is, in a manner, and appears of less moment, than what is unusual and extraordinary. A considerable change of the former kind seems really less to the imagination, than the most trivial alteration of the latter; and by breaking less the continuity of the thought, has less influence in destroying the identity.

We now proceed to explain the nature of *personal identity,* which has become so great a question in philosophy, especially of late years in *England,* where all the abstruser sciences are study'd with a peculiar ardour and application. And here 'tis evident, the same method of reasoning must be continu'd, which has so successfully explain'd the identity of plants, and animals, and ships, and houses, and of all the compounded and changeable productions either of art or nature. The identity, which we ascribe to the mind of man, is only a fictitious one, and of a like kind with that which we ascribe to vegetables and animal bodies. It cannot, therefore, have a different origin, but must proceed from a like operation of the imagination upon like objects.

But lest this argument shou'd not convince the reader; tho' in my opinion perfectly decisive; let him weigh the following reasoning, which is still closer and more immediate. 'Tis evident, that the identity, which we attribute to the human mind, however perfect we may imagine it to be, is not able to run the several different perceptions into one, and make them lose their characters of distinction and difference, which are essential to them. 'Tis still true, that every distinct perception, which enters into the composition of the mind, is a distinct existence, and is different, and distinguishable, and separable from every other perception, either contemporary or successive. But, as, notwithstanding this distinction and separability, we suppose the whole train of perceptions to be united by identity, a question naturally arises concerning this relation of identity; whether it be something that really binds our several perceptions together, or only associates their ideas in the imagination. That is, in other words, whether in pronouncing concerning the identity of a person, we observe some real bond among his perceptions, or only feel one among the ideas we form of them. This question we might easily decide, if we wou'd recollect what has been already prov'd at large, that the understanding never observes any real connexion among objects, and that even the union of cause and effect, when strictly examin'd, resolves itself into a customary association of ideas. For from thence it evidently follows, that identity is nothing really belonging to these different perceptions, and uniting them together; but is merely a quality, which we attribute to them, because of the union of their ideas in the imagination, when we reflect upon them. Now the only qualities, which can give ideas an union in the imagination, are these three relations above-mention'd. These are the uniting principles in the ideal world, and without them every distinct object is separable by mind, and may be separately consider'd, and appears not to have any more connexion with any other object, than if disjoin'd by the greatest difference and remoteness. 'Tis, therefore, on some of these three relations of resemblance, contiguity and causation, that identity depends; and as the very essence of these relations consists in their producing an easy transition of ideas; it follows, that our notions or personal identity, proceed entirely from the smooth and uninterrupted progress of the thought along a train of connected ideas, according to the principles above-explain'd.

The only question, therefore, which remains, is, by what relations this uninterrupted progress of our thought is produc'd, when we consider the successive existence of a mind or thinking person. And here 'tis evident we must confine ourselves to resemblance and causation, and must drop contiguity, which has little or no influence in the present case.

To begin with *resemblance;* suppose we cou'd see clearly into the breast of another, and observe that succession of perceptions, which constitutes his mind or thinking principle, and suppose that he always preserves the memory of a considerable part of past perceptions; 'tis evident that nothing cou'd more contribute to the bestowing a relation on this succession amidst all its variations. For what is the memory but a faculty, by which we raise up the images of past perceptions? And as an image necessarily resembles its object, must not the frequent placing of these resembling perceptions in the chain of thought, convey the imagination more easily from one link to another, and make the whole seem like the continuance of one object? In this particular, then, the memory not only discovers the identity, but also contributes to its production, by producing the relation of resemblance among the perceptions. The case is the same whether we consider ourselves or others.

As to *causation;* we may observe, that the true idea of the human mind, is to consider it as a system of different perceptions or different existences, which are link'd together by the relation of cause and effect, and mutually produce, destroy, influence, and modify each other. Our impressions give rise to their correspondent ideas; and these ideas in their turn produce other impressions. One thought chaces another, and draws after it a third, by which it is expell'd in its turn. In this respect, I cannot compare the soul more properly to any thing than to a republic or commonwealth, in which the several members are united by the reciprocal ties of government and subordination, and give rise to other persons, who propagate the same republic in the incessant changes of its parts. And as the same individual republic may not only change its members, but also its laws and constitutions; in like manner the same person may vary his character and disposition, as well as his impressions and ideas, without losing his identity. Whatever changes he endures, his several parts are still connected by the relation of causation. And in this view our identity with regard to the passions serves to corroborate that with regard to the imagination, by the making our distant perceptions influence each other, and by giving us a present concern for our past or future pains or pleasures.

As memory alone acquaints us with the continuance and extent of this succession of perceptions, 'tis to be consider'd, upon that account chiefly, as the source of personal identity. Had we no memory, we never shou'd have any notion of causation, nor consequently of that chain of causes and effects, which constitute our self or person. But having once acquir'd this notion of causation from the memory, we can extend the same chain of causes, and consequently the identity of our persons beyond our memory, and can comprehend times, and circumstances, and actions, which we have entirely forgot, but suppose in general to have existed. For how few of our past actions are there, of which we have any memory? Who can tell me, for instance, what were his thoughts and actions on the first of *January* 1715, the 11th of *March* 1719, and the 3d of *August* 1733? Or will he affirm, because he has entirely forgot the incidents of these days, that the present self is not the same person with the self of that time; and by that means overturn all the most establish'd notions of personal identity? In this view, therefore, memory does not so much *produce* as *discover* personal identity, by shewing us the relation of cause and effect among our different perceptions. 'Twill be incumbent on those, who affirm that memory produces entirely our personal identity, to give a reason why we can thus extend our identity beyond our memory.

The whole of this doctrine leads us to a conclusion, which is of great importance in the present affair, viz. that all the nice and subtile questions concerning personal identity can never possibly be decided, and are to be regarded rather as grammatical than as philosophical difficulties. Identity depends on the relations of ideas; and these relations produce identity, by means of that easy transition they occasion. But as the relations, and the easiness of the transition may diminish by insensible degrees, we have no just standard, by which we can decide any dispute concerning the time, when they acquire or lose a title to the name of identity. All the disputes concerning the identity of connected objects are merely verbal, except so far as the relation of parts gives rise to some fiction or imaginary principle of union, as we have already observ'd.

What I have said concerning the first origin and uncertainty of our notion of identity, as apply'd to the human mind, may be extended with little or no variation to that of *simplicity*. An object, whose different co-existent parts are bound together by a close relation, operates upon the imagination after much the same manner as one perfectly simple and indivisible, and requires not a much greater stretch of thought in order to its conception. From this similarity of operation we attribute a simplicity to it, and feign a principle of union as the support of this simplicity, and the center of all the different parts and qualities of the object.

Thus we have finish'd our examination of the several systems of philosophy, both of the intellectual and natural world; and in our miscellaneous way of reasoning have been led into several topics; which will either illustrate and confirm some preceding part of this discourse, or prepare the way for our following opinions. 'Tis now time to return to a more close examination of our subject, and to proceed in the accurate anatomy of human nature, having fully explain'd the nature of our judgment and understanding.

Note

1. If the reader is desirous to see how a great genius may be influenc'd by these seemingly trivial principles of the imagination, as well as the mere vulgar, let him read my Lord *Shaftsbury's* reasonings concerning the uniting principle of the universe, and the identity of plants and animals. See his *Moralists:* or, *Philosophical rhapsody*.

The Self and the Future

BERNARD WILLIAMS

Bernard Williams (1929–) is Knightbridge Professor of Philosophy at Cambridge University and a fellow of Kings College. His publications include *Morality* and *Problems of the Self.*

Suppose that there were some process to which two persons, *A* and *B*, could be subjected as a result of which they might be said—question-beggingly—to have *exchanged bodies*. That is to say—less question-beggingly—there is a certain human body which is such that when previously we were confronted with it, we were confronted with person *A*, certain utterances coming from it were expressive of memories of the past experiences of *A*, certain movements of it partly constituted the actions of *A* and were taken as expressive of the character of *A*, and so forth; but now, after the process is completed, utterances coming from this body are expressive of what seem to be just those memories which previously we identified as memories of the past experiences of *B*, its movements partly constitute actions expressive of the character of *B*, and so forth; and conversely with the other body.

There are certain important philosophical limitations on how such imaginary cases are to be constructed, and how they are to be taken when constructed in various ways. I shall mention two principal limitations, not in order to pursue them further here, but precisely in order to get them out of the way.

There are certain limitations, particularly with regard to character and mannerisms, to our ability to imagine such cases even in the most restricted sense of our being disposed to take the later performances of that body which was previously *A*'s as expressive of *B*'s character; if the previous *A* and *B* were extremely unlike one another both physically and psychologically, and if, say, in addition, they were of different sex, there might be grave difficulties in reading *B*'s dispositions in any possible performances of *A*'s body. Let us forget this, and for the present purpose just take *A* and *B* as being sufficiently alike (however alike that has to be) for the difficulty not to arise; after the experiment, persons familiar with *A* and *B* are just *overwhelmingly struck* by the *B*-ish character of the doings associated with what was previously *A*'s body and conversely. Thus the feat of imagining an exchange of bodies is supposed possible in the most restricted sense. But now there is a further limitation which has to be overcome if the feat is to be not merely possible in the most restricted sense but also is to have an outcome which, on serious reflection, we are prepared to describe as *A* and *B* having changed bodies—that is, an outcome where, confronted with what was previously *A*'s body, we are prepared seriously to say that we are now confronted with *B*.

It would seem a necessary condition of so doing that the utterances coming from that body be taken as genuinely expressive of memories of *B*'s past. But memory is a causal notion; and as we actually use it, it seems a necessary condition on *x*'s present knowledge of *x*'s earlier experiences constituting memory of those experiences that the

From the *Philosophical Review* 79, no. 2 (April 1970), pp. 161–80.

causal chain linking the experiences and the knowledge should not run outside *x*'s body. Hence if utterances coming from a given body are to be taken as expressive of memories of the experiences of *B*, there should be some suitable causal link between the appropriate state of that body and the original happening of those experiences to *B*. One radical way of securing that condition in the imagined exchange case is to suppose, with Shoemaker,[1] that the brains of *A* and of *B* are transposed. We may not need so radical a condition. Thus suppose it were possible to extract information from a man's brain and store it in a device while his brain was repaired, or even renewed, the information then being replaced: it would seem exaggerated to insist that the resultant man could not possibly have the memories he had before the operation. With regard to our knowledge of our own past, we draw distinctions between merely recalling, being reminded, and learning again, and those distinctions correspond (roughly) to distinctions between no new input, partial new input, and total new input with regard to the information in question; and it seems clear that the information-parking case just imagined would not count as new input in the sense necessary and sufficient for "learning again." Hence we can imagine the case we are concerned with in terms of information extracted into such devices from *A*'s and *B*'s brains and replaced in the other brain; this is the sort of model which, I think not unfairly for the present argument, I shall have in mind.

We imagine the following. The process considered above exists; two persons can enter some machine, let us say, and emerge changed in the appropriate ways. If *A* and *B* are the persons who enter, let us call the persons who emerge the *A-body-person* and the *B-body-person:* the *A*-body-person is that person (whoever it is) with whom I am confronted when, after the experiment, I am confronted with that body which previously was *A*'s body—that is to say, that person who would naturally be taken for *A* by someone who just saw this person, was familiar with *A*'s appearance before the experiment, and did not know about the happening of the experiment. A non-question-begging description of the experiment will leave it open which (if either) of the persons *A* and *B* the *A*-body-person is; the description of the experiment as "persons changing bodies" of course implies that the *A*-body-person is actually *B*.

We take two persons *A* and *B* who are going to have the process carried out on them. (We can suppose, rather hazily, that they are willing for this to happen; to investigate at all closely at this stage why they might be willing or unwilling, what they would fear, and so forth, would anticipate some later issues.) We further announce that one of the two resultant persons, the *A*-body-person and the *B*-body-person, is going after the experiment to be given $100,000, while the other is going to be tortured. We then ask each *A* and *B* to choose which treatment should be dealt out to which of the persons who will emerge from the experiment, the choice to be made (if it can be) on selfish grounds.

Suppose that *A* chooses that the *B*-body-person should get the pleasant treatment and the *A*-body-person the unpleasant treatment; and *B* chooses conversely (this might indicate that they thought that "changing bodies" was indeed a good description of the outcome). The experimenter cannot act in accordance with both of these sets of perferences, those expressed by *A* and those expressed by *B*. Hence there is one clear sense in which *A* and *B* cannot both get what they want: namely, that if the experimenter, before the experiment, announces to *A* and *B* that he intends to carry out the alternative (for example), of treating the *B*-body-person unpleasantly and the *A*-body-person pleasantly—then *A* can say rightly, "That's just the outcome I chose to happen." So, evidently, *A* and *B* before the experiment can each come to know either that the outcome he chose will be that which will happen, or that the one he chose will not happen, and in that sense they can get or fail to get what they wanted. But is it also true that when the experimenter proceeds *after* the experiment to act in accordance with one of the preferences and not the other, then one of *A* and *B* will have got what he wanted, and the other not?

There seems very good ground for saying so. For suppose the experimenter, having elicited *A*'s and *B*'s preference, says nothing to *A* and *B* about what he will do; conducts the experiment; and then, for example, gives the unpleasant treatment to the *B*-body-person and the pleasant treatment to the *A*-body-person. Then the *B*-body-person will not only complain of the unpleasant treatment as such, but will complain (since he has *A*'s memories) that that was not the outcome he chose, since he chose the *B*-body-person should be well treated; and since *A* made his choice in selfish spirit, he may add that he precisely chose in that way because he did not want the unpleasant things to happen to *him*. The *A*-body-person meanwhile will express satisfaction both at the receipt of the $100,000, and also at the fact that the experimenter has chosen to act in the way that he, *B*, so wisely chose. These facts make a strong case for saying that the experimenter has brought it about that *B* did in the outcome get what he wanted and *A* did not. It is therefore a strong case for saying that the *B*-body-person really is *A*, and the *A*-body-person really is *B;* and therefore for saying that the process of the experiment really is that of changing bodies. For the same reasons it would seem that *A* and *B* in our example really did choose wisely, and that it was *A*'s bad luck that the choice he correctly made was not carried out, *B*'s good luck that the choice he correctly made was carried out. This seems to show that to care about what happens to me in the future is not necessarily to care about what happens to *this* body (the one I now have); and this in turn might be taken to show that in some sense of Descartes's obscure phrase, I and my body are "really distinct" (though, of course, nothing in these considerations could support the idea that I could exist without a body at all).

These suggestions seem to be reinforced if we consider the cases where *A* and *B* make other choices with regard to the experiment. Suppose that *A* chooses that the *A*-body-person should get the money, and the *B*-body-person get the pain, and *B* chooses conversely. Here again there can be no outcome which matches the expressed preferences of both of them: they cannot both get what they want. The experimenter announces, before the experiment, that the *A*-body-person will in fact get the money, and the *B*-body-person will get the pain. So *A* at this stage gets what he wants (the announced outcome matches his expressed preference). After the experiment, the distribution is carried out as announced. Both the *A*-body-person and the *B*-body-person will have to agree that what is happening is in accordance with the preference that *A* originally expressed. The *B*-body-person will naturally express this acknowledgment (since he has *A*'s memories) by saying that this is the distribution he chose; he will recall, among other things, the experimenter announcing this outcome, his approving it as what he chose, and so forth. However, he (the *B*-body-person) certainly does not like what is now happening to him, and would much prefer to be receiving what the *A*-body-person is receiving—namely, $100,000. The *A*-body-person will on the other hand recall choosing an outcome other than this one, but will reckon it good luck that the experimenter did not do what he recalls choosing. It looks, then, as though the *A*-body-person had gotten what he wanted, but not what he chose, while the *B*-body-person has gotten what he chose, but not what he wanted. So once more it looks as though they are, respectively, *B* and *A;* and that in this case the original choices of both *A* and *B* were unwise.

Suppose, lastly, that in the original choice *A* takes the line of the first case and *B* of the second: that is *A* chooses that the *B*-body-person should get the money and the *A*-body-person the pain, and *B* chooses exactly the same thing. In this case, the experimenter would seem to be in the happy situation of giving both persons what they want—or at least, like God, what they have chosen. In this case, the *B*-body-person likes what he is receiving, recalls choosing it, and congratulates himself on the wisdom of (as he puts it) his choice; while the *A*-body-person does not like what he is receiving, recalls choosing it, and is forced to acknowledge that (as he puts it) his choice was unwise. So once more we seem to get results to support the suggestions drawn from the first case.

Let us now consider the question, not of *A* and *B* choosing certain outcomes to take place after the experiment, but of their willingness to engage in the experiment at all. If they were initially inclined to accept the description of the experiment as "changing bodies" then one thing that would interest them would be the character of the other person's body. In this respect also what would happen after the experiment would seem to suggest that "changing bodies" was a good description of the experiment. If *A* and *B* agreed to the experiment, being each not displeased with the appearance, physique, and so forth of the other person's body; after the experiment the *B*-body-person might well be found saying such things as: "When I agreed to this experiment, I thought that *B*'s face was quite attractive, but now I look at it in the mirror, I am not so sure"; or the *A*-body-person might say "When I agreed to this experiment I did not know that *A* had a wooden leg; but now, after it is over, I find that I have this wooden leg, and I want the experiment reversed." It is possible that he might say further that he finds the leg very uncomfortable, and that the *B*-body-person should say, for instance, that he recalls that he found it very uncomfortable at first, but one gets used to it: but perhaps one would need to know more than at least I do about the physiology of habituation to artificial limbs to know whether the *A*-body-person would find the leg uncomfortable: that body, after all, has had the leg on it for some time. But apart from this sort of detail, the general line of the outcome regarded from this point of view seems to confirm our previous conclusions about the experiment.

Now let us suppose that when the experiment is proposed (in non-question-begging terms) *A* and *B* think rather of their psychological advantages and disadvantages. *A*'s thoughts turn primarily to certain sorts of anxiety to which he is very prone, while *B* is concerned with the frightful memories he has of past experiences which still distress him. They each hope that the experiment will in some way result in their being able to get away from these things. They may even have been impressed by philosophical arguments to the effect that bodily continuity is at least a necessary condition of personal identity: *A*, for example, reasons that, granted the experiment comes off, then the person who is bodily continuous with him will not have this anxiety, while the other person will no doubt have some anxiety—perhaps in some sense his anxiety—and at least that person will not be he. The experiment is performed and the experimenter (to whom *A* and *B* previously revealed privately their several difficulties and hopes) asks the *A*-body-person whether he has gotten rid of his anxiety. This person presumably replies that he does not know what the man is talking about; he never had such anxiety, but he did have some very disagreeable memories, and recalls engaging in the experiment to get rid of them, and is disappointed to discover that he still has them. The *B*-body-person will react in a similar way to questions about his painful memories, pointing out that he still has his anxiety. These results seem to confirm still further the description of the experiment as "changing bodies." And all the results suggest that the only rational thing to do, confronted with such an experiment, would be to identify oneself with one's memories, and so forth, and not with one's body. The philosophical arguments designed to show that bodily continuity was at least a necessary condition of personal identity would seem to be just mistaken.

Let us now consider something apparently different. Someone in whose power I am tells me that I am going to be tortured tomorrow. I am frightened, and look forward to tomorrow in great apprehension. He adds that when the time comes, I shall not remember being told that this was going to happen to me, since shortly before the torture something else will be done to me which will make me forget the announcement. This certainly will not cheer me up, since I know perfectly well that I can forget things, and that there is such a thing as indeed being tortured unexpectedly because I had forgotten or been made to forget a prediction of the torture: that will still be a torture which, so long as I do know about the prediction, I look forward to in fear. He then adds that my forgetting the announcement will be only part of a larger process: when the moment of torture comes, I shall not remember any of the things I am now in a position to remember. This does not cheer me up, either, since I can readily conceive of being involved in an accident, for instance, as a result of which I wake up in a completely amnesiac state and also in great pain; that could certainly happen to me, I should not like it to happen to me, nor to know that it was going to happen to me. He now further adds that at the moment of torture I shall not only not remember the things I am now in a position to remember, but will have a different set of impressions of my past, quite different from the memories I now have. I do not think that this would cheer me up, either. For I can at least conceive the possibility, if not the concrete reality, of going completely mad, and thinking perhaps that I am George IV or somebody; and being told that something like that was going to happen to me would have no tendency to reduce the terror of being told authoritatively that I was going to be tortured, but would merely compound the horror. Nor do I see why I should be put into any better frame of mind by the person in charge adding lastly that the impressions of my past with which I shall be equipped on the eve of torture will exactly fit the past of another person now living, and that indeed I shall acquire these impressions by (for instance) information now in his brain being copied into mine. Fear, surely, would still be the proper reaction: and not because one did not know what was going to happen, but because in one vital respect at least one did know what was going to happen—torture, which one can indeed expect to happen to oneself, and to be preceded by certain mental derangements as well.

If this is right, the whole question seems now to be totally mysterious. For what we have just been through is of course merely one side, differently represented, of the transaction which we considered before; and it represents it as a perfectly hateful prospect, while the previous considerations represented it as something one should rationally, perhaps even cheerfully, choose out of the options there presented. It is differently presented, of course, and in two notable respects; but when we look at these two differences of presentation, can we really convince ourselves that the second presentation is wrong or misleading, thus leaving the road open to the first version which at the time seemed so convincing? Surely not.

The first difference is that in the second version the torture is throughout represented as going to happen to *me:* "you," the man in charge persistently says. Thus he is not very neutral. But should he have been neutral? Or, to put it another way, does his use of the second person have a merely emotional and rhetorical effect on me, making me afraid when further reflection would have shown that I had no reason to be? It is certainly not obviously so. The problem just is that through every step of his predictions I seem to be able to follow him successfully. And if I reflect on whether what he has said gives me grounds for fearing that I shall be tortured, I could consider that behind my fears lies some principle such as this: that my undergoing physical pain in the future is not excluded by any psychological state I may be in at the time, with the platitudinous exception of those psychological states which in themselves exclude experiencing pain, notably (if it is a psychological state) unconsciousness. In particular, what impressions I have about the past will not have any effect on whether I undergo the pain or not. This principle seems sound enough.

It is an important fact that not everything I would, as things are, regard as an evil would be something that I should rationally fear as an evil if it were predicted that it would happen to me in the future and also predicted that I should undergo significant psychological changes in the meantime. For the fact that I regard that happening, things being as they are, as an evil can be dependent on factors of belief or character which might themselves be modified by the psychological changes in question. Thus if I am appallingly subject to acrophobia, and am told that I shall find myself on top of a steep mountain in the near future, I shall to that extent be afraid; but if I am told that I shall be psychologically changed in the meantime in such a way as to rid me of my acrophobia (and as with the other prediction, I believe it), then I have no reason to be afraid of the predicted happening, or at least not the same reason. Again, I might look forward to meeting a certain person again with either alarm or excitement because of my memories of our past relations. In some part, these memories operate in connection with my emotion, not only on the present time, but projectively forward: for it is to a meeting itself affected by the presence of those memories that I look forward. If I am convinced that when the time comes I shall not have those memories, then I shall not have just the same reasons as before for looking forward to that meeting with the one emotion or the other. (Spiritualism, incidentally, appears to involve the belief that I have just the same reasons for a given attitude toward encountering people again after I am dead, as I did before: with the one modification that I can be sure it will all be very nice.)

Physical pain, however, the example which for simplicity (and not for any obsessional reason) I have taken, is absolutely minimally dependent on character or belief. No amount of change in my character or my beliefs would seem to affect substantially the nastiness of tortures applied to me; correspondingly, no degree of predicted change in my character and beliefs can unseat the fear of torture which, together with those changes, is predicted for me.

I am not at all suggesting that the *only* basis, or indeed the only rational basis, for fear in the face of these various predictions is how things will be relative to my psychological state in the eventual outcome. I am merely pointing out that this is one component; it is not the only one. For certainly one will fear and otherwise reject the changes themselves, or in very many cases one would. Thus one of the old paradoxes of hedonistic utilitarianism; if one had assurances that undergoing certain operations and being attached to a machine would provide one for the rest of one's existence with an unending sequence of delicious and varied experiences, one might very well reject the option, and react with fear if someone proposed to apply it compulsorily; and that fear and horror would seem appropriate reactions in the second case may help to discredit the interpretation (if anyone has the nerve to propose it) that one's reason for rejecting the option voluntarily would be a consciousness of duties to others which one in one's hedonic state would leave undone. The prospect of contented madness or vegetableness if found by many (not perhaps by all) appalling in ways which are obviously not a function of how things would then be for them, for things would then be for them not appalling. In the case we are at present discussing, these sorts of considerations seem merely to make it clearer that the predictions of the man in charge provide a double ground of horror: at the prospect of torture, and at the prospect of the change in character and in impressions of the past that will precede it. And certainly, to repeat what has already been said, the prospect of the second certainly seems to provide no ground for rejecting or not fearing the prospect of the first.

I said that there were two notable differences between the second presentation of our situation and the first. The first difference, which we have just said something about, was that the man predicted the torture for *me*, a psychologically very changed "me." We have yet to find a reason for saying that he should not have done this, or that I really should be unable to follow him if he does; I seem to be able to follow him only too well. The second difference is that in this presentation he does not mention the other man, except in the somewhat incidental role of being the provenance of the impressions of the past I end up with. He does not mention him at all as someone who will end up with the impressions of the past derived from me (and, incidentally, with $100,000 as well—a consideration which, in the frame of mind appropriate to this version, will merely make me jealous).

But why *should* he mention this man and what is going to happen to him? My selfish concern is to be told what is going to happen to me, and now I know: torture, preceded by changes of character, brain operations, changes in impressions of the past. The knowledge that one other person, or none, or many will be similarly mistreated may affect me in other ways, of sympathy, greater horror at the power of this tyrant, and so forth; but surely it cannot affect my expectations of torture? But—someone will say—this is to leave out exactly the feature which, as the first presentation of the case showed, makes all the difference: for it is to leave out the person who, as the first presentation showed, will be you. It is to leave out not merely a feature which should fundamentally affect your fears, it is to leave out the very person for whom you are fearful. So of course, the objector will say, this makes all the difference.

But can it? Consider the following series of cases. In each case we are to suppose that after what is described, *A* is, as before, to be tortured; we are also to suppose the person *A* is informed beforehand that just these things followed by the torture will happen to him:

(*i*) *A* is subjected to an operation which produces total amnesia;

(*ii*) amnesia is produced in *A*, and other interference leads to certain changes in his character;

(*iii*) changes in his character are produced, and at the same time certain illusory "memory" beliefs are induced in him; these are of a quite fictitious kind and do not fit the life of any actual person;

(*iv*) the same as (*iii*), except that both the character traits and the "memory" impressions are designed to be appropriate to another actual person, *B;*

(*v*) the same as (*iv*), except that the result is produced by putting the information into *A* from the brain of *B,* by a method which leaves *B* the same as he was before;

(*vi*) the same happens to *A* as in (*v*), but *B* is not left the same, since a similar operation is conducted in the reverse direction.

I take it that no one is going to dispute that *A* has reasons, and fairly straightforward reasons, for fear of pain when the prospect is that of situation (*i*); there seems no conceivable reason why this should not extend to situation (*ii*), and the situation (*iii*) can surely introduce no difference of principle—it just seems a situation which for more than one reason we should have grounds for fearing, as suggested above. Situation (*iv*) at least introduces the person *B,* who was the focus of the objection we are now discussing. But it does not seem to introduce him in any way which makes a material difference; if I can expect pain through a transformation which involves new "memory"–impressions, it would seem a purely external fact, relative to that, that the "memory"-impressions had a model. Nor, in (*iv*), do we satisfy a causal condition which I mentioned at the beginning for the "memories" actually being memories; though notice that if the job were done thoroughly, I might well be able to elicit from the *A*-body-person the kinds of remarks about his previous expectations of the experiment—remarks about his previous expectations of the experiment—remarks appropriate to the original *B*—which so impressed us in the first version of the story. I shall have a similar assurance of this being so in situation (*v*), where, moreover, a plausible application of the causal condition is available.

But two things are to be noticed about this situation. First, if we concentrate on *A* and the *A*-body-person, we do not seem to have added anything which from the point of view of his fears makes any material difference; just as, in the move from (*iii*) to (*iv*), it made no relevant difference that the new "memory"-impressions which precede the pain had, as it happened, a model, so in the move from (*iv*) to (*v*) all we have added is that they have a model which is also their cause: and it is still difficult to see why that, to him looking forward, could possibly make the difference between expecting pain and not expecting pain. To illustrate that point from the case of character: if *A* is capable of expecting pain, he is capable of expecting pain preceded by a change in his dispositions—and to that expectation it can make no difference, whether that change in his dispositions is modeled on, or indeed indirectly caused by, the dispositions of some other person. If his fears can, as it were, reach through the change, it seems a mere trimming how the change is in fact induced. The second point about situation (*v*) is that if the crucial question for *A*'s fears with regard to what befalls the *A*-body-person is whether the *A*-body-person is or is not the person *B,*[2] then that condition has not yet been satisfied in situation (*v*): for there we have an undisputed *B* in addition to the *A*-body-person, and certainly those two are not the same person.

But in situation (*vi*), we seemed to think, that is finally what he is. But if *A*'s original fears could reach through the expected changes in (*v*), as they did in (*iv*) and (*iii*), then certainly they can reach through in (*vi*). Indeed, from the point of view of *A*'s expectations and fears, there is less difference between (*vi*) and (*v*) than there is between (*v*) and (*iv*) or between (*iv*) and (*iii*). In those transitions, there were at least differences—though we could not see that they were really relevant differences—in the content and cause of what happened to him; in the present case there is absolutely no difference at all in what happens to him, the only difference being in what happens to someone else. If he can fear pain when (*v*) is predicted, why should he cease to when (*vi*) is?

I can see only one way of relevantly laying great weight on the transition from (*v*) to (*vi*); and this involves a considerable difficulty. This is to deny that, as I put it, the transition from (*v*) to (*vi*) involves merely the addition of something happening to *somebody else;* what rather it does, it will be said, is to involve the reintroduction of *A* himself, as the *B*-body-person; since he has reappeared in this form, it is for this person, and not for the unfortunate *A*-body-person, that *A* will have his expectations. This is to reassert, in effect, the viewpoint emphasized in our first presentation of the experiment. But this surely has the consequence that *A* should not have fears for the *A*-body-person who appeared in situation (*v*). For by the present argument, the *A*-body-person in (*vi*) is not *A;* the *B*-body-person is. But the *A*-body-person in (*v*) is, in character, history, everything, exactly the same as the *A*-body-person in (*vi*); so if the latter is not *A*, then neither is the former. (It is this point, no doubt, that encourages one to speak of the difference that goes with [*vi*] as being, on the present view, the *reintroduction* of *A*.) But no one else in (*v*) has any better claim to be *A*. So in (*v*), it seems, *A* just does not exist. This would certainly explain why *A* should have no fears for the state of things in (*v*)—though he might well have fears for the path to it. But it rather looked earlier as though he could well have fears for the state of things in (*v*). Let us grant, however, that that was an illusion, and that *A* really does not exist in (*v*); then does he exist in (*iv*), (*iii*), (*ii*), or (*i*)? It seems very difficult to deny it for (*i*) and (*ii*); are we perhaps to draw the line between (*iii*) and (*iv*)?

Here someone will say: you must not insist on drawing a line—borderline cases are borderline cases, and you must not push our concepts beyond their limits. But this well-known piece of advice, sensible as it is in many cases, seems in the present case to involve an extraordinary difficulty. It may intellectually comfort observers of *A*'s situation; but what is *A* supposed to make of it? To be told that a future situation is a borderline one for its being myself that is hurt, that it is conceptually undecidable whether it will be me or not, is something which, it seems, I can do nothing with; because, in particular, it seems to have no comprehensible representation in my expectations and the emotions that go with them.

If I expect that a certain situation, *S*, will come about in the future, there is of course a wide range of emotions and concerns, directed on *S*, which I may experience now in relation to my expectation. Unless I am exceptionally egoistic, it is not a condition on my being concerned in relation to this expectation, that I myself will be involved in *S*—where my being "involved" in *S* means that I figure in *S* as someone doing something at that time or having something done to me, or, again, that *S* will have consequences affecting me at that or some subsequent time. There are some emotions, however, which I will feel only if I will be involved in *S*, and fear is an obvious example.

Now the description of *S* under which it figures in my expectations will necessarily be, in various ways, indeterminate; and one way in which it may be indeterminate is that it leave open whether I shall be involved in *S* or not. Thus I may have good reason to expect that one out of us five is going to get hurt, but no reason to expect it to be me rather than one of the others. My present emotions will be correspondingly affected by this indeterminacy. Thus, sticking to the egoistic concern involved in fear, I shall presumably be somewhat more cheerful than if I had been left out altogether. Fear will be mixed with, and qualified by, apprehension; and so forth. These emotions revolve around the thought of the eventual determination of the indeterminacy; moments of straight fear focus on its really turning out to be me, of hope on its turning out not to be me. All the emotions are related to the coming about of what I expect: and what I expect in such a case just cannot come about save by coming about in one of the ways or another.

There are other ways in which indeterminate expectations can be related to fear. Thus I may expect (perhaps neurotically) that something nasty is going to happen to me, indeed expect that when it happens it will take some determinate form, but have no range, or no closed range, of candidates for the determinate form to rehearse in my present thought. Different from this would be the fear of something radically indeterminate—the fear (one might say) of a nameless horror. If somebody had such a fear, one could even say that he had, in a sense, a perfectly determinate expectation: if what he expects indeed comes about, there will be nothing more determinate to be said about it after the event than was said in the expectation. Both these cases of course are cases of *fear* because one thing that is fixed amid the indeterminacy is the belief that it is to me to which the things will happen.

Central to the expectation of *S* is the thought of what it will be like when it happens—thought which may be indeterminate, range over alternatives, and so forth. When *S* involves me, there can be the possibility of a special form of such thought: the thought of how it will be for me, the imaginative projection of myself as participant in *S*.[3]

I do not have to think about *S* in this way, when it involves me; but I may be able to. (It might be suggested that this possibility was even mirrored in the language, in the distinction between "expecting to be hurt'' and ''expecting that I shall be hurt''; but I am very doubtful about this point, which is in any case of no importance.)

Suppose now that there is an *S* with regard to which it is for conceptual reasons undecidable whether it involves me or not, as is proposed for the experimental situation by the line we are discussing. It is important that the expectation of *S* is not *indeterminate* in any of the ways we have just been considering. It is not like the nameless horror, since the fixed point of that case was that it was going to happen to the subject, and that made his state unequivocally fear. Nor is it like the expectation of the man who expects one of the five to be hurt; his fear was indeed equivocal, but its focus, and that of the expectation, was that when *S* came about, it would certainly come about in one way or the other. In the present case, fear (of the torture, that is to say, not of the initial experiment) seems neither appropriate, nor inappropriate, nor appropriately equivocal. Relatedly, the subject has an incurable difficulty about how he may think about *S*. If he engages in projective imaginative thinking (about how it will be for him), he implicitly answers the necessarily unanswerable question; if he thinks that he cannot engage in such thinking, it looks very much as if he also answers it, though in the opposite direction. Perhaps he must just refrain from such thinking; but is he just refraining from it, if it is incurably undecidable whether he can or cannot engage in it?

It may be said that all that these considerations can show is that fear, at any rate, does not get its proper footing in this case; but that there could be some other, more ambivalent, form of concern which would indeed be appropriate to this particular expectation, the expectation of the conceptually undecidable situation. There are, perhaps, analogous feelings that actually occur in actual situations. Thus material objects do occasionally shadow over their identity. Suppose I were sentimentally attached to an object to which this sort of thing then happened; then it might be that I could neither feel about it quite as I did originally, nor be totally indifferent to it, but would have some other and rather ambivalent feeling toward it. Similarly, it may be said, toward the prospective sufferer of pain, my identity relations with whom are conceptually shadowed, I can feel neither as I would if he were certainly me, nor as I would if he were certainly not, but rather some such ambivalent concern.

But this analogy does little to remove the most baffling aspect of the present case—an aspect which has already turned up in what was said about the subject's difficulty in thinking either projectively or non-projectively about the situation. For to regard the prospective pain-sufferer *just* like the transmogrified object of sentiment, and to conceive of my ambivalent distress about his future pain as just like ambivalent distress about some future damage to such an object, is of course to leave him and me clearly distinct from one another, and thus to displace the conceptual shadow from its proper place. I have to get nearer to him than that. But is there any nearer that I can get to him without expecting his pain? If there is, the analogy has not shown us it. We can certainly not get nearer by expecting, as it were, *ambivalent* pain; there is no place at all for that. There seems to be an obstinate bafflement to mirroring in my expectations a situation in which it is conceptually undecidable whether I occur.

The bafflement seems, moreover, to turn to plain absurdity if we move from conceptual undecidability to its close friend and neighbor, conventionalist decision. This comes out if we consider another description, overtly conventionalist, of the series of cases which occasioned the present discussion. This description would reject a point I relied on in an earlier argument—namely, that if we deny that the *A*-body-person in (*vi*) is *A* (because the *B*-body-person is), then we must deny that the *A*-body-person in (*v*) is *A*, since they are exactly the same. ''No,'' it may be said, ''this is just to assume that we say the same in different sorts of situations. No doubt when we have the very good candidate for being *A*—namely, the *B*-body-person—we call him *A;* but this does not mean that we should not call the *A*-body-person *A* in that other situation when we have no better candidate around. Different situations call for different descriptions.'' This line of talk is the sort of thing indeed appropriate to lawyers deciding the ownership of some property which has undergone some bewildering set of transformations; they just have to decide, and in each situation, let us suppose, it has got to go to somebody, on as reasonable grounds as the facts and the law admit. But as a line to deal with a person's fears or expectations about his own future, it seems to have no sense at all. If *A*'s fears can extend to what will happen to the *A*-body-person in (*v*), I do not see how they can be rationally diverted from the fate of the exactly similar person in (*vi*) by his being told that someone would have a reason in the latter situation which he would not have in the former for deciding to call another person *A*.

Thus, to sum up, it looks as though there are two presentations of the imagined experiment and the choice associated with it, each of which carries conviction, and which lead to contrary conclusions. The idea, moreover, that the situation after the experiment is conceptually undecidable in the relevant respect seems not to assist, but rather to increase, the puzzlement; while the idea (so often appealed to in these matters) that it is conventionally decidable is even worse. Following from all that, I am not in the least clear which option it would be wise to take if one were presented with them before the experiment. I find that rather disturbing.

Whatever the puzzlement, there is one feature of the arguments which have led to it which is worth picking out, since it runs counter to something which is, I think, often rather vaguely supposed. It is often recognized that there are "first-personal" and "third-personal" aspects of questions about persons, and that there are difficulties about the relations between them. It is also recognized that "mentalistic" considerations (as we may vaguely call them) and considerations of bodily continuity are involved in questions of personal identity (which is not to say that there are mentalistic and bodily criteria of personal identity). It is tempting to think that the two distinctions run in parallel: roughly, that a first-personal approach concentrates attention on mentalistic considerations, while a third-personal approach emphasizes considerations of bodily continuity. The present discussion is an illustration of exactly the opposite. The first argument, which led to the "mentalistic" conclusion that *A* and *B* would change bodies and that each person should identify himself with the destination of his memories and character, was an argument entirely conducted in third-personal terms. The second argument, which suggested the bodily continuity identification, concerned itself with the first-personal issue of what *A* could expect. That this is so seems to me (though I will not discuss it further here) of some significance.

I will end by suggesting one rather shaky way in which one might approach a resolution of the problem, using only the limited materials already available.

The apparently decisive arguments of the first presentation, which suggested that *A* should identify himself with the *B*-body-person, turned on the extreme neatness of the situation in satisfying, if any could, the description of "changing bodies." But this neatness is basically artificial; it is the product of the will of the experimenter to produce a situation which would naturally elicit, with minimum hesitation, that description. By the sorts of methods he employed, he could easily have left off earlier or gone on further. He could have stopped at situation (*v*), leaving *B* as he was; or he could have gone on and produced two persons each with *A*-like character and memories, as well as one or two with *B*-like characteristics. If he had done either of those, we should have been in yet greater difficulty about what to say; he just chose to make it as easy as possible for us to find something to say. Now if we had some model of ghostly persons in bodies, which were in some sense actually moved around by certain procedures, we could regard the neat experiment just as the *effective* experiment: the one method that really did result in the ghostly persons' changing places without being destroyed, dispersed, or whatever. But we cannot seriously use such a model. The experimenter has not in the sense of that model *induced* a change of bodies; he has rather produced the one situation out of a range of equally possible situations which we should be most disposed to call a change of bodies. As against this, the principle that one's fears can extend to future pain whatever psychological changes precede it seems positively straightforward. Perhaps, indeed, it is not; but we need to be shown what is wrong with it. Until we are shown what is wrong with it, we should perhaps decide that if we were the person *A* then, if we were to decide selfishly, we should pass the pain to the *B*-body-person. It would be risky: that there is room for the notion of a *risk* here is itself a major feature of the problem.

Notes

1. Sydney S. Shoemaker, *Self-knowledge and Self-identity* (Ithaca, N.Y., 1963), p. 23f.
2. This of course does not have to be the crucial question, but it seems one fair way of taking up the present objection.
3. For a more detailed treatment of issues related to this, see Bernard Williams, *Imagination and the Self,* British Academy (London, 1966); reprinted in P.F. Strawson, ed., *Studies in Thought and Action* (Oxford, 1968).

Williams on the Self and Its Future

JOHN PERRY

John Perry (1943–) is professor of philosophy at Stanford University. His publications include *A Dialogue on Personal Identity and Immortality* and, with Jon Barwise, *Situations and Attitudes*.

Williams thinks that persons are material objects. The "most forceful" objection he finds to this is that the identity of persons is not the same as the identity of bodies. . . . When not based on an explicitly Cartesian conception of persons, the motivation for denying that personal identity is just human-body identity usually derives from cases of putative body transfer. Locke's cobbler with the prince's memories, and Sydney Shoemaker's Brownson with Brown's brain and memories and Robinson's body,[1] are perhaps the most famous of such cases. If the same person could at one time have one body, and at another time have a different body, then being the same person cannot amount to having the same body; and then it seems that in some sense (though perhaps not in others) persons are not just bodies. It is Williams's involved and imaginative treatment of these cases . . . that I shall examine.*

Let us begin with what I shall call a "basic case." *A* and *B* are human bodies; such things as "A^t" and "B^{t+n}" mean "the person with body *A* at time *t*" and "the person with body *B* at time *t*+*n*." A basic case involves a person with one of the bodies seeming to have memories of events that happened to the other body. The person who seems to remember I shall sometimes call "the Survivor," the person who seems to be remembered "the Memory Donor," and the unremembered fellow "the Body Donor." We can represent a basic case as follows:

(Basic Case)	A^{t+n} (memories of B^t; none of A^t)	
	A^t	B^t

The problem is, Is A^{t+n} really A^t or just B^t? That is, is the Survivor the Memory Donor or the Body Donor? Is Brownson really Brown or just Robinson? Is the rude-looking fellow making royal pronouncements really the Prince or just the Cobbler?

Even resourceful non-Cartesians such as Shoemaker have been convinced that there are basic cases about which we should say that the Survivor is the Memory Donor and not the Body Donor. This Williams denies. As least he argues tooth and nail against it and won't admit it.

To persuade us that basic cases aren't cases of bodily transfer, Williams asks us, in effect, to consider two sorts of variation on them. The first sort leads to the *reduplication argument*, the second to what I shall call the *nonduplication argument*. For the reduplication argument, we add a second Survivor.

*[Editors' note: Williams's discussion occurs in "The Self and the Future" and other essays in his *Problems of the Self: Philosophical Papers, 1956–1972*. (Cambridge: Cambridge University Press, 1973). Page references in brackets are to "The Self and the Future" (in this volume), while those in parentheses are to *Problems of the Self*.]

From the *Journal of Philosophy* 73, no. 13 (1976), pp. 416–28.

(First Variation)	A^{t+n} (memories of B^t)		C^{t+n} (memories of B^t)
	A^t	B^t	C^t

If Charles gets to be Guy Fawkes in virtue of his putative memories of Fawkes's acts in the basic case, why shouldn't both Charles and his brother get to be Fawkes in the variation in which they both have such putative memories? But clearly, two different Survivors cannot both be identical with one Memory Donor. So the relation that each of the Survivors has to the Memory Donor in the variation is not sufficient for identity. But this is just the relation the sole Survivor had to the Memory Donor in the basic case. So it cannot be sufficient for identity there, either. Williams advanced the reduplication argument in an early paper, "Personal Identity and Individuation." He explores it further in "Personal Identity and Bodily Identity," a reply to some criticisms of the first paper by Robert Coburn, and in "Are Persons Bodies?" I shall defer consideration of it until after examination of the later, more complex argument.

The Nonduplication Argument

Williams advances this argument in a strikingly elegant and forceful essay, "The Self and the Future." He begins by introducing an example whose structure is that of two basic cases superimposed:

(Original Case)	A^{t+n} (remembers B^t)	B^{t+n} (remembers A^t)
	A^t	B^t

Williams then poses a problem for A^t and B^t. Each is asked to choose one of the bodies to be tortured at $t + n$, the other to receive $100,000. This choice is to be made on selfish grounds. Williams assays the results of various possible combinations of choices, and seems to find in them a strong argument for describing the case as one of body transfer. For example, if A^t chose that B^{t+n} be rewarded, and this is done, then B^{t+n} will be happy about a choice he will seem to remember making. It is natural to report this as "Someone got what he wanted," and this someone must be someone who had body *A* and then had body *B*. Indeed, Williams's discussion from page [425] to page [435] puts the case for the possibility of body transfer about as effectively as it has been put.

But then he pulls the rug out from under us. "Let us now consider something apparently different. Someone . . . tells me that I am going to be tortured tomorrow. . . . when the moment of torture comes, I shall not remember any of the things I am now in a position to remember . . . but will have a different set of impressions of my past" [428]. To be tortured is a frightful prospect, and the additional bits of information about loss of memory and acquisition of false belief just make things worse. But this is just a variation on the original case. Instead of adding a character, as in the reduplication argument, character(s) are subtracted. We simply leave off half of the last diagram:

(Second Variation)	A^{t+n} (memories of B^t)
	A^t

(Of course, now the seemingly remembered events may not correspond to anything that happened to anyone.) As Williams says, "For what we have just been through is of course merely one side, differently represented, of the transaction which was considered before; and it represents it as a perfectly hateful prospect, while the previous considerations represented it as something one should rationally, perhaps even cheerfully, choose out of the options there presented." [429].

Williams tells us that these, and other considerations, leave him "not in the least clear which option it would be wise to take if one were presented with them before the experiment" [434]. But his cautious advice is that "if we were the person *A* then, if we were to decide selfishly, we should pass the pain to the *B*-body person" [434].

For the nonduplication argument to work, there must be a certain relation that obtains between A^t and A^{t+n} both in the original case and in the variation that is supposed to be just half of it. The relation will have to be clearly sufficient, in the variation, for the identity of A^t and A^{t+n}. Then the argument will be that the addition of body *B* to make the original case should make no difference (just as adding "B^t" and "B^{t+n}" to the last diagram would leave "A^{t}" and "A^{t+n}" unaffected). A^{t+n} must still be A^{t} and not have suddenly become B^{t} instead.

The plausibility of this argument turns on leaving the details of the original case hazy. I shall argue that filling them in one way leaves the argument with no force, while filling them in the other way leaves the point of the argument obscure, and reduces it to a fancy version of the reduplication argument.

It will help to imagine, for a moment, that Williams is dealing with a Shoemaker type of case, so that A^{t+n} has the actual brain B^{t} had, and B^{t+n} and A^{t}, both in the original case and in the variation in which B is left out, is "having the same body, but not the same brain." But then consider what we should tell A^{t} were we to fully represent to him one side of the transaction: "Tomorrow your brain will be removed from your body. Another man's brain will be put in its place. Then your body will be tortured." This certainly represents a frightening prospect. But it is not at all clear that pain of torture is to be feared, rather than death and defilement. We could, of course, give some surface description that would both be true and inspire fear of pain: "Your body is going to be whipped, and it won't be a corpse when it happens." But the terror inspired might just be a consequence of omission of such details as removal of the brain. The principle, to which Williams appeals in considering this case, is that "one's fears can extend to future pain whatever psychological changes precede it" [434]. It's a little hard to get a grip on how this principle is supposed to work, since it seems that fear can extend to any future pain whatsoever, no matter whose it is, depending on the beliefs of the fearful person. But at any rate the principle would seem only dubiously applicable to the Shoemaker case. Is loss of the brain a "psychological change"? If so, what of loss of the head? I do not mean to suggest that things are simple and straightforward here. (If my body is to be kept "alive" and subjected to electric shock, after removal of my head, should I fear the pain? What if it is just a leg that is to be treated this way after its amputation?) But Williams's argument, that addition of another body to the drama cannot effect the identity of A^{t+n} with A^{t}, shows nothing unless the alleged identity is clear. In one side of a Shoemaker-style original case, it would not be clear at all.

This is perhaps all quite irrelevant, since Williams does not choose to work with the Shoemaker type of case. But I think the same problem arises with the case he does choose.

In setting up his case, Williams emphasizes that "if utterances coming from a given body are to be taken as expressive of memories . . . there should be some suitable causal link between the appropriate state of that body and the original happening" [426]. But one need not imagine, in order to secure this link, so radical a step as the transposition of a brain. "[S]uppose it were possible to extract information from a man's brain and store it in a device while his brain was repaired, or even renewed, the information then being replaced: it would seem exaggerated to insist that the resultant man could not possibly have the memories he had before the operation. . . . Hence we can imagine the case we are concerned with in terms of information extracted into such devices from A's and B's brains and replaced in the other brain" [426].

So A^{t} and A^{t+n} have the same body, and the same brain. But information concerning A^{t}'s life has been extracted from the brain, and other "information" programmed into it.

Consider the variation, in which B is left out. What is the relation between A^{t} and A^{t+n}? Psychological change, through which A^{t}'s fears could appropriately extend? death of A^{t}? or something else? For the nonduplication argument to work, it must be the first. A^{t} would react to the description of what is to happen with fear, because he regards what is to happen to his body as something like *his* forgetting, and assimilates how *he* will be to a "completely amnesiac state" [428].

But "amnesia" is a slippery word. It means one thing to a physician, another to a television writer, and perhaps something still different to Williams. In ordinary fiction amnesia is consistent with, and indeed implies, survival of memory traces. The picture is of a person whose memories are inaccessible, but, in some sense, still there. The disposition to remember is present, but not triggered by the ordinary conditions. Photographs, diaries, and the sight of loved ones will not do the trick; perhaps a fortuitous blow on the head, or electric shock therapy will.

Contrast with this what I shall call a "brain zap." The information in the brain is destroyed. The brain is "wiped clean," to be a suitable receptacle for a completely different set of memory dispositions. Efforts to trigger the disposition to remember would be silly, because the dispositions are not there. This seems to be what Williams means by "amnesia" in this discussion.

If the relation between A^t and A^{t+n} is that the latter has the very brain the former had, but it has been zapped, then the case seems unimportantly different from a case in which they share no brain at all. A surface description of the case might evoke fear of pain, but, when the details are known, fear of death seems more appropriate. If one were tempted to draw a line between the case in which A^t and A^{t+n} do not share a brain and one in which they share a zapped brain, we could appeal to a point of Williams's. He argues that, if the sort of information-parking operation he envisages were possible, "a person could be counted the same if this were done to him, and in the process he were given a new brain (the repairs, let us say, actually required a new part)" (80). Apparently, so long as no transfer of bodies is at issue, it is the retention of information, and not of the brain, that is crucial for survival. Why shouldn't the same be true for nonsurvival? Again, I do not mean to argue that all is clear-cut and unproblematic. But, since the relationship between A^t and A^{t+n} is unclear, it doesn't prove much to point out that the addition of B^t and B^{t+n} to the picture shouldn't change it.

I argue that, if we understand that a brain zap is involved, Williams's nonduplication argument fails. Since it's not clear that A^{t+n} is just the same person as A^t in the variation, it's not clear that he isn't just the same person as B^t in the original case.

Williams suggests that his opponent might claim that, in terrifying Body Donor A^t with his one-sided description of what is to happen, it is the omission of mention of Survivor B^{t+n} that clouds the issue: "[T]his is to leave out exactly the feature which, as the first presentation of the case showed, makes all the difference: for it is to leave out the person who, as the first presentation showed, will be you" [430]. This is not the complaint I have been making. I have been considering just the history of body *A* in the original case and in the variation that omits body *B*. My complaint has been not that Williams keeps what happens to body *B* secret when he presents Body Donor A^t with the tale of future torture, but that he has either changed the details of what happens to body *A* from the original case, or misdescribed them, or misinterpreted them.

I believe this complaint helps to show the reasonableness of the complaint Williams credits to his opponent, however. Again, it will help to think the case through with the Shoemaker example, and then ask whether the Williams model is importantly different. First Body Donor A^t is told that his body will be tortured tomorrow, while alive. He is fearful of the torture. Here my complaint is relevant: his fear would have a different object were he told the details of what is to happen to his body, namely, that the brain is to be removed. Then he would perhaps fear death, not torture. Perhaps he would not know what to think. This fear might still be based on lack of information about body *B*, namely, that Body Donor *A*'s brain will survive in it. Here the kind of complaint Williams credits to his opponent would be relevant, and perfectly reasonable.

I cannot see that the situation is importantly changed when we deal with a brain zap rather than a brain transposition. When it's not clear that A^t's brain will be zapped, he fears torture. When that is clear, but he is left to assume the worst about the survival of the information in his brain, he fears death, or perhaps doesn't know what to fear. When he is told that this information will be appropriately programmed into another brain, itself previously zapped, that might change the focus of his fear considerably.

Williams challenges the objector to draw a line somewhere in the following series. At which point should *A*'s fear of torture give way to anticipation of $100,000?

(i) *A* is subjected to an operation which produces total amnesia;

(ii) amnesia is produced in *A*, and other interference leads to certain changes in his character;

(iii) changes in his character are produced, and at the same time certain illusory "memory" beliefs are induced in him: these are of a quite fictitious kind . . . ;

(iv) the same as (iii), except that both the character traits and the "memory" impressions are designed to be appropriate to another actual person, B;

(v) the same as (iv), except that the result is produced by putting the information into A from the brain of B, by a method which leaves B the same as he was before;

(vi) the same happens to A as in (v), but B is not left the same, since a similar operation is conducted in the reverse direction.

The body-transfer advocate can simply point out, however, that, if a brain zap is involved, "amnesia" in (i)–(v) is simply a euphemism for "death" or at least "ceasing to exist as a person." The use of the pronoun "him" simply begs the questions at issue. In case (vi) the trauma of gaining a new body should probably be feared.

Williams's example need not be interpreted as a brain zap, however. Perhaps he intends a sort of programming of new memory dispositions over the old, in such a way as to leave the old dispositions untriggerable. In introducing the procedure whose consequences he wishes to discuss, he says "Suppose it were possible to extract information. . . ." This is ambiguous. Compare xeroxing a book to ripping its pages out. In either case, one has extracted information from the book. A possible interpretation of Williams is this. The information is extracted, in a way that leaves the brain with all its memory dispositions intact.

But this interpretation would make the point of Williams's whole discussion rather obscure. Let us review the logic of the situation. The interest in cases of putative body transfer is as counterexamples to the necessity of bodily identity as a condition of personal identity. If a case is presented as a counterexample, it's no good to pick another case something like it, but different in essential respects, and point out that this new case is not such a clear-cut counterexample. So I think we have a right to assume that Williams's example is intended to be more or less the same sort of example that advocates of body transfer have offered. Moreover, the fact that he develops his example as a sort of moderate alternative to Shoemaker's (where there is no question of superimposition of one set of memory dispositions over another) and the fact that he speaks of *replacing* the information extracted from each brain with information extracted from the other, suggest that a brain zap is what is involved.

Nevertheless, it's interesting to think of Williams's case interpreted in this new way, as a sort of overlay of new information, for it leads to a complex version of the reduplication argument. A plausible analysis of personal identity in terms of memory will have to be flexible enough to allow for amnesia, even amnesia together with delusions of an alternative past. The memory theorist will then see identity between A^t and A^{t+n} in all six cases. But a problem will emerge at step (v). At this point, we regain all the personnel necessary for a basic case. A^t and A^{t+n} are related, in all relevant respects, just as they are in (iv). But now A^{t+n} is related also, in a way the memory theorist is assumed to find adequate for personal identity, to B^t. That is, if the causal connection that underlies memory is sufficient for personal identity, there are two persons with whom A^{t+n} has the burden of being identical—one by virtue of the accessible memories programmed into his brain, the other by virtue of the inaccessible memories below.

This is simply the variation at the heart of the reduplication argument, stood on its head. Instead of two later persons competing for the identity of an earlier one, we have one later person for whose identity two earlier persons compete. It is the case we would have if Charles remembered being both Guy Fawkes and Guy Fawkes's brother (now, since one of the Memory Donors is also a Body Donor, there is one less body involved than in the original reduplication argument). Moreover, when we move to step (vi), B^{t+n} will have the memory relation to both B^t and A^t. So we will have two sort of upside-down cases of identity competition. Viewed another way, we also have two right-side-up cases. For both B^{t+n} and A^{t+n} have the memory relation to the two Memory Donors, A^t and B^t.

So, interpreted as involving a brain zap, Williams's argument is without much force. Interpreted as involving an overlay of new memories over old, it appears to be a new version of the reduplication argument, to which I now turn.

The Reduplication Argument

The logic of this argument seems to be this. A description of some basic case is given, neutral on questions of personal identity. From this description, we can see that some relation obtains between the Memory Donor and the Survivor. Is this relation sufficient for identity? If it is, changing the example in ways that do not effect it should not effect the question of identity. But certain changes give us a variation in which the relation is clearly not sufficient for identity, namely adding another Survivor with the same relation to the Memory Donor. In "Personal Identity and Individuation" Charles claims to be Guy Fawkes, and supports this claim with detailed memory-like reports of Fawkes's life. "Appears to remember events from Fawkes's life in great detail," is a duplicable relation, which Charles's brother might also have had to Fawkes.

But the relation "appears to remember Fawkes's life in great detail" would surely not be supposed, even by those most sanguine about transfer of bodies, to be sufficient for personal identity. Any inclination to suppose that Charles is Fawkes must be based on the assumption that this relation is good evidence for some other relation, itself sufficient for identity. The real question is the duplicability of this evidenced relationship.

To revert to the Shoemaker example, suppose Charles's behavior leads us to believe he actually has Fawkes's brain, which has somehow survived, unzapped, through the years. The possibility of a competitor with similarly accurate memory impressions is no problem, so long as we believe that only in Charles's case would the memory behavior be linked by this appropriate causal chain to the events in Fawkes's life.

Williams regards it as an advantage of the Shoemaker example that it does not seem to admit of the reduplication problem. But, as he points out, a natural extension of the example does: "if we consider, not the physical transfer of brains, but the transfer of information between brains" (79). That is, if we consider the sort of case involved in the nonduplication argument, we will certainly have on our hands the reduplication problem.

The relevance of this to the Shoemaker example, and to the project of rebutting an argument that personal identity is not bodily identity, is not perfectly clear. The following line of argument is open to Williams. Whatever considerations there are in favor of counting brain transfer as body transfer are also reasons to regard information transfer as body transfer. But the reduplication argument shows we cannot regard information transfer as body transfer, so these reasons must not be good enough. At any rate, as Williams points out, the reduplication argument is certainly an embarrassment to any memory theorist who doesn't want possession of a particular brain to be a condition of personal identity, and the motivations behind memory theories are perhaps such that most would not.

But what sort of embarrassment is it? Williams says the principle of the argument is that "identity is a one-one relation, and that no principle can be a criterion of identity for things of type *T* if it relies only on what is logically a one-many relation between things of type *T*" (21). What the first variation shows (with the details suitably filled in to be relevant to a particular account of personal identity in terms of memory) is that the memory relation proposed as the criterion of identity is not logically one-one.

Does it follow from the fact that identity is logically one-one, that any criterion for identity must be logically one-one? It is not even clear that it follows that it must be, as matter of fact, one-one. For example, "has the same fingerprints" is probably as a matter of fact, but surely not as a matter of logical necessity, a one-one relation, yet this is certainly, in the ordinary sense, a criterion of personal identity. Presumably then some special philosophical notion of "criterion" is at work here. Even if we require some "conceptual" or "logical" connection between the criterion and what it is a criterion for, the inference in question may not hold. Using, for example, Shoemaker's explanation of the term in *Self-knowledge and Self-identity* . . . a criterion for personal identity would be roughly a relation that could not possibly not be good evidence for personal identity. Such a relation wouldn't even have to be one-one as a matter of fact; at most it would have to be one-one *with very few exceptions* in each possible world.

Perhaps a "criterion of identity" is to be some relation between persons which the memory theorist produces as giving an analysis of "the very meaning" of "is the same person as". Williams's remark, that his point could be made more rigorously in terms of "sense and reference of uniquely referring expressions," suggests this (21). Such analyses generally give a relation that obtains among things other than persons, such as perceptions (Hume), total temporary states (Grice), or soul-phases (Quinton). Persons are then taken as being or corresponding to equivalence classes of these entities, generated by the relation given as the "criterion of identity." Williams's demand for a logically one-one relation seems to translate into such a format as a demand that the relation be not just as a matter of fact but logically or necessarily an equivalence relation. It's not clear why it should be. A relation would seem to introduce a set of entities nicely enough so long as it is an equivalence relation in the actual world. That identity of the introduced entities is itself necessarily an equivalence relation, seems to guarantee only that there would not, as a matter of fact, be such entities if the introducing relation were not, as a matter of fact, an equivalence relation. And if the memory theorist is willing to fiddle a little with the mechanics of reference, he can get by with something that falls somewhat short of being a perfect equivalence relation, even as a matter of fact.

Williams, however, probably thinks of a criterion of identity as a relation between persons that is logically sufficient for identity. Such a relation would have to be logically one-one. A memory theorist could manufacture such a relation by adding, to a relation that seemed to pass the other tests for a criterion of identity, the condition that there be no competitors. Thus, in the basic case, but not in the first variation, Charles has the relation "being the *sole* putative rememberer of Fawkes's experiences." In "Personal Identity and Individuation" Williams argues that, in adopting this sort of criterion, we would be making our talk of identity quite vacuous. The reduplication problem forces us to think of ways short of identity of describing Charles's relation to Fawkes; what is added by employing identity, rather than these more cautious alternatives, when there is no competitor? This once seemed to me a telling point: we shouldn't make whether a person did something yesterday or just began to exist today dependent upon whether someone else exists. Terence Leichti, in a work cited below, has shaken my confidence in this argument, by showing that with other kinds of objects we do follow just this sort of procedure.

If we do rule out, as criteria, relations with such noncompetitor clauses, we may find that there are no nontrivial logically sufficient conditions for personal identity in terms of memory. This could be a special embarrassment for the memory theorist only if other candidates for the criterion of personal identity had no problems with the requirement of being logically one-one. But it may seem clear that at least the other main contender, bodily continuity, has a similar problem with the possibility of reduplication.

As Williams observes, one could claim that "even a criterion of identity in terms of spatiotemporal continuity is itself not immune to this possibility. It is possible to imagine a man splitting, amoeba-like, into two simulacra of himself" (23). His discussion of this problem is perplexing: "There's a vital difference between this sort of reduplication . . . and the other sorts of case." The difference is that the procedure of tracing the continuous path between two occurrences of what is taken to be a single person will inevitably reveal the reduplication, if "ideally carried out." But the thorough application of the other criteria would not. "Thus, in this case, but not in the others, the logical possibility of reduplication fails to impugn the status of the criterion of identity" (24). This is puzzling for several reasons. Even if we grant that the spatiotemporal-continuity criterion has the advantage described, having that advantage does not make it "logically one-one." How can such a difference between the spatiotemporal-continuity criterion and others exempt it from what are alleged to be *logical* requirements of a criterion of identity? Perhaps the force of the "logical requirement" simply reduces to the advantage in question. But why should we think, after all, that this advantage is not shared by the memory criterion? Among other things, we should have to know what it is to "ideally carry out" the application of that criterion. Williams asserts that memory is a causal notion (47). As Shoemaker has observed, this seems to suggest that application of the memory criterion, ideally carried out, would disclose the existence of competitors, since the causal chain involved would presumably involve a spatiotemporally continuous chain of events.

I am inclined to think, then, that the reduplication argument is not the compelling refutation of one particular account of personal identity that Williams intended it to be. Nevertheless, Williams has posed an embarrassment for any account that uses as a criterion of identity a conceivably duplicable relation. The problem is not, as he may have thought, that we cannot consistently describe reduplication cases while clinging to our theories of personal identity. A number of ways of doing so have been put forward.[2] But the existence of a number of different ways of describing these cases, internally consistent, mutually incompatible, and individually problematic, is itself an embarrassment. We might seek solace in authority, and agree with Quine that the problem in such cases is that we seek logical force in our words "beyond what our past deeds have invested them with."[3] Reduplication cases are just conceptually indeterminate.

Notes

1. *Self-knowledge and Self-identity* (Ithaca, N.Y.: Cornell, 1963), pp. 23–25, 245–47; "Persons and Their Pasts," *American Philosophical Quarterly,* 7, 4 (October 1970): 269–85, p. 282.
2. Cf. David Wiggins, *Identity and Spatio-temporal Continuity* (New York: Oxford, 1967); Derek Parfit, "Personal Identity," *Philosophical Review,* 80, 1 (January 1971): 3–27; my "Can the Self Divide?", the *Journal of Philosophy,* 69, 16 (September 7, 1972): 463–88; David Lewis, "Survival and Identity," in Amelie Rorty, ed., *The Identities of Persons* (Berkeley and Los Angeles: University of California Press, 1976); Terrence Leichti, *Fission and Identity,* doctoral dissertation, University of California, Los Angeles, 1975.
3. Review of M. Munitz, ed., *Identity and Individuation,* the *Journal of Philosophy,* 69; 16 (September 7, 1972): 488–97, p. 490.

D. FREEDOM AND DETERMINISM

Free Will Is a Myth

BARON D'HOLBACH

Baron d'Holbach (1723–89) was a major thinker of the French Enlightenment. He is the author of *The System of Nature*.

[M]an is a being purely physical; in whatever manner he is considered, he is connected to universal nature, and submitted to the necessary and immutable laws that she imposes on all the beings she contains, according to their peculiar essences or the respective properties with which, without consulting them, she endows each particular species. Man's life is a line that nature commands him to describe upon the surface of the earth, without his ever being able to swerve from it, even for an instant. He is born without his own consent; his organization does in nowise depend upon himself; his ideas come to him involuntarily; his habits are in the power of those who cause him to contract them; he is unceasingly modified by causes, whether visible or concealed, over which he has no control, which necessarily regulate his mode of existence, give the hue to his way of thinking, and determine his manner of acting. He is good or bad, happy or miserable, wise or foolish, reasonable or irrational, without his will being for anything in these various states. . . .

The will . . . is a modification of the brain, by which it is disposed to action, or prepared to give play to the organs. This will is necessarily determined by the qualities, good or bad, agreeable or painful, of the object or the motive that acts upon his senses, or of which the idea remains with him, and is resuscitated by his memory. In consequence, he acts necessarily, his action is the result of the impulse he receives either from the motive, from the object, or from the idea which has modified his brain or disposed his will. When he does not act according to this impulse, it is because there comes some new cause, some new motive, some new idea, which modifies his brain in a different manner, gives him a new impulse, determines his will in another way, by which the action of the former impulse is suspended. . . . This is the mode in which reflection, experience, reason necessarily arrests or suspends the action of man's will: without this he would of necessity have followed the anterior impulse which carried him towards a then desirable object. In all this he always acts according to necessary laws, from which he has no means of emancipating himself. . . .

Man is said to *deliberate*, when the action of the will is suspended; this happens when two opposite motives act alternatively upon him. *To deliberate*, is to hate and to love in succession; it is to be alternatively attracted and repelled; it is to be moved, sometimes by one motive, sometimes by another. . . .

Choice by no means proves the free agency of man: he only deliberates when he does not yet know which to choose of the many objects that move him, he is then in an embarrassment, which does not terminate until his will is decided by the greater advantage he believes he shall find in the

From *The System of Nature*, trans. H. D. Robinson (Boston: J. P. Mendum, 1889), pp. 88–103.

object he chooses, or the action he undertakes. From whence it may be seen, that choice is necessary, because he would not determine for an object, or for an action, if he did not believe that he should find in it some direct advantage. That man should have free agency it were needful that he should be able to will or choose without motive, or that he could prevent motives coercing his will. Action always being the effect of his will once determined, and as his will cannot be determined but by a motive which is not in his own power, it follows that he is never the master of the determination of his own peculiar will; that consequently he never acts as a free agent. . . .

It has been believed that man was a free agent, because it has been imagined that he could at will recall ideas which sometimes suffice to check his most unruly desires. Thus, the idea of a remote evil, frequently prevents him from enjoying a present and actual good: thus remembrance, which is an almost insensible or slight modification of his brain, annihilates, at each instant, the real objects that act upon his will. But he is not master of recalling to himself his ideas at pleasure; their association is independent of him; they are arranged in his brain in despite of him and without his own knowledge, where they have made an impression more or less profound; his memory itself depends upon his organization; its fidelity depends upon the habitual or momentary state in which he finds himself. . . .

If he understood the play of his organs, if he was able to recall to himself all the impulsions they have received, all the modifications they have undergone, all the effects they have produced, he would perceive that all his actions are submitted to that *fatality,* which regulates his own particular system, as it does the entire system of the universe; no one effect in him, any more than in nature, produces itself by *chance;* this, as has been before proved, is a word void of sense. All that passes in him; all that is done by him; as well as all that happens in nature, or that is attributed to her, is derived from necessary causes, which act according to necessary laws, and which produce necessary effects from whence necessarily flow others.

Fatality, is the eternal, the immutable, the necessary order, established in nature; or the indispensable connexion of causes that act, with the effects they operate. Conforming to this order, heavy bodies fall; light bodies rise; that which is analogous in matter reciprocally attracts; that which is heterogeneous mutally repels; man congregates himself in society; modifies each his fellow; becomes either virtuous or wicked; either contributes to his mutual happiness, or reciprocates his misery; either loves his neighbour, or hates his companion necessarily, according to the manner in which one acts upon the other. From whence it may be seen, that the same necessity which regulates the physical, also regulates the moral world, in which everything is in consequence submitted to fatality. Man, in running over, frequently without his own knowledge, often in despite of himself, the route which nature has marked out for him, resembles a swimmer who is obliged to follow the current that carries him along: he believes himself a free agent, because he sometimes consents, sometimes does not consent, to glide with the stream, which, notwithstanding, always hurries him forward; he believes himself the master of his condition, because he is obliged to use his arms under the fear of sinking. . . .

[L]et us then examine if, in the eyes of the disinterested man, who is not entangled by prejudice, who is sensible to the happiness of his species, *the doctrine of fatalism* be useful or dangerous? . . .

The opposers of necessity say: that if all the actions of man are necessary, no right whatever exists to punish bad ones, or even to be angry with those who commit them; that nothing ought to be imputed to them; that the laws would be unjust, if they should decree punishment for necessary actions; in short, that under this system, man could neither have merit nor demerit. . . .

[But] love and anger are modes of existence suitable to modify beings of the human species: when, therefore, man irritates himself against his fellow, he intends to excite his fear, or even to punish him. Moreover, his anger is necessary; it is the result of his nature and of his temperament. The painful sensation produced by a stone that falls on the arm, does not displease the less because it comes from a cause deprived of will, and which acts by the necessity of its nature. In contemplating man as acting necessarily, it is impossible to avoid distinguishing that mode of action or being which is agreeable, which elicits approbation, from that which is affliction, which irritates, which nature obliges him to blame and to prevent. From this it will be seen that the system of fatalism does not in any manner change the actual state of things and is by no means calculated to confound man's ideas of virtue and vice.

Laws are made with a view to maintain society, and to prevent man associated from injuring his neighbour; they are therefore competent to punish those who disturb its harmony, or those who commit actions that are injurous to their fellows; whether these associates may be the agents of necessity, or whether they are free agents, it suffices to know that they are susceptible of modification, and therefore submitted to the operation of the law. . . .

Whatever may be the cause that obliges man to act, society possesses the right to crush the effect: as much as the man whose land would be ruined by a river, has to restrain its waters by a bank, or even, if he is able, to turn its course. It is by virtue of this right, that society has the power to intimidate and to punish, with a view to its own conservation, those who may be tempted to injure it; or those who commit actions which are acknowledged really to interrupt its repose, to be inimical to its security, or repugnant to happiness. . . .

It will perhaps be argued, that society does not usually punish those faults in which the will has no share; that it punishes the will alone; that this it is which decides the nature of the crime, and the degree of its atrocity: that if this will be not free, it ought not to be punished. I reply, that society is an assemblage of sensible beings, susceptible of reason, who desire their own welfare, who fear evil, and seek after good. These dispositions enable their will to be so modified or determined, that they are capable of holding such a conduct as will conduce to the end they have in view. Education, the laws, public opinion, example, habit, fear, are the causes that must modify associated man, influence his will, regulate his passions, restrain the actions of him who is capable of injuring the end of his association, and thereby make him concur to the general happiness. . . .

The fatalist, in consequence of these ideas, will neither be a gloomy misanthrope, nor a dangerous citizen. He will pardon in his brethren those wanderings which their nature vitiated by a thousand causes has rendered necessary; he will offer them consolation; he will endeavour to inspire them with courage; he will be sedulous to undeceive them in their idle notions; in their chimerical ideas; but he will never show them that rancourous animosity which is more suitable to make them revolt from his doctrines than to attract them to reason.

Has the Self "Free Will"?

C. A. CAMPBELL

C. A. Campbell (1897–1974) was a professor of philosophy at the University of Glasgow. His publications include *On Selfhood and Godhood.*

1. . . . It is something of a truism that in philosophic enquiry the exact formulation of a problem often takes one a long way on the road to its solution. In the case of the Free Will problem I think there is a rather special need of careful formulation. For there are many sorts of human freedom; and it can easily happen that one wastes a great deal of labour in proving or disproving a freedom which has almost nothing to do with the freedom which is at issue in the traditional problem of Free Will. The abortiveness of so much of the argument for and against Free Will in contemporary philosophical literature seems to me due in the main to insufficient pains being taken over the preliminary definition of the problem. . . .

Fortunately we can at least make a beginning with a certain amount of confidence. It is not seriously disputable that the kind of freedom in question is the freedom which is commonly recognised to be in some sense a precondition of moral responsibility. Clearly, it is on account of this integral connection with moral responsibility that such exceptional importance has always been felt to attach to the Free Will problem. But in what precise sense is free will a precondition of moral responsibility, and thus a postulate of the moral life in general? This is an exceedingly troublesome question; but until we have satisfied ourselves about the answer to it, we are not in a position to state, let alone decide, the question whether "Free Will" in its traditional, ethical, significance is a reality.

Our first business, then, is to ask, exactly what kind of freedom is it which is required for moral responsibility? And as to method of procedure in this inquiry, there seems to me to be no real choice. I know of only one method that carries with it any hope of success; viz. the critical comparison of those acts for which, on due reflection, we deem it proper to attribute moral praise or blame to the agents, with those acts for which, on due reflection, we deem such judgments to be improper. The ultimate touchstone, as I see it, can only be our moral consciousness as it manifests itself in our more critical and considered moral judgments. . . .

2. The first point to note is that the freedom at issue (as indeed the very name "Free *Will* Problem" indicates) pertains primarily not to overt acts but to inner acts. The nature of things has decreed that, save in the case of one's self, it is only overt acts which one can directly observe. But a very little reflection serves to show that in our moral judgments upon others their overt acts are regarded as significant only in so far as they are the expression of inner acts. We do not consider the acts of a robot to be morally responsible acts; nor do we consider the acts of a man to be so save insofar as they are distinguishable from those of a robot by reflecting an inner life of choice.

From *On Selfhood and Godhood* (London: Allen & Unwin, 1957), pp. 158–65, 167–79.

Similarly, from the other side, if we are satisfied (as we may on occasion be, at least in the case of ourselves) that a person has definitely elected to follow a course which he believes to be wrong, but has been prevented by external circumstances from translating his inner choice into an overt act, we still regard him as morally blameworthy. Moral freedom, then, pertains to *inner* acts.

The next point seems at first sight equally obvious and controversial; but, as we shall see, it has awkward implications if we are in real earnest with it (as almost nobody is). It is the simple point that the act must be one of which the person judged can be regarded as the *sole* author. It seems plain enough that if there are any *other* determinants of the act, external to the self, to that extent the act is not an act which the *self* determines, and to that extent not an act for which the self can be held morally responsible. The self is only part-author of the act, and his moral responsibility can logically extend only to those elements within the act (assuming for the moment that these can be isolated) of which he is the *sole* author.

The awkward implications of this apparent truism will be readily appreciated. For, if we are mindful of the influences exerted by heredity and environment, we may well feel some doubt whether there is any act of will at all of which one can truly say that the self is sole author, sole determinant. No man has a voice in determining the raw material of impulses and capacities that constitute his hereditary endowment, and no man has more than a very partial control of the material and social environment in which he is destined to live his life. Yet it would be manifestly absurd to deny that these two factors do constantly and profoundly affect the nature of a man's choices. That this is so we all of us recognise in our moral judgments when we "make allowances," as we say, for a bad heredity or a vicious environment, and acknowledge in the victim of them a diminished moral responsibility for evil courses. Evidently we do *try,* in our moral judgments, however crudely, to praise or blame a man only in respect of that of which we can regard him as *wholly* the author. And evidently we do recognise that, for a man to be the author of an act in the full sense required for moral responsibility, it is not enough merely that he "wills" or "chooses" the act: since even the most unfortunate victim of heredity or environment does, as a rule, "will" what he does. It is significant, however, that the ordinary man, though well enough aware of the influence upon choices of heredity and environment, does not feel obliged thereby to give up his assumption that moral predicates *are* somehow applicable. Plainly he still believes that there is *something* for which a man is morally responsible, something of which we can fairly say that he is the sole author. *What is this something?* To that question common-sense is not ready with an explicit answer—though an answer is, I think, implicit in the line which its moral judgments take. I shall do what I can to give an explicit answer later in this lecture. Meantime it must suffice to observe that, if we are to be true to the deliverances of our moral consciousness, it is very difficult to deny that *sole* authorship is a necessary condition of the morally responsible act.

Thirdly we come to a point over which much recent controversy has raged. We may approach it by raising the following question. Granted an act of which the agent is sole author, does this "sole authorship" suffice to make the act a morally free act? We may be inclined to think that it does, until we contemplate the possibility that an act of which the agent is sole author might conceivably occur as a necessary expression of the agent's nature; the way in which, e.g. some philosophers have supposed the Divine act of creation to occur. This consideration excites a legitimate doubt, for it is far from easy to see how a person can be regarded as a proper subject for moral praise or blame in respect of an act which he *cannot help* performing—even if it be his own "nature" which necessitates it. Must we not recognise it as a condition of the morally free act that the agent "could have acted otherwise" than he in fact did? It is true, indeed, that we sometimes praise or blame a man for an act about which we are prepared to say, in the light of our knowledge of his established character, that he "could no other." But I think that a little reflection shows that in such cases we are not praising or blaming the man strictly for what he does *now* (or at any rate we ought not to be), but rather for those past acts of his which have generated the firm habit of mind from which his *present* act follows "necessarily." In other words, our praise and blame, so far as justified, are really retrospective, being directed not to the agent *qua* performing *this* act, but to the agent *qua* performing those past acts which have built up his present character, and in respect to which we presume that he *could* have acted otherwise, that there really *were* open possibilities before him. These cases, therefore, seem to me to constitute no valid exception to what I must take to be the rule, viz. that a man can be morally praised or blamed for an act only if he could have acted otherwise.

Now philosophers today are fairly well agreed that it is a postulate of the morally responsible act that the agent "could have acted otherwise" in *some* sense of that phrase. But sharp differences of opinion have arisen over the way in which the phrase ought to be interpreted. There is a strong disposition to water down its apparent meaning by insisting that it is not (as a postulate of moral responsibility) to be understood as a straightforward categorical proposition, but rather as a disguised hypothetical proposition. All that we really require to be assured of, in order to justify our holding X morally responsible for an act, is, we are told, that X could have acted otherwise *if* he had *chosen* otherwise (Moore, Stevenson); or perhaps that X could have acted otherwise *if* he had had a different character, or *if* he had been placed in different circumstances.

I think it is easy to understand, and even, in a measure, to sympathise with, the motives which induce philosophers to offer these counter-interpretations. It is not just the fact that "X could have acted otherwise," as a bald categorical statement, is incompatible with the universal sway of causal law—though this is, to some philosophers, a serious stone of stumbling. The more widespread objection is that it at least looks as though it were incompatible with that causal continuity of an agent's character with his conduct which is implied when we believe (surely with justice) that we can often tell the sort of thing a man will do from our knowledge of the sort of man he is.

We shall have to make our accounts with that particular difficulty later. At this stage I wish merely to show that neither of the hypothetical propositions suggested—and I think the same could be shown for *any* hypothetical alternative—is an acceptable substitute for the categorical proposition "X could have acted otherwise" as the presupposition of moral responsibility.

Let us look first at the earlier suggestion—"X could have acted otherwise *if* he had chosen otherwise." Now clearly there are a great many acts with regard to which we are entirely satisfied that the agent is thus situated. We are often perfectly sure that—for this is all it amounts to—if X had chosen otherwise, the circumstances presented no external obstacle to the translation of that choice into action. For example, we often have no doubt at all that X, who in point of fact told a lie, could have told the truth *if* he had so chosen. But does our confidence on this score allay all legitimate doubts about whether X is really blameworthy? Does it entail that X is free in the sense required for moral responsibility? Surely not. The obvious question immediately arises: "But *could* X have *chosen* otherwise than he did?" It is doubt about the true answer to *that* question which leads most people to doubt the reality of moral responsibility. Yet on this crucial question the hypothetical proposition which is offered as a sufficient statement of the condition justifying the ascription of moral responsibility gives us no information whatsoever.

Indeed this hypothetical substitute for the categorical "X could have acted otherwise" seems to me to lack all plausibility unless one contrives to forget why it is, after all, that we ever come to feel fundamental doubts about man's moral responsibility. Such doubts are born, surely, when one becomes aware of certain reputable world-views in religion or philosophy, or of certain reputable scientific beliefs, which in their several ways imply that man's actions are necessitated, and thus could not be otherwise than they in fact are. But clearly a doubt so based is not even touched by the recognition that a man could very often act otherwise *if* he so chose. That proposition is entirely compatible with the necessitarian theories which generate our doubt: indeed it is this very compatibility that has recommended it to some philosophers, who are reluctant to give up either moral responsibility or Determinism. The proposition which we *must* be able to affirm if moral praise or blame of X is to be justified is the categorical proposition that X could have acted otherwise because—not if—he could have chosen otherwise; or, since it is essentially the inner side of the act that matters, the proposition simply that X could have chosen otherwise.

For the second of the alternative formulae suggested we cannot spare more than a few moments. But its inability to meet the demands it is required to meet is almost transparent. ''X could have acted otherwise,'' as a statement of a precondition of X's moral responsibility, really means (we are told) ''X could have acted otherwise *if* he were differently constituted, or *if* he had been placed in different circumstances.'' It seems a sufficient reply to this to point out that the person whose moral responsibility is at issue is *X*; a specific individual, in a specific set of circumstances. It is totally irrelevant to *X*'s moral responsibility that we should be able to say that some person differently constituted from X, or X in a different set of circumstances, could have done something different from what X did.

3. Let me, then, briefly sum up the answer at which we have arrived to our question about the kind of freedom required to justify moral responsibility. It is that a man can be said to exercise free will in a morally significant sense only insofar as his chosen act is one of which he is the sole cause or author, and only if—in the straightforward, categorical sense of the phrase—he ''could have chosen otherwise''.

I confess that this answer is in some ways a disconcerting one. Disconcerting, because most of us, however objective we are in the actual conduct of our thinking, would *like* to be able to believe that moral responsibility is real: whereas the freedom required for moral responsibility, on the analysis we have given, is certainly far more difficult to establish than the freedom required on the analyses we found ourselves obliged to reject. If, e.g. moral freedom entails only that I could have acted otherwise *if* I had chosen otherwise, there is no real ''problem'' about it at all. I am ''free'' in the normal case where there is no external obstacle to prevent my translating the alternative choice into action, and not free in other cases. Still less is there a problem if all that moral freedom entails is that I could have acted otherwise *if* I had been a differently constituted person, or been in different circumstances. Clearly I am *always* free in *this* sense of freedom. But, as I have argued, these so-called ''freedoms'' fail to give us the pre-conditions of moral responsibility, and hence leave the freedom of the traditional free-will problem, the freedom that people are really concerned about, precisely where it was.

. . . .

5. That brings me to the second, and more constructive, part of this lecture. From now on I shall be considering whether it is reasonable to believe that man does in fact possess a free will of the kind specified in the first part of the lecture. If so, just how and where within the complex fabric of the volitional life are we to locate it?—for although free will must presumably belong (if anywhere) to the volitional side of human experience, it is pretty clear from the way in which we have been forced to define it that it does not pertain simply to volition as such; not even to all volitions that are commonly dignified with the name of ''choices''. It has been, I think, one of the more serious impediments to profitable discussion of the Free Will problem that Libertarians and Determinists alike have so often failed to appreciate the comparatively narrow area within which the free will that is necessary to ''save'' morality is required to operate. It goes without saying that this failure has been gravely prejudicial to the case for Libertarianism. I attach a good deal of importance, therefore, to the problem of locating free will correctly within the volitional orbit. Its solution forestalls and annuls, I believe, some of the more tiresome clichés of Determinist criticism.

We saw earlier that Common Sense's practice of ''making allowances'' in its moral judgments for the influence of heredity and environment indicates Common Sense's conviction, both that a just moral judgment must discount determinants of choice over which the agent has no control, and also (since it still accepts moral judgments as legitimate) that *something* of moral relevance survives which can be regarded as genuinely self-originated. We are now to try to discover what this ''something'' is. And I think we may still usefully take Common Sense as our guide. Suppose one asks the ordinary intelligent citizen *why* he deems it proper to make allowances for X, whose heredity and/or environment are unfortunate. He will tend to reply, I think, in some such terms as these: that X has more and stronger temptations to deviate from what is right than Y or Z, who are normally circumstanced, so that he must put forth a *stronger moral effort* if he is to achieve the same level of external conduct. The intended implication seems to be that X is just as morally praiseworthy as Y or Z *if* he exerts an equivalent moral effort, even though he may not thereby achieve an equal success in conforming his will to the "concrete" demands of duty. And this implies, again, Common Sense's belief that *in moral effort* we have something for which a man is responsible *without qualification,* something that is *not* affected by heredity and environment but depends *solely* upon the self itself.

Now in my opinion Common Sense has here, in principle, hit upon the one and only defensible answer. Here, and here alone, so far as I can see, in the act of deciding whether to put forth or withhold the moral effort required to resist temptation and rise to duty, is to be found an act which is free in the sense required for moral responsibility; an act of which the self is sole author, and of which it is true to say that "it could be" (or, after the event, "could have been") "otherwise." Such is the thesis which we shall now try to establish.

6. The species of argument appropriate to the establishment of a thesis of this sort should fall, I think, into two phases. First, there should be a consideration of the evidence of the moral agent's own inner experience. What *is* the act of moral decision, and what does it imply, from the standpoint of the actual participant? Since there is no way of knowing the act of moral decision—or for that matter any other form of activity—except by actual participation in it, the evidence of the subject, or agent, is on an issue of this kind of palmary importance. It can hardly, however, be taken as in itself conclusive. For even if that evidence should be overwhelmingly to the effect that moral decision does have the characteristics required by moral freedom, the question is bound to be raised—and in view of considerations from other quarters pointing in a contrary direction is *rightly* raised—Can we *trust* the evidence in inner experience? That brings us to what will be the second phase of the argument. We shall have to go on to show, if we are to make good our case, that the extraneous considerations so often supposed to be fatal to the belief in moral freedom are in fact innocuous to it.

In the light of what was said [previously] about the self's experience of moral decision as a *creative* activity, we may perhaps be absolved from developing the first phase of the argument at any great length. The appeal is throughout to one's own experience in the actual taking of the moral decision in the situation of moral temptation. "Is it possible," we must ask, "for anyone so circumstanced to *dis*believe that he could be deciding otherwise?" The answer is surely not in doubt. When we decide to exert moral effort to resist a temptation, we feel quite certain that we *could* withhold the effort; just as, if we decide to withhold the effort and yield to our desires, we feel quite certain that we *could* exert it—otherwise we should not blame ourselves afterwards for having succumbed. It may be, indeed, that this conviction is mere self-delusion. But that is not at the moment our concern. It is enough at present to establish that the act of deciding to exert or to withhold moral effort, as we know it from the inside in actual moral living, belongs to the category of acts which "could have been otherwise."

Mutatis mutandis, the same reply is forthcoming if we ask, "Is it possible for the moral agent in the taking of his decision to *dis*believe that he is the *sole* author of that decision?" Clearly he cannot disbelieve that it is *he* who takes the decision. That, however, is not in itself sufficient to enable him, on reflection, to regard himself as *solely* responsible for the act. For his "character" as so far formed might conceivably be a factor in determining it, and no one can suppose that the constitution of his "character" is uninfluenced by circumstances of heredity and environment with which *he* has nothing to do. But as we pointed out . . . , the very essence of the moral decision as it is experienced is that it is a decision whether or not to *oppose* our character. I think we are entitled to say, therefore, that the act of moral decision is one in which the self is for itself not merely "author" but "sole author."

7. We may pass on, then, to the second phase of our constructive argument; and this will demand more elaborate treatment. Even if a moral agent *qua* making a moral decision in the situa-

tion of "temptation" cannot help believing that he has free will in the sense at issue—a moral freedom between real alternatives, between genuinely open possibilities—are there, nevertheless, objections to a freedom of this kind so cogent that we are bound to distrust the evidence of "inner experience"?

I begin by drawing attention to a simple point whose significance tends, I think, to be underestimated. If the phenomenological analysis we have offered is substantially correct, no one while functioning as a moral agent can help believing that he enjoys free will. Theoretically he may be completely convinced by Determinist arguments, but when actually confronted with a personal situation of conflict between duty and desire he is quite certain that it lies with him here and now whether or not he will rise to duty. It follows that if Determinists could produce convincing theoretical arguments against a free will of this kind, the awkward predicament would ensue that man has to deny as a theoretical being what he had to assert as a practical being. Now I think the Determinist ought to be a good deal more worried about this than he usually is. He seems to imagine that a strong case on general theoretical grounds is enough to prove that the "practical" belief in free will, even if inescapable for us as practical beings, is mere illusion. But in fact it proves nothing of the sort. There is no reason whatever why a belief that we find ourselves obliged to hold *qua* practical beings should be required to give way before a belief which we find ourselves obliged to hold *qua* theoretical beings; or, for that matter, vice versa. All that the theoretical arguments of Determinism can prove, unless they are reinforced by a refutation of the phenomenological analysis that supports Libertarianism, is that there is a radical conflict between the theoretical and the practical sides of man's nature, an antinomy at the very heart of the self. And this is a state of affairs with which no one can easily rest satisfied. I think therefore that the Determinist ought to concern himself a great deal more than he does with phenomenological analysis, in order to show, if he can, that the assurance of free will is not really an inexpungable element in man's practical consciousness. There is just as much obligation upon him, convinced though he may be of the soundness of his theoretical arguments, to expose the errors of the Libertarian's phenomenological analysis, as there is upon us, convinced though we may be of the soundness of the Libertarian's phenomenological analysis, to expose the errors of the Determinist's theoretical arguments.

8. However, we must at once begin the discharge of our own obligation. The rest of this lecture will be devoted to trying to show that the arguments which seem to carry most weight with Determinists are, to say the least of it, very far from compulsive.

Fortunately a good many of the arguments which at an earlier time in the history of philosophy would have been strongly urged against us make almost no appeal to the bulk of philosophers today, and we may here pass them by. That applies to any criticism of "open possibilities" based on a metaphysical theory about the nature of the universe as a whole. Nobody today *has* a metaphysical theory about the nature of the universe as a whole! It applies also, with almost equal force, to criticisms based upon the universality of causal law as a supposed postulate of science. There have always been, in my opinion, sound philosophic reasons for doubting the validity, as distinct from the convenience, of the causal postulate in its universal form, but at the present time, when scientists themselves are deeply divided about the need for postulating causality even within their own special field, we shall do better to concentrate our attention upon criticisms which are more confidently advanced. I propose to ignore also, on different grounds, the type of criticism of free will that is sometimes advanced from the side of religion, based upon religious postulates of Divine Omnipotence and Omniscience. So far as I can see, a postulate of human freedom is every bit as necessary to meet certain religious demands (e.g. to make sense of the "conviction of sin"), as postulates of Divine Omniscience and Omnipotence are to meet certain other religious demands. If so, then it can hardly be argued that religious experience as such tells more strongly against than for the position we are defending; and we may be satisfied, in the present context, to leave the matter there. It will be more profitable to discuss certain arguments which contemporary philosophers do think important, and which recur with a somewhat monotonous regularity in the literature of anti-Libertarianism.

These arguments can, I think, be reduced in principle to no more than two: first, the argument from "predictability"; second, the argument from the alleged meaninglessness of an act supposed to be the self's act and yet not an expression of the self's character. Contemporary criticism of free will seems to me to consist almost exclusively of variations on these two themes. I shall deal with each in turn.

9. On the first we touched in passing at an earlier stage. Surely it is beyond question (the critic urges) that when we know a person intimately we can foretell with a high degree of accuracy how he will respond to at least a large number of practical situations. One feels safe in predicting that one's dog-loving friend will not use his boot to repel the little mongrel that comes yapping at his heels; or again that one's wife will not pass with incurious eyes (or indeed pass at all) the new hat-shop in the city. So to behave would not be (as we say) "in character." But, so the criticism runs, you with your doctrine of "genuinely open possibilities," of a free will by which the self can diverge from its own character, remove all rational basis from such prediction. You require us to make the absurd supposition that the success of countless predictions of the sort in the past has been mere matter of chance. If you *really* believed in your theory, you would not be surprised if tomorrow your friend with the notorious horror of strong drink should suddenly exhibit a passion for whisky and soda, or if your friend whose taste for reading has hitherto been satisfied with the sporting columns of the newspapers should be discovered on a fine Saturday afternoon poring over the works of Hegel. But of course you *would* be surprised. Social life would be sheer chaos if there were not well-grounded social expectations; and social life is not sheer chaos. Your theory is hopelessly wrecked upon obvious facts.

Now whether or not this criticism holds good against some versions of Libertarian theory I need not here discuss. It is sufficient if I can make it clear that against the version advanced in this lecture according to which free will is localised in a relatively narrow field of operation, the criticism has no relevance whatsoever.

Let us remind ourselves briefly of the setting within which, on our view, free will functions. There is X, the course which we believe we ought to follow, and Y, the course towards which we feel our desire is strongest. The freedom which we ascribe to the agent is the freedom to put forth or refrain from putting forth the moral effort required to resist the pressure of desire and do what he thinks he ought to do.

But then there is surely an immense range of practical situations—covering by far the greater part of life—in which there is no question of a conflict within the self between what he most desires to do and what he thinks he ought to do? Indeed such conflict is a comparatively rare phenomenon for the majority of men. Yet over that whole vast range there is nothing whatever in our version of Libertarianism to prevent our agreeing that character determines conduct. In the absence, real or supposed, of any "moral" issue, what a man chooses will be simply that course which, after such reflection as seems called for, he deems most likely to bring him what he most strongly desires; and that is the same as to say the course to which his present character inclines him.

Over by far the greater area of human choices, then, our theory offers no more barrier to successful prediction on the basis of character than any other theory. For where there is no clash of strongest desire with duty, the free will we are defending has no business. There is just nothing for it to do.

But what about the situations—rare enough though they may be—in which there *is* this clash and in which free will does therefore operate? Does our theory entail that there at any rate, as the critic seems to suppose, "anything may happen"?

Not by any manner of means. In the first place, and by the very nature of the case, the range of the agent's possible choices is bounded by what he thinks he ought to do on the one hand, and what he most strongly desires on the other. The freedom claimed for him is a freedom of decision to make or withhold the effort required to do what he thinks he ought to do. There is no question of a freedom to act in some "wild" fashion, out of all relation to his characteristic beliefs and desires. This so-called "freedom of caprice," so often charged against the Libertarian, is, to put it bluntly, a sheer figment of the critic's imagination, with no *habitat* in serious Libertarian theory. Even in situations where free will does come into play it is perfectly possible, on a view like ours, given the appropriate knowledge of a man's character, to predict within certain limits how he will respond.

But "probable" prediction in such situations can, I think, go further than this. It is obvious that where desire and duty are at odds, the felt "gap" (as it were) between the two may vary enormously in breadth in different cases. The moderate drinker and the chronic tippler may each want another glass, and each deem it his duty to abstain, but the felt gap between desire and duty in the case of the former is trivial beside the great gulf which is felt to separate them in the case of the latter. Hence it will take a far harder moral effort for the tippler than for the moderate drinker to achieve the same external result of abstention. So much is matter of common agreement. And we are entitled, I think, to take it into account in prediction, on the simple principle that the harder the moral effort required to resist desire the less likely it is to occur. Thus in the example taken, most people would predict that the tippler will very probably succumb to his desires, whereas there is a reasonable likelihood that the moderate drinker will make the comparatively slight effort needed to resist them. So long as the prediction does not pretend to more than a measure of probability, there is nothing in our theory which would disallow it.

I claim, therefore, that the view of free will I have been putting forward is consistent with predictability of conduct on the basis of character over a very wide field indeed. And I make the further claim that the field will cover all the situations of life concerning which there is any empirical evidence that successful prediction is possible.

10. Let us pass on to consider the second main line of criticism. This is, I think, much the more illuminating of the two, if only because it compels the Libertarian to make explicit certain concepts which are indispensable to him, but which, being desperately hard to state clearly, are apt not to be stated at all. The critic's fundamental point might be stated somewhat as follows:

"Free will as you describe it is completely unintelligible. On your own showing no *reason* can be given, because there just *is* no reason, why a man decides to exert rather than to withhold moral effort, or vice versa. But such an act—or more properly, such an 'occurrence'—it is nonsense to speak of as an act of a *self*. If there is nothing in the self's character to which it is, even in principle, in any way traceable, the self has nothing to do with it. Your so-called 'freedom,' therefore, so far from supporting the self's moral responsibility, destroys it as surely as the crudest Determinism could do."

If we are to discuss this criticism usefully, it is important, I think, to begin by getting clear about two different senses of the word "intelligible".

If, in the first place, we mean by an "intelligible" act one whose occurrence is in principle capable of being inferred, since it follows necessarily from something (though we may not know in fact from what), then it is certainly true that the Libertarian's free will is unintelligible. But that is only saying, is it not, that the Libertarian's "free" act is not an act which follows necessarily from something! This can hardly rank as a *criticism* of Libertarianism. It is just a description of it. That there can be nothing unintelligible in *this* sense is precisely what the Determinist has got to *prove*.

Yet is is surprising how often the critic of Libertarianism involves himself in this circular mode of argument. Repeatedly it is urged against the Libertarian, with a great air of triumph, that on his view he can't say *why* I now decide to rise to duty, or now decide to follow my strongest desire in defiance of duty. Of course he can't. If he could he wouldn't *be* a Libertarian. To "account for" a "free" act is a contradiction in terms. A free will is *ex hypothesi* the sort of thing of which the request for an *explanation* is absurd. The assumption that an explanation must be in principle possible for the act of moral decision deserves to rank as a classic example of the ancient fallacy of "begging the question."

But the critic usually has in mind another sense of the word "unintelligible". He is apt to take it for granted that an act which is unintelligible in the *above* sense (as the morally free act of the Libertarian undoubtedly is) is unintelligible in the *further* sense that we can attach no meaning to it. And this is an altogether more serious matter. If it could really be shown that the Libertarian's "free will" were unintelligible in this sense of being meaningless, that, for myself at any rate, would be the end of the affair. Libertarianism would have been conclusively refuted.

But it seems to me manifest that this can *not* be shown. The critic has allowed himself, I submit, to become the victim of a widely accepted but fundamentally vicious assumption. He has assumed that whatever is meaningful must exhibit its meaningfulness to those who view it from the standpoint of external observation. Now if one chooses thus to limit one's self to the rôle of external observer, it is, I think, perfectly true that one can attach no meaning to an act which is the act of something we call a "self" and yet follows from nothing in that self's character. But then *why should we* so limit ourselves, when what is under consideration is a subjective activity? For the apprehension of subjective acts there is *another* standpoint available, that of *inner experience,* of the practical consciousness in its actual functioning. If our free will should turn out to be something to which we can attach a meaning from *this* standpoint, no more is required. And no more ought to be expected. For I must repeat that only from the inner standpoint of living experience *could* anything of the nature of "activity" be directly grasped. Observation from without is in the nature of the case impotent to apprehend the active *qua* active. We can from without observe sequences of states. If into these we read activity (as we sometimes do), this can only be on the basis of what we discern in ourselves from the inner standpoint. It follows that if anyone insists upon taking his criterion of the meaningful simply from the standpoint of external observation, he is really deciding in advance of the evidence that the notion of activity, and a fortiori the notion of a free will, is "meaningless." He looks for the free act through a medium which is in the nature of the case incapable of revealing it, and then, because inevitably he doesn't find it, he declares that it doesn't exist!

But if, as we surely ought in this context, we adopt the inner standpoint, then (I am suggesting) things appear in a totally different light. From the inner standpoint, it seems to me plain, there is no difficulty whatever in attaching meaning to an act which is the self's act and which nevertheless does not follow from the self's character. So much I claim has been established by the phenomenological analysis . . . of the act of moral decision in face of moral temptation. It is thrown into particularly clear relief where the moral decision is to make the moral effort required to rise to duty. For the very function of moral effort, as it appears to the agent engaged in the act, is to enable the self to act against the line of least resistance, against the line to which his character as so far formed most strongly inclines him. But if the self is thus conscious here of *combating* his formed character, he surely cannot possibly suppose that the act, although his own act, *issues from* his formed character? I submit, therefore, that the self knows very well indeed—from the inner standpoint—what is meant by an act which is the *self's* act and which nevertheless does not follow from the self's *character.*

What this implies—and it seems to me to be an implication of cardinal importance for any theory of the self that aims at being more than superficial—is that the nature of the self is for itself something more than just its character as so far formed. The "nature" of the self and what we commonly call the "character" of the self are by no means the same thing, and it is utterly vital that they should not be confused. The "nature" of the self comprehends, but is not without remainder reducible to, its "character"; it must, if we are to be true to the testimony of our experience of it, be taken as including *also* the authentic creative power of fashioning and re-fashioning "character."

The misguided, and as a rule quite uncritical, belittlement, of the evidence offered by inner experience has, I am convinced, been responsible for more bad argument by the opponents of Free Will than has any other single factor. How often, for example, do we find the Determinist critic saying, in effect, "*Either* the act follows necessarily upon precedent states, *or* it is a mere matter of chance and accordingly of no moral significance." The disjunction is invalid, for it does not exhaust the possible alternatives. It seems to the critic to do so only because he *will* limit himself to the standpoint which is proper, and indeed alone possible, in dealing with the physical world, the standpoint of the external observer. If only he would allow himself to assume the standpoint which is not merely proper for, but necessary to, the apprehension of subjective activity, the inner standpoint of the practical consciousness in its actual functioning, he would find himself obliged to recognise the falsity of his disjunction. Reflection upon the act of moral decision as apprehended from the inner standpoint would force him to recognise a *third* possibility, as remote from chance as from necessity, that, namely, of *creative activity,* in which (as I have ventured to express it) nothing determines the act save the agent's doing of it.

11. There we must leave the matter. But as this lecture has been, I know, somewhat densely packed, it may be helpful if I conclude by reminding you, in bald summary, of the main things I have been trying to say. Let me set them out in so many successive theses.

1. The freedom which is at issue in the traditional Free Will problem is the freedom which is presupposed in moral responsibility.

2. Critical reflection upon carefully considered attributions of moral responsibility reveals that the only freedom that will do is a freedom which permits to inner acts of choice, and that these acts must be acts (*a*) of which the self is *sole* author, and (*b*) which the self could have performed otherwise.

3. From phenomenological analysis of the situation of moral temptation we find that the self as engaged in this situation is inescapably convinced that it possesses a freedom of precisely the specified kind, located in the decision to exert or withhold the moral effort needed to rise to duty where the pressure of its desiring nature is felt to urge it in a contrary direction.

4. Of the two types of Determinist criticism which seem to have most influence today, that based on the predictability of much human behaviour fails to touch a Libertarianism which confines the area of free will as above indicated. Libertarianism so understood is compatible with all the predictability that the empirical facts warrant. And:

5. The second main type of criticism, which alleges the "meaninglessness" of an act which is the self's act and which is yet not determined by the self's character, is based on a failure to appreciate that the standpoint of inner experience is not only legitimate but indispensable where what is at issue is the reality and nature of a subjective activity. The creative act of moral decision is inevitably meaningless to the mere external observer; but from the inner standpoint it is as real, and as significant, as anything in human experience.

Of Liberty and Necessity

DAVID HUME

Part I

It might reasonably be expected in questions which have been canvassed and disputed with great eagerness, since the first origin of science and philosophy, that the meaning of all the terms, at least, should have been agreed upon among the disputants; and our enquiries, in the course of two thousand years, been able to pass from words to the true and real subject of the controversy. For how easy may it seem to give exact definitions of the terms employed in reasoning, and make these definitions, not the mere sound of words, the object of future scrutiny and examination? But if we consider the matter more narrowly, we shall be apt to draw a quite opposite conclusion. From this circumstance alone, that a controversy has been long kept on foot, and remains still undecided, we may presume that there is some ambiguity in the expression, and that the disputants affix different ideas to the terms employed in the controversy. For as the faculties of the mind are supposed to be naturally alike in every individual; otherwise nothing could be more fruitless than to reason or dispute together; it were impossible, if men affix the same ideas to their terms, that they could so long form different opinions of the same subject; especially when they communicate their views, and each party turn themselves on all sides, in search of arguments which may give them the victory over their antagonists. It is true, if men attempt the discussion of questions which lie entirely beyond the reach of human capacity, such as those concerning the origin of worlds, or the economy of the intellectual system or region of spirits, they may long beat the air in their fruitless contests, and never arrive at any determinate conclusion. But if the question regard any subject of common life and experience, nothing, one would think, could preserve the dispute so long undecided but some ambiguous expressions, which keep the antagonists still at a distance, and hinder them from grappling with each other.

This has been the case in the long disputed question concerning liberty and necessity; and to so remarkable a degree that, if I be not much mistaken, we shall find, that all mankind, both learned and ignorant, have always been of the same opinion with regard to this subject, and that a few intelligible definitions would immediately have put an end to the whole controversy. I own that this dispute has been so much canvassed on all hands, and has led philosophers into such a labyrinth of obscure sophistry, that it is no wonder, if a sensible reader indulge his ease so far as to turn a deaf ear to the proposal of such a question, from which he can expect neither instruction or entertainment. But the state of the argument here proposed may, perhaps, serve to renew his attention; as it has more novelty, promises at least some decision of the controversy, and will not much disturb his ease by any intricate or obscure reasoning.

I hope, therefore, to make it appear that all men have ever agreed in the doctrine both of necessity and of liberty, according to any reasonable sense, which can be put on these terms; and that the whole controversy has hitherto turned merely upon words. We shall begin with examining the doctrine of necessity.

It is universally allowed that matter, in all its operations, is actuated by a necessary force, and

From *Enquiries Concerning Human Understanding and Concerning the Principles of Morals,* Selby-Bigge edition (Oxford: Oxford University Press, 1902), pp. 80–103.

that every natural effect is so precisely determined by the energy of its cause that no other effect, in such particular circumstances, could possibly have resulted from it. The degree and direction of every motion is, by the laws of nature, prescribed with such exactness that a living creature may as soon arise from the shock of two bodies as motion in any other degree or direction than what is actually produced by it. Would we, therefore, form a just and precise idea of *necessity,* we must consider whence that idea arises when we apply it to the question of bodies.

It seems evident that, if all the scenes of nature were continually shifted in such a manner that no two events bore any resemblance to each other, but every object was entirely new, without any similitude to whatever had been seen before, we should never, in that case, have attained the least idea of necessity, or of a connexion among these objects. We might say, upon such a supposition, that one object or event has followed another; not that one was produced by the other. The relation of cause and effect must be utterly unknown to mankind. Inference and reasoning concerning the operations of nature would, from that moment, be at an end; and the memory and senses remain the only canals, by which the knowledge of any real existence could possibly have access to the mind. Our idea, therefore, of necessity and causation arises entirely from the uniformity observable in the operations of nature, where similar objects are constantly conjoined together, and the mind is determined by custom to infer the one from the appearance of the other. These two circumstances form the whole of that necessity, which we ascribe to matter. Beyond the constant *conjunction* of similar objects, and the consequent *inference* from one to the other, we have no notion of any necessity or connexion.

If it appear, therefore, that all mankind have ever allowed, without any doubt or hesitation, that these two circumstances take place in the voluntary actions of men, and in the operations of mind; it must follow, that all mankind have ever agreed in the doctrine of necessity, and that they have hitherto disputed, merely for not understanding each other.

As to the first circumstance, the constant and regular conjunction of similar events, we may possibly satisfy ourselves by the following considerations. It is universally acknowledged that there is a great uniformity among the actions of men, in all nations and ages, and that human nature remains still the same, in its principles and operations. The same motives always produce the same actions. The same events follow from the same causes. Ambition, avarice, self-love, vanity, friendship, generosity, public spirit: these passions, mixed in various degrees, and distributed through society, have been, from the beginning of the world, and still are, the source of all the actions and enterprises, which have ever been observed among mankind. Would you know the sentiments, inclinations, and course of life of the Greeks and Romans? Study well the temper and actions of the French and English: You cannot be much mistaken in transferring to the former *most* of the observations which you have made with regard to the latter. Mankind are so much the same, in all times and places, that history informs us of nothing new or strange in this particular. Its chief use is only to discover the constant and universal principles of human nature, by showing men in all varieties of circumstances and situations, and furnishing us with materials from which we may form our observations and become acquainted with the regular springs of human action and behaviour. These records or wars, intrigues, factions, and revolutions, are so many collections of experiments, by which the politician or moral philosopher fixes the principles of his science, in the same manner as the physician or natural philosopher becomes acquainted with the nature of plants, minerals, and other external objects, by the experiments which he forms concerning them. Nor are the earth, water, and other elements, examined by Aristotle, and Hippocrates, more like to those which at present lie under our observation than the men described by Polybius and Tacitus are to those who now govern the world.

Should a traveller, returning from a far country, bring us an account of men, wholly different from any with whom we were ever acquainted; men, who were entirely divested of avarice, ambition, or revenge; who knew no pleasure but friendship, generosity, and public spirit; we should immediately, from these circumstances, detect the falsehood, and prove him a liar, with the same certainty as if he had stuffed his narration with stories of centaurs and dragons, miracles and prodigies. And if we would explode any forgery in history, we cannot make use of a more convincing argument, than to prove, that the actions ascribed to any person are directly contrary to the course of nature, and that no human motives, in such circumstances, could ever induce him to such a conduct. The veracity of Quintus Curtius is as much to be suspected, when he describes the supernatural courage of Alexander, by which he was hurried on singly to attack multitudes, as when he describes his supernatural force and activity, by which he was able to resist them. So readily and universally do we acknowledge a uniformity in human motives and actions as well as in the operations of body.

Hence likewise the benefit of that experience, acquired by long life and a variety of business and company, in order to instruct us in the principles of human nature, and regulate our future conduct, as well as speculation. By means of this guide, we mount up to the knowledge of men's inclinations and motives, from their actions, expressions, and even gestures; and again descend to the interpretation of their actions from our knowledge of their motives and inclinations. The general observations treasured up by a course of experience, give us the clue of human nature, and teach us to unravel all its intricacies. Pretexts and appearances no longer deceive us. Public declarations pass for the specious colouring of a cause. And though virtue and honour be allowed their proper weight and authority, that perfect disinterestedness, so often pretended to, is never expected in multitudes and parties; seldom in their leaders; and scarcely even in individuals of any rank or station. But were there no uniformity in human actions, and were every experiment which we could form of this kind irregular and anomalous, it were impossible to collect any general observations concerning mankind; and no experience, however accurately digested by reflection, would ever serve to any purpose. Why is the aged husbandman more skilful in his calling than the young beginner but because there is a certain uniformity in the operation of the sun, rain, and earth towards the production of vegetables; and experience teaches the old practitioner the rules by which this operation is governed and directed.

We must not, however, expect that this uniformity of human actions should be carried to such a length as that all men, in the same circumstances, will always act precisely in the same manner, without making any allowance for the diversity of characters, prejudices, and opinions. Such a uniformity in every particular, is found in no part of nature. On the contrary, from observing the variety of conduct in different men, we are enabled to form a greater variety of maxims, which still suppose a degree of uniformity and regularity.

Are the manners of men different in different ages and countries? We learn thence the great force of custom and education, which mould the human mind from its infancy and form it into a fixed and established character. Is the behaviour and conduct of the one sex very unlike that of the other? Is it thence we become acquainted with the different characters which nature has impressed upon the sexes, and which she preserves with constancy and regularity? Are the actions of the same person much diversified in the different periods of his life, from infancy to old age? This affords room for many general observations concerning the gradual change of our sentiments and inclinations, and the different maxims which prevail in the different ages of human creatures. Even the characters, which are peculiar to each individual, have a uniformity in their influence; otherwise our acquaintance with the persons and our observation of their conduct could never teach us their dispositions, or serve to direct our behaviour with regard to them.

I grant it possible to find some actions, which seem to have no regular connexion with any known motives, and are exceptions to all the measures of conduct which have ever been established for the government of men. But if we would willingly know what judgement should be formed of such irregular and extraordinary actions, we may consider the sentiments commonly entertained with regard to those irregular events which appear in the course of nature, and the operations of external objects. All causes are not conjoined to their usual effects with like uniformity. An artificer, who handles only dead matter, may be disappointed of his aim, as well as the politician, who directs the conduct of sensible and intelligent agents.

The vulgar, who take things according to their first appearance, attribute the uncertainty of events to such an uncertainty in the causes as makes the latter often fail of their usual influence; though they meet with no impediment in their operation. But philosophers, observing that, almost in every part of nature, there is contained a vast variety of springs and principles, which are hid, by reason of their minuteness or remoteness, find, that it is at least possible the contrariety of events may not proceed from any contingency in the cause, but from the secret operation of contrary causes. This possibility is converted into certainty by farther observation, when they remark that, upon an exact scrutiny, a contrariety of effects always betrays a contrariety of causes, and proceeds from their mutual opposition. A peasant can give no better reason for the stopping of any clock or watch than to say that it does not commonly go right: But an artist easily perceives that the same force in the spring or pendulum has always the same influence on the wheels; but fails of its usual effect, perhaps by reason of a grain of dust, which puts a stop to the whole movement. From the observation of several parallel instances, philosophers form a maxim that the connexion between all causes and effects is equally necessary, and that its seeming uncertainty in some instances proceeds from the secret opposition of contrary causes.

Thus, for instance, in the human body, when the usual symptoms of health or sickness disappoint our expectation; when medicines operate not with their wonted powers; when irregular events follow from any particular cause; the philosopher and physician are not surprised at the matter, nor are even tempted to deny, in general, the necessity and uniformity of those principles by which the animal economy is conducted. They know that a human body is a mighty complicated machine: That many secret powers lurk in it, which are altogether beyond our comprehension: That to us it must often appear very uncertain in its operations: And that therefore the irregular events, which outwardly discover themselves, can be no proof that the laws of nature are not observed with the greatest regularity in its internal operations and government.

The philosopher, if he be consistent, must apply the same reasoning to the actions and volitions of intelligent agents. The most irregular and unexpected resolutions of men may frequently be accounted for by those who know every particular circumstance of their character and situation. A person of an obliging disposition gives a peevish answer: But he has the toothache, or has not dined. A stupid fellow discovers an uncommon alacrity in his carriage: But he has met with a sudden piece of good fortune. Or even when an action, as sometimes happens, cannot be particularly accounted for, either by the person himself or by others; we know, in general, that the characters of men are, to a certain degree, inconstant and irregular. This is, in a manner, the constant character of human nature; though it be applicable, in a more particular manner, to some persons who have no fixed rule for their conduct, but proceed in a continued course of caprice and inconstancy. The internal principles and motives may operate in a uniform manner, notwithstanding these seeming irregularities; in the same manner as the winds, rain, clouds, and other variations of the weather are supposed to be governed by steady principles; though not easily discoverable by human sagacity and enquiry.

Thus it appears, not only that the conjunction between motives and voluntary actions is as regular and uniform as that between the cause and effect in any part of nature; but also that this regular conjunction has been universally acknowledged among mankind, and has never been the subject of dispute, either in philosophy or common life. Now, as it is from past experience that we draw all inferences concerning the future, and as we conclude that objects will always be conjoined together which we find to have always been conjoined; it may seem superfluous to prove that this experienced uniformity in human actions is a source whence we draw *inferences* concerning them. But in order to throw the argument into a greater variety of lights we shall also insist, though briefly, on this latter topic.

The mutual dependence of men is so great in all societies that scarce any human action is entirely complete in itself, or is performed without some reference to the actions of others, which are requisite to make it answer fully the intention of the agent. The poorest artificer, who labours alone, expects at least the protection of the magistrate, to ensure him the enjoyment of the fruits of his labour. He also expects that, when he carries his goods to market, and offers them at a reasonable price, he shall find purchasers, and shall be able, by the money he acquires, to engage others to supply him with those commodities which are requisite for his subsistence. In proportion as men extend their dealings, and render their intercourse with others more complicated, they always comprehend, in their schemes of life, a greater variety of voluntary actions, which they expect, from the proper motives, to co-operate with their own. In all these conclusions they take their measures from past experience, in the same manner as in their reasonings concerning external objects; and firmly believe that men, as well as all the elements, are to continue, in their operations, the same that they have ever found them. A manufacturer reckons upon the labour of his servants for the execution of any work as much as upon the tools which he employs, and would be equally surprised were his expectations disappointed. In short, this experimental inference and reasoning concerning the actions of others enters so much into human life that no man, while awake, is ever a moment without employing it. Have we not reason, therefore, to affirm that all mankind have always agreed in the doctrine of necessity according to the foregoing definition and explication of it?

Nor have philosophers ever entertained a different opinion from the people in this particular. For, not to mention that almost every action of their life supposes that opinion, there are even few of the speculative parts of learning to which it is not essential. What would become of *history,* had we not a dependence on the veracity of the historian according to the experience which we have had of mankind? How could *politics* be a science, if laws and forms of government had not a uniform influence upon society? Where would be the foundation of *morals,* if particular characters had no certain or determinate power to produce particular sentiments, and if these sentiments had no constant operation on actions? And with what pretence could we employ our *criticism* upon any poet or polite author, if we could not pronounce the conduct and sentiments of his actors either natural or unnatural to such characters, and in such circumstances? It seems almost impossible, therefore, to engage either in science or action of any kind without acknowledging the doctrine of necessity, and this *inference* from motive to voluntary actions, from characters to conduct.

And indeed, when we consider how aptly *natural* and *moral* evidence link together, and form only one chain of argument, we shall make no scruple to allow that they are of the same nature, and derived from the same principles. A prisoner who has neither money nor interest, discovers the impossibility of his escape, as well when he considers the obstinacy of the gaoler, as the walls and bars with which he is surrounded; and, in all attempts for his freedom, chooses rather to work upon the stone and iron of the one, than upon the inflexible nature of the other. The same prisoner, when conducted to the scaffold, foresees his death as certainly from the constancy and fidelity of his guards, as from the operation of the axe or wheel. His mind runs along a certain train of ideas: The refusal of the soldiers to consent to his escape; the action of the executioner; the separation of the head and body; bleeding, convulsive motions, and death. Here is a connected chain of natural causes and voluntary actions; but the mind feels no difference between them in passing from one link to another: Nor is less certain of the future event than if it were connected with the objects present to the memory or senses, by a train of causes, cemented together by what we are pleased to call a *physical* necessity. The same experienced union has the same effect on the mind, whether the united objects be motives, volition, and actions; or figure and motion. We may change the name of things; but their nature and their operation on the understanding never change.

Were a man, whom I know to be honest and opulent, and with whom I live in intimate friendship, to come into my house, where I am surrounded with my servants, I rest assured that he is not to stab me before he leaves it in order to rob me of my silver standish; and I no more suspect this event than the falling of the house itself, which is new, and solidly built and founded—*But he may have been seized with a sudden and unknown frenzy.*—So may a sudden earthquake arise, and shake and tumble my house about my ears. I shall therefore change the suppositions. I shall say that I know with certainty that he is not to put his hand into the fire and hold it there till it be consumed: And this event, I think I can foretell with the same assurance, as that, if he throw himself out at the window, and meet with no obstruction, he will not remain a moment suspended in the air. No suspicion of an unknown frenzy can give the least possibility to the former event, which is so contrary to all the known principles of human nature. A man who at noon leaves his purse full of gold on the pavement at Charing-Cross, may as well expect that it will fly away like a feather, as that he will find it untouched an hour after. Above one half of human reasonings contain inferences of a similar nature, attended with more or less degrees of certainty proportioned to our experience of the usual conduct of mankind in such particular situations.

I have frequently considered, what could possibly be the reason why all mankind, though they have ever, without hesitation, acknowledged the doctrine of necessity in their whole practice and reasoning, have yet discovered such a reluctance to acknowledge it in words, and have rather shown a propensity, in all ages, to profess the contrary opinion. The matter, I think, may be accounted for after the following manner. If we examine the operations of body, and the production of effects from their causes, we shall find that all our faculties can never carry us farther in our knowledge of this relation than barely to observe that particular objects are *constantly conjoined* together, and that the mind is carried, by a *customary transition,* from the appearance of one to the belief of the other. But though this conclusion concerning human ignorance be the result of the strictest scrutiny of this subject, men still entertain a strong propensity to believe that they penetrate farther into the powers of nature, and perceive something like a necessary connexion between the cause and the effect. When again they turn their reflections towards the operations of their own minds, and *feel* no such connexion of the motive and the action; they are thence apt to suppose, that there is a difference between the effects which result from material force, and those which arise from thought and intelligence. But being once convinced that we know nothing farther of causation of any kind than merely the *constant conjunction* of objects, and the consequent *inference* of the mind from one to another, and finding that these two circumstances are universally allowed to have place in voluntary actions; we may be more easily led to own the same necessity common to all causes. And though this reasoning may contradict the systems of many philosophers, in ascribing necessity to the determinations of the will, we shall find, upon reflection, that they dissent from it in words only, not in their real sentiment. Necessity, according to the sense in which it is here taken, has never yet been rejected, nor can ever, I think, be rejected by any philosopher. It may only, perhaps, be pretended that the mind can perceive, in the operations of matter, some farther connexion between the cause and effect; and connexion that has not place in voluntary actions of intelligent beings. Now whether it be so or not, can only appear upon examination; and it is incumbent on these philosophers to make good their assertion, by defining or describing that necessity, and pointing it out to us in the operations of material causes.

It would seem, indeed, that men begin at the wrong end of this question concerning liberty and necessity, when they enter upon it by examining the faculties of the soul, the influence of the understanding, and the operations of the will. Let them first discuss a more simple question, namely, the operations of body and of brute unintelligent matter; and try whether they can there form any idea of causation and necessity, except that of a constant conjunction of objects, and subsequent inference of the mind from one to another. If these circumstances form, in reality, the whole of that necessity, which we conceive in matter, and if these circumstances be also universally acknowledged to take place in the operations of the mind, the dispute is at an end; at least, must be owned to be thenceforth merely verbal. But as long as we will rashly suppose, that we have some farther idea of necessity and causation in the operations of external objects; at the same time, that we can find nothing farther in the voluntary actions of the mind; there is no possibility of bringing the question to any determinate issue, while we proceed upon so erroneous a supposition. The only method of undeceiving us is to mount up higher; to examine the narrow extent of science when applied to material causes; and to convince ourselves that all we know of them is the constant conjunction and inference above mentioned. We may, perhaps, find that it is with difficulty we are induced to fix such narrow limits to human understanding: But we can afterwards find no difficulty when we come to apply this doctrine to the actions of the will. For as it is evident that these have a regular conjunction with motives and circumstances and characters, and as we always draw inferences from one to the other, we must be obliged to acknowledge in words that necessity, which we have already avowed, in every deliberation of our lives, and in every step of our conduct and behaviour.[1]

But to proceed in this reconciling project with regard to the question of liberty and necessity; the most contentious question of metaphysics, the most contentious science; it will not require many words to prove, that all mankind have ever agreed in the doctrine of liberty as well as in that of necessity, and that the whole dispute, in this respect also, has been hitherto merely verbal. For what is meant by liberty, when applied to voluntary actions? We cannot surely mean that actions have so little connexion with motives, inclinations, and circumstances, that one does not follow with a certain degree of uniformity from the other, and that one affords no inference by which we can conclude the existence of the other. For these are plain and acknowledged matters of fact. By liberty, then, we can only mean *a power of acting or not acting, according to the determinations of the will;* that is, if we choose to remain at rest, we may; if we choose to move, we also may. Now this hypothetical liberty is universally allowed to belong to every one who is not a prisoner and in chains. Here, then, is no subject of dispute.

Whatever definition we may give of liberty, we should be careful to observe two requisite circumstances; *first,* that it be consistent with plain matter of fact; *secondly,* that it be consistent with itself. If we observe these circumstances, and render our definition intelligible, I am persuaded that all mankind will be found of one opinion with regard to it.

It is universally allowed that nothing exists without a cause of its existence, and that chance, when strictly examined, is a mere negative word, and means not any real power which has anywhere a being in nature. But it is pretended that some causes are necessary, some not necessary. Here then is the advantage of definitions. Let any one *define* a cause, without comprehending, as a part of the definition, a *necessary connexion* with its effect; and let him show distinctly the origin of the idea, expressed by the definition; and I shall readily give up the whole controversy. But if the foregoing explication of the matter be received, this must be absolutely impracticable. Had not objects a regular conjunction with each other, we should never have entertained any notion of cause and effect; and this regular conjunction produces that inference of the understanding, which is the only connexion, that we can have any comprehension of. Whoever attempts a definition of cause, exclusive of these circumstances, will be obliged either to employ unintelligible terms or such as are synonymous to the term which he endeavours to define.[2] And if the definition above mentioned be admitted; liberty, when opposed to necessity, not to constraint, is the same thing with chance; which is universally allowed to have no existence.

Part II

There is no method of reasoning more common, and yet none more blameable, than, in philosophical disputes, to endeavour the refutation of any hypothesis, by a pretence of its dangerous consequences to religion and morality. When any opinion leads to absurdities, it is certainly false; but it is not certain that an opinion is false, because it is of dangerous consequence. Such topics, therefore, ought entirely to be forborne; as serving nothing to the discovery of truth, but only to make the person of an antagonist odious. This I observe in general, without pretending to draw any advantage from it. I frankly submit to an examination of this kind, and shall venture to affirm that the doctrines, both of necessity and of liberty, as above explained, are not only consistent with morality, but are absolutely essential to its support.

Necessity may be defined two ways, conformably to the two definitions of *cause,* of which it makes an essential part. It consists either in the constant conjunction of like objects, or in the inference of the understanding from one object to another. Now necessity, in both these senses, (which, indeed, are at bottom the same) has universally, though tacitly, in the schools, in the pulpit, and in common life, been allowed to belong to the will of man; and no one has ever pretended to deny that we can draw inferences concerning human actions, and that those inferences are founded on the experienced union of like actions, with like motives, inclinations, and circumstances. The only particular in which any one can differ, is, that either, perhaps, he will refuse to give the name of necessity to this property of human actions: But as long as the meaning is understood, I hope the word can do no harm: Or that he will maintain it possible to discover something farther in the operations of matter. But this, it must be acknowledged, can be of no consequence to morality or religion, whatever it may be to natural philosophy or metaphysics. We may here be mistaken in asserting that there is no idea of any other necessity of connexion in the actions of the mind, but what everyone does, and must readily allow of. We change no circumstance in the received orthodox system with regard to the will, but only in that with regard to material objects and causes. Nothing, therefore, can be more innocent, at least, than this doctrine.

All laws being founded on rewards and punishments, it is supposed as a fundamental principle, that these motives have a regular and uniform influence on the mind, and both produce the food and prevent the evil actions. We may give to this influence what name we please; but, as it is usually conjoined with the action, it must be esteemed a *cause,* and be looked upon as an instance of that necessity, which we would here establish.

The only proper object of hatred or vengeance is a person or creature, endowed with thought and consciousness; and when any criminal or injurious actions excite that passion, it is only by their relation to the person, or connexion with him. Actions are, by their very nature, temporary and perishing; and where they proceed not from some *cause* in the character and disposition of the person who performed them, they can neither redound to his honour, if good; nor infamy, if evil. The actions themselves may be blameable; they may be contrary to all the rules of morality and religion: But the person is not answerable for them; and as they proceed from nothing in him that is durable and constant, and leave nothing of that nature behind them, it is impossible he can, upon their account, become the object of punishment or vengeance. According to the principle, therefore, which denies necessity, and consequently causes, a man is as pure and untainted. after having committed the most horrid crime, as at the first moment of his birth, nor is his character anywise concerned in his actions, since they are not derived from it, and the wickedness of the one can never be used as a proof of the depravity of the other.

Men are not blamed for such actions as they perform ignorantly and casually, whatever may be the consequences. Why? but because the principles of these actions are only momentary, and terminate in them alone. Men are less blamed for such actions as they perform hastily and unpremeditately than for such as proceed from deliberation. For what reason? but because a hasty temper, though a constant cause or principle in the mind, operates only by intervals, and infects not the whole character. Again, repentance wipes off every crime, if attended with a reformation of life and manners. How is this to be accounted for? but by asserting that actions render a person criminal merely as they are proofs of criminal principles in the mind; and when, by an alteration of these principles, they cease to be just proofs, they likewise cease to be criminal. But, except upon the doctrine of necessity, they never were just proofs, and consequently never were criminal.

It will be equally easy to prove, and from the same arguments, that *liberty,* according to that definition above mentioned, in which all men agree, is also essential to morality, and that no human actions, where it is wanting, are susceptible of any moral qualities, or can be the objects either of approbation or dislike. For as actions are objects of our moral sentiment, so far only as they are indications of the internal character, passions, and affections; it is impossible that they can give rise either to praise or blame, where they proceed not from these principles, but are derived altogether from external violence.

I pretend not to have obviated or removed all objections to this theory, with regard to necessity and liberty. I can foresee other objections, derived from topics which have not here been treated of. It may be said, for instance, that, if voluntary actions be subjected to the same laws of necessity with the operations of matter, there is a continued chain of necessary causes, pre-ordained and pre-determined, reaching from the original cause of all to every single volition of every human creature. No contingency anywhere in the universe; no indifference; no liberty. While we act, we are, at the same time, acted upon. The ultimate Author of all our volitions is the Creator of the world, who first bestowed motion on this immense machine, and placed all beings in that particular position, whence every subsequent event, by an inevitable necessity, must result. Human actions, therefore, either can have no moral turpitude at all, as proceeding from so good a cause; or if they have any turpitude, they must involve our Creator in the same guilt, while he is acknowledged to be their ultimate cause and author. For as a man, who fired a mine, is answerable for all the consequences whether the train he employed be long or short; so wherever a continued chain of necessary causes is fixed, that Being, either finite or infinite, who produces the first, is likewise the author of all the rest, and must both bear the blame and acquire the praise which belong to them. Our clear and unalterable ideas of morality establish this rule, upon unquestionable reasons, when we examine the consequences of any human action; and these reasons must still have greater force when applied to the volitions and intentions of a Being infinitely wise and powerful. Ignorance or impotence may be pleaded for so limited a creature as man; but those imperfections have no place in our Creator. He foresaw, he ordained, he intended all those actions of men, which we so rashly pronounce criminal. And we must therefore conclude, either that they are not criminal, or that the Deity, not man, is accountable for them. But as either of these positions is absurd and impious, it follows, that the doctrine from which they are deduced cannot possibly be true, as being liable to all the same objections. An absurd consequence, if necessary, proves the original doctrine to be absurd; in the same manner as criminal actions render criminal the original cause, if the connexion between them be necessary and evitable.

This objection consists of two parts, which we shall examine separately; *First,* that, if human actions can be traced up, by a necessary chain, to the Deity, they can never be criminal; on account of the infinite perfection of that Being from whom they are derived, and who can intend nothing but what is altogether good and laudable. Or, *Secondly,* if they be criminal, we must retract the attribute of perfection, which we ascribe to the Deity, and must acknowledge him to be the ultimate author of guilt and moral turpitude in all his creatures.

The answer to the first objection seems obvious and convincing. There are many philosophers who, after an exact scrutiny of all the phenomena of nature, conclude, that the WHOLE, considered as one system, is, in every period of its existence, ordered with perfect benevolence; and that the utmost possible happiness will, in the end, result to all created beings, without any mixture of positive or absolute ill or misery. Every physical ill, say they, makes an essential part of this benevolent system, and could not possibly be removed, even by the Deity himself, considered as a wise agent, without giving entrance to greater ill, or excluding greater good, which will result from it. From this theory, some philosophers, and the ancient *Stoics* among the rest, derived a topic of consolation under all afflictions, while they taught their pupils that those ills under which they laboured were, in reality, goods to the universe; and that to an enlarged view, which could comprehend the whole system of nature, every event became an object of joy and exultation. But though this topic be specious and sublime, it was soon found in practice weak and ineffectual. You would surely more irritate than appease a man lying under the racking pains of the gout by preaching up to him the rectitude of those general laws, which produced the malignant humours in his body, and led them through the proper canals, to the sinews and nerves, where they now excite such acute torments. These enlarged views may, for a moment, please the imagination of a speculative man, who is placed in ease and security; but neither can they dwell with constancy on his mind, even though undisturbed by the emotions of pain or passion; much less can they maintain their ground when attacked by such powerful antagonists. The affections take a narrower and more natural survey of their object; and by an economy, more suitable to the infirmity of human minds, regard alone the beings around us, and are actuated by such events as appear good or ill to the private system.

The case is the same with *moral* as with *physical* ill. It cannot reasonably be supposed, that those remote considerations, which are found of so little efficacy with regard to one, will have a more powerful influence with regard to the other. The mind of man is so formed by nature that, upon the appearance of certain characters, dispositions, and actions, it immediately feels the sentiment of approbation or blame; nor are there any emotions more essential to its frame and constitution. The characters which engage our approbation are chiefly such as contribute to the peace and security of human society; as the characters which excite blame are chiefly such as tend to public detriment and disturbance: Whence it may reasonably be presumed, that the moral sentiments arise, either mediately or immediately, from a reflection of these opposite interests. What though philosophical meditations establish a different opinion or conjecture; that everything is right with regard to the WHOLE, and that the qualities, which disturb society, are, in the main, as beneficial, and are as suitable to the primary intention of nature as those which more directly promote its happiness and welfare? Are such remote and uncertain speculations able to counterbalance the sentiments which arise from the natural and immediate view of the objects? A man who is robbed of a considerable sum; does he find his vexation for the loss anywise diminished by these sublime reflections? Why then should his moral resentment against the crime be supposed incompatible with them? Or why should not the acknowledgment of a real distinction between vice and virtue be reconcilable to all speculative systems of philosophy, as well as that of a real distinction between personal beauty and deformity? Both these distinctions are founded in the natural sentiments of the human mind: And these sentiments are not to be controuled or altered by any philosophical theory or speculation whatsoever.

The *second* objection admits not of so easy and satisfactory an answer; nor is it possible to explain distinctly, how the Deity can be the mediate cause of all the actions of men, without being the author of sin and moral turpitude. These are mysteries, which mere natural and unassisted reason is very unfit to handle; and whatever system she embraces, she must find herself involved in inextricable difficulties, and even contradictions, at every step which she takes with regard to such subjects. To reconcile the indifference and contingency of human actions with prescience; or to defend absolute decrees, and yet free the Deity from being the author of sin, has been found hitherto to exceed all the power of philosophy. Happy, if she be thence sensible of her temerity, when she pries into these sublime mysteries; and leaving a scene so full of obscurities and perplexities, return, with suitable modesty, to her true and proper province, the examination of common life; where she will find difficulties enough to employ her enquiries, without launching into so boundless an ocean of doubt, uncertainty, and contradiction!

Notes

1. The prevalence of the doctrine of liberty may be accounted for, from another cause, viz, a false sensation or seeming experience which we have, or may have, of liberty or indifference, in many of our actions. The necessity of any action, whether of matter or of mind, is not, properly speaking, a quality in the agent, but in any thinking or intelligent being, who may consider the action; and it consists chiefly in the determination of his thoughts to infer the existence of that action from some preceding objects; as liberty, when opposed to necessity, is nothing but the want of that determination, and a certain looseness or indifference, which we feel, in passing, or not passing, from the idea of one object to that of any succeeding one. Now we may observe, that, though, in *reflecting* on human actions, we seldom feel such a looseness, or indifference, but are commonly able to infer them with considerable certainty from their motives, and from the dispositions of the agent; yet it frequently happens, that, in *performing* the actions themselves, we are sensible of something like it: And as all resembling objects are readily taken for each other, this has been employed as a demonstrative and even intuitive proof of human liberty. We feel, that our actions are subject to our will, on most occasions; and imagine we feel, that the will itself is subject to nothing, because, when by a denial of it we are provoked to try, we feel, that it moves easily every way, and produces an im-

age of itself (or a *Velleïty,* as it is called in the schools) even on that side, on which it did not settle. This image, or faint motion, we persuade ourselves, could, at that time, have been compleated into the thing itself; because, should that be denied, we find, upon a second trial, that, at present, it can. We consider not, that the fantastical desire of shewing liberty, is here the motive of our actions. And it seems certain, that, however we may imagine we feel a liberty within ourselves, a spectator can commonly infer our actions from our motives and character; and even where he cannot, he concludes in general, that he might, were he perfectly acquainted with every circumstance of our situation and temper, and the most secret springs of our complexion and disposition. Now this is the very essence of necessity, according to the foregoing doctrine.

2. Thus, if a cause be defined, *that which produces any thing;* it is easy to observe, that *producing* is synonimous to *causing*. In like manner, if a cause be defined, *that by which any thing exists;* this is liable to the same objection. For what is meant by these words, *by which?* Had it been said, that a cause is *that* after which *any thing constantly exists;* we should have understood the terms. For this is, indeed, all we know of the matter. And this constancy forms the very essence of necessity, nor have we any other idea of it.

Moral Luck

THOMAS NAGEL

Kant believed that good or bad luck should influence neither our moral judgment of a person and his actions, nor his moral assessment of himself.

> The good will is not good because of what it effects or accomplishes or because of its adequacy to achieve some proposed end; it is good only because of its willing, i.e., it is good of itself. And, regarded for itself, it is to be esteemed incomparably higher than anything which could be brought about by it in favor of any inclination or even of the sum total of all inclinations. Even if it should happen that, by a particularly unfortunate fate or by the niggardly provision of a stepmotherly nature, this will should be wholly lacking in power to accomplish its purpose, and if even the greatest effort should not avail it to achieve anything of its end, and if there remained only the good will (not as a mere wish but as the summoning of all the means in our power), it would sparkle like a jewel in its own right, as something that had its full worth in itself. Usefulness or fruitlessness can neither diminish nor augment this worth.[1]

He would presumably have said the same about a bad will: whether it accomplishes its evil purposes is morally irrelevant. And a course of action that would be condemned if it had a bad outcome cannot be vindicated if by luck it turns out well. There cannot be moral risk. This view seems to be wrong, but it arises in response to a fundamental problem about moral responsibility to which we possess no satisfactory solution.

The problem develops out of the ordinary conditions of moral judgment. Prior to reflection it is intuitively plausible that people cannot be morally assessed for what is not their fault, or for what is due to factors beyond their control. Such judgment is different from the evaluation of something as a good or bad thing, or state of affairs. The latter may be present in addition to moral judgment, but when we blame someone for his actions we are not merely saying it is bad that they happen, or bad that he exists: we are judging *him,* saying he is bad, which is different from his being a bad thing. This kind of judgment takes only a certain kind of object. Without being able to explain exactly why, we feel that the appropriateness of moral assessment is easily undermined by the discovery that the act or attribute, no matter how good or bad, is not under the person's control. While other evaluations remain, this one seems to lose its footing. So a clear absence of control, produced by involuntary movement, physical force, or ignorance of the circumstances, excuses what is done from moral judgment. But what we do depends in many more ways than these on what is not under our control—what is not produced by a good or a bad will, in Kant's phrase. And external influences in this broader range are not usually thought to excuse what is done from moral judgment, positive or negative.

Let me give a few examples, beginning with the type of case Kant has in mind. Whether we succeed or fail in what we try to do nearly always depends to some extent on factors beyond our control. This is true of murder, altruism, revolution, the sacrifice of certain interests for the

From *Mortal Questions* (Cambridge: Cambridge University Press, 1979), pp. 24–38.

sake of others—almost any morally important act. What has been done, and what is morally judged, is partly determined by external factors. However jewel-like the good will may be in its own right, there is a morally significant difference between rescuing someone from a burning building and dropping him from a twelfth-storey window while trying to rescue him. Similarly, there is a morally significant difference between reckless driving and manslaughter. But whether a reckless driver hits a pedestrian depends on the presence of the pedestrian at the point where he recklessly passes a red light. What we do is also limited by the opportunities and choices with which we are faced, and these are largely determined by factors beyond our control. Someone who was an officer in a concentration camp might have led a quiet and harmless life if the Nazis had never come to power in Germany. And someone who led a quiet and harmless life in Argentina might have become an officer in a concentration camp if he had not left Germany for business reasons in 1930.

I shall say more later about these and other examples. I introduce them here to illustrate a general point. Where a significant aspect of what someone does depends on factors beyond his control, yet we continue to treat him in that respect as an object of moral judgment, it can be called moral luck. Such luck can be good or bad. And the problem posed by this phenomenon, which led Kant to deny its possibility, is that the broad range of external influences here identified seems on close examination to undermine moral assessment as surely as does the narrower range of familiar excusing conditions. If the condition of control is consistently applied, it threatens to erode most of the moral assessments we find it natural to make. The things for which people are morally judged are determined in more ways than we at first realize by what is beyond their control. And when the seemingly natural requirement of fault or responsibility is applied in light of these facts, it leaves few pre-reflective moral judgments intact. Ultimately, nothing or almost nothing about what a person does seems to be under his control.

Why not conclude, then, that the condition of control is false—that it is an initially plausible hypothesis refuted by clear counter-examples? One could in that case look instead for a more refined condition which picked out the *kinds* of lack of control that really undermine certain moral judgments, without yielding the unacceptable conclusion derived from the broader condition, that most or all ordinary moral judgments are illegitimate.

What rules out this escape is that we are dealing not with a theoretical conjecture but with a philosophical problem. The condition of control does not suggest itself merely as a generalization from certain clear cases. It seems *correct* in the future cases to which it is extended beyond the original set. When we undermine moral assessment by considering new ways in which control is absent, we are not just discovering what *would* follow given the general hypothesis, but are actually being persuaded that in itself the absence of control is relevant in these cases too. The erosion of moral judgment emerges not as the absurd consequence of an over-simple theory, but as a natural consequence of the ordinary idea of moral assessment, when it is applied in view of a more complete and precise account of the facts. It would therefore be a mistake to argue from the unacceptability of the conclusions to the need for a different account of the conditions of moral responsibility. The view that moral luck is paradoxical is not a *mistake,* ethical or logical, but a perception of one of the ways in which the intuitively acceptable conditions of moral judgment threaten to undermine it all.

It resembles the situation in another area of philosophy, the theory of knowledge. There too conditions which seem perfectly natural, and which grow out of the ordinary procedures for challenging and defending claims to knowledge, threaten to undermine all such claims if consistently applied. Most skeptical arguments have this quality: they do not depend on the imposition of arbitrarily stringent standards of knowledge, arrived at by misunderstanding, but appear to grow inevitably from the consistent application of ordinary standards.[2] There is a substantive parallel as well, for epistemological skepticism arises from consideration of the respects in which our beliefs and their relation to reality depend on factors beyond our control. External and internal causes produce our beliefs. We may subject these processes to scrutiny in an effort to avoid error, but our conclusions at this next level also result, in part, from influences which we do not control directly. The same will be true no matter how far we carry the investigation. Our beliefs are always, ultimately, due to factors outside our control, and the impossibility of encompassing those factors without being at the mercy of others leads us to doubt whether we know anything. It looks as though, if any of our beliefs are true, it is pure biological luck rather than knowledge.

Moral luck is like this because while there are various respects in which the natural objects of moral assessment are out of our control or influenced by what is out of our control, we cannot reflect on these facts without losing our grip on the judgments.

There are roughly four ways in which the natural objects of moral assessment are disturbingly subject to luck. One is the phenomenon of constitutive luck—the kind of person you are, where this is not just a question of what you deliberately do, but of your inclinations, capacities, and temperament. Another category is luck in one's circumstances—the kind of problems and situations one faces. The other two have to do with the causes and effects of action: luck in how one is determined by antecedent circumstances, and luck in the way one's actions and projects turn out. All of them present a common problem. They are all opposed by the idea that one cannot be more culpable or estimable for anything than one is for that fraction of it which is under one's control. It seems irrational to take or dispense credit or blame for matters over which a person has no control, or for their influence on results over which he has partial control. Such things may create the conditions for action, but action can be judged only to the extent that it goes beyond these conditions and does not just result from them.

Let us first consider luck, good and bad, in the way things turn out. Kant, in the above-quoted passage, has one example of this in mind, but the category covers a wide range. It includes the truck driver who accidentally runs over a child, the artist who abandons his wife and five children to devote himself to painting,[3] and other cases in which the possibilities of success and failure are even greater. The driver, if he is entirely without fault, will feel terrible about his role in the event, but will not have to reproach himself. Therefore this example of agent-regret[4] is not yet a case of *moral* bad luck. However, if the driver was guilty of even a minor degree of negligence—failing to have his brakes checked recently, for example—then if that negligence contributes to the death of the child, he will not merely feel terrible. He will blame himself for the death. And what makes this an example of moral luck is that he would have to blame himself only slightly for the negligence itself if no situation arose which required him to brake suddenly and violently to avoid hitting a child. Yet the *negligence* is the same in both cases, and the driver has no control over whether a child will run into his path.

The same is true at higher levels of negligence. If someone has had too much to drink and his car swerves on the sidewalk, he can count himself morally lucky if there are no pedestrians in its path. If there were, he would be to blame for their deaths, and would probably be prosecuted for manslaughter. But if he hurts no one, although his recklessness is exactly the same, he is guilty of a far less serious legal offence and will certainly reproach himself and be reproached by others much less severely. To take another legal example, the penalty for attempted murder is less than that for successful murder—however similar the intentions and motives of the assailant may be in the two cases. His degree of culpability can depend, it would seem, on whether the victim happened to be wearing a bullet-proof vest, or whether a bird flew into the path of the bullet—matters beyond his control.

Finally, there are cases of decision under uncertainty—common in public and in private life. Anna Karenina goes off with Vronsky, Gauguin leaves his family, Chamberlain signs the Munich agreement, the Decembrists persuade the troops under their command to revolt against the czar, the American colonies declare their independence from Britain, you introduce two people in an attempt at match-making. It is tempting in all such cases to feel that some decision must be possible, in the light of what is known at the time, which will make reproach unsuitable no matter how things turn out. But this is not true; when someone acts in such ways he takes his life, or his moral position, into his hands, because how things turn out determines what he has done. It is possible *also* to assess the decision from the point of view of what could be known at the time, but this is not the end of the story. If the Decembrists had succeeded in overthrowing Nicholas I in 1825 and establishing a constitutional regime, they would be heroes. As it is, not only did they fail and pay for it, but they bore some responsibility for the terrible punishments meted out to the troops who had been persuaded to follow them. If the American Revolution had been a bloody failure resulting in greater repression, then Jefferson, Franklin and Washington would still have made a noble attempt and might not even have regretted it on their way to the scaffold, but they would also have had to blame themselves for what they had helped to bring on their compatriots. (Perhaps peaceful efforts at reform would eventually have succeeded.) If Hitler had not overrun Europe and exterminated millions, but instead had died of a heart attack after occupying the Sudetenland, Chamberlain's action at Munich would still have utterly betrayed the Czechs, but it would not be the great moral disaster that has made his name a household word.[5]

In many cases of difficult choice the outcome cannot be foreseen with certainty. One kind of assessment of the choice is possible in advance, but another kind must await the outcome, because the outcome determines what has been done. The same degree of culpability or estimability in intention, motive, or concern is compatible with a wide range of judgments, positive or negative, depending on what happened beyond the point of decision. The *mens rea* which could have existed in the absence of any consequences does not exhaust the grounds of moral judgment. Actual results influence culpability or esteem in a large class of unquestionably ethical cases ranging from negligence through political choice.

That these are genuine moral judgments rather than expressions of temporary attitude is evident from the fact that one can say *in advance* how the moral verdict will depend on the results. If one negligently leaves the bath running with the baby in it, one will realize, as one bounds up the stairs toward the bathroom, that if the baby has drowned one has done something awful, whereas if it has not one has merely been careless. Someone who launches a violent revolution against an authoritarian regime knows that if he fails he will be responsible for much suffering that is in vain, but if he succeeds he will be justified by the outcome. I do not mean that *any* action can be retroactively justified by history. Certain things are so bad in themselves, or so risky, that no results can make them all right. Nevertheless, when moral judgment does depend on the outcome, it is objective and timeless and not dependent on a change of standpoint produced by success or failure. The judgment after the fact follows from a hypothetical judgment that can be made beforehand, and it can be made as easily by someone else as by the agent.

From the point of view which makes responsibility dependent on control, all this seems absurd. How is it possible to be more or less culpable depending on whether a child gets into the path of one's car, or a bird into the path of one's bullet? Perhaps it is true what is done depends on more than the agent's state of mind or intention. The problem then is, why is it not irrational to base moral assessment on what people do, in this broad sense? It amounts to holding them responsible for the contributions of fate as well as for their own—provided they have made some contribution to begin with. If we look at cases of negligence or attempt, the pattern seems to be that overall culpability corresponds to the product of mental or intentional fault and the seriousness of the outcome. Cases of decision under uncertainty are less easily explained in this way, for it seems that the overall judgment can even shift from positive to negative depending on the outcome. But here too it seems rational to subtract the effects of occurrences subsequent to the choice, that were merely possible at the time, and concentrate moral assessment on the actual decision in light of the probabilities. If the object of moral judgment is the *person,* then to hold him accountable for what he has done in the broader sense is akin to strict liability, which may have its legal uses but seems irrational as a moral position.

The result of such a line of thought is to pare down each act to its morally essential core, an inner act of pure will assessed by motive and intention. Adam Smith advocates such a position in *The Theory of Moral Sentiments,* but notes that it runs contrary to our actual judgments.

> But how well soever we may seem to be persuaded of the truth of this equitable maxim, when we consider it after this manner, in abstract, yet when we come to particular cases, the actual consequences which

> happen to proceed from any action, have a very great effect upon our sentiments concerning its merit or demerit, and almost always either enhance or diminish our sense of both. Scarce, in any one instance, perhaps, will our sentiments be found, after examination, to be entirely regulated by this rule, which we all acknowledge ought entirely to regulate them.[6]

Joel Feinberg points out further that restricting the domain of moral responsibility to the inner world will not immunize it to luck. Factors beyond the agent's control, like a coughing fit, can interfere with his decisions as surely as they can with the path of a bullet from his gun.[7] Nevertheless the tendency to cut down the scope of moral assessment is pervasive, and does not limit itself to the influence of effects. It attempts to isolate the will from the other direction, so to speak, by separating out constitutive luck. Let us consider that next.

Kant was particularly insistent on the moral irrelevance of qualities of temperament and personality that are not under the control of the will. Such qualities as sympathy or coldness might provide the background against which obedience to moral requirements is more or less difficult, but they could not be objects of moral assessment themselves, and might well interfere with confident assessment of its proper object—the determination of the will by the motive of duty. This rules out moral judgment of many of the virtues and vices, which are states of character that influence choice but are certainly not exhausted by dispositions to act deliberately in certain ways. A person may be greedy, envious, cowardly, cold, ungenerous, unkind, vain, or conceited, but *behave* perfectly by a monumental effort of will. To possess these vices is to be unable to help having certain feelings under certain circumstances, and to have strong spontaneous impulses to act badly. Even if one controls the impulses, one still has the vice. An envious person hates the greater success of others. He can be morally condemned as envious even if he congratulates them cordially and does nothing to denigrate or spoil their success. Conceit, likewise, need not be displayed. It is fully present in someone who cannot help dwelling with secret satisfaction on the superiority of his own achievements, talents, beauty, intelligence, or virtue. To some extent such a quality may be the product of earlier choices; to some extent it may be amenable to change by current actions. But it is largely a matter of constitutive bad fortune. Yet people are morally condemned for such qualities, and esteemed for what they are *like*.

To Kant this seems incoherent because virtue is enjoined on everyone and therefore must in principle be possible for everyone. It may be easier for some than for others, but it must be possible to achieve it by making the right choices, against whatever temperamental background.[8] One may want to have a generous spirit, or regret not having one, but it makes no sense to condemn oneself or anyone else for a quality which is not within the control of the will. Condemnation implies that you should not be like that, not that it is unfortunate that you are.

Nevertheless, Kant's conclusion remains intuitively unacceptable. We may be persuaded that these moral judgments are irrational, but they reappear involuntarily as soon as the argument is over. This is the pattern throughout the subject.

The third category to consider is luck in one's circumstances, and I shall mention it briefly. The things we are called upon to do, the moral tests we face, are importantly determined by factors beyond our control. It may be true of someone that in a dangerous situation he would behave in a cowardly or heroic fashion, but if the situation never arises, he will never have the chance to distinguish or disgrace himself in this way, and his moral record will be different.[9]

A conspicuous example of this is political. Ordinary citizens of Nazi Germany had an opportunity to behave heroically by opposing the regime. They also had an opportunity to behave badly, and most of them are culpable for having failed this test. But it is a test to which the citizens of other countries were not subjected, with the result that even if they, or some of them, would have behaved as badly as the Germans in like circumstances, they simply did not and therefore are not similarly culpable. Here again one is morally at the mercy of fate, and it may seem irrational upon reflection, but our ordinary moral attitudes would be unrecognizable without it. We judge people for what they actually do or fail to do, not just for what they would have done if circumstances had been different.[10]

This form of moral determination by the actual

is also paradoxical, but we can begin to see how deep in the concept of responsibility the paradox is embedded. A person can be morally responsible only for what he does; but what he does results from a great deal that he does not do; therefore he is not morally responsible for what he is and is not responsible for. (This is not a contradiction, but it is a paradox.)

It should be obvious that there is a connection between these problems about responsibility and control and an even more familiar problem, that of freedom of the will. That is the last type of moral luck I want to take up, though I can do no more within the scope of this essay than indicate its connection with the other types.

If one cannot be responsible for consequences of one's acts due to factors beyond one's control, or for antecedents of one's acts that are properties of temperament not subject to one's will, or for the circumstances that pose one's moral choices, then how can one be responsible even for the stripped-down acts of the will itself, if *they* are the product of antecedent circumstances outside of the will's control?

The area of genuine agency, and therefore of legitimate moral judgment, seems to shrink under this scrutiny to an extensionless point. Everything seems to result from the combined influence of factors, antecedent and posterior to action, that are not within the agent's control. Since he cannot be responsible for them, he cannot be responsible for their results—though it may remain possible to take up the aesthetic or other evaluative analogues of the moral attitudes that are thus displaced.

It is also possible, of course, to brazen it out and refuse to accept the results, which indeed seem unacceptable as soon as we stop thinking about the arguments. Admittedly, if certain surrounding circumstances had been different, then no unfortunate consequences had been different, then no unfortunate consequences would have followed from a wicked intention, and no seriously culpable act would have been performed; but since the circumstances were *not* different, and the agent *in fact* succeeded in perpetrating a particularly cruel murder, *that* is what he did, and that is what he is responsible for. Similarly, we may admit that if certain antecedent circumstances had been different, the agent would never have developed into the sort of person who would do such a thing; but since he *did* develop (as the inevitable result of those antecedent circumstances) into the sort of swine he is, and into the person who committed such a murder, *that* is what he is blameable for. In both cases one is responsible for what one actually does—even if what one actually does depends in important ways on what is not within one's control. This compatibilist account of our moral judgments would leave room for the ordinary conditions of responsibility—the absence of coercion, ignorance, or involuntary movement—as part of the determination of what someone has done—but it is understood not to exclude the influence of a great deal that he has not done.[11]

The only thing wrong with this solution is its failure to explain how skeptical problems arise. For they arise not from the imposition of an arbitrary external requirement, but from the nature of moral judgment itself. Something in the ordinary idea of what someone does must explain how it can seem necessary to subtract from it anything that merely happens—even though the ultimate consequence of such subtraction is that nothing remains. And something in the ordinary idea of knowledge must explain why it seems to be undermined by any influences on belief not within the control of the subject—so that knowledge seems impossible without an impossible foundation in autonomous reason. But let us leave epistemology aside and concentrate on action, character, and moral assessment.

The problem arises, I believe, because the self which acts and is the object of moral judgment is threatened with dissolution by the absorption of its acts and impulses into the class of events. Moral judgment of a person is judgment not of what happens to him, but of him. It does not say merely that a certain event or state of affairs is fortunate or unfortunate or even terrible. It is not an evaluation of a state of the world, or of an individual as part of the world. We are not thinking just that it would be better if he were different, or did not exist, or had not done some of the things he has done. We are judging *him,* rather than his existence or characteristics. The effect of concentrating on the influence of what is not under his control is to make this responsible self seem to disappear, swallowed up by the order of mere events.

What, however, do we have in mind that a person must *be* to be the object of these moral attitudes? While the concept of agency is easily underminded, it is very difficult to give it a positive characterization. That is familiar from the literature on Free Will.

I believe that in a sense the problem has no solution, because something in the idea of agency is incompatible with actions being events, or people being things. But as the external determinants of what someone has done are gradually exposed, in their effect on consequences, character, and choice itself, it becomes gradually clear that actions are events and people things. Eventually nothing remains which can be ascribed to the responsible self, and we are left with nothing but a portion of the larger sequence of events, which can be deplored or celebrated, but not blamed or praised.

Though I cannot define the idea of the active self that is thus undermined, it is possible to say something about its sources. There is a close connexion between our feelings about ourselves and our feelings about others. Guilt and indignation, shame and contempt, pride and admiration are internal and external sides of the same moral attitudes. We are unable to view ourselves simply as portions of the world, and from inside we have a rough idea of the boundary between what is us and what is not, what we do and what happens to us, what is our personality and what is an accidental handicap. We apply the same essentially internal conception of the self to others. About ourselves we feel pride, shame, guilt, remorse—and agent-regret. We do not regard our actions and our characters merely as fortunate or unfortunate episodes—though they may also be that. We cannot *simply* take an external evaluative view of ourselves—of what we most essentially are and what we do. And this remains true even when we have seen that we are not responsible for our own existence, or our nature, or the choices we have to make, or the circumstances that give our acts the consequences they have. Those acts remain ours and we remain ourselves, despite the persuasiveness of the reasons that seem to argue us out of existence.

It is this internal view that we extend to others in moral judgment—when we judge *them* rather than their desirability or utility. We extend to others the refusal to limit ourselves to external evaluation, and we accord to them selves like our own. But in both cases this comes up against the brutal inclusion of humans and everything about them in a world from which they cannot be separated and of which they are nothing but contents. The external view forces itself on us at the same time that we resist it. One way this occurs is through the gradual erosion of what we do by the subtraction of what happens.[12]

The inclusion of consequences in the conception of what we have done is an acknowledgment that we are parts of the world, but the paradoxical character of moral luck which emerges from this acknowledgment shows that we are unable to operate with such a view, for it leaves us with no one to be. The same thing is revealed in the appearance that determinism obliterates responsibility. Once we see an aspect of what we or someone else does as something that happens, we lose our grip on the idea that it has been done and that we can judge the doer and not just the happening. This explains why the absence of determinism is no more hospitable to the concept of agency than is its presence—a point that has been noticed often. Either way the act is viewed externally, as part of the course of events.

The problem of moral luck cannot be understood without an account of the internal conception of agency and its special connection with the moral attitudes as opposed to other types of value. I do not have such an account. The degree to which the problem has a solution can be determined only by seeing whether in some degree the incompatibility between this conception and the various ways in which we do not control what we do is only apparent. I have nothing to offer on that topic either. But it is not enough to say merely that our basic moral attitudes toward ourselves and others are determined by what is actual; and by the external view of action which forces itself on us when we see how everything we do belongs to a world that we have not created.

Notes

1. *Foundations of the Metaphysics of Morals,* first section, third paragraph.
2. See Thompson Clark, ''The Legacy of Skepticism,'' *Journal of Philosophy,* 69, no. 20 (November 9, 1972), 754–69.

3. Such a case, modelled on the life of Gauguin, is discussed by Bernard Williams in "Moral Luck," *Proceedings of the Aristotelian Society*, supplementary vol. 50 (1976), 115–35 (to which the original version of this essay was a reply). He points out that though success or failure cannot be predicted in advance, Gauguin's most basic retrospective feelings about the decision will be determined by the development of his talent. My disagreement with Williams is that his account fails to explain why such retrospective attitudes can be called moral. If success does not permit Gauguin to justify himself to others, but still determines his most basic feelings, that shows only that his most basic feelings need not be moral. It does not show that morality is subject to luck. If the retrospective judgment were moral, it would imply the truth of a hypothetical judgment made in advance, of the form "If I leave my family and become a great painter, I will be justified by success; if I don't become a great painter, the act will be unforgivable."
4. Williams's term (ibid.).
5. For a fascinating but morally repellent discussion of the topic of justification by history, see Maurice Merleau-Ponty, *Humanisme et Terreur* (Paris: Gallimard, 1947), translated as *Humanism and Terror* (Boston: Beacon Press, 1969).
6. Pt II, sect. 3, Introduction, para. 5.
7. "Problematic Responsibility in Law and Morals," in Joel Feinberg, *Doing and Deserving* (Princeton: Princeton University Press, 1970).
8. "[I]f nature has put little sympathy in the heart of a man, and if he, though an honest man, is by temperament cold and indifferent to the sufferings of others, perhaps because he is provided with special gifts of patience and fortitude and expects or even requires that others should have the same—and such a man would certainly not be the meanest product of nature—would not he find in himself a source from which to give himself a far higher worth than he could have got by having a good-natured temperament?" (*Foundations of the Metaphysics of Morals*, first section, eleventh paragraph).
9. Cf. Thomas Gray, "Elegy Written in a Country Churchyard."

   Some mute inglorious Milton here may rest,
   Some Cromwell, guiltless of his country's blood.

   An unusual example of circumstantial moral luck is provided by the kind of moral dilemma with which someone can be faced through no fault of his own, but which leaves him with nothing to do which is not wrong. See . . . Bernard Williams, "Ethical Consistency," *Proceedings of the Aristotelian Society*, supplementary vol. 39 (1965), reprinted in *Problems of the Self* (Cambridge: Cambridge University Press, 1973), pp. 166–86.
10. Circumstantial luck can extend to aspects of the situation other than individual behavior. For example, during the Vietnam War even U.S. citizens who had opposed their country's actions vigorously from the start often felt compromised by its crimes. Here they were not even responsible; there was probably nothing they could do to stop what was happening, so the feeling of being implicated may seem unintelligible. But it is nearly impossible to view the crimes of one's own country in the same way that one views the crimes of another country, no matter how equal one's lack of power to stop them in the two cases. One is a citizen of one of them, and has a connexion with its actions (even if only through taxes that cannot be withheld)—that one does not have with the other's. This makes it possible to be ashamed of one's country, and to feel a victim of moral bad luck that one was an American in the 1960s.
11. The corresponding position in epistemology would be that knowledge consists of true beliefs formed in certain ways, and that it does not require all aspects of the process to be under the knower's control, actually or potentially. Both the correctness of these beliefs and the process by which they are arrived at would therefore be importantly subject to luck. The Nobel Prize is not awarded to people who turn out to be wrong, no matter how brilliant their reasoning.
12. See P. F. Strawson's discussion of the conflict between the objective attitude and personal reactive attitudes in "Freedom and Resentment," *Proceedings of the British Academy*, 1962, reprinted in *Studies in the Philosophy of Thought and Action*, ed. P. F. Strawson (London: Oxford University Press, 1968), and in P. F. Strawson, *Freedom and Resentment and Other Essays* (London: Methuen, 1974).

V

ETHICS

INTRODUCTION

Almost all of us hold a wide range of moral views. We have views about when it is wrong to lie, cheat, steal, betray a friend, have an abortion, break a law or a promise, kill an adult human being, or threaten to kill one. And we have views about why such acts are wrong when they are. We assess lives, our own and others, as going more or less well or badly. We have views about the contribution to a good life of material well-being, artistic accomplishment, athletic prowess, intellectual curiosity, friendship and love, sex, courage, and so on. We also assess social institutions from a moral perspective. Most of us think that the slavery practiced in the United States in the nineteenth century was unjust. And one has only to pick up the daily newspaper to find views expressed about the fairness or unfairness of the federal tax code.

These views are at many different levels of generality. You may think that your friend was wrong to have cheated on yesterday's exam; and you may also think that if you are faced with saving one life or many, you ought always to save the larger number of lives. Some of these views you may hold with a great deal of confidence, for example, that wanton killing of an adult human being is wrong. Other views you may hold less confidently: this may be true of your assessment of the moral permissibility of abortion. Yet, despite uncertainty, you sometimes must act one way or another. Our moral views are significant to our lives in part because they frequently guide our action.

Moral philosophy begins with reflection on such views. It aims at detecting unsuspected inconsistencies; at articulating and assessing central arguments; at determining the extent to which such views have a defensible, underlying rationale; and, in general, at understanding the nature of morality.

Moral Perplexities

The essays in Section A provide examples of philosophers attempting to reason about relatively specific moral concerns. We begin with Judith Jarvis Thomson's instructive example of how one might critically assess an argument for a moral position. Her target is an often-met argument for the impermissibility of abortion, one that begins with the claim that a fetus has a full-blown right to life. Opponents of this argument typically reject the claim to such a right. However, Thomson argues that even given the claim, there are profound problems with the inference to the conclusion about the impermissibility of abortion, problems that reveal important complexities in the very idea of a right to life.

Philippa Foot discusses the principle of double effect, which is commonly appealed to in discussions of abortion, although it has much wider scope. On this principle it may sometimes be permissible to bring about a harm that one does not intend, even though it would not be permissible to bring about that harm intending to bring it about. We can best understand this principle by considering a pair of examples.

The first example comes from Foot's paper. Suppose you are the driver of a tram whose brakes have failed. The tram is about to rush past the station and slam into five men working on the track. Although you cannot stop the tram, you can steer it onto a side track, thereby preventing it from hitting the five workmen. Unfortunately, you would then run into the one workman who is on that side track. Should you steer the tram onto the side track?

Many answer yes. After all, if you do not steer the tram onto the side track, five persons die; if you do, only one person dies. The principle of the yea-sayers seems to be that if you must choose between five people living and one person dying, and vice versa, you are at least permitted to choose the former. But this principle quickly gets one into trouble. Here is an example suggested by Foot, Gilbert Harman, and others: a doctor may need two lungs, two kidneys, and a heart for organ transplants to save each of five accident victims. Unfortunately, she will not have access to the organs in time to prevent the five deaths. Then, in walks a young stranger seeking a routine checkup. Should the doctor follow the same principle as with the runaway tram and cut up the young man to get his organs to save the five accident victims?

If you think the tram driver should turn onto the side track to save the five workers but that the doctor should not cut up the young man to save the five accident victims, you may be applying the principle of double effect. In the tram case the driver does not intend to kill the one worker as a means to save the five workers, whereas the doctor must kill the young stranger as her means to save the five accident victims. Foot argues that such pairs of examples force us to take the principle of double effect seriously. However, in the end she argues that this principle cannot adequately handle other cases and rejects it in favor of a principle that emphasizes the difference between ''positive'' and ''negative'' duties.

Foot's essay illustrates a kind of dialectical reasoning that is common in philosophy. She begins with examples of actions about the moral status of which many people share fairly clear intuitive judgments. She then seeks a more general principle that systematizes and accounts for these shared intuitions. Finally, she tests this more general principle against further examples. If the principle conflicts with firm views about these further examples, one then considers some alternative principle. This is how Foot is first led to the principle of double effect and then away from it.

In the last two selections in Section A, John M. Taurek and Gregory Kavka show how moral views with which we may be quite comfortable may still be in conflict with other views we hold. Taurek argues that a common view about the importance of the numbers of people affected by different actions is in conflict with other deeply entrenched views. And Kavka argues that our views about deterrent intentions—for example, those that are at the heart of strategies of nuclear deterrence—quickly lead us into paradox.

Moral Theories

Utilitarianism

We now turn to attempts by philosophers to provide systematic approaches to moral issues. Begin by distinguishing two general questions: What makes acts right (or wrong)? What things are good (bad)? *Consequentialist* moral theories treat the second question as basic. Such theories begin by determining what things are good and what things bad. They then see the rightness of an action as determined by the goodness or badness of relevant consequences. (For skepticism about this general framework, see Taurek's essay.)

The most common consequentialist theories are *utilitarian* theories. Such theories suppose that the only thing that has nonderivative value is the *welfare* or *happiness* of sentient beings. It is granted that other things—courage, knowledge, love, and money, for example—have value. But their value is derivative from their contribution to happiness. Jeremy Bentham and John Stuart Mill defend different versions of such a utilitarian perspective. Bentham identifies happiness with pleasure and the absence of pain, and he proceeds to develop a calculus to measure the relative value of different pleasures and pains. He supposes that what makes an act right (or wrong) is the extent to which it increases pleasure or decreases pain. His theory can be called *hedonistic act utilitarianism: hedonistic* because it sees pleasure and pain as the only things with nonderivative value; *act* utilitarianism because, in answering our question about what makes acts right, it applies the test of utility directly to actions.

On one common interpretation, Mill also accepts a version of act utilitarianism. But he differs from Bentham in his view that some pleasures are "higher" than others. Bentham saw happiness as depending only on the felt pleasures and pains of the organism. Mill's emphasis on the "quality" of pleasure seems to make happiness depend also on the satisfaction of certain ideals, for example, those satisfied by a discontented Socrates but not by a contented but unreflective person.

E. F. Carritt argues that such utilitarian theories make "no room for justice." For example, they seem to have the consequence that a prosecutor should frame an innocent person if that is the only way she can prevent a disastrous riot. Act utilitarianism makes the rightness of an action depend solely on *forward-looking* considerations; but the demand that punishment be of the guilty is a *backward-looking* consideration with no clear place in such a theory. A similar point could be made about breaking a solemn promise. Again, cases of lying or even intentionally killing an innocent person as ways in particular circumstances of increasing overall happiness raise similar worries. In such cases the utilitarian requirement to increase happiness as much as possible seems in conflict with common-sense prohibitions on certain ways of treating individuals in the pursuit of overall good. (Such problems are explored in Thomas Nagel's "War and Massacre" and are implicit in Foot's essay.)

J. O. Urmson argues that Mill is better seen as a *rule* rather than an *act* utilitarian: the utilitarian test is to be applied directly only to general rules. A moral rule is shown to be correct by showing that its recognition promotes happiness. An act is right as long as it does not violate some correct moral rule, wrong if it does. The suggestion is that among the correct moral rules will be, for example, a rule generally prohibiting the intentional punishment of innocents; and this is why criticisms along Carritt's lines do not work so easily against Mill's theory.

Rule utilitarianism is a two-tier theory, it sanctions utilitarian reasoning at the level of rules, but not at the level of particular acts. This may seem arbitrary. After all, if happiness is so important, why shouldn't I be able to justify my action by saying that *it* best promotes happiness? As J.J.C. Smart argues, once we accept the main outlines of the utilitarian framework, refusal to allow this form of moral justification may seem like a case of "rule worship."

Carritt's objections to act utilitarianism focus on prohibitions on ways of treating others. Bernard Williams argues that there is another problem, one posed by the value we place on integrity. Finally, Peter Singer shows just how powerful even a weak version of a theory in the spirit of utilitarianism can be by arguing that we are subject to fairly strong moral demands to aid those who are suffering from famine in distant lands.

Kantian Ethics

Utilitarianism supposes that we can determine what things are good independently of an account of what actions are right and then go on to see the rightness of actions as depending on the goodness of consequences. Immanuel Kant argues, in contrast, that the rightness of an action does not depend in this way solely on the goodness of consequences; for the rightness of an action depends on the principle (the "maxim") on which the agent acts.

Kant begins his *Groundwork of the Metaphysic of Morals* with a discussion of "the good will." A person of good will is a morally conscientious person, one who is firmly committed to doing her or his moral duty, come what may. Kant argues that only such a good will is "good without qualification." A person's intelligence, wit, or charm may be a good or a bad thing, depending on other circumstances, or the use to which it is put. But moral conscientiousness "shine[s] like a jewel" in any context, and independently of its actual consequences. (See Nagel's "Moral Luck" in Part IV for a relevant discussion.)

In Chapter 2 Kant tries to determine "the supreme principle of morality." Kant supposes there are objective principles concerning what it is rational to do under certain circumstances. For beings like us who are sometimes tempted to act contrary to reason, these principles are seen as "imperatives." Some imperatives only tell us what to do on the assumption that we have a certain end. These are *hypothetical* imperatives. For example, "you ought to wear a coat outside today" normally expresses only a hypothetical imperative since it tells you what to do on the assumption (let us suppose) that you want to stay warm. You could escape from this imperative by not caring about staying warm. Kant supposes that there are also *categorical* imperatives that tell us what to do without assuming that we have a particular end we could rationally give up. Moral oughts, Kant supposes, must be categorical and not merely hypothetical imperatives. Otherwise we could escape from the demands of morality, just by giving up certain ends. (For challenges to this view of morality, see the selections by David Hume and J. L. Mackie in Section C, "Challenges to Morality.")

Kant supposes that all moral demands on our conduct are grounded in a single basic imperative: The Categorical Imperative. Kant offers three main formulations of this principle (although he argues that these are formulations of the same principle): The Formula of Universal Law (which itself has two different versions); The Formula of the End in Itself; and The Formula of the Kingdom of Ends (which is preceded by a closely related Formula of Autonomy). The first is related to, but importantly different from, the Golden Rule. The second is developed by Onora O'Neill in her discussion of famine problems. And the third can be usefully compared to the framework developed by John Rawls in *A Theory of Justice*. (See the selection below in section 4.)

Kant's theory prohibits my treating a person merely as a means, even when that is necessary to avoid terrible results. For example, our doctor in the emergency room cannot cut up the young stranger as a means to saving the five accident victims. In ''War and Massacre'' Thomas Nagel calls such a theory *absolutist* and explores its nonutilitarian perspective on what we may do in pursuit of wartime objectives.

Aristotelian Ethics

Aristotle turns our attention away from questions of the rightness of particular acts to the question of what we should aim at in trying to live a good human life. His initial answer is that it is *eudaimonia*—here translated as happiness, but sometimes translated as flourishing. In contrast with Bentham, Aristotle does not see human happiness as just a matter of more pleasure and less pain. To say more about what human happiness is he tries to determine the characteristic function *(ergon)* of human beings. As Nagel puts it in his essay, ''the *ergon* of a thing, in general, is what it does that makes it what it is.'' We are complex organisms with many different capacities, capacities that constitute our ''soul.'' Some of these capacities are merely nutritive—for example, capacities for digestion and breathing—and are shared with other animals. But our capacities for rational deliberation and reflection are peculiar to us; their active exercise, Aristotle thought, is our *ergon*. *Eudaimonia*—happiness, flourishing—consists in the active exercise of these rational capacities in accordance with their characteristic virtues or excellences *(arete)*.

Some of our rational activities are theoretical (e.g., the study of mathematics), some concern our day-to-day lives in a world with material needs and social complexities. The virtues (excellences) involved in the first sort of activity Aristole calls intellectual; the latter virtues he calls moral (or practical). Aristotle's Doctrine of the Mean is his theory of what the moral virtues are. This theory is discussed in the essay by J. O. Urmson. Nagel discusses Aristotle's ambivalance concerning the relative importance of theoretical and practical activities to human flourishing. Finally, the Section C, ''Challenges to Morality,'' Hume presents a different approach to the question: Which character traits are virtues? (Also, see Kavka's discussion of the relationship between moral assessments of actions and agents in his essay, ''Some Paradoxes of Deterrence.'')

Theories of Justice

When you criticize slavery or a certain tax system as unjust or unfair, you are assessing certain social institutions, not just certain individuals and their actions. Such social institutions have a deep impact on the ways in which various goods are distributed among the members of a society. When does this impact satisfy the demands of justice?

In the selection from his book, *A Theory of Justice,* John Rawls tries to answer this question for those institutions that constitute the ''basic structure'' of a society. The main idea is that the public principles of justice for this basic structure are those that we would choose in a hypothetical situation that is fair. Thus the label ''Justice as Fairness.''

Rawls calls his specification of such a fair-choice situation ''the original position.'' He supposes that the parties in the situation are rational but are behind a ''veil of ignorance'' that blocks from their view any knowledge that would give its possessor an unfair advantage in choosing basic principles of justice. The parties do not know whether they are rich or poor, male or female. They do not know their racial or ethnic background or their particular talents. They do not even know exactly what in the real world they deem most important. What they do care about, in the original position, is their share of ''primary goods,'' goods that are assumed to have a use whatever a person's particular goals and abilities are. Rawls supposes that among the chief primary goods whose distribution is shaped by the basic structure are various basic liberties (e.g., freedom of speech and association), opportunities (e.g., educational opportunities), and income and wealth. The parties in the original position are to decide on principles that will publically govern the ways in which the basic structure shapes the distribution of such primary goods.

Rawls argues that the parties in the original position would unanimously choose two principles: a principle of maximum, equal basic liberties and a principle that requires that inequalities in the distribution of other social primary goods be to *everyone's* advantage (e.g., not merely to the advantage of the majority) and provide for equality of opportunity. Both principles depart from the utilitarian's overriding concern with maximizing overall happiness.

Robert Nozick would classify Rawls's principles as nonhistorical, end-state principles: they attempt to assess the justice of the social distributions of goods without looking at the actual history of how these distributions came about. Nozick argues that no end-state principle of justice can be continuously realized without serious restrictions on people's liberties. This is the point of his Wilt Chamberlain example. Nozick's alternative is his historical, entitlement theory. This theory aims at three kinds of principles: principles that say when an original acquisition of some good is just; principles that say when the transfer of some good is just; and principles that say what is to be done to rectify past violations of the first two principles. The first principle will involve the Lockean proviso that the appropriation of a previously unowned object must not worsen the situation of others. According to this theory, I am entitled to those goods I possess either through a just original acquisition or through a series of just transfers that begin with a just original acquisition.

Kai Nielsen offers a useful critical discussion of both Nozick and Rawls's theories and argues that his two "socialist principles of justice" are superior to both their theories. Finally, Ronald Dworkin examines a particular and recent controversial issue about justice: Are policies of "reverse discrimination," which are aimed at reducing serious and long-standing social inequalities, themselves unjust?

Challenges to Morality

Morality and Self-interest

Suppose you discovered a way to gain access to the files of any computer system in the country and could change those files at will. Suppose you knew you could do this with no chance of being caught. You could change the grades of anyone at any university. You could change the totals in bank accounts. And so on. You think it would be wrong to do this. But, you still wonder whether you should let that stop you. Why should you let moral considerations prevent you from pursuing what seems to be in your self-interest? Why should you be moral?

Your problem is a high-tech verison of Glaucon's problem of the ring of Gyges, posed in Plato's *Republic.* Since Gyges can treat others unjustly with impunity, wouldn't he live a better life by acting unjustly rather than justly? In the selections reprinted here from Books I through IV of the *Republic,* Socrates argues that it is in a person's interest to be just and against his interest to be unjust. Properly understood, morality and self-interest are not in conflict. Socrates' argument proceeds by way of a famous parallel between the state and an individual and an analysis of the structure of human motivation that leads Socrates to talk of three "parts" of the soul.

We next have excerpts from David Hume's *An Enquiry Concerning the Principles of Morals.* Hume's discussion touches on many issues. His two main questions are: How far do reason and sentiment enter into moral judgment? What character traits are virtues, and why? His answer to the latter question is utilitarian in spirit, seeing character traits as virtues insofar as they are "useful or agreeable to the person himself or to others." We look at his answer to the former question later. We include Hume's *Enquiry* in this section because of its discussions of the relation between morality and self-interest.

Hume's explicit discussion of this issue occurs in Section IX, Part II. Here, he extols the contribution of the moral virtues to the life of their possessor—although, "[t]reating vice with the greatest candour," he does worry that his remarks may not be convincing for the case of justice (which, for Hume, is a virtue primarily concerned with property, honesty, and promisekeeping). But Hume does not think that it is solely because of their contribution to our own interests that we approve of the moral virtues. Rather, Hume argues that as a matter of fact we are all to some extent directly concerned with the interests of others—this is the point of his example of avoiding another's gouty toes. This universal principle of benevolence accounts for our approval of the virtues and is the basis of our moral judgments.

Hume sketches a complex account of the relation between benevolence and self-love. "It is requisite," he says, "that there be an original propensity of some kind, in order to be a basis to self-love, by giving a relish to the objects of its pursuit." Benevolence is itself one such original propensity. Self-love is a "secondary passion," whose concern is with the satisfaction of various original propensities, and these include benevolence, the basis of morality.

In the Prisoner's Dilemma, discussed in Part IV, "Puzzles and Paradoxes," it is in each prisoner's individual interest to confess, even though both prisoners do better if both remain silent than they do if both confess. Prisoners guided solely by a concern with their individual self-interest will each end up worse off than if they were able to cooperate and maintain joint silence. There is a useful analogy here with morality. Consider the moral demand to be truthful. Each person will on occasion be in a situation in which it is in his or her individual interest to lie. Yet, we all do better if everyone is always truthful—even when this conflicts with one's self-interest—than if everyone were to lie whenever this was in one's own interest. A group of people who are guided solely by individual self-interest will each end up worse off than each would have been if they had all been guided by a commitment to honesty. This suggests that there are reasons of self-interest to be moral. In "Morality and Advantage" David Gauthier explores this suggestion, but he concludes that in the end it provides a more limited rationale for being moral than may have been thought.

Finally, J. L. Mackie explores what Richard Dawkins has called "the biology of selfishness and altruism." Mackie suggests that there may be evolutionary reasons to expect the emergence of tendencies toward "reciprocal altruism"—a strategy of tit for tat. Insofar as morality is the expression of such reciprocal altruism, it may be possible to see morality as itself a product of natural selection.

Subjectivism, Relativism, and Skepticism

I believe that wanton torture of an innocent child is wrong; and (I hope) you do, too. Is there some objective fact here—the fact that such conduct is wrong—that is what both of us know? Or, is this merely a case in which we share similar negative attitudes?

In Appendix I of his *An Enquiry Concerning the Principles of Morals* Hume argues that our moral attitudes could not consist merely in the knowledge of facts about the world. Knowledge of facts is not itself sufficient to move us to act. Yet, Hume assumes, our moral views can themselves move us to act. To reach a moral conclusion, then, it is not enough to know that certain acts or character traits have certain effects. We must also have appropriate pro or con attitudes—what Hume calls sentiments—toward those effects. Given our benevolence, we react negatively to torture. But, if (contrary to fact) we were rational but nonbenevolent beings, we could grasp all the facts about torture and yet not react in these ways.

Although there is, for Hume, neither moral knowledge nor moral facts, there is a clear and powerful point of view of morality: the point of view of informed benevolence, which he describes in Section IX, Part I. Hume thinks that his skepticism about the objectivity of morality leaves untouched the importance of this moral point of view for us.

J. L. Mackie develops similar views, and usefully contrasts them with the views of Aristotle and Kant. (See the selections from Aristotle and Kant in Section B, ''Moral Theories.'') Mackie distinguishes three levels of investigation: descriptive ethics, first-order normative ethics, and second-order theories about what moral valuing and moral values are. At the level of descriptive ethics we are only concerned to describe what moral views certain people in fact endorse. At the level of first-order normative ethics we are interested in ourselves making judgments about what is right and what is good. Mackie's main concerns are at the second-order level. He argues that there are no moral facts and no moral knowledge; although he thinks his arguments still allow us to make serious first-order judgments of right and wrong, good and bad, as long as these judgments have been purged of a claim to objectivity.

Mackie thinks that the idea that values are ''part of the fabric of the world'' is deeply embedded in our common-sense thought. But, he offers two main reasons for rejecting such objectivism: the argument from relativity and the argument from queerness. The first begins with a premise from descriptive ethics, but it aims at a second-order conclusion; the second is an extension of Hume's argument from the connection between morality and motivation. Our tendency, nevertheless, to see values as objective is a tendency to project our subjective attitudes and desires onto the objective world.

In his ''Outline of a Decision Procedure for Ethics,'' John Rawls defends the possibility of objective moral knowledge. Rawls suggests that this possibility does not depend on the existence of values that are (in Mackie's phrase) ''part of the fabric of the world.'' Objective moral knowledge is possible if there is a reasonable procedure for justifying the acceptance of various moral judgments. Rawls proceeds to offer and defend a detailed description of such a procedure.

A. MORAL PERPLEXITIES

A Defense of Abortion

JUDITH JARVIS THOMSON

Judith Jarvis Thomson (1929–) is a professor of philosophy at Massachusetts Institute of Technology. Her works include *Acts and Other Events.*

Most opposition to abortion relies on the premise that the fetus is a human being, a person, from the moment of conception. The premise is argued for, but, as I think, not well. Take, for example, the most common argument. We are asked to notice that the development of a human being from conception through birth into childhood is continuous; then it is said that to draw a line, to choose a point in this development and say "before this point the thing is not a person, after this point it is a person" is to make an arbitrary choice, a choice for which in the nature of things no good reason can be given. It is concluded that the fetus is, or anyway that we had better say it is, a person from the moment of conception. But this conclusion does not follow. Similar things might be said about the development of an acorn into an oak tree, and it does not follow that acorns are oak trees, or that we had better say they are. Arguments of this form are sometimes called "slippery slope arguments"—the phrase is perhaps self-explanatory—and it is dismaying that opponents of abortion rely on them so heavily and uncritically.

I am inclined to agree, however, that the prospects for "drawing a line" in the development of the fetus look dim. I am inclined to think also that we shall probably have to agree that the fetus has already become a human person well before birth. Indeed, it comes as a surprise when one first learns how early in its life it begins to acquire human characteristics. By the tenth week, for example, it already has a face, arms and legs, fingers and toes; it has internal organs, and brain activity is detectable.[1] On the other hand, I think that the premise is false, that the fetus is not a person from the moment of conception. A newly fertilized ovum, a newly implanted clump of cells, is no more a person than an acorn is an oak tree. But I shall not discuss any of this. For it seems to me to be of great interest to ask what happens if, for the sake of argument, we allow the premise. How, precisely, are we supposed to get from there to the conclusion that abortion is morally impermissible? Opponents of abortion commonly spend most of their time establishing that the fetus is a person, and hardly any time explaining the step from there to the impermissibility of abortion. Perhaps they think the step too simple and obvious to require much comment. Or perhaps instead they are simply being economical in argument. Many of those who defend abortion rely on the premise that the fetus is not a person, but only a bit of tissue that will become a person at birth; and why pay out more arguments than you have to? Whatever the explanation, I suggest that the step they take is neither easy nor obvious, that it calls for closer examination than it is com-

I am very much indebted to James Thomson for discussion, criticism, and many helpful suggestions.

From *Philosophy & Public Affairs* 1, no. 1 (1971), pp. 47–66.

monly given, and that when we do give it this closer examination we shall feel inclined to reject it.

I propose, then, that we grant that the fetus is a person from the moment of conception. How does the argument go from here? Something like this, I take it. Every person has a right to life. So the fetus has a right to life. No doubt the mother has a right to decide what shall happen in and to her body; everyone would grant that. But surely a person's right to life is stronger and more stringent than the mother's right to decide what happens in and to her body, and so outweighs it. So the fetus may not be killed; an abortion may not be performed.

It sounds plausible. But now let me ask you to imagine this. You wake up in the morning and find yourself back to back in bed with an unconscious violinist. A famous unconscious violinist. He has been found to have a fatal kidney ailment, and the Society of Music Lovers has canvassed all the available medical records and found that you alone have the right blood type to help. They have therefore kidnapped you, and last night the violinist's circulatory system was plugged into yours, so that your kidneys can be used to extract poisons from his blood as well as your own. The director of the hospital now tells you, "Look, we're sorry the Society of Music Lovers did this to you—we would never have permitted it if we had known. But still, they did it, and the violinist now is plugged into you. To unplug you would be to kill him. But never mind, it's only for nine months. By then he will have recovered from his ailment, and can safely be unplugged from you." Is it morally incumbent on you to accede to this situation? No doubt it would be very nice of you if you did, a great kindness. But do you *have* to accede to it? What if it were not nine months, but nine years? Or longer still? What if the director of the hospital says, "Tough luck, I agree, but you've now got to stay in bed, with the violinist plugged into you, for the rest of your life. Because remember this. All persons have a right to life, and violinists are persons. Granted you have a right to decide what happens in and to your body, but a person's right to life outweighs your right to decide what happens in and to your body. So you cannot ever be unplugged from him." I imagine you would regard this as outrageous, which suggests that something really is wrong with that plausible-sounding argument I mentioned a moment ago.

In this case, of course, you were kidnapped; you didn't volunteer for the operation that plugged the violinist into your kidneys. Can those who oppose abortion on the ground I mentioned make an exception for a pregnancy due to rape? Certainly. They can say that persons have a right to life only if they didn't come into existence because of rape; or they can say that all persons have a right to life, but that some have less of a right to life than others, in particular, that those who came into existence because of rape have less. But these statements have a rather unpleasant sound. Surely the question of whether you have a right to life at all, or how much of it you have, shouldn't turn on the question of whether or not you are the product of a rape. And in fact the people who oppose abortion on the ground I mentioned do not make this distinction, and hence do not make an exception in case of rape.

Nor do they make an exception for a case in which the mother has to spend the nine months of her pregnancy in bed. They would agree that would be a great pity, and hard on the mother; but all the same, all persons have a right to life, the fetus is a person, and so on. I suspect, in fact, that they would not make an exception for a case in which, miraculously enough, the pregnancy went on for nine years, or even the rest of the mother's life.

Some won't even make an exception for a case in which continuation of the pregnancy is likely to shorten the mother's life; they regard abortion as impermissible even to save the mother's life. Such cases are nowadays very rare, and many opponents of abortion do not accept this extreme view. All the same, it is a good place to begin: a number of points of interest come out in respect to it.

1. Let us call the view that abortion is impermissible even to save the mother's life "the extreme view." I want to suggest first that it does not issue from the argument I mentioned earlier without the addition of some fairly powerful premises. Suppose a woman has become pregnant, and now learns that she has a cardiac condition such that she will die if she carries the baby to term. What may be done for her? The fetus, being a person, has a right to life, but as the mother is a person too, so has she a right to life.

Presumably they have an equal right to life. How is it supposed to come out that an abortion may not be performed? If mother and child have an equal right to life, shouldn't we perhaps flip a coin? Or should we add to the mother's right to life her right to decide what happens in and to her body, which everybody seems to be ready to grant—the sum of her rights now outweighing the fetus's right to life?

The most familiar argument here is the following. We are told that performing the abortion would be directly killing[2] the child, whereas doing nothing would not be killing the mother, but only letting her die. Moreover, in killing the child, one would be killing an innocent person, for the child has committed no crime, and is not aiming at his mother's death. And then there are a variety of ways in which this might be continued. (1) But as directly killing an innocent person is always and absolutely impermissible, an abortion may not be performed. Or, (2) as directly killing an innocent person is murder, and murder is always and absolutely impermissible, an abortion may not be performed.[3] Or, (3) as one's duty to refrain from directly killing an innocent person is more stringent than one's duty to keep a person from dying, an abortion may not be performed. Or, (4) if one's only options are directly killing an innocent person or letting a person die, one must prefer letting the person die, and thus an abortion may not be performed.[4]

Some people seem to have thought that these are not further premises which must be added if the conclusion is to be reached, but that they follow from the very fact that an innocent person has a right to life.[5] But this seems to me to be a mistake, and perhaps the simplest way to show this is to bring out that while we must certainly grant that innocent persons have a right to life, the theses in (1) through (4) are all false. Take (2), for example. If directly killing an innocent person is murder, and this is impermissible, then the mother's directly killing the innocent person inside her is murder, and thus is impermissible. But it cannot seriously be thought to be murder if the mother performs an abortion on herself to save her life. It cannot seriously be said that she *must* refrain, that she *must* sit passively by and wait for her death. Let us look again at the case of you and the violinist. There you are, in bed with the violinist, and the director of the hospital says to you, "It's all most distressing, and I deeply sympathize, but you see this is putting an additional strain on your kidneys, and you'll be dead within the month. But you *have* to stay where you are all the same. Because unplugging you would be directly killing an innocent violinist, and that's murder, and that's impermissible." If anything in the world is true, it is that you do not commit murder, you do not do what is impermissible, if you reach around to your back and unplug yourself from that violinist to save your life.

The main focus of attention in writings on abortion has been on what a third party may or may not do in answer to a request from a woman for an abortion. This is in a way understandable. Things being as they are, there isn't much a woman can safely do to abort herself. So the question asked is what a third party may do, and what the mother may do, if it is mentioned at all, is deduced, almost as an afterthought, from what it is concluded that third parties may do. But it seems to me that to treat the matter in this way is to refuse to grant to the mother that very status of person which is so firmly insisted on for the fetus. For we cannot simply read off what a person may do from what a third party may do. Suppose you find yourself trapped in a tiny house with a growing child. I mean a very tiny house, and a rapidly growing child—you are already up against the wall of the house and in a few minutes you'll be crushed to death. The child on the other hand won't be crushed to death; if nothing is done to stop him from growing he'll be hurt, but in the end he'll simply burst open the house and walk out a free man. Now I could well understand it if a bystander were to say, "There's nothing we can do for you. We cannot choose between your life and his, we cannot be the ones to decide who is to live, we cannot intervene." But it cannot be concluded that you too can do nothing, that you cannot attack it to save your life. However innocent the child may be, you do not have to wait passively while it crushes you to death. Perhaps a pregnant woman is vaguely felt to have the status of house, to which we don't allow the right of self-defense. But if the woman houses the child, it should be remembered that she is a person who houses it.

I should perhaps stop to say explicitly that I am not claiming that people have a right to do anything whatever to save their lives. I think, rather, that there are drastic limits to the right of self-defense. If someone threatens you with death unless you torture someone else to death, I think you have not the right, even to save your life, to do so. But the case under consideration here is very different. In our case there are only two people involved, one whose life is threatened, and one who threatens it. Both are innocent: the one who is threatened is not threatened because of any fault, the one who threatens does not threaten because of any fault. For this reason we may feel that we bystanders cannot intervene. But the person threatened can.

In sum, a woman surely can defend her life against the threat to it posed by the unborn child, even if doing so involves its death. And this shows not merely that the theses in (1) through (4) are false; it shows also that the extreme view of abortion is false, and so we need not canvass any other possible ways of arriving at it from the argument I mentioned at the outset.

2. The extreme view could of course be weakened to say that while abortion is permissible to save the mother's life, it may not be performed by a third party, but only by the mother herself. But this cannot be right either. For what we have to keep in mind is that the mother and the unborn child are not like two tenants in a small house which has, by an unfortunate mistake, been rented to both: the mothers *owns* the house. The fact that she does adds to the offensiveness of deducing that the mother can do nothing from the supposition that third parties can do nothing. But it does more than this: it casts a bright light on the supposition that third parties can do nothing. Certainly it lets us see that a third party who says "I cannot choose between you" is fooling himself if he thinks this is impartiality. If Jones has found and fastened on a certain coat, which he needs to keep him from freezing, but which Smith also needs to keep him from freezing, then it is not impartiality that says "I cannot choose between you" when Smith owns the coat. Women have said again and again "This body is *my* body!" and they have reason to feel angry, reason to feel that it has been like shouting into the wind. Smith, after all, is hardly likely to bless us if we say to him, "Of course it's your coat, anybody would grant that it is. But no one may choose between you and Jones who is to have it."

We should really ask what it is that says "no one may choose" in the face of the fact that the body that houses the child is the mother's body. It may be simply a failure to appreciate this fact. But it may be something more interesting, namely the sense that one has a right to refuse to lay hands on people, even where it would be just and fair to do so, even where justice seems to require that somebody do so. Thus justice might call for somebody to get Smith's coat back from Jones, and yet you have a right to refuse to be the one to lay hands on Jones, a right to refuse to do physical violence to him. This, I think, must be granted. But then what should be said is not "no one may choose," but only "*I* cannot choose," and indeed not even this, but "*I* will not *act,*" leaving it open that somebody else can or should, and in particular that anyone in a position of authority, with the job of securing people's rights, both can and should. So this is no difficulty. I have not been arguing that any given third party must accede to the mother's request that he perform an abortion to save her life, but only that he may.

I suppose that in some views of human life the mother's body is only on loan to her, the loan not being one which gives her any prior claim to it. One who held this view might well think it impartiality to say "I cannot choose." But I shall simply ignore this possibility. My own view is that if a human being has any just, prior claim to anything at all, he has a just, prior claim to his own body. And perhaps this needn't be argued for here anyway, since, as I mentioned, the arguments against abortion we are looking at do grant that the woman has a right to decide what happens in and to her body.

But although they do grant it, I have tried to show that they do not take seriously what is done in granting it. I suggest the same thing will reappear even more clearly when we turn away from cases in which the mother's life is at stake, and attend, as I propose we now do, to the vastly more common cases in which a woman wants an abortion for some less weighty reason than perserving her own life.

3. Where the mother's life is not at stake, the argument I mentioned at the outset seems to have a much stronger pull. "Everyone has a right to life, so the unborn person has a right to life."

And isn't the child's right to life weightier than anything other than the mother's own right to life, which she might put forward as ground for an abortion?

This argument treats the right to life as if it were unproblematic. It is not, and this seems to me to be precisely the source of the mistake.

For we should now, at long last, ask what it comes to, to have a right to life. In some views having a right to life includes having a right to be given at least the bare minimum one needs for continued life. But suppose that what in fact *is* the bare minimum a man needs for continued life is something he has no right at all to be given? If I am sick unto death, and the only thing that will save my life is the touch of Henry Fonda's cool hand on my fevered brow, then all the same. I have no right to be given the touch of Henry Fonda's cool hand on my fevered brow. It would be frightfully nice of him to fly in from the West Coast to provide it. It would be less nice, though no doubt well meant, if my friends flew out to the West Coast and carried Henry Fonda back with them. But I have no right at all against anybody that he should do this for me. Or again, to return to the story I told earlier, the fact that for continued life that violinist needs the continued use of your kidneys does not establish that he has a right to be given the continued use of your kidneys. He certainly has no right against you that *you* should give him continued use of your kidneys. For nobody has any right to use your kidneys unless you give him such a right; and nobody has the right against you that you shall give him this right—if you do allow him to go on using your kidneys, this is a kindness on your part, and not something he can claim from you as his due. Nor has he any right against anybody else that *they* should give him continued use of your kidneys. Certainly he had no right against the Society of Music Lovers that they should plug him into you in the first place. And if you now start to unplug yourself, having learned that you will otherwise have to spend nine years in bed with him, there is nobody in the world who must try to prevent you, in order to see to it that he is given something he has a right to be given.

Some people are rather stricter about the right to life. In their view, it does not include the right to be given anything, but amounts to, and only to, the right not to be killed by anybody. But here a related difficulty arises. If everybody is to refrain from killing that violinist, then everybody must refrain from doing a great many different sorts of things. Everybody must refrain from slitting his throat, everybody must refrain from shooting him—and everybody must refrain from unplugging you from him. But does he have a right against everybody that they shall refrain from unplugging you from him? To refrain from doing this is to allow him to continue to use your kidneys. It could be argued that he has a right against us that *we* should allow him to continue to use your kidneys. That is, while he had no right against us that we should give him the use of your kidneys, it might be argued that he anyway has a right against us that we shall not now intervene and deprive him of the use of your kidneys. I shall come back to third-party interventions later. But certainly the violinist has no right against you that *you* shall allow him to continue to use your kidneys. As I said, if you do allow him to use them, it is a kindness on your part, and not something you owe him.

The difficulty I point to here is not peculiar to the right to life. It reappears in connection with all the other natural rights; and it is something which an adequate account of rights must deal with. For present purposes it is enough just to draw attention to it. But I would stress that I am not arguing that people do not have a right to life—quite to the contrary, it seems to me that the primary control we must place on the acceptability of an account of rights is that it should turn out in that account to be a truth that all persons have a right to life. I am arguing only that having a right to life does not guarantee having either a right to be given the use of or a right to be allowed continued use of another person's body—even if one needs it for life itself. So the right to life will not serve the opponents of abortion in the very simple and clear way in which they seem to have thought it would.

4. There is another way to bring out the difficulty. In the most ordinary sort of case, to deprive someone of what he has a right to is to treat him unjustly. Suppose a boy and his small brother are jointly given a box of chocolates for Christmas. If the older boy takes the box and refuses to give his brother any of the chocolates, he is unjust to him, for the brother has been given a right to half of them. But suppose that, having learned that otherwise it means nine years in bed with that violinist, you unplug yourself from him. You surely are not being unjust to him, for you gave him no right to use your kidneys, and no one else can have given him any such right. But we have to notice that in unplugging yourself, you are killing him; and violinists, like everybody else, have a right to life, and thus in the view we were considering just now, the right not to be killed. So here you do what he supposedly has a right you shall not do, but you do not act unjustly to him in doing it.

The emendation which may be made at this point is this: the right to life consists not in the right not to be killed, but rather in the right not to be killed unjustly. This runs a risk of circularity, but never mind: it would enable us to square the fact that the violinist has a right to life with the fact that you do not act unjustly toward him in unplugging yourself, thereby killing him. For if you do not kill him unjustly, you do not violate his right to life, and so it is no wonder you do him no injustice.

But if this emendation is accepted, the gap in the argument against abortion stares us plainly in the face: it is by no means enough to show that the fetus is a person, and to remind us that all persons have a right to life—we need to be shown also that killing the fetus violates its right to life, i.e., that abortion is unjust killing. And is it?

I suppose we may take it as a datum that in a case of pregnancy due to rape the mother has not given the unborn person a right to the use of her body for food and shelter. Indeed, in what pregnancy could it be supposed that the mother has given the unborn person such a right? It is not as if there were unborn persons drifting about the world, to whom a woman who wants a child says "I invite you in."

But it might be argued that there are other ways one can have acquired a right to the use of another person's body than by having been invited to use it by that person. Suppose a woman voluntarily indulges in intercourse, knowing of the chance it will issue in pregnancy, and then she does become pregnant; is she not in part responsible for the presence, in fact the very existence, of the unborn person inside her? No doubt she did not invite it in. But doesn't her partial responsibility for its being there itself give it a right to the use of her body?[6] If so, then her aborting it would be more like the boy's taking away the chocolates, and less like your unplugging yourself from the violinist—doing so would be depriving it of what it does have a right to, and thus would be doing it an injustice.

And then, too, it might be asked whether or not she can kill it even to save her own life: If she voluntarily called it into existence, how can she now kill it, even in self-defense?

The first thing to be said about this is that it is something new. Opponents of abortion have been so concerned to make out the independence of the fetus, in order to establish that it has a right to life, just as its mother does, that they have tended to overlook the possible support they might gain from making out that the fetus is *dependent* on the mother, in order to establish that she has a special kind of responsibility for it, a responsibility that gives it rights against her which are not possessed by any independent person—such as an ailing violinist who is a stranger to her.

On the other hand, this argument would give the unborn person a right to its mother's body only if her pregnancy resulted from a voluntary act, undertaken in full knowledge of the chance a pregnancy might result from it. It would leave out entirely the unborn person whose existence is due to rape. Pending the availability of some further argument, then, we would be left with the conclusion that unborn persons whose existence is due to rape have no right to the use of their mothers' bodies, and thus that aborting them is not depriving them of anything they have a right to and hence is not unjust killing.

And we should also notice that it is not at all plain that this argument really does go even as far as it purports to. For there are cases and cases, and the details make a difference. If the room is stuffy, and I therefore open a window to air it, and a burglar climbs in, it would be absurd to say, "Ah, now he can stay, she's given him a right to the use of her house—for she is partially responsible for his presence there, having voluntarily done what enabled him to get in, in full knowledge that there are such things as burglars, and that burglars burgle." It would be still more absurd to say this if I had had bars installed outside my windows, precisely to prevent burglars from getting in, and a burglar got in only because of a defect in the bars. It remains equally absurd if we imagine it is not a burglar who climbs in, but an innocent person who blunders or falls in. Again, suppose it were like this: people-seeds drift about in the air like pollen, and if you open your windows, one may drift in and take root in your carpets or upholstery. You don't want children, so you fix up your windows with fine mesh screens, the very best you can buy. As can happen, however, and on very, very rare occasions does happen, one of the screens is defective; and a seed drifts in and takes root. Does the person-plant who now develops have a right to the use of your house? Surely not—despite the fact that you voluntarily opened your windows, you knowingly kept carpets and upholstered furniture, and you knew that screens were sometimes defective. Someone may argue that you are responsible for its rooting, that it does have a right to your house, because after all you *could* have lived out your life with bare floors and furniture, or with sealed windows and doors. But this won't do—for by the same token anyone can avoid a pregnancy due to rape by having a hysterectomy, or anyway by never leaving home without a (reliable!) army.

It seems to me that the argument we are looking at can establish at most that there are *some* cases in which the unborn person has a right to the use of its mother's body, and therefore *some* cases in which abortion is unjust killing. There is room for much discussion and argument as to precisely which, if any. But I think we should sidestep this issue and leave it open, for at any rate the argument certainly does not establish that all abortion is unjust killing.

5. There is room for yet another argument here, however. We surely must all grant that there may be cases in which it would be morally indecent to detach a person from your body at the cost of his life. Suppose you learn that what the violinist needs is not nine years of your life, but only one hour: all you need do to save his life is to spend one hour in that bed with him. Suppose also that letting him use your kidneys for that one hour would not affect your health in the slightest. Admittedly you were kidnapped. Admittedly you did not give anyone permission to plug him into you. Nevertheless it seems to me plain you *ought* to allow him to use your kidneys for that hour—it would be indecent to refuse.

Again, suppose pregnancy lasted only an hour, and constituted no threat to life or health. And suppose that a woman becomes pregnant as a result of rape. Admittedly she did not voluntarily do anything to bring about the existence of a child. Admittedly she did nothing at all which would give the unborn person a right to the use of her body. All the same it might well be said, as in the newly emended violinist story, that she *ought* to allow it to remain for that hour—that it would be indecent of her to refuse.

Now some people are inclined to use the term "right" in such a way that it follows from the fact that you ought to allow a person to use your body for the hour he needs, that he has a right to use your body for the hour he needs, even though he has not been given that right by any person or act. They may say that it follows also that if you refuse, you act unjustly toward him. This use of the term is perhaps so common that it cannot be called wrong; nevertheless it seems to me to be an unfortunate loosening of what we would do better to keep a tight rein on. Suppose that box of chocolates I mentioned earlier has not been given to both boys jointly, but was given only to the older boy. There he sits, stolidly eating his way through the box, his small brother watching enviously. Here we are likely to say "You ought not to be so mean. You ought to give your brother some of those chocolates." My own view is that it just does not follow from the truth of this that the brother has any right to any of the chocolates. If the boy refuses to give his brother any, he is greedy, stingy, callous—but not unjust. I suppose that the people I have in mind will say it does follow that the brother has a right to some of the chocolates, and thus that the boy does act unjustly if he refuses to give his brother any. But the effect of saying this is to obscure what we should keep distinct, namely the difference between the boy's refusal in this case and the boy's refusal in the earlier case, in which the box was given to both boys jointly, and in which the small brother thus had what was from any point of view clear title to half.

A further objection to so using the term "right" that from the fact that A ought to do a thing for

B, it follows that B has a right against A that A do it for him, is that it is going to make the question of whether or not a man has a right to a thing turn on how easy it is to provide him with it; and this seems not merely unfortunate, but morally unacceptable. Take the case of Henry Fonda again. I said earlier that I had no right to the touch of his cool hand on my fevered brow, even though I needed it to save my life. I said it would be frightfully nice of him to fly in from the West Coast to provide me with it, but that I had no right against him that he should do so. But suppose he isn't on the West Coast. Suppose he has only to walk across the room, place a hand briefly on my brow—and lo, my life is saved. Then surely he ought to do it, it would be indecent to refuse. Is it to be said "Ah, well, it follows that in this case she has a right to the touch of his hand on her brow, and so it would be an injustice in him to refuse"? So that I have a right to it when it is easy for him to provide it, though no right when it's hard? It's rather a shocking idea that anyone's rights should fade away and disappear as it gets harder and harder to accord them to him.

So my own view is that even though you ought to let the violinist use your kidneys for the one hour he needs, we should not conclude that he has a right to do so—we should say that if you refuse, you are, like the boy who owns all the chocolates and will give none away, self-centered and callous, indecent in fact, but not unjust. And similarly, that even supposing a case in which a woman pregnant due to rape ought to allow the unborn person to use her body for the hour he needs, we should not conclude that he has a right to do so; we should conclude that she is self-centered, callous, indecent, but not unjust, if she refuses. The complaints are no less grave; they are just different. However, there is no need to insist on this point. If anyone does wish to deduce "he has a right" from "you ought," then all the same he must surely grant that there are cases in which it is not morally required of you that you allow that violinist to use your kidneys, and in which he does not have a right to use them, and in which you do not do him an injustice if you refuse. And so also for mother and unborn child. Except in such cases as the unborn person has a right to demand it—and we were leaving open the possibility that there may be such cases—nobody is morally *required* to make large sacrifices, of health, of all other interests and concerns, of all other duties and commitments, for nine years, or even for nine months, in order to keep another person alive.

6. We have in fact to distinguish between two kinds of Samaritan: the Good Samaritan and what we might call the Minimally Decent Samaritan. The story of the Good Samaritan, you will remember, goes like this:

> A certain man went down from Jerusalem to Jericho, and fell among thieves, which stripped him of his raiment, and wounded him, and departed, leaving him half dead.
>
> And by chance there came down a certain priest that way; and when he saw him, he passed by on the other side.
>
> And likewise a Levite, when he was at the place, came and looked on him, and passed by on the other side.
>
> But a certain Samaritan, as he journeyed, came where he was; and when he saw him he had compassion on him.
>
> And went to him, and bound up his wounds, pouring in oil and wine, and set him on his own beast, and brought him to an inn, and took care of him.
>
> And on the morrow, when he departed, he took out two pence, and gave them to the host, and said unto him, "Take care of him; and whatsoever thou spendest more, when I come again, I will repay thee."
>
> *(Luke 10:30–35)*

The Good Samaritan went out of his way, at some cost to himself, to help one in need of it. We are not told what the options were, that is, whether or not the priest and the Levite could have helped by doing less than the Good Samaritan did, but assuming they could have, then the fact they did nothing at all shows they were not even Minimally Decent Samaritans, not because they were not Samaritans, but because they were not even minimally decent.

These things are a matter of degree, of course, but there is a difference, and it comes out perhaps most clearly in the story of Kitty Genovese, who, as you will remember, was murdered while thirty-eight people watched or listened, and did nothing at all to help her. A Good Samaritan would have rushed out to give direct assistance against the murderer. Or perhaps we had better allow that it would have been a Splendid Smaritan who did this, on the ground that it would have involved risk of death for himself. But the thirty-eight not only did not do this, they did not even trouble to pick up a phone to call the police. Minimally Decent Samaritanism would call for doing at least that, and their not having done it was monstrous.

After telling the story of the Good Samaritan, Jesus said "Go, and do thou likewise." Perhaps he meant that we are morally required to act as the Good Samaritan did. Perhaps he was urging people to do more than is morally required of them. At all events it seems plain that it was not morally required of any of the thirty-eight that he rush out to give direct assistance at the risk of his own life, and that it is not morally required of anyone that he give long stretches of his life—nine years or nine months—to sustaining the life of a person who has no special right (we were leaving open the possibility of this) to demand it.

Indeed, with one rather striking class of exceptions, no one in any country in the world is *legally* required to do anywhere near as much as this for anyone else. The class of exceptions is obvious. My main concern here is not the state of the law in respect to abortion, but it is worth drawing attention to the fact that in no state in this country is any man compelled by law to be even a Minimally Decent Samaritan to any person; there is no law under which charges could be brought against the thirty-eight who stood by while Kitty Genovese died. By contrast, in most states in this country women are compelled by law to be not merely Minimally Decent Samaritans, but Good Samaritans to unborn persons inside them. This doesn't by itself settle anything one way or the other, because it may well be argued that there should be laws in this country—as there are in many European countries—compelling at least Minimally Decent Samaritanism.[7] But it does show that there is a gross injustice in the existing state of the law. And it shows also that the groups currently working against liberalization of abortion laws, in fact working toward having it declared unconstitutional for a state to permit abortion, had better start working for the adoption of Good Samaritan laws generally, or earn the charge that they are acting in bad faith.

I should think, myself, that Minimally Decent Samaritan laws would be one thing, Good Samaritan laws quite another, and in fact highly improper. But we are not here concerned with the law. What we should ask is not whether anybody should be compelled by law to be a Good Samaritan, but whether we must accede to a situation in which somebody is being compelled—by nature, perhaps—to be a Good Samaritan. We have, in other words, to look now at third-party interventions. I have been arguing that no person is morally required to make large sacrifices to sustain the life of another who has no right to demand them, and this even where the sacrifices do not include life itself; we are not morally required to be Good Samaritans or anyway Very Good Samaritans to one another. But what if a man cannot extricate himself from such a situation? What if he appeals to us to extricate him? It seems to me plain that there are cases in which we can, cases in which a Good Samaritan would extricate him. There you are, you were kidnapped, and nine years in bed with that violinist lie ahead of you. You have your own life to lead. You are sorry, but you simply cannot see giving up so much of your life to the sustaining of his. You cannot extricate yourself, and ask us to do so. I should have thought that—in light of his having no right to the use of your body—it was obvious that we do not have to accede to your being forced to give up so much. We can do what you ask. There is no injustice to the violinist in our doing so.

7. Following the lead of the opponents of abortion, I have throughout been speaking of the fetus merely as a person, and what I have been asking is whether or not the argument we began with, which proceeds only from the fetus's being a person, really does establish its conclusion. I have argued that it does not.

But of course there are arguments and arguments, and it may be said that I have simply fastened on the wrong one. It may be said that what is important is not merely the fact that the fetus is a person, but that it is a person for whom the woman has a special kind of responsibility issuing from the fact that she is its mother. And it might be argued that all my analogies are therefore irrelevant—for you do not have that special kind of responsibility for that violinist, Henry Fonda does not have that special kind of responsibility for me. And our attention might be drawn to the fact that men and women both *are* compelled by law to provide support for their children.

I have in effect dealt (briefly) with this argument in section 4 above; but a (still briefer) recapitulation now may be in order. Surely we do not have any such "special responsibility" for a person unless we have assumed it, explicitly or implicitly. If a set of parents do not try to prevent pregnancy, do not obtain an abortion, and then at the time of birth of the child do not put it out for adoption, but rather take it home with them, then they have assumed responsibility for it, they have given it rights, and they cannot *now* withdraw support from it at the cost of its life because they now find it difficult to go on providing for it. But if they have taken all reasonable precautions against having a child, they do not simply by virtue of their biological relationship to the child who comes into existence have a special responsibility for it. They may wish to assume responsibility for it, or they may not wish to. And I am suggesting that if assuming responsibility for it would require large sacrifices, then they may refuse. A Good Samaritan would not refuse—or anyway, a Splendid Samaritan, if the sacrifices that had to be made were enormous. But then so would a Good Samaritan assume responsibility for that violinist; so would Henry Fonda, if he is a Good Samaritan, fly in from the West Coast and assume responsibility for me.

8. My argument will be found unsatisfactory on two counts by many of those who want to regard abortion as morally permissible. First, while I do argue that abortion is not impermissible, I do not argue that it is always permissible. There may well be cases in which carrying the child to term requires only Minimally Decent Samaritanism of the mother, and this is a standard we must not fall below. I am inclined to think it a merit of my account precisely that it does *not* give a general yes or a general no. It allows for and supports our sense that, for example, a sick and desperately frightened fourteen-year-old schoolgirl, pregnant due to rape, may *of course* choose abortion, and that any law which rules this out is an insane law. And it also allows for and supports our sense that in other cases resort to abortion is even positively indecent. It would be indecent in the woman to request an abortion, and indecent in a doctor to perform it, if she is in her seventh month, and wants the abortion just to avoid the nuisance of postponing a trip abroad. The very fact that the arguments I have been drawing attention to treat all cases of abortion, or even all cases of abortion in which the mother's life is not at stake, as morally on a par ought to have made them suspect at the outset.

Secondly, while I am arguing for the permissibility of abortion in some cases, I am not arguing for the right to secure the death of the unborn child. It is easy to confuse these two things in that up to a certain point in the life of the fetus it is not able to survive outside the mother's body; hence removing it from her body guarantees its death. But they are importantly different. I have argued that you are not morally required to spend nine months in bed, sustaining the life of that violinist; but to say this is by no means to say that if, when you unplug yourself, there is a miracle and he survives, you than have a right to turn round and slit his throat. You may detach yourself even if this costs him his life; you have no right to be guaranteed his death, by some other means, if unplugging yourself does not kill him. There are some people who will feel dissatisfied by this feature of my argument. A woman may be utterly devastated by the thought of a child, a bit of herself, put out for adoption and never seen or heard of again. She may therefore want not merely that the child be detached from her, but more, that it die. Some opponents of abortion are inclined to regard this as beneath contempt—thereby showing insensitivity to what is surely a powerful source of despair. All the same, I agree that the desire for the child's death is not one which anybody may gratify, should it turn out to be possible to detach the child alive.

At this place, however, it should be remembered that we have only been pretending throughout that the fetus is a human being from the moment of conception. A very early abortion is surely not the killing of a person, and so is not dealt with by anything I have said here.

Notes

1. Daniel Callahan, *Abortion: Law, Choice and Morality* (New York, 1970), p. 373. This book gives a fascinating survey of the available information on abortion. The Jewish tradition is surveyed in David M. Feldman, *Birth Control in Jewish Law* (New York, 1968), Part 5; the Catholic tradition in John T. Noonan, Jr., "An Almost Absolute Value in History," in *The Morality of Abortion*, ed. John T. Noonan, Jr. (Cambridge, Mass., 1970).
2. The term "direct" in the arguments I refer to is a technical one. Roughly, what is meant by "direct killing" is either killing as an end in itself, or killing as a means to some end, for example, the end of saving someone else's life. See note 5 for an example of its use.
3. Cf. *Encyclical Letter of Pope Pius XI on Christian Marriage*, St. Paul Editions (Boston, n.d.), p. 32: "[H]owever much we may pity the mother whose health and even life is gravely imperiled in the performance of the duty allotted to her by nature, nevertheless what could ever be a sufficient reason for excusing in any way the direct murder of the innocent? This is precisely what we are dealing with here." Noonan (*The Morality of Abortion*, p. 43) reads this as follows: "What cause can ever avail to excuse in any way the direct killing of the innocent? For it is a question of that."
4. The thesis in (4) is in an interesting way weaker than those in (1), (2), and (3): they rule out abortion even in cases in which both mother *and* child will die if the abortion is not performed. By contrast, one who held the view expressed in (4) could consistently say that one needn't prefer letting two persons die to killing one.
5. Cf. the following passage from Pius XII, *Address to the Italian Catholic Society of Midwives:* "The baby in the maternal breast has the right to life immediately from God.—Hence there is no man, no human authority, no science, no medical, eugenic, social, economic or moral 'indication' which can establish or grant a valid juridical ground for a direct deliberate disposition of an innocent human life, that is a disposition which looks to its destruction either as an end or as a means to another end perhaps in itself not illicit.—The baby, still not born, is a man in the same degree and for the same reason as the mother" (quoted in Noonan, *The Morality of Abortion*, p. 45).
6. The need for a discussion of this agrument was brought home to me by members of the Society for Ethical and Legal Philosophy, to whom this paper was originally presented.
7. For a discussion of the difficulties involved, and a survey of the European experience with such laws, see *The Good Samaritan and the Law*, ed. James M. Ratcliffe (New York, 1966).

The Problem of Abortion and the Doctrine of the Double Effect

PHILIPPA FOOT

Philippa Foot (1920–) is a professor of philosophy at the University of California at Los Angeles and a fellow of Somerville College, Oxford. Her publications include *Virtues and Vices* as well as numerous contributions to philosophical journals.

One of the reasons why most of us feel puzzled about the problem of abortion is that we want, and do not want, to allow to the unborn child the rights that belong to adults and children. When we think of a baby about to be born it seems absurd to think that the next few minutes or even hours could make so radical a difference to its status; yet as we go back in the life of the foetus we are more and more reluctant to say that this is a human being and must be treated as such. No doubt this is the deepest source of our dilemma, but it is not the only one. For we are also confused about the general question of what we may and may not do where the interests of human beings conflict. We have strong intuitions about certain cases; saying, for instance, that it is all right to raise the level of education in our country, though statistics allow us to predict that a rise in the suicide rate will follow, while it is not all right to kill the feeble-minded to aid cancer research. It is not easy, however, to see the principles involved, and one way of throwing light on the abortion issue will be by setting up parallels involving adults or children once born. So we will be able to isolate the "equal rights" issue and should be able to make some advance.

I shall not, of course, discuss all the principles that may be used in deciding what to do where the interests or rights of human beings conflict. What I want to do is to look at one particular theory, known as the "doctrine of the double effect" which is invoked by Catholics in support of their views on abortion but supposed by them to apply elsewhere. As used in the abortion argument this doctrine has often seemed to non-Catholics to be a piece of complete sophistry. In the last number of the *Oxford Review* it was given short shrift by Professor Hart.[1] And yet this principle has seemed to some non-Catholics as well as to Catholics to stand as the only defence against decisions on other issues that are quite unacceptable. It will help us in our difficulty about abortion if this conflict can be resolved.

The doctrine of the double effect is based on a distinction between what a man foresees as a result of his voluntary action and what, in the strict sense, he intends. He intends in the strictest sense both those things that he aims at as ends and those that he aims at as means to his ends. The latter may be regretted in themselves but nevertheless desired for the sake of the end, as we may intend to keep dangerous lunatics confined for the sake of our safety. By contrast a man is said not strictly, or directly, to intend the foreseen consequences of his voluntary actions where these are neither the end at which he is aiming nor the means to this end. Whether the word "intention" should be applied in both cases is not of course

From the *Oxford Review* no. 5 (1967), pp. 5–15.

what matters: Bentham spoke of "oblique intention," contrasting it with the "direct intention" of ends and means, and we may as well follow his terminology. Everyone must recognize that some such distinction can be made, though it may be made in a number of different ways, and it is the distinction that is crucial to the doctrine of the double effect. The words "double effect" refer to the two effects that an action may produce: the one aimed at, and the one foreseen but in no way desired. By "the doctrine of the double effect" I mean the thesis that it is sometimes permissible to bring about by oblique intention what one may not directly intend. Thus the distinction is held to be relevant to moral decision in certain difficult cases. It is said for instance that the operation of hysterectomy involves the death of the foetus as the foreseen but not strictly or directly intended consequence of the surgeon's act, while other operations kill the child and count as the direct intention of taking an innocent life, a distinction that has evoked particularly bitter reactions on the part of non-Catholics. If you are permitted to bring about the death of the child, what does it matter how it is done? The doctrine of the double effect is also used to show why in another case, where a woman in labour will die unless a craniotomy operation is performed, the intervention is not to be condoned. There, it is said, we may not operate but must let the mother die. We foresee her death but do not directly intend it, whereas to crush the skull of the child would count as direct intention of its death.[2]

This last application of the doctrine has been queried by Professor Hart on the ground that the child's death is not strictly a means to saving the mother's life and should logically be treated as an unwanted but foreseen consequence by those who make use of the distinction between direct and oblique intention. To interpret the doctrine in this way is perfectly reasonable given the language that has been used; it would, however, make nonsense of it from the beginning. A certain event may be desired under one of its descriptions, unwanted under another, but we cannot treat these as two different events, one of which is aimed at and the other not. And even if it be argued that there are here two different events—the crushing of the child's skull and its death—the two are obviously much too close for an application of the doctrine of the double effect. To see how odd it would be to apply the principle like this we may consider the story, well known to philosophers, of the fat man stuck in the mouth of the cave. A party of potholers have imprudently allowed the fat man to lead them as they make their way out of the cave, and he gets stuck, trapping the others behind him. Obviously the right thing to do is to sit down and wait until the fat man grows thin; but philosophers have arranged that flood waters should be rising within the cave. Luckily (luckily?) the trapped party have with them a stick of dynamite with which they can blast the fat man out of the mouth of the cave. Either they use the dynamite or they drown. In one version the fat man, whose head is *in* the cave, will drown with them; in the other he will be rescued in due course.[3] Problem: may they use the dynamite or not? Later we will find parallels to this example. Here it is introduced for light relief and because it will serve to show how ridiculous one version of the doctrine of the double effect would be. For suppose that the trapped explorers were to argue that the death of the fat man might be taken as a merely foreseen consequence of the act of blowing him up. ("We didn't want to kill him . . . only to blow him into small pieces" or even ". . . only to blast him out of the mouth of the cave.") I believe that those who use the doctrine of the double effect would rightly reject such a suggestion, though they will, of course, have considerable difficulty in explaining where the line is to be drawn. What is to be the criterion of "closeness" if we say that anything very close to what we are literally aiming at counts as if part of our aim?

Let us leave this difficulty aside and return to the arguments for and against the doctrine, supposing it to be formulated in the way considered most effective by its supporters, and ourselves bypassing the trouble by taking what must on any reasonable definition be clear cases of "direct" or "oblique" intention.

The first point that should be made clear, in fairness to the theory, is that no one is suggesting that it does not matter what you bring about as long as you merely foresee and do not strictly intend the evil that follows. We might think, for instance, of the (actual) case of wicked merchants selling, for cooking, oil they knew to be poisonous and thereby killing a number of innocent people, comparing and contrasting it with that of some unemployed gravediggers, desperate for custom, who got hold of this same oil and sold it (or perhaps *they* secretly gave it away) in order to create orders for graves. They strictly (directly) intend the deaths they cause, while the merchants could say that it was no part of their *plan* that anyone should die. In morality, as in law, the merchants, like the gravediggers, would be considered as murderers; nor are the supporters of the doctrine of the double effect bound to say that there is the least difference between them in respect of moral turpitude. What they are committed to is the thesis that *sometimes* it makes a difference to the permissibility of an action involving harm to others that this harm, although foreseen, is not part of the agent's direct intention. An end such as earning one's living is clearly not such as to justify *either* the direct or oblique intention of the death of innocent people, but in certain cases one is justified in bringing about knowingly what one could not directly intend.

It is now time to say why this doctrine should be taken seriously in spite of the fact that it sounds rather odd, that there are difficulties about the distinction on which it depends, and that it seemed to yield one sophistical conclusion when applied to the problem of abortion. The reason for its appeal is that its opponents have often *seemed* to be committed to quite indefensible views. Thus the controversy has raged around examples such as the following. Suppose that a judge or magistrate is faced with rioters demanding that a culprit be found for a certain crime and threatening otherwise to take their own bloody revenge on a particular section of the community. The real culprit being unknown, the judge sees himself as able to prevent the bloodshed only by framing some innocent person and having him executed. Beside this example is placed another in which a pilot whose aeroplane is about to crash is deciding whether to steer from a more to a less inhabited area. To make the parallel as close as possible it may rather be supposed that he is the driver of a runaway tram which he can only steer from one narrow track on to another; five men are working on one track and one man on the other; anyone on the track he enters is bound to be killed. In the case of the riots the mob have five hostages, so that in both the exchange is supposed to be one man's life for the lives of five. The question is why we should say, without hesitation, that the driver should steer for the less occupied track, while most of us would be appalled at the idea that the innocent man could be framed. It may be suggested that the special feature of the latter case is that it involves the corruption of justice, and this is, of course, very important indeed. But if we remove that special feature supposing that some private individual is to kill an innocent person and pass him off as the criminal, we still find ourselves horrified by the idea. The doctrine of double effect offers us a way out of the difficulty, insisting that it is one thing to steer towards someone foreseeing that you will kill him and another to aim at his death as part of your plan. Moreover there is one very important element of good in what is here insisted. In real life it would hardly ever be certain that the man on the narrow track would be killed. Perhaps he might find a foothold on the side of the tunnel and cling on as the vehicle hurtled by. The driver of the tram does *not* then leap off and brain him with a crowbar. The judge, however, needs the death of the innocent man for his (good) purposes. If the victim proves hard to hang he must see to it that he dies another way. To choose to execute him is to choose that this evil *shall come about,* and this must therefore count as a *certainty* in weighing up the good and evil involved. The distinction between direct and oblique intention is crucial here, and is of great importance in an uncertain world. Nevertheless this is no way to defend the doctrine of the double effect. For the question is whether the difference between aiming at something and obliquely intending it is *in itself* relevant to moral decisions; not whether it is important when correlated with a difference of certainty in the balance of good and evil. Moreover we are particularly interested in the application of the doctrine of the double effect to the question of abortion, and no one can deny that in medicine there are sometimes certainties so complete that is would be a mere quibble to speak of the "probable outcome" of this course of action or that. It is not, therefore, with a merely philosophical interest that we should put aside the uncertainty and scrutinize the examples to test the doctrine of the double effect. Why can we not argue from the case of the steering driver to that of the judge?

Another pair of examples poses a similar problem. We are about to give to a patient who needs it to save his life a massive dose of a certain drug in short supply. There arrive, however, five other patients each of whom could be saved by one-fifth of that dose. We say with regret that we cannot spare our whole supply of the drug for a single patient, just as we should say that we could not spare the whole resources of a ward for one dangerously ill individual when ambulances arrive bringing in the victims of a multiple crash. We feel bound to let one man die rather than many if that is our only choice. Why then do we not feel justified in killing people in the interests of cancer research or to obtain, let us say, spare parts for grafting on to those who need them? We can suppose, similarly, that several dangerously ill people can be saved only if we kill a certain individual and make a serum from his dead body. (These examples are not over fanciful considering present controversies about prolonging the life of mortally ill patients whose eyes or kidneys are to be used for others.) Why cannot we argue from the case of the scarce drug to that of the body needed for medical purposes? Once again the doctrine of the double effect comes up with an explanation. In one kind of case but not the other we aim at the death of the innocent man.

A further argument suggests that if the doctrine of the double effect is rejected this has the consequence of putting us hopelessly in the power of bad men. Suppose for example that some tyrant should threaten to torture five men if we ourselves would not torture one. Would it be our duty to do so, supposing we believed him, because this would be no different from choosing to rescue five men from his torturers rather than one? If so anyone who wants us to do something we think wrong has only to threaten that otherwise he himself will do something we think worse. A mad murderer, known to keep his promises, could thus make it our duty to kill some innocent citizen to prevent him from killing two. From this conclusion we are again rescued by the doctrine of the double effect. If we refuse, we foresee that the greater number will be killed but we do not intend it: it is he who intends (that is strictly or directly intends) the death of innocent persons; we do not.

At one time I thought that these arguments in favour of the doctrine of the double effect were conclusive, but I now believe that the conflict should be solved in another way. The clue that we should follow is that the strength of the doctrine seems to lie in the distinction it makes between what we *do* (equated with direct intention) and what we allow (thought of as obliquely intended). Indeed it is interesting that the disputants tend to argue about whether we are to be held responsible for what we allow as we are for what we do.[4] Yet it is not obvious that this is what they should be discussing, since the distinction between what one does and what one allows to happen is not the same as that between direct and oblique intention. To see this one has only to consider that it is possible *deliberately* to allow something to happen, aiming at it either for its own sake or as part of one's plan for obtaining something else. So one person might want another person dead, and deliberately allow him to die. And again one may be said to *do* things that one does not aim at, as the steering driver would kill the man on the track. Moreover there is a large class of things said to be brought about rather than either done or allowed, and either kind of intention is possible. So it is possible to *bring about* a man's death by getting him to go to sea in a leaky boat, and the intention of his death may be either direct or oblique.

Whatever it may, or may not, have to do with the doctrine of the double effect, the idea of *allowing* is worth looking into in this context. I shall leave aside the special case of giving permission, which involves the idea of authority, and consider the two main divisions into which cases of allowing seem to fall. There is firstly the allowing which is forbearing to prevent. For this we need a sequence thought of as somehow already in train, and something that the agent could do to intervene. (The agent must be able to intervene, but does not do so.) So, for instance, he could warn someone, but *allows* him to walk into a trap. He could feed an animal but *allows* it to die for lack of food. He could stop a leaking tap but *allows* the water to go on flowing. This is the case of allowing with which we shall be concerned, but the other should be mentioned. It is the kind of allowing which is roughly equivalent to *enabling;* the root idea being the removal of some obstacle which is, as it were, holding back a train of events. So someone may remove a plug and *allow* water to flow; open a door and *allow* an animal to get out; or give someone money and *allow* him to get back on his feet.

The first kind of allowing requires an omission, but there is no other general correlation between omission and allowing, commission and bringing about or doing. An actor who fails to turn up for a performance will generally spoil it rather than allow it to be spoiled. I mention the distinction between omission and commission only to set it aside.

Thinking of the first kind of allowing (forebearing to prevent), we should ask whether there is any difference, from the moral point of view, between what one does or causes and what one merely allows. It seems clear that on occasions one is just as bad as the other, as is recognized in both morality and law. A man may murder his child or his aged relatives, by allowing them to die of starvation as well as by giving poison; he may also be convicted of murder on either account. In another case we would, however, make a distinction. Most of us allow people to die of starvation in India and Africa, and there is surely something wrong with us that we do; it would be nonsense, however, to pretend that it is only in law that we make a distinction between allowing people in the underdeveloped countries to die of starvation and sending them poisoned food. There is worked into our moral system a distinction between what we owe people in the form of aid and what we owe them in the way of non-interference. Salmond, in his *Jurisprudence,* expressed as follows the distinction between the two.

> A positive right corresponds to a positive duty, and is a right that he on whom the duty lies shall do some positive act on behalf of the person entitled. A negative right corresponds to a negative duty, and is a right that the person bound shall refrain from some act which would operate to the prejudice of the person entitled. The former is a right to be positively benefited; the latter is merely a right not to be harmed.[5]

As a general account of rights and duties this is defective, since not all are so closely connected with benefit and harm. Nevertheless for our purposes it will do well. Let us speak of negative duties when thinking of the obligation to refrain from such things as killing or robbing, and of the positive duty, e.g., to look after children or aged parents. It will be useful, however, to extend the notion of positive duty beyond the range of things that are strictly called duties, bringing acts of charity under this heading. These are owed only in a rather loose sense, and some acts of charity could hardly be said to be *owed* at all, so I am not following ordinary usage at this point.

Let us now see whether the distinction of negative and positive duties explains why we see differently the action of the steering driver and that of the judge, of the doctors who withhold the scarce durg and those who obtain a body for medical purposes, of those who choose to rescue the five men rather than one man from torture and those who are ready to torture the one man themselves in order to save five. In each case we have a conflict of duties, but what kind of duties are they? Are we, in each case, weighing positive duties against positive, negative against negative, or one against the other? Is the duty to refrain from injury, or rather to bring aid?

The steering driver faces a conflict of negative duties, since it is his duty to avoid injuring five men and also his duty to avoid injuring one. In the circumstances he is not able to avoid both, and it seems clear that he should do the least injury he can. The judge, however, is weighing the duty of not inflicting injury against the duty of bringing aid. He wants to rescue the innocent people threatened with death but can do so only by inflicting injury himself. Since one does not *in general* have the same duty to help people as to refrain from injuring them, it is not possible to argue to a conclusion about what he should do from the steering driver case. It is interesting that, even where the strictest duty of positive aid exists, this still does not weigh as if a negative duty were involved. It is not, for instance, permissible to commit a murder to bring one's starving children food. If the choice is between inflicting injury on one or many there seems only one rational course of action; if the choice is between aid to some at the cost of injury to others, and refusing to inflict the injury to bring the aid, the whole matter is open to dispute. So it is not inconsistent of us to think that the driver must steer for the road on which only one man stands while the judge (or his equivalent) may not kill the innocent person in order to stop the riots. Let us now consider the second pair of examples, which concern the scarce drug on the one hand and on the other the body needed to save lives. Once again we find a difference based on the distinction between the duty to avoid injury and the duty to provide aid. Where one man needs a massive dose of the drug and we withhold it from him in order to save five men, we are weighing aid against aid. But if we consider killing a man in order to use his body to save others, we are thinking of doing him injury to bring others aid. In an interesting variant of the model, we may suppose that instead of killing someone we deliberately let him die. (Perhaps he is a beggar to whom we are thinking of giving food, but then we say "No, they need bodies for medical research.") Here it does seem relevant that in allowing him to die we are aiming at his death, but presumably we are inclined to see this as a violation of negative rather than positive duty. If this is right, we see why we are unable in either case to argue to a conclusion from the case of the scarce drug.

In the examples involving the torturing of one man or five men, the principle seems to be the same as for the last pair. If we are bringing aid (rescuing people about to be tortured by the tyrant), we must obviously rescue the larger rather than the smaller group. It does not follow, however, that we would be justified in inflicting the injury, or getting a third person to do so, in order to save the five. We may therefore refuse to be forced into acting by the threats of bad men. To refrain from inflicting injury ourselves is a stricter duty than to prevent other people from inflicting injury, which is not to say that the other is not a very strict duty indeed.

So far the conclusions are the same as those at which we might arrive following the doctrine of the double effect, but in others they will be different, and the advantage seems to be all on the side of the alternative. Suppose, for instance, that there are five patients in a hospital whose lives could be saved by the manufacture of a certain gas, but that this inevitably releases lethal fumes into the room of another patient whom for some reason we are unable to move. His death, being of no use to us, is clearly a side effect, and not directly intended. Why then is the case different from that of the scarce drug, if the point about that is that we foresaw but did not strictly intend the death of the single patient? Yet it surely is different. The relatives of the gassed patient would presumably be successful if they sued the hospital and the whole story came out. We may find it particularly revolting that someone should be *used* as in the case where he is killed or allowed to die in the interest of medical research, and the fact of *using* may even determine what we would decide to do in some cases, but the principle seems unimportant compared with our reluctance to bring such injury for the sake of giving aid.

My conclusion is that the distinction between direct and oblique intention plays only a quite subsidiary role in determining what we say in these cases, while the distinction between avoiding injury and bringing aid is very important indeed. I have not, of course, argued that there are no other principles. For instance it clearly makes a difference whether our positive duty is a strict duty or rather an act of charity: feeding our own children or feeding those in far away countries. It may also make a difference whether the person about to suffer is one thought of as uninvolved in the threatened disaster, and whether it is his presence that constitutes the threat to the others. In many cases we find it very hard to know what to say, and I have not been arguing for any general conclusion such as that we may never, whatever the balance of good and evil, bring injury to one for the sake of aid to others, even when this injury amounts to death. I have only tried to show that even if we reject the doctrine of the double effect we are not forced to the conclusion that the size of the evil must always be our guide.

Let us now return to the problem of abortion, carrying out our plan of finding parallels involving adults or children rather than the unborn. We must say something about the different cases in which abortion might be considered on medical grounds.

First of all there is the situation in which nothing that can be done will save the life of child and mother, but where the life of the mother can be saved by killing the child. This is parallel to the case of the fat man in the mouth of the cave who is bound to be drowned with the others if nothing is done. Given the certainty of the outcome, as it was postulated, there is no serious conflict of interests here, since the fat man will perish in either case, and it is reasonable that the action that will save someone should be done. It is a great objection to those who argue that the direct intention of the death of an innocent person is never justifiable that the edict will apply even in this case. The Catholic doctrine on abortion must here conflict with that of most reasonable men. Moreover we would be justified in performing the operation whatever the method used, and it is neither a necessary nor a good justification of the special case of hysterectomy that the child's death is not directly intended, being rather a foreseen consequence of what is done. What difference could it make as to how the death is brought about?

Secondly we have the case in which it is possible to perform an operation which will save the mother and kill the child or kill the mother and save the child. This is parallel to the famous case of the shipwrecked mariners who believed that they must throw someone overboard if their boat was not to founder in a storm, and to the other famous case of the two sailors, Dudley and Stephens, who killed and ate the cabin boy when adrift on the sea without food. Here again there is no conflict of interests so far as the decision to act is concerned; only in deciding whom to save. Once again it would be reasonable to act, though one would respect someone who held back from the appalling action either because he preferred to perish rather than do such a thing or because he held on past the limits of reasonable hope. In real life the certainties postulated by philosophers hardly ever exist, and Dudley and Stephens were rescued not long after their ghastly meal. Nevertheless if the certainty were absolute, as it might be in the abortion case, it would seem better to save one than none. Probably we should decide in favour of the mother when weighing her life against that of the unborn child, but it is interesting that, a few years later, we might easily decide it the other way.

The worst dilemma comes in the third kind of example where to save the mother we must kill the child, say by crushing its skull, while if nothing is done the mother will perish but the child can be safely delivered after her death. Here the doctrine of the double effect has been invoked to show that we may not intervene, since the child's death would be directly intended while the mother's would not. On a strict parallel with cases not involving the unborn we might find the conclusion correct though the reason given was wrong. Suppose, for instance, that in later life the presence of a child was certain to bring death to the mother. We would surely not think ourselves justified in ridding her of it by a process that involved its death. For in general we do not think that we can kill one innocent person to rescue another, quite apart from the special care that we feel is due to children once they have prudently got themselves born. What we would be prepared to do when a great many people were involved is another matter, and this is probably the key to one quite common view of abortion on the part of those who take quite seriously the rights of the unborn child. They probably feel that if *enough* people are involved one must be sacrificed, and they think of the mother's life against the unborn child's life as if it were many against one. But of course many people do not view it like this at all, having no inclination to accord to the foetus or unborn child anything like ordinary human status in the matter of rights. I have not been arguing for or against these points of view but only trying to discern some of the currents that are pulling us back and forth. The levity of the examples is not meant to offend.

Notes

1. H. L. A. Hart, "Intention and Punishment," *Oxford Review,* Number 4, Hilary 1967. I owe much to this article and to a conversation with Professor Hart, though I do not know whether he will approve of what follows.
2. For discussions of the Catholic doctrine on abortion see Glanville Williams, *The Sanctity of Life and the Criminal Law* (New York, 1957); also N. St. John Stevas, *The Right to Life* (London, 1963).
3. It was Professor Hart who drew my attention to this distinction.
4. See, e.g., J. Bennett, "Whatever the Consequences," *Analysis,* January 1966, and G. E. M. Anscombe's reply in *Analysis,* June 1966. See also Miss Anscombe's "Modern Moral Philosophy" in *Philosophy,* January 1958.
5. J. Salmond, *Jurisprudence,* 11th edition, p. 283.

Should the Numbers Count?

JOHN M. TAUREK

John M. Taurek (1938–) has taught philosophy at Stanford University, New York University, and the University of California at Los Angeles.

We have resources for bestowing benefits and for preventing harms. But there are limitations. There are many people we are not in a position to help at all. That is one kind of limitation. But there is another kind of limitation we encounter. Often we must choose between bestowing benefits on certain people, or preventing certain harms from befalling them, and bestowing benefits on or preventing harms from befalling certain others. We cannot do both. The general question discussed here is whether we should, in such trade-off situations, consider the relative numbers of people involved as something in itself of significance in determining our course of action.[1] The conclusion I reach is that we should not. I approach this general question by focusing on a particular hypothetical case in which we find ourselves in a position of being able to prevent a certain harm from befalling one person or to prevent a like harm from befalling each of five others, but unable to spare all six from harm.

The situation is that I have a supply of some life-saving drug.[2] Six people will all certainly die if they are not treated with the drug. But one of the six requires all of the drug if he is to survive. Each of the other five requires only one-fifth of the drug. What ought I to do?

To many it seems obvious that in such cases, special considerations apart, one ought to save the greatest number. I cannot accept this view. I believe that at least some of those who do accept it fail to appreciate the difficulty of reconciling their thinking here with other convictions they are inclined to hold with even greater tenacity. First, I want to delineate some of these difficulties. I hope that, in view of them, others might be brought to reflect more critically on the intuitions that underlie this position. I shall then present what seems to me a more appropriate and appealing way of viewing trade-off situations of the kind in question.

Those who think that I ought to distribute my drug in fifths to the five people usually qualify their position. They maintain that "other things being equal, or special considerations apart, one ought to save the greater number." What sort of special considerations to the contrary do they have in mind? What is being ruled out by the "other things being equal" clause?

One thing they have in mind, I think, is the possibility of special facts about the one person that would, in their view, make his death a far worse thing than one might otherwise have supposed. Perhaps he is close to discovering some wonder drug or is on the verge of negotiating a lasting peace in the world's perennial trouble spot. The idea is that it could happen that this one person's continued existence is in some way crucial to the welfare of an unusually large number of

I owe a large debt to Rita V. Lewis, whose views on the issues dealt with in this paper have had a pervasive influence on both its content and style. I should also like to thank Herbert Morris for helpful comments made on an earlier version of this essay.

From *Philosophy & Public Affairs* 6, no. 4 (1977), pp. 293–316.

people. This would make his death a far worse thing in the minds of some than it would otherwise be. Of course, they also have in mind the possibility that special facts about these five persons could make their deaths not nearly so bad a thing after all. They might be five driveling old people or five idiot infants, loved by no one. In light of such facts as these it may well be permissible, perhaps even obligatory in the view of some, to save the one wholesome person instead of the five others. So when people say, "other things being equal, one ought to save the greater number," they mean to rule out such special considerations as these. The thinking here is that, apart from some such considerations, the death of five innocent persons is a worse thing, a greater evil, a greater loss, than the death of one innocent person. Since I am in a position to prevent either of these bad things from happening, but not both, I am morally required to prevent the worst.

Such reasoning seems appealing to many. I find it difficult to understand and even more difficult to see how it is to be reconciled with certain other convictions widely shared by these same people. Suppose this one person, call him David, is someone I know and like, and the others are strangers to me. I might well give all of my drug to him. And I am inclined to think that were I to do so, I would not be acting immorally. I suspect that many share this view with me.

Of course, some people do think that I would be acting immorally. They think it would be wrong to give all the drug to David while the five others die just because David is someone I know and like. They may allow that this could make my action excusable, but on their view it would not make it right.

For the moment, I address myself to those who, while subscribing to the general position, nevertheless share my view that it would not be wrong for me to use my drug to save a person I know and like. They must deny that the original claim, together with the thinking that lies behind it, commits them to the view that I ought to save the five strangers in this case. Perhaps they will object that, in introducing David as someone I know and like, I have introduced another of those special considerations that were meant to be excluded by the "other things being equal" clause. But if this is one of the special considerations meant to be ruled out, it is of a different sort from the special considerations previously mentioned. These were facts about the five persons in light of which it was thought their deaths would not be so bad, after all; or facts about David that would make his death a worse thing than the death of a person of more ordinary credentials. The idea was that these considerations would make a difference to what I ought to do, because in light of them the death of the one person would in fact be a worse thing to have happen than would be the deaths of these five.

But I would not think that the fact that David happens to be someone I know and like would make his death a worse thing in comparison to the deaths of these others than it would be if, by chance, I didn't know him or knew him but happened not to like him. So it is not clear to me how this fact is to make a difference in what I am *morally required* to do in this situation. It is not clear to me how it is to make a difference in the view of those who think that, apart from it, I would have a moral obligation to save the five, an obligation deriving from the fact that it is a worse thing, other things being equal, that these five innocent persons should die than it is that this one should.

Perhaps there are special considerations of a kind different from those described thus far. Suppose that one person had contracted with me in advance to have just this quantity of the drug administered to him at this particular time. It could be thought that such a special obligation to the one party arising out of a contract would override the fact that I would be preventing a far worse thing from happening were I to give the drug to the five. An explicit contract or promise may not be the only source of such special obligations to another person. Perhaps a parent is thought to be thus specially obligated to his child, or a child to his parents. Perhaps a doctor has such a special obligation to his regular patients. Perhaps one might think one has such a special obligation to a benefactor, and so on. It seems reasonable to suppose that the existence of such special obligations to specific individuals involved were also meant to be excluded by the "other things being equal" clause. But can this be helpful to those who wish to reconcile their feeling that I do not do wrong when I give all my drug to a friend with an adherence to the original contention?

This does not seem to be a very promising line. Are we to suppose that I have in this situation an overriding obligation to save this one person, deriving from the fact that he is someone I know and like? Such a supposition does not appear to capture my thinking here at all. The fact is that I would act to save David's life because, knowing him and liking him, my concern for his well-being is simply greater than my concern for the well-being of those others, not because I recognize some overriding obligation to him. Imagine that the situation involved David and only one other person, a stranger. In the absence of any special claim of right possessed by the stranger, I would save David. If asked to explain or justify my choice, I would not think to say that I was *morally required* to give my drug to David in virtue of the fact that I happen to know and like him. The fact that David is a friend explains, naturally enough, my preference for saving him rather than this other person. It is the absence of any moral obligation to save this other person rather than David that makes my choice morally permissible. And, rightly or wrongly, that is how I think of my conduct in the situation under discussion. In securing David's survival I am acting on a purely personal preference. It is the absence of any moral requirement to save these others rather than David that makes my doing so morally permissible.

However, this talk of a special duty to the one person, arising not from any promise, contract or quasi-contractual relationship between us, but somehow from the mere fact that I know and like him, would appear to go too far. For, on such a view, it would be more than simply permissible for me to save David, it would be morally obligatory that I save him rather than these five others. And this is not the thinking of those who feel only that it would not be wrong of me to save David.

On the view in question, one is morally required to save the five instead of the one, other things being equal, because, other things being equal, it is a very much worse thing that these five innocent people should die than it is that this one should. But if this fact constitutes a compelling ground for a moral obligation to give the drug to these five rather than to this one, then I too shall have to acknowledge its moral force. The problem, then, is to explain, especially perhaps to these five people, how it is that merely because I know and like David and am unacquainted with them I can so easily escape the moral requirement to save their lives that would fall on most anyone else in my position. The only relevant consideration here is that I happen to like David more than I like any of them. Imagine my saying to them, "Admittedly, the facts are such that I would be morally obligated to give you this drug, if it didn't happen that I prefer to give it to him." The moral force of such facts must be feeble indeed to be overridden by an appeal as feeble as this.

Contrast this situation with almost any other in which we would be prepared to acknowledge the existence of grounds for a moral requirement to give the drug to these five people. Suppose, for example, that these five had contracted with me in advance to deliver this drug to them at this time and place. It would not seem likely that anyone would think that the fact that I would prefer to give it to someone else instead would alter in any way what I was morally required to do. But of course it might make it harder, psychologically, for me to do what I ought to do. Again, suppose that these five are American soldiers and I am an army doctor with what little is left of the issue of this drug. And let us suppose that this other person is someone I know and like but is a citizen of some other country. Would anyone imagine that the fact that I would prefer to use the drug to save this one person could somehow nullify or lift my obligation to distribute the drug to the five soldiers?

The point is this. Generally, when the facts are such that any impartial person would recognize a moral obligation to do something as important to people as giving this drug to these five would be to them, then an appeal to the fact that one happens to be partial to the interests of some others would do nothing to override the moral obligation. Yet this is the position of those who maintain that in this situation any impartial person would be *morally required* to distribute his drug in fifths to the five. But because I, personally, would prefer to give it to someone else, it is permissible for me to do so.[3]

I am inclined to think, then, that we should either agree that it would be wrong for me to save David in this situation or admit that there are no grounds for a moral requirement on anyone, special obligations apart, to save the five instead of David. Now as I said earlier there are those who will take the view that I do wrong when I give preference to David in this situation. They may feel that what has been said so far only proves the point. So now I would like to say something in support of the opinion that it would be morally permissible for a person in such circumstances to save a friend rather than the five strangers.

Suppose the drug belongs to your friend David. It is his drug, his required dosage. Now there are these five strangers, strangers to David as well as to you. Would you try to persuade David to give his drug to these five people? Do you think you should? Suppose you were to try. How would you begin? You are asking him to give up his life so that each of the five others, all strangers to him, might continue to live.

Imagine trying to reason with David as you would, presumably, have reasoned with yourself were the drug yours. "David, to be sure it is a bad thing, a very bad thing, that you should die. But don't you see it is a far worse thing that these five people should die? Now you are in a position to prevent either of these bad things from happening. Unfortunately you cannot prevent them both. So you ought to insure that the worse thing doesn't happen."

Don't you think that David might demur? Isn't he likely to ask: "Worse for whom?" And it seems natural and relevant that he should continue to put his case in some such way as this: "It is a far worse thing for me that I should die than that they should. I allow that for each of them it would be a worse thing were they all to die while I continue to live than it would be were I to die and they to continue to live. Indeed I wouldn't ask, nor would I expect, any one of them to give up his life so that I, a perfect stranger, might continue to live mine. But why should you, or any one of them, expect me to give up my life so that each of them might continue to live his?"

I think David's question deserves an answer. What could there be about these strangers that might induce David to think it worth giving up his life so that they might continue to live theirs? The usual sort of utilitarian reasoning would be comical if it were not so outrageous. Imagine any one of these five entreating David, "Look here David. Here I am but one person. If you give me one-fifth of your drug I will continue to live. I am confident that I will garner over the long haul a net balance of pleasure over pain, happiness over misery. Admittedly, if this were all that would be realized by your death I should not expect that you would give up your life for it. I mean, it may not be unreasonable to think that you yourself, were you to continue to live, might succeed in realizing at least as favorable a balance of happiness. But here, don't you see, is a second person. If he continues to live he too will accumulate a nice balance of pleasure over pain. And here is yet a third, a fourth, and finally a fifth person. Now, we would not ask you to die to make possible the net happiness realized in the life of any one of us five. For you might well suppose that you could realize as much in your own lifetime. But it would be most unreasonable for you to think that you could realize in your one lifetime anything like as much happiness as we get when we add together our five distinct favorable balances."

Such reasoning coming from some disinterested outside party might be a little less contemptible, but surely not a bit less foolish. But if we recognize the absurdity of trying to sell David on the idea that it would be a worse thing were these five persons to die than it would be were he to die by suggesting he focus on the large sum of their added happinesses as compared to his own, just what kind of reasoning would sound less absurd? Is it less absurd to ask him to focus on the large sum of intrinsic value possessed by five human beings, quite apart from considerations of their happiness, as compared to the value of himself alone?

I cannot imagine that I could give David any reason why *he* should think it better that these five strangers should continue to live than that he should. In using his drug to preserve his own life he acts to preserve what is, understandably, more important to him. He values his own life more than he values any of theirs. This is, of course, not to say that he thinks he is more valuable, period, than any one of them, or than all of them taken together. (Whatever could such a remark mean?) Moreover, and this I would like to stress, in not giving his drug to these five people he does not wrong any of them. He violates no one's rights. None of these five has a legitimate claim on David's drug in this situation, and so the five together have no such claim. Were they to attack David and to take his drug, they would be murderers. Both you and David would be wholly within your rights to defend against any such attempt to deprive him of his drug.

Such, in any case, is my view. I hope that most people would agree with me. But if it is morally permissible for David in this situation to give himself all of his drug, why should it be morally impermissible for me to do the same? It is my drug. It is more important to me that David should continue to live than it is that these five strangers should. I value his life more than I value theirs. None of these five has any special claim to my drug in this situation. None of them can legitimately demand of me that I give him the drug instead of giving it to David. And so the five together have no such special claim. I violate no one's rights when I use my drug to save David's life. Were these five, realizing that I was about to give my drug to David, to attempt to take it from me, I would think myself wholly justified in resisting.

Thus far I have argued that, since it would not be morally impermissible for the one person, David, to use all of his drug to save himself instead of these five others, it cannot be morally impermissible for me, were the drug mine and given that I am under no special obligations to any of these five, to use it all to save David instead of these other five. In so arguing I have committed myself to a view that may strike some as counterintuitive. On my view, if one party, *A*, must decide whether to spare another party, *B*, some loss or harm *H*, or to spare a third party, *C*, some loss or harm *H'*, it cannot be *A*'s moral duty, special obligations apart, to spare *C* harm *H'* unless it would be *B*'s duty, in the absence of special obligations to the contrary, to spare *C* harm *H'* if he could, even at the expense of suffering *H* himself. To put it another way, my thinking here is simply this. If it would be morally permissible for *B* to choose to spare himself a certain loss, *H*, instead of sparing another person, *C*, a loss, *H'*, in a situation where he cannot spare *C* and himself as well, then it must be permissible for someone else, not under any relevant special obligations to the contrary, to take *B*'s perspective, that is, to choose to secure the outcome most favorable to *B* instead of the outcome most favorable to *C*, if he cannot secure what would be best for each.

The following kind of case might be raised as a counterexample. Many of us, perhaps most of us, might agree that were *B* somehow situated so that he could spare *C* the loss of his life, or spare himself the loss of an arm, but could not do both, it would not be morally required, special obligations apart, that he choose to spare *C* the loss of his life. "But," it will be asked, "suppose you are the one who must choose? You can either spare this person, *C*, the loss of his life, or spare *B* the loss of his arm. Even apart from any special obligations to *C*, wouldn't you acknowledge that you ought to spare *C* the loss of his life? Wouldn't it be wrong for you to spare *B* his loss and let *C* die?"

Well, I do not think it would be morally impermissible for me to spare *B* the loss of his arm in such a situation. What exactly would be the ground for such a moral requirement? I am to choose which of two possible outcomes is to be realized: in the one, *B* retains his arm intact and *C* dies; in the other, *B* loses his arm and *C* does not die. If the choice were *B*'s it would be permissible for him to choose the first outcome. But it is not permissible for me to make this same choice? Why exactly is this? By hypothesis, I am under no relevant special obligations in this situation. So what is the difference between *B* and me in virtue of which I am morally required to secure the outcome most favored by *C*, though *B* would not be? Unless it is for some reason morally impermissible for one person to take the same interest in another's welfare as he himself takes in it, it must be permissible for me, in the absence of special obligations to the contrary, to choose the outcome that is in *B*'s best interest. And, of course, this is what I would do if *B*'s welfare were more important to me than *C*'s.

There may well come a point, however, at which the difference between what *B* stands to lose and *C* stands to lose is such that I would spare *C* his loss. But in just these situations I am inclined to think that even if the choice were *B*'s he too should prefer that *C* be spared his loss. For some people such a point of difference may already have been reached in the case where *B* stands to lose an arm, while *C* stands to lose his life. There are profoundly important differences in attitude among people here that I do not know how to reconcile. I personally do not think that anyone should be moved, in the absence of special considerations, to spare me the loss of my life rather than sparing themselves the loss of an arm. Others seem to think that they should.

I suspect that many of those who see in the purported counterexample a forceful objection to my view are people who more than half believe that (ideally) they really should be prepared to spare me the loss of my life even at the expense of losing their arms. Yet they are doubtful that they could bring themselves to make such a choice were it actually to come to that. Sensing this about themselves they are understandably reluctant to openly place such a demand on another. However when they imagine themselves in the role of a third party, who is not especially concerned about *B*, they feel less conflict about sparing *C* the loss of his life. They, after all, will not have to lose their arms. But if this is their thinking, then they are not raising a serious objection to the view I have taken.

Let me return now to a further discussion of the original trade-off situation. It is my conviction that were the drug David's to use, he would do nothing wrong, special obligations apart, were he to use it to save himself instead of giving it up to the five strangers. For the same reasons, I believe that were the drug mine and David someone I know and like, it would not be wrong of me, special obligations apart, to save him rather than the five strangers. And so I feel compelled to deny that any third party, relevant special obligations apart, would be *morally required* to save the five persons and let David die. So what do I think one should do in such a situation in the absence of any special concern for any of the parties involved?

First, let me suggest what I would do in many such cases. Here are six human beings. I can empathize with each of them. I would not like to see any of them die. But I cannot save everyone. Why not give each person an equal chance to survive? Perhaps I could flip a coin. Heads, I give my drug to these five. Tails,I give it to this one. In this way I give each of the six persons a fifty-fifty chance of surviving. Where such an option is open to me it would seem to best express my equal concern and respect for each person. Who among them could complain that I have done wrong? And on what grounds?[4]

The claim that one ought to save the many instead of the few was made to rest on the claim that, other things being equal, it is a worse thing that these five persons should die than that this one should. It is this evaluative judgment that I cannot accept. I do not wish to say in this situation that it is or would be a worse thing were these five persons to die and David to live than it is or would be were David to die and these five to continue to live. I do not wish to say this unless I am prepared to qualify it by explaining to whom or for whom or relative to what purpose it is or would be a worse thing.

I grant that for each one of the five persons, it would be worse were David to survive and they to die than it would be if David were to die and the five to survive. But, of course, from David's perspective the matter is otherwise. For him it would be a worse thing were he to die. From my perspective, I am supposing in this situation that it does not really matter who lives and who dies. My situation is not worsened or bettered by either outcome. No doubt others will be affected differently by what happens. For those who love or need David it would be a better thing were the others to die. But for those especially attached to or dependent on one or the other of these five, it would be better were David to die and these five to live.

Some will be impatient with all this. They will say it is true, no doubt, but irrelevant. They will insist that I say what would be a worse (or a better) thing, period. It seems obvious to them that from the moral point of view, since there is nothing special about any of these six persons, it is a worse thing that these five should die while this one continues to live than for this one to die while these five continue to live. It is a worse thing, not necessarily for anyone in particular, or relative to anyone's particular ends, but just a worse thing in itself.

I cannot give a satisfactory account of the

meaning of judgments of this kind. But there are important differences between them and those judgments which relativize the value ascribed to some particular person or group, purpose or end. When I judge of two possible outcomes that the one would be worse (or better) for this person or this group, I do not, typically, thereby express a preference between these outcomes. Typically, I do not feel constrained to admit that I or anyone *should* prefer the one outcome to the other. But when I evaluate outcomes from an impersonal perspective (perhaps we may say from a moral perspective), matters are importantly different. When I judge that it would be a worse thing, period, were this to happen than were that to happen, then I do, typically, thereby express a preference between these outcomes. Moreover, at the very least, I feel constrained to admit that I *should* have such a preference, even if I do not. It is a moral shortcoming not to prefer what is admittedly in itself a better thing to what is in itself a worse thing.

Hence, I cannot give such an impersonal evaluative judgment as the ground for a decision to give the drug to the five instead of to the one. I could not bring myself to say to this one person, "I give my drug to these five and let you die because, don't you see, it is a worse thing, a far worse thing, that they should die than that you should." I do not expect that David, or anyone in his position, should think it a better thing were he to die and these five others to survive than it would be were he to survive and they to die. I do not think him morally deficient in any way because he prefers the outcome in which he survives and the others die to the outcome in which they survive and he dies.

In a situation where the one person, David, is a friend of mine and the others strangers to me, I do have a preference for the one outcome as against the other, to me a natural and acceptable preference. But since I do not expect everyone to share such a preference I will not elevate its expression to the status of a universally binding evaluation. I do not say to the five strangers that I give all of my drug to my friend because it is a better thing in itself that he should survive than that they should. I do not believe any such thing. Rather, I simply explain that David is my friend. His survival is more important to me than theirs. I would expect them to understand this, provided they were members of a moral community acceptable to me, just as I would were our roles reversed. Further, in securing David's survival I violate no one's rights. No further justification of my action is needed, just as no further justification is needed in a situation where the drug belongs to the one person. He need not, and plainly should not, give as the ground for his decision to use his drug to secure his own survival the judgment that it is better in itself that he should survive than that they should. Who could expect any of them to accept that? He need only point out, as if this really needed remarking, that it is more important to him that he survive than it is to him that they should. Furthermore, in thus securing his own survival he violates none of their rights. What more need be said?

In the trade-off situation as presently conceived, all six persons are strangers to me. I have no special affection for any one of them, no greater concern for one than for any of the others. Further, by hypothesis, my situation will be made neither worse nor better by either outcome. Any preference I might show, therefore, if it is not to be thought arbitrary, would require grounding. Of course this is precisely what an impersonal evaluative judgment of the kind discussed would do. It would provide a reason for the preference I show should I give the drug to the five. But for the reasons given, I cannot subscribe to such an evaluation of these outcomes. Hence, in this situation I have absolutely no reason for showing perference to them as against him, and no reason for showing preference to him as against them. Thus I am inclined to treat each person equally by giving each an equal chance to survive.

Yet I can imagine it will still be said, despite everything, "But surely the numbers must count for something." I can hear the incredulous tones: "Would you flip a coin were it a question of saving fifty persons or saving one? Surely in situations where the numbers are this disproportionate you must admit that one ought to save the many rather than the few or the one."

I would flip a coin even in such a case, special considerations apart. I cannot see how or why the mere addition of numbers should change anything. It seems to me that those who, in situations of the kind in question, would have me count the relative numbers of people involved as something in itself of significance, would have me attach importance to human beings and what happens to them in merely the way I would to objects which I valued. If six objects are threatened by fire and I am in a position to retrieve the five in this room or the one in that room, but unable to get out all six, I would decide what to do in just the way I am told I should when it is human beings who are threatened. Each object will have a certain value in my eyes. If it happens that all six are of equal value, I will naturally preserve the many rather than the one. Why? Because the five objects are together five times more valuable in my eyes than the one.

But when I am moved to rescue human beings from harm in situations of the kind described, I cannot bring myself to think of them in just this way. I empathize with them. My concern for what happens to them is grounded chiefly in the realization that each of them is, as I would be in his place, terribly concerned about what happens to him. It is not my way to think of them as each having a certain *objective* value, determined however it is we determine the objective value of things, and then to make some estimate of the combined value of the five as against the one. If it were not for the fact that these objects were creatures much like me, for whom what happens to them is of great importance, I doubt that I would take much interest in their preservation. As merely intact objects they would mean very little to me, being, as such, nearly as common as toadstools. The loss of an arm of the *Pietà* means something to me not because the *Pietà* will miss it. But the loss of an arm of a creature like me means something to me only because I know he will miss it, just as I would miss mine. It is the loss *to this person* that I focus on. I lose nothing of value to me should he lose his arm. But if I have a concern for him, I shall wish he might be spared his loss.

And so it is in the original situation. I cannot but think of the situation in this way. For each of these six persons it is no doubt a terrible thing to die. Each faces the loss of something among the things he values most. His loss means something to me only, or chiefly, because of what it means to him. It is the loss to the individual that matters to me, not the loss of the individual. But should any one of these five lose his life, his loss is no greater a loss to him because, as it happens, four others (or forty-nine others) lose theirs as well. And neither he nor anyone else loses anything of greater value to him than does David, should David lose his life. Five individuals each losing his life does not add up to anyone's experiencing a loss five times greater than the loss suffered by any one of the five.

If I gave my drug to the five persons and let David die I cannot see that I would thereby have preserved anyone from suffering a loss greater than that I let David suffer. And, similarly, were I to give my drug to David and let the five die I cannot see that I would thereby have allowed anyone to suffer a loss greater than the loss I spared David. Each person's potential loss has the same significance to me, only as a loss to that person alone. Because, by hypothesis, I have an equal concern for each person involved, I am moved to give each of them an equal chance to be spared his loss.

My way of thinking about these trade-off situations consists, essentially, in seriously considering what will be lost or suffered by this one person if I do not prevent it, and in comparing the significance of that *for him* with what would be lost or suffered by anyone else if I do not prevent it. This reflects a refusal to take seriously in these situations any notion of the sum of two persons' separate losses. To me this appears a quite natural extension of the way in which most would view analogous trade-off situations involving differential losses to those involved, indeed even most of those who find my treatment of the cases thus far described paradoxical. Perhaps then, in one last effort to persuade them, it may be helpful to think about a trade-off situation of this kind.

Suppose I am told that if you, a stranger to me, agree to submit to some pain of significant intensity I will be spared a lesser one. Special circumstances apart, I can see no reason whatever why you should be willing to make such a sacrifice. It would be cowardly of me to ask it of you. Now add a second person, also a stranger to you. Again we are told that if you volunteer to undergo this same considerable pain each of us will be spared a lesser one. I feel it would be no less contemptible of me to ask you to make such a sacrifice in this situation. There is no reason you should be willing to undergo such a pain to spare me mine. There is no reason you should be willing to undergo such a pain to spare this other person his. And that is all there is to it.

Now, adding still others to our number, not one of whom will suffer as much as you are asked to bear, will not change things for me. It ought not to change things for any of us. If not one of us can give you a good reason why you should be willing to undergo a greater suffering so that he might be spared a lesser one, then there is simply no good reason why you should be asked to suffer so that the group may be spared. Suffering is not additive in this way. The discomfort of each of a large number of individuals experiencing a minor headache does not add up to anyone's experiencing a migraine. In such a trade-off situation as this we are to compare your pain or your loss, not to our collective or total pain, whatever exactly that is supposed to be, but to what will be suffered or lost by *any given single one of us*.

Perhaps it would not be unseemly for a stranger who will suffer some great agony or terrible loss unless you willingly submit to some relatively minor pain to ask you to consider this carefully, to ask you to empathize with him in what he will have to go through. But to my way of thinking it would be contemptible for any one of us in this crowd to ask you to consider carefully, "not, of course, what I personally will have to suffer. None of us is thinking of himself here! But contemplate, if you will, what *we* the group, will suffer. Think of the awful sum of pain that is in the balance here! There are so very many more of us." At best such thinking seems confused. Typically, I think, it is outrageous.

Yet, just such thinking is engaged in by those who, in situations of the kind described earlier, would be moved to a course of action by a *mere consideration* of the relative numbers of people involved. If the numbers should not be given any significance by those involved in these trade-off situations, why should they count for anyone? Suppose that I am in a position either to spare you your pain or to spare this large number of individuals each his lesser pain, but unable to spare both you and them. Why should I attach any significance to their numbers if none of those involved should? I cannot understand how I am supposed to add up their separate pains and attach significance to that alleged sum in a way that would be inappropriate were any of those involved to do it. If, by allowing you to suffer your pain, I do not see that I can thereby spare a single person any greater pain or, in this case, even as much pain, I did not see why calling my attention to the numbers should move me to spare them instead of you, any more than focusing on the numbers should move you to sacrifice for them collectively when you have no reason to sacrifice for them individually.

It is not my intention to argue that in this situation I ought to spare you rather than them just because your pain is "greater" than would be the pain of any one of them. Rather, I want to make it clear that in reaching a decision in such a case it is natural to focus on a comparison of the pain you will suffer, if I do not prevent it, with the pain that would be suffered by any given individual in this group, if I do not prevent it. I want to stress that it does not seem natural in such a case to attempt to add up their separate pains. I would like to combat the apparent tendency of some people to react to the thought of each of fifty individuals suffering a pain of some given intensity in the same way as they might to the thought of some individual suffering a pain many or fifty times more intense. I cannot but think that some such tendency is at work in the minds of those who attribute significance to the numbers in these trade-off situations.

In the original situation we were to imagine that I must choose between sparing David the loss of his life and sparing five others the loss of their lives. In making my decision I am not to compare his loss, on the one hand, to the collective or total loss to these five, on the other, whatever exactly that is supposed to be. Rather, I should compare what David stands to suffer or lose, if I do not prevent it, to what will be suffered or lost by any other person, if I do not prevent that. Calling my attention to the numbers should not move me to spare them instead of him, any more than focusing on the numbers should move him to sacrifice his life for the group when he has no reason to sacrifice for any individual in the group. The numbers, in themselves, simply do not count for me. I think they should not count for any of us.

I suppose that some will take the apparent absurdity of the following scene as constituting a formidable embarrassment to the opinions I have stated thus far. Volcanic eruptions have placed the lives of many in immediate jeopardy. A large number are gathered at the north end of the island, awaiting evacuation. A handful find themselves on the southern tip. Imagine the captain of the only Coast Guard evacuation ship in the area finding himself midway between. Where shall he head first? Having been persuaded by my argument, to the amazement of his crew and fellow officers, the consternation of the government, and the subsequent outrage in the press, he flips a coin and makes for the south.

Admittedly, it will seem obvious to many people in our moral culture that it is the captain's duty to direct his ship to the north end of the island straightaway with no preliminary coin toss. And I don't wish to deny that this may indeed be his duty. But we must ask what is the source or derivation of his duty? If it is said, simply, that it is the captain's duty to save the many rather than the few because, other things being equal, it is a worse thing that this handful should survive while the many perish than it would be were those few to die and these many to survive, then I would protest. I have said why I think such thinking is unreflective and unacceptable. But I doubt that it is this simple sort of thinking that lies behind the quick and certain judgments of most who, when presented with this case, declare that the captain would be in violation of his duty were he to flip a coin, and then, perhaps, proceed south.

This situation is different in certain important respects from the kind of case I've been discussing up to this point. In this situation, the captain is seen as deploying a resource that is not his own, not exclusively anyway. And though it is not made explicit in the description of the situation, I suspect that in the minds of those who are so quick to judge it is assumed that each of those in jeopardy has a citizen's equal claim to the use or benefit of that resource. For these reasons the Coast Guard captain is seen as *duty-bound* in the situation; duty-bound to behave in accordance with a policy for the use of that resource agreeable to those whose resource it is. Hence the considerations operative here are quite different from those relevant to the decision of a private citizen captaining his own ship or dispensing his own drug or reaching out his hand under no moral constraints but those that would fall on any man.

The recognition of these differences quite obviously colors the judgments of those to whom such a case is presented. Contrast, for example, the way in which most people would judge the Coast Guard captain's conduct with their judgment on the conduct of a private citizen. Were a private citizen to make first for the south end of the island because among the few are some dear to him while among the many are only strangers, most would not raise a hue and cry. Although some might urge that it would have been a better thing had this person gone north to rescue a larger number, they are not likely to think of his action as a violation of his duty to these people. But even if, tragically enough, the Coast Guard captain had friends among the few and none among the many, it will be seen as a breach of his duty should he first see to the safety of his friends. Here it seems that people think of his action as a violation of the rights of those who have a legitimate claim on the resource. How could the Coast Guard captain justify his decision to go first to the south end of the island? How could he justify it to those many at the north end? A justification is owed to them in this case. Personal preferences won't do. For those in the north are seen as having each an equal claim on that resource.

So this case is different from those previously discussed. Still, it may be urged, the point is that the captain *is* thought to be required to secure the safety of the larger number first. It would be wrong of him to flip a coin to decide his course of action. And so isn't this a case of the numbers counting? For what other justification could be given to the handful left to die at the south end of the island except to say: "It would be a worse thing were those many in the north to perish than it would be should only the few of you die."

I think there is a possible alternative justification of the captain's action in this situation that involves no appeal to any such claim as that. It is a more attractive justification. I suspect it comes closer to what most people think (perhaps wrongly) is available in this sort of case. I believe we are inclined to think of the situation in this way. A number of people have joined to invest in a resource, the chief purpose of which is to serve the interests of those who have invested. Whether each has invested an absolutely equal amount, or whether individual investments are scaled to individual resources, is neither here nor there. Theoretically at least, each person's investment (or status) is seen as entitling him to an equal share, an equal claim on the use of that resource or on the benefits from its use. Now a policy for the employment of that resource in just such contingencies as this present trade-off situation must be adopted. And it must be a policy agreeable in advance to all those who are supposed to see their interests as equally served. The captain's duty, then, whatever it is, is seen as deriving from this agreement. Thus, to justify his action to those left behind we need only cite the policy to which they, along with the others, have agreed in advance (theoretically, anyway).

Into the formation of such an agreement or policy, a consideration of the relative numbers in possible future trade-off situations may enter in a way to which I would find no objection; in a way that commits no one to the impersonal, comparative evaluation of the outcomes appealed to in the previous justification of the captain's action. It could well be agreed to by all, in advance, that should a trade-off situation arise the resource is to be used to save the maximum number of those who have equal claims. For we may suppose that none of these people knows, at the time the resource is purchased in their collective name, where in the future he may find himself should a trade-off situation arise, whether among the few or among the many. Hence such a policy might be found acceptable to all these people simply on the ground that such a policy maximizes each individual's chances of benefiting from the resource.

Against the background supposition of such an agreement, a justification of the claim that it is the captain's duty to proceed straightaway to the north end of the island could be given. It would be wholly compatible with my views on how the numbers should *not* count. For in such a justification no appeal is made to any claim that it is, or would be, in itself, a better thing that those few should die and these many survive than it would be were these few to survive and the many to perish. Such a justification requires no one to acknowledge that his life, or that he himself is, from some impersonal, objective (moral?) perspective, worth less than two or three or three hundred others.

I believe that most people would prefer to think that this sort of justification is available in most cases like the one under discussion. Unfortunately, in many cases it is not. For it may happen that the facts are such that a policy of using a resource to benefit the larger number when not all can be benefited could not plausibly be justified by an appeal to each claimant's desire to maximize his chances of benefiting—on the understanding, of course, that equal chances go to each other claim holder. Imagine, for example, that on this island the majority live around the north end while the southern portion is inhabited by relatively few. It is now proposed that everyone on the island invest in an evacuation ship. A policy of using the ship to save the larger number when not all can be saved could not easily be sold to those in the south on the ground that it provides each person with an equal and maximized chance of survival. It will be clear to them that with such a policy an equal investment does not purchase in the south a benefit equal to what it brings in the north. Still, of course, they might be induced to invest equally. Given their circumstances, it may be the best they can do for themselves. But they would not see this as a policy that gives equal weight to the interests of every would-be share holder.

If the bargaining position of the few were sufficiently strong, I believe these southerners might hold out for a more equitable policy, for genuinely equal shares in the benefits of the proposed resource, or for some reduction on their premiums, or for some compensating benefits from elsewhere. Now can we imagine those in the north at this point appealing to morality? "Look here, you are all decent people. Don't you see, if it comes down to it, that it would be a better thing if a larger number of us in the north survive while you perish than it would be were you relatively few to survive while we, the larger number, perish? So be sensible and faithful to the principles of true morality and let us agree that, should a trade-off situation arise, the evacuation ship will be used to save the larger number." Who could waste his time with such sophistries? It might be easier simply to compel the minority to go along with the policy. It would be less hypocritical anyway.[5]

Thus far we have been thinking about a situation in which these people who live on this island have, or are proposing to invest in, an evacuation ship. Each person is supposed to see himself as having an equal claim on this resource, for whatever reasons, whether because he is asked to invest or because of his status as an inhabitant of this island. Since the resource is limited, a situation may develop in which not all of them can be served by it. Hence the need for a policy, some method for determining who will be benefited. Plainly there are many possible policies. But not every policy will allow these people to retain their sense of each having an equal claim on the resource. For example, imagine that it is suggested that medical researchers, high-powered managerial types, and people with IQs over 120, be given first priority. Such a policy, whatever the reasons for adopting it, manifestly does not treat everyone on the island equally. It does not reflect a genuinely equal concern for the survival of each person on this island. Thus, if equal concern is what the inhabitants think they are entitled to, they will reject such a policy.

But under certain conditions, they will reject the policy of using the ship to save the larger number in the event of a trade-off situation, and for the same reasons. The minority who live on the southern tip will not see such a policy as according to each islander an equal claim on the collective resource. Imagine that those in the south know that on the north end there are already more people than the evacuation ship can hold. It is proposed that in the event of a trade-off, the ship is to be used to secure the safety of the larger number. You could hardly expect to convince the southerners that such a policy reflects a genuinely equal concern for the survival of each person on the island, that it accords to them a genuinely equal claim on the resource. You may as well try to convince workers with IQs under 100 that the policy of giving priority to researchers, managers, and to people with IQs over 120 reflects an equal concern for their survival.

Now I think this is how most people will think about these matters when asked to judge a policy governing the use of a resource meant for their benefit. Yet it is curious that many of these same people will not think this way when setting out a policy for using their resource to benefit others. Suppose, for example, that the people on this island have purchased their evacuation ship. On a nearby island, also volcanic, lives another group of people. These people have no means of evacuation because they are too poor, perhaps. The islanders who own the ship are willing, when they themselves are in no danger, to extend aid to those on the other island. Again the question of policy arises. They could, of course, without violating anyone's rights, decide to rescue the other islanders in order of IQ or social importance. But perhaps they want a policy that will treat all equally, that will truly reflect their professedly equal concern for each person's survival. They will then reject a policy that gives preference to those who happen to have higher IQs or more prestigious social positions. It would be incompatible with their desire to show an equal concern for each person's survival. And yet if it happens that most of these inhabitants live around the north end, while a minority dwells in the south, our islanders, if they are like most of us, will adopt the policy of sending their mercy ship first to the north port to evacuate from among the many. True, those who live in the south cannot complain of any violation of their property rights in the vessel. But can such a policy be thought, any more in this case than in the former, to reflect an equal concern for the survival of each, northerner and southerner alike?

Notes

1. The trade-off situations I am focusing on have relatively simple structures. They present us with three relevant options: (1) We may aid a certain person or group of persons. (2) We may aid an entirely different group of persons. (3) We may do nothing at all to aid anyone. (I exclude from consideration this last option, though I do not argue that doing nothing for anyone is impermissible. Whether, why or in what sense it is, are questions best left to another occasion.) Robert Schwartz has caused me some worries about trade-off situations that are as aptly styled as these simpler ones, and that involve different but overlapping groups of possible beneficiaries. For example, perhaps the exercise of one option would bring aid to *A* but none to either *B* or *C*. A second option might bring aid to both *A* and *B* but none to *C*. Yet a third option might be available that would bring aid to *C* but none to either *A* or *B*. It will be seen that it is not completely obvious how one holding the views I present on the simpler trade-off situations would deal with this case and with cases of still greater complexity. After having caused me the worries, Schwartz had the de-

cency to think out an approach to these decision problems that would appear compatible with my thinking about the simpler ones. But I fear that a discussion of these complications would obscure my main argument here, so I have avoided it.

2. This is the case described by Philippa Foot in her paper on "Abortion and the Doctrine of Double Effect," in *Moral Problems,* ed. James Rachels (New York, 1971).
3. There are a number of possible contortions that one might go through in an attempt to reconcile these views. I cannot consider them all here. What I am chiefly interested in stressing is that there are serious difficulties involved in any attempt to reconcile these positions. My hope is that, in view of these difficulties, those who would maintain the original position might be brought to reconsider with an open mind the alleged grounds for the moral requirement to save the greater number of cases where one is in fact impartial in one's concern for those involved.
4. After I had written this paper, my attention was called to Miss Anscombe's note of some years back on this case as put originally by Mrs. Foot. She too was impressed by the fact that in the event a person gave his drug to the one, none of the five others could complain that he had been wronged. Her note is entitled, "Who is Wronged?" *Oxford Review,* no. 5, 1967.
5. To be sure, matters may be far more complex than is supposed here. Perhaps this particular investment in an evacuation ship is but one of many investments made by the entire people of this island through their central government for, as it is commonly put, "the common good." Perhaps, then, it could be said to the southerners that although in this instance the proposed policy for the use of the evacuation ship does not accord to them an equal claim on its benefits, they should not complain. They may well have enjoyed advantages at the expense of the northerners in past instances of "social action," and may look forward, through the intrigues of legislative politics, to yet further advantages in the future. Perhaps it could be argued that somehow it all works out in the long run to everyone's advantage. Maybe even some version of the "majority-rule" principle for policy making could be trotted out in such a context. I despair of finding a clear line of argument in this mare's nest. But if one sets the problem against such a background, the search for a justification of the claim that it is the captain's duty to make straight for the north end of the island will lead back to the general moral underpinnings of government and its functions. And these issues, though related, go beyond the scope of this paper.

Some Paradoxes of Deterrence

GREGORY KAVKA

Gregory Kavka (1947–) is a professor of philosophy at the University of California at Irvine. He has written numerous articles on ethics and related issues.

Deterrence is a parent of paradox. Conflict theorists, notably Thomas Schelling, have pointed out several paradoxes of deterrence: that it may be to the advantage of someone who is trying to deter another to be irrational, to have fewer available options, or to lack relevant information.[1] I shall describe certain new paradoxes that emerge when one attempts to analyze deterrence from a moral rather than a strategic perspective. These paradoxes are presented in the form of statements that appear absurd or incredible on first inspection, but can be supported by quite convincing arguments.

Consider a typical situation involving deterrence. A potential wrongdoer is about to commit an offense that would unjustly harm someone. A defender intends, and threatens, to retaliate should the wrongdoer commit the offense. Carrying out retaliation, if the offense is committed, could well be morally wrong. (The wrongdoer could be insane, or the retaliation could be out of proportion with the offense, or could seriously harm others besides the wrongdoer.) The moral paradoxes of deterrence arise out of the attempt to determine the moral status of the defender's *intention* to retaliate in such cases. If the defender knows retaliation to be wrong, it would appear that this intention is evil. Yet such "evil" intentions may pave the road to heaven, by preventing serious offenses and by doing so without actually harming anyone.

Scrutiny of such morally ambiguous retaliatory intentions reveals paradoxes that call into question certain significant and widely accepted moral doctrines. These doctrines are what I call *bridge principles*. They attempt to link together the moral evaluation of actions and the moral evaluation of agents (and their states) in certain simple and apparently natural ways. The general acceptance, and intuitive appeal, of such principles, lends credibility to the project of constructing a consistent moral system that accurately reflects our firmest moral beliefs about both agents and actions. By raising doubts about the validity of certain popular bridge principles, the paradoxes presented here pose new difficulties for this important project.

I

In this section, a certain class of situations involving deterrence is characterized, and a plausible normative assumption is presented. In the following three sections, we shall see how application of this assumption to these situations yields paradoxes.

An earlier version of this paper was presented at Stanford University. I am grateful to several, especially Robert Merrihew Adams, Tyler Burge, Warren Quinn, and Virginia Warren, for helpful comments on previous drafts. My work was supported, in part, by a Regents' Faculty Research Fellowship from the University of California.

From the *Journal of Philosophy* 75, no. 6 (June 1978), pp. 285–302.

The class of paradox-producing situations is best introduced by means of an example. Consider the balance of nuclear terror as viewed from the perspective of one of its superpower participants, nation *N*. *N* sees the threat of nuclear retaliation as its only reliable means of preventing nuclear attack (or nuclear blackmail leading to world domination) by its superpower rival. *N* is confident such a threat will succeed in deterring its adversary, provided it really intends to carry out that threat. (*N* fears that, if it bluffs, its adversary is likely to learn this through leaks or espionage.) Finally, *N* recognizes it would have conclusive moral reasons *not* to carry out the threatened retaliation, if its opponent were to obliterate *N* with a surprise attack. For although retaliation would punish the leaders who committed this unprecedented crime and would prevent them from dominating the postwar world, *N* knows it would also destroy many millions of innocent civilians in the attacking nation (and in other nations), would set back postwar economic recovery for the world immeasurably, and might add enough fallout to the atmosphere to destroy the human race.

Let us call situations of the sort that nation *N* perceives itself as being in, *Special Deterrent Situations* (SDSs). More precisely, an agent is in an SDS when he reasonably and correctly believes that the following conditions hold. First, it is likely he must intend (conditionally) to apply a harmful sanction to innocent people, if an extremely harmful and unjust offense is to be prevented. Second, such an intention would very likely deter the offense. Third, the amounts of harm involved in the offense and the threatened sanction are very large and of roughly similar quantity (or the latter amount is smaller than the former). Finally, he would have conclusive moral reasons not to apply the sanction if the offense were to occur.

The first condition in this definition requires some comment. Deterrence depends only on the potential wrongdoer's *beliefs* about the prospects of the sanction being applied. Hence, the first condition will be satisfied only if attempts by the defender to bluff would likely be perceived as such by the wrongdoer. This may be the case if the defender is an unconvincing liar, or is a group with a collective decision procedure, or if the wrongdoer is shrewd and knows the defender quite well. Generally, however, bluffing will be a promising course of action. Hence, although it is surely logically and physically possible for an SDS to occur, there will be few actual SDSs. It may be noted, though, that writers on strategic policy frequently assert that nuclear deterrence will be effective only if the defending nation really intends to retaliate.[2] If this is so, the balance of terror may fit the definition of an SDS, and the paradoxes developed here could have significant practical implications.[3] Further, were there no actual SDSs, these paradoxes would still be of considerable theoretical interest. For they indicate that the validity of some widely accepted moral doctrines rests on the presupposition that certain situations that could arise (i.e., SDSs) will not.

Turning to our normative assumption, we begin by noting that any reasonable system of ethics must have substantial utilitarian elements. The assumption that produces the paradoxes of deterrence concerns the role of utilitarian considerations in determining one's moral duty in a narrowly limited class of situations. Let the *most useful* act in a given choice situation be that with the highest expected utility. Our assumption says that the most useful act should be performed whenever a very great deal of utility is at stake. This means that, if the difference in expected utility between the most useful act and its alternatives is extremely large (e.g., equivalent to the difference between life and death for a very large number of people), other moral considerations are overridden by utilitarian considerations.

This assumption may be substantially weakened by restricting in various ways its range of application. I restrict the assumption to apply only when (i) a great deal of *negative* utility is at stake, and (ii) people will likely suffer serious injustices if the agent fails to perform the most useful act. This makes the assumption more plausible, since the propriety of doing one person a serious injustice, in order to produce positive benefits for others, is highly questionable. The justifiability of doing the same injustice to prevent a utilitarian disaster which itself involves grave injustices, seems more in accordance with our moral intuitions.

The above restrictions appear to bring our assumption into line with the views of philosophers such as Robert Nozick, Thomas Nagel, and Richard Brandt, who portray moral rules as "absolutely" forbidding certain kinds of acts, but acknowledge that exceptions might have to be allowed in cases in which such acts are necessary to prevent catastrophe.[4] Even with these restrictions, however, the proposed assumption would be rejected by supporters of genuine Absolutism, the doctrine that there are certain acts (such as vicarious punishment and deliberate killing of the innocent) that are always wrong, whatever the consequences of not performing them. (Call such acts *inherently evil.*) We can, though, accommodate the Absolutists. To do so, let us further qualify our assumption by limiting its application to cases in which (iii) performing the most useful act involves, at most, a small *risk* of performing an inherently evil act. With this restriction, the assumption still leads to paradoxes, yet is consistent with Absolutism (unless that doctrine is extended to include absolute prohibitions on something other than doing acts of the sort usually regarded as inherently evil).[5] The triply qualified assumption is quite plausible; so the fact that it produces paradoxes is both interesting and disturbing.

II

The first moral paradox of deterrence is:

> (P1) There are cases in which, although it would be wrong for an agent to perform a certain act in a certain situation, it would nonetheless be right for him, knowing this, to form the intention to perform that act in that situation.

At first, this strikes one as absurd. If it is wrong and he is aware that it is wrong, how could it be right for him to form the intention to do it? (P1) is the direct denial of a simple moral thesis, the Wrongful Intentions Principle (WIP): *To intend to do what one knows to be wrong is itself wrong.*[6] WIP seems so obvious that, although philosophers never call it into question, they rarely bother to assert it or argue for it. Nevertheless, it appears that Abelard, Aquinas, Butler, Bentham, Kant, and Sidgwick, as well as recent writers such as Anthony Kenny and Jan Narveson, have accepted the principle, at least implicitly.[7]

Why does WIP seem so obviously true? First, we regard the man who fully intends to perform a wrongful act and is prevented from doing so solely by external circumstances (e.g., a man whose murder plan is interrupted by the victim's fatal heart attack) as being just as bad as the man who performs a like wrongful act. Second, we view the man who intends to do what is wrong, and then changes his mind, as having corrected a moral failing or error. Third, it is convenient, for many purposes, to treat a prior intention to perform an act, as the beginning of the act itself. Hence, we are inclined to view intentions as parts of actions and to ascribe to each intention the moral status ascribed to the act "containing" it.

It is essential to note that WIP appears to apply to conditional intentions in the same manner as it applies to nonconditional ones. Suppose I form the intention to kill my neighbor if he insults me again, and fail to kill him only because, fortuitously, he refrains from doing so. I am as bad, or nearly as bad, as if he had insulted me and I had killed him. My failure to perform the act no more erases the wrongness of my intention, than my neighbor's dropping dead as I load my gun would negate the wrongness of the simple intention to kill him. Thus the same considerations adduced above in support of WIP seem to support the formulation: If it would be wrong to perform an act in certain circumstances, then it is wrong to intend to perform that act on the condition that those circumstances arise.

Having noted the source of the strong feeling that (P1) should be rejected, we must consider an instantiation of (P1):

> (P1′) In an SDS, it would be wrong for the defender to apply the sanction if the wrongdoer were to commit the offense, but it is right for the defender to form the (conditional) intention to apply the sanction if the wrongdoer commits the offense.

The first half of (P1′), the wrongness of applying the sanction, follows directly from the last part of the definition of an SDS, which says that the defender would have conclusive moral reasons not to apply the sanction. The latter half of (P1′), which asserts the rightness of forming the intention to apply the sanction, follows from the definition of an SDS and our normative assumption. According to the definition, the defender's forming this intention is likely necessary, and very likely sufficient, to prevent a seriously harmful and unjust offense. Further, the offense and the sanction would each produce very large and roughly commensurate amounts of negative utility (or the latter would produce a smaller amount). It follows that utilitarian considerations heavily favor forming the intention to apply the sanction, and that doing so involves only a small risk of performing an inherently evil act.[8] Applying our normative assumption yields the conclusion that it is right for the defender to form the intention in question.

This argument, if sound, would establish the truth of (P1′), and hence (P1), in contradiction with WIP. It suggests that WIP should not be applied to *deterrent intentions,* i.e., those conditional intentions whose existence is based on the agent's desire to thereby deter others from actualizing the antecedent condition of the intention. Such intentions are rather strange. They are, by nature, self-stultifying: if a deterrent intention fulfills the agent's purpose, it ensures that the intended (and possibly evil) act is not performed, by preventing the circumstances of performance from arising. The unique nature of such intentions can be further explicated by noting the distinction between intending to do something, and desiring (or intending) to intend to do it. Normally, an agent will form the intention to do something because he either desires doing that thing as an end in itself, or as a means to other ends. In such cases, little importance attaches to the distinction between intending and desiring to intend. But in the case of deterrent intentions, the ground of the desire to form the intention is entirely distinct from any desire to carry it out. Thus, what may be inferred about the agent who seeks to form such an intention is this. He desires *having the intention* as a means of deterrence. Also, he is willing, in order to prevent the offense, to accept a certain *risk* that, in the end, he will apply the sanction. But this is entirely consistent with his having a strong desire not to apply the sanction, and no desire at all to apply it. Thus, while the object of his deterrent intention might be an evil act, it does not follow that, in desiring to adopt that intention, he desires to do evil, either as an end or as a means.

WIP ties the morality of an intention exclusively to the moral qualities of its object (i.e., the intended act). This is not unreasonable since, typically, the only significant effects of intentions are the acts of the agent (and the consequences of these acts) which flow from these intentions. However, in certain cases, intentions may have *autonomous effects* that are independent of the intended act's actually being performed. In particular, intentions to act may influence the conduct of other agents. When an intention has important autonomous effects, these effects must be incorporated into any adequate moral analysis of it. The first paradox arises because the autonomous effects of the relevant deterrent intention are dominant in the moral analysis of an SDS, but the extremely plausible WIP ignores such effects.[9]

III

(P1′) implies that a rational moral agent in an SDS should want to form the conditional intention to apply the sanction if the offense is committed, in order to deter the offense. But will he be able to do so? Paradoxically, he will not be. He is a captive in the prison of his own virtue, able to form the requisite intention only by bending the bars of his cell out of shape. Consider the preliminary formulation of this new paradox:

> (P2′) In an SDS, a rational and morally good agent cannot (as a matter of logic) have (or form) the intention to apply the sanction if the offense is committed.[10]

The argument for (P2′) is as follows. An agent in an SDS recognizes that there would be conclusive moral reasons not to apply the sanction if the offense were committed. If he does not regard these admittedly conclusive moral reasons as conclusive reasons for him not to apply the sanction, then he is not moral. Suppose, on the other hand, that he does regard himself as having conclusive reasons not to apply the sanction if the offense is committed. If, nonetheless, he is disposed to apply it, because the reasons for applying it motivate him more strongly than do the conclusive reasons not to apply it, then he is irrational.

But couldn't our rational moral agent recognize, in accordance with (P1′), that he ought to form the intention to apply the sanction? And couldn't he then simply grit his teeth and pledge to himself that he will apply the sanction if the offense is committed? No doubt he could, and this would amount to trying to form the intention to apply the sanction. But the question remains whether he can succeed in forming that intention, by this or any other process, while remaining rational and moral. And it appears he cannot. There are, first of all, psychological difficulties. Being rational, how can he dispose himself to do something that he knows he would have conclusive reasons not to do, when and if the time comes to do it? Perhaps, though, some exceptional people can produce in themselves dispositions to act merely by pledging to act. But even if one could, in an SDS, produce a disposition to apply the sanction in this manner, such a disposition would not count as a *rational intention* to apply the sanction. This is because, as recent writers on intentions have suggested, it is part of the concept of rationally intending to do something, that the disposition to do the intended act be caused (or justified) in an appropriate way by the agent's view of reasons for doing the act.[11] And the disposition in question does not stand in such a relation to the agent's reasons for action.

It might be objected to this that people sometimes intend to do things (and do them) for no reason at all, without being irrational. This is true, and indicates that the connections between the concepts of intending and reasons for action are not so simple as the above formula implies. But it is also true that intending to do something for no reason at all, in the face of recognized significant reasons not to do it, would be irrational. Similarly, a disposition to act in the face of the acknowledged preponderance of reasons, whether called an "intention" or not, could not qualify as rational. It may be claimed that such a disposition, in an SDS, is rational in the sense that the agent knows it would further his aims to form (and have) it. This is not to deny the second paradox, but simply to express one of its paradoxical features. For the point of (P2′) is that the very disposition that *is* rational in the sense just mentioned, is at the same time irrational in an equally important sense. It is a disposition to act in conflict with the agent's own view of the balance of reasons for action.

We can achieve some insight into this by noting that an intention that is deliberately formed, resides at the intersection of two distinguishable actions. It is the beginning of the act that is its object and is the end of the act that is its formation. As such, it may be assessed as rational (or moral) or not, according to whether either of two different acts promotes the agent's (or morality's) ends. Generally, the assessments will agree. But, as Schelling and others have noted, it may sometimes promote one's aims *not* to be disposed to act to promote one's aims should certain contingencies arise. For example, a small country may deter invasion by a larger country if it is disposed to resist any invasion, even when resistance would be suicidal. In such situations, the assessment of the rationality (or morality) of the agent's intentions will depend upon whether these intentions are treated as components of their object-acts or their formation-acts. If treated as both, conflicts can occur. It is usual and proper to assess the practical rationality of an agent, at a given time, according to the degree of correspondence between his intentions and the reasons he has for performing the acts that are the objects of those intentions. As a result, puzzles such as (P2′) emerge when, for purposes of moral analysis, an agent's intentions are viewed partly as components of their formation-acts.

Let us return to the main path of our discussion by briefly summarizing the argument for (P2′). A morally good agent regards conclusive moral reasons for action as conclusive reasons for action *simpliciter*. But the intentions of a rational agent are not out of line with his assessment of the reasons for and against acting. Consequently, a rational moral agent cannot intend to do something that he recognizes there are conclusive moral reasons not to do. Nor can he intend conditionally to do what he recognizes he would have conclusive reasons not to do were that condition to be fulfilled. Therefore, in an SDS, where one has conclusive moral reasons not to apply the sanction, an originally rational and moral agent cannot have the intention to apply it without ceasing to be fully rational or moral; nor can be form the intention (as this entails having it).

We have observed that forming an intention is a process that may generally be regarded as an action. Thus, the second paradox can be reformulated as:

> (P2) There are situations (namely SDSs) in which it would be right for agents to perform certain actions (namely forming the intention to apply the sanction) and in which it is possible for some agents to perform such actions, but impossible for rational and morally good agents to perform them.

(P2), with the exception of the middle clause, is derived from the conjunction of (P1′) and (P2′) by existential generalization. The truth of the middle clause follows from consideration of the vengeful agent, who desires to punish those who commit seriously harmful and unjust offenses, no matter what the cost to others.

(P2) is paradoxical because it says that there are situations in which rationality and virtue preclude the possibility of right action. And this contravenes our usual assumption about the close logical ties between the concepts of right action and agent goodness. Consider the following claim. *Doing something is right if and only if a morally good man would do the same thing in the given situation.* Call this the Right-Good Principle. One suspects that, aside from qualifications concerning the good man's possible imperfections or factual ignorance, most people regard this principle, which directly contradicts (P2), as being virtually analytic. Yet the plight of the good man described in the second paradox does not arise out of an insufficiency of either knowledge or goodness. (P2) says there are conceivable situations in which virtue and knowledge combine with rationality to preclude right action, in which virtue is an obstacle to doing the right thing. If (P2) is true, our views about the close logical connection between right action and agent goodness, as embodied in the Right-Good Principle, require modifications of a sort not previously envisioned.

IV

A rational moral agent in an SDS faces a cruel dilemma. His reasons for intending to apply the sanction if the offense is committed are, according to (P1′), conclusive. But they outrun his reasons for doing it. Wishing to do what is right, he wants to form the intention. However, unless he can substantially alter the basic facts of the situation or his beliefs about those facts, he can do so only by making himself less morally good; that is, by becoming a person who attaches grossly mistaken weights to certain reasons for and against action (e.g., one who prefers retribution to the protection of the vital interests of innocent people).[12] We have arrived at a third paradox:

> (P3) In certain situations, it would be morally right for a rational and morally good agent to deliberately (attempt to) corrupt himself.[13]

(P3) may be viewed in light of a point about the credibility of threats which has been made by conflict theorists. Suppose a defender is worried about the credibility of his deterrent threat, because he thinks the wrongdoer (rightly) regards him as unwilling to apply the threatened sanction. He may make the threat more credible by passing control of the sanction to some *retaliation-agent.* Conflict theorists consider two sorts of retaliation-agents: people known to be highly motivated to punish the offense in question, and machines programmed to retaliate automatically if the offense occurs. What I wish to note is that future selves of the defender himself are a third class of retaliation-agents. If the other kinds are unavailable, a defender may have to create an agent of this third sort (i.e., an altered self willing to apply the sanction), in order to deter the offense. In cases in which applying the sanction would be wrong, this could require self-corruption.

How would a rational and moral agent in an SDS, who seeks to have the intention to apply the sanction, go about corrupting himself so that he may have it? He cannot form the intention simply by pledging to apply the sanction; for, according to the second paradox, his rationality and morality preclude this. Instead, he must seek to initiate a causal process (e.g., a reeducation program) that he hopes will result in his beliefs, attitudes, and values changing in such a way that he can and will have the intention to apply the sanction should the offense be committed. Initiating such a process involves taking a rather odd, though not uncommon attitude toward oneself: viewing oneself as an object to be molded in certain respects by outside influences rather than by inner choices. This is, for example, the attitude of the lazy but ambitious student who enrolls in a fine college, hoping that some of the habits and values of his highly motivated fellow students will "rub off" on him.

We can now better understand the notion of "risking doing *X*" which was introduced in section I. For convenience, let "*X*" be "killing." Deliberately risking killing is different from risking deliberately killing. One does the former when one rushes an ill person to the hospital in one's car at unsafe speed, having noted the danger of causing a fatal accident. One has deliberately accepted the risk of killing by accident. One (knowingly) risks deliberately killing, on the other hand, when one undertakes a course of action that one knows may, by various causal processes, lead to one's later performing a deliberate killing. The mild-mannered youth who joins a violent street gang is an example. Similarly, the agent in an SDS, who undertakes a plan of self-corruption in order to develop the requisite deterrent intention, knowingly risks deliberately performing the wrongful act of applying the sanction.

The above description of what is required of the rational moral agent in an SDS, leads to a natural objection to the argument that supports (P3). According to this objection, an attempt at self-corruption by a rational moral agent is very likely to fail. Hence, bluffing would surely be a more promising strategy for deterrence than trying to form retaliatory intentions by self-corruption. Three replies may be given to this objection. First, it is certainly *conceivable* that, in a particular SDS, undertaking a process of self-corruption would be more likely to result in effective deterrence than would bluffing. Second, and more important, bluffing and attempting to form retaliatory intentions by self-corruption will generally not be mutually exclusive alternatives. An agent in an SDS may attempt to form the retaliatory intention while bluffing, and plan to continue bluffing as a "fall-back" strategy, should he fail. If the offense to be prevented is disastrous enough, the additional expected utility generated by following such a combined strategy (as opposed to simply bluffing) will be very large, even if his attempts to form the intention are unlikely to succeed. Hence, (P3) would still follow from our normative assumption. Finally, consider the rational and *partly corrupt* agent in an SDS who already has the intention to retaliate. (The nations participating in the balance of terror may be examples.) The relevant question about him is whether he ought to act to become less corrupt, with the result that he would lose the intention to retaliate. The present objection does not apply in this case, since the agent already has the requisite corrupt features. Yet, essentially the same argument that produces (P3) leads, when this case is considered, to a slightly different, but equally puzzling, version of our third paradox:

> (P3*) In certain situations, it would be morally wrong for a rational and partly corrupt agent to (attempt to) reform himself and eliminate his corruption.

A rather different objection to (P3) is the claim that its central notion is incoherent. This claim is made, apparently, by Thomas Nagel, who writes:

> The notion that one might sacrifice one's moral integrity justifiably, in the service of a sufficiently worthy end, is an incoherent notion. For if one were justified in making such a sacrifice (or even morally required to make it), then one would not be sacrificing one's moral integrity by adopting that course: one would be preserving it (132/3).

Now the notion of a justified sacrifice of moral virtue (integrity) would be incoherent, as Nagel suggests, if one could sacrifice one's virtue only by doing something wrong. For the same act cannot be both morally justified and morally wrong. But one may also be said to sacrifice one's virtue when one deliberately initiates a causal process that one expects to result, and does result, in one's later becoming a less virtuous person. And, as the analysis of SDSs embodied in

(P1′) and (P2′) implies, one may, in certain cases, be justified in initiating such a process (or even be obligated to initiate it). Hence, it would be a mistake to deny (P3) on the grounds advanced in Nagel's argument.

There is, though, a good reason for *wanting* to reject (P3). It conflicts with some of our firmest beliefs about virtue and duty. We regard the promotion and preservation of one's own virtue as a vital responsibility of each moral agent, and self-corruption as among the vilest of enterprises. Further, we do not view the duty to promote one's virtue as simply one duty among others, to be weighed and balanced against the rest, but rather as a special duty that encompasses the other moral duties. Thus, we assent to the Virtue Preservation Principle: *It is wrong to deliberately lose (or reduce the degree of) one's moral virtue.* To many, this principle seems fundamental to our very conception of morality.[14] Hence the suggestion that duty could require the abandonment of virtue seems quite unacceptable. The fact that this suggestion can be supported by strong arguments produces a paradox.

This paradox is reflected in the ambivalent attitudes that emerge when we attempt to evaluate three hypothetical agents who respond to the demands of SDSs in various ways. The first agent refuses to try to corrupt himself and allows the disastrous offense to occur. We respect the love of virtue he displays, but are inclined to suspect him of too great a devotion to his own purity relative to his concern for the well-being of others. The second agent does corrupt himself to prevent disaster in an SDS. Though we do not approve of his new corrupt aspects, we admire the person that he *was* for his willingness to sacrifice what he loved—part of his own virtue—in the service of others. At the same time, the fact that he succeeded in corrupting himself may make us wonder whether he was entirely virtuous in the first place. Corruption, we feel, does not come easily to a good man. The third agent reluctantly but sincerely tries his best to corrupt himself to prevent disaster, but fails. He may be admired both for his willingness to make such a sacrifice and for having virtue so deeply engrained in his character that his attempts at self-corruption do not succeed. It is perhaps characteristic of the paradoxical nature of the envisioned situation, that we are inclined to admire most the only one of these three agents who fails in the course of action he undertakes.

V

It is natural to think of the evaluation of agents, and of actions, as being two sides of the same moral coin. The moral paradoxes of deterrence suggest they are more like two separate coins that can be fused together only by significantly deforming one or the other. In this concluding section, I shall briefly explain this.

Our shared assortment of moral beliefs may be viewed as consisting of three relatively distinct groups: beliefs about the evaluation of actions, beliefs about the evaluation of agents and their states (e.g., motives, intentions, and character traits), and beliefs about the relationship between the two. An important part of this last group of beliefs is represented by the three bridge principles introduced above: the Wrongful Intentions, Right-Good, and Virtue Preservation principles. Given an agreed-upon set of bridge principles, one could go about constructing a moral system meant to express coherently our moral beliefs in either of two ways: by developing principles that express our beliefs about act evaluation and then using the bridge principles to derive principles of agent evaluation—or vice versa. If our bridge principles are sound and our beliefs about agent and act evaluation are mutually consistent, the resulting systems would, in theory, be the same. If, however, there are underlying incompatibilities between the principles we use to evaluate acts and agents, there may be significant differences between moral systems that are *act-oriented* and those which are *agent-oriented*. And these differences may manifest themselves as paradoxes which exert pressure upon the bridge principles that attempt to link the divergent systems, and the divergent aspects of each system, together.

It seems natural to us to evaluate acts at least partly in terms of their consequences. Hence, act-oriented moral systems tend to involve significant utilitarian elements. The principle of act evaluation usually employed in utilitarian systems is: in a given situation, one ought to perform the most useful act, that which will (or is expected to) produce the most utility. What will maximize utility depends upon the facts of the particular situation. Hence, as various philosophers have pointed out, the above principle could conceivably recommend one's (i) acting from nonutilitarian motives, (ii) advocating some nonutilitarian moral theory, or even (iii) becoming a genuine adherent of some nonutilitarian theory.[15] Related quandaries arise when one considers, from an act-utilitarian viewpoint, the deterrent intention of a defender in an SDS. Here is an intention whose object-act is anti-utilitarian and whose formation-act is a utilitarian duty that cannot be performed by a rational utilitarian.

A utilitarian might seek relief from these quandaries in either of two ways. First, he could defend some form of rule-utilitarianism. But then he would face a problem. Shall he include, among the rules of his system, our normative assumption that requires the performance of the most useful act, whenever an enormous amount of utility is at stake (and certain other conditions are satisfied)? If he does, the moral paradoxes of deterrence will appear within his system. If he does not, it would seem that his system fails to attach the importance to the consequences of particular momentous acts that any reasonable moral, much less utilitarian, system should. An alternative reaction would be to stick by the utilitarian principle of act evaluation, and simply accept (P1)–(P3), and related oddities, as true. Taking this line would require the abandonment of the plausible and familiar bridge principles that contradict (P1)–(P3). But this need not bother the act-utilitarian, who perceives his task as the modification, as well as codification, of our moral beliefs.

Agent-oriented (as opposed to act-oriented) moral systems rest on the premise that what primarily matters for morality are the internal states of a person: his character traits, his intentions, and the condition of his will. The doctrines about intentions and virtue expressed in our three bridge principles are generally incorporated into such systems. The paradoxes of deterrence may pose serious problems for some agent-oriented systems. It may be, for example, that an adequate analysis of the moral virtues of justice, selflessness, and benevolence, would imply that the truly virtuous man would feel obligated to make whatever personal sacrifice is necessary to prevent a catastrophe. If so, the moral paradoxes of deterrence would arise within agent-oriented systems committed to these virtues.

There are, however, agent-oriented systems that would not be affected by our paradoxes. One such system could be called Extreme Kantianism. According to this view, the only things having moral significance are such features of a person as his character and the state of his will. The Extreme Kantian accepts Kant's dictum that morality requires treating oneself and others as ends rather than means. He interprets this to imply strict duties to preserve one's virtue and not to deliberately impose serious harms or risks on innocent people. Thus, the Extreme Kantian would simply reject (P1)–(P3) without qualm.

Although act-utilitarians and Extreme Kantians can view the paradoxes of deterrence without concern, one doubts that the rest of us can. The adherents of these extreme conceptions of morality are untroubled by the paradoxes because their viewpoints are too one-sided to represent our moral beliefs accurately. Each of them is closely attentive to certain standard principles of agent *or* act evaluation, but seems too little concerned with traditional principles of the other sort. For a system of morality to reflect our firmest and deepest convictions adequately, it must represent a middle ground between these extremes by seeking to accommodate the valid insights of both act-oriented and agent-oriented perspectives. The normative assumption set out in section I was chosen as a representative principle that might be incorporated into such a system. It treats utilitarian considerations as relevant and potentially decisive, while allowing for the importance of other factors. Though consistent with the absolute prohibition of certain sorts of acts, it treats the distinction between harms and risks as significant and rules out absolute prohibitions on the latter as unreasonable. It is an extremely plausible middle-ground principle; but, disturbingly, it leads to paradoxes.

That these paradoxes reflect conflicts between commonly accepted principles of agent and act evaluation, is further indicated by the following observation. Consider what initially appears a natural way of viewing the evaluation of acts and agents as coordinated parts of a single moral system. According to this view, reasons for action determine the moral status of acts, agents, and intentions. A right act is an act that accords with the preponderance of moral reasons for action. To have the right intention is to be disposed to perform the act supported by the preponderance of such reasons, because of those reasons. The virtuous agent is the rational agent who has the proper substantive values, i.e., the person whose intentions and actions accord with the preponderance of moral reasons for action. Given these considerations, it appears that it should always be possible for an agent to go along intending, and acting, in accordance with the preponderance of moral reasons; thus ensuring both his own virtue and the rightness of his intentions and actions. Unfortunately, this conception of harmonious coordination between virtue, right intention, and right action, is shown to be untenable by the paradoxes of deterrence. For they demonstrate that, in any system that takes consequences plausibly into account, situations can arise in which the rational use of moral principles leads to certain paradoxical recommendations: that the principles used, and part of the agent's virtue, be abandoned, and that wrongful intentions be formed.

One could seek to avoid these paradoxes by moving in the direction of Extreme Kantianism and rejecting our normative assumption. But to do so would be to overlook the plausible core of act-utilitarianism. This is the claim that, in the moral evaluation of acts, how those acts affect human happiness often is important—the more so as more happiness is at stake—and sometimes is decisive. Conversely, one could move toward accommodation with act-utilitarianism. This would involve qualifying, so that they do not apply in SDSs, the traditional moral doctrines that contradict (P1)–(P3). And, in fact, viewed in isolation, the considerations adduced in section II indicate that the Wrongful Intentions Principle ought to be so qualified. However, the claims of (P2) and (P3): that virtue may preclude right action and that morality may require self-corruption, are not so easily accepted. These notions remain unpalatable even when one considers the arguments that support them.

Thus, tinkering with our normative assumption or with traditional moral doctrines would indeed enable us to avoid the paradoxes, at least in their present form. But this would require rejecting certain significant and deeply entrenched beliefs concerning the evaluation either of agents or of actions. Hence, such tinkering would not go far toward solving the fundamental problem of which the paradoxes are symptoms: the apparent incompatibility of the moral principles we use to evaluate acts and agents. Perhaps this problem can be solved. Perhaps the coins of agent and act evaluation can be successfully fused. But it is not apparent how this is to be done. And I, for one, do not presently see an entirely satisfactory way out of the perplexities that the paradoxes engender.

Notes

1. *The Strategy of Conflict* (New York: Oxford, 1960), chaps. 1–2; and *Arms and Influence* (New Haven, Conn.: Yale, 1966), chap. 2.
2. See, e.g., Herman Kahn, *On Thermonuclear War*, 2nd ed. (Princeton, N.J.: University Press, 1960), p. 185; and Anthony Kenny, "Counterforce and Countervalue," in Walter Stein, ed., *Nuclear Weapons: A Catholic Response* (London: Merlin Press, 1965), pp. 162–64.
3. See, e.g., n. 9, below.
4. Nozick, *Anarchy, State, and Utopia* (New York: Basic Books, 1974), pp. 30/I n; Nagel, "War and Maasacre," *Philosophy & Public Affairs*, 1, no. 2 (Winter 1972): 123–44, p. 126; Brandt, "Utilitarianism and the Rules of War," ibid., 145–65, p. 147, especially n. 3.
5. Extensions of Abolutism that would block some or all of the paradoxes include those which forbid intending to do what is wrong, deliberately making oneself less virtuous, or intentionally risking performing an inherently evil act. (An explanation of the relevant sense of "risking performing an act" will be offered in section IV.)
6. I assume henceforth that, if it would be wrong to do something, the agent knows this. (The agent, discussed in section IV, who has become corrupt may be an exception.) This keeps the discussion of the paradoxes from getting tangled up with the separate problem of whether an agent's duty is to do what is actually right, or what he believes is right.
7. See *Peter Abelard's Ethics*, D. E. Luscombe, trans. (New York: Oxford, 1971), pp. 5–37; Thomas Aquinas, *Summa Theologica*, 1a2ae. 18–20; Joseph Butler, "A Dissertation on the Nature of Virtue," in *Five Sermons* (Indianapolis: Bobbs-Merrill, 1950), p. 83; Immanuel Kant, *Foundations of the Metaphysics of Morals*, first section; Jeremy Bentham, *An Introduction to the Principles of Morals and Legislation*, chap. 9, secs. 13–16; Henry Sidgwick, *The Methods of Ethics* (New York: Dover, 1907), pp. 60/1, 201–4; Kenny, pp. 159,

162; and Jan Narveson, *Morality and Utility* (Baltimore: Johns Hopkins, 1967), pp. 106–8.

8. A qualification is necessary. Although having the intention involves only a small risk of applying the threatened sanction to innocent people, it follows, from points made in section IV, that forming the intention might also involve risks of performing *other* inherently evil acts. Hence, what really follows is that forming the intention is right in those SDSs in which the composite risk is small. This limitation in the scope of (P1′) is to be henceforth understood. It does not affect (P1), (P2), or (P3), since each is governed by an existential quantifier.
9. In *Nuclear Weapons,* Kenny and others use WIP to argue that nuclear deterrence is immoral because it involves having the conditional intention to kill innocent people. The considerations advanced in this section suggest that this argument, at best, is inconclusive, since it presents only one side of a moral paradox, and, at worst, is mistaken, since it applies WIP in just the sort of situation in which its applicability is most questionable.
10. "Rational and morally good" in this and later statements of the second and third paradoxes, means rational and moral in the given situation. A person who usually is rational and moral, but fails to be in the situation in question, could, of course, have the intention to apply the sanction. (P2′) is quite similar to a paradox concerning utilitarianism and deterrence developed by D. H. Hodgson in *Consequences of Utilitarianism* (Oxford: Clarendon Press, 1967), chap. 4.
11. See, e.g., S. Hampshire and H. L. A. Hart, "Decision, Intention and Certainty," *Mind,* 67, 1, 265 (January 1958): 1–12; and G. E. M. Anscombe, *Intention* (Ithaca, N.Y.: Cornell, 1966).
12. Alternatively, the agent could undertake to make himself into an *irrational* person whose intentions are quite out of line with his reasons for action. However, trying to become irrational, in these circumstances, is less likely to succeed than trying to change one's moral beliefs, and, furthermore, might itself constitute self-corruption. Hence, this point does not affect the paradox stated below.
13. As Donald Regan has suggested to me, (P3) can be derived directly from our normative assumption: imagine a villain credibly threatening to kill very many hostages unless a certain good man corrupts himself. I prefer the indirect route to (P3) given in the text, because (P1) and (P2) are interesting in their own right and because viewing the three paradoxes together makes it easier to see what produces them.
14. Its supporters might, of course, allow exceptions to the principle in cases in which only the agent's feelings, and not his acts or dispositions to act, are corrupted. (For example, a doctor "corrupts himself" by suppressing normal sympathy for patients in unavoidable pain, in order to treat them more effectively.) Further, advocates of the doctrine of double-effect might consider self-corruption permissible when it is a "side effect" of action rather than a means to an end. For example, they might approve of a social worker's joining a gang to reform it, even though he expects to assimilate some of the gang's distorted values. Note, however, that neither of these possible exceptions to the Virtue Preservation Principle (brought to my attention by Robert Adams) applies to the agent in an SDS who corrupts his *intentions* as a chosen *means* of preventing an offense.
15. See Hodgson, *Consequences.* Also, Adams, "Motive Utilitarianism," *Journal of Philosophy* 73, 14 (August 12, 1976): 467–81; and Bernard Williams, "A Critique of Utilitarianism," in J. J. C. Smart and Williams, *Utilitarianism: For and Against* (New York: Cambridge, 1973), sec. 6.

B. MORAL THEORIES

1. UTILITARIANISM

The Principle of Utility

JEREMY BENTHAM

Jeremy Bentham (1748–1832) was the founder of utilitarianism. His best-known work is *An Introduction to the Principles of Morals and Legislation.*

Chapter 1 Of the Principle of Utility

I. Nature has placed mankind under the governance of two sovereign masters, *pain* and *pleasure.* It is for them alone to point out what we ought to do, as well as to determine what we shall do. On the one hand the standard of right and wrong, on the other the chain of causes and effects, are fastened to their throne. They govern us in all we do, in all we say, in all we think: every effort we can make to throw off our subjection, will serve but to demonstrate and confirm it. In words a man may pretend to abjure their empire: but in reality he will remain subject to it all the while. The *principle of utility** recognises this subjection, and assumes it for the foundation of that system, the object of which is to rear the fabric of felicity by the hands of reason and law. Systems which attempt to question it, deal in sounds instead of sense, in caprice instead of reason, in darkness instead of light.

But enough of metaphor and declamation: it is not by such means that moral science is to be improved.

II. The principle of utility is the foundation of the present work: it will be proper therefore at the outset to give an explicit and determinate account of what is meant by it. By the principle of utility is meant that principle which approves or disapproves of every action whatsoever, according to the tendency which it appears to have to augment or diminish the happiness of the party whose interest is in question: or, what is the same thing in other words, to promote or to oppose that happiness. I say of every action whatsoever; and

*Note by the Author, July 1822.

To this denomination has of late been added, or substituted, the *greatest happiness* or *greatest felicity* principle: this for shortness, instead of saying at length *that principle* which states the greatest happiness of all those whose interest is in question, as being the right and proper, and only right and proper and universally desirable, end of human action: of human action in every situation, and in particular in that of a functionary or set of functionaries exercising the powers of Government. The word *utility* does not so clearly point to the ideas of *pleasure* and *pain* as the words *happiness* and *felicity* do: nor does it lead us to the consideration of the *number,* of the interests affected; to the *number,* as being the circumstance, which contributes, in the largest proportion, to the formation of the standard here in question; the *standard of right and wrong,* by which alone the propriety of human conduct, in every situation, can with propriety be tried. This want of a sufficiently manifest connexion between the ideas of *happiness* and *pleasure* on the one hand, and the idea of *utility* on the other, I have every now and then found operating, and with but too much efficiency, as a bar to the acceptance, that might otherwise have been given, to this principle. BENTHAM

From *An Introduction to the Principles of Morals and Legislation* (New York: Hafner, 1948), pp. 1–4, 29–32.

therefore not only of every action of a private individual, but of every measure of government.

III. By utility is meant that property in any object, whereby it tends to produce benefit, advantage, pleasure, good, or happiness, (all this in the present case comes to the same thing) or (what comes again to the same thing) to prevent the happening of mischief, pain, evil, or unhappiness to the party whose interest is considered: if that party be the community in general, then the happiness of the community: if a particular individual, then the happiness of that individual.

IV. The interest of the community is one of the most general expressions that can occur in the phraseology of morals: no wonder that the meaning of it is often lost. When it has a meaning, it is this. The community is a fictitious *body*, composed of the individual persons who are considered as constituting as it were its *members*. The interest of the community then is, what?—the sum of the interests of the several members who compose it.

V. It is in vain to talk of the interest of the community without understanding what is the interest of the individual.* A thing is said to promote the interest, or to be *for* the interest, of an individual, when it tends to add to the sum total of his pleasures: or, what comes to the same thing, to diminish the sum total of his pains.

VI. An action then may be said to be conformable to the principle of utility, or, for shortness sake, to utility, (meaning with respect to the community at large) when the tendency it has to augment the happiness of the community is greater than any it has to diminish it.

VII. A measure of government (which is but a particular kind of action, performed by a particular person or persons) may be said to be conformable to or dictated by the principle of utility, when in like manner the tendency which it has to augment the happiness of the community is greater than any which it has to diminish it.

VIII. When an action, or in particular a measure of government, is supposed by a man to be conformable to the principle of utility, it may be convenient, for the purposes of discourse, to imagine a kind of law or dictate, called a law or dictate of utility: and to speak of the action in question, as being conformable to such law or dictate.

IX. A man may be said to be a partizan of the principle of utility, when the approbation or disapprobation he annexes to any action, or to any measure, is determined by and proportioned to the tendency which he conceives it to have to augment or to diminish the happiness of the community: or in other words, to its conformity or unconformity to the laws or dictates of utility.

X. Of an action that is conformable to the principle of utility one may always say either that it is one that ought to be done, or at least that it is not one that ought not to be done. One may say also, that it is right it should be done; at least that it is not wrong it should be done: that it is a right action; at least that it is not a wrong action. When thus interpreted, the words *ought,* and *right* and *wrong,* and others of that stamp, have a meaning: when otherwise, they have none.

XI. Has the rectitude of this principle been ever formally contested? It should seem that it had, by those who have not known what they have been meaning. Is it susceptible of any direct proof? it should seem not: for that which is used to prove every thing else, cannot itself be proved: a chain of proofs must have their commencement somewhere. To give such proof is as impossible as it is needless.

XII. Not that there is or ever has been that human creature breathing, however stupid or perverse, who has not on many, perhaps on most occasions of his life, deferred to it. By the natural constitution of the human frame, on most occasions of their lives men in general embrace this principle, without thinking of it: if not for the ordering of their own actions, yet for the trying of their own actions, as well as of those of other men. There have been, at the same time, not many, perhaps, even of the most intelligent, who have been disposed to embrace it purely and without reserve. There are even few who have not taken some occasion or other to quarrel with it, either on account of their not understanding always how to apply it, or on account of some prejudice or other which they ware afraid to examine into, or could not bear to part with. For such is the stuff that man is made of: in principle and in practice, in a right track and in a wrong

*Interest is one of those words, which not having any superior *genus,* cannot in the ordinary way be defined.

one, the rarest of all human qualities is consistency.

Chapter IV Value of a Lot of Pleasure or Pain, How to Be Measured.

I. Pleasures then, and the avoidance of pains, are the *ends* which the legislator has in view: it behoves him therefore to understand their *value*. Pleasures and pains are the *instruments* he has to work with: it behoves him therefore to understand their force, which is again, in other words, their value.

II. To a person considered *by himself,* the value of a pleasure or pain considered *by itself,* will be greater or less, according to the four following circumstances:

1. Its *intensity*.
2. Its *duration*.
3. Its *certainty* or *uncertainty*.
4. Its *propinquity* or *remoteness*.

III. These are the circumstances which are to be considered in estimating a pleasure or a pain considered each of them by itself. But when the value of any pleasure or pain is considered for the purpose of estimating the tendency of any *act* by which it is produced, there are two other circumstances to be taken into the account; these are,

5. Its *fecundity,* or the chance it has of being followed by sensations of the *same* kind: that is, pleasures, if it be a pleasure: pains, if it be a pain.

6. Its *purity,* or the chance it has of *not* being followed by sensations of the *opposite* kind: that is, pains, if it be a pleasure: pleasures, if it be a pain.

These two last, however, are in strictness scarcely to be deemed properties of the pleasure or the pain itself; they are not, therefore, in strictness to be taken into the account of the value of that pleasure or that pain. They are in strictness to be deemed properties only of the act, or other event, by which such pleasure or pain has been produced; and accordingly are only to be taken into the account of the tendency of such act or such event.

IV. To a *number* of persons, with reference to each of whom the value of a pleasure or a pain is considered, it will be greater or less, according to seven circumstances: to wit, the six preceding ones; viz.

1. Its *intensity*.
2. Its *duration*.
3. Its *certainty* or *uncertainty*.
4. Its *propinquity* or *remoteness*.
5. Its *fecundity*.
6. Its *purity*.

And one other; to wit:

7. Its *extent;* that is, the number of persons to whom it *extends;* or (in other words) who are affected by it.

V. To take an exact account then of the general tendency of any act, by which the interests of a community are affected, proceed as follows. Begin with any one person of those whose interests seem most immediately to be affected by it: and take an account,

1. Of the value of each distinguishable *pleasure* which appears to be produced by it in the *first* instance.

2. Of the value of each *pain* which appears to be produced by it in the *first* instance.

3. Of the value of each pleasure which appears to be produced by it *after* the first. This constitutes the *fecundity* of the first *pleasure* and the *impurity* of the first *pain*.

4. Of the value of each *pain* which appears to be produced by it after the first. This constitutes the *fecundity* of the first *pain,* and the *impurity* of the first pleasure.

5. Sum up all the values of all the *pleasures* on the one side, and those of all the pains on the other. The balance, if it be on the side of pleasure, will give the *good* tendency of the act upon the whole, with respect to the interests of that *individual* person; if on the side of pain, the *bad* tendency of it upon the whole.

6. Take an account of the *number* of persons whose interests appear to be concerned; and repeat the above process with respect to each. *Sum up* the numbers expressive of the degrees of *good* tendency, which the act has, with respect to each individual, in regard to whom the tendency of it is *good* upon the whole: do this again with respect to each individual, in regard to whom the tendency of it is *good* upon the whole: do this again with respect to each individual, in regard to whom the tendency of it is *bad* upon the whole. Take the *balance;* which, if on the side of *plea-*

sure, will give the general *good tendency* of the act, with respect to the total number or community of individuals concerned; if on the side of pain, the general *evil tendency,* with respect to the same community.

VI. It is not to be expected that this process should be strictly pursued previously to every moral judgment, or to every legislative or judicial operation. It may, however, be always kept in view: and as near as the process actually pursued on these occasions approaches to it, so near will such process approach to the character of an exact one.

VII. The same process is alike applicable to pleasure and pain, in whatever shape their appear: and by whatever denomination they are distinguished: to pleasure, whether it be called *good* (which is properly the cause or instrument of pleasure) or *profit* (which is distant pleasure, or the cause or instrument of distant pleasure.) or *convenience,* or *advantage, benefit, emolument, happiness,* and so forth: to pain, whether it be called *evil,* (which corresponds to *good)* or *mischief,* or *inconvenience,* or *disadvantage,* or *loss,* or *unhappiness,* and so forth.

Utilitarianism

JOHN STUART MILL

John Stuart Mill (1806–73) was a leading exponent of utilitarianism and emiricist philosophy. In addition to *Utilitarianism,* his works include *A System of Logic, Examination of Sir William Hamilton's Philosophy, Principles of Political Economy,* and *On Liberty.*

Chapter 1 General Remarks

There are few circumstances among those which make up the present condition of human knowledge, more unlike what might have been expected, or more significant of the backward state in which speculation on the most important subjects still lingers, than the little progress which has been made in the decision of the controversy respecting the criterion of right and wrong. From the dawn of philosophy, the question concerning the *summum bonum,* or, what is the same thing, concerning the foundation of morality, has been accounted the main problem in speculative thought, has occupied the most gifted intellects, and divided them into sects and schools, carrying on a vigorous warfare against one another. And after more than two thousand years the same discussions continue, philosophers are still ranged under the same contending banners, and neither thinkers nor mankind at large seem nearer to being unanimous on the subject, than when the youth Socrates listened to the old Protagoras, and asserted (if Plato's dialogue be grounded on a real conversation) the theory of utilitarianism against the popular morality of the so-called sophist.

. . . .

On the present occasion, I shall, without further discussion of the other theories, attempt to contribute something towards the understanding and appreciation of the Utilitarian or Happiness theory, and towards such proof as it is susceptible of. It is evident that this cannot be proof in the ordinary and popular meaning of the term. Questions of ultimate ends are not amenable to direct proof. Whatever can be proved to be good, must be so by being shown to be a means to something admitted to be good without proof. The medical art is proved to be good by its conducing to health; but how is it possible to prove that health is good? The art of music is good, for the reason, among others, that it produces pleasure; but what proof is it possible to give that pleasure is good? If, then, it is asserted that there is a comprehensive formula, including all things which are in themselves good, and that whatever else is good, is not so as an end, but as a mean, the formula may be accepted or rejected, but is not a subject of what is commonly understood by proof. We are not, however, to infer that its acceptance or rejection must depend on blind impulse, or arbitrary choice. There is a larger meaning of the word proof, in which this question is as amenable to it as any other of the disputed questions of philosophy. The subject is within the cognisance of the rational faculty; and neither does that faculty deal with it solely in the way of intuition. Considerations may be presented capable of determining the intellect either to give or withhold

From *The English Utilitarians,* ed. John Plamenatz (Oxford: Basil Blackwell, 1949), pp. 163, 166–67, 169–74, 179–204.

its assent to the doctrine; and this is equivalent to proof.

We shall examine presently of what nature are these considerations; in what manner they apply to the case, and what rational grounds, therefore, can be given for accepting or rejecting the utilitarian formula. But it is a preliminary condition of rational acceptance or rejection, that the formula should be correctly understood. I believe that the very imperfect notion ordinarily formed of its meaning, is the chief obstacle which impedes its reception; and that could it be cleared, even from only the grosser misconceptions, the question would be greatly simplified, and a large proportion of its difficulties removed. Before, therefore, I attempt to enter into the philosophical grounds which can be given for assenting to the utilitarian standard, I shall offer some illustrations of the doctrine itself; with the view of showing more clearly what it is, distinguishing it from what it is not, and disposing of such of the practical objections to it as either originate in, or are closely connected with, mistaken interpretations of its meaning. Having thus prepared the ground, I shall afterwards endeavour to throw such light as I can upon the question, considered as one of philosophical theory.

Chapter 2 What Utilitarianism Is

. . . The creed which accepts as the foundation of morals, Utility, or the Greatest Happiness Principle, holds that actions are right in proportion as they tend to promote happiness, wrong as they tend to produce the reverse of happiness. By happiness is intended pleasure, and the absence of pain; by unhappiness, pain, and the privation of pleasure. To give a clear view of the moral standard set up by the theory, much more requires to be said; in pacticular, what things it includes in the ideas of pain and pleasure; and to what extent this is left an open question. But these supplementary explanations do not affect the theory of life on which this theory of morality is grounded—namely, that pleasure, and freedom from pain, are the only things desirable as ends; and that all desirable things (which are as numerous in the utilitarian as in any other scheme) are desirable either for the pleasure inherent in themselves, or as means to the promotion of pleasure and the prevention of pain.

Now, such a theory of life excites in many minds, and among them in some of the most estimable in feeling and purpose, inveterate dislike. To suppose that life has (as they express it) no higher end than pleasure—no better and nobler object of desire and pursuit—they designate as utterly mean and grovelling; as a doctrine worthy only of swine, to whom the followers of Epicurus were, at a very early period, contemptuously likened; and modern holders of the doctrine are occasionally made the subject of equally polite comparisons by its German, French, and English assailants.

When thus attacked, the Epicureans have always answered, that it is not they, but their accusers, who represent human nature in a degrading light; since the accusation supposes human beings to be capable of no pleasures except those of which swine are capable. If this supposition were true, the charge could not be gainsaid, but would then be no longer an imputation; for if the sources of pleasure were precisely the same to human beings and to swine, the rule of life which is good enough for the one would be good enough for the other. The comparison of the Epicurean life to that of beasts is felt as degrading, precisely because a beast's pleasures do not satisfy a human being's conceptions of happiness. Human beings have faculties more elevated than the animal appetites, and when once made conscious of them, do not regard anything as happiness which does not include their gratification. I do not, indeed, consider the Epicureans to have been by any means faultless in drawing out their scheme of consequences from the utilitarian principle. To do this in any sufficient manner, many Stoic, as well as Christian elements require to be included. But there is no known Epicurean theory of life which does not assign to the pleasures of the intellect, of the feelings and imagination, and of the moral sentiments, a much higher value as pleasures than to those of mere sensation. It must be admitted, however, that utilitarian writers in general have placed the superiority of mental over bodily pleasures chiefly in the greater permanency, safety, uncostliness, etc., of the former—that is, in their circumstantial advantages rather than in their intrinsic nature. And on all these points utilitarians have fully proved their case; but they might have taken the other, and, as it may be called, higher ground, with entire consistency. It is quite compatible with the principle of utility to recognise the fact, that some *kinds* of pleasure are more desirable and more valuable than others. It would be absurd that while, in estimating all other things, quality is considered as well as quantity, the estimation of pleasures should be supposed to depend on quantity alone.

If I am asked, what I mean by difference of quality in pleasures, or what makes one pleasure more valuable than another, merely as a pleasure, except its being greater in amount, there is but one possible answer. Of two pleasures, if there be one to which all or almost all who have experience of both give a decided preference, irrespective of any feeling of moral obligation to prefer it, that is the more desirable pleasure. If one of the two is, by those who are competently acquainted with both, placed so far above the other that they prefer it, even though knowing it to be attended with a greater amount of discontent, and would not resign it for any quantity of the other pleasure which their nature is capable of, we are justified in ascribing to the preferred enjoyment a superiority in quality, so far outweighing quantity as to render it, in comparison, of small account.

Now it is an unquestionable fact that those who are equally acquainted with, and equally capable of appreciating and enjoying, both, do give a most marked preference to the manner of existence which employs their higher faculties. Few human creatures would consent to be changed into any of the lower animals, for a promise of the fullest allowance of a beast's pleasures; no intelligent human being would consent to be a fool, no instructed person would be an ignoramus, no person of feeling and conscience would be selfish and base, even though they should be persuaded that the fool, the dunce, or the rascal is better satisfied with his lot than they are with theirs. They would not resign what they possess more than he for the most complete satisfaction of all the desires which they have in common with him. If they ever fancy they would, it is only in cases of unhappiness so extreme, that to escape from it they would exchange their lot for almost any other, however undesirable in their own eyes. A being of higher faculties requires more to make him happy, is capable probably of more acute suffering, and certainly accessible to it at more points, than one of an inferior type; but in spite of these liabilities, he can never really wish to sink into what he feels to be a lower grade of existence. We may give what explanation we please of this unwillingness; we may attribute it to pride, a name which is given indiscriminately to some of the most and to some of the least estimable feelings of which mankind are capable: we may refer it to the love of liberty and personal independence, an appeal to which was with the Stoics one of the most effective means for the inculcation of it; to the love of power, or to the love of excitement, both of which do really enter into and contribute to it: but its most appropriate appellation is a sense of dignity, which all human beings possess in one form or other, and in some, though by no means in exact, proportion to their higher faculties, and which is so essential a part of the happiness of those in whom it is strong, that nothing which conflicts with it could be, otherwise than momentarily, an object of desire to them. Whoever supposes that this preference takes place at a sacrifice of happiness—that the superior being, in anything like equal circumstances, is not happier than the inferior—confounds the two very different ideas, of happiness, and content. It is indisputable that the being whose capacities of enjoyment are low, has the greatest chance of having them fully satisfied; and a highly endowed being will always feel that any happiness which he can look for, as the world is constituted, is imperfect. But he can learn to bear its imperfections, if they are at all bearable; and they will not make him envy the being who is indeed unconscious of the imperfections, but only because he feels not at all the good which those imperfections qualify. It is better to be a human being dissatisfied than a pig satisfied; better to be Socrates dissatisfied than a fool satisfied. And if the fool, or the pig, are of a different opinion, it is because they only know their own side of the question. The other party to the comparison knows both sides.

It may be objected, that many who are capable

of the higher pleasures, occasionally, under the influence of temptation, postpone them to the lower. But this is quite compatible with a full appreciation of the intrinsic superiority of the higher. Men often, from infirmity of character, make their election for the nearer good, though they know it to be the less valuable; and this no less when the choice is between two bodily pleasures, than when it is between bodily and mental. They pursue sensual indulgences to the injury of health, though perfectly aware that health is the greater good. It may be further objected, that many who begin with youthful enthusiasm for everything noble, as they advance in years sink into indolence and selfishness. But I do not believe that those who undergo this very common change, voluntarily choose the lower description of pleasures in preference to the higher. I believe that before they devote themselves exclusively to the one, they have already become incapable of the other. Capacity for the nobler feelings is in most natures a very tender plant, easily killed, not only by hostile influences, but by mere want of sustenance; and in the majority of young persons it speedily dies away if the occupations to which their position in life has devoted them, and the society into which it has thrown them, are not favourable to keeping that higher capacity in exercise. Men lose their high aspirations as they lose their intellectual tastes, because they have not time or opportunity for indulging them; and they addict themselves to inferior pleasures, not because they deliberately prefer them, but because they are either the only ones to which they have access, or the only ones which they are any longer capable of enjoying. It may be questioned whether any one who has remained equally susceptible to both classes of pleasures, ever knowingly and calmly preferred the lower; though many, in all ages, have broken down in an ineffectual attempt to combine both.

From this verdict of the only competent judges, I apprehend there can be no appeal. On a question which is the best worth having of two pleasures, or which of two modes of existence is the most grateful to the feelings, apart from its moral attributes and from its consequences, the judgment of those who are qualified by knowledge of both, or, if they differ, that of the majority among them, must be admitted as final. And there needs be the less hesitation to accept this judgment respecting the quality of pleasures, since there is no other tribunal to be referred to even on the question of quantity. What means are there of determining which is the acutest of two pains, or the intensest of two pleasurable sensations, except the general suffrage of those who are familiar with both? Neither pains nor pleasures are homogeneous, and pain is always heterogeneous with pleasure. What is there to decide whether a particular pleasure is worth purchasing at the cost of a particular pain, except the feelings and judgment of the experienced? When, therefore, those feelings and judgment declare the pleasures derived from the higher faculties to be preferable *in kind,* apart from the question of intensity, to those of which the animal nature, disjoined from the higher faculties, is susceptible, they are entitled on this subject to the same regard.

I have dwelt on this point, as being a necessary part of a perfectly just conception of Utility or Happiness, considered as the directive rule of human conduct. But it is by no means an indispensable condition to the acceptance of the utilitarian standard; for that standard is not the agent's own greatest happiness, but the greatest amount of happiness altogether; and if it may possibly be doubted whether a noble character is always the happier for its nobleness, there can be no doubt that it makes other people happier, and that the world in general is immensely a gainer by it. Utilitarianism, therefore, could only attain its end by the general cultivation of nobleness of character, even if each individual were only benefited by the nobleness of others, and his own, so far as happiness is concerned, were a sheer deduction from the benefit. But the bare enunciation of such an absurdity as this last, renders refutation superfluous.

According to the Greatest Happiness Principle, as above explained, the ultimate end, with reference to and for the sake of which all other things are desirable (whether we are considering our own good or that of other people), is an existence exempt as far as possible from pain, and as rich as possible in enjoyments, both in point of quantity and quality; the test of quality, and the rule for measuring it against quantity, being the preference felt by those who in their opportunities of experience, to which must be added their habits of self-consciousness and self-observation, are best furnished with the means of comparison. This, being, according to the utilitarian opinion, the end of human action, is necessarily also the standard of morality; which may accordingly be defined, the rules and precepts for human conduct, by the observance of which an existence such as has been described might be, to the greatest extent possible, secured to all mankind; and not to them only, but, so far as the nature of things admits, to the whole sentient creation.

. . . .

I must again repeat, what the assailants of utilitarianism seldom have the justice to acknowledge, that the happiness which forms the utilitarian standard of what is right in conduct, is not the agent's own happiness, but that of all concerned. As between his own happiness and that of others, utilitarianism requires him to be as strictly impartial as a disinterested and benevolent spectator. In the golden rule of Jesus of Nazareth, we read the complete spirit of the ethics of utility. To do as you would be done by, and to love your neighbour as yourself, constitute the ideal perfection of utilitarian morality. As the means of making the nearest approach to this ideal, utility would enjoin, first, that laws and social arrangements should place the happiness, or (as speaking practically it may be called) the interest, of every individual, as nearly as possible in harmony with the interest of the whole; and secondly, that education and opinion, which have so vast a power over human character, should so use that power as to establish in the mind of every individual an indissoluble association between his own happiness and the good of the whole; especially between his own happiness and the practice of such modes of conduct, negative and positive, as regard for the universal happiness prescribes; so that not only he may be unable to conceive the possibility of happiness to himself, consistently with conduct opposed to the general good, but also that a direct impulse to promote the general good may be in every individual one of the habitual motives of action, and the sentiments connected therewith may fill a large and prominent place in every human being's sentient existence. If the impugners of the utilitarian morality represented it to their own minds in this its true character, I know not what recommendation possessed by any other morality they could possibly affirm to be wanting to it; what more beautiful or more exalted developments of human nature any other ethical system can be supposed to foster, or what springs of action, not accessible to the utilitarian, such systems rely on for giving effect to their mandates.

The objectors to utilitarianism cannot always be charged with representing it in a discreditable light. On the contrary, those among them who entertain anything like a just idea of its disinterested character, sometimes find fault with its standard as being too high for humanity. They say it is exacting too much to require that people shall always act from the inducement of promoting the general interests of society. But this is to mistake the very meaning of a standard of morals, and confound the rule of action with the motive of it. It is the business of ethics to tell us what are our duties, or by what test we may know them; but no system of ethics requires that the sole motive of all we do shall be a feeling of duty; on the contrary, ninety-nine hundredths of all our actions are done from other motives, and rightly so done, if the rule of duty does not condemn them. It is the most unjust to utilitarianism that this particular misapprehension should be made a ground of objection to it, inasmuch as utilitarian moralists have gone beyond almost all others in affirming that the motive has nothing to do with the morality of the action, though much with the worth of the agent. He who saves a fellow creature from drowning does what is morally right, whether his motive be duty, or the hope of being paid for his trouble; he who betrays the friend that trusts him, is guilty of a crime, even if his object be to serve another friend to whom he is under greater obligations. But to speak only of actions done from the motive of duty, and in direct obedience to principle: it is a misapprehension of the utilitarian mode of thought, to conceive it as implying that people should fix their minds upon so wide a generality as the world, or society at large. The great majority of good actions are intended not for the benefit of the world, but for that of individuals, of which the good of the world is made up; and the thoughts of the most virtuous man need not on these occasions travel beyond the particular persons concerned, except so far as is necessary to assure himself that in benefiting them he is not violating the rights, that is, the legitimate and authorised expectations, of any one else. The multiplication of happiness is, according to the utilitarian ethics, the object of virtue: the occasions on which any person (except one in a thousand) has it in his power to do this on an extended scale, in other words to be a public benefactor, are but exceptional; and on these occasions alone is he called on to consider public utility; in every other case, private utility, the interest or happiness of some few persons, is all he has to attend to. Those alone the influence of whose actions extends to society in general, need concern themselves habitually about so large an object. In the case of abstinences indeed—of things which people forbear to do from moral considerations, though the consequences in the particular case might be beneficial—it would be unworthy of an intelligent agent not to be consciously aware that the action is of a class which, if practised generally, would be generally injurious, and that this is the ground of the obligation to abstain from it. The amount of regard for the public interest implied in this recognition, is no greater than is demanded by every system of morals, for they all enjoin to abstain from whatever is manifestly pernicious to society.

The same considerations dispose of another reproach against the doctrine of utility, founded on a still grosser misconception of the purpose of a standard of morality, and of the very meaning of the words right and wrong. It is often affirmed that utilitarianism renders men cold and unsympathising; that it chills their moral feelings towards individuals; that it makes them regard only the dry and hard consideration of the consequences of actions, not taking into their moral estimate the qualities from which those actions emanate. If the assertion means that they do not allow their judgment respecting the rightness or wrongness of an action to be influenced by their opinion of the qualities of the person who does it, this is a complaint not against utilitarianism, but against having any standard of morality at all; for certainly no known ethical standard decides an action to be good or bad because it is done by a good or a bad man, still less because done by an amiable, a brave, or a benevolent man, or the contrary. These considerations are relevant, not to the estimation of actions, but of persons; and there is nothing in the utilitarian theory inconsistent with the fact that there are other things which interest us in persons besides the rightness and wrongness of their actions. The Stoics, indeed, with the paradoxical misuse of language which was part of their system, and by which they strove to raise themselves above all concern about anything but viture, were fond of saying, that he who has that has everything; that he, and only he, is rich, is beautiful, is a king. But no claim of this description is made for the virtuous man by the utilitarian doctrine. Utilitarians are quite aware that there are other desirable possessions and qualities besides virtue, and are perfectly willing to allow to all of them their full worth. They are also aware that a right action does not necessarily indicate a virtuous character, and that actions which are blamable, often proceed from qualities entitled to praise. When this is apparent in any particular case, it modifies their estimation, not certainly of the act, but of the agent. I grant that they are, notwithstanding, of opinion, that in the long run the best proof of a good character is good actions; and resolutely refuse to consider any mental disposition as good, of which the predominant tendency is to produce bad conduct. This makes them unpopular with many people; but it is an unpopularity which they must share with every one who regards the distinction between right and wrong in a serious light; and the reproach is not one which a conscientious utilitarian need be anxious to repel.

If no more be meant by the objection than that many utilitarians look on the morality of actions, as measured by the utilitarian standard, with too exclusive a regard, and do not lay sufficient stress upon the other beauties of character which go towards making a human being lovable or admirable, this may be admitted. Utilitarians who have cultivated their moral feelings, but not their sympathies nor their artistic perceptions, do fall into this mistake; and so do all other moralists under the same conditions. What can be said in excuse for other moralists is equally available for them, namely, that, if there is to be any error, it is better that it should be on that side. As a matter of fact, we may affirm that among utilitarians as among adherents of other systems, there is every imaginable degree of rigidity and of laxity in the application of their standard: some are even puritanically rigorous, while others are as indulgent as can possibly be desired by sinner or by sentimentalist. But on the whole, a doctrine which brings prominently forward the interest that man kind have in the repression and prevention of conduct which violates the moral law, is likely to be inferior to no other in turning the sanctions of opinion against such violations. It is true, the question, What does violate the moral law? is one on which those who recognise different standards of morality are likely now and then to differ. But difference of opinion on moral questions was not first introduced into the world by utilitarianism, while that doctrine does supply, if not always an easy, at all events a tangible and intelligible mode of deciding such differences.

It may not be superfluous to notice a few more of the common misapprehensions of utilitarian ethics, even those which are so obvious and gross that it might appear impossible for any person of candour and intelligence to fall into them; since persons, even of considerable mental endowments, often give themselves so little trouble to understand the bearings of any opinion against which they entertain a prejudice, and men are in general so little conscious of this voluntary ignorance as a defect, that the vulgarest misunderstandings of ethical doctrines are continually met with in the deliberate writings of persons of the greatest pretensions both to high principle and to philosophy. We not uncommonly hear the doctrine of utility inveighed against as a *godless* doctrine. If it be necessary to say anything at all against so mere an assumption, we may say that the question depends upon what idea we have formed of the moral character of the Deity. If it be a true belief that God desires, above all things, the happiness of his creatures, and that this was his purpose in their creation, utility is not only not a godless doctrine, but more profoundly religious than any other. If it be meant that utilitarianism does not recognise the revealed will of God as the supreme law of morals, I answer, that a utilitarian who believes in the perfect goodness and wisdom of God, necessarily believes that whatever God has thought fit to reveal on the subject of morals, must fulfil the requirements of utility in a supreme degree. But others besides utilitarians have been of opinion that the Christian revelation was intended, and is fitted, to inform the hearts and minds of mankind with a spirit which should enable them to find for themselves what is right, and incline them to do it when found, rather than to tell them, except in a very general way, what it is; and that we need a doctrine of ethics, carefully followed out, to *interpret* to us the will of God. Whether this opinion is correct or not, it is superfluous here to discuss; since whatever aid religion, either natural or revealed, can afford to ethical investigation, is as open to the utilitarian moralist as to any other. He can use it as the testimony of God to the usefulness or hurtfulness of any given course of action, by as good a right as others can use it for the indication of a transcendental law, having no connexion with usefulness or with happiness.

Again, Utility is often summarily stigmatised as an immoral doctrine by giving it the name of Expediency, and taking advantage of the popular use of that term to contrast it with Principle. But the Expedient, in the sense in which it is opposed to the Right, generally means that which is expedient for the particular interest of the agent himself; as when a minister sacrifices the interests of his country to keep himself in place. When it means anything better than this, it means that which is expedient for some immediate object, some temporary purpose, but which violates a rule whose observance is expedient in a much higher degree. The Expedient, in this sense, instead of being the same thing with the useful, is a branch of the hurtful. Thus, it would often be expedient, for the purpose of getting over some momentary embarrassment, or attaining some object immediately useful to ourselves or others, to tell a lie. But inasmuch as the cultivation in ourselves of a sensitive feeling on the subject of veracity, is one of the most useful, and the enfeeblement of that feeling one of the most hurtful, things to which our conduct can be instrumental; and inasmuch as any, even unintentional, deviation from truth, does that much towards weakening the trustworthiness of human assertion, which is not only the principal support of all present social well-being, but the insufficiency of which does more than any one thing that can be named to keep back civilisation, virtue, everything on which human happiness on the largest scale depends; we feel that the violation, for a present advantage, of a rule of such transcendent expediency, is not expedient, and that he who, for the sake of a convenience to himself or to some other individual, does what depends on him to deprive mankind of the good, and inflict upon them the evil, involved in the greater or less reliance which they can place in each other's word, acts the part of one of their worst enemies. Yet that even this rule, sacred as it is, admits of possible exceptions, is acknowledged by all moralists; the chief of which is when the withholding of some fact (as of information from a malefactor, or of bad news from a person dangerously ill) would save an individual (especially an individual other than oneself) from great and unmerited evil, and when the withholding can only be effected by denial. But in order that the exception may not extend itself beyond the need, and may have the least possible effect in weakening reliance on veracity, it ought to be recognised, and, if possible, its limits defined; and if the principle of utility is good for anything, it must be good for weighing these conflicting utilities against one another, and marking out the region within which one or the other preponderates.

Again, defenders of utility often find themselves called upon to reply to such objections as this—that there is not time, previous to action, for calculating and weighing the effects of any line of conduct on the general happiness. This is exactly as if any one were to say that it is impossible to guide our conduct by Christianity, because there is not time, on every occasion on which anything has to be done, to read through the Old and New Testaments. The answer to the objection is, that there has been ample time, namely, the whole past duration of the human species. During all that time, mankind have been learning by experience the tendencies of actions; on which experience all the prudence, as well as all the morality of life, are dependent. People talk as if the commencement of this course of experience had hitherto been put off, and as if, at the moment when some man feels tempted to meddle with the property or life of another, he had to begin considering for the first time whether murder and theft are injurious to human happiness. Even then I do not think that he would find the question very puzzling; but, at all events, the matter is now done to his hand. It is truly a whimsical supposition that, if mankind were agreed in considering utility to be the test of morality, they would remain without any agreement as to what *is* useful, and would take no measures for having their notions on the subject taught to the young, and enforced by law and opinion. There is no difficulty in proving any ethical standard whatever to work ill, if we suppose universal idiocy to be conjoined with it; but on any hypothesis short of that, mankind must by this time have acquired positive beliefs as to the effects of some actions on their happiness; and the beliefs which have thus come down are the rules of morality for the multitude, and for the philosopher until he has succeeded in finding better. That philosophers might easily do this, even now, on many subjects; that the received code of ethics is by no means of divine right; and that mankind have still much to learn as to the effects of actions on the general happiness, I admit, or rather, earnestly maintain. The corollaries from the principle of utility, like the precepts of every practical art, admit of indefinite improvement, and, in a progressive state of the human mind, their improvement is perpetually going on. But to consider the rules of morality as improvable, is one thing; to pass over the intermediate generalisations entirely, and endeavour to test each individual action directly by the first principle, is another. It is a strange notion that the acknowledgment of a first principle is inconsistent with the admission of secondary ones. To inform a traveller respecting the place of his ultimate destination, is not to forbid the use of landmarks and direction-posts on the way. The proposition that happiness is the end and aim of morality does not mean that no road ought to be laid down to that goal, or that persons going thither should not be advised to take one direction rather than another. Men really ought to leave off talking a kind of nonsense on this subject, which they would neither talk nor listen to on other matters of practical concernment. Nobody argues that the art of navigation is not founded on astronomy, because sailors cannot wait to calculate the Nautical Almanack. Being rational creatures, they go to sea with it ready calculated; and all rational creatures go out upon the sea of life with their minds made up on the common questions of right and wrong, as well as on many of the far more difficult questions of wise and foolish. And this, as long as foresight is a human quality, it is to be presumed they will continue to do. Whatever we adopt as the fundamental principle of morality, we require subordinate principles to apply it by; the impossibility of doing without them, being common to all systems, can afford no argument against any one in particular; but gravely to argue as if no such secondary principles could be had, and as if mankind had remained till now, and always must remain, without drawing any general conclusions from the experience of human life, is as high a pitch, I think, as absurdity has ever reached in philosophical controversy.

The remainder of the stock arguments against utilitarianism mostly consist in laying to its charge the common infirmities of human nature, and the general difficulties which embarrass conscientious persons in shaping their course through life. We are told that a utilitarian will be apt to make his own particular case an exception to moral rules, and, when under temptation, will see a utility in the breach of a rule, greater than he will see in its observance. But is utility the only creed which is able to furnish us with excuses for evil doing, and means of cheating our own conscience? They are afforded in abundance by all doctrines which recognise as a fact in morals the existence of conflicting considerations; which all doctrines do, that have been believed by sane persons. It is not the fault of any creed, but of the complicated nature of human affairs, that rules of conduct cannot be so framed as to require no exceptions, and that hardly any kind of action can safely be laid down as either always obligatory or always condemnable. There is no ethical creed which does not temper the rigidity of its laws, by giving a certain latitude, under the moral responsibility of the agent, for accommodation to peculiarities of circumstances; and under every creed, at the opening thus made, self-deception and dishonesty casuistry get in. There exists no moral system under which there do not arise unequivocal cases of conflicting obligations. These are the real difficulties, the knotty points both in the theory of ethics, and in the conscientious guidance of personal conduct. They are overcome practically, with greater or with less success, according to the intellect and virtue of the individual; but it can hardly be pretended that any one will be the less qualified for dealing with them, from possessing an ultimate standard to which conflicting rights and duties can be referred. If utility is the ultimate source of moral obligations, utility may be invoked to decide between them when their demands are incompatible. Though the application of the standard may be difficult, it is better than none at all: while in other systems, the moral laws all claiming independent authority, there is no common umpire entitled to interfere between them; their claims to precedence one over another rest on little better than sophistry, and unless determined, as they generally are, by the unacknowledged influence of considerations of utility, afford a free scope for the action of personal desires and partialities. We must remember that only in these cases of conflict between secondary principles is it requisite that first principles should be appealed to. There is no case of moral obligation in which some secondary principle is not involved; and if only one, there can seldom by any real doubt which one it is, in the mind of any person by whom the principle itself is recognised.

Chapter 3 Of the Ultimate Sanction of the Principle of Utility

The question is often asked, and properly so, in regard to any supposed moral standard—What is its sanction? what are the motives to obey it? or more specifically, what is the source of its obligation? whence does it derive its binding force? It is a necessary part of moral philosophy to provide the answer to this question; which, though frequently assuming the shape of an objection to the utilitarian morality, as if it had some special applicability to that above others, really arises in regard to all standards. It arises, in fact, whenever a person is called on to *adopt* a standard, or refer morality to any basis on which he has not been accustomed to rest it. For the customary morality, that which education and opinion have consecrated, is the only one which presents itself to the mind with the feeling of being *in itself* obligatory; and when a person is asked to believe that this morality *derives* its obligation from some general principle round which custom has not thrown the same halo, the assertion is to him a paradox; the supposed corollaries seem to have a more binding force than the original theorem; the superstructure seems to stand better without, than with, what is represented as its foundation. He says to himself, I feel that I am bound not to rob or murder, betray or deceive; but why am I bound to promote the general happiness? If my own happiness lies in something else, why may I not give that the preference?

If the view adopted by the utilitarian philosophy of the nature of the moral sense be correct, this difficulty will always present itself, until the influences which form moral character have taken the same hold of the principle which they have taken of some of the consequences—until, by the improvement of education, the feeling of unity with our fellow-creatures shall be (what it cannot be denied that Christ intended it to be) as deeply rooted in our character, and to our own consciousness as completely a part of our nature, as the horror of crime is in an ordinarily well brought up young person. In the meantime, however, the difficulty has no pecualir application to the doctrine of utility, but is inherent in every attempt to analyse morality and reduce it to principles; which, unless the principle is already in men's minds invested with as much sacredness as any of its applications, always seems to divest them of a part of their sanctity.

The principle of utility either has, or there is no reason why it might not have, all the sanctions which belong to any other system or morals. Those sanctions are either external or internal. Of the external sanctions it is not necessary to speak at any length. They are, the hope of favour and the fear of displeasure, from our fellow-creatures or from the Ruler of the Universe along with whatever we may have of sympathy or affection for them, or of love and awe of Him, inclining us to do His will independently of selfish consequences. There is evidently no reason why all these motives for observance should not attach themselves to the utilitarian morality, as completely and as powerfully as to any other. Indeed, those of them which refer to our fellow-creatures are sure to do so, in proportion to the amount of general intelligence; for whether there be any other ground of moral obligation than the general happiness or not, men do desire happiness; and however imperfect may be their own practice, they desire and commend all conduct in others towards themselves, by which they think their happiness is promoted. With regard to the religious motive, if men believe, as most profess to do, in the goodness of God, those who think that conduciveness to the general happiness is the essence, or even only the criterion of good, must necessarily believe that it is also that which God approves. The whole force therefore of external reward and punishment, whether physical or moral, and whether proceeding from God or from our fellow men, together with all that the capacities of human nature admit of disinterested devotion to either, become available to enforce the utilitarian morality, in proportion as that morality is recognised; and the more powerfully, the more the appliances of education and general cultivation are bent to the purpose.

So far as to external sanctions. The internal sanction of duty, whatever our standard of duty may be, is one and the same—a feeling in our own mind; a pain, more or less intense, attendant on violation of duty, which in properly cultivated moral natures rises, in the more serious cases, into shrinking from it as an impossibility. This feeling, when disinterested, and connecting itself with the pure idea of duty, and not with some particular form of it, or with any of the merely accessory circumstances, is the essence of Conscience; though in that complex phenomenon as it actually exists, the simple fact is in general all encrusted over with collateral associations, derived from sympathy, from love, and still more from fear; from all the forms of religious feeling; from the recollections of childhood and of all our past life; from self-esteem, desire of the esteem of others, and occasionally even self-abasement. This extreme complication is, I apprehend, the origin of the sort of mystical character which, by a tendency of the human mind of which there are many other examples, is apt to be attributed to the idea of moral obligation, and which leads people to believe that the idea cannot possibly attach itself to any other objects than those which, by a supposed mysterious law, are found in our present experience to excite it. Its binding force, however, consists in the existence of a mass of feeling which must be broken through in order to do what violates our standard of right, and which, if we do nevertheless violate that standard, will probably have to be encountered afterwards in the form of remorse. Whatever theory we have of the nature or origin of conscience, this is what essentially constitutes it.

The ultimate sanction, therefore, of all morality (external motives apart) being a subjective feeling in our own minds, I see nothing embarrassing to those whose standard is utility, in the question, what is the sanction of that particular standard? We may answer, the same as of all other moral standards—the conscientious feelings of mankind. Undoubtedly this sanction has no binding efficacy on those who do not possess the feelings it appeals to; but neither will these persons be more obedient to any other moral principle than to the utilitarian one. On them morality of any kind has no hold but through the external sanctions. Meanwhile the feelings exist, a fact in human nature, the reality of which, and the great power with which they are capable of acting on those in whom they have been duly cultivated, are proved by experience. No reason has ever been shown why they may not be cultivated to as great intensity in connexion with the utilitarian, as with any other rule of morals.

There is, I am aware, a disposition to believe that a person who sees in moral obligation a transcendental fact, an objective reality belonging to the province of "Things in themselves," is likely to be more obedient to it than one who believes it to be entirely subjective, having its seat in human consciousness only. But whatever a person's opinion may be on this point of Ontology, the force he is really urged by is his own subjective feeling, and is exactly measured by its strength. No one's belief that duty is an objective reality is stronger than the belief that God is so; yet the belief in God, apart from the expectation of actual reward and punishment, only operates on conduct through, and in proportion to, the subjective religious feeling. The sanction, so far as it is disinterested, is always in the mind itself; and the notion therefore of the transcendental moralists must be, that this sanction will not exist *in* the mind unless it is believed to have its root out of the mind; and that if a person is able to say to himself, This which is restraining me, and which is called my conscience, is only a feeling in my own mind, he may possibly draw the conclusion that when the feeling ceases the obligation ceases, and that if he find the feeling inconvenient, he may disregard it, and endeavour to get rid of it. But is this danger confined to the utilitarian morality? Does the belief that moral obligation has its seat outside the mind make the feeling of it too strong to be got rid of? The fact is so far otherwise, that all moralists admit and lament the ease with which, in the generality of minds, conscience can be silenced or stifled. The question, Need I obey my conscience? is quite as often put to themselves by persons who never heard of the principle of utility, as by its adherents. Those whose conscientious feelings are so weak as to allow of their asking this question, if they answer it affirmatively, will not do so because they believe in the transcendental theory, but because of the external sanctions.

It is not necessary, for the present purpose, to decide whether the feeling of duty is innate or implanted. Assuming it to be innate, it is an open question to what objects it naturally attaches itself; for the philosophic supporters of that theory are now agreed that the intuitive perception is of principles of morality and not of the details. If there be anything innate in the matter, I see no reason why the feeling which is innate should not be that of regard to the pleasures and pains of others. If there is any principle of morals which is intuitively obligatory, I should say it must be that. If so, the intuitive ethics would coincide with the utilitarian, and there would be no further quarrel between them. Even as it is, the intuitive moralists, though they believe that there are other intuitive moral obligations, do already believe this to be one; for they unanimously hold that a large *portion* of morality turns upon the consideration due to the interests of our fellow-creatures. Therefore, if the belief in the transcendental origin of moral obligation gives any additional efficacy to the internal sanction, it appears to me that the utilitarian principle has already the benefit of it.

On the other hand, if, as is my own belief, the moral feelings are not innate, but acquired, they are not for that reason the less natural. It is natural to man to speak, to reason, to build cities, to cultivate the ground, though these are acquired faculties. The moral feelings are not indeed a part of our nature, in the sense of being in any perceptible degree present in all of us; but this, unhappily, is a fact admitted by those who believe the most strenuously in their transcendental origin. Like the other acquired capacities above referred to, the moral faculty, if not a part of our nature, is a natural outgrowth from it; capable, like them, in a certain small degree, of springing up spontaneously; and susceptible of being brought by cultivation to a high degree of development. Unhappily it is also susceptible, by a sufficient use of the external sanctions and of the force of early impressions, of being cultivated in almost any direction: so that there is hardly anything so absurd or so mischievous that it may not, by means of these influences, be made to act on the human mind with all the authority of conscience. To doubt that the same potency might be given by the same means to the principle of utility, even if it had no foundation in human nature, would be flying in the face of all experience.

But moral associations which are wholly of artificial creation, when intellectual culture goes on, yield by degrees to the dissolving force of analysis: and if the feeling of duty, when associated with utility, would appear equally arbitrary; if there were no leading department of our nature, no powerful class of sentiments, with which that association would harmonise, which would make us feel it congenial, and incline us not only to foster it in others (for which we have abundant interested motives), but also to cherish it in ourselves; if there were not, in short, a natural basis of sentiment for utilitarian morality, it might well happen that this association also, even after it had been implanted by education, might be analysed away.

But there *is* this basis of powerful natural sentiment; and this it is which, when once the general happiness is recognised as the ethical standard, will constitute the strength of the utilitarian morality. This firm foundation is that of the social feelings of mankind; the desire to be in unity with our fellow creatures, which is already a powerful principle in human nature, and happily one of those which tend to become stronger, even without express inculcation, from the influences of advancing civilisation. The social state is at once so natural, so necessary, and so habitual to man, that, except in some unusual circumstances or by an effort of voluntary abstraction, he never conceives himself otherwise than as a member of a body; and this association is riveted more and more, as mankind are further removed from the stage of savage independence. Any condition, therefore, which is essential to a state of society, becomes more and more an inseparable part of every person's conception of the state of things which he is born into, and which is the destiny of a human being. Now, society between human beings, except in the relation of master and slave, is manifestly impossible on any other footing than that the interests of all are to be consulted. Society between equals can only exist on the understanding that the interests of all are to be regarded equally. And since in all states of civilisation, every person, except an absolute monarch, has equals, every one is obliged to live on these terms with somebody; and in every age some advance is made towards a state in which it will be impossible to live permanently on other terms with anybody. In this way people grow up unable to conceive as possible to them a state of total disregard of other people's interests. They are under a necessity of conceiving themselves as at least abstaining from all the grosser injuries, and (if only for their own protection) living in a state of constant protest against them. They are also familiar with the fact of co-operating with others, and proposing to themselves a collective, not an individual interest as the aim (at least for the time being) of their actions. So long as they are co-operating, their ends are identified with those of others; there is at least a temporary feeling that the interests of others are their own interests. Not only does all strengthening of social ties, and all healthy growth of society, give to each individual a stronger personal interest in practically consulting the welfare of others; it also leads him to identify his *feelings* more and more with their good, or at least with an even greater degree of practical consideration for it. He comes, as though instinctively, to be conscious of himself as a being who *of course* pays regard to others. The good of others becomes to him a thing naturally and necessarily to be attended to, like any of the physical conditions of our existence. Now, whatever amount of this feeling a person has, he is urged by the strongest motives both of interest and of sympathy to demonstrate it, and to the utmost of his power encourage it in others;

and even if he has none of it himself, he is as greatly interested as any one else that others should have it. Consequently the smallest germs of the feeling are laid hold of and nourished by the contagion of sympathy and the influences of education; and a complete web of corroborative association is woven round it, by the powerful agency of the external sanctions. This mode of conceiving ourselves and human life, as civilisation goes on, is felt to be more and more natural. Every step in political improvement renders it more so, by removing the sources of opposition of interest, and levelling those inequalities of legal privilege between individuals or classes, owing to which there are large portions of mankind whose happiness it is still practicable to disregard. In an improving state of the human mind, the influences are constantly on the increase, which tend to generate in each individual a feeling of unity with all the rest; which, if perfect, would make him never think of, or desire, any beneficial condition for himself, in the benefits of which they are not included. If we now suppose this feeling of unity to be taught as a religion, and the whole force of education, of institutions, and of opinion, directed, as it once was in the case of religion, to make every person grow up from infancy surrounded on all sides both by the profession and the practice of it, I think that no one, who can realise this conception, will feel any misgiving about the sufficiency of the ultimate sanction for the Happiness morality. To any ethical student who finds the realisation difficult, I recommend, as a means of facilitating it, the second of M. Comte's two principal works, the *Traité de politique positive*. I entertain the strongest objections to the system of politics and morals set forth in that treatise; but I think it has superabundantly shown the possibility of giving to the service of humanity, even without the aid of belief in a Providence, both the psychological power and the social efficacy of a religion; making it take hold of human life, and colour all thought, feeling, and action, in a manner of which the greatest ascendancy ever exercised by any religion may be but a type and foretaste; and of which the danger is, not that it should be insufficient, but that it should be so excessive as to interfere unduly with human freedom and individuality.

Neither is it necessary to the feeling which constitutes the binding force of the utilitarian morality on those who recognise it, to wait for those social influences which would make its obligation felt by mankind at large. In the comparatively early state of human advancement in which we now live, a person cannot indeed feel that entireness of sympathy with all others, which would make any real discordance in the general direction of their conduct in life impossible; but already a person in whom the social feeling is at all developed, cannot bring himself to think of the rest of his fellow-creatures as struggling rivals with him for the means of happiness, whom he must desire to see defeated in their object in order that he may succeed in his. The deeply rooted conception which every individual even now has of himself as a social being, tends to make him feel it one of his natural wants that there should be harmony between his feelings and aims and those of his fellow-creatures. If differences of opinion and of mental culture make it impossible for him to share many of their actual feelings—perhaps make him denounce and defy those feelings—he still needs to be conscious that his real aim and theirs do not conflict; that he is not opposing himself to what they really wish for, namely their own good, but is, on the contrary, promoting it. This feeling in most individuals is much inferior in strength to their selfish feelings, and is often wanting altogether. But to those who have it, it possesses all the characters of a natural feeling. It does not present itself to their minds as a superstition of education, or a law despotically imposed by the power of society, but as an attribute which it would not be well for them to be without. This conviction is the ultimate sanction of the greatest happiness morality. This it is which makes any mind, of well-developed feelings, work with, and not against, the outward motives to care for others, afforded by what I have called the external sanctions; and when those sanctions are wanting, or act in an opposite direction, constitutes in itself a powerful internal binding force, in proportion to the sensitiveness and thoughtfulness of the character; since few but those whose mind is a moral blank, could bear to lay out their course of life on the plan of paying no regard to others except so far as their own private interest compels.

Chapter 4 Of What Sort of Proof the Principle of Utility Is Susceptible

It has already been remarked, that questions of ultimate ends do not admit of proof, in the ordinary acceptation of the term. To be incapable of proof by reasoning is common to all first principles; to the first premises of our knowledge, as well as to those of our conduct. But the former, being matters of fact, may be the subject of a direct appeal to the faculties which judge of fact—namely, our senses, and our internal consciousness. Can an appeal be made to the same faculties on questions of practical ends? Or by what other faculty is cognisance taken of them?

Questions about ends are, in other words, questions what things are desirable. The utilitarian doctrine is, that happiness is desirable, and the only thing desirable, as an end; all other things being only desirable as means to that end. What ought to be required of this doctrine—what conditions is it requisite that the doctrine should fulfil—to make good its claim to be believed?

The only proof capable of being given that an object is visible, is that people actually see it. The only proof that a sound is audible, is that people hear it: and so of the other sources of our experience. In like manner, I apprehend, the sole evidence it is possible to produce that anything is desirable, is that people do actually desire it. If the end which the utilitarian doctrine proposes to itself were not, in theory and in practice, acknowledged to be an end, nothing could ever convince any person that it was so. No reason can be given why the general happiness is desirable, except that each person, so far as he believes it to be attainable, desires his own happiness. This, however, being a fact, we have not only all the proof which the case admits of, but all which it is possible to require, that happiness is a good: that each person's happiness is a good to that person, and the general happiness, therefore, a good to the aggregate of all persons. Happiness has made out its title as *one* of the ends of conduct, and consequently one of the criteria of morality.

But it has not, by this alone, proved itself to be the sole criterion. To do that, it would seem, by the same rule, necessary to show, not only that people desire happiness, but that they never desire anything else. Now it is palpable that they do desire things which, in common language, are decidedly distinguished from happiness. They desire, for example, virtue, and the absence of vice, no less really than pleasure and the absence of pain. The desire of virtue is not as universal, but it is as authentic a fact, as the desire of happiness. And hence the opponents of the utilitarian standard deem that they have a right to infer that there are other ends of human action besides happiness, and that happiness is not the standard of approbation and disapprobation.

But does the utilitarian doctrine deny that people desire virtue, or maintain that virtue is not a thing to be desired? The very reverse. It maintains not only that virtue is to be desired, but that it is to be desired disinterestedly, for itself. Whatever may be the opinion of utilitarian moralists as to the original conditions by which virtue is made virtue; however they may believe (as they do) that actions and dispositions are only virtuous because they promote another end than virtue; yet this being granted, and it having been decided, from considerations of this description, what *is* virtuous, they not only place virtue at the very head of the things which are good as means to the ultimate end, but they also recognise as a psychological fact the possibility of its being, to the individual, a good in itself, without looking to any end beyond it; and, hold, that the mind is not in a right state, not a state conformable to Utility, not in the state most conducive to the general happiness, unless it does love virtue in this manner—as a thing desirable in itself, even although, in the individual instance, it should not produce those other desirable consequences which it tends to produce, and on account of which it is held to be virtue. This opinion is not, in the smallest degree, a departure from the Happiness principle. The ingredients of happiness are very various, and each of them is desirable in itself, and not merely when considered as swelling an aggregate. The principle of utility does not mean that any given pleasure, as music, for instance, or any given exemption from pain, as for example health, is to be looked upon as means to a collective something termed happiness, and to be desired on that account. They are desired and desirable in and for themselves; besides being means, they are a part of the end. Virtue, according to the utilitarian doctrine, is not naturally and originally part of the end, but it is capable of becoming so; and in those who love it disinterestedly it has become so, and is desired and cherished, not as a means to happiness, but as a part of their happiness.

To illustrate this farther, we may remember that virtue is not the only thing, originally a means, and which if it were not a means to anything else, would be and remain indifferent, but which by association with what it is a means to, comes to be desired for itself, and that too with the utmost intensity. What, for example, shall we say of the love of money? There is nothing originally more desirable about money than about any heap of glittering pebbles. Its worth is solely that of the things which it will buy; the desires for other things than itself, which it is a means of gratifying. Yet the love of money is not only one of the strongest moving forces of human life, but money is, in many cases, desired in and for itself; the desire to possess it is often stronger than the desire to use it, and goes on increasing when all the desires which point to ends beyond it, to be compassed by it, are falling off. It may, then, be said truly, that money is desired not for the sake of an end, but as part of the end. From being a means to happiness, it has come to be itself a principal ingredient of the individual's conception of happiness. The same may be said of the majority of the great objects of human life—power, for example, or fame; except that to each of these there is a certain amount of immediate pleasure annexed, which has at least the semblance of being naturally inherent in them; a thing which cannot be said of money. Still, however, the strongest natural attraction, both of power and of fame, is the immense aid they give to the attainment of our other wishes; and it is the strong association thus generated between them and all our objects of desire, which gives to the direct desire of them the intensity it often assumes, so as in some characters to surpass in strength all other desires. In these cases the means have become a part of the end, and a more important part of it than any of the things which they are means to. What was once desired as an instrument for the attainment of happiness, has come to be desired for its own sake. In being desired for its own sake it is, however, desired as *part* of happiness. The person is made, or thinks he would be made, happy by its mere possession; and is made unhappy by failure to obtain it. The desire of it is not a different thing from the desire of happiness, any more than the love of music, or the desire of health. They are included in happiness. They are some of the elements of which the desire of happiness is made up. Happiness is not an abstract idea, but a concrete whole; and these are some of its parts. And the utilitarian standard sanctions and approves their being so. Life would be a poor thing, very ill provided with sources of happiness, if there were not this provision of nature, by which things originally indifferent, but conducive to, or otherwise associated with, the satisfaction of our primitive desires, become in themselves sources of pleasure more valuable than the primitive pleasures, both in permanency, in the space of human existence that they are capable of covering, and even in intensity.

Virtue, according to the utilitarian conception, is a good of this description. There was no original desire of it, or motive to it, save its conduciveness to pleasure, and especially to protection from pain. But through the association thus formed, it may be felt a good in itself, and desired as such with as great intensity as any other good; and with this difference between it and the love of money, of power, or of fame, that all of these may, and often do, render the individual noxious to the other members of society to which he belongs, whereas there is nothing which makes him so much a blessing to them as the cultivation of the disinterested love of virtue. And consequently, the utilitarian standard, while it tolerates and approves those other acquired desires, up to the point beyond which they would be more injurious to the general happiness than promotive of it, enjoins and requires the cultivation of the love of virtue up to the greatest strength possible, as being above all things important to the general happiness.

It results from the preceding considerations, that there is in reality nothing desired except happiness. Whatever is desired otherwise than as a means to some end beyond itself, and ultimately to happiness, is desired as itself a part of happiness, and is not desired for itself until it has become so. Those who desire virtue for its own sake, desire it either because the consciousness of it is a pleasure, or because the consciousness of being without it is a pain, or for both reasons united; as in truth the pleasure and pain seldom exist separately, but almost always together, the same person feeling pleasure in degree of virtue attained, and pain in not having attained more. If one of these give him no pleasure, and the other no pain, he would not love or desire virtue, or would desire it only for the other benefits which it might produce to himself or to persons whom he cared for.

We have now, then, an answer to the question, of what sort of proof the principle of utility is susceptible. If the opinion which I have now stated is psychologically true—if human nature is so constituted as to desire nothing which is not either a part of happiness or a means of happiness, we can have no other proof, and we require no other, that these are the only things desirable. If so, happiness is the sole end of human action, and the promotion of it the test by which to judge of all human conduct; from whence it necessarily follows that it must be the criterion of morality, since a part is included in the whole.

And now to decide whether this is really so; whether mankind do desire nothing for itself but that which is a pleasure to them or of which the absence is a pain; we have evidently arrived at a question of fact and experience, dependent, like all similar questions, upon evidence. It can only be determined by practised self-consciousness and self-observation, assisted by observation of others. I believe that these sources of evidence, impartially consulted, will declare that desiring a thing and finding it pleasant, aversion to it and thinking of it as painful, are phenomena entirely inseparable, or rather two parts of the same phenomenon; in strictness of language, two different modes of naming the same psychological fact: that to think of an object as desirable (unless for the sake of its consequences), and to think of it as pleasant, are one and the same thing; and that to desire anything, except in proportion as the idea of it is pleasant, is a physical and metaphysical impossibility.

So obvious does this appear to me, that I expect it will hardly be disputed: and the objection made will be, not that desire can possibly be directed to anything ultimately except pleasure and exemption from pain, but that the will is a different thing from desire; that a person of confirmed virtue, or any other person whose purposes are fixed, carries out his purposes without any thought of the pleasure he has in contemplating them, or expects to derive from their fulfilment; and persists in acting on them, enough though these pleasures are much diminished, by changes in his character or decay of his passive sensibilities, or are outweighed by the pains which the pursuit of the purposes may bring upon him. All this I fully admit, and have stated it elsewhere, as positively and emphatically as any one. Will, the active phenomenon, is a different thing from desire, the state of passive sensibility, and though originally an offshoot from it, may in time take root and detach itself from the parent stock; so much so, that in the case of an habitual purpose, instead of willing the thing because we desire it, we often desire it only because we will it. This, however, is but an instance of that familiar fact, the power of habit, and is nowise confined to the case of virtuous actions. Many indifferent things, which men originally did from a motive of some sort, they continue to do from habit. Sometimes this is done unconsciously, the consciousness coming only after the action; at other times with conscious volition, but volition which has become habitual, and is put in operation by the force of habit, in opposition perhaps to the deliberate preference, as often happens wih those who have contracted habits of vicious or hurtful indulgence. Third and last comes the case in which the habitual act of will in the individual instance is not in contradiction to the general intention prevailing at other times, but in fulfilment of it; as in the case of the person of confirmed virtue, and of all who pursue deliberately and consistently any determinate end. The distinction between will and desire thus understood is an authentic and highly important psychological fact; but the fact consists solely in this—that will, like all other parts of our constitution, is amenable to habit, and that we may will from habit what we no longer desire for itself, or desire only because we will it. It is not the less true that will, in the beginning, is entirely produced by desire; including in that term the repelling influence of pain as well as the attractive one of pleasure. Let us take into consideration, no longer the person who has a confirmed will to do right, but him in whom that virtuous will is still feeble, conquerable by temptation, and not to be fully relied on; by what means can it be strengthened? How can the will to be virtuous, where it does not exist in sufficient force, be implanted or awakened? Only by making the person *desire* virtue—by making him think of it in a pleasurable light, or of its absence in a painful one. It is by associating the doing right with pleasure, or the doing wrong with pain, or by eliciting and impressing and bringing home to the person's experience the pleasure naturally involved in the one or the pain in the other, that it is possible to call forth that will to be virtuous, which, when confirmed, acts without any thought of either pleasure or pain. Will is the child of desire, and passes out of the dominion of its parent only to come under that of habit. That which is the result of habit affords no presumption of being intrinsically good; and there would be no reason for wishing that the purpose of virtue should become independent of pleasure and pain, were it not that the influence of the pleasurable and painful associations which prompt to virtue is not sufficiently to be depended on for unerring constancy of action until it has acquired the support of habit. Both in feeling and in conduct, habit is the only thing which imparts certainty; and it is because of the importance to others of being able to rely absolutely on one's feelings and conduct, and to oneself of being able to rely on one's own, that the will to do right ought to be cultivated into this habitual independence. In other words, this state of the will is a means to good, not intrinsically a good; and does not contradict the doctrine that nothing is a good to human beings but in so far as it is either itself pleasurable, or a means of attaining pleasure or averting pain.

But if this doctrine be true, the principle of utility is proved. Whether it is so or not, must now be left to the consideration of the thoughtful reader.

Criticisms of Utilitarianism

E. F. CARRITT

E. F. Carritt (1876–1964) was a Fellow of University College, Oxford. His publications include *The Theory of Morals: An Introduction to Ethical Philosophy.*

(1) One criticism frequently brought against utilitarianism seems to me invalid. It is said that pleasures and pains cannot be measured or weighed like proteins or money and therefore cannot be compared, so that I can never tell whether I shall produce an overbalance of pleasure in this way or in that. I cannot weigh the pleasure of a starving man whom I feed on bread against my own in eating strawberries and say that his is twice as great as mine. Such an argument might seem hardly worth serious discussion had it not been used in defence of applying to conduct a theory of abstract economics: "There is no scientific criterion which would enable us to compare or assess the relative importance of needs of different persons . . . illegitimate inter-personal comparison,"[1] and "There is no means of testing the magnitude of A's satisfaction as compared with B's."[2]

But this argument, though those who use it are not ready to admit so much, really should apply against any comparison of my own desires and needs. I cannot say that two glasses of beer will give me twice as much pleasure as one, and still less that hearing a concert will give me three times or half as much; yet I may know very well indeed which will give me *more,* and may act upon the knowledge, since the two things though not measurable are comparable. It is true that, not being measurable, they are less easy to discriminate precisely, where the difference is not great, than physical objects; I may be unable to say whether the smell of roasting coffee or of bacon fried gives me the greater pleasure (mixed with some pain of appetite) even at two successive moments. It is no doubt often easier to read off the luminosity of two very similar surfaces on a pointer than to say which looks brighter, though in the end I have to trust my eyes for the pointer. As we have admitted, the mere existence of other minds is not demonstrable, still less is the intensity of their desires. But if in self-regarding acts I am sometimes prepared to spend my money in the belief that I shall desire to-morrow's bread more than to-morrow's jam, the utilitarian is justified, on his principles, in believing that it is his duty to provide bread for the starving sooner than jam for the well fed.

In fact it would be no commendation of an ethical theory if, on its showing, moral or even beneficent choice were always clear, since in practice we know that it is not. We often wonder if we can do more for the happiness, even the immediate happiness, of our parents or of our children; the former seem more in need of enjoyments, the latter have a keener capacity but a quicker recovery from diappointment. Utilitarianism has no need to stake its case on the possibility of an accurate "hedonistic (or agathistic) calculus." We have a well-founded belief that starvation hurts most people more than a shortage of grape-fruit, and no *knowledge how much* more it will hurt even ourselves to-morrow; and it is on such beliefs that we have to act; we can

From *Ethical and Political Thinking* (Oxford: Oxford University Press, 1950), pp. 61–65.

never know either our objective duty or our objective long-run interest.

(2) The second objection to the utilitarians is serious and indeed fatal. They make no room for justice. Most of them really admitted this when they found it hard on their principle to allow for the admitted obligation to distribute happiness "fairly," that is either equally or in proportion to desert. This led them to qualify their definition of duty as "promoting the greatest amount of happiness," by adding "of the greatest number," and to emphasize this by the proviso "every one count for one and no more." They can hardly have meant by this merely that it did not matter to whom I gave the happiness so long as I produced the most possible, for this they had already implied. They must at least have meant that if I could produce the same amount either in equal shares or in unequal I ought to prefer the former; and this means that I ought to be just as well as generous. The other demand of justice, that we should take account of past merit in our distribution, I think they would have denied, or rather explained away by the argument that to reward beneficence was to encourage such behaviour by example, and therefore a likely way to increase the total of happiness.

(3) A third criticism, incurred by some utilitarians[3] in the attempt to accommodate their theory to our moral judgements, was that of inconsistency in considering differences of quality or kind, as well as of amount, among pleasures when determming what we ought to do. It seems clear that people do not feel the same obligation to endow the art of cookery or pot-boiling as that of poetry or music, and this not because they are convinced that the one causes keener and more constant pleasure to a greater number than the other. Yet the recognition of a stronger obligation to promote "higher" or "better" pleasures implies that we think something good, say musical or poetic experience, not merely in proportion to its general pleasantness but by its own nature. The attempt to unite this "qualification of pleasures" with hedonistic utilitarianism is like saying 'I care about nothing but money, but I would not come by it dishonestly.' The fundamental fact is that we do not think some pleasures, such as that of cruelty, good at all.

(4) Though the inconsistency of modifying their theory in these two ways seems to have escaped the notice of most utilitarians, they could not help seeing that they were bound to meet a fourth criticism by giving some account of the universal belief that we have obligations to keep our promises. It is obvious that the payment of money to a rich creditor may not immediately result in so much satisfaction as the keeping of it by a poor debtor or the giving of it to a useful charity, and that yet it may, under most circumstances, be judged a duty and always an obligation. The argument of utilitarians to explain this has usually been as follows: It is true that a particular instance of justice may not directly increase the sum of human happiness but quite the contrary, and yet we often approve such an instance. This is becuase the *general* practice of such good faith, with the consequent possibility of credit and contract, is supremely conducive to happiness, and therefore so far as any violation of a bargain impairs this confidence, it is, indirectly and in the long run, pernicious.

Such an attempt to bring promise-keeping under the utilitarian formula breaks down because it only applies where the promise and its performance or neglect would be public and therefore serve as an example to others.

Suppose the two explorers in the Artic have only enough food to keep one alive till he can reach the base, and one offers to die if the other will promise to educate his children. No other person can know that such a promise was made, and the breaking or keeping of it cannot influence the future keeping of promises. On the utilitarian theory, then, it is the duty of the returned traveller to act precisely as he ought to have acted if no bargain had been made: to consider how he can spend his money most expediently for the happiness of mankind, and, if he thinks his own child is a genius, to spend it upon him.

Or, to take a different kind of justice, the utilitarian must hold that we are justified in inflicting pain always and only in order to prevent worse pain or bring about greater happiness. This, then, is all we need consider in so-called punishment, which must be purely preventive. But if some kind of very cruel crime becomes common, and none of the criminals can be caught, it might be highly expedient, as an example, to hang an innocent man, if a charge against him could be so framed that he were universally thought guilty; indeed this would only fail to be an ideal instance of utilitarian "punishment" because the victim himself would not have been so likely as a real felon to commit such a crime in the future, in all other respects it would be perfectly deterrent and therefore felicific.

In short, utilitarianism has forgotten rights; it allows no right to a man because he is innocent or because he has worked hard or has been promised or injured, or because he stands in any other special relation to us. It thinks only of duties or rather of a single duty, to dump happiness wherever we most conveniently can. If it speaks of rights at all it could only say all men have one and the same right, namely that all men should try to increase the total happiness. And this is a manifest misuse of language.

Notes

1. Hayek, *Collectivist Economic Planning,* p. 25.
2. Robbins, *Nature and Significance of Economic Science,* pp. 122–4. Cf. Jay, *The Socialist Case,* ch. 2.
3. E.g., J. S. Mill. Bentham more consistently held that the pleasure of push-pin is as good as the pleasure of poetry."

The Interpretation of the Moral Philosophy of J. S. Mill

J. O. URMSON

J. O. Urmson (1915–) is Emeritus Henry Waldgrave Stuart Professor at Stanford University and a fellow of Corpus Christi College, Oxford. A leader of the ordinary language movement, his works include *Philosophical Analysis, Berkeley,* and *The Emotive Theory of Ethics.*

It is a matter which should be of great interest to those who study the psychology of philosophers that the theories of some great philosophers of the past are studied with the most patient and accurate scholarship, while those of others are so burlesqued and travestied by critics and commentators that it is hard to believe that their works are ever seriously read with a sympathetic interest, or even that they are read at all. Amongst those who suffer most in this way John Stuart Mill is an outstanding example. . . .

. . . Mill, in his *Utilitarianism* attempts to do two things; first, he attempts to state the place of the conception of a *summum bonum* in ethics, secondly, he attempts to give an account of the nature of this ultimate end. We shall be concerned only with the first of these two parts of Mill's ethical theory; we shall not ask what Mill thought the ultimate end was, and how he thought that his view on this point could be substantiated, but only what part Mill considered that the notion of an ultimate end, whatever it be, must play in a sound ethical theory. This part of Mill's doctrine is logically independent of his account of happiness.

Two Mistaken Interpretations of Mill

Some of Mill's expositors and critics have thought that Mill was attempting to analyse or define the notion of right in terms of the *summum bonum*. Thus Mill is commonly adduced as an example of an ethical naturalist by those who interpret his account of happiness naturalistically, as being one who defined rightness in terms of the natural consequences of actions. Moore, for example, while criticising Mill's account of the ultimate end says: "In thus insisting that what is right must mean what produces the best possible results Utilitarianism is fully justified."[1] Others have been less favourable in their estimation of this alleged view of Mill's. But right or wrong, it seems clear to me that Mill did not hold it. Mill's only reference to this analytic problem is on page 27 (of the Everyman edition, to which all references will be made), where he refers to a person "who sees in moral obligation a transcendent fact, an objective reality belonging to the province of 'Things in themselves'," and goes on to speak of this view as an irrelevant opinion "on this point of Ontology," as though the analysis of ethical terms was

From *Philosophical Quarterly* 3 (1953), pp. 33–39.

no part of ethical philosophy at all as he conceived it, but part of ontology. It seems clear that when Mill speaks of his quest being for the "criterion of right and wrong" (p. 1), "concerning the foundation of morality" (p. 1) for a "test of right or wrong" (p. 2), he is looking for a "means of ascertaining what is right or wrong" (p. 2), not for a definition of these terms. We shall not, therefore, deal further with this interpretation of Mill; if a further refutation of it is required it should be sought in the agreement of the text with the alternative exposition shortly to be given.

The other mistaken view avoids the error of this first view, and indeed is incompatible with it. It is, probably, the received view. On this interpretation Mill is looking for a test of right or wrong as the ultimate test by which one can justify the ascription of rightness or wrongness to courses of action, rightness and wrongness being taken to be words which we understand. This test is taken to be whether the course of action does or does not tend to promote the ultimate end (which Mill no doubt says is the general happiness). So far there is no cause to quarrel with the received view, for it is surely correct. But in detail the view is wrong. For it is further suggested that for Mill this ultimate test is also the immediate test; the rightness or wrongness of any particular action is to be decided by considering whether it promotes the ultimate end. We may, it might be admitted, on Mill's view sometimes act, by rule of thumb or in a hurry, without actually raising this question; but the actual justification if there is one, must be directly in terms of consequences, including the consequences of the example that we have set. On this view, then, Mill holds that an action, a particular action, is right if it promotes the ultimate end better than any alternative, and otherwise it is wrong. However we in fact make up our minds in moral situations, so far as justification goes no other factor enters into the matter. It is clear that on this interpretation Mill is immediately open to two shattering objections; first, it is obviously and correctly urged, if one has, for example, promised to do something it is one's duty to do it at least partly because one has promised to do it and not merely because of consequences, even if these consequences are taken to include one's example in promise-breaking. Secondly, it is correctly pointed out that on this view a man who, *ceteris paribus,* chooses the inferior of two musical comedies for an evening's entertainment has done a moral wrong, and this is preposterous.[2] If this were in fact the view of Mill, he would indeed be fit for little more than the halting eristic of philosophical infants.

A Revised Interpretation of Mill

I shall now set out in a set of propositions what I take to be in fact Mill's view and substantiate them afterwards from the text. This will obscure the subtleties but will make clearer the main lines of interpretation.

A. A particular action is justified as being right by showing that it is in accord with some moral rule. It is shown to be wrong by showing that it trangresses some moral rule.

B. A moral rule is shown to be correct by showing that the recognition of that rule promotes the ultimate end.

C. Moral rules can be justified only in regard to matters in which the general welfare is more than negligibly affected.

D. Where no moral rule is applicable the question of the rightness or wrongness of particular acts does not arise, though the worth of the actions can be estimated in other ways.

As a terminological point it should be mentioned that where the phrase "moral rule" occurs above Mill uses the phrase "secondary principle" more generally, though he sometimes says "moral law." By these terms, whichever is preferred, Mill is referring to such precepts as "Keep promises," "Do no murder," or "Tell no lies." A list of which Mill approves is to be found in *On Liberty* (p. 135).

There is, no doubt, need of further explanation of these propositions; but that, and some caveats, can best be given in the process of establishing that these are in fact Mill's views. First, then, to establish from the text that in Mill's view particular actions are shown to be right or wrong by showing that they are or are not in accord with some moral rule. (i) He says with evident approbation on p.2: "The intuitive, no less than what may be termed the inductive, school of ethics, insists on the necessity of general laws. They both agree that the morality of an individual action is not a question of direct perception, but of the application of a law to an individual case. They recognise also, to a great extent, the same moral laws.'' Mill reproaches these schools only with being unable to give a unifying rationale of these laws (as he will do in proposition B). (ii) He says on page 22; ''But to consider the rules of morality as improvable is one thing; to pass over the intermediate generalisations entirely, and endeavour to test each individual action directly by the first principle, is another. It is a strange notion that the acknowledgement of a first principle is inconsistent with the admission of secondary ones.'' He adds, with feeling: ''Men really ought to leave off talking a kind of nonsense on this subject which they would neither talk nor listen to on other matters of practical concernment.'' (iii) Having admitted on p. 23 that ''rules of conduct cannot be so framed as to require no exceptions,'' he adds (p. 24) ''We must remember that only in these cases of conflict between secondary principles is it requisite that first principles should be appealed to. There is no case of moral obligation in which some secondary principle is not involved; and if only one, there can seldom be any real doubt which one it is, in the mind of any person by whom the principle itself is recognised.'' This quotation supports both propositions A and D. It shows that for Mill moral rules are not merely rules of thumb which aid the unreflective man in making up his mind, but an essential part of moral reasoning. The revelance of a moral rule is the criterion of whether we are dealing with a case of right or wrong or some other moral or prudential situation. (iv) The last passage which we shall select to establish this interpretation of Mill (it would be easy to find more) is also a joint confirmation of propositions A and D, showing that our last was not an *obiter dictum* on which we have placed too much weight. In the chapter entitled ''On the connection between justice and utility,'' Mill has maintained that it is a distinguishing mark of a just act that it is one required by a specific rule or law, positive or moral, carrying also liability to penal sanctions. He then writes this important paragraph (p. 45), which in view of its importance and the neglect that it has suffered must be quoted at length: ''The above is, I think, a true account, as far as it goes, of the origin and progressive growth of the idea of justice. But we must observe, that it contains, as yet, nothing to distinguish that obligation from moral obligation in general. For the truth is, that the idea of penal sanction, which is the essence of law, enters not only into the conception of injustice, but into that of any kind of wrong. We do not call anything wrong, unless we mean to imply that a person ought to be punished in some way or other for doing it; if not by law, by the opinion of his fellow-creatures; if not by opinion, by the reproaches of his own conscience. This seems to be the real turrning point of the distinction between morality and simple expediency. It is a part of the notion of Duty in every one of its forms, that a person may rightfully be compelled to fulfil it. Duty is a thing which may be exacted from a person, as one exacts a debt. Unless we think that it may be exacted from him, we do not call it his duty. . . . There are other things, on the contrary, which we wish that people should do, which we like or admire them for doing, perhaps dislike or despise them for not doing, but yet admit that they are not bound to do; it is not a case of moral obligation; we do not blame them, that is, we do not think that they are proper objects of punishment. . . . I think there is no doubt that this distinction lies at the bottom of the notions of right and wrong; that we call any conduct wrong, or employ, instead, some other term of dislike or disparagement, according as we think that the person ought, or ought not, to be punished for it; and we say, it would be right to do so and so, or merely that it would be desirable or laudable, according as we would wish to see the person whom it concerns, compelled, or only persuaded and exhorted, to act in that manner.'' How supporters of the received view have squared it with this passage I do not know; they do not mention it. If they have noticed it at all it is, presumably, regarded as an example of Mill's inconsistent eclecticism. Mill here makes it quite clear that in his view right and wrong are derived from moral rules; in other cases where the ultimate end is no doubt affected appraisal of conduct must be made in other ways. For example, if one's own participation in the ultimate end is impaired without breach of moral law, it is ([*On*] *Liberty*, p. 135) imprudence or lack of self respect, it is not wrong-doing. So much for the establishment of this interpretation of Mill, in a positive way, as regards points A and D. We must now ask whether there is anything in Mill which is inconsistent with it and in favour of the received view.

It is impossible to show positively that there is nothing in Mill which favours the received view against the interpretation here given, for it would require a complete review of everything that Mill says. We shall have to be content with examining two points which might be thought to tell in favour of the received view.

(a) On p. 6 Mill says: "The creed which accepts as the foundation of morals, Utility, or the Greatest Happiness Principle, holds that actions are right in proportion as they tend to promote happiness, wrong as they tend to promote the reverse of Happiness." This seems to be the well-known sentence which is at the bottom of the received interpretation. Of course, it could be taken as a loose and inaccurate statement of the received view, if the general argument required it. But note that strictly one can say that a certain action tends to produce a certain result only if one is speaking of type- rather than token-actions. Drinking alcohol may tend to promote exhilaration, but my drinking this particular glass either does or does not produce it. It seems, then, that Mill can well be interpreted here as regarding moral rules as forbidding or enjoining types of action, in fact as making the point that the right moral rules are the ones which promote the ultimate end (my proposition B), not as saying something contrary to proposition A. And this, or something like it, is the interpretation which consistency requires. Mill's reference to "tendencies of actions" at the top of p. 22 supports the stress here laid on the word "tend," and that context should be examined by those who require further conviction.

(b) Mill sometimes refers to moral rules as "intermediate generalisations" (e.g., p. 22) from the supreme principle, or as "corollaries" of it (also p. 22). These are proably the sort of phrases which lead people to think that they play a purely heuristic role in ethical thinking for Mill. As for the expression "intermediate generalisation," Mill undoubtedly thinks that we should, and to some extent do, arrive at and improve our moral rules by such methods as observing that a certain type of action has had bad results of a social kind in such an overwhelming majority of cases that it ought to be banned. But this is an over-simplification; see the note on p. 58 on how we ought to arrive at moral rules, and the pessimistic account of how we in fact arrive at them in *[On] Liberty,* ([p]p. 69–70). But this account of the genesis of moral rules does not require us to interpret them as being anything but rules when once made. It really seems unnecessary to say much of the expression "corollary"; Mill obviously cannot wish it to be taken literally; in fact it is hard to state the relation of moral rules to a justifying principle with exactitude and Mill, in a popular article in *Fraser,* did not try very hard to do so.

Moral Rules and the Ultimate End

We have already been led in our examination of possible objections to proposition A to say something in defence of the view that Mill thought that a moral rule is shown to be correct by showing that the recognition of that rule promotes the ultimate end (proposition B). A little more may be added on this point, though it seems fairly obvious that if we are right in saying that the supreme principle is not to be evoked, in Mill's view, in the direct justification of particular right acts, it must thus come in in an indirect way in view of the importance that Mill attached to it. And it is hard to think what the indirect way is if not this. (i) On p. 3 Mill reproaches other moral philosophers with not giving a satisfactory account of moral rules in terms of a fundamental principle, though they have correctly placed moral rules as governing particular actions. It would be indeed the mark of an inconsistent philosopher if he did not try to repair the one serious omission which he ascribes to others. (ii) Mill ascribes to Kant (p. 4) the use of utilitarian arguments because Mill alleges, he in fact supports the rules of morality by showing the evil consequences of not adopting them or adopting alternatives. Thus Mill is here regarding as distinctively utilitarian the justification or rejection of moral rules on the ground of consequences. He could hardly have wished to suggest that Kant would directly justify, even inadvertently, particular actions on such grounds. But it is perhaps not to the point to argue this matter more elaborately. If anyone has been convinced by what has gone before, he will not need much argument on this point; with others it is superfluous to make the attempt.

In What Fields Are Moral Rules of Right and Wrong Applicable?

The applicability of moral rules is, says Mill, "the characteristic difference which marks off, not justice, but morality in general, from the remaining provinces of Expediency and Worthiness" (p. 46). Mill says little or nothing in *Utilitarianism* about the boundary between morality and worthiness (surely it would be better to have said the boundary between right and wrong on the one hand and other forms of both moral and non-moral appraisal on the other?). It seems reasonable to suppose that he would have recognised that the use of moral rules must be confined to matters in which the kind of consequence is sufficiently invariable for there not to be too many exceptions. But this is a pragmatic limitation; Mill does have something to say about a limitation in principle in [*On*] *Liberty* which I have crudely summarised in my proposition C—moral rules can be justifiably maintained in regard only to matters in which the general welfare is more than negligibly affected.

It is important to note that Mill in *Liberty* is concerned with freedom from moral sanctions as well as the sanctions of positive law. The distinction between self-regarding and other actions is regarded by him as relevant to moral as well as to political philosophy. The most noteworthy passage which bears on the scope of moral rules is on page 135. Here he mentions such things as encroachment on the rights of others as being "fit objects of moral reprobation, and, in grave cases, of moral retribution and punishment." But self-regarding faults (low tastes and the like) are "not properly immoralities and to whatever pitch they are carried, do not constitute wickedness. . . . The term duty to oneself, when it means anything more than prudence, means self-respect or self-development." Self-regarding faults render the culprit "necessarily and properly a subject of distaste, or, in extreme cases, even of contempt," but this is in the sphere of worthiness not of right and wrong.

So much then for Mill's account of the logic of moral reasoning. It must be emphasised that no more has been attempted than a skeleton plan of Mill's answer, and that Mill puts the matter more richly and more subtly in his book. Even on the question of general interpretation more store must be laid on the effect of a continuous reading in the light of the skeleton plan than on the effect of the few leading quotations introduced in this paper. It is emphaticaly not the contention of this paper that Mill has given a finally correct account of these matters which is immune to all criticism; an attempt has been made only to give a sympathetic account without any criticism favourable or unfavourable. But I certainly do maintain that the current interpretations of Mill's *Utilitarianism* are so unsympathetic and so incorrect that the majority of criticisms which have in fact been based on them are irrelevant and worthless.

Notes

1. *Principia Ethica,* reprinted 1948, p. 106.
2. For one example of this interpretation of Mill and the first and more important objection, see Carritt, *The Theory of Morals,* Ch. 4.

Extreme and Restricted Utilitarianism

J. J. C. Smart

J. J. C. Smart (1920–) is professor of philosophy at the Institute of Advanced Studies of the Australian National University. Influential in a wide variety of areas, he has several publications to his name, including *Philosophy and Scientific Realism* and *Between Science and Philosophy.*

I

Utilitarianism is the doctrine that the rightness of actions is to be judged by their consequences. What do we mean by "actions" here? Do we mean particular actions or do we mean classes of actions? According to which way we interpret the word "actions" we get two different theories, both of which merit the appellation "utilitarian."

(1) If by "actions" we mean particular individual actions we get the sort of doctrine held by Bentham, Sidgwick, and Moore. According to this doctrine we test individual actions by their consequences, and general rules, like "keep promises," are mere rules of thumb which we use only to avoid the necessity of estimating the probable consequences of our actions at every step. The rightness or wrongness of keeping a promise on a particular occasion depends only on the goodness or badness of the consequences of keeping or of breaking the promise on that particular occasion. Of course part of the consequences of breaking the promise, and a part to which we will normally ascribe decisive importance, will be the weakening of faith in the institution of promising. However, if the goodness of the consequences of breaking the rule is *in toto* greater than the goodness of the consequences of keeping it, then we must break the rule, irrespective of whether the goodness of the consequences of *everybody's* obeying the rule is or is not greater than the consequences of *everybody's* breaking it. To put it shortly, rules do not matter, save *per accidens* as rules of thumb and as *de facto* social institutions with which the utilitarian has to reckon when estimating consequences. I shall call this doctrine "extreme utilitarianism."

(2) A more modest form of utilitarianism has recently become fashionable. The doctrine is to be found in Toulmin's book *The Place of Reason in Ethics,* in Nowell-Smith's *Ethics* (though I think Nowell-Smith has qualms), in John Austin's *Lectures on Jurisprudence* (Lecture II), and even in J. S. Mill, if Urmson's interpretation of him is correct (*Philosophical Quarterly,* Vol. 3, pp. 3–39, 1953). Part of its charm is that it appears to resolve the dispute in moral philosophy between intuitionists and utilitarians in a way which is very neat. The above philosophers hold, or seem to hold, that moral rules are more than rules of thumb. In general the rightness of an action is *not* to be tested by evaluating its consequences but only by considering whether or not it falls under a certain rule. Whether the rule is to be con-

Based on a paper read to the Victorian Branch of the Australasian Association of Psychology and Philosophy, October 1955. [The article is discussed in J. H. McCloskey, "An Examination of Restricted Utilitarianism" *Philosophical Review* (1957); also by D. Lyons, *Forms and Limits of Utilitarianism* (Clarendon Press, Oxford, 1965). Ed. *(in original)*]

From *Theories of Ethics,* ed. Philippa Foot (Oxford: Oxford University Press, 1967), pp. 171–83.

sidered an acceptable moral rule, is, however, to be decided by considering the consequences of adopting the rule. Broadly, then, actions are to be tested by rules and rules by consequences. The only cases in which we must test an individual action directly by its consequences are *(a)* when the action comes under two different rules, one of which enjoins it and one of which forbids it, and *(b)* when there is no rule whatever that governs the given case. I shall call this doctrine ''restricted utilitarianism.''

It should be noticed that the distinction I am making cuts across, and is quite different from, the distinction commonly made between hedonistic and ideal utilitarianism. Bentham was an extreme hedonistic utilitarian and Moore an extreme ideal utilitarian, and Toulmin (perhaps) could be classified as a restricted ideal utilitarian. A hedonistic utilitarian holds that the goodness of the consequences of an action is a function only of their pleasurableness and an ideal utilitarian, like Moore, holds that pleasurableness is not even a necessary condition of goodness. Mill seems, if we are to take his remarks about higher and lower pleasures seriously, to be neither a pure hedonistic nor a pure ideal utilitarian. He seems to hold that pleasurableness is a necessary condition for goodness, but that goodness is a function of other qualities of mind as well. Perhaps we can call him a quasi-ideal utilitarian. When we say that a state of mind is good I take it that we are expressing some sort of *rational preference*. When we say that it is pleasurable I take it that we are saying that it is enjoyable, and when we say that something is a higher pleasure I take it that we are saying that it is more truly, or more deeply, enjoyable. I am doubtful whether ''more deeply enjoyale'' does not just mean ''more enjoyable, even though not more enjoyable on a first look,'' and so I am doubtful whether quasi-ideal utilitarianism, and possibly ideal utilitarianism too, would not collapse into hedonistic utilitarianism on a closer scrutiny of the logic of words like ''preference,'' ''pleasure,'' ''enjoy,'' ''deeply enjoy,'' and so on. However, it is beside the point of the present paper to go into these questions. I am here concerned only with the issue between extreme and restricted utilitarianism and am ready to concede that both forms of utilitarianism can be either hedonistic or non-hedonistic.

The issue between extreme and restricted utilitarianism can be illustrated by considering the remark ''But suppose everyone did the same.'' (Cf. A. K. Stout's article in *The Australasian Journal of Philosophy,* Vol. 32, pp. 1–29.) Stout distinguishes two forms of the universalization principle, the causal forms and the hypothetical form. To say that you ought not to do an action A because it would have bad results if everyone (or many people) did action A may be merely to point out that while the action A would otherwise be the optimific one, nevertheless when you take into account that doing A will probably cause other people to do A too, you can see that A is not, on a broad view, really optimific. If this causal influence could be avoided (as may happen in the case of a secret desert island promise) then we would disregard the universalization principle. This is the causal form of the principle. A person who accepted the universalization principle in its hypothetical form would be one who was concerned only with what would happen *if* everyone did the action A: he would be totally unconcerned with the question of whether in fact everyone would do the action A. That is, he might say that it would be wrong not to vote because it would have bad results if everyone took this attitude, and he would be totally unmoved by arguments purporting to show that my refusing to vote has no effect whatever on other people's propensity to vote. Making use of Stout's distinction, we can say that an extreme utilitarian would apply the universalization principle in the causal form, while a restricted utilitarian would apply it in the hypothetical form.

How are we to decide the issue between extreme and restricted utilitarianism? I wish to repudiate at the outset that milk and water approach which describes itself sometimes as ''investigating what is implicit in the common moral consciousness'' and sometimes as ''investigating how people ordinarily talk about morality.'' We have only to read the newspaper correspondence about capital punishment or about what should be done with Formosa to realize that the common moral consciousness is in part made up of superstitious elements, of morally bad elements, and of logically confused elements. I address myself to good hearted and benevolent people and so I hope that if we rid ourselves of the logical confusion the superstitious and morally bad elements will largely fall away. For even among good hearted and benevolent people it is possible to find superstitious and morally bad reasons for moral beliefs. These superstitious and morally bad reasons hide behind the protective screen of logical confusion. With people who are not logically confused but who are openly superstitious or morally bad I can of course do nothing. That is, our ultimate pro-attitudes may be different. Nevertheless I propose to rely on *my own* moral consciousness and to appeal to *your* moral consciousness and to forget about what people ordinarily say. "The obligation to obey a rule," says Nowell-Smith (*Ethics,* p. 239), "does not, *in the opinion of ordinary men,*" (my italics), "rest on the beneficial consequences of obeying it in a particular case." What does this prove? Surely it is more than likely that ordinary men are confused here. Philosophers should be able to examine the question more rationally.

II

For an extreme utilitarian moral rules are rules of thumb. In practice the extreme utilitarian will mostly guide his conduct by appealing to the rules ("do not lie," "do not break promises," etc.) of common sense morality. This is not because there is anything sacrosanct in the rules themselves but because he can argue that probably he will most often act in an extreme utilitarian way if he does not think as a utilitarian. For one thing, actions have frequently to be done in a hurry. Imagine a man seeing a person drowning. He jumps in and rescues him. There is no time to reason the matter out, but usually this will be the course of action which an extreme utilitarian would recommend if he did reason the matter out. If, however, the man drowning had been drowning in a river near Berchtesgaden in 1938, and if he had had the well-known black forelock and moustache of Adolf Hitler, an extreme utliitarian would, if he had time, work out the probability of the man's being the villainous dictator, and if the probability were high enough he would, on extreme utilitarian grounds, leave him to drown. The rescuer, however, has not time. He trusts to his instincts and dives in and rescues the man. And this trusting to instincts and to moral rules can be justified on extreme utilitarian grounds. Furthermore, an extreme utilitarian who knew that the drowning man was Hitler would nevertheless praise the rescuer, not condemn him. For by praising the man he is strengthening a courageous and benevolent disposition of mind, and in general this disposition has great positive utility. (Next time, perhaps, it will be Winston Churchill that the man saves!) We must never forget that an extreme utilitarian may praise actions which he knows to be wrong. Saving Hitler was wrong, but it was a member of a class of actions which are generally right, and the motive to do actions of this class is in general an optimific one. In considering questions of praise and blame it is not the expediency of the praised or blamed action that is at issue, but the expediency of the praise. It can be expedient to praise an inexpedient action and inexpedient to praise an expedient one.

Lack of time is not the only reason why an extreme utilitarian may, on extreme utilitarian principles, trust to rules of common-sense morality. He knows that in particular cases where his own interests are involved his calculations are likely to be biased in his own favour. Suppose that he is unhappily married and is deciding whether to get divorced. He will in all probability greatly exaggerate his own unhappiness (and possibly his wife's) and greatly underestimate the harm done to his children by the break up of the family. He will probably also underestimate the likely harm done by the weakening of the general faith in marriage vows. So probably he will come to the correct extreme utilitarian conclusion if he does not in this instance think as an extreme utilitarian but trusts to common-sense morality.

There are many more and subtle points that could be made in connexion with the relation between extreme utilitarianism and the morality of common sense. All those that I have just made and many more will be found in Book IV Chapters 3–5 of Sidgwick's *Methods of Ethics.* I think that this book is the best book ever written on ethics, and that these chapters are the best chapters of the book. As they occur so near the end of a very long book they are unduly neglected. I refer the reader, then, to Sidgwick for the classical exposition of the relation between (extreme) utilitarianism and the morality of common sense. One further point raised by Sidgwick in this connexion is whether an (extreme) utilitarian ought on (extreme) utilitarian principles to propagate (extreme) utilitarianism among the public. As most people are not very philosophical and not good at empirical calculations, it is probable that they will most often act in an extreme utilitarian way if they do not try to think as extreme utilitarians. We have seen how easy it would be to misapply the extreme utilitarian criterion in the case of divorce. Sidgwick seems to think it quite probable that an extreme utilitarian should not propagate his doctrine too widely. However, the great danger to humanity comes nowadays on the plane of public morality—not private morality. There is a greater danger to humanity from the hydrogen bomb than from an increase of the divorce rate, regrettable though that might be, and there seems no doubt that extreme utilitarianism makes for good sense in international relations. When France walked out of the United Nations because she did not wish Morocco discussed, she said that she was within her rights because Morocco and Algiers are part of her metropolitan territory and nothing to do with U.N. This was clearly a legalistic if not superstitious argument. We should not be concerned with the so-called "rights" of France or any other country but with whether the cause of humanity would best be served by discussing Morocco in U.N. (I am not saying that the answer to this is "Yes." There are good grounds for supposing that more harm than good would have come by such a discussion.) I myself have no hesitation in saying that on extreme utilitarian principles we ought to propagate extreme utilitarianism as widely as possible. But Sidgwick had respectable reasons for suspecting the opposite.

The extreme utilitarian, then, regards moral rules as rules of thumb and as sociological facts that have to be taken into account when deciding what to do, just as facts of any other sort have to be taken into account. But in themselves they do not justify any action.

III

The restricted utilitarian regards moral rules as more than rules of thumb for short-circuiting calculations of consequences. Generally, he argues, consequences are not relevant at all when we are deciding what to do in a particular case. In general, they are relevant only to deciding what rules are good reasons for acting in a certain way in particular cases. This doctrine is possibly a good account of how the modern unreflective twentieth century Englishman often thinks about morality, but surely it is monstrous as an account of how it is most rational to think about morality. Suppose that there is a rule *R* and that in 99 percent of cases the best possible results are obtained by acting in accordance with *R*. Then clearly *R* is a useful rule of thumb; if we have not time or are not impartial enough to assess the consequences of an action it is an extremely good bet that the thing to do is to act in accordance with *R*. But is it not monstrous to suppose that if we *have* worked out the consequences and if we have perfect faith in the impartiality of our calculations, and if we *know* that in this instance to break *R* will have better results than to keep it, we should nevertheless obey the rule? Is it not to erect *R* into a sort of idol if we keep it when breaking it will prevent, say, some avoidable misery? Is not this a form of superstitious rule-worship (easily explicable psychologically) and not the rational thought of a philosopher?

The point may be made more clearly if we consider Mill's comparison of moral rules to the tables in the nautical almanack. (*Utilitarianism,* Everyman Edition, pp. 22–23). This comparison of Mill's is adduced by Urmson as evidence that Mill was a restricted utilitarian, but I do not think that it will bear this interpretation at all. (Though I quite agree with Urmson that many other things said by Mill are in harmony with restricted rather than extreme utilitarianism. Probably Mill had never thought very much about the distinction and was arguing for utilitarianism, restricted or extreme, against other and quite non-utilitarian forms of moral argument.) Mill says: "Nobody argues that the art of navigation is not founded on astronomy, because sailors cannot wait to calculate the Nautical Almanack. Being rational creatures, they go out upon the sea of life with their minds made up on the common questions of right and wrong, as well as on many of the far more difficult questions of wise and foolish. . . . Whatever we adopt as the fundamental principle of morality, we require subordinate principles to apply it." Notice that this is, as it stands, only an argument for subordinate principles as rules of thumb. The example of the nautical almanack is misleading because the informaton given in the almanack is in all cases the same as the information one would get if one made a long and laborious calculation from the original astronomical data on which the almanack is founded. Suppose, however, that astronomy were different. Suppose that the behaviour of the sun, moon and planets was very nearly as it is now, but that on rare occasions there were peculiar irregularities and discontinuities, so that the almanack gave us rules of the form "in 99 percent of cases where the observations are such and such you can deduce that your position is so and so." Furthermore, let us suppose that there were methods which enabled us, by direct and laborious calculation from the original astronomical data, not using the rough and ready tables of the almanack, to get our correct position in 100 percent of cases. Seafarers might use the almanack because they never had time for the long calculations and they were content with the 99 percent chance of success in calculating their positions. Would it not be absurd, however, if they *did* make the direct calculation, and finding that it disagreed with the almanack calculation, nevertheless they ignored it and stuck to the almanack conclusion? Of course the case would be altered if there were a high enough probability of making slips in the direct calculation: then we might stick to the almanack result, liable to error though we knew it to be, simply because the direct calculation would be open to error for a different reason, the fallibility of the computer. This would be analogous to the case of the extreme utilitarian who abides by the conventional rule against the dictates of his utilitarian calculations simply because he thinks that his calculations are probably affected by personal bias. But if the navigator were sure of his direct calculations would he not be foolish to abide by his almanack? I conclude, then, that if we change our suppositions about astronomy and the almanack (to which there are no exceptions) to bring the case into line with that of morality (to whose rules there are exceptions), Mill's example loses its appearance of supporting the restricted form of utilitarianism. Let me say once more that I am not here concerned with how ordinary men think about morality but with how they ought to think. We could quite well imagine a race of sailors who acquired a superstitious reverence for their almanack, even though it was only right in 99 percent of cases, and who indignantly threw overboard any man who mentioned the possibility of a direct calculation. But would this behaviour of the sailors be rational?

Let us consider a much discussed sort of case in which the extreme utilitarian might go against the conventional moral rule. I have promised to a friend, dying on a desert island from which I am subsequently rescued, that I will see that his fortune (over which I have control) is given to a jockey club. However, when I am rescued I decide that it would be better to give the money to a hospital, which can do more good with it. It may be argued that I am wrong to give the money to the hospital. But why? (*a*) The hospital can do more good with the money than the jockey club can. (*b*) The present case is unlike most cases of promising in that no one except me knows about the promise. In breaking the promise I am doing so with complete secrecy and am doing nothing to weaken the general faith in promises. That is, a factor, which would normally keep the extreme utilitarian from promise breaking even in otherwise unoptimific cases, does not at present operate. (*c*) There is no doubt a slight weakening in my own character as an habitual promise keeper, and moreover psychological tensions will be set up in me every time I am asked what the man made me promise him to do. For clearly I shall have to say that he made me promise to give the money to the hospital, and, since I am an habitual truth teller, this will go very much against the grain with me. Indeed I am pretty sure that in practice I myself would keep the promise. But we are not discusing what my moral habits would probably make me do; we are discussing what I ought to do. Moreover, we must not forget that even if it would be most rational of me to give the money to the hospital it would also be most rational of you to punish or condemn me if you did, most improbably, find out the truth (e.g. by finding a note washed ashore in a bottle). Furthermore, I would agree that though it was most rational of me to give the money to the hospital it would be most rational of you to condemn me for it. We revert again to Sidgwick's distinction between the utility of the action and the utility of the praise of it.

Many such issues are discussed by A. K. Stout in the article to which I have already referred. I do not wish to go over the same ground again, especially as I think that Stout's arguments support my own point of view. It will be useful, however, to consider one other example that he gives. Suppose that during hot weather there is an edict that no water must be used for watering gardens. I have a garden and I reason that most people are sure to obey the edict, and that as the amount of water that I use will be by itself negligible no harm will be done if I use the water secretly. So I do use the water, thus producing some lovely flowers which give happiness to various people. Still, you may say, though the action was perhaps optimific, it was unfair and wrong.

There are several matters to consider. Certainly my action should be condemned. We revert once more to Sidgwick's distinction. A right action may be rationally condemned. Furthermore, this sort of offence is normally found out. If I have a wonderful garden when everybody else's is dry and brown there is only one explanation. So if I water my garden I am weakening my respect for law and order, and as this leads to bad results an extreme utilitarian would agree that I was wrong to water the garden. Suppose now that the case is altered and that I can keep the thing secret: there is a secluded part of the garden where I grow flowers which I give away anonymously to a home for old ladies. Are you still so sure that I did the wrong thing by watering my garden? However, this is still a weaker case than that of the hospital and the jockey club. There will be tensions set up within myself: my secret knoweldge that I have broken the rule will make it hard for me to exhort others to keep the rule. These psychological ill effects in myself may not be inconsiderable: directly and indirectly they may lead to harm which is at least of the same order as the happiness that the old ladies get from the flowers. You can see that on an extreme utilitarian view there are two sides to the question.

So far I have been considering the duty of an extreme utilitarian in a predominantly non-utilitarian society. The case is altered if we consider the extreme utilitarian who lives in a society every member, or most members, of which can be expected to reason as he does. Should he water his flowers now? (Granting, what is doubtful, that in the case already considered he would have been right to water his flowers.) As a first approximation, the answer is that he should not do so. For since the situation is a completely symmetrical one, what is rational for him is rational for others. Hence, by a *reductio ad absurdum* argument, it would seem that watering his garden would be rational for none. Nevertheless, a more refined analysis shows that the above argument is not quite correct, though it is correct enough for practical purposes. The argument considers each person as confronted with the choice either of watering his garden or of not watering it. However there is a third possibility, which is that each person should, with the aid of a suitable randomizing device, such as throwing dice, give himself a certain probability of watering his garden. This would be to adopt what in the theory of games is called "a mixed strategy." If we could give numerical values to the private benefit of garden watering and to the public harm done by 1 2, 3, etc., persons using the water in this way, we could work out a value of the probability of watering his garden that each extreme utilitarian should give himself. Let a be the value which each extreme utilitarian gets from watering his garden, and let $f(1)$, $f(2)$, $f(3)$, etc., be the public harm done by exactly 1, 2, 3, etc., persons respectively watering their gardens. Suppose that p is the probability that each person gives himself of watering his garden. Then we can easily calculate, as functions of p, the probabilities that exactly 1, 2, 3, etc., persons will water their gardens. Let these probabilities be $p_1, p_2, \ldots p_n$. Then the total net probable benefit can be expresed as

$$V = p_1(a - f(1)) + p_2(2a - f(2)) + \ldots p_n(na - f(n))$$

Then if we know the function of $f(x)$ we can calculate the value of p for which $(dV/dp) = 0$. This gives the value of p which it would be rational for each extreme utilitarian to adopt. The present argument does not of course depend on a perhaps unjustified assumption that the values in question are measurable, and in a practical case such as that of the garden watering we can doubtless assume that p will be so small that we can take it near enough as equal to zero. However the argument is of interest for the theoretical underpinning of extreme utilitarianism, since the possibility of a mixed strategy is usually neglected by critics of utilitarianism, who wrongly assume that the only relevant and symmetrical alternatives are of the form "everybody does *X*" and "nobody does *X*."[1]

I now pass on to a type of case which may be thought to be the trump card of restricted utilitarianism. Consider the rule of the road. It may be said that since all that matters is that everyone should do the same it is indifferent which rule we have, "go on the left-hand side" or "go on the right-hand side." Hence the only *reason* for going on the left-hand side in British countries is that this is the rule. Here the rule does seem to be a reason, in itself, for acting in a certain way. I wish to argue against this. The rule in itself is not a reason for our actions. We would be perfectly justified in going on the right-hand side if (*a*) we knew that the rule was to go on the left-hand side, and (*b*) we were in a country peopled by super-anarchists who always on principle did the opposite of what they were told. This shows that the rule does not give us a reason for acting so much as an indication of the probable actions of others, which helps us to find out what would be our own most rational course of action. If we are in a country not peopled by anarchists, but by non-anarchist extreme Utilitarians, we expect, other things being equal, that they will keep rules laid down for them. Knoweldge of the rule enables us to predict their behaviour and to harmonize our own actions with theirs. The rule "keep to the left-hand side," then, is not a logical *reason* for action but an anthropological *datum* for planning actions.

I conclude that in every case if there is a rule *R* the keeping of which is in general optimific, but such that in a special sort of circumstances the optimific behaviour is to break *R*, then in these circumstances we should break *R*. Of course we must consider all the less obvious effects of breaking *R*, such as reducing people's faith in the moral order, before coming to the conclusion that to break *R* is right: in fact we shall rarely come to such a conclusion. Moral rules, on the extreme utilitarian view, are rules of thumb only, but they are not bad rules of thumb. But if we *do* come to the conclusion that we should break the rule and if we have weighed in the balance of our own fallibility and liability to personal bias, what good reason remains for keeping the rule? I can understand "it is optimific" as a reason for action, but why should "it is a member of a class of actions which are usually optimific" or "it is a member of a class of actions which as a class are more optimific than any alternative general class" be a good reason? You might as well say that a person ought to be picked to play for Australia just because all his brothers have been, or that the Australian team should be compose entirely of the Harvey family because this would be better than composing it entirely of any other family. The extreme utilitarian does not appeal to artificial feelings, but only to our feelings of benevolence, and what better feelings can there be to appeal to? Admittedly we can have a pro-attitude to anything, even to rules, but such artificially begotten pro-attitudes smack of superstition. Let us get down to realities, human happiness and misery, and make these the objects of our pro-attitudes and anti-attitudes.

The restricted utilitarian might say that he is talking only of *morality,* not of such things as rules of the road. I am not sure how far this objection, if valid, would affect my argument, but in any case I would reply that as a philosopher I conceive of ethics as the study of how it would be *most rational* to act. If my opponent wishes to restrict the word "morality" to a narrower use he can have the word. The fundamental question is the question of rationality of action *in general.* Similarly if the restricted utilitarian were to appeal to ordinary usage and say "it might be most rational to leave Hitler to drown but it would surely not be *wrong* to rescue him," I should again let him have the words "right" and "wrong" and should stick to "rational" and "irrational." We already saw that it would be rational to praise Hitler's rescuer, even though it would have been most rational not to have rescued Hitler. In ordinary language, no doubt, "right" and "wrong" have not only the meaning "most rational to do" and "not most rational to do" but also have the meaning "praiseworthy" and "not praiseworthy." Usually to the utility of an action corresponds utility of praise of it, but as we saw, this is not always so. Moral language could thus do with tidying up, for example by reserving "right" for "most rational" and "good" as an epithet of praise for the motive from which the action sprang. It would be more becoming in a philosopher to try to iron out illogicalities in moral language and to make suggestions for its reform than to use it as a court of appeal whereby to perpetuate confusions.

One last defence of restricted utilitarianism might be as follows. "Act optimifically" might be regarded as itself one of the rules of our system (though it would be odd to say that this rule was justified by its optimificality). According to Toulmin (*The Place of Reason in Ethics,* pp. 146–8) if "keep promises," say, conflicts with another rule we are allowed to argue the case on its merits, as if we were extreme utilitarians. If "act optimifically" is itself one of our rules then there will always be a conflict of rules whenever to keep a rule is not itself optimific. If this is so, restricted utilitarianism collapses into extreme utilitarianism. And no one could read Toulmin's book or Urmson's article on Mill without thinking that Toulmin and Urmson are of the opinion that they have thought of a doctrine which does *not* collapse into extreme utilitarianism, but which is, on the contrary, an improvement on it.

Note

1. [This paragraph has been substantially emended by the author. Ed. *(in original)*]

Utilitarianism and Integrity

BERNARD WILLIAMS

[L]et us look more concretely at two examples, to see what utilitarianism might say about them, what we might say about utilitarianism and, most importantly of all, what would be implied by certain ways of thinking about the situations. The examples are inevitably schematized, and they are open to the objection that they beg as many questions as they illuminate. There are two ways in particular in which examples in moral philosophy tend to beg important questions. One is that, as presented, they arbitrarily cut off and restrict the range of alternative courses of action—this objection might particularly be made against the first of my two examples. The second is that they inevitably present one with the situation as a going concern, and cut off questions about how the agent got into it, and correspondingly about moral considerations which might flow from that: this objection might perhaps specially arise with regard to the second of my two situations. These difficulties, however, just have to be accepted, and if anyone finds these examples cripplingly defective in this sort of respect, then he must in his own thought rework them in richer and less question-begging form. If he feels that no presentation of any imagined situation can ever be other than misleading in morality, and that there can never be any substitute for the concrete experienced complexity of actual moral situations, then this discussion, with him, must certainly grind to a halt: but then one may legitimately wonder whether every discussion with him about conduct will not grind to a halt, including any discussion about the actual situations, since discussion about how one would think and feel about situations somewhat different from the actual (that is to say, situations to that extent imaginary) plays an important role in discussion of the actual.

(I) George, who has just taken his Ph.D. in chemistry, finds it extremely difficult to get a job. He is not very robust in health, which cuts down the number of jobs he might be able to do satisfactorily. His wife has to go out to work to keep them, which itself causes a great deal of strain, since they have small children and there are severe problems about looking after them. The results of all this, especially on the children, are damaging. An older chemist, who knows about this situation, says that he can get George a decently paid job in a certain laboratory, which pursues research into chemical and biological warfare. George says that he cannot accept this, since he is opposed to chemical and biological warfare. The older man replies that he is not too keen on it himself, come to that, but after all George's refusal is not going to make the job or the laboratory go away; what is more, he happens to know that if George refuses the job, it will certainly go to a contemporary of George's who is not inhibited by any such scruples and is likely if appointed to push along the research with greater zeal than George would. Indeed, it is not merely concern for George and his family, but (to speak frankly and in confidence) some alarm about this other man's excess of zeal, which had led the older man to offer to use his influence to get George the job. . . . George's wife, to whom he is deeply attached, has views (the details of which need not concern us) from which it follows that at least there is nothing particularly

From *Utilitarianism: For and Against,* ed. J. J. C. Smart and B. Williams (Cambridge: Cambridge University Press, 1973), pp. 96–117.

wrong with research into CBW. What should he do?

(2) Jim finds himself in the central square of a small South American town. Tied up against the wall are a row of twenty Indians, most terrified, a few defiant, in front of them several armed men in uniform. A heavy man in a sweat-stained khaki shirt turns out to be the captain in charge and, after a good deal of questioning of Jim which establishes that he got there by accident while on a botanical expedition, explains that the Indians are a random group of the inhabitants who, after recent acts of protest against the government, are just about to be killed to remind other possible protestors of the advantages of not protesting. However, since Jim is an honoured visitor from another land, the captain is happy to offer him a guest's privilege of killing one of the Indians himself. If Jim accepts, then as a special mark of the occasion, the other Indians will be let off. Of course, if Jim refuses, then there is no special occasion, and Pedro here will do what he was about to do when Jim arrived, and kill them all. Jim, with some desperate recollection of schoolboy fiction, wonders whether if he got hold of a gun, he could hold the captain, Pedro and the rest of the soldiers to threat, but it is quite clear from the set-up that nothing of that kind is going to work: any attempt at that sort of thing will mean that all the Indians will be killed, and himself. The men against the wall, and the other villagers, understand the situation, and are obviously begging him to accept. What should he do?

To these dilemmas, it seems to me that utilitarianism replies, in the first case, that George should accept the job, and in the second, that Jim should kill the Indian. Not only does utilitarianism give these answers but, if the situations are essentially as described and there are no further special factors, it regards them, it seems to me, as *obviously* the right answers. But many of us would certainly wonder whether, in (I), that could possibly be the right answer at all; and in the case of (2), even one who came to think that perhaps that was the answer, might well wonder whether it was obviously the answer. Nor is it just a question of the rightness or obviousness of these answers. It is also a question of what sort of considerations come into finding the answer. A feature of utilitarianism is that it cuts out a kind of consideration which for some others makes a difference to what they feel about such cases: a consideration involving the idea, as we might first and very simply put it, that each of us is specially responsible for what *he* does, rather than for what other people do. This is an idea closely connected with the value of integrity. It is often suspected that utilitarianism, at least in its direct forms, makes integrity as a value more or less unintelligible. I shall try to show that this suspicion is correct. Of course, even if that is correct, it would not necessarily follow that we should reject utilitarianism; perhaps, as utilitarians sometimes suggest, we should just forget about integrity, in favour of such things as a concern for the general good. However, if I am right, we cannot merely do that, since the reason why utilitarianism cannot understand integrity is that it cannot coherently describe the relations between a man's projects and his actions.

Two Kinds of Remoter Effect

A lot of what we have to say about this question will be about the relations between my projects and other people's projects. But before we get on to that, we should first ask whether we are assuming too hastily what the utilitarian answers to the dilemmas will be. In terms of more direct effects of the possible decisions, there does not indeed seem much doubt about the answer in either case; but it might be said that in terms of more remote or less evident effects counterweights might be found to enter the utilitarian scales. Thus the effect on George of a decision to take the job might be invoked, or its effect on others who might know of his decision. The possibility of there being more beneficent labours in the future from which he might be barred or disqualified, might be mentioned; and so forth. Such effects—in particular, possible effects on the agent's character, and effects on the public at large—are often invoked by utilitarian writers dealing with problems about lying or promise-breaking, and some similar considerations might be invoked here.

There is one very general remark that is worth making about arguments of this sort. The certainty that attaches to these hypotheses about possible effects is usually pretty low; in some cases, indeed, the hypothesis invoked is so implausible that it would scarcely pass if it were not being used to deliver the respectable moral answer, as in the standard fantasy that one of the effects of one's telling a particular lie is to weaken the disposition of the world at large to tell the truth. The demands on the certainty or probability of these beliefs as beliefs about particular actions are much milder than they would be on beliefs favouring the unconventional course. It may be said that this is as it should be, since the presumption must be in favour of the conventional course: but that scarcely seems a *utilitarian* answer, unless utilitarianism has already taken off in the direction of not applying the consequences to the particular act at all.

Leaving aside that very general point, I want to consider now two types of effect that are often invoked by utilitarians, and which might be invoked in connexion with these imaginary cases. The attitude or tone involved in invoking these effects may sometimes seem peculiar; but that sort of peculiarity soon becomes familiar in utilitarian discussions, and indeed it can be something of an achievement to retain a sense of it.

First, there is the psychological effect on the agent. Our descriptions of these situations have not so far taken account of how George or Jim will be after they have taken the one course or the other; and it might be said that if they take the course which seemed at first the utilitarian one, the effects on them will be in fact bad enough and extensive enough to cancel out the initial utilitarian advantages of that course. Now there is one version of this effect in which, for a utilitarian, some confusion must be involved, namely that in which the agent feels bad, his subsequent conduct and relations are crippled and so on, *because he thinks that he has done the wrong thing*—for if the balance of outcomes was as it appeared to be *before* invoking this effect, then he has not (from the utilitarian point of view) done the wrong thing. So that version of the effect, for a rational and utilitarian agent, could not possibly make any difference to the assessment of right and wrong. However, perhaps he is not a thoroughly rational agent, and is disposed to have bad feelings, whichever he decided to do. Now such feelings, which are from a strictly utilitarian point of view irrational—nothing, a utilitarian can point out, is advanced by having them—cannot, consistently, have any great weight in a utilitarian calculation. I shall consider in a moment an argument to suggest that they should have no weight at all in it. But short of that, the utilitarian could reasonably say that such feelings should not be encouraged, even if we accept their existence, and that to give them a lot of weight is to encourage them. Or, at the very best, even if they are straightforwardly and without any discount to be put into the calculation, their weight must be small: they are after all (and at best) one man's feelings.

That consideration might seem to have particular force in Jim's case. In George's case, his feelings represent a larger proportion of what is to be weighed, and are more commensurate in character with other items in the calculation. In Jim's case, however, his feelings might seem to be of very little weight compared with other things that are at stake. There is a powerful and recognizable appeal that can be made on this point: as that a refusal by Jim to do what he has been invited to do would be a kind of self-indulgent squeamishness. That is an appeal which can be made by other than utilitarians—indeed, there are some uses of it which cannot be consistently made by utilitarians, as when it essentially involves the idea that there is something dishonourable about such self-indulgence. But in some versions it is a familiar, and it must be said a powerful, weapon of utilitarianism. One must be clear, though, about what it can and cannot accomplish. The most it can do, so far as I can see, is to invite one to consider how seriously, and for what reasons, one feels that what one is invited to do is (in these circumstances) wrong, and in particular, to consider that question from the utilitarian point of view. When the agent is not seeing the situation from a utilitarian point of view, the appeal cannot force him to do so; and if he does come round to seeing it from a utilitarian point of view, there is virtually nothing left for the appeal to do. If he does not see it from a utilitarian point of view, he will not see his resistance to the invitation, and the unpleasant feelings he associates with accepting it, *just* as disagreeable experiences of his; they figure rather as emotional expressions of a thought that to accept would be wrong. He may be asked, as by the appeal, to consider whether he is right, and indeed whether he is fully serious, in thinking that. But the assertion of the appeal, that he is being self-indulgently squeamish, will not itself answer that question, or even help to answer it, since it essentially tells him to regard his feelings just as unpleasant experiences of his, and he cannot, by doing that, answer the question they pose when they are precisely not so regarded, but are regarded as indications of what he thinks is right and wrong. If he does come round fully to the utilitarian point of view then of course he will regard these feelings just as unpleasant experiences of his. And once Jim—at least—has come to see them in that light, there is nothing left for the appeal to do, since *of course* his feelings so regarded, are of virtually no weight at all in relation to the other things at stake. The "squeamishness" appeal is not an argument which adds in a hitherto neglected consideration. Rather, it is an invitation to consider the situation, and one's own feelings, from a utilitarian point of view.

The reason why the squeamishness appeal can be very unsettling, and one can be unnerved by the suggestion of self-indulgence in going against utilitarian considerations, is not that we are utilitarians who are uncertain what utilitarian value to attach to our moral feelings, but that we are partially at least not utilitarians, and cannot regard our moral feelings merely as objects of utilitarian value. Because our moral relation to the world is partly given by such feelings, and by a sense of what we can or cannot "live with," to come to regard those feelings from a purely utilitarian point of view, that is to say, as happenings outside one's moral self, is to lose a sense of one's moral identity; to lose, in the most literal way, one's integrity. At this point utilitarianism alienates one from one's moral feelings; we shall see a little later how, more basically, it alienates one from one's actions as well.

If, then, one is really going to regard one's feelings from a strictly utilitarian point of view, Jim should give very little weight at all to his; it seems almost indecent, in fact, once one has taken that point of view, to suppose that he should give any at all. In George's case one might feel that things were slightly different. It is interesting, though, that one reason why one might think that—namely that one person principally affected is his wife—is very dubiously available to a utilitarian. George's wife has some reason to be interested in George's integrity and his sense of it; the Indians, quite properly, have no interest in Jim's. But it is not at all clear how utilitarianism would describe that difference.

There is an argument, and a strong one, that a strict utilitarian should give not merely small extra weight, in calculations of right and wrong, to feelings of this kind, but that he should give absolutely no weight to them at all. This is based on the point, which we have already seen, that if a course of action is, before taking these sorts of feelings into account, utilitarianly preferable, then bad feelings about that kind of action will be from a utilitarian point of view irrational. Now it might be thought that even if that is so, it would not mean that in a utilitarian calculation such feelings should not be taken into account; it is after all a well-known boast of utilitarianism that it is a realistic outlook which seeks the best in the world as it is, and takes any form of happiness or unhappiness into account. While a utilitarian will no doubt seek to diminish the incidence of feelings which are utilitarianly irrational—or at least of disagreeable feelings which are so—he might be expected to take them into account while they exist. This is without doubt classical utilitarian doctrine, but there is good reason to think that utilitarianism cannot stick to it without embracing results which are startlingly unacceptable and perhaps self-defeating.

Suppose that there is in a certain society a racial minority. Considering merely the ordinary interests of the other citizens, as opposed to their sentiments, this minority does no particular harm; we may suppose that it does not confer any very great benefits either. Its presence is in those terms neutral or mildly beneficial. However, the other citizens have such prejudices that they find the sight of this group, even the knowledge of its presence, very disagreeable. Proposals are made for removing in some way this minority. If we assume various quite plausible things (as that programmes to change the majority sentiment are likely to be protracted and ineffective) then even if the removal would be unpleasant for the minority, a utilitarian calculation might well end up favouring this step, especially if the minority were a rather small minority and the majority were very severely prejudiced, that is to say, were made very severely uncomfortable by the presence of the minority.

A utilitarian might find that conclusion embarrassing; and not merely because of its nature, but because of the grounds on which it is reached. While a utilitarian might be expected to take into account certain other sorts of consequences of the prejudice, as that a majority prejudice is likely to be displayed in conduct disagreeable to the minority, and so forth, he might be made to wonder whether the unpleasant experiences of the prejudiced people should be allowed, *merely as such,* to count. If he does count them, merely as such, then he has once more separated himself from a body of ordinary moral thought which he might have hoped to accommodate; he may also have started on the path of defeating his own view of things. For one feature of these sentiments is that they are from the utilitarian point of view itself irrational, and a thoroughly utilitarian person would either not have them, or if he found that he did tend to have them, would himself seek to discount them. Since the sentiments in question are such that a rational utilitarian would discount them in himself, it is reasonable to suppose that he should discount them in his calculations about society; it does seem quite unreasonable for him to give just as much weight to feelings—considered just in themselves, one must recall, as experiences of those that have them—which are essentially based on views which are from a utilitarian point of view irrational, as to those which accord with utilitarian principles. Granted this idea, it seems reasonable for him to rejoin a body of moral thought in other respects congenial to him, and discount those sentiments, just considered in themselves, totally, on the principle that no pains or discomforts are to count in the utilitarian sum which their subjects have just because they hold views which are by utilitarian standards irrational. But if he accepts that, then in the cases we are at present considering no extra weight at all can be put in for bad feelings of George or Jim about their choices, if those choices are, leaving out those feelings, on the first round utilitarianly rational.

The psychological effect on the agent was the first of two general effects considered by utilitarians, which had to be discussed. The second is in general a more substantial item, but it need not take so long, since it is both clearer and has little application to the present cases. This is the *precedent effect*. As Burke rightly emphasized, this effect can be important: that one morally *can* do what someone has actually done, is a psychologically effective principle, if not a deontically valid one. For the effect to operate, obviously some conditions must hold on the publicity of the act and on such things as the status of the agent (such considerations weighed importantly with Sir Thomas More); what these may be will vary evidently with circumstances.

In order for the precedent effect to make a difference to a utilitarian calculation, it must be based upon a confusion. For suppose that there is an act which would be the best in the circumstances, except that doing it will encourage by precedent other people to do things which will not be the best things to do. Then the situation of those other people must be relevantly different from that of the original agent; if it were not, then in doing the same as what would be the best course for the original agent, they would necessarily do the best thing themselves. But if the situations are in this way relevantly different, it must be a confused perception which takes the first situation, and the agent's course in it, as an adequate precedent for the second.

However, the fact that the precedent effect, if it really makes a difference, is in this sense based on a confusion, does not mean that it is not perfectly real, nor that it is to be discounted: social effects are by their nature confused in this sort of way. What it does emphasize is that calculations of the precedent effect have got to be realistic, involving considerations of how people are actually likely to be influenced. In the present examples, however, it is very implausible to think that the precedent effect could be invoked to make any difference to the calculation. Jim's case is extraordinary enough, and it is hard to imagine who the recipients of the effect might be supposed to be; while George is not in a sufficiently public situation or role for the question to arise in that form, and in any case one might suppose that the motivations of others on such an issue were quite likely to be fixed one way or another already.

No appeal, then, to these other effects is going

to make a difference to what the utilitarian will decide about our examples. Let us now look more closely at the structure of those decisions.

Integrity

The situations have in common that if the agent does not do a certain disagreeable thing, someone else will, and in Jim's situation at least the result, the state of affairs after the other man has acted, if he does, will be worse than after Jim has acted, if Jim does. The same, on a smaller scale, is true of George's case. I have already suggested that it is inherent in consequentialism that it offers a strong doctrine of negative responsibility: if I know that if I do *X*, O_1 will eventuate, and if I refrain from doing *X*, O_2 will, and that O_2 is worse than O_1, then I am responsible for O_2 if I refrain voluntarily from doing *X*. "You could have prevented it," as will be said, and truly, to Jim, if he refuses, by the relatives of the other Indians. . . .

In the present cases, the situation of O_2 includes another agent bringing about results worse than O_1. So far as O_2 has been identified up to this point—merely as the worse outcome which will eventuate if I refrain from doing *X*—we might equally have said that what that other brings about is O_2; but that would be to underdescribe the situation. For what occurs if Jim refrains from action is not solely twenty Indians dead, but *Pedro's killing twenty Indians,* and that is not a result which Pedro brings about, though the death of the Indians is. We can say: what one does is not included in the outcome of what one does, while what another does can be included in the outcome of what one does. For that to be so, as the terms are now being used, only a very weak condition has to be satisfied: for Pedro's killing the Indians to be the outcome of Jim's refusal, it only has to be causally true that if Jim had not refused, Pedro would not have done it.

That may be enough for us to speak, in some sense, of Jim's responsibility for that outcome, if it occurs; but it is certainly not enough, it is worth noticing, for us to speak of Jim's *making* those things happen. For granted this way of their coming about, he could have made them happen only by making Pedro shoot, and there is no acceptable sense in which his refusal makes Pedro shoot. If the captain had said on Jim's refusal, "you leave me with no alternative," he would have been lying, like most who use that phrase. While the deaths, and the killing, may be the outcome of Jim's refusal, it is misleading to think, in such a case, of Jim having an *effect* on the world through the medium (as it happens) of Pedro's acts; for this is to leave Pedro out of the picture in his essential role of one who has intentions and projects, projects for realizing which Jim's refusal would leave an opportunity. Instead of thinking in terms of supposed effects of Jim's projects on Pedro, it is more revealing to think in terms of the effects of Pedro's projects on Jim's decision. This is the direction from which I want to criticize the notion of negative responsibility.

. . . .

What projects does a utilitarian agent have? As a utilitarian, he has the general project of bringing about maximally desirable outcomes; how he is to do this at any given moment is a question of what causal levers, so to speak, are at that moment within reach. The desirable outcomes, however, do not just consist of agents carrying out *that* project; there must be other more basic or lower-order projects which he and other agents have, and the desirable outcomes are going to consist, in part, of the maximally harmonious realization of those projects ("in part," because one component of a utilitarianly desirable outcome may be the occurrence of agreeable experiences which are not the satisfaction of anybody's projects). Unless there were first-order projects, the general utilitarian project would have nothing to work on, and would be vacuous. What do the more basic or lower-order projects comprise? Many will be the obvious kinds of desires for things for oneself, one's family, one's friends, including basic necessities of life, and in more relaxed circumstances, objects of taste. Or there may be pursuits and interests of an intellectual, cultural or creative character. I introduce those as a separate class not because the objects of them lie in a separate class, and provide—as some utilitarians, in their churchy way, are fond of saying—"higher" pleasures. I introduce them separately because the agent's identification with them may be of a different order. It does not have to be: cultural and aesthetic interests just belong, for many, along with any other taste; but some people's commitment to these kinds of interests just is at once more thoroughgoing and serious than their pursuit of various objects of taste, while it is more individual and permeated with character than the desire for the necessities for life.

Beyond these, someone may have projects connected with his support of some cause: Zionism, for instance, or the abolition of chemical and biological warfare. Or there may be projects which flow from some more general disposition towards human conduct and character, such as a hatred of injustice, or of cruelty, or of killing.

It may be said that this last sort of disposition and its associated project do not count as (logically) "lower-order" relative to the higher-order project of maximizing desirable outcomes; rather, it may be said, it is itself a "higher-order" project. The vital question is not, however, how it is to be classified, but whether it and similar projects are to count among the projects whose satisfaction is to be included in the maximizing sum, and, correspondingly, as contributing to the agent's happiness. If the utilitarian says "no" to that, then he is almost certainly committed to a version of utilitarianism as absurdly superficial and shallow as Benthamite versions have often been accused of being. For this project will be discounted, presumably, on the ground that it involves, in the specification of its object, the mention of other people's happiness or interests: thus it is the kind or project which (unlike the pursuit of food for myself) presupposes a reference to other people's projects. But that criterion would eliminate any desire at all which was not blankly and in the most straightforward sense egoistic.[1] Thus we should be reduced to frankly egoistic first-order projects, and—for all essential purposes—the one second-order utilitarian project of maximally satisfying first-order projects. Utilitarianism has a tendency to slide in this direction, and to leave a vast hole in the range of human desires, between egoistic inclinations and necessities at one end, and impersonally benevolent happiness-management at the other. But the utilitarianism which has to leave this hole is the most primitive form, which offers a quite rudimentary account of desire. Modern versions of the theory are supposed to be neutral with regard to what sorts of things make people happy or what their projects are. Utilitarianism would do well then to acknowledge the evident fact that among the things that make people happy is not only making other people happy, but being taken up or involved in any of a vast range of projects, or—if we waive the evangelical and moralizing associations of the word—commitments. One can be committed to such things as a person, a cause, an institution, a career, one's own genius, or the pursuit of danger.

Now none of these is itself the *pursuit of happiness:* by an exceedingly ancient platitude, it is not at all clear that there could be anything which was just that, or at least anything that had the slightest chance of being successful. Happiness, rather, requires being involved in, or at least content with, something else.[2] It is not impossible for utilitarianism to accept that point: it does not have to be saddled with a naïve and absurd philosophy of mind about the relation between desire and happiness. What it does have to say is that if such commitments are worth while, then pursuing the projects that flow from them, and realizing some of those projects, will make the person for whom they are worth while, happy. It may be that to claim that is still wrong: it may well be that a commitment can make sense to a man (can make sense of his life) without his supposing that it will make him *happy*. But that is not the present point; let us grant to utilitarianism that all worthwhile human projects must conduce, one way or another, to happiness. The point is that even if that is true, it does not follow, nor could it possibly be true, that those projects are themselves projects of pursuing happiness. One has to believe in, or at least want, or quite minimally, be content with, other things, for there to be anywhere that happiness can come from.

Utilitarianism, then, should be willing to agree that its general aim of maximizing happiness does not imply that what everyone is doing is just pursuing happiness. On the contrary, people have to be pursuing other things. What those other things may be, utilitarianism, sticking to its professed empirical stance, should be prepared just to find out. No doubt some possible projects it will want to discourage, on the grounds that their being pursued involves a negative balance of happiness to others: though even there, the unblinking accountant's eye of the strict utilitarian will have something to put in the positive column, the satisfactions of the destructive agent. Beyond that, there will be a vast variety of generally beneficent or at least harmless projects; and some no doubt, will take the form not just of tastes or fancies, but of what I have called "commitments." It may even be that the utilitarian researcher will find that many of those with commitments, who have really identified themselves with objects outside themselves, who are thoroughly involved with other persons, or institutions, or activities or causes, are actually happier than those whose projects and wants are not like that. If so, that is an important piece of utilitarian empirical love.

. . . .

Let us now go back to the agent as utilitarian, and his higher-order project of maximizing desirable outcomes. At this level, he is committed only to that: what the outcome will actually consist of will depend entirely on the facts, on what persons with what projects and what potential satisfactions there are within calculable reach of the causal levers near which he finds himself. His own substantial projects and commitments come into it, but only as one lot among others—they potentially provide one set of satisfactions among those which he may be able to assist from where he happens to be. He is the agent of the satisfaction system who happens to be at a particular point at a particular time: in Jim's case, our man in South America. His own decisions as a utilitarian agent are a function of all the satisfactions which he can affect from where he is: and this means that the projects of others, to an indeterminately great extent, determine his decision.

This may be so either positively or negatively. It will be so positively if agents within the causal field of his decision have projects which are at any rate harmless, and so should be assisted. It will equally be so, but negatively, if there is an agent within the causal field whose projects are harmful, and have to be frustrated to maximize desirable outcomes. So it is with Jim and the soldier Pedro. On the utilitarian view, the undesirable projects of other people as much determine, in this negative way, one's decisions as the desirable ones do positively: if those people were not there, or had different projects, the causal nexus would be different, and it is the actual state of the causal nexus which determines the decision. The determination to an indefinite degree of my decisions by other people's projects is just another aspect of my unlimited responsibility to act for the best in a causal framwork formed to a considerable extent by their projects.

The decision so determined is, for utilitarianism, the right decision. But what if it conflicts with some project of mine? This, the utilitarian will say, has already been dealt with: the satisfaction to you of fulfilling your project, and any satisfactions to others of your so doing, have already been through the calculating device and have been found inadequate. Now in the case of many sorts of projects, that is a perfectly reasonable sort of answer. But in the case of projects of the sort I have called "commitments," those with which one is more deeply and extensively involved and identified, this cannot just by itself be an adequate answer, and there may be no adequate answer at all. For, to take the extreme sort of case, how can a man, as a utilitarian agent, come to regard as one satisfaction among others, and a dispensable one, a project or attitude round which he has built his life, just because someone else's projects have so structured the causal scene that that is how the utilitarian sum comes out?

The point here is not, as utilitarians may hasten to say, that if the project or attitude is that central to his life, then to abandon it will be very disagreeable to him and great loss of utility will be involved. I have already argued [earlier] that it is not like that; on the contrary, once he is prepared to look at it like that, the argument in any serious case is over anyway. The point is that he is identified with his actions as flowing from projects and attitudes which in some cases he takes seriously at the deepest level, as what his life is about (or, in some cases, this section of his life—seriousness is not necessarily the same as persistence). It is absurd to demand of such a man, when the sums come in from the utility network which the projects of others have in part determined, that he should just step aside from his own project and decision and acknowledge the decision which utilitarian calculation requires. It is to alienate him in a real sense from his actions and the source of his action in his own convictions. It is to make him into a channel between the input of everyone's projects, including his own, and an output of optimific decision; but this is to neglect the extent to which *his* actions and *his* decisions have to be seen as the actions and decisions which flow from the projects and attitudes with which he is most closely identified. It is thus, in the most literal sense, an attack on his integrity.

Notes

1. On the subject of egoistic and non-egoistic desires, see 'Egoism and altruism', in *Problems of the Self* (Cambridge University Press, London, 1973).
2. This does not imply that there is no such thing as the project of pursuing pleasure. Some writers who have correctly resisted the view that all desires are desires for pleasure, have given an account of pleasure so thoroughly adverbial as to leave it quite unclear how there could be a distinctively hedonist way of life at all. Some room has to be left for that, though there are important difficulties both in defining it and living it. Thus (particularly in the case of the very rich) it often has highly ritual aspects, apparently part of a strategy to counter boredom.

Famine, Affluence, and Morality

PETER SINGER

Peter Singer (1946–) is a professor of philosophy at Monash University. His publications include *Democracy and Disobedience, Animal Liberation,* and *Practical Ethics.*

As I write this, in November 1971, people are dying in East Bengal from lack of food, shelter, and medical care. The suffering and death that are occurring there now are not inevitable, not unavoidable in any fatalistic sense of the term. Constant poverty, a cyclone, and a civil war have turned at least nine million people into destitute refugees; nevertheless, it is not beyond the capacity of the richer nations to give enough assistance to reduce any further suffering to very small proportions. The decisions and actions of human beings can prevent this kind of suffering. Unfortunately, human beings have not made the necessary decisions. At the individual level, people have, with very few exceptions, not responded to the situation in any significant way. Generally speaking, people have not given large sums to relief funds; they have not written to their parliamentary representatives demanding increased government assistance; they have not demonstrated in the streets, held symbolic fasts, or done anything else directed toward providing the refugees with the means to satisfy their essential needs. At the government level, no government has given the sort of massive aid that would enable the refugees to survive for more than a few days. Britain, for instance, has given rather more than most countries. It has, to date, given £14,750,000. For comparative purposes, Britain's share of the nonrecoverable development costs of the Anglo-French Concorde project is already in excess of £275,000,000, and on present estimates will reach £440,000,000. The implication is that the British government values a supersonic transport more than thirty times as highly as it values the lives of the nine million refugees. Australia is another country which, on a per capita basis, is well up in the "aid to Bengal" table. Australia's aid, however, amounts to less than one-twelfth of the cost of Sydney's new opera house. The total amount given, from all sources, now stands at about £65,000,000. The estimated cost of keeping the refugees alive for one year is £464,000,000. Most of the refugees have now been in the camps for more than six months. The World Bank has said that India needs a minimum of £300,000,000 in assistance from other countries before the end of the year. It seems obvious that assistance on this scale will not be forthcoming. India will be forced to choose between letting the refugees starve or diverting funds from her own development program, which will mean that more of her own people will starve in the future.[1]

These are the essential facts about the present situation in Bengal. So far as it concerns us here, there is nothing unique about this situation except its magnitude. The Bengal emergency is just the latest and most acute of a series of major emergencies in various parts of the world, arising both from natural and from man-made causes. There are also many parts of the world in which people die from malnutrition and lack of food independent of any special emergency. I take Ben-

From *Philosophy & Public Affairs* 1, (no. 3 1972), pp. 229–43.

gal as my example only because it is the present concern, and because the size of the problem has ensured that it has been given adequate publicity. Neither individuals nor governments can claim to be unaware of what is happening there.

What are the moral implications of a situation like this? In what follows, I shall argue that the way people in relatively affluent countries react to a situation like that in Bengal cannot be justified; indeed, the whole way we look at moral issues—our moral conceptual scheme—needs to be altered, and with it, the way of life that has come to be taken for granted in our society.

In arguing for this conclusion I will not, of course, claim to be morally neutral. I shall, however, try to argue for the moral position that I take, so that anyone who accepts certain assumptions, to be made explicit, will, I hope, accept my conclusion.

I begin with the assumption that suffering and death from lack of food, shelter, and medical care are bad. I think most people will agree about this, although one may reach the same view by different routes. I shall not argue for this view. People can hold all sorts of eccentric positions, and perhaps from some of them it would not follow that death by starvation is in itself bad. It is difficult, perhaps impossible, to refute such positions, and so for brevity I will henceforth take this assumption as accepted. Those who disagree need read no further.

My next point is this: if it is in our power to prevent something bad from happening, without thereby sacrificing anything of comparable moral importance, we ought, morally, to do it. By "without sacrificing anything of comparable moral importance" I mean without causing anything else comparably bad to happen, or doing something that is wrong in itself, or failing to promote some moral good, comparable in significance to the bad thing that we can prevent. This principle seems almost as uncontroversial as the last one. It requires us only to prevent what is bad, and not to promote what is good, and it requires this of us only when we can do it without sacrificing anything that is, from the moral point of view, comparably important. I could even, as far as the application of my argument to the Bengal emergency is concerned, qualify the point so as to make it: if it is in our power to prevent something very bad from happening, without thereby sacrificing anything morally significant, we ought, morally, to do it. An application of this principle would be as follows: if I am walking past a shallow pond and see a child drowning in it, I ought to wade in and pull the child out. This will mean getting my clothes muddy, but this is insignificant, while the death of the child would presumably be a very bad thing.

The uncontroversial appearance of the principle just stated is deceptive. If it were acted upon, even in its qualified form, our lives, our society, and our world would be fundamentally changed. For the principle takes, firstly, no account of proximity or distance. It makes no moral difference whether the person I can help is a neighbor's child ten yards from me or a Bengali whose name I shall never know, ten thousand miles away. Secondly, the principle makes no distinction between cases in which I am the only person who could possibly do anything and cases in which I am just one among millions in the same position.

I do not think I need to say much in defense of the refusal to take proximity and distance into account. The fact that a person is physically near to us, so that we have personal contact with him, may make it more likely that we *shall* assist him, but this does not show that we *ought* to help him rather than another who happens to be further away. If we accept any principle of impartiality, universalizability, equality, or whatever, we cannot discriminate against someone merely because he is far away from us (or we are far away from him). Admittedly, it is possible that we are in a better position to judge what needs to be done to help a person near to us than one far away, and perhaps also to provide the assistance we judge to be necessary. If this were the case, it would be a reason for helping those near to us first. This may once have been a justification for being more concerned with the poor in one's own town than with famine victims in India. Unfortunately for those who like to keep their moral responsibilities limited, instant communication and swift transportation have changed the situation. From the moral point of view, the development of the world into a "global village" has made an important, though still unrecognized, difference to our moral situation. Expert observers and supervisors, sent out by famine relief organizations or permanently stationed in famine-prone areas, can direct our aid to a refugee in Bengal almost as effectively as we could get it to someone in our own block. There would seem, therefore, to be no possible justification for discriminating on geographical grounds.

There may be a greater need to defend the second implication of my principle—that the fact there are millions of other people in the same position, in respect to the Bengali refugees, as I am, does not make the situation significantly different from a situation in which I am the only person who can prevent something very bad from occurring. Again, of course, I admit that there is a psychological difference between the cases; one feels less guilty about doing nothing if one can point to others, similarly placed, who have also done nothing. Yet this can make no real difference to our moral obligations.[2] Should I consider that I am less obliged to pull the drowning child out of the pond if on looking around I see other people, no further away than I am, who have also noticed the child but are doing nothing? One has only to ask this question to see the absurdity of the view that numbers lessen obligation. It is a view that is an ideal excuse for inactivity; unfortunately most of the major evils—poverty, overpopulation, pollution—are problems in which everyone is almost equally involved.

The view that numbers do make a difference can be made plausible if stated in this way: if everyone in circumstances like mine gave £5 to the Bengal Relief Fund, there would be enough to provide food, shelter, and medical care for the refugees; there is no reason why I should give more than anyone else in the same circumstances as I am; therefore I have no obligation to give more than £5. Each premise in this argument is true, and the argument looks sound. It may convince us, unless we notice that it is based on a hypothetical premise, although the conclusion is not stated hypothetically. The argument would be sound if the conclusion were: if everyone in circumstances like mine were to give £5, I would have no obligation to give more than £5. If the conclusion were so stated, however, it would be obvious that the argument has no bearing on a situation in which it is not the case that everyone else gives £5. This, of course, is the actual situation. It is more or less certain that not everyone in circumstances like mine will give £5. So there will not be enough to provide the needed food, shelter, and medical care. Therefore by giving more than £5 I will prevent more suffering than I would if I gave just £5.

It might be thought that this argument has an absurd consequence. Since the situation appears to be that very few people are likely to give substantial amounts, it follows that I and everyone else in similar circumstances ought to give as much as possible, that is, at least up to the point at which by giving more one would begin to cause serious suffering for oneself and one's dependents—perhaps even beyond this point to the point of marginal utility, at which by giving more one would cause oneself and one's dependents as much suffering as one would prevent in Bengal. If everyone does this, however, there will be more than can be used for the benefit of the refugees, and some of the sacrifice will have been unnecessary. Thus, if everyone does what he ought to do, the result will not be as good as it would be if everyone did a little less than he ought to do, or if only some do all that they ought to do.

The paradox here arises only if we assume that the actions in question—sending money to the relief funds—are performed more or less simultaneously, and are also unexpected. For if it is to be expected that everyone is going to contribute something, then clearly each is not obliged to give as much as he would have been obliged to had others not been giving too. And if everyone is not acting more or less simultaneously, then those giving later will know how much more is needed, and will have no obligation to give more than is necessary to reach this amount. To say this is not to deny the principle that people in the same circumstances have the same obligations, but to point out that the fact that others have given, or may be expected to give, is a relevant circumstance: those giving after it has become known that many others are giving and those giving before are not in the same circumstances. So the seemingly absurd consequence of the principle I have put forward can occur only if people are in error about the actual circumstances—that is, if they think they are giving when others are not, but in fact they are giving when others are. The result of everyone doing what he really ought to do cannot be worse than the result of everyone doing less than he ought to do, although the result of everyone doing what he reasonably believes he ought to do could be.

If my argument so far has been sound, neither our distance from a preventable evil nor the number of other people who, in respect to that evil, are in the same situation as we are, lessens our obligation to mitigate or prevent that evil. I shall therefore take as established the principle I asserted earlier. As I have already said, I need to assert it only in its qualified form: if it is in our power to prevent something very bad from happening, without thereby sacrificing anything else morally significant, we ought, morally, to do it.

The outcome of this argument is that our traditional moral categroies are upset. The traditional distinction between duty and charity cannot be drawn, or at least, not in the place we normally draw it. Giving money to the Bengal Relief Fund is regarded as an act of charity in our society. The bodies which collect money are known as "charities." These organizations see themselves in this way—if you send them a check, you will be thanked for your "generosity." Because giving money is regarded as an act of charity, it is not thought that there is anything wrong with not giving. The charitable man may be praised, but the man who is not charitable is not condemmed. People do not feel in any way ashamed or guilty about spending money on new clothes or a new car instead of giving it to famine relief. (Indeed, the alternative does not occur to them.) This way of looking at the matter cannot be justified. When we buy new clothes not to keep ourselves warm but to look "well-dressed" we are not providing for any important need. We would not be sacrificing anything significant if we were to continue to wear our old clothes, and give the money to famine relief. By doing so, we would be preventing another person from starving. It follows from what I have said earlier that we ought to give money away, rather than spend it on clothes which we do not need to keep us warm. To do so is not charitable, or generous. Nor is it the kind of act which philosophers and theologians have called "supererogatory"—an act which it would be good to do, but not wrong not to do. On the contrary, we ought to give the money away, and it is wrong not to do so.

I am not maintaining that there are no acts which are charitable, or that there are no acts which it would be good to do but not wrong not to do. It may be possible to redraw the distinction between duty and charity in some other place. All I am arguing here is that the present way of drawing the distinction, which makes it an act of charity for a man living at the level of affluence which most people in the "developed nations" enjoy to give money to save someone else from starvation, cannot be supported. It is beyond the scope of my argument to consider whether the distinction should be redrawn or abolished altogether. There would be many other possible ways of drawing the distinction—for instance, one might decide that it is good to make other people as happy as possible, but not wrong not to do so.

Despite the limited nature of the revision in our moral conceptual scheme which I am proposing, the revision would, given the extent of both affluence and famine in the world today, have radical implications. These implications may lead to further objections, distinct from those I have already considered. I shall discuss two of these.

One objection to the position I have taken might be simply that it is too drastic a revision of our moral scheme. People do not ordinarily judge in the way I have suggested they should. Most people reserve their moral condemnation for those who violate some moral norm, such as the norm against taking another person's property. They do not condemn those who indulge in luxury instead of giving to famine relief. But given that I did not set out to present a morally neutral description of the way people make moral judgments, the way people do in fact judge has nothing to do with the validity of my conclusion. My conclusion follows from the principle which I advanced earlier, and unless that principle is rejected, or the arguments shown to be unsound, I think the conclusion must stand, however strange it appears.

It might, nevertheless, be interesting to consider why our society, and most other societies, do judge differently from the way I have suggested they should. In a well-known article, J. O. Urmson suggests that the imperatives of duty, which tell us what we must do, as distinct from what it would be good to do but not wrong not to do, function so as to prohibit behavior that is intolerable if men are to live together in society.[3] This may explain the origin and continued existence of the present division between acts of duty and acts of charity. Moral attitudes are shaped by the needs of society, and no doubt society needs people who will observe the rules that make social existence tolerable. From the point of view of a particular society, it is essential to prevent violations of norms against killing, stealing, and so on. It is quite inessential, however, to help people outside one's own society.

If this is an explanation of our common distinction between duty and supererogation, however, it is not a justification of it. The moral point of view requires us to look beyond the interests of our own society. Previously, as I have already mentioned, this may hardly have been feasible, but it is quite feasible now. From the moral point of view, the prevention of the starvation of millions of people outside our society must be considered at least as pressing as the upholding of property norms within our society.

It has been argued by some writers, among them Sidgwick and Urmson, that we need to have a basic moral code which is not too far beyond the capacities of the ordinary man, for otherwise there will be a general breakdown of compliance with the moral code. Crudely stated, this argument suggests that if we tell people that they ought to refrain from murder and give everything they do not really need to famine relief, they will do neither, whereas if we tell them that they ought to refrain from murder and that it is good to give to famine relief but not wrong not to do so, they will at least refrain from murder. The issue here is: Where should we draw the line between conduct that is required and conduct that is good although not required, so as to get the best possible result? This would seem to be an empirical question, although a very difficult one. One objection to the Sidgwick–Urmson line of argument is that it takes insufficient account of the effect that moral standards can have on the decisions we make. Given a society in which a wealthy man who gives five percent of his income to famine relief is regarded as most generous, it is not surprising that a proposal that we all ought to give away half our incomes will be thought to be absurdly unrealistic. In a society which held that no man should have more than enough while others have less then they need, such a proposal might seem narrow-minded. What it is possible for a man to do and what he is likely to do are both, I think, very greatly influenced by what people around him are doing and expecting him to do. In any case, the possibility that by spreading the idea that we ought to be doing very much more than we are to relieve famine we shall bring about a general breakdown of moral behavior seems remote. If the stakes are an end to widespread starvation, it is worth the risk. Finally, it should be emphasized that these considerations are relevant only to the issue of what we should require from others, and not to what we ourselves ought to do.

The second objection to my attack on the present distinction between duty and charity is one which has from time to time been made against utilitarianism. It follows from some forms of utilitarian theory that we all ought, morally, to be working full time to increase the balance of happiness over misery. The position I have taken here would not lead to this conclusion in all circumstances, for if there were no bad occurrences that we could prevent without sacrificing something of comparable moral importance, my argument would have no application. Given the present conditions in many parts of the world, however, it does follow from my argument that we ought, morally, to be working full time to relieve great suffering of the sort that occurs as a result of famine or other disasters. Of course, mitigating circumstances can be adduced—for instance, that if we were ourselves out through overwork, we shall be less effective than we would otherwise have been. Nevertheless, when all considerations of this sort have been taken into account, the conclusion remains: we ought to be preventing as much suffering as we can without sacrificing something else of comparable moral importance. This conclusion is one which we may be reluctant to face. I cannot see, though, why it should be regarded as a criticism of the position for which I have argued, rather than a criticism of our ordinary standards of behavior. Since most people are self-interested to some degree, very few of us are likely to do everything that we ought to do. It would, however, hardly be honest to take this as evidence that it is not the case that we ought to do it.

It may still be thought that my conclusions are so wildly out of line with what everyone else thinks and has always thought that there must be something wrong with the argument somewhere. In order to show that my conclusions, while certainly contrary to contemporary Western moral standards, would not have seemed so extraordinary at other times and in other places, I would like to quote a passage from a writer not normally thought of as a way-out radical, Thomas Aquinas.

> Now, according to the natural order instituted by divine providence, material goods are provided for the satisfaction of human needs. Therefore the division and appropriation of property, which proceeds from human law, must not hinder the satisfaction of man's necessity from such goods. Equally, whatever a man has in superabundance is owed, of natural right, to the poor for their sustenance. So Ambrosius says, and it is also to be found in the *Decretum Gratiani:* "The bread which you withhold belongs to the hungry; the clothing you shut away, to the naked; and the money you bury in the earth is the redemption and freedom of the penniless."[4]

I now want to consider a number of points, more practical than philosophical, which are relevant to the application of the moral conclusion we have reached. These points challenge not the idea that we ought to be doing all we can to prevent starvation, but the idea that giving away a great deal of money is the best means to this end.

It is sometimes said that overseas aid should be a government responsibility, and that therefore one ought not to give to privately run charities. Giving privately, it is said, allows the government and the noncontributing members of society to escape their responsibilities.

This argument seems to assume that the more people there are who give to privately organized famine relief funds, the less likely it is that the government will take over full responsibility for such aid. This assumption is unsupported, and does not strike me as at all plausible. The opposite view—that if no one gives voluntarily, a government will assume that its citizens are uninterested in famine relief and would not wish to be forced into giving aid—seems more plausible. In any case, unless there were a definite probability that by refusing to give one would be helping to bring about massive government assistance, people who do refuse to make voluntary contributions are refusing to prevent a certain amount of suffering without being able to point to any tangible beneficial consequence of their refusal. So the onus of showing how their refusal will bring about government action is on those who refuse to give.

I do not, of course, want to dispute the contention that governments of affluent nations should be giving many times the amount of genuine, no-strings-attached aid that they are giving now. I agree, too, that giving privately is not enough, and that we ought to be compaigning actively for entirely new standards for both public and private contributions to famine relief. Indeed, I would sympathize with someone who thought that compaigning was more important than giving oneself, although I doubt whether preaching what one does not practice would be very effective. Unfortunately, for many people the idea that "it's the government's responsibility" is a reason for not giving which does not appear to entail any political action either.

Another, more serious reason for not giving to famine relief funds is that until there is effective population control, relieving famine merely postpones starvation. If we save the Bengal refugees now, others, perhaps the children of these refugees, will face starvation in a few years' time. In support of this, one may cite the now well-known facts about the population explosion and the relatively limited scope for expanded production.

This point, like the previous one, is an argument against relieving suffering that is happening now, because of a belief about what might happen in the future; it is unlike the previous point in that very good evidence can be adduced in support of this belief about the future. I will not go into the evidence here. I accept that the earth cannot support indefinitely a population rising at the present rate. This certainly poses a problem for anyone who thinks it important to prevent famine. Again, however, one could accept the argument without drawing the conclusion that it absolves one from any obligation to do anything to prevent famine. The conclusion that should be drawn is that the best means of preventing famine, in the long run, is population control. It would then follow from the position reached earlier that one ought to be doing all one can to promote population control (unless one held that all forms of population control were wrong in themselves, or would have significantly bad consequences). Since there are organizations working specifically for population control, one would then support them rather than more orthodox methods of preventing famine.

A third point raised by the conclusion reached earlier relates to the question of just how much we all ought to be giving away. One possibility, which has already been mentioned, is that we ought to give until we reach the level of marginal utility—that is, the level at which, by giving more, I would cause as much suffering to myself or my dependents as I would relieve by my gift. This would mean, of course, that one would reduce oneself to very near the material circumstances of a Bengali refugee. It will be recalled that earlier I put forward both a strong and a moderate version of the principle of preventing bad occurrences. The strong version, which required us to prevent bad things from happening unless in doing so we would be sacrificing something of comparable moral significance, does seem to require reducing ourselves to the level of marginal utility. I should also say that the strong version seems to me to be the correct one. I proposed the more moderate version—that we should prevent bad occurrences unless, to do so, we had to sacrifice something morally significant—only in order to show that even on this surely undeniable principle a great change in our way of life is required. On the more moderate principle, it may not follow that we ought to reduce ourselves to the level of marginal utility, for one might hold that to reduce oneself and one's family to this level is to cause something significantly bad to happen. Whether this is so I shall not discuss, since, as I have said, I can see no good reason for holding the moderate version of the principle rather than the strong version. Even if we accepted the principle only in its moderate form, however, it should be clear that we would have to give away enough to ensure that the consumer society, dependent as it is on people spending on trivia rather than giving to famine relief, would slow down and perhaps disappear entirely. There are several reasons why this would be desirable in itself. The value and necessity of economic growth are now being questioned not only by conservationists, but by economists as well.[5] There is no doubt, too, that the consumer society has had a distorting effect on the goals and purposes of its members. Yet looking at the matter purely from the point of view of overseas aid, there must be a limit to the extent to which we should deliberately slow down our economy; for it might be the case that if we gave away, say, forty percent of our Gross National Product, we would slow down the economy so much that in absolute terms we would be giving less than if we gave twenty-five percent of the much larger GNP that we would have if we limited our contribution to this smaller percentage.

I mention this only as an indication of the sort of factor that one would have to take into account in working out an ideal. Since Western societies generally consider one percent of the GNP an acceptable level for overseas aid, the matter is entirely academic. Nor does it affect the question of how much an individual should give in a society in which very few are giving substantial amounts.

It is sometimes said, though less often now than it used to be, that philosophers have no special role to play in public affairs, since most public issues depend primarily on an assessment of facts. On questions of fact, it is said, philosophers as such have no special expertise, and so it has been possible to engage in philosophy without committing oneself to any position on major public issues. No doubt there are some issues of social policy and foreign policy about which it can truly be said that a really expert assessment of the facts is required before taking sides or acting, but the issue of famine is surely not one of these. The facts about the existence of suffering are beyond dispute. Nor, I think, is it disputed that we can do something about it, either through orthodox methods of famine relief or through population control or both. This is therefore an issue on which philosophers are competent to take a position. The issue is one which faces everyone who has more money than he needs to support himself and his dependents, or who is in a position to take some sort of political action. These categories must include practically every teacher and student of philosophy in the universities of the Western world. If philosophy is to deal with matters that are relevant to both teachers and students, this is an issue that philosophers should discuss.

Discussion, though, is not enough. What is the point of relating philosophy to public (and personal) affairs if we do not take our conclusions seriously? In this instance, taking our conclusion seriously means acting upon it. The philosopher will not find it any easier than anyone else to alter his attitudes and way of life to the extent that, if I am right, is involved in doing everything that we ought to be doing. At the very least, though, one can make a start. The philosopher who does so will have to sacrifice some of the benefits of the consumer society, but he can find compensation in the satisfaction of a way of life in which theory and practice, if not yet in harmony, are at least coming together.

Notes

1. There was also a third possibility: that India would go to war to enable the refugees to return to their lands. Since I wrote this paper, India has taken this way out. The situation is no longer that described above, but this does not affect my argument, as the next paragraph indicates.
2. In view of the special sense philosophers often give to the term, I should say that I use "obligation" simply as the abstract noun derived from "ought," so that "I have an obligation to" means no more, and no less, than "I ought to." This usage is in accordance with the definition of "ought" given by the *Shorter Oxford English Dictionary:* "the general verb to express duty or obligation." I do not think any issue of substance hangs on the way the term is used; sentences in which I use "obligation" could all be rewritten, although somewhat clumsily, as sentences in which a clause containing "ought" replaces the term "obligation."
3. J.O. Urmson, "Saints and Heroes," in *Essays in Moral Philosophy,* ed. Abraham I. Melden (Seattle and London, 1958), p. 214. For a related but significantly different view see also Henry Sidgwick, *The Methods of Ethics,* 7th ed. (London, 1907), pp. 220–1, 492–3.
4. *Summa Theologica,* II–II, Question 66, Article 7, in *Aquinas, Selected Political Writings,* ed. A. P. d'Entreves, trans. J. G. Dawson (Oxford, 1948), p. 171.
5. See, for instance, John Kenneth Galbraith, *The New Industrial State* (Boston, 1967); and E.J. Mishan, *The Costs of Economic Growth* (London, 1967).

2. KANTIAN ETHICS

Groundwork of the Metaphysic of Morals

IMMANUEL KANT

Immanuel Kant (1724–1804) was one of the most important philosophers in the history of Western thought. His major works include *The Critique of Pure Reason* (1781), *The Critique of Practical Reason* (1788), and *Groundwork of the Metaphysic of Morals* (1785).

Chapter 1
Passage from Ordinary Rational Knowledge of Morality to Philosophical

[The Good Will.]

It is impossible to conceive anything at all in the world, or even out of it, which can be taken as good without qualification, except a **good will**. Intelligence, wit, judgement, and any other *talents* of the mind we may care to name, or courage, resolution, and constancy of purpose, as qualities of *temperament,* are without doubt good and desirable in many respects; but they can also be extremely bad and hurtful when the will is not good which has to make use of these gifts of nature, and which for this reason has the term "*character*" applied to its peculiar quality. It is exactly the same with *gifts of fortune*. Power, wealth, honour, even health and that complete well-being and contentment with one's state which goes by the name of "*happiness*", produce boldness, and as a consequence often over-boldness as well, unless a good will is present by which their influence on the mind—and so too the whole principle of action—may be corrected and adjusted to universal ends; not to mention that a rational and impartial spectator can never feel approval in contemplating the uninterrupted prosperity of a being graced by no touch of a pure and good will, and that consequently a good will seems to constitute the indispensable condition of our very worthiness to be happy.

Some qualities are even helpful to this good will itself and can make its task very much easier. They have none the less no inner unconditioned worth, but rather presuppose a good will which sets a limit to the esteem in which they are rightly held and does not permit us to regard them as absolutely good. Moderation in affections and passions, self-control, and sober reflexion are not only good in many respects: they may even seem to constitute part of the *inner* worth of a person. Yet they are far from being properly described as good without qualification (however unconditionally they have been commended by the ancients). For without the principles of a good will they may become exceedingly bad; and the very coolness of a scoundrel makes him, not merely more dangerous, but also immediately more abominable in our eyes than we should have taken him to be without it.

[The Good Will and Its Results.]

A good will is not good because of what it effects or accomplishes—because of its fitness for attaining some proposed end: it is good through

From *Groundwork of the Metaphysic of Morals* trans. J. J. Paton (London: Hutchinson's University Library), pp. 61–62, 64–67, 74, 80–92, 95–107.

its willing alone—that is, good in itself. Considered in itself it is to be esteemed beyond comparison as far higher than aything it could ever bring about merely in order to favour some inclination or, if you like, the sum total of inclinations. Even if, by some special disfavour of destiny or by the niggardly endowment of stepmotherly nature, this will is entirely lacking in power to carry out its intentions; if by its utmost effort it still accomplishes nothing, and only good will is left (not, admittedly, as a mere wish, but as the straining of every means so far as they are in our control); even then it would still shine like a jewel for its own sake as something which has its full value in itself. Its usefulness or fruitlessness can neither add to, nor subtract from, this value. Its usefulness would be merely, as it were, the setting which enables us to handle it better in our ordinary dealings or to attract the attention of those not yet sufficiently expert, but not to commend it to experts or to determine its value.

. . . .

[The Good Will and Duty.]

We have now to elucidate the concept of a will estimable in itself and good apart from any further end. This concept, which is already present in a naturally sound understanding and requires not so much to be taught as merely to be clarified, always holds the highest place in estimating the total worth of our actions and constitutes the condition of all the rest. We will therefore take up the concept of **duty**, which includes that of a good will, exposed, however, to certain subjective limitations and obstacles. These, so far from hiding a good will or disguising it, rather bring it out by contrast and make it shine forth more brightly.

[The Motive of Duty.]

I will here pass over all actions already recognized as contrary to duty, however useful they may be with a view to this or that end; for about these the question does not even arise whether they could have been done *for the sake of duty* inasmuch as they are directly opposed to it. I will also set aside actions which in fact accord with duty, yet for which men have *no immediate inclination,* but perform them because impelled to do so by some other inclination. For there it is easy to decide whether the action which accords with duty has been done *from duty* or from some purpose of self-interest. This distinction is far more difficult to perceive when the action accords with duty and the subject has in addition an *immediate* inclination to the action. For example, it certainly accords with duty that a grocer should not overcharge his inexperienced customer; and where there is much competition a sensible shopkeeper refrains from so doing and keeps to a fixed and general price for everybody so that a child can buy from him just as well as anyone else. Thus people are served *honestly;* but this is not nearly enough to justify us in believing that the shopkeeper has acted in this way from duty or from principles of fair dealing; his interests required him to do so. We cannot assume him to have in addition an immediate inclination towards his customers, leading him, as it were out of love, to give no man preference over another in the matter of price. Thus the action was done neither from duty nor from immediate inclination, but solely from purposes of self-interest.

On the other hand, to preserve one's life is a duty, and besides this every one has also an immediate inclination to do so. But on account of this the often anxious precautions taken by the greater part of mankind for this purpose have no inner worth, and the maxim of their action is without moral content. They do protect their lives *in conformity with duty,* but not *from the motive of duty.* When, on the contrary, disappointments and hopeless misery have quite taken away the taste for life; when a wretched man, strong in soul and more angered at his fate than faint-hearted or cast down, longs for death and still preserves his life without loving it—not from inclination or fear but from duty; then indeed his maxim has a moral content.

To help others where one can is a duty, and besides this there are many spirits of so sympathetic a temper that, without any further motive of vanity or self-interest, they find an inner pleasure in spreading happiness around them and can take delight in the contentment of others as their own work. Yet I maintain that in such a case an action of this kind, however right and however amiable it may be, has still no genuinely moral worth. It stands on the same footing as other inclinations—for example, the inclination for honour, which if fortunate enough to hit on something beneficial and right and consequently honourable, deserves praise and encouragement, but not esteem; for its maxim lacks moral content, namely, the performance of such actions, not from inclination, but *from duty*. Suppose then that the mind of this friend of man was overclouded by sorrows of his own which extinguished all sympathy with the fate of others, but that he still had power to help those in distress, though no longer stirred by the need of others because sufficiently occupied with his own; and suppose that, when no longer moved by any inclination, he tears himself out of this deadly insensibility and does the action without any inclination for the sake of duty alone; then for the first time his action has its genuine moral worth. Still further: if nature had implanted little sympathy in this or that man's heart; if (being in other respects an honest fellow) he were cold in temperament and indifferent to the sufferings of others—perhaps because, being endowed with the special gift of patience and robust endurance in his own sufferings, he assumed the like in others or even demanded it; if such a man (who would in truth not be the worst product of nature) were not exactly fashioned by her to be a philanthropist, would he not still find in himself a source from which he might draw a worth far higher than any that a good-natured temperament can have? Assuredly he would. It is precisely in this that the worth of character begins to show—a moral worth and beyond all comparison the highest—namely that he does good, not from inclination, but from duty.

To assure one's own happiness is a duty (at least indirectly); for discontent with one's state, in a press of cares and amidst unsatisfied wants, might easily become a great *temptation to the transgression of duty*. But here also, apart from regard to duty, all men have already of themselves the strongest and deepest inclination towards happiness, because precisely in this Idea of happiness there is combined the sum total of inclinations. The prescription for happiness is, however, often so constituted as greatly to interfere with some inclinations, and yet men cannot form under the name of "happiness" any determinate and assured conception of the satisfaction of all inclinations as a sum. Hence it is not to be wondered at that a single inclination which is determinate as to what it promises and as to the time of its satisfaction may outweigh a wavering Idea; and that a man, for example, a sufferer from gout, may choose to enjoy what he fancies and put up with what he can—on the ground that on balance he has here at least not killed the enjoyment of the present moment because of some possibly groundless expectations of the good fortune supposed to attach to soundness of health. But in this case also, when the universal inclination towards happiness has failed to determine his will, when good health, at least for him, has not entered into his calculations as so necessary, what remains over, here as in other cases, is a law—the law of furthering his happiness, not from inclination, but from duty—and in this for the first time his conduct has a real moral worth.

It is doubtless in this sense that we should understand too the passages from Scripture in which we are commanded to love our neighbour and even our enemy. For love out of inclination cannot be commanded; but kindness done from duty—although no inclination impels us, and even although natural and unconquerable disinclination stands in our way—is *practical*, and not *pathological*, love, residing in the will and not in the propensions of feeling, in principles of action and not of melting compassion; and it is this practical love alone which can be an object of command.

. . . .

Chapter II
Passage from Popular Moral Philosophy to a Metaphysic of Morals

. . . .

[Imperatives in General.]

Everything in nature works in accordance with laws. Only a rational being has the power to act *in accordance with his idea* of laws—that is, in accordance with principles—and only so has he a *will*. Since *reason* is required in order to derive actions from laws, the will is nothing but practical reason. If reason infallibly determines the will, then in a being of this kind the actions which are recognized to be objectively necessary are also subjectively necessary—that is to say, the will is then a power to choose *only that* which reason independently of inclination recognizes to be practically necessary, that is, to be good. But if reason solely by itself is not sufficient to determine the will; if the will is exposed also to subjective conditions (certain impulsions) which do not always harmonize with the objective ones; if, in a word, the will is not *in itself* completely in accord with reason (as actually happens in the case of men); then actions which are recognized to be objectively necessary are subjectively contingent, and the determining of such a will in accordance with objective laws is *necessitation*. That is to say, the relation of objective laws to a will not good through and through is conceived as one in which the will of a rational being, although it is determined by principles of reason, does not necessarily follow these principles in virtue of its own nature.

The conception of an objective principle so far as this principle is necessitating for a will is called a command (of reason), and the formula of this command is called an **Imperative**.

All imperatives are expressed by an *"ought" (Sollen)*. By this they mark the relation of an objective law of reason to a will which is not necessarily determined by this law in virtue of its subjective constitution (the relation of necessitation). They say that something would be good to do or to leave undone; only they say it to a will which does not always do a thing because it has been informed that this is a good thing to do. The practically *good* is that which determines the will by concepts of reason, and therefore not by subjective causes, but objectively—that is, on grounds valid for every rational being as such. It is distinguished from the *pleasant* as that which influences the will, not as a principle of reason valid for every one, but solely through the medium of sensation by purely subjective causes valid only for the senses of this person or that.[1]

A perfectly good will would thus stand quite as much under objective laws (laws of the good), but it could not on this account be conceived as *necessitated* to act in conformity with law, since of itself, in accordance with its subjective constitution, it can be determined only by the concept of the good. Hence for the *divine* will, and in general for a *holy* will, there are no imperatives: *"I ought"* is here out of place, because *"I will"* is already of itself necessarily in harmony with the law. Imperatives are in consequence only formulae for expressing the relation of objective laws of willing to the subjective imperfection of the will of this or that rational being—for example, of the human will.

[Classification of Imperatives.]

All *imperatives* command either *hypothetically* or *categorically*. Hypothetical imperatives declare a possible action to be practically necessary as a means to the attainment of something else that one wills (or that one may will). A categorical imperative would be one which represented an action as objectively necessary in itself apart from its relation to a further end.

Every practical law represents a possible action as good and therefore as necessary for a subject whose actions are determined by reason. Hence all imperatives are formulae for determining an action which is necessary in accordance with the principle of a will in some sense good. If the action would be good solely as a means *to something else,* the imperative is *hypothetical;* if the action is represented as good *in itself* and therefore as necessary, in virtue of its principle, for a will which of itself accords with reason, then the imperative is *categorical*.

An imperative therefore tells me which of my possible actions would be good; and it formulates a practical rule for a will that does not perform an action straight away because the action is good—whether because the subject does not always know that it is good or because, even if he did know this, he might still act on maxims contrary to the objective principles of practical reason.

A hypothetical imperative thus says only that an action is good for some purpose or other, either *possible* or *actual*. In the first case it is a **problematic** practical principle; in the second case an **assertoric** practical principle. A categorical imperative, which declares an action to be objectively necessary in itself without reference to some purpose—that is, even without any further end—ranks as an **apodeictic** practical principle.

Everything that is possible only through the efforts of some rational being can be conceived as a possible purpose of some will; and consequently there are in fact innumerable principles of action so far as action is thought necessary in order to achieve some possible purpose which can be effected by it. All sciences have a practical part consisting of problems which suppose that some end is possible for us and of imperatives which tell us how it is to be attained. Hence the latter can in general be called imperatives of **skill**. Here there is absolutely no question about the rationality or goodness of the end, but only about what must be done to attain it. A prescription required by a doctor in order to cure his man completely and one required by a poisoner in order to make sure of killing him are of equal value so far as each serves to effect its purpose perfectly. Since in early youth we do not know what ends may present themselves to us in the course of life, parents seek above all to make their children learn things *of many kinds;* they provide carefully for *skill* in the use of means to all sorts of *arbitrary* ends, of none of which can they be certain that it could not in the future become an actual purpose of their ward, while it is always *possible* that he might adopt it. Their care in this matter is so great that they commonly neglect on this account to form and correct the judgement of their children about the worth of things which they might possibly adopt as ends.

There is, however, *one* end that can be presupposed as actual in all rational beings (so far as they are dependent beings to whom imperatives apply); and thus there is one purpose which they not only *can* have, but which we can assume with certainty that they all *do* have by a natural necessity—the purpose, namely, of *happiness.* A hypothetical imperative which affirms the practical necessity of an action as a means to the furtherance of happiness is **assertoric**. We may represent it, not simply as necessary to an uncertain, merely possible purpose, but as necessary to a purpose which we can presuppose a priori and with certainty to be present in every man because it belongs to his very being. Now skill in the choice of means to one's own greatest well-being can be called *prudence*[2] in the narrowest sense. Thus an imperative concerned with the choice of means to one's own happiness—that is, a precept of prudence—still remains *hypothetical:* an action is commanded, not absolutely, but only as a means to a further purpose.

Finally, there is an imperative which, without being based on, and conditioned by, any further purpose to be attained by a certain line of conduct, enjoins this conduct immediately. This imperative is **categorical**. It is concerned, not with the matter of the action and its presumed results, but with its form and with the principle from which it follows; and what is essentially good in the action consists in the mental disposition, let the consequences be what they may. This imperative may be called the imperative of **morality**.

Willing in accordance with these three kinds of principle is also sharply distinguished by a *dissimilarity* in the necessitation of the will. To make this dissimilarity obvious we should, I think, name these kinds of principle most appropriately in their order if we said they were either *rules* of skill or *counsels* of prudence or *commands (laws)* of morality. For only *law* carries with it the concept of an *unconditioned,* and yet objective and so universally valid, *necessity;* and commands are laws which must be obeyed—that is, must be followed even against inclination. *Counsel* does indeed involve necessity, but necessity valid only under a subjective and contingent condition—namely, if this or that man counts this or that as belonging to his happiness. As against this, a categorical imperative is limited by no condition and can quite precisely be called a command, as being absolutely, although practically, necessary. We could also call imperatives of the first kind *technical* (concerned with art); of the second kind *pragmatic*[3] (concerned with well-being); of the third kind *moral* (concerned with free conduct as such—that is, with morals).

[How Are Imperatives Possible?]

The question now arises "How are all these imperatives possible?" This question does not ask how we can conceive the execution of an action commanded by the imperative, but merely how we can conceive the necessitation of the will expressed by the imperative in setting us a task. How an imperative of skill is possible requires no special discussion. Who wills the end, wills (so far as reason has decisive influence on his actions) also the means which are indispensably necessary and in his power. So far as willing is concerned, this proposition is analytic: for in my willing of an object as an effect there is already conceived the causality of myself as an acting cause—that is, the use of means; and from the concept of willing an end the imperative merely extracts the concept of actions necessary to this end. (Synthetic propositions are required in order to determine the means to a proposed end, but these are concerned, not with the reason for performing the act of will, but with the cause which produces the object.) That in order to divide a line into two equal parts on a sure principle I must from its ends describe two intersecting arcs—this is admittedly taught by mathematics only in synthetic propositions; but when I know that the aforesaid effect can be produced only by such an action, the proposition "If I fully will the effect, I also will the action required for it" is analytic; for it is one and the same thing to conceive something as an effect possible in a certain way through me and to conceive myself as acting in the same way with respect to it.

If it were only as easy to find a determinate concept of happiness, the imperatives of prudence would agree entirely with those of skill and would be equally analytic. For here as there it could alike be said "Who wills the end, wills also (necessarily, if he accords with reason) the sole means which are in his power." Unfortunately, however, the concept of happiness is so indeterminate a concept that although every man wants to attain happiness, he can never say definitely and in unison with himself what it really is that he wants and wills. The reason for this is that all the elements which belong to the concept of happiness are without exception empirical—that is, they must be borrowed from experience; but that none the less there is required for the Idea of happiness an absolute whole, a maximum of well-being in my present, and in every future, state. Now it is impossible for the most intelligent, and at the same time most powerful, but nevertheless finite, being to form here a determinate concept of what he really wills. Is it riches that he wants? How much anxiety, envy, and pestering might he not bring in this way on his own head! Is it knowledge and insight? This might perhaps merely give him an eye so sharp that it would make evils at present hidden from him and yet unavoidable seem all the more frightful, or would add a load of still further needs to the desires which already give him trouble enough. Is it long life? Who will guarantee that it would not be a long misery? Is it at least health? How often has infirmity of body kept a man from excesses into which perfect health would have let him fall!—and so on. In short, he has no principle by which he is able to decide with complete certainty what will make him truly happy, since for this he would require omniscience. Thus we cannot act on determinate principles in order to be happy, but only on empirical counsels, for example, of diet, frugality, politeness, reserve, and so on—things which experience shows contribute most to well-being on the average. From this it follows that imperatives of prudence, speaking strictly, do not command at all—that is, cannot exhibit actions objectively as practically *necessary;* that they are rather to be taken as recommendations *(consilia),* than as commands *(praecepta),* of reason; that the problem of determining certainly and universally what action will promote the happiness of a rational being is completely insoluble; and consequently that in regard to this there is no imperative possible which in the strictest sense could command us to do what will make us happy, since happiness is an Ideal, not of reason, but of imagination—an Ideal resting merely on empirical grounds, of which it is vain to expect that they should determine an action by which we could attain the totality of a series of consequences which is in fact infinite. Nevertheless, if we assume that the means to happiness could be discovered with certainty, this imperative of prudence would be an analytic practical proposition; for it differs from the imperative of skill only in this—that in the latter the end is merely possible, while in the former the end is given. In spite of this difference, since both command solely the means to something assumed to be willed as an end, the imperative which commands him who wills the end to will the means is in both cases analytic. Thus there is likewise no difficulty in regard to the possibility of an imperative of prudence.

As against this, the question "How is the imperative of *morality* possible?" is the only one in need of a solution; for it is in no way hypothetical, and consequently we cannot base the objective necessity which it affirms on any presupposition, as we can with hypothetical imperatives. Only we must never forget here that it is impossible to settle *by an example,* and so empirically, whether there is any imperative of this kind at all: we must rather suspect that all imperatives which seem to be categorical may none the less be covertly hypothetical. Take, for example, the saying "Thou shalt make no false promises." Let us assume that the necessity for this abstention is no mere advice for the avoidance of some further evil—as it might be said "You ought not to make a lying promise lest, when this comes to light, you destroy your credit." Let us hold, on the contrary, that an action of this kind must be considered as bad in itself, and that the imperative of prohibition is therefore categorical. Even so, we cannot with any certainty show by an example that the will is determined here solely by the law without any further motive, although it may appear to be so; for it is always possible that fear of disgrace, perhaps also hidden dread of other risks, may unconsciously influence the will. Who can prove by experience that a cause is not present? Experience shows only that it is not perceived. In such a case, however, the so-called moral imperative, which as such appears to be categorical and unconditioned, would in fact be only a pragmatic prescription calling attention to our advantage and merely bidding us take this into account.

We shall thus have to investigate the possibility of a *categorical* imperative entirely a priori, since here we do not enjoy the advantage of having its reality given in experience and so of being obliged merely to explain, and not to establish, its possibility. So much, however, can be seen provisionally—that the categorical imperative alone purports to be a practical **law**, while all the rest may be called *principles* of the will but not laws; for an action necessary merely in order to achieve an arbitrary purpose can be considered as in itself contingent, and we can always escape from the precept if we abandon the purpose; whereas an unconditioned command does not leave it open to the will to do the opposite at its discretion and therefore alone carries with it that necessity which we demand from a law.

In the second place, with this categorical imperative or law of morality the reason for our difficulty (in comprehending its possibility) is a very serious one. We have here a synthetic a priori practical proposition;[4] and since in theoretical knowledge there is so much difficulty in comprehending the possibility of propositions of this kind, it may readily be gathered that in practical knowledge the difficulty will be no less.

[The Formula of Universal Law.]

In this task we wish first to enquire whether perhaps the mere concept of a categorical imperative may not also provide us with the formula containing the only proposition that can be a categorical imperative; for even when we know the purport of such an absolute command, the question of its possibility will still require a special and troublesome effort, which we postpone to the final chapter.

When I conceive a *hypothetical* imperative in general, I do not know beforehand what it will contain—until its condition is given. But if I conceive a *categorical* imperative, I know at once what it contains. For since besides the law this imperative contains only the necessity that our maxim[5] should conform to this law, while the law, as we have seen, contains no condition to limit it, there remains nothing over to which the maxim has to conform except the universality of a law as such; and it is this conformity alone that the imperative properly asserts to be necessary.

There is therefore only a single categorical imperative and it is this: *"Act only on that maxim through which you can at the same time will that it should become a universal law."*

Now if all imperatives of duty can be derived from this one imperative as their principle, then even although we leave it unsettled whether what we call duty may not be an empty concept, we shall still be able to show at least what we understand by it and what the concept means.

[The Formula of the Law of Nature.]

Since the universality of the law governing the production of effects constitutes what is properly called *nature* in its most general sense (nature as regards its form)—that is, the existence of things so far as determined by universal laws—the universal imperative of duty may also run as follows: *"Act as if the maxim of your action were to become through your will a* UNIVERSAL LAW OF NATURE."

[Illustrations.]

We will now enumerate a few duties, following their customary division into duties towards self and duties towards others and into perfect and imperfect duties.[6]

1. A man feels sick of life as the result of a series of misfortunes that has mounted to the point of despair, but he is still so far in possession of his reason as to ask himself whether taking his own life may not be contrary to his duty to himself. He now applies the test "Can the maxim of my action really become a universal law of nature?" His maxim is "From self-love I make it my principle to shorten my life if its continuance threatens more evil than it promises pleasure." The only further question to ask is whether this principle of self-love can become a universal law of nature. It is then seen at once that a system of nature by whose law the very same feeling whose function *(Bestimmung)* is to stimulate the furtherance of life should actually destroy life would contradict itself and consequently could not subsist as a system of nature. Hence this maxim cannot possibly hold as a universal law of nature and is therefore entirely opposed to the supreme principle of all duty.

2. Another finds himself driven to borrowing money because of need. He well knows that he will not be able to pay it back; but he sees too that he will get no loan unless he gives a firm promise to pay it back within a fixed time. He is inclined to make such a promise; but he has still enough conscience to ask "Is it not unlawful and contrary to duty to get out of difficulties in this way?" Supposing, however, he did resolve to do so, the maxim of his action would run thus: "Whenever I believe myself short of money, I will borrow money and promise to pay it back, though I know that this will never be done." Now this principle of self-love or personal advantage is perhaps quite compatible with my own entire future welfare; only there remains the question "Is it right?" I therefore transform the demand of self-love into a universal law and frame my question thus: "How would things stand if my maxim became a universal law?" I then see straight away that this maxim can never rank as a universal law and be self-consistent, but must necessarily contradict itself. For the universality of a law that every one believing himself to be in need may make any promise he pleases with the intention not to keep it would make promising, and the very purpose of promising, itself impossible, since no one would believe he was being promised anything, but would laugh at utterances of this kind as empty shams.

3. A third finds in himself a talent whose cultivation would make him a useful man for all sorts of purposes. But he sees himself in comfortable circumstances, and he prefers to give himself up to pleasure rather than to bother about increasing and improving his fortunate natural aptitudes. Yet he asks himself further "Does my maxim of neglecting my natural gifts, besides agreeing in itself with my tendency to indulgence, agree also with what is called duty?" He then sees that a system of nature could indeed always subsist under such a universal law, although (like the South Sea Islanders) every man should let his talents rust and should be bent on devoting his life solely to idleness, indulgence, procreation, and, in a word, to enjoyment. Only he cannot possibly **will** that this should become a universal law of nature or should be implanted in us as such a law by a natural instinct. For as a rational being he necessarily wills that all his powers should be developed, since they serve him, and are given him, for all sorts of possible ends.

4. Yet a *fourth* is himself flourishing, but he sees others who have to struggle with great hardships (and whom he could easily help); and he thinks "What does it matter to me? Let every one be as happy as Heaven wills or as he can make himself; I won't deprive him of anything; I won't even envy him; only I have no wish to contribute anything to his well-being or to his support in distress!" Now admittedly if such an attitude were a universal law of nature, mankind could get on perfectly well—better no doubt than if everybody prates about sympathy and good will, and even takes pains, on occasion, to practise them, but on the other hand cheats where he can, traffics in human rights, or violates them in other ways. But although it is possible that a universal law of nature could subsist in harmony with this maxim, yet it is impossible to **will** that such a principle should hold everywhere as a law of nature. For a will which decided in this way would be at variance with itself, since many a situation

might arise in which the man needed love and sympathy from others, and in which, by such a law of nature sprung from his own will, he would rob himself of all hope of the help he wants for himself.

[The Canon of Moral Judgement.]

These are some of the many actual duties—or at least of what we take to be such—whose derivation from the single principle cited above leaps to the eye. We must *be able to will* that a maxim of our action should become a universal law—this is the general canon for all moral judgement of action. Some actions are so constituted that their maxim cannot even be *conceived* as a universal law of nature without contradiction, let alone be *willed* as what *ought* to become one. In the case of others we do not find this inner impossibility, but it is still impossible to *will* that their maxim should be raised to the universality of a law of nature, because such a will would contradict itself. It is easily seen that the first kind of action is opposed to strict or narrow (rigorous) duty, the second only to wider (meritorious) duty; and thus that by these examples all duties—so far as the type of obligation is concerned (not the object of dutiful action)—are fully set out in their dependence on our single principle.

If we now attend to ourselves whenever we transgress a duty, we find that we in fact do not will that our maxim should become a universal law—since this is impossible for us—but rather that its opposite should remain a law universally: we only take the liberty of making an *exception* to it for ourselves (or even just for this once) to the advantage of our inclination. Consequently if we weighed it all up from one and the same point of view—that of reason—we should find a contradiction in our own will, the contradiction that a certain principle should be objectively necessary as a universal law and yet subjectively should not hold universally but should admit of exceptions. Since, however, we first consider our action from the point of view of a will wholly in accord with reason, and then consider precisely the same action from the point of view of a will affected by inclination, there is here actually no contradiction, but rather an opposition of inclination to the precept of reason *(antagonismus)*, whereby the universality of the principle *(universalitas)* is turned into a mere generality *(generalitas)* so that the practical principle of reason may meet our maxim half-way. This procedure, though in our own impartial judgement it cannot be justified, proves none the less that we in fact recognize the validity of the categorical imperative and (with all respect for it) merely permit ourselves a few exceptions which are, as we pretend, inconsiderable and apparently forced upon us.

We have thus at least shown this much—that if duty is a concept which is to have meaning and real legislative authority for our actions, this can be expressed only in categorical imperatives and by no means in hypothetical ones. At the same time—and this is already a great deal—we have set forth distinctly, and determinately for every type of application, the content of the categorical imperative, which must contain the principle of all duty (if there is to be such a thing at all). But we are still not so far advanced as to prove a priori that there actually is an imperative of this kind—that there is a practical law which by itself commands absolutely and without any further motives, and that the following of this law is duty.

. . . .

[The Formula of the End in Itself.]

The will is conceived as a power of determining oneself to action *in accordance with the idea of certain laws.* And such a power can be found only in rational beings. Now what serves the will as a subjective ground of its self-determination is an *end;* and this, if it is given by reason alone, must be equally valid for all rational beings. What, on the other hand, contains merely the ground of the possibility of an action whose effect is an end is called a *means.* The subjective ground of a desire is an *impulsion (Triebfeder);* the objective ground of a volition is a *motive (Bewegungsgrund).* Hence the difference between subjective ends, which are based on impulsions, and objective ends, which depend on motives valid for every rational being. Practical principles are *formal* if they abstract from all subjective ends; they are *material,* on the other hand, if they are based on such ends and consequently on certain impulsions. Ends that a rational being adopts arbitrarily as *effects* of his action (material ends) are in every case only relative; for it is solely their relation to special characteristics in the subject's power of appetition which gives them their value. Hence this value can provide no universal principles, no principles valid and necessary for all rational beings and also for every volition—that is, no practical laws. Consequently all these relative ends can be the ground only of hypothetical imperatives.

Suppose, however, there were something *whose existence* has *in itself* an absolute value, something which as *an end in itself* could be a ground of determinate laws; then in it, and in it alone, would there be the ground of a possible categorical imperative—that is, of a practical law.

Now I say that man, and in general every rational being, *exists* as an end in himself, *not merely as a means* for arbitrary use by this or that will: he must in all his actions, whether they are directed to himself or to other rational beings, always be viewed *at the same time as an end.* All the objects of inclination have only a conditioned value; for if there were not these inclinations and the needs grounded on them, their object would be valueless. Inclinations themselves, as sources of needs, are so far from having an absolute value to make them desirable for their own sake that it must rather be the universal wish of every rational being to be wholly free from them. Thus the value of all objects that can *be produced* by our action is always conditioned. Beings whose existence depends, not on our will, but on nature, have none the less, if they are non-rational beings, only a relative value as means and are consequently called *things.* Rational beings, on the other hand, are called *persons* because their nature already marks them out as ends in themselves—that is, as something which ought not to be used merely as a means—and consequently imposes to that extent a limit on all arbitrary treatment of them (and is an object of reverence). Persons, therefore, are not merely subjective ends whose existence as an effect of our actions has a value *for us:* they are *objective ends*—that is, things whose existence is in itself an end, and indeed an end such that in its place we can put no other end to which they should serve *simply* as means; for unless this is so, nothing at all of *absolute* value would be found anywhere. But if all value were conditioned—that is, contingent—then no supreme principle could be found for reason at all.

If then there is to be a supreme practical principle and—so far as the human will is concerned—a categorical imperative, it must be such that from the idea of something which is necessarily an end for every one because it is an *end in itself* it forms an *objective* principle of the will and consequently can serve as a practical law. The ground of this principle is: *Rational nature exists as an end in itself.* This is the way in which a man necessarily conceives his own existence: it is therefore so far a *subjective* principle of human actions. But it is also the way in which every other rational being conceives his existence on the same rational ground which is valid also for me;[7] hence it is at the same time an *objective* principle, from which, as a supreme practical ground, it must be possible to derive all laws for the will. The practical imperative will therefore be as follows: *Act in such a way that you always treat humanity, whether in your own person or in the person of any other, never simply as a means, but always at the same time as an end.* We will now consider whether this can be carried out in practice.

[Illustrations.]

Let us keep to our previous examples.

First, as regards the concept of necessary duty to oneself, the man who contemplates suicide will ask "Can my action be compatible with the Idea of humanity *as an end in itself?*" If he does away with himself in order to escape from a painful situation, he is making use of a person merely as a *means* to maintain a tolerable state of affairs till the end of his life. But man is not a thing—not something to be used *merely* as a means: he must always in all his actions be regarded as an end in himself. Hence I cannot dispose of man in my person by maiming, spoiling, or killing. (A more precise determination of this principle in order to avoid all misunderstanding—for example, about having limbs amputated to save myself or about exposing my life to danger in order to preserve it, and so on—I must here forego: this question belongs to morals proper.)

Secondly, so far as necessary or strict duty to

others is concerned, the man who has a mind to make a false promise to others will see at once that he is intending to make use of another man *merely as a means* to an end he does not share. For the man whom I seek to use for my own purposes by such a promise cannot possibly agree with my way of behaving to him, and so cannot himself share the end of the action. This incompatibility with the principle of duty to others leaps to the eye more obviously when we bring in examples of attempts on the freedom and property of others. For then it is manifest that a violator of the rights of man intends to use the person of others merely as a means without taking into consideration that, as rational beings, they ought always at the same time to be rated as ends—that is, only as beings who must themselves be able to share in the end of the very same action.[8]

Thirdly, in regard to contingent (meritorious) duty to oneself, it is not enough that an action should refrain from conflicting with humanity in our own person as an end in itself: it must also *harmonize with this end.* Now there are in humanity capacities for greater perfection which form part of nature's purpose for humanity in our person. To neglect these can admittedly be compatible with the *maintenance* of humanity as an end in itself, but not with the *promotion* of this end.

Fourthly, as regards meritorious duties to others, the natural end which all men seek is their own happiness. Now humanity could no doubt subsist if everybody contributed nothing to the happiness of others but at the same time refrained from deliberately impairing their happiness. This is, however, merely to agree negatively and not positively with *humanity as an end in itself* unless every one endeavours also, so far as in him lies, to further the ends of others. For the ends of a subject who is an end in himself must, if this conception is to have its *full* effect in me, be also, as far as possible, *my* ends.

[The Formula of Autonomy.]

This principle of humanity, and in general of every rational agent, *as an end in itself* (a principle which is the supreme limiting condition of every man's freedom of action) is not borrowed from experience; firstly, because it is universal, applying as it does to all rational beings as such, and no experience is adequate to determine universality; secondly, because in it humanity is conceived, not as an end of man (subjectively)—that is, as an object which, as a matter of fact, happens to be made an end—but as an objective end—one which, be our ends what they may, must, as a law, constitute the supreme limiting condition of all subjective ends and so must spring from pure reason. That is to say, the ground for every enactment of practical law lies *objectively in the rule* and in the form of universality which (according to our first principle) makes the rule capable of being a law (and indeed a law of nature); *subjectively,* however, it lies in the *end;* but (according to our second principle) the subject of all ends is to be found in every rational being as an end in himself. From this there now follows our third practical principle for the will—as the supreme condition of the will's conformity with universal practical reason—namely, the Idea *of the will of every rational being as a will which makes universal law.*

By this principle all maxims are repudiated which cannot accord with the will's own enactment of universal law. The will is therefore not merely subject to the law, but is so subject that it must be considered as also *making the law* for itself and precisely on this account as first of all subject to the law (of which it can regard itself as the author).

[The Exclusion of Interest.]

Imperatives as formulated above—namely, the imperative enjoining conformity of actions to universal law on the analogy of a *natural order* and that enjoining the universal *supremacy* of rational beings in themselves *as ends*—did, by the mere fact that they were represented as categorical, exclude from their sovereign authority every admixture of interest as a motive. They were, however, merely *assumed* to be categorical because we were bound to make this assumption if we wished to explain the concept of duty. That there were practical propositions which commanded categorically could not itself be proved, any more than it can be proved in this chapter generally; but one thing could have been done—namely, to show that in willing for the sake of duty renunciation of all interest, as the specific mark distinguishing a categorical from a hypothetical imperative, was expressed in the very imperative itself by means of some determination inherent in it. This is what is done in the present third formulation of the principle—namely, in the Idea of the will of every rational being as *a will which makes universal law.*

Once we conceive a will of this kind, it becomes clear that while a will *which is subject to law* may be bound to this law by some interest, nevertheless a will which is itself a supreme law-giver cannot possibly as such depend on any interest; for a will which is dependent in this way would itself require yet a further law in order to restrict the interest of self-love to the condition that this interest should itself be valid as a universal law.

Thus the *principle* that every human will is *a will which by all its maxims enacts universal law*[9]—provided only that it were right in other ways—would be *well suited* to be a categorical imperative in this respect: that precisely because of the Idea of making universal law it is *based on no interest* and consequently can alone among all possible imperatives be *unconditioned.* Or better still—to convert the proposition—if there is a categorical imperative (that is, a law for the will of every rational being), it can command us only to act always on the maxim of such a will in us as can at the same time look upon itself as making universal law; for only then is the practical principle and the imperative which we obey unconditioned, since it is wholly impossible for it to be based on any interest.

We need not now wonder, when we look back upon all the previous efforts that have been made to discover the principle of morality, why they have one and all been bound to fail. Their authors saw man as tied to laws by his duty, but it never occurred to them that he is subject only to *laws which are made by himself* and yet are *universal,* and that he is bound only to act in accordance with a will which is his own but has for its natural purpose the function of making universal law. For when they thought of man merely as subject to a law (whatever it might be), the law had to carry with it some interest in order to attract or compel, because it did not spring as a law from *his own* will: in order to conform with the law his will had to be necessitated by *something else* to act in a certain way. This absolutely inevitable conclusion meant that all the labour spent in trying to find a supreme principle of duty was lost beyond recall; for what they discovered was never duty, but only the necessity of acting from a certain interest. This interest might be one's own or another's; but on such a view the imperative was bound to be always a conditioned one and could not possibly serve as a moral law. I will therefore call my principle the principle of the **Autonomy** of the will in contrast with all others, which I consequently class under **Heteronomy**.

[The Formula of the Kingdom of Ends.]

The concept of every rational being as one who must regard himself as making universal law by all the maxims of his will, and must seek to judge himself and his actions from this point of view, leads to a closely connected and very fruitful concept—namely, that of *a kingdom of ends.*

I understand by a *''kingdom''* a systematic union of different rational beings under common laws. Now since laws determine ends as regards their universal validity, we shall be able—if we abstract from the personal differences between rational beings, and also from all the content of their private ends—to conceive a whole of all ends in systematic conjunction (a whole both of rational beings as ends in themselves and also of the personal ends which each may set before himself); that is, we shall be able to conceive a kingdom of ends which is possible in accordance with the above principles.

For rational beings all stand under the *law* that each of them should treat himself and all others, *never merely as a means,* but always *at the same time as an end in himself.* But by so doing there arises a systematic union of rational beings under common objective laws—that is, a kingdom. Since these laws are directed precisely to the relation of such beings to one another as ends and means, this kingdom can be called a kingdom of ends (which is admittedly only an Ideal).

A rational being belongs to the kingdom of ends as a *member,* when, although he makes its universal laws, he is also himself subject to these laws. He belongs to it as its *head,* when as the maker of laws he is himself subject to the will of no other.

A rational being must always regard himself as making laws in a kingdom of ends which is possible through freedom of the will—whether it be as member or as head. The position of the latter he can maintain, not in virtue of the maxim of his will alone, but only if he is a completely independent being, without needs and with an unlimited power adequate to his will.

Thus morality consists in the relation of all action to the making of laws whereby alone a kingdom of ends is possible. This making of laws must be found in every rational being himself and must be able to spring from his will. The principle of his will is therefore never to perform an action except on a maxim such as can also be a universal law, and consequently such *that the will can regard itself as at the same time making universal law by means of its maxim.* Where maxims are not already by their very nature in harmony with this objective principle of rational beings as makers of universal law, the necessity of acting on this principle is practical necessitation—that is, *duty*. Duty does not apply to the head in a kingdom of ends, but it does apply to every member and to all members in equal measure.

The practical necessity of acting on this principle—that is, duty—is in no way based on feelings, impulses, and inclinations, but only on the relation of rational beings to one another, a relation in which the will of a rational being must always be regarded as *making universal law,* because otherwise he could not be conceived as *an end in himself.* Reason thus relates every maxim of the will, considered as making universal law, to every other will and also to every action towards oneself: it does so, not because of any further motive or future advantage, but from the Idea of the *dignity* of a rational being who obeys no law other than that which he at the same time enacts himself.

[The Dignity of Virtue.]

In the kingdom of ends everything has either a *price* or a *dignity*. If it has a price, something else can be put in its place as an *equivalent;* if it is exalted above all price and so admits of no equivalent, then it has a dignity.

What is relative to universal human inclinations and needs has a *market price;* what, even without presupposing a need, accords with a certain taste—that is, with satisfaction in the mere purposeless play of our mental powers—has a *fancy price (Affektionspreis);* but that which constitutes the sole condition under which anything can be an end in itself has not merely a relative value—that is, a price— but has an intrinsic value—that is, *dignity*.

Now morality is the only condition under which a rational being can be an end in himself; for only through this is it possible to be a law-making member in a kingdom of ends. Therefore morality, and humanity so far as it is capable of morality, is the only thing which has dignity. Skill and diligence in work have a market price; wit, lively imagination, and humour have a fancy price; but fidelity to promises and kindness based on principle (not on instinct) have an intrinsic worth. In default of these, nature and art alike contain nothing to put in their place; for their worth consists, not in the effects which result from them, not in the advantage or profit they produce, but in the attitudes of mind—that is, in the maxims of the will—which are ready in this way to manifest themselves in action even if they are not favoured by success. Such actions too need no recommendation from any subjective disposition or taste in order to meet with immediate favour and approval; they need no immediate propensity or feeling for themselves; they exhibit the will which performs them as an object of immediate reverence; nor is anything other than reason required to *impose* them upon the will, not to *coax* them from the will—which last would anyhow be a contradiction in the case of duties. This assessment reveals as dignity the value of such a mental attitude and puts it infinitely above all price, with which it cannot be brought into reckoning or comparison without, as it were, a profanation of its sanctity.

What is it then that entitles a morally good attitude of mind—or virtue—to make claims so high? It is nothing less than the *share* which it affords to a rational being *in the making of universal law,* and which therefore fits him to be a member in a possible kingdom of ends. For this he was already marked out in virtue of his own proper nature as an end in himself and consequently as a maker of laws in the kingdom of ends—as free in respect of all laws of nature, obeying only those laws which he makes himself and in virtue of which his maxims can have their part in the making of universal law (to which he at the same time subjects himself). For nothing can have a value other than that determined for it by the law. But the law-making which determines all value must for this reason have a dignity—that is, an unconditioned and incomparable worth—for the appreciation of which, as necessarily given by a rational being, the word *"reverence"* is the only becoming expression. *Autonomy* is therefore the ground of the dignity of human nature and of every rational nature.

[Review of the Formulae.]

The aforesaid three ways of representing the principle of morality are at bottom merely so many formulations of precisely the same law, one of them by itself containing a combination of the other two. There is nevertheless a difference between them, which, however, is subjectively rather than objectively practical: that is to say, its purpose is to bring an Idea of reason nearer to intuition (in accordance with a certain analogy) and so nearer to feeling. All maxims have, in short,

1. a *form,* which consists in their universality; and in this respect the formula of the moral imperative is expressed thus: "Maxims must be chosen as if they had to hold as universal laws of nature";

2. a *matter*— that is, an end; and in this respect the formula says: "A rational being, as by his very nature an end and consequently an end in himself, must serve for every maxim as a condition limiting all merely relative and arbitrary ends";

3. a *complete determination* of all maxims by the following formula, namely: "All maxims as proceeding from our own making of law ought to harmonize with a possible kingdom of ends as a kingdom of nature."[10] This progression may be said to take place through the categories of the *unity* of the form of will (its universality); of the *multiplicity* of its matter (its objects—that is, its ends); and of the *totality* or completeness of its systems of ends. It is, however, better if in moral *judgement* we proceed always in accordance with the strictest method and take as our basis the universal formula of the categorical imperative: *"Act on the maxim which can at the same time be made a universal law."* If, however, we wish also to secure acceptance for the moral law, it is very useful to bring one and the same action under the above-mentioned three concepts and so, as far as we can, to bring the universal formula nearer to intuition.

[Review of the Whole Argument.]

We can now end at the point from which we started out at the beginning—namely, the concept of an unconditionally good will. The *will* is *absolutely good* if it cannot be evil—that is, if its maxim, when made into a universal law, can never be at variance with itself. This principle is therefore also its supreme law: "Act always on that maxim whose universality as a law you can at the same time will." This is the one principle on which a will can never be at variance with itself, and such an imperative is categorical. Because the validity of the will as a universal law for possible actions is analogous to the universal interconnexion of existent things in accordance with universal laws—which constitutes the formal aspect of nature as such—we can also express the categorical imperative as follows: *"Act on that maxim which can at the same time have for its object itself as a universal law of nature."* In this way we provide the formula for an absolutely good will.

Rational nature separates itself out from all other things by the fact that it sets itself an end. An end would thus be the matter of every good will. But in the Idea of a will which is absolutely good—good without any qualifying condition (namely, that it should attain this or that end)—there must be complete abstraction from every end that has to be *produced* (as something which would make every will only relatively good). Hence the end must here be conceived, not as an end to be produced, *but as a self-existent* end. It must therefore be conceived only negatively—that is, as an end against which we should never act, and consequently as one which in all our willing we must never rate *merely* as a means, but always at the same time as an end. Now this end can be nothing other than the subject of all possible ends himself, because this subject is also the subject of a will that may be absolutely good; for such a will cannot without contradiction be subordinated to any other object. The principle "So act in relation to every rational being (both to yourself and to others) that he may at the same time count in your maxim as an end in himself" is thus at bottom the same as the principle "Act on a maxim which at the same time contains in itself its own universal validity for every rational being." For to say that in using means to every end I ought to restrict my maxim by the condition that it should also be universally valid as a law for every subject is just the same as to say this—that a subject of ends, namely, a rational being himself, must be made the ground for all maxims of action, never *merely* as a means, but as a supreme condition restricting the use of every means—that is, always also as an end.

Now from this it unquestionably follows that every rational being, as an end in himself, must be able to regard himself as also the maker of universal law in respect of any law whatever to which he may be subjected; for it is precisely the fitness of his maxims to make universal law that marks him out as an end in himself. It follows equally that this dignity (or prerogative) of his above all the mere things of nature carries with it the necessity of always choosing his maxims from the point of view of himself—and also of every other rational being—as a maker of law (and this is why they are called persons). It is in this way that a world of rational beings *(mundus intelligibilis)* is possible as a kingdom of ends—possible, that is, through the making of their own laws by all persons as its members. Accordingly every rational being must so act as if he were through his maxims always a law-making member in the universal kingdom of ends. The formal principle of such maxims is "So act as if your maxims had to serve at the same time as a universal law (for all rational beings)." Thus a kingdom of ends is possible only on the analogy of a kingdom of nature; yet the kingdom of ends is possible only through maxims—that is, self-imposed rules—while nature is possible only through laws concerned with causes whose action is necessitated from without. In spite of this difference, we give to nature as a whole, even although it is regarded as a machine, the name of a "kingdom of nature" so far as—and for the reason that—it stands in a relation to rational beings as its ends. Now a kingdom of ends would actually come into existence through maxims which the categorical imperative prescribes as a rule for all rational beings, *if these maxims were universally followed.* Yet even if a rational being were himself to follow such a maxim strictly, he cannot count on everybody else being faithful to it on this ground, nor can he be confident that the kingdom of nature and its purposive order will work in harmony with him, as a fitting member, towards a kingdom of ends made possible by himself—or, in other words, that it will favour his expectation of happiness. But in spite of this the law "Act on the maxims of a member who makes universal laws for a merely possible kingdom of ends" remains in full force, since its command is categorical. And precisely here we encounter the paradox that without any further end or advantage to be attained the mere dignity of humanity, that is, of rational nature in man—and consequently that reverence for a mere Idea—should function as an inflexible precept for the will; and that it is just this freedom from dependence on interested motives which constitutes the sublimity of a maxim and the worthiness of every rational subject to be a law-making member in the kingdom of ends; for otherwise he would have to be regarded as subject only to the law of nature—the law of his own needs. Even if it were thought that both the kingdom of nature and the kingdom of ends were united under one head and that thus the latter kingdom ceased to be a mere Idea and achieved genuine reality, the Idea would indeed gain by this the addition of a strong motive, but never any increase in its intrinsic worth; for, even if this were so, it would still be necessary to conceive the unique and absolute lawgiver himself as judging the worth of rational beings solely by the disinterested behaviour they prescribed to themselves in virtue of this Idea alone. The essence of things does not vary with their external relations; and where there is something which, without regard to such relations, constitutes by itself the absolute worth of man, it is by this that man must also be judged by everyone whatsoever—even by the Supreme Being.

Thus *morality* lies in the relation of actions to the autonomy of the will—that is, to a possible making of universal law by means of its maxims. An action which is compatible with the autonomy of the will is *permitted;* one which does not harmonize with it is *forbidden.* A will whose maxims necessarily accord with the laws of autonomy is a *holy,* or absolutely good, will. The dependence of a will not absolutely good on the principle of autonomy (that is, moral necessitation) is *obligation.* Obligation can thus have no reference to a holy being. The objective necessity to act from obligation is called *duty.*

From what was said a little time ago we can now easily explain how it comes about that, although in the concept of duty we think of subjection to the law, yet we also at the same time attribute to the person who fulfils all his duties a certain sublimity and *dignity.* For it is not in so far as he is *subject* to the law that he has sublimity, but rather in so far as, in regard to this very same law, he is at the same time its *author* and is subordinated to it only on this ground. We have also shown above how neither fear nor inclination, but solely reverence for the law, is the motive which can give an action moral worth. Our own will, provided it were to act only under the condition of being able to make universal law by means of its maxims—this ideal will which can be ours is the proper object of reverence; and the dignity of man consists precisely in his capacity to make universal law, although only on condition of being himself also subject to the law he makes.

Notes

1. The dependence of the power of appetition on sensations is called an inclination, and thus an inclination always indicates a *need.* The dependence of a contingently determinable will on principles of reason is called an *interest.* Hence an interest is found only where there is a dependent will which in itself is not always in accord with reason: to a divine will we cannot ascribe any interest. But even the human will can *take an interest* in something without therefore *acting from interest.* The first expression signifies *practical* interest in the action; the second *pathological* interest in the object of the action. The first indicates only dependence of the will on principles of reason by itself; the second its dependence on principles of reason at the service of inclination—that is to say, where reason merely supplies a practical rule for meeting the need of inclination. In the first case what interests me is the action; in the second case what interests me is the object of the action (so far as this object is pleasant to me). We have seen in Chapter I that in an action done for the sake of duty we must have regard, not to interest in the object, but to interest in the action itself and in its rational principle (namely, the law).
2. The word "prudence" *(Klugheit)* is used in a double sense: in one sense it can have the name of "worldly wisdom" *(Weltklugheit);* in a second sense that of "personal wisdom" *(Privatklugheit).* The first is the skill of a man in influencing others in order to use them for his own ends. The second is sagacity in combining all these ends to his own lasting advantage. The latter is properly that to which the value of the former can itself be traced; and of him who is prudent in the first sense, but not in the second, we might better say that he is clever and astute, but on the whole imprudent.
3. It seems to me that the proper meaning of the word *"pragmatic"* can be defined most accurately in this way. For those *Sanctions* are called Pragmatic which, properly speaking, do not spring as necessary laws from the Natural Right of States, but from *forethought* in regard to the general welfare. A *history* is written pragmatically when it teaches *prudence*—that is, when it instructs the world of to-day how to provide for its own advantage better than, or at least as well as, the world of other times.
4. Without presupposing a condition taken from some inclination I connect an action with the will a priori and therefore necessarily (although only objectively so—that is, only subject to the Idea of a reason having full power over all subjective impulses to action). Here we have a practical proposition in which the willing of an action is not derived analytically from some other willing already presupposed (for we do not possess any such perfect will), but is on the contrary connected immediately with the concept of the will of a rational being as something which is not contained in this concept.
5. A *maxim* is a subjective principle of action and must be distinguished from an *objective principle*—namely, a practical law. The former contains a practical rule determined by reason in accordance with the conditions of the subject (often his ignorance or again his inclinations): it is thus a principle on which the subject *acts.* A law, on the other hand, is an objective principle valid for every rational being; and it is a principle on which he *ought to act*—that is, an imperative.
6. It should be noted that I reserve my division of duties entirely for a future *Metaphysic of Morals* and that my present division is therefore put forward as arbitrary (merely for the purpose of arranging my examples). Further, I understand here by a perfect duty one which allows no exception in the interests of inclination, and so I recognize among *perfect duties,* not only outer ones, but also inner. This

is contrary to the accepted usage of the schools, but I do not intend to justify it here, since for my purpose it is all one whether this point is conceded or not.

7. This proposition I put forward here as a postulate. The grounds for it will be found in the final chapter. [Editors' note: This final chapter is omitted here.]

8. Let no one think that here the trivial *"quod tibi non vis fieri, etc."* can serve as a standard or principle. For it is merely derivative from our principle, although subject to various qualifications: it cannot be a universal law since it contains the ground neither of duties to oneself nor of duties of kindness to others (for many a man would readily agree that others should not help him if only he could be dispensed from affording help to them), nor finally of strict duties towards others; for on this basis the criminal would be able to dispute with the judges who punish him, and so on.

9. I may be excused from bringing forward examples to illustrate this principle, since those which were first used as illustrations of the categorical imperative and its formula can all serve this purpose here.

10. Teleology views nature as a kingdom of ends; ethics views a possible kingdom of ends as a kingdom of nature. In the first case the kingdom of ends is a theoretical Idea used to explain what exists. In the second case it is a practical Idea used to bring into existence what does not exist but can be made actual by our conduct—and indeed to bring it into existence in conformity with this Idea.

Kantian Approaches to Some Famine Problems

ONORA O'NEILL

Onora O'Neill (1941–) is a professor of philosophy at the University of Essex. Her works include *Acting on Principle*.

§22 A Simplified Account of Kant's Ethics

Kant's moral theory has acquired the reputation of being forbiddingly difficult to understand and, once understood, excessively demanding in its requirements. I don't believe that this reputation has been wholly earned, and I am going to try to undermine it. In §§23–26 I shall try to reduce some of the difficulties, and in §§27–[29] I shall try to show the implications of a Kantian moral theory for action toward those who do or may suffer famine. Finally, I shall compare Kantian and utilitarian approaches and assess their strengths and weaknesses.

The main method by which I propose to avoid some of the difficulties of Kant's moral theory is by explaining only one part of the theory. This does not seem to me to be an irresponsible approach in this case. One of the things that makes Kant's moral theory hard to understand is that he gives a number of different versions of the principle that he calls the Supreme Principle of Morality, and these different versions don't look at all like one another. They also don't look at all like the utilitarians' Greatest Happiness Principle. But the Kantian principle is supposed to play a similar role in arguments about what to do.

Kant calls his Supreme Principle the *Categorical Imperative;* its various versions also have sonorous names. One is called the Formula of Universal Law; another is the Formula of the Kingdom of Ends. The one on which I shall concentrate is known as the *Formula of the End in Itself.* To understand why Kant thinks that these picturesquely named principles are equivalent to one another takes quite a lot of close and detailed analysis of Kant's philosophy. I shall avoid this and concentrate on showing the implications of this version of the Categorical Imperative.

§23 The Formula of the End in Itself

Kant states the Formula of the End in Itself as follows:

> Act in such a way that you always treat humanity, whether in your own person or in the person of any other, never simply as a means but always at the same time as an end.[1]

To understand this we need to know what it is to treat a person as a means or as an end. According to Kant, each of our acts reflects one or more *maxims.* The maxim of the act is the principle on which one sees oneself as acting. A maxim expresses a person's policy, or if he or she has no settled policy, the principle underlying the particular intention or decision on which he or she

From *Matters of Life and Death,* ed. T. Regan (New York: Random House, 1980), pp. 285–94.

acts. Thus, a person who decides "This year I'll give 10 percent of my income to famine relief" has as a maxim the principle of tithing his or her income for famine relief. In practice, the difference between intentions and maxims is of little importance, for given any intention, we can formulate the corresponding maxim by deleting references to particular times, places, and persons. In what follows I shall take the terms "maxim" and "intention" as equivalent.

Whenever we act intentionally, we have at least one maxim and can, if we reflect, state what it is. (There is of course room for self-deception here—"I'm only keeping the wolf from the door" we may claim as we wolf down enough to keep ourselves overweight, or, more to the point, enough to feed someone else who hasn't enough food.)

When we want to work out whether an act we propose to do is right or wrong, according to Kant, we should look at our maxims and not at how much misery or happiness the act is likely to produce, and whether it does better at increasing happiness than other available acts. We just have to check that the act we have in mind will not use anyone as a mere means, and, if possible, that it will treat other persons as ends in themselves.

§24 Using Persons as Mere Means

To use someone as a *mere means* is to involve them in a scheme of action *to which they could not in principle consent.* Kant does not say that there is anything wrong about using someone as a means. Evidently we have to do so in any cooperative scheme of action. If I cash a check I use the teller as a means, without whom I could not lay my hands on the cash; the teller in turn uses me as a means to earn his or her living. But in this case, each party consents to her or his part in the transaction. Kant would say that though they use one another as means, they do not use one another as *mere* means. Each person assumes that the other has maxims of his or her own and is not just a thing or a prop to be manipulated.

But there are other situations where one person uses another in a way to which the other could not in principle consent. For example, one person may make a promise to another with every intention of breaking it. If the promise is accepted, then the person to whom it was given must be ignorant of what the promisor's intention (maxim) really is. If one knew that the promisor did not intend to do what he or she was promising, one would, after all, not accept or rely on the promise. It would be as though there had been no promise made. Successful false promising depends on deceiving the person to whom the promise is made about what one's real maxim is. And since the person who is deceived doesn't know that real maxim, he or she can't in principle consent to his or her part in the proposed scheme of action. The person who is deceived is, as it were, a prop or a tool—a mere means—in the false promisor's scheme. A person who promises falsely treats the acceptor of the promise as a prop or a thing and not as a person. In Kant's view, it is this that makes false promising wrong.

One standard way of using others as mere means is by deceiving them. By getting someone involved in a business scheme or a criminal activity on false pretenses, or by giving a misleading account of what one is about, or by making a false promise or a fraudulent contract, one involves another in something to which he or she in principle cannot consent, since the scheme requires that he or she doesn't know what is going on. Another standard way of using others as mere means is by coercing them. If a rich or powerful person threatens a debtor with bankruptcy unless he or she joins in some scheme, then the creditor's intention is to coerce; and the debtor, if coerced, cannot consent to his or her part in the creditor's scheme. To make the example more specific: If a moneylender in an Indian village threatens not to renew a vital loan unless he is given the debtor's land, then he uses the debtor as a mere means. He coerces the debtor, who cannot truly consent to this "offer he can't refuse." (Of course the outward form of such transactions may look like ordinary commercial dealings, but we know very well that some offers and demands couched in that form are coercive.)

In Kant's view, acts that are done on maxims that require deception or coercion of others, and so cannot have the consent of those others (for consent precludes both deception and coercion), are wrong. When we act on such maxims, we treat others as mere means, as things rather than as ends in themselves. If we act on such maxims, our acts are not only wrong but unjust: such acts wrong the particular others who are deceived or coerced.

§25 Treating Persons as Ends in Themselves

Duties of justice are, in Kant's view (as in many others'), the most important of our duties. When we fail in these duties, we have used some other or others as mere means. But there are also cases where, though we do not use others as mere means, still we fail to use them as ends in themselves in the fullest possible way. To treat someone as an end in him or herself requires in the first place that one not use him or her as mere means, that one respect each as a rational person with his or her own maxims. But beyond that, one may also seek to foster others' plans and maxims by sharing some of their ends. To act beneficently is to seek others' happiness, therefore to intend to achieve some of the things that those others aim at with their maxims. If I want to make others happy, I will adopt maxims that not merely do not manipulate them but that foster some of their plans and activities. Beneficent acts try to achieve what others want. However, we cannot seek everything that others want; their wants are too numerous and diverse, and, of course, sometimes incompatible. It follows that beneficence has to be selective.

There is then quite a sharp distinction between the requirements of justice and of beneficence in Kantian ethics. Justice requires that we act on *no* maxims that use others as mere means. Beneficence requires that we act on *some* maxims that foster others' ends, though it is a matter for judgment and discretion which of their ends we foster. Some maxims no doubt ought not to be fostered because it would be unjust to do so. Kantians are not committed to working interminably through a list of happiness-producing and misery-reducing acts; but there are some acts whose obligatoriness utilitarians may need to debate as they try to compare total outcomes of different choices, to which Kantians are stringently bound. Kantians will claim that they have done nothing wrong if none of their acts is unjust, and that their duty is complete if in addition their life plans have in the circumstances been reasonably beneficent.

In making sure that they meet all the demands of justice, Kantians do not try to compare all available acts and see which has the best effects. They consider only the proposals for action that occur to them and check that these proposals use no other as mere means. If they do not, the act is permissible; if omitting the act would use another as mere means, the act is obligatory. Kant's theory has less scope than utilitarianism. Kantians do not claim to discover whether acts whose maxims they don't know fully are just. They may be reluctant to judge others' acts or policies that cannot be regarded as the maxim of any person or institution. They cannot rank acts in order of merit. Yet, the theory offers more precision than utilitarianism when data are scarce. One can usually tell whether one's act would use others as mere means, even when its impact on human happiness is thoroughly obscure.

§26 Kantian Deliberations on Famine Problems

The theory I have just sketched may seem to have little to say about famine problems. For it is a theory that forbids us to use others as mere means but does not require us to direct our benevolence first to those who suffer most. A conscientious Kantian, it seems, has only to avoid being unjust to those who suffer famine and can then be beneficent to those nearer home. He or she would not be obliged to help the starving, even if no others were equally distressed.

Kant's moral theory does make less massive demands on moral agents than utilitarian moral theory. On the other hand, it is somewhat clearer just what the more stringent demands are, and they are not negligible. We have here a contrast between a theory that makes massive but often indeterminate demands and a theory that makes fewer but less unambiguous demands and leaves other questions, in particular the allocation of beneficence, unresolved. We have also a contrast between a theory whose scope is comprehensive and one that is applicable only to persons acting intentionally and to those institutions that adopt policies, and so maxims. Kantian ethics is silent about the moral status of unintentional action;

utilitarians seek to assess all consequences regardless of the intentions that led to them.

§27 Kantian Duties of Justice in Times of Famine

In famine situations, Kantian moral theory requires unambiguously that we do no injustice. We should not act on any maxim that uses another as mere means, so we should neither deceive nor coerce others. Such a requirement can become quite exacting when the means of life are scarce, when persons can more easily be coerced, and when the advantage of gaining more than what is justly due to one is great. I shall give a list of acts that on Kantian principles it would be unjust to do, but that one might be strongly tempted to do in famine conditions.

I will begin with a list of acts that one might be tempted to do as a member of a famine-stricken population. First, where there is a rationing scheme, one ought not to cheat and seek to get more than one's share—any scheme of cheating will use someone as mere means. Nor may one take advantage of others' desperation to profiteer or divert goods onto the black market or to accumulate a fortune out of others' misfortunes. Transactions that are outwardly sales and purchases can be coercive when one party is desperate. All the forms of corruption that deceive or put pressure on others are also wrong: hoarding unallocated food, diverting relief supplies for private use, corruptly using one's influence to others' disadvantage. Such requirements are far from trivial and frequently violated in hard times. In severe famines, refraining from coercing and deceiving may risk one's own life and require the greatest courage.

Second, justice requires that in famine situations one still try to fulfill one's duties to particular others. For example, even in times of famine, a person has duties to try to provide for dependents. These duties may, tragically, be unfulfillable. If they are, Kantian ethical theory would not judge wrong the acts of a person who had done her or his best. There have no doubt been times in human history where there was nothing to be done except abandon the weak and old or to leave children to fend for themselves as best they might. But providing the supporter of dependents acts on maxims of attempting to meet their claims, he or she uses no others as mere means to his or her own survival and is not unjust. A conscientious attempt to meet the particular obligations one has undertaken may also require of one many further maxims of self-restraint and of endeavor—for example, it may require a conscientious attempt to avoid having (further) children; it may require contributing one's time and effort to programs of economic development. Where there is no other means to fulfill particular obligations, Kantian principles may require a generation of sacrifice. They will not, however, require one to seek to maximize the happiness of later generations but only to establish the modest security and prosperity needed for meeting present obligations.

The obligations of those who live with or near famine are undoubtedly stringent and exacting; for those who live further off it is rather harder to see what a Kantian moral theory demands. Might it not, for example, be permissible to do nothing at all about those suffering famine? Might one not ensure that one does nothing unjust to the victims of famine by adopting no maxims whatsoever that mention them? To do so would, at the least, require one to refrain from certain deceptive and coercive practices frequently employed during the European exploration and economic penetration of the now underdeveloped world and still not unknown. For example, it would be unjust to "purchase" valuable lands and resources from persons who don't understand commercial transactions or exclusive property rights or mineral rights, so do not understand that their acceptance of trinkets destroys their traditional economic pattern and way of life. The old adage "trade follows the flag" reminds us to how great an extent the economic pentration of the less-developed countries involved elements of coercion and deception, so was on Kantian principles unjust (regardless of whether or not the net effect has benefited the citizens of those countries).

Few persons in the developed world today find themselves faced with the possibility of adopting on a grand scale maxims of deceiving or coercing persons living in poverty. But at least some people find that their jobs require them to make decisions about investment and aid policies that enormously affect the lives of those nearest to famine. What does a commitment to Kantian moral theory demand of such persons?

It has become common in writings in ethics and social policy to distinguish between one's *personal responsibilities* and one's *role responsibilities*. So a person may say, "As an individual I sympathize, but in my official capacity I can do nothing"; or we may excuse persons' acts of coercion because they are acting in some particular capacity—e.g., as a soldier or a jailer. On the other hand, this distinction isn't made or accepted by everyone. At the Nuremberg trials of war criminals, the defense "I was only doing my job" was disallowed, at least for those whose command position meant that they had some discretion in what they did. Kantians generally would play down any distinction between a person's own responsibilities and his or her role responsibilities. They would not deny that in any capacity one is accountable for certain things for which as a private person one is not accountable. For example, the treasurer of an organization is accountable to the board and has to present periodic reports and to keep specified records. But if she fails to do one of these things for which she is held accountable she will be held responsible for that failure—it will be imputable to her as an individual. When we take on positions, we *add* to our responsibilities those that the job requires; but we do not lose those that are already required of us. Our social role or job gives us, on Kant's view, no license to use others as mere means; even business executives and aid officials and social revolutionaries will act unjustly, so wrongly, if they deceive or coerce—however benevolent their motives.

If persons are responsible for all their acts, it follows that it would be unjust for aid officials to coerce persons into accepting sterilization, wrong for them to use coercive power to achieve political advantages (such as military bases) or commercial advantages (such as trade agreements that will harm the other country). It would be wrong for the executives of large corporations to extort too high a price for continued operation employment and normal trading. Where a less-developed country is pushed to exempt a multinational corporation from tax laws, or to construct out of its meager tax revenues the infrastructure of roads, harbors, or airports (not to mention executive mansions) that the corporation—but perhaps not the country—needs, then one suspects that some coercion has been involved.

The problem with such judgments—and it is an immense problem—is that it is hard to identify coercion and deception in complicated institutional settings. It is not hard to understand what is coercive about one person threatening another with serious injury if he won't comply with the first person's suggestion. But it is not at all easy to tell where the outward forms of political and commercial negotiation—which often involve an element of threat—have become coercive. I can't here explore this fascinating question. But I think it is at least fairly clear that the preservation of the outward forms of negotiation, bargaining, and voluntary consent do *not* demonstrate that there is no coercion, especially when one party is vastly more powerful or the other in dire need. Just as our judiciary has a long tradition of voiding contracts and agreements on grounds of duress or incompetence of one of the parties, so one can imagine a tribunal of an analogous sort rejecting at least some treaties and agreements as coercive, despite the fact that they were negotiated between "sovereign" powers or their representatives. In particular, where such agreements were negotiated with some of the cruder deceptions and coercion of the early days of European economic expansion or the subtler coercions and deceptions of contemporary superpowers, it seems doubtful that the justice of the agreement could be sustained.

Justice, of course, is not everything, even for Kantians. But its demands are ones that they can reasonably strive to fulfill. They may have some uncertain moments—for example, does advocating cheap raw materials mean advocating an international trade system in which the less developed will continue to suffer the pressures of the developed world—or is it a benevolent policy that will maximize world trade and benefit all parties, while doing no one an injustice? But for Kantians, the important moral choices are above all those in which one acts directly, not those in which one decides which patterns of actions to encourage in others or in those institutions that one can influence. And such moral decisions include decisions about the benevolent acts that one will or will not do.

§28 Kantian Duties of Beneficence in Times of Famine

The grounds of duties of beneficence are that such acts not merely don't use others as mere means but are acts that develop or promote others' ends and that, in particular, foster others' capacities to pursue ends, to be autonomous beings.

Clearly there are many opportunities for beneficence. But one area in which the *primary* task of developing others' capacity to pursue their own ends is particularly needed is in the parts of the world where extreme poverty and hunger leave people unable to pursue *any* of their other ends. Beneficence directed at putting people in a position to pursue whatever ends they may have has, for Kant, a stronger claim on us than beneficence directed at sharing ends with those who are already in a position to pursue varieties of ends. It would be nice if I bought a tennis racquet to play with my friend who is tennis mad and never has enough partners; but it is more important to make people able to plan their own lives to a minimal extent. It is nice to walk a second mile with someone who requests one's company; better to share a cloak with someone who may otherwise be too cold to make any journey. Though these suggestions are not a detailed set of instructions for the allocation of beneficence by Kantians, they show that relief of famine must stand very high among duties of beneficence.

§29 The Limits of Kantian Ethics: Intentions and Results

Kantian ethics differs from utilitarian ethics both in its scope and in the precision with which it guides action. Every action, whether of a person or of an agency, can be assessed by utilitarian methods, provided only that information is available about all the consequences of the act. The theory has unlimited scope, but, owing to a lack of data, often lacks precision. Kantian ethics has a more restricted scope. Since it assesses actions by looking at the maxims of agents, it can only assess intentional acts. This means that it is most at home in assessing individuals' acts; but it can be extended to assess acts of agencies that (like corporations and governments and student unions) have decision-making procedures. It can do nothing to assess patterns of action that reflect no intention or policy, hence it cannot assess the acts of groups lacking decision-making procedures, such as the student movement, the women's movement, or the consumer movement.

It may seem a great limitation of Kantian ethics that it concentrates on intentions to the neglect of results. It might seem that all conscientious Kantians have to do is to make sure that they never intend to use others as mere means, and that they sometimes intend to foster others' ends. And, as we all know, good intentions sometimes lead to bad results, and correspondingly, bad intentions sometimes do no harm, or even produce good. If Hardin is right, the good intentions of those who feed the starving lead to dreadful results in the long run. If some traditional arguments in favor of capitalism are right, the greed and selfishness of the profit motive have produced unparalleled prosperity for many.

But such discrepancies between intentions and results are the exception and not the rule. For we cannot just *claim* that our intentions are good and do what we will. Our intentions reflect what we expect the immediate results of our action to be. Nobody credits the "intentions" of a couple who practice neither celibacy nor contraception but still insist "we never meant to have (more) children." Conception is likely (and known to be likely) in such cases. Where people's expressed intentions ignore the normal and predictable results of what they do, we infer that (if they are not amazingly ignorant) their words do not express their true intentions. The Formula of the End in Itself applies to the intentions on which one acts—not to some prettified version that one may avow. Provided this intention—the agent's real intention—uses no other as mere means, he or she does nothing unjust. If some of his or her intentions foster others' ends, then he or she is sometimes beneficent. It is therefore possible for people to test their proposals by Kantian arguments even when they lack the comprehensive causal knowledge that utilitarianism requires. Conscientious Kantians can work out whether they will be doing wrong by some act even though they know that their foresight is limited and that they may cause some harm or fail to cause some benefit. But they will not cause harms that they can foresee without this being reflected in their intentions.

Note

1. I. Kant, *Groundwork of the Metaphysic of Morals*, trans. H. H. Paton (New York: Harper Torchbooks, 1964), p. 96.

War and Massacre

THOMAS NAGEL

From the apathetic reaction to atrocities committed in Vietnam by the United States and its allies, one may conclude that moral restrictions on the conduct of war command almost as little sympathy among the general public as they do among those charged with the formation of U.S. military policy.[1] Even when restrictions on the conduct of warfare are defended, it is usually on legal grounds alone: their moral basis is often poorly understood. I wish to argue that certain restrictions are neither arbitrary nor merely conventional, and that their validity does not depend simply on their usefulness. There is, in other words, a moral basis for the rules of war, even though the conventions now officially in force are far from giving it perfect expression.

I

No elaborate moral theory is required to account for what is wrong in cases like the Mylai massacre, since it did not serve, and was not intended to serve, any strategic purpose. Moreover, if the participation of the United States in the Indo-Chinese war is entirely wrong to begin with, then that engagement is incapable of providing a justification for *any* measures taken in its pursuit—not only for the measures which are atrocities in every war, however just its aims.

But this war has revealed attitudes of a more general kind, which influenced the conduct of earlier wars as well. After it has ended, we shall still be faced with the problem of how warfare may be conducted, and the attitudes that have resulted in the specific conduct of this war will not have disappeared. Moreover, similar problems can arise in wars or rebellions fought for very different reasons, and against very different opponents. It is not easy to keep a firm grip on the idea of what is not permissible in warfare, because while some military actions are obvious atrocities, other cases are more difficult to assess, and the general principles underlying these judgments remain obscure. Such obscurity can lead to the abandonment of sound intuitions in favor of criteria whose rationale may be more obvious. If such a tendency is to be resisted, it will require a better understanding of the restrictions than we now have.

I propose to discuss the most general moral problem raised by the conduct of warfare: the problem of means and ends. In one view, there are limits on what may be done even in the service of an end worth pursuing—and even when adherence to the restriction may be very costly. A person who acknowledges the force of such restrictions can find himself in acute moral dilemmas. He may believe, for example, that by torturing a prisoner he can obtain information necessary to prevent a disaster, or that by obliterating one village with bombs he can halt a campaign of terrorism. If he believes that the gains from a certain measure will clearly outweigh its costs, yet still supects that he ought not to adopt it, then he is in a dilemma produced by the conflict between two disparate categories of moral reason: categories that may be called *utilitarian* and *absolutist*.

Utilitarianism gives primacy to a concern with what will *happen*. Absolutism gives primacy to a concern with what one is *doing*. The conflict between them arises because the alternatives we

From *Mortal Questions* (Cambridge: Cambridge University Press, 1979), pp. 53–74.

face are rarely just choices between *total outcomes:* they are also choices between alternative pathways or measures to be taken. When one of the choices is to do terrible things to another person, the problem is altered fundamentally; it is no longer merely a question of which outcome would be worse.

Few of us are completely immune to either of these types of moral intuition, though in some people, either naturally or for doctrinal reasons, one type will be dominant and the other suppressed or weak. But it is perfectly possible to feel the force of both types of reason very strongly; in that case the moral dilemma in certain situations of crisis will be acute, and it may appear that every possible course of action or inaction is unacceptable for one reason or another.

II

Although it is this dilemma that I propose to explore, most of the discussion will be devoted to its absolutist component. The utilitarian component is straightforward by comparison, and has a natural appeal to anyone who is not a complete skeptic about ethics. Utilitarianism says that one should try, either individually or through institutions, to maximize good and minimize evil (the definition of these categories need not enter into the schematic formulation of the view), and that if faced with the possibility of preventing a great evil by producing a lesser, one should choose the lesser evil. There are certainly problems about the formulation of utilitarianism, and much has been written about it, but its intent is morally transparent. Nevertheless, despite the additions and refinements, it continues to leave large portions of ethics unaccounted for. I do not suggest that some form of absolutism can account for them all, only that an examination of absolutism will lead us to see the complexity, and perhaps the incoherence, of our moral ideas.

Utilitarianism certainly justifies *some* restrictions on the conduct of warfare. There are strong utilitarian reasons for adhering to any limitation which seems natural to most people—particularly if the limitation is widely accepted already. An exceptional measure which seems to be justified by its results in a particular conflict may create a precedent with disastrous long-term effects.[2] It may even be argued that war involves violence on such a scale that it is never justified on utilitarian grounds—the consequences of refusing to go to war will never be as bad as the war itself would be, even if atrocities were not committed. Or in a more sophisticated vein it might be claimed that a uniform policy of never resorting to military force would do less harm in the long run, if followed consistently, than a policy of deciding each case on utilitarian grounds (even though on occasion particular applications of the pacifist policy might have worse results than a specific utilitarian decision). But I shall not consider these arguments, for my concern is with reasons of a different kind, which may remain when reasons of utility and interest fail.[3]

In the final analysis, I believe that the dilemma cannot always be resolved. While not every conflict between absolutism and utilitarianism creates an insoluble dilemma, and while it seems to me certainly right to adhere to absolutist restrictions unless the utilitarian considerations favoring violation are overpoweringly weighty and extremely certain—nevertheless, when that special condition is met, it may become impossible to adhere to an absolutist position. What I shall offer, therefore, is a somewhat qualified defense of absolutism. I believe it underlies a valid and fundamental type of moral judgment—which cannot be reduced to or overridden by other principles. And while there may be other principles just as fundamental, it is particularly important not to lose confidence in our absolutist intuitions, for they are often the only barrier before the abyss of utilitarian apologetics for large-scale murder.

III

One absolutist position that creates no problems of interpretation is pacifism: the view that one may not kill another person under any circumstances, no matter what good would be achieved or evil averted thereby. The type of absolutist position that I am going to discuss is different. Pacifism draws the conflict with utilitarian considerations very starkly. But there are other views according to which violence may be undertaken, even on a large scale, in a clearly just cause, so long as certain absolute restrictions on the character and direction of that violence are observed. The line is drawn somewhat closer to the bone, but it exists.

The philosopher who has done most to advance contemporary philosophical discussion of such a view, and to explain it to those unfamiliar with its extensive treatment in Roman Catholic moral theology, is G. E. M. Anscombe. In 1958 Miss Anscombe published a pamphlet entitled *Mr. Truman's Degree,*[4] on the occasion of the award by Oxford University of an honorary doctorate to Harry Truman. The pamphlet explained why she had opposed the decision to award that degree, recounted the story of her unsuccessful opposition, and offered some reflections on the history of Truman's decision to drop atom bombs on Hiroshima and Nagasaki, and on the difference between murder and allowable killing in warfare. She pointed out that the policy of deliberately killing large numbers of civilians either as a means or as an end in itself did not originate with Truman, and was common practice among all parties during World War II for some time before Hiroshima. The Allied area bombings of German cities by conventional explosives included raids which killed more civilians than did the atomic attacks; the same is true of certain fire-bomb raids on Japan.

The policy of attacking the civilian population in order to induce an enemy to surrender, or to damage his morale, seems to have been widely accepted in the civilized world, and seems to be accepted still, at least if the stakes are high enough. It gives evidence of a moral conviction that the deliberate killing of noncombatants—women, children, old people—is permissible if enough can be gained by it. This follows from the more general position that any means can in principle be justified if it leads to a sufficiently worthy end. Such an attitude is evident not only in the more spectacular current weapons systems but also in the day-to-day conduct of the nonglobal war in Indo-China: the indiscriminate destructiveness of antipersonnel weapons, napalm, and aerial bombardment; cruelty to prisoners; massive relocation of civilians; destruction of crops; and so forth. An absolutist position opposes to this the view that certain acts cannot be justified no matter what the consequences. Among those acts is murder—the deliberate killing of the harmless: civilians, prisoners of war, and medical personnel.

In the present war such measures are sometimes said to be regrettable, but they are generally defended by reference to military necessity and the importance of the long-term consequences of success or failure in the war. I shall pass over the inadequacy of this consequentialist defense in its own terms. (That is the dominant form of moral criticism of the war, for it is part of what people mean when they ask, "Is it worth it?") I am concerned rather to account for the inappropriateness of offering any defense of that kind for such actions.

Many people feel, without being able to say much more about it, that something has gone seriously wrong when certain measures are admitted into consideration in the first place. The fundamental mistake is made there, rather than at the point where the overall benefit of some monstrous measure is judged to outweigh its disadvantages, and it is adopted. An account of absolutism might help us to understand this. If it is not allowable to *do* certain things, such as killing unarmed prisoners or civilians, then no argument about what will happen if one does not do them can show that doing them would be all right.

Absolutism does not, of course, require one to ignore the consequences of one's acts. It operates as a limitation on utilitarian reasoning, not as a substitute for it. An absolutist can be expected to try to maximize good and minimize evil, so long as this does not require him to transgress an absolute prohibition like that against murder. But when such a conflict occurs, the prohibition takes complete precedence over any consideration of consequences. Some of the results of this view are clear enough. It requires us to forgo certain potentially useful military measures, such as the slaughter of hostages and prisoners or indiscriminate attempts to reduce the enemy civilian population by starvation, epidemic infectious diseases like anthrax and bubonic plague, or mass incineration. It means that we cannot deliberate on whether such measures are justified by the fact that they will avert still greater evils, for as intentional measures they cannot be justified in terms of any consequences whatever.

Someone unfamiliar with the events of this century might imagine that utilitarian arguments, or arguments of national interest, would suffice to deter measures of this sort. But it has become evident that such considerations are insufficient to prevent the adoption and employment of enormous antipopulation weapons once their use is considered a serious moral possibility. The same is true of the piecemeal wiping out of rural civilian populations in airborne antiguerrilla warfare. Once the door is opened to calculations of utility and national interest, the usual speculations about the future of freedom, peace, and economic prosperity can be brought to bear to ease the consciences of those responsible for a certain number of charred babies.

For this reason alone it is important to decide what is wrong with the frame of mind which allows such arguments to begin. But it is also important to understand absolutism in the cases where it genuinely conflicts with utility. Despite its appeal, it is a paradoxical position, for it can require that one refrain from choosing the lesser of two evils when that is the only choice one has. And it is additionally paradoxical because, unlike pacifism, it permits one to do horrible things to people in some circumstances but not in others.

IV

Before going on to say what, if anything, lies behind the position, there remain a few relatively technical matters which are best discussed at this point.

First, it is important to specify as clearly as possible the kind of thing to which absolutist prohibitions can apply. We must take seriously the proviso that they concern what we deliberately do to people. There could not, for example, without incoherence, be an absolute prohibition against *bringing about* the death of an innocent person. For one may find oneself in a situation in which, no matter what one does, some innocent people will die as a result. I do not mean just that there are cases in which someone will die no matter what one does, because one is not in a position to affect the outcome one way or the other. That, it is to be hoped, is one's relation to the deaths of most innocent people. I have in mind, rather, a case in which someone is bound to die, but who it is will depend on what one does. Sometimes these situations have natural causes, as when too few resources (medicine, lifeboats) are available to rescue everyone threatened with a certain catastrophe. Sometimes the situations are manmade, as when the only way to control a campaign of terrorism is to employ terrorist tactics against the community from which it has arisen. Whatever one does in cases such as these, some innocent people will die as a result. If the absolutist prohibition forbade doing what would result in the deaths of innocent people, it would have the consequence that in such cases nothing one could do would be morally permissible.

This problem is avoided, however, because what absolutism forbids is *doing* certain things to people, rather than bringing about certain *results*. Not everything that happens to others as a result of what one does is something that one has *done* to them. Catholic moral theology seeks to make this distinction precise in a doctrine known as the law of double effect, which asserts that there is a morally relevant distinction between bringing about or permitting the death of an innocent person deliberately, either as an end in itself or as a means, and bringing it about or permitting it as a side effect of something else one does deliberately. In the latter case, even if the outcome is foreseen, it is not murder, and does not fall under the absolute prohibition, though of course it may still be wrong for other reaons (reasons of utility, for example). Briefly, the principle states that one is sometimes permitted knowingly to bring about or permit as a side-effect of one's actions something which it would be absolutely impermissible to bring about or permit deliberately as an end or as a means. In application to war or revolution, the law of double effect permits a certain amount of civilian carnage as a side-effect of bombing munitions plants or attacking enemy soldiers. And even this is permissible only if the cost is not too great to be justified by one's objectives.

However, despite its importance and its usefulness in accounting for certain plausible moral judgments, I do not believe that the law of double effect is a generally applicable test for the consequences of an absolutist position. Its own application is not always clear, so that it introduces uncertainty where there need not be uncertainty.

In Indo-China, for example, there is a great deal of aerial bombardment, strafing, spraying of napalm, and employment of pellet- or needle-spraying antipersonnel weapons against rural villages in which guerrillas are suspected to be hiding, or from which small-arms fire has been received. The majority of those killed and wounded in these aerial attacks are reported to be women and children, even when some combatants are caught as well. However, the government regards these civilian casualties as a regrettable side-effect of what is a legitimate attack against an armed enemy.

It might be thought easy to dismiss this as sophistry: if one bombs, burns, or strafes a village containing a hundred people, twenty of whom one believes to be guerrillas, so that by killing most of them one will be statistically likely to kill most of the guerrillas, then is not one's attack on the group of one hundred a *means* of destroying the guerrillas, pure and simple? If one makes no attempt to discriminate between guerrillas and civilians, as is impossible in an aerial attack on a small village, then one cannot regard as a mere side-effect the deaths of those in the group that one would not have bothered to kill if more selective means had been available.

The difficulty is that this argument depends on one particular description of the act, and the reply might be that the means used against the guerrillas is not: killing everybody in the village—but rather: obliteration bombing of the *area* in which the twenty guerrillas are known to be located. If there are civilians in the area as well, they will be killed as a side-effect of such action.[5]

Because of casuistical problems like this, I prefer to stay with the original, unanalyzed distinction between what one does to people and what merely happens to them as a result of what one does. The law of double effect provides an approximation to that distinction in many cases, and perhaps it can be sharpened to the point where it does better than that. Certainly the original distinction itself needs clarification, particularly since some of the things we do to people involve things happening to them as a result of other things we do. In a case like the one discussed, however, it is clear that by bombing the village one slaughters and maims the civilians in it. Whereas by giving the only available medicine to one of two sufferers from a disease, one does not kill the other or deliberately allow him to die, even if he dies as a result.

The second technical point is this. The absolutist focus on actions rather than outcomes does not merely introduce a new, outstanding item into the catalogue of evils. That is, it does not say that the worst thing in the world is the deliberate murder of an innocent person. For if that were all, then one could presumably justify one such murder on the ground that it would prevent several others, or ten thousand on the ground that they would prevent a hundred thousand more. That is a familiar argument. But if this is allowable, then there is no absolute prohibition against murder after all. Absolutism requires that we *avoid* murder at all costs, not that we *prevent* it at all costs.

It would also be possible to adopt a deontological position less stringent than absolutism, without falling into utilitarianism. There are two ways in which someone might acknowledge the moral relevance of the distinction between deliberate and nondeliberate killing, without being an absolutist. One would be to count murder as a specially bad item in the catalogue of evils, much worse than accidental death or nondeliberate killing. But the other would be to say that deliberately killing an innocent is impermissible unless it is the only way to prevent some very large evil (say the deaths of fifty innocent people). Call this the *threshold* at which the prohibition against murder is overriden. The position is not absolutist, obviously, but it is also not equivalent to an assignment of utilitarian disvalue to murder equal to the disvalue of the threshold. This is easily seen. If a murder had the disvalue of fifty accidental deaths, it would still be permissible on utilitarian grounds to commit a murder to prevent one other murder, plus some lesser evil like a broken arm. Worse still, we would be required on utilitarian grounds to prevent one murder even at the cost of forty-nine accidental deaths that we could otherwise have prevented. These are not in fact consequences of a deontological prohibition against murder with a threshold, because it does not say that the occurrence of a certain kind of act is a bad thing, and therefore to be prevented, but rather tells everyone to *refrain* from such acts, except under certain conditions. In fact, it is perfectly compatible with a deontological prohibition against murder to hold that, considered as an outcome, a murder has *no* more disvalue than an accidental death. While the admission of thresholds would reduce the starkness of the conflicts discussed here, I do not think it would make them disappear, or change their basic character. They would persist in the clash between any deontological requirement and utilitarian values somewhat lower than its threshold.

Finally, let me remark on a frequent criticism of absolutism that depends on a misunderstanding. It is sometimes suggested that such prohibitions depend on a kind of moral self-interest, a primary obligation to preserve one's own moral purity, to keep one's hands clean no matter what happens to the rest of the world. If this were the position, it might be exposed to the charge of self-indulgence. After all, what gives one man a right to put the purity of his soul or the cleanness of his hands above the lives or welfare of large numbers of other people? It might be argued that a public servant like Truman has no right to put himself first in that way; therefore if he is convinced that the alternatives would be worse, he must give the order to drop the bombs, and take the burden of those deaths on himself, as he must do other distasteful things for the general good.

But there are two confusions behind the view that moral self-interest underlies moral absolutism. First, it is a confusion to suggest that the need to preserve one's moral purity might be the *source* of an obligation. For if by committing murder one sacrifices one's moral purity or integrity, that can only be because there is *already* something wrong with murder. The general reason against committing murder cannot therefore be merely that it makes one an immoral person. Secondly, the notion that one might sacrifice one's moral integrity justifiably, in the service of a sufficiently worthy end, is an incoherent notion. For if one were justified in making such a sacrifice (or even morally required to make it), then one would not be sacrificing one's moral integrity by adopting that course: one would be preserving it.

Moral absolutism is not unique among moral theories in requiring each person to do what will preserve his own moral purity in all circumstances. This is equally true of utilitarianism, or of any other theory which distinguishes between right and wrong. Any theory which defines the right course of action in various circumstances and asserts that one should adopt that course, ipso facto asserts that one should do what will preserve one's moral purity, simply because the right course of action *is* what will preserve one's moral purity in those circumstances. Of course utilitarianism does not assert that this is *why* one should adopt that course, but we have seen that the same is true of absolutism.

V

It is easier to dispose of false explanations of absolutism than to produce a true one. A positive account of the matter must begin with the observation that war, conflict, and aggression are relations between persons. The view that it can be wrong to consider merely the overall effect of one's actions on the general welfare comes into prominence when those actions involve relations with others. A man's acts usually affect more people than he deals with directly, and those effects must naturally be considered in his decisions. But if there are special principles governing the manner in which he should *treat* people, that will require special attention to the particular persons toward whom the act is directed, rather than just to its total effect.

Absolutist restrictions in warfare appear to be of two types: restrictions on the class of persons at whom aggression or violence may be directed and restrictions on the manner of attack, given that the object falls within that class. These can be combined, however, under the principle that hostile treatment of any person must be justified in terms of something *about that person* which makes the treatment appropriate. Hostility is a personal relation, and it must be suited to its target. One consequence of this condition will be that certain persons may not be subjected to hostile treatment in war at all, since nothing about them justifies such treatment. Others will be proper objects of hostility only in certain circumstances, or when they are engaged in certain pursuits. And the appropriate manner and extent of hostile treatment will depend on what is justified by the particular case.

A coherent view of this type will hold that extremely hostile behavior toward another is compatible with treating him as a person—even perhaps as an end in himself. This is possible only if one has not automatically stopped treating him as a person as soon as one starts to fight with him. If hostile, aggressive, or combative treatment of others always violated the condition that they be treated as human beings, it would be difficult to make further distinctions on that score *within* the class of hostile actions. That point of view, on the level of international relations, leads to the position that if complete pacifism is not accepted, no holds need be barred at all, and we may slaughter and massacre to our hearts' content, if it seems advisable. Such a position is often expressed in discussions of war crimes.

But the fact is that ordinary people do not believe this about conflicts, physical or otherwise, between individuals, and there is no more reason why it should be true of conflicts between nations. There seems to be a perfectly natural conception of the distinction between fighting clean and fighting dirty. To fight dirty is to direct one's hostility or aggression not at its proper object, but at a peripheral target which may be more vulnerable, and through which the proper object can be attacked indirectly. This applies in a fist fight, an election campaign, a duel, or a philosophical argument. If the concept is general enough to apply to all these matters, it should apply to war—both to the conduct of individual soldiers and to the conduct of nations.

Suppose that you are a candidate for public office, convinced that the election of your opponent would be a disaster, that he is an unscrupulous demagogue who will serve a narrow range of interests and seriously infringe the rights of those who disagree with him; and suppose you are convinced that you cannot defeat him by conventional means. Now imagine that various unconventional means present themselves as possibilities: you possess information about his sex life which would scandalize the electorate if made public; or you learn that his wife is an alcoholic or that in his youth he was associated for a brief period with a proscribed political party, and you believe that this information could be used to blackmail him into withdrawing his candidacy; or you can have a team of your supporters flatten the tires of a crucial subset of his supporters on election day; or you are in a position to stuff the ballot boxes; or, more simply, you can have him assassinated. What is wrong with these methods, given that they will achieve an overwhelmingly desirable result?

There are, of course, many things wrong with them: some are against the law; some infringe the procedures of an electoral process to which you are presumably committed by taking part in it; very importantly, some may backfire, and it is in the interest of all political candidates to adhere to an unspoken agreement not to allow certain personal matters to intrude into a campaign. But that is not all. We have in addition the feeling that these measures, these methods of attack, are *irrelevant* to the issue between you and your opponent, that in taking them up you would not be directing yourself to that which makes him an object of your opposition. You would be directing your attack not at the true target of your hostility, but at peripheral targets that happen to be vulnerable.

The same is true of a fight or argument outside the framework of any system of regulations or law. In an altercation with a taxi driver over an excessive fare, it is inappropriate to taunt him about his accent, flatten one of his tires, or smear chewing gum on his windshield; and it remains inappropriate even if he casts aspersions on your race, politics, or religion, or dumps the contents of your suitcase into the street.[6]

The importance of such restrictions may vary with the seriousness of the case; and what is unjustifiable in one case may be justified in a more extreme one. But they all derive from a single principle: that hostility or aggression should be directed at its true object. This means both that it should be directed at the person or persons who provoke it and that it should aim more specifically at what is provocative about them. The second condition will determine what form the hostility may appropriately take.

It is evident that some idea of the relation in which one should stand to other people underlies this principle, but the idea is difficult to state. I believe it is roughly this: whatever one does to another person intentionally must be aimed at him as a subject, with the intention that he receive it as a subject. It should manifest an attitude to *him* rather than just to the situation, and he should be able to recognize it and identify himself as its object. The procedures by which such an attitude is manifested need not be addressed to the person directly. Surgery, for example, is not a form of personal confrontation but part of a medical treatment that can be offered to a patient face to face and received by him as a response to his needs and the natural outcome of an attitude toward *him*.

Hostile treatment, unlike surgery, is already addressed *to* a person, and does not take its interpersonal meaning from a wider context. But hostile acts can serve as the expression or implementation of only a limited range of attitudes to the person who is attacked. Those attitudes in turn have as objects certain real or presumed characteristics or activities of the person which are thought to justify them. When this background is absent, hostile or aggressive behavior can no longer be intended for the reception of the victim as a subject. Instead it takes on the character of a purely bureaucratic operation. This occurs when one attacks someone who is not the true object of one's hostility—the true object may be someone else, who can be attacked through the victim; or one may not be manifesting a hostile attitude toward anyone, but merely using the easiest available path to some desired goal. One finds oneself not facing or addressing the victim at all, but operating on him—without the larger context of personal interaction that surrounds a surgical operation.

If absolutism is to defend its claim to priority over considerations of utility, it must hold that the maintenance of a direct interpersonal response to the people one deals with is a requirement which no advantages can justify one in abandoning. The requirement is absolute only if it rules out any calculation of what would justify its violation. I have said earlier that there may be circumstances so extreme that they render an absolutist position untenable. One may find then that one has no choice but to do something terrible. Nevertheless, even in such cases absolutism retains its force in that one cannot claim *justification* for the violation. It does not become *all right*.

As a tentative effort to explain this, let me try to connect absolutist limitations with the possibility of justifying *to the victim* what is being done to him. If one abandons a person in the course of rescuing several others from a fire or a sinking ship, one *could* say to him, "You understand, I have to leave you to save the others." Similarly, if one subjects an unwilling child to a painful surgical procedure, one can say to him, "If you could understand, you would realize that I am doing this to help you." One could *even* say, as one bayonets an enemy soldier, "It's either you or me." But one cannot really say while torturing a prisoner, "You understand, I have to pull out your finger-nails because it is absolutely essential that we have the names of your confederates"; nor can one say to the victims of Hiroshima, "You understand, we have to incinerate you to provide the Japanese government with an incentive to surrender."

This does not take us very far, of course, since a utilitarian would presumably be willing to offer justifications of the latter sort to his victims, in cases where he thought they were sufficient. They are really justifications to the world at large, which the victim, as a reasonable man, would be expected to appreciate. However, there seems to me something wrong with this view, for it ignores the possibility that to treat someone else horribly puts you in a special relation to him, which may have to be defended in terms of other features of your relation to him. The suggestion needs much more development; but it may help us to understand how there may be requirements which are absolute in the sense that there can be no justification for violating them. If the justification for what one did to another person had to be such that it could be offered to him specifically, rather than just to the world at large, that would be a significant source of restraint.

If the account is to be deepened, I would hope for some results along the following lines. Absolutism is associated with a view of oneself as a small being interacting with others in a large world. The justifications it requires are primarily interpersonal. Utilitarianism is associated with a view of oneself as a benevolent bureaucrat distributing such benefits as one can control to countless other beings, with whom one may have various relations or none. The justifications it requires are primarily administrative. The argument between the two moral attitudes may depend on the relative priority of these two conceptions.[7]

VI

Some of the restrictions on methods of warfare which have been adhered to from time to time are to be explained by the mutual interests of the involved parties: restrictions on weaponry, treatment of prisoners, etc. But that is not all there is to it. The conditions of directness and relevance which I have argued apply to relations of conflict and aggression apply to war as well. I have said that there are two types of absolutist restrictions on the conduct of war: those that limit the legitimate targets of hostility and those that limit its character, even when the target is acceptable. I shall say something about each of these. As will become clear, the principle I have sketched does not yield an unambiguous answer in every case.

First let us see how it implies that attacks on some people are allowed, but not attacks on others. It may seem paradoxical to assert that to fire a machine gun at someone who is throwing hand grenades at your emplacement is to treat him as a human being. Yet the relation with him is direct and straightforward.[8] The attack is aimed specifically against the threat presented by a dangerous adversary, and not against a peripheral target through which he happens to be vulnerable but which has nothing to do with that threat. For example, you might stop him by machine-gunning his wife and children, who are standing nearby, thus distracting him from his aim of blowing you up and enabling you to capture him. But if his wife and children are not threatening your life, that would be to treat them as means with a vengeance.

This, however, is just Hiroshima on a smaller scale. One objection to weapons of mass annihilation—nuclear, thermonuclear, biological, or chemical—is that their indiscriminateness disqualifies them as direct instruments for the expression of hostile relations. In attacking the civilian population, one treats neither the military enemy nor the civilians with that minimal respect which is owed to them as human beings. This is clearly true of the direct attack on people who present no threat at all. But it is also true of the character of the attack on those who *are* threatening you, i.e., the government and military forces of the enemy. Your aggression is directed against an area of vulnerability quite distinct from any threat presented by them which you may be justified in meeting. You are taking aim at them through the mundane life and survival of their countrymen, instead of aiming at the destruction of their military capacity. And of course it does not require hydrogen bombs to commit such crimes.

This way of looking at the matter also helps us to understand the importance of the distinction between combatants and noncombatants, and the irrelevance of much of the criticism offered against its intelligibility and moral significance. According to an absolutist position, deliberate killing of the innocent is murder, and in warfare the role of the innocent is filled by noncombatants. This has been thought to raise two sorts of problems: first, the widely imagined difficulty of making a division, in modern warfare, between combatants and noncombatants; second, problems deriving from the connotation of the word ''innocence''.

Let me take up the latter question first.[9] In the absolutist position, the operative notion of innocence is not moral innocence, and it is not opposed to moral guilt. If it were, then we would be justified in killing a wicked but noncombatant hairdresser in an enemy city who supported the evil policies of his government, and unjustified in killing a morally pure conscript who was driving a tank toward us with the profoundest regrets and nothing but love in his heart. But moral innocence has very little to do with it, for in the definition of murder ''innocent'' means ''currently harmless'', and it is opposed not to ''guilty'' but to ''doing harm''. It should be noted that such an analysis has the consequence that in war we may often be justified in killing people who do not deserve to die, and unjustified in killing people who do deserve to die, if anyone does.

So we must distinguish combatants from noncombatants on the basis of their immediate threat or harmfulness. I do not claim that the line is a sharp one, but it is not so difficult as is often supposed to place individuals on one side of it or the other. Children are not combatants even though they may join the armed forces if they are allowed to grow up. Women are not combatants just because they bear children or offer comfort to the soldiers. More problematic are the supporting personnel, whether in or out of uniform, from drivers of munitions trucks and army cooks to civilian munitions workers and farmers. I believe they can be plausibly classified by applying the condition that the prosecution of conflict must direct itself to the cause of danger, and not to what is peripheral. The threat presented by an army and its members does not consist merely in the fact that they are men, but in the fact that they are armed and are using their arms in the pursuit of certain objectives. Contributions to their arms and logistics are contributions to this threat; contributions to their mere existence as men are not. It is therefore wrong to direct an attack against those who merely serve the combatants' needs as human beings, such as farmers and food suppliers, even though survival as a human being is a necessary condition of efficient functioning as a soldier.

This brings us to the second group of restrictions: those that limit what may be done even to combatants. These limits are harder to explain clearly. Some of them may be arbitrary or conventional, and some may have to be derived from other sources; but I believe that the condition of directness and relevance in hostile relations accounts for them to a considerable extent.

Consider first a case which involves both a protected class of noncombatants and a restriction of the measures that may be used against combatants. One provision of the rules of war which is universally recognized, though it seems to be turning into a dead letter in Vietnam, is the special status of medical personnel and the wounded in warfare. It might be more efficient to shoot medical officers on sight and to let the enemy wounded die rather than be patched up to fight another day. But someone with medical insignia is supposed to be left alone and permitted to tend and retrieve the wounded. I believe this is because medical attention is a species of attention to completely general human needs, not specifically the needs of a combat soldier, and our conflict with the soldier is not with his existence as a human being.

By extending the application of this idea, one can justify prohibitions against certain particularly cruel weapons: starvation, poisoning, infectious diseases (supposing they could be inflicted on combatants only), weapons designed to maim or disfigure or torture the opponent rather than merely to stop him. It is not, I think, mere casuistry to claim that such weapons attack the men, not the soldiers. The effect of dum-dum bullets, for example, is much more extended than necessary to cope with the combat situation in which they are used. They abandon any attempt to discriminate in their effects between the combatant and the human being. For this reason the use of flamethrowers and napalm is an atrocity in all circumstances that I can imagine, whoever the target may be. Burns are both extremely painful and extremely disfiguring—far more than any other category of wound. That this well-known fact plays no (inhibiting) part in the determination of U.S. weapons policy suggests that moral sensitivity among public officials has not increased markedly since the Spanish Inquisition.[10]

Finally, the same condition of appropriateness to the true object of hostility should limit the scope of attacks on an enemy country: its economy, agriculture, transporation system, and so forth. Even if the parties to a military conflict are considered to be not armies or governments but entire nations (which is usually a grave error), that does not justify one nation in warring against every aspect or element of another nation. That is not justified in a conflict between individuals, and nations are even more complex than individuals, so the same reasons apply. Like a human being, a nation is engaged in countless other pursuits while waging war, and it is not in those respects that it is an enemy.

The burden of the argument has been that absolutism about murder has a foundation in principles governing all one's relations to other persons, whether aggressive or amiable, and that these principles and that absolutism, apply to warfare as well, with the result that certain measures are impermissible no matter what the consequences.[11] I do not mean to romanticize war. It is sufficiently utopian to suggest that when nations conflict they might rise to the level of limited barbarity that typically characterizes violent conflict between individuals, rather than wallowing in the moral pit where they appear to have settled, surrounded by enormous arsenals.

VI

Having described the elements of the absolutist position, we must now return to the conflict between it and utilitarianism. Even if certain types of dirty tactics become acceptable when the stakes are high enough, the most serious of the prohibited acts, like murder and torture, are not just supposed to require unusually strong justification. They are supposed *never* to be done, because no quantity of resulting benefit is thought capable of *justifying* such treatment of a person.

The fact remains that when an absolutist knows or believes that the utilitarian cost of refusing to adopt a prohibited course will be very high, he may hold to his refusal to adopt it, but he will find it difficult to feel that a moral dilemma has been satisfactorily resolved. The same may be true of someone who rejects an absolutist requirement and adopts instead the course yielding the most acceptable consequences. In either case, it is possible to feel that one has acted for reasons insufficient to justify violation of the opposing principle. In situations of deadly conflict, particularly where a weaker party is threatened with annihilation or enslavement by a stronger one, the argument for resorting to atrocities can be powerful, and the dilemma acute.

There may exist principles, not yet codified, which would enable us to resolve such dilemmas. But then again there may not. We must face the pessimistic alternative that these two forms of moral intuition are not capable of being brought together into a single, coherent moral system, and that the world can present us with situations in which there is no honorable or moral course for a man to take, no course free of guilt and responsibility for evil.[12]

The idea of a moral blind alley is a perfectly intelligible one. It is possible to get into such a situation by one's own fault, and people do it all the time. If, for example, one makes two incompatible promises or commitments—becomes engaged to two people, for example—then there is no course one can take which is not wrong, for one must break one's promise to at least one of them. Making a clean breast of the whole thing will not be enough to remove one's reprehensibility. The existence of such cases is not morally disturbing, however, because we feel that the situation was not unavoidable: one had to do something wrong in the first place to get into it. But what if the world itself, or someone else's actions, could face a previously innocent person with a choice between morally abominable courses of action, and leave him no way to escape with his honor? Our intuitions rebel at the idea, for we feel that the constructibility of such a case must show a contradiction in our moral views. But it is not in itself a contradiction to say that someone can do X or not do X, and that for him to take either course would be wrong. It merely contradicts the supposition that *ought* implies *can*—since presumably one ought to refrain from what is wrong, and in such a case it is impossible to do so.[13] Given the limitations on human action, it is naïve to suppose that there is a solution to every moral problem with which the world can face us. We have always known that the world is a bad place. It appears that it may be an evil place as well.

Notes

1. This essay was completed in 1971. Direct U.S. military involvement in the Vietnam War lasted from 1961 to 1973. Hence the present tense.
2. Straightforward considerations of national interest often tend in the same direction: the inadvisability of using nuclear weapons seems to be overdetermined in this way.
3. These reasons, moreover, have special importance in that they are available even to one who denies the appropriateness of utilitarian considerations in international matters. He may acknowledge limitations on what may be done to the soldiers and civilians of other countries in pursuit of his nation's military objectives, while denying that one country should in general consider the interests of nationals of other countries in determining its policies.
4. (Privately printed.) See also her essay "War and Murder," in *Nuclear Weapons and Christian Conscience,* ed. Walter Stein (London: The Merlin Press, 1961). The present paper is much indebted to these two essays throughout. These and related subjects are extensively treated by Paul Ramsey in *The Just War* (New York: Scribners, 1968). Among recent writings that bear on the moral problem are Jonathan Bennett, "Whatever the Consequences," *Analysis,* 26, no. 3 (1966), 83–102; and Philippa Foot, "The Problem of Abortion and the Doctrine of the Double Effect," *Oxford Review,* 5 (1967), 5–15. Miss Anscombe's replies are "A Note on Mr. Bennett," *Analysis,* 26, no. 3 (1966), 208 and "Who Is Wronged?" *Oxford Review,* 5 (1967), 16–17.
5. This counter-argument was suggested by Rogers Albritton.
6. Why, on the other hand, does it seem appropriate, rather than irrelevant, to punch someone in the mouth if he insults you? The answer is that in our culture it is an insult to punch someone in the mouth, and

not just an injury. This reveals, by the way, a perfectly unobjectionable sense in which convention may play a part in determining exactly what falls under an absolutist restriction and what does not. I am indebted to Robert Fogelin for this point.

7. Finally, I should mention a different possibility, suggested by Robert Nozick: that there is a strong general presumption against benefiting from the calamity of another, whether or not it has been deliberately inflicted for that or any other reason. This broader principle may well lend its force to the absolutist position.
8. Marshall Cohen once remarked that, according to my view, shooting at someone establishes an I–thou relationship.
9. What I say on this subject derives from Anscombe.
10. Beyond this I feel uncertain. Ordinary bullets, after all, can cause death, and nothing is more permanent than that. I am not at all sure why we are justified in trying to kill those who are trying to kill us (rather than merely in trying to stop them with force which may also result in their deaths). It is often argued that incapacitating gases are a relatively humane weapon (when not used, as in Vietnam, merely to make people easier to shoot). Perhaps the legitimacy of restrictions against them must depend on the dangers of escalation, and the great utility of maintaining *any* conventional category of restriction so long as nations are willing to adhere to it.

    Let me make clear that I do not regard my argument as a defense of the moral immutability of the Hague and Geneva Conventions. Rather, I believe that they rest partly on a moral foundation, and that modifications of them should also be assessed on moral grounds.
11. It is possible to draw a more radical conclusion, which I shall not pursue here. Perhaps the technology and organization of modern war are such as to make it impossible to wage as an acceptable form of interpersonal or even international hostility. Perhaps it is too impersonal and large-scale for that. If so, then absolutism would in practice imply pacifism, given the present state of things. On the other hand, I am skeptical about the unstated assumption that a technology dictates its own use.
12. In his reply to this essay ("Rules of War and Moral Reasoning," *Philosophy & Public Affairs,* I, no. 2 [Winter, 1972], 167), R. M. Hare pointed out the apparent discrepancy between my acceptance of such a possibility here and my earlier claim in section IV that absolutism must be formulated so as to avoid the consequence that in certain cases nothing one could do would be morally permissible. The difference is that in those cases the moral incoherence would result from the application of a single principle, whereas the dilemmas described here result from a conflict between two fundamentally different types of principle.
13. This was first pointed out to me by Christopher Boorse. The point is also made in E. J. Lemmon's "Moral Dilemmas," *Philosophical Review,* 71 (April, 1962), 150.

3. ARISTOTELIAN ETHICS

Nicomachean Ethics

ARISTOTLE

Aristotle (384–322 B.C.) was a student of Plato's who, some think, surpassed his teacher to become the greatest philosopher of all. His works include *Metaphysics, Categories, Physics,* and many others in addition to the *Nicomachean Ethics.*

Book I

1 Every art and every inquiry, and similarly every
1094a action and pursuit, is thought to aim at some good; and for this reason the good has rightly been declared to be that at which all things aim. But a certain difference is found among ends; some are activities, others are products apart from the activities that produce them. Where there are ends apart from the actions, it is the nature of the products to be better than the activities. Now, as there are many actions, arts, and sciences, their ends also are many; the end of the medical art is health, that of shipbuilding a vessel, that of strategy victory, that of economics wealth. But where such arts fall under a single capacity—as bridle-making and the other arts concerned with the equipment of horses fall under the art of riding, and this and every military action under strategy, in the same way other arts fall under yet others—in all of these the ends of the master arts are to be preferred to all the subordinate ends; for it is for the sake of the former that the latter are pursued. It makes no difference whether the activities themselves are the ends of the actions, or something else apart from the activities, as in the case of the sciences just mentioned.

If, then, there is some end of the things we 2
do, which we desire for its own sake (everything else being desired for the sake of this), and if we do not choose everything for the sake of something else (for at that rate the process would go on to infinity, so that our desire would be empty and vain), clearly this must be the good and the chief good. Will not the knowledge of it, then, have a great influence on life? Shall we not, like archers who have a mark to aim at, be more likely to hit upon what is right? If so, we must try, in outline at least, to determine what it is, and of which of the sciences or capacitites it is the object. It would seem to belong to the most authoritative art and that which is most truly the master art. And politics appears to be of this nature; for
it is this that ordains which of the sciences should 1094b
be studied in a state, and which each class of citizens should learn and up to what point they should learn them; and we see even the most highly esteemed of capacities to fall under this, e.g. strategy, economics, rhetoric; now, since politics uses the rest of the sciences, and since, again, it legislates as to what we are to do and what we are to abstain from, the end of this science must include those of the others, so that this end must be the good for man. For even if the

From *Nicomachean Ethics,* trans. W. D. Ross (Oxford: Oxford University Press, 1925), pp. 1094a1–1096a10, 1097a15–1099b8, 1102a5–1109b27, 1177a11–1179a32.

end is the same for a single man and for a state, that of the state seems at all events something greater and more complete whether to attain or to preserve; though it is worth while to attain the end merely for one man, it is finer and more godlike to attain it for a nation or for city-states. These, then, are the ends at which our inquiry aims, since it is political science, in one sense of that term.

3 Our discussion will be adequate if it has as much clearness as the subject-matter admits of, for precision is not to be sought for alike in all discussions, any more than in all the products of the crafts. Now fine and just actions, which political science investigates, admit of much variety and fluctuation of opinion, so that they may be thought to exist only by convention, and not by nature. And goods also give rise to a similar fluctuation because they bring harm to many people; for before now men have been undone by reason of their wealth, and others by reason of their courage. We must be content, then, in speaking of such subjects and with such premisses to indicate the truth roughly and in outline, and in speaking about things which are only for the most part true and with premisses of the same kind to reach conclusions that are no better. In the same spirit, therefore, should each type of statement be *received;* for it is the mark of an educated man to look for precision in each class of things just so far as the nature of the subject admits; it is evidently equally foolish to accept probable reasoning from a mathematician and to demand from a rhetorician scientific proofs.

1095[a] Now each man judges well the things he knows, and of these he is a good judge. And so the man who has been educated in a subject is a good judge of that subject, and the man who has received an all-round education is a good judge in general. Hence a young man is not a proper hearer of lectures on political science; for he is inexperienced in the actions that occur in life, but its discussions start from these and are about these; and, further, since he tends to follow his passions, his study will be vain and unprofitable, because the end aimed at is not knowledge but action. And it makes no difference whether he is young in years or youthful in character; the defect does not depend on time, but on his living, and pursuing each successive object, as passion directs. For to such persons, as to the incontinent, knowledge brings no profit; but to those who desire and act in accordance with a rational principle knowledge about such matters will be of great benefit.

These remarks about the student, the sort of treatment to be expected, and the purpose of the inquiry, may be taken as our preface.

Let us resume our inquiry and state, in view 4
of the fact that all knowledge and every pursuit aims at some good, what it is that we say political science aims at and what is the highest of all goods achievable by action. Verbally there is very general agreement; for both the general run of men and people of superior refinement say that it is happiness, and identify living well and doing well with being happy; but with regard to what happiness is they differ, and the many do not give the same account as the wise. For the former think it is some plain and obvious thing, like pleasure, wealth, or honour; they differ, however, from one another—and often even the same man identifies it with different things, with health when he is ill, with wealth when he is poor; but, conscious of their ignorance, they admire those who proclaim some great ideal that is above their comprehension. Now some thought that apart from these many goods there is another which is self-subsistent and causes the goodness of all these as well. To examine all the opinions that have been held were perhaps somewhat fruitless; enough to examine those that are most prevalent or that seem to be arguable.

Let us not fail to notice, however, that there is a difference between arguments from and those to the first principles. For Plato, too, was right in raising this question and asking, as he used to do, "are we on the way from or to the first principles?" There is a difference, as there is in a racecourse between the course from the judges to the turning-point and the way back. For, while we must begin with what is known, things are objects of knowledge in two senses—some to us, some without qualification. Presumably, then, *we* must begin with things known to *us*. Hence any one who is to listen intelligently to lectures about what is noble and just and, generally, about the subjects of political science must have been brought up in good habits. For the fact is the starting-point, and if this is sufficiently plain to him, he will not at the start need the reason as well; and the man who has been well brought up has or can easily get starting-points. And as for him who neither has nor can get them, let him hear the words of Hesiod:

Far best is he who knows all things himself;
Good, he that hearkens when men counsel right;
But he who neither knows, nor lays to heart
Another's wisdom, is a useless wight.

5 Let us, however, resume our discussion from the point at which we digressed. To judge from the lives that men lead, most men, and men of the most vulgar type, seem (not without some ground) to identify the good, or happiness, with pleasure; which is the reason why they love the life of enjoyment. For there are, we may say, three prominent types of life—that just mentioned, the political, and thirdly the contemplative life. Now the mass of mankind are evidently quite slavish in their tastes, preferring a life suitable to beasts, but they get some ground for their view from the fact that many of those in high places share the tastes of Sardanapallus. A consideration of the prominent types of life shows that people of superior refinement and of active disposition identify happiness with honour; for this is, roughly speaking, the end of the political life. But it seems too superficial to be what we are looking for, since it is thought to depend on those who bestow honour rather than on him who receives it, but the good we divine to be something proper to a man and not easily taken from him. Further, men seem to pursue honour in order that they may be assured of their goodness; at least it is by men of practical wisdom that they seek to be honoured, and among those who know them, and on the ground of their virtue; clearly, then, according to them, at any rate, virtue is better. And perhaps one might even suppose this to be, rather than honour, the end of the political life. But even this appears somewhat incomplete; for possession of virtue seems actually compatible with being asleep, or with lifelong inactivity, and, further,
1096a with the greatest sufferings and misfortunes; but a man who was living so no one would call happy, unless he were maintaining a thesis at all costs. Third comes the contemplative life, which we shall consider later. But enough of this; for the subject has been sufficiently treated even in the current discussions.

The life of money-making is one undertaken under compulsion, and wealth is evidently not the good we are seeking; for it is merely useful and for the sake of something else. And so one might rather take the aforenamed objects to be ends; for they are loved for themselves. But it is evident that not even these are ends; yet many arguments have been thrown away in support of them. Let us leave this subject, then.

. . . .

Let us again return to the good we are seek- 7
ing, and ask what it can be. It seems different in different actions and arts; it is different in medicine, in strategy, and in the other arts likewise. What then is the good of each? Surely that for whose sake everything else is done. In medicine this is health, in strategy victory, in architecture a house, in any other sphere something else, and in every action and pursuit the end; for it is for the sake of this that all men do whatever else they do. Therefore, if there is an end for all that we do, this will be the good achievable by action, and if there are more than one, these will be the goods achievable by action.

So the argument has by a different course reached the same point; but we must try to state this even more clearly. Since there are evidently more than one end, and we choose some of these (e.g. wealth, flutes, and in general instruments) for the sake of something else, clearly not all ends are final ends; but the chief good is evidently something final. Therefore, if there is only one final end, this will be what we are seeking, and if there are more than one, the most final of these will be what we are seeking. Now we call that which is in itself worthy of pursuit more final than that which is worthy of pursuit for the sake of something else, and that which is never desirable for the sake of something else more final than the things that are desirable both in themselves and for the sake of that other thing, and therefore we call final without qualification that which is always desirable in itself and never for the sake of something else.

Now such a thing happiness, above all else, is 1097b
held to be; for this we choose always for itself and never for the sake of something else, but

honour, pleasure, reason, and every virtue we choose indeed for themselves (for if nothing resulted from them we should still choose each of them), but we choose them also for the sake of happiness, judging that by means of them we shall be happy. Happiness, on the other hand, no one chooses for the sake of these, nor, in general, for anything other than itself.

From the point of view of self-sufficiency the same result seems to follow; for the final good is thought to be self-sufficient. Now by self-sufficient we do not mean that which is sufficient for a man by himself, for one who lives a solitary life, but also for parents, children, wife, and in general for his friends and fellow citizens, since man is born for citizenship. But some limit must be set to this; for if we extend our requirement to ancestors and descendants and friends' friends we are in for an infinite series. Let us examine this question, however, on another occasion; the self-sufficient we now define as that which when isolated makes life desirable and lacking in nothing; and such we think happiness to be; and further we think it most desirable of all things, without being counted as one good thing among others—if it were so counted it would clearly be made more desirable by the addition of even the least of goods; for that which is added becomes an excess of goods, and of goods the greater is always more desirable. Happiness, then, is something final and self-sufficient, and is the end of action.

Presumably, however, to say that happiness is the chief good seems a platitude, and a clearer account of what it is is still desired. This might perhaps be given, if we could first ascertain the function of man. For just as for a flute-player, a sculptor, or any artist, and, in general, for all things that have a function or activity, the good and the "well" is thought to reside in the function, so would it seem to be for man, if he has a function. Have the carpenter, then, and the tanner certain functions or activities, and has man none? Is he born without a function? Or as eye, hand, foot, and in general each of the parts evidently has a function, may one lay it down that man similarly has a function apart from all these? What then can this be? Life seems to be common even to plants, but we are seeking what is peculiar to man. Let us exclude, therefore, the life of
1098a nutrition and growth. Next there would be a life of perception, but *it* also seems to be common even to the horse, the ox, and every animal. There remains, then, an active life of the element that has a rational principle; of this, one part has such a principle in the sense of being obedient to one, the other in the sense of possessing one and exercising thought. And, as "life of the rational element" also has two meanings, we must state that life in the sense of activity is what we mean; for this seems to be the more proper sense of the term. Now if the function of man is an activity of soul which follows or implies a rational principle, and if we say "a so-and-so" and "a good so-and-so" have a function which is the same in kind, e.g. a lyre-player and a good lyre-player, and so without qualification in all cases, eminence in respect of goodness being added to the name of the function (for the function of a lyre-player is to play the lyre, and that of a good lyre-player is to do so well): if this is the case, [and we state the function of man to be a certain kind of life, and this to be an activity or actions of the soul implying a rational principle, and the function of a good man to be the good and noble performance of these, and if any action is well performed when it is performed in accordance with the appropriate excellence: if this is the case,] human good turns out to be activity of soul in accordance with virtue, and if there are more than one virtue, in accordance with the best and most complete.

But we must add "in a complete life." For one swallow does not make a summer, nor does one day; and so too one day, or a short time, does not make a man blessed and happy.

Let this serve as an outline of the good; for we must presumably first sketch it roughly, and then later fill in the details. But it would seem that any one is capable of carrying on and articulating what has once been well outlined, and that time is a good discoverer or partner in such a work; to which facts the advances of the arts are due; for any one can add what is lacking. And we must also remember what has been said before, and not look for precision in all things alike, but in each class of things such precision as accords with the subject-matter, and so much as is appropriate to the inquiry. For a carpenter and a geometer investigate the right angle in different ways; the former does so in so far as the right angle is useful for his work, while the latter inquires what it is or what sort of thing it is; for he is a spectator of the truth. We must act in the same way, then, in all other matters as well, that our main task may not be subordinated to minor questions. Nor must we demand the cause in all matters alike; it 8b is enough in some cases that the *fact* be well established, as in the case of the first principles; the fact is the primary thing or first principle. Now of first principles we see some by induction, some by perception, some by a certain habituation, and others too in other ways. But each set of principles we must try to investigate in the natural way, and we must take pains to state them definitely, since they have a great influence on what follows. For the beginning is thought to be more than half of the whole, and many of the questions we ask are cleared up by it.

8 We must consider it, however, in the light not only of our conclusion and our premisses, but also of what is commonly said about it; for with a true view all the data harmonize, but with a false one the facts soon clash. Now goods have been divided into three classes, and some are described as external, others as relating to soul or to body; we call those that relate to soul most properly and truly goods, and psychical actions and activities we class as relating to soul. Therefore our account must be sound, at least according to this view, which is an old one and agreed on by philosophers. It is correct also in that we identify the end with certain actions and activities; for thus it falls among goods of the soul and not among external goods. Another belief which harmonizes with our account is that the happy man lives well and does well; for we have practically defined happiness as a sort of good life and good action. The characteristics that are looked for in happiness seem also, all of them, to belong to what we have defined happiness as being. For some identify happiness with virtue, some with practical wisdom, others with a kind of philosophic wisdom, others with these, or one of these, accompanied by pleasure or not without pleasure; while others include also external prosperity. Now some of these views have been held by many men and men of old, others by a few eminent persons; and it is not probable that either of these should be entirely mistaken, but rather that they should be right in at least some one respect or even in most respects.

With those who identify happiness with virtue or some one virtue our account is in harmony; for to virtue belongs virtuous activity. But it makes, perhaps, no small difference whether we place the chief good in possession or in use, in state of mind or in activity. For the state of mind may exist without producing any good result, as 1099a in a man who is asleep or in some other way quite inactive, but the activity cannot; for one who has the activity will of necessity be acting, and acting well. And as in the Olympic Games it is not the most beautiful and the strongest that are crowned but those who compete (for it is some of these that are victorious), so those who act win, and rightly win, the noble and good things in life.

Their life is also in itself pleasant. For pleasure is a state of *soul,* and to each man that which he is said to be a lover of is pleasant; e.g. not only is a horse pleasant to the lover of horses, and a spectacle to the lover of sights, but also in the same way just acts are pleasant to the lover of justice and in general virtuous acts to the lover of virtue. Now for most men their pleasures are in conflict with one another because these are not by nature pleasant, but the lovers of what is noble find pleasant the things that are by nature pleasant; and virtuous actions are such, so that these are pleasant for such men as well as in their own nature. Their life, therefore, has no further need of pleasure as a sort of adventitious charm, but has its pleasure in itself. For, besides what we have said, the man who does not rejoice in noble actions is not even good; since no one would call a man just who did not enjoy acting justly, nor any man liberal who did not enjoy liberal actions; and similarly in all other cases. If this is so, virtuous actions must be in themselves pleasant. But they are also *good* and *noble,* and have each of these attributes in the highest degree, since the good man judges well about these attributes; his judgement is such as we have described. Happiness then is the best, noblest, and most pleasant thing in the world, and these attributes are not severed as in the inscription at Delos—

Most noble is that which is justest, and best is
  health;
But pleasantest is it to win what we love.

For all these properties belong to the best activities; and these, or one—the best—of these, we identify with happiness.

1099b Yet evidently, as we said, it needs the external goods as well; for it is impossible, or not easy, to do noble acts without the proper equipment. In many actions we use friends and riches and political power as instruments; and there are some things the lack of which takes the lustre from happiness, as good birth, goodly children, beauty; for the man who is very ugly in appearance or ill-born or solitary and childless is not very likely to be happy, and perhaps a man would be still less likely if he had thoroughly bad children or friends or had lost good children or friends by death. As we said, then, happiness seems to need this sort of prosperity in addition; for which reason some identify happiness with good fortune, though others identify it with virtue.

. . . .

13 Since happiness is an activity of soul in accordance with perfect virtue, we must consider the nature of virtue; for perhaps we shall thus see better the nature of happiness. The true student of politics, too, is thought to have studied virtue above all things; for he wishes to make his fellow citizens good and obedient to the laws. As an example of this we have the lawgivers of the Cretans and the Spartans, and any others of the kind that there may have been. And if this inquiry belongs to political science, clearly the pursuit of it will be in accordance with our original plan. But clearly the virtue we must study is human virtue; for the good we were seeking was human good and the happiness human happiness. By human virtue we mean not that of the body but that of the soul; and happiness also we call an activity of soul. But if this is so, clearly the student of politics must know somehow the facts about soul, as the man who is to heal the eyes or the body as a whole must know about the eyes or the body; and all the more since politics is more prized and better than medicine; but even among doctors the best educated spend much labour on acquiring knowledge of the body. The student of politics, then, must study the soul, and must study it with these objects in view, and do so just to the extent which is sufficient for the questions we are discussing; for further precision is perhaps something more laborious than our purposes require.

Some things are said about it, adequately enough, even in the discussions outside our school, and we must use these; e.g. that one element in the soul is irrational and one has a rational principle. Whether these are separated as the parts of the body or of anything divisible are, or are distinct by definition but by nature inseparable, like convex and concave in the circumference of a circle, does not affect the present question.

Of the irrational element one division seems to be widely distributed, and vegetative in its nature, I mean that which causes nutrition and growth; for it is this kind of power of the soul that one must assign to all nurslings and to em- 110
bryos, and this same power to full-grown creatures; this is more reasonable than to assign some different power to them. Now the excellence of this seems to be common to all species and not specifically human; for this part or faculty seems to function most in sleep, while goodness and badness are least manifest in sleep (whence comes the saying that the happy are no better off than the wretched for half their lives; and this happens naturally enough, since sleep is an inactivity of the soul in that respect in which it is called good or bad), unless perhaps to a small extent some of the movements actually penetrate to the soul, and in this respect the dreams of good men are better than those of ordinary people. Enough of this subject, however; let us leave the nutritive faculty, alone, since it has by its nature no share in human excellence.

There seems to be also another irrational element in the soul—one which in a sense, however, shares in a rational principle. For we praise the rational principle of the continent man and of the incontinent, and the part of their soul that has such a principle, since it urges them aright and towards the best objects; but there is found in them also another element naturally opposed to the rational principle, which fights against and resists that principle. For exactly as paralysed limbs when we intend to move them to the right turn on the contrary to the left, so is it with the soul; the impulses of incontinent people move in contrary directions. But while in the body we see that which moves astray, in the soul we do not. No doubt, however, we must none the less suppose that in the soul too there is something contrary to the rational principle, resisting and opposing it. In what sense it is distinct from the other elements does not concern us. Now even this seems to have a share in a rational principle, as we said; at any rate in the continent man it obeys the rational principle—and presumably in the temperate and brave man it is still more obedient; for in him it speaks, on all matters, with the same voice as the rational principle.

Therefore the irrational element also appears to be twofold. For the vegetative element in no way shares in a rational principle, but the appetitive and in general the desiring element in a sense shares in it, in so far as it listens to and obeys it; this is the sense in which we speak of "taking account" of one's father or one's friends, not that in which we speak of "accounting" for a mathematical property. That the irrational element is in some sense persuaded by a rational principle is indicated also by the giving of advice and by
103[a] all reproof and exhortation. And if this element also must be said to have a rational principle, that which has a rational principle (as well as that which has not) will be twofold, one subdivision having it in the strict sense and in itself, and the other having a tendency to obey as one does one's father.

Virtue too is distinguished into kinds in accordance with this difference; for we say that some of the virtues are intellectual and others moral, philosophic wisdom and understanding and practical wisdom being intellectual, liberality and temperance moral. For in speaking about a man's character we do not say that he is wise or has understanding but that he is good-tempered or temperate; yet we praise the wise man also with respect to his state of mind; and of states of mind we call those which merit praise virtues.

Book II

1 Virtue, then, being of two kinds, intellectual and moral, intellectual virtue in the main owes both its birth and its growth to teaching (for which reason it requires experience and time), while moral virtue comes about as a result of habit, whence also its name (ἠθική) is one that is formed by a slight variation from the word ἔθος (habit). From this it is also plain that none of the moral virtues arises in us by nature; for nothing that exists by nature can form a habit contrary to its nature. For instance the stone which by nature moves downwards cannot be habituated to move upwards, not even if one tries to train it by throwing it up ten thousand times; nor can fire be habituated to move downwards, nor can anything else that by nature behaves in one way be trained to behave in another. Neither by nature, then, nor contrary to nature do the virtues arise in us; rather we are adapted by nature to receive them, and are made perfect by habit.

Again, of all the things that come to us by nature we first acquire the potentiality and later exhibit the activity (this is plain in the case of the senses; for it was not by often seeing or often hearing that we got these senses, but on the contrary we had them before we used them, and did not come to have them by using them); but the virtues we get by first exercising them, as also happens in the case of the arts as well. For the things we have to learn before we can do them, we learn by doing them, e.g. men become builders by building and lyre-players by playing the lyre; so too we become just by doing just acts, temperate by doing temperate acts, brave by doing brave acts.

This is confirmed by what happens in states; 1103[b]
for legislators make the citizens good by forming habits in them, and this is the wish of every legislator, and those who do not effect it miss their mark, and it is in this that a good constitution differs from a bad one.

Again, it is from the same causes and by the same means that every virtue is both produced and destroyed, and similarly every art; for it is from playing the lyre that both good and bad lyre-players are produced. And the corresponding statement is true of builders and of all the rest; men will be good or bad builders as a result of building well or badly. For if this were not so, there would have been no need of a teacher, but all men would have been born good or bad at their craft. This, then, is the case with the virtues also; by doing the acts that we do in our transactions with other men we become just or unjust, and by doing the acts that we do in the presence of danger, and being habituated to feel fear or confidence, we become brave or cowardly. The same is true of appetites and feelings of anger; some men become temperate and good-tempered, others self-indulgent and irascible, by behaving in one way or the other in the appropriate circumstances. Thus, in one word, states of character arise out of like activities. This is why the activities we exhibit must be of a certain kind; it is because the states of character correspond to the differences between these. It makes no small difference, then, whether we form habits of one kind or of another from our very youth; it makes a very great difference, or rather *all* the difference.

2 Since, then, the present inquiry does not aim at theoretical knowledge like the others (for we are inquiring not in order to know what virtue is, but in order to become good, since othewise our inquiry would have been of no use), we must examine the nature of actions, namely how we ought to do them; for these determine also the nature of the states of character that are produced, as we have said. Now, that we must act according to the right rule is a common principle and must be assumed—it will be discussed later, i.e. both what the right rule is, and how it is related to the other
1104a virtues. But this must be agreed upon beforehand, that the whole account of matters of conduct must be given in outline and not precisely, as we said at the very beginning that the accounts we demand must be in accordance with the subject-matter; matters concerned with conduct and questions of what is good for us have no fixity, any more than matters of health. The general account being of this nature, the account of particular cases is yet more lacking in exactness; for they do not fall under any art or precept but the agents themselves must in each case consider what is appropriate to the occasion, as happens also in the art of medicine or of navigation.

But though our present account is of this nature we must give what help we can. First, then, let us consider this, that it is the nature of such things to be destroyed by defect and excess, as we see in the case of strength and of health (for to gain light on things impreceptible we must use the evidence of sensible things); both excessive and defective exercise destroys the strength, and similarly drink or food which is above or below a certain amount destroys the health, while that which is proportionate both produces and increases and preserves it. So too is it, then, in the case of temperance and courage and the other virtues. For the man who flies from and fears everything and does not stand his ground against anything becomes a coward, and the man who fears nothing at all but goes to meet every danger becomes rash; and similarly the man who indulges in every pleasure and abstains from none becomes self-indulgent, while the man who shuns every pleasure, as boors do, becomes in a way insensible; temperance and courage, then, are destroyed by excess and defect, and preserved by the mean.

But not only are the sources and causes of their origination and growth the same as those of their destruction, but also the sphere of their actualization will be the same; for this is also true of the things which are more evident to sense, e.g. of strength; it is produced by taking much food and undergoing much exertion, and it is the strong man that will be most able to do these things. So too is it with the virtues; by abstaining from pleasures we become temperate, and it is when we have become so that we are most able to abstain from them; and similarly too in the case of
courage; for by being habituated to despise things 1104b
that are terrible and to stand our ground against them we become brave, and it is when we have become so that we shall be most able to stand our ground against them.

We must take as a sign of states of character 3
the pleasure or pain that ensues on acts; for the man who abstains from bodily pleasures and delights in this very fact is temperate, while the man who is annoyed at it is self-indulgent, and he who stands his ground against things that are terrible and delights in this or at least is not pained is brave, while the man who is pained is a coward. For moral excellence is concerned with pleasures and pains; it is on account of the pain that we abstain from noble ones. Hence we ought to have been brought up in a particular way from our very youth, as Plato says, so as both to delight in and to be pained by the things that we ought; for this is the right education.

Again, if the virtues are concerned with actions and passions, and every passion and every action is accompanied by pleasure and pain, for this reason also virtue will be concerned with pleasures and pains. This is indicated also by the fact that punishment is inflicted by these means; for it is a kind of cure, and it is the nature of cures to be effected by contraries.

Again, as we said but lately, every state of soul has a nature relative to and concerned with the kind of things by which it tends to be made worse or better; but it is by reason of pleasures and pains that men become bad, by pursuing and avoiding these—either the pleasures and pains they ought not or when they ought not or as they ought not, or by going wrong in one of the other similar ways that may be distinguished. Hence men even define the virtues as certain states of impassivity and rest; not well, however, because they speak absolutely, and do not say "as one ought" and "as one ought not" and "when one ought or ought not," and the other things that may be added. We assume, then, that this kind of excellence tends to do what is best with regard to pleasures and pains, and vice does the contrary.

The following facts also may show us that virtue and vice are concerned with these same things. There being three objects of choice and three of avoidance, the noble, the advantageous, the pleasant, and their contraries, the base, the injurious, the painful, about all of these the good man tends to go right and the bad man to go wrong, and especially about pleasure; for this is common to the animals, and also it accompanies all objects of choice; for even the noble and the advantageous appear pleasant.

105a Again, it has grown up with us all from our infancy; this is why it is difficult to rub off this passion, engrained as it is in our life. And we measure even our actions, some of us more and others less, by the rule of pleasure and pain. For this reason, then, our whole inquiry must be about these; for to feel delight and pain rightly or wrongly has no small effect on our actions.

Again, it is harder to fight with pleasure than with anger, to use Heraclitus' phrase, but both art and virtue are always concerned with what is harder; for even the good is better when it is harder. Therefore for this reason also the whole concern both of virtue and of political science is with pleasures and pains; for the man who uses these well will be good, he who uses them badly bad.

That virtue, then, is concerned with pleasures and pains, and that by the acts from which it arises it is both increased and, if they are done differently, destroyed, and that the acts from which it arose are those in which it actualizes itself—let this be taken as said.

The question might be asked, what we mean 4
by saying that we must become just by doing just acts, and temperate by doing temperate acts; for if men do just and temperate acts, they are already just and temperate, exactly as, if they do what is in accordance with the laws of grammar and of music, they are grammarians and musicians.

Or is this not true even of the arts? It is possible to do something that is in accordance with the laws of grammar, either by chance or at the suggestion of another. A man will be a grammarian, then, only when he has both done something grammatical and done it grammatically; and this means doing it in accordance with the grammatical knowledge in himself.

Again, the case of the arts and that of the virtues are not similar; for the products of the arts have their goodness in themselves, so that it is enough that they should have a certain character, but if the acts that are in accordance with the virtues have themselves a certain character it does not follow that they are done justly or temperately. The agent also must be in a certain condition when he does them; in the first place he must have knowledge, secondly he must choose the acts, and choose them for their own sakes, and thirdly his action must proceed from a firm
and unchangeable character. These are not reck- 1105b
oned in as conditions of the possession of the arts, except the bare knowledge; but as a condition on the possession of the virtues knowledge has little or no weight, while the other conditions count not for a little but for everything, i.e. the very conditions which result from often doing just and temperate acts.

Actions, then, are called just and temperate when they are such as the just or the temperate man would do; but it is not the man who does these that is just and temperate, but the man who also does them *as* just and temperate men do them.

It is well said, then, that it is by doing just acts that the just man is produced, and by doing temperate acts the temperate man; without doing these no one would have even a prospect of becoming good.

But most people do not do these, but take refuge in theory and think they are being philosophers and will become good in this way, behaving somewhat like patients who listen attentively to their doctors, but do none of the things they are ordered to do. As the latter will not be made well in body by such a course of treatment, the former will not be made well in soul by such a course of philosophy.

5 Next we must consider what virtue is. Since things that are found in the soul are of three kinds—passions, faculties, states of character, virtue must be one of these. By passions I mean appetite, anger, fear, confidence, envy, joy, friendly feeling, hatred, longing, emulation, pity, and in general the feelings that are accompanied by pleasure or pain; by faculties the things in virtue of which we are said to be capable of feeling these, e.g. of becoming angry or being pained or feeling pity; by states of character the things in virtue of which we stand well or badly with reference to the passions, e.g. with reference to anger we stand badly if we feel it violently or too weakly, and well if we feel it moderately; and similarly with reference to the other passions.

Now neither the virtues nor the vices are *passions,* because we are not called good or bad on the ground of our passions, but are so called on the ground of our virtues and our vices, and because we are neither praised nor blamed for our passions (for the man who feels fear or anger is not praised, nor is the man who simply feels anger blamed, but the man who feels it in a certain way), but for our virtues and our vices we *are* praised or blamed.

1106a Again, we feel anger and fear without choice, but the virtues are modes of choice or involve choice. Further, in respect of the passions we are said to be moved, but in respect of the virtues and the vices we are said not to be moved but to be disposed in a particular way.

For these reasons also they are not *faculties;* for we are neither called good nor bad, nor praised nor blamed, for the simple capacity of feeling the passions; again, we have the faculties by nature, but we are not made good or bad by nature; we have spoken of this before.

If, then, the virtues are neither passions nor faculties, all that remains is that they should be *states of character.*

Thus we have stated what virtue is in respect of its genus.

We must, however, not only describe virtue as 6
a state of character, but also say what sort of state it is. We may remark, then, that every virtue or excellence both brings into good condition the thing of which it is the excellence and makes the work of that thing be done well; e.g. the excellence of the eye makes both the eye and its work good; for it is by the excellence of the eye that we see well. Similarly the excellence of the horse makes a horse both good in itself and good at running and at carrying its rider and at awaiting the attack of the enemy. Therefore, if this is true in every case, the virtue of man also will be the state of character which makes a man good and which makes him do his own work well.

How this is to happen we have stated already, but it will be made plain also by the following consideration of the specific nature of virtue. In everything that is continuous and divisible it is possible to take more, less, or an equal amount, and that either in terms of the thing itself or relatively to us; and the equal is an intermediate between excess and defect. By the intermediate in the object I mean that which is equidistant from each of the extremes, which is one and the same for all men; by the intermediate relatively to us that which is neither too much nor too little—and this is not one, nor the same for all. For instance, if ten is many and two is few, six is the intermediate, taken in terms of the object; for it exceeds and is exceeded by an equal amount; this is intermediate according to arithmetical proportion. But the intermediate relatively to us is not to be taken so; if ten pounds are too much for a 11
particular person to eat and two too little, it does not follow that the trainer will order six pounds; for this also is perhaps too much for the person who is to take it, or too little—too little for Milo, too much for the beginner in athletic exercises. The same is true of running and wrestling. Thus a master of any art avoids excess and defect, but

seeks the intermediate and chooses this—the intermediate not in the object but relatively to us.

If it is thus, then, that every art does its work well—by looking to the intermediate and judging its works by this standard (so that we often say of good works of art that it is not possible either to take away or to add anything, implying that excess and defect destroy the goodness of works of art, while the mean preserves it; and good artists, as we say, look to this in their work), and if, further, virtue is more exact and better than any art, as nature also is, then virtue must have the quality of aiming at the intermediate. I mean moral virtue; for it is this that is concerned with passions and actions, and in these there is excess, defect, and the intermediate. For instance, both fear and confidence and appetite and anger and pity and in general pleasure and pain may be felt both too much and too little, and in both cases not well; but to feel them at the right times, with reference to the right objects, towards the right people, with the right motive, and in the right way, is what is both intermediate and best, and this is characteristic of virtue. Similarly with regard to actions also there is excess, defect, and the intermediate. Now virtue is concerned with passions and actions, in which excess is a form of failure, and so is defect, while the intermediate is praised and is a form of success; and being praised and being successful are both characteristics of virtue. Therefore virtue is a kind of mean, since, as we have seen, it aims at what is intermediate.

Again, it is possible to fail in many ways (for evil belongs to the class of the unlimited, as the Pythagoreans conjectured, and good to that of the limited), while to succeed is possible only in one way (for which reason also one is easy and the other difficult—to miss the mark easy, to hit it difficult); for these reasons also, then, excess and defect are characteristic of vice, and the mean of virtue;

For men are good in but one way, but bad in many.

1107a Virtue, then, is a state of character concerned with choice, lying in a mean, i.e., the mean relative to us, this being determined by a rational principle, and by that principle by which the man of practical wisdom would determine it. Now it is a mean between two vices, that which depends on excess and that which depends on defect; and again it is a mean because the vices respectively fall short of or exceed what is right in both passions and actions, while virtue both finds and chooses that which is intermediate. Hence in respect of its substance and the definition which states its essence virtue is a mean, with regard to what is best and right an extreme.

But not every action nor every passion admits of a mean; for some have names that already imply badness, e.g. spite, shamelessness, envy, and in the case of actions adultery, theft, murder; for all of these and suchlike things imply by their names that they are themselves bad, and not the excesses or deficiencies of them. It is not possible, then, ever to be right with regard to them; one must always be wrong. Nor does goodness or badness with regard to such things depend on committing adultery with the right woman, at the right time, and in the right way, but simply to do any of them is to go wrong. It would be equally absurd, then, to expect that in unjust, cowardly, and voluptuous action there should be a mean, an excess, and a deficiency; for at that rate there would be a mean of excess and of deficiency, an excess of excess, and a deficiency of deficiency. But as there is no excess and deficiency of temperance and courage because what is intermediate is in a sense an extreme, so too of the actions we have mentioned there is no mean nor any excess and deficiency, but however they are done they are wrong; for in general there is neither a mean of excess and deficiency, nor excess and deficiency of a mean.

We must, however, not only make this general 7
statement, but also apply it to the individual facts. For among statements about conduct those which are general apply more widely, but those which are particular are more genuine, since conduct has to do with individual cases, and our statements must harmonize with the facts in these cases. We may take these cases from our table. With regard
to feelings of fear and confidence courage is the 1107b
mean; of the people who exceed, he who exceeds in fearlessness has no name (many of the states have no name), while the man who exceeds in confidence is rash, and he who exceeds in fear and falls short in confidence is a coward.

With regard to pleasures and pains—not all of them, and not so much with regard to the pains—the mean is temperance, the excess self-indulgence. Persons deficient with regard to the pleasures are not often found; hence such persons also have received no name. But let us call them "insensible."

With regard to giving and taking of money the mean is liberality, the excess and the defect prodigality and meanness. In these actions people exceed and fall short in contrary ways; the prodigal exceeds in spending and falls short in taking, while the mean man exceeds in taking and falls short in spending. . . . With regard to money there are also other dispositions—a mean, magnificence (for the magnificent man differs from the liberal man; the former deals with large sums, the latter with small ones), an excess, tastelessness and vulgarity, and a deficiency, niggardliness; these differ from the states opposed to liberality. . . .

With regard to honour and dishonour the mean is proper pride, the excess is known as a sort of "empty vanity," and the deficiency is undue humility; and as we said liberality was related to magnificence, differing from it by dealing with small sums, so there is a state similarly related to proper pride, being concerned with small honours while that is concerned with great. For it is possible to desire honour as one ought, and more than one ought, and less, and the man who exceeds in his desires is called ambitious, the man who falls short unambitious, while the intermediate person has no name. The dispositions also are nameless, except that that of the ambitious man is called ambition. Hence the people who are at the extremes lay claim to the middle place; and we ourselves sometimes call the intermediate person ambitious and sometimes unambitious, and sometimes praise the ambitious man and sometimes the unambitious. . . . [N]ow let us speak of the remaining states according to the method which has been indicated.

1108[a] With regard to anger also there is an excess, a deficiency, and a mean. Although they can scarcely be said to have names, yet since we call the intermediate person good-tempered let us call the mean good temper; of the persons at the extremes let the one who exceeds be called irascible, and his vice irascibility, and the man who falls short an inirascible sort of person, and the deficiency inirascibility.

There are also theree other means, which have a certain likeness to one another, but differ from one another: for they are all concerned with intercourse in words and actions, but differ in that one is concerned with truth in this sphere, the other two with pleasantness; and of this one kind is exhibited in giving amusement, the other in all the circumstances of life. We must therefore speak of these too, that we may the better see that in all things the mean is praiseworthy, and the extremes neither praiseworthy nor right, but worthy of blame. Now most of these states also have no names, but we must try, as in the other cases, to invent names ourselves so that we may be clear and easy to follow. With regard to truth, then, the intermediate is a truthful sort of person and the mean may be called truthfulness, while the pretence which exaggerates is boastfulness and the person characterized by it a boaster, and that which understates is mock modesty and the person characterized by it mock-modest. With regard to pleasantness in the giving of amusement the intermediate person is ready-witted and the disposition ready wit, the excess is buffoonery and the person characterized by it a buffoon, while the man who falls short is a sort of boor and his state is boorishness. With regard to the remaining kind of pleasantness, that which is exhibited in life in general, the man who is pleasant in the right way is friendly and the mean is friendliness, while the man who exceeds is an obsequious person if he has no end in view, a flatterer if he is aiming at his own advantage, and the man who falls short and is unpleasant in all circumstances is a quarrelsome and surly sort of person.

There are also means in the passions and concerned with the passions; since shame is not a virture, and yet praise is extended to the modest man. For even in these matters one man is said to be intermediate, and another to exceed, as for instance the bashful man who is ashamed of everything; while he who falls short or is not ashamed of anything at all is shameless, and the intermediate person is modest. Righteous indignation is a mean between envy and spite, and these states are concerned with the pain and pleasure 1108[b]
that are felt at the fortunes of our neighbours; the

man who is characterized by righteous indignation is pained at undeserved good fortune, the envious man, going beyond him, is pained at all good fortune, and the spiteful man falls so far short of being pained that he even rejoices. . . .

8 There are three kinds of disposition, then, two of them vices, involving excess and deficiency respectively, and one a virtue, viz. the mean, and all are in a sense opposed to all; for the extreme states are contrary both to the intermediate state and to each other, and the intermediate to the extremes; as the equal is greater relatively to the less, less relatively to the greater, so the middle states are excessive relatively to the deficiencies, deficient relatively to the excesses, both in passions and in actions. For the brave man appears rash relatively to the coward, and cowardly relatively to the rash man; and similarly the temperate man appears self-indulgent relatively to the insensible man, insensible relatively to the self-indulgent, and the liberal man prodigal relatively to the mean man, mean relatively to the prodigal. Hence also the people at the extremes push the intermediate man each over to the other, and the brave man is called rash by the coward, cowardly by the rash man, and correspondingly in the other cases.

These states being thus opposed to one another, the greatest contrariety is that of the extremes to each other, rather than to the intermediate; for these are further from each other than from the intermediate, as the great is further from the small and the small from the great than both are from the equal. Again, to the intermediate some extremes show a certain likeness, as that of rashness to courage and that of prodigality to liberality; but the extremes show the greatest unlikeness to each other; now contraries are defined as the things that are furthest from each other, so that things that are further apart are more contrary.

1109[a] To the mean in some cases the deficiency, in some the excess is more opposed; e.g. it is not rashness, which is an excess, but cowardice, which is a deficiency, that is more opposed to courage, and not insensibility, which is a deficiency, but self-indulgence, which is an excess, that is more opposed to temperance. This happens from two reasons, one being drawn from the thing itself; for because one extreme is nearer and liker to the intermediate, we oppose not this but rather its contrary to the intermediate. E.g., since rashness is thought liker and nearer to courage, and cowardice more unlike, we oppose rather the latter to courage; for things that are further from the intermediate are thought more contrary to it. This, then, is one cause, drawn from the thing itself; another is drawn from ourselves; for the things to which we ourselves more naturally tend seem more contrary to the intermediate. For instance, we ourselves tend more naturally to pleasures, and hence are more easily carried away towards self-indulgence than towards propriety. We describe as contrary to the mean, then, rather the directions in which we more often go to great lengths; and therefore self-indulgence, which is an excess, is the more contrary to temperance.

That moral virtue is a mean, then, and in what 9
sense it is so, and that it is a mean between two vices, the one involving excess, the other deficiency, and that it is such because its character is to aim at what is intermediate in passions and in actions, has been sufficiently stated. Hence also it is no easy task to be good. For in everything it is no easy task to find the middle, e.g. to find the middle of a circle is not for every one but for him who knows; so, too, any one can get angry—that is easy—or to give or spend money; but to do this to the right person, to the right extent, at the right time, with the right motive, and in the right way, *that* is not for every one, nor is it easy; wherefore goodness is both rare and laudable and noble.

Hence he who aims at the intermediate must first depart from what is the more contrary to it, as Calypso advises—

Hold the ship out beyond that surf and spray.

For of the extremes one is more erroneous, one less so; therefore, since to hit the mean is hard in the extreme, we must as a second best, as people say, take the least of the evils; and this will be done best in the way we describe.

But we must consider the things towards which 1109[b]
we ourselves also are easily carried away; for some of us tend to one thing, some to another; and this will be recognizable from the pleasure and the pain we feel. We must drag ourselves away to the

contrary extreme; for we shall get into the intermediate state by drawing well away from error, as people do in straightening sticks that are bent.

Now in everything the pleasant or pleasure is most to be guarded against; for we do not judge it impartially. We ought, then, to feel towards pleasure as the elders of the people felt towards Helen, and in all circumstances repeat their saying; for if we dismiss pleasure thus we are less likely to go astray. It is by doing this, then, (to sum the matter up) that we shall best be able to hit the mean.

But this is no doubt difficult, and especially in individual cases; for it is not easy to determine both how and with whom and on what provocation and how long one should be angry; for we too sometimes praise those who fall short and call them good-tempered, but sometimes we praise those who get angry and call them manly. The man, however, who deviates little from goodness is not blamed, whether he do so in the direction of the more or of the less, but only the man who deviates more widely; for *he* does not fail to be noticed. But up to what point and to what extent a man must deviate before he becomes blameworthy it is not easy to determine by reasoning, any more than anything else that is perceived by the senses; such things depend on particular facts, and the decision rests with perception. So much, then, is plain, that the intermediate state is in all things to be praised, but that we must incline sometimes towards the excess, sometimes towards the deficiency; for so shall we most easily hit the mean and what is right.

. . . .

Book X

7 If happiness is activity in accordance with virtue, it is reasonable that it should be in accordance with the highest virtue; and this will be that of the best thing in us. Whether it be reason or something else that is this element which is thought to be our natural ruler and guide and to take thought of things noble and divine, whether it be itself also divine or only the most divine element in us, the activity of this in accordance with its proper virtue will be perfect happiness. That this activity is contemplative we have already said.

Now this would seem to be in agreement both with what we said before and with the truth. For, firstly, this activity is the best (since not only is reason the best thing in us, but the objects of reason are the best of knowable objects); and, secondly, it is the most continuous, since we can contemplate truth more continuously than we can *do* anything. And we think happiness has pleasure mingled with it, but the activity of philosophic wisdom is admittedly the pleasantest of virtuous activities; at all events the pursuit of it is thought to offer pleasures marvellous for their purity and their enduringness, and it is to be expected that those who know will pass their time more pleasantly than those who inquire. And the self-sufficiency that is spoken of must belong most to the contemplative activity. For while a philosopher, as well as a just man or one possessing any other virtue, needs the necessaries of life, when they are sufficiently equipped with things of that sort the just man needs people towards whom and with whom he shall act justly, and the temperate man, the brave man, and each of the others is in the same case, but the philosopher, even when by himself, can contemplate truth, and the better the wiser he is; he can perhaps do so better if he has fellow-workers, but still he is the most self-sufficient. And this activity alone would 117
seem to be loved for its own sake; for nothing arises from it apart from the contemplating, while from practical activities we gain more or less apart from the action. And happiness is thought to depend on leisure; for we are busy that we may have leisure, and make war that we may live in peace. Now the activity of the practical virtues is exhibited in political or military affairs, but the actions concerned with these seem to be unleisurely. Warlike actions are completely so (for no one chooses to be at war, or provokes war, for the sake of being at war; any one would seem absolutely murderous is he were to make enemies of his friends in order to bring about battle and slaughter); but the action of the statesman is also unleisurely, and—apart from the political action itself—aims at despotic power and honours, or at all events happiness, for him and his fellow citizens—a happiness different from political ac-

tion, and evidently sought as being different. So if among virtuous actions political and military actions are distinguished by nobility and greatness, and these are unleisurely and aim at an end and are not desirable for their own sake, but the activity of reason, which is contemplative, seems both to be superior in serious worth and to aim at no end beyond itself, and to have its pleasure proper to itself (and this augments the activity), and the self-sufficiency, leisureliness, unweariedness (so far as this is possible for man), and all the other attributes ascribed to the supremely happy man are evidently those connected with this activity, it follows that this will be the complete happiness of man, if it be allowed a complete term of life (for none of the attributes of happiness is *in*complete).

But such a life would be too high for man; for it is not in so far as he is man that he will live so, but in so far as something divine is present in him; and by so much as this is superior to our composite nature is its activity superior to that which is the exercise of the other kind of virtue. If reason is divine, then, in comparison with man, the life according to it is divine in comparison with human life. But we must not follow those who advise us, being men, to think of human things, and, being mortal, of mortal things, but must, so far as we can, make ourselves immortal, and strain every nerve to live in accordance with the best thing in us; for even if it be small
1178[a] in bulk, much more does it in power and worth surpass everything. This would seem, too, to be each man himself, since it is the authoritative and better part of him. It would be strange, then, if he were to choose not the life of his self but that of something else. . . [T]hat which is proper to each thing is by nature best and most pleasant for each thing; for man, therefore, the life according to reason is best and pleasantest, since reason more than anything else *is* man. This life therefore is also the happiest.

8 But in a secondary degree the life in accordance with the other kind of virtue is happy; for the activities in accordance with this befit our human estate. Just and brave acts, and other virtuous acts, we do in relation to each other, observing our respective duties with regard to contracts and services and all manner of actions and with regard to passions; and all of these seem to be typically human. Some of them seem even to arise from the body, and virtue of character to be in many ways bound up with the passions. Practical wisdom, too, is linked to virtue of character, and this to practical wisdom, since the principles of practical wisdom are in accordance with the moral virtues and rightness in morals is in accordance with practical wisdom. Being connected with the passions also, the moral virtues must belong to our composite nature; and the virtues of our composite nature are human; so, therefore, are the life and the happiness which correspond to these. The excellence of the reason is a thing apart; we must be content to say this much about it, for to describe it precisely is a task greater than our purpose requires. It would seem, however, also to need external equipment but little, or less than moral virtue does. Grant that both need the necessaries, and do so equally, even if the statesman's work is the more concerned with the body and things of that sort; for there will be little difference there; but in what they need for the exercise of their activities there will be much difference. The liberal man will need money for the doing of his liberal deeds, and the just man too will need it for the returning of services (for wishes are hard to discern, and even people who are not just pretend to wish to act justly); and the brave man will need power if he is to accomplish any of the acts that correspond to his virtue, and the temperate man will need opportunity; for how else is either he or any of the others to be recognized? It is debated, too, whether the will or the deed is more essential to virtue, which is assumed to involve both; it is surely clear that its perfection involves both; but for deeds many
things are needed, and more, the greater and 1178[b]
nobler the deeds are. But the man who is contemplating the truth needs no such thing, at least with a view to the exercise of his activity; indeed they are, one may say, even hindrances, at all events to his contemplation; but in so far as he is a man and lives with a number of people, he chooses to do virtuous acts; he will therefore need such aids to living a human life..

But that perfect happiness is a contemplative activity will appear from the following consideration as well. We assume the gods to be above all other beings blessed and happy; but what sort of actions must we assign to them? Acts of justice? Will not the gods seem absurd if they make contracts and return deposits, and so on? Acts of a brave man, then, confronting dangers and running risks because it is noble to do so? Or liberal acts? To whom will they give? It will be strange if they are really to have money or anything of the kind. And what would their temperate acts be? Is not such praise tasteless, since they have no bad appetites? If we were to run through them all, the circumstances of action would be found trivial and unworthy of gods. Still, every one supposes that they *live* and therefore that they are active; we cannot suppose them to sleep like Endymion. Now if you take away from a living being action, and still more production, what is left but contemplation? Therefore the activity of God, which surpasses all others in blessedness, must be contemplative; and of human activities, therefore, that which is most akin to this must be most of the nature of happiness.

This is indicated, too, by the fact that the other animals have no share in happiness, being completely deprived of such activity. For while the whole life of the gods is blessed, and that of men too in so far as some likeness of such activity belongs to them, none of the other animals is happy, since they in no way share in contemplation. Happiness extends, then, just so far as contemplation does, and those to whom contemplation more fully belongs are more truly happy, not as a mere concomitant but in virtue of the contemplation; for this is in itself precious. Happiness, therefore, must be some form of contemplation.

But, being a man, one will also need external prosperity; for our nature is not self-sufficient for the purpose of contemplation, but our body also must be healthy and must have food and other
1179a attention. Still, we must not think that the man who is to be happy will need many things or great things, merely because he cannot be supremely happy without external goods; for self-sufficiency and action do not involve excess, and we can do noble acts without ruling earth and sea; for even with moderate advantages one can act virtuously (this is manifest enough; for private persons are thought to do worthy acts no less than despots—indeed even more); and it is enough that we should have so much as that; for the life of the man who is active in accordance with virtue will be happy. Solon, too, was perhaps sketching well the happy man when he described him as moderately furnished with externals but as having done (as Solon thought) the noblest acts, and lived temperately; for one can with but moderate possessions do what one ought. Anaxagoras also seems to have supposed the happy man not to be rich nor a despot, when he said that he would not be surprised if the happy man were to seem to most people a strange person; for they judge by externals, since these are all they perceive. The opinions of the wise seem, then, to harmonize with our arguments. But while even such things carry some conviction, the truth in practical matters is discerned from the facts of life; for these are the decisive factor. We must therefore survey what we have already said, bringing it to the test of the facts of life, and if it harmonizes with the facts we must accept it, but if it clashes with them we must suppose it to be mere theory. Now he who exercises his reason and cultivates it seems to be both in the best state of mind and most dear to the gods. For if the gods have any care for human affairs, as they are thought to have, it would be reasonable both that they should delight in that which was best and most akin to them (i.e. reason) and that they should reward those who love and honour this most, as caring for the things that are dear to them and acting both rightly and nobly. And that all these attributes belong most of all to the philosopher is manifest. He, therefore, is the dearest to the gods. And he who is that will presumably be also the happiest; so that in this way too the philosopher will more than any other be happy.

Aristotle's Doctrine of the Mean

J. O. URMSON

Aristotle's account of excellence of character, of which the doctrine of the mean is a part, seems to me to be both interesting and bold. In spite of some difficulties in detail, it is quite possibly true. However, in many current interpretations of the doctrine Aristotle is made to say things that are either uninteresting, or manifestly false, or both false and uninteresting. It will, therefore, be as well to begin by offering an interpretation of what he has to say on this topic. But I shall spend the minimum of time attacking alternative interpretations and on points that are primarily of philological interest; I want to get on to the question whether what Aristotle, as interpreted by me, says is true.

Though Aristotle has said that the *end* of ethical philosophy is practical, the doctrine of the mean is not introduced by Aristotle as a piece of moral advice but as part of the definition of excellence of character *(ethike arete)*. At 1105b 19 he asks, "What is excellence?" which is his regular, formal way of setting the question of definition (in the Aristotelian, not the modern, sense of "definition"). To give a definition one must first state the genus and then the differentia of the kind of thing to be defined. Accordingly Aristotle immediately shows that excellence is a settled state *(hexis)*, and says (1106a 12) that this is the genus. He then starts at once to look for the differentia, for merely to know the genus does not get us very far. For intellectual excellence is also a settled state, and so is badness of character. What distinguishes excellence of character from all other settled states is, in his own words, that it is "concerned with choice, lying in a mean, i.e., the mean relative to us, this being determined by the rational procedures by which a wise man *(phronimos)* would determine it." Like badness of character, but unlike intellectual excellence, it is a settled state concerned with choice; unlike all other states, it is in a mean relative to us.

Now there are, according to Artistotle, six possible states of character. At the top of the list, in order of merit, there is heroic excellence (NE, Bk. VII, ch. 1). Second comes (ordinary) excellence. Third comes *enkrateia* or self-control, the state of the man who, unlike the previous two, wants to act badly but makes himself act as they would. Fourth comes *akrasia,* or lack of self-control, the state of man who wants to act badly, tries to act properly, but fails. Fifth comes badness of character, the state of the man who wants to act badly and does so without resistance, thinking it to be a good way to act. Finally there is brutishness, the state of the man who from congenital defect or disease has to be regarded as sub-human and not a proper object of normal moral appraisal. So the doctrine of the mean, as part of the differentia of excellence of character, ought to enable us to distinguish it from all the other five states of character that have just been listed. In fact Aristotle gives us no indication how heroic excellence could be distinguished from ordinary excellence as a different state; it seems to be merely ordinary excellence to the highest possible degree. But this perhaps does not matter, since Aristotle makes no serious use of the notion of heroic excellence. I think that we may safely ignore it as being merely part of a Kant-like architectonic, something brought in to be the opposite of brutishness. But we must certainly be

From the *American Philosophical Quarterly*, 10, no. 3 (July 1973), pp. 223–30.

able to distinguish excellence of character from all the other states, if Aristotle's account of the mean is to be vindicated.

Now we cannot distinguish the good man, the man with an excellent character, from the self-controlled man either by his actions or by his beliefs and reasoning. They both act in the same way, and do so under the guidance of the same practical thinking. The only way in which the good man differs from the self-controlled man is that he wants to act in the way that he does, whereas the self-controlled man does so with difficulty. In this one way, indeed, the good man is like the bad, though in all other ways they are at opposite extremes; both the good man and the bad act as they want to act, without any internal conflict.

In the *Nicomachean Ethics* Aristotle discusses excellence and badness of character fully before he more than incidentally mentions those who have or lack self-control. None the less, as he very well realizes, he has to make room for them, and does so. Interpreters who forget this tend to underemphasize or misinterpret two points about excellence of character which Aristotle makes very clearly, but the significance of which he does not fully explain. These two points are that (1) excellence of character is concerned with both emotions (*pathe,* passions) and actions, not with actions alone. In the *Eudemean Ethics,* indeed, Aristotle says simply that it is concerned with emotions, without mentioning actions (e.g., EE 1106b, 16); (2) excellence of character is concerned with likes and dislikes (*hedonai* and *lupai,* traditionally translated as "pleasures and pains").

When Aristotle says that excellence of character is concerned with emotions and actions he does not mean that it has two distinct fields. He means that (temporarily neglecting the complicated cases of self-control and lack of it) an action can be regarded as manifesting and embodying some emotion. As emotions, he says (NE 1105b 21) he has in mind desire, anger, fear, confidence, envy, joy, friendship, hatred, longing, emulation, pity and, in general, conditions that involve likes and dislikes. Whenever one acts in a way that displays character, Aristotle believes, one will be manifesting one or another of these and similar emotions. If we cease to put the complicated case of self-control on one side, we can now see one way in which to distinguish the good man from the self-controlled man; whereas the action of the good man is a natural manifestation of his emotion and he therefore acts in accordance with his likes and dislikes, the action of the self-controlled man is not. He makes himself act contrary to his emotions and therefore contrary to his likes and dislikes.

We can readily imagine a situation in which the bad man, the self-controlled man, and the good man all act in the same way. If this is so, it can only be that the bad man is externally compelled to act that way—otherwise he would act differently. The self-controlled man will make himself act that way. Neither of them wants to act that way, neither likes acting that way, neither enjoys acting that way, neither takes pleasure in acting that way. But the good man is, without friction, manifesting and responding to his emotion. So he does it liking it, wanting to, enjoying it, taking pleasure in it. So Aristotle can say (NE 1104b 3ff.) that a criterion of the nature of the state is the liking, enjoyment, or pleasure with which an act is performed or the dislike, distress, or distaste with which it is done. If, say, one abstains from some bodily indulgence, liking and wanting to abstain, that shows that one has a character of a certain sort. So excellence of character is concerned with likes and dislikes in this way: if a man has excellence of character he likes acting in a proper way, feeling emotions which he can manifest with pleasure, since there is no internal struggle.

One can get confused at this point because there is one special excellence, temperance, which is concerned with certain pleasures, bodily pleasures, in a quite different way. In the way in which bodily pleasure and distress are the field of temperance, other special excellences have as their field, not pleasure and distress or likes and dislikes, but emotions like anger and fear. So temperance is doubly concerned with pleasure or enjoyment. As is the case with all excellences, temperance is concerned with the pleasure or dislike with which you act; but, unlike other excellences, it is concerned with the pleasure or dislike which you find in indulgence in bodily pleasures. If you are temperate you will like abstaining from orgies.

We have here, incidentally, one very good reason in addition to many others for not accepting the thoughtless traditional translation of *ethike arete* and *kakia* as "moral virtue" and "vice." No doubt the fact that the great translator Cicero translated *kakia* as *vitium* should be enough to warn us off those English translations. For in classical Latin *vitium* does not mean "vice." But, more relevantly, it is an insult to Aristotle's good sense to make him say that taking insufficient pleasure in the pleasure of food, drink, and sex is a moral vice, though he regards it as an *ethike kakia*. Moreover the encratic man can be said to have moral virtue with as good or better reason than the Aristotelian man of excellent character. Thus the man who makes himself stand and fight the enemy, while longing to run away, is at least as entitled to be regarded as possessing the moral virtue of courage as the man who takes his stand without inner conflict. But, for Aristotle, having to make oneself behave properly, however admirable the deed, betrays a defect of character. Excellence of character is not the triumph of grace over the old Adam; it is that state of character which entitles a man to be called *eudaemon*. Clearly one is more *eudaemon* if one acts properly without friction, without effort, enjoying it, than if one has to struggle to do so through faulty education. That is how Adam would have acted when *eudaemon* before the fall.

So in the case of excellence of character both emotions and actions are in a mean, whatever that signifies; in the case of self-control actions, but not emotions, are in a mean; in the case of bad character neither actions nor emotions are in a mean. But what is it for emotions and actions to be in a mean?

If one takes the doctrine of the mean to claim that one should always feel and exhibit a moderate, though (since it is a relative mean) not a mathematically fixed quantity of a given emotion, the doctrine is plainly absurd. It is perfectly plain that in any given situation one should feel and exhibit a zero amount of almost every emotion. Let us suppose that is a normal context you invite me to dinner with you; how much anger, fear, pity, and confidence should I exhibit as my reaction? Plainly, in normal circumstances, none. Or should we take Aristotle as saying that when some amount of a certain emotion is appropriate the right amount is always a moderate amount? But this is very stupid. If you are trivially rude to me should I be moderately angry with you, and also when you torture my wife? To be moderately angry would be absurd on both occasions.

It is perfectly plain, in fact, that for Aristotle what is primarily in a mean is a settled state of character. In his definition he says that excellence of character is a settled state in a mean; thus an emotion or action is in a mean if it exhibits a settled state that is in a mean. The man whose character is such that he feels only mild annoyance at a trivial slight and is enraged by torture has a character which is in a mean between one which exhibits rage on trivial as well as important occasions and one which can coolly contemplate the greatest outrages. On each occasion his reaction exhibits a mean state and thus his actions are on each occasion in a mean.

To have one's emotions and actions in a mean, says Aristotle, is to feel and manifest each emotion when, on what matters, toward such people, for what reasons and in such a manner as is proper. To diverge from the mean in the direction of deficiency is as much not to experience and exhibit emotions at all when one should, or not about matters about which one should, or not toward people toward whom one should as it is to exhibit the emotions to the wrong degree. The same holds of the defect of excess, *mutatis mutandis*. The point of the doctrine being of the *mean,* and not merely the doctrine that excellence of character is a settled state of exhibiting the *proper* amount of emotion, is sufficiently obvious. One's character may err in two opposed ways; one may exhibit an emotion too often, or too rarely; about too many or too few things; toward too many or too few people; for too many or for too few reasons; when it is uncalled for, and not even when it is called for. A point that Aristotle, who admits to be talking in outline only, fails to notice is that it is possible, if unlikely, that one's character should exhibit deficiency in some respects, the mean in others, and excess in others, even with regard to a single specific excellence.

One could summarize the point which has just been made by saying that Aristotle holds excellence of character to be a mean or intermediate disposition regarding emotions and actions, not that it is a disposition towards mean or intermediate emotions and actions. This latter view is, as we have seen, absurd, if taken strictly. Interpreted more charitably it is the doctrine of moderation, the view that *medio tutissimus ibis.* No doubt Aristotle was, in general, like most Greek sages, inclined to accept a doctrine of moderation, though in Bk. X of the *Nicomachean Ethics* he seems to believe in a rather immoderate indulgence in contemplation of the immutable. But no doubt he was inclined to hold that usually, when some people said "None of that at any price" and others "As much of that as possible," the sanest view would be that a fair amount was all right, but one should always go easy on it. So Aristotle was probably a believer in the doctrine of moderation, sensibly interpreted. But what I wish to emphasize is that the doctrine of moderation is no part of the doctrine of the mean, nor is it a consequence of the doctrine of the mean, though it is perfectly compatible with it. The doctrine of moderation holds that a character in a mean state will never, or very rarely, require such extreme action as some people are sometimes inclined to believe. Everyone would agree that one should be very angry, for example, at extreme gratuitous cruelty; but extreme emotion and action is far less often justified than one may be inclined to believe. So the doctrine of moderation is a doctrine about where the mean lies; as such it is a partial sketch of how the man of wisdom would determine where the mean lies, which is quite a different thing from the doctrine that excellence is in a mean to be determined by the wise man (perhaps making use of the principle of moderation).

That the doctrine of the mean does not reqiire the doctrine of moderation can be easily shown. Let us suppose that I were to hold that one should rarely drink alcohol, but that when one did one should make a real night of it, while you held that a regular daily glass of wine was in order but one should never take much. Presumably your view is more in line with the doctrine of moderation than mine. But we can both readily assent to the doctrine of the mean as part of the differentia of excellence of character. Both can allow that the right way lies between two errors of excess and deficiency. I for my part can recognize that regular nightly swilling was excess and total abstention a deficiency. We certainly disagree about what the wise man would regard as proper, which is important but quite a different matter.

If the foregoing is correct it must be wrong to hold that Aristotle thought that we should decide how to act on particular occasions by working in from the extremes. For this view clearly supposes that Aristotle viewed excellence of character as a disposition toward the mean, not a mean disposition. If one were to ask Aristotle how to decide how to act on particular occasions his initial answer would be that one must do so by bringing to bear the intellectual excellence of (practical) wisdom. If we then ask in what wisdom consists we shall get a long answer about it involving, among other things, planning ability, experience, ability to appreciate a situation, and executive ability *(deinotes).* There is no simple decision procedure for the wise man to use. How could there be when there are so many variables? If one is generous one has a settled disposition to do gladly whatever is found to be the generous thing; but what the generous thing to do is depends on a full appreciation of all the factors in the situation by an experienced man who has acquired sound general principles. As Aristotle was well aware, the doctrine of the mean does not begin to answer the question of how rationally to decide how to act, a topic to which most of Bk. VI of the *Nicomachean Ethics* is devoted.

Aristotle's account of excellence of character is then, in summary form, as follows:

(1) For each specific excellence of character that we recognize there will be some specific emotion whose field it is.

(2) In the case of each such emotion it is possible to be disposed to exhibit it to the right amount, which is excellence.

(3) In the case of every such emotion it is possible to be disposed to exhibit it either too much or too little, and each of these dispositions is a defect of character.

(4) "Too much" includes "on too many occasions" and similar possibilities as well as "too violently"; "too little" includes "on too few occasions" and similar possibilities as well as "too weakly."

I believe that Aristotle is prepared to go even further and also accept the following proposition:

(5) There is no emotion that one should never exhibit.

The ground for attributing this view to him is that he considers certain emotions and actions that are alleged always to be wrong and claims that this is because they are in fact cases of excessive emotion, of which it would be proper to exhibit a proper amount (NE 1107a 9–26). Another is that if there were emotions in regard to which excellence was not in a mean Aristotle's definition of excellence of character would be defective.

The differences between excellence of character, self-control, lack of self-control, and badness of character can be schematically displayed with reference to the doctrine of the mean as follows:

	Emotion displaying mean state	Action displaying mean state	Choice displaying mean state
Excellence of character	Yes	Yes	Yes
Self-control	No	Yes	Yes
Lack of self-control	No	No	Yes
Badness of character	No	No	No

In saying, in the above table, that the acratic man makes the same correct choice as the excellent man I am obviously saying something over-simple, which would require much qualification, but not retraction, in a full discussion of Bk. VII of the *Nicomachean Ethics*.

So much for exposition of the doctrine of the mean. The exposition has been selective; nothing has been said about the difference between relative and mathematical means or the theory that the doctrine is related to certain theories to be found in the *Physics,* among other omissions. But I hope that the positive view that I wish to attribute to Aristotle has emerged with reasonable clarity.

I now turn from exposition of Aristotle to critical discussion. I have claimed that the doctrine of the mean is interesting and bold; if any reader should disagree with me on this point I should be very perplexed but should not wish to argue. I have also claimed that it is very possibly true. But it is certainly not obviously true and certain difficulties in it need examination.

Aristotle's attempt to show that the doctrine is true takes the form of running through a quite large set of specific excellences of character and showing that the doctrine of the mean fits them all. But in doing so he gets into some serious difficulties, some of which he notices and some of which he does not. It is by no means clear that he succeeds in clearing up even the difficulties that he does notice.

. . . .

We have already noted that Aristotle appears to claim that not only some defects of character are excesses or deficiencies with respect to some emotion but that all are. Thus Aristotle appears to hold that every emotion is in itself capable of being legitimate; there is no emotion that one should never experience—it is only a matter of avoiding over- and under-indulgence in each. He duly notes that certain actions such as murder, adultery, and theft, and certain emotions such as spite, shamelessness, and envy are *ex vi terminorum* bad (NE 1107a 9ff.), which might seem to contradict this. But he goes on to claim that all these are simply names for excesses and deficiencies. Envy is necessarily bad since it is the name for an excess of an emotion which one may have to a proper extent.

This is a very bold doctrine, though Aristotle must in consistency hold it. To some extent it presents no very serious difficulty. Theft would normally be an excessive desire for goods, adultery is excessive sexual activity, and murder may exhibit excessive anger. But how about *epikhairekakia,* usually translated "spite" but literally meaning "rejoicing in others' misfortunes," and envy? What Aristotle says about these two is very odd (NE 1108b 1ff.): *nemesis* is a mean between envy and spite, and their field is distress and pleasure about the fortunes of one's neighbors. The man of *nemesis* experiences distress when people fare well undeservedly, the envious man goes beyond him and is distressed when anyone fares well, while the spiteful man so far falls short of distress as to rejoice.

Now this will not do at all. First, it is arbitrary and absurd to call rejoicing a deficiency of distress. Secondly, Aristotle incredibly says that the spiteful man rejoices when others fare well, when in fact he rejoices when others fare ill; and it is hard to see how this could be the deficiency of an emotion of which envy is an excess. Aristotle, as Ross notes in his translation, has made a careless slip, but it is not clear how he would rectify it.

If one had to try to find some related triad, it might seem best to start from the requirement that the field be that of pleasure and distress about the fortune of neighbors. The man in a mean state would presumably both rejoice and be sorry to the right extent and on the right occasions about their fortunes. He will rejoice at deserved good and bad fortune and regret undeserved good and bad fortune, to the right extent and on the right occasions. Now we could imagine a man who was too concerned about his neighbors' fortunes, who rejoiced and sorrowed about them too much and inappropriately; he could be said to be in excess, similarly we could imagine a man whose concern about neighbors' fortunes was deficient. But neither bears the slightest resemblance to the envious or spiteful man; one is simply over-involved emotionally and the other under-involved. If we consider envy to be regret at neighbors' good fortune and spitefulness to be rejoicing in their bad fortune neither seems to be particularly in excess or deficient with regard to any common feeling or emotion.

So it is hard to see how envy and spite could be seen as excess and deficiency of some emotion of which a proper amount could be felt. Nor could it have seemed obvious to Aristotle that he was right since in the *Eudemean Ethics* he gives a table in which envy is said to be an excess where *nemesis* is the mean and the deficiency is said to have no name. It is surely possible and even likely that the same man should be both envious and spiteful, as Aristotle himself notes in *Rhetoric* (II, ix, 5). Nor can I think of two emotions of which envy and spite are wrong amounts, though unconnected, nor can I see why either should be called an excess or deficiency rather than vice versa.

It might seem then that we have found two faults of character that are not excesses or deficiencies, two emotions that are always a mark of a bad character, if felt in any degree. If this is so, then the doctrine of the mean cannot be an all-embracing account of good and bad character. But the matter is not clear, because of a passage in the *Nicomachean Ethics* which may safeguard Aristotle on this point, but is by no means easy to interpret.

In ch. vii of Bk. II of the *Nicomachean Ethics* Aristotle has rapidly run through the trilogies of excellences and defects, roughly sorted into similar groups. Having given a group concerned with cooperation in words and deeds, he goes on: "There are means both in pathemata and concerning emotions. For shame is not an excellence, though the modest person is praised (NE 1108a 30ff)." In the sphere of shame the extremes are said to be bashfulness and shamelessness. If shame is not an excellence of character then the extremes are presumably not defects of character, though no doubt blameworthy in some way. The bogus trilogy of envy, *nemesis,* and rejoicing in the misfortunes of others immediately follows. It is thus a reasonable hypothesis that the bogus triology is also not one of excellence and related defects of character. If so, then though Aristotle's treatment of envy and rejoicing in misfortune may not be satisfactory, the flaw will not be in his account of goodness and badness of character.

But why are shame and, presumably, *nemesis* not excellences of character? Aristotle gives us no further account of *nemesis* and related defects, but he does tell us more about shame in the last chapter of Bk. IV of the *Nicomachean Ethics*. Shame, we are there told, is a largely physiological reaction to ill-repute, manifested in such ways as a tendency to blush. Aristotle also says that it is an emotion, not a settled state or *hexis;* but then no emotion is a settled state. I take him to mean that whereas in the case of some emotions there can be a settled state in which one regularly manifests them of a proper or improper degree, in the case of shame, a mere reaction, there is no associated settled state of choice. At EE. 1234a Aristotle explicitly says that such feelings are not excellences of character because they are without choice. Let us see if we can develop this meager clue.

Aristotle's list of emotions in Bk. II, ch. V, begins with desire. Could it be that all the emotions manifested in character are to be regarded as forms of desire or motivation? Certainly Aristotle was prepared to define anger as something like desire for retaliatory suffering (*De Anima* 403a 30). Can we regard fear as essentially involving a desire for safety and pity as involving desire that the misfortunes of those pitied should end? These emotions can then be regarded as at least having an appetitive component and thus suitable to be embodied in choice and action. Again, in *akrasia* or lack of self-control the errant emotion could hardly conflict with rational choice if it did not include some form of desire.

But in the case of, say, shame and rejoicing over the misfortunes of others we seem to be faced with a mere passive reaction involving no desire. Shame is largely a physiological reaction; and rejoicing in misfortune is merely to take a nasty pleasure in contemplation of the misery of others and does not involve procuring their misery. Neither is a motive to action. Shame may, indeed, hold me back from action; but perhaps we have to distinguish a desire not to do something from an inability to bring oneself to do it.

It would be excessive to claim that these speculations are either clearly true or clearly what Aristotle had in mind. But, if tentatively accepted, they would constitute a defense of Aristotle's position. He could still claim that all states of character were connected with some specific emotion and that every emotion that embodies desire might be exhibited to an excessive or proper or deficient extent. Such feelings or non-appetitive emotions as shame and envy and rejoicing in misfortune would fall outside his theory of excellence of character. But his few short remarks about envy, *nemesis,* and rejoicing in misfortune certainly cannot be defended as they stand.

I wish finally to consider a further difficulty in the doctrine of the mean which has been raised, as exemplified in the account of bravery *(andreia).* Ross considered that rashness was not an opposite extreme to cowardice, and suggested that Aristotle's triad should be replaced by two dyads:

Defect or "vice"	*Excellence or "virtue"*
Rashness	Caution
Cowardice	Courage

I agree with Ross in finding Aristotle's triad unsatisfactory, but would prefer, in accordance with Aristotle's general theory, to replace his one triad with two triads. For if rashness is, as Ross says, an insufficiency of caution, is there not also a possible fault, not very uncommon, which is excess of caution, over-cautiousness? If we can think of *tharros* as an indeterminate degree of daring, then one can be over-daring, over-bold, or rash, insufficiently daring or over-cautious, or also daring to the right degree. If one is daring to the right degree then one will be called cautious in comparison with the over-bold man or bold in comparison with the over-cautious man, as Aristotle explains in Bk. II, ch. viii. The same form of behavior can be called either, depending on which extreme it is being contrasted with.

Now cowardice is not the same thing as excessive caution. One might be brave but over-cautious temperamentally. Unwillingness to take a proper risk need not result from excessive fear, or from fear at all. *Andreia* as opposed to *deileia* or cowardice is not courage but bravery or valor. One may be called courageous if one masters one's fears, but there is a fearless bravery which is quite different, and it is this that Aristotle would count as an excellence of character. In a well-known story, Socrates was left unmolested by the enemy during the retreat from Potidaea because he was clearly, from his demeanor, not afraid of them. Now Aristotle says, rightly, that there are things that any sane man would fear; to be totally fearless is to be a lunatic. But probably there are some men who would not fear some things that a well-integrated man of sense would fear. If a man is not afraid under heavy fire there is something wrong with him, as there is if he is afraid to cross a road in a rear area, lest some stray shell should hit him. There is here, too, the possibility of excess and deficiency, even if excessive fearlessness is rare. So we have here two triads:

Defect	*Excellence*	*Defect*
over-caution	caution	rashness
cowardice	bravery	insensitive fearlessness

We should distinguish these two triads and not run them together as Aristotle does. But he incorrectly applies his theory, rather than, as Ross suggests, applying an incorrect theory.

Aristotle, then, makes mistakes. . . . He is inclined to look for a different emotion for each different excellence, whereas empty vanity and graspingness are better seen as showing the same emotion toward different objects—greed for honor and greed for money. He gives a very unsatisfactory account of envy and spite. He confounds two triads in one when he discusses *andreia*. But provided that we realize that he is discussing that excellence of character that is manifested in the practical life of the *eudaemon,* not Christian virtues, I cannot see that the mistakes we have noted are major, or render his account seriously inadequate in principle. At the very least it is a substantial doctrine worthy of Aristotle's genius.

Aristotle on *Eudaimonia*

THOMAS NAGEL

The *Nicomachean Ethics* exhibits indecision between two accounts of *eudaimonia*—a comprehensive and an intellectualist account. According to the intellectualist account, stated in Book X Chap. 7, *eudaimonia* is realized in the activity of the most divine part of man, functioning in accordance with its proper excellence. This is the activity of theoretical contemplation. According to the comprehensive account (described as "secondary" at 1178 a 9), *eudaimonia* essentially involves not just the activity of the theoretical intellect, but the full range of human life and action, in accordance with the broader excellences of moral virtue and practical wisdom. This view connects *eudaimonia* with the conception of human nature as composite, i.e. as involving the interaction of reason, emotion, perception, and action in an ensouled body.

The *Eudemian Ethics* exhibits a similar indecision, less elaborately expressed. Most of the work expounds a comprehensive account, but the following passage appears at its close:

> Therefore whatever mode of choosing and of acquiring things good by nature—whether goods of body or wealth or friends or the other goods—will best promote the contemplation of God, that is the best mode, and that standard is the finest; and any mode of choice and acquisition that either through deficiency or excess hinders us from serving and from contemplating God—that is a bad one. This is how it is for the soul, and this is the soul's best standard—to be as far as possible unconscious of the irrational part of the soul, as such. (1249 b 17–24)

Although this passage is admittedly somewhat isolated, it seems to support the conclusion that Aristotle was tempted by an intellectualist (or perhaps spiritualist) account of the ends of life in the *Eudemian Ethics*. In fact, considering the emphasis on the divine element in our nature at the end of the *Nicomachean Ethics* (1178 b 7–33), it does not seem out of line to bring God into the matter at the end of the *Eudemian*. "Intellectualist" may be rather too dry a term for the almost Augustinian sentiments which can be detected in both works.

Since the philosophical issue between these two positions arises in virtue of the ambivalence of the *Nicomachean Ethics* alone, I shall discuss it largely in that setting. I shall also comment on the relation of this issue to the psychology of the *De Anima*. There is a connection between intellectualist tendencies in the *Ethics* and Aristotle's view of the relation between *nous* and the rest of the soul. But the latter view appears to me to contain as much indecision as the former. It is because he is not sure who we are that Aristotle finds it difficult to say unequivocally in what our *eudaimonia* consists, and how the line is to be drawn between its constituents and its necessary conditions. Moreover I shall argue that intellectualism has strong defenses even without a two-substance theory of human beings.

Aristotle's program is compactly set out in NE

These remarks derive from comments on a paper by John M. Cooper, "Intellectualism and Practical Reasoning in Aristotle's Moral Philosophy," presented at a meeting of the Society for Ancient Greek Philosophy, in New York, December 28, 1969. My research was supported in part by the National Science Foundation.

From *Phronesis* 17 (1972), 252–59.

I 7, beginning at 1097 b 22. If we are not to stop with the truism that the supreme human good is *eudaimonia,* we must inquire into the *ergon* of man, since if something has an *ergon,* that thing's good is a function of its *ergon.* The *ergon* of a thing, in general, is what it does that makes it what it is. Not everything has an *ergon,* for there are things to be which is not to do anything. But when something has an *ergon,* that thing's good is specified by it. The proper *ergon* of man, by which human excellence is measured, is that which makes him a man rather than anything else. Humans do a great many things, but since some are done equally well, or better, by plants, fish, and animals, they are not among the things to do which is to be human.

This lands us immediately in difficulty, for the inference seems unsound. If the feature of life unique to humans could exist in the absence of those features which humans share with the beasts, the result would be not a human being but something else. And why should we take the highest good of a rarefied individual like that as the ultimate end for complicated and messy individuals like ourselves? One would expect at the very least that the *interaction* between the function that differentiates us from animals, and the functions that we share with them, would play a role in the definition of *eudaimonia.* This would mean including the *practical* exercise of the rational faculty as well as the contemplative.

Suppose we pursue this line of criticism further, however, by asking whether we should not demand the inclusion of still more functions in the definition of human *ergon* and hence of human good. What about health, for example, or fertility? It will be objected that these fail to meet an essential condition for inclusion: the condition of autonomy.[1] This condition states that the fundamental elements of human good cannot be due simply to luck. And health, for example, can be the result of sheer good fortune, rather than a man's own efforts.

But the basis of this objection must be examined. It stems, presumably, from the condition that good is tied to *ergon* or functioning, and what simply *befalls* a thing, whether that thing be a man or a plant, is not an instance of its functioning or malfunctioning. Therefore if I contract cholera, the intrusion of the hostile bacilli is a calamity, but not a malfunction of mine, hence not to be weighed in counting me *eudaimon* or not. Its *effect* on me, however, is certainly a malfunction. And why should this purely physical malfunction not be *in itself* a deviation from my human well-being (rather than just because of its deleterious effects on the life of reason)? If it is excluded on the ground that sweating, throwing up, and shuddering with fever are not things that *I do,* then the question has been begged. For the issue is precisely whether the account of what a person is and does should include or exclude the bodily functions that he shares with animals and even plants. If digesting, for instance, is something a clam does, why is it not something a human does as well—and something to do which is part of being human, even though it does not require *effort?*

In neither the *De Anima* nor the *Nicomachean Ethics* is the nutritive element excluded from the human soul, yet it is not one of the aspects of human functioning that Aristotle is willing to regard as a measure of *eudaimonia.* This position has considerable intuitive appeal. If we could see why nutrition is assigned such a low status, we might have a clue to the train of thought which tempts Aristotle to pare away everything except the intellect, till the only thing which intrinsically bears on *eudaimonia* is the quality of contemplative activity.[2]

Let me introduce a homely example. A combination corkscrew and bottle-opener has the function of removing corks and caps from bottles. This is a simple *ergon,* which allows us to evaluate the implement in terms of its capacity for successful performance. However, it does not seem simple enough to escape the question Aristotle has raised. It removes bottle-caps, to be sure. But since it has that function in common with any mere bottle-opener, *that* cannot be the special *ergon (to idion)* of our implement—the *ergon* by which its excellence is judged. So, by elimination, to *idion* must be removing corks. Unfortunately that is a capacity it shares with mere corkscrews, so that can't be part of its special *ergon* either. Obviously this argument is no good. The thing must have a simple conjunctive *ergon,* and its excellence is a function of both conjuncts.

Why won't such a reduction work for the case

of the human soul and *eudaimonia?* We have dispensed with digestion and procreation on the ground that clams do it too. Sensation and desire are common to dogs. So we are left with reason. But the gods have reason without having these other capacities, so *that* isn't the peculiar *ergon* of man, either. Therefore we must abandon this method of arguing by elimination, and acknowledge that man has a conjunctive *ergon* which overlaps the *erga* of gods and dogs, as a combination corkscrew and bottle-opener combines the functions of corkscrews and bottle-openers. They just happen to find themselves in the same *ergon* box.

If this argument were correct, it would support not just a comprehensive position extending to non-intellectual areas of consciousness and activity, but the inclusion of all the lower life functions in the measure of human excellence. But in fact the conjunctive picture of the component capacities of the human soul is absurd, and if we can say why it is absurd, we may be able to understand why Aristotle accords to reason the title of *ergon idion* of man, despite the fact that it, like digestion, might be shared by other beings as well.

The operative idea is evidently that of a hierarchy of capacities. The life capacities of a complex organism are not all on a level: some serve to support others. This is not so easy to account for clearly. Take for example the prima facie subservience of nutrition to perception and locomotion. That might be a ground for denying that nutrition was part of the special *ergon* of a higher animal. But perception and locomotion e.g. in a giraffe, largely serve the ends of nutrition and reproduction, so the case is unclear. What is the point of being a giraffe? A giraffe leads a certain type of active life, supported by complex metabolic, digestive, and circulatory processes, and ordered in such a way as to permit those processes to proceed efficiently. One thing is clear: its walking and seeing and digesting are not simply three separate activities going on side by side in the same individual, like a doll that wets, cries, and closes its eyes. A giraffe is one organism and its functions are coherently organized. Its proper excellence is not just the conjunction of the special excellences of its component functions, but the optimal functioning of the total system in the giraffe's *life*. And the highest-level account of this will be concerned not with blood pressure and peristalsis but with activity—some of which, admittedly, helps to control blood pressure and provide material for peristalsis.

The main difference between a human being and a giraffe is that a human being has reason, and that his entire complex of organic functions supports rational as well as irrational activity. There is of course feedback as well: in humans, not only perception and locomotion, but also reason, is employed in the service of nutrition and reproduction. Reason is also involved in the control of perception, locomotion, and desire. Nevertheless the highest-level account of a human life puts all the other functions into a supportive position in relation to rational activity. And although reason helps us to get enough to eat and move around, it is not subservient to those lower functions. Occasionally it may have to serve as the janitor or pimp of the passions, but that is not basically what it is *for*. On one plausible view reason, despite its continual service to the lower functions, is what human life is all about. The lower functions serve it, provide it with a setting, and are to some extent under its control, but the dominant characterization of a human being must refer to his reason. This is why intellectualism tempts Aristotle, and why a conjunctive position, which lets various other aspects of life into the measure of good, is less plausible. Neither a conjunctive nor a disjunctive view about *eudaimonia* is adequate to these facts. The supreme good for man must be measured in terms of that around which all other human functions are organized.

But at this point it is essential to recall that much of the practical employment of reason is in the service of lower functions. Is this a proper exercise of that faculty, or does it have a point beyond the uses of cleverness, prudence, and courage, beyond the rational calculation of the most sensible way to spend one's time and money, or to organize society? This question prompts Aristotle to pass from the vague characterization that human life, as opposed to other life, is rational, to a consideration of the *objects* best suited for the exercise of this capacity. This is a peculiar question, which did not arise about giraffes. The nonrational activity of giraffes and its feedback on the metabolic functions seems at first sight a perfectly satisfactory model, and we might be tempted to apply it to humans. Why can't we reach a parallel account of proper human functioning by just adding reason to the top of the class of capacities that cooperate in an organized fashion to further the life of the individual? Why should there be any doubt that the use of reason to earn a living or procure food should belong to the central function of man?

The answer is as follows. Human possibilities reveal that reason has a use beyond the ordering of practical life. The circle of mutual support between reason, activity, and nutrition is not completely closed. In fact all of it, including the practical employment of reason, serves to support the individual for an activity that completely transcends these wordly concerns. The model of feedback does not work for the *ergon* of humans, because the best and purest employment of reason has nothing to do with daily life. Aristotle believes, in short, that human life is not important enough for humans to spend their lives on. A person should seek to transcend not only his individual practical concerns, but also those of society or humanity as a whole.

In *NE* VI 7, while arguing that *sophia* is the highest type of knowledge, and knowledge of the highest objects, he says (1141 a 21–23): "For it is absurd to think that Political Science or Prudence is the loftiest kind of knowledge, inasmuch as man is not the highest thing in the universe." Theoretical and practical matters must compete for the attention of the rational faculty; and the capacity which enables humans to concentrate on subjects more elevated than themselves at the same time spoils them for lowlier concerns. The imperfection of applications of reason to practical matters is that these applications make human life the primary object of rational attention, whereas with reason man has become the only creature capable of concentrating on what is higher than himself and thereby sharing in it to some extent. His time is, so to speak, too valuable to waste on anything so insignificant as human life.

This does not mean that there is no distinction between excellence and depravity in the practical domain. It is certainly better to exercise reason well in providing for one's needs and in dealing with others—i.e. to have moral virtue—than to exercise it badly. But this is essentially a caretaker function of reason, in which it is occupied with matters—i.e. the sordid details of the life of a complex person—far below those which it might be considering if it had more time and were less called upon merely to *manage*.

It is this point of view, I believe, which dominates Chapters 7 and 8 of Book X, where the intellectualist account of *eudaimonia* receives its strongest endorsement. Even there the possibility of doubt is acknowledged. Aristotle appears uncertain whether the result is to be described as a strictly human good. Having argued the claims of the contemplative life on a variety of grounds, he breaks in at 1177 b 27 with the remark that such a life would be higher than human. It is achieved not in virtue simply of being a man, but in virtue of something divine of which men partake. Nevertheless this divine element, which gives us the capacity to think about things higher than ourselves, is the highest aspect of our souls, and we are not justified in foregoing its activities to concentrate on lowlier matters, viz. our own lives, unless the demands in the latter area threaten to make contemplation impossible. As he says at 1177 b 33, we should not listen to those who urge that a human should think human thoughts and a mortal mortal ones. Rather we should cultivate that portion of our nature that promises to transcend the rest. If anyone insists that the rest belongs to a complete account of human life, then the view might be put, somewhat paradoxically, by saying that comprehensive human good isn't everything, and should not be the main human goal. We must identify with the highest part of ourselves rather than with the whole. The other functions, including the practical employment of reason itself, provide support for the highest form of activity, but do not enter into our proper excellence as primary component factors. This is because men are not simply the most complex species of animal, but possess as their essential nature a capacity to transcend themselves and become like gods. It is in virtue of this capacity that they are capable of *eudaimonia,* whereas animals are incapable of it, children have not achieved it, and certain adults, e.g. slaves, are prevented from reaching it.

Perhaps this is an unsatisfactory view of human nature and hence an unsatisfactory view of what it is for a human being to flourish. I believe it is a compelling position, however, and one that does not have to depend on a denial of the hylomorphic doctrine of the soul. It might be challenged in either of two ways. One might simply deny that the *ergon* of man is single, and allege that it is a collection of sub-*erga* without orderings of priority and support—like those of a manybladed knife. This leaves us uncertain how to draw the line against good digestion as a component of *eudaimonia* (rather than just as a contribution to it.) A second method would be to preserve the assumption that the *ergon* of man is one, but to offer a different account of its organization, according to which the highest-level specification of human capacities was not just intellectual but involved both theoretical and practical concerns. While this seems to me the most promising line of attack, I shall not pursue it here.

Notes

1. Cooper is responsible for pointing out the importance of this condition. His paper cites three textual statements of it: *EE* 1215 a 12–19, *NE* 1099 b 18–25, and most explicitly *Politics* 1323 b 24–29.

2. This conclusion would require explanation even if a two-substance reading of the *Ethics* were correct. That is, even if the psychology of the *Nicomachean Ethics* included a soul composed of both a form or primary actuality of the body and a pure intellect which was distinct from this, we would still have to ask why the proper function of the hylomorphic section was not counted in the assessment of *eudaimonia*. And I suspect that any account which made sense of the restriction in light of the two-substance theory, could be applied with equal success to justify corresponding restrictions on what counts toward *eudaimonia* on a purely hylomorphic theory of persons, where *nous*, instead of being another soul, was just the highest type of first-order actuality in the complex—distinguishable only in thought from the other parts of the soul, and not really *distinct* from them. That Aristotle shares this view is shown by a parenthetical remark in *NE* I 13, where he is considering which part of the soul possesses the excellence which is to be identified with *eudaimonia*.

   Whether these two parts are really distinct in the sense that the parts of the body or of any other divisible whole are distinct, or whether though distinguishable in thought as two they are inseparable in reality, like the convex and concave sides of a curve, is a question of no importance for the matter in hand. (1102 a 30–34).

4. THEORIES OF JUSTICE

A Theory of Justice

JOHN RAWLS

John Rawls (1921–) is John Cowles Professor of Philosophy at Harvard University. His book *A Theory of Justice* is one of the most influential twentieth-century works on ethics and political philosophy.

Chapter I. Justice as Fairness

. . . .

1. The Role of Justice

Justice is the first virtue of social institutions, as truth is of systems of thought. A theory however elegant and economical must be rejected or revised if it is untrue; likewise laws and institutions no matter how efficient and well arranged must be reformed or abolished if they are unjust. Each person possesses an inviolability founded on justice that even the welfare of society as a whole cannot override. For this reason justice denies that the loss of freedom for some is made right by a greater good shared by others. It does not allow that the sacrifices imposed on a few are outweighed by the larger sum of advantages enjoyed by many. Therefore in a just society, the liberties of equal citizenship are taken as settled; the rights secured by justice are not subject to political bargaining or to the calculus of social interests. The only thing that permits us to acquiesce in an erroneous theory is the lack of a better one; analogously, an injustice is tolerable only when it is necessary to avoid an even greater injustice. Being first virtues of human activities, truth and justice are uncompromising.

These propositions seem to express our intuitive conviction of the primacy of justice. No doubt they are expressed too strongly. In any event I wish to inquire whether these contentions or others similar to them are sound, and if so how they can be accounted for. To this end it is necessary to work out a theory of justice in the light of which these assertions can be interpreted and assessed. I shall begin by considering the role of the principles of justice. Let us assume, to fix ideas, that a society is a more or less self-sufficient association of persons who in their relations to one another recognize certain rules of conduct as binding and who for the most part act in accordance with them. Suppose further that these rules specify a system of cooperation designed to advance the good of those taking part in it. Then, although a society is a cooperative venture for mutual advantage, it is typically marked by a conflict as well as by an identity of interests. There is an identity of interests since social cooperation makes possible a better life for all than any would have if each were to live solely by his own efforts. There is a conflict of interests since persons are not indifferent as to how the greater

From *A Theory of Justice* (Cambridge: Harvard University Press, 1971), pp. 3–5, 7, 11–15, 17–27, 60–65, 150–56.

benefits produced by their collaboration are distributed, for in order to pursue their ends they each prefer a larger to a lesser share. A set of principles is required for choosing among the various social arrangements which determine this division of advantages and for underwriting an agreement on the proper distributive shares. These principles are the principles of social justice: they provide a way of assigning rights and duties in the basic institutions of society and they define the appropriate distribution of the benefits and burdens of social cooperation.

Now let us say that a society is well ordered when it is not only designed to advance the good of its members but when it is also effectively regulated by a public conception of justice. That is, it is a society in which (1) everyone accepts and knows that the others accept the same principles of justice, and (2) the basic social institutions generally satisfy and are generally known to satisfy these principles. In this case while men may put forth excessive demands on one another, they nevertheless acknowledge a common point of view from which their claims may be adjudicated. If men's inclination to self-interest makes their vigilance against one another necessary, their public sense of justice makes their secure association together possible. Among individuals with disparate aims and purposes a shared conception of justice establishes the bonds of civic friendship; the general desire for justice limits the pursuit of other ends. One may think of a public conception of justice as constituting the fundamental charter of a well-ordered human association.

. . . .

2. The Subject of Justice

Many different kinds of things are said to be just and unjust: not only laws, institutions, and social systems, but also particular actions of many kinds, including decisions, judgments, and imputations. We also call the attitudes and dispositions of persons, and persons themselves, just and unjust. Our topic, however, is that of social justice. For us the primary subject of justice is the basic structure of society, or more exactly, the way in which the major social institutions distribute fundamental rights and duties and determine the division of advantages from social cooperation. By major institutions I understand the political constitution and the principal economic and social arrangements. Thus the legal protection of freedom of thought and liberty of conscience, competitive markets, private property in the means of production, and the monogamous family are examples of major social institutions. Taken together as one scheme, the major institutions define men's rights and duties and influence their life-prospects, what they can expect to be and how well they can hope to do. The basic structure is the primary subject of justice because its effects are so profound and present from the start. The intuitive notion here is that this structure contains various social positions and that men born into different positions have different expectations of life determined, in part, by the political system as well as by economic and social circumstances. In this way the institutions of society favor certain starting places over others. These are especially deep inequalities. Not only are they pervasive, but they affect men's initial chances in life; yet they cannot possibly be justified by an appeal to the notions of merit or desert. It is these inequalities, presumably inevitable in the basic structure of any society, to which the principles of social justice must in the first instance apply. These principles, then regulate the choice of a political constitution and the main elements of the economic and social system. The justice of a social scheme depends essentially on how fundamental rights and duties are assigned and on the economic opportunities and social conditions in the various sectors of society.

. . . .

3. The Main Idea of the Theory of Justice

My aim is to present a conception of justice which generalizes and carries to a higher level of abstraction the familiar theory of the social contract as found, say, in Locke, Rousseau, and Kant. In order to do this we are not to think of the original contract as one to enter a particular society or to set up a particular form of government. Rather, the guiding idea is that the principles of justice for the basic structure of society are the object of the original agreement. They are the principles that free and rational persons concerned to further their own interests would accept in an initial position of equality as defining the fundamental terms of their association. These principles are to regulate all further agreements; they specify the kinds of social cooperation that can be entered into and the forms of government that can be established. This way of regarding the principles of justice I shall call justice as fairness.

Thus we are to imagine that those who engage in social cooperation choose together, in one joint act, the principles which are to assign basic rights and duties and to determine the division of social benefits. Men are to decide in advance how they are to regulate their claims against one another and what is to be the foundation charter of their society. Just as each person must decide by rational reflection what constitutes his good, that is, the system of ends which it is rational for him to pursue, so a group of persons must decide once and for all what is to count among them as just and unjust. The choice which rational men would make in this hypothetical situation of equal liberty, assuming for the present that this choice problem has a solution, determines the principles of justice.

In justice as fairness the original position of equality corresponds to the state of nature in the traditional theory of the social contract. This original position is not, of course, thought of as an actual historical state of affairs, much less as a primitive condition of culture. It is understood as a purely hypothetical situation characterized so as to lead to a certain conception of justice. Among the essential features of this situation is that no one knows his place in society, his class position or social status, nor does any one know his fortune in the distribution of natural assets and abilities, his intelligence, strength, and the like. I shall even assume that the parties do not know their conceptions of the good or their special psychological propensities. The principles of justice are chosen behind a veil of ignorance. This ensures that no one is advantaged or disadvantaged in the choice of principles by the outcome of natural chance or the contingency of social circumstances. Since all are similarly situated and no one is able to design principles to favor his particular condition, the principles of justice are the result of a fair agreement or bargain. For given the circumstances of the original position, the symmetry of everyone's relations to each other, this initial situation is fair between individuals as moral persons, that is, as rational beings with their own ends and capable, I shall assume, of a sense of justice. The original position is, one might say, the appropriate initial status quo, and thus the fundamental agreements reached in it are fair. This explains the propriety of the name "justice as fairness": it conveys the idea that the principles of justice are agreed to in an initial situation that is fair. The name does not mean that the concepts of justice and fairness are the same, any more than the phrase "poetry as metaphor" means that the concepts of poetry and metaphor are the same.

Justice as fairness begins, as I have said, with one of the most general of all choices which persons might make together, namely, with the choice of the first principles of a conception of justice which is to regulate all subsequent criticism and reform of instititutions. Then, having chosen a conception of justice, we can suppose that they are to choose a constitution and a legislature to enact laws, and so on, all in accordance with the principles of justice initially agreed upon. Our social situation is just if it is such that by this sequence of hypothetical agreements we would have contracted into the general system of rules which defines it. Moreover, assuming that the original position does determine a set of principles (that is, that a particular conception of justice would be chosen), it will then be true that whenever social institutions satisfy these principles those engaged in them can say to one another that they are cooperating on terms to which they would agree if they were free and equal persons whose relations with respect to one another were fair. They could all view their arrangements as meeting the stipulations which they would acknowledge in an initial situation that embodies widely accepted and reasonable constraints on the choice of principles. The general recognition of this fact would provide the basis for a public acceptance of the corresponding principles of justice. No society can, of course, be a scheme of cooperation which men enter voluntarily in a literal sense; each person finds himself placed at birth in some particular position in some particular society, and the nature of this position materially affects his life prospects. Yet a society satisfying the principles of justice as fairness comes as close as a society can to being a voluntary scheme, for it meets the principles which free and equal persons would assent to under circumstances that are fair. In this sense its members are autonomous and the obligations they recognize self-imposed.

One feature of justice as fairness is to think of the parties in the initial situation as rational and mutually disinterested. This does not mean that the parties are egoists, that is, individuals with only certain kinds of interests, say in wealth, prestige, and domination. But they are conceived as not taking an interest in one another's interests. They are to presume that even their spiritual aims may be opposed, in the way that the aims of those of different religions may be opposed. Moreover, the concept of rationality must be interpreted as far as possible in the narrow sense, standard in economic theory, of taking the most effective means to given ends. . . . [O]ne must try to avoid introducing into it any controversial ethical elements. The initial situation must be characterized by stipulations that are widely accepted.

In working out the conception of justice as fairness one main task clearly is to determine which principles of justice would be chosen in the original position. To do this we must describe this situation in some detail and formulate with care the problem of choice which it presents. . . . It may be observed, however, that once the principles of justice are thought of as arising from an original agreement in a situation of equality, it is an open question whether the principle of utility would be acknowledged. Offhand it hardly seems likely that persons who view themselves as equals, entitled to press their claims upon one another, would agree to a principle which may require lesser life prospects for some simply for the sake of a greater sum of advantages enjoyed by others. Since each desires to protect his interests, his capacity to advance his conception of the good, no one has a reason to acquiesce in an enduring loss for himself in order to bring about a greater net balance of satisfaction. In the absence of strong and lasting benevolent impulses, a rational man would not accept a basic structure merely because it maximized the algebraic sum of advantages irrespective of its permanent effects on his own basic rights and interests. Thus it seems that the principle of utility is incompatible with the conception of social cooperation among equals for mutual advantage. It appears to be inconsistent with the idea of reciprocity implicit in the notion of a well-ordered society. Or, at any rate, so I shall argue.

I shall maintain instead that the persons in the initial situation would choose two rather different principles: the first requires equality in the assignment of basic rights and duties, while the second holds that social and economic inequalities, for example inequalities of wealth and authority, are just only if they result in compensating benefits for everyone, and in particular for the least advantaged members of society. These principles rule out justifying institutions on the grounds that the hardships of some are offset by a greater good in the aggregate. It may be expedient but it is not just that some should have less in order that others may prosper. But there is no injustice in the greater benefits earned by a few provided that the situation of persons not so fortunate is thereby improved. The intuitive idea is that since everyone's well-being depends upon a scheme of cooperation without which no one could have a satisfactory life, the division of advantages should be such as to draw forth the willing cooperation of everyone taking part in it, including those less well situated. Yet this can be expected only if reasonable terms are proposed. The two principles mentioned seem to be a fair agreement on the basis of which those better endowed, or more fortunate in their social position, neither of which we can be said to deserve, could expect the willing cooperation of others when some workable scheme is a necessary condition of the welfare of all. Once we decide to look for a conception of justice that nullifies the accidents of natural endowment and the contingencies of social circumstance as counters in quest for political and economic advantage, we are led to these principles. They express the result of leaving aside those aspects of the social world that seem arbitrary from a moral point of view.

. . . .

4. The Original Position and Justification

I have said that the original position is the appropriate initial status quo which insures that the fundamental agreements reached in it are fair. This fact yields the name "justice as fairness." It is clear, then, that I want to say that one conception of justice is more reasonable than another, or justifiable with respect to it, if rational persons in the initial situation would choose its principles over those of the other for the role of justice. Conceptions of justice are to be ranked by their acceptability to persons so circumstanced. Understood in this way the question of justification is settled by working out a problem of deliberation: we have to ascertain which principles it would be rational to adopt given the contractual situation. This connects the theory of justice with the theory of rational choice.

If this view of the problem of justification is to succeed, we must, of course, describe in some detail the nature of this choice problem. A problem of rational decision has a definite answer only if we know the beliefs and interests of the parties, their relations with respect to one another, the alternatives between which they are to choose, the procedure whereby they make up their minds, and so on. As the circumstances are presented in different ways, correspondingly different principles are accepted. The concept of the original position, as I shall refer to it, is that of the most philosophically favored interpretation of this initial choice situation for the purposes of a theory of justice.

But how are we to decide what is the most favored interpretation? I assume, for one thing, that there is a broad measure of agreement that principles of justice should be chosen under certain conditions. To justify a particular description of the initial situation one shows that it incorporates these commonly shared presumptions. One argues from widely accepted but weak premises to more specific conclusions. Each of the presumptions should by itself be natural and plausible; some of them may seem innocuous or even trivial. The aim of the contract approach is to establish that taken together they impose significant bounds on acceptable principles of justice. The ideal outcome would be that these conditions determine a unique set of principles; but I shall be satisfied if they suffice to rank the main traditional conceptions of social justice.

One should not be misled, then, by the somewhat unusual conditions which characterize the original position. The idea here is simply to make vivid to ourselves the restrictions that it seems reasonable to impose on arguments for principles of justice, and therefore on these principles themselves. Thus it seems reasonable and generally acceptable that no one should be advantaged or disadvantaged by natural fortune or social circumstances in the choice of principles. It also seems widely agreed that it should be impossible to tailor principles to the circumstances of one's own case. We should insure further that particular inclinations and aspirations, and persons' conceptions of their good do not affect the principles adopted. The aim is to rule out those principles that it would be rational to propose for acceptance, however little the chance of success, only if one knew certain things that are irrelevant from the standpoint of justice. For example, if a man knew that he was wealthy, he might find it rational to advance the principle that various taxes for welfare measures be counted unjust; if he knew that he was poor, he would most likely propose the contrary principle. To represent the desired restrictions one imagines a situation in which everyone is deprived of this sort of information. One excludes the knowledge of those contingencies which sets men at odds and allows them to be guided by their prejudices. In this manner the veil of ignorance is arrived at in a natural way. This concept should cause no difficulty if we keep in mind the constraints on arguments that it is meant to express. At any time we can enter the original position, so to speak, simply by following a certain procedure, namely, by arguing for principles of justice in accordance with these restrictions.

It seems reasonable to suppose that the parties in the original position are equal. That is, all have the same rights in the procedure for choosing principles; each can make proposals, submit reasons for their acceptance, and so on. Obviously the purpose of these conditions is to represent equality between human beings as moral persons, as creatures having a conception of their good and capable of a sense of justice. The basis of equality is taken to be similarity in these two respects. Systems of ends are not ranked in value; and each man is presumed to have the requisite ability to understand and to act upon whatever principles are adopted. Together with the veil of ignorance, these conditions define the principles of justice as those which rational persons concerned to advance their interests would consent to as equals when none are known to be advantaged or disadvantaged by social and natural contingencies.

There is, however, another side to justifying a particular description of the original position. This is to see if the principles which would be chosen match our considered convictions of justice or extend them in an acceptable way.*

. . . .

By going back and forth, sometimes altering the conditions of the contractual circumstances, at others withdrawing our judgments and conforming them to principle, I assume that eventually we shall find a description of the initial situation that both expresses reasonable conditions and yields principles which match our considered judgments duly pruned and adjusted. This state of affairs I refer to as reflective equilibirum. It is an equilibirum because at last our principles and judgments coincide; and it is reflective since we know to what principles our judgments conform and the premises of their derivation.

. . . .

A final comment. We shall want to say that certain principles of justice are justified because they would be agreed to in an initial situation of equality. I have emphasized that this original position is purely hypothetical. It is natural to ask why, if this agreement is never actually entered into, we should take any interest in these principles, moral or otherwise. The answer is that the conditions embodied in the description of the original position are ones that we do in fact accept. Or if we do not, then perhaps we can be persuaded to do so by philosophical reflection. Each aspect of the contractual situation can be given supporting grounds. Thus what we shall do is to collect together into one conception a number of conditions on principles that we are ready upon due consideration to recognize as reasonable. These constraints express what we are prepared to regard as limits on fair terms of social cooperation. One way to look at the idea of the original position, therefore, is to see it as an expository device which sums up the meaning of these conditions and helps us to extract their consequences. On the other hand, this conception is also an intuitive notion that suggests its own elaboration, so that led on by it we are drawn to define more clearly the standpoint from which we can best interpret moral relationships. We need a conception that enables us to envision our objective from afar: the intuitive notion of the original position is to do this for us.

5. Classical Utilitarianism

. . . [T]he kind of utilitarianism I shall describe here is the strict classical doctrine which receives perhaps its clearest and most accessible formulation in Sidgwick. The main idea is that society is rightly ordered, and therefore just, when its major institutions are arranged so as to achieve the greatest net balance of satisfaction summed over all the individuals belonging to it.

We may note first that there is, indeed, a way of thinking of society which makes it easy to suppose that the most rational conception of justice is utilitarian. For consider: each man in realizing his own interests is certainly free to balance his own losses against his own gains. We may impose a sacrifice on ourselves now for the sake of a greater advantage later. A person quite properly acts, at least when others are not affected, to achieve his own greatest good, to advance his rational ends as far as possible. Now why should not a society act on precisely the same principle applied to the group and therefore regard that which is rational for one man as right for an association of men? Just as the well-being of a person is constructed from the series of satisfactions that are experienced at different moments in the course of his life, so in very much the same way the well-being of society is to be constructed from the fulfillment of the systems of desires of the many individuals who belong to it. Since the principle for an individual is to advance as far as possible his own welfare, his own system of desires, the principle for society is to advance as far as possible the welfare of the group, to realize to the greatest extent the comprehensive system of desire arrived at from the desires of its members. Just as an individual balances present and future gains against present and future losses, so a society may balance satisfac-

*[Editors' note: For an elaboration of this remark, see Rawls's "Outline of a Decision Procedure for Ethics," pp. 779–86.

tions and dissatisfactions between different individuals. And so by these reflections one reaches the principle of utility in a natural way: a society is properly arranged when its institutions maximize the net balance of satisfaction. The principle of choice for an association of men is interpreted as an extension of the principle of choice for one man. Social justice is the principle of rational prudence applied to an aggregative conception of the welfare of the group. . . .

This idea is made all the more attractive by a further consideration. The two main concepts of ethics are those of the right and the good; the concept of a morally worthy person is, I believe, derived from them. The structure of an ethical theory is, then, largely determined by how it defines and connects these two basic notions. Now it seems that the simplest way of relating them is taken by teleological theories: the good is defined independently from the right, and then the right is defined as that which maximizes the good. More precisely, those institutions and acts are right which of the available alternatives produce the most good, or at least as much good as any of the other institutions and acts open as real possibilities (a rider needed when the maximal class is not a singleton). Teleological theories have a deep intuitive appeal since they seem to embody the idea of rationality. It is natural to think that rationality is maximizing something and that in morals it must be maximizing the good. Indeed, it is tempting to suppose that it is self-evident that things should be arranged so as to lead to the most good.

It is essential to keep in mind that in a teleological theory the good is defined independently from the right. This means two things. First, the theory accounts for our considered judgments as to which things are good (our judgments of value) as a separate class of judgments intuitively distinguishable by common sense, and then proposes the hypothesis that the right is maximizing the good as already specified. Second, the theory enables one to judge the goodness of things without referring to what is right. For example, if pleasure is said to be the sole good, then presumably pleasures can be recognized and ranked in value by criteria that do not presuppose any standards of right, or what we would normally think of as such. Whereas if the distribution of goods is also counted as a good, perhaps a higher order one, and the theory directs us to produce the most good (including the good of distribution among others), we no longer have a teleological view in the classical sense. The problem of distribution falls under the concept of right as one intuitively understands it, and so the theory lacks an independent definition of the good. The clarity and simplicity of classical teleological theories derives largely from the fact that they factor our moral judgments into two classes, the one being characterized separately while the other is then connected with it by a maximizing principle.

Teleological doctrines differ, pretty clearly, according to how the conception of the good is specified. If it is taken as the realization of human excellence in the various forms of culture, we have what may be called perfectionism. This notion is found in Aristotle and Nietzsche, among others. If the good is defined as pleasure, we have hedonism; if as happiness, eudaimonism, and so on. I shall understand the principle of utility in its classical form as defining the good as the satisfaction of desire, or perhaps better, as the satisfaction of rational desire. This accords with the view in all essentials and provides, I believe, a fair interpretation of it. The appropriate terms of social cooperation are settled by whatever in the circumstances will achieve the greatest sum of satisfaction of the rational desires of individuals. It is impossible to deny the initial plausibility and attractiveness of this conception.

The striking feature of the utilitarian view of justice is that it does not matter, except indirectly, how this sum of satisfactions is distributed among individuals any more than it matters, except indirectly, how one man distributes his satisfactions over time. The correct distribution in either case is that which yields the maximum fulfillment. Society must allocate its means of satisfaction whatever these are, rights and duties, opportunities and privileges, and various forms of wealth, so as to achieve this maximum if it can. But in itself no distribution of satisfaction is better than another except that the more equal distribution is to be preferred to break ties. It is true that certain common-sense precepts of justice, particularly those which concern the protection of liberties and rights, or which express the claims of desert, seem to contradict this contention. But from a utilitarian standpoint the explanation of these precepts and of their seemingly stringent character is that they are those precepts which experience shows should be strictly respected and departed from only under exceptional circumstances if the sum of advantages is to be maximized. Yet, as with all other precepts, those of justice are derivative from the one end of attaining the greatest balance of satisfaction. Thus there is no reason in principle why the greater gains of some should not compensate for the lesser losses of others; or more importantly, why the violation of the liberty of a few might not be made right by the greater good shared by many. It simply happens that under most conditions, at least in a reasonably advanced stage of civilization, the greatest sum of advantages is not attained in this way. No doubt the strictness of common-sense precepts of justice has a certain usefulness in limiting men's propensities to injustice and to socially injurious actions, but the utilitarian believes that to affirm this strictness as a first principle of morals is a mistake. For just as it is rational for one man to maximize the fulfillment of his system of desires, it is right for a society to maximize the net balance of satisfaction taken over all of its members.

The most natural way, then, of arriving at utilitarianism (although not, of course, the only way of doing so) is to adopt for society as a whole the principle of rational choice for one man. Once this is recognized, the place of the impartial spectator and the emphasis on sympathy in the history of utilitarian thought is readily understood. For it is by the conception of the impartial spectator and the use of sympathetic identification in guiding our imagination that the principle for one man is applied to society. It is this spectator who is conceived as carrying out the required organization of the desires of all persons into one coherent system of desire; it is by this construction that many persons are fused into one. Endowed with ideal powers of sympathy and imagination, the impartial spectator is the perfectly rational individual who identifies with and experiences the desires of others as if these desires were his own. In this way he ascertains the intensity of these desires and assigns them their appropriate weight in the one system of desire the satisfaction of which the ideal legislator then tries to maximize by adjusting the rules of the social system. On this conception of society separate individuals are thought of as so many different lines along which rights and duties are to be assigned and scarce means of satisfaction allocated in accordance with rules so as to give the greatest fulfillment of wants. The nature of the decision made by the ideal legislator is not, therefore, materially different from that of an entrepreneur deciding how to maximize his profit by producing this or that commodity, or that of a consumer deciding how to maximize his satisfaction by the purchase of this or that collection of goods. In each case there is a single person whose system of desires determines the best allocation of limited means. The correct decision is essentially a question of efficient administration. This view of social cooperation is the consequence of extending to society the principle of choice for one man, and then, to make this extension work, conflating all persons into one through the imaginative acts of the impartial sympathetic spectator. Utilitarianism does not take seriously the distinction between persons.

. . . .

11. Two Principles of Justice

I shall now state in a provisional form the two principles of justice that I believe would be chosen in the original position. . . .

The first statement of the two principles reads as follows.

First: each person is to have an equal right to the most extensive basic liberty compatible with a similar liberty for others.

Second: social and economic inequalities are to be arranged so that they are both (a) reasonably expected to be to everyone's advantage, and (b) attached to positions and offices open to all.

. . . .

By way of general comment, these principles primarily apply, as I have said, to the basic structure of society. They are to govern the assignment of rights and duties and to regulate the distribution of social and economic advantages. As their formulation suggests, these principles presuppose that the social structure can be divided into two more or less distinct parts, the first principle applying to the one, the second to the other. They distinguish between those aspects of the social system that define and secure the equal liberties of citizenship and those that specify and establish social and economic inequalities. The basic liberties of citizens are, roughly speaking, political liberty (the right to vote and to be eligible for public office) together with freedom of speech and assembly; liberty of conscience and freedom of thought; freedom of the person along with the right to hold (personal) property; and freedom from arbitrary arrest and seizure as defined by the concept of the rule of law. These liberties are all required to be equal by the first principle, since citizens of a just society are to have the same basic rights.

The second principle applies, in the first approximation, to the distribution of income and wealth and to the design of organizations that make use of differences in authority and responsibility, or chains of command. While the distribution of wealth and income need not be equal, it must be to everyone's advantage, and at the same time, positions of authority and offices of command must be accessible to all. One applies the second principle by holding positions open, and then, subject to this constraint, arranges social and economic inequalities so that everyone benefits.

These principles are to be arranged in a serial order with the first principle prior to the second. This ordering means that a departure from the institutions of equal liberty required by the first principle cannot be justified by, or compensated for, by greater social and economic advantages. The distribution of wealth and income, and the hierarchies of authority, must be consistent with both the liberties of equal citizenship and equality of opportunity.

It is clear that these principles are rather specific in their content, and their acceptance rests on certain assumptions that I must eventually try to explain and justify. A theory of justice depends upon a theory of society in ways that will become evident as we proceed. For the present, it should be observed that the two principles (and this holds for all formulations) are a special case of a more general conception of justice that can be expressed as follows.

> All social values—liberty and opportunity, income and wealth, and the bases of self-respect—are to be distributed equally unless an unequal distribution of any, or all, of these values is to everyone's advantage.

Injustice, then, is simply inequalities that are not to the benefit of all. Of course, this conception is extremely vague and requires interpretation.

As a first step, suppose that the basic structure of society distributes certain primary goods, that is, things that every rational man is presumed to want. These goods normally have a use whatever a person's rational plan of life. For simplicity, assume that the chief primary goods at the disposition of society are rights and liberties, powers and opportunities, income and wealth. (Later on in Part Three the primary good of self-respect has a central place.) These are the social primary goods. Other primary goods such as health and vigor, intelligence and imagination, are natural goods; although their possession is influenced by the basic structure, they are not so directly under its control. Imagine, then, a hypothetical initial arrangement in which all the social primary goods are equally distributed: everyone has similar rights and duties, and income and wealth are evenly shared. This state of affairs provides a benchmark for judging improvements. If certain inequalities of wealth and organizational powers would make everyone better off than in this hypothetical starting situation, then they accord with the general conception.

Now it is possible, at least theoretically, that by giving up some of their fundamental liberties men are sufficiently compensated by the resulting social and economic gains. The general conception of justice imposes no restrictions on what sort of inequalities are permissible; it only requires that everyone's position be improved. We need not suppose anything so drastic as consenting to a condition of slavery. Imagine instead that men forego certain political rights when the economic returns are significant and their capacity to influence the course of policy by the exercise of these rights would be marginal in any case. It is this kind of exchange which the two principles as stated rule out; being arranged in serial order they do not permit exchanges between basic liberties and economic and social gains. The serial ordering of principles expresses an underlying preference among primary social goods. When this preference is rational so likewise is the choice of these principles in this order.

. . . .

Now the second principle insists that each person benefit from permissible inequalities in the basic structure. This means that it must be reasonable for each relevant representative man defined by this structure, when he views it as a going concern, to prefer his prospects with the inequality to his prospects without it. One is not allowed to justify differences in income or organizational powers on the ground that the disadvantages of those in one position are outweighed by the greater advantages of those in another. Much less can infringements of liberty be counterbalanced in this way. Applied to the basic structure, the principle of utility would have us maximize the sum of expectations of representative men (weighted by the number of persons they represent, on the classical view); and this would permit us to compensate for the losses of some by the gains of others. Instead, the two principles require that everyone benefit from economic and social inequalities.

. . . .

26. The Reasoning Leading to the Two Principles of Justice

In this [section] I take up the choice between the two principles of justice and the principle of average utility. Determining the rational preference between these two options is perhaps the central problem in developing the conception of justice as fairness as a viable alternative to the utilitarian tradition. I shall begin in this section by presenting some intuitive remarks favoring the two principles. I shall also discuss briefly the qualitative structure of the argument that needs to be made if the case for these principles is to be conclusive.

It will be recalled that the general conception of justice as fairness requires that all primary social goods be distributed equally unless an unequal distribution would be to everyone's advantage. No restrictions are placed on exchanges of these goods and therefore a lesser liberty can be compensated for by greater social and economic benefits. Now looking at the situation from the standpoint of one person selected arbitrarily, there is no way for him to win special advantages for himself. Nor, on the other hand, are there grounds for his acquiescing in special disadvantages. Since it is not reasonable for him to expect more than an equal share in the division of social goods, and since it is not rational for him to agree to less, the sensible thing for him to do is to acknowledge as the first principle of justice one requiring an equal distribution. Indeed, this principle is so obvious that we would expect it to occur to anyone immediately.

Thus, the parties start with a principle establishing equal liberty for all, including equality of opportunity, as well as an equal distribution of income and wealth. But there is no reason why this acknowledgment should be final. If there are inequalities in the basic structure that work to make everyone better off in comparison with the benchmark of initial equality, why not permit them? The immediate gain which a greater equality might allow can be regarded as intelligently invested in view of its future return. If, for example, these inequalities set up various incentives which succeed in eliciting more productive efforts, a person in the original position may look upon them as necessary to cover the costs of training and to encourage effective performance. One might think that ideally individuals should want to serve one another. But since the parties are assumed not to take an interest in one another's interests, their acceptance of these inequalities is only the acceptance of the relations in which men stand in the circumstances of justice. They have no grounds for complaining of one another's motives. A person in the original position would, therefore, concede the justice of these inequalities. Indeed, it would be shortsighted of him not to do so. He would hesitate to agree to these regularities only if he would be dejected by the bare knowledge or perception that others were better situated; and I have assumed that the parties decide as if they are not moved by envy. In order to make the principle regulating inequalities determinate, one looks at the system from the standpoint of the least advantaged representative man. Inequalities are permissible when they maximize, or at least all contribute to, the long-term expectations of the least fortunate group in society.

Now this general conception imposes no constraints on what sorts of inequalities are allowed, whereas the special conception, by putting the two principles in serial order (with the necessary adjustments in meaning) forbids exchanges between basic liberties and economic and social benefits. I shall not try to justify this ordering here. . . . But roughly, the idea underlying this ordering is that if the parties assume that their basic liberties can be effectively exercised, they will not exchange a lesser liberty for an improvement in economic well-being. It is only when social conditions do not allow the effective establishment of these rights that one can concede their limitation; and these restrictions can be granted only to the extent that they are necessary to prepare the way for a free society. The denial of equal liberty can be defended only if it is necessary to raise the level of civilization so that in due course these freedoms can be enjoyed. Thus in adopting a serial order we are in effect making a special assumption in the original position, namely, that the parties know that the conditions of their society, whatever they are, admit the effective realization of the equal liberties. The serial ordering of the two principles of justice eventually comes to be reasonable if the general conception is consistently followed. This lexical ranking is the long-run tendency of the general view. For the most part I shall assume that the requisite circumstances for the serial order obtain.

It seems clear from these remarks that the two principles are at least a plausible conception of justice. The question, though, is how one is to argue for them more systematically. Now there are several things to do. One can work out their consequences for institutions and note their implications for fundamental social policy. In this way they are tested by a comparison with our considered judgments of justice. . . . But one can also try to find arguments in their favor that are decisive from the standpoint of the original position. In order to see how this might be done, it is useful as a heuristic device to think of the two principles as the maximin solution to the problem of social justice. There is an analogy between the two principles and the maximin rule for choice under uncertainty. This is evident from the fact that the two principles are those a person would choose for the design of a society in which his enemy is to assign him his place. The maximin rule tells us to rank alternatives by their worst possible outcomes: we are to adopt the alternative the worst outcome of which is superior to the worst outcomes of the others. The persons in the original position do not, of course, assume that their initial place in society is decided by a malevolent opponent. As I note below, they should not reason from false premises. The veil of ignorance does not violate this idea, since an absence of information is not misinformation. But that the two principles of justice would be chosen if the parties were forced to protect themselves against such a contingency explains the sense in which this conception is the maximin solution. And this analogy suggests that if the original position has been described so that it is rational for the parties to adopt the conservative attitude expressed by this rule, a conclusive argument can indeed be constructed for these principles. Clearly the maximin rule is not, in general, a suitable guide for choices under uncertainty. But it is attractive in situations marked by certain special features. My aim, then, is to show that a good case can be made for the two principles based on the fact that the original position manifests these features to the fullest possible degree, carrying them to the limit, so to speak.

Consider the gain-and-loss table below. It represents the gains and losses for a situation which is not a game of strategy. There is no one playing against the person making the decision; instead he is faced with several possible circumstances which may or may not obtain. Which circumstances happen to exist does not depend upon what the person choosing decides or whether he announces his moves in advance. The numbers in the table are monetary values (in hundreds of dollars) in comparison with some initial situation. The gain (g) depends upon the individual's decision (d) and the circumstances (c). Thus $g = f(d, c)$. Assuming that there are three possible decisions and three possible circumstances, we might have this gain-and-loss table.

	Circumstances		
Decisions	C_1	C_2	C_3
d_1	−7	8	12
d_2	−8	7	14
d_3	5	6	8

The maximin rule requires that we make the third decision. For in this case the worst that can happen is that one gains five hundred dollars, which is better than the worst for the other actions. If we adopt one of these we may lose either eight or seven hundred dollars. Thus, the choice of d_3 maximizes f(d,c) for that value of c, which for a given d, minimizes f. The term "maximin" means the *maximum minimorum;* and the rule directs our attention to the worst that can happen under any proposed course of action, and to decide in the light of that.

Now there appear to be three chief features of situations that give plausibility to this unusual rule. First, since the rule takes no account of the likelihoods of the possible circumstances, there must be some reason for sharply discounting estimates of these probabilities. Offhand, the most natural rule of choice would seem to be to compute the expectation of monetary gain for each decision and then to adopt the course of action with the highest prospect. (This expectation is defined as follows: let us suppose that g_{ij} represent the numbers in the gain-and-loss table, where i is the row index and j is the column index; and let p_j, $j = 1, 2, 3$, be the likelihoods of the circumstances, with $\Sigma p_j = 1$. Then the expectation for the ith decision is equal to $\Sigma p_j g_{ij}$.) Thus it must be, for example, that the situation is one in which a knowledge of likelihoods is impossible, or at best extremely insecure. In this case it is unreasonable not to be skeptical of probabilistic calculations unless there is no other way out, particularly if the decision is a fundamental one that needs to be justified to others.

The second feature that suggests the maximin rule is the following: the person choosing has a conception of the good such that he cares very little, if anything, for what he might gain above the minimum stipend that he can, in fact, be sure of by following the maximin rule. It is not worthwhile for him to take a chance for the sake of a further advantage, expecially when it may turn out that he loses much that is important to him. This last provision brings in the third feature, namely, that the rejected alternatives have outcomes that one can hardly accept. The situation involves grave risks. Of course these features work most effectively in combination. The paradigm situation for following the maximin rule is when all three features are realized to the highest degree. This rule does not, then, generally apply, nor of course is it self-evident. Rather, it is a maxim, a rule of thumb, that comes into its own in special circumstances. Its application depends upon the qualitative structure of the possible gains and losses in relation to one's conception of the good, all this against a background in which it is reasonable to discount conjectural estimates of likelihoods.

It should be noted, as the comments on the gain-and-loss table say, that the entries in the table represent monetary values and not utilities. This difference is significant since for one thing computing expectations on the basis of such objective values is not the same thing as computing expected utility and may lead to different results. The essential point though is that in justice as fairness the parties do not know their conception of the good and cannot estimate their utility in the ordinary sense. In any case, we want to go behind de facto preferences generated by given conditions. Therefore expectations are based upon an index of primary goods and the parties make their choice accordingly. The entries in the example are in terms of money and not utility to indicate this aspect of the contract doctrine.

Now, as I have suggested, the original position has been defined so that it is a situation in which the maximin rule applies. In order to see this, let us review briefly the nature of this situation with these three special features in mind. To begin with, the veil of ignorance excludes all but the vaguest knowledge of likelihoods. The parties have no basis for determining the probable nature of their society, or their place in it. Thus they have strong reasons for being wary of probability calculations if any other course is open to them. They must also take in account the fact that their choice of principles should seem reasonable to others, in particular their descendants, whose rights will be deeply affected by it. There are further grounds for discounting that I shall mention as we go along. For the present it suffices to note that these considerations are strengthened by the fact that the parties know very little about the gain-and-loss table. Not only are they unable to conjecture the likelihoods of the various possible circumstances, they cannot say much about what the possible circumstances are, much less enumerate them and foresee the outcome of each alternative available. Those deciding are much more in the dark than the illustration by a numerical table suggests. It is for this reason that I have spoken of an analogy with the maximin rule.

Several kinds of arguments for the two principles of justice illustrate the second feature. Thus, if we can maintain that these principles provide a workable theory of social justice, and that they are compatible with reasonable demands of efficiency, then this conception guarantees a satisfactory minimum. There may be, on reflection, little reason for trying to do better. . . .

Finally, the third feature holds if we can assume that other conceptions of justice may lead to institutions that the parties would find intolerable. For example, it has sometimes been held that under some conditions the utility principle (in either form) justifies, if not slavery or serfdom, at any rate serious infractions of liberty for the sake of greater social benefits. We need not consider here the truth of this claim, or the likelihood that the requisite conditions obtain. For the moment, this contention is only to illustrate the way in which conceptions of justice may allow for outcomes which the parties may not be able to accept. And having the ready alternative of the two principles of justice which secure a satisfactory minimum, it seems unwise, if not irrational, for them to take a chance that these outcomes are not realized.

Justice and Entitlement

ROBERT NOZICK

Robert Nozick (1938–) is a professor of philosophy at Harvard University. His publications include *Anarchy, State, and Utopia* and *Philosophical Explanations*.

Chapter 7
Distributive Justice

. . . .

The term "distributive justice" is not a neutral one. Hearing the term "distribution," most people presume that some thing or mechanism uses some principle or criterion to give out a supply of things. Into this process of distributing shares some error may have crept. So it is an open question, at least, whether *re*distribution should take place; whether we should do again what has already been done once, though poorly. However, we are not in the position of children who have been given portions of pie by someone who now makes last minute adjustments to rectify careless cutting. There is no *central* distribution, no person or group entitled to control all the resources, jointly deciding how they are to be doled out. What each person gets, he gets from others who give to him in exchange for something, or as a gift. In a free society, diverse persons control different resources, and new holdings arise out of the voluntary exchanges and actions of persons. There is no more a distributing or distribution of shares than there is a distributing of mates in a society in which persons choose whom they shall marry. The total result is the product of many individual decisions which the different individuals involved are entitled to make. . . . We shall speak of people's holdings; a principle of justice in holdings describes (part of) what justice tells us (requires) about holdings. I shall state first what I take to be the correct view about justice in holdings, and then turn to the discussion of alternate views.

The Entitlement Theory

The subject of justice in holdings consists of three major topics. The first is the *original acquisition of holdings,* the appropriation of unheld things. This includes the issues of how unheld things may come to be held, the process, or processes, by which unheld things may come to be held, the things that may come to be held by these processes, the extent of what comes to be held by a particular process, and so on. We shall refer to the complicated truth about this topic, which we shall not formulate here, as the principle of justice in acquisition. The second topic concerns the *transfer of holdings* from one person to another. By what processes may a person transfer holdings to another? How may a person acquire a holding from another who holds it? Under this topic come general descriptions of voluntary exchange, and gift and (on the other hand) fraud, as well as reference to particular conventional details fixed upon in a given society. The complicated truth about this subject (with placeholders for conventional details) we shall call the principle of justice in transfer. (And we shall suppose it also includes principles governing how a person may divest himself of a holding, passing it into an unheld state.)

From *Anarchy, State, and Utopia* (New York: Basic Books, 1974), pp. 149–57, 160–63, 174–75, 177–82.

If the world were wholly just, the following inductive definition would exhaustively cover the subject of justice in holdings.

1. A person who acquires a holding in accordance with the principle of justice in acquisition is entitled to that holding.
2. A person who acquires a holding in accordance with the principle of justice in transfer, from someone else entitled to the holding, is entitled to the holding.
3. No one is entitled to a holding except by (repeated) applications of 1 and 2.

The complete principle of distributive justice would say simply that a distribution is just if everyone is entitled to the holdings they possess under the distribution.

A distribution is just if it arises from another just distribution by legitimate means. The legitimate means of moving from one distribution to another are specified by the principle of justice in transfer. The legitimate first "moves" are specified by the principle of justice in acquisition.[1] Whatever arises from a just situation by just steps is itself just. The means of change specified by the principle of justice in transfer preserve justice. As correct rules of inference are truth preserving, and any conclusion deduced via repeated application of such rules from only true premisses is itself true, so the means of transition from one situation to another specified by the principle of justice in transfer are justice preserving, and any situation actually arising from repeated transitions in accordance with the principle from a just situation is itself just. The parallel between justice-preserving transformations and truth-preserving transformations illuminates where it fails as well as where it holds. That a conclusion could have been deduced by truth-preserving means from premisses that are true suffices to show its truth. That from a just situation a situation *could* have arisen via justice-preserving means does *not* suffice to show its justice. The fact that a thief's victims voluntarily *could* have presented him with gifts does not entitle the thief to his ill-gotten gains. Justice in holdings is historical; it depends upon what actually has happened. We shall return to this point later.

Not all actual situations are generated in accordance with the two principles of justice in holdings: the principle of justice in acquisition and the principle of justice in transfer. Some people steal from others, or defraud them, or enslave them, seizing their product and preventing them from living as they choose, or forcibly exclude others from competing in exchanges. None of these are permissible modes of transition from one situation to another. And some persons acquire holdings by means not sanctioned by the principle of justice in acquisition. The existence of past injustice (previous violations of the first two principles of justice in holdings) raises the third major topic under justice in holdings: the rectification of injustice in holdings. If past injustice has shaped present holdings in various ways, some identifiable and some not, what now, if anything, ought to be done to rectify these injustices? What obligations do the performers of injustice have toward those whose position is worse than it would have been had the injustice not been done? Or, than it would have been had compensation been paid promptly? How, if at all, do things change if the beneficiaries and those made worse off are not the direct parties in the act of injustice, but, for example, their descendants? Is an injustice done to someone whose holding was itself based upon an unrectified injustice? How far back must one go in wiping clean the historical slate of injustices? What may victims of injustice permissibly do in order to rectify the injustices being done to them, including the many injustices done by persons acting through their government? I do not know of a thorough or theoretically sophisticated treatment of such issues. Idealizing greatly, let us suppose theoretical investigation will produce a principle of rectification. This principle uses historical information about previous situations and injustices done in them (as defined by the first two principles of justice and rights against interference), and information about the actual course of events that flowed from these injustices, until the present, and it yields a description (or descriptions) of holdings in the society. The principle of rectification presumably will make use of its best estimate of subjunctive information about what would have occurred (or a probability distribution over what might have occurred, using the expected value) if the injustice had not taken place. If the actual description of holdings turns out not to be one of the descriptions yielded by the principle, then one of the descriptions yielded must be realized.[2]

The general outlines of the theory of justice in holdings are that the holdings of a person are just if he is entitled to them by the principles of justice in acquisition and transfer, or by the principle of rectification of injustice (as specified by the first two principles). If each person's holdings are just, then the total set (distribution) of holdings is just. To turn these general outlines into a specific theory we would have to specify the details of each of the three principles of justice in holdings: the principle of acquisition of holdings, the principle of transfer of holdings, and the principle of rectification of violations of the first two principles. I shall not attempt that task here. (Locke's principle of justice in acquisition is discussed below.)

Historical Principles and End-result Principles

The general outlines of the entitlement theory illuminate the nature and defects of other conceptions of distributive justice. The entitlement theory of justice in distribution is *historical;* whether a distribution is just depends upon how it came about. In contrast, *current time-slice principles* of justice hold that the justice of a distribution is determined by how things are distributed (who has what) as judged by some *structural* principle(s) of just distribution. A utilitarian who judges between any two distributions by seeing which has the greater sum of utility and, if the sums tie, applies some fixed equality criterion to choose the more equal distribution, would hold a current time-slice principle of justice. As would someone who had a fixed schedule of trade-offs between the sum of happiness and equality. According to a current time-slice principle, all that needs to be looked at, in judging the justice of a distribution, is who ends up with what; in comparing any two distributions one need look only at the matrix presenting the distributions. No further information need be fed into a principle of justice. It is a consequence of such principles of justice that any two structurally identical distributions are equally just. (Two distributions are structurally identical if they present the same profile, but perhaps have different persons occupying the particular slots. My having ten and your having five, and my having five and your having ten are structurally identical distributions.) Welfare economics is the theory of current time-slice principles of justice. The subject is conceived as operating on matrices representing only current information about distribution. This, as well as some of the usual conditions (for example, the choice of distribution is invariant under relabeling of columns), guarantees that welfare economics will be a current time-slice theory, with all of its inadequacies.

Most persons do not accept current time-slice principles as constituting the whole story about distributive shares. They think it relevant in assessing the justice of a situation to consider not only the distribution it embodies, but also how that distribution came about. If some persons are in prison for murder or war crimes, we do not say that to assess the justice of the distribution in the society we must look only at what this person has, and that person has, and that person has, . . . at the current time. We think it relevant to ask whether someone did something so that he *deserved* to be punished, deserved to have a lower share. Most will agree to the relevance of further information with regard to punishments and penalties. Consider also desired things. One traditional socialist view is that workers are entitled to the product and full fruits of their labor; they have earned it; a distribution is unjust if it does not give the workers what they are entitled to. Such entitlements are based upon some past history. No socialist holding this view would find it comforting to be told that because the actual distribution *A* happens to coincide structurally with the one he desires *D, A* therefore is no less just that *D;* it differs only in that the "parasitic" owners of capital receive under *A* what the workers are entitled to under *D,* and the workers receive under *A* what the owners are entitled to under *D,* namely very little. This socialist rightly, in my view, holds onto the notions of earning, producing, entitlement, desert, and so forth, and he rejects current time-slice principles that look only to the structure of the resulting set of holdings. (The set of holdings resulting from what? Isn't it implausible that how holdings are produced and come to exist has no effect at all on who should hold what?) His mistake lies in his view of what entitlements arise out of what sorts of productive processes.

We construe the position we discuss too narrowly by speaking of *current* time-slice principles. Nothing is changed if structural principles operate upon a time sequence of current time-slice profiles and, for example, give someone more now to counterbalance the less he has had earlier. A utilitarian or an egalitarian or any mixture of the two over time will inherit the difficulties of his more myopic comrades. He is not helped by the fact that *some* of the information others consider relevant in assessing a distribution is reflected, unrecoverably, in past matrices. Henceforth, we shall refer to such unhistorical principles of distributive justice, including the current time-slice principles, as *end-result principles* or *end-state principles*.

In contrast to end-result principles of justice, *historical principles* of justice hold that past circumstances or actions of people can create differential entitlements or differential deserts to things. An injustice can be worked by moving from one distribution to another structurally identical one, for the second, in profile the same, may violate people's entitlements or deserts; it may not fit the actual history.

Patterning

The entitlement principles of justice in holdings that we have sketched are historical principles of justice. To better understand their precise character, we shall distinguish them from another subclass of the historical principles. Consider, as an example, the principle of distribution according to moral merit. This principle requires that total distributive shares vary directly with moral merit; no person should have a greater share than anyone whose moral merit is greater. (If moral merit could be not merely ordered but measured on an interval or ratio scale, stronger principles could be formulated.) Or consider the principle that results by substituting "usefulness to society" for "moral merit" in the previous principle. Or instead of "distribute according to moral merit," or "distribute according to usefulness to society," we might consider "distribute according to the weighted sum of moral merit, usefulness to society, and need," with the weights of the different dimensions equal. Let us call a principle of distribution *patterned* if it specifies that a distribution is to vary along with some natural dimension, weighted sum of natural dimensions, or lexicographic ordering of natural dimensions. And let us say a distribution is patterned if it accords with some patterned principle. (I speak of natural dimensions, admittedly without a general criterion for them, because for any set of holdings some artificial dimensions can be gimmicked up to vary along with the distribution of the set.) The principle of distribution in accordance with moral merit is a patterned historical principle, which specifies a patterned distribution. "Distribute according to I.Q." is a patterned principle that looks to information not contained in distributional matrices. It is not historical, however, in that it does not look to any past actions creating differential entitlements to evaluate a distribution; it requires only distributional matrices whose columns are labeled by I.Q. scores. The distribution in a society, however, may be composed of such simple patterned distributions, without itself being simply patterned. Different sectors may operate different patterns, or some combination of patterns may operate in different proportions across a society. A distribution composed in this manner, from a small number of patterned distributions, we also shall term "patterned." And we extend the use of "pattern" to include the overall designs put forth by combinations of end-state principles.

Almost every suggested principle of distributive justice is patterned: to each according to his moral merit, or needs, or marginal product, or how hard he tries, or the weighted sum of the foregoing, and so on. The principle of entitlement we have sketched is *not* patterned. There is no one natural dimension or weighted sum or combination of a small number of natural dimensions that yields the distributions generated in accordance with the principle of entitlement. The set of holdings that results when some persons receive their marginal products, others win at gambling, others receive a share of their mate's income, others receive gifts from foundations, others receive interest on loans, others receive gifts from admirers, others receive returns on investment, others make for themselves much of what they have, others find things, and so on, will not be patterned.

. . . .

How Liberty Upsets Patterns

It is not clear how those holding alternative conceptions of distributive justice can reject the entitlement conception of justice in holdings. For suppose a distribution favored by one of these nonentitlement conceptions is realized. Let us suppose it is your favorite one and let us call this distribution D_1; perhaps everyone has an equal share, perhaps shares vary in accordance with some dimension you treasure. Now suppose that Wilt Chamberlain is greatly in demand by basketball teams, being a great gate attraction. (Also suppose contracts run only for a year, with players being free agents.) He signs the following sort of contract with a team: In each home game, twenty-five cents from the price of each ticket of admission goes to him. (We ignore the question of whether he is "gouging" the owners, letting them look out for themselves.) The season starts, and people cheerfully attend his team's games; they buy their tickets, each time dropping a separate twenty-five cents of their admission price into a special box with Chamberlain's name on it. They are excited about seeing him play; it is worth the total admission price to them. Let us suppose that in one season one million persons attend his home games, and Wilt Chamberlain winds up with $250,000, a much larger sum than the average income and larger even than anyone else has. Is he entitled to this income? Is this new distribution D_2, unjust? If so, why? There is *no* question about whether each of the people was entitled to the control over the resources they held in D_1; because that was the distribution (your favorite) that (for the purposes of argument) we assumed was acceptable. Each of these persons *chose* to give twenty-five cents of their money to Chamberlain. They could have spent it on going to the movies, or on candy bars, or on copies of *Dissent* magazine, or of *Monthly Review*. But they all, at least one million of them, converged on giving it to Wilt Chamberlain in exchange for watching him play basketball. If D_1 was a just distribution, and people voluntarily moved from it to D_2, transferring parts of their shares they were given under D_1 (what was it for if not to do something with?), isn't D_2 also just? If the people were entitled to dispose of the resources to which they were entitled (under D_1), didn't this include their being entitled to give it to, or exchange it with, Wilt Chamberlain? Can anyone else complain on grounds of justice? Each other person already has his legitimate share under D_1. Under D_1, there is nothing that anyone has that anyone else has a claim of justice against. After someone transfers something to Wilt Chamberlain, third parties *still* have their legitimate shares; *their* shares are not changed. By what process could such a transfer among two persons give rise to a legitimate claim of distributive justice on a portion of what was transferred, by a third party who had no claim of justice on any holding of the others *before* the transfer?

. . . .

The general point illustrated by the Wilt Chamberlain example . . . is that no end-state principle or distributional-patterned principle of justice can be continuously realized without continuous interference with people's lives. Any favored pattern would be transformed into one unfavored by the principle, by people choosing to act in various ways; for example, by people exchanging goods and services with other people, or giving things to other people, things the transferrers are entitled to under the favored distributional pattern. To maintain a pattern one must either continually interfere to stop people from transferring resources as they wish to, or continually (or periodically) interfere to take from some persons resources that others for some reason chose to transfer to them.

. . . .

Locke's Theory of Acquisition

. . . [W]e must introduce an additional bit of complexity into the structure of the entitlement theory. This is best approached by considering Locke's attempt to specify a principle of justice in acquisition. Locke views property rights in an unowned object as originating through someone's mixing his labor with it. This gives rise to many questions. What are the boundaries of what labor is mixed with? If a private astronaut clears a place on Mars, has he mixed his labor with (so that he comes to own) the whole planet, the whole uninhabited universe, or just a particular plot? Which plot does an act bring under ownership? The minimal (possibly disconnected) area such that an act decreases entropy in that area, and not elsewhere? Can virgin land (for the purposes of ecological investigation by high-flying airplane) come under ownership by a Lockean process? Building a fence around a territory presumably would make one the owner of only the fence (and the land immediately underneath it).

Why does mixing one's labor with something make one the owner of it? Perhaps because one owns one's labor, and so one comes to own a previously unowned thing that becomes permeated with what one owns. Ownership seeps over into the rest. But why isn't mixing what I own with what I don't own a way of losing what I own rather than a way of gaining what I don't? If I own a can of tomato juice and spill it in the sea so that its molecules (made radioactive, so I can check this) mingle evenly throughout the sea, do I thereby come to own the sea, or have I foolishly dissipated my tomato juice? Perhaps the idea, instead, is that laboring on something improves it and makes it more valuable; and anyone is entitled to own a thing whose value he has created. (Reinforcing this, perhaps, is the view that laboring is unpleasant. If some people made things effortlessly, as the cartoon characters in *The Yellow Submarine* trail flowers in their wake, would they have lesser claim to their own products whose making didn't *cost* them anything?) Ignore the fact that laboring on something may make it less valuable (spraying pink enamel paint on a piece of driftwood that you have found). Why should one's entitlement extend to the whole object rather than just to the *added value* one's labor has produced? (Such reference to value might also serve to delimit the extent of ownership; for example, substitute "increases the value of" for "decreases entropy in" in the above entropy criterion.) No workable or coherent value-added property scheme has yet been devised, and any such scheme presumably would fall to objections (similar to those) that fell the theory of Henry George.

It will be implausible to view improving an object as giving full ownership to it, if the stock of unowned objects that might be improved is limited. For an object's coming under one person's ownership changes the situation of all others. Whereas previously they were at liberty (in Hohfeld's sense) to use the object, they now no longer are. This change in the situation of others (by removing their liberty to act on a previously unowned object) need not worsen their situation. If I appropriate a grain of sand from Coney Island, no one else may now do as they will with *that* grain of sand. But there are plenty of other grains of sand left for them to do the same with. Or if not grains of sand, then other things. Alternatively, the things I do with the grain of sand I appropriate might improve the position of others, counterbalancing their loss of the liberty to use that grain. The crucial point is whether appropriation of an unowned object worsens the situation of others.

Locke's proviso that there be "enough and as good left in common for others" (sect. 27) is meant to ensure that the situation of others is not worsened.

. . . .

Is the situation of persons who are unable to appropriate (there being no more accessible and useful unowned objects) worsened by a system allowing appropriation and permenent property? Here enter the various familiar social considerations favoring private property: it increases the social product by putting means of production in the hands of those who can use them most efficiently (profitably); experimentation is encouraged, because with separate persons controlling resources, there is no one person or small group whom someone with a new idea must convince to try it out; private property enables people to decide on the pattern and types of risks they wish to bear, leading to specialized types of risk bearing; private property protects future persons by leading some to hold back resources from current consumption for future markets; it provides alternate sources of employment for unpopular persons who don't have to convince any one person or small group to hire them, and so on. These considerations enter a Lockean theory to support the claim that appropriation of private property satisfies the intent behind the "enough and as good left over" proviso, *not* as a utilitarian justification of property. They enter to rebut the claim that because the proviso is violated no natural right to private property can arise by a Lockean process. The difficulty in working such an argument to show that the proviso is satisfied is in fixing the appropriate baseline for comparison. Lockean appropriation makes people no worse off than they would be *how?* This question of fixing the baseline needs more detailed investigation than we are able to give it here.

. . . .

The Proviso

Whether or not Locke's particular theory of appropriation can be spelled out so as to handle various difficulties, I assume that any adequate theory of justice in acquisition will contain a proviso similar to the weaker of the ones we have attributed to Locke. A process normally giving rise to a permanent bequeathable property right in a previously unowned thing will not do so if the position of others no longer at liberty to use the thing is thereby worsened. It is important to specify *this* particular mode of worsening the situation of others, for the proviso does not encompass other modes. It does not include the worsening due to more limited opportunities to appropriate . . . , and it does not include how I "worsen" a seller's position if I appropriate materials to make some of what he is selling, and then enter into competition with him. Someone whose appropriation otherwise would violate the proviso still may appropriate provided he compensates the others so that their situation is not thereby worsened; unless he does compensate these others, his appropriation will violate the proviso of the principle of justice in acquisition and will be an illegitimate one. A theory of appropriation incorporating this Lockean proviso will handle correctly the cases (objections to the theory lacking the proviso) where someone appropriates the total supply of something necessary for life.

A theory which includes this proviso in its principle of justice in acquisition must also contain a more complex principle of justice in transfer. Some reflection of the proviso about appropriation constrains later actions. If my appropriating all of a certain substance violates the Lockean proviso, then so does my appropriating some and purchasing all the rest from others who obtained it without otherwise violating the Lockean proviso. If the proviso excludes someone's appropriating all the drinkable water in the world, it also excludes his purchasing it all. (More weakly, and messily, it may exclude his charging certain prices for some of his supply.) This proviso (almost?) never will come into effect; the more someone acquires of a scarce substance which others want, the higher the price of the rest will go, and the more difficult it will become for him to acquire it all. But still, we can imagine, at least, that something like this occurs: someone makes simultaneous secret bids to the separate owners of a substance, each of whom sells assuming he can easily purchase more from the other owners; or some natural catastrophe destroys all of the supply of something except that in one person's possession. The total supply could not be permissibly appropriated by one person at the beginning. His later acquisition of it all does not show that the original appropriation violated the proviso. . . . Rather, it is the combination of the original appropriation *plus* all the later transfers and actions that violates the Lockean proviso.

Each owner's title to his holding includes the historical shadow of the Lockean proviso on appropriation. This excludes his transferring it into an agglomeration that does violate the Lockean proviso and excludes his using it in a way, in coordination with others or independently of them, so as to violate the proviso by making the situation of others worse than their baseline situation. Once it is known that someone's ownership runs afoul of the Lockean proviso, there are stringent limits on what he may do with (what it is difficult any longer unreservedly to call) "his property." Thus a person may not appropriate the only water hole in a desert and charge what he will. Nor may he charge what he will if he possesses one, and unfortunately it happens that all the water holes in the desert dry up, except for his. This unfortunate circumstance, admittedly no fault of his, brings into operation the Lockean proviso and limits his property rights. Similarly, an owner's property right in the only island in an area does not allow him to order a castaway from a shipwreck off his island as a trespasser, for this would violate the Lockean proviso.

. . . .

The fact that someone owns the total supply of something necessary for others to stay alive does *not* entail that his (or anyone's) appropriation of anything left some people (immediately or later) in a situation worse than the baseline one. A medical researcher who synthesizes a new substance that effectively treats a certain disease and who refuses to sell except on his terms does not worsen the situation of others by depriving them of whatever he has appropriated. The others easily can possess the same materials he appropriated; the researcher's appropriation or purchase of chemicals didn't make those chemicals scarce in a way so as to violate the Lockean proviso. Nor would someone else's purchasing the total supply of the synthesized substance from the medical researcher. The fact that the medical researcher uses easily available chemicals to synthesize the drug no more violates the Lockean proviso than does the fact that the only surgeon able to perform a particular operation eats easily obtainable food in order to stay alive and to have the energy to work. This shows that the Lockean proviso is not an "end-state principle"; it focuses on a particular way that appropriative actions affect others, and not on the structure of the situation that results.

Intermediate between someone who takes all of the public supply and someone who makes the total supply out of easily obtainable substances is someone who appropriates the total supply of something in a way that does not deprive the others of it. For example, someone finds a new substance in an out-of-the-way place. He discovers that it effectively treats a certain disease and appropriates the total supply. He does not worsen the situation of others; if he did not stumble upon the substance no one else would have, and the others would remain without it. However, as time passes, the likelihood increases that others would have come across the substance; upon this fact might be based a limit to his property right in the substance so that others are not below their baseline position; for example, its bequest might be limited. The theme of someone worsening another's situation by depriving him of something he otherwise would possess may also illuminate the example of patents. An inventor's patent does not deprive others of an object which would not exist if not for the inventor. Yet patents would have this effect on others who independently invent the object. Therefore, these independent inventors, upon whom the burden of proving independent discovery may rest, should not be excluded from utilizing their own invention as they wish (including selling it to others). Furthermore, a known inventor drastically lessens the chances of actual independent invention. For persons who know of an invention usually will not try to reinvent it, and the notion of independent discovery here would be murky at best. Yet we may assume that in the absence of the original invention, sometime later someone else would have come up with it. This suggests placing a time limit on patents, as a rough rule of thumb to approximate how long it would have taken, in the absence of knowledge of the invention, for independent discovery.

I believe that the free operation of a market system will not actually run afoul of the Lockean proviso. . . .

Notes

1. Applications of the principle of justice in acquisition may also occur as part of the move from one distribution to another. You may find an unheld thing now and appropriate it. Acquisitions also are to be understood as included when, to simplify, I speak only of transitions by transfers.
2. If the principle of rectification of violations of the first two principles yields more than one description of holdings, then some choice must be made as to which of these is to be realized. Perhaps the sort of considerations about distributive justice and equality that I argue against play a legitimate role in *this* subsidiary choice. Similarly, there may be room for such considerations in deciding which otherwise arbitrary features a statute will embody, when such features are unavoidable because other considerations do not specify a precise line; yet a line must be drawn.

Capitalism, Socialism and Justice

KAI NIELSEN

Kai Nielsen (1925–) is a professor of philosophy at the University of Calgary. He has written many articles on political philosophy and the philosohy of religion.

I

There is, understandably, a not inconsiderable amount of argument about justice under capitalism and socialism as well as much argument about what principles of justice, if any, would characterize these socio-economic systems. When we reflect on capitalist and socialist societies, when we think about fundamental alternatives in our social world, we want to gain, if we can, a sense of which societies, particularly under optimal conditions, would be the juster societies and which would answer most fully to the needs and legitimate aspirations of human beings. However, before we can even begin to approach these questions, we should say something about what capitalism and socialism are.

I shall characterize capitalism and socialism in their "pure" forms and then contrast them with what some regard as perversions and others simply as mutations of these pure forms. These perversions/mutations are State capitalism, on the one hand, and State socialism, on the other. There is a strong tendency on the part of both many socialists and some capitalists to regard these Statist forms as not being "genuine socialism" or "genuine capitalism."

I shall not here make any such stipulations, though I am inclined to view with sympathy, as my argument will make clear, the view that State socialism is a flawed version of socialism. It is perhaps unavoidable under certain circumstances, but it still is a long way from the idea or (if you will) the ideal of a socialist society.

A common view of the difference between capitalism and socialism simply equates capitalism with the private ownership of capital and socialism with the public or State ownership of capital. The basic distinction is drawn in terms of the legal ownership of the means or instruments of production. It is, however, a mistake to characterize either capitalism or socialism solely in terms of legal relations of ownership. We also need to take note of forms of effective control and power, as well as different class formations and different conceptions of democracy. Capitalism is a system in which a class of owners (the capitalists), typically a numerically very small class, owns and controls most of the means of production and buys the labour power—where that labour power is a commodity—of workers. These workers (the proletariat) typically are the greater majority of the people in the society. The capitalists use the proletariat's labour power to produce wealth, i.e. to produce profits and accumulate capital, which in turn is owned and controlled by the capitalist. Capitalism is thus a system of wage labour with private ownership and control of the means of production, and, as a consequence, a capitalist society is a class society divided into two principal classes—classes that Marxists regard as antagonistic classes—the cap-

From *And Justice for All*, ed. T. Regan and D. Van De Veer (Totowa, N.J.: Rowman & Littelfield, 1982), pp. 264–80, 282–85.

italist class, which owns and controls the major means of production and buys labour power, and the working class (the proletariat), which either owns no means of production or very little and sells its labour power to the capitalist for wages.

A socialist society by contrast is a society in which all ablebodied people are, except during periods of childhood and retirement, workers. In its pure form it is, no more than capitalism, a state ownership and control of the means of production. It is rather a form of social ownership and control of the means of production. This means that the workers collectively have effective control of their own workplaces. This further requires that a socialist society be a worker's democracy which in turn means that it will, unlike a capitalist society, which is at best a political democracy, also be an economic and industrial democracy, with workers, in the form of worker's councils and the like, owning and controlling their own means of production and workplace and deciding, in consultation and cooperation with other workers, who similarly own and control their means of production and workplace, what is to be produced, how much is to be produced, what is to be done with what is to be produced and what the working hours and conditions are to be.

Such a society will be decentralized with participatory control for the individuals, though the various working units will also be centrally coordinated by democratically elected and recallable worker's representatives from the various working units. The inequalities of wealth, power and control characteristic of all capitalist societies (pure and impure) could not obtain in a socialist society of the pure and paradigmatic form I have just described. In a socialist society the needs of everyone are considered alike and the ultimate community unit is all of humankind.

A socialist society would be a society in which every able-bodied adult person would be required to work—he who does not work does not eat—and labour contribution would be according to ability. But the wage relation would be abolished—no one would or could sell their labour power as a commodity, for here would be no one to buy it—and the workers would be in cooperative control of their own instruments of production in a society in which the cleavage between physical and mental labour would gradually be overcome, through the all around development of human beings. It must be borne in mind, however, that the construction of a socialist society takes time and that I am, in the above description, describing socialism in a very developed form after the springs of social wealth flow freely and the capitalist mentality is a thing of the past.

It is important to recognize that we probably do not have anywhere at the present time any very good exemplars of either capitalism or socialism in its pure form. The plain reality is that in extant industrial societies (though in varying degrees and in somewhat different kinds) we have State capitalism and State socialism, the perversions or mutations of the pure forms. In advanced capitalist countries, such as West Germany, Sweden, and France, we have State capitalism in fairly developed forms with what is called a "mixed economy." What makes such societies State capitalist societies is not essentially that there are some State owned branches of production, but that the State has taken on the responsibility of regulating and managing the entire economy. Laissez-faire capitalism is a thing of the past (if indeed it ever existed in anything like a pure form then). However, unlike a socialist society, even a State socialist society, the State owned production sectors in State capitalist countries still, like the private sectors of the economy, produce to maximize profit and capital accumulation. The crucial thing that distinguishes them from the pure forms of capitalism is State regulation of the economy, including, of course, the private sector as well as the public sector. It is this that makes it appropriate to refer to such societies as *State* capitalist societies. All the major capitalist countries are now, though in degrees that vary somewhat, State capitalist societies.

However, it is also the case that the Soviet Union, the Eastern European countries in economic union with the Soviet Union, China and Cuba are all—again in varying degrees—State socialist societies. In these countries we have (again in varying degrees) stratified, bureaucratic, hierarchical societies "in which the maximization of material goods production—subject to the constraint of preserving hierarchical control—is a primary objective."[1] The State apparatus, with its few leaders, is at the pinnacle of such bureaucratic hierarchies. It is they, in the name of the workers, and not the workers themselves, who exert the principal control over the economy.

. . . .

II

The four socio-economic systems previously discussed (1) capitalism (laissez-faire, competitive capitalism), (2) State capitalism, (3) State socialism and (4) socialism may be viewed as models both for how industrial societies *can* be organized and for how they *ought* to be organized. State capitalism and State socialism—both in various forms and degrees—are not only models; they are also social realities. Lassez-faire capitalism and socialism (participatory socialism if you will) remain at present only ideals: conceptions of what some people think a just or a truly human society would be like.

What I would like to do now is to articulate, particularly where they have strong philosophical representation, what some of those alternative conceptions and accounts of justice are when they are matched with these four distinct systems for organizing society, beginning with laissez-faire capitalism, especially as this view is defended by this century's leading philosophical spokesman for libertarianism, Robrt Nozick.

For libertarians individual liberty is the cardinal moral conception. It can never be sacrificed or traded off or even be diminished to attain a greater equality or even to attain a more extensive overall system of secure basic liberties. It is, for libertarians, the highest value in the firmament of values.

Liberty for libertarians is negative liberty. They would indeed be happy, as an initial rough characterization, with J. S. Mill's conception of liberty as that of a person having the right, free from interference, to pursue what that person takes to be her own good in her own way as long as her actions do not interfere with the similar liberties of others. In a free society, we must not be interfered with in the doing of what we want to do as long as we do not violate the rights of others. To be free is to be able to choose your own life plans according to your own lights and to be free from governmental and other institutional interference or regulation.

The conception of justice that goes with that libertarian stress on freedom—a conception defended most elaborately by Robert Nozick—claims that justice exists to protect an individual's liberty. Given this conception, it is taken by libertarians to be an evident corollary that whatever economic arrangements we freely consent to are thereby just, if they do not involve fraud, deceit or the appropriation of something already justly appropriated or acquired.[2] Contrary to orthodox liberal assumptions—Welfare State capitalist assumptions—there is no particular *pattern of distribution* that justice requires. And since there is no pattern of distribution that justice requires, it cannot be the case, unless it can be shown that extensive rectifications of past injustices are in order, that justice demands extensive economic redistribution.

Not only do libertarians conceive of liberty negatively as the right to choose as one will, free from interference, they also, in stressing, as they do, individual rights, stress negative rights. Indeed it is very likely that "negative rights" for a libertarian is redundant. They are the only kind of genuine rights except for contractually acquired. There are things we have a right to do and have, if we can do them or get them, where we, in these activities, are not to be interfered with by others. There are boundaries between people that just *must* not be crossed.

The rights that people have that must not be transgressed are *negative rights* because they require, vis-à-vis the person having the rights, others to refrain from interfering with the person exercising those rights. Bu they do not require others to do anything for that person. They are *only* morally required not to interfere with the exercise of those rights. They are not required to do anything positive for the rights-bearer which will in anyway help him to exercise those rights.

The central thing to see is that there are negative rights that all human beings have that can never, according to such an account, justly or rightly be overridden. But no one is obliged or in anyway morally required to do anything for anyone, unless they have agreed to do so or they have already harmed that person and must rectify a past violation of rights. Even when the society has the industrial and technical capacity to do so, there is no obligation at all to provide people with material goods they might urgently need or with health care or with education or with meaningful, satisfying or even gainful work. There is no obligation in any circumstances (where there has been no violation of rights) to meet even the most basic subsistence needs of other persons, even when it is not difficult for the agent to whom a plea for aid is directed to do so. The appropriate way to view human beings, on a libertarian account, is as autonomous and responsible individuals capable of fending for themselves. We must, of course, not harm them but we need not help them no matter how dire their straights unless we are responsible for their being in such straights. What is to be done, according to libertarians, is to create a social environment in which human beings are left to fashion their own lives free from the interference of others. We neither need a big daddy nor a big brother and we have a right to be free from any such paternalistic interference with our lives. It is evident enough that libertarianism is a radical individualism.

It is a deeply embedded libertarian belief that *only* by an acknowledgment of this near absolute right to negative liberty, to choose without interference how one is to live one's life, and what social arrangements one will make, can the distinctiveness or separateness of individuals as persons be respected. Such a conception, when translated into a social theory, involves a rejection of anything like the Welfare State and involves either a rejection of state authority altogether, and the acceptance of *individualistic* anarchism, or the commitment to the accepting as legitimate a minimal, night watchman state. It involves endorsing the minimal state and rejecting the legitimacy of any more extensive state control or state functions. The State, for example, has no right to tax us and to take that money—money in reality stolen from us—and use it for its redistributive schemes, no matter how benevolent they may be. This remains the case even when the redistributive schemes are enlightened and humane and would relieve considerable misery. The States' legitimate functions are limited to protecting the negative rights of its citizens. That is to say, it is to protect them from theft, fraud, violence, coercion and the like. But it has no right to get into the redistribution business. It can and should play a night watchman role but it is not to play a paternalistic role.

It is called the minimal state because its authority is so severely restricted and it is called the night watchman state because of the minimal legitimate functions it has.

Libertarians are also committed to a parallel economic doctrine, namely laissez-faire capitalism. Just as they reject the Welfare State and defend a minimal State, they reject contemporary corporate or State capitalism and defend laissez-faire (free market, competitive) capitalism. To disturb the free market, on their view, is to tread on liberty and to redistribute wealth through taxation is to engage in coercive practices which in effect utilize forced labour. It is, on the libertarian view, quite incompatible with justice to do anything like that.

There is, as the above indicates, an unequivocal commitment to an utterly free market economic system on the part of libertarians. A genuine respect for liberty will, when thought through, generate, on their view, a moral commitment to the priority of liberty. But then we cannot rightly prevent capitalist acts between consenting adults. . . .

. . . .

III

Robert Nozick in the middle sections of his *Anarchy, State, and Utopia* develops, as a further specification of this libertarian social theory, a distinctive *entitlement* theory of justice. What this means can be explained as follows.

Justice, for Nozick, as for libertarians generally, is a backward-looking virtue concerned with who, because of his past acts, is entitled to what. It is not, for him, a forward-looking virtue concerned with what distributive or redistributive patterns to achieve or to maintain.[3] Instead, an entitlement theory is concerned most fundamentally with (1) justice in original acquisition, (2) justice in transfer, as in a voluntary exchange from a just original acquisition, and (3), where some injustice in acquisition or transfer has already taken place, justice in rectification. In determining what is just, it is almost always crucial to ascertain what happened in the past: how some state of arrairs came about. This is why Nozick calls the entitlement theory an historical theory. Whether a certain distribution of benefits and burdens is just does not depend *at all* on what the actual pattern of distribution is but on how the pattern came about. *Any* pattern of holdings is just, if the distributive pattern results from just original acquisitions and just transfers, or, where in the past some violation in the justice of original acquisition has occurred or something like fraud in transfer has occurred, rectification is required and the pattern meets those requirements.

Our common talk—at least common in roughly liberal circles—of "distributive justice" is not, on Nozick's view, ideologically neutral. It gives us a skewed picture of what justice is. If we are held captive by that theory, we will, when we think of what is just or unjust, operate with a picture something like that of an adult in a position of authority seeking to make a fair division of a pie to children. But in our social life there is no authority, no central distribution centre, which is "entitled to control all the resources" and decide "how they are to be doled out" in what this authority takes to be a fair way. We should reject such paternalistic political images. The morally appropriate picture is one of a society in which each person gets what he gets from his own efforts or from others who give to him these things in exchange or as a gift. . . .

For such an account one plain and very central question is *how do we,* if indeed we can at all, *identify a just original acquisition?*

In trying to specify a principle of justice in original acquisition, Nozick turns to John Locke's theory of acquisition and his conception of property rights. Nozick finds all sorts of difficulties in it. Some of them seem to me to be genuine while others seem laboured. Yet he accepts what he regards as the core of Locke's account here, though he does have his own special interpretation of it.[4] My interest is not whether it is a correct description of Locke but with whether it is an adequate specification of justice in initial acquisition.

This Lockean account of justice in initial acquisition gives us an account of when we came to have a property right in some unowned object. *We gain a property right in such an object, we are entitled to such an object, when (a) we mix our labour with it and (b) when there is "enough and as good left in common for others."* (B is called *Locke's proviso.*) If (a) and (b) obtain we have justly acquired it. We are now entitled to it; it is now a holding of ours and, as something which is ours, we are entitled to do with it what we like as long as we do not harm others in doing so. Thus, if I find a stick in an unowned forest and I fashion it into a spear (thus mixing my labour with it), it is thereby mine, if there are enough other sticks of similar quality lying around for others to use. I now own it and can do with it what I will, short of harming others with it by, for example, running them through.

Mixing one's labour with something previously unowned is a *necessary* but not a *sufficient* condition for coming to own such an object in an original just acquisition. We do not automatically get full ownership over something if "the stock of unowned objects that might be improved is limited. When this condition obtains, it is crucial to ask whether the appropriation of the unowned object worsens the situation of others."[5] The Lockean proviso that there be "enough and as good left in common for others" is "meant to ensure that the situation of others is not worsened."[6] This, for Nozick, understandably enough, is an utterly crucial condition. Yet it is subject to at least two readings and only on one of those two readings can it be utilized by Nozick in a way that would make sense of his account.

On the first reading of "being made worse off by another's appropriation" (the one Nozick does not intend) one loses one's chance to improve one's situation by that appropriation. Suppose I am in the truffle-selling business and there is an unowned stand of forest with lots of truffles. Pierre appropriates it before me and I lose my chance for a new source of comparatively cheap truffles. This is one way I may be made worse off by another's appropriation. I have simply lost an opportunity to improve my situation. On the second reading of "being made worse off by another's appropriation" (the one Nozick does intend) one is made worse off because after the appropriation one is no longer able to use freely what one previously could. Considering the baseline from where one started, one is now worse off.

The first way of taking the Lockean proviso seems too strong. An acquisition which violates it does not seem plainly unfair or, in many instances, otherwise morally questionable. Indeed, if the Lockean proviso were read in that strong way, it would make just acquisition almost impossible. Thus the second way seems to be more appropriate.

Taking that second understanding of "being made worse off," we should now ask whether the situation of persons being unable to appropriate, because there are no more accessible and useful unowned objects, is worsened, by a system allowing appropriation and permanent property? Nozick thinks not because he believes that the social product is increased by putting the means of production in the hands of those who can use it most efficiently.

Nozick is trying to show us that even in situations where there are no more accessible and unowned objects, the *intent* behind Locke's proviso of "enough and as good left" is not violated. It is not violated because the situation of the non-owners is not worsened, for, with the capitalist system—the system emerging out of these acquisitions—people, even without ownership, are not worse off than they were before in the important sense that they are still free to do as much as they were previously able to do before the question of such acquisition arose. Moreover, with the increase of the social product, their general material condition is not worsened but improved.

What we are not justified in doing by any original acquisition, either with or without any combination of transfers, is to bring about a situation where the person, making the acquisition or the transfer, "violates the proviso by making the situation of others worse *than their baseline situation*."[7] A person cannot "appropriate the only water hole in a desert and charge what he will. Nor may he charge what he will, if he possesses one, and unfortunately it happens that all the water holes in the desert dry up, except for his."[8] Similarly, an owner's "property right in the only island in the area does not allow him to order a castaway from a shipwreck off his island as a trespasser."[9] All these violate the Lockean proviso. But a "medical researcher who synthesizes a new substance that effectively treats a certain disease and who refuses to sell except on his terms does not worsen the situation of others by depriving them of whatever he has appropriated."[10] He has a right, not to be overridden, to refuse to sell it.

. . . .

IV

Nozick's conception of how we determine whether original aquisitions are just is subject to an array of criticisms, criticisms which reflect back on his entitlement theory generally and on the very foundations of libertarianism.

For Nozick an acquisition is a just acquisition of an unowned object only if it doesn't make people worse off than they were before the acquisition. Suppose we have a system of property relations that bring about a state of affairs S in which many people remain miserable and are worked very hard at very low wages, but still are not worse off, everything considered, than they were prior to the institution of those property relations. However, the situation is one in which another state of affairs S' could be brought about in which there is generally much less misery and exploitation. But to bring about S' requires some overriding of that system of private property, i.e. those just initial acquisitions. It requires, that is, the end of a system of private property rights in the *means of production* and the institution of a social ownership and control of the means of production. Even if this new situation S' would provide better work at a better pay scale and be a situation in which there was far less misery than in S, still, on Nozick's account, we should stick with S and take property rights as inalienable and absolute as long as the Lockean proviso is met. Such a judgment conflicts in a radical way with my considered judgments. It seems to me just wrong, indeed evil, to stick with inalienable *property* rights in such a situation: a situation where by sanctioning them we ensure far more misery than would otherwise obtain. Nozick, no doubt, would reply that here I am simply invoking an "end-state principle" of a roughly utilitarian sort. I would reply that whatever we should say *in general* about utilitarian reasoning it is morally arbitrary not to so reason here. We have a duty to prevent misery where we reasonably can. To treat some *property* rights, particularly property rights in the means of production, as inalienable when by overriding them great suffering for many people can be alleviated is, morally speaking, monstrous.[11]

An actual example might help make vivid the moral point I am trying to make. The *Latifundia* system of land tenure and property ownership in Latin America sustains and legally protects a highly inefficient system of agriculture where, conservatively speaking, 1 percent of all farm families control at least one-half of all farm land.[12] Millions of landless peasants live in circumstances of misery and degradation. Even if they are not worse off than they were before such property acquisitions were made and even if the initial acquisitions were just, to treat such property rights as inalienable in such circumstances in through and through evil. It may be important, as Nozick stresses again and again, to consider, where justice is at issue, how the holdings came about. But that cannot be the whole story. Even if the holdings came about justly it may be unjust and indeed deeply evil to persist in claiming those holdings.

To see what is involved in such a judgment consider the case of the medical researcher who effectively synthesizes a new substance which will effectively cure cancer. Nozick rightly remarks that if he refuses to sell it except on his own terms, he does not violate the Lockean proviso, even if he does sell it at such a high price that few can purchase it and many will die from cancer who otherwise would not if they had had the drug. Nozick says that if the researcher so acts he has done nothing wrong. He can do what he likes with his property as long as he doesn't use it in such a way that he harms others. By so acting, he doesn't harm others, though he admittedly doesn't help them, for without the new drug they would have died anyway. They are no worse off than they otherwise would be if he hadn't made the invention. So by making the invention, by acquiring that particular bit of property, he hasn't done them any harm. I say such behaviour on the part of the researcher is morally monstrous. To have a drug that will save lives and prevent extensive misery and yet to withhold it from those who need it is simply vile. In such a situation there are moral obligations to provide *mutual aid* and to relieve suffering; if the researcher is not willing to make the drug available, property which he owns or not, he should be forced to do so by the State or by social pressure.

Nozick would respond that such state intervention would be too destructive of human freedom to be morally acceptable. But why should this be so if we interfere with freedom in *such cases?* Why should we think this would start a slippery slope that would lead to our interfering with freedom all over the place? There are no good grounds for believing that that will be the upshot of overriding property rights in such a circumstance.

There is also a distinct lack of realism in Nozick's account. He gives us what in effect in an inapplicable model. For any of the property relations that now actually obtain, we do not know, or even have any reasonable grounds for believing, that they were acquired by an original just acquisition meeting anything like the Lockean proviso. What we do know is that, if we go back far enough, there were plenty of unowned objects around that could have been initially acquired under conditions that would meet the Lockean proviso. At one time there must have been more than enough to go around and as good in kind or nearly so. But what the original transfers were like we do not know. It is, of course, *logically* possible that they could have been just transfers but it is far more likely that plunder, the use of violence, force, and deceit were there from the very beginning. In many cases it surely must be the case that we can hardly properly speak of anything like a contractual transfer, but just of marauders seizing other people's holdings. . . .

V

This hard-hearted doctrine which would deny that there are duties to mutual aid or duties of beneficence and which conceptualizes things as if there were only one form of wrong doing, namely the violation of rights, does rest on a foundation of sorts or at least has a rationale. Nozick believes that if in deciding what we *must* do—what morality requires of us—we count the consequences in terms of human happiness or the misery resulting from the working of his system of individual rights, it will not infrequently *require* some persons to contribute to the assistance of others, but this, Nozick maintains, violates their moral autonomy and commits the fundamental utilitarian error of not having regard for the separateness of persons. It fails to acknowledge the inviolability of persons. It is on this insistence on the moral centrality of a regard for the separateness of persons that this rights-based theory has its foundations. On consequentialist conceptions, as kindly as they may seem, people are violated and sacrificed for others. And this, to return my compliment, is itself morally monstrous.

However, as H. L. A. Hart has pointed out, Nozick engages in some rather hysterical hyperbole here.[13] It is plainly violating the integrity of a person to kill him, to take one of his vital organs, to force him to marry another person against his will, to silence him in his expression of his convictions, but it is altogether another thing again to tax a very rich person's income to save others from great suffering or to require that a person's invention (say a cure for cancer) be publicly available where its availability would relieve great suffering and save lives. Taking your vital organs without your permission just does make you a resource for others, taking some of your very great income to meet very basic needs of others is not so treating you. Such redistributive measures do not sacrifice people, violate their integrity or treat them as means only.

. . . The rights and liberties that Nozick takes to be morally required are a very restrictive list. We have an inviolable right not to be interfered with in certain determinate ways. That is, others must abstain from murdering us, assaulting us, stealing from us, breaching contracts with us and the like. These rights are what have been called *negative* rights and they require abstension from certain things on the part of others. But to limit rights to negative rights is an arbitrary move. Why should people not have a right to have their basic needs met (health needs, needs for security and decent housing, needs for meaningful work and for education) where these needs can be met? It is simply morally arbitrary (to put it minimally) to claim that a person has an absolute, permanent, exclusive, inheritable and unmodifiable right to own and control productive property (say a factory) and to deny, in a society of reasonable affluence, that a person has any right at all to an education, to health care and to be protected from starvation. It is meaningless to talk of the protection of an individual's right to a meaningful life which he shapes himself while denying him the right to the necessary means to live such a life. . . .

VI

Nozick is a trenchant critic of egalitarianism of both a Welfare State sort and a socialist sort. To press home his point, and make it vividly concrete, he develops his Wilt Chamberlain parable, a parable many, on first reading at least, find quite compelling.

Nozick asks us to suppose we are living in an egalitarian society operating under an egalitarian principle of justice—a principle which specifies that a certain patterned end-result is to obtain. Suppose Wilt Chamberlain lives in that society as well as many avid basketball fans who are very keen on seeing Wilt play. Suppose further he signs the following contract with a professional basketball team. In each home game twenty-five cents added to the price of each ticket will go to him. The season starts and the home fans cheerfully attend the games quite willing to pay the extra twenty-five cents to see Wilt play basketball. During the course of the season Wilt gains a very considerable additional income—say $250,000—upsetting the previously egalitarian income patterns in our egalitarian society. But isn't he plainly entitled to the extra income? He freely contracted for it, he worked for it, and the fans freely and happily paid the extra twenty-five cents to see him play. It was their money, on a previously equal distribution, to do with what they wanted to as long as they did not so use it as to harm others. In this instance, they simply disposed of their resources as they wanted to and people who didn't go to the games cannot complain that any injustice has been done to them, for they still have what they were entitled to (their rightful "shares") under the egalitarian distributional pattern. To keep an egalitarian pattern would, Nozick claims, be too destructive of individual liberty. We must, in the name of liberty and a respect for people's rights and moral integrity, reject patterned end-state principles of justice. . . .

VII

This argument of Nozick's has been, I believe, refuted by G. A. Cohen and in the course of his refutation Cohen also makes plain how a socialist society would not undermine liberty in the way Nozick fears.[14]

I shall set out and examine some of the core portions of Cohen's argument. He first points out that the Chamberlain parable, as Nozick presents it, seems morally innocuous. What could be wrong, we ask ourselves, with the fans so financially compensating Chamberlain? They get to see him play, which is what they want, and he gets some more money, which is what he wants. And he doesn't get it by stealing from them or by defrauding them or coercing them or exploiting them, for they voluntarily transfer some of their holdings to him to get what they want. This respects both their freedom and his freedom. If the initial situation is just, which *ex hypothesis* it is, the resulting situation of just transfers must also be just. If we have respect for liberty and believe that justice requires liberty, we will not view it as morally right to require (by some deliberate social policy) a redistribution so as to return to the *initial* status quo before Chamberlain made his wad. It seems morally arbitrary to require such a redistribution.

Cohen argues that actually it is not and that there is a rationale for such a redistribution that respecters of liberty should acknowledge. The reason why we should limit the amount that Wilt Chamberlain, or any individual should have a right to hold, is to prevent them or their heirs from acquiring through such holdings an unacceptable amount of power and control over others. Through their enhanced wealth, which will tend to go on accumulating (the rich tend to get richer), they will gain power, in a previously egalitarian society, the possession of which tends to undermine the liberty of others. Because of this accrual of power to the rich, the non-rich have rather less control over their lives than they otherwise would have.[15] Even if, as in this case, the Wilt Chamberlain types come to hold what they hold in a morally innocuous way, the effects of their coming to have these holdings, whatever their intentions, are going to be anything but innocuous. It is slightly hysterical to get worried about Wilt Chamberlain per se but the effect of a number of people so acquiring holdings in that way is to create a situation in which there will be a large power differential between this class of people and others. And this will translate into a differential in their respective liberty, one which is plainly harmful to democracy. If we prize moral autonomy we will not favor such situations. In short, what Cohen shows is that the Chamberlain transaction is not, as Nozick presents it, beneficial or even harmless to everyone with an interest in it. Quite to the contrary, "it threatens to generate a situation in which some have unacceptable amounts of power over others."[16] Indeed it is very likely to worsen the situation of many people.

. . . .

Nozick seems to take as absolute, or nearly so, the fans' entitlement to dispose of their resources (in this instance their money) as they deem fit, as long as they do not harm others. But why should this right be so absolute? Their rights would be violated only if they are taken to be absolute. But why not take all rights as prima facie and as defeasible? They can be overridden without being violated, if certain conditions obtain. Nozick has not shown that any restrictions which would forbid the Chamberlain transaction must be unjustified. Although it might turn out that sanctioning *that* transaction will not be particularly harmful, if we do so in that case, we must sanction such transcations in relevantly similar cases. But if we do allow such arrangements it is likely that they will generate an inordinate power and consequent control in the hands of a few. With that power we have at least the very real possibility of the control of the many by the few with the big holdings.

. . . .

VIII

. . . Our next question is whether, as Welfare State liberals believe, but socialist critics deny, a Welfare State capitalist society would be as just or juster than a non-Statist socialist system. We shall explore this question by concentrating on *A Theory of Justice,* the seminal work by Nozick's colleague at Harvard, John Rawls.

IX

I shall begin by examining some of the core arguments between Rawls and his socialist critics in an attempt to see if we can get a grip on whether, under conditions of material abundance, ideal but still achievable forms of socialism are, or are not, juster social systems than ideal but still achievable forms of Welfare State capitalism.

I shall first simply state fundamental liberal principles of justice and fundamental socialist principles of justice—and then turn to commentary on them. The liberal principles are in Rawls's formulation and the socialist principles are my own.

Liberal Principles of Justice: Justice as Fairness

(1) Each person is to have an equal right to the most extensive total system of equal basic liberties compatible with a similar system of liberty for all.

(2) Social and economic inequalities are to be arranged so that they are both:

(a) to the greatest benefit of the least advantaged consistent with the just savings principle, and

(b) attached to offices and positions open to all under conditions of fair equality of opportunity.

Socialist Principles of Justice: Justice as Equality

(1) Each person is to have an equal right to the most extensive total system of equal basic liberties and opportunities (including equal opportunities for meaningful work, for self-determination and political and economic participation) compatible with a like treatment of all. (This principle gives expression to a commitment to attain and/or sustain equal moral autonomy and equal self-respect.)

(2) After provisions are made for common social (community) values, for capital overhead to preserve the society's productive capacity, allowances are made for differing unmanipulated needs and preferences, and due weight is given to the just entitlements of individuals, the income and wealth (the common stock of means) is to be so divided that each person will have a right to an equal share. The necessary burdens requisite to enhance human well-being are also to be equally shared, subject, of course, to limitations by differing abilities and differing situations (natural environment not class position).[17]

I have put Rawls's principles and my socialist principles cheek to jowl for ease of comparison. I shall now consider the comparative merits of these respective principles. (These principles, of course, need to be related, as the argument unfolds, to their characteristic theories.) In this way we can get before us some of the case for and against liberal justice and socialist justice.[18]

Both the Liberal Principles and the Socialist Principles (as I shall refer to them henceforth) build on what is, in societies such as ours, the pervasive and deep conviction that there is a link between fairness and equality and a belief in the importance of liberty.

The first principle of Liberal Justice (Rawls's first principle), *the equal liberty principle,* and a key part of his second principle, *the difference principle,* i.e. social and economic inequalities are to be arranged so that they are to the greatest benefit of the least advantaged, are very attractive and very plausible sounding principles indeed. They seem to encapsulate the essence of liberal justice.[19]

The equal liberty principle can be seen as a principle which directs us to try to bring into existence a society where everyone can do what he or she likes, where each can, as fully as possible, satisfy his or her desires, subject only to the restriction that doing what they like be compatible with everyone's being able to do what he or she likes. In other words, people can do what they like except where doing that undermines a like liberty for others, i.e., prevents others from being able to do what they like. In fine, liberty can only justifiably be restricted, when the restriction of some particular liberty or liberties would be necessary, to protect the most extensive system possible of equal liberties. It is Rawls's belief that liberty can be sacrificed, in circumstances of relative affluence, *only* to ensure or protect a still greater liberty *for all.*

There are certain qualifications that we should make to this claim, but it remains, all the same, an attractive ideal. Would we not, if we reflect carefully on the matter, want a world in which each and every person could do, to the fullest extent possible, whatever it is they want—where everyone could most fully realize their aims and ideals, achieve their hopes, live their lives as they really wish to, subject only to the restriction, that their so living be compatible with a like condition of life for their fellow human beings? This is surely a very attractive conception.

Secondly—and here is where the *difference* principle comes into play—if there must be some inequalities, as apparently there must, what fairer or better arrangement could be devised than an arrangement in which the inequalities are justified *when, and only when,* the positions of relative advantage can be fairly competed for and the resultant inequalities benefit everyone, or, where they cannot benefit everyone, or where we cannot ascertain that they benefit everyone, they benefit, more than any alternative arrangement, the most disadvantaged stratum of society? What could be *fairer,* where we must allow some inequalities, then to allow inequalities only when they, more than any other arrangement, are to the advantage of the most disadvantaged? It is bad enough that some people have to be disadvantaged: it is still worse when they do *not* get the maximal advantages that could go with their being in that disadvantaged position. The humane and just thing to do is to try to ensure that the inequalities that exist will be such that they mitigate, as much as possible, the situation of the most disadvantaged. This is Rawls's essential reasoning about the *difference* principle. It surely seems humane and reasonable and it is a core ideal of liberal egalitarianism.

Someone arguing for the Socialist Principles could very well begin their critique of the Liberal Principles by starting with the *difference* principle, namely with the claim that inequalities are just, or at least are justified, only if they maximally benefit the worst off under the constraints articulated by Rawls. For it could be the case, as Rawls allows, that the Liberal Principles are in force, that they actually are being correctly applied, and that we would, if we reasoned in accordance with them, still be committed to accepting as *just* a not inconsiderable disparity in total life prospects between children of entrepreneurs and the professional class, on the one hand, and children of unskilled labourers or people on welfare, on the other, even when those children are equally talented, equally energetic and the like.

This seems manifestly unjust. It is unfair that one child's life prospects are such that, when he starts out in life, it is close to inevitable that he will end up working (if he has any work at all) all his life in a factory, a mine or the like, while another child's life prospects are such that it makes it almost inevitable that he will enter the professional or entrepreneurial strata of society. Such disparities in life prospects are basically unfair or unjust, unless they are unalterable or the costs of their cure are worse than the grave ills they perpetuate. Given that such disparities in total life prospects are such plain ills *and* that they do not appear to be unalterable, the burden of proof is surely on the defender of the capitalist order to show that they cannot be altered or that the costs of breaking down these disparities are too high.

The liberal Rawlsian response is that they are necessary evils that we have to live with, even in affluent societies, to avoid still greater evils. It is, such liberals would plausibly argue, bad enough that such inequalities in total life prospects must exist, but it is still worse, by narrowing them, to make the children of unskilled workers still worse off. It is, everything considered, juster and more decent, to accept these not inconsiderable disparities in life and apply the *difference* principle, accepting only such reductions in these disparities as are sanctioned by the *difference* principle.

If we start, as defenders of both the Liberal Principles and the Socialist Principles insist, with the deep underlying commitment that in the design of institutions all people are to have *a right to equal concern and respect,* and if we believe that liberation from class society is possible, we will not be satisfied with the *difference* principle, even when it is surrounded by Rawls's safeguards, for, where such differences in whole life prospects obtain, there will be differences in power and control in society riding with these differences in life prospects. Differences, recall, sanctioned by the *difference* principle. These in turn will make it impossible for the most disadvantaged effectively to exercise anything like fully equal citizenship and this in turn will undermine their standing on a footing of equal liberty with the more advantaged, e.g. the capitalists and the professional elite. Moreover, much work in capitalist society is degrading and undermining of human autonomy, and, where the worker sees her condition with any clarity, undermining of self-respect. This could be lessened in capitalist society but not obliterated, for in the capitalist production process workers are simply told to carry out certain tasks. In that very important area of their lives, they lack autonomy. They work for a salary and do what they are told; they, generally, have no alternative, except the even more degrading alternative of going on the dole.

Where this is seen by people subjected to alienated labour, there is a tendency to suffer a loss of self-respect, a loss not certain to be made good by abiding by Rawls's *difference* principle. Contrary to Rawls, then, it is arguable that in a society of material abundance the most disadvantaged would, where fully informed and rational, choose, the second Socialist Principle rather than the *difference* principle, if they prize the good of self-respect and autonomy as much as Rawls believes they would and should. They would prefer, under these circumstances, a somewhat lesser income (lesser material wealth) if this would enable them to have a greater control over their own lives—a fuller realization of liberty and the good of self-respect. They would not and should not accept the differences in power and control acceptable under the *difference* principle.

It is not envy or irrationality that leads to such a Socialist insistence on levelling, but a commitment to the fullest achievement possible of equal liberty, i.e. equal control for each person over the design of his life.

A socialist belief is that this cannot be attained in class society with its inevitable differences in power and control in society. State capitalist societies, committed to Liberal Principles, can ameliorate this condition and they are an advance over laissez-faire capitalism with its commitment to libertarianism. But in class society—any class society—equal citizenship, equal liberty and equal opportunity cannot be attained. Thus, if they are otherwise obtainable, a capitalist society (even a Social Democratically oriented Liberal Welfare State Capitalism) cannot be a fully just society. It is the claim of socialism that there are such alternatives: that there is a liberation, or at least the reasonable hope of liberation, from class society.

. . . .

X

I bring this essay to its final section with the frustrated awareness that the dialectic of the argument is not nearly at an end in the great debate between liberalism and socialism. That is hardly surprising in that it is the most important moral and social issue of our time. As religion once did, it divides and touches our deepest hopes for ourselves and for our children. The issue will be fought out in the next few decades in a long and complicated and many leveled struggle. Given the complexity of what is involved here, it is hardly to be wondered that there are myriads of issues crying for discussion that I have not even touched on. Indeed, even for the two issues I shall discuss in this last section, there are many loose ends which must remain.

(1) In comparing the Liberal Principles and the Socialist Principles, I have argued that the socialist second principle ought to be accepted rather than the *difference* principle, but I have said nothing in favour of the first principle, either to distinguish it from the first liberal principle or to show why, as both the liberal formulation and the socialist formulation do, such stress should be placed on the attainment and protection of equal liberty and moral autonomy.

It is crucial first to recognize that neither Rawls nor I even try to articulate eternal principles of justice to be accepted in all historical epochs and circumstances. Our equal liberty principles, for example, only have application in conditions of moderate scarcity or relative abundance. Brecht's "Eats first, morality afterwards" should never be forgotten.

It is also the case that the liberal first principle and the socialist first principle are very alike in that they call for the widest possible system of equal liberty, though the socialist principle makes more explicit what is involved. It is not basic differences over whether to accept something like an equal liberty principle that divide liberals and socialists.

However there are people (some utilitarians among them) who would not accept the equal liberty principle. Why, they would ask, even in situations of abundance, give such weight to liberty, to self-determination, and to something as obscure and airy-fairy as the good of self-respect? Why care so much about equal citizenship, equal autonomy, and the good of self-respect? The answer, I believe, lies in recognizing that the value of moral autonomy and the good of self-respect are rooted in deeply felt considered judgments and beliefs about what it is to live a human life. It is tied up, I believe, with our deepest hopes about ourselves and about what it would be to live a life with integrity.

The need to have some control over one's own existence, to be able to direct and orient one's own life according to a conception chosen by oneself from alternatives that seem meaningful to one, is a very powerful and persistent need indeed and becomes more powerful the more securely one's basic subsistence needs are met and the more leisured one is from endless backbreaking toil. That in barest outline is why the attainment and protection of equal liberty and autonomy are so important.

(2) I have argued for socialism over laissez-faire capitalism. But suppose I am wrong and socialism is not a reasonable non-fanciful possibility and our actual choices are only between State capitalism and State socialism. Then is it not reasonable to believe that, not State capitalism *sans phrase,* but Liberal Welfare State capitalism is a juster and better social system than *any form* of State socialism? Isn't Sweden clearly a better society to live in than Cuba?

It is not unreasonable to be skeptical about whether the aims of socialism are attainable. If it is not reasonable to believe that they are, should we opt for the reformist aims of social democracy or State socialism?

Now, in view of the Liberal Principles and Socialist Principles of justice I have articulated, we readily can see that even the best forms of State capitalism and State socialism are flawed in terms of liberty, the good of self-respect, equal citizenship, equality and industrial democracy, and that they both are hierarchical, bureaucratic societies with elites and with paternalistic control.

However, unlike some actual State capitalist and State socialist societies, there is no reason at all why possible forms of each could not be political democracies, have respect for rights and civil liberties and be societies of plenty. Assuming this much, what grounds, if any, in terms of justice and morality, do we have for choosing one of these social systems over the other? Thee reasons can be given for choosing State socialism. First, State socialism is committed to maximally, and equally, satisfy needs and to foster capital accumulations as instrumental only to that. State capitalism, by contrast, has no such underlying rationale. Second, State capitalism rests on its class structure. State socialism will indeed produce elites, but (a) its belief system cannot justify their existence, except as temporary expedients, and (b) the elites lack the clear structural means of the capitalist class for intragenerationally passing on their privileges. Third, since socialists are committed to attaining classlessness and to taking the standpoint of labour, there are strong grounds, in terms of social legitimization in the socialist belief system, to push for a greater equality and for the expansion of liberty.

There is, of course, much more to be said on this topic. There are normative points and normative-cum-factual points to be made on both sides; but, in the above arguments, we still have reason, where the choice is so narrowed, to prefer State socialism in its *best forms* to State capitalism in its best forms.

However, the core of my defense has been of socialism and not of State socialism. Conventional wisdom—a very ideologically convenient conventional wisdom—identifies commitment to it with a belief in a Marxist fairy tale, a possibly pleasant dream but not something which could come to have a real social exemplification. It is, we are given to understand, the secular equivalent of pie-in-the-sky-by-and-by, for those who cannot bear to look at social reality straight in the face, but who can no longer accept Jewish or Christian fairy tales. I have not tried to show that socialism is on the historical agenda, let alone that it is inevitable. But I have tried to provide some reason for believing that the popular "political realism" and cultural pessimism are forms of ideological posturing *and* that socialism remains a *reasonable possibility.* If it is such a possibility, then I think that close reflection on justice and morality will give a person of humane sentiments and a reasonable grasp of the relevant facts good grounds indeed to struggle to make that possibility a reality.

Notes

1. Richard C. Edwards, Michael Reich and Thomas E. Weisskopf (eds.) *The Capitalist System,* (Second Edition), (Prentice Hall, Inc.: Englewood Cliffs, N.J., 1978), p. xii. This is an excellent source for the political, economic, sociological, and other empirical issues essential for understanding the issues argued in this essay.
2. That this economic doctrine is actually such a corollary of liberty is powerfully challenged by G. A. Cohen in his "Capitalism, Freedom and the Proletariat" in *The Idea of Freedom,* Alan Ryan (ed.) (Oxford University Press: Oxford, 1979), pp. 9–25 and by John Exdell, "Liberty, Equality and Capitalism," *Canadian Journal of Philosophy,* (1981).
3. Rorbert Nozick argues this is the middle section of *Anarchy, State, and Utopia* (Basic Books Inc.: New York, 1974) and it has been argued by Antony Flew is "Equality *or* Justice," *Midwest Studies in Philosophy,* Vol. 3 (1978), pp. 176–194 and "A Theory of Social Justice" in *Contemporary British Philosophy,* H. D. Lewis (ed.) (Humanities Press: New York, 1976), pp. 69–85. I have criticized such accounts in my "Impediments to Radical Egalitarianism," *American Philosophical Quarterly,* (1981) and my "A Rationale for Egalitarianism," *Social Research,* (1981).
4. Virginia Held, "John Locke on Robert Nozick," *Social Research,* Vol. 43 (1976) pp. 169–95 and Shadia Drury, "Robert Nozick and the Right to Property" in *Theories of Property,* Anthony Parel and Thomas Flanagan (eds.) (Wilfred Laurier University Press: Waterloo, Ontario, 1979), pp. 361–79. Among other things, these authors, in their perceptive criticisms of Nozick, show how far he departs here from Locke. Filmer is his genuine antecedent.
5. Nozick, *op. cit.*, pp. 175–76.
6. *Ibid.*
7. *Ibid.* H. L. A. Hart points out that the baseline situation Nozick assumes is the "state of nature," but, aside from not having any very clear conception of what this is, no reason is given for taking such a low baseline. H. L. A. Hart, "Between Utility and Rights" in *The Idea of Freedom.*
8. Nozick, *op. cit.*, pp. 179–80.
9. *Ibid.*, pp. 180–81.
10. *Ibid.*
11. George Kateb, "The Night Watchman State," *American Scholar* (1977), pp. 816–25.
12. Ernest Feder, "Latifundia and Agricultural Labour in Latin America" in *Peasants and Peasant Societies* in Teodor Shanin (ed.) (Penguin Books Ltd.: Harmondworth, Middlesex, England, 1971) p. 83.
13. Hart, *op. cit.*
14. G. A. Cohen, "Robert Nozick and Wilt Chamberlain: How Patterns Preserve Liberty" in *Justice and Economic Distribution,* J. Arthur and W. H. Shaw (eds.) (Prentice-Hall, Inc.: Englewood Cliffs, N.J., 1978) pp. 246–62. See also his essay cited in footnote 2.
15. Cohen, "Robert Nozick and Wilt Chamberlain: How Patterns Preserve Liberty," p. 251.
16. *Ibid.*
17. It might be thought that there is a qualifying element in my second principle of socialist justice that gives everything away to the libertarian. Things are to be divided equally *only after due weight is given to the just entitlements of individuals.* What more could Nozick ask for? But the catch here is on the reading to be given to "due weight." As my discussion of the principle makes clear, as well as my discussion of Nozick's principles of justice, entitlements cannot be legitimately insisted on in situations where insisting on them would cause great harm and suffering or in an undermining of human liberty, e.g. one cannot rightly hold on to one's patent rights and let thousands die as a result of hanging on to them, and one cannot hold on to productive property where having that property gives one power over the lives of others such that whole life prospects of people are radically unequal. Thus, "due weight" is accorded one's entitlements by recognizing that to have an entitlement to something is to have a prima facie right to it and that we have a prima facie obligation not to interfere with the exercising of that right. Such a recognition is giving "due weight." However, in order to maintain patterns which preserve liberty, we will occasionally be required to override a particular entitlement, just as we will also disallow some entitlements (e.g. no one is allowed privately to own productive property) in order to maintain patterns which perserve liberty. This is consistent with insisting that we can never rightly ignore the claims of entitlement.
18. Kai Nielsen "Class and Justice" in *Justice and Economic Distribution* and "Radical Egalitarian Justice: Justice as Equality," *Social Theory and Practice,* Vol. 5 No. 2 (1979).
19. Stuart Hampshire, "What Is the Just Society?", *New York Review of Books,* Vol. 18 No 3 (February 24, 1972), pp 34–39.

Reverse Discrimination

RONALD DWORKIN

Ronald Dworkin (1931–) is a professor of jurisprudence at Oxford University. His publications include *Taking Rights Seriously* and various contributions to legal and philosophical journals.

1

In 1945 a black man named Sweatt applied to the University of Texas Law School, but was refused admission because state law provided that only whites could attend. The Supreme Court declared that this law violated Sweatt's rights under the Fourteenth Amendment to the United States Constitution, which provides that no state shall deny any man the equal protection of its laws.[1] In 1971 a Jew named DeFunis applied to the University of Washington Law School; he was rejected although his test scores and college grades were such that he would have been admitted if he had been a black or a Filipino or a Chicano or an American Indian. DeFunis asked the Supreme Court to declare that the Washington practice, which required less exacting standards of minority groups, violated his rights under the Fourteenth Amendment.[2]

The Washington Law School's admission procedures were complex. Applications were divided into two groups. The majority—those not from the designated minority groups—were first screened so as to eliminate all applicants whose predicted average, which is a function of college grades and aptitude test scores, fell below a certain level. Majority applicants who survived this initial cut were then placed in categories that received progressively more careful consideration. Minority-group applications, on the other hand, were not screened; each received the most careful consideration by a special committee consisting of a black professor of law and a white professor who had taught in programs to aid black law students. Most of the minority applicants who were accepted in the year in which DeFunis was rejected had predicted averages below the cutoff level, and the law school conceded that any minority applicant with his average would certainly have been accepted.

The *DeFunis* case split those political action groups that have traditionally supported liberal causes. The B'nai Brith Anti-Defamation League and the AFL-CIO, for example, filed briefs as *amici curiae* in support of DeFunis's claim, while the American Hebrew Women's Council, the UAW, and the UMWA filed briefs against it.

These splits among old allies demonstrate both the practical and the philosophical importance of the case. In the past liberals held, within one set of attitudes, three propositions: that racial classification is an evil in itself; that every person has a right to an educational opportunity commensurate with his abilities; and that affirmative state action is proper to remedy the serious inequalities of American society. In the last decade, however, the opinion has grown that these three liberal propositions are in fact not compatible, because the most effective programs of state action are those that give a competitive advantage to minority racial groups.

From *Taking Rights Seriously* (Cambridge: Harvard University Press, 1977), pp. 223–39.

That opinion has, of course, been challenged. Some educators argue that benign quotas are ineffective, even self-defeating, because preferential treatment will reinforce the sense of inferiority that many blacks already have. Others make a more general objection. They argue that any racial discrimination, even for the purpose of benefiting minorities, will in fact harm those minorities, because prejudice is fostered whenever racial distinctions are tolerated for any purpose whatever. But these are complex and controversial empirical judgments, and it is far too early, as wise critics concede, to decide whether preferential treatment does more harm or good. Nor is it the business of judges, particularly in constitutional cases, to overthrow decisions of other officials because the judges disagree about the efficiency of social policies. This empirical criticism is therefore reinforced by the moral argument that even if reverse discrimination does benefit minorities and does reduce prejudice in the long run, it is nevertheless wrong because distinctions of race are inherently unjust. They are unjust because they violate the rights of individual members of groups not so favored, who may thereby lose a place as DeFunis did.

DeFunis presented this moral argument, in the form of a constitutional claim, to the courts. The Supreme Court did not, in the end, decide whether the argument was good or bad. DeFunis had been admitted to the law school after one lower court had decided in his favor, and the law school said that he would be allowed to graduate however the case was finally decided. The Court therefore held that the case was moot and dismissed the appeal on that ground. But Mr. Justice Douglas disagreed with this neutral disposition of the case; he wrote a dissenting opinion in which he argued that the Court should have upheld DeFunis's claim on the merits. Many universities and colleges have taken Justice Douglas's opinion as handwriting on the wall, and have changed their practices in anticipation of a later Court decision in which his opinion prevails. In fact, his opinion pointed out that law schools might achieve much the same result by a more sophisticated policy than Washington used. A school might stipulate, for example, that applicants from all races and groups would be considered together, but that the aptitude tests of certain minority applicants would be graded differently, or given less weight in overall predicted average, because experience had shown that standard examinations were for different reasons a poorer test of the actual ability of these applicants. But if this technique is used deliberately to achieve the same result, it is devious, and it remains to ask why the candid program used by the University of Washington was either unjust or unconstitutional.

2

DeFunis plainly had no constitutional right that the state provide him a legal education of a certain quality. His rights would not be violated if his state did not have a law school at all, or if it had a law school with so few places that he could not win one on intellectual merit. Nor does he have a right to insist that intelligence be the exclusive test of admission. Law schools do rely heavily on intellectual tests for admission. That seems proper, however, not because applicants have a right to be judged in that way, but because it is reasonable to think that the community as a whole is better off if its lawyers are intelligent. That is, intellectual standards are justified, not because they reward the clever, but because they seem to serve a useful social policy.

Law schools sometimes serve that policy better, moreover, by supplementing intelligence tests with other sorts of standards: they sometimes prefer industrious applicants, for example, to those who are brighter but lazier. They also serve special policies for which intelligence is not relevant. The Washington Law School, for example, gave special preference not only to the minority applicants but also to veterans who had been at the school before entering the military, and neither DeFunis nor any of the briefs submitted in his behalf complained of that preference.

DeFunis does not have an absolute right to a law school place, nor does he have a right that only intelligence be used as a standard for admission. He says he nevertheless has a right that race *not* be used as a standard, no matter how well a racial classification might work to promote the general welfare or to reduce social and economic inequality. He does not claim, however, that he has this right as a distinct and independent political right that is specifically protected by the Constitution, as is his right to freedom of speech and religion. The Constitution does not condemn racial classification directly, as it does condemn censorship or the establishment of a state religion. DeFunis claims that his right that race not be used as a criterion of admission follows from the more abstract right of equality that is protected by the Fourteenth Amendment, which provides that no state shall deny to any person the equal protection of the law.

But the legal arguments made on both sides show that neither the text of the Constitution nor the prior decisions of the Supreme Court decisively settle the question whether, as a matter of law, the Equal Protection Clause makes all racial classifications unconstitutional. The Clause makes the concept of equality a test of legislation, but it does not stipulate any particular conception of that concept. Those who wrote the Clause intended to attack certain consequences of slavery and racial prejudice, but it is unlikely that they intended to outlaw all racial classifications, or that they expected such a prohibition to be the result of what they wrote. They outlawed whatever policies would violate equality, but left it to others to decide, from time to time, what that means. There cannot be a good legal argument in favor of DeFunis, therefore, unless there is a good moral argument that all racial classifications, even those that make society as a whole more equal, are inherently offensive to an individual's right to equal protection for himself.

There is nothing paradoxical, of course, in the idea that an individual's right to equal protection may sometimes conflict with an otherwise desirable social policy, including the policy of making the community more equal overall. Suppose a law school were to charge a few middle-class students, selected by lot, double tuition in order to increase the scholarship fund for poor students. It would be serving a desirable policy—equality of opportunity—by means that violated the right of the students selected by lot to be treated equally with other students who could also afford the increased fees. It is, in fact, part of the importance of DeFunis's case that it forces us to acknowledge the distinction between equality as a policy and equality as a right, a distinction that political theory has virtually ignored. He argues that the Washington Law School violated his individual right to equality for the sake of a policy of greater equality overall, in the same way that double tuition for arbitrarily chosen students would violate their rights for the same purpose.

We must therefore concentrate our attention on that claim. We must try to define the central concept on which it turns, which is the concept of an individual right to equality made a constitutional right by the Equal Protection Clause. What rights to equality do citizens have as individuals which might defeat programs aimed at important economic and social policies, including the social policy of improving equality overall?

There are two different sorts of rights they may be said to have. The first is the right to *equal treatment,* which is the right to an equal distribution of some opportunity or resource or burden. Every citizen, for example, has a right to an equal vote in a democracy; that is the nerve of the Supreme Court's decision that one person must have one vote even if a different and more complex arrangement would better secure the collective welfare. The second is the right to *treatment as an equal,* which is the right, not to receive the same distribution of some burden or benefit, but to be treated with the same respect and concern as anyone else. If I have two children, and one is dying from a disease that is making the other uncomfortable, I do not show equal concern if I flip a coin to decide which should have the remaining dose of a drug. This example shows that the right to treatment as an equal is fundamental, and the right to equal treatment, derivative. In some circumstances the right to treatment as an equal will entail a right to equal treatment, but not, by any means, in all circumstances.

DeFunis does not have a right to equal treatment in the assignment of law school places; he does not have a right to a place just because others are given places. Individuals may have a right to equal treatment in elementary education, because someone who is denied elementary education is unlikely to lead a useful life. But legal education is not so vital that everyone has an equal right to it.

DeFunis does have the second sort of right—a right to treatment as an equal in the decision as to which admissions standards should be used. That is, he has a right that his interests be treated as fully and sympathetically as the interests of any others when the law school decides whether to count race as a pertinent criterion for admission. But we must be careful not to overstate what that means.

Suppose an applicant complains that his right to be treated as an equal is violated by tests that place the less intelligent candidates at a disadvantage as against the more intelligent. A law school might properly reply in the following way. Any standard will place certain candidates at a disadvantage as against others, but an admission policy may nevertheless be justified if it seems reasonable to expect that the overall gain to the community exceeds the overall loss, and if no other policy that does not provide a comparable disadvantage would produce even roughly the same gain. An individual's right to be treated as an equal means that his potential loss must be treated as a matter of concern, but that loss may nevertheless be outweighed by the gain to the community as a whole. If it is, then the less intelligent applicant cannot claim that he is cheated of his right to be treated as an equal just because he suffers a disadvantage others do not.

Washington may make the same reply to DeFunis. Any admissions policy must put some applicants at a disadvantage, and a policy of preference for minority applicants can reasonably be supposed to benefit the community as a whole, even when the loss to candidates such as DeFunis is taken into account. If there are more black lawyers, they will help to provide better legal services to the black community, and so reduce social tensions. It might well improve the quality of legal education for all students, moreover, to have a greater number of blacks as classroom discussants of social problems. Further, if blacks are seen as successful law students, then other blacks who do meet the usual intellectual standards might be encouraged to apply, and that, in turn, would raise the intellectual quality of the bar. In any case, preferential admissions of blacks should decrease the difference in wealth and power that now exists between different racial groups, and so make the community more equal overall. It is, as I said, controversial whether a preferential admissions program will in fact promote these various policies, but it cannot be said to be implausible that it will. The disadvantage to applicants such as DeFunis is, on that hypothesis, a cost that must be paid for a greater gain; it is in that way like the disadvantage to less intelligent students that is the cost of ordinary admissions policies.[3]

We now see the difference between DeFunis's case and the case we imagined, in which a law school charged students selected at random higher fees. The special disadvantage to these students was not necessary to achieve the gain in scholarship funds, because the same gain would have been achieved by a more equal distribution of the cost amongst all the students who could afford it. That is not true of DeFunis. He did suffer from the Washington policy more than those majority applicants who were accepted. But that discrimination was not arbitrary; it was a consequence of the meritocratic standards he approves. DeFunis's argument therefore fails. The Equal Protection Clause gives constitutional standing to the right to be treated as an equal, but he cannot find, in that right, any support for his claim that the clause makes all racial classifications illegal.

3

If we dismiss DeFunis's claim in this straightforward way, however, we are left with this puzzle. How can so many able lawyers, who supported his claim both in morality and law, have made that mistake? These lawyers all agree that intelligence is a proper criterion for admission to law schools. They do not suppose that anyone's constitutional right to be treated as an equal is compromised by that criterion. Why do they deny that race, in the circumstances of this decade, may also be a proper criterion?

They fear, perhaps, that racial criteria will be misused; that such criteria will serve as an excuse for prejudice against the minorities that are not favored, such as Jews. But that cannot explain their opposition. Any criteria may be misused, and in any case they think that racial criteria are wrong in principle and not simply open to abuse.

Why? The answer lies in their belief that, in theory as well as in practice, *DeFunis* and *Sweatt* must stand or fall together. They believe that it is illogical for liberals to condemn Texas for raising a color barrier against Sweatt, and then applaud Washington for raising a color barrier against DeFunis. The difference between these two cases, they suppose, must be only the subjective preference of liberals for certain minorities now in fashion. If there is something wrong with racial classifications, then it must be something that is wrong with racial classifications as such, not just classifications that work against those groups currently in favor. That is the inarticulate premise behind the slogan, relied on by defendants of DeFunis, that the Constitution is color blind. That slogan means, of course, just the opposite of what it says: it means that the Constitution is so sensitive to color that it makes any institutional racial classification invalid as a matter of law.

It is of the greatest importance, therefore, to test the assumption that Sweatt and DeFunis must stand or fall together. If that assumption is sound, then the straightforward argument against DeFunis must be fallacious after all, for no argument could convince us that segregation of the sort practiced against Sweatt is justifiable or constitutional.[4] Superficially, moreover, the arguments against DeFunis do indeed seem available against Sweatt, because we can construct an argument that Texas might have used to show that segregation benefits the collective welfare, so that the special disadvantage to blacks is a cost that must be paid to achieve an overall gain.

Suppose the Texas admissions committee, though composed of men and women who themselves held no prejudices, decided that the Texas economy demanded more white lawyers than they could educate, but could find no use for black lawyers at all. That might have been, after all, a realistic assessment of the commercial market for lawyers in Texas just after World War II. Corporate law firms needed lawyers to serve booming business but could not afford to hire black lawyers, however skillful, because the firms' practices would be destroyed if they did. It was no doubt true that the black community in Texas had great need of skillful lawyers, and would have preferred to use black lawyers if these were available. But the committee might well have thought that the commercial needs of the state as a whole outweighed that special need.

Or suppose the committee judged, no doubt accurately, that alumni gifts to the law school would fall off drastically if it admitted a black student. The committee might deplore that fact, but nevertheless believe that the consequent collective damage would be greater than the damage to black candidates excluded by the racial restriction.

It may be said that these hypothetical arguments are disingenuous, because any policy of excluding blacks would in fact be supported by a prejudice against blacks as such, and arguments of the sort just described would be rationalization only. But if these arguments are, in fact, sound, then they might be accepted by men who do not have the prejudices the objection assumes. It therefore does not follow from the fact that the admissions officers were prejudiced, if they were, that they would have rejected these arguments if they had not been.

In any case, arguments such as those I describe were in fact used by officials who might have been free from prejudice against those they excluded. Many decades ago, as the late Professor Bickel reminds us in his brief for the B'nai Brith, President Lowel of Harvard University argued in favor of a quota limiting the number of Jews who might be accepted by his university. He said that if Jews were accepted in numbers larger than their proportion of the population, as they certainly would have been if intelligence were the only test, then Harvard would no longer be able to provide to the world men of the qualities and temperament it aimed to produce, men, that is, who were more well-rounded and less exclusively intellectual than Jews tended to be, and who, therefore, were better and more likely leaders of other men, both in and out of government. It was no doubt true, when Lowell spoke, that Jews were less likely to occupy important places in government or at the heads of large public companies. If Harvard wished to serve the general welfare by improving the intellectual qualities of the nation's leaders, it was rational not to allow its classes to be filled up with Jews. The men who reached that conclusion might well prefer the company of Jews to that of the Wasps who were more likely to become senators. Lowell suggested he did, though perhaps the responsibilities of his office prevented him from frequently indulging his preference.

It might now be said, however, that discrimination against blacks, even when it does serve some plausible policy, is nevertheless unjustified because it is invidious and insulting. The briefs opposing DeFunis make just that argument to distinguish his claim from Sweatt's. Because blacks were the victims of slavery and legal segregation, they say, any discrimination that excludes blacks will be taken as insulting by them, whatever arguments of general welfare might be made in its support. But it is not true, as a general matter, that any social policy is unjust if those whom it puts at a disadvantage feel insulted. Admission to law school by intelligence is not unjust because those who are less intelligent feel insulted by their exclusion. Everything depends upon whether the feeling of insult is produced by some more objective feature that would disqualify the general welfare, even when the disadvantage to blacks is fully taken into account, and if no other reason can be found why segregation is nevertheless unjustified, then the insult blacks feel, while understandable, must be based on misperception.

It would be wrong, in any case, to assume that men in the position of DeFunis will not take *their* exclusion to be insulting. They are very likely to think of themselves . . . as members of some other minority, such as Jews or Poles or Italians, whom comfortable and successful liberals are willing to sacrifice in order to delay more violent social change. If we wish to distinguish *DeFunis* from *Sweatt* on some argument that uses the concept of an insult, we must show that the treatment of the one, but not the other, is in fact unjust.

4

So these familiar arguments that might distinguish the two cases are unconvincing. That seems to confirm the view that Sweatt and DeFunis must be treated alike, and therefore that racial classification must be outlawed altogether. But fortunately a more successful ground of distinction can be found to support our initial sense that the cases are in fact very different. This distinction does not rely, as these unconvincing arguments do, on features peculiar to issues of race or segregation, or even on features peculiar to issues of educational opportunity. It relies instead on further analysis of the idea, which was central to my argument against DeFunis, that in certain circumstances a policy which puts many individuals at a disadvantage is nevertheless justified because it makes the community as a whole better off.

Any institution which uses that idea to justify a discriminatory policy faces a series of theoretical and practical difficulties. There are, in the first place, two distinct senses in which a community may be said to be better off as a whole, in spite of the fact that certain of its members are worse off, and any justification must specify which sense is meant. It may be better off in a *utilitarian* sense, that is, because the average or collective level of welfare in the community is improved even though the welfare of some individuals falls. Or it may be better off in an *ideal* sense, that is, because it is more just, or in some other way closer to an ideal society, whether or not average welfare is improved. The University of Washington might use either utilitarian or ideal arguments to justify its racial classification. It might argue, for example, that increasing the number of black lawyers reduces racial tensions, which improves the welfare of almost everyone in the community. That is a utilitarian argument. Or it might argue that, whatever effect minority preference will have on average welfare, it will make the community more equal and therefore more just. That is an ideal, not a utilitarian, argument.

The University of Texas, on the other hand, cannot make an ideal argument for segregation. It cannot claim that segregation makes the community more just whether it improves the average welfare or not. The arguments it makes to defend segregation must therefore all be utilitarian arguments. The arguments I invented, like the argument that white lawyers could do more than black lawyers to improve commercial efficiency in Texas, are utilitarian, since commercial efficiency makes the community better off only if it improves average welfare.

Utilitarian arguments encounter a special difficulty that ideal arguments do not. What is meant by average or collective welfare? How can the welfare of an individual be measured, even in principle, and how can gains in the welfare of different individuals be added and then compared with losses, so as to justify the claim that gains outweigh losses overall? The utilitarian argument that segregation improves average welfare presupposes that such calculations can be made. But how?

Jeremy Bentham, who believed that only utilitarian arguments could justify political decisions, gave the following answer. He said that the effect of a policy on an individual's welfare could be determined by discovering the amount of pleasure or pain the policy brought him, and that effect of the policy on the collective welfare could be calculated by adding together all the pleasure and subtracting all of the pain it brought to everyone. But, as Bentham's critics insisted, it is doubtful whether there exists a simple psychological state of pleasure common to all those who benefit from a policy or of pain common to all those who lose by it; in any case it would be impossible to identify, measure, and add the different pleasures and pains felt by vast numbers of people.

Philosophers and economists who find utilitarian arguments attractive, but who reject Bentham's psychological utilitarianism, propose a different concept of individual and overall welfare. They suppose that whenever an institution or an official must decide upon a policy, the members of the community will each prefer the consequences of one decision to the consequences of others. DeFunis, for example, prefers the consequences of the standard admissions policy to the policy of minority preference Washington used, while the blacks in some urban ghetto might each prefer the consequences of the latter policy to the former. If it can be discovered what each individual prefers, and how intensely, then it might be shown that a particular policy would satisfy on balance more preferences, taking into account their intensity, than alternative policies. On this concept of welfare, a policy makes the community better off in a utilitarian sense if it satisfies the collection of preferences better than alternative policies would, even though it dissatisfies the preferences of some.[5]

Of course, a law school does not have available any means of making accurate judgments about the preferences of all those whom its admissions policies will affect. It may nevertheless make judgments which, though speculative, cannot be dismissed as implausible. It is, for example, plausible to think that in post-War Texas, the preferences of the people were overall in favor of the consequences of segregation in law schools, even if the intensity of the competing preference for integration, and not simply the number of those holding that preference, is taken into account. The officials of the Texas law school might have relied upon voting behavior, newspaper editorials, and simply their own sense of their community in reaching that decision. Though they might have been wrong, we cannot now say, even with the benefit of hindsight, that they were.

So even if Bentham's psychological utilitarianism is rejected, law schools may appeal to preference utilitarianism to provide at least a rough and speculative justification for admissions policies that put some classes of applicants at a disadvantage. But once it is made clear that these utilitarian arguments are based on judgments about the actual preferences of members of the community, a fresh and much more serious difficulty emerges.

The utilitarian argument, that a policy is justified if it satisfies more preferences overall, seems at first sight to be an egalitarian argument. It seems to observe strict impartiality. If the community has only enough medicine to treat some of those who are sick, the argument seems to recommend that those who are sickest be treated first. If the community can afford a swimming pool or a new theater, but not both, and more people want the pool, then it recommends that the community build the pool, unless those who want the theater can show that their preferences are so much more intense that they have more weight in spite of the numbers. One sick man is not to be preferred to another because he is worthier of official concern; the tastes of the theater audience are not to be preferred because they are more admirable. In Bentham's phrase, each man is to count as one and no man is to count as more than one.

These simple examples suggest that the utilitarian argument not only respects, but embodies, the right of each citizen to be treated as the equal of any other. The chance that each individual's preferences have to succeed, in the competition for social policy, will depend upon how important his preference is to him, and how many others share it, compared to the intensity and number of competing preferences. His chance will not be affected by the esteem or contempt of either officials or fellow citizens, and he will therefore not be subservient or beholden to them.

But if we examine the range of preferences that individuals in fact have, we shall see that the apparent egalitarian character of a utilitarian argument is often deceptive. Preference utilitarianism asks officials to attempt to satisfy people's preferences so far as this is possible. But the preferences of an individual for the consequences of a particular policy may be seen to reflect, on further analysis, either a *personal* preference for his own enjoyment of some goods or opportunities, or an *external* preference for the assignment of goods and opportunities to others, or both. A white law school candidate might have a personal preference for the consequences of segregation, for example, because the policy improves his own chances of success, or an external preference for those consequences because he has contempt for blacks and disapproves social situations in which the races mix.

The distinction between personal and external preferences is of great importance for this reason. If a utilitarian argument counts external preferences along with personal preferences, then the egalitarian character of that argument is corrupted, because the chance that anyone's preferences have to succeed will then depend, not only on the demands that the personal preferences of others make on scarce resources, but on the respect or affection they have for him or for his way of life. If external preferences tip the balance, then the fact that a policy makes the community better off in a utilitarian sense would *not* provide a justification compatible with the right of those it disadvantages to be treated as equals.

This corruption of utilitarianism is plain when some people have external preferences because they hold political theories that are themselves contrary to utilitarianism. Suppose many citizens, who are not themselves sick, are racists in political theory, and therefore prefer that scarce medicine be given to a white man who needs it rather than a black man who needs it more. If utilitarianism counts these political preferences at face value, then it will be, from the standpoint of personal preferences, self-defeating, because the distribution of medicine will then not be, from that standpoint, utilitarian at all. In any case, self-defeating or not, the distribution will not be egalitarian in the sense defined. Blacks will suffer, to a degree that depends upon the strength of the racist preference, from the fact that others think them less worthy of respect and concern.

There is a similar corruption when the external preferences that are counted are altruistic or moralistic. Suppose many citizens, who themselves do not swim, prefer the pool to the theater because they approve of sports and admire athletes, or because they think that the theater is immoral and ought to be repressed. If the altruistic preferences are counted, so as to reinforce the personal preferences of swimmers, the result will be a form of double counting: each swimmer will have the benefit not only of his own preference, but also of the preference of someone else who takes pleasure in his success. If the moralistic preferences are counted, the effect will be the same: actors and audiences will suffer because their preferences are held in lower respect by citizens whose personal preferences are not themselves engaged.

In these examples, external preferences are independent of personal preferences. But of course political, altruistic, and moralistic preferences are often not independent, but grafted on to the personal preferences they reinforce. If I am white and sick, I may also hold a racist political theory. If I want a swimming pool for my own enjoyment I may also be altruistic in favor of my fellow athlete, or I may also think that the theater is immoral. The consequences of counting these external preferences will be as grave for equality as if they were independent of personal preference, because those against whom the external preferences run might be unable or unwilling to develop reciprocal external preferences that would right the balance.

External preferences therefore present a great difficulty for utilitarianism. That theory owes much of its popularity to the assumption that it embodies the right of citizens to be treated as equals. But if external preferences are counted in overall preferences, then this assumption is jeopardized. That is, in itself, an important and neglected point in political theory; it bears, for example, on the liberal thesis, first made prominent by Mill, that the government has no right to enforce popular morality by law. It is often said that this liberal thesis is inconsistent with utilitarianism, because if the preferences of the majority that homosexuality should be repressed, for example, are sufficiently strong, utilitarianism must give way to their wishes. But the preference against homosexuality is an external preference, and the present argument provides a general reason why utilitarians should not count external preferences of any form. If utilitarianism is suitably reconstituted so as to count only personal preferences, then the liberal thesis is a consequence, not an enemy, of that theory.

It is not always possible, however, to reconstitute a utilitarian argument so as to count only personal preferences. Sometimes personal and external preferences are so inextricably tied together, and so mutually dependent, that no practical test for measuring preferences will be able to discriminate the personal and external elements in any individual's overall preference. That is especially true when preferences are affected by prejudice. Consider, for example, the associational preference of a white law student for white classmates. This may be said to be a personal preference for an association with one kind of colleague rather than another. But it is a personal preference that is parasitic upon external preferences: except in very rare cases a white student prefers the company of other whites because he has racist, social, and political convictions, or because he has contempt for blacks as a group. If these associational preferences are counted in a utilitarian argument used to justify segregation, then the egalitarian character of the argument is destroyed just as if the underlying external preferences were counted directly. Blacks would be denied their right to be treated as equals because the chance that their preferences would prevail in the design of admissions policy would be crippled by the low esteem in which others hold them. In any community in which prejudice against a particular minority is strong, then the personal preferences upon which a utilitarian argument must fix will be saturated with that prejudice; it follows that in such a community no utilitarian argument purporting to justify a disadvantage to that minority can be fair.[6]

This final difficulty is therefore fatal to Texas's utilitarian arguments in favor of segregation. The preferences that might support any such argument are either distinctly external, like the preferences of the community at large for racial separation, or are inextricably combined with and dependent upon external preferences, like the associational preferences of white students for white classmates and white lawyers for white colleagues. These external preferences are so widespread that they must corrupt any such argument. Texas's claim, that segregation makes the community better off in a utilitarian sense, is therefore incompatible with Sweatt's right to treatment as an equal guaranteed by the Equal Protection Clause.

It does not matter, to this conclusion, whether external preferences figure in the justification of a fundamental policy or in the justification of derivative policies designed to advance a more fundamental policy. Suppose Texas justifies segregation by pointing to the apparently neutral economic policy of increasing community wealth, which satisfies the personal preferences of everyone for better homes, food, and recreation. If the argument that segregation will improve community wealth depends upon the fact of external preference; if the argument notices, for example, that because of prejudice industry will run more efficiently if factories are segregated; then the argument has the consequence that the black man's personal preferences are defeated by what others think of him. Utilitarian arguments that justify a disadvantage to members of a race against whom prejudice runs will always be unfair arguments, unless it can be shown that the same disadvantage would have been justified in the absence of the prejudice. If the prejudice is widespread and pervasive, as in fact it is in the case of blacks, that can never be shown. The preferences on which any economic argument justifying segregation must be based will be so intertwined with prejudice that they cannot be disentangled to the degree necessary to make any such contrary-to-fact hypothesis plausible.

We now have an explanation that shows why any form of segregation that disadvantages blacks is, in the United States, an automatic insult to them, and why such segregation offends their right to be treated as equals. The argument confirms our sense that utilitarian arguments purporting to justify segregation are not simply wrong in detail but misplaced in principle. This objection to utilitarian arguments is not, however, limited to race or even prejudice. There are other cases in which counting external preferences would offend the rights of citizens to be treated as equals and it is worth briefly noticing these, if only to protect the argument against the charge that it is constructed ad hoc for the racial case. I might have a moralistic preference against professional women, or an altruistic preference for virtuous men. It would be unfair for any law school to count preferences like these in deciding whom to admit to law schools; unfair because these preferences, like racial prejudices, make the success of the personal preferences of an applicant depend on the esteem and approval, rather than on the competing personal preferences, of others.

The same objection does not hold, however, against a utilitarian argument used to justify admission based on intelligence. That policy need not rely, directly or indirectly, on any community sense that intelligent lawyers are intrinsically more worthy of respect. It relies instead upon the law school's own judgment, right or wrong, that intelligent lawyers are more effective in satisfying personal preferences of others, such as the preference for wealth or winning law suits. It is true that law firms and clients prefer the services of intelligent laywers; that fact might make us suspicious of any utilitarian argument that is said not to depend upon that preference, just as we are suspicious of any argument justifying segregation that is said not to depend upon prejudice. But the widespread preference for intelligent lawyers is, by and large, not parasitic on external preferences: law firms and clients prefer intelligent lawyers because they also hold the opinion that such lawyers will be more effective in serving their personal preferences. Instrumental preferences, of that character, do not themselves figure in utilitarian arguments, though a law school may accept, on its own responsibility, the instrumental hypothesis upon which such preferences depend.[7]

5

We therefore have the distinctions in hand necessary to distinguish *DeFunis* from *Sweatt*. The arguments for an admissions program that discriminates against blacks are all utilitarian arguments, and they are all utilitarian arguments that rely upon external preferences in such a way as to offend the constitutional right of blacks to be treated as equals. The arguments for an admissions program that discriminates in favor of blacks are both utilitarian and ideal. Some of the utilitarian arguments do rely, at least indirectly, on external preferences, such as the preference of certain blacks for lawyers of their own race; but the utilitarian arguments that do not rely on such preferences are strong and may be sufficient. The ideal arguments do not rely upon preferences at all, but on the independent argument that a more equal society is a better society even if its citizens prefer inequality. That argument does not deny anyone's right to be treated as an equal himself.

We are therefore left, in *DeFunis,* with the simple and straightforward argument with which we began. Racial criteria are not necessarily the right standards for deciding which applicants should be accepted by law schools. But neither are intellectual criteria, nor indeed, any other set of criteria. The fairness—and constitutionality—of any admissions program must be tested in the same way. It is justified if it serves a proper policy that respects the right of all members of the community to be treated as equals, but not otherwise. The criteria used by schools that refused to consider blacks failed that test, but the criteria used by the Washington University Law School do not.

We are all rightly suspicious of racial classifications. They have been used to deny, rather than to respect, the right of equality, and we are all conscious of the consequent injustice. But if we misunderstand the nature of that injustice because we do not make the simple distinctions that are necessary to understand it, then we are in danger of more injustice still. It may be that preferential admissions programs will not, in fact, make a more equal society, because they may not have the effects their advocates believe they will. That strategic question should be at the center of debate about these programs. But we must not corrupt the debate by supposing that these programs are unfair even if they do work. We must take care not to use the Equal Protection Clause to cheat ourselves of equality.

Notes

1. *Sweatt v. Painter,* 339 U.S. 629, 70 S. Ct. 848.
2. *DeFunis v. Odegaard,* 94 S. Ct. 1704 (1974).
3. I shall argue later in this Chapter that there are circumstances in which a policy violates someone's right to be treated as an equal in spite of the fact that the social gains from that policy may be said to outweigh the losses. These circumstances arise when the gains that outweigh the losses include the satisfaction of prejudices and other sorts of preferences that it is improper for officials or institutions to take into account at all. But the hypothetical social gains described in this paragraph do not include gains of that character. Of course, if DeFunis had some other right, beyond the right to be treated as an equal, which the Washington policy violated, then the fact that the policy might achieve an overall social gain would not justify the violation. . . . If the Washington admissions procedure included a religious test that violated his right to religious freedom, for example, it woud offer no excuse that using such a test might make the community more cohesive. But DeFunis does not rely on any distinct right beyond his right to equality protected by the Equal Protection Clause.
4. In the actual *Sweatt* decision, the Supreme Court applied the old rule which held that segregation was constitutionally permitted if facilities were provided for blacks that were "separate but equal." Texas had provided a separate law school for blacks, but the Court held that that school was by no means the equal of the white school. *Sweattf* was decided before the famous *Brown* case in which the Court finally rejected the "separate but equal" rule, and there is no doubt that an all-white law school would be unconstitutional today, even if an all-black law school were provided that was, in a material sense, the equal of that provided for whites.
5. Many economists and philosophers challenge the intelligibility of preference utilitarianism as well as psychological utilitarianism. They argue that there is no way, even in principle, to calculate and compare the intensity of individual preferences. Since I wish to establish a different failing in certain utilitarian arguments, I assume, for purposes of this essay, that at least rough and speculative calculations about overall community preferences can be made.
6. The argument of this paragraph is powerful, but it is not, in itself, sufficient to disqualify all utilitarian arguments that produce substantial disadvantages to minorities who suffer from prejudice. Suppose the government decides, on a utilitarian argument, to allow unemployment to increase because the loss to those who lose their jobs is outweighed by the gain to those who would otherwise suffer from inflation. The burden of this policy will fall disproportionately on blacks, who will be fired first because prejudice runs against them. But though prejudice in this way affects the consequences of the policy of unemployment, it does not figure, even indirectly, in the utilitarian argument that supports that policy. (It figures, if at all, as a utilitarian argument against it.) We cannot say, therefore, that the special damage blacks suffer from a high unemployment policy is unjust for the reasons described in this essay. It may well be unjust for other reasons; if John Rawls is right, for example, it is unjust because the policy improves the condition of the majority at the expense of those already worse off.
7. No doubt the preference that some men and women have for intellectual companions is parasitic on external preferences; they value these companions not as a means to anything else, but because they think that intelligent people are better, and more worthy of honor, than others. If such preferences were sufficiently strong and pervasive we might reach the same conclusion here that we reached about segregation: that no utilitarian argument pruporting to justify discrimination against less intelligent men and women could be trusted to be fair. But there is no reason to assume that the United States is that intellectualistic; certainly no reason to think that it is intellectualistic to the degree that it is racist.

C. CHALLENGES TO MORALITY

1. MORALITY AND SELF-INTEREST

The Republic

PLATO

Plato (ca. 428–ca. 348 B.C.) is regarded by many as the greatest philosopher of all time; it has been said that all philosophy is merely a footnote to his work. His *Republic* was but one of many dialogues he wrote on a wide variety of philosophical topics.

Part I
(Book I)
Some Current Views of Justice

Chapter I
(I. 327–331 D)
Cephalus: Justice as Honesty in Word and Deed

The whole imaginary conversation is narrated by Socrates to an unspecified audience. The company who will take part in it assemble at the house of Cephalus, a retired manufacturer living at the Piraeus, the harbour town about five miles from Athens. It includes, besides Plato's elder brothers, Glaucon and Adeimantus, Cephalus' sons, Polemarchus, Lysias, well known as a writer of speeches, and Euthydemus; Thrasymachus of Chalcedon, a noted teacher of rhetoric, who may have formulated the definition of justice as 'the interest of the stronger,' though hardly any evidence about his opinions exists outside the Republic; *and a number of Socrates' young friends. The occasion is the festival of Bendis, a goddess whose cult had been imported from Thrace. Cephalus embodies the wisdom of a long life honourably spent in business. He is well-to-do, but values money as a means to that peace of mind which comes of honesty and the ability to render to gods and men their due. This is what he understands by 'right' conduct or justice.*

SOCRATES. I walked down to the Piraeus yesterday with Glaucon, the son of Ariston, to make my prayers to the goddess. As this was the first celebration of her festival, I wished also to see how the ceremony would be conducted. The Thracians, I thought, made as fine a show in the procession as our own people, though they did well enough. The prayers and the spectacle were over, and we were leaving to go back to the city, when from some way off Polemarchus, the son of Cephalus, caught sight of us starting homewards and sent his slave running to ask us to wait for him. The boy caught my garment from behind and gave me the message.

I turned round and asked where his master was.

There, he answered; coming up behind. Please wait.

Very well, said Glaucon; we will.

From the Republic trans. F. MacDonald Cornford (New York: Oxford University Press 1974), pp. 2–7, 9–40, 42–66, 102–5, 119–43.

A minute later Polemarchus joined us, with Glaucon's brother, Adeimantus, and Niceratus, the son of Nicias, and some others who must have been at the procession.

Socrates, said Polemarchus, I do believe you are starting back to town and leaving us.

You have guessed right, I answered.

Well, he said, you see what a large party we are?

I do.

Unless you are more than a match for us, then, you must stay here.

Isn't there another alternative? said I; we might convince you that you must let us go.

How will you convince us, if we refuse to listen?

We cannot, said Glaucon.

Well, we shall refuse; make up your minds to that.

Here Adeimantus interposed: Don't you even know that in the evening there is going to be a torch-race on horseback in honour of the goddess?

On horseback! I exclaimed; that is something new. How will they do it? Are the riders going to race with torches and hand them on to one another?

Just so, said Polemarchus. Besides, there will be a festival lasting all night, which will be worth seeing. We will go out after dinner and look on. We shall find plenty of young men there and we can have a talk. So please stay, and don't disappoint us.

It looks as if we had better stay, said Glaucon.

Well, said I, if you think so, we will.

Accordingly, we went home with Polemarchus; and there we found his brothers, Lysias and Euthydemus, as well as Thrasymachus of Chalcedon, Charmantides of Paeania, and Cleitophon, the son of Aristonymus. Polemarchus' father, Cephalus, was at home too. I had not seen him for some time, and it struck me that he had aged a good deal. He was sitting in a cushioned chair, wearing a garland, as he had just been conducting a sacrifice in the courtyard. There were some chairs standing round, and we sat down beside him.

As soon as he saw me, Cephalus greeted me. You don't often come down to the Piraeus to visit us, Socrates, he said. But you ought to. If I still had the strength to walk to town easily, you would not have to come here; we would come to you. But, as things are, you really ought to come here oftener. I find, I can assure you, that in proportion as bodily pleasures lose their savour, my appetite for the things of the mind grows keener and I enjoy discussing them more than ever. So you must not disappoint me. Treat us like old friends, and come here often to have a talk with these young men.

To tell the truth, Cephalus, I answered, I enjoy talking with very old people. They have gone before us on a road by which we too may have to travel, and I think we do well to learn from them what it is like, easy or difficult, rough or smooth. And now that you have reached an age when your foot, as the poets say, is on the threshold, I should like to hear what report you can give and whether you find it a painful time of life.

I will tell you by all means what it seems like to me, Socrates. Some of us old men often meet, true to the old saying that people of the same age like to be together. Most of our company are very sorry for themselves, looking back with regret to the pleasures of their young days, all the delights connected with love affairs and merry-making. They are vexed at being deprived of what seems to them so important; life was good in those days, they think, and now they have no life at all. Some complain that their families have no respect for their years, and make that a reason for harping on all the miseries old age has brought. But to my mind, Socrates, they are laying the blame on the wrong shoulders. If the fault were in old age, so far as that goes, I and all who have ever reached my time of life would have the same experience; but in point of fact, I have met many who felt quite differently. For instance, I remember someone asking Sophocles, the poet, whether he was still capable of enjoying a woman. "Don't talk that way," he answered; "I am only too glad to be free of all that; it is like escaping from bondage to a raging madman." I thought that a good answer at the time, and I still think so; for certainly a great peace comes when age sets us free from passions of that sort. When they weaken and relax their hold, most certainly it means, as Sophocles said, a release from servitude to many forms of madness. All these troubles, Socrates, including the complaints about not being respected, have only one cause; and that is not old age, but a man's character. If you have a contented mind at peace with itself, age is no intolerable burden; without that, Socrates, age and youth will be equally painful.

I was charmed with these words and wanted him to go on talking; so I tried to draw him out. I fancy, Cephalus, said I, most people will not accept that account; they imagine that it is not character that makes your burden light, but your wealth. The rich, they say, have many consolations.

That is true, he replied; they do not believe me; and there is something in their suggestion, though not so much as they suppose. When a man from Seriphus taunted Themistocles and told him that his fame was due not to himself but to his country, Themistocles made a good retort: "Certainly, if I had been born a Seriphian, I should not be famous; but no more would you, if you had been born at Athens." And so one might say to men who are not rich and feel old age burdensome: If it is true that a good man will not find it easy to bear old age and poverty combined, no more will riches ever make a bad man contented and cheerful.

And was your weath, Cephalus, mostly inherited or have you made your own fortune?

Made my fortune, Socrates? As a man of business I stand somewhere between my grandfather and my father. My grandfather, who was my namesake, inherited about as much property as I have now and more than doubled it; whereas my father Lysanias reduced it below its present level. I shall be content if I can leave these sons of mine not less than I inherited, and perhaps a little more.

I asked, said I, because you strike me as not caring overmuch about money; and that is generally so with men who have not made their own fortune. Those who have are twice as fond of their possessions as other people. They have the same affection for the money they have earned that poets have for their poems, or fathers for their children: they not merely find it useful, as we all do, but it means much to them as being of their own creation. That makes them disagreeable company; they have not a good word for anything but riches.

That is quite true.

It is indeed, I said; but one more question: what do you take to be the greatest advantage you have got from being wealthy?

One that perhaps not many people would take my word for. I can tell you, Socrates, that, when the prospect of dying is near at hand, a man begins to feel some alarm about things that never troubled him before. He may have laughed at those stories they tell of another world and of punishments there for wrongdoing in this life; but now the soul is tormented by a doubt whether they may not be true. Maybe from the weakness of old age, or perhaps because, now that he is nearer to what lies beyond, he begins to get some glimpse of it himself—at any rate he is beset with fear and misgiving; he begins thinking over the past: is there anyone he has wronged? If he finds that his life has been full of wrongdoing, he starts up from his sleep in terror like a child, and his life is haunted by dark forebodings; whereas, if his conscience is clear, that "sweet Hope" that Pindar speaks of is always with him to tend his age. Indeed, Socrates, there is great charm in those lines describing the man who has led a life of righteousness:

> Hope is his sweet companion, she who guides
> Man's wandering purpose, warms his heart
> And nurses tenderly his age.

That is admirably expressed, admirably. Now in this, as I believe, lies the chief value of wealth, not for everyone, perhaps, but for the right-thinking man. It can do much to save us from going to that other world in fear of having cheated or deceived anyone even unintentionally or of being in debt to some god for sacrifice or to some man for money. Wealth has many other uses, of course; but, taking one with another, I should regard this as the best use that can be made of it by a man of sense.

You put your case admirably, Cephalus, said I. But take this matter of doing right: can we say that it really consists in nothing more nor less than telling the truth and paying back anything we may have received? Are not these very actions sometimes right and sometimes wrong? Suppose, for example, a friend who had lent us a weapon were to go mad and then ask for it back, surely anyone would say we ought not to return it. It would not be "right" to do so; nor yet to tell the truth without reserve to a madman.

No, it would not.

Right conduct, then, cannot be defined as telling the truth and restoring anything we have been trusted with.

Yes, it can, Polemarchus broke in, at least if we are to believe Simonides.

Well, well, said Cephalus, I will bequeath the argument to you. It is time for me to attend to the sacrifice.

Your part, then, said Polemarchus, will fall to me as your heir.

By all means, said Cephalus with a smile; and with that he left us, to see to the sacrifice.

Chapter II (I. 331 E–336 A)
POLEMARCHUS: JUSTICE AS HELPING FRIENDS AND HARMING ENEMIES

. . . .

Then, said I, if you are to inherit this discussion, tell me, what is this saying of Simonides about right conduct which you approve?

That it is just to render every man his due. That seems to me a fair statement.

It is certainly hard to question the inspired wisdom of a poet like Simonides; but what this saying means you may know, Polemarchus, but I do not. Obviously it does not mean what we were speaking of just now—returning something we have been entrusted with to the owner even when he has gone out of his mind. And yet surely it is his due, if he asks for it back?

Yes.

But it is out of the question to give it back when he has gone mad?

True.

Simonides, then, must have meant something different from that when he said it was just to render a man his due.

Certainly he did; his idea was that, as between friends, what one owes to another is to do him good, not harm.

I see, said I; to repay money entrusted to one is not to render what is due, if the two parties are friends and the repayment proves harmful to the lender. That is what you say Simonides meant?

Yes, certainly.

And what about enemies? Are we to render whatever is their due to them?

Yes certainly, what really is due to them; which means, I suppose, what is appropriate to an enemy—some sort of injury.

It seems, then, that Simonides was using words with a hidden meaning, as poets will. He really meant to define justice as rendering to everyone what is appropriate to him; only he called that his "due."

Well, why not?

But look here, said I. Suppose we could question Simonides about the art of medicine—whether a physician can be described as rendering to some object what is due or appropriate to it; how do you think he would answer?

That the physician administers the appropriate diet or remedies to the body.

And the art of cookery—can that be described in the same way?

Yes; the cook gives the appropriate seasoning to his dishes.

Good. And the practice of justice?

If we are to follow those analogies, Socrates, justice would be rendering services or injuries to friends or enemies.

So Simonides means by justice doing good to friends and harm to enemies?

I think so.

And in matters of health who would be the most competent to treat friends and enemies in that way?

A physician.

And on a voyage, as regards the dangers of the sea?

A ship's captain.

In what sphere of action, then, will the just man be the most competent to do good or harm?

In war, I should imagine; when he is fighting on the side of his friends and against his enemies.

I see. But when we are well and staying on shore, the doctor and the ship's captain are of no use to us.

True.

Is it also true that the just man is useless when we are not at war?

I should not say that.

So justice has its uses in peace-time too?

Yes.

Like farming, which is useful for producing crops, or shoemaking, which is useful for providing us with shoes. Can you tell me for what purposes justice is useful or profitable in time of peace?

For matters of business, Socrates.

In a partnership, you mean?

Yes.

But if we are playing draughts, or laying bricks, or making music, will the just man be as good and helpful a partner as an expert draught-player, or a builder, or a musician?

No.

Then in what kind of partnership will he be more helpful?

Where money is involved, I suppose.

Except, perhaps, Polemarchus, when we are putting our money to some use. If we are buying or selling a horse, a judge of horses would be a better partner; or if we are dealing in ships, a shipwright or a sea-captain.

I suppose so.

Well, when will the just man be sepcially useful in handling our money?

When we want to deposit it for safe-keeping.

When the money is to lie idle, in fact?

Yes.

So justice begins to be useful only when our money is out of use?

Perhaps so.

And in the same way, I suppose, if a pruning-knife is to be used, or a shield, or a lyre, then a vine-dresser, or a soldier, or a musician will be of service; but justice is helpful only when these things are to be kept safe. In fact justice is never of any use in using things; it becomes useful when they are useless.

That seems to follow.

If that is so, my friend, justice can hardly be a thing of much value. And here is another point. In boxing or fighting of any sort skill in dealing blows goes with skill in keeping them off; and the same doctor that can keep us from disease would also be clever at producing it by stealth; or again, a general will be good at keeping his army safe, if he can also cheat the enemy and steal his plans and dispositions. So a man who is expert in keeping things will always make an expert thief.

Apparently.

The just man, then, being good at keeping money safe, will also be good at stealing it.

That seems to be the conclusion, at any rate.

So the just man turns out to be a kind of thief. You must have learnt that from Homer, who showed his predilection for Odysseus' grandfather Autolycus by remarking that he surpassed all men in cheating and perjury. Justice, according to you and Homer and Simonides, turns out to be a form of skill in cheating, provided it be to help a friend or harm an enemy. That was what you meant?

Good God, no, he protested; but I have forgotten now what I did mean. All the same, I do still believe that justice consists in helping one's friends and harming one's enemies.

. . . .

Which do you mean by a man's friends and enemies—those whom he believes to be good honest people and the reverse, or those who really are, though they may not seem so?

Naturally, his loves and hates depend on what he believes.

But don't people often mistake an honest man for a rogue, or a rogue for an honest man; in which case they regard good people as enemies and bad people as friends?

No doubt.

But all the same, it will then be right for them to help the rogue and to injure the good man?

Apparently.

And yet a good man is one who is not given to doing wrong.

True.

According to your account, then, it is right to ill-treat a man who does no wrong.

No, no, Socrates; that can't be sound doctrine.

It must be the wrongdoers, then, that it is right to injure, and the honest that are to be helped.

That sounds better.

Then, Polemarchus, the conclusion will be that for a bad judge of character it will often be right to injure his friends, when they really are rogues, and to help his enemies, when they really are honest men—the exact opposite of what we took Simonides to mean.

That certainly does follow, he said. We must

shift our ground. Perhaps our definition of friend and enemy was wrong.

What definition, Polemarchus?

We said a friend was one whom we believe to be an honest man.

And how are we to define him now?

As one who really is honest as well as seeming so. If he merely seems so, he will be only a seeming friend. And the same will apply to enemies.

On this showing, then, it is the good people that will be our friends, the wicked our enemies.

Yes.

You would have us, in fact, add something to our original definition of justice: it will not mean merely doing good to friends and harm to enemies, but doing good to friends who are good, and harm to enemies who are wicked.

Yes, I think that is all right.

Can it really be a just man's business to harm any human being?

Certainly; it is right for him to harm bad men who are his enemies.

But does not harming a horse or a dog mean making it a worse horse or dog, so that each will be a less perfect creature in its own special way?

Yes.

Isn't that also true of human beings—that to harm them means making them worse men by the standard of human excellence?

Yes.

And is not justice a peculiarly human excellence?

Undoubtedly.

To harm a man, then, must mean making him less just.

I suppose so.

But a musician or a riding-master cannot be exercising his special skill, if he makes his pupils unmusical or bad riders.

No.

Whereas the just man is to exercise his justice by making men unjust? Or, in more general terms, the good are to make men bad by exercising their virtue? Can that be so?

No, it cannot.

It can no more be the function of goodness to do harm than of heat to cool or of drought to produce moisture. So if the just man is good, the business of harming people, whether friends or not, must belong to his opposite, the unjust.

I think that is perfectly true, Socrates.

So it was not a wise saying that justice is giving every man his due, if that means that harm is due from the just man to his enemies, as well as help to his friends. That is not true; because we have found that it is never right to harm anyone.

I agree.

Then you and I will make common cause against anyone who attributes that doctrine to Simonides or to any of the old canonical sages, like Bias or Pittacus.

Yes, he said, I am prepared to support you.

Do you know, I think that account of justice, as helping friends and harming enemies, must be due to some despot, so rich and powerful that he thought he could do as he liked—someone like Periander, or Perdiccas, or Xerxes, or Ismenias of Thebes.

That is extremely probable.

Very good, said I; and now that we have disposed of that definition of justice, can anyone suggest another?

Chapter III (I. 336 B–347 E)
Thrasymachus: Justice as the Interest of the Stronger

. . . .

All this time Thrasymachus had been trying more than once to break in upon our conversation; but his neighbours had restrained him, wishing to hear the argument to the end. In the pause after my last words he could keep quiet no longer; but gathering himself up like a wild beast he sprang at us as if he would tear us in pieces. Polemarchus and I were frightened out of our wits, when he burst out to the whole company:

What is the matter with you two, Socrates? Why do you go on in this imbecile way, politely deferring to each other's nonsense? If you really want to know what justice means, stop asking questions and scoring off the answers you get. You know very well it is easier to ask questions than to answer them. Answer yourself, and tell us what you think justice means. I won't have you telling us it is the same as what is obligatory or useful or advantageous or profitable or expedient; I want a clear and precise statement; I won't put up with that sort of verbiage.

I was amazed by this onslaught and looked at him in terror. If I had not seen this wolf before he saw me, I really believe I should have been struck dumb; but fortunately I had looked at him earlier, when he was beginning to get exasperated with our argument; so I was able to reply, though rather tremulously:

Don't be hard on us, Thrasymachus. If Polemarchus and I have gone astray in our search, you may be quite sure the mistake was not intentional. If we had been looking for a piece of gold, we should never have deliberately allowed politeness to spoil our chance of finding it; and now when we are looking for justice, a thing much more precious than gold, you cannot imagine we should defer to each other in that foolish way and not do our best to bring it to light. You must believe we are in earnest, my friend; but I am afraid the task is beyond our powers, and we might expect a man of your ability to pity us instead of being so severe.

Thrasymachus replied with a burst of sardonic laughter.

Good Lord, he said; Socrates at his old trick of shamming ignorance! I knew it; I told the others you would refuse to commit yourself and do anything sooner than answer a question.

Yes, Thrasymachus, I replied; because you are clever enough to know that if you asked someone what are the factors of the number twelve, and at the same time warned him: "Look here, you are not to tell me that 12 is twice 6, or 3 times 4, or 6 times 2, or 4 times 3; I won't put up with any such nonsense"—you must surely see that no one would answer a question put like that. He would say: "What do you mean, Thrasymachus? Am I forbidden to give any of these answers, even if one happens to be right? Do you want me to give a wrong one?" What would you say to that?

Humph! said he. As if that were a fair analogy!

I don't see why it is not, said I; but in any case, do you suppose our barring a certain answer would prevent the man from giving it, if he thought it was the truth?

Do you mean that you are going to give me one of those answers I barred?

I should not be surprised, if it seemed to me true, on reflection.

And what if I give you another definition of justice, better than any of those? What penalty are you prepared to pay?[1]

The penalty deserved by ignorance, which must surely be to receive instruction from the wise. So I would suggest that as a suitable punishment.

I like your notion of a penalty! he said; but you must pay the costs as well.

I will, when I have any money.

That will be all right, said Glaucon; we will all subscribe for Socrates. So let us have your definition, Thrasymachus.

Oh yes, he said; so that Socrates may play the old game of questioning and refuting someone else, instead of giving an answer himself!

But really, I protested, what can you expect from a man who does not know the answer or profess to know it, and, besides that, has been forbidden by no mean authority to put forward any notions he may have? Surely the definition should naturally come from you, who say you do know the answer and can tell it us. Please do not disappoint us. I should take it as a kindness, and I hope you will not be chary of giving Glaucon and the rest of us the advantage of your instruction.

Glaucon and the others added their entreaties to mine. Thrasymachus was evidently longing to win credit, for he was sure he had an admirable answer ready, though he made a show of insisting that I should be the one to reply. In the end he gave way and exclaimed:

So this is what Socrates' wisdom comes to! He refuses to teach, and goes about learning from others without offering so much as thanks in return.

I do learn from others, Thrasymachus; that is quite true; but you are wrong to call me ungrateful. I give in return all I can—praise; for I have no money. And how ready I am to applaud any idea that seems to me sound, you will see in a moment, when you have stated your own; for I am sure that will be sound.

Listen then, Thrasymachus began. What I say is that "just" or "right" means nothing but what is to the interest of the stronger party. Well, where is your applause? You don't mean to give it me.

I will, as soon as I understand, I said. I don't see yet what you mean by right being the interest of the stronger party. For instance, Polydamas, the athlete, is stronger than we are, and it is to his interest to eat beef for the sake of his muscles; but surely you don't mean that the same diet would be good for weaker men and therefore be right for us?

You are trying to be funny, Socrates. It's a low trick to take my words in the sense you think will be most damaging.

No, no, I protested; but you must explain.

Don't you know, then, that a state may be ruled by a despot, or a democracy, or an aristocracy?

Of course.

And that the ruling element is always the strongest?

Yes.

Well then, in every case the laws are made by the ruling party in its own interest; a democracy makes democratic laws, a despot autocratic ones, and so on. By making these laws they define as "right" for their subjects whatever is for their own interest, and they call anyone who breaks them a "wrongdoer" and punish him accordingly. That is what I mean: in all states alike "right" has the same meaning, namely what is for the interest of the party established in power, and that is the strongest. So the sound conclusion is that what is "right" is the same everywhere: the interest of the stronger party.

Now I see what you mean, said I; whether it is true or not, I must try to make out. When you define right in terms of interest, you are yourself giving one of those answers you forbade to me; though, to be sure, you add "to the stronger party."

An insignificant addition, perhaps!

Its importance is not clear yet; what is clear is that we must find out whether your definition is true. I agree myself that right is in a sense a matter of interest; but when you add "to the stronger party," I don't know about that. I must consider.

Go ahead, then.

I will. Tell me this. No doubt you also think it is right to obey the men in power?

I do.

Are they infallible in every type of state, or can they sometimes make a mistake?

Of course they can make a mistake.

In framing laws, then, they may do their work well or badly?

No doubt.

Well, that is to say, when the laws they make are to their own interest; badly, when they are not?

Yes.

But the subjects are to obey any law they lay down, and they will then be doing right?

Of course.

If so, by your account, it will be right to do what is not to the interest of the stronger party, as well as what is so.

What's that you are saying?

Just what you said, I believe; but let us look again. Haven't you admitted that the rulers, when they enjoin certain acts on their subjects, sometimes mistake their own best interests, and at the same time that it is right for the subjects to obey, whatever they may enjoin?

Yes, I suppose so.

Well, that amounts to admitting that it is right to do what is not to the interest of the rulers or the stronger party. They may unwittingly enjoin what is to their own disadvantage; and you say it is right for the others to do as they are told. In that case, their duty must be the opposite of what you said, because the weaker will have been ordered to do what is against the interest of the stronger. You with your intelligence must see how that follows.

Yes, Socrates, said Polemarchus, that is undeniable.

No doubt, Cleitophon broke in, if you are to be a witness on Socrates' side.

No witness is needed, replied Polemarchus; Thrasymachus himself admits that rulers sometimes ordain acts that are to their own disadvantage, and that it is the subjects' duty to do them.

That is because Thrasymachus said it was right to do what you are told by the men in power.

Yes, but he also said that what is to the interest of the stronger party is right; and, after making both these assertions, he admitted that the stronger sometimes command the weaker subjects to act against their interests. From all which it follows that what is in the stronger's interest is no more right than what is not.

No, said Cleitophon; he meant whatever the stronger *believes* to be in his own interest. That is what the subject must do, and what Thrasymachus meant to define as right.

That was not what he said, rejoined Polemarchus.

No matter, Polemarchus, said I; if Thrasymachus says so now, let us take him in that sense. Now, Thrasymachus, tell me, was that what you intended to say—that right means what the stronger thinks is to his interest, whether it really is so or not?

Most certainly not, he replied. Do you suppose I should speak of a man as "stronger" or "superior" at the very moment when he is making a mistake?

I did think you said as much when you admitted that rulers are not always infallible.

That is because you are a quibbler, Socrates. Would you say a man deserves to be called a physician at the moment when he makes a mistake in treating his patient and just in respect of that mistake; or a mathematician, when he does a sum wrong and just in so far as he gets a wrong result? Of course we do commonly speak of a physician or a mathematician or a scholar having made a mistake; but really none of these, I should say, is ever mistaken, in so far as he is worthy of the name we give him. So strictly speaking—and you are all for being precise—no one who practices a craft makes mistakes. A man is mistaken when his knowledge fails him; and at that moment he is no craftsman. And what is true of craftsmanship or any sort of skill is true of the ruler: he is never mistaken so long as he is acting as a ruler; though anyone might speak of a ruler making a mistake, just as he might of a physician. You must understand that I was talking in that loose way when I answered your question just now; but the precise statement is this. The ruler, in so far as he is acting as a ruler, makes no mistakes and consequently enjoins what is best for himself; and that is what the subject is to do. So, as I said at first, "right" means doing what is to the interest of the stronger.

Very well, Thrasymachus, said I. So you think I am quibbling?

I am sure you are.

You believe my questions were maliciously designed to damage your position?

I know it. But you will gain nothing by that. You cannot outwit me by cunning, and you are not the man to crush me in the open.

Bless your soul, I answered, I should not think of trying. But, to prevent any more misunderstanding, when you speak of that ruler or stronger party whose interest the weaker ought to serve, please make it clear whether you are using the words in the ordinary way or in that strict sense you have just defined.

I mean a ruler in the strictest possible sense. Now quibble away and be as malicious as you can. I want no mercy. But you are no match for me.

Do you think me mad enough to beard a lion or try to outwit a Thrasymachus?

You did try just now, he retorted, but it wasn't a success.

. . . .

Enough of this, said I. Now tell me about the physician in that strict sense you spoke of: is it his business to earn money or to treat his patients? Remember, I mean your physician who is worthy of the name.

To treat his patients.

And what of the ship's captain in the true sense? Is he a mere seaman or the commander of the crew?

The commander.

Yes, we shall not speak of him as a seaman just because he is on board a ship. That is not the point. He is called captain because of his skill and authority over the crew.

Quite true.

And each of these people has some special interest?[2]

No doubt.

And the craft in question exists for the very purpose of discovering that interest and providing for it?

Yes.

Can it equally be said of any craft that it has an interest, other than its own greatest possible perfection?

What do you mean by that?

Here is an illustration. If you ask me whether it is sufficient for the human body just to be itself, with no need of help from without, I should say, Certainly not; it has weaknesses and defects, and its condition is not all that it might be. That is precisely why the art of medicine was invented: it was designed to help the body and provide for its interests. Would not that be true?

It would.

But now take the art of medicine itself. Has that any defects or weaknesses? Does any art stand in need of some further perfection, as the eye would be imperfect without the power of vision or the ear without hearing, so that in their case an art is required that will study their interests and provide for their carrying out those functions? Has the art itself any corresponding need of some further art to remedy its defects and look after its interests; and will that further art require yet another, and so on for ever? Or will every art look after its own interests? Or, finally, is it not true that no art needs to have its weaknesses remedied or its interests studied either by another art or by itself, because no art has in itself any weakness or fault, and the only interest it is required to serve is that of its subject-matter? In itself, an art is sound and flawless, so long as it is entirely true to its own nature as an art in the strictest sense—and it is the strict sense that I want you to keep in view. Is not that true?

So it appears.

Then, said I, the art of medicine does not study its own interest, but the needs of the body, just as a groom shows his skill by caring for horses, not for the art of grooming. And so every art seeks, not its own advantage—for it has no deficiencies—but the interest of the subject on which it is exercised.

It appears so.

But surely, Thrasymachus, every art has authority and superior power over its subject.

To this he agreed, though very reluctantly.

So far as arts are concerned, then, no art ever studies or enjoins the interest of the superior or stronger party, but always that of the weaker over which it has authority.

Thrasymachus assented to this at last, though he tried to put up a fight. I then went on:

So the physician, as such, studies only the patient's interest, not his own. For as we agreed, the business of the physician, in the strict sense, is not to make money for himself, but to exercise his power over the patient's body; and the ship's captain, again, considered strictly as no mere sailor, but in command of the crew, will study and enjoin the interest of his subordinates, not his own.

He agreed reluctantly.

And so with government of any kind: no ruler, in so far as he is acting as ruler, will study or enjoin what is for his own interest. All that he says and does will be said and done with a view to what is good and proper for the subject for whom he practises his art.

. . . .

At this point, when everyone could see that Thrasymachus' definition of justice had been turned inside out, instead of making any reply, he said:

Socrates, have you a nurse?

Why do you ask such a question as that? I said. Wouldn't it be better to answer mine?

Because she lets you go about sniffling like a child whose nose wants wiping. She hasn't even taught you to know a shepherd when you see one, or his sheep either.

What makes you say that?

Why, you imagine that a herdsman studies the interests of his flocks or cattle, tending and fattening them up with some other end in view than his master's profit or his own; and so you don't see that, in politics, the genuine ruler regards his subjects exactly like sheep, and thinks of nothing else, night and day, but the good he can get out of them for himself. You are so far out in your notions of right and wrong, justice and injustice, as not to know that "right" actually means what is good for someone else, and to be "just" means serving the interest of the stronger who rules, at the cost of the subject who obeys; whereas injustice is just the reverse, asserting its authority over those innocents who are called just, so that they minister solely to their master's advantage and happiness, and not in the least degree to their own. Innocent as you are yourself, Socrates, you must see that a just man always has the worst of it. Take a private business: when a partnership is wound up, you will never find that the more honest of two partners comes off with the larger share; and in their relations to the state, when there are taxes to be paid, the honest man will pay more than the other on the same amount of property; or if there is money to be distributed, the dishonest will get it all. When either of them hold some public office, even if the just man loses in no other way, his private affairs at any rate will suffer from neglect, while his principles will not allow him to help himself from the public funds; not to mention the offence he will give to his friends and relations by refusing to sacrifice those principles to do them a good turn. Injustice has all the opposite advantages. I am speaking of the type I described just now, the man who can get the better of other people on a large scale: you must fix your eye on him, if you want to judge how much it is to one's own interest not to be just. You can see that best in the most consummate form of injustice, which rewards wrongdoing with supreme welfare and happiness and reduces its victims, if they won't retaliate in kind, to misery. That form is despotism, which uses force or fraud to plunder the goods of others, public or private, sacred or profane, and to do it in a wholesale way. If you are caught committing any one of these crimes on a small scale, you are punished and disgraced; they call it sacrilege, kidnapping, burglary, theft and brigandage. But if, besides taking their property, you turn all your countrymen into slaves, you will hear no more of those ugly names; your countrymen themselves will call you the happiest of men and bless your name, and so will everyone who hears of such a complete triumph of injustice; for when people denounce injustice, it is because they are afraid of suffering wrong, not of doing it. So true is it, Socrates, that injustice, on a grand enough scale, is superior to justice in strength and freedom and autocratic power; and "right," as I said at first, means simply what serves the interest of the stronger party; "wrong" means what is for the interest and profit of oneself.

Having deluged our ears with this torrent of words, as the man at the baths might empty a bucket over one's head, Thrasymachus meant to take himself off; but the company obliged him to stay and defend his position. I was specially urgent in my entreaties.

My good Thrasymachus, said I, do you propose to fling a doctrine like that at our heads and then go away without explaining it properly or letting us point out to you whether it is true or not? Is it so small a matter in your eyes to determine the whole course of conduct which every one of us must follow to get the best out of life?

Don't I realize it is a serious matter? he retorted.

Apparently not, said I; or else you have no consideration for us, and do not care whether we shall lead better or worse lives for being ignorant of this truth you profess to know. Do take the trouble to let us into your secret; if you treat us handsomely, you may be sure it will be a good investment; there are so many of us to show our gratitude. I will make no secret of my own conviction, which is that injustice is not more profitable than justice, even when left free to work its will unchecked. No; let your unjust man have full power to do wrong, whether by successful violence or by escaping detection; all the same he will not convince me that he will gain more than he would by being just. There may be others here who feel as I do, and set justice above injustice. It is for you to convince us that we are not well advised.

How can I? he replied. If you are not convinced by what I have just said, what more can I do for you? Do you want to be fed with my ideas out of a spoon?

God forbid! I exclaimed; not that. But I do want you to stand by your own words; or, if you shift your ground, shift it openly and stop trying to hoodwink us as you are doing now. You see, Thrasymachus, to go back to your earlier argument, in speaking of the shepherd you did not think it necessary to keep to that strict sense you laid down when you defined the genuine physician. You represent him, in his character of shepherd, as feeding up his flock, not for their own sake but for the table or the market, as if he were out to make money as a caterer or a cattle-dealer, rather than a shepherd. Surely the sole concern of the shepherd's art is to do the best for the charges put under its care; its own best interest is sufficiently provided for, so long as it does not fall short of all that shepherding should imply. On that principle it followed, I thought, that any kind of authority, in the state or in private life, must, in its character of authority, consider solely what is best for those under its care. Now what is your opinion? Do you think that the men who govern states—I mean rulers in the strict sense—have no reluctance to hold office?

I don't think so, he replied; I know it.

Well, but haven't you noticed, Thrasymachus, that in other positions of authority no one is willing to act unless he is paid wages, which he demands on the assumption that all the benefit of his action will go to his charges? Tell me: Don't we always distinguish one form of skill from another by its power to effect some particular result? Do say what you really think, so that we may get on.

Yes, that is the distinction.

And also each brings us some benefit that is peculiar to it: medicine gives health, for example; the art of navigation, safety at sea; and so on.

Yes.

And wage-earning brings us wages; that is its distinctive product. Now, speaking with that precision which you proposed, you would not say that the art of navigation is the same as the art of medicine, merely on the ground that a ship's captain regained his health on a voyage, because the sea air was good for him. No more would you identify the practice of medicine with wage-earning because a man may keep his health while earning wages, or a physician attending a case may receive a fee.

No.

And, since we agreed that the benefit obtained by each form of skill is peculiar to it, any common benefit enjoyed alike by all these practitioners must come from some further practice common to them all?

It would seem so.

Yes, we must say that if they all earn wages, they get that benefit in so far as they are engaged in wage-earning as well as in practising their several arts.

He agreed reluctantly.

This benefit, then—the receipt of wages—does not come to a man from his special art. If we are to speak strictly, the physician, as such, produces health; the builder, a house; and then each, in his further capacity of wage-earner, gets his pay. Thus every art has its own function and benefits its proper subject. But suppose the practitioner is not paid; does he then get any benefit from his art?

Clearly not.

And is he doing no good to anyone either, when he works for nothing?

No, I suppose he does some good.

Well then, Thrasymachus, it is now clear that no form of skill or authority provides for its own benefit. As we were saying some time ago, it always studies and prescribes what is good for its subject—the interest of the weaker party, not of the stronger. And that, my friend, is why I said that no one is willing to be in a position of authority and undertake to set straight other men's troubles, without demanding to be paid; because, if he is to do his work well, he will never, in his capacity of ruler, do, or command others to do, what is best for himself, but only what is best for the subject. For that reason, if he is to consent, he must have his recompense, in the shape of money or honour, or of punishment in case of refusal.

What do you mean, Socrates? asked Glaucon. I recognize two of your three kinds of reward; but I don't understand what you mean by speaking of punishment as a recompense.

Then you don't understand the recompense required by the best type of men, or their motive for accepting authority when they do consent. You surely know that a passion for honours or for money is rightly regarded as something to be ashamed of.

Yes, I do.

For that reason, I said, good men are unwilling to rule, either for money's sake or for honour. They have no wish to be called mercenary for demanding to be paid, or thieves for making a secret profit out of their office; nor yet will honours tempt them, for they are not ambitious. So they must be forced to consent under threat of penalty; that may be why a readiness to accept power under no such constraint is thought discreditable. And the heaviest penalty for declining to rule is to be ruled by someone inferior to yourself. That is the fear, I believe, that makes decent people accept power; and when they do so, they face the prospect of authority with no idea that they are coming into the enjoyment of a comfortable berth; it is forced upon them because they can find no one better than themselves, or even as good, to be entrusted with power. If there could ever be a society of perfect men, there might well be as much competition to evade office as there now is to gain it; and it would then be clearly seen that the genuine ruler's nature is to seek only the advantage of the subject, with the consequence that any man of understanding would sooner have another to do the best for him than be at the pains to do the best for that other himself. On this point, then, I entirely disagree with Thrasymachus' doctrine that right means what is to the interest of the stronger.

Chapter IV (I. 347 E–354 C)
Thrasymachus: Is Injustice More profitable Than Justice?

. . . .

However, I continued, we may return to that question later. Much more important is the position Thrasymachus is asserting now: that a life of injustice is to be preferred to a life of justice. Which side do you take, Glaucon? Where do you think the truth lies?

I should say that the just life is the better worth having.

You heard Thrasymachus' catalogue of all the good things in store for injustice?

I did, but I am not convinced.

Shall we try to convert him, then, supposing we can find some way to prove him wrong?

By all means.

We might answer Thrasymachus' case in a set speech of our own, drawing up a corresponding list of the advantages of justice; he would then have the right to reply, and we should make our final rejoinder; but after that we should have to count up and measure the advantages on each list, and we should need a jury to decide between us. Whereas, if we go on as before, each securing the agreement of the other side, we can combine the functions of advocate and judge. We will take whichever course you prefer.

I prefer the second, said Glaucon.

Come then, Thrasymachus, said I, let us start afresh with our questions. You say that injustice pays better than justice, when both are carried to the furthest point?

I do, he replied; and I have told you why.

And how would you describe them? I suppose you would call one of them an excellence and the other a defect?

Of course.

Justice an excellence, and injustice a defect?

Now is that likely, when I am telling you that injustice pays, and justice does not?

Then what do you say?

The opposite.

That justice is a defect?

No; rather the mark of a good-natured simpleton.

Injustice, then, implies being ill-natured?

No; I should call it good policy.

Do you think the unjust are positively superior in character and intelligence, Thrasymachus?

Yes, if they are the sort that can carry injustice to perfection and make themselves masters of whole cities and nations. Perhaps you think I was talking of pickpockets. There is profit even in that trade, if you can escape detection; but it doesn't come to much as compared with the gains I was describing.

I understand you now on that point, I replied. What astonished me was that you should class injustice with superior character and intelligence and justice with the reverse.

Well, I do, he rejoined.

That is a much more stubborn position, my friend; and it is not so easy to see how to assail it. If you would admit that injustice, however well it pays, is nevertheless, as some people think, a defect and a discreditable thing, then we could argue on generally accepted principles. But now that you have gone so far as to rank it with superior character and intelligence, obviously you will say it is an admirable thing as well as a source of strength, and has all the other qualities we have attributed to justice.

You read my thoughts like a book, he replied.

However, I went on, it is no good shirking; I must go through with the argument, so long as I can be sure you are really speaking your mind. I do believe you are not playing with us now, Thrasymachus, but stating the truth as you conceive it.

Why not refute the doctrine? he said. What does it matter to you whether I believe it or not?

It does not matter, I replied.

. . . .

Thrasymachus' assent was dragged out of him with a reluctance of which my account gives no idea. He was sweating at every pore, for the weather was hot; and I saw then what I had never seen before—Thrasymachus blushing. However, now that we had agreed that justice implies superior character and intelligence, injustice a deficiency in both respects, I went on:

Good; let us take that as settled. But we were also saying that injustice was a source of strength. Do you remember, Thrasymachus?

I do remember; only your last argument does not satisfy me, and I could say a good deal about that. But if I did, you would tell me I was haranguing you like a public meeting. So either let me speak my mind at length, or else, if you want to ask questions, ask them, and I will nod or shake my head, and say "Hm?" as we do to encourage an old woman telling us a story.

No, please, said I; don't give your assent against your real opinion.

Anything to please you, he rejoined, since you won't let me have my say. What more do you want?

Nothing. I replied. If that is what you mean to do, I will go on with my questions.

Go on, then.

Well, to continue where we left off. I will repeat my question: What is the nature and quality of justice as compared with injustice? It was suggested, I believe, that injustice is the stronger and more effective of the two; but now we have seen that justice implies superior character and intelligence, it will not be hard to show that it will also be superior in power to injustice, which implies ignorance and stupidity; that must be obvious to anyone. However, I would rather look deeper into this matter than take it as settled offhand. Would you agree that a state may be unjust and may try to enslave other states or to hold a number of others in subjection unjustly?

Of course it may, he said; above all if it is the best sort of state, which carries injustice to perfection.

I understand, said I; that was your view. But I am wondering whether a state can do without justice when it is asserting its superior power over another in that way.

Not if you are right, that justice implies intelligence; but if I am right, injustice will be needed.

I am delighted with your answer, Thrasymachus; this is much better than just nodding and shaking your head.

It is all to oblige you.

Thank you. Please add to your kindness by telling me whether any set of men—a state or an army or a band of robbers or thieves—who were acting together for some unjust purpose would be likely to succeed, if they were always trying to injure one another. Wouldn't they do better, if they did not?

Yes, they would.

Because, of course, such injuries must set them quarrelling and hating each other. Only fair treatment can make men friendly and of one mind.

Be it so, he said; I don't want to differ from you.

Thank you once more, I replied. But don't you agree that, if injustice has this effect of implanting hatred wherever it exists, it must make any set of people, whether freemen or slaves, split into factions, at feud with one another and incapable of any joint action?

Yes.

And so with any two individuals: injustice will set them at variance and make them enemies to each other as well as to everyone who is just.

It will.

And will it not keep its character and have the same effect, if it exists in a single person?

Let us suppose so.

The effect being, apparently, wherever it occurs—in a state or a family or an army or anywhere else—to make united action impossible because of factions and quarrels, and moreover to set whatever it resides in at enmity with itself as well as with any opponent and with all who are just.

Yes, certainly.

Then I suppose it will produce the same natural results in an individual. He will have a divided mind and be incapable of action, for lack of singleness of purpose; and he will be at enmity with all who are just as well as with himself?

Yes.

And "all who are just" surely includes the gods?

Let us suppose so.

The unjust man, then, will be a god-forsaken creature; the good-will of heaven will be for the just.

Enjoy your triumph, said Thrasymachus. You need not fear my contradicting you. I have no wish to give offence to the company.

. . . .

You will make my enjoyment complete, I replied, if you will answer my further questions in the same way. We have made out so far that just men are superior in character and intelligence and more effective in action. Indeed without justice men cannot act together at all; it is not strictly true to speak of such people as ever having effected any strong action in common. Had they been thoroughly unjust, they could not have kept their hands off one another; they must have had some justice in them, enough to keep them from injuring one another at the same time with their victims. This it was that enabled them to achieve what they did achieve: their injustice only partially incapacitated them for their career of wrongdoing; if perfect, it would have disabled them for any action whatsoever. I can see that all this is true, as against your original position. But there is a further question which we postponed: Is the life of justice the better and happier life? What we have said already leaves no doubt in my mind; but we ought to consider more carefully, for this is no light matter: it is the question, what is the right way to live?

Go on, then.

I will, said I. Some things have a function;[3] a horse, for instance, is useful for certain kinds of work. Would you agree to define a thing's function in general as the work for which that thing is the only instrument or the best one?

I don't understand.

Take an example. We can see only with the eyes, hear only with the ears; and seeing and hearing might be called the functions of those organs.

Yes.

Or again, you might cut vine-shoots with a carving-knife or a chisel or many other tools, but with none so well as with a pruning-knife made for the purpose; and we may call that its function.

True.

Now, I expect, you see better what I meant by suggesting that a thing's function is the work that it alone can do, or can do better than anything else.

Yes, I will accept that definition.

Good, said I; and to take the same examples, the eye and the ear, which we said have each its particular function: have they not also a specific excellence or virtue? Is not that always the case with things that have some appointed work to do?

Yes.

Now consider: is the eye likely to do its work well, if you take away its peculiar virtue and substitute the corresponding defect?

Of course not, if you mean substituting blindness for the power of sight.

I mean whatever its virtue may be; I have not come to that yet. I am only asking, whether it is true of things with a function—eyes or ears or anything else—that there is always some specific virtue which enables them to work well; and if they are deprived of that virtue, they work badly.

I think that is true.

Then the next point is this. Has the soul a function that can be performed by nothing else? Take for example such actions as deliberating or taking charge and exercising control: is not the soul the only thing of which you can say that these are its proper and peculiar work?

That is so.

And again, living—is not that above all the function of the soul?

No doubt.

And we also speak of the soul as having a certain specific excellence or virtue?

Yes.

Then, Thrasymachus, if the soul is robbed of its peculiar virtue, it cannot possibly do its work well. It must exercise its power of controlling and taking charge well or ill according as it is itself in a good or a bad state.

That follows.

And did we not agree that the virtue of the soul is justice, and injustice its defect?

We did.

So it follows that a just soul, or in other words a just man, will live well; the unjust will not.

Apparently, according to your argument.

But living well involves well-being and happiness.

Naturally.

Then only the just man is happy; injustice will involve unhappiness.

Be it so.

But you cannot say it pays better to be unhappy.

Of course not.

Injustice then, my dear Thrasymachus, can never pay better than justice.

Well, he replied, this is a feast-day, and you

may take all this as your share of the entertainment.

For which I have to thank you, Thrasymachus; you have been so gentle with me since you recovered your temper. It is my own fault if the entertainment has not been satisfactory. I have been behaving like a greedy guest, snatching a taste of every new dish that comes round before he has properly enjoyed the last. We began by looking for a definition of justice; but before we had found one, I dropped that question and hurried on to ask whether or not it involved superior character and intelligence; and then, as soon as another idea cropped up, that injustice pays better, I could not refrain from pursuing that.

So now the whole conversation has left me completely in the dark; for so long as I do not know what justice is, I am hardly likely to know whether or not it is a virtue, or whether it makes a man happy or unhappy.

Part II (Books II–IV, 445 B) Justice in the State and in the Individual

Chapter V (II. 357 A–367 E) The Problem Stated

. . . .

I thought that, with these words, I was quit of the discussion; but it seems this was only a prelude. Glaucon, undaunted as ever, was not content to let Thrasymachus abandon the field.

Socrates, he broke out, you have made a show of proving that justice is better than injustice in every way. Is that enough, or do you want us to be really convinced?

Certainly I do, if it rests with me.

Then you are not going the right way about it. I want to know how you classify the things we call good. Are there not some which we should wish to have, not for their consequences, but just for their own sake, such as harmless pleasures and enjoyments that have no further result beyond the satisfaction of the moment?

Yes, I think there are good things of that description.

And also some that we value both for their own sake and for their consequences—things like knowledge and health and the use of our eyes?

Yes.

And a third class which would include physical training, medical treatment, earning one's bread as a doctor or otherwise—useful, but burdensome things, which we want only for the sake of the profit or other benefit they bring.

Yes, there is that third class. What then?

In which class do you place justice?

I should say, in the highest, as a thing which anyone who is to gain happiness must value both for itself and for its results.

Well, that is not the common opinion. Most people would say it was one of those things, tiresome and disagreeable in themselves, which we cannot avoid practising for the sake of reward or a good reputation.

I know, said I; that is why Thrasymachus has been finding fault with it all this time and praising injustice. But I seem to be slow in seeing his point.

Listen to me, then, and see if you agree with mine. There was no need, I think, for Thrasymachus to yield so readily. like a snake you had charmed into submission; and nothing so far said about justice and injustice has been established to my satisfaction. I want to be told what each of them really is, and what effect each has, in itself, on the soul that harbours it, when all rewards and consequences are left out of account. So here is my plan, if you approve, I shall revive Thrasymachus' theory. First, I will state what is commonly held about the nature of justice and its origin; secondly, I shall maintain that it is always practised with reluctance, not as good in itself, but as a thing one cannot do without; and thirdly, that this reluctance is reasonable, because the life of injustice is much the better life of the two—so people say. That is not what I think myself, Socrates; only I am bewildered by all that Thrasymachus and ever so many others have dinned into my ears; and I have never yet heard the case for justice stated as I wish to hear it. You, I believe, if anyone, can tell me what is to be said in praise of justice in and for itself; that is what I want. Accordingly, I shall set you an example by glorifying the life of injustice with all the energy that I hope you will show later in denouncing it and exalting justice in its stead. Will that plan suit you?

Nothing could be better, I replied. Of all subjects this is one on which a sensible man must always be glad to exchange ideas.

Good, said Glaucon. Listen then, and I will begin with my first point: the nature and origin of justice.

What people say is that to do wrong is, in itself, a desirable thing; on the other hand, it is not at all desirable to suffer wrong, and the harm to the sufferer outweighs the advantage to the doer. Consequently, when men have had a taste of both, those who have not the power to seize the advantage and escape the harm decide that they would be better off if they made a compact neither to do wrong nor to suffer it. Hence they began to make laws and covenants with one another; and whatever the law prescribed they called lawful and right. That is what right or justice is and how it came into existence; it stands half-way between the best thing of all—to do wrong with impunity— and the worst, which is to suffer wrong without the power to retaliate. So justice is accepted as a compromise, and valued, not as good in itself, but for lack of power to do wrong; no man worthy of the name, who had that power, would ever enter into such a compact with anyone; he would be mad if he did. That, Socrates, is the nature of justice according to this account, and such the circumstances in which it arose.

The next point is that men practice it against the grain, for lack of power to do wrong. How true that is, we shall best see if we imagine two men, one just, the other unjust, given full license to do whatever they like, and then follow them to observe where each will be led by his desires. We shall catch the just man taking the same road as the unjust; he will be moved by self-interest, the end which it is natural to every creature to pursue as good, until forcibly turned aside by law and custom to respect the principle of equality.

Now, the easiest way to give them that complete liberty of action would be to imagine them possessed of the talisman found by Gyges, the ancestor of the famous Lydian. The story tells how he was a shepherd in the King's service. One day there was a great storm, and the ground where his flock was feeding was rent by an earthquake. Astonished at the sight, he went down into the chasm and saw, among other wonders of which the story tells, a brazen horse, hollow, with windows in its sides. Peering in, he saw a dead body, which seemed to be of more than human size. It was naked save for a gold ring, which he took from the finger and made his way out. When the shepherds met, as they did every month, to send an account to the King of the state of his flocks, Gyges came wearing the ring. As he was sitting with the others, he happened to turn the bezel of the ring inside his hand. At once he became invisible, and his companions, to his surprise, began to speak of him as if he had left them. Then, as he was fingering the ring, he turned the bezel outwards and became visible again. With that, he set about testing the ring to see if it really had this power, and always with the same result: according as he turned the bezel inside or out he vanished and reappeared. After this discovery he contrived to be one of the messengers sent to the court. There he seduced the Queen, and with her help murdered the King and seized the throne.

Now suppose there were two such magic rings, and one were given to the just man, the other to the unjust. No one, it is commonly believed, would have such iron strength of mind as to stand fast in doing right or keep his hands off other men's goods, when he could go to the market-place and fearlessly help himself to anything he wanted, enter houses and sleep with any woman he chose, set prisoners free and kill men at his pleasure, and in a word go about among men with the powers of a god. He would behave no better than the other; both would take the same course. Surely this would be strong proof that men do right only under compulsion; no individual thinks of it as good for him personally, since he does wrong whenever he finds he has the power. Every man believes that wrongdoing pays him personally much better, and, according to this theory, that is the truth. Granted full licence to do as he liked, people would think him a miserable fool if they found him refusing to wrong his neighbours or to touch their belongings, though in public they would keep up a pretence of praising his conduct, for fear of being wronged themselves. So much for that.

Finally, if we are really to judge between the two lives, the only way is to contrast the extremes of justice and injustice. We can best do that by imagining our two men to be perfect types, and crediting both to the full with the qualities they need for their respective ways of life. To begin with the unjust man: he must be like any consummate master of a craft, a physician or a captain, who, knowing just what his art can do, never tries to do more, and can always retrieve a false step. The unjust man, if he is to reach perfection, must be equally discreet in his criminal attempts, and he must not be found out, or we shall think him a bungler; for the highest pitch of injustice is to seem just when you are not. So we must endow our man with the full complement of injustice; we must allow him to have secured a spotless reputation for virtue while committing the blackest crimes; he must be able to retrieve any mistake, to defend himself with convincing eloquence if his misdeeds are denounced, and, when force is required, to bear down all opposition by his courage and strength and by his command of friends and money.

Now set beside this paragon the just man in his simplicity and nobleness, one who, in Aeschylus' words, ''would be, not seem, the best.'' There must, indeed, be no such seeming; for if his character were apparent, his reputation would bring him honours and rewards, and then we should not know whether it was for their sake that he was just or for justice's sake alone. He must be stripped of everything but justice, and denied every advantage the other enjoyed. Doing no wrong, he must have the worst reputation for wrong-doing, to test whether his virtue is proof against all that comes of having a bad name; and under this lifelong imputation of wickedness, let him hold on his course of justice unwavering to the point of death. And so, when the two men have carried their justice and injustice to the last extreme, we may judge which is the happier.

My dear Glaucon, I exclaimed, how vigorously you scour these two characters clean for inspection, as if you were burnishing a couple of statues!

I am doing my best, he answered. Well, given two such characters, it is not hard, I fancy, to describe the sort of life that each of them may expect; and if the description sounds rather coarse, take it as coming from those who cry up the merits of injustice rather than from me. They will tell you that our just man will be thrown into prison, scourged and racked, will have his eyes burnt out, and, after every kind of torment, be impaled. That will teach him how much better it is to seem virtuous than to be so. In fact those lines of Aeschylus I quoted are more fitly applied to the unjust man, who, they say, is a realist and does not live for appearances: ''he would be, not seem'' unjust,

> reaping the harvest sown
> In those deep furrows of the thoughtful heart
> Whence wisdom springs.

With his reputation for virtue, he will hold offices of state, ally himself by marriage to any family he may choose, become a partner in any business, and, having no scruples about being dishonest, turn all these advantages to profit. If he is involved in a lawsuit, public or private, he will get the better of his opponents, grow rich on the proceeds, and be able to help his friends and harm his enemies. Finally, he can make sacrifices to the gods and dedicate offerings with due magnificence, and, being in a much better position than the just man to serve the gods as well as his chosen friends, he may reasonably hope to stand higher in the favour of heaven. So much better, they say, Socrates, is the life prepared for the unjust by gods and men.

Here Glaucon ended, and I was meditating a reply, when his borther Adeimantus exclaimed:

Surely, Socrates, you cannot suppose that that is all there is to be said.

Why, isn't it? said I.

The most essential part of the case has not been mentioned, he replied.

Well, I answered, there is a proverb about a brother's aid. If Glaucon has failed, it is for you to make good his shortcomings; though, so far as I am concerned, he has said quite enough to put me out of the running and leave me powerless to rescue the cause of justice.

Nonsense, said Adeimantus; there is more to be said, and you must listen to me. If we want a clear view of what I take to be Glaucon's meaning, we must study the opposite side fo the case, the arguments used when justice is praised and injustice condemned. When children are told by their fathers and all their pastors and masters that it is a good thing to be just, what is commended is not justice in itself but the respectability it brings. They are to let men see how just they are, in order to gain high positions and marry well and win all the other advantages which Glaucon mentioned, since the just man owes all these to his good reputation.

In this matter of having a good name, they go farther still: they throw in the favourable opinion of heaven, and can tell us of no end of good things with which they say the gods reward piety. There is the good old Hesiod, who says the gods make the just man's oak-trees "bear acorns at the top and bees in the middle; and their sheep's fleeces are heavy with wool," and a great many other blessings of that sort. And Homer speaks in the same strain:

> As when a blameless king fears the gods and upholds right judgment; then the dark earth yields wheat and barley, and the trees are laden with fruit; the young of his flocks are strong, and the sea gives abundance of fish.

Musaeus and his son Eumolpus enlarge in still more spirited terms upon the rewards from heaven they promise to the righteous. They take them to the other world and provide them with a banquet of the Blest, where they sit for all time carousing with garlands on their heads, as if virtue could not be more nobly recompensed than by an eternity of intoxication. Others, again, carry the rewards of heaven yet a stage farther: the pious man who keeps his oaths is to have children's children and to leave a posterity after him. When they have sung the praises of justice in that strain, with more to same effect, they proceed to plunge the sinners and unrighteous men into a pool of mud in the world below, and set them to fetch water in a sieve. Even in this life, too, they give them a bad name, and make out that the unjust suffer all those penalties which Glaucon described as falling upon the good man who has a bed reputation: they can think of no others. That is how justice is recommended and injustice denounced.

Besides all this, think of the way in which justice and injustice are spoken of, not only in ordinary life, but by the poets. All with one voice reiterate that self-control and justice, admirable as they may be, are difficult and irksome, whereas vice and injustice are pleasant and very easily to be had; it is mere convention to regard them as discreditable. They tell us that dishonesty generally pays better than honesty. They will cheerfully speak of a bad man as happy and load him with honours and social esteem, provided he be rich and otherwise powerful; while they despise and disregard one who has neither power nor wealth, though all the while they acknowledge that he is the better man of the two.

Most surprising of all is what they say about the gods and virtue: that heaven itself often allots misfortunes and a hard life to the good man, and gives prosperity to the wicked. Mendicant priests and soothsayers come to the rich man's door with a story of a power they possess by the gift of heaven to atone for any offence that he or his ancestors have committed with incantations and sacrifice, agreeably accompanied by feasting. If he wishes to injure an enemy, he can, at a trifling expense, do him a hurt with equal case, whether he be an honest man or not, by means of certain invocations and spells which, as they profess, prevail upon the gods to do their bidding. In support of all these claims they call the poets to witness. Some, by way of advertising the easiness of vice, quote the words: "Unto wickedness men attain easily and in multitudes; smooth is the way and her dwelling is very near at hand. But the gods have ordained much sweat upon the path to virtue" and a long road that is rough and steep.

Others, to show that men can turn the gods from their purpose, cite Homer: "Even the gods themselves listen to entreaty. Their hearts are turned by the entreaties of men with sacrifice and humble prayers and libation and burnt offering, whensoever anyone transgresses and does amiss." They produce a whole farrago of books in which Musaeus and Orpheus, described as descendants of the Muses and the Moon, prescribe their ritual; and they persuade entire communities, as well as individuals, that, both in this life and after death, wrongdoing may be absolved and purged away by means of sacrifices and agreeable performances which they are pleased to call rites of initiation. These deliver us from punishment in the other world, where awful things are in store for all who neglect to sacrifice.

Now, my dear Socrates, when all this stuff is talked about the estimation in which virtue and vice are held by heaven and by mankind, what effect can we suppose it has upon the mind of a young man quick-witted enough to gather honey from all these flowers of popular wisdom and to draw his own conclusions as to the sort of person he should be and the way he should go in order to lead the best possible life? In all likelihood he would ask himself, in Pindar's words: "Will the way of right or the by-paths of deceit lead me to the higher fortress," where I may entrench myself for the rest of my life? For, according to what they tell me, I have nothing to gain but trouble and manifest loss from being honest, unless I also get a name for being so; whereas, if I am dishonest and provide myself with a reputation for honesty, they promise me a marvellous career. Very well, then; since "outward seeming," as wise men inform me, "overpowers the truth" and decides the question of happiness, I had better go in for appearances wholeheartedly. I must ensconce myself behind an imposing facade designed to look like virtue, and trail the fox behind me, "the cunning shifty fox"—Archilochus knew the world as well as any man. You may say it is not so easy to be wicked without ever being found out. Perhaps not; but great things are never easy. Anyhow, if we are to reach happiness, everything we have been told points to this as the road to be followed. We will form secret socieites to save us from exposure; besides, there are men who teach the art of winning over popular assemlies and courts of law; so that, one way or another, by persuasion or violence, we shall get the better of our neighbours without being punished. You might object that the gods are not to be deceived and are beyond the reach of violence. But suppose that there are no gods, or that they do not concern themselves with the doings of men; why should we concern ourselves to deceive them? Or, if the gods do exist and care for mankind, all we know or have ever heard about them comes from current tradition and from the poets who recount their family history, and these same authorities also assure us that they can be won over and turned from their purpose "by sacrifice and humble prayers" and votive offerings. We must either accept both these statements or neither. If we are to accept both, we had better do wrong and use part of the proceeds to offer sacrifice. By being just we may escape the punishment of heaven, but we shall be renouncing the profits of injustice; whereas by doing wrong we shall make our profit and escape punishment into the bargain, by means of those entreaties which win over the gods when we transgress and do amiss. But then, you will say, in the other world the penalty for our misdeeds on earth will fall either upon us or upon our children's children. We can counter that objection by reckoning on the great efficacy of mystic rites and the divinities of absolution, vouched for by the most advanced societies and by the descendants of the gods who have appeared as poets and spokesmen of heavenly inspiration.

What reason, then, remains for preferring justice to the extreme of injustice, when common belief and the best authorities promise us the fulfilment of our desires in this life and the next, if only we conceal our ill-doing under a veneer of decent behaviour? The upshot is, Socrates, that no man possessed of superior powers of mind or person or rank or wealth will set any value on justice; he is more likely to laugh when he hears it praised. So, even one who could prove my case false and were quite sure that justice is best, far from being indignant with the unjust, will be very ready to excuse them. He will know that, here and there, a man may refrain from wrong because it revolts some instinct he is graced with or because he has come to know the truth; no one else is virtuous of his own will; it is only lack of spirit or the infirmity of age or some other weakness that makes men condemn the iniquities they have not the strength to practise. This is easily seen: give such a man the power, and he will be the first to use it to the utmost.

What lies at the bottom of all this is nothing but the fact from which Glaucon, as well as I, started upon this long discourse. We put it to you, Scorates, with all respect, in this way. All you who profess to sing the praises of right conduct, from the ancient heroes whose legends have survived down to the men of the present day, have never denounced injustice or praised justice apart from the reputation, honours, and rewards they bring; but what effect either of them in itself has upon its possessor when it dwells in his soul unseen of gods or men, no poet or ordinary man has ever yet explained. No one has proved that a soul can harbour no worse evil than injustice, no greater good that justice. Had all of you said that from the first and tried to convince us from our youth up, we should not be keeping watch upon our neighbours to prevent them from doing wrong to us, but everyone would keep a far more effectual watch over himself, for fear lest by wronging others he should open his doors to the worst of all evils.

That, Socrates, is the view of justice and injustice which Thrasymachus and, no doubt, others would state, perhaps in even stronger words. For myself, I believe it to be a gross perversion of their true worth and effect; but, as I must frankly confess, I have put the case with all the force I could muster because I want to hear the other side from you. You must not be content with proving that justice is superior to injustice; you must make clear what good or what harm each of them does to its possessor, taking it simply in itself and, as Glaucon required, leaving out of account the reputation it bears. For unless you deprive each of its true reputation and attach to it the false one, we shall say that you are praising or denouncing nothing more than the appearances in either case, and recommending us to do wrong without being found out; and that you hold with Thrasymachus that right means what is good for someone else, being the interest of the stronger, and wrong is what really pays, serving one's own interest at the expense of the weaker. You have agreed that justice belongs to that highest class of good things which are worth having not only for their consequences, but much more for their own sakes—things like sight and hearing, knowledge, and health, whose value is genuine and intrinsic, not dependent on opinion. So I want you, in commending justice, to consider only how justice, in itself, benefits a man who has it in him, and how injustice harms him, leaving rewards and reputation out of account. I might put up with others dwelling on those outward effects as a reason for praising the one and condemning the other; but from you, who have spent your life in the study of this question, I must beg leave to demand something better. You must not be content merely to prove that justice is superior to injustice, but explain how one is good, the other evil, in virtue of the intrinsic effect each has on its possessor, whether gods or men see it or not.

Chapter VI (II. 367 E—372 A) The Rudiments of Social Organization

. . . .

I was delighted with these speeches from Glaucon and Adeimantus, whose gifts I had always admired. How right, I exclaimed, was Glaucon's lover to begin that poem of his on your exploits at the battle of Megara by describing you two as the

sons divine
Of Ariston's noble line!

Like father, like sons: there must indeed be some divine quality in your nature, if you can plead the cause of injustice so eloquently and still not be convinced yourselves that it is better than justice. That you are not really convinced I am sure from all I know of your dispositions, though your words might well have left me in doubt. But the more I trust you, the harder I find it to reply. How can I come to the rescue? I have no faith in my own powers, when I remember that you were not satisfied with the proof I thought I had given to Thrasymachus that it is better to be just. And yet I cannot stand by and hear justice reviled without lifting a finger. I am afraid to commit a sin by holding aloof while I have breath and strength to say a word in its defence. So there is nothing for it but to do the best I can.

Glaucon and the others begged me to step into the breach and carry through our inquiry into the real nature of justice and injustice, and the truth about their respective advantages. So I told them what I thought. This is a very obscure question, I said, and we shall need keen sight to see our way. Now, as we are not remarkably clever, I will make a suggestion as to how we should proceed. Imagine a rather short-sighted person told to read an inscription in small letters from some way off. He would think it a godsend if someone pointed out that the same inscription was written up elsewhere on a bigger scale, so that he could first read the larger characters and then make out whether the smaller ones were the same.

No doubt, said Adeimantus; but what analogy do you see in that to our inquiry?

I will tell you. We think of justice as a quality that may exist in a whole community as well as in an individual, and the community is the bigger of the two. Possibly, then, we may find justice there in larger proportions, easier to make out. So I suggest that we should begin by inquiring what justice means in a state. Then we can go on to look for its counterpart on a smaller scale in the individual.

That seems a good plan, he agreed.

Well then, I continued, suppose we imagine a state coming into being before our eyes. We might then be able to watch the growth of justice or of injustice within it. When that is done, we may hope it will be easier to find what we are looking for.

Much easier.

Shall we try, then, to carry out this scheme? I fancy it will be no light undertaking; so you had better think twice.

No need for that, said Adeimantus. Don't waste any more time.

My notion is, said I, that a state comes into existence because no individual is self-sufficing; we all have many needs. But perhaps you can suggest some different origin for the foundation of a community?

No, I agree with you.

So, having all these needs, we call in one another's help to satisfy our various requirements; and when we have collected a number of helpers and associates to live together in one place, we call that settlement a state.

Yes.

So if one man gives another what he has to give in exchange for what he can get, it is because each finds that to do so is for his own advantage.

Certainly.

Very well, said I. Now let us build up our imaginary state from the beginning. Apparently, it will owe its existence to our needs, the first and greatest need being the provision of food to keep us alive. Next we shall want a house; and thirdly, such things as clothing.

True.

How will our state be able to supply all these demands? We shall need at least one man to be a farmer, another a builder, and a third a weaver. Will that do, or shall we add a shoemaker and one or two more to provide for our personal wants?

By all means.

The minimum state, then, will consist of four or five men.

Apparently.

Now here is a further point. Is each one of them to bring the product of his work into a common stock? Should our one farmer, for example, provide food enough for four people and spend the whole of his working time in producing corn, so as to share with the rest; or should he take no notice of them and spend only a quarter of his time on growing just enough corn for himself, and divide the other three-quarters between building his house, weaving his clothes, and making his shoes, so as to save the trouble of sharing with others and attend himself to all his own concerns?

The first plan might be the easier, replied Adeimantus.

That may very well be so, said I; for, as you spoke, it occurred to me, for one thing, that no two people are born exactly alike. There are innate differences which fit them for different occupations.

I agree.

And will a man do better working at many trades, or keeping to one only?

Keeping to one.

And there is another point: obviously work may be ruined, if you let the right time go by. The workman must wait upon the work; it will not wait upon his leisure and allow itself to be done in a spare moment. So the conclusion is that more things will be produced and the work be more easily and better done, when every man is set free from all other occupations to do, at the right time, the one thing for which he is naturally fitted.

That is certainly true.

We shall need more than four citizens, then, to supply all those necessaries we mentioned. You see, Adeimantus, if the farmer is to have a good plough and spade and other tools, he will not make them himself. No more will the builder and weaver and shoemaker make all the many implements they need. So quite a number of carpenters and smiths and other craftsmen must be enlisted. Our miniature state is beginning to grow.

It is.

Still, it will not be very large, even when we have added cowherds and shepherds to provide the farmers with oxen for the plough, and the builders as well as the farmers with draught-animals, and the weavers and shoemakers with wool and leather.

No; but it will not be so very small either.

And yet, again, it will be next to impossible to plant our city in a territory where it will need no imports. So there will have to be still another set of people, to fetch what it needs from other countries.

There will.

Moreover, if these agents take with them nothing that those other countries require in exchange, they will return as empty-handed as they went. So, besides everything wanted for consumption at home, we must produce enough goods of the right kind for the foreigners whom we depend on to supply us. That will mean increasing the number of farmers and craftsmen.

Yes.

And then, there are these agents who are to import and export all kinds of goods—merchants, as we call them. We must have them; and if they are to do business overseas, we shall need quite a number of ship-owners and others who know about that branch of trading.

We shall.

Again, in the city itself how are the various sets of producers to exchange their products? That was our object, you will remember, in forming a community and so laying the foundation of our state.

Obviously, they must buy and sell.

That will mean having a market-place, and a currency to serve as a token for purposes of exchange.

Certainly.

Now suppose a farmer, or an artisan, brings some of his produce to market at a time when no one is there who wants to exchange with him. Is he to sit there idle, when he might be at work?

No, he replied; there are people who have seen an opening here for their services. In well-ordered communities they are generally men not strong enough to be of use in any other occupation. They have to stay where they are in the market-place and take goods for money from those who want to sell, and money for goods from those who want to buy.

That, then, is the reason why our city must include a class of shopkeepers—so we call these people who sit still in the market-place to buy and sell, in contrast with merchants who travel to other countries.

Quite so.

There are also the services of yet another class, who have the physical strength for heavy work, though on intellectual grounds they are hardly worth including in our society—hired labourers, as we call them, because they sell the use of their strength for wages. They will go to make up our population.

Yes.

Well, Adeimantus, has our state now grown to its full size?

Perhaps.

Then, where in it shall we find justice or injustice? If they have come in with one of the elements we have been considering, can you say with which one?

I have no idea, Socrates; unless it be somewhere in their dealings with one another.

You may be right, I answered. Anyhow, it is a question which we shall have to face.

Chapter VII (II 372 A–374 E)
The Luxurious State

. . . .

Let us begin, then, with a picture of our citizens' manner of life, with the provision we have made for them. They will be producing corn and wine, and making clothes and shoes. When they have built their houses, they will mostly work without their coats or shoes in summer, and in winter be well shod and clothed. For their food, they will prepare flour and barley-meal for kneading and baking, and set out a grand spread of loaves and cakes on rushes or fresh leaves. Then they will lie on beds of myrtle-boughs and bryony and make merry with their children, drinking their wine after the feast with garlands on their heads and singing the praises of the gods. So they will live pleasantly together; and a prudent fear of poverty or war will keep them from begetting children beyond their means.

Here Glaucon interrupted me: You seem to expect your citizens to feast on dry bread.

True, I said; I forgot that they will have something to give it a relish, salt, no doubt, and olives, and cheese, and country stews of roots and vegetables. And for dessert we will give them figs and peas and beans; and they shall roast myrtle-berries and acorns at the fire, while they sip their wine. Leading such a healthy life in peace, they will naturally come to a good old age, and leave their children to live after them in the same manner.

That is just the sort of provender you would supply, Socrates, if you were founding a community of pigs.

Well, how are they to live, then, Glaucon?

With the ordinary comforts. Let them lie on couches and dine off tables on such dishes and sweets as we have nowadays.

Ah, I see, said I; we are to study the growth, not just of a state, but of a luxurious one. Well, there may be no harm in that; the consideration of luxury may help us to discover how justice and injustice take root in society. The community I have described seems to me the ideal one, in sound health as it were: but if you want to see one suffering from inflammation, there is nothing to hinder us. So some people, it seems, will not be satisfied to live in this simple way; they must have couches and tables and furniture of all sorts; and delicacies too, perfumes, unguents, courtesans, sweetmeats, all in plentiful variety. And besides, we must not limit ourselves now to those bare necessaries of house and clothes and shoes; we shall have to set going the arts of embroidery and painting, and collect rich materials, like gold and ivory.

Yes.

Then we must once more enlarge our community. The healthy one will not be big enough now; it must be swollen up with a whole multitude of callings not ministering to any bare necessity: hunters and fishermen, for instance; artists in sculpture, painting, and music; poets with their attendant train of professional reciters, actors, dancers, producers; and makers of all sorts of household gear, including everything for women's adornment. And we shall want more servants: children's nurses and attendants, lady's maids, barbers, cooks and confectioners. And then swineherds—there was no need for them in our original state, but we shall want them now; and a great quantity of sheep and cattle too, if people are going to live on meat.

Of course.

And with this manner of life physicians will be in much greater request.

No doubt.

The country, too, which was large enough to support the original inhabitants, will now be too small. If we are to have enough pasture and plough land, we shall have to cut off a slice of our neighbours' territory; and if they too are not content with necessaries, but give themselves up to getting unlimited wealth, they will want a slice of ours.

That is inevitable, Socrates.

So the next thing will be, Glaucon, that we shall be at war.

No doubt.

We need not say yet whether war does good or harm, but only that we have discovered its origin in desires which are the most fruitful source of evils both to individuals and to states.

Quite true.

This will mean a considerable addition to our community—a whole army, to go out to battle with any invader, in defence of all this property and of the citizens we have been describing.

Why so? Can't they defend themselves?

Not if the principle was right, which we all accepted in framing our society. You remember we agreed that no one man can practise many trades or arts satisfactorily.

True.

Well, is not the conduct of war an art, quite as important as shoemaking?

Yes.

But we would not allow our shoemaker to try to be also a farmer or weaver or builder, because we wanted our shoes well made. We gave each man one trade, for which he was naturally fitted; he would do good work, if he confined himself to that all his life, never letting the right moment slip by. Now in no form of work is efficiency so important as in war; and fighting is not so easy a business that a man can follow another trade, such as farming or shoemaking, and also be an efficient soldier. Why, even a game like draughts or dice must be studied from childhood; no one can become a fine player in his spare moments. Just taking up a shield or other weapon will not make a man capable of fighting that very day in any sort of warfare, any more than taking up a tool or implement of some kind will make a man a craftsman or an athlete, if he does not understand its use and has never been properly trained to handle it.

No; if that were so, tools would indeed be worth having.

These guardians of our state, then, inasmuch as their work is the most important of all, will need the most complete freedom from other occupations and the greatest amount of skill and practice.

I quite agree.

And also a native aptitude for their calling.

Certainly.

So it is our business to define, if we can, the natural gifts that fit men to be guardians of a commonwealth, and to select them accordingly. It will certainly be a formidable task; but we must grapple with it to the best of our power.

Yes.

Chapter VIII (II. 375 A–376 E)
The Guardian's Temperament

. . . .

Don't you think then, said I, that, for the purpose of keeping guard, a young man should have much the same temperament and qualities as a well-bred watch-dog? I mean, for instance, that both must have quick senses to detect an enemy, swiftness in pursuing him, and strength, if they have to fight when they have caught him.

Yes, they will need all those qualities.

And also courage, if they are to fight well.

Of course.

And courage, in dog or horse or any other creature, implies a spirited disposition. You must have noticed that a high spirit is unconquerable. Every soul possessed of it is fearless and indomitable in the face of any danger.

Yes, I have noticed that.

So now we know what physical qualities our Guardian must have, and also that he must be of a spirited temper.

Yes.

Then, Glaucon, how are men of that natural disposition to be kept from behaving pugnaciously to one another and to the rest of their countrymen?

It is not at all easy to see.

And yet they must be gentle to their own people and dangerous only to enemies; otherwise they will destroy themselves without waiting till others destroy them.

True.

What are we to do, then? If gentleness and a high temper are contraries, where shall we find a character to combine them? Both are necessary to make a good Guardian, but it seems they are incompatible. So we shall never have a good Guardian.

It looks like it.

Here I was perplexed, but on thinking over what we had been saying, I remarked that we deserved to be puzzled, because we had not followed up the comparison we had just drawn.

What do you mean? he asked.

We never noticed that, after all, there are natures in which these contraries are combined. They are to be found in animals, and not least in the kind we compared to our Guardian. Well-bred dogs, as you know, are by instinct perfectly gentle to people whom they know and are accustomed to, and fierce to strangers. So the combination of qualities we require for our Guardian is, after all, possible and not against nature.

Evidently.

Do you further agree that, besides this spirited temper, he must have a philosophical element in his nature?

I don't see what you mean.

This is another trait you will see in the dog. It is really remarkable how the creature gets angry at the mere sight of a stranger and welcomes anyone he knows, though he may never have been treated unkindly by the one or kindly by the other. Did that never strike you as curious?

I had not thought of it before; but that certainly is how a dog behaves.

Well, but that shows a fine instinct, which is philosophic in the true sense.

How so?

Because the only mark by which he distinguishes a friendly and an unfriendly face is that he knows the one and does not know the other; and if a creature makes that the test of what it finds congenial or otherwise, how can you deny that it has a passion for knowledge and understanding?

Of course, I cannot.

And that passion is the same thing as philosphy—the love of wisdom.

Yes.

Shall we boldly say, then, that the same is true of human beings? If a man is to be gentle towards his own people whom hs knows, he must have an instinctive love of wisdom and understanding.

Agreed.

So the nature required to make a really noble Guardian of our commonwealth will be swift and strong, spirited, and philosophic.

Quite so. . . .

. . . .

Chapter X (III. 412 B–IV. 421 C) Selection of Rulers: The Guardians' Manner of Living

. . . .

What is the next point to be settled? Is it not the question, which of these Guardians are to be rulers and which are to obey?

No doubt.

Well, it is obvious that the elder must have authority over the young, and that the rulers must be the best.

Yes.

And as among farmers the best are those with a natural turn for farming, so, if we want the best among our Guardians, we must take those naturally fitted to watch over a commonwealth. They must have the right sort of intelligence and ability; and also they must look upon the commonwealth as their special concern—the sort of concern that is felt for something so closely bound up with oneself that its interests and fortunes, for good or ill, are held to be identical with one's own.

Exactly.

So the kind of men we must choose from among the Guardians will be those who, when we look at the whole course of their lives, are found to be full of zeal to do whatever they believe is for the good of the commonwealth and never willing to act against its interest.

Yes, they will be the men we want.

We must watch them, I think, at every age and see whether they are capable of preserving this conviction that they must do what is best for the community, never forgetting it or allowing themselves to be either forced or bewitched into throwing it over.

How does this throwing over come about?

I will explain. When a belief passes out of the mind, a man may be willing to part with it, if it is false and he has learnt better, or unwilling, if it is true.

I see how he might be willing to let it go; but you must explain how he can be unwilling.

Where is your difficulty? Don't you agree that men are unwilling to be deprived of good, though ready enough to part with evil? Or that to be deceived about the truth is evil, to possess it good? Or don't you think that possessing truth means thinking of things as they really are?

You are right. I do agree that men are unwilling to be robbed of a true belief.

When that happens to them, then, it must be by theft, or violence, or bewitchment.

Again I do not understand.

Perhaps my metaphors are too high-flown. I call it theft when one is persuaded out of one's belief or forgets it. Argument in the one case, and time in the other, steal it away without one's knowing what is happening. You understand now?

Yes.

And by violence I mean being driven to change one's mind by pain or suffering.

That too I understand, and you are right.

And bewitchment, as I think you would agree, occurs when a man is beguiled out of his opinion by the allurements of pleasure or scared out of it under the spell of panic.

Yes, all delusions are like a sort of bewitchment.

As I said just now, then, we must find out who are the best guardians of this inward conviction that they must always do what they believe to be best for the commonwealth. We shall have to watch them from earliest childhood and set them tasks in which they would be most likely to forget or to be beguilded out of this duty. We shall then choose only those whose memory holds firm and who are proof against delusion.

Yes.

We must also subject them to ordeals of toil and pain and watch for the same qualities there. And we must observe them when exposed to the test of yet a third kind of bewitchment. As people lead colts up to alarming noises to see whether they are timid, so these young men must be brought into terrifying situations and then into scenes of pleasure, which will put them to severer proof than gold tied in the furnace. If we find one bearing himself well in all these trials and resisting every enchantment, a true guardian of himself, preserving always that perfect rhythm and harmony of being which he has acquired from his training in music and poetry, such a one will be of the greatest service to the commonwealth as well as to himself. Whenever we find one who has come unscathed through every test in childhood, youth, and manhood, we shall set him as a Ruler to watch over the commonwealth; he will be honoured in life, and after death receive the highest tribute of funeral rites and other memorials. All who do not reach this standard we must reject. And that, I think, my dear Glaucon, may be taken as an outline of the way in which we shall select Guardians to be set in authority as Rulers.

I am very much of your mind.

These, then, may properly be called Guardians in the fullest sense, who will ensure that neither foes without shall have the power, nor friends within the wish, to do harm. Those young men whom up to now we have been speaking of as Guardians, will be better described as Auxiliaries, who will enforce the decisions of the Rulers.

I agree.

. . . .

Chapter XII (IV. 427 C–434 D) The Virtues in the State

. . . .

So now at last, son of Ariston, said I, your commonwealth is established. The next thing is to bring to bear upon it all the light you can get from any quarter, with the help of your brother and Polemarchus and all the rest, in the hope that we may see where justice is to be found in it and where injustice, how they differ, and which of the two will bring happiness to its possessor, no matter whether gods and men see that he has it or not.

Nonsense, said Glaucon; you promised to conduct the search yourself, because it would be a sin not to uphold justice by every means in your power.

That is true; I must do as you say, but you must all help.

We will.

I suspect, then, we may find what we are looking for in this way. I take it that our state, having been founded and built up on the right lines, is good in the complete sense of the word.

It must be.

Obviously, then, it is wise, brave, temperate, and just.

Obviously.

Then if we find some of these qualities in it, the remainder will be the one we have not found. It is as if we were looking somewhere for one of any four things: if we detected that one immediately, we should be satisfied; whereas if we recognized the other three first, that would be enough to indicate the thing we wanted; it could only be the remaining one. So here we have four qualities. Had we not better follow that method in looking for the one we want?

Surely.

To begin then: the first quality to come into view in our state seems to be its wisdom; and there appears to be something odd about this quality.[4]

What is there odd about it?

I think the state we have described really has wisdom; for it will be prudent in counsel, won't it?

Yes.

And prudence in counsel is clearly a form of knowledge; good counsel cannot be due to ignorance and stupidity.

Clearly.

But there are many and various kinds of knowledge in our commonwealth. There is the knowledge possessed by the carpenters or the smiths, and the knowledge how to raise crops. Are we to call the state wise and prudent on the strength of these forms of skill?

No; they would only make it good at furniture-making or working in copper or agriculture.

Well then, is there any form of knowledge,

possessed by some among the citizens of our new-founded commonwealth, which will enable it to take thought, not for some particular interest, but for the best possible conduct of the state as a whole in its internal and external relations?

Yes, there is.

What is it, and where does it reside?

It is precisely that art of guardianship which resides in those Rulers whom we just now called Guardians in the full sense.

And what would you call the state on the strength of that knowledge?

Prudent and truly wise.

And do you think there will be more or fewer of these genuine Guardians in our state than there will be smiths?

Far fewer.

Fewer, in fact, than any of those other groups who are called after the kind of skill they possess?

Much fewer.

So, if a state is constituted on natural principles, the wisdom it possesses as a whole will be due to the knowledge residing in the smallest part, the one which takes the lead and governs the rest. Such knowledge is the only kind that deserves the name of wisdom, and it appears to be ordained by nature that the class privileged to possess it should be the smallest of all.

Quite true.

Here then we have more or less made out one of our four qualities and its seat in the structure of the commonwealth.

To my satisfaction, at any rate.

Next there is courage. It is not hard to discern that quality or the part of the community in which it resides so as to entitle the whole to be called brave.

Why do you say so?

Because anyone who speaks of a state as either brave or cowardly can only be thinking of that part of it which takes the field and fights in its defence; the reason being, I imagine, that the character of the state is not determined by the bravery or cowardice of the other parts.

No.

Courage, then, is another quality which a community owes to a certain part of itself. And its being brave will mean that, in this part, it possesses the power of preserving, in all circumstances, a conviction about the sort of things that it is right to be afraid of—the conviction implanted by the education which the law-giver has established. Is not that what you mean by courage?

I do not quite understand. Will you say it again?

I am saying that courage means preserving something.

Yes, but what?

The conviction, inculcated by lawfully established education, about the sort of things which may rightly be feared. When I added "in all circumstances," I meant preserving it always and never abandoning it, whether under the influence of pain or of pleasure, of desire or of fear. If you like, I will give an illustration.

Please do.

You know how dyers who want wool to take a purple dye, first select the white wool from among all the other colours, next treat it very carefully to make it take the dye in its full brilliance, and only then dip it in the vat. Dyed in that way, wool gets a fast colour, which no washing, even with soap, will rob of its brilliance; whereas if they choose wool of any colour but white, or if they neglect to prepare it, you know what happens.

Yes, it looks washed-out and ridiculous.

That illustrates the result we were doing our best to achieve when we were choosing our fighting men and training their minds and bodies. Our only purpose was to contrive influences whereby they might take the colour of our insitutions like a dye, so that, in virtue of having both the right temperament and the right education, their convictions about what ought to be feared and on all other subjects might be indelibly fixed, never to be washed out by pleasure and pain, desire and fear, solvents more terribly effective than all the soap and fuller's earth in the world. Such a power of constantly preserving, in accordance with our institutions, the right conviction about the things which ought, or ought not, to be feared, is what I call courage. That is my position, unless you have some objection to make.

None at all, he replied; if the belief were such as might be found in a slave or an animal—correct, but not produced by education—you would hardly describe it as in accordance with our institutions, and you would give it some other name than courage.

Quite true.

Then I accept your account of courage.

You will do well to accept it, at any rate as applying to the courage of the ordinary citizen; if you like we will go into it more fully some other time. At present we are in search of justice, rather than of courage; and for that purpose we have said enough.

I quite agree.

Two qualities, I went on, still remain to be made out in our state, temperance and the object of our whole inquiry, justice. Can we discover justice without troubling ourselves further about temperance?

I do not know, and I would rather not have justice come to light first, if that means that we should not go on to consider temperance. So if you want to please me, take temperance first.

Of course I have every wish to please you.

Do go on then.

I will. At first sight, temperance seems more like some sort of concord or harmony than the other qualities did.

How so?

Temperance surely means a kind of orderliness, a control of certain pleasures and appetites. People use the expression, ''master of oneself,'' whatever that means, and various other phrases that point the same way.

Quite true.

Is not ''master of oneself'' an absured expression? A man who was master of himself would presumably be also subject to himself, and the subject would be master; for all these terms apply to the same person.

No doubt.

I think, however, the phrase means that within the man himself, in his soul, there is a better part and a worse; and that he is his own master when the part which is better by nature has the worse under its control. It is certainly a term of praise; whereas it is considered a disgrace, when, through bad breeding or bad company, the better part is overwhelmed by the worse, like a small force outnumbered by a multitude. A man in that condition is called a slave to himself and intemperate.

Probably that is what is meant.

Then now look at our newly founded state and you will find one of these two conditions realized there. You will agree that it deserves to be called master of itself, if temperance and self-mastery exist where the better part rules the worse.

Yes, I can see that is true.

It is also true that the great mass of multifarious appetites and pleasures and pains will be found to occur chiefly in children and women and slaves, and, among free men so called, in the inferior multitude; whereas the simple and moderate desires which, with the aid of reason and right belief, are guided by reflection, you will find only in a few, and those with the best inborn dispositions and the best educated.

Yes, certainly.

Do you see that this state of things will exist in your commonwealth, where the desires of the inferior multitude will be controlled by the desires and wisdom of the superior few? Hence, if any society can be called master of itself and in control of pleasures and desires, it will be ours.

Quite so.

On all these grounds, then, we may describe it as temperate. Furthermore, in our state, if anywhere, the governors and the governed will share the same conviction on the question who ought to rule. Don't you think so?

I am quite sure of it.

Then, if that is their state of mind, in which of the two classes of citizens will temperance reside—in the governors or in the governed?

In both, I suppose.

So we were not wrong in divining a resemblance between temperance and some kind of harmony. Temperance is not like courage and wisdom, which made the state wise and brave by residing each in one particular part. Temperance works in a different way; it extends throughout the whole gamut of the state, producing a consonance of all its elements from the weakest to the strongest as measured by any standard you like to take—wisdom, bodily strength, numbers, or wealth. So we are entirely justified in identifying with temperance this unanimity or harmonious agreement between the naturally superior and inferior elements on the question which of the two should govern, whether in the state or in the individual.

I fully agree.

Good, said I. We have discovered in our commonwealth three out of our four qualities, to the best of our present judgment. What is the remaining one, required to make up its full complement of goodness? For clearly this will be justice.

Clearly.

Now is the moment, then, Glaucon, for us to keep the closest watch, like huntsmen standing round a covert, to make sure that justice does not slip through and vanish undetected. It must certainly be somewhere hereabouts; so keep your eyes open for a view of the quarry, and if you see it first, give me the alert.

I wish I could, he answered; but you will do better to give me a lead and not count on me for more than eyes to see what you show me.

Pray for luck, then, and follow me.

I will, if you will lead on.

The thicket looks rather impenetrable, said I; too dark for it to be easy to start up the game. However, we must push on.

Of course we must.

Here I gave the view halloo. Glaucon, I exclaimed, I believe we are on the track and the quarry is not going to escape us altogether.

That is good news.

Really, I said, we have been extremely stupid. All this time the thing has been under our very noses from the start, and we never saw it. We have been as absurd as a person who hunts for something he has all the time got in his hand. Instead of looking at the thing, we have been staring into the distance. No doubt that is why it escaped us.

What do you mean?

I believe we have been talking about the thing all this while without ever understanding that we were giving some sort of account of it.

Do come to the point. I am all ears.

Listen, then, and judge whether I am right. You remember how, when we first began to establish our commonwealth and several times since, we have laid down, as a universal principle, that everyone ought to perform the one function in the community for which his nature best suited him. Well, I believe that that principle, or some form of it, is justice.

We certainly laid that down.

Yes, and surely we have often heard people say that justice means minding one's own business and not meddling with other men's concerns; and we have often said so ourselves.

We have.

Well, my friend, it may be that this minding of one's own business, when it takes a certain form, is actually the same thing as justice. Do you know what makes me think so?

No, tell me.

I think that this quality which makes it possible for the three we have already considered, wisdom, courage, and temperance, to take their place in the commonwealth, and so long as it remains present secures their continuance, must be the remaining one. And we said that, when three of the four were found, the one left over would be justice.

It must be so.

Well now, if we had to decide which of these qualities will contribute most to the excellence of our commonwealth, it would be hard to say whether it was the unanimity of rulers and subjects or the soldier's fidelity to the established conviction about what is, or is not, to be feared, or the watchful intelligence of the Rulers; or whether its excellence were not above all due to the observance by everyone, child or woman, slave or freeman or artisan, ruler or ruled, of this principle that each one should do his own proper work without interfering with others.

It would be hard to decide, no doubt.

It seems, then, that this principle can at any rate claim to rival wisdom, temperance, and courage as conducing to the excellence of a state. And would you not say that the only possible competitor of these qualities must be justice?

Yes, undoubtedly.

Here is another thing which points to the same conclusion. The judging of law-suits is a duty that you will lay upon your Rulers, isn't it?

Of course.

And the chief aim of their decisions will be that neither party shall have what belongs to another or be deprived of what is his own.

Yes.

Because that is just?

Yes.

So here again justice admittedly means that a man should possess and concern himself with what properly belongs to him.

True.

Again, do you agree with me that no great harm

would be done to the community by a general interchange of most forms of work, the carpenter and the cobbler exchanging their positions and their tools and taking on each other's jobs, or even the same man undertaking both?

Yes, there would not be much harm in that.

But I think you will also agree that another kind of interchange would be disastrous. Suppose, for instance, someone whom nature designed to be an artisan or tradesman should be emboldened by some advantage, such as wealth or command of votes or bodily strength, to try to enter the order of fighting men; or some member of that order should aspire, beyond his merits, to a seat in the council-chamber of the Guardians. Such interference and exchange of social positions and tools, or the attempt to combine all these forms of work in the same person, would be fatal to the commonwealth.

Most certainly.

Where there are three orders, then, any plurality of functions or shifting from one order to another is not merely utterly harmful to the community, but one might fairly call it the extreme of wrongdoing. And you will agree that to do the greatest of wrongs to one's own community is injustice.

Surely.

This, then, is injustice. And, conversely, let us repeat that when each order—tradesman, Auxiliary, Guardian—keeps to its own proper business in the commonwealth and does its own work, that is justice and what makes a just society.

I entirely agree.

Chapter XIII (IV. 434 D–441 C)
The Three Parts of the Soul

. . . .

We must not be too positive yet, said I. If we find that this same quality when it exists in the individual can equally be identified with justice, then we can at once give our assent; there will be no more to be said; otherwise, we shall have to look further. For the moment, we had better finish the inquiry which we began with the idea that it would be easier to make out the nature of justice in the individual if we first tried to study it in something on a larger scale. That larger thing we took to be a state, and so we set about constructing the best one we could, being sure of finding justice in a state that was good. The discovery we made there must now be applied to the individual. If it is confirmed, all will be well; but if we find that justice in the individual is something different, we must go back to the state and test our new result. Perhaps if we brought the two cases into contact like flint and steel, we might strike out between them the spark of justice, and in its light confirm the conception in our own minds.

A good method. Let us follow it.

Now, I continued, if two things, one large, the other small, are called by the same name, they will be alike in that respect to which the common name applies. Accordingly, in so far as the quality of justice is concerned, there will be no difference between a just man and a just society.

No.

Well, but we decided that a society was just when each of the three types of human character it contained performed its own function; and again, it was temperate and brave and wise by virtue of certain other affections and states of mind of those same types.

True.

Accordingly, my friend, if we are to be justified in attributing those same virtues to the individual, we shall expect to find that the individual soul contains the same three elements and that they are affected in the same way as are the corresponding types in society.

That follows.

Here, then, we have stumbled upon another little problem: Does the soul contain these three elements or not?

Not such a very little one, I think. It may be a true saying, Socrates, that what is worth while is seldom easy.

Apparently; and let me tell you, Glaucon, it is my belief that we shall never reach the exact truth in this matter by following our present methods of discussion; the road leading to that goal is longer and more laborious. However, perhaps we can find an answer that will be up to the standard we have so far maintained in our speculations.

Is not that enough? I should be satisfied for the moment.

Well, it will more than satisfy me, I replied.

Don't be disheartened, then, but go on.

Surely, I began, we must admit that the same elements and characters that appear in the state must exist in every one of us; where else could they have come from? It would be absurd to imagine that among peoples with a reputation for a high-spirited character, like the Thracians and Scythians and northerners generally, the states have not derived that character from their individual members; or that it is otherwise with the love of knowledge, which would be ascribed chiefly to our own part of the world, or with the love of money, which one would specially connect with Phoenicia and Egypt.

Certainly.

So far, then, we have a fact which is easily recognized. But here the difficulty begins. Are we using the same part of ourselves in all these three experiences, or a different part in each? Do we gain knowledge with one part, feel anger with another, and with yet a third desire the pleasures of food, sex, and so on? Or is the whole soul at work in every impulse and in all these forms of behaviour? The difficulty is to answer that question satisfactorily.

I quite agree.

Let us approach the problem whether these elements are distinct or identical in this way. It is clear that the same thing cannot act in two opposite ways or be in two opposite states at the same time, with respect to the same part of itself, and in relation to the same object. So if we find such contradictory actions or states among the elements concerned, we shall know that more than one must have been involved.

Very well.

Consider this proposition of mine, then. Can the same thing, at the same time and with respect to the same part of itself, be at rest and in motion?

Certainly not.

We had better state this principle in still more precise terms, to guard against misunderstanding later on. Suppose a man is standing still, but moving his head and arms. We should not allow anyone to say that the same man was both at rest and in motion at the same time, but only that part of him was at rest, part in motion. Isn't that so?

Yes.

An ingenious objector might refine still further and argue that a peg-top, spinning with its peg fixed at the same spot, or indeed any body that revolves in the same place, is both at rest and in motion as a whole. but we should not agree, because the parts in respect of which such a body is moving and at rest are not the same. It contains an axis and a circumference; and in respect of the axis it is at rest inasmuch as the axis is not inclined in any direction, while in respect of the circumference it revolves; and if, while it is spinning, the axis does lean out of the perpendicular in all directions, then it is in no way at rest.

That is true.

No objection of that sort, then, will disconcert us or make us believe that the same thing can ever act or be acted upon in two opposite ways, or be two opposite things, at the same time, in respect of the same part of itself, and in relation to the same object.

I can answer for myself at any rate.

Well, anyhow, as we do not want to spend time in reviewing all such objections to make sure that they are unsound, let us proceed on this assumption, with the understanding that, if we ever come to think otherwise, all the consequences based upon it will fall to the ground.

Yes, that is a good plan.

Now, would you class such things as assent and dissent, striving after something and refusing it, attraction and repulsion, as pairs of opposite actions or states of mind—no matter which?

Yes, they are opposites.

And would you not class all appetites such as hunger and thirst, and again willing and wishing, with the affirmative members of those pairs I have just mentioned? For instance, you would say that the soul of a man who desires something is striving after it, or trying to draw to itself the thing it wishes to possess, or again, in so far as it is willing to have its want satisfied, it is giving its assent to its own longing, as if to an inward question.

Yes.

And, on the other hand, disinclination, unwillingness, and dislike, we should class on the negative side with acts of rejection or repulsion.

Of course.

That being so, shall we say that appetites form one class, the most conspicuous being those we call thirst and hunger?

Yes.

Thirst being desire for drink, hunger for food?

Yes.

Now, is thirst, just in so far as it is thirst, a desire in the soul for anything more than simply drink? Is it, for instance, thirst for hot drink or for cold, for much drink or for little, or in a word for drink of any particular kind? Is it not rather true that you will have a desire for cold drink only if you are feeling hot as well as thirsty, and for hot drink only if you are feeling cold; and if you want much drink or little, that will be because your thirst is a great thirst or a little one? But, just in itself, thirst or hunger is a desire for nothing more than its natural object, drink or food, pure and simple.

Yes, he agreed, each desire, just in itself, is simply for its own natural object. When the object is of such and such a particular kind, the desire will be correspondingly qualified.[5]

We must be careful here, or we might be troubled by the objection that no one desires mere food and drink, but always wholesome food and drink. We shall be told that what we desire is always something that is good; so if thirst is a desire, its object must be, like that of any other desire, something—drink or whatever it may be—that will be good for one.[6]

Yes, there might seem to be something in that objection.

But surely, wherever you have two correlative terms, if one is qualified, the other must always be qualified too; whereas if one is unqualified, so is the other.

I don't understand.

Well, "greater" is a relative term; and the greater is greater than the less; if it is much greater, then the less is much less; if it is greater at some moment, past or future, then the less is less at that same moment. The same principle applies to all such correlatives, like "more" and "fewer," "double" and "half"; and again to terms like "heavier" and "lighter," "quicker" and "slower," and to things like hot and cold.

Yes.

Or take the various branches of knowledge: is it not the same there? The object of knowledge pure and simple is the knowable—if that is the right word—without any qualification; whereas a particular kind of knowledge has an object of a particular kind. For example, as soon as men learnt how to build houses, their craft was distinguished from others under the name of architecture, because it had a unique character, which was itself due to the character of its object; and all other branches of craft and knowledge were distinguished in the same way.

True.

This, then, if you understand me now, is what I meant by saying that, where there are two correlatives, the one is qualified if, and only if, the other is so. I am not saying that the one must have the same quality as the other—that the science of health and disease is itself healthy and diseased, or the knowledge of good and evil is itself good and evil—but only that, as soon as you have a knowledge that is restricted to a particular kind of object, namely health and disease, the knowledge itself becomes a particular kind of knowledge. Hence we no longer call it merely knowledge, which would have for its object whatever can be known, but we add the qualification and call it medical science.

I understand now and I agree.

Now, to go back to thirst: is not that one of these relative terms? It is essentially thirst for something.

Yes, for drink.

And if the drink desired is of a certain kind, the thirst will be correspondingly qualified. But thirst which is just simply thirst is not for drink of any particular sort—much or little, good or bad—but for drink pure and simple.

Quite so.

We conclude, then, that the soul of a thirsty man, just in so far as he is thirsty, has no other wish than to drink. That is the object of its craving, and towards that it is impelled.

That is clear.

Now if there is ever something which at the same time pulls it the opposite way, that something must be an element in the soul other than the one which is thirsting and driving it like a beast to drink; in accordance with our principle that the same thing cannot behave in two opposite ways at the same time and towards the same object with the same part of itself. It is like an archer drawing the bow: it is not accurate to say that his hands are at the same time both pushing and pulling it. One hand does the pushing, the other the pulling.

Exactly.

Now, is it sometimes true that people are thirsty and yet unwilling to drink?

Yes, often.

What, then, can one say of them, if not that their soul contains something which urges them to drink and something which holds them back, and that this latter is a distinct thing and overpowers the other?

I agree.

And is it not true that the intervention of this inhibiting principle in such cases always has its origin in reflection; whereas the impulses driving and dragging the soul are engendered by external influences and abnormal conditions?

Evidently.

We shall have good reason, then, to assert that they are two distinct principles. We may call that part of the soul whereby it reflects, rational; and the other, with which it feels hunger and thirst and is distracted by sexual passion and all the other desires, we will call irrational appetite, associated with pleasure in the replenishment of certain wants.

Yes, there is good ground for that view.

Let us take it, then, that we have now distinguished two elements in the soul. What of that passionate element which makes us feel angry and indignant? Is that a third, or identical in nature with one of those two?

It might perhaps be identified with appetite.

I am more inclined to put my faith in a story I once heard about Leontius, son of Aglaion. On his way up from the Piraeus outside the north wall, he noticed the bodies of some criminals lying on the ground, with the executioner standing by them. He wanted to go and look at them, but at the same time he was disgusted and tried to turn away. He struggled for some time and covered his eyes, but at last the desire was too much for him. Opening his eyes wide, he ran up to the bodies and cried, 'There you are, curse you; feast yourselves on this lovely sight!'

Yes, I have heard that story too.

The point of it surely is that anger is sometimes in conflict with appetite, as if they were two distinct principles. Do we not often find a man whose desires would force him to go against his reason, reviling himself and indignant with this part of his nature which is trying to put constraint on him? It is like a struggle between two factions, in which indignation takes the side of reason. But I believe you have never observed, in yourself or anyone else, indignation make common cause with appetite in behaviour which reason decides to be wrong.

No, I am sure I have not.

Again, take a man who feels he is in the wrong. The more generous his nature, the less can he be indignant at any suffering, such as hunger and cold, inflicted by the man he has injured. He recognizes such treatment as just, and, as I say, his spirit refuses to be roused against it.

That is true.

But now contrast one who thinks it is he that is being wronged. His spirit boils with resentment and sides with the right as he conceives it. Persevering all the more for the hunger and cold and other pains he suffers, it triumphs and will not give in until its gallant struggle has ended in success or death; or until the restraining voice of reason, like a shepherd calling off his dog, makes it relent.

An apt comparison, he said; and in fact it fits the relation of our Auxiliaries to the Rulers: they were to be like watch-dogs obeying the shepherds of the commonwealth.

Yes, you understand very well what I have in mind. But do you see how we have changed our view? A moment ago we were supposing this spirited element to be something of the nature of appetite; but now it appears that, when the soul is divided into factions, it is far more ready to be up in arms on the side of reason.

Quite true.

Is it, then, distinct from the rational element or only a particular form of it, so that the soul will contain no more than two elements, reason and appetite? Or is the soul like the state, which had three orders to hold it together, traders, Auxiliaries, and counsellors? Does the spirited element make a third, the natural auxiliary of reason, when not corrupted by bad upbringing?

It must be a third.

Yes, I said, provided it can be shown to be distinct from reason, as we saw it was from appetite.

That is easily proved. You can see that much in children: they are full of passionate feelings from their very birth; but some, I should say, never become rational, and most of them only late in life.

A very sound observation, said I, the truth of which may also be seen in animals. And beside, there is the witness of Homer in that line I quoted before: "He smote his breast and spoke, chiding his heart." The poet is plainly thinking of the two elements as distinct, when he makes the one which has chosen the better course after reflection rebuke the other for its unreasoning passion.

I entirely agree.

Chapter XIV (IV. 441 C–445 B)
The Virtues in the Individual

. . . .

And so, after a stormy passage, we have reached the land. We are farily agreed that the same three elements exist alike in the state and in the individual soul.

That is so.

Does it not follow at once that state and individual will be wise or brave by virtue of the same element in each and in the same way? Both will possess in the same manner any quality that makes for excellence.

That must be true.

Then it applies to justice: we shall conclude that a man is just in the same way that a state was just. And we have surely not forgotten that justice in the state meant that each of the three orders in it was doing its own proper work. So we may henceforth bear in mind that each one of us likewise will be a just person, fulfilling his proper function, only if the several parts of our nature fulfil theirs.

Certainly.

And it will be the business of reason to rule with wisdom and forethought on behalf of the entire soul; while the spirited element ought to act as its subordinate and ally. The two will be brought into accord, as we said earlier, by that combination of mental and bodily training which will tune up one string of the instrument and relax the other, nourishing the reasoning part on the study of noble literature and allaying the other's wildness by harmony and rhythm. When both have been thus nurtured and trained to know their own true functions, they must be set in command over the appetites, which form the greater part of each man's soul and are by nature insatiably covetous. They must keep watch lest this part, by battening on the pleasures that are called bodily, should grow so great and powerful that it will no longer keep to its own work, but will try to enslave the others and usurp a dominion to which it has no right, thus turning the whole of life upside down. At the same time, those two together will be the best of guardians for the entire soul and for the body against all enemies from without: the one will take counsel, while the other will do battle, following its ruler's commands and by its own bravery giving effect to the ruler's designs.

Yes, that is all true.

And so we call an individual brave in virtue of this spirited part of his nature, when, in spite of pain or pleasure, it holds fast to the injunctions of reason about what he ought or ought not to be afraid of.

True.

And wise in virtue of that small part which rules and issues these injunctions, possessing as it does the knowledge of what is good for each of the three elements and for all of them in common.

Certainly.

And, again, temperate by reason of the unanimity and concord of all three, when there is no internal conflict between the ruling element and its two subjects, but all are agreed that reason should be ruler.

Yes, that is an exact account of temperance, whether in the state or in the individual.

Finally, a man will be just by observing the principle we have so often stated.

Necessarily.

Now is there any indistinctness in our vision of justice, that might make it seem somehow different from what we found it to be in the state?

I don't think so.

Because, if we have any lingering doubt, we might make sure by comparing it with some commonplace notions. Suppose, for instance, that a sum of money were entrusted to our state or to an individual of corresponding character and training, would anyone imagine that such a person would be specially likely to embezzle it?

No.

And would he not be incapable of sacrilege and theft, or of treachery to friend or country; never false to an oath or any other compact; the last to be guilty of adultery or of neglecting parents or the due service of the gods?

Yes.

And the reason for all this is that each part of his nature is exercising its proper function, of ruling or of being ruled.

Yes, exactly.

Are you satisfied, then, that justice is the power which produces states or individuals of whom that is true, or must we look further?

There is no need; I am quite satisfied.

And so our dream has come true—I mean the inkling we had that, by some happy chance, we had lighted upon a rudimentary form of justice from the very moment when we set about founding our commonwealth. Our principle that the born shoemaker or carpenter had better stick to his trade turns out to have been an adumbration of justice; and that is why it has helped us. But in reality justice, though evidently analogous to this principle, is not a matter of external behaviour, but of the inward self and of attending to all that is, in the fullest sense, a man's proper concern. The just man does not allow the several elements in his soul to usurp one another's functions; he is indeed one who sets his house in order, by self-mastery and discipline coming to be at peace with himself, and bringing into tune those three parts, like the terms in the proportion of a musical scale, the highest and lowest notes and the mean between them, with all the intermediate intervals. Only when he has linked these parts together in well-tempered harmony and has made himself one man instead of many, will he be ready to go about whatever he may have to do, whether it be making money and satisfying bodily wants, or business transactions, or the affairs of state. In all these fields when he speaks of just and honourable conduct, he will mean the behaviour that helps to produce and to preserve this habit of mind; and by wisdom he will mean the knowledge which presides over such conduct. Any action which tends to break down this habit will be for him unjust; and the notions governing it he will call ignorance and folly.

That is perfectly true, Socrates.

Good, said I. I believe we should not be thought altogether mistaken, if we claimed to have discovered the just man and the just state, and wherein their justice consists.

Indeed we should not.

Shall we make that claim, then?

Yes, we will.

So be it, said I. Next, I suppose, we have to consider injustice.

Evidently.

This must surely be a sort of civil strife among the three elements, whereby they usurp and encroach upon one another's functions and some one part of the soul rises up in rebellion against the whole, claiming a supremacy to which it has no right because its nature fits it only to be the servant of the ruling principle. Such turmoil and aberration we shall, I think, identify with injustice, intemperance, cowardice, ignorance, and in a word with all wickedness.

Exactly.

And now that we know the nature of justice and injustice, we can be equally clear about what is meant by acting justly and again by unjust action and wrongdoing.

How do you mean?

Plainly, they are exactly analogous to those wholesome and unwholesome activities which respectively produce a healthy or unhealthy condition in the body; in the same way just and unjust conduct produce a just or unjust character. Justice is produced in the soul, like health in the body, by establishing the elements concerned in their natural relations of control and subordination, whereas injustice is like disease and means that this natural order is inverted.

Quite so.

It appears, then, that virtue is as it were the health and comeliness and well-being of the soul, as wickedness is disease, deformity, and weakness.

True.

And also that virtue and wickedness are brought about by one's way of life, honourable or disgraceful.

That follows.

So now it only remains to consider which is the more profitable course: to do right and live honourably and be just, whether or not anyone knows what manner of man you are, or to do wrong and be unjust, provided that you can escape the chastisement which might make you a better man.

But really, Socrates, it seems to me ridiculous to ask that question now that the nature of justice and injustice has been brought to light. People think that all the luxury and wealth and power in the world cannot make life worth living when the bodily constitution is going to rack and ruin; and are we to believe that, when the very principle whereby we live is deranged and corrupted, life will be worth living so long as a man can do as he will, and wills to do anything rather than to free himself from vice and wrongdoing and to win justice and virtue?

Yes, I replied, it is a ridiculous question.

Notes

1. In certain lawsuits the defendant, if found guilty, was allowed to propose a penalty alternative to that demanded by the prosecution. The judges then decided which should be inflicted. The "costs" here means the fee which the sophist, unlike Socrates, expected from his pupils.
2. All the persons mentioned have some interest. The craftsman *qua* craftsman has an interest in doing his work as well as possible, which is the same thing as serving the interest of the subjects on whom his craft is exercised; and the subjects have their interest, which the craftsman is there to promote.
3. The word translated "function" is the common word for "work." Hence the need for illustrations to confine it to the narrower sense of "function," here defined for the first time.
4. Because the wisdom of the whole resides in the smallest part, as explained below.
5. The object of the following subtle argument about relative terms is to distinguish thirst as a mere blind craving for drink from a more complex desire whose object includes the pleasure or health expected to result from drinking. We thus forestall the objection that all desires have "the good" (apparent or real) for their object and include an intellectual or rational element, so that the conflict of motives might be reduced to an intellectual debate, in the same "part" of the soul, on the comparative values of two incompatible ends.
6. If this objection were admitted, it would follow that the desire would always be correspondingly qualified. It is necessary to insist that we do experience blind cravings which can be isolated from any judgement about the goodness of their object.

An Enquiry Concerning the Principles of Morals

DAVID HUME

Section I
Of the General Principles of Morals

Disputes with men, pertinaciously obstinate in their principles, are, of all others, the most irksome; except, perhaps, those with persons, entirely disingenuous, who really do not believe the opinions they defend, but engage in the controversy, from affectation, from a spirit of opposition, or from a desire of showing wit and ingenuity, superior to the rest of mankind. The same blind adherence to their own arguments is to be expected in both; the same contempt of their antagonists; and the same passionate vehemence, in inforcing sophistry and falsehood. And as reasoning is not the source, whence either disputant derives his tenets; it is in vain to expect, that any logic, which speaks not to the affections, will ever engage him to embrace sounder principles.

Those who have denied the reality of moral distinctions, may be ranked among the disingenuous disputants; nor is it conceivable, that any human creature could ever seriously believe, that all characters and actions were alike entitled to the affection and regard of everyone. The difference, which nature has placed between one man and another, is so wide, and this difference is still so much farther widened, by education, example, and habit, that, where the opposite extremes come at once under our apprehension, there is no scepticism so scrupulous, and scarce any assurance so determined, as absolutely to deny all distinction between them. Let a man's insensibility be ever so great, he must often be touched with the images of Right and Wrong; and let his prejudices be ever so obstinate, he must observe, that others are susceptible of like impressions. The only way, therefore, of converting an antagonist of this kind, is to leave him to himself. For, finding that nobody keeps up the controversy with him, it is probable he will, at last, of himself, from mere weariness, come over to the side of common sense and reason.

There has been a controversy started of late, much better worth examination, concerning the general foundation of Morals; whether they be derived from Reason, or from Sentiment; whether we attain the knowledge of them by a chain of argument and induction, or by an immediate feeling and finer internal sense; whether, like all sound judgement of truth and falsehood, they should be the same to every rational intelligent being; or whether, like the perception of beauty and deformity, they be founded entirely on the particular fabric and constitution of the human species.

The ancient philosophers, though they often affirm, that virtue is nothing but conformity to reason, yet, in general, seem to consider morals as deriving their existence from taste and sentiment. On the other hand, our modern enquirers, though they also talk much of the beauty of virtue, and deformity of vice, yet have commonly endeavoured to account for these distinctions by

From *Enquiries Concerning Human Understanding and Concerning the Principles of Morals,* Selby-Bigge edition, rev. by P. H. Nidditch (Oxford: Oxford University Press, 1975), pp. 169–76, 178–88, 190–92, 212–21, 225–32, 268, 270–76, 278–91, 293–98, 300–302.

metaphysical reasonings, and by deductions from the most abstract principles of the understanding. Such confusion reigned in these subjects, that an opposition of the greatest consequence could prevail between one system and another, and even in the parts of almost each individual system; and yet nobody, till very lately, was ever sensible of it. The elegant Lord Shaftesbury, who first gave occasion to remark this distinction, and who, in general, adhered to the principles of the ancients, it not, himself, entirely free from the same confusion.

It must be acknowledged, that both sides of the question are susceptible of specious arguments. Moral distinctions, it may be said, are discernible by pure *reason*: else, whence the many disputes that reign in common life, as well as in philosophy, with regard to this subject: the long chain of proofs often produced on both sides; the examples cited, the authorities appealed to, the analogies employed, the fallacies detected, the inferences drawn, and the several conclusions adjusted to their proper principles. Truth is disputable; not taste: what exists in the nature of things is the standard of our judgement; what each man feels within himself is the standard of sentiment. Propositions in geometry may be proved, systems in physics may be controverted; but the harmony of verse, the tenderness of passion, the brilliancy of wit, must give immediate pleasure. No man reasons concerning another's beauty; but frequently concerning the justice or injustice of his actions. In every criminal trail the first object of the prisoner is to disprove the facts alleged, and deny the actions imputed to him: the second to prove, that, even if these actions were real, they might be justified, as innocent and lawful. It is confessedly by deductions of the understanding, that the first point is ascertained: how can we suppose that a different faculty of the mind is employed in fixing the other?

On the other hand, those who would resolve all moral determinations into *sentiment,* may endeavour to show, that it is impossible for reason ever to draw conclusions of this nature. To virtue, say they, it belongs to be *amiable,* and vice *odious.* This forms their very nature or essence. But can reason or argumentation distribute these different epithets to any subjects, and pronounce beforehand, that this must produce love, and that hatred? Or what other reason can we ever assign for these affections, but the original fabric and formation of the human mind, which is naturally adapted to receive them?

The end of all moral speculations is to teach us our duty; and, by proper representations of the deformity of vice and beauty of virtue, beget correspondent habits, and engage us to avoid the one, and embrace the other. But is this ever to be expected from inferences and conclusions of the understanding, which of themselves have no hold of the affections nor set in motion the active powers of men? They discover truths: but where the truths which they discover are indifferent, and beget no desire or aversion, they can have no influence on conduct and behaviour. What is honourable, what is fair, what is becoming, what is noble, what is generous, takes possession of the heart, and animates us to embrace and maintain it. What is intelligible, what is evident, what is probable, what is true, procures only the cool assent of the understanding; and gratifying a speculative curiosity, puts an end to our researches.

Extinguish all the warm feelings and prepossessions in favour of virtue, and all disgust or aversion to vice: render men totally indifferent towards these distinctions; and morality is no longer a practical study, nor has any tendency to regulate our lives and actions.

These arguments on each side (and many more might be produced) are so plausible, that I am apt to suspect, they may, the one as well as the other, be solid and satisfactory, and that *reason* and *sentiment* concur in almost all moral determinations and conclusions. The final sentence, it is probable, which pronounces characters and actions amiable or odious, praise-worthy or blameable; that which stamps on them the mark of honour or infamy, approbation or censure; that which renders morality an active principle and constitutes virtue our happiness, and vice our misery: it is probable, I say, that this final sentence depends on some internal sense or feeling, which nature has made universal in the whole species. For what else can have an influence of this nature? But in order to pave the way for such a sentiment, and give a proper discernment of its object, it is often necessary, we find, that much reasoning should precede, that nice distinctions be made, just conclusions drawn, distant comparisons formed, complicated relations examined, and general facts fixed and ascertained. Some species of beauty, especially the natural kinds, on their first appearance, command our affection and approbation; and where they fail of this effect, it is impossible for any reasoning to redress their influence, or adapt them better to our taste and sentiment. But in many orders of beauty, particularly those of the finer arts, it is requisite to employ much reasoning, in order to feel the proper sentiment; and a false relish may frequently be corrected by argument and reflection. There are just grounds to conclude, that moral beauty partakes much of this latter species, and demands the assistance of our intellectual faculties, in order to give it a suitable influence on the human mind.

But though this question, concerning the general principles of morals, be curious and important, it is needless for us, at present, to employ further care in our researches concerning it. For if we can be so happy, in the course of this enquiry, as to discover the true origin of morals, it will then easily appear how far either sentiment or reason enters into all determinations of this nature.[1] In order to attain this purpose, we shall endeavour to follow a very simple method: we shall analyse that complication of mental qualities, which form what, in common life, we call Personal Merit: we shall consider every attribute of the mind, which renders a man an object either of esteem and affection, or of hatred and contempt; every habit or sentiment or faculty, which, if ascribed to any person, implies either praise or blame, and may enter into any panegyric or satire of his character and manners. The quick sensibility, which, on this head, is so universal among mankind, gives a philosopher sufficient assurance, that he can never be considerably mistaken in framing the catalogue, or incur any danger of misplacing the objects of his contemplation: he needs only enter into his own breast for a moment, and consider whether or not he should desire to have this or that quality ascribed to him, and whether such or such an imputation would proceed from a friend or an enemy. The very nature of language guides us almost infallibly in forming a judgement of this nature; and as every tongue possesses one set of words which are taken in a good sense, and another in the opposite, the least acquaintance with the idiom suffices, without any reasoning, to direct us in collecting and arranging the estimable or blameable qualities of men. The only object of reasoning is to discover the circumstances on both sides, which are common to these qualities; to observe that particular in which the estimable qualities agree on the one hand, and the blameable on the other; and thence to reach the foundation of ethics, and find those universal principles, from which all censure or approbation is ultimately derived. As this is a question of fact, not of abstract science, we can only expect success, by following the experimental method, and deducing general maxims from a comparison of particular instances. The other scientific method, where a general abstract principle is first established, and is afterwards branched out into a variety of inferences and conclusions, may be more perfect in itself, but suits less the imperfection of human nature, and is a common source of illusion and mistake in this as well as in other subject. Men are now cured of their passion for hypotheses and systems in natural philosophy, and will hearken to no arguments but those which are derived from experience. It is full time they should attempt a like reformation in all moral disquisitions; and reject every system of ethics, however subtle or ingenious, which is not founded on fact and observation.

We shall begin our enquiry on this head by the consideration of the social virtues, Benevolence and Justice. The explication of them will probably give us an opening by which the others may be accounted for.

Section II
Of Benevolence

Part I

It may be esteemed, perhaps, a superfluous task to prove, that the benevolent or softer affections are estimable; and wherever they appear, engage the approbation and good-will of mankind. The epithets *sociable, good-natured, humane, merciful, grateful, friendly, generous, beneficent,* or their equivalents, are known in all languages, and universally express the highest merit, which *human nature* is capable of attaining. Where these amiable qualities are attended with birth and power and eminent abilities, and display themselves in the good government or useful instruction of mankind, they seem even to raise the possessors of them above the rank of *human nature,* and make them approach in some measure to the divine. Exalted capacity, undaunted courage, prosperous success; these may only expose a hero or politician to the envy and ill-will of the public: but as soon as the praises are added of humane and beneficent; when instances are displayed of lenity, tenderness or friendship; envy itself is silent, or joins the general voice of approbation and applause.

. . . .

Part II

We may observe that, in displaying the praises of any humane, beneficent man, there is one circumstance which never fails to be amply insisted on, namely, the happiness and satisfaction, derived to society from his intercourse and good offices. To his parents, we are apt to say, he endears himself by his pious attachment and duteous care still more than by the connexions of nature. His children never feel his authority, but when employed for their advantage. With him, the ties of love are consolidated by beneficence and friendship. The ties of friendship approach, in a fond observance of each obliging office, to those of love and inclination. His domestics and dependants have in him a sure resource; and no longer dread the power of fortune, but so far as she exercises it over him. From him the hungry receive food, the naked clothing, the ignorant and slothful skill and industry. Like the sun, an inferior minister of providence he cheers, invigorates, and sustains the surrounding world.

If confined to private life, the sphere of his activity is narrower; but his influence is all benign and gentle. If exalted into a higher station, mankind and posterity reap the fruit of his labours.

As these topics of praise never fail to be employed, and with success, where we would inspire esteem for any one; may it not thence be concluded, that the utility, resulting from the social virtues, forms, at least, a *part* of their merit, and is one source of that approbation and regard so universally paid to them?

. . . .

In all determinations of morality, this circumstance of public utility is ever principally in view; and wherever disputes arise, either in philosophy or common life, concerning the bounds of duty, the question cannot, by any means, be decided with greater certainty, than by ascertaining, on any side, the true interests of mankind. If any false opinion, embraced from appearances, has been found to prevail; as soon as farther experience and sounder reasoning have given us juster notions of human affairs, we retract our first sentiment, and adjust anew the boundaries of moral good and evil.

Giving alms to common beggars is naturally praised; because it seems to carry relief to the distressed and indigent: but when we observe the encouragement thence arising to idleness and debauchery, we regard that species of charity rather as a weakness than a virtue.

Tyrannicide, or the assassination of usurpers and oppressive princes, was highly extolled in ancient times; because it both freed mankind from many of these monsters, and seemed to keep the others in awe, whom the sword or poinard could not reach. But history and experience having since convinced us, that this practice increases the jealously and cruelty of princes, a Timoleon and a Brutus, though treated with indulgence on account of the prejudices of their times, are now considered as very improper models for imitation.

Liberality in princes is regarded as a mark of beneficence, but when it occurs, that the homely bread of the honest and industrious is often thereby converted into delicious cates for the idle and the prodigal, we soon retract our heedless praises. The regrets of a prince, for having lost a day, were noble and generous: but had he intended to have spent it in acts of generosity to his greedy courtiers, it was better lost than misemployed after that manner.

Luxury, or a refinement on the pleasures and conveniencies of life, had long been supposed the source of every corruption in government, and the immediate cause of faction, sedition, civil wars, and the total loss of liberty. It was, therefore, universally regarded as a vice, and was an object of declamation to all satirists, and severe moralists. Those, who prove, or attempt to prove, that such refinements rather tend to the increase of industry, civility, and arts regulate anew our *moral* as well as *political* sentiments, and represent, as laudable or innocent, what had formerly been regarded as pernicious and blameable.

Upon the whole, then, it seems undeniable, *that* nothing can bestow more merit on any human creature than the sentiment of benevolence in an eminent degree; and *that* a *part,* at least, of its merit arises from its tendency to promote the interests of our species, and bestow happiness on human society. We carry our view into the salutary consequences of such a character and disposition; and whatever has so benign an influence, and forwards so desirable an end, is beheld with complacency and pleasure. The social virtues are never regarded without their beneficial tendencies, nor viewed as barren and unfruitful. The happiness of mankind, the order of society, and harmony of families, the mutual support of friends, are always considered as the result of their gentle dominion over the breasts of men.

How considerable a *part* of their merit we ought to ascribe to their utility, will better appear from future disquisitions[2]; as well as the reason, why this circumstance has such a command over our esteem and approbation.[3]

Section III
Of Justice

Part I

That Justice is useful to society, and consequently that *part* of its merit, at least, must arise from that consideration, it would be a superfluous undertaking to prove. That public utility is the *sole* origin of justice, and that reflections on the beneficial consequences of this virtue are the *sole* foundation of its merit; this proposition, being more curious and important, will better deserve our examination and enquiry.

Let us suppose that nature has bestowed on the human race such profuse *abundance* of all *external* conveniencies, that, without any uncertainty in the event, without any care or industry on our part, every individual finds himself fully provided with whatever his most voracious appetites can want, or luxurious imagination wish or desire. His natural beauty, we shall suppose, surpasses all acquired ornaments: the perpetual clemency of the seasons renders useless all clothes or covering: the raw herbage affords him the most delicious fare; the clear fountain, the richest beverage. No laborious occupation required: no tillage: no navigation. Music, poetry, and contemplation form his sole business: conversation, mirth, and friendship his sole amusement.

It seems evident that, in such a happy state, every other social virtue would flourish, and receive tenfold increase; but the cautious, jealous virtue of justice would never once have been dreamed of. For what purpose make a partition of goods, where every one has already more than enough? Why give rise to property, where there cannot possibly be any injury? Why call this object *mine,* when upon the seizing of it by another, I need but stretch out my hand to possess myself of what is equally valuable? Justice, in that case, being totally useless, would be an idle ceremonial, and could never possibly have place in the catalogue of virtues.

We see, even in the present necessitous condition of mankind, that, wherever any benefit is bestowed by nature in an unlimited abundance, we leave it always in common among the whole human race, and make no subdivisions of right and property. Water and air, though the most necessary of all objects, are not challenged as the property of individuals; nor can any man commit injustice by the most lavish use and enjoyment of these blessings. In fertile extensive countries, with few inhabitants, land is regarded on the same footing. And no topic is so much insisted on by those, who defend the liberty of the seas, as the unexhausted use of them in navigation. Were the advantages, procured by navigation, as inexhaustible, these reasoners had never had any adversaries to refute; nor had any claims ever been advanced of a separate, exclusive dominion over the ocean.

It may happen, in some countries, at some periods, that there be established a property in water, none in land; if the latter be in greater abundance than can be used by the inhabitants, and the former be found, with difficulty, and in very small quantities.

Again; suppose, that, though the necessities of human race continue the same as the present, yet the mind is so enlarged, and so replete with friendship and generosity, that every man has the utmost tenderness for every man, and feels no more concern for his own interest than for that of his fellows; it seems evident, that the use of justice would, in this case, be suspended by such an extensive benevolence, nor would the divisions and barriers of property and obligation have ever been thought of. Why should I bind another, by a deed or promise, to do me any good office, when I know that he is already prompted, by the strongest inclination, to seek my happiness, and would, of himself, perform the desired service; except the hurt, he thereby receives, be greater than the benefit accruing to me? in which case, he knows, that, from my innate humanity and friendship, I should be the first to oppose myself to his imprudent generosity. Why raise land-marks between my neighbour's field and mine, when my heart has made no division between our interests; but shares all his joys and sorrows with the same force and vivacity as if originally my own? Every man, upon this supposition, being a second self to another, would trust all his interests to the discretion of every man; without jealousy, without partition, without distinction. And the whole human race would form only one family; where all would lie in common, and be used freely, without regard to property; but cautiously too, with as entire regard to the necessities of each individual, as if our own interests were most intimately concerned.

In the present disposition of the human heart, it would, perhaps, be difficult to find complete instances of such enlarged affections; but still we may observe, that the case of families approaches towards it; and the stronger the mutual benevolence is among the individuals, the nearer it approaches; till all distinction of property be, in a great measure, lost and confounded among them. Between married persons, the cement of friendship is by the laws supposed so strong as to abolish all division of possessions; and has often, in reality, the force ascribed to it. And it is observable, that, during the ardour of new enthusiasms, when every principle is inflamed into extravagance, the community of goods has frequently been attempted; and nothing but experience of its inconveniencies, from the returning or disguised selfishness of men, could make the imprudent fanatics adopt anew the ideas of justice and of separate property. So true is it, that this virtue derives its existence entirely from its necessary *use* to the intercourse and social state of mankind.

To make this truth more evident, let us reverse the foregoing suppositions; and carrying everything to the opposite extreme, consider what would be the effect of these new situations. Suppose a society to fall into such want of all common necessaries, that the utmost frugality and industry cannot preserve the greater number from perishing, and the whole from extreme misery; it will readily, I believe, be admitted, that the strict laws of justice are suspended, in such a pressing emergence, and give place to the stronger motives of necessity and self-preservation. Is it any crime, after a shipwreck, to seize whatever means or instrument of safety one can lay hold of, without regard to former limitations of property? Or if a city besieged were perishing with hunger; can we imagine, that men will see any means of preservation before them, and lose their lives, from a scrupulous regard to what, in other situations, would be the rules of equity and justice? The use and tendency of that virtue is to procure happiness and security, by preserving order in society: but where the society is ready to perish from extreme necessity, no greater evil can be dreaded from violence and injustice; and every man may now provide for himself by all the means which prudence can dictate, or humanity permit. The public, even in less urgent necessities, opens granaries, without the consent of proprietors; as justly supposing, that the authority of magistracy may, consistent with equity, extend so far: but were any number of men to assemble, without the tie of laws or civil jurisdiction; would an equal partition of bread in a famine, though effected by power and even violence, be regarded as criminal or injurious?

Suppose likewise, that it should be a virtuous man's fate to fall into the society of ruffians, remote from the protection of laws and government; what conduct must he embrace in that melancholy situation? He sees such a desperate rapaciousness prevail; such a disregard to equity, such contempt of order, such stupid blindness to future consequences, as must immediately have the most tragical conclusion, and must terminate in destruction to the greater number, and in a total dissolution of society to the rest. He, meanwhile, can have no other expedient than to arm himself, to whomever the sword he seizes, or the buckler, may belong: To make provision of all means of defence and security: And his particular regard to justice being no longer of use to his own safety or that of others, he must consult the dictates of self-preservation alone, without concern for those who no longer merit his care and attention.

When any man, even in political society, renders himself by his crimes, obnoxious to the public, he is punished by the laws in his goods and person; that is, the ordinary rules of justice are, with regard to him, suspended for a moment, and it becomes equitable to inflict on him, for the *benefit* of society, what otherwise he could not suffer without wrong or injury.

The rage and violence of public war; what is it but a suspension of justice among the warring parties, who perceive, that this virtue is now no longer of any *use* or advantage to them? The laws of war, which then succeed to those of equity and justice, are rules calculated for the *advantage* and *utility* of that particular state, in which men are now placed. And were a civilized nation engaged with barbarians, who observed no rules even of war, the former must also suspend their observance of them, where they no longer serve to any purpose; and must render every action or rencounter as bloody and pernicious as possible to the first aggressors.

Thus, the rules of equity or justice depend entirely on the particular state and condition in which men are placed, and owe their origin and existence to that utility, which results to the public from their strict and regular observance. Reverse, in any considerable circumstance, the condition of men: Produce extreme abundance or extreme necessity: Implant in the human breast perfect moderation and humanity, or perfect rapaciousness and malice: By rendering justice totally *useless,* you thereby totally destroy its essence, and suspend its obligation upon mankind.

The common situation of society is a medium amidst all these extremes. We are naturally partial to ourselves, and to our friends; but are capable of learning the advantage resulting from a more equitable conduct. Few enjoyments are given us from the open and liberal hand of nature; but by art, labour, and industry, we can extract them in great abundance. Hence the ideas of property become necessary in all civil society: Hence justice derives its usefulness to the public: And hence alone arises its merit and moral obligation.

. . . .

The more we vary our views of human life, and the newer and more unusual the lights are in which we survey it, the more shall we be convinced, that the origin here assigned for the virtue of justice is real and satisfactory.

Were there a species of creatures intermingled with men, which, though rational, were possessed of such inferior strength, both of body and mind, that they were incapable of all resistance, and could never, upon the highest provocation, make us feel the effects of their resentment; the necessary consequence, I think, is that we should be bound by the laws of humanity to give gentle usage to these creatures, but should not, properly speaking, lie under any restraint of justice with regard to them, nor could they possess any right or property, exclusive of such arbitrary lords. Our intercourse with them could not be called society, which supposes a degree of equality; but absolute command on the one side, and servile obedience on the other. Whatever we covet, they must instantly resign: Our permission is the only tenure, by which they hold their possessions: Our compassion and kindness the only check, by which they curb our lawless will: And as no inconvenience ever results from the exercise of a power, so firmly established in nature, the restraints of justice and property, being totally *useless,* would never have place in so unequal a confederacy.

This is plainly the situation of men, with regard to animals; and how far these may be said to possess reason, I leave it to others to determine. The great superiority of civilized Europeans above barbarous Indians, tempted us to imagine ourselves on the same footing with regard to them, and made us throw off all restraints of justice, and even of humanity, in our treatment of them. In many nations, the female sex are reduced to like slavery, and are rendered incapable for all property, in opposition to their lordly masters. But though the males, when united, have in all countries bodily force sufficient to maintain this severe tyranny, yet such are the insinuation, address, and charms of their fair companions, that women are commonly able to break the confederacy, and share with the other sex in all the rights and privileges of society.

Were the human species so framed by nature as that each individual possessed within himself every faculty, requisite both for his own preservation and for the propagation of his kind: Were all society and intercourse cut off between man and man, by the primary intention of the supreme Creator: It seems evident, that so solitary a being would be as much incapable of justice, as of social discourse and conversation. Where mutual regards and forbearance serve to no manner of purpose, they would never direct the conduct of any reasonable man. The headlong course of the passions would be checked by no reflection on future consequences. And as each man is here supposed to love himself alone, and to depend only on himself and his own activity for safety and happiness, he would, on every occasion, to the utmost of his power, challenge the preference above every other being, to none of which he is bound by any ties, either of nature or of interest.

But suppose the conjunction of the sexes to be established in nature, a family immediately arises; and particular rules being found requisite for its subsistence, these are immediately embraced; though without comprehending the rest of mankind within their prescriptions. Suppose that several families unite together into one society, which is totally disjoined from all others, the rules, which preserve peace and order, enlarge themselves to the utmost extent of that society; but becoming then entirely useless, lose their force when carried one step farther. But again suppose, that several distinct societies maintain a kind of intercourse for mutual convenience and advantage, the boundaries of justice still grow larger, in proportion to the largeness of men's views, and the force of their mutual connexions. History, experience, reason sufficiently instruct us in this natural progress of human sentiments, and in the gradual enlargement of our regards to justice, in proportion as we become acquainted with the extensive utility of that virtue.

. . . .

Section V
Why Utility Pleases

Part I

It seems so natural a thought to ascribe to their utility the praise, which we bestow on the social virtues, that one would expect to meet with this principle everywhere in moral writers, as the chief foundation of their reasoning and enquiry. In common life, we may observe, that the circumstance of utility is always appealed to; nor is it supposed, that a greater eulogy can be given to any man, than to display his usefulness to the public, and enumerate the services, which he has performed to mankind and society. What praise, even of an inanimate form, if the regularity and elegance of its parts destroy not its fitness for any useful purpose! And how satisfactory an apology for any disproportion or seeming deformity, if we can show the necessity of that particular construction for the use intended! A ship appears more beautiful to an artist, or one moderately skilled in navigation, where its prow is wide and swelling beyond its poop, than if it were framed with a precise geometrical regularity, in contradiction to all the laws of mechanics. A building, whose doors and windows were exact squares, would hurt the eye by that very proportion; as ill adapted to the figure of a human creature, for whose service the fabric was intended. What wonder then, that a man, whose habits and conduct are hurtful to society, and dangerous or pernicious to every one who has an intercourse with him, should, on that account, be an object of disapprobation, and communicate to every spectator the strongest sentiment of disgust and hatred.

But perhaps the difficulty of accounting for these effects of usefulness, or its contrary, has kept philosophers from admitting them into their systems of ethics, and has induced them rather to employ any other principle, in explaining the origin of moral good and evil. But it is no just reason for rejecting any principle, confirmed by experience, that we cannot give a satisfactory account of its origin, nor are able to resolve it into other more general principles. And if we would employ a little thought on the present subject, we need be at no loss to account for the influence of utility, and to deduce it from principles, the most known and avowed in human nature.

From the apparent usefulness of the social virtues, it has readily been inferred by sceptics, both ancient and modern, that all moral distinctions arise from education, and were, at first, invented, and afterwards encouraged, by the art of politicians, in order to render men tractable, and subdue their natural ferocity and selfishness, which incapacitated them for society. This principle, indeed, of precept and education, must so far be owned to have a powerful influence, that it may frequently increase or diminish, beyond their natural standard, the sentiments of approbation or dislike; and may even, in particular instances, create, without any natural principle, a new sentiment of this kind; as is evident in all superstitious practices and observances: But that *all* moral affection or dislike arises from this origin, will never surely be allowed by any judicious enquirer. Had nature made no such distinction, founded on the original constitution of the mind, the words, *honourable* and *shameful, lovely* and *odious, noble* and *despicable,* had never had place in any language; nor could politicians, had they invented these terms, ever have been able to render them intelligible, or make them convey any idea to the audience. So that nothing can be more superficial than this paradox of the sceptics; and it were well, if, in the abstruser studies of logic and metaphysics, we could as easily obviate the cavils of that sect, as in the practical and more intelligible sciences of politics and morals.

The social virtues must, therefore, be allowed to have a natural beauty and amiableness, which, at first, antecedent to all precept or education, recommends them to the esteem of uninstructed mankind, and engages their affections. And as the public utility of these virtues is the chief circumstance, whence they derive their merit, it follows, that the end, which they have a tendency to promote, must be some way agreeable to us, and take hold of some natural affection. It must please, either from considerations of self-interest, or from more generous motives and regards.

It has often been asserted, that, as every man has a strong connexion with society, and perceives the impossibility of his solitary subsistence, he becomes, on that account, favourable to all those habits or principles, which promote order in society, and insure to him the quiet possession of so inestimable a blessing. As much as we value our own happiness and welfare, as much must we applaud the practice of justice and humanity, by which alone the social confederacy can be maintained, and every man reap the fruits of mutual protection and assistance.

This deduction of morals from self-love, or a regard to private interest, is an obvious thought, and has not arisen wholly from the wanton sallies and sportive assaults of the sceptics. To mention no others, Polybius, one of the gravest and most judicious, as well as most moral writers of antiquity, has assigned this selfish origin to all our sentiments of virtue. But though the solid practical sense of that author, and his aversion to all vain subtilties, render his authority on the present subject very considerable; yet is not this an affair to be decided by authority, and the voice of nature and experience seems plainly to oppose the selfish theory.

We frequently bestow praise on virtuous actions, performed in very distant ages and remote countries; where the utmost subtilty of imagination would not discover any appearance of self-interest, or find any connexion of our present happiness and security with events so widely separated from us.

A generous, a brave, a noble deed, performed by an adversary, commands our approbation; while in its consequences it may be acknowledged prejudicial to our particular interest.

Where private advantage concurs with general affection for virtue, we readily perceive and avow the mixture of these distinct sentiments, which have a very different feeling and influence on the mind. We praise, perhaps, with more alacrity, where the generous humane action contributes to our particular interest: But the topics of praise, which we insist on, are very wide of this circumstance. And we may attempt to bring over others to our sentiments, without endeavouring to convince them, that they reap any advantage from the actions which we recommend to their approbation and applause.

Frame the model of a praiseworthy character, consisting of all the most amiable moral virtues: Give instances, in which these display themselves after an eminent and extraordinary manner: You readily engage the esteem and approbation of all your audience, who never so much as enquire in what age and country the person lived, who possessed these noble qualities: A circumstance, however, of all others, the most material to self-love, or a concern for our own individual happiness.

Once on a time, a statesman, in the shock and contest of parties, prevailed so far as to procure, by his eloquence, the banishment of an able adversary; whom he secretly followed, offering him money for his support during his exile, and soothing him with topics of consolation in his misfortunes. *Alas !* cries the banished statesman, *with what regret must I leave my friends in this city, where even enemies are so generous!* Virtue, though in an enemy, here pleased him: And we also give it the just tribute of praise and approbation; nor do we retract these sentiments, when we hear, that the action passed at Athens, about two thousand years ago, and that the persons names were Eschines and Demosthenes.

What is that to me? There are few occasions, when this question is not pertinent: And had it that universal, infallible influence supposed, it would turn into ridicule every composition, and almost every conversation, which contain any praise or censure of men and manners.

It is but a weak subterfuge, when pressed by these facts and arguments, to say, that we transport ourselves, by the force of imagination, into distant ages and countries, and consider the advantage, which we should have reaped from these characters, had we been contemporaries, and had any commerce with the persons. It is not conceivable, how a *real* sentiment or passion can ever arise from a known *imaginary* interest; especially when our *real* interest is still kept in view, and is often acknowledged to be entirely distinct from the imaginary, and even sometimes opposite to it.

A man, brought to the brink of a precipice, cannot look down without trembling; and the sentiment of *imaginary* danger actuates him, in opposition to the opinion and belief of *real* safety. But the imagination is here assisted by the presence of a striking object; and yet prevails not, except to be also aided by novelty, and the unusual appearance of the object. Custom soon reconciles us to heights and precipices, and wears off these false and delusive terrors. The reverse is observable in the estimates which we form of characters and manners; and the more we habituate ourselves to an accurate scrutiny of morals, the more delicate feeling do we acquire of the most minute distinctions between vice and virtue. Such frequent occasion, indeed, have we, in common life, to pronounce all kinds of moral determinations, that no object of this kind can be new or unusual to us; nor could any *false* views or prepossessions maintain their ground against an experience, so common and familiar. Experience being chiefly what forms the associations of ideas, it is impossible that any association could establish and support itself, in direct opposition to that principle.

Usefulness is agreeable, and engages our approbation. This is a matter of fact, confirmed by daily observation. But, *useful?* For what? For somebody's interest, surely. Whose interest then? Not our own only: For our approbation frequently extends farther. It must, therefore, be the interest of those, who are served by the character or action approved of; and these we may conclude, however remote, are not totally indifferent to us. By opening up this principle, we shall discover one great source of moral distinctions.

Part II

Self-love is a principle in human nature of such extensive energy, and the interest of each individual is, in general, so closely connected with that of the community, that those philosophers were excusable, who fancied that all our concern for the public might be resolved into a concern for our own happiness and preservation. They saw every moment, instances of approbation or blame, satisfaction or displeasure towards characters and actions; they denominated the objects of these sentiments, *virtues,* or *vices;* they observed, that the former had a tendency to increase the happiness, and the latter the misery of mankind; they asked, whether it were possible that we could have any general concern for society, or any disinterested resentment of the welfare or injury of others; they found it simpler to consider all these sentiments as modifications of self-love; and they discovered a pretence, at least, for this unity of principle, in that close union of interest, which is so observable between the public and each individual.

But notwithstanding this frequent confusion of interests, it is easy to attain what natural philosophers, after Lord Bacon, have affected to call the *experimentum crucis,* or that experiment which points out the right way in any doubt or ambiguity. We have found instances, in which private interest was separate from public; in which it was even contrary: And yet we observed the moral sentiment to continue, notwithstanding this disjunction of interests. And wherever these distinct interests sensibly concurred, we always found a sensible increase of the sentiment, and a more warm affection to virtue, and detestation of vice, or what we properly call, *gratitude* and *revenge.* Compelled by these instances, we must renounce the theory, which accounts for every moral sentiment by the principle of self-love. We must adopt a more public affection, and allow, that the interests of society are not, even on their own account, entirely indifferent to us. Usefulness is only a tendency to a certain end; and it is a contradiction in terms, that anything pleases as means to an end, where the end itself no wise affects us. If usefulness, therefore, be a source of moral sentiment, and if this usefulness be not always considered with a reference to self; it follows, that everything, which contributes to the happiness of society, recommends itself directly to our approbation and good-will. Here is a principle, which accounts, in great part, for the origin of morality: And what need we seek for abstruse and remote systems, when there occurs one so obvious and natural?[4]

Have we any difficulty to comprehend the force of humanity and benevolence? Or to conceive, that the very aspect of happiness, joy, prosperity, gives pleasure; that of pain, suffering, sorrow, communicates uneasiness? The human countenance, says Horace, borrows smiles or tears from the human countenance. Reduce a person to solitude, and he loses all enjoyment, except either of the sensual or speculative kind; and that because the movements of his heart are not forwarded by correspondent movements in his fellow-creatures. The signs of sorrow and mourning, though arbitrary, affect us with melancholy; but the natural symptoms, tears and cries and groans, never fail to infuse compassion and uneasiness. And if the effects of misery touch us in so lively a manner; can we be supposed altogether insensible or indifferent towards its causes; when a malicious or treacherous character and behaviour are presented to us?

We enter, I shall suppose, into a convenient, warm, well-contrived apartment: We necessarily receive a pleasure from its very survey; because it presents us with the pleasing ideas of ease, satisfaction, and enjoyment. The hospitable, good-humoured, humane landlord appears. This circumstance surely must embellish the whole; nor can we easily forbear reflecting, with pleasure, on the satisfaction which results to every one from his intercourse and good-offices.

His whole family, by the freedom, ease, confidence, and calm enjoyment, diffused over their countenances, sufficiently express their happiness. I have a pleasing sympathy in the prospect of so much joy, and can never consider the source of it, without the most agreeable emotions.

He tells me, that an oppressive and powerful neighbour had attempted to dispossess him of his inheritance, and had long disturbed all his innocent and social pleasures. I feel an immediate indignation arise in me against such violence and injury.

But it is no wonder, he adds, that a private wrong should proceed from a man, who had enslaved provinces, depopulated cities, and made the field and scaffold stream with human blood. I am struck with horror at the prospect of so much misery, and am actuated by the strongest antipathy against its author.

In general, it is certain, that, wherever we go, whatever we reflect on or converse about, everything still presents us with the view of human happiness or misery, and excites in our breast a sympathetic movement of pleasure or uneasiness. In our serious occupations, in our careless amusements, this principle still exerts its active energy.

. . . .

If any man from a cold insensibility, or narrow selfishness of temper, is unaffected with the images of human happiness or misery, he must be equally indifferent to the images of vice and virtue: As, on the other hand, it is always found, that a warm concern for the interests of our species is attended with a delicate feeling of all moral distinctions; a strong resentment of injury done to men; a lively approbation of their welfare. In this particular, though great superiority is observable of one man above another; yet none are so entirely indifferent to the interest of their fellow-creatures, as to perceive no distinctions of moral good and evil, in consequence of the different tendencies of actions and principles. How, indeed, can we suppose it possible in any one, who wears a human heart, that if there be subjected to his censure, one character or system of conduct, which is beneficial, and another which is pernicious, to his species or community, he will not so much as give a cool preference to the former, or ascribe to it the smallest merit or regard? Let us suppose such a person ever so selfish; let private interest have ingrossed ever so much his attention; yet in instances, where that is not concerned, he must unavoidably feel *some* propensity to the good of mankind, and make it an object of choice, if everything else be equal. Would any man, who is walking along, tread as willingly on another's gouty toes, whom he has no quarrel with, as on the hard flint and pavement? There is here surely a difference in the case. We surely take into consideration the happiness and misery of others, in weighing the several motives of action, and incline to the former, where no private regards draw us to seek our own promotion or advantage by the injury of our fellow-creatures. And if the principles of humanity are capable, in many instances, of influencing our actions, they must, at all times, have *some* authority over our sentiments, and give us a general approbation of what is useful to society, and blame of what is dangerous or pernicious. The degrees of these sentiments may be the subject of controversy; but the reality of their existence, one should think, must be admitted in every theory or system.

. . . .

A statesman or patriot, who serves our own country in our own time, has always a more passionate regard paid to him, than one whose beneficial influence operated on distant ages or remote nations; where the good, resulting from his generous humanity, being less connected with us, seems more obscure, and affects us with a less lively sympathy. We may own the merit to be equally great, though our sentiments are not raised to an equal height, in both cases. The judgment here corrects the inequalities of our internal emotions and perceptions; in like manner, as it preserves us from error, in the several variations of images, presented to our external senses. The same object, at a double distance, really throws on the eye a picture of but half the bulk; yet we imagine that it appears of the same size in both situations; because we know that on our approach to it, its image would expand on the eye, and that the difference consists not in the object itself, but in our position with regard to it. And, indeed, without such a correction of appearances, both in internal and external sentiment, men could never think or talk steadily on any subject; while their fluctuating situations produce a continual variation on objects, and throw them into such different and contrary lights and positions.[5]

The more we converse with mankind, and the greater social intercourse we maintain, the more shall we be familiarized to these general preferences and distinctions, without which our conversation and discourse could scarcely be rendered intelligible to each other. Every man's interest is peculiar to himself, and the aversions and desires, which result from it, cannot be supposed to affect others in a like degree. General language, therefore, being formed for general use, must be moulded on some more general views, and must affix the epithets of praise or blame, in conformity to sentiments, which arise from the general interests of the community. And if these sentiments, in most men, be not so strong as those, which have a reference to private good; yet still they must make some distinction, even in persons the most depraved and selfish; and must attach the notion of good to a beneficient conduct, and of evil to the contrary. Sympathy, we shall allow, is much fainter than our concern for ourselves, and sympathy with persons remote from us much fainter than that with persons near and contiguous; but for this very reason it is necessary for us, in our calm judgements and discourse concerning the characters of men, to neglect all these differences, and render our sentiments more public and social. Besides, that we ourselves often change our situation in this particular, we every day meet with persons who are in a situation different from us, and who could never converse with us were we to remain constantly in that position and point of view, which is peculiar to ourselves. The intercourse of sentiments, therefore, in society and conversation, makes us form some general unalterable standard, by which we may approve or disapprove of characters and manners. And though the heart takes not part entirely with those general notions, nor regulates all its love and hatred, by the universal abstract differences of vice and virtue, without regard to self, or the persons with whom we are more intimately connected; yet have these moral differences a considerable influence, and being sufficient, at least, for discourse, serve all our purposes in company, in the pulpit, on the theatre, and in the schools.

Thus, in whatever light we take this subject, the merit, ascribed to the social virtues, appears still uniform, and arises chiefly from that regard, which the natural sentiment of benevolence engages us to pay to the interests of mankind and society. If we consider the principles of the human make, such as they appear to daily experience and observation, we must, a priori, conclude it impossible for such a creature as man to be totally indifferent to the well or ill-being of his fellow-creatures, and not readily, of himself, to pronounce, where nothing gives him any particular bias, that what promotes their happiness is good, what tends to their misery is evil, without any farther regard to consideration. Here then are the faint rudiments, at least, or outlines, of a *general* distinction between actions; and in proportion as the humanity of the person is supposed to encrease, his connexion with those who are injured or benefited, and his lively conception of their misery or happiness; his consequent censure or approbation acquires proportionable vigour. There is no necessity, that a generous action, barely mentioned in an old history or remote gazette, should communicate any strong feelings of applause and admiration. Virtue, placed at such a distance, is like a fixed star, which, though to the eye of reason it may appear as luminous as the sun in his meridian, is so infinitely removed as to affect the senses, neither with light nor heat. Bring this virtue nearer, by our acquaintance or connexion with the persons, or even by an eloquent recital of the case; our hearts are immediately caught, our sympathy enlivened, and our cool approbation converted into the warmest sentiments of friendship and regard. These seem necessary and infallible consequences of the general principles of human nature, as discovered in common life and practice.

Again; reverse these views and reasonings: Consider the matter a posteriori; and weighing the consequences, enquire if the merit of social virtue be not, in a great measure, derived from the feelings of humanity, with which it affects the spectators. It appears to be matter of fact, that the circumstance of *utility,* in all subjects, is a source of praise and approbation: That it is constantly appealed to in all moral decisions concerning the merit and demerit of actions: That it is the *sole* source of that high regard paid to justice, fidelity, honour, allegiance, and chastity: That it is inseparable from all the other social virtues, humanity, generosity, charity, affability, lenity, mercy, and moderation: And, in a word, that it is a foundation of the chief part of morals, which has a reference to mankind and our fellow-creatures.

It appears also, that, in our general approbation of characters and manners, the useful tendency of the social virtues moves us not by any regards to self-interest, but has an influence much more universal and extensive. It appears that a tendency to public good, and to the promoting of peace, harmony, and order in society, does always, by affecting the benevolent principles of our frame, engage us on the side of the social virtues. And it appears, as an additional confirmation, that these principles of humanity and sympathy enter so deeply into all our sentiments, and have so powerful an influence, as may enable them to excite the strongest censure and applause. The present theory is the simple result of all these inferences, each of which seems founded on uniform experience and observation.

Were it doubtful, whether there were any such principle in our nature as humanity or a concern for others, yet when we see, in numberless instances, that whatever has a tendency to promote the interests of society, is so highly approved of, we ought thence to learn the force of the benevolent principle; since it is impossible for anything to please as means to an end, where the end is totally indifferent. On the other hand, were it doubtful, whether there were, implanted in our nature, any general principle of moral blame and approbation, yet when we see, in numberless instances, the influence of humanity, we ought thence to conclude, that it is impossible, but that everything which promotes the interest of society must communicate pleasure, and what is pernicious give uneasiness. But when these different reflections and observations concur in establishing the same conclusion, must they not bestow an undisputed evidence upon it?

. . . .

Section IX
Conclusion

Part I

It may justly appear surprising that any man in so late an age, should find it requisite to prove, by elaborate reasoning, that Personal Merit consists altogether in the possession of mental qualities, *useful* or *agreeable* to the *person himself* or to *others*. It might be expected that this principle would have occurred even to the first rude, unpractised enquirers concerning morals, and been received from its own evidence, without any argument or disputation. Whatever is valuable in any kind, so naturally classes itself under the division of *useful* or *agreeable,* the *utile* or the *dulce,* that it is not easy to imagine why we should ever seek further, or consider the question as a matter of nice research or inquiry. And as every thing useful or agreeable must possess these qualities with regard either to the *person himself* or to *others,* the complete delineation or description of merit seems to be performed as naturally as a shadow is cast by the sun, or an image is reflected upon water.

. . . .

And as every quality which is useful or agreeable to ourselves or others is, in common life, allowed to be a part of personal merit; so no other will ever be received, where men judge of things by their natural, unprejudiced reason, without the delusive glosses of superstition and false religion. Celibacy, fasting, penance, mortification, self-denial, humility, silence, solitude, and the whole train of monkish virtues; for what reason are they everywhere rejected by men of sense, but because they serve to no manner of purpose; neither advance a man's fortune in the world, nor render him a more valuable member of society; neither qualify him for the entertainment of company, nor increase his power of self-enjoyment? We observe, on the contrary, that they cross all these desirable ends; stupify the understanding and harden the heart, obscure the fancy and sour the temper. We justly, therefore, transfer them to the opposite column, and place them in the catalogue of vices; nor has any superstition force sufficient among men of the world, to pervert entirely these natural sentiments. A gloomy, hair-brained enthusiast, after his death, may have a place in the calendar; but will scarcely ever be admitted, when alive, into intimacy and society, except by those who are as delirious and dismal as himself.

It seems a happiness in the present theory, that it enters not into that vulgar dispute concerning the *degrees* of benevolence or self-love, which prevail in human nature; a dispute which is never likely to have any issue, both because men, who have taken part, are not easily convinced, and because the phenomena, which can be produced on either side, are so dispersed, so uncertain, and subject to so many interpretations, that it is scarcely possible accurately to compare them, or draw from them any determinate inference or conclusion. It is sufficient for our present purpose, if it be allowed, what surely, without the greatest absurdity cannot be disputed, that there is some benevolence, however small, infused into our bosom; some spark of friendship for human kind; some particle of the dove kneaded into our frame, along with the elements of the wolf and serpent. Let these generous sentiments be supposed ever so weak; let them be insufficient to move even a hand or finger of our body, they must still direct the determinations of our mind, and where everything else is equal, produce a cool preference of what is useful and serviceable to mankind, above what is pernicious and dangerous. A *moral distinction,* therefore, immediately arises; a general sentiment of blame and approbation; a tendency, however faint, to the objects of the one, and a proportionable aversion to those of the other. Nor will those reasoners, who so earnestly maintain the predominant selfishness of human kind, be any wise scandalized at hearing of the weak sentiments of virtue implanted in our nature. On the contrary, they are found as ready to maintain the one tenet as the other; and their spirit of satire (for such it appears, rather than of corruption) naturally gives rise to both opinions; which have, indeed, a great and almost an indissoluble connexion together.

Avarice, ambition, vanity, and all passions vulgarly, though improperly, comprised under the denomination of *self-love,* are here excluded from our theory concerning the origin of morals, not because they are too weak, but because they have not a proper direction for that purpose. The notion of morals implies some sentiment common to all mankind, which recommends the same object to general approbation, and makes every man, or most men, agree in the same opinion or decision concerning it. It also implies some sentiment, so universal and comprehensive as to extend to all mankind, and render the actions and conduct, even of the persons the most remote, an object of applause or censure, according as they agree or disagree with that rule of right which is established. These two requisite circumstances belong alone to the sentiment of humanity here insisted on. The other passions produce in every breast, many strong sentiments of desire and aversion, affection and hatred; but these neither are felt so much in common, nor are so comprehensive, as to be the foundation of any general system and established theory of blame or approbation.

When a man denominates another his *enemy,* his *rival,* his *antagonist,* his *adversary,* he is understood to speak the language of self-love, and to express sentiments, peculiar to himself, and arising from his particular circumstances and situation. But when he bestows on any man the epithets of *vicious* or *odious* or *depraved,* he then speaks another language, and expresses sentiments, in which he expects all his audience are to concur with him. He must here, therefore, depart from his private and particular situation, and must choose a point of view, common to him with others; he must move some universal principle of the human frame, and touch a string to which all mankind have an accord and symphony. If he mean, therefore, to express that this man possesses qualities, whose tendency is pernicious to society, he has chosen this common point of view, and has touched the principle of humanity, in which every man, in some degree, concurs. While the human heart is compounded of the same elements as at present, it will never be wholly indifferent to public good, nor entirely unaffected with the tendency of characters and manners. And though this affection of humanity may not generally be esteemed so strong as vanity or ambition, yet, being common to all men, it can alone be the foundation of morals, or of any general system of blame or praise. One man's ambition is not another's ambition, nor will the same event or object satisfy both; but the humanity of one man is the humanity of every one, and the same object touches this passion in all human creatures.

But the sentiments, which arise from humanity, are not only the same in all human creatures, and produce the same approbation or censure; but they also comprehend all human creatures; nor is there any one whose conduct or character is not, by their means, an object to every one of censure or approbation. On the contrary, those other passions, commonly denominated selfish, both produce different sentiments in each individual, according to his particular situation; and also contemplate the greater part of mankind with the utmost indifference and unconcern. Whoever has a high regard and esteem for me flatters my vanity; whoever expresses contempt mortifies and displeases me; but as my name is known but to a small part of mankind, there are few who come within the sphere of this passion, or excite, on its account, either my affection or disgust. But if you represent a tyrannical, insolent, or barbarous behaviour, in any country or in any age of the world, I soon carry my eye to the pernicious tendency of such a conduct, and feel the sentiment of repugnance and displeasure towards it. No character can be so remote as to be, in this light, wholly indifferent to me. What is beneficial to society or to the person himself must still be preferred. And every quality or action, of every human being, must, by this means, be ranked under some class or denomination, expressive of general censure or applause.

What more, therefore, can we ask to distinguish the sentiments, dependent on humanity, from those connected with any other passion, or to satisfy us, why the former are the origin of morals, not the latter? Whatever conduct gains my approbation, by touching my humanity, procures also the applause of all mankind, by affecting the same principle in them; but what serves my avarice or ambition pleases these passions in me alone, and affects not the avarice and ambition of the rest of mankind. There is no circumstance of conduct in any man, provided it have a beneficial tendency, that is not agreeable to my humanity, however remote the person; but every man, so far removed as neither to cross nor serve my avarice and ambition, is regarded as wholly indifferent by those passions. The distinction, therefore, between these species of sentiment being so great and evident, language must soon be moulded upon it, and must invent a peculiar set of terms, in order to express those universal sentiments of censure or approbation, which arise from humanity, or from views of general usefulness and its contrary. Virtue and Vice become then known; morals are recognized; certain general ideas are framed of human conduct and behaviour; such measures are expected from men in such situations. This action is determined to be conformable to our abstract rule; that other, contrary. And by such universal principles are the particular sentiments of self-love frequently controlled and limited.

From instances of popular tumults, seditions, factions, panics, and of all passions, which are shared with a multitude, we may learn the influence of society in exciting and supporting any emotion; while the most ungovernable disorders are raised, we find, by that means, from the slightest and most frivolous occasions. Solon was no very cruel, though, perhaps, an unjust legislator, who punished neuters in civil wars; and few, I believe, would, in such cases, incur the penalty, were their affection and discourse allowed sufficient to absolve them. No selfishness, and scarce any philosophy, have there force sufficient to support a total coolness and indifference; and he must be more or less than man, who kindles not in the common blaze. What wonder then, that moral sentiments are found of such influence in life; though springing from principles, which may appear, at first sight, somewhat small and delicate? But these principles, we must remark, are social and universal; they form, in a manner, the *party* of humankind against vice or disorder, its common enemy. And as the benevolent concern for others is diffused, in a greater or less degree, over all men, and is the same in all, it occurs more frequently in discourse, is cherished by society and conversation, and the blame and approbation, consequent on it, are thereby roused from that lethargy into which they are probably lulled, in solitary and uncultivated nature. Other passions, though perhaps originally stronger, yet being selfish and private, are often overpowered by its force, and yield the dominion of our breast to those social and public principles.

. . . .

Part II

Having explained the moral *approbation* attending merit or virtue, there remains nothing but briefly to consider our interested *obligation* to it, and to inquire whether every man, who has any regard to his own happiness and welfare, will not best find his account in the practice of every moral duty. If this can be clearly ascertained from the foregoing theory, we shall have the satisfaction to reflect, that we have advanced principles, which not only, it is hoped, will stand the test of reasoning and inquiry, but may contribute to the amendment of men's lives, and their improvement in morality and social virtue. And though the philosophical truth of any proposition by no means depends on its tendency to promote the interests of society; yet a man has but a bad grace, who delivers a theory, however true, which, he must confess, leads to a practice dangerous and pernicious. Why rake into those corners of nature which spread a nuisance all around? Why dig up the pestilence from the pit in which it is buried? The ingenuity of your researches may be admired, but your systems will be detested; and mankind will agree, if they cannot refute them, to sink them, at least, in eternal silence and oblivion. Truths which are *pernicious* to society, if any such there be, will yield to errors which are salutary and *advantageous*.

But what philosophical truths can be more advantageous to society, than those here delivered, which represent virtue in all her genuine and most engaging charms, and make us approach her with ease, familiarity, and affection? The dismal dress falls off, with which many divines, and some philosophers, have covered her; and nothing appears but gentleness, humanity beneficence, affability; nay, even at proper intervals, play, frolic, and gaiety. She talks not of useless austerities and rigours, suffering and self-denial. She declares that her sole purpose is to make her votaries and all mankind, during every instant of their existence, if possible, cheerful and happy; nor does she ever willingly part with any pleasure but in hopes of ample compensation in some other period of their lives. The sole trouble which she demands, is that of just calculation, and a steady preference of the greater happiness. And if any austere pretenders approach her, enemies to joy and pleasure, she either rejects them as hypocrites and deceivers; or, if she admit them in her train, they are ranked, however, among the least favoured of her votaries.

And, indeed, to drop all figurative expression, what hopes can we ever have of engaging mankind to a practice which we confess full of austerity and rigour? Or what theory of morals can ever serve any useful purpose, unless it can show, by a particular detail, that all the duties which it recommends, are also the true interest of each individual? The peculiar advantage of the foregoing system seems to be, that it furnishes proper mediums for that purpose.

That the virtues which are immediately *useful* or *agreeable* to the person possessed of them, are desirable in a view of self-interest, it would surely be superfluous to prove. Moralists, indeed, may spare themselves all the pains which they often take in recommending these duties. To what purpose collect arguments to evince that temperance is advantageous, and the excesses of pleasure hurtful. When it appears that these excesses are only denominated such, because they are hurtful; and that, if the unlimited use of strong liquors, for instance, no more impaired health or the faculties of mind and body than the use of air or water, it would not be a whit more vicious or blameable.

It seems equally superfluous to prove, that the *companionable* virtues of good manners and wit, decency and genteelness, are more desirable than the contrary qualities. Vanity alone, without any other consideration, is a sufficient motive to make us wish for the possession of these accomplishments. No man was ever willingly deficient in this particular. All our failures here proceed from bad education, want of capacity, or a perverse and unpliable disposition. Would you have your company coveted, admired, followed; rather than hated, despised, avoided? Can any one seriously deliberate in the case? As no enjoyment is sincere, without some reference to company and society; so no society can be agreeable, or even tolerable, where a man feels his presence unwelcome, and discovers all around him symptoms of disgust and aversion.

But why, in the greater society or confederacy of mankind, should not the case be the same as in particular clubs and companies? Why is it more doubtful, that the enlarged virtues of humanity, generosity, beneficence, are desirable with a view to happiness and self-interest, than the limited endowments of ingenuity and politeness? Are we apprehensive lest those social affections interfere, in a greater and more immediate degree than any other pursuits, with private utility, and cannot be gratified, without some important sacrifice of honour and advantage? If so, we are but ill-instructed in the nature of the human passions, and are more influenced by verbal distinctions than by real differences.

Whatever contradiction may vulgarly be supposed between the *selfish* and *social* sentiments or dispositions, they are really no more opposite than selfish and ambitious, selfish and revengeful, selfish and vain. It is requisite that there be an original propensity of some kind, in order to be a basis to self-love, by giving a relish to the objects of its pursuit; and none more fit for this purpose than benevolence or humanity. The goods of fortune are spent in one gratification or another: the miser who accumulates his annual income, and lends it out at interest, has really spent it in the gratification of his avarice. And it would be difficult to show why a man is more a loser by a generous action, than by any other method of expense; since the utmost which he can attain by the most elaborate selfishness, is the indulgence of some affection.

Now if life, without passion, must be altogether insipid and tiresome; let a man suppose that he has full power of modelling his own disposition, and let him deliberate what appetite or desire he would choose for the foundation of his happiness and enjoyment. Every affection, he would observe, when gratified by success, gives a satisfaction proportioned to its force and violence; but besides this advantage, common to all, the immediate feeling of benevolence and friendship, humanity and kindness, is sweet, smooth, tender, and agreeable, independent of all fortune and accidents. These virtues are besides attended with a pleasing consciousness or remembrance, and keep us in humour with ourselves as well as others; while we retain the agreeable reflection of having done our part towards mankind and society. And though all men show a jealousy of our success in the pursuits of avarice and ambition; yet are we almost sure of their good-will and good wishes, so long as we persevere in the paths of virtue, and employ ourselves in the execution of generous plans and purposes. What other passion is there where we shall find so many advantages united; an agreeable sentiment, a pleasing consciousness, a good reputation? But of these truths, we may observe, men are, of themselves, pretty much convinced; nor are they deficient in their duty to society, because they would not wish to be generous, friendly, and humane; but because they do not feel themselves such.

Treating vice with the greatest candour, and making it all possible concessions, we must acknowledge that there is not, in any instance, the smallest pretext for giving it the preference above virtue, with a view to self-interest; except, perhaps, in the case of justice, where a man, taking things in a certain light, may often seem to be a loser by his integrity. And though it is allowed that, without a regard to property, no society could subsist; yet according to the imperfect way in which human affairs are conducted, a sensible knave, in particular incidents, may think that an act of iniquity or infidelity will make a considerable addition to his fortune, without causing any considerable breach in the social union and confederacy. That *honesty is the best policy,* may be a good general rule, but is liable to many exceptions; and he, it may perhaps be thought, conducts himself with most wisdom, who observes the general rule, and takes advantage of all the exceptions.

I must confess that, if a man think that this reasoning much requires an answer, it will be a little difficult to find any which will to him appear satisfactory and convincing. If his heart rebel not against such pernicious maxims, if he feel no reluctance to the thoughts of villainy or baseness, he has indeed lost a considerable motive to virtue; and we may expect that his practice will be answerable to his speculation. But in all ingenuous natures, the antipathy to treachery and roguery is too strong to be counter-balanced by any views of profit or pecuniary advantage. Inward peace of mind, consciousness of integrity, a satisfactory review of our own conduct; these are circumstances, very requisite to happiness, and will be cherished and cultivated by every honest man, who feels the importance of them.

Such a one has, besides, the frequent satisfaction of seeing knaves, with all their pretended cunning and abilities, betrayed by their own maxims; and while they purpose to cheat with moderation and secrecy, a tempting incident occurs, nature is frail, and they give into the snare; whence they can never extricate themselves, without a total loss of reputation, and the forfeiture of all future trust and confidence with mankind.

But were they ever so secret and successful, the honest man, if he has any tincture of philosophy, or even common observation and reflection, will discover that they themselves are, in the end, the greatest dupes, and have sacrificed the invaluable enjoyment of a character, with themselves at least, for the acquisition of worthless toys and gewgaws. How little is requisite to supply the *necessities* of nature? And in a view to *pleasure,* what comparison between the unbought satisfaction of conversation, society, study, even health and the common beauties of nature, but above all the peaceful reflection on one's own conduct; what comparison, I say, between these and the feverish, empty amusements of luxury and expense? These natural pleasures, indeed, are really without price; both because they are below all price in their attainment, and above it in their enjoyment.

Appendix I

Concerning Moral Sentiment

If the foregoing hypothesis be received, it will now be easy for us to determine the question first started,[6] concerning the general principles of morals; and though we postponed the decision of that question, lest it should then involve us in intricate speculations, which are unfit for moral discourses, we may resume it at present, and examine how far either *reason* or *sentiment* enters into all decisions of praise or censure.

One principal foundation of moral praise being supposed to lie in the usefulness of any quality or action, it is evident that *reason* must enter for a considerable share in all decisions of this kind; since nothing but that faculty can instruct us in the tendency of qualities and actions, and point out their beneficial consequences to society and to their possessor. In many cases this is an affair liable to great controversy: doubts may arise; opposite interests may occur; and a preference must be given to one side, from very nice views, and a small overbalance of utility. This is particularly remarkable in questions with regard to justice; as is, indeed, natural to suppose, from that species of utility which attends this virtue. Were every single instance of justice, like that of benevolence, useful to society; this would be a more simple state of the case, and seldom liable to great controversy. But as single instances of justice are often pernicious in their first and immediate tendency, and as the advantage to society results only from the observance of the general rule, and from the concurrence and combination of several persons in the same equitable conduct; the case here becomes more intricate and involved. The various circumstances of society; the various consequences of any practice; the various interests which may be proposed; these, on many occasions, are doubtful, and subject to great discussion and inquiry. The object of municipal laws is to fix all the questions with regard to justice: the debates of civilians; the reflections of politicians; the precedents of history and public records, are all directed to the same purpose. And a very accurate *reason* or *judgement* is often requisite, to give the true determination, amidst such intricate doubts arising from obscure or opposite utilities.

But though reason, when fully assisted and improved, be sufficient to instruct us in the pernicious or useful tendency of qualities and actions; it is not alone sufficient to produce any moral blame or approbation. Utiity is only a tendency to a certain end; and were the end totally indifferent to us, we should feel the same indifference towards the means. It is requisite a *sentiment* should here display itself, in order to give a preference to the useful above the pernicious tendencies. This sentiment can be no other than a feeling for the happiness of mankind, and a resentment of their misery; since these are the different ends which virtue and vice have a tendency to promote. Here therefore *reason* instructs us in the several tendencies of actions, and *humanity* makes a distinction in favour of those which are useful and beneficial.

This partition between the faculties of understanding and sentiment, in all moral decisions, seems clear from the preceding hypothesis. But I shall suppose that hypothesis false: it will then be requisite to look out for some other theory that may be satisfactory; and I dare venture to affirm that none such will ever be found, so long as we suppose reason to be the sole source of morals. To prove this, it will be proper to weigh the . . . following considerations.

I. It is easy for a false hypothesis to maintain some appearance of truth, while it keeps wholly in generals, makes use of undefined terms, and employs comparisons, instead of instances. This is particularly remarkable in that philosophy, which ascribes the discernment of all moral distinctions to reason alone, without the concurrence of sentiment. It is impossible that, in any particular instance, this hypothesis can so much as be rendered intelligible, whatever specious figure it may make in general declamations and discourses. Examine the crime of *ingratitude,* for instance; which has place, wherever we observe good-will, expressed and known, together with good-offices performed, on the one side, and a return of ill-will or indifference, with ill-offices or neglect on the other: anatomize all these circumstances, and examine, by your reason alone, in what consists the demerit or blame. You never will come to any issue or conclusion.

Reason judges either of *matter of fact* or of *relations.* Enquire then, *first,* where is that matter of fact which we here call *crime;* point it out; determine the time of its existence; describe its essence of nature; explain the sense or faculty to which it discovers itself. It resides in the mind of the person who is ungrateful. He must, therefore, feel it, and be conscious of it. But nothing is there, except the passion of ill-will or absolute indifference. You cannot say that these, of themselves, always, and in all circumstances, are crimes. No, they are only crimes when directed towards persons who have before expressed and displayed good-will towards us. Consequently, we may infer, that the crime of ingratitude is not any particular individual *fact;* but arises from a complication of circumstances, which, being presented to the spectator, excites the *sentiment* of blame, by the particular structure and fabric of his mind.

This representation, you say, is false. Crime, indeed, consists not in a particular *fact,* of whose reality we are assured by *reason;* but it consists in certain *moral relations,* discovered by reason, in the same manner as we discover by reason the truths of geometry or algebra. But what are the relations, I ask, of which you here talk? In the case stated above, I see first good-will and good-offices in one person; then ill-will and ill-offices in the other. Between these, there is a relation of *contrariety.* Does the crime consist in that relation? But suppose a person bore me ill-will or did me ill-offices; and I, in return, were indifferent towards him, or did him good-offices. Here is the same relation of *contrariety;* and yet my conduct is often highly laudable. Twist and turn this matter as much as you will, you can never rest the morality on relation; but must have recourse to the decisions of sentiment.

When it is affirmed that two and three are equal to the half of ten, this relation of equality I understand perfectly. I conceive, that if ten be divided into two parts, of which one has as many units as the other; and if any of these parts be compared to two added to three, it will contain as many units as that compound number. But when you draw thence a comparison to moral relations, I own that I am altogether at a loss to understand you. A moral action, a crime, such as ingratitude, is a complicated object. Does the morality consist in the relation of its parts to each other? How? After what manner? Specify the relation: be more particular and explicit in your propositions, and you will easily see their falsehood.

No, say you, the morality consists in the relation of actions to the rule of right; and they are denominated good or ill, according as they agree or disagree with it. What then is this rule of right? In what does it consist? How is it determined? By reason, you say, which examines the moral relations of actions. So that moral relations are determined by the comparison of action to a rule. And that rule is determined by considering the moral relations of objects. Is not this fine reasoning?

All this is metaphysics, you cry. That is enough; there needs nothing more to give a strong presumption of falsehood. Yes, reply I, here are metaphysics surely; but they are all on your side, who advance an abstruse hypothesis, which can never be made intelligible, nor quadrate with any particular instance or illustration. The hypothesis which we embrace is plain. It maintains that morality is determined by sentiment. It defines virtue to be *whatever mental action or quality gives to a spectator the pleasing sentiment of approbation;* and vice the contrary. We then proceed to examine a plain matter of fact, to wit, what actions have this influence. We consider all the circumstances in which these actions agree, and thence endeavour to extract some general observations with regard to these sentiments. If you call this metaphysics, and find anything abstruse here, you need only conclude that your turn of mind is not suited to the moral sciences.

II. When a man, at any time, deliberates concerning his own conduct (as, whether he had better, in a particular emergence, assist a brother or a benefactor), he must consider these separate relations, with all the circumstances and situations of the persons, in order to determine the superior duty and obligation; and in order to determine the proportion of lines in any triangle, it is necessary to examine the nature of that figure, and the relations which its several parts bear to each other. But notwithstanding this appearing similarity in the two cases, there is, at bottom, an extreme difference between them. A speculative reasoner concerning triangles or circles considers the several known and given relations of the parts of these figures, and thence infers some unknown relation, which is dependent on the former. But in moral deliberations we must be acquainted beforehand with all the objects, and all their relations to each other; and from a comparison of the whole, fix our choice or approbation. No new fact to be ascertained; no new relation to be discovered. All the circumstances of the case are supposed to be laid before us, ere we can fix any sentence of blame or approbation. If any material circumstance be yet unknown or doubtful, we must first employ our inquiry or intellectual faculties to assure us of it; and must suspend for a time all moral decision or sentiment. While we are ignorant whether a man were aggressor or not, how can we determine whether the person who killed him be criminal or innocent? But after every circumstance, every relation is known, the understanding has no further room to operate, nor any object on which it could employ itself. The approbation or blame which then ensues, cannot be the work of the judgement, but of the heart; and is not a speculative proposition or affirmation, but an active feeling or sentiment. In the disquisitions of the understanding, from known circumstances and relations, we infer some new and unknown. In moral decisions, all the circumstances and relations must be previously known; and the mind, from the contemplation of the whole, feels some new impression of affection or disgust, esteem or contempt, approbation or blame.

Hence the great difference between a mistake of *fact* and one of *right;* and hence the reason why the one is commonly criminal and not the other. When Oedipus killed Laius, he was ignorant of the relation, and from circumstances, innocent and involuntary, formed erroneous opinions concerning the action which he committed. But when Nero killed Agrippina, all the relations between himself and the person, and all the circumstances of the fact, were previously known to him; but the motive of revenge, or fear, or interest, prevailed in his savage heart over the sentiments of duty and humanity. And when we express that detestation against him to which he himself, in a little time, became insensible, it is not that we see any relations, of which he was ignorant; but that, from the rectitude of our disposition, we feel sentiments against which he was hardened from flattery and a long perseverance in the most enormous crimes. In these sentiments then, not in a discovery of relations of any kind, do all moral determinations consist. Before we can pretend to form any decision of this kind, everything must be known and ascertained on the side of the object or action. Nothing remains but to feel, on our part, some sentiment of blame or approbation; whence we pronounce the action criminal or virtuous.

. . . .

V. It appears evident that the ultimate ends of human actions can never, in any case, be accounted for by *reason,* but recommend themselves entirely to the sentiments and affections of mankind, without any dependance on the intellectual faculties. Ask a man *why he uses exercise;* he will answer, *because he desires to keep his health.* If you then enquire, *why he desires health,* he will readily reply, *because sickness is painful.* If you push your enquiries farther, and desire a reason *why he hates pain,* it is impossible he can ever give any. This is an ultimate end, and is never referred to any other object.

Perhaps to your second question, *why he desires health,* he may also reply, that *it is necessary for the exercise of his calling.* If you ask, *why he is anxious on that head,* he will answer, *because he desires to get money.* If you demand *Why? It is the instrument of pleasure,* says he. And beyond this it is an absurdity to ask for a reason. It is impossible there can be a progress *in infinitum;* and that one thing can always be a reason why another is desired. Something must be desirable on its own account, and because of its immediate accord or agreement with human sentiment and affection.

Now as virtue is an end, and is desirable on its own account, without fee or reward, merely for the immediate satisfaction which it conveys; it is requisite that there should be some sentiment which it touches, some internal taste or feeling, or whatever you please to call it, which distinguishes moral good and evil, and which embraces the one and rejects the other.

Thus the distinct boundaries and offices of *reason* and of *taste* are easily ascertained. The former conveys the knowledge of truth and falsehood: the latter gives the sentiment of beauty and deformity, vice and virtue. The one discovers objects as they really stand in nature, without addition or diminution: the other has a productive faculty, and gilding or staining all natural objects with the colours, borrowed from internal sentiment, raises in a manner a new creation. Reason being cool and disengaged, is no motive to action, and directs only the impulse received from appetite or inclination, by showing us the means of attaining happiness or avoiding misery: Taste, as it gives pleasure or pain, and thereby constitutes happiness or misery, becomes a motive to action, and is the first spring or impulse to desire and volition. From circumstances and relations, known or supposed, the former leads us to the discovery of the concealed and unknown: after all circumstances and relations are laid before us, the latter makes us feel from the whole a new sentiment of blame or approbation. The standard of the one, being founded on the nature of things, is eternal and inflexible, even by the will of the Supreme Being: the standard of the other, arising from the internal frame and constitution of animals, is ultimately derived from that Supreme Will, which bestowed on each being its peculiar nature, and arranged the several classes and orders of existence.

Appendix II

Of Self-love

There is a principle, supposed to prevail among many, which is utterly incompatible with all virtue or moral sentiment; and as it can proceed from nothing but the most depraved disposition, so in its turn it tends still further to encourage that depravity. This principle is, that all *benevolence* is mere hypocrisy, friendship a cheat, public spirit a farce, fidelity a snare to procure trust and confidence; and that while all of us, at bottom, pursue only our private interest, we wear these fair disguises, in order to put others off their guard, and expose them the more to our wiles and machinations. What heart one must be possessed of who professes such principles, and who feels no internal sentiment that belies so pernicious a theory, it is easy to imagine: and also what degree of affection and benevolence he can bear to a species whom he represents under such odious colours, and supposes so little susceptible of gratitude or any return of affection. Or if we should not ascribe these principles wholly to a corrupted heart, we must at least account for them from the most careless and precipitate examination. Superficial reasoners, indeed, observing many false pretences among mankind, and feeling, perhaps, no very strong restraint in their own disposition, might draw a general and a hasty conclusion that all is equally corrupted, and that men, different from all other animals, and indeed from all other species of existence, admit of no degrees of good or bad, but are, in every instance, the same creatures under different disguises and appearances.

There is another principle, somewhat resembling the former; which has been much insisted on by philosophers, and has been the foundation of many a system; that, whatever affection one may feel, or imagine he feels for others, no passion is, or can be disinterested; that the most generous friendship, however sincere, is a modification of self-love; and that, even unknown to ourselves, we seek only our own gratification, while we appear the most deeply engaged in schemes for the liberty and happiness of mankind. By a turn of imagination, by a refinement of reflection, by an enthusiasm of passion, we seem to take part in the interests of others, and imagine ourselves divested of all selfish considerations: but, at bottom, the most generous patriot and most niggardly miser, the bravest hero and most abject coward, have, in every action, an equal regard to their own happiness and welfare.

Whoever concludes from the seeming tendency of this opinion, that those, who make profession of it, cannot possibly feel the true sentiments of benevolence, or have any regard for genuine virtue, will often find himself, in practice, very much mistaken. Probity and honour were no strangers to Epicurus and his sect. Atticus and Horace seem to have enjoyed from nature, and cultivated by reflection, as generous and friendly dispositions as any disciple of the austerer schools. And among the modern, Hobbes and Locke, who maintained the selfish system of morals, lived irreproachable lives; though the former lay not under any restraint of religion which might supply the defects of his philosophy.

An Epicurean or a Hobbist readily allows, that there is such a thing as friendship in the world, without hypocrisy or disguise; though he may attempt, by a philosophical chymistry, to resolve the elements of this passion, if I may so speak, into those of another, and explain every affection to be self-love, twisted and moulded, by a particular turn of imagination, into a variety of appearances. But as the same turn of imagination prevails not in every man, nor gives the same direction to the original passion; this is sufficient even according to the selfish system to make the widest difference in human characters, and denominate one man virtuous and humane, another vicious and meanly interested. I esteem the man whose self-love, by whatever means, is so directed as to give him a concern for others, and render him serviceable to society: as I hate or despise him, who has no regard to any thing beyond his own gratifications and enjoyments. In vain would you suggest that these characters, though seemingly opposite, are at bottom the same, and that a very inconsiderable turn of thought forms the whole difference between them. Each character, notwithstanding these inconsiderable differences, appears to me, in practice, pretty durable and untransmutable. And I find not in this more than in other subjects, that the natural sentiments arising from the general appearances of things are easily destroyed by subtile reflections concerning the minute origin of these appearances. Does not the lively, cheerful colour of a countenance inspire me with complacency and pleasure; even though I learn from philosophy that all difference of complexion arises from the most minute differences of thickness, in the most minute parts of the skin; by means of which a superficies is qualified to reflect one of the original colours of light, and absorb the others?

But though the question concerning the universal or partial selfishness of man be not so material as is usually imagined to morality and practice, it is certainly of consequence in the speculative science of human nature, and is a proper object of curiosity and enquiry. It may not, therefore, be unsuitable, in this place, to bestow a few reflections upon it.[7]

The most obvious objection to the selfish hypothesis is, that, as it is contrary to common feeling and our most unprejudiced notions, there is required the highest stretch of philosophy to establish so extraordinary a paradox. To the most careless observer there appear to be such dispositions as benevolence and generosity; such affections as love, friendship, compassion, gratitude. These sentiments have their causes, effects, objects, and operations, marked by common language and observation, and plainly distinguished from those of the selfish passions. And as this is the obvious appearance of things, it must be admitted, till some hypothesis be discovered, which by penetrating deeper into human nature, may prove the former affections to be nothing but modifications of the latter. All attempts of this kind have hitherto proved fruitless, and seem to have proceeded entirely from that love of *simplicity* which has been the source of much false reasoning in philosophy. I shall not here enter into any detail on the present subject. Many able philosophers have shown the insufficiency of these systems. And I shall take for granted what, I believe, the smallest reflection will make evident to every impartial enquirer.

. . . .

. . . Tenderness to their offspring, in all sensible beings, is commonly able alone to counterbalance the strongest motives of self-love, and has no manner of dependance on that affection. What interest can a fond mother have in view, who loses her health by assiduous attendance on her sick child, and afterwards languishes and dies of grief, when freed, by its death, from the slavery of that attendance?

Is gratitude no affection of the human breast, or is that a word merely, without any meaning or reality? Have we no satisfaction in one man's company above another's, and no desire of the welfare of our friend, even though absence or death should prevent us from all participation in it? Or what is it commonly, that gives us any participation in it, even while alive and present, but our affection and regard to him?

These and a thousand other instances are marks of a general benevolence in human nature, where no *real* interest binds us to the object. And how an *imaginary* interest known and avowed for such, can be the origin of any passion or emotion, seems difficult to explain. No satisfactory hypothesis of this kind has yet been discovered; nor is there the smallest probability that the future industry of men will ever be attended with more favourable success.

But farther, if we consider rightly of the matter, we shall find that the hypothesis which allows of a disinterested benevolence, distinct from self-love, has really more *simplicity* in it, and is more conformable to the analogy of nature than that which pretends to resolve all friendship and humanity into this latter principle. There are bodily wants or appetites acknowledged by every one, which necessarily precede all sensual enjoyment, and carry us directly to seek possession of the object. Thus, hunger and thirst have eating and drinking for their end; and from the gratification of these primary appetites arises a pleasure, which may become the object of another species of desire or inclination that is secondary and interested. In the same manner there are mental passions by which we are impelled immediately to seek particular objects, such as fame or power, or vengeance without any regard to interest; and when these objects are attained a pleasing enjoyment ensues, as the consequence of our indulged affections. Nature must, by the internal frame and constitution of the mind, give an original propensity to fame, ere we can reap any pleasure from that acquisition, or pursue it from motives of self-love, and a desire of happiness. If I have no vanity, I take no delight in praise: if I be void of ambition, power gives me no enjoyment: if I be not angry, the punishment of an adversary is totally indifferent to me. In all these cases there is a passion which points immediately to the object, and constitutes it our good or happiness; as there are other secondary passions which afterwards arise and pursue it as a part of our happiness, when once it is constituted such by our original affections. Were there no appetite of any kind antecedent to self-love, that propensity could scarcely ever exert itself; because we should, in that case, have felt few and slender pains or pleasures, and have little misery or happiness to avoid or to pursue.

Now where is the difficulty in conceiving, that this may likewise be the case with benevolence and friendship, and that, from the original frame of our temper, we may feel a desire of another's happiness or good, which, by means of that affection, becomes our own good, and is afterwards pursued, from the combined motives of benevolence and self-enjoyment? Who sees not that vengeance, from the force alone of passion, may be so eagerly pursued, as to make us knowingly neglect every consideration of ease, interest, or safety; and, like some vindictive animals, infuse our very souls into the wounds we give an enemy; and what a malignant philosophy must it be, that will not allow to humanity and friendship the same privileges which are undisputably granted to the darker passions of enmity and resentment? Such a philosophy is more like a satyr than a true delineation or description of human nature; and may be a good foundation for paradoxical wit and raillery, but is a very bad one for any serious argument or reasoning.

Notes

1. See Appendix I.
2. Sect. III and IV.
3. Sect. V.
4. It is needless to push our researches so far as to ask, why we have humanity or a fellow-feeling with others. It is sufficient, that this is experienced to be a principle in human nature. We must stop somewhere in our examination of causes; and there are, in every science, some general principles, beyond which we cannot hope to find any principle more general. No man is absolutely indifferent to the happiness and misery of others. The first has a natural tendency to give pleasure; the second, pain. This every one may find in himself. It is not probable, that these principles can be resolved into principles more simple and universal, whatever attempts may have been made to that purpose. But if it were possible, it belongs not to the present subject; and we may here safely consider these principles as original: happy, if we can render all the consequences sufficiently plain and perspicious!
5. For a like reason, the tendencies of actions and characters, not their real accidental consequences, are alone regarded in our moral determinations or general judgements; though in our real feeling or sentiment, we cannot help paying greater regard to one whose station, joined to virtue, renders him really useful to society, than to one, who exerts the social virtues only in good intentions and benevolent affections. Separating the character from the fortune, by an easy and necessary effort of thought, we pronounce these persons alike, and give them the same general praise. The judgement corrects or endeavours to correct the appearance: But is not able entirely to prevail over sentiment.

   Why is this peach-tree said to be better than that other; but because it produces more or better fruit? And would not the same praise be given it, though snails or vermin had destroyed the peaches, before they came to full maturity? In morals too, is not *the tree known by the fruit?* And cannot we easily distinguish between nature and accident, in the one case as well as in the other?
6. Sect. I.
7. Benevolence naturally divides into two kinds, the *general* and the *particular*. The first is, where we have no friendship or connexion or esteem for the person, but feel only a general sympathy with him or a compassion for his pains, and a congratulation with his pleasures. The other species of benevolence is founded on an opinion of virtue, on services done us, or on some particular connexions. Both these sentiments must be allowed real in human nature: but whether they will resolve into some nice considerations of self-love, is a question more curious than important. The former sentiment, to wit, that of general benevolence, or humanity, or sympathy, we shall have occasion frequently to treat of in the course of this enquiry; and I assume it as real, from general experience, without any other proof.

Morality and Advantage

DAVID GAUTHIER

David Gauthier (1932–) is a professor of philosophy at the University of Pittsburgh. His publications include *The Logic of Leviathan* and the forthcoming *Morals by Agreement*.

I

Hume asks, rhetorically, "what theory of morals can ever serve any useful purpose, unless it can show, by a particular detail, that all the duties which it recommends, are also the true interest of each individual?"[1] But there are many to whom this question does not seem rhetorical. Why, they ask, do we speak the language of morality, impressing upon our fellows their duties and obligations, urging them with appeals to what is right and good, if we could speak to the same effect in the language of prudence, appealing to considerations of interest and advantage? When the poet, Ogden Nash, is moved by the muse to cry out:

O Duty,
Why hast thou not the visage of a sweetie or a cutie?[2]

we do not anticipate the reply:

O Poet,
I really am a cutie and I think you ought to know it.

The belief that duty cannot be reduced to interest, or that morality may require the agent to subordinate all considerations of advantage, is one which has withstood the assaults of contrary-minded philosophers from Plato to the present. Indeed, were it not for the conviction that only interest and advantage can motivate human actions, it would be difficult to understand philosophers contending so vigorously for the identity, or at least compatibility, of morality with prudence.

Yet if morality is not true prudence it would be wrong to suppose that those philosophers who have sought some connection between morality and advantage have been merely misguided. For it is a truism that we should all expect to be worse off if men were to substitute prudence, even of the most enlightened kind, for morality in all of their deliberations. And this truism demands not only some connection between morality and advantage, but a seemingly paradoxical connection. For if we should all expect to suffer, were men to be prudent instead of moral, then morality must contribute to advantage in a unique way, a way in which prudence—following reasons of advantage—cannot.

Thomas Hobbes is perhaps the first philosopher who tried to develop this seemingly paradoxical connection between morality and advantage. But since he could not admit that a man might ever reasonably subordinate considerations of advantage to the dictates of obligation, he was led to deny the possibility of real conflict between morality and prudence. So his argument

From *The Philosophical Review* 76 (October 1967), pp. 460–75.

fails to clarify the distinction between the view that claims of obligation reduce to considerations of interest and the view that claims of obligation promote advantage in a way in which considerations of interest cannot.

More recently, Kurt Baier has argued that "being moral is following rules designed to overrule self-interest whenever it is in the interest of everyone alike that everyone should set aside his interest."[3] Since prudence is following rules of (enlightened) self-interest, Baier is arguing that morality is designed to overrule prudence when it is to everyone's advantage that it do so—or, in other words, that morality contributes to advantage in a way in which prudence cannot.[4]

Baier does not actually demonstrate that morality contributes to advantage in this unique and seemingly paradoxical way. Indeed, he does not ask how it is possible that morality should do this. It is this possibility which I propose to demonstrate.

II

Let us examine the following proposition, which will be referred to as "the thesis": *Morality is a system of principles such that it is advantageous for everyone if everyone accepts and acts on it, yet acting on the system of principles requires that some persons perform disadvantageous acts.*[5]

What I wish to show is that this thesis *could be true,* that morality could possess those characteristics attributed to it by the thesis. I shall not try to show that the thesis is true—indeed, I shall argue in Section V that it presents at best an inadequate conception of morality. But it is plausible to suppose that a modified form of the thesis states a necessary, although not a sufficient, condition for a moral system.

Two phrases in the thesis require elucidation. The first is "advantageous for everyone." I use this phrase to mean that *each* person will do better if the system is accepted and acted on than if *either* no system is accepted and acted on *or* a system is accepted and acted on which is similar, save that it never requires any person to perform disadvantageous acts.

Clearly, then, the claim that it is advantageous for everyone to accept and act on the system is a very strong one; it may be so strong that no system of principles which might be generally adopted could meet it. But I shall consider in Section V one among the possible ways of weakening the claim.

The second phrase requiring elucidation is "disadvantageous acts." I use this phrase to refer to acts which, in the context of their performance, would be less advantageous to the performer than some other act open to him in the same context. The phrase does not refer to acts which merely impose on the performer some short-term disadvantage that is recouped or outweighed in the long run. Rather it refers to acts which impose a disadvantage that is never recouped. It follows that the performer may say to himself, when confronted with the requirement to perform such an act, that it would be better *for him* not to perform it.

It is essential to note that the thesis, as elucidated, does not maintain that morality is advantageous for everyone in the sense that each person will do *best* if the system of principles is accepted and acted on. Each person will do better than if no system is adopted, or than if the one particular alternative mentioned above is adopted, but not than if any alternative is adopted.

Indeed, for each person required by the system to perform some disadvantageous act, it is easy to specify a better alternative—namely, the system modified so that it does not require *him* to perform any act disadvantageous to himself. Of course, there is no reason to expect such an alternative to be better than the moral system for everyone, or in fact for anyone other than the person granted the special exemption.

A second point to note is that each person must gain more from the disadvantageous acts performed by others than he loses from the disadvantageous acts performed by himself. If this were not the case, then some person would do better if a system were adopted exactly like the moral system save that it never requires *any* person to perform disadvantageous acts. This is ruled out by the force of "advantageous for everyone."

This point may be clarified by an example. Suppose that the system contains exactly one principle. Everyone is always to tell the truth. It follows from the thesis that each person gains more from those occasions on which others tell the truth, even though it is disadvantageous to them to do so, than he loses from those occasions on which he tells the truth even though it is disadvantageous to him to do so.

Now this is not to say that each person gains by telling others the truth in order to ensure that in return they tell him the truth. Such gains would merely be the result of accepting certain short-term disadvantages (those associated with truth-telling) in order to reap long-term benefits (those associated with being told the truth). Rather, what is required by the thesis is that those disadvantages which a person incurs in telling the truth, when he can expect neither short-term nor long-term benefits to accrue to him from truth-telling, are outweighed by those advantages he receives when others tell him the truth when they can expect no benefits to accrue to them from truth-telling.

The principle enjoins truth-telling in those cases in which whether one tells the truth or not will have no effect on whether others tell the truth. Such cases include those in which others have no way of knowing whether or not they are being told the truth. The thesis requires that the disadvantages one incurs in telling the truth in these cases are less than the advantages one receives in being told the truth by others in parallel cases; and the thesis requires that this holds for everyone.

Thus we see that although the disadvantages imposed by the system on any person are less than the advantages secured him through the imposition of disadvantages on others, yet the disadvantages are real in that incurring them is *unrelated* to receiving the advantages. The argument of long-term prudence, that I ought to incur some immediate disadvantage *so that* I shall receive compensating advantages later on, is entirely inapplicable here.

III

It will be useful to examine in some detail an example of a system which possesses those characteristics ascribed by the thesis to morality. This example, abstracted from the field of international relations, will enable us more clearly to distinguish, first, conduct based on immediate interest; second, conduct which is truly prudent; and third, conduct which promotes mutual advantage but is not prudent.

A and *B* are two nations with substantially opposed interests, who find themselves engaged in an arms race against each other. Both possess the latest in weaponry, so that each recognizes that the actual outbreak of full-scale war between them would be mutually disastrous. This recognition leads *A* and *B* to agree that each would be better off if they were mutually disarming instead of mutually arming. For mutual disarmament would preserve the balance of power between them while reducing the risk of war.

Hence *A* and *B* enter into a disarmament pact. The pact is advantageous for both if both accept and act on it, although clearly it is not advantageous for either to act on it if the other does not.

Let *A* be considering whether or not to adhere to the pact in some particular situation, whether or not actually to perform some act of disarmament. *A* will quite likely consider the act to have disadvantageous consequences. *A* expects to benefit, not by its own acts of disarmament, but by *B*'s acts. Hence if *A* were to reason simply in terms of immediate interest, *A* might well decide to violate the pact.

But *A*'s decision need be neither prudent nor reasonable. For suppose first that *B* is able to determine whether or not *A* adheres to the pact. If *A* violates, then *B* will detect the violation and will then consider what to do in the light of *A*'s behavior. It is not to *B*'s advantage to disarm alone; *B* expects to gain, not by its own acts of disarmament, but by *A*'s acts. Hence *A*'s violation, if known to *B*, leads naturally to *B*'s counter-violation. If this continues, the effect of the pact is entirely undone, and *A* and *B* return to their mutually disadvantageous arms race. *A*, foreseeing this when considering whether or not to adhere to the pact in the given situation, must therefore conclude that the truly prudent course of action is to adhere.

Now suppose that *B* is unable to determine whether or not *A* adheres to the pact in the particular situation under consideration. If *A* judges adherence to be in itself disadvantageous, then it will decide, both on the basis of immediate interest and on the basis of prudence, to violate the pact. Since *A*'s decision is unknown to *B*, it cannot affect whether or not *B* adheres to the pact, and so the advantage gained by *A*'s violation is not outweighed by any consequent loss.

Therefore if *A* and *B* are prudent they will adhere to their disarmament pact whenever violation would be detectable by the other, and violate the pact whenever violation would not be detectable by the other. In other words, they will adhere openly and violate secretly. The disarmament pact between *A* and *B* thus possesses two of the characteristics ascribed by the thesis to morality. First, accepting the pact and acting on it is more advantageous for each than making no pact at all. Second, in so far as the pact stipulates that each must disarm even when disarming is undetectable by the other, it requires each to perform disadvantageous acts—acts which run counter to considerations of prudence.

One further condition must be met if the disarmament pact is to possess those characteristics ascribed by the thesis to a system of morality. It must be the case that the requirement that each party perform disadvantageous acts be essential to the advantage conferred by the pact; or, to put the matter in the way in which we expressed it earlier, both *A* and *B* must do better to adhere to this pact than to a pact which is similar save that it requires no disadvantageous acts. In terms of the example, *A* and *B* must do better to adhere to the pact than to a pact which stipulates that each must disarm only when disarming is detectable by the other.

We may plausibly suppose this condition to be met. Although *A* will gain by secretly retaining arms itself, it will lose by *B*'s similar acts, and its losses may well outweigh its gains. *B* may equally lose more by *A*'s secret violations than it gains by its own. So, despite the fact that prudence requires each to violate secretly, each may well do better if both adhere secretly than if both violate secretly. Supposing this to be the case, the disarmament pact is formally analogous to a moral system, as characterized by the thesis. That is, acceptance of and adherence to the pact by *A* and *B* is more advantageous for each, either than making no pact at all or than acceptance of and adherence to a pact requiring only open disarmament, and the pact requires each to perform acts of secret disarmament which are disadvantageous.

Some elementary notation, adapted for our purposes from the mathematical theory of games, may make the example even more perspicuous. Given a disarmament pact between *A* and *B*, each may pursue two pure strategies—adherence and violation. There are, then, four possible combinations of strategies, each determining a particular outcome. These outcomes can be ranked preferentially for each nation; we shall let the numerals 1 to 4 represent the ranking from first to fourth preference. Thus we construct a simple matrix,[6] in which *A*'s preferences are stated first:

		B	
		adheres	*violates*
A	adheres	2, 2	4, 1
	violates	1, 4	3, 3

The matrix does not itself show that agreement is advantageous to both, for it gives only the rankings of outcomes given the agreement. But it is plausible to assume that *A* and *B* would rank mutual violation on a par with no agreement. If we assume this, we can then indicate the value to each of making and adhering to the pact by reference to the matrix.

The matrix shows immediately that adherence to the pact is not the most advantageous possiblity for either, since each prefers the outcome, if it alone violates, to the outcome of mutual adherence. It shows also that each gains less from its own violations than it loses from the other's, since each ranks mutual adherence above mutual violation.

Let us now use the matrix to show that, as we argued previously, public adherence to the pact is prudent and mutually advantageous, whereas private adherence is not prudent although mutually advantageous. Consider first the case where adherence—and so violation—are open and public.

If adherence and violation are open, then each knows the strategy chosen by the other, and can adjust its own strategy in the light of this knowledge—or, in other words, the strategies are interdependent. Suppose that each initially chooses the strategy of adherence. *A* notices that if it switches to violation it gains—moving from 2 to 1 in terms of preference ranking. Hence immediate interest dictates such a switch. But it notices further that if it switches, then *B* can also be expected to switch—moving from 4 to 3 on its preference scale. The eventual outcome would be stable, in that neither could benefit from switching from violation back to adherence. But the eventual outcome would represent not a gain for *A* but a loss—moving from 2 to 3 on its preference scale. Hence prudence dictates no change from the strategy of adherence. This adherence is mutually advantageous; *A* and *B* are in precisely similar positions in terms of their pact.

Consider now the case when adherence and violation are secret and private. Neither nation knows the strategy chosen by the other, so the two strategies are independent. Suppose *A* is trying to decide which strategy to follow. It does not know *B*'s choice. But it notices that if *B* adheres, then it pays *A* to violate, attaining 1 rather than 2 in terms of preference ranking. If *B* violates, then again it pays *A* to violate, attaining 3 rather than 4 on its preference scale. Hence, no matter which strategy *B* chooses, *A* will do better to violate, and so prudence dictates violation.

B of course reasons in just the same way. Hence each is moved by considerations of prudence to violate the pact, and the outcome assigns each rank 3 on its preference scale. This outcome is mutually disadvantageous to *A* and *B*, since mutual adherence would assign each rank 2 on its preference scale.

If *A* and *B* are both capable only of rational prudence, they find themselves at an impasse. The advantage of mutual adherence to the agreement when violations would be secret is not available to them, since neither can find it in his own overall interest not to violate secretly. Hence, strictly prudent nations cannot reap the maximum advantage possible from a pact of the type under examination.

Of course, what *A* and *B* will no doubt endeavor to do is eliminate the possibility of secret violations of their pact. Indeed, barring additional complications, each must find it to his advantage to make it possible for the other to detect his own violations. In other words, each must find it advantageous to ensure that their choice of strategies is interdependent, so that the pact will always be prudent for each to keep. But it may not be possible for them to ensure this, and to the extent that they cannot, prudence will prevent them from maximizing mutual advantage.

IV

We may now return to the connection of morality with advantage. Morality, if it is a system of principles of the type characterized in the thesis, requires that some persons perform acts genuinely disadvantageous to themselves, as a means to greater mutual advantage. Our example shows sufficiently that such a system is possible, and indicates more precisely its character. In particular, by an argument strictly parallel to that which we have pursued, we may show that men who are merely prudent will not perform the required disadvantageous acts. But in so violating the principles of morality, they will disadvantage themselves. Each will lose more by the violations of others than he will gain by his own violations.

Now this conclusion would be unsurprising if it were only that no man can gain if he alone is moral rather than prudent. Obviously such a man loses, for he adheres to moral principles to his own disadvantage, while others violate them also to his disadvantage. The benefit of the moral system is not one which any individual can secure for himself, since each man gains from the sacrifices of others.

What is surprising in our conclusion is that no man can ever gain if he is moral. Not only does he not gain by being moral if others are prudent, but he also does not gain by being moral if others are moral. For although he now receives the advantage of others' adherence to moral principles, he reaps the disadvantage of his own adherence. As long as his own adherence to morality is independent of what others do (and this is required to distinguish morality from prudence), he must do better to be prudent.

If all men are moral, all will do better than if all are prudent. But any one man will always do better if he is prudent than if he is moral. There is no real paradox in supposing that morality is advantageous, even though it requires the performance of disadvantageous acts.

On the supposition that morality has the characteristics ascribed to it by the thesis, is it possible to answer the question "Why should we be moral?" where "we" is taken distributively, so that the question is a compendious way of asking, for each person, "Why should I be moral?"

More simply, is it possible to answer the question "Why should I be moral?"

I take it that this question, if asked seriously, demands a reason for being moral other than moral reasons themselves. It demands that moral reasons be shown to be reasons for acting by a noncircular argument. Those who would answer it, like Baier, endeavor to do so by the introduction of considerations of advantage.

Two such considerations have emerged from our discussion. The first is that if all are moral, all will do better than if all are prudent. This will serve to answer the question "Why should we be moral?" if this question is interpreted rather as "Why should we all be moral—rather than all being something else?" If we must all be the same, then each person has a reason—a prudential reason—to prefer that we all be moral.

But, so interpreted, "Why should we be moral?" is not a compendious way of asking, for each person, "Why should I be moral?" Of course, if everyone is to be whatever I am, then I should be moral. But a general answer to the question "Why should I be moral?" cannot presuppose this.

The second consideration is that any individual always does better to be prudent rather than moral, provided his choice does not determine other choices. But in so far as this answers the question "Why should I be moral?" it leads to the conclusion "I should not be moral." One feels that this is not the answer which is wanted.

We may put the matter otherwise. The individual who needs a reason for being moral which is not itself a moral reason cannot have it. There is nothing surprising about this; it would be much more surprising if such reasons could be found. For it is more than apparently paradoxical to suppose that considerations of advantage could ever of themselves justify accepting a real disadvantage.

V

I suggested in Section II that the thesis, in modified form, might provide a necessary, although not a sufficient, condition for a moral system. I want now to consider how one might characterize the man who would quality as moral according to the thesis—I shall call him the "moral" man—and then ask what would be lacking from this characterization, in terms of some of our commonplace moral views.

The rationally prudent man is incapable of moral behavior, in even the limited sense defined by the thesis. What difference must there be between the prudent man and the "moral" man? Most simply, the "moral" man is the prudent but trustworthy man. I treat trustworthiness as the capacity which enables its possessor to adhere, and to judge that he ought to adhere, to a commitment which he has made, without regard to considerations of advantage.

The prudent but trustworthy man does not possess this capacity completely. He is capable of trustworthy behavior only in so far as he regards his *commitment* as advantageous. Thus he differs from the prudent man just in the relevant respect; he accepts arguments of the form "If it is advantageous for me to agree[7] to do x, and I do agree to do x, then I ought to do x, whether or not it then proves advantageous for me to do x."

Suppose that *A* and *B*, the parties to the disarmament pact, are prudent but trustworthy. *A*, considering whether or not secretly to violate the agreement, reasons that its advantage in making and keeping the agreement, provided *B* does so as well, is greater than its advantage in not making it. If it can assume that *B* reasons in the same way, then it is in a position to conclude that it ought not to violate the pact. Although violation would be advantageous, consideration of this advantage is ruled out by *A*'s trustworthiness, given the advantage in agreeing to the pact.

The prudent but trustworthy man meets the requirements implicitly imposed by the thesis for the "moral" man. But how far does this "moral" man display two characteristics commonly associated with morality—first, a willingness to make sacrifices, and second, a concern with fairness?

Whenever a man ignores his own advantage for reasons other than those of greater advantage, he may be said to make some sacrifice. The "moral" man, in being trustworthy, is thus required to make certain sacrifices. But these are extremely limited. And—not surprisingly, given the general direction of our argument—it is quite possible that they limit the advantages which the "moral" man can secure.

Once more let us turn to our example. *A* and *B* have entered into a disarmament agreement and, being prudent but trustworthy, are faithfully carrying it out. The government of *A* is now informed by its scientists, however, that they have developed an effective missile defense, which will render *A* invulnerable to attack by any of the weapons actually or potentially at *B*'s disposal, barring unforeseen technological developments. Furthermore, this defense can be installed secretly. The government is now called upon to decide whether to violate its agreement with *B*, install the new defense, and, with the arms it has retained through its violation, establish its dominance over *B*.

A is in a type of situation quite different from that previously considered. For it is not just that *A* will do better by secretly violating its agreement. *A* reasons not only that it will do better to violate no matter what *B* does, but that it will do better if both violate than if both continue to adhere to the pact. *A* is now in a position to gain from abandoning the agreement; it no longer finds mutual adherence advantageous.

We may represent this new situation in another matrix:

		B	
		adheres	*violates*
A	adheres	3, 2	4, 1
	violates	1, 4	2, 3

We assume again that the ranking of mutual violation is the same as that of no agreement. Now had this situation obtained at the outset, no agreement would have been made, for *A* would have had no reason to enter into a disarmament pact. And of course had *A* expected this situation to come about, no agreement—or only a temporary agreement—would have been made; *A* would no doubt have risked the short-term dangers of the continuing arms race in the hope of securing the long-run benefit of predominance over *B* once its missile defense was completed. On the contrary, *A* expected to benefit from the agreement, but now finds that, because of its unexpected development of a missile defense, the agreement is not in fact advantageous to it.

The prudent but trustworthy man is willing to carry out his agreements, and judges that he ought to carry them out, in so far as he considers them advantageous. *A* is prudent but trustworthy. But is *A* willing to carry out its agreement to disarm, now that it no longer considers the agreement advantageous?

If *A* adheres to its agreement in this situation, it makes a sacrifice greater than any advantage it receives from the similar sacrifices of others. It makes a sacrifice greater in kind than any which can be required by a mutually advantageous agreement. It must, then, possess a capacity for trustworthy behavior greater than that ascribed to the merely prudent but trustworthy man (or nation). This capacity need not be unlimited; it need not extend to a willingness to adhere to any commitment no matter what sacrifice is involved. But it must involve a willingness to adhere to a commitment made in the expectation of advantage, should that expectation be disappointed.

I shall call the man (or nation) who is willing to adhere, and judges that he ought to adhere, to his prudentially undertaken agreements even if they prove disadvantageous to him, the trustworthy man. It is likely that there are advantages available to trustworthy men which are not available to merely prudent but trustworthy men. For there may be situations in which men can make agreements which each expects to be advantageous to him, provided he can count on the others' adhering to it whether or not their expectation of advantage is realized. But each can count on this only if all have the capacity to adhere to commitments regardless of whether the commitment actually proves advantageous. Hence, only trustworthy men who know each other to be such will be able rationally to enter into, and so to benefit from, such agreements.

Baier's view of morality departs from that stated in the thesis in that it requires trustworthy, and not merely prudent but trustworthy, men. Baier admits that "a person might do better for himself by following enlightened self-interest rather than morality."[8] This admission seems to require that morality be a system of principles which each person may expect, initially, to be advantageous to him, if adopted and adhered to by everyone, but not a system which actually is advantageous to everyone.

Our commonplace moral views do, I think, support the view that the moral man must be trustworthy. Hence, we have established one modification required in the thesis, if it is to provide a more adequate set of conditions for a moral system.

But there is a much more basic respect in which the "moral" man falls short of our expectations. He is willing to temper his single-minded pursuit of advantage only by accepting the obligation to adhere to prudentially undertaken commitments. He has no real concern for the advantage of others, which would lead him to modify his pursuit of advantage when it conflicted with the similar pursuits of others. Unless he expects to gain, he is unwilling to accept restrictions on the pursuit of advantage which are intended to equalize the opportunitites open to all. In other words, he has no concern with fairness.

We tend to think of the moral man as one who does not seek his own well-being by means which would deny equal well-being to his fellows. This marks him off clearly from the "moral" man, who differs from the prudent man only in that he can overcome the apparent paradox of prudence and obtain those advantages which are available only to those who can display real restraint in their pursuit of advantage.

Thus a system of principles might meet the conditions laid down in the thesis without taking any account of considerations of fairness. Such a system would contain principles for ensuring increased advantage (or expectation of advantage) to everyone, but no further principle need be present to determine the distribution of this increase.

It is possible that there are systems of principles which, if adopted and adhered to, provide advantages which strictly prudent men, however rational, cannot attain. These advantages are a function of the sacrifices which the principles impose on their adherents.

Morality may be such a system. If it is, this would explain our expectation that we should all be worse off were we to substitute prudence for morality in our deliberations. But to characterize morality as a system of principles advantageous to all is not to answer the question "Why should I be moral?" nor is it to provide for those considerations of fairness which are equally essential to our moral understanding.

Notes

1. David Hume, *An Enquiry Concerning the Principles of Morals,* sec. ix, pt. ii.
2. Ogden Nash, "Kind of an Ode to Duty."
3. Kurt Baier, *The Moral Point of View: A Rational Basis of Ethics* (Ithaca, 1958), p. 314.
4. That this, and only this, is what he is entitled to claim may not be clear to Baier, for he supposes his account of morality to answer the question "Why should we be moral?," interpreting "we" distributively. This, as I shall argue in Sec. IV, is quite mistaken.
5. The thesis is not intended to state Baier's view of morality. I shall suggest in Sec. V that Baier's view would require substituting "everyone can expect to benefit" for "it is advantageous to everyone." The thesis is stronger and easier to discuss.
6. Those familiar with the theory of games will recognize the matrix as a variant of the Prisoner's Dilemma. In a more formal treatment, it would be appropriate to develop the relation between morality and advantage by reference to the Prisoner's Dilemma. This would require reconstructing the disarmament pact and the moral system as proper games. Here I wish only to suggest the bearing of game theory on our enterprise.
7. The word "agree" requires elucidation. It is essential not to confuse an advantage in agreeing to do x with an advantage in saying that one will do x. If it is advantageous for me to agree to do x, then there is some set of actions open to me which includes both saying that I will do x and doing x, and which is more advantageous to me than any set of actions open to me which does not include saying that I will do x. On the other hand, if it is advantageous for me to say that I will do x, then there is some set of actions open to me which includes saying that I will do x, and which is more advantageous to me than any set which does not include saying that I will do x. But this set need not include doing x.
8. Baier, *op. cit.*, p. 314.

The Law of the Jungle: Moral Alternatives and Principles of Evolution

J. L. MACKIE

J. L. Mackie (1917–81) taught philosophy at University College, Oxford. His writings were influential in a number of areas of philosophy, including ethics and metaphysics. They include *The Cement of the Universe* and *Ethics: Inventing Right and Wrong.*

When people speak of "the law of the jungle," they usually mean unrestrained and ruthless competition, with everyone out solely for his own advantage. But the phrase was coined by Rudyard Kipling, in *The Second Jungle Book,* and he meant something very different. His law of the jungle is a law that wolves in a pack are supposed to obey. His poem says that "the strength of the Pack is the Wolf, and the strength of the Wolf is the Pack," and it states the basic principles of social co-operation. Its provisions are a judicious mixture of individualism and collectivism, prescribing graduated and qualified rights for fathers of families, mothers with cubs, and young wolves, which constitute an elementary system of welfare services. Of course, Kipling meant his poem to give moral instruction to human children, but he probably thought it was at least roughly correct as a description of the social behaviour of wolves and other wild animals. Was he right, or is the natural world the scene of unrestrained competition, of an individualistic struggle for existence?

Views not unlike those of Kipling have been presented by some recent writers on ethology, notably Robert Ardrey and Konrad Lorenz. These writers connect their accounts with a view about the process of evolution that has brought this behaviour, as well as the animals themselves, into existence. They hold that the important thing in evolution is the good of the species, or the group, rather than the good of the individual. Natural selection favours those groups and species whose members tend, no doubt through some instinctive programming, to co-operate for a common good; this would, of course, explain why wolves, for example, behave co-operatively and generously towards members of their own pack, if indeed they do.

However, this recently popular view has been keenly attacked by Richard Dawkins in his admirable and fascinating book, *The Selfish Gene.*[1] He defends an up-to-date version of the orthodox Darwinian theory of evolution, with special reference to "the biology of selfishness and altruism." One of his main theses is that there is no such thing as group selection, and that Lorenz and others who have used this as an explanation are simply wrong. This is a question of some interest to moral philosophers, particularly those who have been inclined to see human morality itself as the product of some kind of natural evolution.[2]

It is well, however, to be clear about the issue. It is not whether animals ever behave for the good of the group in the sense that this is their conscious subjective goal, that they *aim* at the well-being or survival of the whole tribe or pack: the question of motives in this conscious sense does not arise. Nor is the issue whether animals

From *Philosophy* 53 (1978), 455–61, 463–64.

ever behave in ways which do in fact promote the well-being of the group to which they belong, or which help the species of which they are members to survive: of course they do. The controversial issue is different from both of these: it is whether the good of the group or the species would ever figure in a correct evolutionary account. That is, would any correct evolutionary account take either of the following forms?

(i) The members of this species tend to do these things which assist the survival of this species because their ancestors were members of a sub-species whose members had an inheritable tendency to do these things, and as a result that sub-species survived, whereas other sub-species of the ancestral species at that time had members who tended not to do these things and as a result their sub-species did not survive.

(ii) The members of this species tend to do these things which help the group of which they are members to flourish because some ancestral groups happened to have members who tended to do these things and these groups, as a result, survived better than related groups of the ancestral species whose members tended not to do these things.

In other words, the issue is this: is there natural selection by and for group survival or species survival as opposed to selection by and for individual survival (or, as we shall see, gene survival)? Is behaviour that helps the group or the species, rather than the individual animal, rewarded by the natural selection which determines the course of evolution?

However, when Dawkins denies that there is selection by and for group or species survival, it is not selection by and for individual survival that he puts in its place. Rather it is selection by and for the survival of each single gene—the genes being the unit factors of inheritance, the portions of chromosomes which replicate themselves, copy themselves as cells divide and multiply. Genes, he argues, came into existence right back at the beginning of life on earth, and all more complex organisms are to be seen as their products. We are, as he picturesquely puts it, gene-machines: our biological function is just to protect our genes, carry them around, and enable them to reproduce themselves. Hence the title of his book, *The Selfish Gene*. Of course what survives is not a token gene: each of these perishes with the cell of which it is a part. What survives is a gene-type, or rather what we might call a gene-clone, the members of a family of token genes related to one another by simple direct descent, by replication. The popularity of the notions of species selection and group selection may be due partly to confusion on this point. Since clearly it is only types united by descent, not individual organisms, that survive long enough to be of biological interest, it is easy to think that selection must be by and for species survival. But this is a mistake: genes, not species, are the types which primarily replicate themselves and are selected. Since Dawkins roughly defines the gene as "a genetic unit which is small enough to last for a number of generations and to be distributed around in the form of many copies," it is (as he admits) practically a tautology that the gene is the basic unit of natural selection and therefore, as he puts it, "the fundamental unit of self-interest," or, as we might put it less picturesquely, the primary beneficiary of natural selection. But behind this near-tautology is a synthetic truth, that this basic unit, this primary beneficiary, is a small bit of chromosome. The reason why this is so, why what is differentially effective and therefore subject to selection is a small bit of a chromosome, lies in the mechanism of sexual reproduction by way of meiosis, with crossing over between chromosomes. When male and female cells each divide before uniting at fertilization, it is not chromosomes as a whole that are randomly distributed between the parts, but sections of chromosomes. So sections of chromosomes can be separately inherited, and therefore can be differentially selected by natural selection.

The issue between gene selection, individual selection, group selection, and species selection might seem to raise some stock questions in the philosophy of science. Many thinkers have favoured reductionism of several sorts, including methodological individualism. Wholes are made up of parts, and therefore in principle whatever happens in any larger thing depends upon and is explainable in terms of what happens in and between its smaller components. But though this metaphysical individualism is correct, methodological individualism does not follow from it. It does not follow that we must always conduct our investigations and construct our explanations in terms of component parts, such as the individual members of a group or society. Scientific accounts need not be indefinitely reductive. Some wholes are obviously more accessible to us than their components. We can understand what a human being does without analysing this in terms of how each single cell in his body or his brain behaves. Equally we can often understand what a human society does without analysing this in terms of the behaviour of each of its individual members. And the same holds quite generally: we can often understand complex wholes as units, without analysing them into their parts. So if, in the account of evolution, Dawkins's concentration upon genes were just a piece of methodological individualism or reductionism, it would be inadequately motivated. But it is not: there is a special reason for it. Dawkins's key argument is that species, populations, and groups, and individual organisms too, are as genetic units too temporary to qualify for natural selection. "They are not stable through evolutionary time. Populations are constantly blending with other populations and so losing their identity," and, what is vitally important, "are also subject to evolutionary change from within" (p. 36).

This abstract general proposition may seem obscure. But it is illustrated by a simple example which Dawkins gives (pp. 197–201).

A species of birds is parasitized by dangerous ticks. A bird can remove the ticks from most parts of its own body, but, having only a beak and no hands, it cannot get them out of the top of its own head. But one bird can remove ticks from another bird's head: there can be mutual grooming. Clearly if there were an inherited tendency for each bird to take the ticks out of any other bird's head, this would help the survival of any group in which that tendency happened to arise—for the ticks are dangerous: they can cause death. Some who believe in group selection would, therefore, expect this tendency to be favoured and to evolve and spread for this reason. But Dawkins shows that it would not. He gives appropriate names to the different "strategies," that is, the different inheritable behavioural tendencies. The strategy of grooming anyone who needs it he labels "Sucker." The strategy of accepting grooming from anyone, but never grooming anyone else, even someone who has previously groomed you, is called "Cheat." Now if in some population both these tendencies or strategies, and only these two, happen to arise, it is easy to see that the cheats will always do better than the suckers. They will be groomed when they need it, and since they will not waste their time pecking out other birds' ticks, they will have more time and energy to spare for finding food, attracting mates, building nests, and so on. Consequently the gene for the Sucker strategy will gradually die out. So the population will come to consist wholly of cheats, despite the fact that this is likely to lead to the population itself becoming extinct, if the parasites are common enough and dangerous enough, whereas a population consisting wholly of suckers would have survived. The fact that the group is open to evolutionary change from within, because of the way the internal competition between Cheat and Sucker genes works out, prevents the group from developing or even retaining a feature which would have helped the group as a whole.

This is just one illustration among many, and Dawkins's arguments on this point seem pretty conclusive. We need, as he shows, the concept of an *evolutionarily stable strategy* or *ESS* (p. 74 *et passim*). A strategy is evolutionarily stable, in relation to some alternative strategy or strategies, if it will survive indefinitely in a group in competition with those alternatives. We have just seen that where Cheat and Sucker alone are in competition, Cheat is an ESS but Sucker is not. We have also seen, from this example, that an ESS may not help a group, or the whole species, to survive and multiply. Of course we must not leap to the conclusion that an ESS never helps a group or a species: if that were so we could not explain much of the behaviour that actually occurs. Parents sacrifice themselves for their children, occasionally siblings for their siblings, and with the social insects, bees and ants and termites, their whole life is a system of communal service. But the point is that these results are not to be explained in terms of group selection. They can and must be explained as consequences of the selfishness of genes, that is, the fact that gene-clones are selected for whatever helps each gene-clone itself to survive and multiply.

But now we come to another remarkable fact. Although the gene is the hero of Dawkins's book, it is not unique either in principle or in fact. It is not the only possible subject of evolutionary natural selection, nor is it the only actual one. What is important about the gene is just that it has a certain combination of logical features. It is a replicator: in the right environment it is capable of producing multiple copies of itself; but in this process of copying some mistakes occur; and even mistaken copies—mutations—will also produce copies of themselves; and, finally, the copies produced may either survive or fail to survive. Anything that has these formal, logical, features is a possible subject of evolution by natural selection. As we have seen, individual organisms, groups, and species do not have the required formal features, though many thinkers have supposed that they do. They cannot reproduce themselves with sufficient constancy of characteristics. But Dawkins, in his last chapter, introduces another sort of replicators. These are what are often called cultural items or traits; Dawkins christens them *memes*—to make a term a bit like "genes"—because they replicate by memory and imitation (mimesis). Memes include tunes, ideas, fashions, and techniques. They require, as the environment in which they can replicate, a collection of minds, that is, brains that have the powers of imitation and memory. These brains (particularly though not exclusively human ones) are themselves the products of evolution by gene selection. But once the brains are there gene selection has done its work: given that environment, memes can themselves evolve and multiply in much the same way as genes do, in accordance with logically similar laws. But they can do so more quickly. Cultural evolution may be much faster than biological evolution. But the basic laws are the same. Memes are selfish in the same sense as genes. The explanation of the widespread flourishing of a certain meme, such as the idea of a god or the belief in hell fire, may be simply that it is an efficiently selfish meme. Something about it makes it well able to infect human minds, to take root and spread in and among them, in the same way that something about the smallpox virus makes it well able to take root and spread in human bodies. There is no need to explain the success of a meme in terms of any benefit it confers on individuals or groups; it is a replicator in its own right. Contrary to the optimistic view often taken of cultural evolution, this analogy shows that a cultural trait can evolve, not because it is advantageous to society, but simply because it is advantageous to itself. It is ironical that Kipling's phrase "the law of the jungle" has proved itself a more efficient meme than the doctrine he tried to use it to propogate.

So far I have been merely summarizing Dawkins's argument. We can now use it to answer the question from which I started. Who is right about the law of the jungle? Kipling, or those who have twisted his phrase to mean almost the opposite of what he intended? The answer is that neither party is right. The law by which nature works is not unrestrained and ruthless competition between individual organisms. But neither does it turn upon the advantages to a group, and its members, of group solidarity, mutual care and respect, and co-operation. It turns upon the self-preservation of gene-clones. This has a strong tendency to express itself in individually selfish behaviour, simply because each agent's genes are more certainly located in him than in anyone else. But it can and does express itself also in certain forms of what Broad called self-referential altruism, including special care for one's own children and perhaps one's siblings, and, as we shall see, reciprocal altruism, helping those (and only those) who help you.

But now I come to what seems to be an exception to Dawkins's main thesis, though it is generated by his own argument and illustrated by one of his own examples. We saw how, in the example of mutual grooming, if there are only suckers and cheats around, the strategy Cheat is evolutionarily stable, while the strategy Sucker is not. But Dawkins introduces a third strategy, Grudger. A grudger is rather like you and me. A grudger grooms anyone who has previously groomed him, and any stranger, but he remembers and bears a grudge against anyone who cheats him—who refuses to groom him in return for having been groomed— and the grudger refuses to groom the cheat ever again. Now when all three strategies are in play, both Cheat and Grudger are evolutionarily stable. In a population consisting largely of cheats, the cheats will do better than the others, and both suckers and grudgers will die out. But in a population that starts off with more than a certain critical proportion of grudgers, the cheats will first wipe out the suckers, but will then themselves become rare and eventually extinct: cheats can flourish only while they have suckers to take advantage of, and yet by doing so they tend to eliminate those suckers.

It is obvious, by the way, that a population containing only suckers and grudgers, in any proportions, but no cheats, would simply continue as it was. Suckers and grudgers behave exactly like one another as long as there are no cheats around, so there would be no tendency for either the Sucker or the Grudger gene to do better than the other. But if there is any risk of an invasion of Cheat genes, either through mutation or through immigration, such a pattern is not evolutionarily stable, and the higher the proportion of suckers, the more rapidly the cheats would multiply.

So we have two ESSs, Cheat and Grudger. But there is a difference between these two stable strategies. If the parasites are common enough and dangerous enough, the population of cheats will itself die out, having no defence against ticks in their heads, whereas a separate population of grudgers will flourish indefinitely. Dawkins says, "If a population arrives at an ESS which drives it extinct, then it goes extinct, and that is just too bad" (p. 200). True: *but is this not group selection after all?* Of course, this will operate only if the populations are somehow isolated. But if the birds in question were distributed in geographically isolated regions, and Sucker, Cheat and Grudger tendencies appeared (after the parasites became plentiful) in randomly different proportions in these different regions, then some populations would become pure grudger populations, and others would die out, so that eventually all surviving birds would be grudgers. And they would be able to re-colonize the areas where cheat populations had perished.

Another name for grudgers is "reciprocal altruists." They act as if on the maxim "Be done by as you did." One implication of this story is that this strategy is not only evolutionarily stable within a population, it is also viable for a population as a whole. The explanation of the final situation, where all birds of this species are grudgers, lies partly in the non-viability of a population of pure cheats. So this is, as I said, a bit of group selection after all.

. . . .

What implications for human morality have such biological facts about selfishness and altruism? One is that the possibility that morality is itself a product of natural selection is not ruled out, but care would be needed in formulating a plausible speculative account of how it might have been favoured. Another is that the notion of an ESS may be a useful one for discussing questions of practical morality. Moral philosophers have already found illumination in such simple items of game theory as the Prisoners' Dilemma; perhaps these rather more complicated evolutionary "games" will prove equally instructive. Of course there is no simple transition from "is" to "ought," no direct argument from what goes on in the natural world and among non-human animals to what human beings ought to do. Dawkins himself explicitly warns against any simple transfer of conclusions. At the very end of the book he suggests that conscious foresight may enable us to develop radically new kinds of behaviour. "We are built as gene-machines and cultured as meme-machines, but we have the power to turn against our creators. We, alone on earth, can rebel against the tyranny of the selfish replicators" (p. 215). This optimistic suggestion needs fuller investigation. It must be remembered that the human race as a whole cannot act as a unit with conscious foresight. Arrow's Theorem shows that even quite small groups of rational individuals may be unable to form coherently rational preferences, let alone to act rationally. Internal competition, which in general prevents a group from being a possible subject of natural selection, is even more of an obstacle to its being a rational agent. And while we can turn against some memes, it will be only with the help and under the guidance of other memes.

This is an enormous problematic area. For the moment I turn to a smaller point. In the mutal grooming model, we saw that the Grudger strategy was, of the three strategies considered, the only one that was healthy in the long run. Now something closely resembling this strategy, reciprocal altrusim, is a well-known and long-established tendency in human life. It is expressed in such formulae as that justice consists in giving everyone his due, interpreted, as Polemarchus interprets it in the first book of Plato's *Republic,* as doing good to one's friends and harm to one's enemies, or repaying good with good and evil with evil. Morality itself has been seen, for example by Edward Westermarck, as an outgrowth from the retributive emotions. But some moralists, including Socrates and Jesus, have recommended something very different from this, turning the other cheek and repaying evil with good. They have tried to substitute "Do as you would be done by" for "Be done by as you did." Now this, which in human life we characterize as a Christian spirit or perhaps as saintliness, is roughly equivalent to the strategy Dawkins has unkindly labelled "Sucker." Suckers are saints, just as grudgers are reciprocal altruists, while cheats are a hundred per cent selfish. And as Dawkins points out, the presence of suckers endangers the healthy Grudger strategy. It allows cheats to prosper, and could make them multiply to the point where they would wipe out the grudgers, and ultimately bring about the extinction of the whole population. This seems to provide fresh support for Neitzsche's view of the deplorable influence of moralities of the Christian type. But in practice there may be little danger. After two thousand years of contrary moral teaching, recriprocal altrusim is still dominant in all human societies; thoroughgoing cheats and thoroughgoing saints (or suckers) are distinctly rare. The sucker slogan is an efficient meme, but the sucker behaviour pattern far less so. Saintliness is an attractive topic for preaching, but with little practical persuasive force. Whether in the long run this is to be deplored or welcomed, and whether it is alterable or not, is a larger question. To answer it we should have carefully to examine our specifically human capabilities and the structure of human societies, and also many further alternative strategies. We cannot simply apply to the human situation conclusions drawn from biological models. Nevertheless they are significant and challenging as models; it will need to be shown how and where human life diverges from them.

Notes

1. R. Dawkins, *The Selfish Gene* (Oxford, 1976).
2. I am among these: see p. 113 of my *Ethics: Inventing Right and Wrong* (Penguin, Harmondsworth, 1977).

2. SUBJECTIVISM, RELATIVISM, AND SKEPTICISM

The Subjectivity of Values

J. L. MACKIE

1. Moral Scepticism

There are no objective values. This is a bald statement of the thesis of this chapter, but before arguing for it I shall try to clarify and restrict it in ways that may meet some objections and prevent some misunderstanding.

The statement of this thesis is liable to provoke one of the three very different reactions. Some will think it not merely false but pernicious; they will see it as a threat to morality and to everything else that is worthwhile, and they will find the presenting of such a thesis in what purports to be a book on ethics paradoxical or even outrageous. Others will regard it as a trivial truth, almost too obvious to be worth mentioning, and certainly too plain to be worth much argument. Others again will say that it is meaningless or empty, that no real issue is raised by the question whether values are or are not part of the fabric of the world. But, precisely because there can be these three different reactions, much more needs to be said.

The claim that values are not objective, are not part of the fabric of the world, is meant to include not only moral goodness, which might be most naturally equated with moral value, but also other things that could be more loosely called moral values or disvalues—rightness and wrongness, duty, obligation, an action's being rotten and contemptible, and so on. It also includes nonmoral values, notably aesthetic ones, beauty and various kinds of artistic merit. I shall not discuss these explicitly, but clearly much the same considerations apply to aesthetic and to moral values, and there would be at least some initial implausibility in a view that gave the one a different status from the other.

Since it is with moral values that I am primarily concerned, the view I am adopting may be called moral scepticism. But this name is likely to be misunderstood: "moral scepticism" might also be used as a name for either of two first order views, or perhaps for an incoherent mixture of the two. A moral sceptic might be the sort of person who says "All this talk of morality is tripe," who rejects morality and will take no notice of it. Such a person may be literally rejecting all moral judgments; he is more likely to be making moral judgments of his own, expressing a positive moral condemnation of all that conventionally passes for morality; or he may be confusing these two logically incompatible views, and saying that he rejects all morality, while he is in fact rejecting only a particular morality that is current in that society in which he has grown up. But I am not at present concerned with the merits or faults of such a position. These are first order moral views, positive or negative: the person who adopts either of them is taking a certain practical, normative, stand. By contrast, what I am discussing is a second order view, a view about the status of moral values and the nature of moral valuing, about where and how they fit into the world. These first and second order views are not merely distinct but completely independent:

From *Ethics: Inventing Right and Wrong* (Harmondsworth: Penguin Books, 1977), pp. 15–18, 25–48 one could be a second order moral sceptic without being a first order one, or again the other way round. A man could hold strong moral views, and indeed ones whose content was thoroughly conventional, while believing that they were simply attitudes and policies with regard to conduct that he and other people held. Conversely, a man could reject all established morality while believing it to be an objective truth that it was evil or corrupt.

With another sort of misunderstanding moral scepticism would seem not so much pernicious as absurd. How could anyone deny that there is a difference between a kind action and a cruel one, or that a coward and a brave man behave differently in the face of danger? Of course, this is undeniable; but it is not to the point. The kinds of behaviour to which moral values and disvalues are ascribed are indeed part of the furniture of the world, and so are the natural, descriptive, differences between them; but, not perhaps, their differences in value. It is a hard fact that cruel actions differ from kind ones, and hence that we can learn, as in fact we all do, to distinguish them fairly well in practice, and to use the words "cruel" and "kind" with fairly clear descriptive meanings; but is it an equally hard fact that actions which are cruel in such a descriptive sense are to be condemned? The present issue is with regard to the objectivity specifically of value, not with regard to the objectivity of those natural, factual, differences on the basis of which differing values are assigned.

2. Subjectivism

Another name often used, as an alternative to "moral scepticism," for the view I am discussing is "subjectivism." But this too has more than one meaning. Moral subjectivism too could be a first order, normative, view, namely that everyone really ought to do whatever he thinks he should. This plainly is a (systematic) first order view; on examination it soon ceases to be plausible, but that is beside the point, for it is quite independent of the second order thesis at present under consideration. What is more confusing is that different second order views compete for the name "subjectivism". Several of these are doctrines about the meaning of moral terms and moral statements. What is often called moral subjectivism is the doctrine that, for example, "This action is right" *means* "I approve of this action", or more generally that moral judgments are equivalent to reports of the speaker's own feelings or attitudes. But the view I am now discussing is to be distinguished in two vital respects from any such doctrine as this. First, what I have called moral scepticism is a negative doctrine, not a positive one: it says what there isn't, not what there is. It says that there do not exist entities or relations of a certain kind, objective values or requirements, which many people have believed to exist. Of course, the moral sceptic cannot leave it at that. If his position is to be at all plausible, he must give some account of how other people have fallen into what he regards as an error, and this account will have to include some positive suggestions about how values fail to be objective, about what has been mistaken for, or has led to false beliefs about, objective values. But this will be a development of his theory, not its core: its core is the negation. Secondly, what I have called moral subjectivism, is an ontological thesis, not a linguistic or conceptual one. It is not, like the other doctrine often called moral subjectivism, a view about the meanings of moral statements. Again, no doubt, if it is to be at all plausible, it will have to give some account of their meanings, and I shall say something about this in Section 7 of this chapter. . . . But this too will be a development of the theory, not its core.

It is true that those who have accepted the moral subjectivism which is the doctrine that moral judgments are equivalent to reports of the speaker's own feelings or attitudes have usually presupposed what I am calling moral scepticism. It is because they have assumed that there are no objective values that they have looked elsewhere for an analysis of what moral statements might mean, and have settled upon subjective reports. Indeed, if all our moral statements were such subjective reports, it would follow that, at least so far as we are aware, there are no objective moral values. If we were aware of them, we would say something about them. In this sense this sort of subjectivism entails moral scepticism. But the converse entailment does not hold. The denial that there are objective values does not commit one to any particular view about what moral statements mean, and certainly not to the view that they are equivalent to subjective reports. No doubt if moral values are not objective they are in some very broad sense subjective, and for this reason I would accept "moral subjectivism" as an alternative name to "moral scepticism". But subjectivism in this broad sense must be distinguished from the specific doctrine about meaning referred to above. Neither name is altogether satisfactory: we simply have to guard against the (different) misinterpretations which each may suggest.

. . . .

5. Standards of Evaluation

One way of stating the thesis that there are no objective values is to say that value statements cannot be either true or false. But this formulation, too, lends itself to misinterpretation. For there are certain kinds of value statements which undoubtedly can be true or false, even if, in the sense I intend, there are no objective values. Evaluations of many sorts are commonly made in relation to agreed and assumed standards. The classing of wool, the grading of apples, the awarding of prizes at sheepdog trials, flower shows, skating and diving championships, and even the marking of examination papers are carried out in relation to standards of quality or merit which are peculiar to each particular subject-matter or type of contest, which may be explicitly laid down but which, even if they are nowhere explicitly stated, are fairly well understood and agreed by those who are recognized as judges or experts in each particular field. Given any sufficiently determinate standards, it will be an objective issue, a matter of truth and falsehood, how well any particular specimen measures up to those standards. Comparative judgments in particular will be capable of truth and falsehood: it will be a factual question whether this sheepdog has performed better than that one.

The subjectivist about values, then, is not denying that there can be objective evalutions relative to standards, and these are as possible in the aesthetic and moral fields as in any of those just mentioned. More than this, there is an objective distinction which applies in many such fields, and yet would itself be regarded as a peculiarly moral one: the distinction between justice and injustice. In one important sense of the word it is a paradigm case of injustice if a court declares someone to be guilty of an offence of which it knows him to be innocent. More generally, a finding is unjust if it is at variance with what the relevant law and the facts together require, and particularly if it is known by the court to be so. More generally still, any award of marks, prizes, or the like is unjust if it is at variance with the agreed standards for the contest in question: if one diver's performance in fact measures up better to the accepted standards for diving than another's, it will be unjust if the latter is awarded higher marks or the prize. In this way the justice or injustice of decisions relative to standards can be a thoroughly objective matter, though there may still be a subjective element in the interpretation or application of standards. But the statement that a certain decision is thus just or unjust will not be objectively prescriptive: in so far as it can be simply true it leaves open the question whether there is any objective requirement to do what is just and to refrain from what is unjust, and equally leaves open the practical decision to act in either way.

Recognizing the objectivity of justice in relation to standards, and of evaluative judgments relative to standards, then, merely shifts the question of the objectivity of values back to the standards themselves. The subjectivist may try to make his point by insisting that there is no objective validity about the choice of standards. Yet he would clearly be wrong if he said that the choice of even the most basic standards in any field was completely arbitrary. The standards used in sheepdog trials clearly bear some relation to the work that sheepdogs are kept to do, the standards for grading apples bear some relation to what people generally want in or like about apples, and so on. On the other hand, standards are not as a rule strictly validated by such purposes. The appropriateness of standards is neither fully determinate nor totally indeterminate in relation to independently specifiable aims or desires. But however determinate it is, the objective appropriateness of standards in relation to aims or desires is no more of a threat to the denial of objective values than is the objectivity of evaluation relative to standards. In fact it is logically no different from the objectivity of goodness relative to desires. Something may be called good simply in so far as it satisfies or is such as to satisfy a certain desire; but the objectivity of such relations of satisfaction does not constitute in our sense an objective value.

6. Hypothetical and Categorical Imperatives

We may make this issue clearer by referring to Kant's distinction between hypothetical and categorical imperatives, though what he called imperatives are more naturally expressed as "ought" statements than in the imperative mood. "If you want *X*, do *Y*" (or "You ought to do *Y*") will be a hypothetical imperative if it is based on the supposed fact that *Y* is, in the circumstances, the only (or the best) available means to *X*, that is, on a causal relation between *Y* and *X*. The reason for doing *Y* lies in its causal connection with the desired end, *X*; the oughtness is contingent upon the desire. But "You ought to do *Y*" will be a categorical imperative if you ought to do *Y* irrespective of any such desire for any end to which *Y* would contribute, if the oughtness is not thus contingent upon any desire. But this distinction needs to be handled with some care. An "ought"-statement is not in this sense hypothetical merely because it incorporates a conditional clause. "If you promised to do *Y*, you ought to do *Y*" is not a hypothetical imperative merely on account of the stated if-clause; what is meant may be either a hypothetical or a categorical imperative, depending upon the implied reason for keeping the supposed promise. If this rests upon some such further unstated conditional as "If you want to be trusted another time," then it is a hypothetical imperative; if not, it is categorical. Even a desire of the agent's can figure in the antecedent of what, though conditional in grammatical form, is still in Kant's sense a categorical imperative. "If you are strongly attracted sexually to young children you ought not to go in for shcool teaching" is not, in virtue of what it explicitly says, a hypothetical imperative: the avoidance of school teaching is not being offered as a means to the satisfaction of the desires in question. Of course, it could still be a hypothetical imperative, if the implied reason were a prudential one; but it could also be a categorical imperative, a moral requirement where the reason for the recommended action (strictly, avoidance) does not rest upon that action's being a means to the satisfaction of any desire that the agent is supposed to have. Not every conditional ought-statement or command, then, is a hypothetical imperative; equally, not every non-conditional one is a categorical imperative. An appropriate if-clause may be left unstated. Indeed, a simple command in the imperative mood, say a parade-ground order, which might seem most literally to qualify for the title of a categorical imperative, will hardly ever be one in the sense we need here. The implied reason for complying with such an order will almost always be some desire of the person addressed, perhaps simply the desire to keep out of the trouble. If so, such an apparently categorical order will be in our sense a hypothetical imperative. Again, an imperative remains hypothetical even if we change the "if" to "since": the fact that the desire for *X* is actually present does not alter the fact that the reason for doing *Y* is contingent upon the desire for *X* by way of *Y*'s being a means to *X*. In Kant's own treatment, while imperatives of skill relate to desires which an agent may or may not have, imperatives of prudence relate to the desire for happiness which, Kant assumes, everyone has. So construed, imperatives of prudence are no less hypothetical than imperatives of skill, no less contingent upon desires that the agent has at the time the imperatives are addressed to him. But if we think rather of a counsel of prudence as being related to the agent's future welfare, to the satisfaction of desires that he does not yet have—not even to a present desire that his future desires should be satisfied—then a counsel of prudence is a categorical imperative, different indeed from a moral one, but analogous to it.

A categorical imperative, then, would express a reason for acting which was unconditional in the sense of not being contingent upon any present desire of the agent to whose satisfaction the recommended action would contribute as a means—or more directly: "You ought to dance," if the implied reason is just that you want to dance or like dancing, is still a hypothetical imperative. Now Kant himself held that moral judgements are categorical imperatives, or perhaps are all applications of one categorical imperative, and it can plausibly be maintained at least that many moral judgments contain a categorically imperative element. So far as ethics is concerned, my thesis that there are no objective values is specifically the denial that any such categorically imperative element is objectively valid. The objective values which I am denying would be action-directing absolutely, not contingently (in the way indicated) upon the agent's desires and inclinations.

Another way of trying to clarify this issue is to refer to moral reasoning or moral arguments. In practice, of course, such reasoning is seldom fully explicit: but let us suppose that we could make explicit the reasoning that supports some evaluative conclusion, where this conclusion has some action-guiding force that is not contingent upon desires or purposes or chosen ends. Then what I am saying is that somewhere in the input to this argument—perhaps in one or more of the premises, perhaps in some part of the form of the argument—there will be something which cannot be objectively validated—some premiss which is not capable of being simply true, or some form of argument which is not valid as a matter of general logic, whose authority or cogency is not objective, but is constituted by our choosing or deciding to think in a certain way.

7. The Claim to Objectivity

If I have succeeded in specifying precisely enough the moral values whose objectivity I am denying, my thesis may now seem to be trivially true. Of course, some will say, valuing, preferring, choosing, recommending, rejecting, condemning, and so on, are human activities, and there is no need to look for values that are prior to and logically independent of all such activities. There may be widespread agreement in valuing, and particular value-judgments are not in general arbitrary or isolated: they typically cohere with others, or can be criticized if they do not, reasons can be given for them, and so on: but if all that the subjectivist is maintaining is that desires, ends, purposes, and the like figure somewhere in the system of reasons, and that no ends or purposes are objective as opposed to being merely inter-subjective, then this may be conceded without much fuss.

But I do not think that this should be conceded so easily. As I have said, the main tradition of European moral philosophy includes the contrary claim, that there are objective values of just the sort I have denied. I have referred already to Plato, Kant, and Sidgwick. Kant in particular holds that the categorical imperative is not only categorical and imperative but objectively so: though a rational being gives the moral law to himself, the law that he thus makes is determinate and necessary. Aristotle begins the *Nicomachean Ethics* by saying that the good is that at which all things aim, and that ethics is part of a science which he calls "politics," whose goal is not knowledge but practice; yet he does not doubt that there can be *knowledge* of what is the good for man, nor, once he has identified this as well-being or happiness, *eudaimonia,* that it can be known, rationally determined, in what happiness consists; and it is plain that he thinks that this happiness is intrinsically desirable, not good simply because it is desired. The rationalist Samuel Clarke holds that

> these eternal and necessary differences of things make it *fit and reasonable* for creatures so to act . . . even separate from the consideration of these rules being the *positive will* or *command of God;* and also antecedent to any respect or regard, expectation or apprehension, of any *particular private and personal advantage or disadvantage, reward or punishment,* either present or future. . . .

Even the sentimentalist Hutcheson defines moral goodness as "some quality apprehended in actions, which procures approbation . . . ," while saying that the moral sense by which we perceive virtue and vice has been given to us (by the Author of nature) to direct our actions. Hume indeed was on the other side, but he is still a witness to the dominance of the objectivist tradition, since he claims that when we "see that the distinction of vice and virtue is not founded merely on the relations of objects, nor is perceiv'd by reason," this "wou'd subvert all the vulgar systems of morality." And Richard Price insists that right and wrong are "real characters of actions," not "qualities of our minds," and are perceived by the understanding; he criticizes the notion of moral sense on the ground that it would make virtue an affair of taste, and moral right and wrong "nothing in the objects themselves"; he rejects Hutcheson's view because (perhaps mistakenly) he sees it as collapsing into Hume's.

But this objectivism about values is not only a feature of the philosophical tradition. It has also a firm basis in ordinary thought, and even in the meanings of moral terms. No doubt it was an extravagance for Moore to say that "good" is the name of a non-natural quality, but it would not be so far wrong to say that in moral contexts it is used as if it were the name of a supposed non-natural quality, where the description "non-natural" leaves room for the peculiar evaluative, prescriptive, intrinsically action-guiding aspects of this supposed quality. . . . Someone in a state of moral perplexity, wondering whether it would be wrong for him to engage, say, in research related to bacteriological warfare, wants to arrive at some judgement about this concrete case, his doing this work at this time in these actual circumstances; his relevant characteristics will be part of the subject of the judgment, but no relation between him and the proposed action will be part of the predicate. The question is not, for example, whether he really wants to do this work, whether it will satisfy or dissatisfy him, whether he will in the long run have a pro-attitude towards it, or even whether this is an action of a sort that he can happily and sincerely recommend in all relevantly similar cases. Nor is he even wondering just whether to recommend such action in all relevantly similar cases. He wants to know whether this course of action would be wrong in itself. Something like this is the everyday objectivist concept of which talk about non-natural qualities is a philosopher's reconstruction.

The prevalence of this tendency to objectify values—and not only moral ones—is confirmed by a pattern of thinking that we find in existentialists and those influenced by them. The denial of objective values can carry with it an extreme emotional reaction, a feeling that nothing matters at all, that life has lost its purpose. Of course this does not follow; the lack of objective values is not a good reason for abandoning subjective concern or for ceasing to want anything. But the abandonment of a belief in objective values can cause, at least temporarily, a decay of subjective concern and sense of purpose. That it does so is evidence that the people in whom this reaction occurs have been tending to objectify their concerns and purposes, have been giving them a fictitious external authority. A claim to objectivity has been so strongly associated with their subjective concerns and purposes that the collapse of the former seems to undermine the latter as well.

This view, that conceptual analysis would reveal a claim to objectivity, is sometimes dramatically confirmed by philosophers who are officially on the other side. Bertrand Russell, for example, says that "ethical propositions should be expressed in the optative mood, not in the indicative"; he defends himself effectively against the charge of inconsistency in both holding ultimate ethical valuations to be subjective and expressing emphatic opinions on ethical questions. Yet at the end he admits:

> Certainly there *seems* to be something more. Suppose, for example, that some one were to advocate the introduction of bull-fighting in this country. In opposing the proposal, I should *feel,* not only that I was expressing my desires, but that my desires in the matter are *right,* whatever that may mean. As a matter of argument, I can, I think, show that I am not guilty of any logical inconsistency in holding to the above interpretation of ethics and at the same time expressing strong ethical preferences. But in feeling I am not satisfied.

But he concludes, reasonably enough, with the remark: "I can only say that, while my own opinions as to ethics do not satisfy me, other people's satisfy me still less."

I conclude, then, that ordinary moral judgments include a claim to objectivity, an assumption that there are objective values in just the sense in which I am concerned to deny this. And I do not think it is going too far to say that this assumption has been incorporated in the basic, conventional, meanings of moral terms. Any analysis of the meanings of moral terms which omits this claim to objective, intrinsic, prescriptivity is to that extent incomplete. . . .

If second order ethics were confined, then, to linguistic and conceptual analysis, it ought to conclude that moral values at least are objective:

that they are so is part of what our ordinary moral statements mean: the traditional moral concepts of the ordinary man as well as of the main line of western philosophers are concepts of objective value. But it is precisely for this reason that linguistic and conceptual analysis is not enough. The claim to objectivity, however ingrained in our language and thought, is not self-validating. It can and should be questioned. But the denial of objective values will have to be put forward not as the result of an analytic approach, but as an "error theory," a theory that although most people in making moral judgements implicitly claim, among other things, to be pointing to something objectively prescriptive, these claims are all false. It is this that makes the name "moral scepticism" appropriate.

But since this is an error theory, since it goes against assumptions ingrained in our thought and built into some of the ways in which language is used, since it conflicts with what is sometimes called common sense, it needs very solid support. It is not something we can accept lightly or casually and then quietly pass on. If we are to adopt this view, we must argue explicitly for it. Traditionally it has been supported by arguments of two main kinds, which I shall call the argument from relativity and the argument from queerness, but these can, as I shall show, be supplemented in several ways.

8. The Argument from Relativity

The argument from relativity has as its premiss the well-known variation in moral codes from one society to another and from one period to another, and also the differences in moral beliefs between different groups and classes within a complex community. Such variation is in itself merely a truth of descriptive morality, a fact of anthropology which entails neither first order nor second order ethical views. Yet it may indirectly support second order subjectivism: radical differences between first order moral judgements make it difficult to treat those judgements as apprehensions of objective truths. But it is not the mere occurrence of disagreements that tells against the objectivity of values. Disagreement on questions in history or biology or cosmology does not show that there are no objective issues in these fields for investigators to disagree about. But such scientific disagreement results from speculative inferences or explanatory hypotheses based on inadequate evidence; and it is hardly plausible to interpret moral disagreement in the same way. Disagreement about moral codes seems to reflect people's adherence to and participation in different ways of life. The causal connection seems to be mainly that way round: it is that people approve of monogamy because they participate in a monogamous way of life rather than that they participate in a monogamous way of life because they approve of monogamy. Of course, the standards may be an idealization of the way of life from which they arise: the monogamy in which people participate may be less complete, less rigid, than that of which it leads them to approve. This is not to say that moral judgements are purely conventional. Of course there have been and are moral heretics and moral reformers, people who have turned against the established rules and practices of their own communities for moral reasons, and often for moral reasons that we would endorse. But this can usually be understood as the extension, in ways which, though new and unconventional, seemed to them to be required for consistency, of rules to which they already adhered as arising out of an existing way of life. In short, the argument from relatively has some force simply because the actual variations in the moral codes are more readily explained by the hypothesis that they reflect ways of life than by the hypothesis that they express perceptions, most of them seriously inadequate and badly distorted, of objective values.

But there is a well-known counter to this argument from relativity, namely to say that the items for which objective validity is in the first place to be claimed are not specific moral rules or codes but very general basic principles which are recognized at least implicitly to some extent in all society—such principles as provide the foundations of what Sidgwick has called different methods of ethics: the principle of universalizability, perhaps, or the rule that one ought to conform to the specific rules of any way of life in which one takes part, from which one profits, and on which one relies, or some utilitarian principle of doing what tends, or seems likely, to promote the general happiness. It is easy to show that such general principles, married with differing concrete circumstances, different existing social patterns or different preferences, will beget different specific moral rules; and there is some plausibility in the claim that the specific rules thus generated will vary from community to community or from group to group in close agreement with the actual variations in accepted codes.

The argument from relativity can be only partly countered in this way. To take this line the moral objectivist has to say that it is only in these principles that the objective moral character attaches immediately to its descriptively specified ground or subject: other moral judgments are objectively valid or true, but only derivatively and contingently—if things had been otherwise, quite different sorts of actions would have been right. And despite the prominence in recent philosophical ethics of universalization, utilitarian principles, and the like, these are very far from constituting the whole of what is actually affirmed as basic in ordinary moral thought. Much of this is concerned rather with what Hare calls "ideals" or, less kindly, "fanaticism." That is, people judge that some things are good or right, and others are bad or wrong, not because—or at any rate not only because—they exemplify some general principle for which widespread implicit acceptance could be claimed, but because something about those things arouses certain responses immediately in them, though they would arouse radically and irresolvably different responses in others. "Moral sense" or "intuition" is an initially more plausible description of what supplies many of our basic moral judgments than "reason." With regard to all these starting points of moral thinking the argument from relativity remains in full force.

9. The Argument from Queerness

Even more important, however, and certainly more generally applicable, is the argument from queerness. This has two parts, one metaphysical, the other epistemological. If there were objective values, then they would be entities or qualities or relations of a very strange sort, utterly different from anything else in the universe. Correspondingly, if we were aware of them, it would have to be by some special faculty of moral perception or intuition, utterly different from our ordinary ways of knowing everything else. These points were recognized by Moore when he spoke of non-natural qualities, and by the intuitionists in their talk about a "faculty of moral intuition." Intuitionism has long been out of favour, and it is indeed easy to point out its implausibilities. What is not so often stressed, but is more important, is that the central thesis of intuitionism is one to which any objectivist view of values is in the end committed: intuitionism merely makes unpalatably plain what other forms of objectivism wrap up. Of course the suggestion that moral judgements are made or moral problems solved by just sitting down and having an ethical intuition is a travesty of actual moral thinking. But, however complex the real process, it will require (if it is to yield authoritatively prescriptive conclusions) some input of this distinctive sort, either premises or forms of argument or both. When we ask the awkward question, how we can be aware of this authoritative prescriptivity, of the truth of these distinctively ethical premisses or of the cogency of this distinctively ethical pattern of reasoning, none of our ordinary accounts of sensory perception or introspection or the framing and confirming of explanatory hypotheses or inference or logical construction or conceptual analysis, or any combination of these, will provide a satisfactory answer; "a special sort of intuition" is a lame answer, but it is the one to which the clearheaded objectivist is compelled to resort.

Indeed, the best move for the moral objectivist is not to evade this issue, but to look for companions in guilt. For example, Richard Price argues that it is not moral knowledge alone that such an empiricism as those of Locke and Hume is unable to account for, but also our knowledge and even our ideas of essence, number, identity, diversity, solidity, inertia, substance, the necessary existence and infinite extension of time and space, necessity and possibility in general, power, and causation. If the understanding, which Price defines as the faculty within us that discerns truth, is also a source of new simple ideas of so many other sorts, may it not also be a power of immediately perceiving right and wrong, which yet are real characters of actions?

This is an important counter to the argument from queerness. The only adequate reply to it would be to show how, on empiricist foundations, we can construct an account of the ideas and beliefs and knowledge that we have of all these matters. I cannot even begin to do that here, though I have undertaken some parts of the task elsewhere. I can only state my belief that satisfactory accounts of most of these can be given in empirical terms. If some supposed metaphysical necessities or essences resist such treatment, then they too should be included, along with objective values, among the targets of the argument from queerness.

. . . .

Plato's Forms give a dramatic picture of what objective values would have to be. The Form of the Good is such that knowledge of it provides the knower with both a direction and an overriding motive; something's being good both tells the person who knows this to pursue it and makes him pursue it. An objective good would be sought by anyone who was acquainted with it, not because of any contingent fact that this person, or every person, is so constituted that he desires this end, but just because the end has to-be-pursuedness somehow built into it. Similarly, if there were objective principles of right and wrong, any wrong (possible) course of action would have not-to-be-doneness somehow built into it. Or we should have something like Clarke's necessary relations of fitness between situations and actions, so that a situation would have a demand for such-and-such an action somehow built into it.

The need for an argument of this sort can be brought out by reflection on Hume's argument that "reason"—in which at this stage he includes all sorts of knowing as well as reasoning—can never be an "influencing motive of the will." Someone might object that Hume has argued unfairly from the lack of influencing power (not contingent upon desires) in ordinary objects of knowledge and ordinary reasoning, and might maintain that values differ from natural objects precisely in their power, when known, automatically to influence the will. To this Hume could, and would need to, reply that this objection involves the postulating of value-entities or value-features of quite a different order from anything else with which we are acquainted, and of a corresponding faculty with which to detect them. That is, he would have to supplement his explicit argument with what I have called the argument from queerness.

Another way of bringing out this queerness is to ask, about anything that is supposed to have some objective moral quality, how this is linked with its natural features. What is the connection between the natural fact that an action is a piece of deliberate cruelty—say, causing pain just for fun—and the moral fact that it is wrong? It cannot be an entailment, a logical or semantic necessity. Yet it is not merely that the two features occur together. The wrongness must somehow be "consequential" or "supervenient"; it is wrong because it is a piece of deliberate cruelty. But just what *in the world* is signified by this "because"? And how do we know the relation that it signifies, if this is something more than such actions being socially condemned, and condemned by us too, perhaps through our having absorbed attitudes from our social environment? It is not even sufficient to postulate a faculty which "sees" the wrongness: something must be postulated which can see at once the natural features that constitute the cruelty, and the wrongness, and the mysterious consequential link between the two. Alternatively, the intuition required might be the perception that wrongness is a higher order property belonging to certain natural properties; but what is this belonging of properties to other properties, and how can we discern it? How much simpler and more comprehensible the situation would be if we could replace the moral quality with some sort of subjective response which could be causally related to the detection of the natural features on which the supposed quality is said to be consequential.

. . . .

10. Patterns of Objectification

Considerations of these kinds suggest that it is in the end less paradoxical to reject than to retain the common-sense belief in the objectivity of moral values, provided that we can explain how this belief, if it is false, has become established and is so resistant to criticisms. This priviso is not difficult to satisfy.

On a subjectivist view, the supposedly objective values will be based in fact upon attitudes which the person has who takes himself to be recognizing and responding to those values. If we admit what Hume calls the mind's "propensity to spread itself on external objects," we can understand the supposed objectivity of moral qualities as arising from what we can call the projection or objectification of moral attitudes. This would be analogous to what is called the "pathetic fallacy," the tendency to read our feelings into their objects. If a fungus, say, fills us with disgust, we may be inclined to ascribe to the fungus itself a non-natural quality of foulness. But in moral contexts there is more than this propensity at work. Moral attitudes themselves are at least partly social in origin: socially established—and socially necessary—patterns of behaviour put pressure on individuals, and each individual tends to internalize these pressures and to join in requiring these patterns of behaviour of himself and of others. The attitudes that are objectified into moral values have indeed an external source, though not the one assigned to them by the belief in their absolute authority. Moreover, there are motives that would support objectification. We need morality to regulate interpersonal relations, to control some of the ways in which people behave towards one another, often in opposition to contrary inclinations. We therefore want our moral judgments to be authoritative for other agents as well as for ourselves: objective validity would give them the authority required. Aesthetic values are logically in the same position as moral ones; much the same metaphysical and epistemological considerations apply to them. But aesthetic values are less strongly objectified than moral ones; their subjective status, and an "error theory" with regard to such claims to objectivity as are incorporated in aesthetic judgments, will be more readily accepted, just because the motives for their objectification are less compelling.

But it would be misleading to think of the objectification of moral values as primarily the projection of feelings, as in the pathetic fallacy. More important are wants and demands. As Hobbes says, "whatsoever is the object of any man's Appetite or Desire, that is it, which he for his part calleth *Good*"; and certainly both the adjective "good" and the noun "goods" are used in non-moral contexts of things because they are such as to satisfy desires. We get the notion of something's being objectively good, or having intrinsic value, by reversing the direction of dependence here, by making the desire depend upon the goodness, instead of the goodness on the desire. And this is aided by the fact that the desired thing will indeed have features that make it desired, that enable it to arouse a desire or that make it such as to satisfy some desire that is already there. It is fairly easy to confuse the way in which a thing's desirability is indeed objective with its having in our sense objective value. The fact that the word "good" serves as one of our main moral terms is a trace of this pattern of objectification.

Similarly related uses of words are covered by the distinction between hypothetical and categorical imperatives. The statement that someone "ought to" or, more strongly, "must" do such-and-such may be backed up explicitly or implicitly by reference to what he wants or to what his purposes and objects are. Again, there may be a reference to the purposes of someone else, perhaps the speaker: "You must do this"—"Why?"—"Because I want such-and-such." The moral categorical imperative which could be expressed in the same words can be seen as resulting from the suppression of the conditional clause in a hypothetical imperative without its being replaced by any such reference to the speaker's wants. The action in question is still required in something like the way in which it would be if it were appropriately related to a want, but it is no longer admitted that there is any contingent want upon which its being required depends. Again this move can be understood when we remember that at least our central and basic moral judgments represent social demands, where the source of the demand is indeterminate and diffuse. Whose demands or wants are in question, the agent's, or the speaker's, or those of an indefinite multitude of other people? All of these in a way, but there are advantages in not specifying them precisely. The speaker is expressing demands which he makes as a member of a community, which he has developed in and by participation in a joint way of life; also, what is required of this particular agent would be required of any other in a relevantly similar situation; but the agent too is expected to have internalized the relevant demands, to act as if the ends for which the action is required were his own. By suppressing any explicit reference to demands and making the imperatives categorical we facilitate conceptual moves from one such demand relation to another. The moral uses of such words as "must" and "ought" and "should", all of which are used also to express hypothetical imperatives, are traces of this pattern of objectification.

It may be objected that this explanation links normative ethics too closely with descriptive morality, with the mores or socially enforced patterns of behaviour that anthropologists record. But it can hardly be denied that moral thinking starts from the enforcement of social codes. Of course it is not confined to that. But even when moral judgements are detached from the mores of any actual society they are liable to be framed with reference to an ideal community of moral agents, such as Kant's kingdom of ends, which but for the need to give God a special place in it would have been better called a commonwealth of ends.

Another way of explaining the objectification of moral values is to say that ethics is a system of law from which the legislator has been removed. This might have derived either from the positive law of a state or from a supposed system of divine law. There can be no doubt that some features of modern European moral concepts are traceable to the theological ethics of Christianity. The stress on quasi-imperative notions, on what ought to be done or on what is wrong in a sense that is close to that of "forbidden", are surely relics of divine commands. Admittedly, the central ethical concepts for Plato and Aristotle also are in a broad sense prescriptive or intrinsically action-guiding, but in concentrating rather on "good" than on "ought" they show that their moral thought is an objectification of the desired and the satisfying rather than of the commanded. Elizabeth Anscombe has argued that modern, non-Aristotelian, concepts of *moral* obligation, *moral* duty, of what is *morally* right and wrong, and of the *moral* sense of "ought" are survivals outside the framework of thought that made them really intelligible, namely the belief in divine law. She infers that "ought" has "become a word of mere mesmeric force," with only a "delusive appearance of content," and that we would do better to discard such terms and concepts altogether, and go back to Aristotelian ones.

There is much to be said for this view. But while we can explain some distinctive features of modern moral philosophy in this way, it would be a mistake to see the whole problem of the claim to objective prescriptivity as merely local and unnecessary, as a post-operative complication of a society from which a dominant system of theistic belief has recently been rather hastily excised. As Cudworth and Clarke and Price, for example, show, even those who still admit divine commands, or the positive law of God, may believe moral values to have an independent objective but still action-guiding authority. Responding to Palto's *Euthyphro* dilemma, they believe that God commands what he commands because it is in itself good or right, not that it is good or right merely because and in that he commands it. Otherwise God himself could not be called good. Price asks, "What can be more preposterous, than to make the Deity nothing but will; and to exalt this on the ruins of all his attributes?" The apparent objectivity of moral value is a widespread phenomenon which has more than one source: the persistence of a belief in something like divine law when the belief in the divine legislator has faded out is only one factor among others. There are several different patterns of the objectification, all of which have left characteristic traces in our actual moral concepts and moral language.

11. The General Goal of Human Life

The argument of the preceding sections is meant to apply quite generally to moral thought, but the terms in which it has been stated are largely those of the Kantian and post-Kantian tradition of English moral philosophy. To those who are more familiar with another tradition, which runs through Aristotle and Aquinas, it may seem wide of the mark. For them, the fundamental notion is that of the good for man, or the general end or goal of human life, or perhaps of a set of basic goods or primary human purposes. Moral reasoning consists partly in achieving a more adequate understanding of this basic goal (or set of goals), partly in working out the best way of pursuing and realizing it. But this approach is open to two radically different interpretations. According to one, to say that something is the good for man or the general goal of human life is just to say that this is what men in fact pursue or will find ultimately satisfying, or perhaps that it is something which, if postulated as an implicit goal, enables us to make sense of actual human strivings and to detect a coherent pattern in what would otherwise seem to be a chaotic jumble of conflicting purposes. According to the other interpretation, to say that something is the good for man or the general goal of human life is to say that this is man's proper end, that this is what he ought to be striving after, whether he in fact is or not. On the first interpretation we have a descriptive statement, on the second a normative or evaluative or prescriptive one. But this approach tends to combine the two interpretations, or to slide from one to the other, and to borrow support for what are in effect claims of the second sort from the plausibility of statements of the first sort.

I have no quarrel with this notion interpreted in the first way, I would only insert a warning that there may well be more diversity even of fundamental purposes, more variation in what different human beings will find ultimately satisfying, than the terminology of "*the* good for man" would suggest. Nor indeed, have I any quarrel with the second, prescriptive, interpretation, provided that it is recognized as subjectively prescriptive, that the speaker is here putting forward his own demands or proposals, or those of some movement that he represents, though no doubt linking these demands or proposals with what he takes to be already in the first, descriptive, sense fundamental human goals. . . . But if it is claimed that something is objectively the right or proper goal of human life, then this is tantamount to the assertion of something that is objectively categorically imperative, and comes fairly within the scope of our previous arguments. Indeed, the running together of what I have here called the two interpretations is yet another pattern of objectification: a claim to objective prescriptivity is constructed by combining the normative element in the second interpretation with the objectivity allowed by the first, by the statement that such and such are fundamentally pursued or ultimately satisfying human goals. The argument from relativity still applies: the radical diversity of the goals that men actually pursue and find satisfying makes it implausible to construe such pursuits as resulting from an imperfect grasp of a unitary true good. So too does the argument from queerness; we can still ask what this objectively prescriptive rightness of the true goal can be, and how this is linked on the one hand with the descriptive features of this goal and on the other with the fact that it is to *some extent* an actual goal of human striving.

To meet these difficulties, the objectivist may have recourse to the purpose of God: the true purpose of human life is fixed by what God intended (or, intends) men to do and to be. Actual human strivings and satisfactions have some relation to this true end because God made men for this end and made them such as to pursue it—but only *some* relation, because of the inevitable imperfection of created beings.

I concede that if the requisite theological doctrine could be defended, a kind of objective ethical prescriptively could be thus introduced. Since I think that theism cannot be defended, I do not regard this as any threat to my argument. . . . Those who wish to keep theism as a live option can read the arguments of the intervening chapters hypothetically, as a discussion of what we can make of morality without recourse to God, and hence of what we can say about morality if, in the end, we dispense with religious belief.

. . . .

Outline of a Decision Procedure for Ethics

JOHN RAWLS

1.1 The question with which we shall be concerned can be stated as follows: Does there exist a reasonable decision procedure which is sufficiently strong, at least in some cases, to determine the manner in which competing interests should be adjudicated, and, in instances of conflict, one interest given preference over another; and, further, can the existence of this procedure, as well as its reasonableness, be established by rational methods of inquiry? In order to answer both parts of this question in the affirmative, it is necessary to describe a reasonable procedure and then to evidence that it satisfies certain criteria. This I attempt to do beginning at 2.1 below.

1.2 It should be noted that we are concerned here only with the existence of a reasonable method, and not with the problem of how to make it psychologically effective in the settling of disputes. How much allegiance the method is able to gain is irrelevant for our present purposes.

1.3 The original question has been framed the way it is because the objectivity or the subjectivity of moral knowledge turns, not on the question whether ideal value entities exist or whether moral judgments are caused by emotions or whether there is a variety of moral codes the world over, but simply on the question: does there exist a reasonable method for validating and invalidating given or proposed moral rules and those decisions made on the basis of them? For to say of scientific knowledge that it is objective is to say that the propositions expressed therein may be evidenced to be true by a reasonable and reliable method, that is, by the rules and procedures of what we may call "inductive logic"; and, similarly, to establish the objectivity of moral rules, and the decisions based upon them, we must exhibit the decision procedure, which can be shown to be both reasonable and reliable, at least in some cases, for deciding between moral rules and lines of conduct consequent to them.

2.1 For the present, we may think of ethics as being more analogous to the study of inductive logic than to any other established inquiry. Just as in inductive logic we are concerned with discovering reasonable criteria which, when we are given a proposition, or theory, together with the empirical evidence for it, will enable us to decide the extent to which we ought to consider it to be true so in ethics we are attempting to find reasonable principles which, when we are given a proposed line of conduct and the situation in which it is to be carried out and the relevant interests which it effects, will enable us to determine whether or not we ought to carry it out and hold it to be just and right.

2.2 There is no way of knowing ahead of time how to find and formulate these reasonable principles. Indeed, we cannot even be certain that they exist, and it is well known that there are no mechanical methods of discovery. In what follows, however, a method will be described, and it remains for the reader to judge for himself to what extent it is, or can be, successful.

2.3 First it is necessary to define a class of competent moral judges as follows: All those persons having to a certain requisite degree each of the following characteristics, which can, if desired, be made more determinate:

(i) A competent moral judge is expected to have a certain requisite degree of intelligence, which may be thought of as that ability which intelligence tests are designed to measure. The degree of this ability required should not be set too high,

From *The* Philosophical Review 60, no. 2 (April 1951), 177–90.

on the assumption that what we call "moral insight" is the possession of the normally intelligent man as well as of the more brilliant. Therefore I am inclined to say that a competent moral judge need not be more than normally intelligent.

(ii) A competent judge is required to know those things concerning the world about him and those consequences of frequently performed actions, which it is reasonable to expect the average intelligent man to know. Further, a competent judge is expected to know, in all cases whereupon he is called to express his opinion, the peculiar facts of those cases. It should be noted that the kind of knowledge here referred to is to be distinguished from sympathetic knowledge discussed below

(iii) A competent judge is required to be a reasonable man as this characteristic is evidenced by his satisfying the following tests: First, a reasonable man shows a willingness, if not a desire, to use the criteria of inductive logic in order to determine what is proper for him to believe. Second, a reasonable man, whenever he is confronted with a moral question, shows a disposition to find reasons for and against the possible lines of conduct which are open to him. Third, a reasonable man exhibits a desire to consider questions with an open mind, and consequently, while he may already have an opinion on some issue, he is always willing to reconsider it in the light of further evidence and reasons which may be presented to him in discussion. Fourth, a reasonable man knows, or tries to know, his own emotional, intellectual, and moral predilections and makes a conscientious effort to take them into account in weighing the merits of any question. He is not unaware of the influences of prejudice and bias even in his most sincere efforts to annul them; nor is he fatalistic about their effect so that he succumbs to them as being those factors which he thinks must sooner or later determine his decision.

(iv) Finally, a competent judge is required to have a sympathetic knowledge of those human interests which, by conflicting in particular cases, give rise to the need to make a moral decision. The presence of this characteristic is evidenced by the following: First, by the person's direct knowledge of those interests gained by experiencing, in his own life, the goods they represent. The more interests which a person can appreciate in terms of his own direct experience, the greater the extent to which he satisfies this first test. Yet it is obvious that no man can know all interests directly, and therefore the second test is that, should a person not be directly acquainted with an interest, his competency as a judge is seen, in part, by his capacity to give that interest an appraisal by means of an imaginative experience of it. This test also requires of a competent judge that he must not consider his own de facto preferences as the necessarily valid measure of the actual worth of those interests which come before him, but that he be both able and anxious to determine, by imaginative appreciation, what those interests mean to persons who share them, and to consider them accordingly. Third, a competent judge is required to have the capacity and the desire to lay before himself in imagination all the interests in conflict, together with the relevant facts of the case, and to bestow upon the appraisal of each the same care which he would give to it if that interest were his own. He is required to determine what he would think to be just and unjust if each of the interests were as thoroughly his own as they are in fact those of other persons, and to render his judgment on the case as he feels his sense of justice requires after he has carefully framed in his mind the issues which are to be decided.

2.4 Before considering the next step in the development of the method here adopted, it is necessary to make some comments on the previous remarks. First, the tests for defining and determining the class of competent moral judges are vague; that is, given a group of persons, there would be, in all probability, instances in which we could not decide whether a person is a competent moral judge or not. Yet we do recognize in everyday life the pattern of characteristics discussed above; we do think that certain individuals exhibit them to a comparatively pre-eminent degree, and these individuals we call "reasonable" or "impartial"; it is men of their character whom we want to decide any case in which our interests are at stake. Thus, while the foregoing tests are admittedly not precise, they do describe and select a recognized type of person; and those persons who do satisfy them beyond any reasonable doubt, will be called "competent moral judges."

Second, it is important to note that a competent judge has not been defined by what he says in particular cases, not by what principles he expresses or adopts. Competence is determined solely by the possession of certain characteristics, some of which may be said to be capacities and achievements (intelligence and knowledge), while others may be said to be virtues (thus, the intellectual virtues of reasonableness.) It will become clear in later sections why we cannot define a competent judge, at least at the beginning of our inquiry, as one who accepts certain principles. The reason is that we wish to say of some principles for adjudicating interests that one ground for accepting them as reasonable principles is that competent judges seem to apply them intuitively to decide moral issues. Obviously if a competent judge were defined as one who applies those principles, this reasoning would be circular. Thus a competent judge must not be defined in terms of what he says or by what principles he uses.

Third, one should note the kind of characteristics which have been used to define a competent moral judge: namely, those characteristics which, in the light of experience, show themselves as necessary conditions for the reasonable expectation that a given person may come to know something. Thus, we think of intelligence as being such a condition in all types of inquiry; and similarly with knowledge, since the more a man knows, the greater the likelihood of his success in further inquiry. Again, not only is it necessary to have certain abilities and achievements but, to be a good investigator, a person must develop those habits of mind and thought which we may call "intellectual virtues" (cf. 2.3 [iii]). Finally, there are those habits and capacities of thought and imagination which were described in connection with sympathetic knowledge of human interests. Just as intellectual capacities and virtues are found to foster the conditions necessary for successful inquiry of whatever type, so these habits and capacities are believed to be necessary for making fair decisions on moral issues. We may call them the "virtues of moral insight" with the understanding that they do not define either the content or the nature of moral insight, but, assuming it exists, simply represent those habits and capacities which secure the conditions under which we believe it most likely to assert itself effectively. Thus the defining characteristics of a competent judge have not been selected arbitrarily, but in each case there is a reason for choosing them which accords with the purpose of coming to know.

Finally, we can make these remarks clearer if we consider other methods of choosing the class of competent judges. It is one of the marks of an ideology that it violates the above criteria. Ideologies, of whatever type, claim a monopoly of the knowledge of truth and justice for some particular race, or social class, or institutional group, and competence is defined in terms of racial and/or sociological characteristics which have no known connection with coming to know. In the present method care has been exercised to select the class of competent moral judges according to those characteristics which are associated with coming to know something, and not by means of characteristics which are the privileged possession of any race, class, or group, but which can and often do belong, at least to certain degree, to men everywhere.

2.5 The next step in the development of our procedure is to define the class of considered moral judgments, the determining characteristics of which are as follows:

(i) It is required that the judgment on a case be given under such conditions that the judge is immune from all of the reasonably foreseeable consequences of the judgment. For example, he will not be punished for deciding the case one way rather than another.

(ii) It is required that the conditions be such that the integrity of the judge can be maintained. So far as possible, the judge must not stand to gain in any immediate and personal way by his decision. These two tests are designed to exclude judgments wherein a person must weigh the merit of one of his own interests. The imposition of these conditions is justified on the grounds that fear and partiality are recognized obstructions in the determination of justice.

(iii) It is required that the case, on which the judgment is given, be one in which there is an actual conflict of interests. Thus, all judgments on hypothetical cases are excluded. In addition, it is preferable that the case be not especially difficult and be one that is likely to arise in ordinary life. These restrictions are desirable in order that the judgments in question be made in the effort to settle problems with which men are familiar and whereupon they have had an opportunity to reflect.

(iv) It is required that the judgment be one which has been preceded by a careful inquiry into the facts of the question at issue, and by a fair opportunity for all concerned to state their side of the case. This requirement is justified on the ground that it is only by chance that a just decision can be made without a knowledge of the relevant facts.

(v) It is required that the judgment be felt to be certain by the person making it. This characteristic may be called "certitude" and it is to be sharply distinguished from certainty, which is a logical relation between a proposition, or theory, and its evidence. This test is justified on the ground that it seems more profitable to study those judgments which are felt to be correct than those which seem to be wrong or confused even to those who make them.

(vi) It is required that the judgment be stable, that is, that there be evidence that at other times and at other places competent judges have rendered the same judgment on similar cases, understanding similar cases to be those in which the relevant facts and the competing interests are similar. The stability must hold, by and large, over the class of competent judges and over their judgments at different times. Thus, if on similar cases of a certain type, competent judges decided one way one day, and another the next, or if a third of them decided one way, a third the opposite way, while the remaining third said they did not know how to decide the cases, then none of these judgments would be stable judgments, and therefore none would be considered judgments. These restrictions are justified on the grounds that it seems unreasonable to have any confidence that a judgment is correct if competent persons disagree about it.

(vii) Finally, it is required that the judgment be intuitive with respect to ethical principles, that is, that it should not be determined by a conscious application of principles so far as this may be evidenced by introspection. By the term "intuitive" I do not mean the same as that expressed by the terms "impulsive" and "instinctive." An intuitive judgment may be consequent to a thorough inquiry into the facts of the case, and it may follow a series of reflections on the possible effects of different decisions, and even the application of a common sense rule, e.g., promises ought to be kept. What is required is that the judgment not be determined by a systematic and conscious use of ethical principles. The reason for this restriction will be evident if one keeps in mind the aim of the present inquiry, namely, to describe a decision procedure whereby principles, by means of which we may justify specific moral decisions, may themselves be shown to be justifiable. Now part of this procedure will consist in showing that these principles are implicit in the considered judgments of competent judges. It is clear that if we allowed these judgments to be determined by a conscious and systematic application of these principles, then the method is threatened with circularity. We cannot test a principle honestly by means of judgments wherein it has been consciously and systematically used to determine the decision.

2.6 Up to this point I have defined, first, a class of competent judges and, second, a class of considered judgments. If competent judges are those persons most likely to make correct decisions, then we should take care to abstract those judgments of theirs which, from the conditions and circumstances under which they are made, are most likely to be correct. With the exception of certain requirements, which are needed to prevent circularity, the defining characteristics of considered judgments are such that they select those judgments most likely to be decided by the habits of thought and imagination deemed essential for a competent judge. One can say, then, that those judgments which are relevant for our present purposes are the considered judgments of competent judges as these are made from day to day on the moral issues which continually arise. No other judgments, for reasons previously stated, are of any concern.

3.1 The next step in the present method is as follows: once the class of considered judgments of competent judges has been selected, there remains to discover and formulate a satisfactory explication of the total range of these judgments. This process is understood as being a heuristic device which is likely to yield reasonable and justifiable principles.

3.2 The term "explication" is given meaning somewhat graphically as follows: Consider a group of competent judges making considered judgments in review of a set of cases which would be likely to arise in ordinary life. Then an explication of these judgments is defined to be a set of principles, such that, if any competent man were to apply them intelligently and consistently to the same cases under review, his judgments, made systematically nonintuitive by the explicit and conscious use of the principles, would be, nevertheless, identical, case by case, with the considered judgments of the group of competent judges. The range of an explication is specified by stating precisely those judgments which it is designed to explicate, and any given explication which successfully explicates its specified range is satisfactory.

3.3 The next objective, then, in the development of the present method is to discover and formulate an explication which is satisfactory, by and large, over the total range of the considered judgments of competent moral judges as they are made from day to day in ordinary life, and as they are found embodied in the many dictates of common-sense morality, in various aspects of legal procedure, and so on. If reasonable principles exist for deciding moral questions, there is a presumption that the principles of a satisfactory explication of the total range of the considered judgments of competent judges will at least approximate them. On the basis of this presumption the explication of these judgments is designed to be a heuristic device for discovering reasonable principles. Therefore, while explication is an empirical inquiry, it is felt that it is likely to be a way of finding reasonable and justifiable principles in view of the nature of the class of judgments which make up its range.

3.4 Since the concept of an explication may not be clear, I shall try to clarify it by stating some of the things that an explication is not. First, an explication is not an analysis of the meaning of the ethical terms used in the judgments constituting its range. An explication attempts to do nothing more than that explictly stated above, and in no way concerns itself with the sense of ethical expressions or with their linguistic meaning.

Second, an explication is not concerned with what people intend to assert when they use ethical expressions or make moral judgments in particular cases.

Third, an explication is not a theory about the actual causes of the considered judgments of competent judges, and this fact, in addition to the restriction to a specified class of judgments, sharply distinguishes it from a phychological or a sociological study of moral judgments. The only sense in which explication, as here defined, is concerned with causes is that a satisfactory explication can be a cause, or could be a cause, of the judgments in its range, i.e., the explicit and conscious adoption of the principles of the explication would yield the same judgments. Since explication is not concerned with the actual causes of judgments, it is immaterial whether the judgments in its range are caused by the intuition of nonnatural ethical characteristics, or by the response of intentional feelings to directly experienced value qualities, or by emotional attitudes which may in turn have been caused by certain specifiable psychological and sociological determinants. Questions about the actual causes, while interesting, are irrelevant from the standpoint of the present method. That such questions are irrelevant is also clear from the fact, previously stated, that the objectivity or subjectivity of moral judgments depends not on their causes, in any of the senses just listed, but solely on whether a reasonable decision procedure exists which is sufficiently strong to decide, at least in some cases, whether a given decision, and the conduct consequent thereto, is reasonable.

Finally, there is only one way of showing an explication to be unsatisfactory, and that is to show that there exist considered judgments of competent judges on specifiable cases for which it either fails to yield any judgments at all or leads one to make judgments inconsistent with them. Conversely, the only way to show that an explication is satisfactory is to evidence that its explicit and conscious application can be, or could be, a cause of the judgments in its range.

3.5 Having noted some of the things that an explication is not, I consider some positive features thereof. First, an explication must be such that it can be applied intelligently by a competent judge; and since a competent judge is not required to have a special training in logic and mathematics, an explication either must be formulated or formulatable in ordinary language and its principles must be capable of an interpretation which the average competent man can grasp.

Second, an explication must be stated in the form of principles, the reason for this demand lying in the use of explication as a heuristic device. The typical form of a considered judgment is as follows: since *A, B, C*, ..., and *M, N, O*, ..., are the facts of the case and the interests in conflict, *M* is to be given preference over *N, O*, . . . A considered judgment does not provide any reasons for the decision. It simply states the felt preference in view of the facts of the case and the interests competing therein. The principles of an explication must be general directives, expressible in ordinary language, such that, when applied to specific cases, they yield the preferences expressed in considered judgments.

Finally, an explication, to be completely successful, must be comprehensive; that is, it must explicate, in view of the explication itself (for this proviso, see below, 4.3), all considered judgments; and it is expected to do this with the greatest possible simplicity and elegance. The requirement of simplicity means that, other things being equal, an explication is more or less satisfactory according to the number of principles which it uses; and although this demand is difficult to state precisely, it is clear that nothing is gained if we require a separate principle for each case or for each class of cases.

3.6 The attempt to discover a comprehensive explication may be thought of as the attempt to express the invariant in the considered judgments of competent judges in the sense that, given the wide variety of cases on which considered judgments are made at different times and places, the principles of the explication are such that the conscious and systematic application of them could have been a common factor in the determination of the multiplicity of considered judgments as made on the wide variety of cases. Whether such an explication exists or not, one cannot know at present, and opinions vary; but the belief that such an explication does exist is perhaps a prerequisite for the finding of it, should it exist, for the reason that one who does not so believe is not likely to exert the great effort which is surely required to find it.

4.1 Perhaps the principal aim of ethics is the formulation of justifiable principles which may be used in cases wherein there are conflicting interests to determine which one of them should be given preference. Therefore it remains to consider what is meant by the terms "justifiable principle" and a "rational judgment" in a particular case.

4.2 Consider the simpler question first, namely, what is the test of whether a judgment in a particular case is rational? The answer is that a judgment in a particular case is evidenced to be rational by showing that, given the facts and the conflicting interests of the case, the judgment is capable of being explicated by a justifiable principle (or set of principles). Thus if the explicit and conscious adoption of a justifiable principle (or set of principles) can be, or could have been, the ground of the judgment, or if the judgment expresses that preference which justifiable principles would yield if applied to the case, then the judgment is rational. Clearly the justification of particular judgments, if the above is correct, depends upon the use of justifiable principles. But how do we know whether a principle is justifiable? Four criteria for answering this question are considered below.

4.3 In what follows we shall assume that a satisfactory and comprehensive explication of the considered judgments of competent judges is already known (note proviso under fourth test below). Now consider the question as to what reasons we can have for accepting these principles as justifiable.

The first reason for accepting them has already been touched upon: namely, since the principles explicate the considered judgments of competent judges, and since these judgments are more likely than any other judgments to represent the mature convictions of competent men as they have been worked out under the most favorable existing conditions, the invariant in what we call "moral insight," if it exists, is more likely to be approximated by the principles of a successful explication than by principles which a man might fashion out of his own head. Individual predilections will tend to be canceled out once the explication has included judgments of many persons made on a wide variety of cases. Thus the fact that the principles constitute a comprehensive explication of the considered judgments of competent judges is a reason for accepting them. That this should be so is understandable if we reflect, to take the contrary case, how little confidence we would have in principles which should happen to explicate the judgments of men under strong emotional or physical duress, or of those mentally ill. Hence the type of judgments which make up the range of the explication is the first ground for accepting the principles thereof.

Secondly, the reasonableness of a principle is tested by seeing whether it shows a capacity to become accepted by competent moral judges after they have freely weighed its merits by criticism and open discussion, and after each has thought it over and compared it with his own considered judgments. It is hoped that some principles will exhibit a capacity to win free and willing allegiance and be able to implement a gradual convergence of uncoerced opinion.

Thirdly, the reasonableness of a principle is tested by seeing whether it can function in existing instances of conflicting opinion, and in new cases causing difficulty, to yield a result which, after criticism and discussion, seems to be acceptable to all, or nearly all, competent judges, and to conform to their intuitive notion of a reasonable decision. For example, the problem of punishment has been a troublesome moral issue for some time, and if a principle or set of principles should be formulated which evidenced a capacity to settle this problem to the satisfaction of all, or nearly all, competent judges, then this principle, or set of principles, would meet this test in one possible instance of its application. In general, a principle evidences its reasonableness by being able to resolve moral perplexities which existed at the time of its formulation and which will exist in the future. This test is somewhat analogous to a test which we impose upon an empirical theory: namely, its ability to foresee laws and facts hitherto unknown, and to explain facts and laws hitherto unexplainable.

Finally, the reasonableness of a principle is tested by seeing whether it shows a capacity to hold its own (that is, to continue to be felt reasonable), against a subclass of the considered judgments of competent judges, as this fact may be evidenced by our intuitive conviction that the considered judgments are incorrect rather than the principle, when we confront them with the principle. A principle satisfies this test when a subclass of considered judgments, rather than the principle, is felt to be mistaken when the principle fails to explicate it. For example, it often happens that competent persons, in judging the moral worth of character, blame others in conflict with the rule that a man shall not be morally condemned for the possession of characteristics which would not have been otherwise even if he had so chosen. Frequently, however, when we point out that their judgments conflict with this rule, these persons, upon reflection, will decide that their judgments are incorrect, and acknowledge the principle. To the extent that principles exhibit this capacity to alter what we think to be our considered judgments in cases of conflict, they satisfy the fourth test. It is, of course, desirable, although not essential, that whenever a principle does successfully militate against what is taken to be a considered judgment, some convincing reason can be found to account for the anomaly. We should like to find that the once accepted intuitive conviction is actually caused by a mistaken belief as to a matter of fact of which we were unaware or fostered by what is admittedly a narrow bias of some kind. The rationale behind this fourth test is that while the considered judgments of competent judges are the most likely repository of the working out of men's sense of right and wrong, a more likely one, for example, than that of any particular individual's judgments alone, they may, nevertheless, contain certain deviations, or confusions, which are best discovered by comparing the considered judgments with principles which pass the first three tests and seeing which of the two tends to be felt incorrect in the light of reflection. The previous proviso (3.5) is to be understood in connection with the above discussion of the fourth test.

4.4 A principle is evidenced to be reasonable to the extent that it satisfies jointly all of the foregoing tests. In practice, however, we are wise if we expect less than this. We are not likely to find easily a comprehensive explication which convinces all competent judges, which resolves all existing difficulties, and which, should there be anomalies in the considered judgments themselves, always tends to overcome them. We should expect satisfactory explications of but delimited areas of the considered judgments. Ethics must, like any other discipline, work its way piece by piece.

4.5 It is worthwhile to note that the present method of evidencing the reasonableness of ethical principles is analogous to the method used to establish the reasonableness of the criteria of inductive logic. In the latter study what we attempt to do is to explicate the full variety of our intuitive judgments of credibility which we make in daily life and in science in connection with a proposition, or theory, given the evidence for it. In this way we hope to discover the principles of weighing evidence which are actually used and which seem to be capable of winning the assent of competent investigators. The principles so gained can be tested by seeing how well they can resolve our perplexity about how we ought to evaluate evidence in particular cases, and by how well they can stand up against what appear to be anomalous, but nevertheless settled, ways of appraising evidence, provided these anomalies exist. Thus each test above (4.3) has its parallel, or analogy, in the tests which are applied to inductive criteria. If we make the assumption that men have a capacity for knowing right and wrong, as they have for knowing what is true and false, then the present method is a likely way of developing a procedure for determining when we posses that knowledge; and we should be able to evidence the reasonableness of ethical principles in the same manner that we evidence the reasonableness of inductive criteria. On the other hand, just as the development of science and the method of science evidences the capacity to know what is true and false, so the actual formulation of ethical principles and the method whereby they can be tested, as this formulation is shown in the existence of satisfactory and reasonable explications, will evidence the capacity to know what is right and wrong as well as the validity of the objective distinction between the two.

. . . .

PART VI

PUZZLES AND PARADOXES

INTRODUCTION

Puzzles and paradoxes have played an important role in the history of philosophy and are both challenging and fun to think about. Of course, any philosophical problem can be considered a puzzle. But, we have in mind problems expressed in relatively few words that immediately reveal some puzzling aspect of things to which there is no obvious and clearly satisfactory solution. Most of these puzzles can be stated in the form of *paradoxes*. A paradox is an argument that *appears* to derive self-contradictory or otherwise absurd conclusions by valid reasoning from acceptable premises.

When a paradox becomes well-enough understood, whether as the result of a few moments work by an individual or the insights of successive generations of thinkers, the appearance of a valid derivation of an absurdity should disappear. In some cases, when properly understood the conclusion will cease to seem absurd. In other cases the premises will no longer seem acceptable or the reasoning will no longer seem valid. In the essay that concludes Part VI, W. V. Quine calls paradoxes of the first sort *veridical,* those of the second sort *falsidical,* and those for which we can neither accept the conclusion nor spot the mistake *antinomies*. All three kinds are represented here.

Some of our puzzles are presented as paradoxes, whereas others are simply set forth as problems or puzzles. In deciding what to say about these latter problems or puzzles, students will usually find they can state their reasoning in the form of a paradox.

There is extensive literature on each of these puzzles, and we cite some of it. But, we think puzzles are most interesting if students approach them, at least at first, as occasions for unfettered thought rather than as scholarly projects. For example, in the case of Newcomb's problem, we urge students to first decide what they would do in the imagined circumstances, to construct arguments justifying their choice, and, then, to try to find flaws or loopholes in their arguments—perhaps with the aid of students who support the opposite strategy. This approach is more rewarding than going to the library and looking up what the experts have said about the problem.

A. ASSORTED PUZZLES AND PARADOXES

1. ZENO'S PARADOXES

Zeno of Elea was born around 490 B.C. He was a supporter of the philosopher Parmenides, founder of the Eleatic School of Greek philosophy, who held that the particularity of individual things is an illusion. Zeno supported this view by producing arguments to show that plurality and change are really self-contradictory notions. Because most philosophers have regarded the conclusions of Zeno's arguments as absurd, they are known as paradoxes. Some fragments of Zeno's writings that contain arguments against plurality survive; the arguments against motion are known almost entirely through Aristotle's account of them in his *Physics*.

There is an excellent discussion of Zeno and his paradoxes by Gregory Vlastos in Paul Edwards's *Encyclopedia of Philosophy*. This article also contains a good bibliography. Max Black's treatment of Zeno's arguments in his *Problems of Analysis* (Ithaca, N.Y., 1954) and Adolf Grünbaum's *Modern Science and Zeno's Paradoxes* (Middletown, Conn., 1967) might be particularly useful to the student wishing to learn about these paradoxes. Here, we give versions of two of the paradoxes of motion and one of plurality. The statement of the plurality puzzle is that of Carl Ginet, professor of philosophy at Cornell University.

Achilles and the Tortoise

Suppose that Achilles and the tortoise are having a race. Because Achilles is faster, we give the tortoise a head start of 10 yards. We suppose that the tortoise can run 1 yard in a second and that Achilles can run 10 yards in a second. It seems that Achilles will certainly catch and pass the tortoise. However, in order to pass the tortoise, Achilles must perform an endless sequence of tasks, one after the other. But it is easily seen that this is impossible.

The first task Achilles must perform is to reach the point where the tortoise starts. Call this Point 1. This takes one second. But, after Achilles does this, the tortoise is still 1 yard ahead, at what we will call Point 2.

The second task Achilles must perform is to reach Point 2, the point that the tortoise is at after Achilles completes the first task. When Achilles completes this second task, though, the tortoise is still ahead by 0.1 yard, at Point 3.

The third task Achilles must perform is to reach Point 3. After Achilles does this, though, the tortoise will still be ahead by 0.01 yard at Point 4.

We can see that after each task of this sort that Achilles performs, the tortoise will still be ahead, and there will be another task of the same sort still facing Achilles. That is, for any *n* (no matter how large), after Achilles has completed *n* tasks of this sort, he still won't have caught up with the tortoise, who will still be ahead by $1/10^{n-1}$ yards. But Achilles can never complete more tasks than there are numbers because we never run out of numbers. So Achilles will never catch the tortoise.

The Racecourse

It seems embarrassing enough for the advocates of motion and change that a runner so fast as Achilles can never catch a runner so slow as the tortoise. But things are worse. Achilles cannot even win a one-man race, for wherever the finish line is, he will never reach it.

Suppose Achilles is to run from the starting point *S* to the goal *G*. To do this, he must do all of the following:

1. Run to the point halfway from *S* to *G*.
2. Run from that point to the point halfway between it and *G*.
3. Run from that point to the point halfway between it and *G*.
4. Run from that point to the point halfway between it and *G*, etc.

The "etc." clearly goes on forever. That is, the first point is only halfway to *G*, the second point only three-fourths of the way to *G*, the third point only seven-eighths of the way to *G*, the fourth point only fifteen-sixteenths of the way to *G*, and, in general, the *n*th point will be only $2^n - 1/2^n$ of the way to *G*. Hence, Achilles will never make it to *G*.

The Argument Against Plurality

A. The Main Argument:

1. If a finite spatial interval is divisible (i.e., composed of a plurality of parts), then it can be endlessly divided into ever-larger numbers of ever-smaller distinct and equal parts.

2. Therefore, any such interval is composed of infinitely many distinct and equal parts.

3. Each of these parts either (a) has some length or (b) has no length.

4. If (a), then the whole finite interval must be infinitely long.

5. If (b), then the whole finite interval must have no length.

6. Therefore, if a finite spatial interval is divisible, then either it is infinitely long or it has no length.

7. But every finite interval has a non-zero finite length.

8. Therefore, a finite spatial interval is not divisible.

B. An Argument for A.5:

1. If a finite spatial interval is composed of lengthless points, then its length must be the sum of the lengths of those points.

2. The length of any such point is zero.

3. The sum of any number of zeros (even infinitely many) is zero.

4. Therefore, if a finite spatial interval is composed of lengthless points, then its length is zero.

2. MISCELLANEOUS PUZZLES AND PARADOXES

The Paradox of Identity

Problems about the notion of identity through change have played a long and important role in philosophy. Heraclitus, a Greek philosopher of the fifth century, B.C. claimed that one could not step in the same river twice because new waters were always rushing in. This supported his general view of things, which was the opposite of that of Parmenides and Zeno. They thought that Being was one thing that didn't change; he thought that Being was an incredible plurality in constant flux. Many centuries later, David Hume argued that all attributions of identity over time were based on confusion. The following argument for the absurd conclusion that nothing persists through time, although perhaps cruder than either of these great philosophers would accept, captures some of the spirit of their line of thinking about identity.

By *identity,* we mean that relation that obtains between each thing and itself and that never obtains between a thing and anything else. So if *A* is identical with *B,* there is just one thing that is both *A* and *B*. For example, the man who coached the Stanford football team to Bowl victories in the mid-1970s is identical with the man who coached the San Francisco Forty-Niners to a Super Bowl victory in 1982. Thus, there is one man (Bill Walsh) who did both things. That is, there is one man who is the man who coached the Stanford football team to Bowl victories in the mid-1970s and who is the man who coached the San Francisco Forty-Niners to a Super Bowl victory in 1982.

Note that *identity* is not always used in ordinary English with this precise meaning. Sometimes, it is used to mean something like *exactly similar* or *exactly similar with respect to some important property*. Given *our* use of *identity,* for example, the term *identical twins* is self-contradictory. If *A* and *B* are twins, *A* and *B* are two individuals who are not identical in *our* official sense.

Now, given this sense of identity, there is one important principle that should be completely noncontroversial:

> If *A* is identical with *B,* then *A* and *B* have exactly the same properties.

We can call this principle *The indiscernibility of the identical.* It should not be confused with Leibniz's principle of the identity of the indiscernible:

> If *A* and *B* have exactly the same properties, then *A* is identical with *B*.

This latter principle is controversial. But the first should not be. For, if *A* and *B* are identical, then there is just one thing that is both *A* and *B,* and the principle just requires that it has the properties it has, which is utterly trivial.

But, given this principle, it follows that no individual persists through time.

First, note that our principle has the consequence that no individual persists through change and that the very example we used to illustrate the concept of identity makes no sense. For,

> The coach of the Stanford football team has the property of being the coach of the Stanford football team. (Obviously)
> The coach of the San Francisco Forty-

> Niners does not have the property of being the coach of the Stanford football team. (It would be a violation of NCAA rules.)

But, then, it is obvious that, contrary to our example, the first cannot be identical with the second.

But, note that any individual who is alive at a certain time moment *(t)* has a certain exact age *(n)*—where *n* is the number of moments the individual has been alive, up to and including *t*. But a moment later, at *t*′, this individual will no longer have this exact age. But, then, we see that the whole idea of persistence makes no sense, for to persist from moment to moment an individual has to change in respect to his or her exact age, but we have seen that change is ruled out.

So there is no persistence through change; no individual existing at any given time *t* is identical with any individual existing at any earlier or later time *t*′. Not only is there no individual who coached Stanford at one time and the Forty-Niners at some later time, there is not even an individual who coached Stanford to Bowl victories in different years, nor even one who coached them successive days, nor even through a single practice.

The Paradox of the Heap

This is an ancient paradox, that is most flexible. Here, we first use it to "show" that there is no such thing as a heap. Then, we use the same sort of reasoning to "show" that there is no such thing as baldness and that if it is wrong to have an abortion toward the end of a pregnancy, it is always wrong. This paradox can be used to "show" many other things. When versions of this paradox are set out as a chain of syllogisms, they have the form known in Aristotelian logic as the Sorities; the paradox is often just called by that name.

One grain of sand is not a heap of sand. If something is not a heap of sand, addition (or diminution) by one grain will not make it a heap. But, then, nothing is a heap. For, by starting with one grain of sand and adding to it a grain at a time, we will never have a heap. If something arrived at by such a method is not a heap, then nothing just like it, arrived at by some other method, is a heap either. So there are no heaps of sand and the whole idea is incoherent.

Given a person who is not bald, plucking one hair never makes that person bald. For, the person is already bald before the last hair is plucked. Plucking one hair from a person who is not bald will never make that person bald. So, if we started with a man or woman with a full head of hair and plucked his or her hairs one at a time, we would never make that person bald. Thus, the whole idea of baldness is incoherent.

Everyone agrees that it is wrong to have an abortion on the last day of a normal pregnancy. But, surely, if it is wrong to have an abortion on a given day (or at a certain minute of a pregnancy or at a certain second of a pregnancy), it is equally wrong to have it the day (minute, second) before. But, then, it is equally wrong to have an abortion at each point in a pregnancy, and so, by our opening assumption, always wrong.

The Surprise Examination

W. V. Quine reports that this puzzle has been around since 1943. He discusses it in his essay "On a Supposed Antinomy," in *The Ways of Paradox* (New York, 1966). Richard Montague and David Kaplan discuss it in "A Paradox Regained," in Montague's *Formal Philosophy,* edited by R. H. Thomason, (New Haven, Conn., 1974). Both of these discussions contain bibliographies. The student who consults the literature will find it quickly gets intricate. Yet, the problem is easily grasped. Note that it is easy to generate analogous puzzles involving hangings (the version Quine discusses), air-raid drills, and other events whose unpleasantness is enhanced when they are a surprise. The version involving an examination seems most relevant to the philosophy student.

Professor *X* announces at the end of class on Friday that there will be a surprise hour-examination the following week. Student *Y* contemplates spending the weekend in study, but he hits on an argument that shows there can be no such examination. Here is her argument.

> The exam cannot be on Friday. For, then, I would know Thursday after class that it was going to be on Friday, for it would not have been on Monday, Tuesday, Wednesday, or Thursday. But, then, it would not be a surprise, for I would know in advance when it was.
>
> But, because it cannot be on Friday, it cannot be given on Thursday either. For, given that it cannot be on Friday, if it is not given Monday, Tuesday, or Wednesday, it has to be given on Thursday. So I would know after Wednesday's class that it was going to be given on Thursday, and it would not be a surprise.
>
> But, because it cannot be given on Thursday or Friday, by similar reasoning it cannot be given on Wednesday either. And, indeed, the same reasoning works for Tuesday and Monday, too. So there will be no surprise examination, and I can relax this weekend.

Student *Y* does not study. The following Wednesday Professor *X* hands out an exam. Student *Y* is surprised, and she does quite poorly.

The Prisoner's Dilemma

This problem has been discussed in the literature on rational action for many years. The following statement is that of Carl Ginet.

Two men suspected of comitting a crime together are arrested and placed in separate cells. They are not permitted to communicate with one another. Each of them is told the following:

1. You may either confess to the crime or refuse to confess.
2. If one of you confesses but the other does not, then, the one who confesses will go free and the other one will go to jail for four years.
3. If both of you confess, then, you will both go to jail for three years.
4. If neither of you confesses, then, you will both go to jail for one year.
5. The other one of you is being told these same things.

Assume that each prisoner is concerned solely with his own welfare and knows that the fewer years he spends in jail the better off he will be. Assume also that each knows that the other is likewise concerned only with minimizing his own jail term.

In these circumstances, which alternative, to confess or to refuse to confess, should each prisoner choose? That is, given what each prisoner knows, which alternative would it be more rational for him to choose?

Newcomb's Problem

This problem is posed by William Newcomb, a physicist. The philosophical world first heard of it from Robert Nozick in his ''Newcomb's Problem and Two Principles of Choice,'' which appeared in *Essays in Honor of Carl. G. Hempel,* edited by Nicholas Rescher (Dordrecht, The Netherlands: Reidel, 1970).

A psychology professor at your school has a reputation for being brilliant as well as possessed of an enormous fortune she has dedicated to her research. One day you get a request to report to her office at a certain hour. On a table are two boxes. One of them, labeled *A,* is transparent; in it you can see an enormous pile of $100 bills. The other, labeled *B,* is opaque. She tells you that there is $10,000 in transparent box *A* and that in box *B* there is either $1,000,000 or nothing. She tells you that she is going to give you a choice between:

(1) Taking just what is in box B.
(2) Taking what is in both boxes.

(Think about what you would choose given this much information.)

Then, she tells you that this is part of an experiment. During registration at the beginning of the quarter, you walked under a peculiar device that reminded you of the machines at airports that are used to prevent hijacking. You didn't think much about it at the time. But, she now informs you that this machine was something she designed and that it recorded an instant profile of your basic personality and character traits. On the basis of your profile, she made a prediction about what choice you would make, and she decided what to put in Box *B* on the basis of this prediction:

(1) If she predicted you would take both, she put nothing in Box *B*.

(2) If she predicted you would take only Box *B,* she put $1,000,000 in it.

(Now, think about what you would do given this much information.)

At this point you ask her how accurate her predictions have been. She says that 1,000 students have been given the choice, and she has only been wrong once. In all the other cases, students who chose both boxes got only $10,000, whereas those who chose only box B got $1,000,000. Then she tells you to choose. What do you do?

Goodman's New Riddle of Induction

This paradox is based on a problem introduced by Nelson Goodman in his book *Fact, Fiction and Forecast,* 2nd ed. (Indianapolis, Ind., 1965). He explains his own approach in this book, and his discussion has given rise to a voluminous literature.

We ordinarily assume that we can confirm a general hypothesis by examination of instances and that this process of induction is useful in conducting our lives. For example, we assume that repeated observations of green emeralds and failure to observe any that are not green supports the hypothesis that all emeralds are green. Thus, it is reasonable to expect the next emerald we examine to be green if we have no other evidence to go on. But, actually, such confirmation provides no basis for forming expectations at all, and induction is quite useless.

Suppose that it is January 1, 1987, and that all emeralds examined have been green. This seems to support the hypothesis that all emeralds are green and to make it rational, other things being equal, to expect the next emerald we examine to also be green.

But, let the word *grue* apply to things just in case:

(1) They are examined before January 1, 1987, and are green.

(2) They have not been examined before January 1, 1987, and are blue.

All of the emeralds examined before January 1, 1987, are grue as well as green. Hence, our observations up to that time support the hypothesis that all emeralds are grue every bit as much as the hypothesis that all emeralds are green. Hence, our observations give us as much reason to expect the next emerald we examine to be grue as to expect it to be green. But, if the next emerald we examine is grue, it is also blue, and not green. So our observations give us as much reason to expect the next emerald we examine to be blue as they do to expect that it will be green. But, obviously, we could repeat the same argument to show that we have as much reason to expect the next emerald we examine to be any color other than green. E.g., we could repeat the argument by using the predicate *gred,* which applies to things examined before January 1, 1987, if they are green and to other things if they are red. So our observations give us no more reason to expect the next emerald we examine to be green than they do to expect it to be blue or red or any other color. So, contrary to what we assumed to be plausible, induction is totally useless.

3. PARADOXES OF LOGIC, SET THEORY, AND SEMANTICS

Paradoxes have played an important role in the history of logic and the related disciplines of set theory and semantics. These paradoxes as well as some others are discussed by Quine in his essay "The Ways of Paradox," at the end of Part VI.

The Paradox of the Liar

Here are two basic principles of logic:

NC—THE PRINCIPLE OF NONCONTRADICTION: No statement is both true and false.

EM—THE PRINCIPLE OF THE EXCLUDED MIDDLE: Every statement is either true or false.

But now consider this statement:

(1) Statement (1) is false.

By EM (1) is either true or false. Suppose (1) is true. Then (1) is false, for this is what (1) says. But then (1) is both true and false, contrary to NC. Thus, the supposition that (1) is true leads to a contradiction and must be denied. So we must suppose that (1) is false. But if (1) is false, then what (1) says is so, for what (1) says is that (1) is false. But then (1) is true. But then (1) is both false and true, contrary to NC. So the supposition that (1) is false leads to a contradiction and must be denied. But now we have a contradiction. For by EM (1) is either true or false; but, by our argument, (1) is neither true nor false.

Other Versions of the Liar

There are many different versions of the liar paradox, which the student may wish to think about after coming up with some hypotheses about what to say about the first version. Here are some of them.

*****

(1) Statement (2) is true.
(2) Statement (1) is false.

****

(1) Statement (1) is not true

****

The Statement in Box *A* is not true

Box *A*

****

''yields a falsehood when appended to its own quotation'' yields a falsehood when appended to its own quotation.

(Quine, ''The Ways of Paradox'')

Russell's Paradox

This paradox, which Quine calls the most celebrated of all antinomies, was discovered by Bertrand Russell in 1901. Here is Quine's statement:

> Some classes are members of themselves; some are not. For example, the class of all classes that have more than five members clearly has more than five classes as members; therefore the class is a member of itself. On the other hand, the class of all men is not a member of itself, not being a man. What of the class of all classes that are not members of themselves? Since its members are the non-self-members, it qualifies as a member of itself if and only if it is not.

Grelling's Paradox

Consider the relation of describing between adjectives and objects. *Red* describes an object x if and only if x is red, *Tall* describes an object if and only if X is tall, and so forth.

Among adjectives are those that describe words. For example, *7-lettered* describes the word *example* and *ambiguous* describes the word *bank*. This raises the possibility of adjectives that describe themselves, and there are many of them. For example, *14-charactered* describes itself, as do *English, short, ambiguous,* and *polysyllabic*. Let us call these words *autological.*

There are also lots of adjectives that do not apply to themselves. Among these are *long, German, monosyllabic,* and *50-lettered.* Let us call such adjectives *heterological.* That is, an adjective A is heterological if and only if A does not describe A.

Is *heterlogical* heterological?

B. PARADOXES AND ANTINOMIES

The Ways of Paradox

W. V. QUINE

Willard Van Orman Quine (1908–) is Emeritus Pierce Professor of Philosophy at Harvard University. One of the most influential and original twentieth-century philosophers, he has written a number of works, including *Mathematical Logic, Word and Object,* and *From a Logical Point of View.*

Frederic, protagonist of *The Pirates of Penzance,* has reached the age of 21 after passing only five birthdays. Several circumstances conspire to make this possible. Age is reckoned in elapsed time, whereas a birthday has to match the date of birth; and February 29 comes less frequently than once a year.

Granted that Frederic's situation is possible, wherein is it paradoxical? Merely in its initial air of absurdity. The likelihood that a man will be more than *n* years old on his *n*th birthday is as little as 1 to 1,460, or slightly better if we allow for seasonal trends; and this likelihood is so slight that we easily forget its existence.

May we say in general, then, that a paradox is just any conclusion that at first sounds absurd but that has an argument to sustain it? In the end I think this account stands up pretty well. But it leaves much unsaid. The argument that sustains a paradox may expose the absurdity of a buried premise or of some preconception previously reckoned as central to physical theory, to mathematics, or to the thinking process. Catastrophe may lurk, therefore, in the most innocent-seeming paradox. More than once in history the discovery of paradox has been the occasion for major reconstruction at the foundations of thought. For some decades, indeed, studies of the foundation of mathematics have been confounded and greatly stimulated by confrontation with two paradoxes, one propounded by Bertrand Russell in 1901 and the other by Kurt Gödel in 1931.

As a first step onto this dangerous ground, let us consider another paradox: that of the village barber. This is not Russell's great paradox of 1901, to which we shall come, but a lesser one that Russell attributed to an unnamed source in 1918. In a certain village there is a man, so the paradox runs, who is a barber; this barber shaves all and only those men in the village who do not shave themselves. Query: Does the barber shave himself?

Any man in this village is shaved by the barber if and only if he is not shaved by himself. Therefore in particular the barber shaves himself if and only if he does not. We are in trouble if we say the barber shaves himself and we are in trouble if we say he does not.

Now compare the two paradoxes. Frederic's situation seemed absurd at first, but a simple argument sufficed to make us acquiesce in it for good. In the case of the barber, on the other hand,

From *The Ways of Paradox and Other Essays* (New York: Random House, 1966), pp. 3–10.
[Quine] presented this as a lecture at the University of Akron, November 1961, and again at a Shop Club at Harvard. It was published under the title "Paradox" in *Scientific American* (Volume 206, 1962).

the conclusion is too absurd to acquiesce in at any time.

What are we to say to the argument that goes to prove this unacceptable conclusion? Happily it rests on assumptions. We are asked to swallow a story about a village and a man in it who shaves all and only those men in the village who do not shave themselves. This is the source of our trouble; grant this and we end up saying, absurdly, that the barber shaves himself if and only if he does not. The proper conclusion to draw is just that there is no such barber. We are confronted with nothing more mysterious than what logicians have been referring to for a couple of thousand years as a reductio ad absurdum. We disprove the barber by assuming him and deducing the absurdity that he shaves himself if and only if he does not. The paradox is simply a proof that no village can contain a man who shaves all and only those men in it who do not shave themselves. This sweeping denial at first sounds absurd; why should there not be such a man in a village? But the argument shows why not, and so we acquiesce in the sweeping denial just as we acquiesced in the possibility, absurd on first exposure, of Frederic's being so much more than 5 years old on his 5th birthday.

Both paradoxes are alike, after all, in sustaining prima facie absurdities by conclusive argument. What is strange but true in the one paradox is that one can be $4n$ years old on one's nth birthday; what is strange but true in the other paradox is that no village can contain a man who shaves all and only those men in the village who do not shave themselves.

Still, I would not limit the word "paradox" to cases where what is purportedly established is true. I shall call these, more particularly, veridical, or truth-telling, paradoxes. For the name of paradox is suited equally to falsidical ones. (This word is not so barbarous as it sounds; *falsidicus* occurs twice in Plautus and twice in earlier writers.)

The Frederic paradox is a veridical one if we take its proposition not as something about Frederic but as the abstract truth that a man can be $4n$ years old on his nth birthday. Similarly, the barber paradox is a veridical one if we take its proposition as being that no village contains such a barber. A falsidical paradox, on the other hand, is one whose proposition not only seems at first absurd but also is false, there being a fallacy in the purported proof. Typical falsidical paradoxes are the comic misproofs that $2=1$. Most of us have heard one or another such. Here is the version offered by Augustus De Morgan: Let $x=1$. Then $x^2=x$. So $x^2-1=x-1$. Dividing both sides by $x-1$, we conclude that $x+1=1$; that is, since $x=1$, $2=1$. The fallacy comes in the division by $x-1$, which is 0.

Instead of "falsidical paradox" could I say simply "fallacy"? Not quite. Fallacies can lead to true conclusions as well as false ones, and to unsurprising conclusions as well as surprising ones. In a falsidical paradox there is always a fallacy in the argument, but the proposition purportedly established has furthermore to seem absurd and to be indeed false.

Some of the ancient paradoxes of Zeno belong under the head of falsidical paradoxes. Take the one about Achilles and the tortoise. Generalized beyond these two fictitious characters, what the paradox purports to establish is the absurd proposition that so long as a runner keeps running, however slowly, another runner can never overtake him. The argument is that each time the pursure reaches a spot where the pursued has been, the pursued has moved a bit beyond. When we try to make this argument more explicit, the fallacy that emerges is the mistaken notion that any infinite succession of intervals of time has to add up to all eternity. Actually when an infinite succession of intervals of time is so chosen that the succeeding intervals become shorter and shorter, the whole succession may take either a finite or an infinite time. It is a question of a convergent series.

Grelling's Paradox

The realm of paradox is not clearly exhausted even by the verdical and falsidical paradoxes together. The most startling of all paradoxes are not clearly assignable to either of these domains. Consider the paradox, devised by Kurt Grelling in 1908, concerning the heterological, or non-self-descriptive, adjectives.

To explain this paradox requires first a definition of the autological, or self-descriptive, adjective. The adjective "short" is short; the adjective "English" is English; the adjective "adjectival" is adjectival; the adjective "polysyllabic" is polysyllabic. Each of these adjectives is, in Grelling's terminology, autological: each is true of itself. Other adjectives are heterological; thus "long", which is not a long adjective; "German", which is not a German adjective; "monosyllabic", which is not a monosyllabic one.

Grelling's paradox arises from the query: Is the adjective "heterological" an autological or a heterological one? We are as badly off here as we were with the barber. If we decide that "heterological" is autological, then the adjective is true of itself. But that makes it heterological rather than autological, since whatever the adjective "heterological" is true of is heterological. If we therefore decide that the adjective "heterological" is heterological, then it is true of itself, and that makes it autological.

Our recourse in a comparable quandry over the village barber was to declare a reductio ad absurdum and conclude that there was no such barber. Here, however, there is no interim premise to disavow. We merely defined the adjective "heterological" and asked if it was heterological. In fact, we can get the paradox just as well without the adjective and its definition. "Heterological" was defined as meaning "not true of self"; we can therefore ask if the adjectival phrase "not true of self" is true of itself. We find that it is if and only if it is not, hence that it is and it is not; and so we have our paradox.

Thus viewed, Grelling's paradox seems unequivocally falsidical. Its proposition is a self-contradictory compound proposition to the effect that our adjective is and is not true of itself. But this paradox contrasts strangely with the falsidical paradoxes of Zeno, or of "2 = 1", in that we are at a loss to spot the fallacy in the argument. It may for this reason be best seen as representing a third class of paradoxes, separate from the veridical and falsidical ones.

Antinomies

The paradoxes of this class are called antinomies, and it is they that bring on the crises in thought. An antinomy produces a self-contradiction by accepted ways of reasoning. It establishes that some tacit and trusted pattern of reasoning must be made explicit and henceforward be avoided or revised.

Take Grelling's paradox, in the form in which it shows the adjective phrase "not true of self" to be both true and false of itself. What tacit principles of reasoning does the argument depend on? Notably this one: the adjective "red" is true of a thing if and only if the thing is red; the adjective "big" is true of a thing if and only if the thing is big; the adjective "not true of self" is true of a thing if and only if the thing is not true of itself; and so on. This last case of the principle is the case that issues directly in the paradox.

There is no denying that this principle is constantly used, tacitly, when we speak of adjectives as true of things: the adjective "red" is true of a thing if and only if the thing is red, and correspondingly for all adjectives. This principle simply reflects what we mean in saying that adjectives are true of things. It is a hard principle to distrust, and yet it is obviously the principle that is to blame for our antinomy. The antinomy is directly a case of this principle. Take the adjective in the principle as the adjectival phrase "not true of self" instead of the adjective "red", and take the "thing" in the principle, of which the adjective is to be true, as that adjective over again; thereupon the principle says outright that "not true of self" is true of itself if and only if it is not true of itself. So the principle must be abandoned or at least somehow restricted.

Yet so faithfully does the principle reflect what we mean in calling adjectives true of things that we cannot abandon it without abjuring the very expression "true of" as pernicious nonsense. We could still go on using the adjectives themselves that had been said to be true of things; we could go on attributing them to things as usual; what we would be cutting out in "true of" is merely a special locution for talking about the attribution of the adjectives to the things.

This special locution, however, has its conveniences, and it would be missed. In fact, we do not have to do without it altogether. Speaking of adjectives as true or not true of things has made trouble in one special case, involving one special adjective, namely the phrase "not true of self", in attribution to one special thing, namely that same phrase over again. If we forswear the use of the locution ''true of'' in connection with this particular phrase in relation to itself as object, we thereby silence our antinomy and may go on blithely using the locution ''true of'' in other cases as always, pending the discovery of further antinomies.

Actually related antinomies are still forthcoming. To inactivate the lot we have to cut a little deeper than our one case; we have to forswear the use of ''true of'' not only in connection with ''not true of self'' but also in connection with various other phrases relating to truth; and in such connections we have to forswear the use not only of ''true of'' but also of various other truth locutions. First let us look at some of the antinomies that would otherwise threaten.

The Paradox of Epimenides

There is the ancient paradox of Epimenides the Cretan, who said that all Cretans were liars. If he spoke the truth, he was a liar. It seems that this paradox may have reached the ears of St. Paul and that he missed the point of it. He warned, in his epistle to Titus: ''One of themselves, even a prophet of their own, said, The Cretans are always liars.''

Actually the paradox of Epimenides is untidy; there are loopholes. Perhaps some Cretans were liars, notably Epimenides, and others were not; perhaps Epimenides was a liar who occasionally told the truth; either way it turns out that the contradiction vanishes. Something of paradox can be salvaged with a little tinkering; but we do better to switch to a different and simpler rendering, also ancient, of the same idea. This is the *pseudomenon,* which runs simply: ''I am lying''. We can even drop the indirectness of a personal reference and speak directly of the sentence: ''This sentence is false''. Here we seem to have the irreducible essence of antinomy: a sentence that is true if and only if it is false.

In an effort to clear up this antinomy it has been protested that the phrase ''This sentence'', so used, refers to nothing. This is claimed on the ground that you cannot get rid of the phrase by supplying a sentence that is referred to. For what sentence does the phrase refer to? The sentence ''This sentence is false''. If, accordingly, we supplant the phrase ''This sentence'' by a quotation of the sentence referred to, we get: '' ''This sentence is false'' is false''. But the whole outside sentence here attributes falsity no longer to itself but merely to something other than itself, thereby engendering no paradox.

If, however, in our perversity we are still bent on constructing a sentence that does attribute falsity unequivocally to itself, we can do so thus: '' ''Yields a falsehood when appended to its own quotation'' yields a falsehood when appended to its own quotation''. This sentence specifies a string of nine words and says of this string that if you put it down twice, with quotation marks around the first of the two occurrences, the result is false. But that result is the very sentence that is doing the telling. The sentence is true if and only if it is false, and we have our antinomy.

This is a genuine antinomy, on a par with the one about ''heterological'', or ''false of self'', or ''not true of self'', being true of itself. But whereas that earlier one turned on ''true of'', through the construct ''not true of self'', this new one turns merely on ''true'', through the construct ''falsehood'', or ''statement not true''. We can avoid both antinomies, and others related to them, by ceasing to use ''true of'' and ''true'' and their equivalents and derivatives, or at any rate ceasing to apply such truth locutions to adjectives or sentences that themselves contain such truth locutions.

This restriction can be relaxed somewhat by admitting a hierarchy of truth locutions, as suggested by the work of Bertrand Russell and Alfred Tarski. The expressions ''true'', ''true of'', ''false'', and related ones can be used with numerical subscripts ''0,'' ''1,'' ''2,'' and so on always attached or imagined; thus ''true_0'', ''true_1'', ''true_2'', ''false_0'', and so on. Then we can avoid the antimonies by taking care, when a truth locution T is applied to a sentence or other expression S, that the subscript on T is higher than any subscript inside S. Violations of this restriction would be treated as meaningless, or ungrammatical, rather than as true or false sentences. For instance, we could meaningfully ask whether the adjectives ''long'' and ''short'' are true_0 of themselves; the answers are respectively no and yes. But we could not meaningfully speak of the phrase ''not true_0 of self'' as true_0 or false_0 of itself; we would have to ask whether it is true_1

or $false_1$ of itself, and this is a question that leads to no antinomy. Either way the question can be answered with a simple and unpenalized negative.

This point deserves to be restated: Whereas "long" and "short" are adjectives that can meaningfully be applied to themselves, falsely in the one case and truly in the other, on the other hand "$true_0$ of self" and "not $true_0$ of self" are adjectival phrases that cannot be applied to themselves meaningfully at all, truly or falsely. Therefore to the question "Is "$true_0$ of self" $true_1$ of itself?" the answer is no; the adjectival phrase "$true_0$ of itself" is meaningless of itself rather than $true_1$ of itself.

Next let us consider, in terms of subscripts, the most perverse version of the *pseudomenon*. We have now, for meaningfulness, to insert subscripts on the two occurrences of the word "falsehood", and in ascending order, thus: " "Yields a $falsehood_0$ when appended to its own quotation" yields a $falsehood_1$ when appended to its own quotation." Thereupon paradox vanishes. This sentence is unequivocally false. What it tells us is that a certain described form of words is $false_1$, namely the form of words " "Yields a $falsehood_0$ when appended to its own quotation" yields a $falsehood_0$ when appended to its own quotation." But in fact this form of words is not $false_1$; it is meaningless. So the preceeding sentence, which said that this form of words was $false_1$, is false. It is $false_2$.

This may seem an extravagant way of eliminating antinomies. But it would be much more costly to drop the word "true", and related locutions, once and for all. At an intermediate cost one could merely leave off applying such locutions to expressions containing such locutions. Either method is less economical than this method of subscripts. The subscripts do enable us to apply truth locutions to expressions containing such locutions, although in a manner disconcertingly at variance with custom. Each resort is desperate; each is an artificial departure from natural and established usage. Such is the way of antinomies.

A veridical paradox packs a surprise, but the surprise quickly dissipates itself as we ponder the proof. A falsidical paradox packs a surprise, but it is seen as a false alarm when we solve the underlying fallacy. An antinomy, however, packs a surprise that can be accommodated by nothing less than a repudiation of part of our conceptual heritage.

Revision of a conceptual scheme is not unprecedented. It happens in a small way with each advance in science, and it happens in a big way with the big advances, such as the Copernican revolution and the shift from Newtonian mechanics to Einstein's theory of relativity. We can hope in time even to get used to the biggest such changes and to find the new schemes natural. There was a time when the doctrine that the earth revolves around the sun was called the Copernican paradox, even by the men who accepted it. And perhaps a time will come when truth locutions without implicit subscripts, or like safeguards, will really sound as nonsensical as the antinomies show them to be.

Conversely, the falsidical paradoxes of Zeno must have been, in his day, genuine antinomies. We in our latter-day smugness point to a fallacy: the notion that an infinite succession of intervals must add up to an infinite interval. But surely this was part and parcel of the conceptual scheme of Zeno's day. Our recognition of convergent series, in which an infinite number of segments add up to a finite segment, is from Zeno's vantage point an artificiality comparable to our new subscripts on truth locutions. Perhaps these subscripts will seem as natural to our descendants of A.D. 4000, granted the tenuous hypothesis of there being any, as the convergent series does to us. One man's antinomy is another man's falsidical paradox, give or take a couple of thousand years.

I have not, by the way, exhausted the store of latter-day antinomies. Another good one is attributed by Russell to a librarian named G. G. Berry. Here the theme is numbers and syllables. Ten has a one-syllable name. Seventy-seven has a five-syllable name. The seventh power of seven hundred seventy-seven has a name that, if we were to work it out, might run to 100 syllables or so; but this number can also be specified more briefly in other terms. I have just specified it in 15 syllables. We can be sure, however, that there are no end of numbers that resist all specification, by name or description, under 19 syllables. There is only a finite stock of syllables altogether, and hence only a finite number of names or phrases of less than 19 syllables, whereas there are an infinite number of positive integers. Very well, then; of those numbers not specifiable in less than 19 syllables, there must be a least. And here is our antinomy: the least number not specifiable in less than nineteen syllables is specifiable in 18 syllables. I have just so specified it.

This antinomy belongs to the same family as the antinomies that have gone before. For the key word of this antinomy, "specifiable", is interdefinable with "true of". It is one more of the truth locutions that would take on subscripts under the Russell–Tarski plan. The least number not specifiable_0 in less than 19 syllables is indeed specifiable_1 in 18 syllables, but it is not specifiable_0 in less than 19 syllables; for all I know it is not specifiable_0 in less than 23. This resolution of Berry's antinomy is the one that would come through automatically if we paraphrase "specifiable" in terms of "true of" and then subject "true of" to the subscript treatment.

Russell's Antinomy

Not all antinomies belong to this family. The most celebrated of all antinomies, discovered by Russell in 1901, belongs outside this family. It has to do with self-membership of classes. Some classes are members of themselves; some are not. For example, the class of all classes that have more than five members clearly has more than five classes as members; therefore the class is a member of itself. On the other hand, the class of all men is not a member of itself, not being a man. What of the class of all classes that are not members of themselves? Since its members are the non-self-members, it qualifies as member of itself if and only if it is not. It is and it is not: antinomy's by now familiar face.

Russell's antinomy bears a conspicuous analogy to Grelling's antinomy of "not true of self", which in fact it antedates. But Russell's antinomy does not belong to the same family as the Epimenides antinomy and those of Berry and Grelling. By this I mean that Russell's antinomy cannot be blamed on any of the truth locutions, nor is it resolved by subjecting those locutions to subscripts. The crucial words in Russell's antinomy are "class" and "member", and neither of these is definable in terms of "true", "true of", or the like.

I said earlier that an antinomy establishes that some tacit and trusted pattern of reasoning must be made explicit and be henceforward avoided or revised. In the case of Russell's antinomy, the tacit and trusted pattern of reasoning that is found wanting is this: for any condition you can formulate, there is a class whose members are the things meeting the condition.

This principle is not easily given up. The almost invariable way of specifying a class is by stating a necessary and sufficient condition for belonging to it. When we have stated such a condition, we feel that we have "given" the class and can scarcely make sense of there not being such a class. The class may be empty, yes; but how could there not be such a class at all? What substance can be asked for it that the membership condition does not provide? Yet such exhortations avail us nothing in the face of the antinomy, which simply proves the principle untenable. It is a simple point of logic, once we look at it, that there is no class, empty or otherwise, that has as members precisely the classes that are not members of themselves. It would have to have itself as member if and only if it did not.

Russell's antinomy came as a shock to Gottlob Frege, founder of mathematical logic. In his *Grundgesetze der Arithmetik* Frege thought that he had secured the foundations of mathematics in the self-consistent laws of logic. He received a letter from Russell as the second volume of this work was on its way to press. "Arithmetic totters," Frege is said to have written in answer. An appendix that he added to the volume opens with the words: "A scientist can hardly encounter anything more undesirable than to have the foundation collapse just as the work is finished. I was put in this position by a letter from Bertrand Russell. . . ."

In Russell's antinomy there is more than a hint of the paradox of the barber. The parallel is, in truth, exact. It was a simple point of logic that there was in no village a man who shaved all and only those men in the village who did not shave themselves; he would shave himself if and only if he did not. The barber paradox was a veridical paradox showing that there is no such barber. Why is Russell's antinomy then not a veridical paradox showing that there is no class whose members are all and only the non-self-members? Why does it count as an antinomy and the barber paradox not? The reason is that there has been in our habits of thought an overwhelming presumption of there being such a class but no presumption of there being such a barber. The barber paradox barely qualifies as paradox in that we are mildly surprised at being able to exclude the barber on purely logical grounds by reducing him to absurdity. Even this surprise ebbs as we review the argument; and anyway we had never positively believed in such a barber. Russell's paradox is a genuine antinomy because the principle of class existence that it compels us to give up is so fundamental. When in a future century the absurdity of that principle has become a commonplace, and some substitute principle has enjoyed long enough tenure to take on somewhat the air of common sense, perhaps we can begin to see Russell's paradox as no more than a veridical paradox, showing that there is no such class as that of the non-self-members. One man's antinomy can be another man's veridical paradox, and one man's veridical paradox can be another man's platitude.

Russell's antinomy made for a more serious crisis still than did Grelling's and Berry's and the one about Epimenides. For these strike at the semantics of truth and denotation, but Russell's strikes at the mathematics of classes. Classes are appealed to in an auxiliary way in most branches of mathematics, and increasingly so as passages of mathematical reasoning are made more explicit. The basic principle of classes that is tacitly used, at virtually every turn where classes are involved at all, is precisely the class-existence principle that is discredited by Russell's antinomy.

I spoke of Grelling's antinomy and Berry's and the Epimenides as all in a family, to which Russell's antinomy does not belong. For its part, Russell's antinomy has family connections of its own. In fact, it is the first of an infinite series of antinomies, as follows. Russell's antinomy shows that there is no class whose members are precisely the classes that are not members of themselves. Now there is a parallel antinomy that shows there is no class whose members are precisely the classes that are not members of members of themselves. Further, there is an antinomy that shows there is no class whose members are precisely the classes that are not members of members of members of themselves. And so on ad infinitum

All these antinomies, and other related ones, can be inactivated by limiting the guilty principle of class existence in a very simple way. The principle is that for any membership condition you can formulate there is a class whose members are solely the things meeting the condition. We get Russell's antinomy and all the others of its series by taking the condition as non-membership in self, or non-membership in members of self, or the like. Each time the trouble comes of taking a membership condition that itself talks in turn of membership and non-membership. If we withhold our principle of class existence from cases where the membership condition mentions membership, Russell's antinomy and related ones are no longer forthcoming. This restriction on class existence is parallel to a restriction on the truth locutions that we contemplated for a while, before bringing in the subscripts; namely, not to apply the truth locutions to expressions containing any of the truth locutions.

Happily we can indeed withhold the principle of class existence from cases where the membership condition mentions membership, without unsettling those branches of mathematics that make only incidental use of classes. This is why it has been possible for most branches of mathematics to go on blithely using classes as auxiliary apparatus in spite of Russell's and related antinomies.

The Mathematics of Classes

There is a particular branch of mathematics in which the central concern is with classes; general set theory. In this domain one deals expressly with classes of classes, classes of classes of classes, and so on, in ways that would be paralyzed by the restriction just now contemplated: withholding the principle of class existence from cases where the membership condition mentions membership. So one tries in general set theory to manage with milder restrictions.

General set theory is rich in paradox. Even the endless series of antinomies that I mentioned above, of which Russell's was the first, by no means exhausts this vein of paradox. General set theory is primarily occupied with infinity—infinite classes, infinite numbers—and so is involved in paradoxes of the infinite. A rather tame old paradox under this head is that you can exhaust the members of a whole class by correlating them with the members of a mere part of the class. For instance, you can correlate all the positive integers with the multiples of 10, thus: 1 with 10, 2 with 20, 3 with 30, and so on. Every positive integer gets disposed of; there are as many multiples of 10 as integers altogether. This is no antinomy but a veridical paradox. Among adepts in the field it even loses the air of paradox altogether, as is indeed the way of veridical paradox.

Georg Cantor, the nineteenth-century pioneer in general set theory and infinite arithmetic, proved that there are always more classes of things of a given kind than there are things of that kind; more classes of cows than cows. A distinct air of paradox suffuses his proof of this.

First note the definition of "more". What it means when one says there are more things of one kind than another is that every correlation of things of the one kind to things of the other fails to exhaust the things of the one kind. So what Cantor is proving is that no correlation of cow classes to cows accommodates all the cow classes. The proof is as follows. Suppose a correlation of cow classes to cows. It can be any arbitrary correlation; a cow may or may not belong to the class correlated with her. Now consider the cows, if any, that do not belong to the classes correlated with them. These cows themselves form a cow class, empty or not. And it is a cow class that is not correlated with any cow. If the class were so correlated, that cow would have to belong to the class if and only if she did not.

This argument is typical of the arguments in general set theory that would be sacrificed if we were to withhold the principle of class existence from cases where the membership condition mentions membership. The recalcitrant cow class that clinched the proof was specified by a membership condition that mentioned membership. The condition was non-membership in the correlated cow class.

But what I am more concerned to bring out, regarding the cow-class argument, is its air of paradox. The argument makes its negative point in much the same way that the veridical barber paradox showed there to be no such barber, and in much the same way that Russell's antinomy showed there to be no class of all and only the non-self-members. So in Cantor's theorem—a theorem not only about cows and their classes but also about things of any sort and their classes—we see paradox, or something like it, seriously at work in the advancement of theory. His theorem establishes that for every class, even every infinite class, there is a larger class: the class of its subclasses.

So far, no antinomy. But now it is a short step to one. If for every class there is a larger class, what of the class of everything? Such is Cantor's antinomy. If you review the proof of Cantor's theorem in application directly to this disastrous example—speaking therefore not of cows but of everything—you will quickly see that Cantor's antinomy boils down, after all, to Russell's.

So the central problem in laying the foundations of general set theory is to inactivate Russell's antinomy and its suite. If such theorems as Cantor's are to be kept, the antinomies must be inactivated by milder restrictions than the total withholding of the principle of class existence from cases where the membership condition mentions membership. One tempting line is a scheme of subscripts analogous to the scheme used in avoiding the antinomies of truth and denotation. Something like this line was taken by Russell himself in 1908, under the name of the theory of logical types. A very different line was proposed in the same year by Ernst Zermelo, and further variations have been advanced in subsequent years.

All such foundations for general set theory have as their point of departure the counsel of the antinomies; namely, that a given condition, advanced as a necessary and sufficient condition of membership in some class, may or may not really have a class corresponding to it. So the various alternative foundations for general set theory differ from one another with respect to the membership conditions to which they do and do not guarantee corresponding classes. Non-self-membership is of course a condition to which none of the theories accord corresponding classes. The same holds true for the condition of not being a member of any own member; and for the conditions that give all the further antinomies of the series that began with Russell's; and for any membership condition that would give rise to any other antinomy, if we can spot it.

But we cannot simply withhold each antinomy-producing membership condition and assume classes corresponding to the rest. The trouble is that there are membership conditions corresponding to each of which, by itself, we can innocuously assume a class, and yet these classes together can yield a contradiction. We are driven to seeking optimum consistent combinations of existence assumptions, and consequently there is a great variety of proposals for the foundations of general set theory. Each proposed scheme is unnatural, because the natural scheme is the unrestricted one that the antinomies discredit; and each has advantages, in power or simplicity or in attractive consequences in special directions, that each of its rivals lacks.

I remarked earlier that the discovery of antinomy is a crisis in the evolution of thought. In general set theory the crisis began 60 years ago and is not yet over.

Gödel's Proof

Up to now the heroes or villains of this piece have been the antinomies. Other paradoxes have paled in comparison. Other paradoxes have been less startling to us, anyway, and more readily adjusted to. Other paradoxes have not precipitated 60 year crises, at least not in our time. When any of them did in the past precipitate crises that durable (and surely the falsidical paradoxes of Zeno did), they themselves qualified as antinomies.

Let me, in closing, touch on a latter-day paradox that is by no means an antinomy but is strictly a veridical paradox, and yet is comparable to the antinomies in the pattern of its proof, in the surprisingness of the result and even in its capacity to precipitate a crisis. This is Gödel's proof of the incompletability of number theory.

What Kurt Gödel proved, in that great paper of 1931, was that no deductive system, with axioms however arbitrary, is capable of embracing among its theorems all the truths of the elementary arithmetic of positive integers unless it discredits itself by letting slip some of the falsehoods too. Gödel showed how, for any given deductive system, he could construct a sentence of elementary number theory that would be true if and only if not provable in that system. Every such system is therefore either incomplete, in that it misses a relevant truth, or else bankrupt, in that it proves a falsehood.

Gödel's proof may conveniently be related to the Epimenides paradox or the *pseudomenon* in the ''yields a falsehood'' version. For ''falsehood'' read ''non-theorem'', thus: '' ''Yields a non-theorem when appended to its own quotation'' yields a non-theorem when appended to its own quotation''.

This statement no longer presents an antinomy, because it no longer says of itself that it is false. What it does say of itself is that it is not a theorem (of some deductive theory that I have not yet specified). If it is true, here is one truth that that deductive theory, whatever it is, fails to include as a theorem. If the statement is false, it is a theorem, in which event that deductive theory has a false theorem and so is discredited.

What Gödel proceeds to do, in getting his proof of the incompletability of number theory, is the following. He shows how the sort of talk that occurs in the above statement—talk of non-theoremhood and of appending things to quotations—can be mirrored systematically in arithmetical talk of integers. In this way, with much ingenuity, he gets a sentence purely in the arithmetical vocabulary of number theory that inherits that crucial property of being true if and only if not a theorem of number theory. And Gödel's trick works for any deductive system we may choose as defining ''theorem of number theory''.

Gödel's discovery is not an antinomy but a veridical paradox. That there can be no sound and complete deductive systematization of elementary number theory, much less of pure mathematics generally, is true. It is decidedly paradoxical, in the sense that it upsets crucial preconceptions. We used to think that mathematical truth consisted in provability.

Like any veridical paradox, this is one we can get used to, thereby gradually sapping its quality of paradox. But this one takes some sapping. And mathematical logicians are at it, most assiduously. Gödel's result started a trend of research that has grown in 30 years to the proportions of a big and busy branch of mathematics sometimes called proof theory, having to do with recursive functions and related matters, and embracing indeed a general abstract theory of machine computation. Of all the ways of paradoxes, perhaps the quaintest is their capacity on occasion to turn out to be so very much less frivolous than they look.

APPENDIX: READING PHILOSOPHY

To read philosophy well one must read slowly and aggressively. There is a lot of emphasis today on reading fast. This is the age of information, we are told. To take advantage of the information available to us (even to cope with it) or to master that which is important for our job, for responsible citizenship, or for a full life—or at any rate for the final or the midterm—one must learn to absorb large amounts of information in limited amounts of time. The college student, one hears, must learn to read at a minimum of 1,000 words a minute. And 2,000 or 3,000 words is better; and those who really want to get ahead should read so fast that the only limiting factor in the speed with which they read is the speed with which they can turn pages.

These skills may be suitable for some types of reading, but not for philosophy. Good philosophers develop arguments and theories of some intricacy: arguments that are designed to convince the reader of the author's position on important issues. Reading such works is valuable insofar as one grapples with the ideas—fighting not only to understand the author but also, once one does, fighting with him or her for control of one's mind. One should not be easily convinced of one position or another on issues so weighty as the existence of God, the indirectness of our knowledge of the external world, or the nature of justice.

Of course, all generalizations are a bit suspect. When one is reading for pleasure or to absorb straightforward information from a reliable source, speed-reading can be fine. But, if one derives pleasure from reading philosophy, it should be the pleasure of grappling with important and sublime ideas, not the exhilaration of racing through a thriller. And, when one learns from reading philosophy, it should be a result of being forced to think through new ideas and grasp new concepts, not simply the uploading of a data file from the text to the mind.

College students will have learned that mathematics and other technical material cannot be read in overdrive. But, philosophy can be deceptive. It cannot be claimed that good philosophy always makes good reading, but some philosophy does. A lot of philosophy, including a good portion of the famous historical works included in this anthology, make pleasnat reading. They do not contain symbols, equations, charts, or other obvious signs of technicality and intricacy. One can just sit down and read Hume, or even Descartes, getting a feel for the author's position and style and the historical perspective of the work. When these texts are assigned in courses that survey the literature of various periods—with an eye toward getting a sense of the flow of ideas and concerns—as parts of larger assignments that cover hundreds of pages a week, one may have little choice but to read philosophy in this way, that is, just to get a feel for what is going on.

But appearances to the contrary, philosophy is inevitably technical. The philosopher constructs arguments, theories, positions, or criticisms in an attempt to persuade his or her most intelligent and perceptive opponents. The ideas and issues dealt with have a long history: to say something new, interesting, and persuasive, the philosopher must build his or her case with care. The result may be understood on various levels; to understand it at the deepest level, the reader must adopt the stance of the intelligent and perceptive opponent, thus coming to understand the case the philosopher is trying to make. This is what we mean by reading aggressively.

To read philosophy in this way, one should imagine oneself in a dialogue with the philosopher—as if the philosopher were one's roommate (or an intelligent and articulate new roommate) trying to convince one of a startling new idea.

To see this approach at work, let's consider an example. Here is a passage from Descartes's "First Meditation."

> Today, then, having rid myself of worries and having arranged for some peace and quiet, I withdraw alone, free at last earnestly and wholeheartedly to overthrow all my beliefs.
>
> To do this, I do not need to show each of my beliefs to be false; I may never be able to do that. But, since reason now convinces me that I ought to withhold my assent just as carefully from what is not obviously certain and indubitable as from what is obviously false, I can justify the rejection of all my beliefs if I can find some ground for doubt in each. And, to do this, I need not take on the endless task of running through my beliefs one by one: since a building collapses when its foundation is cut out from under it, I will go straight to the principles on which all my former beliefs rested.

Let's start with the second paragraph. The first place to pause is the word *this*. Whenever one encounters a demonstrative pronoun or other device by which the author refers back to something earlier, one should pause and make sure one knows to what it refers.

DESCARTES: To do this . . .

YOU: Wait a minute. To do what? Oh yes, I see, *to overthrow all your beliefs*.

But what is is to overthrow one's beliefs? This sort of phrase ought immediately to occasion a demand for clarification.

Y: What do you mean, "Overthrow all your beliefs, anyway?" Every one of them? You must be kidding? You are trying to make yourself believe everything you now believe is false? Can that really be what you mean?

Of course, Descartes isn't your roommate and, in fact, is long dead. So he can't respond to you. Still, you should mentally—or on the margin of your book—note this question.

Y: Well, of course you can't respond. But this sounds pretty odd. I will keep my eye open for clarification of just what it is you are trying to do.

D: As I was saying: To do this, I do not need to show each of my beliefs to be false; I may never be able to do that.

Y: Well, I didn't have to wait long. It's a relief that you aren't going to show all of your beliefs to be false. Still, it sounds as if this is something you want to do but simply don't think you could. The point of even wanting to seems a bit obscure. Go ahead.

D: But, as reason now convinces me . . .

Y: Reason. Reason. I wonder what exactly you mean by that. Hmm, this is the first use of the word. I mean, I know the meaning of the word *reason,* but it sounds as if you have something rather definite in mind. Actually, I use the word as a verb rather than a noun. Maybe I had better look it up in the dictionary. Here we are: "A statement offered in explanation." That doesn't seem to fit. *Motive, cause,* likewise. *Sanity*. That must be as in, "He has lost his reason." Or *intelligence*. One of these must be the closest. The latter seems better. So you are saying that your intelligence convinces you that you should be a great deal more cautious about what you believe—that's what this seems to amount to. Still, I have a hunch that more is packed into your use of the word *reason* than I can get out of the dictionary. The prof said you were a rationalist and that they put great emphasis on the power of reason. I'll keep in mind that this is a key word and look for other clues as to exactly what you mean by it.

D: . . . That I ought to withhold my assent just as carefully from what is not obviously certain and indubitable as from what is obviously false. I can justify the rejection of all my beliefs if I can find some ground for doubt in each.

Y: Wait a minute. You just said a mouthful. Let me try to sort it out. Let's see. *Withhold my assent*. So you said you were going to overthrow your beliefs at the end of the last paragraph. Then, you said to do this you don't need to show that they are false. So *withholding assent* must be how you describe the in-between position—you have quit believing something, although you haven't shown it false, you don't believe the opposite either.

Wait a minute. Does that make sense? If I don't believe that $3+5=8$, don't I automatically believe that it's not the case that $3+5=8$? Hmm. I guess not. Suppose it was $358+267$. Until I add it up, I neither believe it does equal 625 nor believe that doesn't. So I guess that's where one is at when one is *withholding assent.*

Here is another mouthful: "Not obviously certain and indubitable." I'll look up the last word. *Unquestionable: Too evident to be doubted.* How is that different from certain? If your *Meditations* is one of the all-time classics, why are you being redundant in this show-offy way? Maybe I should give you the benefit of the doubt.

Let's see, the contrast is between *certain and indubitable*—no, wait, *obviously certain and indubitable*—and *obviously false.* Clearly one withholds one's assent from what is obviously false. So what you are saying is that you are going to do the same for *everything,* except that which is obviously clear and indubitable. And your reason, which seems to amount to your intelligence, is what leads you to do this. OK, proceed.

D: . . . I can justify the rejection of all my beliefs . . .

Y: You seem to go back and forth between a pretty sensible position—not believing what you aren't really sure of—and something that sounds a bit weird. Before you said you were going to try to overthrow *all* your beliefs; now, you are trying to justify rejecting *all* your beliefs. I must admit, even though you have quite a reputation as a philosopher, this project strikes me as sort of extreme.

D: . . . If I can find some ground for doubt in each . . .

Y: Oh dear, another technical sounding phrase: *ground for doubt.* I better pull out my *Webster's* again. Well, you aren't using *ground* to mean dirt and you don't mean the bottom of a body of water, so you must mean *basis for belief or argument.* It sounds as if you are going to look for some basis for an argument *against* every single one of your beliefs. *That* sounds like quite a project. I wonder how come your *Meditations* is so short if you are really going to go through each one of your beliefs.

D: And, to do this, I need not take on the endless task of running through my beliefs one by one . . .

Y: Well, that's a relief.

D: . . . Because a building collapses when its foundation is cut out from under it, I will go straight to the principles on which all my former beliefs rested.

Y: Relying on a metaphor at a crucial point, eh? I thought the prof said that was a dubious practice. She said we should look at the assumptions underlying the appropriateness of the metaphor. So it looks like you think your beliefs form a *structure* with a *foundation.* The foundation is principles. All your beliefs rest on—i.e., I suppose, depend on in some way—certain principles. For this all to make sense, these principles must be beliefs. So what you are saying is that you are going to isolate certain beliefs, on which the rest depend. If you have a ground for doubt for a principle, you will quit believing it, not in the sense of taking it to be false or believing the opposite, but in the sense of withholding your assent. In so doing, you will automatically have a ground for doubt for all the other beliefs that depend on the dubious principle.

Well, I guess that's an intelligible project. It still seems like it ought to take a lot longer than 50 pages. We shall see . . .

This is what it is like to read aggressively.